Prentice Hall
LITERATURE
Timeless Voices, Timeless Themes

The British Tradition

PRENTICE HALL
Upper Saddle River, New Jersey
Needham, Massachusetts
Glenview, Illinois

ISBN 0-13-050280-4

2 3 4 5 6 7 8 9 10   03 02 01 00 99

PRENTICE HALL

ACKNOWLEDGMENTS

Grateful acknowledgment is made to the following for permission to reprint copyrighted material:

Georges Borchardt, Inc.
"The First Year of My Life" from *The Stories of Muriel Spark.* Copyright © 1985 by Copyright Administration. Reprinted by permission of Georges Borchardt, Inc. for the author.

Cambridge University Press
Excerpt from "Letter to Thomas Flower Ellis from Thomas Babington Macaulay on the Passing of the Reform Bill" written in 1831, from *The Selected Letters of Thomas Babington Macaulay,* ed. Thomas Pinney, 5 vols.(Cambridge: Cambridge University Press, 1974–80). Reprinted by permission of the publisher.

(Acknowledgments continue on p.1252.)

Prentice Hall

LITERATURE
Timeless Voices, Timeless Themes

Copper

Bronze

Silver

Gold

Platinum

The American Experience

The British Tradition

World Masterpieces

National Program Advisors

The program advisors provided ongoing input throughout the development of Prentice Hall Literature: Timeless Voices, Timeless Themes. *Their valuable insights ensure that the perspectives of teachers throughout the country are represented within this literature series.*

Diane Cappillo
Language Arts Department Chair
Barbara Goleman Senior High
  School
Miami, Florida

Anita Clay
English Instructor
Gateway Institute of Technology
St. Louis, Missouri

Nancy M. Fahner
Language Arts Instructor
Charlotte High School
Charlotte, Michigan

Terri Fields
Language Arts and Communication
  Arts Teacher, Author
Sunnyslope High School
Phoenix, Arizona

V. Pauline Hodges
Teacher and Educational Consultant
Forgan High School
Forgan, Oklahoma

Jennifer Huntress
Secondary Language Arts Coordinator
Putnam City Schools
Oklahoma City, Oklahoma

Angelique McMath Jordan
English Teacher
Dunwoody High School
Dunwoody, Georgia

Nancy L. Monroe
English and Speed Reading Teacher
Bolton High School
Alexandria, Louisiana

Rosemary A. Naab
English Chairperson
Ryan High School
Archdiocese of Philadelphia
Philadelphia, Pennsylvania

Ann Okamura
English Teacher
Laguna Creek High School
Elk Grove, California

Jonathan L. Schatz
English Teacher/Team Leader
Tappan Zee High School
Orangeburg, New York

John Scott
English Teacher
Hampton High School
Hampton, Virginia

Ken Spurlock
Assistant Principal
Boone County High School
Florence, Kentucky

Multicultural Review Board

Contributing Writers

Amy K. Duer
Former English Teacher, Expert on
  Special Needs
Palm Beach Lakes High School
West Palm Beach, Florida

Carroll Moulton
Former English Teacher
Stoughton High School
Stoughton, Massachusetts

Emily Hutchinson
Former English Teacher
Los Angeles Unified School District
Los Angeles, California

Lois Markham
Former English Teacher
Fort Lee High School
Fort Lee, New Jersey

Eileen Oshinsky
Former ESL Teacher
New York City Public Schools
Brooklyn, New York

Joan Hefele
Research Writing Instructor
College of Mount Saint Vincent
Riverdale, New York

Robert McIlwaine
Instructor of Literature
Duke University
Durham, North Carolina

Academic Reviewers

Thomas J. Heffernan
Professor, Department of English
Adjunct Professor of
  Religious Studies
University of Tennessee at Knoxville
Knoxville, Tennessee

Susan Navarette
Professor, Department of English
University of North Carolina
Chapel Hill, North Carolina

Patrick Brantlinger
Professor, Department of English
Indiana University
Bloomington, Indiana

Lee T. Hamilton
Professor, Department of English
The University of Texas—
  Pan American
Edinburg, Texas

Introductory Overview of British Literature

From Legend to History:
The Old English and Medieval Periods (449–1485)

Celebrating Humanity:
The English Renaissance Period (1485–1625)

PART 3   FOCUS ON LITERARY FORMS: DRAMA

Unit

3

A Turbulent Time:
The Seventeenth and Eighteenth Centuries (1625–1798)

Unit 3

PART 4   FOCUS ON LITERARY FORMS: THE ESSAY

Rebels and Dreamers:
The Romantic Period (1798–1832)

Unit 4

PART 3   THE STORY OF BRITAIN: THE REACTION TO SOCIETY'S ILLS

Progress and Decline:
The Victorian Period (1833–1901)

Unit 5

A Time of Rapid Change:
The Modern and Postmodern Periods (1901–Present)

Unit 6

PART 2 THE STORY OF BRITAIN: CONFLICTS ABROAD AND AT HOME

PART 3   FOCUS ON LITERARY FORMS:
           THE SHORT STORY

Joseph Conrad   **The Lagoon** . . . . Short Story 1034

James Joyce   **Araby** . . . . Short Story 1044

Virginia Woolf   **The Lady in the Looking Glass: A Reflection** . . . Short Story 1054

Muriel Spark   **The First Year of My Life** . . . . Short Story 1058

D. H. Lawrence   **The Rocking-Horse Winner** . . . . Short Story 1068

Graham Greene   **A Shocking Accident** . . . . Short Story 1078

                      Connections to World Literature

Jorge Luis Borges   **The Book of Sand** . . . . Short Story 1085

                     Writing Process Workshop: Short Story 1089
                     Applying Language Skills: Writing Dialogue;
                     Using Active Voice 1090, 1091

                     Student Success Workshop:
                     Research Skills: Organizing Information Gathered Through Research 1092

PART 4   FROM THE NATIONAL TO THE GLOBAL

Additional Readings and Resources

ANALYZING REAL-WORLD TEXTS

Introductory Overview of British Literature

Connecting Literature to the Historical Context

Two Funerals

To get the whole of British literature in your mind, you might begin with two funerals. These ceremonies occur 1,500 years apart, but each honors a person of great importance. Between these two solemn public events—one real and one possibly fictional—the story of British literature unfolds. Even before you study that literature in detail, you can "read" its effects in descriptions of these two ceremonies.

One occurred on Saturday, September 6, 1997. It was the funeral of Diana, Princess of Wales. You yourself might have been among the estimated 2.5 billion people worldwide to watch the services for Diana, killed in a tragic auto accident.

The other funeral, from the beginnings of British history and literature, honored Beowulf. He was the king of a Germanic tribe living in southern Sweden, probably during the early sixth century A.D. His death came, after a glorious lifetime of killing enemies and monsters, in a desperate battle with a dragon. Beowulf's funeral was not broadcast round the world on television. It did not even take place in Britain. However, it was described at the end of the first great storytelling poem in British literature, named *Beowulf* after its legendary hero.

The first listeners to this poem—for it was sung or chanted—were British Christians living in the eighth century A.D. They were hearing what their non-Christian ancestors, or fictional characters like them, did some 200 years earlier. However, they were probably stirred by the hero's death just as more than two billion viewers were stirred by the funeral of Princess Diana.

Epic Poem and News Story The similarities and differences between these two funerals reveal much about the history of Britain and its literature.

from **Beowulf**

Translated by Seamus Heaney
In memory of George Mackay Brown

The Geat people built a pyre for Beowulf,
stacked it four-square from the ground up,
and hung helmets on it, as he had instructed,
surrounding it with war-shields and shining mail.
5 Then his warriors laid him in the middle of it,
mourning a lord who had been far-famed and
  beloved.
On a height they kindled the biggest ever
funeral fire; fumes of woodsmoke
billowed darkly up, the blaze roared
10 and drowned out their weeping, wind died down
and flames wrought havoc in the hot bone-house,
burning it to the core. They were disconsolate
and wailed aloud for their lord's decease.
A Geat woman too sang out in grief;
15 with hair bound up, she unburdened herself
of her sorrows, telling again and again
of the dread that possessed her: her people
  invaded,
enemies on the rampage, bodies in piles,
slavery and abasement. Heaven swallowed the
  smoke.
20 Then the Geat people began to construct
a mound on a headland, high and imposing,
a marker that sailors could see from far away,
and in ten days they had done the work.
It was their hero's monument; what remained
  from the fire
25 they bestowed inside it, behind a wall
as worthy of him as their workmanship could
  make it.
And they buried torques in the barrow, and jewels
and a trove of such things as trespassing men
had once dared to drag from the hoard.
30 They let the ground keep that ancestral treasure,
gold under gravel, gone to earth,
as useless to men as it ever was.
Then twelve warriors rode around the tomb,
chieftains' sons, champions in battle,
35 all of them distraught, chanting in dirges,
mourning his loss as a man and a king.
They extolled his heroic nature and exploits
and gave thanks for his greatness; which was the
  proper thing
for a man should praise a lord who is dear
40 and cherish his memory when that moment comes
when he has to be conveyed from his bodily home.

from "A Farewell to the 'People's Princess'"

by Dan Balz
(The Washington Post)

LONDON, Sept. 6—In precedent-shattering ceremonies that were at once sorrowful and uplifting, Diana, Princess of Wales, was remembered today as a woman of "natural nobility" whose life of compassion and style transcended sometimes abusive press coverage and even the royal family itself. Later she was laid to rest on her family's estate, concluding one of the most extraordinary weeks in the modern history of Britain.

Diana's flag-draped coffin, resplendent in the summer sun and topped with three wreaths—one carrying the simple notation "Mummy"—was carried this morning from the gates of Kensington Palace through the streets of central London in a silent, solemn 105-minute procession to the doors of Westminster Abbey, the historic burial place of British monarchs.

The ceremonies brought out one of the largest crowds in London since the end of World War II. More than a million people filled the streets, squares and parks to watch the procession and the funeral, which was beamed onto two gigantic screens in Hyde Park.

Just past its midpoint, the cortege was joined by Diana's two sons, Prince William and Prince Harry, along with their father, Prince Charles, Diana's former husband and heir to the British throne; their grandfather, the Duke of Edinburgh; and their uncle and Diana's brother, the Earl Spencer. With heads bowed, they accompanied the coffin to the abbey.

There Spencer delivered a barbed and biting tribute to the late princess, who died in an automobile accident in Paris last Sunday. Spencer castigated the media and warned the royal family that Diana's family will make sure her two sons continue to be raised with the openness and spirit she wanted.

Beowulf

- of the nobility; a king
- honored by public ceremonies
- a man known for his honor, bravery, and loyalty in a warrior society that valued these qualities
- his funeral and memorial emphasize extraordinary achievements of which very few can boast
- his fame was spread by word of mouth and by poets who sang of his deeds

Princess Diana

- of the nobility; a princess
- honored by public ceremonies
- a woman known for her honesty about her feelings and her devotion to charities
- her funeral emphasizes "natural nobility," qualities of caring that we can all share
- her fame was spread by the press, radio, and television

A Story Told in Literature This comparison shows that in 1,500 years, warring male-centered tribes that valued physical courage and loyalty became a nation of male and female citizens who valued concern for all those in need and the honest expression of feelings as much as physical courage. British literature both recorded and influenced this dramatic change. Christian values, the Renaissance, Romanticism, Modernism—these beliefs and literary movements all helped to shape the literature of Britain, as the following pages will reveal. In turn, this literature influenced the men and women who heard and read it.

Furthermore, English is now a worldwide language, and British literature is therefore the basis for work being produced in America, Australia, Canada, the Caribbean, India, Ireland, Jamaica, Nigeria, and South Africa. Among the living Nobel laureates who owe a debt to British literature are Saul Bellow and Toni Morrison from America, Seamus Heaney from Ireland, Derek Walcott from St. Lucia in the Caribbean, Wole Soyinka from Nigeria, and Nadine Gordimer from South Africa. In coming years, these writers and others like them will continue to study works in the British tradition as they create a world literature in English.

▲ Critical Viewing This shoulder clasp, made of gold, garnet, and glass, comes from the Sutton Hoo estate in Suffolk, England, the site of a seventh-century grave or commemorative tomb for an Anglo-Saxon king. It is comparable to items buried with Beowulf. Why do you think Anglo-Saxons buried such items with their royal dead? [Infer]

The Old English Period
and the Medieval Period:

From Legend to History (A.D. 449 to 1485)

Connecting Literature to the Historical Context

Change in Society

Geoffrey Chaucer (1343–1400), the greatest English poet of the Middle Ages, is popularly regarded as "the father of English poetry." In Chaucer's day, a feudal society was becoming a nation. For example, what must have seemed like an unending war with France, the Hundred Years' War (1337–1453), began as a feudal struggle between competing dynasties but ended as something quite different. In 1337, Edward III of England declared war on Philip VI of France. Edward wanted to claim the French throne and to prevent the French king from seizing English holdings in France. At first, the war was rather like a dispute between noble cousins. English rulers had come from France, and they owned so much French land that no one could tell what was English and what was French.

By the time the Hundred Years' War ended, the English had won many victories but had lost nearly all of their French possessions. England and France were starting to look like they do on today's maps. As part of this process, the population of each country had been drawn into a national struggle, not just an aristocratic quarrel.

The Yeoman and the Longbow In England, independent farmers, called yeomen, took up the struggle. Using the new longbow, these yeomen bested the mounted knight, symbol of the feudal order. The longbow, which probably originated in Wales, was about 6 feet tall and required a force of about 100 pounds to draw it. It could send arrows about 200 yards, the length of two modern football fields. Infantrymen with longbows changed the face of medieval warfare, practicing together as professionals even during intervals of peace. Aristocratic warriors were being replaced by professional soldiers.

The longbow was especially effective for the English at the Battle of Agincourt (1415), one of the greatest English victories in the Hundred Years' War. On a thickly wooded battlefield in northern France, English archers used the longbow to repel attacks by mounted French knights. Then the highly maneuverable archers used their swords and axes to attack the flanks of the main French force. The English sustained hardly any casualties, but the French suffered the loss of about 1,500 knights and about 4,500 other soldiers.

The Use of English National feeling stirred by the wars also promoted the use of the English language. It sounds surprising, but English had not been the country's official language since the Norman invasion. The Normans were descendants of Vikings (Normans = North Men) who had successfully invaded England in 1066 and then ruled the country. Under the Normans, French had been the language of the ruling classes, used for law and politics, while Latin remained the language of the church and of learning. English was still widely used by commoners, even though it had lost its official status. However, English victories on the battlefield during the Hundred Years' War influenced the field of education. A few years after the English victory at Crécy, France (1346), grammar-school teachers began to translate sentences from Latin into English, not into French. In effect, arrows launched from victorious English longbows had carried all the way to the classrooms! A little more than a decade later, English replaced French in courts of law. Then it was introduced into the proceedings of Parliament in the Statute of Pleading (1361).

Parliament itself, the basis of England's democratic government, gained new powers as a result of the wars with France. Dependent on Parliament for raising war money, English kings had to give the legislative body powers and privileges in return.

More Deadly Than the Longbow

Far more deadly than the longbow was the flea. In a relatively short period in the middle of the fourteenth century, this creature helped to spread the Black Death, a particular type of the disease known as the plague. Before this epidemic struck England in 1348, the country's population was close to 3.2 million. By the early 1400's, after the ravages of the plague, the population was closer to 1.7 million!

To bring home the dramatic effects of this disaster, picture what would happen if the United States lost half its population in just a few decades. In medieval England, the plague killed rich and poor alike. However, it decisively changed the nature of work for poorer people—servants and laborers. Those who survived could ask for and get higher wages. However, attempts by landlords to freeze wages, together with taxes levied on poor laborers, helped provoke the Peasants' Revolt of 1381.

A Fourteen-Year-Old King

Led by Wat Tyler and Jack Straw, a ragtag "army" of peasants actually reached the capital city of London. There, after a spate of riots, looting, and murder, they were stopped by a fourteen-year-old. That young man was the King of England, Richard II, who appeared before the discontented peasants and promised to reform the feudal system. Although the rioters believed him and dispersed, Richard II did not keep his word.

Whatever the king did or did not do, the feudal system was dying and being replaced by an early version of a capitalist system based on trade, industry, and the exchange of money. The need for money to finance the Hundred Years' War and the agricultural downturn resulting from the Black Death caused the government to take

from "The Parson's Prologue," The Canterbury Tales
by Geoffrey Chaucer

Translation by Nevill Coghill	Original Middle English
"But trust me truly, I'm a southern man,	"But trusteth wel, I am a Southren man,
I can't romance with rum-ram-ruf by letter,	I kan nat geeste 'rum, ram, ruf,' by lettre,
And rhyme, God knows, I hold but little better;	Ne, God woot, rym holde I but litel bettre;
I won't embellish things with tricks like those	And therfore, if yow list—I wol nat glose—
5 If you'll excuse me, but I'll speak in prose,	I wol yow telle a myrie tale in prose
A happy thing, to knit and make an end	To knytte up al this feeste, and make an ende.
Of all our feast. Jesu in mercy send	And Jhesu, for his grace, wit me sende
Me wit to guide your way one further stage	To shewe yow the wey, in this viage,
Upon that perfect, glorious pilgrimage	Of thilke parfit glorious pilgrymage
10 Called the celestial, to Jerusalem.	That highte Jerusalem celestial.
These are my thoughts; if you approve of them	And if ye vouche sauf, anon I shal
I'll start my tale at once, so tell me pat	Bigynne upon my tale, for which I preye
If you agree. I can't say more than that. . . ."	Telle youre avys, I kan no bettre seye. . . ."

a more active role in the economy. It taxed the export of wool to raise funds. It also took measures to support the country's textile industry, which manufactured cloth from wool. That industry began to operate in a more modern way, with different stages of production handled by different contractors. A rising class of merchants and manufacturers was thriving in the big cities.

Poet and Merchant's Son

Poet Geoffrey Chaucer was born into the merchant class that was adding to the wealth of London and the nation. Chaucer's father was a wine merchant, and young Geoffrey grew up amid the bustle of a successful international business. As a young teenager, he entered an aristocratic household as a servant. This apprenticeship led to a career in which he served the nobility as a capable administrator. Chaucer's perch in society, just below the aristocracy, gave him a perfect vantage point for observing all kinds of people.

Eye and Ear for Character

Nowhere does Chaucer display his keen powers of observation better than in *The Canterbury Tales* (see p. A4). This work, planned as an exchange of tales among pilgrims journeying to the shrine of martyr Thomas à Beckett at Canterbury, gave Chaucer the opportunity to show a cross section of medieval society. In doing so, he moved literature beyond the themes of courtly love and knightly adventure that dominated so many medieval tales called romances. His compassionate humor and lively realism make him one of the first modern writers.

A Variety of Tales

Although Chaucer completed only 20 of the 120 tales promised in the Prologue to *The Canterbury Tales*, these 20 allow for a wide variety. They include the tale of chivalry told by the Knight, the *fabliaux* (French for "short stories") told by the Miller and Reeve, the animal fable told by the Nun's Priest, and the story based on a fairy tale that is told by the Merchant. The highly moral Parson, when asked to contribute a tale, declines

Frontispiece from Chaucer's Troilus—Chaucer reading "Troilus and Cressida" to the court, The Master and Fellows of Corpus Christi College, Cambridge

▲ **Critical Viewing** This illustration at the beginning of an early edition of Chaucer's *Troilus and Cressida* shows Chaucer reading this tale in verse to the court. What does the scene indicate about Chaucer's position at court? Why? [Interpret]

to tell an "idle story" like those of the other pilgrims. In the Prologue to his tale, quoted on p. A4, he promises a "happy thing" but actually delivers a treatise on the seven deadly sins.

This passage shows how Chaucer introduces a greater dimension of realism by having his fictional storytellers describe their tales and react to previous ones. The Parson is a simple, good parish priest living in poverty "Yet . . . rich in holy thought and work." It is therefore natural that he would decline to tell a story of love or chivalry, as other pilgrims have done. "I can't romance with rum-ram-ruf by letter, / And rhyme, God knows, I hold but little better" (lines 2–3), he states rather flatly. Chaucer probably enjoyed the irony of having this prosy character reject rhyme in rhyme.

The "rum-ram-ruf" is a reference to the alliteration used by such well-known romances of the time as *Sir Gawain and the Green Knight*. The Parson's impatient little phrase both imitates this alliteration, with nonsensical *r* sounds, and dismisses it at the same time.

Chaucer himself was a teller of tales in rhyme and, of course, the master storyteller behind all the tales told by the pilgrims, including the romances. However, notice the way Chaucer makes himself disappear in this passage, allowing the character to have his say. Chaucer's ability to lose himself in the life of his characters is what makes him such a great writer. He can even take sides against himself!

The Final Tale   This was to be the final tale on the outward journey toward Canterbury. Even though Chaucer had probably planned additional tales for the way back, he may have realized that his masterwork and his writing career were reaching a conclusion. What better way to end *The Canterbury Tales*, therefore, than with a prose sermon on sin—for this is the "tale" that the Parson will tell. The journey of the pilgrims to the holy site of Canterbury begins to merge with the spiritual journey that every good person must make: "that perfect, glorious pilgrimage / Called the celestial, to Jerusalem" (lines 9–10). Chaucer, the mischievous storyteller, was a devout Christian, too. In this sense, the Parson is also one of his true voices.

Connecting Art to the Historical Context

King Arthur and His Knights at the Round Table, colored woodcut, 1488

King Arthur: From History to Legend

Among the other important works to be born during the medieval period were the legends of King Arthur. The actual King Arthur appears in historical accounts as early as the sixth century; however, Arthur gained increasing popularity as a mythical figure during the twelfth century. The people of England were in need of a "hero-king," and the tales of good, brave, and just Arthur fueled the national spirit. By the fifteenth century, Arthur and his "Knights of the Round Table" had become the center of a body of romantic literature and the subjects of many tales of chivalry and works of art, like this woodcut from 1488.

Analyze (a) What details in the woodcut show that Arthur is a well-liked king?
(b) What political and social conditions contributed to the people's need for a hero during the Medieval period?

The English Renaissance:

Celebrating Humanity (1485 to 1625)

The Rise of the Drama in a Dramatic Age

In medieval times, books were not widely available and most people were illiterate. They learned about the Christian religion by participating in the regular drama of church services. In addition, at festivals like Whitsuntide or Corpus Christi, they could see enactments of Christianity's most important events—from the loss of the Garden of Eden all the way through the life of Christ. These dramas were called mystery plays because they revealed religious mysteries. A mystery cycle might include scores of individual plays, giving viewers the sense of witnessing the whole of time unfolding before them.

These mysteries were performed by medieval guilds, close-knit organizations of those who worked in the same trade. Each guild might specialize in performing a particular play in the mystery cycle, possibly one that related to their trade. Carpenters, for example, might perform the building of Noah's ark. For a stage, guild members often used a wagon. They would give the same performance repeatedly in different sections of a town, rolling the wagon on when they finished. As an alternative, they could give a single performance on a stage built in the center of a town.

In an era when life was hard and entertainment sparse, these performances gave people a great deal of pleasure. This pleasure was heightened by the humor and down-to-earth dialogue of these dramas. For example, townspeople might see their local blacksmith hamming it up in a portrayal of the biblical strongman Samson.

These mystery plays gradually died out. However, it would have been theoretically possible for William Shakespeare, England's greatest poet and playwright, born in 1564, to have seen the last performance of the mystery cycle at the town of Chester in 1575.

Morality Plays Another kind of medieval drama, also based in religion, was the morality play. Instead of focusing on the whole span of time, like the mysteries, the morality play dramatized the story of an individual Christian's life, with its choices and temptations. Using allegory, it represented as characters such qualities as Beauty, Strength, and Knowledge. Then, in the play's action, it showed the roles that these qualities played in a Christian's journey to salvation. Perhaps the most famous of these plays is *Everyman*, whose title suggests the universal lessons it sought to teach.

Briefer morality plays, called interludes, were also popular in the early Renaissance. They were a favorite pastime of Thomas More, a Renaissance scholar and advisor to King Henry VIII, who not only wrote interludes but acted in them.

Classical Roots More was strongly influenced by humanism, the Renaissance movement that took a renewed interest in ancient Greek and Latin authors. Dramas by these authors were also an important influence on Elizabethan playwriting, together with the native English tradition of mystery and morality plays. Sometimes schoolmasters would write plays to help students learn about ancient Roman comedies. Playwrights also looked to ancient tragedies as models, especially to the work of the Roman dramatist Seneca. The Senecan qualities they imitated were his lofty style, his sense of the conflict between the demands of public and private life, and his tendency to expose unflinching heroes to treachery and bloody betrayal. As far as Elizabethan audiences were concerned, the bloodier the better.

Thomas Kyd took advantage of the Senecan fashion with his popular play *The Spanish Tragedy*. Featuring a character driven to madness by his son's murder, it takes place in a dangerous and corrupt Renaissance palace. This tragedy helped establish a tradition for plays dealing with the theme of revenge. Shakespeare's *Hamlet*, with its own corrupt court and hero bent on revenge, is a much more sophisticated treatment of the theme.

Vagabonds and Actors Despite the religious and classical roots of drama, plays and players had a somewhat unsavory reputation. Actors were lumped together with vagabonds, rapscallions, and rebels. (Acting was a male profession, with boys playing female parts.) Increased enclosure of open grazing lands and other changes were driving peasants from the countryside, creating a class of wanderers. Elizabeth I was concerned that these men, with no place in society, could be molded into a rebellious mob. Actors, who traveled from town to town or innyard to innyard putting on plays, seemed to be part of this same dangerous group. That's why acting companies often tried to gain the protection of a nobleman, whose livery or uniform they could wear. Such sponsorship would make them legitimate servants rather than suspicious characters.

Shakespeare's company, for instance, showed that it had the right sponsorship by calling itself the Lord Chamberlain's Men. Even so, the company was aware of the London city government's dislike of the acting profession. In the late 1590's, therefore, the company built a new theater, called the Globe, on the south bank of the Thames River. This location put them out of reach of the London city government, which might not approve of their performances, but within reach of a London audience. It also placed them in the middle of a neighborhood known for such disreputable spectacles as bull- and bear-baiting. The latter "sport," which seems cruel to us, involved a battle between a tied-up bear and dogs.

Shakespeare's Globe has recently been restored, and attending a play there reveals some important aspects of Elizabethan theater. The tourists who now watch the performance may be better behaved than the spectators who paid a minimum admission to watch the play while milling around the stage that

◀ **Critical Viewing** This photograph shows the interior of the recently restored Globe theater in London. Where are the balconies from which nobles viewed the play, the place where spectators who paid a minimum admission could stand, and the portion of the stage that projected outward into the standing crowd? **[Analyze]**

projected into their midst. These spectators were probably the very image of the
mob that Elizabethan rulers feared. The
tourists are probably even better behaved
than the nobles who watched from the
surrounding balconies. However, the
closeness of players and audience, with
thousands jammed into the small wooden
circle of the theater, is evident even today.
It's clear that if a play disappointed them,
the Elizabethan audience would react
swiftly. In fact, audiences were known to
stop a play and demand to see one they
preferred that had been produced the
week before!

Hard-Working Words Plays were
performed in the middle of the afternoon,
outdoors, and with no special lighting
effects. There were theatrical devices, such
as trapdoors leading down into the "lower

regions" and up into the "heavens." Also,
the columns and facades on stage might
be richly decorated. However, the words
themselves had to do most of the work.
Shakespeare's words packed the theater
and satisfied the patrons, day after day,
week after week, year after year.

There is a missing connection, however,
between the stilted language of Kyd and
the vivid words of Shakespeare. That connection is the explosive Christopher Marlowe, bad boy and brilliant poet. Marlowe
led a brief and troubled life. A shoemaker's
son, he attended Cambridge University on
a religious scholarship. His extracurricular activities probably included service
for the queen as a spy against Catholic
plotters, and he died in a fight before he
was thirty. However, he also found time
to change the English theater forever.
Marlowe fashioned unrhymed iambic

Connecting Art to the Historical Context

Royals of the English Renaissance

The period known as the English Renaissance spanned the rule of several monarchs
and saw the growth of the arts, especially
drama. Henry VIII reigned as King of England from 1509 to 1547. While Henry was
king, Sir Thomas More published *Utopia*
and the poet Thomas Wyatt introduced the
sonnet to England. However, it was Henry's
daughter Elizabeth, crowned in 1558, whose
reign saw a full flourishing of the arts. Her
name would become forever associated
with the growth of drama and other literature—the period became known as the
Elizabethan Age.

Make an Inference What details of this
painting by Hans Holbein indicate that
Henry VIII valued art?

Henry VIII, Hans Holbein

pentameter (blank verse) into a powerful means for portraying character on stage.

However, William Shakespeare (see p. 268) is the playwright who most fully exploited the resources of Elizabethan theater. He wrote 38 plays (counting *The Two Noble Kinsmen,* which he appears to have coauthored), including:

- Dramas about English history and its conflicts
- Comedies that explore love, imagination, and transformation
- Tragedies that depict the downfall of highly placed men and women
- Romances that deal with the theme of reconciliation

The excerpts on page A11 come from the prologue to a history play, *King Henry the Fifth,* and from one of the famous late romances, *The Tempest.* They show the playwright reflecting on his own theatrical tradition.

King Henry V, the subject of Shakespeare's history play, lived in the early fifteenth century, about two hundred years before the play was produced (ca. 1600). However, Shakespeare's history plays are not just entertaining versions of very old events. These plays reflect the concerns and conflicts of Shakespeare's own time. The Tudors, whose dynasty had begun with the reign of Henry VII in 1485, thought of themselves as bringing a new order and stability to England. They viewed Henry V as a hero whose short-lived but successful reign was a forerunner of the more sustained Tudor success.

Patriotism
Even as late as 1600, Henry V's victories in France would have sounded a patriotic note, for the English had still not relinquished their claims to French land. Moreover, Henry's great victory at Agincourt (1415) would have recalled Elizabeth I's victory over the Spanish armada in 1588. In fact, the war with Spain was still dragging on, so that Henry V was relevant to current events. The play would also serve a patriotic purpose more than 300 years later, when Sir Laurence Olivier adapted it to film during World War II.

The speech from *Henry V* is spoken by an actor as part of a prologue, an introduction to the play. Shakespeare's use of a prologue reflects the influence of both classical drama and the mystery and morality plays. All these types of drama used prologues to tell the audience certain facts they should know before the play begins. Here, the prologue informs the audience that they will see an account of Henry V and his famous victory at Agincourt. However, they would have known that from the play's title, and the prologue seems designed less to inform than to apologize for the deficiencies of the Elizabethan theater. In its little "wooden O," it cannot show even the "casques" (helmets) of the men who fought in France. To make up for these deficiencies, the audience must use its "imaginary forces." In other words, the prologue is rallying the audience's support just as Henry V, in a later speech, will rally the support of his few but gallant soldiers on the battlefield.

Magnificent Words
Yet even in this apology, you can hear Shakespeare showing off his language, the magnificent words that will re-create history in this little theater. Lines 1–8, in denying the presence of the real thing, still manage to summon it into being with verve and energy. These lines take off like a glorious rocket: "O for a Muse of fire that would ascend / The brightest heaven of invention. . . ."

By contrast, the speech from *The Tempest* reads like a sweet lullaby, as it puts to sleep not only the play that the speaker has staged but the world itself. *The Tempest,* which may have been Shakespeare's last play, is often regarded as his farewell to the theater. This speech is spoken by the magician Prospero, sometimes identified with Shakespeare. After being deposed from power, Prospero and his daughter, Miranda, found refuge on the magical island that is the setting for the play. When his former enemies, among others, are shipwrecked on the island, he has the opportunity to take his bloodless revenge. Here, he has just staged an elaborate play-within-a-play, and then quickly ended it in recalling what he still must do to thwart his enemies.

In referring to the scenery of the vision he has created, he could be talking about the scenery of a play or about the features of a world: "The cloud-capp'd towers, the gorgeous palaces, / The solemn temples, the great globe itself . . ." (lines 6–7). This double meaning is supported by his pun on the word *globe*, which could refer to the globe of the Earth or to the Globe theater where so many of Shakespeare's plays were staged.

In good Elizabethan fashion, he equates life with theater, at the same time suggesting the illusory quality of life. When its "revels . . . are ended," the scenery of reality will "dissolve" as we embark on our "sleep" of death. It's almost as if life itself were a dream. However, there is still a further dimension. Shakespeare's language is the source of true reality in the plays, more so than any painted facades or costumes. Now this language and its image-making power are coming to an end. Just as words had power to summon a whole world, they are here dismissing and dissolving it.

from King Henry the Fifth, Prologue

by William Shakespeare

O for a Muse of fire, that would ascend
The brightest heaven of invention,
A kingdom for a stage, princes to act,
And monarchs to behold the swelling scene!
5 Then should the warlike Harry, like himself,
Assume the port of Mars, and at his heels
(Leash'd in, like hounds) should famine,
    sword, and fire
Crouch for employment. But pardon,
    gentles all,
The flat, unraised spirits that hath dar'd
10 On this unworthy scaffold to bring forth
So great an object. Can this cockpit hold
The vasty fields of France? Or may we cram
Within this wooden O the very casques
That did affright the air at Agincourt?
15 O, pardon! since a crooked figure may
Attest in little place a million,
And let us, ciphers to this great accompt,
On your imaginary forces work.
Suppose within the girdle of these walls
20 Are now confin'd two mighty monarchies,
Whose high upreared and abutting fronts
The perilous narrow ocean parts asunder.
Piece out our imperfection with your thoughts. . . .

from The Tempest, Act IV, Scene 1

by William Shakespeare

. . . Be cheerful, sir.
Our revels now are ended. These our actors,
As I foretold you, were all spirits and
Are melted into air, into thin air;
5 And, like the baseless fabric of this vision,
The cloud-capp'd towers, the gorgeous
    palaces,
The solemn temples, the great globe itself,
Yea, all which it inherit, shall dissolve,
And, like this insubstantial pageant faded,
10 Leave not a rack behind. We are such stuff
As dreams are made on, and our little life
Is rounded with a sleep. . . .

The Seventeenth and Eighteenth Centuries:

A Turbulent Time (1625–1798)

Connecting Literature to the Historical Context

John Milton, the English Civil War, and *Paradise Lost*

Charles I acted his kingly role with a winning dignity when, in January 1649, Parliament and the army had him beheaded. The problem is that this occasion is the only time when he seemed to understand his role. On taking power in 1625, he had little idea that the job description of an English king had changed since the era of the Tudors. New money and the rise of the merchant class were creating new centers of power in the cities, especially London. In religion, the need for authority was as great as ever, but differences among Catholics, Anglicans, and Puritans about the source of that authority created bitter disputes. Catholics looked for leadership to the pope, head of the Roman Catholic Church. Anglicans were members of the Church of England, the national church that King Henry VIII had established in defiance of the Pope. Puritans were those who wanted to purify and reform the Church of England.

Parliament, propelled by social change and conflict, was questioning more and more the power and prerogatives of the king. An up-to-date, early-seventeenth-century king would have found ways to placate Parliament and calm religious disputes. Yet Charles, his crowned head in the clouds, went on trying to be an old-fashioned absolute monarch.

Civil War Charles's mismanagement and his increasingly vicious conflicts with Parliament eventually resulted in something that few had foreseen and many did not really want: the execution of a king. Leading to that revolutionary event was an armed struggle—from 1642 to 1646 and again in 1648—between supporters of the king, called Royalists or Cavaliers, and supporters of Parliament, called Roundheads or Puritans. The Cavaliers, who tended to come from the north of England, represented upper-class supporters of the king and the Anglican establishment. Puritans, who came from the south and east, included merchants, independent farmers, and religious dissenters who supported the rights of Parliament.

Oliver Cromwell, who emerged from this conflict as the leader of the Puritan army, ruled England from 1649 to 1658. Although he refused the title of king, he was kingly in nature. He was also a successful military man and a deeply religious Puritan.

During the nearly ten years of his rule, he maintained relative peace at home and enhanced English power abroad. Yet try as he might, he could not create new institutions to replace the king-and-Parliament machinery that had broken down. It is not surprising, therefore, that the revolution died with him in 1658. After two years of struggle, including an unsuccessful bid for power by Cromwell's son Richard, Parliament summoned to power the exiled King Charles II.

The Puritans had wanted a government of "saints," but apparently there were many "sinners" in the cheering crowds

The Battle of Preston and Walton, August 17th, 1648, Harris Museum and Art Gallery, Preston, Lancashire, UK

▲ **Critical Viewing** This painting by Charles Cattermole is entitled *The Battle of Preston and Walton, August 17th, 1648.* In the battle, which took place August 17–25, 1648, 9,000 troops led by Oliver Cromwell defeated 24,000 troops led by Royalist James Hamilton. In what part of the painting do the two sides seem to be directly engaged? Explain. [Infer]

that welcomed the Stuart king back to London. However, the period of the Interregnum, the time between kings when Cromwell ruled, had brought important changes. For one thing, it signaled a shift in the balance of power between king and Parliament. No matter how loudly the people welcomed their new ruler, a king had been beheaded, and nothing would ever be the same again.

John Milton One man who didn't lift his voice to celebrate royalty restored was John Milton. He had not fought for Cromwell on the battlefields of Marston Moor and Naseby, but he had been a scholar-warrior in the pamphlet wars. Scholars all over Europe had furiously debated the rights and wrongs of regicide, the execution of a king. Milton, who was a Cambridge-trained scholar and proven pamphleteer, had been given the job of defending the Commonwealth's decision

to execute King Charles. Sadly, as a result of this new labor, his eyestrain worsened and he began to go blind.

The young John Milton had not planned to be a pamphleteer. He had prepared himself to be a great poet, training for this role just as a young person today might train to be a great athlete. At Cambridge University, which he attended from 1625 to 1632, he mastered Greek, Latin, and Hebrew, as well as modern languages. Then he gave himself a competitive advantage by traveling in Europe, as Chaucer had done many years before.

For a Christian humanist like Milton, the training program for a great poet included "sprints" with lyric poems. These would be good warm-ups for the "long-distance run" of the most ambitious poetic form, the epic.

However, Milton was overtaken by the events leading up to the Civil War. He put aside his poetic ambitions to take part in the controversies of the day. This decision was not totally surprising for someone with Milton's beliefs. Renaissance humanists, like Thomas More, believed that scholars should participate in public affairs.

Dangers In 1660, however, Milton might not have regarded the previous twenty years with enthusiasm. Disputes among various factions on the Puritan side, together with the restoration of Charles II, put an end to his political hopes. For a time, the Restoration even seemed to hold personal danger for the man who had defended the murder of kings. The disillusioned poet had not only gone blind from his services to the Commonwealth, but he was also wounded in spirit.

Then Milton did something that only very great writers can do. He did not dismiss or avoid the problems that he and his nation faced. Instead, he used those problems to create a powerful work of art. In this work, an epic, he would explain the events of the past twenty years in the largest possible context, the story of how our ancestors, Adam and Eve, lost their place in paradise. Telling this story, in *Paradise Lost*, would enable him to explain and justify God's plan for humans and the importance of human choice in this plan.

Milton had to draw upon his vast and many-sided learning to achieve success. From classical epics—particularly Virgil's *Aeneid*, the story of Rome's founding—he took elements like these:

- Invocations, or calls to heavenly powers for help in writing his poem
- The technique of starting in the middle of events (*in medias res*), and then telling what happened earlier
- Scenes of great battles

To these classical elements, he added Christian beliefs and a Christian narrative. Moreover, he composed his poem after he had gone blind, dictating it orally to a daughter who acted as his secretary.

from Paradise Lost, Book 3 by John Milton

Hail, holy Light, offspring of Heaven first-born,
Or of the Eternal coeternal° beam   °Eternal, as God is.
May I express thee unblamed? since God is light,
And never but in unapproachèd light
5   Dwelt from eternity, dwelt then in thee,
Bright effluence of bright essence increate.°   °Eternal because uncreated.
Or hear'st thou rather° pure ethereal stream,   °Would you rather be called.
Whose fountain who shall tell? Before the sun,
Before the Heavens, thou wert, and at the voice
10   Of God, as with a mantle didst invest°   °Clothe; cover.
The rising world of waters dark and deep,
Won from the void and formless infinite.
Thee I revisit now with bolder wing,
Escaped the Stygian pool,° though long detained   °The region of Hell.
15   In that obscure sojourn, while in my flight
Through utter and through middle darkness° borne   °Through Hell and Chaos.
With other notes than to the Orphean lyre°   °Orpheus had visited the
I sung of Chaos and eternal Night,   underworld.
Taught by the Heavenly Muse° to venture down   °Urania.
20   The dark descent, and up to reascend,
Though hard and rare. Thee I revisit safe,
And feel thy sovran° vital lamp; but thou   °Sovereign—supreme; greatest.
Revisit'st not these eyes, that roll in vain
To find thy piercing ray, and find no dawn;
25   So thick a drop serene hath quenched their orbs,
Or dim suffusion° veiled. Yet not the more   °Medical terms for his blindness.
Cease I to wander where the Muses haunt

The Story Milton's story, told in twelve books (which are more like chapters), begins in the middle of the narrative with the fall of the rebel angels from Heaven. In a flashback, readers later learn about the events leading up to this fall. The main tale, however, concerns the temptation of Adam and Eve by Satan, the leader of the rebelling angels. This temptation is Satan's attempt to seek revenge against God. Satan is successful in getting the first two humans to disobey God's commandment and thereby lose the right to remain in Paradise. However, even this success does not disturb God's plan for the world. According to this plan, humans must always have the freedom to choose. At the end of the poem, Adam and Eve face up to what they have done, accept their freedom of choice, and slowly leave the timeless and beautiful garden of Paradise to begin human history. For Milton, this ending is sober but certainly not tragic. It is a reaffirmation of his belief in human freedom, tempered by devotion to God.

The first two books of *Paradise Lost* describe the rebel angels in Hell. Stunned by their fiery fall, they recover enough to build their palace of Pandemonium and scheme against Adam and Eve. As Book 2 ends, Satan is headed toward Paradise to put their plan into action. The passage below is the invocation that begins Book 3.

This is not the first invocation, or call for heavenly aid, in *Paradise Lost*. At the beginning of the poem, Milton invokes the help of Urania, the Greek goddess of astronomy, as well as that of the Holy Spirit. The twofold invocation indicates Milton's debt to both classical tradition

	Clear spring, or shady grove, or sunny hill,	
	Smit with the love of sacred song; but chief	
30	Thee, Sion,° and the flowery brooks beneath	°Mountain in the Bible.
	That wash thy hallowed feet, and warbling flow,	
	Nightly I visit; nor sometimes forget°	°I never forget.
	Those other two equaled with me in fate,°	°Also blind.
	So were I equaled with them in renown,	
35	Blind Thamyris and blind Maeonides,°	°Poets Thamyris and Homer.
	And Tiresias and Phineus,° prophets old:	°Two ancient blind prophets.
	Then feed on thoughts, that voluntary move	
	Harmonious numbers, as the wakeful bird	
	Sings darkling,° and in shadiest covert hid	°The nightingale, singing in
40	Tunes her nocturnal note. Thus with the year	darkness.
	Seasons return; but not to me returns	
	Day, or the sweet approach of even or morn,	
	Or sight of vernal bloom, or summer's rose,	
	Or flocks, or herds, or human face divine;	
45	But cloud instead and ever-during° dark	°Everlasting.
	Surrounds me, from the cheerful ways of men	
	Cut off, and for the book of knowledge fair	
	Presented with a universal blank	
	Of Nature's works to me expunged and razed,°	°Erased.
50	And wisdom at one entrance quite shut out.	
	So much the rather thou, celestial Light,	
	Shine inward, and the mind through all her powers	
	Irradiate, there plant eyes, all mist from thence	
	Purge and disperse, that I may see and tell	
55	Of things invisible to mortal sight.	

and Christianity. The invocation here, at the start of Book 3, is addressed to "holy Light" (line 1), which is closely associated with God. Not only is it "coeternal" (line 2) with Him, but it is an essential part of His identity: "God is light" (line 3).

It is no accident that Milton calls for the help of "holy Light" just at this moment in the poem. The first two books have been spent in the "dungeon horrible" and "darkness visible" of Hell. In this darkness, the fallen angels have displayed their meanness, fear, and pride, scheming against God and His creation. Now, after following Satan's long flight through Hell and Chaos, the poem emerges into daylight. Just as darkness is the proper medium for Satan and his crew, light is the medium of God.

An epic usually is not regarded as a personal poem. Yet in this moving invocation, Milton sounds a personal note. He mentions his own blindness: ". . . but thou/Revisit'st not these eyes, that roll in vain . . ." (lines 22–23). Even so, he connects his blindness with that of ancient poets and prophets (lines 35–36). Their infirmities were traditionally associated with their special talents or genius. Milton's blindness is a kind of bodily wound, incurred in the service of the Commonwealth. Yet it may also be a symbol of the spiritual wound that the Civil Wars inflicted on the poet. If so, he calls on the aid of spiritual light, inwardly visible, to heal that wound by helping him tell his great story. Because it involves heavenly matters, this story requires spiritual insight rather than bodily sight.

Although his blindness cuts him off "from the cheerful ways of men" (line 46), he still can look inward to learn the ways of God. In *Paradise Lost*, he will therefore be able to "justify the ways of God to men" (Book 1, line 26).

Connecting Art to the Historical Context

Ben Jonson and the Moral Duty of the Poet

A contemporary of Milton, Ben Jonson also saw the conflict of his age—revealed in violence, persecutions, and religious conflict. In his writing, Jonson worked to live up to the moral responsibilities he felt as a poet. In fact, Jonson once said that a person could not be "the good poet without first being a good man." Jonson used his position as a poet to give good advice in some poems; to honor worthy men and women in others; and in his plays, to satirize the corruption and immorality he saw around him.

Make a Connection What details of this engraving show that Jonson took himself as seriously as he took his role as a poet?

Engraving of Ben Jonson (1573–1637), English School (18th century)

# The Romantic Period:

Rebels and Dreamers (1798–1832)

Connecting Literature to the Historical Context

Revolution and Romanticism

- A love of nature and an appreciation for spectacular scenery
- The importance of discovering one's personal identity
- A belief that children behave more naturally than adults do

These common ideas and feelings are only part of our inheritance from the Romantic period. That we take them for granted is evidence that we still look at the world through the lenses of Romanticism, even though this way of thinking and feeling developed two hundred years ago or more.

The Neoclassical Ideal In the middle of the eighteenth century, no one knew that Romanticism was about to be born. The neoclassical ideal allowed for the permanence, order, and stability associated with the term *Nature.* Reason, as exemplified by Sir Isaac Newton, was shedding its light on the world's mysteries, revealing the laws that governed the movements of all heavenly and earthly bodies. Indeed, this age was called the Enlightenment, and its political ideals are built into our Constitution.

Yet this age of reason and light had its dark side as well. Hidden in this darkness were all the *un*reasonable qualities that the age had disqualified and dispossessed: fear, wonder, brooding sadness, and a host of other emotions. Romantic writers would embrace these qualities and use them to create a more complete picture of human nature than the Enlightenment had offered. Before Romanticism existed, however, there were twinges of awareness that important things had somehow been forgotten.

The Beauty of the Sublime One such "twinge," for example, was a new idea about what was beautiful. In the late 1750's, Edmund Burke wrote about the "terror," "astonishment," and "awe" excited by the sublime, a type of beauty discussed by ancient authors but not previously emphasized in the Age of Reason. According to Burke, the sublime caused a suspension of reason in the face of "whatever is fitted in any sort to excite the ideas of pain, and danger, that is to say, whatever is in any sort terrible." Such natural features and phenomena as lofty mountains, deep gorges, and thunderstorms might be sources of this emotion.

The sublime allowed the age an outlet for some of the feelings it had suppressed. Now one could put aside the mask of reason, at least for a moment, and shiver at nature's grandeur. Over the years, hardy travelers began to pursue the pleasing shivers of the sublime in journeys to mountain ranges, like the Alps. Formerly, mountains had been viewed as irregularities on the otherwise perfect roundness of the globe. As the taste for the sublime became fashionable, however, the craggy immensity of mountains became an attraction rather than a sign of imperfection. The urge to climb mountains, so popular today, can be traced back to this new appreciation of the sublime.

The Graveyard School   In addition to influencing tastes in natural scenery, the emphasis on terror and astonishment helped foster two new types of literature: the "Graveyard School" of poets and Gothic fiction. Graveyard poets, as their name suggests, had a preference for gloom. Their poems are often set in grave- yards, typically at night, and they brood on the certainty of death and the promise of immortality. The most famous of these works is Thomas Gray's "Elegy Written in a Country Churchyard," which ends with an epitaph for "A youth, to Fortune and to Fame unknown." (An elegy is a formal or ceremonious poem about the death of a person.) Gray's solitary nighttime musings are far from the sparkling witticisms of Alexander Pope's neoclassical verse.

Spooky Fictional Funhouses
Gothic novels, named for the medieval castles in which they were often set, were like spooky fictional funhouses designed to give readers a thrill. With their ghosts, dark corridors, underground passages, innocent heroines, and evil lords, they fed a new craze for the supernatural. In some ways, they resembled today's horror movies. Just as these movies allow mod- ern viewers to scream with pleasure, Gothic fiction permitted eighteenth- century readers to indulge feelings that had been suppressed or ignored in the age's pursuit of reason. Horace Walpole is credited with creating the Gothic genre in *The Castle of Otranto* (1765).

In addition to novelists and poets, certain philosophers also challenged the Enlightenment's belief in the supremacy of reason. Chief among these was the Frenchman Jean-Jacques Rousseau (1712–1778). He brought to the abstrac- tions offered by the thinkers of the day his own varied and rich experience. The son of a Geneva watchmaker, he had left home as a teenager and wandered through Europe. His travels and talents gave him the opportunity to play an almost dizzying array of roles—from servant to botanist to musician to mathematician. Rousseau's

basic theory was that humans are good by nature, although they are corrupted by society.

However, Rousseau did not advocate a return to a primitive state of existence. Instead, he showed how important natural surroundings are to our well-being and how we, crave them as a release, if only a brief one, from life in cities. He also showed how, through new methods of education and the establishment of rep- resentative democracy, people could achieve a more natural way of life. His educational ideas, which stressed the potential already in children, ran counter to previous notions that learning should be instilled in a child.

New Ideas From Germany   German philosophers built upon Rousseau's ideas as they attempted to replace Enlighten- ment theories. The philosophers Schiller, Hegel, and Schelling each spoke of a lost paradise, where humans were in harmony with nature and with themselves. Rational thought and the development of culture had destroyed this natural harmony. It had produced a society in which, accord- ing to Schiller, individuals were only "fragments" or pieces of "an ingenious clockwork." However, like Rousseau, these thinkers believed that there was no going back to a more primitive existence. In- stead, people could regain a sense of harmony through the exercise of all their powers, experiencing themselves not as rational machines but as growing organ- isms. In fact, the living organism, which defies reason by mysteriously combining opposite qualities in its growth, would become the master image for the Romantic period.

An Agricultural Revolution   While writers and thinkers were questioning the assumptions of the Enlightenment, the world itself was changing so dramatically that the old truths began to seem insuffi- cient. It was as if the use of reason to solve selected problems was producing a society that was spinning out of reason's

The Taking of the Bastille, 14th July 1789, Jean-Pierre Houel, Musée Carnavalet, Paris, France

▲ **Critical Viewing** Jean-Pierre Houel's *The Taking of the Bastille, 14th July 1789* commemorates the capture of the Bastille prison by a Parisian mob at the beginning of the French Revolution. For the attackers, the Bastille was a symbol of the monarchy that oppressed them. How would most middle- and upper-class English citizens have reacted to a picture like this in the late 1790's? Why? **[Infer]**

control. For example, innovations in agriculture were changing age-old ways of working the land and boosting production. These developments helped the average consumer, who could now afford a diet of white bread and roast beef. They also helped the wealthy farmers, who had gained more and more land from the enclosure of village fields that had once been open to all. However, the small farmers, who could no longer pasture their livestock on communal lands, were not able to compete. They had to give up their farms, becoming impoverished laborers either in the country or in the expanding cities of the Midlands, a region of central England.

An Industrial Revolution Meanwhile, the production of goods was changing more in a few decades than it had in the previous thousand years. The ancient process of weaving was transformed by such inventions as the flying shuttle (1733), which enabled one worker to move threads quickly from side to side rather than having to pass them to another worker.

Traditionally, textile work had been done by individuals working at home on hand looms. That is why textiles had been called a cottage industry. Now, the sheer size of the new machines required that the work be done in factories. These factories drew the rural poor to cities, providing them with low-paying jobs and weaving their lives into the coarse fabric of urban poverty.

People today might think of steam as a wispy cloud that whistles harmlessly from a teakettle. In the eighteenth century, however, steam was a dynamic new form of energy. Inventors saw in clouds of steam a force greater than human shoulders or the power of horses or the flow of wind or water. Inventors like James Watt, Matthew Boulton, and Richard Trivithick devoted themselves to improving the steam engine and adapting it to various industrial purposes.

The achievement of higher steam pressures by Trivithick led to the use of steam engines in trains and in pumps for coal mines. Coal was becoming important in the manufacture of iron, and the iron industry was moving to the northern cities near the coal fields. It seemed as if the furious, whistling force in steam was pumping the poor from the countryside and spinning them into these grimy cities. There, men and women and young children labored for long hours in the factories, like parts of some great machine. Production was up. Profits were up—for the factory owners. Yet the life of the worker was a spinning, never-catch-up round of poverty.

Political Revolutions The age's belief in reason was intangible, but reason proved to be a force as powerful as steam. Locke's political ideas prompted the wording of the American Declaration of Independence just as surely as steam power drove a piston. If political bonds are established by reasonable consent, they can also be dissolved in the same way: "When in the course of human events, it becomes necessary for one people to dissolve the political bands which have connected them with another . . ." Reason, in other words, can lead to revolution.

Revolutions have a way of being contagious. The American Revolution inspired other rebellions, which were similar to it in some ways and different in others. In America, the struggle was directed against a colonial power but also involved a civil war because a substantial minority of Americans were Loyalists who supported England. Before it ended, the struggle also became an international war. Countries like Spain and France entered the war against England, giving America the sea power and munitions that it needed. The American victory replaced a monarchy with a constitutional republic. This change was a significant one, but it did not arise from a conflict among different economic classes and it did not endanger property rights. The French Revolution, which began eight years after the war in America ended, did involve a struggle among classes and did threaten property rights. Those factors, combined with the desire of French radicals to spread revolution by means of armed struggle, sent a wave of fear through England and the monarchies of Europe.

The French Revolution In the period from 1789 to 1791, however, the reforms introduced by the new French National Assembly were greeted with enthusiasm by liberals in England. Subsequent events propelled the revolution in a more radical direction. King Louis XVI attempted to flee the country and was captured. The civil war between royalist supporters of the monarchy and republicans was aggravated by France's war with Austria, Prussia, and England. These countries, especially England, sought to aid the French royalists. Republicans countered in 1793 by executing the king and, in a Reign of Terror, by executing aristocrats and all so-called "enemies of the revolution." Furthermore, they continued to battle against foreign foes, threatening to spread their revolutionary ideas throughout Europe.

Many English liberals who had initially supported the French Revolution found themselves caught in the middle. They could no longer sympathize with an increasingly violent revolution, but neither could they endorse an increasingly repressive English government. Two such men were the young poets William Wordsworth (1770–1850) and Samuel Taylor Coleridge (1772–1834).

A Pioneer in Poetry Wordsworth had been born into a middle-class family living in England's northwestern Lake District, a region about thirty miles in diameter. As its name suggests, this district is extremely beautiful. Its main attractions are the lakes for which it was named—Windermere, Ullswater, and others—but it also boasts picturesque waterfalls and several of England's highest mountains, such as Scafell Pike and Helvellyn (both more than three thousand feet high). In the poet's time, the Lake District was still untouched and not the tourist destination it is today. It was a region of small villages and farms but certainly not a ghostly or forgotten place. Its mines, quarries, and farms were busy centers of activity. Wordsworth pays tribute to the district in *The Prelude* (1805), a long poem about the growth of his mind: "Fair seed-time had my soul, and I grew up / Foster'd alike by beauty and by fear; / Much favored in my birthplace . . ." (This poem is an autobiography and shows the importance that the Romantics gave to the development of individual consciousness.)

▲ **Critical Viewing** Just as Wordsworth and Coleridge led the Romantic movement in literature, the painter J.M.W. Turner (1775–1851) brought Romanticism to the visual arts. His painting *The Fighting Téméraire Tugged to Her Last Berth to Be Broken Up* honors the old sailing vessels that were being replaced by steam-powered ships. In what ways does this painting demonstrate the preference of Romantics for the picturesque, the historic, and the sublime? **[Interpret]**

Where Is Home? Yet the young poet, living in such a glorious place, was still uncertain about home. Wordsworth's mother died when he was about eight, a tragedy that led to the breakup of the family. His sister Dorothy, with whom he was close, moved away to live with relatives, and William and his brother Richard were sent to a school in another section of the Lake District. At one blow, Wordsworth had been separated from his mother, father, and sister. Then, when Wordsworth was only thirteen, his father died as well. Though Wordsworth loved his school and the surrounding area, he was also an orphan who had lost his original

family home. Later, in his poetry, he would consider the contradictions arising from this experience: the sense that he was at home in nature, combined with the feeling that an original home or paradise was forever lost to him. By way of compensation, he would seek shelter for himself in poems that explored this dilemma. He would also offer a refuge in poetry for all the poor, who had been excluded from eighteenth-century neoclassical verse and left out in the cold.

His "co-conspirator" in writing the *Lyrical Ballads*, Coleridge, must have felt somewhat out in the cold himself. The fourteenth child of a country clergyman, he had been his father's favorite. However, he was just nine when his father died and therefore had an experience of early loss similar to Wordsworth's. Perhaps loneliness and loss drove him to conversational performances that would surround him with listening friends. After a brief period at Cambridge University and a disastrous episode in the cavalry, Coleridge began planning an ideal community in faraway Pennsylvania. His partner in this day-dream was the poet Robert Southey. In the excitement of this experiment, Coleridge even married the sister of the young woman to whom Southey was engaged. However, the dream of utopia fizzled, and Coleridge was left with an incompatible wife. It was about this time that Coleridge met Wordsworth and sought solace in their friendship for his disappointments. In 1797, they began the collaboration that would lead to the publication of *Lyrical Ballads* (1798).

A Revolution in Poetry Unlike Coleridge, Wordsworth did not have immediate reasons for personal unhappiness. However, he did share his fellow poet's frustration at political developments in France and England. Only those who can understand the joy with which these poets and other liberals greeted news of the French Revolution in 1789 can understand the bitterness of their later frustration. By 1797, however, the violence of the revolution had disappointed the hopes of liberals, and England had become a fearful and repressive society, wary of French invasion.

Connecting Art to the Historical Context

The Second Generation of Romantic Poets

Wordsworth and Coleridge's revolution in poetry blazed the way for another generation of poets that included Byron, Shelley, and Keats. Like his predecessors, John Keats saw the appreciation of beauty as an end in itself, and he made the pursuit of beauty the goal of his writing. In fact, his lyric poems seek to find beauty in the most ordinary circumstances. **Speculate** Look at this painting of Hampstead Heath, a park near Keats's London home. If a romantic were to respond to this scene in a journal, what tone or mood might the writing reveal?

Hampstead Heath, John Constable, Victoria & Albert Museum, London, UK

Yet bitterness was turning back to bliss as the two poets shared ideas for poems on long walks through the countryside of southwestern England. They were joyfully plotting a revolution in poetry that would make up for the lost political revolution.

Coleridge wrote some of his greatest work, including "The Rime of the Ancient Mariner," a poem that Wordsworth helped plan. The book that was born of their collaboration, *Lyrical Ballads*, came out in 1798, with Wordworth finishing "Lines Composed a Few Miles Above Tintern Abbey" just in time to include it. When a revised version of the book was published in January 1801 (but dated 1800), Wordsworth supplied a preface that explained the revolution in poetry that he and Coleridge had made (see below).

To understand how radical these statements were, imagine how a neoclassical writer like Pope would have reacted to them. To Pope, subjects "from common life," especially "rustic life," would have seemed more appropriate for satire or low comedy than for a serious poem. Why would anyone be interested in what insignificant country people thought, much less in their uneducated language?

As for "social vanity," Pope would have asserted that the skillful use of society's polished language is what distinguishes a poet. It is the country clown, not the man-about-town, who suffers from "the sameness and narrow circle" of acquaintance. Moreover, the notion that trees and lakes and mountains, as opposed to landscaped gardens, can inspire nobler feelings (Pope might have said) is utterly ludicrous.

As this imaginary reaction suggests, Wordsworth was turning neoclassical values topsy-turvy. He was praising in his poetry men and women who were so apparently insignificant that they would never have been allowed into a neoclassical poem, except perhaps to be satirized. They were like the oppressed peasants in whose name the French revolutionaries had toppled the aristocracy.

In "The Old Cumberland Beggar," on page A24, notice how Wordsworth uses phrases that emphasize the lowliness of the beggar: "On the ground" (line 2), "along the ground" (line 4), "one little span of earth" (line 7), and "for ever on the ground" (line 9). He also uses simple, repetitive language that seems to creep along and even double back on itself—

from Preface to *Lyrical Ballads* (1800)
by William Wordsworth

The principal object, then, proposed in these Poems, was to choose incidents and situations from common life, and to relate or describe them throughout, as far as was possible, in a selection of language really used by men . . . Humble and rustic life was generally chosen, because in that condition the essential passions of the heart find a better soil in which they can attain their maturity, are less under restraint, and speak a plainer and more emphatic language; because in that condition of life our elementary feelings co-exist in a state of greater simplicity, and . . . because in that condition the passions of men are incorporated with the beautiful and permanent forms of nature. The language, too, of these men has been adopted (purified indeed from what appear to be its real defects, from all lasting and rational causes of dislike or disgust), because such men hourly communicate with the best objects from which the best part of language is originally derived; and because, from their rank in society and the sameness and narrow circle of their intercourse, being less under the influence of social vanity, they convey their feelings and notions in simple and unelaborated expressions. Accordingly, such a language, arising out of repeated experience and regular feelings, is a more permanent, and a far more philosophical language, than that which is frequently substituted for it by Poets. . . .

". . . seeing still, / And seldom knowing that he sees" (lines 10 and 11)—imitating the beggar's slow progress.

Unlike Pope, Wordsworth does not use rhymes to call out witty and memorable couplets. Such proud, self-advertising devices would not be in keeping with his humble subject. Wordsworth rejects the adornments of rhyme in favor of blank-verse sentences that wind their way across line ends. These sentences adapt themselves both to the beggar's movements and to the poet's indignant attack on those who would scorn such a lowly man (lines 15–25).

Equally important, the gradual winding of the blank verse (unrhymed iambic pentameter) down the page imitates the process by which the old man, in the course of his wanderings, "binds / Past deeds and offices of charity." He is not only a broken-down human figure but also a living record book of charity in which people can read their own past kindnesses (lines 27–29). Thus, Wordsworth has turned the beggar's apparently insignificant movement through space into a highly significant movement through time.

Further, he has demonstrated that a situation from "Humble and rustic life" and "plainer . . . language" can convey an enduring and heartfelt truth.

from "The Old Cumberland Beggar"
by William Wordsworth

He travels on, a solitary Man;
His age has no companion. On the
  ground
His eyes are turned, and, as he moves
  along
They move along the ground; and,
  evermore,
5 Instead of common and habitual sight
Of fields with rural works, of hill and
  dale,
And the blue sky, one little span of
  earth
Is all his prospect. Thus, from day to
  day,
Bow-bent, his eyes for ever on the
  ground,
10 He plies his weary journey; seeing still,
And seldom knowing that he sees, some
  straw,
Some scattered leaf, or marks which, in
  one track,
The nails of cart or chariot-wheel have
  left
Impressed on the white road . . .
15   But deem not this Man useless.—
  Statesmen! ye
Who are so restless in your wisdom, ye

Who have a broom still ready in your
  hands
To rid the world of nuisances; ye proud,
Heart-swoln, while in your pride ye
  contemplate
20 Your talents, power, or wisdom, deem
  him not
A burthen of the earth! 'Tis Nature's
  law
That none, the meanest of created
  things,
Or forms created the most vile and
  brute,
The dullest or most noxious, should
  exist
25 Divorced from good . . .
    . . . While from door to door,
This old Man creeps, the villagers in
  him
Behold a record which together binds
Past deeds and offices of charity,
30 Else unremembered, and so keeps alive
The kindly mood in hearts which lapse
  of years,
And that half-wisdom half-experience
  gives,
Make slow to feel . . .

The Victorian Period:
Progress and Decline (1833–1901)

Challenges to Values in Victorian England

The Victorian period, which followed Romanticism, is tied closely to a historical fact: the sixty-four-year reign of Queen Victoria, from 1837 to 1901. (Sometimes the period is said to have begun early in the 1830's, to include the 1832 Reform Bill, an important piece of social legislation; similarly, the end of the period is sometimes pushed back to 1914, the beginning of World War I.) Nevertheless, the handy adjective *Victorian* applied to literature and thought of as that time can be misleading. It may suggest that these sixty-plus years were all of a piece. Actually, historians divide this period into three eras:

- Time of Troubles: 1830's and 1840's
- Mid-Victorian Period: 1848–1870
- Late Victorian Period: 1870–1901

As its name suggests, the Time of Troubles was a period when working people who could barely make a living in the newly industrialized cities agitated for economic and political reforms. Often the conditions in which they lived and worked were so bad as to be almost beyond imagining. The Factory Act of 1833 was an attempt to improve working conditions, especially for children in the textile industry, but even a list of its main provisions suggests how severe those conditions were. This act declared that:

- No child under nine years of age could be employed.
- No child under thirteen could work more than nine hours a day.
- No child under eighteen could work longer than twelve hours a day.
- Inspectors were directed to enforce these provisions.

Not only were the working classes treated almost like slave labor, but they were denied political representation as well. Most workers were barred from voting, and many of the large industrial cities—including Leeds, Manchester, and Birmingham—were not represented in Parliament at all. At the same time, many of the districts that *were* represented in Parliament had few inhabitants. The elections in these so-called "rotten boroughs" were manipulated through bribery and political influence, thereby allowing a relatively small number of wealthy and powerful men to dominate the nation's affairs.

In addition, the Corn Laws (the English use the word *corn* to refer to wheat and other grains as well) made it difficult for the poor to buy enough bread. These laws had been passed to help wealthy farmers rather than consumers. By raising the tax on imported grain, they ensured that such farmers would not have to compete with low-priced imports and could therefore sell their grain for a higher price. However, these laws also ensured that the price of bread would remain high.

Threat of Revolution Often barely able to subsist, the working classes were also more vulnerable than the middle or upper classes to the economic downturns or depressions that occurred periodically. One such depression, for example, caused widespread unemployment in the early 1840's. This unemployment led to riots that threatened to boil over into a full-scale political revolution.

During these dangerous times, memories of the French Revolution haunted the British imagination. Mobs like the one that had seized control of the Bastille prison in Paris on July 14, 1789, might also surge through London and the industrial cities of the north and west. That is why the demands of the Chartist movement aroused such concern. These demands, which were incorporated into a "People's Charter" (1838), included granting to all males the right to vote and eliminating property requirements for those who wanted to serve in Parliament. Such demands do not seem revolutionary to modern readers, but the Chartists promoted their ideas at large rallies that frightened the middle and upper classes.

The country's political system, controlled by landowning aristocrats together with wealthy merchants and manufacturers, could not or would not respond to the terrible problems brought about by industrialization. However, not everyone ignored or exploited economic and political injustices. Many campaigned to bridge the gap between what politician and novelist Benjamin Disraeli had called "The Two Nations"—that of the rich and that of the poor. For example, an Anti-Corn Law League was organized in 1839 to establish free trade in grain. In 1846, Tory Prime Minister Robert Peel went against the policy of his own party and repealed the Corn Laws. Peel acted when a poor domestic harvest threatened to make grain extremely scarce. He knew that Britain would have to rely on imported grain in order to avoid famine. Soon, however, he became convinced that free trade was a worthy policy in itself.

Some Reform Additional factory legislation also helped to correct abuses caused by the Industrial Revolution. Also, the Reform Bill of 1832—which was resisted by the aristocratic chamber of Parliament, the House of Lords—made the political system more democratic, although it did not go far enough. It granted seats in Parliament to industrial centers that had not been represented, and it eliminated a number of rotten boroughs. It also increased the voting rolls, but it restricted the right to vote to males owning property with an annual rental value of at least £10. Only about one of every seven adult males could vote. Women and the working classes were still disenfranchised.

The cumulative effect of these and other reforms was neither to create a fully representative democracy nor to correct all the problems caused by the Industrial Revolution. Terrible poverty persisted throughout the Victorian era, even during the so-called prosperous years of 1848 to 1870. However, the nation would no longer feel the imminent threat of armed rebellion, as it did in the 1830's and 1840's.

The Mid-Victorian Years This period saw a rapid expansion of industry and technology, major advances in scientific thought, the continued development of the middle classes and their influence, and Britain's involvement in several international conflicts. Britain was now a great manufacturing center, known as the "workshop of the world." It also had the world's most powerful navy, which protected its trade with colonies and with other nations.

In 1851, the Great Exhibition held in London reflected the confidence of Mid-Victorian Britain. The first modern world's fair, it was meant to celebrate progress toward a world united by trade and advancing technology. Among the exhibits were the latest in machines and manufactured goods from different countries.

Perhaps more impressive than any of the individual exhibits was the structure in which they were housed, the Crystal Palace. A daring advance in architecture, it was designed by Sir Joseph Paxton and violated the assumption of the time that buildings needed thick outer walls as supports. This large but lightweight building, assembled from prefabricated parts, was made of glass walls and linking iron rods.

The palace symbolized the technological

▲ **Critical Viewing** Edmund Thomas's painting is entitled *The Coronation of Queen Victoria, 1837*. Do any details in this scene reveal that the 1830's and 1840's were a "time of troubles"? Why or why not? **[Evaluate]**

achievements of Mid-Victorian Britain. However, during this period, scientists were making breakthroughs in theory as well. In 1859, for example, Charles Darwin published *The Origin of Species*, in which he offered evidence that living organisms had evolved through natural processes. This book inaugurated modern biological science. In 1862, the Scottish physicist James Clerk Maxwell proposed a new theory of light, linking it to such phenomena as electricity and magnetism. To many Victorians, it must have seemed that science was building its own Crystal Palace of theory, which would soon embrace and explain all natural phenomena.

During the 1850's, Britain's position as a world power lured it into several international conflicts. Britain, for example, had already gained control over much of India and was therefore concerned about any Russian expansion that might threaten British interests in that subcontinent. When war broke out between Turkey and Russia, Britain therefore joined France in defending Turkey. The resulting conflict was known as the Crimean War (1853–1856) because it was centered on the Crimean peninsula in southern Russia.

Perhaps the only good to come from this war was the attention it won for the profession of nursing. The English nurse Florence Nightingale took a group of thirty-eight nurses to the battlefields in order to care for sick and wounded soldiers. Her courage and compassion became widely known, and after the war she was able to collect enough money to establish the Nightingale School and Home for training nurses. In 1915, not long after her death, the British government erected the Crimean Monument—not to celebrate the war but to honor the humanity of Florence Nightingale.

On the domestic front, the Reform Bill of 1867 added to the measures introduced by the Reform Bill of 1832 and almost doubled the number of voters. Property requirements for voting were now so low that they included most working-class men. However, if nearly every British male had the vote, women would still have to wait until the twentieth century to gain complete equality with men at the ballot box.

Because almost every man could vote, it became more important to ensure that voters were educated. The Reform Bill of 1867, therefore, led to the passage of the Education Act of 1870. This act gave local governments the right to set up public schools that would be supported by tax money and by fees paid by students. However, poor students could attend these schools without charge.

A sense of prosperity and well-being, at least for the upper and middle classes, persisted into the late Victorian period. These three decades were punctuated by the Jubilees of 1887 and 1897, celebrations of the fiftieth and sixtieth anniversaries of Queen Victoria's reign. In celebrating these anniversaries, the British were also paying tribute to themselves and their empire.

Empire-Building The final decades of the century saw a concerted attempt by the British to expand their empire—partly as a result of competition with other colonial powers. Ireland, a colony that was also a neighbor, had been a source of conflict for many hundreds of years. Queen Elizabeth had brutally suppressed a number of Irish rebellions, and her successor, James I, had forcibly colonized the six northern counties of Ireland with Protestant settlers from England and Scotland. This policy created a constituency in

A Steam Hammer at Work, 1871, James Nasmyth

▲ **Critical Viewing** Does James Nasmyth's painting *A Steam Hammer at Work, 1871*, suggest the confidence and prosperity of the mid-Victorian years? Explain. **[Assess]**

Northern Ireland that often felt alienated from Irish Catholics and looked to Britain for support. English oppression had led to chronic poverty for many of the Irish, and from 1845 to 1849, failed potato harvests led to widespread famine that caused more than a million Irish to emigrate while perhaps another million starved to death. In the 1870's, a temporary period of political quiet was broken when Irish nationalists again began agitating for independence from Britain.

As the nineteenth century neared its end, writers seemed to reflect a world-weariness and a pessimism about reforming society. If art critic John Ruskin (1819–1900) had once championed social reform, his counterpart in the next generation, Walter Pater (1839–1894), narrowed his focus to the individual. Pater believed that in a world of quickly passing impressions, the best that individuals could hope for was to learn how to enjoy these sensations. Social theories and ideas could only be a distraction from "gathering all we are into one desperate effort to see and touch."

The following sections illustrate how major writers responded to issues and events that challenged Victorian values.

"The Two Nations"

It was a novelist and future prime minister who summed up the ills of society in a telling phrase. In his novel *Sybil* (1845), Disraeli writes of "the two nations" living side by side, one in poverty and one in wealth. Other novelists addressed this issue in a compelling way, including Mrs. Elizabeth Gaskell. Her book *North and South* (1855) offers another perspective on the two nations. It contrasts the wealthy landowning classes of southern England with the energetic but ungentlemanly manufacturers and struggling workers of northern England.

Charles Dickens (1812–1870), the most influential and widely read novelist of Victorian times, dramatized this contrast between the rich and the poor vividly. For example, in his novel *Bleak House* (1853), which focuses on the corruption of the Victorian legal system, he portrays both aristocrats and paupers. His description of Sir Leicester Dedlock, whose very name suggests death and inaction, seems to praise the man but actually condemns him (see box at right).

Notice Dickens's ironic use of the word *conscience*, which at first seems to indicate that Dedlock might want to right social wrongs. As the sentence continues, however, it becomes clear that he is more concerned with protecting his reputation for "integrity" than for helping others.

In a different section of the novel, Dickens addresses "obstinate . . . intensely prejudiced, perfectly unreasonable" men and women like Dedlock. He describes for them—and for those who are more sympathetic—the death of a poor crossing sweeper named Jo, a child of the slums (see box at right).

This passage shows Dickens speaking from the novel in his own voice, angry and indignant. He is saying, "How can we call

from Bleak House
by Charles Dickens

Sir Leicester Dedlock

Sir Leicester Dedlock is only a baronet, but there is no mightier baronet than he. His family is as old as the hills, and infinitely more respectable. He has a general opinion that the world might get on without hills but would be done up without Dedlocks. He would on the whole admit nature to be a good idea (a little low, perhaps, when not enclosed with a park-fence), but an idea dependent for its execution on your great county families. He is a gentleman of strict conscience, disdainful of all littleness and meanness and ready on the shortest notice to die any death you may please to mention rather than give occasion for the least impeachment of his integrity. He is an honorable, obstinate, truthful, high-spirited, intensely prejudiced, perfectly unreasonable man.

The Death of Jo

The light is come upon the dark benighted way. Dead! Dead, your Majesty. Dead, my lords and gentlemen. Dead, right reverends and wrong reverends of every order. Dead, men and women, born with heavenly compassion in your hearts. And dying thus around us every day.

ourselves compassionate yet permit the poor to suffer in this way?"

The Novel Comes of Age

The English novel, born in the eighteenth century, came of age in the nineteenth. The rising middle classes provided a wide readership, enabling talented novelists like Charles Dickens and Wilkie Collins to thrive as professional writers. Also, Dickens helped to pioneer a new method of serial publication. This method involved publishing the parts of a novel in sequence, like a series of magazines. Each part, consisting of several chapters, might appear monthly over a period of a year or more.

By ending each part at a suspenseful moment, the novelist could build interest for the next part of the story. In addition, as word circulated that the story was a good one, an increasing number of readers would buy each new section. Finally, the publisher could capitalize on reader interest by republishing the completed work in book form.

Not all novels were published in this way, but serial publication did strongly influence both the writing and reading of novels. Writers, for example, had to plan their works to fit neatly into three- and four-chapter sections. In addition, writers could now get their audience's reaction while the work was in progress, as if it were a long-running play. Writers might even make changes based on that reaction. For readers as well, a serial novel was somewhat like a play, because everyone in the audience was experiencing it at the same time.

A Writer's Nerves Dickens was skillful at completing each new part according to schedule, yet sometimes even he would feel the deadline pressure. Once, in a store, he overheard some people gossiping about a novel he was writing. The next part was due out soon, and they were wondering how he would handle a certain outcome. Not having written the part yet, he wondered a little nervously how he would handle those events!

The same middle-class public that supported novelists like Dickens—his work often sold in editions of 40,000—could exert a subtle kind of control over their writing. Dickens, as previously mentioned, was fearless in calling his audience's attention to the problems of society. However, he would be cautious and proper in his description of relationships between men and women, always aware that his novels were being read by middle-class parents together with their children.

One quality that especially appealed to the Victorian reading public was sentimentality, often in the form of tear-provoking descriptions of innocents suffering in a cruel world. However, it is not necessarily the case that the public forced sentimentality on writers. Dickens, for example, seemed to share his readers' love of tearful scenes. The most famous of these is the death of Little Nell in *The Old Curiosity Shop* (1841). A young girl fleeing the corrupt city in the company of her grandfather, Nell dies in her quest for a refuge. Dickens emphasized the sadness of her death, and his audience loved the experience of weeping for innocent Nell.

Dickens was the most famous Victorian novelist but certainly not the only one in this novel-writing and novel-reading age. Two writers who joined Dickens in condemning hypocrisy were William Makepeace Thackeray (1811–1863) and Anthony Trollope (1815–1882). Thackeray's *Vanity Fair* (1848) is named for a fair that symbolizes worldly corruption in Puritan John Bunyan's allegory *Pilgrim's Progress* (1678, 1679). The novel describes the rise of Becky Sharp from governess to woman of society and reveals the immoral side of upper-class life. In *Barchester Towers* (1857), Trollope satirizes hypocrisy and scheming in the community linked with a cathedral.

Women Novelists As the novel came into its own, so did women novelists. Women had already achieved success in this genre. Aphra Behn (1640–1689), perhaps England's first self-supporting woman author, wrote fictional narratives. Later, Jane Austen (1775–1817) wrote finely crafted novels like *Sense and Sensibility* (1811), *Pride and Prejudice* (1813), and *Emma* (1815). In these works and others, she explored with intelligence, humor, and compassion the choices made by women in an upper-class country environment. Austen's works continue to attract readers today, and they have repeatedly been adapted for film. The same is true of *Frankenstein* (1818) by Mary Wollstonecraft Shelley. However, the Victorian era saw the emergence of even greater numbers of distinguished women novelists.

Some of these authors wrote about serious social issues like "the two nations" problem. Among them were Frances Trollope (1780–1863), the mother of Anthony Trollope; Charlotte Elizabeth Tonna (1790–1846); and the previously mentioned Elizabeth Gaskell. Dickens had enormous respect for Gaskell's work in calling attention to the abuses of industrialization. Writing in his magazine *Household Words*, he commented that "there is no living English writer whose aid I would desire to enlist in preference to the authoress of *Mary Barton*." (This was the name of a novel by Gaskell that focused on life in industrial Manchester.)

Using the pen name George Eliot, Mary Ann Evans (1819–1880) wrote novels that fellow-novelist Henry James hailed as true works of art. Eliot evoked everyday settings with a careful attention to detail and focused on her characters' inner lives. *Middlemarch* (1872), often considered her greatest work, describes the slow and painful maturation of its central character, Dorothea Brooke.

The Brontës Remarkably, two of the greatest women novelists of the Victorian era were sisters, Emily (1818–1848) and Charlotte Brontë (1816–1855). They were among six children raised by their father and aunt in the isolation of a northern English village. Bright and imaginative, these children relied on one another for entertainment and encouragement. They

Connecting Art to the Historical Context

Changing Sensibilities in Victorian Art

Just as the late nineteenth century found many writers skeptical about social reform and the values that characterized Victorian England, the period also saw a reformation in art. In response to the artistic style of the day, Dante Gabriel Rossetti (1828–1882), both a poet and a painter, took a major role in founding the Pre-Raphaelite Brotherhood, a group of artists whose work sought to emulate work created by Italian painters in the early 1500's—the simple style of an earlier time. Pre-Raphaelites paid close attention to natural detail in their paintings of romantic, moral, and religious subjects. Rossetti is known for his portraits, which combined physical beauty with a sad spirituality. Although the Brotherhood lasted only five years, the artists' mode of painting set in motion lasting changes in British art.

Make an Inference What does this painting reveal about the Pre-Raphaelites' views of Victorian society?

Day Dream, 1880, Dante Gabriel Rossetti, Victoria & Albert Museum, London, UK

read great authors like Shakespeare and Byron, wrote verse and prose, and created fantasy worlds with names like Gondal and Angria. Emily and Charlotte later drew on these vivid childhood experiences to create powerful works of fiction.

Wuthering Heights (1847), by Emily Brontë, is perhaps the Victorian novel that was most influenced by Romanticism. Set in the wild Yorkshire country that Emily Brontë knew firsthand, the book has at its center a dramatic love affair between Catherine Earnshaw and Heathcliff, a boy adopted by Catherine's father. Heathcliff is an embittered character, somewhat like the brooding heroes in poems by the Romantic poet Lord Byron. With its focus on isolated characters whose feelings are like natural forces, this novel differs sharply from the many Victorian novels concerned with the relations between individuals and society. Yet in addition to conveying the power of her central characters, Brontë skillfully contrasts them with other, far different characters. Also, she adeptly uses two different narrators—one a participant and one an outsider—to introduce new perspectives on events.

In *Jane Eyre* (1847), by Emily's sister Charlotte, the central characters, Jane and Rochester, are not quite so cut off from the world as Catherine and Heathcliff are in *Wuthering Heights.* Nor are Jane and Rochester larger than life in the same way that Emily Brontë's characters are. However, *Jane Eyre* is a vivid description of a woman's determination to achieve a fulfilling and independent life.

When the novel opens, ten-year-old Jane is an orphan being raised by Mrs. Reed, the wife of her deceased uncle. Oppressed by Mrs. Reed and her children alike, Jane is miserable in this household. When she stands up to fourteen-year-old John Reed and bests him in a fight, Mrs. Reed decides to send her away to a school for orphan girls called Lowood. Then, in an interview with Mr. Brocklehurst, the head of the school, Mrs. Reed tells him what a bad girl Jane is. He, in turn, gives Jane a book about a young girl punished for lying. Finally, Jane and her guardian are alone together. At this moment, young Jane shows the fierce spirit that will guide her quest for independence throughout the book (see box at left).

In this passage, Brontë skillfully foreshadows other crucial moments in which Jane Eyre will assert what she knows to be true, despite the views of others. Brontë also conveys the struggle within Jane between obedience and self-assertion by describing her movement first toward the door and then toward Mrs. Reed: "I got up, I went to the door; I came back again . . ."

Not only was Brontë challenging readers' expectations by describing an independent heroine, but she was violating a taboo by writing such a serious work at all.

Women would make further strides in the new century and win the right to vote. Ironically, their victories would come *after* a world war had called into question the Victorian belief in material and spiritual progress.

from Jane Eyre, Chapter IV

by Charlotte Brontë

Mrs. Reed looked up from her work; her eye settled on mine, her fingers at the same time suspended their nimble movements.

"Go out of the room; return to the nursery," was her mandate. My look or something else must have struck her as offensive, for she spoke with extreme, though suppressed irritation. I got up, I went to the door; I came back again; I walked to the window, across the room, then close up to her.

Speak I must; I had been trodden on severely, and *must* turn: but how? What strength had I to dart retaliation at my antagonist? I gathered my energies and launched them in this blunt sentence:—"I am not deceitful: if I were, I should say I loved *you;* but I declare I do not love you: I dislike you the worst of anybody in the world except John Reed; and this book about the liar, you may give to your girl, Georgiana, for it is she who tells lies, and not I."

VI The Modern and Postmodern Periods:

A Time of Rapid Change (1901–Present)

World War I

Chronologically speaking, a century ends on the midnight of its final year. However, dramatic events can give the impression that a century ends earlier or later than the chronology dictates. In the case of the nineteenth century, the beginning of World War I (1914) may seem like a truer end than December 31, 1899 (or 1900). The mechanized violence of this war, together with its terrible cost in casualties, marked a turning point in history. In a sense, therefore, the brief period from 1900 to 1914 is a kind of extension of the nineteenth century. It is also a period in which a number of great writers who were born in the nineteenth century continued to produce significant works. These writers—including Thomas Hardy, George Bernard Shaw, and Joseph Conrad—worked in an atmosphere of increasing political and social unrest.

The simple facts of royal succession—the reign of Victoria's son, Edward VII (1901–1910), followed by that of his own son, George V (1910–1936)—do not suggest the record of domestic and foreign conflicts that preceded the war. In 1906, the Liberal party decisively beat the Tories in an election and began to implement a program of social reform. The Liberals were a party that developed after the Reform Bill of 1832 and consisted of elements of the old Whig party, combined with members of the new business interests. Liberal efforts at reform were consistently blocked by conservative aristocrats in the House of Lords. Eventually, this battle resulted in a loss of power by the House of Lords.

Stalled Reforms Delays in reform, however, led to protests on the part of workers, many of whom were now organized in unions. A major nationwide strike, supported by many unions, was avoided only by the outbreak of World War I. Another controversy of the time related to the failure of Parliament to grant women the right to vote. When no political party supported woman suffrage, activists took to the streets. Although Liberals began to work on a solution to this problem, the issue was still unresolved when World War I began.

A troubling issue in foreign policy involved Irish Home Rule. When Liberals introduced a Home Rule bill in Parliament, Protestants in Northern Ireland asserted that they would not obey such a law even if it were passed. They were afraid that the Catholic South would dominate an Irish Parliament. Both Catholics and Protestants began to organize military groups, and King George V called a conference to keep the peace. Violence seemed to threaten but, once again, it was the outbreak of World War I, a greater violence, that postponed this crisis.

The Response of Writers The major writers of the time responded in various ways, and to a greater or lesser extent, to a society in which social and political agreements were unraveling. Thomas Hardy (1840–1928) had written his final and greatest novels at the end of the nineteenth century: *Tess of the D'Urbervilles* (1891) and *Jude the Obscure* (1896). Both novels portray poor, rural characters defeated by social conventions. Now, in the new century, Hardy was pursuing an equally distinguished career as a poet, establishing a native English tradition on which later writers, like Philip Larkin, would draw.

In verse as in prose, however, Hardy's outlook was bleak. He wrote of the indifferent forces of the universe, in whose hands humans are playthings. In "The Convergence of the Twain," for example, he describes the fateful meeting in 1912 of the great ship *Titanic* and the iceberg that sank it. Hardy's deep pessimism was not merely a response to the current events of 1906 to 1914. He could certainly sympathize with the frustrations of the poor, however, even though he had focused in his novels on the rural poor rather than the industrial working classes. Also, his sense of an ominous fate, revealed in his *Titanic* poem, seemed almost to anticipate the impending disaster of World War I.

Witty Playwright The playwright George Bernard Shaw (1856–1950) was much more directly engaged in public issues than Hardy was. Shaw was one of the founders of the Fabian Society, an organization that promoted socialism, and he used his witty plays as a means of encouraging social reform. The often surprising statements that his characters make are meant to challenge the audience and to force them to reexamine their preconceived ideas about society and its organization. For example, in *Pygmalion*, which was later adapted as the musical *My Fair Lady*, one character asserts that a poor girl can pass herself off as a duchess merely by speaking in a refined way. This notion suggests the superficiality of class distinctions.

For novelist Joseph Conrad (1857–1924), English was a third language, after Polish and French. He was Polish by birth, and his father was a leader in the struggle against the Russian rule of Poland. However, three years after his father's death, fifteen-year-old Conrad decided that he wanted to be a sailor. Eventually, he saw service on an English ship, rose to the rank of master in the British merchant service, and became an English citizen. Much of his fiction takes the sea as its setting, and an important theme in his work is the way in which human courage and loyalty are tested by the dangers of the sea. In his story "The Secret Sharer," written several years before World War I, he tells how a young man passes such a test in his first experience of commanding a ship.

War as a Test Many young men in England and elsewhere regarded the war as a noble test of manhood, at least before its horrors became apparent. They were inspired by strong feelings of patriotism and national allegiance. Such feelings had been especially intense for almost fifty years before the war. During the period 1870 to 1914, nationalism and colonial competition among European powers had led to a number of conflicts and created a system of opposing international alliances. On the one side were Germany and Austria, and on the other were France, Britain, and Russia. The assassination of the heir to the Austrian throne on June 28, 1914, set off a series of events that, by the middle of August, involved these two alliances in a world war.

The European theater of the war was known as the Western Front. There, Germany swept through Belgium and invaded France, where its invasion was finally halted by French armies and an assisting British force. The war settled down to a stalemate with large armies in trenches facing each other across the battlefield. Meanwhile, on the Eastern Front, German and Austrian forces inflicted defeats and

▲ **Critical Viewing** What does this photograph reveal about the way in which World War I was fought? [Deduce]

enormous casualties on the Russian armies. These setbacks caused increasing discontent in Russia and helped lead to the Russian Revolution of 1917, in which the Bolsheviks, led by Lenin, overthrew the czarist regime. When Lenin seized control of Russia, he withdrew its armies from the war. However, the loss of Russia as an ally by France and Britain was more than compensated for when the United States entered the war on their side in 1917. In November 1918, Germany and Austria surrendered to the allies, ending the war.

The effectiveness of modern artillery, machine guns, and poison gas resulted in a huge number of casualties for armies attacking enemy trenches. It is estimated that 8,500,000 soldiers died in the war either from wounds or disease, a figure that greatly exceeded the number of military deaths in any previous war. A whole generation of young men was wiped out.

Young men who experienced this inferno aged quickly. In addition, they quickly lost their sense of Romanticism or any notion of military glory. This was so for poets like Wilfred Owen (1893–1918) and Siegfried Sassoon (1886–1967). Owen, for example, entered the war as a Keatsian Romantic, but he soon began writing poetry with a disillusioned, modern spirit. It was the guns that "modernized" him in the few years he lived, changing his work

more effectively than any literary critique. Owen was living a harsh new reality in which his compassion for fellow soldiers was much more real than abstractions like patriotism. In the preface to his book of poems, Owen asserts that he will not write about conventional ideas like "glory, honor, might, majesty." He declares, "My subject is War, and the pity of War." That pity is revealed in poems like "Futility" (see below).

In this quiet but deeply grieving poem, a soldier tries to make sense of a comrade's death. At first, in his distraction, he wants to move the body "into the sun." He knows that the sun cannot "rouse" the man "now," but he denies this knowledge. Something inside him wants to believe that the sun as the source of all earthly life can restore a soldier who seems to be sleeping. Then, in lines 10–11, he admits the finality of death. This acknowledgment, however, leads him to question the purpose and meaning of life (lines 12–14).

Futility
by Wilfred Owen

Move him into the sun—
Gently its touch awoke him once,
At home, whispering of fields
    unsown.
Always it woke him, even in
    France,
5 Until this morning and this snow.
If anything might rouse him now
The kind old sun will know.

Think how it wakes the seeds,—
Woke, once, the clays of a cold
    star.
10 Are limbs, so dear-achieved, are
    sides,
Full-nerved—still warm—too hard
    to stir?
Was it for this the clay grew tall?
—O what made fatuous sunbeams
    toil
To break earth's sleep at all?

Owen is famous for his use of consonantal rhymes, in which consonants match but vowel sounds are different—for example *grained* and *ground*. Perhaps this type of rhyming provided an off-kilter music suitable for the off-kilter reality of the wartime scenes he described. At any rate, such consonantal rhyming is evident in this poem. Two examples are *seeds/sides* (lines 8/10) and *star/stir* (lines 9/11).

The three-beat lines at the beginning and end of each stanza contrast with the four-beat lines in the rest of the stanza. At the end of the poem, the final, briefer line emphasizes the breaking off of the poem in a sense of "futility."

Connecting Literature to the Historical Context

Modernism

The widespread destruction and loss of life caused by World War I made many people feel disillusioned and cynical. Not only did they question the nineteenth-century belief in progress, but they doubted the worth of civilization itself. After all, higher ideals and values had been unable to prevent the most destructive war in history. Prompted by such feelings, some people lived for the moment and enjoyed the 1920's era that became known as the Roaring Twenties. One form of music they enjoyed was jazz, imported from America, where it had been created by African Americans. They also engaged in flashy new dances like the Charleston.

World War I had postponed the resolution of social and political conflicts within Britain. In the case of political democracy, the war eventually made reforms easier. Women defense workers had contributed so much to the war effort that it now seemed unjust to deny women the vote. In 1918, the Representation of the Peoples Act extended suffrage to women thirty and older who had a minimum amount of property. The same act nearly abolished property requirements for male voters, making it possible for nearly all working-class males to vote. (Later, in 1928, the voting rights of men and women were equalized.)

After the war, the working classes, now represented by the Labor party and various unions, continued to assert their rights. Unions went on strike, even during the economic boom of the immediate post-war years (1919–1920). As the 1920's continued, however, an economic downturn replaced the boom, and millions became unemployed. This situation worsened in 1929, when the collapse of the American stock market and the subsequent worldwide depression brought increased economic hardship to Britain.

A small number of Irish patriots had ventured an armed rebellion against Britain in the Easter Rising of 1916. However, Britain quickly suppressed the revolt, which went unsupported by the majority of Irish. From 1919 to 1920, however, Irish nationalists under Michael Collins fought a successful underground war against British forces. The negotiations to end this conflict led to the formation of the Irish Free State in 1921. In 1922, a civil war broke out in Ireland between those who supported the Free State and those who opposed it. By the end of the year, however, the Free State was established.

A Sense of Unrest Meanwhile, the Versailles peace treaty, which the victorious Allies had imposed on Germany (1919), required it to disarm and to pay $32 billion in war reparations. The severity of these terms created bitter feelings in Germany and laid the basis for Hitler's rise to power and still another world war.

All these conflicts, domestic and international, created a sense of unrest, as did the quickening pace of change in daily life. Many new inventions—including the radio, the telephone, and the automobile—were linking people more closely and speeding up the transmission of information. On the one hand, these inventions gave people the sense that they were more in control of their lives and had the world at their fingertips. For example, they only had to pick up a telephone in order to speak with a friend or business associate. On the other hand, these inventions made it necessary to change habits and routines, a process that could generate anxiety. In addition, these advances in technology required people to assimilate more information in a briefer period of time.

Still Life, Pablo Picasso, Prado, Madrid, Spain

▲ **Critical Viewing** What elements in *Still Life* by Pablo Picasso indicate that it is a Modernist work of art? Why? **[Analyze]**

Inventions like the telephone and the automobile were becoming a part of every-day life. Less tangible but influential nevertheless were dramatic discoveries in science. These breakthroughs were changing the ways in which people thought of themselves.

By the early twentieth century, most areas of the Earth had been explored. However, the Viennese psychologist Sigmund Freud (1856–1939) had discovered a whole new continent within the human mind. He called it the unconscious, expounding his theories in books like *The Interpretation of Dreams* (1900). Freud wrote in German, but his disciple, the English psychologist Ernest Jones, helped to popularize his ideas in the English-speaking world. For Freud, the unconscious was an irrational realm that could be understood through dreams and slips of the tongue. Ordinarily, people were unaware of the unconscious, yet it could exert a great deal of control over human decisions and actions. His theories made it seem as if humans were less in control of their lives than was previously believed. However, unconscious motivations might be the key to explaining the widespread slaughter of a world war.

At the same time that Freud was exploring primitive and irrational elements within the human mind, anthropologist Sir James George Frazer (1854–1941) was studying the folklore and magic of primitive peoples. His book *The Golden Bough*, first published in 1890, appeared in an abridged one-volume edition in the 1920's. Frazer's explorations of primitive rituals influenced T. S. Eliot's great Modernist poem *The Waste Land* (see page A39).

Albert Einstein's (1879–1955) theories of special and general relativity also made the world seem a stranger and more mysterious place—even for those who did not fully understand them. Newton's theory of gravity, proposed in 1687, had not been seriously challenged in more than 200 years, although scientists were aware of certain problems that this theory did not resolve. Einstein's theory of special relativity (1905) did resolve those problems and demonstrated that the laws of physics applied uniformly throughout the universe. However, Einstein showed that the universe did not have a master frame of reference from which all events could be observed. Consequently, two observers moving uniformly *relative* to one another would disagree about measurements of length and time. In addition, Einstein showed that solid matter could, under certain circumstances, be converted to energy and vice versa ($E=mc^2$). The general theory of relativity (about 1916) was even harder for nonscientists to understand. It suggested that gravity, previously thought of as a force, was more like a curvature in what Einstein called space-time.

Modernism

Modernism Disillusionment, social conflicts, economic depression, the pace of technological change, and dramatic new scientific discoveries all contributed to the artistic movement known as Modernism. This movement influenced a number of art forms, including the visual arts and music as well as literature. It arose in a number of different places and at different times, both before and after World War I. Wherever it appeared, it tended to be self-consciously experimental and defied agreed-upon conventions in order to capture the fast pace and fragmentation of modern life. In prewar Paris, for example, artists like Pablo Picasso (1881–1973) and Georges Braque (1882–1963) abandoned the traditional use of perspective and realistic subject matter. (See painting on page A37.) They developed a system in which three-dimensional objects were broken into pieces and viewed from several perspectives at once. Early critics, noticing the cubelike shapes in their work, called this style of painting Cubism. Just as Einstein had eliminated Newton's single frame of reference, the Cubists did away with a single, realistic perspective.

Similarly, James Joyce (1882–1941) and Virginia Woolf (1882–1941) rejected the realistic framework of Victorian fiction. That framework consisted of a well-described external reality through which recognizable characters move in the patterns of a well-defined plot. To Joyce and Woolf, however, these fictional conventions reflected a nineteenth-century notion of the world that was no longer valid. Woolf presented twentieth-century reality in a 1925 essay entitled "Modern Fiction" (see below).

The style that Joyce and Woolf developed to capture the "luminous halo . . . of consciousness" was called stream-of-consciousness, a term first used by the American psychologist William James. In a stream-of-consciousness novel like Woolf's *Mrs. Dalloway* (1925), readers

---

from Modern Fiction
by Virginia Woolf

. . . Examine for a moment an ordinary mind on an ordinary day. The mind receives a myriad impressions—trivial, fantastic, evanescent [short-lived], or engraved with the sharpness of steel. From all sides they come, an incessant shower of innumerable atoms; and as they fall, as they shape themselves into the life of Monday or Tuesday, the accent falls differently from of old; the moment of importance came not here but there; so that, if a writer were a free man and not a slave, if he could write what he chose, not what he must, if he could base his work upon his own feeling and not upon convention, there would be no plot, no comedy, no tragedy, no love interest or catastrosphe in the accepted style, and perhaps not a single button sewn on as the Bond Street [London street with clothing stores] tailors would have it. Life is not a series of gig-lamps [carriage-lamps] symmetrically arranged; life is a luminous halo, a semi-transparent envelope surrounding us from the beginning of consciousness to the end. Is it not the task of the novelist to convey this varying, this unknown and uncircumscribed [unlimited] spirit, whatever aberration [deviation from the norm] or complexity it may display, with as little mixture of the alien and external as possible? . . .

from Mrs. Dalloway

by Virginia Woolf

For it was the middle of June. The War was over, except for some one like Mrs. Foxcroft at the Embassy last night eating her heart out because that nice boy was killed and now the old Manor House must go to a cousin; or Lady Bexborough who opened a bazaar, they said, with the telegram in her hand, John, her favorite, killed; but it was over; thank Heaven—over. It was June. The King and Queen were at the Palace. And everywhere, though it was still so early, there was a beating, a stirring of galloping ponies, tapping of cricket bats . . .

are plunged immediately into the character's mind. In this mysterious inner world, fast-paced and fragmentary, impressions of external reality and ideas combine and recombine (see box above).

The central character, Mrs. Dalloway, is walking through London on a June morning not long after the end of World War I. She focuses on the time, "the middle of June," and then on the fact that "[t]he War was over." This thought makes her recall Mrs. Foxcroft who, at a party the previous night, had mourned for a boy killed in the war. She then thinks of another woman, Lady Bexborough, who suffered a great loss in the war. Then Mrs. Dalloway returns to the thought that the war "was over; thank Heaven—over." She thinks again of the month and of the fact that the royal couple are "at the Palace." Then, possibly stimulated by the sight of horse-drawn carriages, she imagines polo ponies and people playing polo and cricket.

Throughout, however, Woolf does not use phrases like *she thought* or *this reminded her.* Instead, she tries to reproduce the actual flow of thoughts in Mrs. Dalloway's mind.

Poets also experimented with Modernist devices, eliminating explanations and placing side by side voices from different

from The Waste Land

by T. S. Eliot

I. The Burial of the Dead

April is the cruellest month, breeding
Lilacs out of the dead land, mixing
Memory and desire, stirring
Dull roots with spring rain.
5   Winter kept us warm, covering
Earth in forgetful snow, feeding
A little life with dried tubers.
Summer surprised us, coming over the Starnbergersee°   °Lake near Munich, Germany.
With a shower of rain; we stopped in the colonnade,
10   And went on in sunlight, into the Hofgarten,°   °Public park in Munich.
And drank coffee, and talked for an hour.
Bin gar keine Russin, stamm' aus Litauen, echt deutsch.°   °German for "I'm not Russian, I come from Lithuania, I am a real German."
And when we were children, staying at the archduke's,
My cousin's, he took me out on a sled,
15   And I was frightened. He said, Marie,
Marie, hold on tight. And down we went.
In the mountains, there you feel free.
I read, much of the night, and go south in the winter.

times and places. The most famous Modernist poem was perhaps T. S. Eliot's (1888–1965) *The Waste Land.* Instead of trying to understand it on a first reading, just listen for its nervous and shifting music (see page A39).

The poem as a whole is 434 lines and consists of four parts in addition to Part I, "The Burial of the Dead," whose beginning appears here. As the title indicates, Eliot was portraying postwar Western civilization as a spiritual waste land. He adds dimensions of meaning to his portrayal with references to literary works and events from other historical eras.

The first seven lines, which describe the coming of spring, are spoken by the poem's first voice. Spring should be a time of rebirth and rejoicing, and these lines recall the joyous beginning of Chaucer's *Canterbury Tales:* "When in April the sweet showers fall . . ." However, the voice in *The Waste Land* resents the awakening of spring: "April is the cruellest month . . ."

This voice, not wanting to be reborn, prefers the forgetfulness and warmth of winter burial: "Winter kept us warm. . . ."

The next voice in the poem (lines 8–11, 13–18) is that of Countess Marie Larisch, whose autobiography *My Past* (1913) was the source of details and episodes in these lines. Without making any explanations, Eliot begins speaking in this other voice. He expects readers to find a common thread between these lines and lines 1–7. Marie is a member of the aristocracy who seems to be living a sheltered, well-pampered, perhaps fearful life ("And I was frightened"). In this respect, she resembles the first speaker, who would rather be buried than reborn. Line 12 seems to reproduce the speech of someone Marie meets in a Munich park. This person, too, is fearful and anxious to establish his or her identity as a "real German."

This whole first section, then, deals with people who are in retreat from life, perhaps even spiritually dead. By letting the

Connecting Art to the Historical Context

Head of a Woman, Pablo Picasso, Fitzwilliam Museum, University of Cambridge, UK

Picasso: Breaking With Tradition

Like Eliot's *The Waste Land,* Pablo Picasso's work also reflected the despair of the Modernist Age. When Picasso was nineteen, he broke with traditional styles and began what is known as his "Blue Period." He painted whole works in shades of blue to communicate a sense of loneliness and alienation. The painting on this page, with its contrasting blocks of blue and tan, is an example of Picasso's innovative style that critics called Cubism. This style was highly experimental and unusual in Picasso's time.

Make an Inference (a) Why do you think Picasso and his contemporaries broke away from traditional artistic styles and techniques? (b) In what ways does the Cubist style reflect the times in which Picasso lived?

reader hear their voices, without explanation or intervention, Eliot adds to the immediacy of the reader's experience. The shift from voice to voice even accentuates the anxiety that each voice conveys. Modernist devices enable the poet to short-circuit rational responses by re-creating, rather than explaining, the spiritual condition of modern society.

Connecting Literature to the Historical Context

Postmodernism: A Conclusion and a New Beginning

During the 1930's, the indecision of Britain and other democracies allowed externally aggressive totalitarian regimes like those of Germany, Italy, and Japan to expand their power. Finally, Britain and France declared war on Germany when that country invaded Poland in 1939. In the ensuing world war, France quickly fell to Germany. Britain continued the fight and, joined by the United States and the Soviet Union, defeated Germany, Italy, and Japan. Although Britain emerged victorious from the war, it lost its empire and its status as a world power. As if in response to a diminished nationhood, postmodern writers like Philip Larkin (1922–1985) found it more difficult to make imaginative claims for their work.

Postwar Britain Larkin felt he could not stand apart from and above everyday life, as some of the great Modernist writers like W. B. Yeats (1865–1939) had done. Like any other citizen of a diminished postwar Britain, Larkin lived in an everyday world that his poetry would have to acknowledge.

However, in Larkin's imagination, there was still a faint trace of the Romantic and Modernist desire to go beyond ordinary life and find a greater, higher truth. His poetry therefore looks at the ordinary world and sees it with great clarity, but it is also haunted by a faint sense of something out of the ordinary.

A World of Language This conflict, which Larkin embodies in his work, does not exhaust the possibilities of post-Modernism in English. Fiction and poetry from England's former colonies reflect a greater sense of possibility. Writers in (or from) the Caribbean, Australia, Ireland, India, and Nigeria are bestowing new riches on the English language.

The Story of British Literature— To Be Continued This story of English literature began with the fictional funeral of a tribal chieftain, described in the Old English poem *Beowulf*. It has continued to the end of the twentieth century, when a global audience witnessed the funeral of an English princess on television. These two funerals, about a millennium and a half apart, indicate that the basic facts of human life have not changed. People are born and die, and in the ceremonies marking a death, they try to speak meaningful and deeply felt words.

If the basic facts of human life have not altered, what people make of those facts *has* changed considerably. Literature is the record of that change. It shows men and women defining and redefining in deeply felt words what is important to them. Over the past 1,500 years, writers in English have engaged in this effort. Taken together, their poems, plays, and fiction record the transformation of a society of warriors into a democratic nation of citizens. At the same time, the English language itself has evolved from the Old English spoken by Germanic tribes to the modern English that is spoken by people of diverse backgrounds throughout the world.

The story of English literature will continue into the twenty-first century and beyond. It is a living record that readers can consult as they decide what to value in their own lives. Furthermore, it is a record that will never become dated, because even the oldest stories and poems show people creating meaning from the unchanging facts of human existence.

Sir Gawain and the Green Knight, Bodleian Library, Oxford

From Legend to History:

The Old English and Medieval Periods (449–1485)

Who pulleth out this sword of
this stone and anvil, is rightwise king
born of all England.

—Sir Thomas Malory,
from *Morte d'Arthur*

Timeline

449–1485

British Events

- **449** Anglo-Saxon invasion. ▼

- **597** St. Augustine founds Christian monastery at Canterbury, Kent.

- **664** Synod of Whitby establishes Roman Church in England.
- **731** **Bede** completes *A History of the English Church and People*.
- **c. 750** Surviving version of *Beowulf* composed.
- **792** Vikings attack Lindisfarne. ▼

- **843** Scottish ruler Kenneth MacAlprin unites Scots and Picts.
- **871** Alfred the Great becomes King of Wessex. ▼

- **c. 930** Howel the Good unites kingdom of Wales.
- **c. 975** Saxon monks copy Old English poems into *The Exeter Book*.
- **991** English defeated by Danes at Battle of Maldon.
- **1002** Brian Boru unites kingdom of Ireland.
- **1034** Duncan I inherits Scottish throne.
- **1040** Macbeth murders Duncan I.
- **1042** Edward the Confessor becomes king of Saxons.
- **1066** Normans defeat Saxons at Hastings; William the Conqueror becomes king of England. ▼

World Events

- **476** Western Europe: Fall of Western Roman Empire.
- **493** Italy: Theodoric the Great establishes Ostrogothic kingdom.
- **496** France: Clovis, king of Franks, converts to Christianity.
- **542** Constantinople: Plague kills half the population.
- **c. 550** Mexico: Toltecs defeat Mayas.
- **552** Japan: Buddhism introduced. ▶
- **591** China: Beginning of book printing.

- **637** Middle East: Jerusalem conquered by Arabs.
- **641** Egypt: Library at Alexandria destroyed.
- **712** Spain: Seville conquered by Moors.
- **732** France: Charles Martel defeats Moors.
- **771** France: Charlemagne becomes king. ▲
- **800** Peru: Incas build city of Machu Picchu.
- **c. 810** Persia: Algebra devised.
- **c. 830** France: Einhard writes *Life of Charlemagne*.
- **861** North Atlantic: Vikings discover Iceland.
- **c. 882** Russia: Nation founded by Vikings.

- **c. 900** Western Europe: Feudalism develops.
- **911** France: Normans establish Normandy.
- **982** Greenland: Eric the Red establishes first Viking colony.
- **1009** Middle East: Moslems destroy Holy Sepulcher in Jerusalem.
- **c. 1020** America: Viking explorer Leif Ericson explores Canadian coast.
- **1045** Spain: Birth of El Cid, national hero who fought Moors.
- **1053** Italy: Normans conquer Sicily.

British Events

- **1073** Canterbury becomes England's religious center.
- **c. 1075** Construction on Tower of London begins.
- **1100** Henry I becomes king.
- **c. 1130** Oxford becomes a center for learning.
- **1170** Thomas Becket, Archbishop of Canterbury, murdered. ▼
- **1171** Henry II conquers south-eastern Ireland.
- **1180** Glass windows first used in private homes.

- **1215** King John forced to sign Magna Carta.
- **1218** First Newgate prison built in London.

- **c. 1209** Cambridge University founded.
- **1233** First coal mined at Newcastle.
- **1258** First commoners allowed in Parliament.
- **1272** Edward I becomes king.
- **1282** England conquers Wales.
- **1295** Edward I assembles Model Parliament.
- **1337** Beginning of the Hundred Years' War with France.
- **1348** Black Death begins sweeping through England. ▼

- **1361** Bible first translated into English.
- **c. 1375** Surviving version of *Sir Gawain and the Green Knight* written.

- **1381** Peasants' Revolt.
- **1386 Chaucer** begins writing *The Canterbury Tales.* ▶
- **1455** Beginning of the Wars of the Roses.
- **1460** Richard of York killed at Battle of Wakefield.
- **c. 1470 Thomas Malory** writes *Morte d'Arthur.*
- **1476** William Caxton builds first English printing press.

World Events

- **1096** Europe and Middle East: First Crusade begins.
- **c. 1100** France: *Song of Roland* written.
- **c. 1130** Portugal: Alfonso VII defeats Moors.
- **c. 1150** Spain: First paper made.
- **1174** Italy: Tower of Pisa built.
- **1192** Austria: Duke Leopold imprisons Richard I of England.
- **1194** Iceland: *Elder Edda*, a collection of Norse myths and legends, first appears.
- **1214** China: Mongol leader Genghis Khan captures Peking.

- **1221** Italy: First known sonnet appears.
- **1231** Europe: Pope Gregory IX establishes Inquisition.
- **1241** Eastern Europe: Mongols withdraw from Poland and Hungary.
- **1275** China: Marco Polo visits court of Kublai Khan.
- **1291** Europe and Middle East: End of Crusades.
- **1307** Italy: Dante begins writing *The Divine Comedy.*
- **1327** Mexico: Aztecs establish Mexico City and create a dating system with a solar year of 365 days. ▲
- **1332** India: Bubonic plague begins.
- **1341** Italy: Petrarch crowned poet laureate of Rome.
- **1346** France: English defeat French at Crecy.

- **c. 1400** Italy: Beginning of Medici rule.
- **1429** France: Joan of Arc leads French in breaking siege of Orleans. ▼
- **c.1450** North America: Iroquois nations unite.
- **1453** France: Hundred Years' War with England ends.
- **1453** Germany: First Gutenberg Bible printed.

- **1461** France: François Villon writes *Grand Testament.*
- **1483** Portugal: John II refuses to finance Columbus.
- **1484** Italy: Botticelli paints *Birth of Venus.*
- **1485** Peru: Incan empire reaches its zenith.

The Story of the Times

(A.D. 449–1485)

▲ **Compare and Contrast** How are these housekeys from the Viking era similar to and different from those you use today?

▲ **Draw Conclusions** From looking at the details in this illuminated drawing what conclusions can you draw about the trade of shoeing horses during this era?

Historical Background

The Conquest of Britain Between 800 and 600 B.C., two groups of Celts from southern Europe invaded the British Isles. One group, who called themselves Brythons (now spelled "Britons"), settled on the largest island, Britain. The other, known as Gaels, settled on the second largest island, known to us as Ireland.

The Celts were farmers and hunters. They organized themselves into tightly knit clans, each with a fearsome loyalty to its chieftain. When these clans fell into disagreement with one another, they often looked to a class of priests known as Druids to settle their disputes.

The next conquerors of Britain were the far more sophisticated Romans. In 55 B.C. and again the next year, the Roman general Julius Caesar made hasty invasions. The true conquest of Britain, however, occurred nearly one hundred years later. Disciplined Roman legions spread out over the island, establishing camps that soon grew into towns.

Roman rule of Britain lasted for more than 300 years. It ended only when northern European tribes invaded Italy and increased pressure on Rome itself. The last Roman legions departed from Britain to defend Rome in A.D. 407. By that time, the Britons faced a new set of invaders.

The next invaders were the Anglo-Saxons, from what is now Germany. Some Anglo-Saxons appear to have been deep-sea fishermen; others seem to have been farmers, perhaps seeking soil richer than the sandy or marshy land at home. Gradually, the newcomers took over more and more of what today is England.

The Coming of Christianity During the fourth century, the Romans had accepted Christianity and introduced it to Britain. A century later, when the Celts fled the Anglo-Saxons, they took their Christian faith with them. Although Rome fell to barbarian tribes in A.D. 476, the Celtic Christian church continued to thrive.

In the late sixth century, a soldier and abbot named Columba, along with some monks, gained converts to Christianity and established monasteries in the north.

In 597, the Roman cleric Saint Augustine (not the early Christian Church father) arrived in southeast England and converted King Ethelbert of Kent to Christianity. Augustine set up a monastery at Canterbury in Kent and began preaching his faith to other rulers as well. By providing counsel to quarreling rulers, the Church promoted peace and helped to unify the English people.

Danish Invasion In the ninth century, the Norse of Norway and the Danes of Denmark were beset with a rising population and took to the seas. These Vikings carried their piracy to the British Isles. The Norse set their sights on Northumbria, Scotland, Wales, and Ireland, whereas the Danes targeted eastern and southern England.

Viking invaders sacked and plundered monasteries, destroyed manuscripts, and stole sacred religious objects. They burned entire communities and put villagers to the sword. Although the English fought back valiantly, the Danes made broad inroads. By the middle of the ninth century, most of northern, eastern, and central England had fallen to the invaders.

In 871, a king ascended to the Wessex throne who would become the only ruler in England's history ever to be honored with the epithet "the Great." His name was Alfred, and he earned the title partly by resisting further Danish encroachment. Under a truce concluded in 886, England was formally divided: the Saxons acknowledged Danish rule in the east and north, but the Danes agreed to respect Saxon rule in the south. Alfred the Great became a national hero.

Alfred's achievements went far beyond the field of battle, however. Not only was he instrumental in preserving the remnants of pre-Danish civilization in Britain, but he encouraged a rebirth of learning and education.

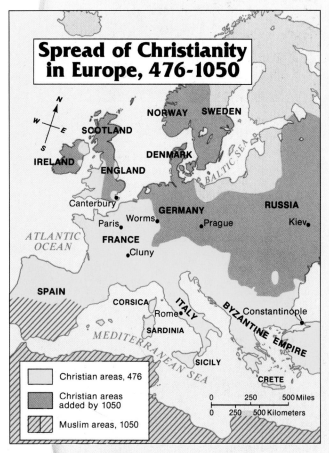

Spread of Christianity in Europe, 476–1050

Christian areas, 476
Christian areas added by 1050
Muslim areas, 1050

0   250   500 Miles
0   250   500 Kilometers

▲ **Analyze Causes and Effects** This map shows the spread of Christianity throughout Europe. What effects might this religious conversion have had on daily life?

▲ **Draw a Conclusion** The Bayeux Tapestry is a piece of embroidery (230 feet by 20 inches) that tells the story of King Harold's defeat at Hastings in 1066. This small section of the tapestry shows the Normans preparing a meal after their channel crossing. What conclusions can you draw from this scene about the Normans and their way of life?

▶ **Make an Inference** What can you infer about Viking society and technology by studying this sword?

Toward the close of the tenth century, however, more Danes from Europe attempted to recapture and widen the Danelaw, the eastern and northern sections of England under Danish control. Once they succeeded, they forced the Saxons to select Danish kings.

Then, in 1042, the line of succession returned to a descendant of Alfred the Great. This king, Edward, had gained the title "the Confessor" because he was a deeply religious Christian. His death in 1066 led to the end of the Anglo-Saxon period of history.

The Norman Conquest The Normans, or "north men," were descendants of Vikings who had invaded the coast of France in the ninth century. William, Duke of Normandy, had family ties to Edward the Confessor, the English king. When Edward died in 1066, the Saxon council of elders chose Harold II as king. William of Normandy, meanwhile, claimed that Edward had promised him the throne and he crossed the English Channel to assert his claim by force. At the Battle of Hastings near a seaside village in southern England, Harold was killed, and William emerged victorious.

Over the next five years William suppressed the Anglo-Saxon nobility and confiscated their lands. He saw to it that Normans controlled government and that business was conducted in Norman French or Latin. The Normans gradually remade England along feudal lines.

Feudalism had taken root on the European continent at a time when no central government was strong enough to keep order. The feudal system involved an exchange of property for personal service. In theory, all the land belonged to the king, who parceled out land among his powerful supporters. He gave these supporters noble titles—usually "Baron"—and special privileges. As a vassal of his overlord, each baron paid certain fees, or taxes, and supplied a specified number of knights—professional soldiers—should the king require them. In return for their services, knights usually received smaller parcels of land, called manors. The peasants who worked these manors were the lowest class in the feudal system, the serfs.

Reign of the Plantagenets Although Norman influence continued for centuries, Norman rule ended in 1154 when Henry Plantagenet, Count of Anjou, came to the throne as Henry II. Henry founded the royal house of Plantagenet and established a record as one of England's ablest kings.

Henry's concern with legal matters led him into direct conflict with the Church. When the archbishop's seat at Canterbury fell vacant, he appointed his friend Thomas Becket to the position, expecting Becket to go along with royal policy. Instead, Becket defied the king and appealed to the Pope. The Pope sided with Becket, provoking Henry to rage.

Some of Henry's knights misunderstood the royal wrath. In 1170, four of them murdered Becket in his cathedral. Henry quickly condemned the crime and tried to atone for it by making a holy journey, or pilgrimage, to Becket's tomb. Thereafter, a pilgrimage to Becket's shrine at Canterbury became a common English means of showing religious devotion.

The Magna Carta The next king, Richard I, spent most of his reign staging military expeditions overseas. His activities proved costly, and his successor, King John, inherited the debts. John tried to raise money by ordering new taxes on the barons. The barons resisted these measures, bringing England to the edge of civil war. To avert further trouble, King John at last agreed to certain of the barons' conditions by putting his seal to the Magna Carta (Latin for "Great Charter").

In this document, the king promised not to tax land without first meeting with the barons. The Magna Carta produced no radical changes in government. Yet many historians believe that the document's restrictions on royal power marked the beginning of constitutional government in England.

The Lancasters, Yorks, and Tudors During the fourteenth and fifteenth centuries, the house of Lancaster replaced the Plantagenets on the throne, only to be replaced in turn by the house of York. The Lancastrian kings were Henry IV, Henry V, and Henry VI, all of whom later became central figures in the historical dramas of Shakespeare.

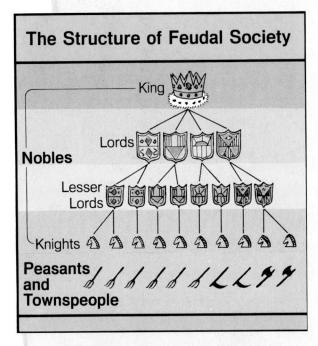

The Structure of Feudal Society

King
Nobles — Lords
Lesser Lords
Knights
Peasants and Townspeople

▲ **Relate** What aspects of feudal society, as diagrammed here, are similar to aspects of modern-day America? What class of modern people are equivalent to the class of knights in feudal society?

▲ **Deduce** From the evidence in this picture, what can you deduce about women's duties and chores?

▲ **Speculate** Dance is an important part of most cultures: celebrations, entertainment, and religious rituals usually involve some form of dancing. Speculate about the nature of the medieval dance portrayed in this picture.

The Decline of the Feudal System After the great plague, called the Black Death, swept across England in 1348 and 1349, a massive labor shortage increased the value of a peasant's work. Landowners began paying their farmers in cash, giving these workers a greater sense of freedom. Along with freedom went frustration, as peasants began to complain about discriminatory laws and heavy taxation. Finally, in 1381, peasants in southern England staged a revolt, demanding an end to serfdom. Although the revolt was crushed, many of its causes continued, and so did the peasants' discontent.

The conflicts known as the Wars of the Roses began in 1453, pitting the house of York against the house of Lancaster. Eventually, Henry Tudor, a distant cousin and supporter of the Lancastrian kings, led a rebellion against the unpopular Yorkist king Richard III and killed him. Tudor, crowned Henry VII, later married Richard's niece, uniting the houses of York and Lancaster and ending the Wars of the Roses.

Literature of the Period

Saxon Literature Anglo-Saxon literature began not with books, but with spoken verse and incantations. The reciting of poems often occurred on ceremonial occasions, such as the celebration of military victories.

This early verse falls mainly into two categories: heroic poetry, recounting the achievements of warriors, and elegiac poetry, lamenting the deaths of loved ones and the loss of the past. The long poem *Beowulf* is the most famous example of heroic poetry, and a famous elegiac poem is "The Wanderer."

Beowulf is an epic—a long heroic poem. It tells the story of a great pagan warrior renowned for his courage, strength, and dignity. Because it is the first such work composed in the English language, it is considered the national epic of England.

Before the reign of Alfred the Great, all important prose written in the British Isles was composed in Latin. The monks who transcribed these works regarded the vernacular, the language of the common people, as a "vulgar tongue." The greatest of England's Latin scholars was the Venerable Bede, whose *A History of the English Church and People* gives an account of England from the Roman invasion to his own time (673–735).

Another great work of prose from this time is *The Anglo-Saxon Chronicles*, the name given to a group of historical journals written and compiled in monasteries. Unlike Bede's *History*, these records were written in Old English.

Literature of the English Middle Ages Lyric poems of this period fall into two major categories—secular and religious. The usual topics of secular poetry are love and nature. Another popular poetic form was the ballad, a folk song that told a story. One surviving series of ballads, for example, concerns the exploits of the legendary outlaw Robin Hood.

During early Norman times, the Church often sponsored plays as part of religious services. In time, these plays moved from the church to the churchyard and then to the marketplace. The earliest dramas were miracle plays, or mystery plays, that retold stories from the Bible or dealt with some aspect of the lives of saints.

During the turbulent fifteenth century, a new kind of drama arose: the morality play. Morality plays depicted the life of an ordinary person and taught a moral lesson.

An Emerging National Identity In 1454, a German silversmith, Johann Gutenberg, perfected a process of printing from movable type. Printing then spread rapidly throughout Europe, and, in 1476, William Caxton set up the first movable-type press in England. English literature no longer needed to be hand copied by church scribes.

One of Caxton's first projects was the printing of Geoffrey Chaucer's *The Canterbury Tales*, a series of verse stories told by pilgrims on their way to the tomb of Thomas Becket. Chaucer wrote in Middle English, a language quite close to English as it is spoken today. After centuries of the ebb and flow of conquerors and their languages, the island of England had finally settled on a national identity of its own.

▲ **Infer** During this time, folk medicines were widely used to treat diseases. What does this representation of head surgery suggest about the surgical techniques of the period?

▲ **Speculate** In the late fifteenth century, the movable type press began to play an important role in society. This set of letters and designed border were created by William Caxton's printing device. Speculate about the effect this device had on English society.

The Changing English Language

THE BEGINNINGS OF ENGLISH

by Richard Lederer

English

The rise of English as a planetary language is an unparalleled success story that begins long ago, in the middle of the fifth century A.D. Several large tribes of sea rovers, the Angles, Saxons, and Jutes, lived along the continental North Sea coast, from Denmark to Holland. Around A.D. 449, these Teutonic plunderers sailed across the water and invaded the islands then known as Britannia. (See the map of invasions on this page.) They found the land pleasant and the people easy to conquer, so they remained there. They brought with them a Low Germanic tongue that, in its new setting, became Anglo-Saxon, or Old English. In A.D. 827, King Egbert first named Britannia *Englaland,* "land of the Angles," after the chief people there.

The language came to be called *Englisc.* Old Englisc differs so much from modern English that it is harder for us to learn than German or Latin. Still, we can recognize a number of Anglo-Saxon words: *bedd, candel, eorth, faederm froendscipe, healf, healp, mann, moder,* and *waeter.*

Middle English

A dramatic evolution in the language came after yet another conquest of England, this one by the Norman French two centuries after the rule of

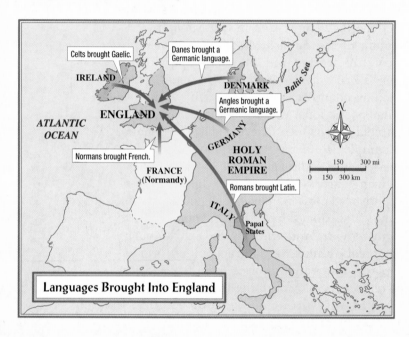

Languages Brought Into England

Celts brought Gaelic.
Danes brought a Germanic language.
IRELAND
DENMARK
Angles brought a Germanic language.
ENGLAND
ATLANTIC OCEAN
Normans brought French.
GERMANY
HOLY ROMAN EMPIRE
FRANCE (Normandy)
Romans brought Latin.
ITALY
Papal States
Baltic Sea
N
0   150   300 mi
0   150   300 km

Egbert. The new conquerors came from Normandy, a province of France across the English Channel. These Normans (shortened from *Northmen*) had originally been Viking freebooters from Scandinavia, but they now spoke French and had taken to French customs. Their *triouveurs,* or minstrels, sang the *Song of Roland* and the legends of King Charlemagne.

In 1066, under William, Duke of Normandy, the Normans invaded England. In a bloody battle at Hastings they conquered the Saxons and Danes who resisted them, killed the Saxon king, Harold, and forced the nobles to choose Duke William as king of England.

One result was that Old Englisc changed rapidly as many of the French words used by the Normans flooded the vocabulary of their adopted tongue. Examples include *sir* and *madam; courtesy, honor,* and *chivalry; dine, table,* and *roast;* and *court* and *royal.* From this infusion of French words emerged a tongue that we today call Middle English.

Activity

Read the opening verse of the Prologue to Geoffrey Chaucer's *Canterbury Tales* and look for the words *March, shires,* and *martyr.* Research the origins of these words to gain a fuller understanding of their meanings. Also, write briefly about what the diverse origins of these words suggests about the history of the English language.

PART **1** *Earthly Exile,*
Heavenly Home

Arrival of William at Penvesy (detail from Bayeux Tapestry)

Guide for Interpreting

The Exeter Book

Before *Star Wars* A family gathers with a group of friends to see the latest installment of their favorite drama. The following day, almost everyone in town is discussing the event and reenacting exciting passages. This event may sound to you like the opening of the latest movie thriller, but it also accurately describes a popular form of entertainment during Britain's Anglo-Saxon period.

> *Anglo-Saxon communities gathered to listen to storytellers weave tales of enchantment, heroes, and the everyday.*

Telling the Story Very few people were able to read during this period. As a result, an oral tradition flourished in which traveling storytellers, known as *scops,* would entertain the masses. Through the years, many stories ceased to be told and were lost. Others, however, have been preserved because they were eventually written down.

The Exeter Book "The Seafarer," "The Wanderer," and "The Wife's Lament" were all discovered in a collection of manuscripts called *The Exeter Book.* The book was probably compiled by monks during the reign of Alfred the Great, between 871 and 899. The history of *The Exeter Book* is a mystery to scholars, but it has evidently survived some rough treatment. The book has a large burn in the manuscript, several stains from a drinking mug, and marks that look almost as if the book had been used as a cutting board! Without *The Exeter Book,* many stories that came out of the oral tradition would have been lost to us forever.

◆ Background for Understanding

CULTURE: THE MEANING OF EXILE

To be in exile is to be forced to leave one's home. We cannot understand what exile meant to Anglo-Saxons until we understand what they meant by "home." While we identify ourselves as citizens of a certain country, an Anglo-Saxon warrior viewed himself as the follower of a particular lord or king. The notion of loyalty toward one's country, called patriotism today, did not exist. It was the lord himself who commanded allegiance: He dispensed bread, fruit, and goods won in raids and skirmishes. Perhaps even more important, he guaranteed the security of his followers in a dangerous and uncertain world.

The most important symbol of home for Anglo-Saxon warriors was the mead-hall (mead was an alcoholic beverage made of honey and water), where the lord and his followers shared the warmth of fire, food and drink, and entertainment

such as hearing poetry recited. The pleasures of poetry were especially welcome when the *scop* praised the heroism of the listening warriors. Enlivened with a feeling of fellowship, the mead-hall was smoky, noisy, smelly, and crowded. It was home.

Journal Writing Suppose that you were forced to leave your home. List some of the things that you would miss the most.

◆ Literature and Your Life

CONNECT YOUR EXPERIENCE

You are forced to leave home and live among strangers in another country. You don't know the language or customs, nor do you like the food served in this country. All you dream of is returning home, but you can't.

In the poems you're about to read, three speakers tell the story of how they came to live in exile and how they survived.

THEMATIC FOCUS: EARTHLY EXILE, HEAVENLY HOME

When these poems were written, it was not uncommon for people to lose their family, friends, and home following a great battle. How do you think they coped with such devastating losses?

◆ Build Vocabulary

RELATED WORDS: FORMS OF *GRIEVOUS*

"The Wanderer" contains the word *grievous*, which is related to the verb *grieve*, meaning "to feel deep sorrow or distress." By knowing the meaning of the verb, you can determine that the adjective *grievous* means "causing sorrow" or "hard to bear."

admonish
sentinel
fervent
rancor
compassionate
grievous
rapture
redress
blithe

WORD BANK

Before you read, preview this list of words from the poems.

◆ Grammar and Style

COMPOUND PREDICATES

One characteristic of Anglo-Saxon poetry is the use of **compound predicates**. A predicate is the sentence part that says something about the subject; it includes the verb and its modifiers. When a sentence or poetic line contains more than one verb that has the same subject, it has a compound predicate.

In this example, the subject is *sea*. The three verbs in the compound predicate are in italics. Notice how the compound predicate creates a rolling effect that mirrors the motion of the sea.

> ...It tells/How the sea *took* me, *swept* me back/And forth in sorrow and fear and pain,/*Showed* me suffering in a hundred ships,/In a thousand ports, and in me....

◆ Literary Focus

ANGLO-SAXON LYRICS

A **lyric poem** expresses the thoughts and feelings of a single speaker, usually by recounting events in the speaker's life. One type of lyric poem is the elegy, in which the loss of someone or something is mourned. All three poems that follow are elegies.

Because **Anglo-Saxon lyrics** sprang from the oral tradition, they were composed in a way that made them easy to memorize. The poems have been translated with an effort to preserve the rhythms and imagery of the original versions.

Most Anglo-Saxon poetry contained lines with regular rhythms, usually four strong beats or stresses to a line. In "The Wanderer" and "The Wife's Lament," a sound break called a **caesura** appears in the middle of each line, indicating a pause for breath in the reading. This caesura was probably a useful device for scops who had to recite hundreds of lines of poetry.

Another notable feature of Anglo-Saxon poetry is the **kenning,** a two-word metaphorical name for something, such as "whales' home" for the sea. Kennings were clever ways of renaming familiar things; for example, a modern kenning might be "bird's nest" for someone's messy hair.

Reading for Success

Literal Comprehension Strategies

To fully appreciate literature, you first must have a clear understanding of the basics: What's happening and to whom? Where is it happening? Why is it happening? Often the answers to these questions are found in the text of the story, poem, or piece of nonfiction. Successful readers use a few simple strategies to make sense of confusing or difficult passages of literature.

Use one of the following strategies to unlock the meaning of troublesome passages you encounter:

Connect the work to its historical context and recognize the characteristics of the period.

Knowing about the period from which a work comes will help you comprehend the writer's words and ideas. The introduction to this unit provides background on the period.

Reread or read ahead.

▶ Reread a sentence or a paragraph to find the connections among the words or to connect the ideas in several sentences.

▶ Read ahead. A confusing detail may become clear further on.

Break down long or confusing sentences.

▶ Figure out the subject of the sentence and what the sentence is saying about the subject. You may need to rearrange the parts of a sentence or to take other groups of words out of the way to do this.

Use context clues.

Context refers to the words, phrases, and sentences that surround a word. You can often use clues in the context to figure out the meaning of an unfamiliar word.

. . . Who could understand / . . . what we others suffer / As the paths of exile stretch endlessly on?

The words "suffer" and "stretch endlessly" provide clues that exile is something that involves long suffering.

Restate for understanding.

▶ Paraphrase, or restate a sentence or a paragraph in your own words.

▶ Summarize; review and state the main points of what has happened.

As you read "The Seafarer," read the side notes, which demonstrate how to apply these strategies to a work of early English literature.

The Seafarer

Translated by Burton Raffel

Ships With Three Men, Fish
Bodleian Library, Oxford

Critical Viewing ▶
Which elements in this picture are true to the seafarer's experience? Which elements are stylized? **[Classify]**

Read ahead to understand that the speaker is a sailor who is speaking about his life on the sea.

This tale is true, and mine. It tells
How the sea took me, swept me back
And forth in sorrow and fear and pain,
Showed me suffering in a hundred ships,
5 In a thousand ports, and in me. It tells
Of smashing surf when I sweated in the cold
Of an anxious watch, perched in the bow
As it dashed under cliffs. My feet were cast

In icy bands, bound with frost,
10 With frozen chains, and hardship groaned
Around my heart. Hunger tore
At my sea-weary soul. No man sheltered
On the quiet fairness of earth can feel
How wretched I was, drifting through winter
15 On an ice-cold sea, whirled in sorrow,
Alone in a world blown clear of love,
Hung with icicles. The hailstorms flew.
The only sound was the roaring sea,
The freezing waves. The song of the swan
20 Might serve for pleasure, the cry of the sea-fowl,
The death-noise of birds instead of laughter,
The mewing of gulls instead of mead.[1]
Storms beat on the rocky cliffs and were echoed
By icy-feathered terns and the eagle's screams;
25 No kinsman could offer comfort there,
To a soul left drowning in desolation.
        And who could believe, knowing but
The passion of cities, swelled proud with wine
And no taste of misfortune, how often, how wearily,
30 I put myself back on the paths of the sea.
Night would blacken; it would snow from the north;
Frost bound the earth and hail would fall,
The coldest seeds. And how my heart
Would begin to beat, knowing once more
35 The salt waves tossing and the towering sea!
The time for journeys would come and my soul
Called me eagerly out, sent me over
The horizon, seeking foreigners' homes.
        But there isn't a man on earth so proud,
40 So born to greatness, so bold with his youth,
Grown so brave, or so graced by God,
That he feels no fear as the sails unfurl,
Wondering what Fate has willed and will do.
No harps ring in his heart, no rewards,
45 No passion for women, no worldly pleasures,
Nothing, only the ocean's heave;
But longing wraps itself around him.
Orchards blossom, the towns bloom,
Fields grow lovely as the world springs fresh,
50 And all these admonish that willing mind
Leaping to journeys, always set
In thoughts traveling on a quickening tide.
So summer's sentinel, the cuckoo, sings

---

1. **mead:** Liquor made from fermented honey and water.

Paraphrase lines 12–17 to clarify their meaning: No landlubber can understand my misery. All winter long I was sailing on the cold sea. I was filled with sorrow and felt alone in a loveless, cold world.

Use context clues to figure out the meaning of *terns* (l. 24); "icy-feathered" helps you see that terns are a kind of bird.

Break down and **restate** this long, confusing passage (lines 47–52): The loveliness of one's home in spring serves to scold a person who is always looking for adventure in places other than home.

Recognize the **characteristics of the period** in lines 64–80: Anglo-Saxons were new to Christianity, and religious themes and ideas pervade their literature and philosophy.

Connect to **historical context.** In lines 81–86, the speaker mourns the passage of a golden era. The Anglo-Saxons lived in a world of confusion and uncertainty.

In his murmuring voice, and our hearts mourn
55 As he urges. Who could understand,
In ignorant ease, what we others suffer
As the paths of exile stretch endlessly on?
        And yet my heart wanders away,
My soul roams with the sea, the whales'
60 Home, wandering to the widest corners
Of the world, returning ravenous with desire,
Flying solitary, screaming, exciting me
To the open ocean, breaking oaths
On the curve of a wave.
                        Thus the joys of God
65 Are <u>fervent</u> with life, where life itself
Fades quickly into the earth. The wealth
Of the world neither reaches to Heaven nor remains.
No man has ever faced the dawn
Certain which of Fate's three threats
70 Would fall: illness, or age, or an enemy's
Sword, snatching the life from his soul.
The praise the living pour on the dead
Flowers from reputation: plant
An earthly life of profit reaped
75 Even from hatred and <u>rancor</u>, of bravery
Flung in the devil's face, and death
Can only bring you earthly praise
And a song to celebrate a place
With the angels, life eternally blessed
80 In the hosts of Heaven.
                        The days are gone
When the kingdoms of earth flourished in glory;
Now there are no rulers, no emperors,
No givers of gold, as once there were,
When wonderful things were worked among them
85 And they lived in lordly magnificence.
Those powers have vanished, those pleasures are dead.
The weakest survives and the world continues,
Kept spinning by toil. All glory is tarnished.
The world's honor ages and shrinks,
90 Bent like the men who mold it. Their faces
Blanch as time advances, their beards
Wither and they mourn the memory of friends.
The sons of princes, sown in the dust.
The soul stripped of its flesh knows nothing
95 Of sweetness or sour, feels no pain,
Bends neither its hand nor its brain. A brother
Opens his palms and pours down gold
On his kinsman's grave, strewing his coffin

◆ Build Vocabulary

admonish (ad män´ ish) v.: Advise; caution

sentinel (sen´ ti nəl) n.: Person or animal that guards or watches over

fervent (fʉr´ vənt) adj.: Having or showing great warmth of feeling

rancor (raŋ´ kər) n.: Ill will

▲ **Critical Viewing** How well does this painting capture the theme of exile as it is treated in the poem? **[Evaluate]**

With treasures intended for Heaven, but nothing
100 Golden shakes the wrath of God
For a soul overflowing with sin, and nothing
Hidden on earth rises to Heaven.
         We all fear God. He turns the earth,
He set it swinging firmly in space,
105 Gave life to the world and light to the sky.
Death leaps at the fools who forget their God.
He who lives humbly has angels from Heaven
To carry him courage and strength and belief.
A man must conquer pride, not kill it,
110 Be firm with his fellows, chaste for himself,
Treat all the world as the world deserves,
With love or with hate but never with harm,
Though an enemy seek to scorch him in hell,

> **Paraphrase** lines
> 103–124: We should
> think about heaven
> and how we might
> earn eternal life and
> happiness, which is
> given through loving
> God and living a
> Christian life.

Or set the flames of a funeral pyre
115 Under his lord. Fate is stronger
And God mightier than any man's mind.
Our thoughts should turn to where our home is,
Consider the ways of coming there,
Then strive for sure permission for us
120 To rise to that eternal joy,
That life born in the love of God
And the hope of Heaven. Praise the Holy
Grace of Him who honored us,
Eternal, unchanging creator of earth. Amen.

Science Connection

Early Navigation "My soul roams with the sea" says the speaker of "The Seafarer." In order to roam the seas, he had to rely upon early navigation techniques. The earliest sailors used landmarks to help guide short trips. For longer ocean voyages, a sailor used the temperature of the wind to determine direction— a cold wind came from the north and a warm wind came from the south. Early sailors also guided themselves by observing celestial bodies, noting the directions of sunrise and sunset, shadows cast by the noon-day sun, and the rising and setting of the night stars. Finally, navigators recorded all their methods of plotting courses, making it possible for others to follow the same routes. When you take a trip, what aids do you use to help you follow your course?

Guide for Responding

◆ Literature and Your Life

Reader's Response Do you agree that "Fate is stronger . . . than any man's mind"? Why or why not?

Thematic Focus In what ways is the seafarer in exile? How do his ideas of heaven compare with his earthly experience?

Questions for Research "The Seafarer" is rich in Christian imagery and phrases, but Christianity originated far away in the eastern Mediterranean basin. How did the religion come to Great Britain?

☑ Check Your Comprehension

1. To what is the speaker constantly drawn?
2. To what does the speaker compare the relationship of man and the sea?
3. What does the seafarer miss about the days of the past?
4. According to the speaker, what qualities might earn a person a place in heaven?

◆ Critical Thinking

INTERPRET

1. What are three images the poet uses in the first stanza to convey his sense of isolation? **[Support]**
2. How might you explain the mixed feelings about the sea that the poet seems to feel? **[Interpret]**
3. What contrast is implied in lines 80–102? **[Compare and Contrast]**

APPLY

4. Explain how a person can dislike something as much as the seafarer dislikes life at sea and yet keep going back to it. **[Hypothesize]**

◆ Literary Focus

ANGLO-SAXON LYRICS: KENNING

One interesting element in Anglo-Saxon is the **kenning,** a two-word metaphorical name for something, like "summer's sentinel" for "cuckoo." Locate two more kennings in "The Seafarer." Explain how each enhances the poem's meaning.

The WANDERER

Translated by Charles W. Kennedy

Sketch for Hadleigh Castle, John Constable

▲ **Critical Viewing** Every picture tells a story. What might have happened in this setting to cause its ruined and desolate condition? **[Hypothesize]**

Oft to the wanderer,   weary of exile,
Cometh God's pity,   compassionate love,
Though woefully toiling   on wintry seas
With churning oar   in the icy wave,
5 Homeless and helpless   he fled from fate.
Thus saith the wanderer   mindful of misery,
Grievous disasters,   and death of kin:

"Oft when the day broke, oft at the dawning,
Lonely and wretched I wailed my woe.
10 No man is living, no comrade left.
To whom I dare fully unlock my heart.
I have learned truly the mark of a man
Is keeping his counsel and locking his lips,
Let him think what he will! For, woe of heart
15 Withstandeth not fate: a failing spirit
Earneth no help. Men eager for honor
Bury their sorrow deep in the breast.
    "So have I also, often in wretchedness
Fettered[1] my feelings, far from my kin,
20 Homeless and hapless,[2] since days of old,
When the dark earth covered my dear lord's face,
And I sailed away with sorrowful heart,
Over wintry seas, seeking a gold-lord,
If far or near lived one to befriend me
25 With gift in the mead-hall and comfort for grief.
    "Who bears it, knows what a bitter companion,
Shoulder to shoulder, sorrow can be,
When friends are no more. His fortune is exile,
Not gifts of fine gold; a heart that is frozen,
30 Earth's winsomeness[3] dead. And he dreams of the hall-men,
The dealing of treasure, the days of his youth,
When his lord bade welcome to wassail[4] and feast.
But gone is that gladness, and never again
Shall come the loved counsel of comrade and king.
35 "Even in slumber his sorrow assaileth,
And, dreaming he claspeth his dear lord again,
Head on knee, hand on knee, loyally laying,
Pledging his liege[5] as in days long past.
Then from his slumber he starts lonely-hearted,
40 Beholding gray stretches of tossing sea.
Sea-birds bathing, with wings outspread,
While hailstorms darken, and driving snow.
Bitterer then is the bane of his wretchedness,
The longing for loved one: his grief is renewed.

---

1. **fettered** (fet´ ərd): Chained; restrained.
2. **hapless** (hap´ lis): Unlucky.
3. **winsomeness** (win´ səm nəs): Pleasantness; delightfulness.
4. **wassail** (wäs´ əl): A toast in drinking a person's health, or a celebration at which such toasts are made.
5. **liege** (lēj): Loyalty.

◆ Build Vocabulary

compassionate (kəm pash´ ən it) *adj*.: Sympathizing; pitying

grievous (grēv´ əs) *adj*.: Causing sorrow; hard to bear

45 The forms of his kinsmen   take shape in the silence:
In rapture he greets them;   in gladness he scans
Old comrades remembered.   But they melt into air
With no word of greeting   to gladden his heart.
Then again surges   his sorrow upon him;
50 And grimly he spurs   his weary soul
Once more to the toil   of the tossing sea.
        "No wonder therefore,   in all the world,
If a shadow darkens   upon my spirit
When I reflect   on the fates of men—
55 How one by one   proud warriors vanish
From the halls that knew them,   and day by day
All this earth ages   and droops unto death.
No man may know wisdom   till many a winter
Has been his portion.   A wise man is patient,
60 Not swift to anger,   nor hasty of speech,
Neither too weak,   nor too reckless, in war,
Neither fearful nor fain,[6]   nor too wishful of wealth,
Nor too eager in vow—   ere he know the event.
A brave man must bide[7]   when he speaketh his boast
65 Until he know surely   the goal of his spirit.
        "A wise man will ponder   how dread is that doom
When all this world's wealth   shall be scattered and waste
As now, over all,   through the regions of earth,
Walls stand rime-covered[8]   and swept by the winds.
70 The battlements crumble,   the wine-halls decay;
Joyless and silent   the heroes are sleeping
Where the proud host fell   by the wall they defended.
Some battle launched   on their long, last journey;
One a bird bore   o'er the billowing sea:
75 One the gray wolf slew;   one a grieving earl
Sadly gave   to the grave's embrace.
The Warden of men   hath wasted this world
Till the sound of music   and revel is stilled,
And these giant-built structures   stand empty of life.
80   "He who shall muse   on these moldering ruins,
And deeply ponder   this darkling life,
Must brood on old legends   of battle and bloodshed,
And heavy the mood   that troubles his heart:
'Where now is the warrior?   Where is the war horse?
85 Bestowal of treasure,   and sharing of feast?
Alas! the bright ale-cup,   the byrny-clad[9] warrior,
The prince in his splendor—   those days are long sped
In the night of the past,   as if they never had been!'
And now remains only,   for warriors' memorial,
90 A wall wondrous high   with serpent shapes carved.
Storms of ash-spears   have smitten the earls,

---

6. **fain** (fān): Archaic word meaning "eager"; In this context it means "too eager."
7. **bide** (bīd): Wait.
8. **rime** (rīm)**-covered**: Covered with frost.
9. **byrny** (bər´ nē)**-clad**: Dressed in a coat of chain-mail armor.

Carnage of weapon,   and conquering fate.
"Storms now batter   these ramparts of stone;
    Blowing snow   and the blast of winter
95 Enfold the earth;   night-shadows fall
Darkly lowering,   from the north driving
Raging hail   in wrath upon men.
Wretchedness fills   the realm of earth,
And fate's decrees   transform the world.
100 Here wealth is fleeting,   friends are fleeting,
Man is fleeting,   maid is fleeting;
All the foundation   of earth shall fail!"
    Thus spake the sage   in solitude pondering.
Good man is he   who guardeth his faith.
105 He must never too quickly   unburden his breast
Of its sorrow, but eagerly   strive for redress;
And happy the man   who seeketh for mercy
From his heavenly Father,   our fortress and strength.

◆ **Build Vocabulary**

rapture (rap´ chər) *n.*: Expression of joy or pleasure

redress (ri dres´) *n.*: Compensation, as for a wrong

Guide for Responding

◆ Literature and Your Life

Reader's Response In what ways is the wanderer someone to whom you can relate?

Thematic Focus Explain how the wanderer experiences exile, both emotionally and physically. In what ways do his ideas about heaven comfort him?

Group Discussion In a group of four, quickly explore the types of exile a person can experience. For example, exile might be self-imposed; it could be a frame of mind; it could be for a short duration. You can use situations from fiction, television, movies, or real life.

☑ Check Your Comprehension

1. What event causes the wanderer to go into exile?
2. What is the goal of the wanderer's search?
3. What is the wanderer's outlook on life?

◆ Critical Thinking

INTERPRET

1. This poem contains two speakers. Identify the points at which the speaker changes, and explain how the change affects the poem. **[Distinguish]**
2. What images does the poet use to convey isolation and despair? **[Analyze]**
3. Explain the wanderer's attitude toward wisdom. Give details to support your answer. **[Analyze]**
4. What is the message of this poem? **[Draw Conclusions]**

COMPARE LITERARY WORKS

5. Reread the final verses of these two poems and compare them for the notes of hopefulness or despair with which each author ends his poem. **[Compare and Contrast]**

◆ Literary Focus

ANGLO-SAXON LYRICS: RHYTHM

Most Anglo-Saxon lyrics contain a distinct **rhythm.** Examine the poetic structure of "The Wanderer."

1. How many strong beats per line are there?
2. What effect might this rhythm have on the listener?

Susannah in Bath, (detail), Albrecht Altdorfer
Wasserholendes Madchen, Munchen, Alte Pinakothek

▲ **Critical Viewing** Compare the woman in this picture with the speaker in the poem. [**Compare and Contrast**]

The WIFE'S LAMENT

Translated by Ann Stanford

I make this song   about me full sadly
my own wayfaring.   I a woman tell
what griefs I had   since I grew up
new or old   never more than now.
5 Ever I know   the dark of my exile.

First my lord went out   away from his people
over the wave-tumult.   I grieved each dawn
wondered where my lord   my first on earth might be.
Then I went forth   a friendless exile
10 to seek service   in my sorrow's need.
My man's kinsmen   began to plot
by darkened thought   to divide us two
so we most widely   in the world's kingdom
lived wretchedly   and I suffered longing.

15 My lord commanded me   to move my dwelling here.
I had few loved ones   in this land
or faithful friends.   For this my heart grieves:
that I should find the man   well matched to me
hard of fortune   mournful of mind
20 hiding his mood   thinking of murder.

Blithe was our bearing   often we vowed
that but death alone   would part us two
naught else.   But this is turned round
now . . .   as if it never were
25 our friendship.   I must far and near
bear the anger   of my beloved.
The man sent me out   to live in the woods
under an oak tree   in this den in the earth.
Ancient this earth hall.   I am all longing.

30 The valleys are dark   the hills high
the yard overgrown   bitter with briars
a joyless dwelling.   Full oft the lack of my lord
seizes me cruelly here.   Friends there are on earth
living beloved   lying in bed

35   while I at dawn   am walking alone
     under the oak tree   through these earth halls.
     There I may sit   the summerlong day
     there I can weep   over my exile
     my many hardships.   Hence I may not rest
40   from this care of heart   which belongs to me ever
     nor all this longing   that has caught me in this life.

     May that young man   be sad-minded always
     hard his heart's thought   while he must wear
     a blithe bearing   with care in the breast
45   a crowd of sorrows.   May on himself depend
     all his world's joy.   Be he outlawed far
     in a strange folk-land—   that my beloved sits
     under a rocky cliff   rimed with frost
     a lord dreary in spirit   drenched with water
50   in a ruined hall.   My lord endures
     much care of mind.   He remembers too often
     a happier dwelling.   Woe be to them
     that for a loved one   must wait in longing.

◆ Build Vocabulary

blithe (blīth) *adj.*: Cheerful

Guide for Responding

◆ Literature and Your Life

Reader's Response In what ways do you think the wife is justified in her anger and sorrow?

Thematic Focus Why was a sense of belonging or home important to the Anglo-Saxons? Why was exile such a prominent theme in their stories?

Letter to the Wife Write a brief letter to the wife in which you give advice on how she could overcome her feelings of abandonment, anger, and loss.

☑ Check Your Comprehension

1. To whom does the wife refer as "her lord"?
2. Why is the wife unhappy?
3. Why was the wife commanded to leave her home?

◆ Critical Thinking

INTERPRET

1. What does the wife mean by the phrase "grew up" in line 3? **[Interpret]**
2. What is meant by the line "I must far and near bear the anger of my beloved"? **[Interpret]**
3. If the husband were to return, do you think the wife would be welcoming? **[Make Predictions]**

EVALUATE

4. Does the poem effectively portray the wife as a believable person? **[Evaluate]**

◆ Literary Focus

ANGLO-SAXON LYRICS: THE CAESURA

One feature of Anglo-Saxon poetry is the **caesura,** which divides each line into two parts.

Identify three examples of caesura in "The Wife's Lament." Explain how the caesura makes the poem easier to recite.

Guide for Responding (continued)

◆ Reading for Success

LITERAL COMPREHENSION STRATEGIES

Review the reading strategies and the notes showing how to comprehend a writer's words and intention. Then apply them to answer the following questions.

1. Explain how context clues help reveal the meaning of *flourished*, in line 82 of "The Seafarer."
2. Paraphrase lines 14–16 from "The Wanderer":

> . . . For, woe of heart
> Withstandeth not fate: a failing spirit
> Earneth no help. . . .

3. What context clues enabled you to decode the meaning of *ramparts* in line 93?
4. Summarize "The Wife's Lament."

◆ Build Vocabulary

USING FORMS OF *GRIEVOUS*

Grievous, which means "causing sorrow" or "hard to bear," is related to a variety of other words that are similar in meaning. Match each form of *grievous* to its definition.

1. grievance   **a.** one in sorrow or distress
2. aggrieved   **b.** a serious complaint
3. griever   **c.** offended or wronged
4. grief   **d.** sorrow

USING THE WORD BANK: Synonyms

Replace each italicized word with a synonym from the Word Bank. You may change the form of the word.

1. Before being exiled by the king, we were *carefree* and in a state of *bliss*.
2. Being left with nothing, my husband and I sought *compensation*.
3. Our queen was *sympathetic* when she learned of our *distressing* loss.
4. The queen *scolded* the king and, out of *spite,* repealed our banishment.
5. A(An) *ardent* believer in justice, the queen appointed a *guard* to accompany us on our return home.

◆ Literary Focus

ANGLO-SAXON LYRICS

All these poems are **lyrics**—poems that express the thoughts and feelings of a single speaker.

1. An **elegy** is a specific type of lyric in which the loss of something or someone is mourned. Explain why each poem is an example of an elegy.
2. All these lyrics sprang from the Anglo-Saxon oral tradition. Find three elements in these poems that would have helped people remember and recite the poems. Explain each example.

◆ Grammar and Style

COMPOUND PREDICATES

Compound predicates help the writers of these poems provide detailed descriptions of events.

> A predicate is a sentence part that contains the verb and states the action or condition of the subject. A **compound predicate** has two or more verbs or verb phrases that relate to the same subject.

Practice In your notebook, write the verbs or verb phrases in the compound predicate in each of the following sentences.

1. The world's honor ages and shrinks, . . .
2. He who shall muse on these moldering ruins, / And deeply ponder this darkling life, / Must brood on old legends of battle and bloodshed. . . .
3. A brother / Opens his palm and pours down gold / On his kinsman's grave, . . .
4. The soul . . . knows nothing / Of sweetness, or sour, feels no pain, / Bends neither its hand nor its brain.
5. All this earth ages and droops unto death.

Writing Application Rewrite each group of sentences as one sentence with a compound predicate.

1. She walked to the wharf. She watched the ships dock. She scanned faces in the crowd.
2. The lord mounted his horse. He ordered a siege on the castle. He claimed victory.

Build Your Portfolio

 ## Idea Bank

Writing

1. Funeral Oration Write a funeral oration, describing the speaker of one of the poems. In your speech, mourn the loss of the speaker.

2. Analysis of Theme Each of these poems deals with the themes of exile and loneliness. Write an analysis of one of the poems, explaining how its theme is conveyed through imagery and symbols.

3. Comparison and Contrast In both "The Seafarer" and "The Wanderer," several religious passages are interwoven with the narrative. Compare and contrast the religious philosophies presented in the two poems.

Speaking, Listening, and Viewing

4. Demonstration of Caesuras With a partner, take turns reading portions of these poems aloud. Then discuss how the caesura—the break within each line—helps readers understand the poem's meaning and helps reciters present the poem to an audience. **[Performing Arts Link]**

5. Oral Interpretation Assume the role of a *scop,* or traveling storyteller, and perform one of these poems for the class. Capture the emotions of the speaker. **[Performing Arts Link]**

Researching and Representing

6. Help Wanted The speakers in these poems had ordinary occupations—as a wife, a sailor, and a soldier. Investigate Anglo-Saxon occupations. Then create a Help Wanted page listing the positions to be filled as well as the job requirements. **[Career Link]**

7. Portrait Choose one of the speakers from these poems to portray visually. Display your portrait in the classroom. **[Art Link]**

Online Activity **www.phlit.phschool.com**

 ## Guided Writing Lesson

Song

"The Seafarer," "The Wanderer," and "The Wife's Lament" are all lyric poems that tell of each speaker's misery and loss. Choose one of the speakers' stories to re-create in the form of a song. Include a verse in which a story is told, as well as a refrain, which is repeated throughout the song and captures its essence or theme. You may also include sound devices such as rhyme, rhythm, and alliteration. Keep this strategy in mind as you write.

Writing Skills Focus: Sequence of Events

Because you're retelling a story through song, be specific about the **sequence of events.** Transitions such as *first, then, next,* and *later* clarify the connections among the events. In this passage from "The Wife's Lament," transitions make the sequence of events clear.

Model From the Poem

First my lord went out away . . .
Then I went forth a friendless exile

Prewriting Reread the poem you want to retell and take notes about the sequence of events that led to the speaker's state of misery. Identify a major event or a dominant theme and create a refrain, or chorus, to repeat throughout your song.

Drafting Draft the verses of your song, laying out the speaker's story in its proper sequence. Each verse should tell a part of the story. Alternate the refrain with the verses.

Revising Add transitions such as *then* and *next* wherever necessary to make the sequence of events more clear. Add sound devices like alliteration to make your song more memorable.

CONNECTIONS TO WORLD LITERATURE

from Tristia
Ovid

Far Corners of Earth
Tu Fu

Thematic Connection

THE THEME OF EXILE

Exile can be experienced in many ways, in many degrees, and for many reasons. For example, in "The Seafarer," the exile is self-imposed; the seafarer cannot resist the lure of the sea and all its dangers. "The Wanderer," however, experiences exile due to the death in battle of his lord and comrades. In "The Wife's Lament," exile is enforced on the woman by her husband and his conniving relatives.

The following poems also deal with the theme of exile. For Tu Fu, exile is not to be wholly reviled; in some ways, Tu Fu finds himself as a poet when banished from government service.

The same cannot be said of Ovid. For him, exile was perhaps more cruel than death. The verses in *Tristia* echo the deeply felt sorrow and longing he felt for his beloved Rome.

OVID
(43 B.C.–A.D. 17)

Born in Sulmona, Italy, Publius Ovidius Naso, known to us as Ovid, was educated for a career in law. Preferring to be a writer, Ovid became the author of numerous elegies as well as the narrative poem *Metamorphoses*, in which he recounted legends involving miraculous transformations of form since the beginning of time. Ovid lived and wrote chiefly in Rome, a city he loved and in which he was celebrated and favored. In A.D. 8, however, Ovid offended Emperor Augustus with his satires and was banished from Rome to Tomis, near the Black Sea. Despite numerous pleas for forgiveness, Ovid was to remain in exile until his death. *Tristia*, a lament, was written while Ovid was in exile.

TU FU
(712–770)

The son of a prominent scholar and an emperor's great-granddaughter, the poet Tu Fu had connections to people of power and influence. His background appears to be a mix of the traditional and unexpected: Although classically educated, he left home at a very early age to travel alone through China. He eventually ended up in the nation's capital and took a test for government service, failing it several times. He finally passed the exam in 752, and in 755 was granted a position in the palace of the crown-prince. The next few years of Tu Fu's life are a blur of political upheavals: Rebel forces send the emperor into exile; Tu Fu himself is exiled; Tu Fu flees into the country with his family to live in poverty and write; Tu Fu returns to a government position; and so on. The bulk of Tu Fu's poetry was written in the last eleven years of his life, when he left his government position and traveled in poverty with his family through the vast countryside of China.

from TRISTIA

Ovid, Translated by L. R. Lind

BOOK 10

Since I've been here in the Pontus the Danube has frozen thrice over,
    The waves of the Euxine ocean have hardened as well three times.
And it seems now I've been far from my country just so long a time
    As Dardanian Troy was besieged by the Grecian Army—ten years.
5 So slowly the time goes you'd think it was standing still in its traces
    And the year takes its way as though it were dragging its footsteps along.
The summer solstice deprives me of nothing at all from the nighttime
    Nor does the winter solstice make shorter each of my days.

Can it be in my case that nature has taken unusual posture
10   And does she make everything long as the wearisome length of my cares?
Or does that time common to all pursue its accustomed progress
    While the time that's peculiar to me is simply more harsh in my life,
I whom the shore of the Euxine, the sea that is falsely denoted,
    Holds now and the left (and ill-omened) land of the Scythian strait?

15 The numberless races around me menace with terrible warfare,
    These people who think it is shameful to live without plundering men;
Nothing beyond me lacks danger; the hill is defended around it
    By the slightest of walls, the strategic position that favors the place.
Whenever you least expect it, like a bird the enemy gathered
20   In a dense mass flies past us and, scarce seen, drives its booty along.
Often inside of the walls when the gates have been shut quite securely,
    We have picked up their poisoned arrows flung into the midst of the roads.
It's a rare farmer who dares to till his acres, and he with
    One hand (poor devil) goes plowing, with the other he handles his sword.
25 Under his helmet the shepherd blows on straws joined with pitch-gum
    And instead of a wolf the trembling sheep stand in dread of war.
We are scarcely defended within the fortress and even within it
    The barbarous crowd mixed with Greeks still inspires our hearts with fear.
In fact, the barbarians live with us without discrimination
30   And they possess more than half of the houses which shelter us.
Even though you don't fear them you would hate them all when you see them,
    Their chests covered over with hides and their heads with long hanging hair.
And even those men who're believed to descend from Greek colonizers
    Wear Persian trousers instead of the garments their own nation wears.

Roman Forum at the Height of the Empire

◄ **Critical Viewing** Judging from this picture of Rome, why might Ovid have missed it so much while in exile? **[Speculate]**

35 They carry on their relations by means of their common language
        While I am reduced to communication by making signs.
    Here I am the barbarian, and I'm understood by no one,
        And the stupid Getae make fun of the Latin words which I speak;
    And openly often they speak ill of me and with perfect freedom,
40   Perhaps even holding against me the fact that I'm exiled from Rome.
    And as it happens, they think I am crazy when to their jabber
        I nod my head to say "yes" and shake it to signify "no."
    Add that an unjust justice is enforced with the rigid sword blade
        And wounds are frequently given in the midst of the market place.

45 O harsh Lachesis, who gave me, born under a star that's unlucky,
        The threads of a life that were not shorter than those which are mine!
    The fact that I lack the sight of my fatherland and of my comrades
        And that I live here among the Scythian race I lament:
    Both of these penalties are grave, but I deserved the loss of my City;
50   Perhaps I did not deserve to be punished in such a place.
    Why do I speak? I'm a madman. I deserved to lose even my life then
        When I did injury to the power of Caesar the god.

Guide for Responding

◆ Literature and Your Life

Reader's Response What do you think of the speaker's attitude toward the people who surround him in his new home?

Thematic Focus Which do you think is worse for the poet—death or exile? Explain.

☑ Check Your Comprehension

1. Why is the speaker unhappy?
2. How long has the speaker been in exile?
3. Under what conditions is the speaker forced to live?

◆ Critical Thinking

INTERPRET
1. How does Ovid distinguish between a civilized person and a barbarian? **[Distinguish]**
2. What does this passage suggest about the meaning of exile for Ovid? **[Interpret]**

EVALUATE
3. Which details are especially effective in conveying Ovid's distress? Why? **[Criticize]**

APPLY
4. If Ovid were a contemporary writer, where might he live? Why? **[Hypothesize]**

FAR CORNERS OF *Earth* Tu Fu

Translated by David Hinton

Evening in Spring Hills, Chinese, Metropolitan Museum of Art

Chiang-han mountains looming, impassable,
A cloud drifts over this far corner of earth.
Year after year, nothing familiar, nothing
Anywhere but one further end of the road.

5 Here, Wang Ts'an found loss and confusion,
And Ch'ü Yüan cold grief. My heart already
Broken in quiet times—and look at me,
Each day wandering a new waste of highway.

▲ **Critical Viewing** In what ways does this painting depict isolation and solitude? **[Analyze]**

Guide for Responding

◆ *Literature and Your Life*

Reader's Response What mood does this poem evoke in you?

Thematic Focus What type of exile does the speaker of this poem experience? How does exile affect the outlook of the speaker?

Additional Stanza Write another stanza to this poem, extending the mood already established by Tu Fu.

☑ Check Your Comprehension

1. As the poem begins, what does the poet see before him?
2. What is the poet doing "Each day"?

◆ Critical Thinking

INTERPRET
1. Explain how details from the landscape contribute to the mood of the poem. **[Analyze]**
2. What seems to be the hardest thing about exile for Tu Fu? Why? **[Interpret]**

EVALUATE
3. What is the intended effect of beginning the poem with a description of the landscape? Explain. **[Criticize]**

APPLY
4. What sort of person in modern life might experience a life similar to Tu Fu's? Explain. **[Relate]**

Thematic Connection

THE THEME OF EXILE

Tristia and "Far Corners of Earth" both deal with the theme of exile, or expulsion from home or society. This theme can be found throughout world literature, in just about every era of history.

1. Compare Ovid's treatment of exile with its treatment in "The Wanderer" or "The Wife's Lament." Consider the use of symbols to represent the life of an exile and the speaker's attitude toward exile.

2. Name three current examples of people who live in exile. Draw these examples from the news, from songs, or from books and movies.

3. In Tu Fu's "Far Corners of Earth," the line "Year after year, nothing familiar" gets at the essence of what it's like to be without a home. Show how this same idea is expressed in "The Seafarer" and "The Wanderer." Cite specific passages from the poems to illustrate the points you're making.

 Idea Bank

Writing

1. **Screenplay Treatment** Reread the excerpt from *Tristia* and think of a few camera shots you could use to accompany a reading of this poem. For each shot, explain why it would be effective. **[Media Link]**

2. **Comparison and Contrast** *Tristia* is a poem lamenting Ovid's exile from Rome. In the Anglo-Saxon poems, however, the characters are fictional. Choose one of these fictional characters and compare his or her attitudes and emotional state with Ovid's.

3. **Symbols of Exile** A symbol is a person, place, or thing that stands for an idea. In "Far Corners of Earth," for example, the endless highway symbolizes the monotony of a journey never ended or the life of a permanent exile looking for a home. Reexamine the three Anglo-Saxon poems and look for symbols of exile. Analyze each symbol and explain why it is or isn't effective.

Speaking, Listening, and Viewing

4. **Monologue of an Exile** Write a brief monologue for the speaker in Tu Fu's poem. Borrow the situation laid out in "Far Corners of Earth" and expand upon it in the monologue, conveying the sense of despair and monotony that Tu Fu has captured in his poem. Perform your monologue for the class. **[Performing Arts Link]**

Researching and Representing

5. **Exile's Map** Draw a map that illustrates China in Tu Fu's time or the Roman empire in Ovid's. Use labels to show what Tu Fu's or Ovid's exile meant in geographical terms. **[Social Studies Link; Art Link]**

6. **Timeline** Ovid was exiled from Rome after angering Emperor Augustus. Research other actions by this emperor and create a timeline that shows significant events during his reign. **[Social Studies Link]**

Online Activity **www.phlit.phschool.com**

Writing Process Workshop

The lyric poems in this unit resemble **dramatic monologues**; in the poems, an imaginary character speaks to a silent listener, revealing his or her innermost self, often at a moment of crisis. Similarly, in a dramatic monologue, a character speaks to a silent listener about something that concerns him or her. The character might reflect on life or express fears, beliefs, or desires.

Write a dramatic monologue in which you tell the story of your speaker—a character living during the Anglo-Saxon or medieval periods, or someone from our own time. Your speaker might respond in the monologue to something that has just occurred in his or her life. Use the following skills to bring the speaker of your poem to life.

Writing Skills Focus

▶ **Follow a sequence of events** to make the speaker's story clear. Decide on the type of conflict that will propel the story. (See p. 27.)

▶ **Develop your character's personality** through his or her speech patterns and vocabulary.

▶ **Try free verse form**—verse without a regular rhythm or rhyme scheme—to emphasize the content and mood of your poem.

The following passage from "The Wanderer" contains many elements found in dramatic monologues.

MODEL FROM LITERATURE

from "The Wanderer"

① Oft when the day broke, oft at the
    dawning,
② Lonely and wretched I wailed my woe.
③ No man is living, no comrade is left,
    To whom I dare fully unlock my heart.

① This passage is spoken by the wanderer, the character who's telling the story.

② The speaker begins by telling what's happened in the past.

③ Here, the speaker moves forward in time to reveal his present thoughts.

Applying LANGUAGE SKILLS: Using Verb Tenses

Because a dramatic monologue often tells a story, it's important to use correct verb tenses to keep the story events clear and logical. Use the **present tense** to express an action or state of being that is ongoing or taking place now. Use the **past tense** to express an action or state of being that has already happened. Use the **future tense** to express an action or state of being that will happen.

Present: I am jumping overboard.

Past: I jumped overboard.

Future: I will jump overboard if the storm continues.

Practice Identify the tenses of the italicized verbs.

Madness *overtook* me as the ship's captain was swept away. I *shudder* now when I think back on it. Tomorrow, I *will continue* my long journey homeward, over land.

Writer's Solution Connection Language Lab

For more on using verb tenses, see the Principal Parts of Verbs and Verb Tense lessons in the Sharpening Language Skills section.

Prewriting

Choosing a Topic Whose story would make an interesting monologue? Consider characters from literature or movies, legendary figures, or characters you create yourself.

Selection-Related Writing Ideas

- The "seafarer" debates the merits of life at sea
- The "wanderer" recounts the battle in which his lord was killed, leaving him alone in the world
- The "wife" spills out her anger and fears when her husband finally returns

---

Map Out a Sequence of Events Create a diagram to illustrate the sequence of events in your dramatic monologue.

Beginning: The husband tells his wife of his journey home after being away for a year.

Middle: He reveals that the ship he was traveling in was battered by a storm and took on water.

High Point: The husband tells how he spotted the shoreline and imagined that his wife was waving a welcome to him.

End: The husband bursts into tears and expresses his love for his wife.

Develop Character Through Speech Choose a manner of speaking that will fit your character. To do this, experiment with different ways of saying the same thing. For example, would your character say "I don't want to go back" or " Wild horses couldn't drag me home"?

Drafting

Let the Character Tell the Story Now that you've sketched out your character's situation and personality, take a moment to "assume your character's identity" and let the character take over as you write.

Draft Free Verse As you draft, rough out the form your poem will take. Break lines by instinct, and let the character you've created and the emotional situation guide the structure of your poem. For example, if your character is angry, you might explore creating short, choppy lines to emphasize that emotion. If your character is recalling a pleasant experience, the lines of your poem could be long, like an uninterrupted dream.

Revising

Connect Sequence of Events In the drafting stage, your character took you on a dramatic journey. Now, make sure that your readers can follow along. Insert transitions such as *then, immediately after*, and *before*, to connect the story events.

Strengthen Characterization Read your monologue aloud and replace any words or phrases that seem out of character. Following are tips for strengthening character through speech.

▶ Choose vocabulary appropriate to the time period and personality of the speaker:

> **Draft:** I was *devastated* when *my lord exiled* me.
> **Revision:** I was *depressed* when *my boss fired* me.

▶ Change complete sentences into fragments wherever it seems natural to do so:

> **Draft:** The waves broke over my head in a fury.
> **Revision:** The waves! The fury!

Revise Structure to Enhance a Poem's Meaning Review the lines of your poem and revise line breaks and line lengths to match the events and emotional content of your dramatic monologue.

In the following example, lines of free verse were revised to mirror the desperate efforts of the speaker's struggle.

Draft

> My heart pounded
> furiously as I struggled to free myself from the tenacious grasp of the murderous sea.

Revision

> My heart pounded furiously
> as I
> struggled to free myself
> from the
> tenacious grasp
> of the murderous sea.

Publishing

▶ **Performing** Read your dramatic monologue aloud to the class.
▶ **Group Activity** With a group of friends, put on a production of dramatic monologues.
▶ **Cross-Disciplinary Activity** Draw a portrait of the speaker of your dramatic monologue. Post the portrait and the monologue on a bulletin board.

APPLYING LANGUAGE SKILLS: Punctuating Free Verse

Because free verse contains no consistent structure or rhyme scheme, punctuation takes on added importance. Use commas to indicate short pauses, ellipsis points to indicate breaks in thought, periods to indicate full stops, and dashes to indicate interruptions.

Draft	**Revision**
Fist of sand	Fist of sand . . .
Waves lapping, lapping lapping	Waves lapping, lapping, lapping,
Gently lifting, then dropping exhausted legs	Gently lifting, then dropping exhausted legs.

Writing Application Review your dramatic monologue, and then insert or revise punctuation as needed to enhance your poem's meaning or mood.

Writer's Solution Connection Writing Lab

To help you develop your character, use the Character Trait Word Bin in the Writing Lab tutorial on Creative Writing.

Student Success Workshop

Vocabulary Development

Using Reference Materials

Strategies for Success

As you read widely in increasingly demanding texts, you will encounter words you don't know. To learn the meanings of these words, you may start with a dictionary, but other resources are also helpful, such as a glossary, the Internet, a thesaurus, an encyclopedia, or even a specialized dictionary. Using these resources will build your vocabulary and increase your reading comprehension:

Use Glossaries and Dictionaries Both glossaries and dictionaries include definitions. A glossary is an alphabetical list of difficult or technical words with the meanings used in that particular book. Technical, scientific, instructional, and translated texts often have glossaries. A dictionary provides all of a word's meanings, and it gives you information that a glossary may not, such as multiple meanings, pronunciation, part of speech, the word's derivation, definitions of prefixes and suffixes, and information about the correct use of the word.

Choose the Best Reference When you see an unfamilar word, look for its definition in the glossary if one is provided; otherwise, use a dictionary. For more in-depth information, search specific reference materials: If you want the meaning of a French phrase, check a dictionary of foreign words and phrases; if you're looking for word origins, try an etymological dictionary; if you want synonyms and antonyms, look in a thesaurus; if you need information about a person, place, or field of knowledge, an encyclopedia may be your best choice.

Use Specialized Resources Specialized terms, such as words used in science articles or professional journals, can be difficult to figure out.

When you come across such a word, turn to specialized resources. Internet Web pages and CD-ROMs are appropriate if you know that your source is valid. For example, NASA's Web pages provide reliable definitions and explanations of scientific terms related to space exploration, sonic booms, the ozone layer, and much more.

Apply the Strategies

Read this passage and answer the questions that follow.

Congress held a campaign finance reform meeting yesterday. Many congressional representatives said their constituents favored the elimination of soft money donations to political party caucuses. In an attempt to expedite passage of a bill and avoid partisan squabbles, a bipartisan team of reform advocates plans to push for a plenary session on putting an end to soft money.

1. Which reference source would you use to find the meaning of the word *constituents*? What kind of information does this particular resource give you?

2. Where would you look to find words with meanings similar to the word *partisan*?

3. If you wanted the meaning of the term *plenary* and information about its origins, where would you look?

4. How would you begin an Internet search for the meaning of the term *soft money*?

✔ You may find reference materials helpful in situations like these:
▶ Doing a crossword puzzle
▶ Planning a debate or speech
▶ Watching a science program on television

PART 2 *Focus on Literary Forms:* *The Epic*

Beowulf on the Funeral Pyre, Rockwell Kent

From the fifth through fifteenth centuries, England was a place of upheaval and uncertainty. Invasions, plagues, and political battles raged, and people looked for reassurance in the form of heroes who embodied strength, honor, and virtue. This need for heroes is met in epic tales, such as *Beowulf,* which follows.

Guide for Interpreting

About Beowulf

Origins of a Legend Long before there were books, stories and poems were passed along by word of mouth. In Anglo-Saxon England, traveling minstrels known as *scops* captivated audiences with entertaining presentations of long narrative poems. One of these poems was *Beowulf*, which was told and retold to audiences throughout England over hundreds of years. Although the action takes place in sixth-century Scandinavia, *Beowulf* was originally told in Old English. When *Beowulf* was finally written down in the eleventh century, it marked the beginning of English literature.

> **Beowulf *is not only an important historical record, but also a hair-raising tale that has electrified readers through the centuries.***

Beowulf, a Geat from a region that is today southern Sweden, sets sail from his homeland to try to free Danish King Hrothgar's great banquet hall, Herot, of a monster that has been ravaging it for twelve years. The monster, Grendel, is a terrifying swampland creature of enormous size whose eyes burn "with gruesome light." The struggle between Beowulf, a young adventurer eager for fame, and Grendel, a fierce and bloodthirsty foe, is the first of three mortal battles in the long poem.

From Oral Tradition to Cyberspace The only original manuscript of the complete 3,182-line poem comes to us from Sir Robert Cotton's (1571–1631) collection of medieval manuscripts. In 1731, the manuscript was saved from a fire but did not escape damage—the edges of 2,000 letters crumbled away.

Fortunately, the computer age has made it possible to prevent additional damage to the manuscript. Thanks to an initiative called the Electronic *Beowulf* Project, the manuscript has been preserved and made available electronically. Not only is the legend of *Beowulf* timeless, but the Old English manuscript has proved its adaptability to the computer age.

◆ Background for Understanding

HISTORY: PAGANISM AND CHRISTIANITY

Before Christianity began taking hold of the nation in the seventh century, England was a pagan society. People believed that their lives were completely in the hands of fate, and they told tales of monsters and other shadowy creatures that lurked in the depths of the forest. These pagan beliefs contrasted sharply with the Christian beliefs in a single deity, in the freedom of individuals to determine their own path, and in the clear distinction between good and evil.

At the time when *Beowulf* was written, England was in the process of changing from a pagan culture to a Christian society. Not surprisingly, *Beowulf* reflects both pagan and Christian ideals. For example, Grendel is reminiscent of monsters found in pagan legends, yet the battle of Beowulf and Grendel captures the Christian ideal of good conquering the forces of evil.

from Beowulf

◆ *Literature and Your Life*

CONNECT YOUR EXPERIENCE

A defiant hero battles an arch-enemy in a deadly struggle. This ever-popular combination of villain and hero in literature and media can be traced to a poem composed more than twelve hundred years ago. Like the heroes of today, Beowulf fights for the safety of society.

THEMATIC FOCUS: PERILS AND ADVENTURES

The adventures of Beowulf are legendary, whereas the adventures of Charlemagne were actual. What characteristics do actual and legendary adventurers share?

Journal Writing Describe the types of problems that heroes of today's world confront.

◆ Build Vocabulary

LATIN WORD ROOTS: -sol-

In *Beowulf*, the Danes are unable to find solace from their misfortunes. The word *solace* is built upon the Latin root -sol-, which means "to comfort." Solace is an easing of grief, loneliness, or discomfort.

WORD BANK

Before you read, preview this list of words from the story.

reparation
solace
purge
writhing
massive
loathsome

◆ Grammar and Style

APPOSITIVES AND APPOSITIVE PHRASES

Throughout *Beowulf*, the poet uses **appositive phrases**—nouns or pronouns with modifiers that identify, explain, or rename other nouns or pronouns—to provide important information about the characters and setting. In the following lines, an appositive phrase, in italics, gives additional information about Beowulf:

In his far-off home Beowulf, *Higlac's*
Follower and the strongest of the Geats—

As you read *Beowulf*, notice how appositives and appositive phrases provide information without hindering the flow of the story.

◆ Literary Focus

THE EPIC

An **epic** is a long narrative poem, sometimes developed orally, that celebrates the deeds of a legendary or heroic figure. Typically, an epic is presented in a serious manner, often through the use of elevated language. The hero of an epic battles the forces of evil and represents widespread national, cultural, or religious values.

Epics such as *Beowulf* also contain elements of Anglo-Saxon poetry like the **kenning** and **caesura.** (For more about these, see p. 13.) Look for elements of the epic as you read *Beowulf*.

◆ Reading Strategy

PARAPHRASE

Although *Beowulf* has been translated into modern English, its long, involved sentences may be difficult to follow. To aid your understanding, **paraphrase**—identify key ideas and details and restate them in your own words. Look at the following example:

High on a wall a Danish watcher / Patrolling along the cliffs saw / The travelers crossing to the shore, their shields / Raised and shining; . . .

Paraphrased

A Danish guard saw strangers with raised shields come ashore.

from BEOWULF

Translated by Burton Raffel

The selection opens during an evening of celebration at Herot, the banquet hall of the Danish king Hrothgar (hroth´gär). Outside in the darkness, however, lurks the monster Grendel, a murderous creature who poses a great danger to the people inside the banquet hall.

The Wrath of Grendel

A powerful monster, living down
In the darkness, growled in pain, impatient
As day after day the music rang
Loud in that hall,[1] the harp's rejoicing

5   Call and the poet's clear songs, sung
Of the ancient beginnings of us all, recalling
The Almighty making the earth, shaping
These beautiful plains marked off by oceans,
Then proudly setting the sun and moon

10   To glow across the land and light it;
The corners of the earth were made lovely with trees
And leaves, made quick with life, with each
Of the nations who now move on its face. And then
As now warriors sang of their pleasure:

15   So Hrothgar's men lived happy in his hall
Till the monster stirred, that demon, that fiend,
Grendel, who haunted the moors, the wild
Marshes, and made his home in a hell
Not hell but earth. He was spawned in that slime,

20   Conceived by a pair of those monsters born
Of Cain,[2] murderous creatures banished
By God, punished forever for the crime
Of Abel's death. The Almighty drove
Those demons out, and their exile was bitter,

25   Shut away from men; they split
Into a thousand forms of evil—spirits
And fiends, goblins, monsters, giants,
A brood forever opposing the Lord's
Will, and again and again defeated.

1. hall: Herot.

2. Cain: Oldest son of Adam and Eve, who murdered his brother Abel.

Grendel (Frontispiece from *Beowulf*), Patten Wilson, The British Library

▲ Critical Viewing Analyze the artist's use of details
to make Grendel look fearsome. **[Analyze]**

30 Then, when darkness had dropped, Grendel
 Went up to Herot, wondering what the warriors
 Would do in that hall when their drinking was done.
 He found them sprawled in sleep, suspecting
 Nothing, their dreams undisturbed. The monster's
35 Thoughts were as quick as his greed or his claws:
 He slipped through the door and there in the silence
 Snatched up thirty men, smashed them
 Unknowing in their beds and ran out with their bodies,
 The blood dripping behind him, back
40 To his lair, delighted with his night's slaughter.
  At daybreak, with the sun's first light, they saw
 How well he had worked, and in that gray morning
 Broke their long feast with tears and laments
 For the dead. Hrothgar, their lord, sat joyless
45 In Herot, a mighty prince mourning
 The fate of his lost friends and companions,
 Knowing by its tracks that some demon had torn
 His followers apart. He wept, fearing
 The beginning might not be the end. And that night
50 Grendel came again, so set
 On murder that no crime could ever be enough,
 No savage assault quench his lust
 For evil. Then each warrior tried
 To escape him, searched for rest in different
55 Beds, as far from Herot as they could find,
 Seeing how Grendel hunted when they slept.
 Distance was safety; the only survivors
 Were those who fled him. Hate had triumphed.
  So Grendel ruled, fought with the righteous,
60 One against many, and won; so Herot
 Stood empty, and stayed deserted for years,
 Twelve winters of grief for Hrothgar, king
 Of the Danes, sorrow heaped at his door
 By hell-forged hands. His misery leaped
65 The seas, was told and sung in all
 Men's ears: how Grendel's hatred began,
 How the monster relished his savage war
 On the Danes, keeping the bloody feud
 Alive, seeking no peace, offering
70 No truce, accepting no settlement, no price
 In gold or land, and paying the living
 For one crime only with another. No one
 Waited for reparation from his plundering claws:
 That shadow of death hunted in the darkness,
75 Stalked Hrothgar's warriors, old
 And young, lying in waiting, hidden
 In mist, invisibly following them from the edge
 Of the marsh, always there, unseen.
  So mankind's enemy continued his crimes,
80 Killing as often as he could, coming
 Alone, bloodthirsty and horrible. Though he lived

◆ Build Vocabulary

reparation (rep′ə rā′ shən)
n.: Making up for wrong
or injury

solace (säl′ is) *n.*: Comfort; relief

In Herot, when the night hid him, he never
Dared to touch king Hrothgar's glorious
Throne, protected by God—God,
85 Whose love Grendel could not know. But Hrothgar's
Heart was bent. The best and most noble
Of his council debated remedies, sat
In secret sessions, talking of terror
And wondering what the bravest of warriors could do.
90 And sometimes they sacrificed to the old stone gods,
Made heathen vows, hoping for Hell's
Support, the Devil's guidance in driving
Their affliction off. That was their way,
And the heathen's only hope, Hell
95 Always in their hearts, knowing neither God
Nor His passing as He walks through our world, the Lord
Of Heaven and earth; their ears could not hear
His praise nor know His glory. Let them
Beware, those who are thrust into danger,
100 Clutched at by trouble, yet can carry no <u>solace</u>
In their hearts, cannot hope to be better! Hail
To those who will rise to God, drop off
Their dead bodies and seek our Father's peace!

The Coming of Beowulf

So the living sorrow of Healfdane's son[3]
105 Simmered, bitter and fresh, and no wisdom
Or strength could break it: that agony hung
On king and people alike, harsh
And unending, violent and cruel, and evil.
In his far-off home Beowulf, Higlac's[4]
110 Follower and the strongest of the Geats—greater
And stronger than anyone anywhere in this world—
Heard how Grendel filled nights with horror
And quickly commanded a boat fitted out,
Proclaiming that he'd go to that famous king.
115 Would sail across the sea to Hrothgar,
Now when help was needed. None
Of the wise ones regretted his going, much
As he was loved by the Geats: the omens were good,
And they urged the adventure on. So Beowulf
120 Chose the mightiest men he could find,
The bravest and best of the Geats, fourteen
In all, and led them down to their boat;
He knew the sea, would point the prow
Straight to that distant Danish shore.
125   Then they sailed, set their ship
Out on the waves, under the cliffs.
Ready for what came they wound through the currents,
The seas beating at the sand, and were borne
In the lap of their shining ship, lined
130 With gleaming armor, going safely

3. Healfdane's (hā´ alf den´ nez) **son:** Hrothgar.

4. Higlac's (hig´ laks): Higlac was the king of the Geats (gā´ ats) and Beowulf's feudal lord and uncle.

In that oak-hard boat to where their hearts took them.
The wind hurried them over the waves,
The ship foamed through the sea like a bird
Until, in the time they had known it would take,
135 Standing in the round-curled prow they could see
Sparkling hills, high and green
Jutting up over the shore, and rejoicing
In those rock-steep cliffs they quietly ended
Their voyage. Jumping to the ground, the Geats
140 Pushed their boat to the sand and tied it
In place, mail[5] shirts and armor rattling
As they swiftly moored their ship. And then
They gave thanks to God for their easy crossing.
    High on a wall a Danish watcher
145 Patrolling along the cliffs saw
The travelers crossing to the shore, their shields
Raised and shining; he came riding down,
Hrothgar's lieutenant, spurring his horse,
Needing to know why they'd landed, these men
150 In armor. Shaking his heavy spear
In their faces he spoke:

                    "Whose soldiers are you,
You who've been carried in your deep-keeled ship
Across the sea-road to this country of mine?
Listen! I've stood on these cliffs longer
155 Than you know, keeping our coast free
Of pirates, raiders sneaking ashore
From their ships, seeking our lives and our gold.
None have ever come more openly—
And yet you've offered no password, no sign
160 From my prince, no permission from my people for your landing
Here. Nor have I ever seen,
Out of all the men on earth, one greater
Than has come with you; no commoner carries
Such weapons, unless his appearance, and his beauty,
165 Are both lies. You! Tell me your name,
And your father's; no spies go further onto Danish
Soil than you've come already. Strangers,
From wherever it was you sailed, tell it,
And tell it quickly, the quicker the better,
170 I say, for us all. Speak, say
Exactly who you are, and from where, and why."
    Their leader answered him, Beowulf unlocking

5. mail: Flexible body armor made of metal.

◆ **Literary Focus**
Is the kenning *sea-road* an effective description of the ocean? Explain.

The Oseberg Ship (Viking artifact, c. A.D. 850)
Viking Ship Museum, Bygdoy, Oslo

Words from deep in his breast:

                    "We are Geats,
Men who follow Higlac. My father

175   Was a famous soldier, known far and wide
As a leader of men. His name was Edgetho.
His life lasted many winters;
Wise men all over the earth surely
Remember him still. And we have come seeking

180   Your prince, Healfdane's son, protector
Of this people, only in friendship: instruct us,
Watchman, help us with your words! Our errand
Is a great one, our business with the glorious king
Of the Danes no secret; there's nothing dark

185   Or hidden in our coming. You know (if we've heard
The truth, and been told honestly) that your country
Is cursed with some strange, vicious creature
That hunts only at night and that no one
Has seen. It's said, watchman, that he has slaughtered

190   Your people, brought terror to the darkness. Perhaps
Hrothgar can hunt, here in my heart,
For some way to drive this devil out—
If anything will ever end the evils
Afflicting your wise and famous lord.

195   Here he can cool his burning sorrow.
Or else he may see his suffering go on
Forever, for as long as Herot towers
High on your hills."

                  The mounted officer
Answered him bluntly, the brave watchman:

200   "A soldier should know the difference between words
And deeds, and keep that knowledge clear
In his brain. I believe your words, I trust in
Your friendship. Go forward, weapons and armor
And all, on into Denmark. I'll guide you

205   Myself—and my men will guard your ship,
Keep it safe here on our shores,
Your fresh-tarred boat, watch it well,
Until that curving prow carries
Across the sea to Geatland a chosen

210   Warrior who bravely does battle with the creature
Haunting our people, who survives that horror
Unhurt, and goes home bearing our love."

    Then they moved on. Their boat lay moored,
Tied tight to its anchor. Glittering at the top

215   Of their golden helmets wild boar heads gleamed,
Shining decorations, swinging as they marched,
Erect like guards, like sentinels, as though ready
To fight. They marched, Beowulf and his men
And their guide, until they could see the gables

220   Of Herot, covered with hammered gold
And glowing in the sun—that most famous of all dwellings,
Towering majestic, its glittering roofs

> ◆ **Reading Strategy**
> Paraphrase lines 179–198, giving Beowulf's reasons for coming to the Danish land.

Visible far across the land.
Their guide reined in his horse, pointing
225 To that hall, built by Hrothgar for the best
And bravest of his men; the path was plain,
They could see their way . . .

Beowulf and his men arrive at Herot and are about to be escorted in to see King Hrothgar.

Beowulf arose, with his men
230 Around him, ordering a few to remain
With their weapons, leading the others quickly
Along under Herot's steep roof into Hrothgar's
Presence. Standing on that prince's own hearth,
Helmeted, the silvery metal of his mail shirt
235 Gleaming with a smith's high art, he greeted
The Danes' great lord:

          "Hail, Hrothgar!
Higlac is my cousin[6] and my king; the days
Of my youth have been filled with glory. Now Grendel's
Name has echoed in our land: sailors
240 Have brought us stories of Herot, the best
Of all mead-halls,[7] deserted and useless when the moon
Hangs in skies the sun had lit,
Light and life fleeing together.
My people have said, the wisest, most knowing
245 And best of them, that my duty was to go to the Danes'
Great king. They have seen my strength for themselves,
Have watched me rise from the darkness of war,
Dripping with my enemies' blood. I drove
Five great giants into chains, chased
250 All of that race from the earth. I swam
In the blackness of night, hunting monsters
Out of the ocean, and killing them one
By one; death was my errand and the fate
They had earned. Now Grendel and I are called
255 Together, and I've come. Grant me, then,
Lord and protector of this noble place,
A single request! I have come so far,
Oh shelterer of warriors and your people's loved friend,
That this one favor you should not refuse me—
260 That I, alone and with the help of my men,
May purge all evil from this hall. I have heard,
Too, that the monster's scorn of men
Is so great that he needs no weapons and fears none.
Nor will I. My lord Higlac
265 Might think less of me if I let my sword
Go where my feet were afraid to, if I hid
Behind some broad linden[8] shield: my hands
Alone shall fight for me, struggle for life
Against the monster. God must decide

Gilt silver brooch from Gotland (Pre-Viking Scandinavia) Statens Historiska Museet, Stockholm

6. cousin: Here, used as a general term for relative.

7. mead-halls: To reward his thanes, the king in heroic literature would build a hall where mead (a drink made from fermented honey) was served.

8. linden: Very sturdy type of wood.

270   Who will be given to death's cold grip.
        Grendel's plan, I think, will be
        What it has been before, to invade this hall
        And gorge his belly with our bodies. If he can,
        If he can. And I think, if my time will have come,
275   There'll be nothing to mourn over, no corpse to prepare
        For its grave: Grendel will carry our bloody
        Flesh to the moors, crunch on our bones
        And smear torn scraps of our skin on the walls
        Of his den. No, I expect no Danes
280   Will fret about sewing our shrouds, if he wins.
        And if death does take me, send the hammered
        Mail of my armor to Higlac, return
        The inheritance I had from Hrethel, and he
        From Wayland.[9] Fate will unwind as it must!"

<aside>

◆ **Reading Strategy**

To follow what happens when Beowulf and Grendel meet, paraphrase lines 264–279, describing their plans of action.

</aside>

<aside>

9. Wayland: From Germanic folklore, an invisible blacksmith.

</aside>

The Battle with Grendel

That night Beowulf and his men take the places of Hrothgar and the Danes inside Herot. While his men sleep, Beowulf lies awake, eager to meet with Grendel.

285   Out from the marsh, from the foot of misty
        Hills and bogs, bearing God's hatred,
        Grendel came, hoping to kill
        Anyone he could trap on this trip to high Herot.
        He moved quickly through the cloudy night,
290   Up from his swampland, sliding silently
        Toward that gold-shining hall. He had visited Hrothgar's
        Home before, knew the way—
        But never, before nor after that night,
        Found Herot defended so firmly, his reception
295   So harsh. He journeyed, forever joyless,
        Straight to the door, then snapped it open,
        Tore its iron fasteners with a touch
        And rushed angrily over the threshold.
        He strode quickly across the inlaid
300   Floor, snarling and fierce: his eyes
        Gleamed in the darkness, burned with a gruesome
        Light. Then he stopped, seeing the hall
        Crowded with sleeping warriors, stuffed
        With rows of young soldiers resting together.
305   And his heart laughed, he relished the sight,
        Intended to tear the life from those bodies
        By morning; the monster's mind was hot
        With the thought of food and the feasting his belly
        Would soon know. But fate, that night, intended
310   Grendel to gnaw the broken bones
        Of his last human supper. Human

<aside>

◆ **Build Vocabulary**

purge (pʉrj) *v.*: Purify; cleanse

</aside>

Eyes were watching his evil steps,
Waiting to see his swift hard claws.
Grendel snatched at the first Geat
315 He came to, ripped him apart, cut
His body to bits with powerful jaws,
Drank the blood from his veins and bolted
Him down, hands and feet; death
And Grendel's great teeth came together,
320 Snapping life shut. Then he stepped to another
Still body, clutched at Beowulf with his claws,
Grasped at a strong-hearted wakeful sleeper
—And was instantly seized himself, claws
Bent back as Beowulf leaned up on one arm.
325   That shepherd of evil, guardian of crime,
Knew at once that nowhere on earth
Had he met a man whose hands were harder;
His mind was flooded with fear—but nothing
Could take his talons and himself from that tight
330 Hard grip. Grendel's one thought was to run
From Beowulf, flee back to his marsh and hide there:
This was a different Herot than the hall he had emptied.
But Higlac's follower remembered his final
Boast and, standing erect, stopped
335 The monster's flight, fastened those claws
In his fists till they cracked, clutched Grendel
Closer. The infamous killer fought
For his freedom, wanting no flesh but retreat,
Desiring nothing but escape; his claws
340 Had been caught, he was trapped. That trip to Herot
Was a miserable journey for the writhing monster!
    The high hall rang, its roof boards swayed,
And Danes shook with terror. Down
The aisles the battle swept, angry
345 And wild. Herot trembled, wonderfully
Built to withstand the blows, the struggling
Great bodies beating at its beautiful walls;
Shaped and fastened with iron, inside
And out, artfully worked, the building
350 Stood firm. Its benches rattled, fell
To the floor, gold-covered boards grating
As Grendel and Beowulf battled across them.
Hrothgar's wise men had fashioned Herot
To stand forever; only fire,
355 They had planned, could shatter what such skill had put
Together, swallow in hot flames such splendor
Of ivory and iron and wood. Suddenly
The sounds changed, the Danes started
In new terror, cowering in their beds as the terrible
360 Screams of the Almighty's enemy sang
In the darkness, the horrible shrieks of pain
And defeat, the tears torn out of Grendel's
Taut throat, hell's captive caught in the arms

♦ Literature
and Your Life
How does this
scene compare
with those you
have seen in
horror movies?

Of him who of all the men on earth

365 Was the strongest.

That mighty protector of men
Meant to hold the monster till its life
Leaped out, knowing the fiend was no use
To anyone in Denmark. All of Beowulf's
Band had jumped from their beds, ancestral

370 Swords raised and ready, determined
To protect their prince if they could. Their courage
Was great but all wasted: they could hack at Grendel
From every side, trying to open
A path for his evil soul, but their points

375 Could not hurt him, the sharpest and hardest iron
Could not scratch at his skin, for that sin-stained demon
Had bewitched all men's weapons, laid spells
That blunted every mortal man's blade. And yet his time had come, his days

380 Were over, his death near; down
To hell he would go, swept groaning and helpless
To the waiting hands of still worse fiends.
Now he discovered—once the afflictor
Of men, tormentor of their days—what it meant

385 To feud with Almighty God: Grendel
Saw that his strength was deserting him, his claws
Bound fast, Higlac's brave follower tearing at
His hands. The monster's hatred rose higher,
But his power had gone. He twisted in pain,

390 And the bleeding sinews deep in his shoulder
Snapped, muscle and bone split
And broke. The battle was over, Beowulf
Had been granted new glory: Grendel escaped,
But wounded as he was could flee to his den,

395 His miserable hole at the bottom of the marsh,
Only to die, to wait for the end
Of all his days. And after that bloody
Combat the Danes laughed with delight.
He who had come to them from across the sea,

400 Bold and strong-minded, had driven affliction
Off, purged Herot clean. He was happy,
Now, with that night's fierce work; the Danes
Had been served as he'd boasted he'd serve them; Beowulf,
A prince of the Geats, had killed Grendel,

405 Ended the grief, the sorrow, the suffering
Forced on Hrothgar's helpless people
By a bloodthirsty fiend. No Dane doubted
The victory, for the proof, hanging high
From the rafters where Beowulf had hung it, was the monster's

410 Arm, claw and shoulder and all.

◆ **Build Vocabulary**

writhing (rīth′ iŋ) *adj.*: Making twisting or turning motions

Hrothgar and his host celebrate Beowulf's victory over the monster Grendel. That night, however, Grendel's mother kidnaps and kills Hrothgar's closest friend and carries off the claw that Beowulf tore from her child. The next day the horrified king tells Beowulf about the two monsters and their underwater lair.

The Monsters' Lair

"I've heard that my people, peasants working
In the fields, have seen a pair of such fiends
Wandering in the moors and marshes, giant
Monsters living in those desert lands.
415 And they've said to my wise men that, as well as they could see,
One of the devils was a female creature.
The other, they say, walked through the wilderness
Like a man—but mightier than any man.
They were frightened, and they fled, hoping to find help
420 In Herot. They named the huge one Grendel:
If he had a father no one knew him,
Or whether there'd been others before these two,
Hidden evil before hidden evil.
They live in secret places, windy
425 Cliffs, wolf-dens where water pours
From the rocks, then runs underground, where mist
Steams like black clouds, and the groves of trees
Growing out over their lake are all covered
With frozen spray, and wind down snakelike
430 Roots that reach as far as the water
And help keep it dark. At night that lake
Burns like a torch. No one knows its bottom,
No wisdom reaches such depths. A deer,
Hunted through the woods by packs of hounds,
435 A stag with great horns, though driven through the forest
From faraway places, prefers to die
On those shores, refuses to save its life
In that water. It isn't far, nor is it
A pleasant spot! When the wind stirs
440 And storms, waves splash toward the sky,
As dark as the air, as black as the rain
That the heavens weep. Our only help,
Again, lies with you. Grendel's mother
Is hidden in her terrible home, in a place
445 You've not seen. Seek it, if you dare! Save us,
Once more, and again twisted gold,
Heaped-up ancient treasure, will reward you
For the battle you win!"

Golden horn, National Museet, Copenhagen

The Battle With Grendel's Mother

Beowulf resolves to kill the "lady monster." Arriving at the lake under which she lives, Beowulf and his companions see serpents in the water and sea beasts on the rocks. The young hero kills one of the beasts with an arrow and then prepares to fight Grendel's mother.

Then Edgetho's brave son[10] spoke:

"Remember,

450   Hrothgar, Oh knowing king, now
When my danger is near, the warm words we uttered,
And if your enemy should end my life
Then be, oh generous prince, forever
The father and protector of all whom I leave
455   Behind me, here in your hands, my beloved
Comrades left with no leader, their leader
Dead. And the precious gifts you gave me,
My friend, send them to Higlac. May he see
In their golden brightness, the Geats' great lord
460   Gazing at your treasure, that here in Denmark
I found a noble protector, a giver
Of rings whose rewards I won and briefly
Relished. And you, Unferth,[11] let
My famous old sword stay in your hands:
465   I shall shape glory with Hrunting, or death
Will hurry me from this earth!"

As his words ended
He leaped into the lake, would not wait for anyone's
Answer; the heaving water covered him
Over. For hours he sank through the waves;
470   At last he saw the mud of the bottom.
And all at once the greedy she-wolf
Who'd ruled those waters for half a hundred
Years discovered him, saw that a creature
From above had come to explore the bottom
475   Of her wet world. She welcomed him in her claws,
Clutched at him savagely but could not harm him,
Tried to work her fingers through the tight
Ring–woven mail on his breast, but tore
And scratched in vain. Then she carried him, armor
480   And sword and all, to her home; he struggled
To free his weapon, and failed. The fight
Brought other monsters swimming to see
Her catch, a host of sea beasts who beat at
His mail shirt, stabbing with tusks and teeth
485   As they followed along. Then he realized, suddenly,
That she'd brought him into someone's battle-hall,

10. Edgetho's brave son: Beowulf. Elsewhere he is identified by such phrases as "the Geats' proud prince" and "the Geats' brave prince." These different designations add variety and interest to the poem.

11. Unferth: Danish warrior who had questioned Beowulf's bravery before the battle with Grendel.

And there the water's heat could not hurt him.
Nor anything in the lake attack him through
The building's high-arching roof. A brilliant
490 Light burned all around him, the lake
Itself like a fiery flame.
                                        Then he saw
The mighty water witch and swung his sword,
His ring-marked blade, straight at her head;
The iron sang its fierce song,
495 Sang Beowulf's strength. But her guest
Discovered that no sword could slice her evil
Skin, that Hrunting could not hurt her, was useless
Now when he needed it. They wrestled, she ripped
And tore and clawed at him, bit holes in his helmet,
500 And that too failed him; for the first time in years
Of being worn to war it would earn no glory;
It was the last time anyone would wear it. But
    Beowulf
Longed only for fame, leaped back
Into battle. He tossed his sword aside,
505 Angry; the steel-edged blade lay where
He'd dropped it. If weapons were useless he'd use
His hands, the strength in his fingers. So fame
Comes to the men who mean to win it
And care about nothing else! He raised
510 His arms and seized her by the shoulder; anger
Doubled his strength, he threw her to the floor.
She fell, Grendel's fierce mother, and the Geats'
Proud prince was ready to leap on her. But she rose
At once and repaid him with her clutching claws,
515 Wildly tearing at him. He was weary, that best
And strongest of soldiers; his feet stumbled
And in an instant she had him down, held helpless.
Squatting with her weight on his stomach, she drew
A dagger, brown with dried blood, and prepared
520 To avenge her only son. But he was stretched
On his back, and her stabbing blade was blunted
By the woven mail shirt he wore on his chest.
The hammered links held; the point
Could not touch him. He'd have traveled to the bottom of the earth,
525 Edgetho's son, and died there, if that shining
Woven metal had not helped—and Holy
God, who sent him victory, gave judgment
For truth and right, Ruler of the Heavens,
Once Beowulf was back on his feet and fighting.

530   Then he saw, hanging on the wall, a heavy
Sword, hammered by giants, strong
And blessed with their magic, the best of all weapons
But so <u>massive</u> that no ordinary man could lift
Its carved and decorated length. He drew it
535 From its scabbard, broke the chain on its hilt,

*Silver pendant showing the
helmet of the Vendel*
(Early Viking period, 10th century), Statens
Historiska Museet, Stockholm

◆ **Build Vocabulary**

massive (mas´ iv) *adj.*:
Big and solid

loathsome (lōth´ səm)
adj.: Disgusting

And then, savage, now, angry
And desperate, lifted it high over his head
And struck with all the strength he had left,
Caught her in the neck and cut it through,
540 Broke bones and all. Her body fell
To the floor, lifeless, the sword was wet
With her blood, and Beowulf rejoiced at the sight.
    The brilliant light shone, suddenly,
As though burning in that hall, and as bright as Heaven's
545 Own candle, lit in the sky. He looked
At her home, then following along the wall
Went walking, his hands tight on the sword,
His heart still angry. He was hunting another
Dead monster, and took his weapon with him
550 For final revenge against Grendel's vicious
Attacks, his nighttime raids, over
And over, coming to Herot when Hrothgar's
Men slept, killing them in their beds,
Eating some on the spot, fifteen
555 Or more, and running to his loathsome moor
With another such sickening meal waiting
In his pouch. But Beowulf repaid him for those visits,
Found him lying dead in his corner,
Armless, exactly as that fierce fighter
560 Had sent him out from Herot, then struck off
His head with a single swift blow. The body
jerked for the last time, then lay still.
    The wise old warriors who surrounded Hrothgar,
Like him staring into the monsters' lake,
565 Saw the waves surging and blood
Spurting through. They spoke about Beowulf,
All the graybeards, whispered together
And said that hope was gone, that the hero
Had lost fame and his life at once, and would never
570 Return to the living, come back as triumphant
As he had left; almost all agreed that Grendel's
Mighty mother, the she-wolf, had killed him.
The sun slid over past noon, went further
Down. The Danes gave up, left
575 The lake and went home, Hrothgar with them.
The Geats stayed, sat sadly, watching,
Imagining they saw their lord but not believing
They would ever see him again.
                                    —Then the sword
Melted, blood-soaked, dripping down
580 Like water, disappearing like ice when the world's
Eternal Lord loosens invisible
Fetters and unwinds icicles and frost
As only He can, He who rules
Time and seasons, He who is truly
585 God. The monsters' hall was full of
Rich treasures, but all that Beowulf took

Was Grendel's head and the hilt of the giants'
Jeweled sword; the rest of that ring-marked
Blade had dissolved in Grendel's steaming
590 Blood, boiling even after his death.
And then the battle's only survivor
Swam up and away from those silent corpses;
The water was calm and clean, the whole
Huge lake peaceful once the demons who'd lived in it
595 Were dead.
    Then that noble protector of all seamen
Swam to land, rejoicing in the heavy
Burdens he was bringing with him. He
And all his glorious band of Geats
Thanked God that their leader had come back unharmed;
600 They left the lake together. The Geats
Carried Beowulf's helmet, and his mail shirt.
Behind them the water slowly thickened
As the monsters' blood came seeping up.
They walked quickly, happily, across
605 Roads all of them remembered, left
The lake and the cliffs alongside it, brave men
Staggering under the weight of Grendel's skull,
Too heavy for fewer than four of them to handle—
Two on each side of the spear jammed through it—
610 Yet proud of their ugly load and determined
That the Danes, seated in Herot, should see it.
Soon, fourteen Geats arrived
At the hall, bold and warlike, and with Beowulf,
Their lord and leader, they walked on the mead-hall
615 Green. Then the Geats' brave prince entered
Herot, covered with glory for the daring
Battles he had fought; he sought Hrothgar
To salute him and show Grendel's head.
He carried that terrible trophy by the hair,
620 Brought it straight to where the Danes sat,
Drinking, the queen among them. It was a weird
And wonderful sight, and the warriors stared.

◆ **Reading Strategy**
Paraphrase lines
596–622, which
describe what hap-
pens after Grendel's
mother dies.

The Last Battle

*After being honored by Hrothgar, Beowulf and his fellow Geats
return home. He is welcomed by the king, his uncle Higlac, and
later becomes king himself when Higlac and his son have died.
Beowulf rules Geatland for fifty years. Then a dragon menaces
his kingdom. Although he is an old man, Beowulf determines to
slay the beast. Before going into battle, he tells the men who have
accompanied him about the history of the royal house and his exploits in its service.*

And Beowulf uttered his final boast:
"I've never known fear, as a youth I fought

The Dragon for "The High Kings," George Sharp

625   In endless battles. I am old, now,
      But I will fight again, seek fame still,
      If the dragon hiding in his tower dares
      To face me."
                Then he said farewell to his followers,
      Each in his turn, for the last time:
630   "I'd use no sword, no weapon, if this beast
      Could be killed without it, crushed to death
      Like Grendel, gripped in my hands and torn
      Limb from limb. But his breath will be burning
      Hot, poison will pour from his tongue.
635   I feel no shame, with shield and sword
      And armor, against this monster: when he comes to me
      I mean to stand, not run from his shooting
      Flames, stand till fate decides
      Which of us wins. My heart is firm,
640 My hands calm: I need no hot

▲ **Critical Viewing**
What characteristics do this dragon and Grendel have in common? **[Compare and Contrast]**

Words. Wait for me close by, my friends.
We shall see, soon, who will survive
This bloody battle, stand when the fighting
Is done. No one else could do

645 What I mean to, here, no man but me
Could hope to defeat this monster. No one
Could try. And this dragon's treasure, his gold
And everything hidden in that tower, will be mine
Or war will sweep me to a bitter death!"

650   Then Beowulf rose, still brave, still strong,
And with his shield at his side, and a mail shirt on his breast,
Strode calmly, confidently, toward the tower, under
The rocky cliffs: no coward could have walked there!
And then he who'd endured dozens of desperate

655 Battles who'd stand boldly while swords and shields
Clashed, the best of kings, saw
Huge stone arches and felt the heat
Of the dragon's breath, flooding down
Through the hidden entrance, too hot for anyone

660 To stand, a streaming current of fire
And smoke that blocked all passage. And the Geats'
Lord and leader, angry, lowered
His sword and roared out a battle cry,
A call so loud and clear that it reached through

665 The hoary rock, hung in the dragon's
Ear. The beast rose, angry,
Knowing a man had come—and then nothing
But war could have followed. Its breath came first.
A steaming cloud pouring from the stone,

670 Then the earth itself shook. Beowulf
Swung his shield into place, held it
In front of him, facing the entrance. The dragon
Coiled and uncoiled, its heart urging it
Into battle. Beowulf's ancient sword

675 Was waiting, unsheathed, his sharp and gleaming
Blade. The beast came closer; both of them
Were ready, each set on slaughter. The Geats'
Great prince stood firm, unmoving, prepared
Behind his high shield, waiting in his shining

680 Armor. The monster came quickly toward him,
Pouring out fire and smoke, hurrying
To its fate. Flames beat at the iron
Shield, and for a time it held, protected
Beowulf as he'd planned; then it began to melt,

685 And for the first time in his life that famous prince
Fought with fate against him, with glory
Denied him. He knew it, but he raised his sword
And struck at the dragon's scaly hide.
The ancient blade broke, bit into

690 The monster's skin, drew blood, but cracked
And failed him before it went deep enough, helped him
Less than he needed. The dragon leaped

◆ **Literary Focus**
In lines 644–649, how does Beowulf show himself to be a true epic hero?

Detail of a dragon head on the Mammen horse collar (Viking artifact, 10th century), National Museum, Denmark

With pain, thrashed and beat at him, spouting
Murderous flames, spreading them everywhere.
695 And the Geats' ring-giver did not boast of glorious
Victories in other wars: his weapon
Had failed him, deserted him, now when he needed it
Most, that excellent sword. Edgetho's
Famous son stared at death,
700 Unwilling to leave this world, to exchange it
For a dwelling in some distant place—a journey
Into darkness that all men must make, as death
Ends their few brief hours on earth.
     Quickly, the dragon came at him, encouraged
705 As Beowulf fell back; its breath flared,
And he suffered, wrapped around in swirling
Flames—a king, before, but now
A beaten warrior. None of his comrades
Came to him, helped him, his brave and noble
710 Followers; they ran for their lives, fled
Deep in a wood. And only one of them
Remained, stood there, miserable, remembering,
As a good man must, what kinship should mean.

     His name was Wiglaf, he was Wexstan's son
715 And a good soldier; his family had been Swedish,
Once. Watching Beowulf, he could see
How his king was suffering, burning. Remembering
Everything his lord and cousin had given him,
Armor and gold and the great estates
720 Wexstan's family enjoyed, Wiglaf's
Mind was made up; he raised his yellow
Shield and drew his sword—an ancient
Weapon that had once belonged to Onela's
Nephew, and that Wexstan had won, killing
725 The prince when he fled from Sweden, sought safety
With Herdred, and found death.[12] And Wiglaf's father
Had carried the dead man's armor, and his sword,
To Onela, and the king had said nothing, only
Given him armor and sword and all,
730 Everything his rebel nephew had owned

**12. Onela's/Nephew . . .
found death:** When Onela
seized the throne of Swe-
den, his two nephews
sought shelter with the
king of Geatland, Herdred.
Wiglaf's father, Wexstan,
killed the older nephew
for Onela.

Gilt bronze winged dragon
(Swedish artifact, 8th century),
Statens Historiska Museet,
Stockholm

And lost when he left this life. And Wexstan
Had kept those shining gifts, held them
For years, waiting for his son to use them,
Wear them as honorably and well as once
735 His father had done; then Wexstan died
And Wiglaf was his heir, inherited treasures
And weapons and land. He'd never worn
That armor, fought with that sword, until Beowulf
Called him to his side, led him into war.
740 But his soul did not melt, his sword was strong;
The dragon discovered his courage, and his weapon,
When the rush of battle brought them together.
    And Wiglaf, his heart heavy, uttered
The kind of words his comrades deserved:
745   "I remember how we sat in the mead-hall, drinking
And boasting of how brave we'd be when Beowulf
Needed us, he who gave us these swords
And armor: all of us swore to repay him,
When the time came, kindness for kindness
750 —With our lives, if he needed them. He allowed us to
        join him,
Chose us from all his great army, thinking
Our boasting words had some weight, believing
Our promises, trusting our swords. He took us
For soldiers, for men. He meant to kill
755 This monster himself, our mighty king,
Fight this battle alone and unaided,
As in the days when his strength and daring dazzled
Men's eyes. But those days are over and gone
And now our lord must lean on younger
760 Arms. And we must go to him, while angry
Flames burn at his flesh, help
Our glorious king! By almighty God,
I'd rather burn myself than see
Flames swirling around my lord.
765 And who are we to carry home
Our shields before we've slain his enemy
And ours, to run back to our homes with Beowulf
So hard-pressed here? I swear that nothing
He ever did deserved an end
770 Like this, dying miserably and alone,
Butchered by this savage beast: we swore
That these swords and armor were each for us all!"
    Then he ran to his king, crying encouragement
As he dove through the dragon's deadly fumes.

The Spoils

Together, Wiglaf and Beowulf kill the dragon, but the old king is mortally wounded. As a last request, Beowulf asks Wiglaf to bring him the treasure that the dragon was guarding.

775   Then Wexstan's son went in, as quickly
      As he could, did as the dying Beowulf
      Asked, entered the inner darkness
      Of the tower, went with his mail shirt and his sword.
      Flushed with victory he groped his way,
780 A brave young warrior, and suddenly saw
      Piles of gleaming gold, precious
      Gems, scattered on the floor, cups
      And bracelets, rusty old helmets, beautifully
      Made but rotting with no hands to rub
785 And polish them. They lay where the dragon left them;
      It had flown in the darkness, once, before fighting
      Its final battle. (So gold can easily
      Triumph, defeat the strongest of men,
      No matter how deep it is hidden!) And he saw,
790 Hanging high above, a golden
      Banner, woven by the best of weavers
      And beautiful. And over everything he saw
      A strange light, shining everywhere,
      On walls and floor and treasure. Nothing
795 Moved, no other monsters appeared;
      He took what he wanted, all the treasures
      That pleased his eye, heavy plates
      And golden cups and the glorious banner,
      Loaded his arms with all they could hold.
800 Beowulf's dagger, his iron blade,
      Had finished the fire-spitting terror
      That once protected tower and treasures
      Alike; the gray-bearded lord of the Geats
      Had ended those flying, burning raids
805 Forever.
           Then Wiglaf went back, anxious
      To return while Beowulf was alive, to bring him
      Treasure they'd won together. He ran,
      Hoping his wounded king, weak
      And dying, had not left the world too soon.
810 Then he brought their treasure to Beowulf, and found
      His famous king bloody, gasping
      For breath. But Wiglaf sprinkled water
      Over his lord, until the words
      Deep in his breast broke through and were heard.
815 Beholding the treasure he spoke, haltingly:
        "For this, this gold, these jewels, I thank
      Our Father in Heaven, Ruler of the Earth—
      For all of this, that His grace has given me,
      Allowed me to bring to my people while breath

♦ *Literature and Your Life*

What type of rewards do modern heroes receive?

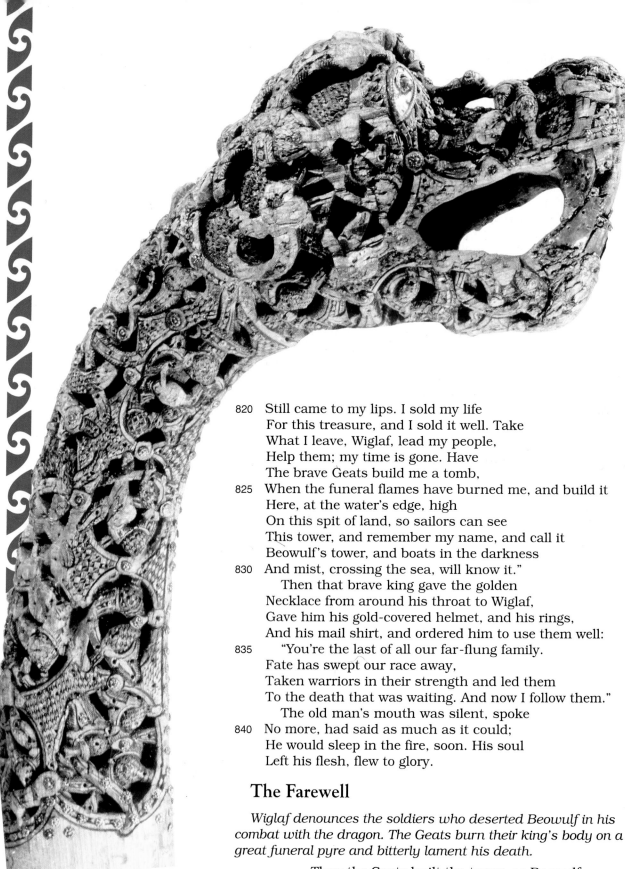

820 Still came to my lips. I sold my life
For this treasure, and I sold it well. Take
What I leave, Wiglaf, lead my people,
Help them; my time is gone. Have
The brave Geats build me a tomb,
825 When the funeral flames have burned me, and build it
Here, at the water's edge, high
On this spit of land, so sailors can see
This tower, and remember my name, and call it
Beowulf's tower, and boats in the darkness
830 And mist, crossing the sea, will know it."
    Then that brave king gave the golden
Necklace from around his throat to Wiglaf,
Gave him his gold-covered helmet, and his rings,
And his mail shirt, and ordered him to use them well:
835   "You're the last of all our far-flung family.
Fate has swept our race away,
Taken warriors in their strength and led them
To the death that was waiting. And now I follow them."
    The old man's mouth was silent, spoke
840 No more, had said as much as it could;
He would sleep in the fire, soon. His soul
Left his flesh, flew to glory.

The Farewell

Wiglaf denounces the soldiers who deserted Beowulf in his combat with the dragon. The Geats burn their king's body on a great funeral pyre and bitterly lament his death.

        Then the Geats built the tower, as Beowulf

Head of carved post from the ship burial at Oseberg

Had asked, strong and tall, so sailors
845 Could find it from far and wide; working
For ten long days they made his monument,
Sealed his ashes in walls as straight
And high as wise and willing hands
Could raise them. And the riches he and Wiglaf
850 Had won from the dragon, rings, necklaces,
Ancient, hammered armor—all
The treasures they'd taken were left there, too,
Silver and jewels buried in the sandy
Ground, back in the earth, again
855 And forever hidden and useless to men.
And then twelve of the bravest Geats
Rode their horses around the tower,
Telling their sorrow, telling stories
Of their dead king and his greatness, his glory,
860 Praising him for heroic deeds, for a life
As noble as his name. So should all men
Raise up words for their lords, warm
With love, when their shield and protector leaves
His body behind, sends his soul
865 On high. And so Beowulf's followers
Rode, mourning their beloved leader,
Crying that no better king had ever
Lived, no prince so mild, no man
So open to his people, so deserving of praise.

Guide for Responding

◆ Literature and Your Life

Reader's Response What part of the poem did you find most thrilling? Why?

Thematic Focus Explain how Beowulf grows in stature as a hero as he meets peril.

Discussion of Cultures In a small group, list people who are the heroes of various cultures. Compare and contrast each to Beowulf.

☑ Check Your Comprehension

1. What does Grendel do when he first goes to Herot?
2. What is Beowulf's plan for fighting Grendel?
3. How does Grendel die?
4. Describe the battle with Grendel's mother.
5. What happens to Beowulf during his fight with the dragon?

Guide for Responding (continued)

◆ Critical Thinking

INTERPRET

1. At the beginning of the poem, Hrothgar's warriors are happy, whereas Grendel is consumed by hatred. What causes these differences in attitude? **[Analyze]**
2. What traits of Beowulf and Grendel raise the fight between them to an epic struggle between good and evil? **[Interpret]**
3. Compare and contrast the three battles described in these excerpts. In what ways are all three different versions of the poem's main conflict? **[Compare and Contrast]**

EVALUATE

4. Critics have praised the *Beowulf* poet's skill at describing various settings. (a) Find a passage in which the poet displays this skill. (b) Explain what makes the description so effective. **[Evaluate]**

EXTEND

5. What can you infer about Anglo-Saxon beliefs and life from the poem? Support your answer with details. **[Social Studies Link]**

◆ Build Vocabulary

USING THE LATIN ROOT -sol-

Considering that *solace*, with the Latin root *-sol-*, means "to comfort," answer the following.
1. Which characters in *Beowulf* would receive a *consolation* prize?
2. Which character is *inconsolable* and seeks revenge?

USING THE WORD BANK: Antonyms

On your paper, write the letter of the word that is the antonym, the word opposite in meaning, to the first word.
1. loathsome: (a) disgusting, (b) delightful, (c) angry
2. massive: (a) tremendous, (b) average, (c) flimsy
3. purge: (a) pollute, (b) purify, (c) complete
4. reparation: (a) renewal, (b) destruction, (c) reimbursement
5. writhing: (a) valor, (b) moving, (c) still
6. solace: (a) comfort, (b) resentment, (c) aggravation

◆ Reading Strategy

PARAPHRASE

By **paraphrasing**—restating passages in your own words—you can better understand the main events in a work like *Beowulf*.
Paraphrase lines 238–243 from *Beowulf*.

◆ Literary Focus

THE EPIC

Beowulf is an **epic**—a long narrative poem, presented in an elevated style, that celebrates episodes in a people's heroic tradition. An **epic hero** battles forces of evil as he fights for the good of society.
1. Find three details in lines 109–116 that show Beowulf in a heroic light.
2. Epics usually center on a battle between good and evil. Find evidence in lines 173–198 that indicates Beowulf is battling for the forces of good.
3. Through Beowulf's deeds, you can infer the qualities that make him a hero. In what specific ways does Beowulf demonstrate loyalty and valor?

◆ Grammar and Style

APPOSITIVES AND APPOSITIVE PHRASES

An **appositive** is a noun or pronoun placed near another noun or pronoun to identify or explain it. An **appositive phrase** is an appositive with modifiers.

Practice Identify the appositive phrases in the following lines from *Beowulf*.
1. "We are Geats, / Men who follow Higlac. My father / Was a famous soldier, known far and wide"
2. "Grendel escaped. / But wounded as he was could flee to his den, / His miserable hole at the bottom of the marsh . . ."
3. " . . . And we have come seeking / Your prince, Healfdane's son, protector / Of this people, only in friendship: instruct us . . ."

Writing Application Use appositive phrases to combine each set of sentences into one.
1. Hrothgar welcomed Beowulf and his men to Herot. Herot was the strongest hall ever built.
2. Beowulf gave the monster's arm to Hrothgar. Beowulf was a prince of Geats. Hrothgar was king of the Danes.

Build Your Portfolio

 ## Idea Bank

Writing

1. **Memo** Write a memo from Beowulf to Hrothgar, reporting on your victory in a businesslike manner. Include the following heads at the top: *To, From, Re* (about), and *Date*. **[Career Link]**

2. **Comparison and Contrast** Choose another courageous hero from literature and compare and contrast that hero with Beowulf.

3. **Response to Criticism** Burton Raffel remarked that "of all the many-sided excellences of *Beowulf*," one of the most satisfying "is the poet's insight into people." Agree or disagree with this observation in a brief paper.

Speaking, Listening, and Viewing

4. **Performance** Present a dramatic reading of "The Battle With Grendel." Create dramatic effects by emphasizing key words.
   [Performing Arts Link]

5. **Visual Presentation** Prepare a visual presentation that offers images of mythical creatures and monsters from various cultures. Write captions that tell about the background and the significance of each creature within its specific culture. **[Artz Link]**

Researching and Representing

6. **Multimedia Presentation** Prepare a presentation that follows the history of superheroes. Find illustrations from older comic books and more current computer animation to show how characters have changed. **[Media Link]**

7. **Sculpture** Create a sculpture of Grendel's mother or the dragon. Refer to details in the poem as you create your sculpture. **[Art Link]**

Online Activity www.phlit.phschool.com

 ## Guided Writing Lesson

Press Release for Grendel

Give Grendel the opportunity to present the events of this epic poem from his point of view. Prepare a statement that Grendel might read at a press conference to inform the public of his side of the story.

Use the following skill to guide you as you prepare your statement.

**Writing Skills Focus:
Grab Readers' Attention**

Grab your readers' attention by surprising them: Present Grendel with human qualities. For example, in the following passage, Grendel describes his feelings about being left out of the festivities at Herot.

> Every day I listen to the happy noises at Herot and weep alone. Why do they leave me out? What have I ever done to them?

Prewriting Review the scenes that involve Grendel. Choose a scene that your readers would find surprising if presented from the monster's point of view. Jot down what Grendel might be feeling at the time and why you think he feels this way.

Drafting Using your notes, write a rough draft of the statement to be read at the press conference. As Grendel, state your main grievances, and support each one with examples. Remembering your audience (your press) and your purpose (to win sympathy), choose details and examples that will show you in a positive light.

Revising Read your draft to a classmate and ask for his or her response. If at any point the statement does not hold your reader's attention, consider adding details to enhance Grendel's human qualities.

CONNECTIONS TO WORLD LITERATURE

from *Gilgamesh*
Translated by David Ferry

from the *Iliad*
Homer, Translated by Richmond Lattimore

Literary Connection

THE EPIC

If you enjoy watching movies or reading books about heroes battling the forces of evil, you have a lot in common with audiences of thousands of years ago. These audiences would thrill to heroic stories sung and chanted by poet-performers.

Often these heroic tales were **epics**—long narrative poems that celebrated the adventures of legendary heroes. Epics provided not only a roller-coaster ride of nonstop thrills, but also examples of how to behave properly in all kinds of situations. The heroes were role models, and as you read about their exploits today, you can learn about the values and behaviors that ancient societies admired. The legendary fighter who served as a model for the English was Beowulf, whose exploits are described in the poem named for him. (See p. 38.)

Other, even earlier, epics in world literature are the epic of *Gilgamesh*, an ancient Near Eastern poem about 4,000 years old, and the *Iliad*, a Greek poem that is almost 3,000 years old. This section contains the Prologue to *Gilgamesh* and the most famous battle scene from the *Iliad*.

Front of a lyre from the tomb of Queen Pu-abi, Ur, (detail), The British Museum

▲ **Critical Viewing** Music often accompanied the telling of epics, such as *Gilgamesh* and the *Iliad*. Does the appearance of this lyre seem appropriate for the telling of an epic? **[Make a Judgment]**

GILGAMESH

Gilgamesh is a long narrative poem about a Sumerian king named Gilgamesh who lived between 2700 and 2500 B.C. Unlike modern books, this epic does not have a single author. Stories about King Gilgamesh were told and handed down by Sumerians for hundreds of years after his death. When the Babylonians conquered the Sumerians, they inherited the Sumerian cultural tradition. A Babylonian author, borrowing from some of these tales, created a unified epic about the legendary Sumerian king.

HOMER

The ancient Greeks ascribed the *Iliad* and the *Odyssey,* their two oldest epic poems, to Homer, whom they called "The Poet." Nothing certain is known about Homer's life.

Although Homer's birth and death dates are uncertain, the *Iliad* was probably composed late in the eighth century B.C. The epic tells about a legendary war that occurred hundreds of years earlier, in which Greek forces had attacked the city of Troy in Asia Minor.

from GILGAMESH
The Prologue
Translated by David Ferry

Hero and Animals, Impression from a Sumerian cylinder seal of about 2750 B.C.

The Story

of him who knew the most of all men know;
who made the journey; heartbroken; reconciled;

who knew the way things were before the Flood
the secret things, the mystery; who went

5 to the end of the earth, and over; who returned,
and wrote the story on a tablet of stone.

He built Uruk.[1] He built the keeping place
of Anu and Ishtar.[2] The outer wall

shines in the sun like brightest copper; the inner
10 wall is beyond the imagining of kings.

Study the brickwork, study the fortification;
climb the great ancient staircase to the terrace;

study how it is made; from the terrace see
the planted and fallow fields, the ponds and orchards.

1. **Uruk** (o͞o′ ro͝ok):
Ancient Sumerian city.
2. **Anu and Ishtar**
(ä′ no͞o; ish′ tär): Anu
is the father of the
Babylonian gods and
god of the sky; Ishtar
is the Babylonian
goddess of love.

15   This is Uruk, the city of Gilgamesh
      the Wild Ox, son of Lugalbanda, son

      of the Lady Wildcow Ninsun, Gilgamesh
      the vanguard and the rear guard of the army,

      Shadow of Darkness over the enemy field,
20   the Web, the Flood that rises to wash away

      the walls of alien cities, Gilgamesh
      the strongest one of all, the perfect, the terror.

      It is he who opened passes through the mountains;
      and he who dug deep wells on the mountainsides;

25   who measured the world; and sought out Utnapishtim[3]
      beyond the world; it is he who restored the shrines;

      two-thirds a god, one-third a man, the king.
      Go to the temple of Anu and Ishtar:

      open the copper chest with the iron locks;
30   the tablet of lapis lazuli[4] tells the story.

3. Utnapishtim
(o͞ot nə pēsh´ təm): The
Mesopotamian Noah, sur-
vivor of the great flood.

4. lapis lazuli
(lap´ is laz´ yo͞o lĭ´): An
azure-blue, opaque,
semiprecious stone.

Guide for Responding

◆ Literature and Your Life

Reader's Response Which achievements of
King Gilgamesh do you think were most important?
Explain.

Thematic Focus What parts of the Prologue
hint at the adventures of Gilgamesh?

☑ Check Your Comprehension

1. Where did Gilgamesh write his story?
2. What qualities of Gilgamesh does the Prologue
praise?
3. What are Gilgamesh's accomplishments?

◆ Critical Thinking

INTERPRET
1. What does the prologue suggest about the values of ancient Mesopotamia? **[Infer]**
2. Gilgamesh is described as being "two-thirds a
god" and "one-third a man." What conflicts might
arise from such a combination? **[Infer]**

EVALUATE
3. Does the Prologue help build your anticipation for
what is to come? Why or why not? **[Evaluate]**

EXTEND
4. Compare Gilgamesh and Beowulf as protectors
of their people. **[Literature Link]**

from the ILIAD

Homer, Translated by Richmond Lattimore

During the war between the Greeks and the Trojans over Helen of Troy, Achilleus, the greatest warrior of the Greeks, faces Hektor, the best warrior of the Trojans. Hektor has brutally killed *Achilleus' friend Patroklos, who was wearing Achilleus' armor. As the scene opens, Hektor and Achilleus meet for battle.*

'My brother, it is true our father and the lady our mother, taking
my knees in turn, and my companions about me, entreated
that I stay within, such was the terror upon all of them.
But the heart within me was worn away by hard sorrow for you.
5   But now let us go straight on and fight hard, let there be no sparing
of our spears, so that we can find out whether Achilleus
will kill us both and carry our bloody war spoils back
to the hollow ships, or will himself go down under your spear.'
   So Athene[1] spoke and led him on by beguilement.
10   Now as the two in their advance were come close together,
first of the two to speak was tall helm-glittering Hektor:
'Son of Peleus, I will no longer run from you, as before this
I fled three times around the great city of Priam, and dared not
stand to your onfall. But now my spirit in turn has driven me
15   to stand and face you. I must take you now, or I must be taken.
Come then, shall we swear before the gods? For these are the highest
who shall be witnesses and watch over our agreements.
Brutal as you are I will not defile you, if Zeus[2] grants
to me that I can wear you out, and take the life from you.
20   But after I have stripped your glorious armour, Achilleus,
I will give your corpse back to the Achaians.[3] Do you do likewise.'
   Then looking darkly at him swift-footed Achilleus answered:
'Hektor, argue me no agreements. I cannot forgive you.
As there are no trustworthy oaths between men and lions,
25   nor wolves and lambs have spirit that can be brought to agreement
but forever these hold feelings of hate for each other,
so there can be no love between you and me, nor shall there be
oaths between us, but one or the other must fall before then
to glut with his blood Ares the god who fights under the shield's guard.
30   Remember every valour of yours, for now the need comes
hardest upon you to be a spearman and a bold warrior.
There shall be no more escape for you, but Pallas Athene
will kill you soon by my spear. You will pay in a lump for all those
sorrows of my companions you killed in your spear's fury.'
35   So he spoke, and balanced the spear far shadowed, and threw it;

1. Athene (ə thē´ nə): Daughter of Zeus. She is associated with victory in war and clever thinking and speaking. She protects the Greeks.

2. Zeus (zoos): The most powerful of the gods, known as "father of men and gods."
3. Achaians (ə kē´ ənz): Greeks.

but glorious Hektor kept his eyes on him, and avoided it,
for he dropped, watchful, to his knee, and the bronze spear flew over his shoulder
and stuck in the ground, but Pallas Athene snatched it, and gave it
back to Achilleus, unseen by Hektor shepherd of the people.
40   But now Hektor spoke out to the blameless son of Peleus:
'You missed; and it was not, o Achilleus like the immortals,
from Zeus that you knew my destiny; but you thought so; or rather
you are someone clever in speech and spoke to swindle me,
to make me afraid of you and forget my valour and war strength.
45   You will not stick your spear in my back as I run away from you
but drive it into my chest as I storm straight in against you;
if the god gives you that; and now look out for my brazen
spear. I wish it might be taken full length in your body.
And indeed the war would be a lighter thing for the Trojans
50   if you were dead, seeing that you are their greatest affliction.
    So he spoke, and balanced the spear far shadowed, and threw it,
and struck the middle of Peleïdes' shield, nor missed it,
but the spear was driven far back from the shield, and Hektor was angered
because his swift weapon had been loosed from his hand in a vain cast.
55   He stood discouraged, and had no other ash spear; but lifting
his voice he called aloud on Deïphobos[4] of the pale shield,
and asked him for a long spear, but Deïphobos was not near him.
And Hektor knew the truth inside his heart, and spoke aloud:
'No use. Here at last the gods have summoned me deathward.
60   I thought Deïphobos the hero was here close beside me,
but he is behind the wall and it was Athene cheating me,
and now evil death is close to me, and no longer far away,
and there is no way out. So it must long since have been pleasing
to Zeus, and Zeus' son who strikes from afar, this way; though before this
65   they defended me gladly. But now my death is upon me.
Let me at least not die without a struggle, inglorious,
but do some big thing first, that men to come shall know of it.'
    So he spoke, and pulling out the sharp sword that was slung
at the hollow of his side, huge and heavy, and gathering
70   himself together, he made his swoop, like a high-flown eagle
who launches himself out of the murk of the clouds on the flat land
to catch away a tender lamb or a shivering hare; so
Hektor made his swoop, swinging his sharp sword, and Achilleus
charged, the heart within him loaded with savage fury.
75   In front of his chest the beautiful elaborate great shield
covered him, and with the glittering helm with four horns
he nodded; the lovely golden fringes were shaken about it
which Hephaistos[5] had driven close along the horn of the helmet.
And as a star moves among stars in the night's darkening,
80   Hesper,[6] who is the fairest star who stands in the sky, such
was the shining from the pointed spear Achilleus was shaking
in his right hand with evil intention toward brilliant Hektor.
He was eyeing Hektor's splendid body, to see where it might best
give way, but all the rest of the skin was held in the armour,
85   brazen and splendid, he stripped when he cut down the strength of Patroklos;[7]
yet showed where the collar-bones hold the neck from the shoulders,
the throat, where death of the soul comes most swiftly; in this place
brilliant Achilleus drove the spear as he came on in fury,

4. Deïphobos (dā i fō′ bōs): Son of Priam; powerful Trojan fighter.

5. Hephaistos (hē fes′ təs): God of fire and the forge. He made Achilleus' armor.
6. Hesper (hes′ pər): The evening star.
7. Patroklos (pə träk′ lōs): Companion and henchman to Achilleus.

and clean through the soft part of the neck the spearpoint was driven.

90 Yet the ash spear heavy with bronze did not sever the windpipe,
so that Hektor could still make exchange of words spoken.
But he dropped in the dust, and brilliant Achilleus vaunted above him:
'Hektor, surely you thought as you killed Patroklos you would be
safe, and since I was far away you thought nothing of me,

95 o fool, for an avenger was left, far greater than he was,
behind him and away by the hollow ships. And it was I;
and I have broken your strength; on you the dogs and the vultures
shall feed and foully rip you; the Achaians will bury Patroklos.'
In his weakness Hektor of the shining helm spoke to him:

100 'I entreat you, by your life, by your knees, by your parents,
do not let the dogs feed on me by the ships of the Achaians,
but take yourself the bronze and gold that are there in abundance,
those gifts that my father and the lady my mother will give you,
and give my body to be taken home again, so that the Trojans

105 and the wives of the Trojans may give me in death my rite of burning.'
But looking darkly at him swift-footed Achilleus answered:
'No more entreating of me, you dog, by knees or parents.
I wish only that my spirit and fury would drive me
to hack your meat away and eat it raw for the things that

110 you have done to me. So there is no one who can hold the dogs off
from your head, not if they bring here and set before me ten times
and twenty times the ransom, and promise more in addition,
not if Priam son of Dardanos should offer to weigh out
your bulk in gold; not even so shall the lady your mother

115 who herself bore you lay you on the death-bed and mourn you:
no, but the dogs and the birds will have you all for their feasting.'
Then, dying, Hektor of the shining helmet spoke to him:
'I know you well as I look upon you, I know that I could not
persuade you, since indeed in your breast is a heart of iron.

120 Be careful now; for I might be made into the gods' curse
upon you, on that day when Paris and Phoibos Apollo[8]
destroy you in the Skaian gates,[9] for all your valour.'
He spoke, and as he spoke the end of death closed in upon him,
and the soul fluttering free of the limbs went down into Death's house

125 mourning her destiny, leaving youth and manhood behind her.
Now though he was a dead man brilliant Achilleus spoke to him:
'Die: and I will take my own death at whatever time
Zeus and the rest of the immortals choose to accomplish it.'

Shield of Achilles: gold and silver
sculpture, John Flaxman

▲ Critical Viewing
In what ways is
this shield suitable
for a great warrior
like Achilleus?
[Analyze]

8. **Paris and Phoibus
Apollo** (par´ is; fē´ bəs;
ə pôl´ ō): Paris, son of King
Priam, and Apollo, the
archer god: a god of light
and of healing who favors
and protects the Trojans.

9. **Skaian gates** (skē´ ən):
The northwest gates of Troy.

Guide for Responding

◆ Literature and Your Life

Reader's Response Who do you think acts
more heroically—Hektor or Achilleus? Explain.

Thematic Focus Like most epics, the *Iliad* has its
roots in historical events. What are the legendary
and mythological aspects of the battle scene between Hektor and Achilleus?

☑ Check Your Comprehension

1. Briefly summarize the battle between Hektor
and Achilleus.
2. What does Hektor ask of Achilleus after he is
mortally wounded? How does Achilleus respond?

◆ Critical Thinking

INTERPRET

1. What role does the goddess Athene play in this battle? **[Infer]**
2. In what ways does Achilleus appear more warriorlike than Hektor? Explain. **[Infer]**
3. Hektor pleads with Achilleus not to defile his corpse. What does Achilleus' refusal suggest about the Greek warrior? **[Infer]**

EVALUATE

4. Is Achilleus more brutal than he needs to be, even in avenging the death of a friend? Explain. **[Evaluate]**

EXTEND

5. Would a warrior like Achilleus function well in a modern army? Why or why not? **[Career Link]**

Literary Connection

THE EPIC

Like the English poem *Beowulf*, *Gilgamesh* and the *Iliad* are examples of **epics**—long narrative poems about the deeds of legendary heroes. You can read these poems not only for their action scenes, but for what they reveal about the societies that created them. Hektor's concern about the fate of his body after death, for example, discloses the importance of burial ceremonies to the ancient Greeks.

1. Why do you think the "rite of burning" was important to ancient Greek warriors? **[Infer]**
2. What does the Prologue to *Gilgamesh* suggest about the duties of a Sumerian king? **[Infer]**
3. Would Beowulf and Achilleus have been successful as Sumerian kings? Explain. **[Speculate]**
4. Compare and contrast an action hero of today with Gilgamesh, Achilleus, or Beowulf. Consider both the deeds and the values of the heroes you're comparing. **[Compare and Contrast]**

 Idea Bank

Writing

1. **Classified Ad** As an employer of heroes, create a print advertisement that will attract candidates with the characteristics of Beowulf, Achilleus, or Gilgamesh. **[Career Link]**

2. **Adventure** Write your own episode for *Gilgamesh*—in prose or in verse—based on the information in the Prologue.

3. **Response to Criticism** N. K. Sandars declared that epic poetry "is a mixture of pure adventure, of mortality, and of tragedy." Respond to this statement by identifying elements of adventure, mortality, and tragedy in the excerpts from *Beowulf*, *Gilgamesh*, and the *Iliad*.

Speaking, Listening, and Viewing

4. **Song for an Epic Hero** Write a modern song—rock, rap, blues, or any other style—about one of these ancient epic heroes. Compose the music for it or set it to a tune that you already know. Then perform it for the class. **[Performing Arts Link]**

Researching and Representing

5. **Comic Book** Create a comic book adventure for an epic hero of your own. Illustrate your comic book by drawing pictures, clipping photos from magazines, or using computer graphics. **[Media Link; Art Link]**

Online Activity ▶ www.phlit.phschool.com

Writing Process Workshop

To defeat his foes, Beowulf may have researched information about their battle techniques and areas of weakness. **Research writing**—writing based on information gathered from outside resources—gives you the power to become an expert on any subject. Researchers use text and technical resources, including databases and the Internet.

Write a research paper in which you share with your audience what you have learned from your research.

Writing Skills Focus

▶ Begin your paper with a startling fact, an anecdote, a question, or a quotation to **grab your readers' attention**. (See p. 63.)

▶ Organize the information you have gathered so it has a **clear beginning, middle,** and **end**.

▶ **Keep a clear and consistent purpose.** Decide what you want to accomplish in the paper before you begin writing. Then keep to that purpose as you plan, write, and revise your report.

Notice how these skills work together in the following model.

WRITING MODEL

Imagine being judged a "barbarian" because you are wearing pants! ① During the Anglo-Saxon period, trousers distinguished the Germanic settlers from Greeks and Romans, who wore loose, gownlike garments called togas. Also, different styles of trousers—loose or tight, slit at the ankle or with belt loops— were not just a matter of personal taste but often indicated a tribal tradition. By examining the clothing of the Anglo-Saxons, we can learn more about Anglo-Saxon society, especially its various social groups and the types of work done by men and women. ②

① Beginning with a startling fact that grabs readers' attention and makes them want to find out more.

② This thesis statement tells readers what the middle of the report will explore in greater detail and clarifies the writer's purpose.

Applying Language Skills: Punctuating Quotations

When you incorporate quoted material into your research paper, use the following guidelines.

• Use quotation marks to enclose passages taken from another writer. If an end mark is part of a quotation, place it inside the closing quotation marks. Otherwise, place the end mark outside. When using a period, though, always place it inside the closing quotation marks.

• If you introduce a quotation with words like *stated that* or *wrote that,* don't use a comma:

• The professor stated that "advertising is our greatest export."

• When you use a quotation of four lines or more, introduce it with a colon, don't use quotation marks, and set it off from the rest of your report.

Writing Application In your research report, check that you have punctuated quotations correctly.

Writer's Solution Connection
Writing Lab

For more help in using the computer and other research tools to gather information, see the Research Writing tutorial.

Prewriting

Choose a Topic Choose a general topic that interests you, like clothing or sports. Then apply it to the discipline about which you're writing.

Selection-Related Ideas
- Beowulf and John Gardner's Grendel
- Anglo-Saxon superstitions about dragons
- The strange fate of the Beowulf manuscript

Generate Researchable Questions Guide your research by generating relevant, interesting, and researchable questions.

Identify Your Purpose Identify the goal you want to accomplish with your research paper. Use a K-W-L chart like the one below to help you determine this goal.

Locate Appropriate Information Before you go to a library, consider the text and technical resources, including databases and the Internet, that would be appropriate. Evaluate the credibility of your sources.

Formulate a Thesis Statement After organizing your notes according to the topics you will cover in your paper, develop a thesis statement that sums up your main idea.

What I Know	What I Want To Know	What I Learned
I know that clothing can indicate a person's culture and background.	I want to know what Anglo-Saxon clothing can tell us about that time.	Anglo-Saxon clothing reflected the wearer's social status.

Drafting

Write a Strong Introduction An effective introduction conveys your own interest in your topic. Include your thesis statement and grab readers' attention with an anecdote, a startling fact, a question, or a quotation.

Write Body Paragraphs In the body of your paper, you develop your ideas with facts and details. Each body paragraph should contain a topic sentence and should examine one aspect of your thesis.

Write a Conclusion In your conclusion, restate your main points and leave your readers with a recommendation, a provocative statement, or a question.

Revising

Use a Writing Skills Checklist Go back to the Writing Skills Focus on page 71 and use the items as a checklist to evaluate and revise your research paper. Make revisions that will

▶ Grab readers' attention

▶ Make them aware of your purpose

▶ Provide a clear beginning, middle, and end of your report

REVISION MODEL

Although we may not like to believe that we ^Do you judge others by

① ? Most people do and
their appearance ^this type of evaluation has been occurring

② during the Anglo-
Saxon period has
as long as clothing has existed. What was worn ^provided us

with information on the roles the German tribes and Romans

and Greeks had in society. Today's clothing is much more

interesting than Anglo-Saxon clothing.③

① The writer begins her concluding paragraph with a question that will grab readers' attention.

② The writer adds a phrase to clarify her meaning.

③ The writer deletes a sentence that distracts readers from her conclusion.

Publishing

▶ **Classroom Presentation** Present your paper orally to your classmates. Do not read it directly, but present the key points in a clear and engaging manner. You may opt to use visual prompts to make your report come alive for your peers.

▶ **Paper Exchange** Exchange papers with a group of classmates and read one another's work. Then meet for a friendly discussion of your findings.

▶ **Internet** Post your report to a message board in a news group about your topic. Be sure to credit all the sources you've used before you post your work.

APPLYING LANGUAGE SKILLS: Using Transitions to Show Importance

Use transitions to show the order of importance among ideas. You can use the following phrases:

First of all, most of all, more importantly, less significantly, primarily, secondarily, best of all, worst of all, the main reason, more outstanding, the most vital

Practice Rewrite the following passage, using order-of-importance transitions.

Space science, medicine, and engineering have been greatly changed by computers. Business and industry have also experienced significant change. Personal home computers also affect people's lives.

Writing Application Review your paper and add transitions to show order-of-importance relationships and to create a smooth, logical flow of ideas.

Writer's Solution Connection Language Lab

For more help using transitions in your writing, use the Composition lesson in the Writing Style section.

Student Success Workshop

Real-World Reading Skills

Evaluating the Credibility of Information Sources

Strategies for Success

Computer modems, electronic mail, and satellite television have made it possible to communicate information very quickly. An increase in the speed of communication, however, does not necessarily mean an increase in its quality. When you get information—even from the newest media—you need to evaluate its credibility, to examine it for bias, accuracy, and completeness.

Look for Bias Bias is a prejudice for or against a person or idea. When you evaluate information, be alert for signs that your source may be biased, rather than balanced and impartial. Signs of bias include emotionally loaded words, personal attacks, unsupported generalizations, and oversimplified either/or reasoning.

Consider *who* is speaking. Does the person or group providing information have an interest in the outcome? If so, that interest may lead to bias.

Consider what the writer does *not* say. Omitting details can slant information in a particular direction. This, too, is a form of bias.

Evaluate the Facts Make sure that the information is accurate and complete. Ask yourself these questions:

▶ Am I aware of facts that seem to contradict this information? Are the sources of this information reliable and up to date?

▶ Is the information complete? Is there evidence that important facts and contradictory opinions were left out?

▶ If the information is a statistical sample, is it representative?

VOTE NO!!!

Let's not fool ourselves. If it is passed, the bond issue for a new town library will raise your taxes. Some homeowners will pay a great deal more every year. And that's just the beginning. Hidden maintenance costs may triple the annual tax bite within three to five years. The old library has served the town well and can continue to do so. SAY NO ON OCTOBER 19! VOTE THE SPENDTHRIFT LIBRARY BOND ISSUE DOWN!!

Apply the Strategies

1. List any of the following signs of bias that you find in the flier: emotionally loaded language, unsupported generalizations, and oversimplified reasoning. Explain for each sign you list how the flier exemplifies it.

2. Does the information in the flier seem accurate and complete? Why?

✔ *Here are other sources of information that you need to evaluate carefully:*
▶ Campaign posters and speeches
▶ Sales messages in all media
▶ News stories in print and on television

PART **3**   *A National Spirit*

Four Kings of England, British Library, London, Great Britain

Despite invasions by Romans, Vikings, Anglo-Saxons, and Normans, by the fifteenth century, England began to come together as a nation as its peoples expanded their concerns and loyalties beyond the boundaries of villages and towns. The two pieces in this section, Bede's *History* and *The Anglo-Saxon Chronicle,* are both notable documents that capture and preserve the newly developing English identity.

Guide for Interpreting

Bede (673–735)

Though he lived all his life in a tiny corner of northeastern England, Bede's influence spread across Europe and down the ages. Born in Wearmouth (now the city of Sunderland), Bede entered the monastic school of Jarrow in northeastern England. He was a diligent student and stayed on at the monastery as a priest and scholar. Bede lived his whole life at Jarrow, but he wrote in Latin, so his work was accessible to scholars throughout the West. His pupils carried his writings to Europe. Famous in his own lifetime for his scholarship, after his death he was honored with the title "the Venerable Bede."

A Respected Historian Modern historians still turn to Bede's book, *A History of the English Church and People,* to learn about England before A.D. 700. To tell the story of England's warring kings and of the spread of Christianity, Bede used not only the documents assembled in his monastery's rich library, but also the learning and research of knowledgeable monks in other parts of England.

The Anglo-Saxon Chronicle

Except for Bede's *History*, the story of Britain's past was fragmentary in the years before the ninth century: a poem passed from one person to another; a parchment listing the names of old kings; a soldier's memories of a battle. During the renaissance of scholarship in King Alfred's reign (A.D. 871–899), a group of monks decided to knit together this fragmentary story. Their efforts resulted in *The Anglo-Saxon Chronicle,* the most important English historical record of the time.

Putting the Pieces Together In writing the *Chronicle,* these monks pulled together parts of Bede's *History,* existing chronologies, royal genealogies (family trees), and other historical documents. They wrote their new manuscript out by hand and sent copies to several other monasteries.

A Letter to the Future For the following two centuries, members of these monasteries added news to the Chronicle—ranging from gossip about a local baron to the battles of kings. *The Anglo-Saxon Chronicle* became a kind of chain letter from one generation to the next.

◆ Background for Understanding

HISTORY: THE FIGHT TO PRESERVE LEARNING

It was as if the lights had gone out. In the fifth century, two hundred years or so before Bede's time, Rome had abandoned Britain. The empire that had been ruled from Rome, Italy, was the most advanced civilization in the West. As part of the Roman empire, Britain had been connected with a larger world of trade and culture; the Roman army had patrolled Britain's borders. With Britain now isolated, threatened by invasion from without and by strife from within, who in Britain would continue the traditions of reading, learning, and teaching?

Monks, particularly in Ireland, kept knowledge alive during these dark times, studying Latin and copying books (which were rare and expensive) during the centuries of Anglo-Saxon rule. Through their work and, later, with the encouragement of King Alfred the Great (849–899), learning endured and prospered.

from A History of the English Church and People
◆ from The Anglo-Saxon Chronicle ◆

◆ *Literature and Your Life*

CONNECT YOUR EXPERIENCE

What sources might the students of the future use to learn about life in your time? How accurate a picture would those sources give?

Our best sources of information about life in early England include the two histories excerpted here. They were handwritten on parchment and treasured for generations in monasteries.

Journal Writing In a journal entry, list the sources that students of the future might use to learn about the present.

THEMATIC FOCUS: A NATIONAL SPIRIT

How do these works of history reflect a new sense of regional identity?

◆ Literary Focus

HISTORICAL WRITING

Historical writing tells the story of past events using evidence, such as documents from the time, that the writer has evaluated for reliability. Examining the evidence is one way in which writers of history take a step back from the shared beliefs of those around them.

You can sense this special historical "step back" at work in a sentence from Bede's *History:* "Britain, formerly known as Albion, is an island in the ocean. . . ." The moment Bede writes that sentence, he has left behind the tiny corner of England in which he lived his life and entered a wider world. He writes not just for his neighbors, but for those who may never have heard of Britain before.

◆ Grammar and Style

COMPOUND SENTENCES

Bede uses **compound sentences**, which contain two or more independent clauses (groups of words, with subjects and predicates, that can stand alone as sentences). In a compound sentence, the clauses can be joined by *and, or, but,* or a semicolon.

independent clause
There are many land and sea birds of various species, and

independent clause
it is well known for its plentiful springs and rivers abounding in fish.

◆ Reading Strategy

BREAK DOWN SENTENCES

Break down sentences—identify the key part of a sentence—to aid your understanding of long, complex sentences like Bede's.

As time went on, *Britain received a third nation*, that of the Scots, who migrated from Ireland under their chieftain Reuda, and by a combination of force and treaty, obtained from the Picts the settlements that they still hold.

The independent clause expressing the main action is italicized. Once you have identified this clause, it is easier to see how each of the "leftover" clauses explains the *when, where, how, why,* and *who* of the main action.

◆ Build Vocabulary

LATIN SUFFIXES: *-ade*

In *The Anglo-Saxon Chronicle,* a nobleman occupied a large house and "barricaded" its gate against his enemies. Knowing that the Latin suffix *-ade* often means "the act of" or "people involved in," you can figure out that *barricade* means "the act of barring the way."

WORD BANK

Before you read, preview this list of words from the selections.

| promontories |
| innumerable |
| stranded |
| barricaded |
| ravaged |

from

A History of the English Church and People

Bede
Translated by Leo Sherley-Price

The Situation of Britain and Ireland: *Their Earliest Inhabitants*

Britain, formerly known as Albion, is an island in the ocean, facing between north and west, and lying at a considerable distance from the coasts of Germany, Gaul, and Spain, which together form the greater part of Europe. It extends 800 miles northwards, and is 200 in breadth, except where a number of <u>promontories</u> stretch farther, the coastline round which extends to 3,675 miles. To the south lies Belgic Gaul,[1] from the nearest shore of which travelers can see the city known as Rutubi Portus, which the English have corrupted to Reptacestir.[2] The distance from there across the sea to Gessoriacum,[3] the nearest coast of the Morini, is 50 miles or, as some write it, 450 furlongs.[4] On the opposite side of Britain, which lies open to the boundless ocean, lie the isles of the Orcades.[5] Britain is rich in grain and timber; it has good pasturage for cattle and draft animals,[6] and vines are cultivated in various localities. There are many land and sea birds of various species, and it is well known for its plentiful springs and rivers abounding in fish. There are salmon and eel fisheries, while seals, dolphins, and sometimes whales are caught. There are also many varieties of shellfish, such as mussels, in which are often found excellent pearls of several colors: red, purple, violet, and green, but mainly white. Cockles[7] are abundant, and a beautiful scarlet dye is extracted from them which remains unfaded by sunshine or rain; indeed, the older the cloth, the more beautiful its color. The country has both salt and hot springs, and the waters flowing from them provide hot baths, in which the people bathe separately according to age and sex. As Saint Basil says: "Water receives its heat when it flows across certain metals, and becomes hot, and even scalding." The land has rich veins of many metals, including copper, iron, lead, and silver. There is also much black jet[8] of fine quality, which sparkles in firelight. When burned, it drives away snakes, and, like amber, when it is warmed by friction, it clings to whatever is applied to it. In old times, the country had twenty-eight noble cities, and <u>innumerable</u> castles, all of which were guarded by walls, towers, and barred gates.

Since Britain lies far north toward the pole, the nights are short in summer, and at midnight it is hard to tell whether the evening twilight still lingers or whether dawn is approaching; for in these northern latitudes the sun does not remain long below the horizon at night. Consequently both summer days and winter nights are long, and when the sun withdraws southwards, the winter nights last

> ◆ **Literary Focus**
> Find an example of a fact and a superstition in this passage.

---

1. **Belgic Gaul:** France.
2. **Reptacestir:** Richborough, part of the city of Sandwich.
3. **Gessoriacum:** Boulogne, France.
4. **furlongs:** Units for measuring distance; a furlong is equal to one eighth of a mile.

---

5. **Orcades:** Orkney Isles.
6. **draft animals:** Animals used for pulling loads.
7. **cockles:** Edible shellfish with two heart-shaped shells.
8. **jet** *n.:* Type of coal.

eighteen hours. In Armenia,[9] Macedonia,[10] and Italy, and other countries of that latitude, the longest day lasts only fifteen hours and the shortest nine.

At the present time there are in Britain, in harmony with the five books of the divine law, five languages and four nations —English, British, Scots, and Picts. Each of these have their own language, but all are united in their study of God's truth by the fifth, Latin, which has become a common medium through the study of the scriptures. The original inhabitants of the island were the Britons, from whom it takes its name, and who, according to tradition, crossed into Britain from Armorica,[11] and occupied the southern parts. When they had spread northwards and possessed the greater part of the islands, it is said that some Picts from Scythia[12] put to sea in a few long ships and were driven by storms around the coasts of Britain, arriving at length on the north coast of Ireland. Here they found the nation of the Scots, from whom they asked permission to settle, but their request was refused. Ireland is the largest island after Britain, and lies to the west. It is shorter than Britain to the north, but extends far beyond it to the south towards the northern coasts of Spain, although a wide sea separates them. These Pictish seafarers, as I have said, asked for a grant of land to make a settlement. The Scots replied that there was not room for them both, but said: "We can give you good advice. There is another island not far

◆ **Reading Strategy**
Break down this sentence to find the core ideas.

Cotton Ms Tiberius C II Folio 5 Verso
Page of Bede's *History*, The British Library

▲ **Critical Viewing** Bede's fellow monks spent years creating books filled with pages such as this one. What can you infer about the values of the society that produced such work? **[Infer]**

to the east, which we often see in the distance on clear days. Go and settle there if you wish; should you meet resistance, we will come to your help." So the Picts crossed into Britain, and began to settle in the north of the island, since the Britons were in possession of the south. Having no women with them, these Picts asked wives of the Scots, who consented on condition that, when any dispute arose, they should choose a king from the female royal line rather than the male. This custom continues among the Picts to this day. As time went on, Britain received a third nation, that of the Scots, who migrated from Ireland under their chieftain Reuda, and by a combination of force and treaty, obtained from the Picts the settlements that they still hold. From the name of this chieftain, they are still known as Dalreudians, for in their tongue *dal* means a division.

Ireland is broader than Britain, and its mild

---

9. Armenia: Region between the Black and the Caspian seas, now divided between the nations of Armenia and Turkey.

10. Macedonia: Region in the eastern Mediterranean, divided among Greece, Yugoslavia, and Bulgaria.

11. Armorica: Brittany, France.

12. Scythia: Ancient region in southeastern Europe.

◆ **Build Vocabulary**

promontories (prä´ mən tôr´ ēz) *n.*: Parts of high land sticking out into the sea or other body of water

innumerable (i noo´ mər ə bəl) *adj.*: Too many to count

Monks, Bodleian Library, Oxford

▲ **Critical Viewing** The picture shows two events that occurred at different times. Speculate about medieval ideas of time. In what sense is time like a straight line for Bede? **[Speculate]**

and healthy climate is superior. Snow rarely lies longer than three days, so that there is no need to store hay in summer for winter use or to build stables for beasts. There are no reptiles, and no snake can exist there, for although often brought over from Britain, as soon as the ship nears land, they breathe its scented air and die. In fact, almost everything in this isle enjoys immunity to poison, and I have heard that folk suffering from snakebite have drunk water in which scrapings from the leaves of books from Ireland had been steeped, and that this remedy checked the spreading poison and reduced the swelling. The island abounds in milk and honey, and there is no lack of vines, fish, and birds, while deer and goats are widely hunted. It is the original home of the Scots, who, as already mentioned, later migrated and joined the Britons and Picts in Britain. There is a very extensive arm of the sea, which originally formed the boundary between the Britons and the Picts. This runs inland from the west for a great distance as far as the strongly fortified British city of Alcuith.[13] It was to the northern shores of this firth[14] that the Scots came and established their new homeland.

13. **Alcuith:** Dumbarton, Scotland.
14. **firth:** Narrow arm of the sea.

Guide for Responding

♦ Literature and Your Life

Reader's Response List three details that you found interesting in Bede's history of England.
Thematic Focus Find two details of Bede's account that give a sense of national pride.

☑ Check Your Comprehension

1. (a) In Bede's time, what were the four nations of Britain? (b) What united them?

2. (a) Who were the original inhabitants of Britain? (b) Who were the later settlers?

♦ Critical Thinking

INTERPRET

1. Write down two conclusions that Bede's explanation of scarlet dye suggests to you about the lifestyle of the people of Britain. **[Infer]**

2. Bede states that Britain once "had twenty-eight noble cities guarded by walls, towers, and barred gates." What does this statement suggest about the political situation at the time? **[Interpret]**

3. (a) Why does Bede think learning Latin is important? (b) According to Bede, what factor is most important in uniting people and giving them a common identity? **[Draw Conclusions]**

from The ANGLO-SAXON CHRONICLE

—————— Translated by Anne Savage ——————

896 In the summer of this year, the force[1] split up, one part in East Anglia,[2] one part in Northumbria;[3] and those who were without property got themselves ships and went south over the sea to the Seine.

The force had not, by the grace of God, utterly broken down the English; but they were more greatly broken in those three years by the slaughter of cattle and men, most of all by the fact that many of the king's best thanes[4] in the land had died in those three years. One of them was Swithulf, bishop of Rochester; also Ceolmund, ealdorman[5] in Kent, Beorhtulf, ealdorman in Essex, Wulfred, ealdorman in Hampshire, Ealhheard, bishop of Dorchester, Eadulf, king's thane in Sussex, Beornulf, reeve[6] of Winchester, Ecgulf, king's horse-thane, and many others also, though I have named the most distinguished.

The same year, the forces in East Anglia and Northumbria greatly harassed Wessex along the south coast with raiding bands, most of all with the ash-ships[7] they had built many years before. Then king Alfred commanded longships to be built against the ash-ships. They were nearly twice as long as the others; some had sixty oars, some more. They were both swifter and steadier, also higher than the others; nor were they in the Frisian[8] manner or the Danish, but as he himself thought might be most useful.

As it fell out, at a certain time in the same year, six ships came to the Isle of Wight and did much evil there, both in Devon and everywhere along the sea-coast. Then the king commanded men to go there with nine of the new ships, and they went in front of them at the river's mouth in the open sea. The Danes went out with three ships against them, and three stood higher up the river's mouth, beached on dry land; the men from them had gone inland. The English took two of their three ships at the river's mouth, further out, killed the men, and one ship got away—and also on that all the men were killed but five. They got away because the other ships ran aground. They were very awkwardly aground: three were <u>stranded</u> on the same side of the deep water as the Danish ships, and the others all on the other side. But when the tide

> ◆ **Literary Focus**
> Find details in this passage that indicate which side the author favors.

ANGLO-SAXON PRONUNCIATIONS

General Rules

There are no silent letters in Old English. Most consonants are pronounced as in modern English.

Example: *Eadulf* can be pronounced a´ əd o͞olf´.

H before a vowel is pronounced as it is in modern English. Before a consonant or at the end of a word, it has a "throat-clearing" sound, as in the Scottish *loch.*

Example: *Beorhtulf* was probably pronounced bā´ ōrkh to͞olf´.

Specific Vowel and Consonant Pronunciations

ae = *a* in *ash*
c before or after *i* and *e*, or after *a* = *ch*;
    otherwise, *c* = *k*
cg = *j*
ea = *a* in *ash* + ə
f between two vowels = *v*
g before or after *i* or *e*, or after *ae* = *y* as in *year*;
    otherwise, *g* = *g* in *get*
sc = *sh* in *ship*
y = *u* in French *tu* or German *grün*

---

1. **the force:** Danish settlers in England; Vikings.
2. **East Anglia:** Kingdom of Anglo-Saxon England in the East, including modern Norfolk and Suffolk.
3. **Northumbria:** Kingdom of Anglo-Saxon England in the North, including the city of York.
4. **thanes:** Lords in Anglo-Saxon society, ranking below the members of a king's family.
5. **ealdorman:** Official who managed specific areas of a kingdom.
6. **reeve:** Official who collected his subjects' taxes.
7. **ash-ships:** Ships used by Vikings, propelled by oar and sail.
8. **Frisian:** Relating to people originally from Frisia, a region now divided between the Netherlands and Germany.

had ebbed many furlongs[9] from the ships, the Danes went out from their three ships to the other three that were stranded on their side and there fought with them. There were killed Lucumon the king's reeve, Wulfheard the Frisian, Aebbe the Frisian, Aethelhere the Frisian, Athelferth of the king's household, and in all, Frisians and English, sixty-two, and one hundred and twenty of the Danes.

The tide, however, came to the Danish ships before the Christians[10] could shove out, and in this way they rowed out. They were all so damaged that they could not row around Sussex; but there the sea threw two of them to land, and the men were led to Winchester, to the king. He commanded them to be hanged. The men who were on the one ship badly wounded came to East Anglia. The same summer no less than twenty ships perished with men and all along the south coast. The same year Wulfric the king's horse-thane died; he was also the Welsh-reeve.

900 Alfred, son of Aethelwulf, passed away, six nights before All Saints' Day. He was king over all the English, except for that part which was under Danish rule; and he held that kingdom for one and a half years less than thirty. Then his son Edward received the kingdom, Aethelwald, his father's brother's son, took over the manors at Wimbourne and at Christchurch, without the leave of the king and his counsellors. Then the king rode with the army until he camped at Badbury Rings near Wimbourne, and Aethelwald occupied the manor with those men who were loyal to him, and had barricaded all the gates against them; he said that he would stay there, alive or dead. Then he stole himself away under the cover of night, and sought the force in Northumbria. The king commanded them to ride after, but he could not be overtaken. They captured the woman he had seized without the king's leave and against the bishop's command, because she was hallowed[11] as a nun.

In the same year, Aethelred passed away, who was an ealdorman in Devon, four weeks before king Alfred.

902 Athelwald came here over the sea with all the ships he could get, and in Essex they submitted to him.

903 Aethelwald lured the East Anglian force into breaking the peace, so that they ravaged over the land of Mercia, until they came to Cricklade,

◆ **Reading Strategy** Break down this sentence into smaller sentences to clarify its meaning.

went over the Thames there, seized all they could carry off both in and around Braydon and then went home-ward again. Then king Edward went after them, as quickly as he could gather his army, and ravaged all their land between Devil's Dyke and Fleam Dyke and the Ouse, and everything up to the northern fens.[12] When he meant to leave there, he had it announced to the army that they would all leave together. The Kentish[13] stayed on there against his command and seven messages he had sent to them. The force came upon them there, and they fought; ealdorman Sigulf was killed there, ealdorman Sigelm, Eadwold the king's thane, abbot[14] Cenulf, Sigebriht son of Sigulf, Eadwald son of Acca, and many besides them although I have named the most distinguished. On the Danish side were killed Eohric their king, atheling[15] Aethelwald, who had lured them into peacebreaking, Byrhtsige son of the atheling Beornoth, hold Ysopa, hold Oscytel, and very many besides them we might not now name. On either hand much slaughter was made, and of the Danes there were more killed, though they had the battlefield. Ealhswith

---

9. **furlongs:** Units for measuring distance; a furlong is equal to one eighth of a mile.
10. **the Christians:** Referring here to the English and Frisian forces, in contrast to the unconverted Danes.
11. **hallowed:** Made holy; given over, in a ceremony, to religious purposes.

---

12. **Dyke . . . fens:** Dykes are barriers made of earth; fens are areas of peaty land covered with water.
13. **The Kentish:** Inhabitants of Kent, an English kingdom ruled by the kings of Wessex after 825.
14. **abbot:** Leader of a monastery; chief monk.
15. **atheling:** Anglo-Saxon noble, especially one related to the kings of Wessex.

◆ **Build Vocabulary**

stranded (stran´ did) v.: Forced into shallow water or onto a beach, reef, or other land; left helpless

barricaded (ber´ i ka´ did) v.: Blocked

ravaged (rav´ ijd) v.: Destroyed

▶ **Critical Viewing** Locate on the map the kingdoms of East Anglia, Wessex, and Kent. **[Interpret]**

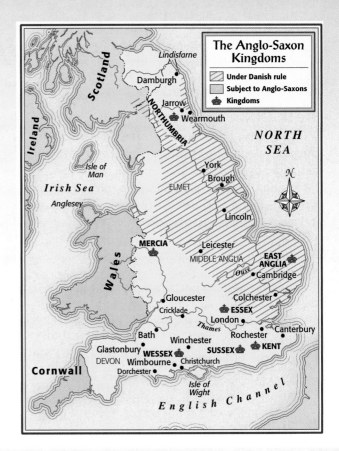

passed away. That same year was the fight at The Holme between the Kentish and the Danes. Ealdorman Aethelwulf died, brother of Ealh-swith, king Alfred's mother; and abbot Virgilus of the Scots, and the mass-priest Grimbold. In the same year a new church in Chester was hallowed, and the relics of St. Judoc[16] brought there.

904 The moon darkened.

905 A comet appeared on October 20th.

906 Alfred died, who was town-reeve at Bath; and in the same year the peace was fastened at Tiddingford, just as king Edward advised, both with the East Anglians and the Northumbrians.

---

16. **relics of St. Judoc:** Objects associated with Saint Josse, patron of harvests and ships.

Guide for Responding

◆ *Literature and Your Life*

Reader's Response Was life interesting in the ninth and tenth centuries? Explain.

Thematic Focus In what way do the authors of the *Chronicle* display a national spirit?

Questions for Research According to the *Chronicle*, the English fought with the Danes over Britain. What were the Danes doing there? How long were they in Britain? Did they contribute anything to British culture?

☑ Check Your Comprehension

1. Who are the main warring peoples in this excerpt?
2. What technological innovation does Alfred introduce?
3. What part of England did Alfred rule by the end of his reign?
4. How would you characterize relations between Edward and his cousin Aethelwald?
5. What other kinds of events besides battles does the *Chronicle* relate?

◆ Critical Thinking

INTERPRET

1. (a) Judging from this excerpt, how strong was Edward's authority? (b) How united was England under his reign? **[Draw Conclusions]**
2. Some of the king's followers have the title "bishop" or "abbot." What does this suggest about the society of the time? **[Infer]**
3. Not very much is recorded for the years 904 and 905. What does this suggest about the way in which the *Chronicle* was created? **[Infer]**

EVALUATE

4. In what ways does this excerpt succeed as a historical record? What are its shortcomings? **[Make a Judgment]**

EXTEND

5. Name three facts reported by *The Anglo-Saxon Chronicle* and the methods a modern historian might use to check whether or not they are true. **[Social Studies Link]**

Guide for Responding (continued)

◆ Reading Strategy

BREAK DOWN SENTENCES

As you read the sentence in *The Anglo-Saxon Chronicle* introducing "the force," you may have been distracted by unfamiliar place names and secondary information. Look at the sentence again and **break it down** to find a clause that can stand on its own and expresses the main action:

> In the summer of this year, the force split up, one part in East Anglia, one part in Northumbria, and those who were without property got themselves ships and went south over the sea to the Seine.

1. What is the main action of the sentence?
2. When did it happen?
3. Name the three parts of the force that were involved in the main action. Tell where each one went.

◆ Build Vocabulary

USING THE LATIN SUFFIX *-ade*

Knowing that the Latin suffix *-ade* means "the act of, the people involved in an action, or the product of a raw material," write the definition of these words (use the clues provided in parentheses):

1. lemonade
2. motorcade
3. cannonade
4. ambuscade (related to the word *ambush*)
5. cavalcade (related to the word *cavalier,* meaning "horseman")

USING THE WORD BANK: Sentence Completions

Choose words from the Word Bank to complete the following paragraph:

High on the _____?_____, the king could see his ships entering the firth. The ships were only a few furlongs away from safety. Suddenly, a fleet of Viking ships appeared and began to ____?____ the king's ships. Several of the king's ships were ____?____ on the beach. Others tried to sail back out to sea, but the Viking ships had ____?____ the mouth of the harbor.

◆ Literary Focus

HISTORICAL WRITING

Authors of **historical writing** use evidence as they tell the story of past events. Even as they strive to be objective, however, they may reveal their own opinions and biases. For example, when the authors of the *Chronicle* write that the Vikings did not "by the grace of God" defeat the English, they reveal their loyalty to the Anglo-Saxon cause.

1. (a) List three details from either the *Chronicle* or Bede's *A History of the English Church and People* that show the writers' opinions. (b) Explain how each detail indicates the writer's bias.
2. (a) Name three types of details that Bede's *History* or the *Chronicle* leaves out but which a modern historian would have included. (b) Explain your choices.

◆ Grammar and Style

COMPOUND SENTENCES

The conjunction or punctuation that joins the parts of a **compound sentence** expresses the relationship between the parts.

> A **compound sentence** contains two or more independent clauses joined by *and, or, but,* or a semicolon.

and or a semicolon: addition; further details or support; sequence; explanation
but: contrast; opposition; exception
or: alternative

Practice Rewrite the following pairs of sentences as a single compound sentence. Use the conjunction that suggests the indicated relation between ideas.
1. Alfred did not set out to rule England. Events dictated otherwise. [Contrast]
2. Later, Northumbria was taken over by Viking raiders. Bede lived in Northumbria when it was still a center for Anglo-Saxon learning. [Sequence]
3. It is a fact that there are no snakes in Ireland. Bede writes that Ireland has an immunity to poison. [Explanation]
4. We call them Vikings. The Anglo-Saxons referred to them as the Danes. [Contrast]

Build Your Portfolio

Idea Bank

Writing

1. **Details That Identify You** Bede gives details that identify the island of Britain. List key details about your hometown and the groups to which you belong.

2. **Weekly Chronicle** Write a "history" of your school week—either from the point of view of students or from the point of view of teachers. **[Social Studies Link]**

3. **Fantasy History** Write a brief history, following Bede's model, of a land of your own invention. Include maps and, if you like, drawings of buildings and people. **[Social Studies Link]**

Speaking, Listening, and Viewing

4. **Interview With Bede** Referring to the details of Bede's history, create a radio interview between a reporter and Bede. With a partner, perform your interview for the class. **[Performing Arts Link]**

5. **Illuminated Manuscripts** Look closely at the illustrated page from a Medieval book on page 79. Research the subject of illuminated manuscripts, noting especially the changes in this art form over time. Prepare a report illustrated with examples taken from your research. **[Art Link]**

Researching and Representing

6. **Tour of a Viking Ship** Research Danish sea-faring technology, and construct a set of diagrams of a Viking ship. Once you have "built" your ship, take your class on a tour of it. **[Art Link; Science Link; Social Studies Link]**

7. **Evening Newscast From the Tenth Century** Using information from these selections, write an evening newscast for a day in the tenth century, and present it to your class. **[Media Link]**

Online Activity www.phlit.phschool.com

Guided Writing Lesson

Regional History

Like the Anglo-Saxons who appear in Bede's *History* and in *The Anglo-Saxon Chronicle,* the ancestors of most American citizens crossed an ocean to live in a new land. With a new home came a new identity.

Write a history of a place such as a park or a sports arena that has helped define your identity. To help your reader follow the connections, organize your ideas coherently.

Writing Skills Focus: Coherence

Coherence in writing involves tying individual details to general ideas and clearly showing the order in which events occurred. In a coherent essay, paragraphs are arranged according to an obvious plan, with clear connections between ideas. For example, Bede creates coherence by first dealing with Britain's physical characteristics, then discussing the people who inhabit it.

Prewriting Gather facts, examples, quotations, and other details for your history. You may conduct original research by interviewing someone connected with the subject of your paper. Organize and record this new information before you write, arranging it in outline form.

Drafting Refer to your outline as you write, and use transitions to show: order in time (*before, after, soon*), order in space (*above, below, beside*), order of importance (*first, second, finally*), cause and effect (*because, therefore, so*).

Revising Read your draft critically, making sure that it is coherent. If the links between ideas are unclear as you reread your draft, add transitions to clarify these connections. Also, double-check all your facts for accuracy, and delete any passages in which you display bias or an opinion.

Guide for Interpreting

Geoffrey Chaucer
(1343?–1400)

From Page to Poet Son of a merchant, page in a royal house, soldier, diplomat, and royal clerk, Geoffrey Chaucer saw quite a bit of the medieval world. His varied experiences helped prepare him to write *The Canterbury Tales.* It provides the best contemporary picture we have of fourteenth-century England.

Gathering together characters from different walks of life, Chaucer takes the reader on a journey across medieval society.

The exact date of Geoffrey Chaucer's birth is unknown, but official records furnish many details of his active life. In 1359, while serving in the English army in France, Chaucer was captured and held prisoner. The king paid a £16 (sixteen-pound) ransom for his release (eight times what a simple laborer might make in a year). In 1366, Chaucer married Philippa Pan, a lady-in-waiting to the queen. Their eldest child, Thomas, continued his father's rise in the world, marrying a noblewoman and acquiring great wealth.

The Poet Matures While Chaucer was rising through the ranks of medieval society, he managed to practice and hone his skills as a poet. Chaucer began writing in his twenties and continued into his old age.

His early poems were based on the works of European poets. He also wrote translations of French poetry. As he grew older, he developed a mature style of his own. In *Troilus and Criseyde,* a later poem drawn from the Greek legend of the Trojan War, Chaucer displays penetrating insight into human character.

The Canterbury Tales Chaucer wrote *The Canterbury Tales* in his later years. Only 24 of the projected 124 tales were finished, but these 24 stand together as a complete work.

In this masterwork, each character tells a tale on the pilgrimage to the cathedral of Canterbury. Even as the tellers of *The Canterbury Tales* come from the length and breadth of medieval society, the tales themselves take you on a trip through medieval literature: romances and comedies; stories in rhyme and stories in prose; crude humor and religious mysteries.

The Father of English Poetry In his own lifetime, Geoffrey Chaucer was considered the greatest English poet. Since his death, his poems have never gone out of print. Each new generation of poets writing in English has studied Chaucer's work.

Chaucer lies buried in Westminster Abbey. The Abbey's honorary burial area for distinguished writers, the Poet's Corner, was established around his tomb.

◆ Background for Understanding

HISTORY: PILGRIMAGES

In medieval Christianity, pilgrimages—long trips to holy places—were popular. Every year, pilgrims would travel great distances, sometimes as far as Rome or the Holy Land (the modern Middle East), to tombs of saints and other shrines. Some came to ask for divine assistance, such as a miraculous cure, or to give thanks for that already received. Others came to do penance or simply to show devotion.

Canterbury, a town about fifty miles southeast of London, was a major destination for English pilgrims. The cathedral in Canterbury was the site of Archbishop Thomas à Becket's murder in 1170. Days after the murder, and three years before Becket officially was made a saint, people began flocking to the cathedral to pay their respects.

from The Canterbury Tales: The Prologue

◆ *Literature and Your Life*

CONNECT YOUR EXPERIENCE

Trips taken for the purpose of renewal or inspiration, even if they are not religious, can loosely be called pilgrimages. Think about a pilgrimage you've taken or would like to take. The Prologue to *The Canterbury Tales* describes a group of people who are setting out on a pilgrimage.

Journal Writing Briefly describe your fellow "pilgrims" on a "pilgrimage" you have taken.

THEMATIC FOCUS: A NATIONAL IDENTITY

Each of Chaucer's characters represents a different social type—from knights to plowmen. As you read, notice all the different ways of "being English" in Chaucer's day.

◆ Build Vocabulary

LATIN SUFFIXES: *-tion*

One of Chaucer's characters has a gift for *prevarication*. The Latin suffix *-tion,* which means "the action of," gives a clue to the meaning of *prevarication*. To *prevaricate* means "to distort the truth." One way to define *prevarication* is "the act of distorting the truth."

WORD BANK

Before you read, preview this list of words from the Prologue to *The Canterbury Tales*.

solicitous
garnished
absolution
commission
sanguine
avouches
prevarication

◆ Grammar and Style

PAST AND PAST PERFECT TENSES

Like most storytellers, Chaucer tells his tales in the **past tense,** a verb form showing an action or a condition that began and ended at a given time in the past. Chaucer uses the **past perfect tense** to indicate an action or condition that ended before another past action began. The past perfect tense is formed by using the helping verb *had* before the past participle of the main verb. Here are examples from *The Canterbury Tales*:

Past Tense: It *happened* in that season that one day . . .

Past Perfect Tense: In fifteen mortal battles he *had been* . . . (He had been in these battles before the time of the story.)

◆ Literary Focus

CHARACTERIZATION

Characterization is the act of creating and developing the personality of a character. Authors use **direct characterization** when they make direct statements about characters. They use **indirect characterization** when they reveal a character's personality through his or her actions, thoughts, and words.

Chaucer delighted audiences with his skillful characterizations. For example, when he says the Knight "followed chivalry/Truth, honor . . .", he is describing this character directly. He uses indirect characterization when he says, "he was not gaily dressed," which suggests the man is poor or severe.

◆ Reading Strategy

ANALYZE DIFFICULT SENTENCES

When reading works of literature, **analyze difficult sentences** by asking yourself what information they express.

To understand the eighteen-line sentence at the beginning of the Prologue, for example, ask yourself *when, who,* and *what:*

When: in April

Who: people; palmers

What: long to go on pilgrimages

from The Canterbury Tales
The Prologue

Geoffrey Chaucer
Translated by Nevill Coghill

✦

Chaucer wrote in what we now call Middle English. The first eighteen lines of the Prologue are presented here in Middle English, followed by the entire Prologue in a modern translation.

✦

Whan that Aprill with his shourës sootë
The droghte of March hath percëd to the rootë
And bathëd every veyne in swich licour
Of which vertu engendrëd is the flour,
5 Whan Zephirus eek with his sweetë breeth
Inspirëd hath in every holt and heeth
The tendrë croppës, and the yongë sonnë
Hath in the Ram his half cours y-ronnë,
And smalë fowelës maken melodyë
10 That slepen al the nyght with open eye,
So priketh hem Nature in hir corages,
Than longen folk to goon on pilgrymages,
And palmeres for to seken straungë strondës,
To fernë halwës kouthe in sondry londës.
15 And specially, from every shirës endë
Of Engelond, to Caunterbury they wendë,
The holy, blisful martir for to seke
That hem hath holpen whan that they were seekë.

When in April the sweet showers fall
And pierce the drought of March to the root, and all
The veins are bathed in liquor of such power
As brings about the engendering of the flower,
5 When also Zephyrus[1] with his sweet breath
Exhales an air in every grove and heath
Upon tender shoots, and the young sun
His half-course in the sign of the Ram[2] has run,
And the small fowl are making melody
10 That sleep away the night with open eye

1. **Zephyrus** (zef′ ə rəs): The west wind.
2. **Ram:** Aries, the first sign of the zodiac. The pilgrimage began on April 11, 1387.

The Tabard Inn, Arthur Szyk for The Canterbury Tales

▲ Critical Viewing In what ways does the rhythm of lines and patterns capture the mood of the poem's opening? **[Analyze]**

(So nature pricks them and their heart engages)
Then people long to go on pilgrimages
And palmers[3] long to seek the stranger strands[4]
Of far-off saints, hallowed in sundry lands,
15 And specially, from every shire's end
In England, down to Canterbury they wend
To seek the holy blissful martyr,[5] quick
To give his help to them when they were sick.
　　It happened in that season that one day
20 In Southwark,[6] at The Tabard,[7] as I lay
Ready to go on pilgrimage and start
For Canterbury, most devout at heart,
At night there came into that hostelry
Some nine and twenty in a company
25 Of sundry folk happening then to fall
In fellowship, and they were pilgrims all
That towards Canterbury meant to ride.
The rooms and stables of the inn were wide;
They made us easy, all was of the best.
30 And shortly, when the sun had gone to rest,
By speaking to them all upon the trip
I soon was one of them in fellowship
And promised to rise early and take the way
To Canterbury, as you heard me say.
35 　　But nonetheless, while I have time and space,
Before my story takes a further pace,
It seems a reasonable thing to say

3. **palmers:** Pilgrims who wore two crossed palm leaves to show that they had visited the Holy Land.
4. **strands:** Shores.
5. **martyr:** St. Thomas à Becket, the Archbishop of Canterbury, who was murdered in Canterbury Cathedral in 1170.
6. **Southwark** (suth´ ərk): Suburb of London at the time.
7. **The Tabard** (ta´ bərd): An inn.

What their condition was, the full array
Of each of them, as it appeared to me
40 According to profession and degree,
And what apparel they were riding in;
And at a Knight I therefore will begin.
There was a *Knight*, a most distinguished man,
Who from the day on which he first began
45 To ride abroad had followed chivalry,
Truth, honor, generousness and courtesy.
He had done nobly in his sovereign's war
And ridden into battle, no man more,
As well in Christian as heathen places,
50 And ever honored for his noble graces.
    When we took Alexandria,[8] he was there.
He often sat at table in the chair
Of honor, above all nations, when in Prussia.
In Lithuania he had ridden, and Russia,
55 No Christian man so often, of his rank.
When, in Granada, Algeciras sank
Under assault, he had been there, and in
North Africa, raiding Benamarin;
In Anatolia he had been as well
60 And fought when Ayas and Attalia fell,
For all along the Mediterranean coast
He had embarked with many a noble host.
In fifteen mortal battles he had been
And jousted for our faith at Tramissene
65 Thrice in the lists, and always killed his man.
This same distinguished knight had led the van[9]
Once with the Bey of Balat,[10] doing work
For him against another heathen Turk;
He was of sovereign value in all eyes.
70 And though so much distinguished, he was wise
And in his bearing modest as a maid.
He never yet a boorish thing had said
In all his life to any, come what might;
He was a true, a perfect gentle-knight.
75 Speaking of his equipment, he possessed
Fine horses, but he was not gaily dressed.
He wore a fustian[11] tunic stained and dark
With smudges where his armor had left mark;
Just home from service, he had joined our ranks
80 To do his pilgrimage and render thanks.
    He had his son with him, a fine young *Squire*,
A lover and cadet, a lad of fire
With locks as curly as if they had been pressed.
He was some twenty years of age, I guessed.
85 In stature he was of a moderate length,
With wonderful agility and strength.
He'd seen some service with the cavalry
In Flanders and Artois and Picardy[12]
And had done valiantly in little space

8. Alexandria: Site of one of the campaigns fought by Christians against groups who posed a threat to Europe during the fourteenth century. The place names that follow refer to other battle sites in these campaigns, or crusades.

◆ **Reading Strategy**
According to lines 56–65, what has the knight done?

9. van: The part of the army that goes before the rest (short for vanguard).
10. Bey of Balat: Pagan leader.

11. fustian (fus´ chən) *n.*: Coarse cloth of cotton and linen.

12. Flanders . . . Picardy: Regions in Belgium and France.

The Yeoman, Arthur Szyk for *The Canterbury Tales*

▶ **Critical Viewing** Compare this portrait with Chaucer's description of the Yeoman. What details did the artist choose to change or omit? **[Compare and Contrast]**

90   Of time, in hope to win his lady's grace.
        He was embroidered like a meadow bright
        And full of freshest flowers, red and white.
        Singing he was, or fluting all the day;
        He was as fresh as is the month of May.
95   Short was his gown, the sleeves were long and wide;
        He knew the way to sit a horse and ride.
        He could make songs and poems and recite,
        Knew how to joust and dance, to draw and write.
        He loved so hotly that till dawn grew pale
100   He slept as little as a nightingale.
        Courteous he was, lowly and serviceable,
        And carved to serve his father at the table.
          There was a *Yeoman*[13] with him at his side,
        No other servant; so he chose to ride.
105   This Yeoman wore a coat and hood of green,
        And peacock-feathered arrows, bright and keen
        And neatly sheathed, hung at his belt the while
        —For he could dress his gear in yeoman style,
        His arrows never drooped their feathers low—
110   And in his hand he bore a mighty bow.
        His head was like a nut, his face was brown.
        He knew the whole of woodcraft up and down.
        A saucy brace[14] was on his arm to ward

13. Yeoman (yō´ mən) *n.*: Attendant.

14. brace: Bracelet.

It from the bow-string, and a shield and sword
115 Hung at one side, and at the other slipped
A jaunty dirk,[15] spear-sharp and well-equipped.
A medal of St. Christopher[16] he wore
Of shining silver on his breast, and bore
A hunting-horn, well slung and burnished clean,
120 That dangled from a baldric[17] of bright green.
He was a proper forester I guess.
　　　There also was a *Nun*, a Prioress.[18]
Her way of smiling very simple and coy.
Her greatest oath was only "By St. Loy!"[19]
125 And she was known as Madam Eglantyne.
And well she sang a service,[20] with a fine
Intoning through her nose, as was most seemly,
And she spoke daintily in French, extremely,
After the school of Stratford-atte-Bowe;[21]
130 French in the Paris style she did not know.
At meat her manners were well taught withal;
No morsel from her lips did she let fall,
Nor dipped her fingers in the sauce too deep;
But she could carry a morsel up and keep
135 The smallest drop from falling on her breast.
For courtliness she had a special zest,
And she would wipe her upper lip so clean
That not a trace of grease was to be seen
Upon the cup when she had drunk; to eat,
140 She reached a hand sedately for the meat.
She certainly was very entertaining,
Pleasant and friendly in her ways, and straining
To counterfeit a courtly kind of grace,
A stately bearing fitting to her place,
145 And to seem dignified in all her dealings.
As for her sympathies and tender feelings,
She was so charitably solicitous
She used to weep if she but saw a mouse
Caught in a trap, if it were dead or bleeding.
150 And she had little dogs she would be feeding
With roasted flesh, or milk, or fine white bread.
And bitterly she wept if one were dead
Or someone took a stick and made it smart;
She was all sentiment and tender heart.
155 Her veil was gathered in a seemly way,
Her nose was elegant, her eyes glass-gray;
Her mouth was very small, but soft and red,
Her forehead, certainly, was fair of spread,
Almost a span[22] across the brows, I own;
160 She was indeed by no means undergrown.
Her cloak, I noticed, had a graceful charm.

15. **dirk** *n.*: Dagger.
16. **St. Christopher:** Patron saint of forests and travelers.
17. **baldric** *n.*: Belt worn over one shoulder and across the chest to support a sword.
18. *Prioress* *n.*: In an abbey, the nun ranking just below the abbess.
19. **St. Loy:** St. Eligius, patron saint of goldsmiths and courtiers.
20. **service:** Daily prayer.
21. **Stratford-atte-Bowe:** Nunnery near London.

22. **span:** Nine inches.

◆ **Build Vocabulary**

solicitous (sə lis′ ə təs) *adj.*: Showing care or concern

The Monk
Arthur Szyk for *The Canterbury Tales*

◀ **Critical Viewing** What can you infer from this picture about the Monk's style of living? List three details supporting your conclusion. **[Infer]**

She wore a coral trinket on her arm,
A set of beads, the gaudies[23] tricked in green,
Whence hung a golden brooch of brightest sheen
165 On which there first was graven a crowned A,
And lower, *Amor vincit omnia.*[24]
    Another *Nun,* the chaplain at her cell,
Was riding with her, and *three Priests* as well.
    A *Monk* there was, one of the finest sort
170 Who rode the country; hunting was his sport.
A manly man, to be an Abbot able;
Many a dainty horse he had in stable.

23. gaudies: Large green beads that marked certain prayers on a set of prayer beads.
24. *Amor vincit omnia* (ä môr´ wink´ it ôm´ nē ä): "Love conquers all" (Latin).

His bridle, when he rode, a man might hear
Jingling in a whistling wind as clear,
175   Aye, and as loud as does the chapel bell
Where my lord Monk was Prior of the cell.
The Rule of good St. Benet or St. Maur[25]
As old and strict he tended to ignore;
He let go by the things of yesterday
180   And took the modern world's more spacious way.
He did not rate that text at a plucked hen
Which says that hunters are not holy men
And that a monk uncloistered is a mere
Fish out of water, flapping on the pier,
185   That is to say a monk out of his cloister.
That was a text he held not worth an oyster;
And I agreed and said his views were sound;
Was he to study till his head went round
Poring over books in cloisters? Must he toil
190   As Austin[26] bade and till the very soil?
Was he to leave the world upon the shelf?
Let Austin have his labor to himself.
        This Monk was therefore a good man to horse;
Greyhounds he had, as swift as birds, to course.
195   Hunting a hare or riding at a fence
Was all his fun, he spared for no expense.
I saw his sleeves were garnished at the hand
With fine gray fur, the finest in the land,
And on his hood, to fasten it at his chin
200   He had a wrought-gold cunningly fashioned pin;
Into a lover's knot it seemed to pass.
His head was bald and shone like looking-glass;
So did his face, as if it had been greased.
He was a fat and personable priest;
205   His prominent eyeballs never seemed to settle.
They glittered like the flames beneath a kettle;
Supple his boots, his horse in fine condition.
He was a prelate fit for exhibition,
He was not pale like a tormented soul.
210   He liked a fat swan best, and roasted whole.
His palfrey[27] was as brown as is a berry.
        There was a *Friar*, a wanton[28] one and merry
A Limiter,[29] a very festive fellow.
In all Four Orders[30] there was none so mellow
215   So glib with gallant phrase and well-turned speech.
He'd fixed up many a marriage, giving each
Of his young women what he could afford her.
He was a noble pillar to his Order.
Highly beloved and intimate was he
220   With County folk[31] within his boundary,
And city dames of honor and possessions;
For he was qualified to hear confessions,
Or so he said, with more than priestly scope;
He had a special license from the Pope.

◆ Literary Focus
What does the comparison of the two sounds (lines 173–176) suggest about the Monk?

25. St. Benet or St. Maur: St. Benedict, author of monastic rules, and St. Maurice, one of his followers. Benet and Maur are French versions of Benedict and Maurice.

26. Austin: English version of St. Augustine, who criticized lazy monks.

27. palfrey *n.*: Saddle horse.
28. wanton *adj.*: Jolly.
29. Limiter: Friar who is given begging rights for a certain limited area.
30. Four Orders: There were four orders of friars who supported themselves by begging: Dominicans, Franciscans, Carmelites, and Augustinians.
31. County folk: The phrase refers to rich landowners.

225   Sweetly he heard his penitents at shrift[32]
        With pleasant <u>absolution</u>, for a gift.
        He was an easy man in penance-giving
        Where he could hope to make a decent living;
        It's a sure sign whenever gifts are given
230   To a poor Order that a man's well shriven,[33]
        And should he give enough he knew in verity
        The penitent repented in sincerity.
        For many a fellow is so hard of heart
        He cannot weep, for all his inward smart.
235   Therefore instead of weeping and of prayer
        One should give silver for a poor Friar's care.
        He kept his tippet[34] stuffed with pins for curls,
        And pocket-knives, to give to pretty girls.
        And certainly his voice was gay and sturdy,
240   For he sang well and played the hurdy-gurdy.[35]
        At sing-songs he was champion of the hour.
        His neck was whiter than a lily-flower
        But strong enough to butt a bruiser down.
        He knew the taverns well in every town
245   And every innkeeper and barmaid too
        Better than lepers, beggars and that crew,
        For in so eminent a man as he
        It was not fitting with the dignity
        Of his position, dealing with a scum
250   Of wretched lepers; nothing good can come
        Of dealings with the slum-and-gutter dwellers,
        But only with the rich and victual-sellers.
        But anywhere a profit might accrue
        Courteous he was and lowly of service too.
255   Natural gifts like his were hard to match.
        He was the finest beggar of his batch,
        And, for his begging-district, payed a rent;
        His brethren did no poaching where he went.
        For though a widow mightn't have a shoe,
260   So pleasant was his holy how-d'ye-do
        He got his farthing from her just the same
        Before he left, and so his income came
        To more than he laid out. And how he romped,
        Just like a puppy! He was ever prompt
265   To arbitrate disputes on settling days
        (For a small fee) in many helpful ways,
        Not then appearing as your cloistered scholar
        With threadbare habit hardly worth a dollar,
        But much more like a Doctor or a Pope.
270   Of double-worsted was the semi-cope[36]
        Upon his shoulders, and the swelling fold
        About him, like a bell about its mold
        When it is casting, rounded out his dress.
        He lisped a little out of wantonness
275   To make his English sweet upon his tongue.
        When he had played his harp, or having sung,

32. shrift *n*.: Confession.

33. well shriven *adj*.: Absolved of his sins.

34. tippet *n*.: Hood.

35. hurdy-gurdy: Stringed instrument played by cranking a wheel.

◆ **Literary Focus**
In this sentence (lines 244–252), is Chaucer using direct or indirect characterization, or both?

36. semi-cope: Cape.

◆ **Build Vocabulary**
garnished (gär′ nisht) *adj*.: Decorated; trimmed

absolution (ab sə loo′ shən) *n*.: Act of freeing someone of a sin or of a criminal charge

His eyes would twinkle in his head as bright
As any star upon a frosty night.
This worthy's name was Hubert, it appeared.
280   There was a *Merchant* with a forking beard
And motley dress, high on his horse he sat,
Upon his head a Flemish[37] beaver hat
And on his feet daintily buckled boots.
He told of his opinions and pursuits
285   In solemn tones, and how he never lost.
The sea should be kept free at any cost
(He thought) upon the Harwich-Holland range,[38]
He was expert at currency exchange.

37. Flemish: From Flanders.

38. Harwich-Holland range: The North Sea between England and Holland.

The Student
Arthur Szyk for *The Canterbury Tales*

◀ **Critical Viewing** What can you infer from this picture about the Oxford Cleric's style of living? List three details supporting your conclusion. **[Infer]**

	This estimable Merchant so had set
290	His wits to work, none knew he was in debt,
	He was so stately in negotiation,
	Loan, bargain and commercial obligation.
	He was an excellent fellow all the same;
	To tell the truth I do not know his name.
295	An *Oxford Cleric*, still a student though,
	One who had taken logic long ago,
	Was there; his horse was thinner than a rake,
	And he was not too fat, I undertake,
	But had a hollow look, a sober stare;
300	The thread upon his overcoat was bare.
	He had found no preferment in the church
	And he was too unworldly to make search
	For secular employment. By his bed
	He preferred having twenty books in red
305	And black, of Aristotle's[39] philosophy,
	To having fine clothes, fiddle or psaltery.[40]
	Though a philosopher, as I have told,
	He had not found the stone for making gold.[41]
	Whatever money from his friends he took
310	He spent on learning or another book
	And prayed for them most earnestly, returning
	Thanks to them thus for paying for his learning.
	His only care was study, and indeed
	He never spoke a word more than was need,
315	Formal at that, respectful in the extreme,
	Short to the point, and lofty in his theme.
	The thought of moral virtue filled his speech
	And he would gladly learn, and gladly teach.
	A *Sergeant at the Law* who paid his calls,
320	Wary and wise, for clients at St. Paul's[42]
	There also was, of noted excellence.
	Discreet he was, a man to reverence,
	Or so he seemed, his sayings were so wise.
	He often had been Justice of Assize
325	By letters patent, and in full commission.
	His fame and learning and his high position
	Had won him many a robe and many a fee.
	There was no such conveyancer[43] as he;
	All was fee-simple[44] to his strong digestion,
330	Not one conveyance could be called in question.
	Nowhere there was so busy a man as he;
	But was less busy than he seemed to be.
	He knew of every judgment, case and crime
	Recorded, ever since King William's time.
335	He could dictate defenses or draft deeds;

♦ *Literature and Your Life*

Name a modern type of person who resembles the Cleric.

39. Aristotle's (ar′ is tät′ əlz): Referring to the Greek philosopher (384–322 B.C.).

40. psaltery (sôl′ tər ē): Ancient stringed instrument.

41. stone . . . gold: At the time, alchemists believed that a "philosopher's stone" existed that could turn base metals into gold.

42. St. Paul's: London cathedral near which lawyers often met to discuss their cases.

43. conveyancer: One who draws up documents for transferring ownership of property.

44. fee-simple: Unrestricted ownership.

♦ **Build Vocabulary**

commission (kə mish′ ən) *n*.: Authorization; act of giving authority to an individual

No one could pinch a comma from his screeds,[45]
And he knew every statute off by rote.
He wore a homely parti-colored coat
Girt with a silken belt of pin-stripe stuff;
340   Of his appearance I have said enough.
    There was a *Franklin*[46] with him, it appeared;
White as a daisy-petal was his beard.
A sanguine man, high-colored and benign,
He loved a morning sop[47] of cake in wine.
345   He lived for pleasure and had always done,
For he was Epicurus'[48] very son,
In whose opinion sensual delight
Was the one true felicity in sight.
As noted as St. Julian[49] was for bounty
350   He made his household free to all the County.
His bread, his ale were the finest of the fine
And no one had a better stock of wine.
His house was never short of bake-meat pies,
Of fish and flesh, and these in such supplies
355   It positively snowed with meat and drink
And all the dainties that a man could think.
According to the seasons of the year
Changes of dish were ordered to appear.
He kept fat partridges in coops, beyond,
360   Many a bream and pike were in his pond.
Woe to the cook whose sauces had no sting
Or who was unprepared in anything!
And in his hall a table stood arrayed
And ready all day long, with places laid.
365   As Justice at the Sessions[50] none stood higher;
He often had been Member for the Shire.[51]
A dagger and a little purse of silk
Hung at his girdle, white as morning milk.
As Sheriff he checked audit, every entry.
370   He was a model among landed gentry.
    A *Haberdasher*, a *Dyer*, a *Carpenter*,
A *Weaver* and a *Carpet-maker* were
Among our ranks, all in the livery
Of one impressive guild-fraternity.[52]
375   They were so trim and fresh their gear would pass
For new. Their knives were not tricked out with brass
But wrought with purest silver, which avouches
A like display on girdles and on pouches.
Each seemed a worthy burgess,[53] fit to grace
380   A guild-hall with a seat upon the dais.
Their wisdom would have justified a plan
To make each one of them an alderman;

45. **screeds:** Long, boring speeches or pieces of writing.

46. **Franklin:** Wealthy landowner.

47. **sop:** Piece.

48. **Epicurus'** (ep´ i kyoor´ əs): Referring to a Greek philosopher (342?–270 B.C.) who believed that happiness is the most important goal in life.
49. **St. Julian:** Patron saint of hospitality.

50. **Sessions:** Court sessions.
51. **Member . . . Shire:** Parliamentary representative for the county.

52. **guild-fraternity:** In the Middle Ages, associations of men practicing the same craft or trade, called guilds, set standards for workmanship and protected their members by controlling competition.
53. **burgess:** Member of a legislative body.

◆ **Build Vocabulary**

sanguine (saŋ´ gwin) *adj.*: Confident; cheerful

avouches (ə vouch´ ez) *v.*: Asserts positively; affirms

They had the capital and revenue,
Besides their wives declared it was their due.
385 And if they did not think so, then they ought;
To be called "*Madam*" is a glorious thought,
And so is going to church and being seen
Having your mantle carried like a queen.
       They had a *Cook* with them who stood alone
390 For boiling chicken with a marrow-bone,
Sharp flavoring-powder and a spice for savor.
He could distinguish London ale by flavor,
And he could roast and seethe and broil and fry,
Make good thick soup and bake a tasty pie.
395 But what a pity—so it seemed to me,
That he should have an ulcer on his knee.
As for blancmange,[54] he made it with the best.
       There was a *Skipper* hailing from far west;
He came from Dartmouth, so I understood.
400 He rode a farmer's horse as best he could,
In a woolen gown that reached his knee.
A dagger on a lanyard[55] falling free
Hung from his neck under his arm and down.
The summer heat had tanned his color brown,
405 And certainly he was an excellent fellow.
Many a draught of vintage, red and yellow,
He'd drawn at Bordeaux, while the trader snored.
The nicer rules of conscience he ignored.
If, when he fought, the enemy vessel sank,
410 He sent his prisoners home; they walked the plank.
As for his skill in reckoning his tides,
Currents and many another risk besides,
Moons, harbors, pilots, he had such dispatch
That none from Hull to Carthage was his match.
415 Hardy he was, prudent in undertaking;
His beard in many a tempest had its shaking,
And he knew all the havens as they were
From Gottland to the Cape of Finisterre,
And every creek in Brittany and Spain;
420 The barge he owned was called *The Maudelayne*.
       A *Doctor* too emerged as we proceeded;
No one alive could talk as well as he did
On points of medicine and of surgery,
For, being grounded in astronomy,
425 He watched his patient's favorable star
And, by his Natural Magic, knew what are
The lucky hours and planetary degrees
For making charms and magic effigies.
The cause of every malady you'd got
430 He knew, and whether dry, cold, moist or hot;[56]
He knew their seat, their humor and condition.
He was a perfect practicing physician.
These causes being known for what they were,

54. blancmange (blə mänzh´): At the time, a creamy chicken dish.

55. lanyard: Loose rope around the neck.

◆ **Reading Strategy**
How does the Doctor attempt to heal patients (lines 421–428)?

56. The cause . . . hot: It was believed that the body was composed of four "humors" (cold and dry, hot and moist, hot and dry, cold and moist) and that diseases resulted from a disturbance of one of these "humors."

He gave the man his medicine then and there.

435 All his apothecaries[57] in a tribe
Were ready with the drugs he would prescribe,
And each made money from the other's guile;
They had been friendly for a goodish while.
He was well-versed in Esculapius[58] too

440 And what Hippocrates and Rufus knew
And Dioscorides, now dead and gone,
Galen and Rhazes, Hali, Serapion,
Averroes, Avicenna, Constantine,
Scotch Bernard, John of Gaddesden, Gilbertine.[59]

445 In his own diet he observed some measure;
There were no superfluities for pleasure,
Only digestives, nutritives and such.
He did not read the Bible very much.
In blood-red garments, slashed with bluish-gray

450 And lined with taffeta,[60] he rode his way;
Yet he was rather close as to expenses
And kept the gold he won in pestilences.
Gold stimulates the heart, or so we're told.

57. apothecaries (ə päth´ə ker´ ēz): Persons who prepared medicines.

58. Esculapius (es´ kyoo lā´ pē əs): In Greek mythology, the god of medicine and healing.

59. Hippocrates . . . Gilbertine: Famous physicians and medical authorities.

60. taffeta (taf´ i tə): Fine silk fabric.

◀ **Critical Viewing** What does the Wife of Bath's body language convey about her character? [Analyze]

The Wife of Bath
Arthur Szyk for *The Canterbury Tales*

He therefore had a special love of gold.

455   A worthy *woman* from beside Bath[61] city
Was with us, somewhat deaf, which was a pity.
In making cloth she showed so great a bent
She bettered those of Ypres and of Ghent.[62]
In all the parish not a dame dared stir
460 Towards the altar steps in front of her,
And if indeed they did, so wrath was she
As to be quite put out of charity.
Her kerchiefs were of finely woven ground;[63]
I dared have sworn they weighed a good ten pound,
465 The ones she wore on Sunday, on her head.
Her hose were of the finest scarlet red
And gartered tight; her shoes were soft and new.
Bold was her face, handsome, and red in hue.
A worthy woman all her life, what's more
470 She'd had five husbands, all at the church door,
Apart from other company in youth;
No need just now to speak of that, forsooth.
And she had thrice been to Jerusalem,
Seen many strange rivers and passed over them;
475 She'd been to Rome and also to Boulogne,
St. James of Compostella and Cologne,[64]
And she was skilled in wandering by the way.
She had gap-teeth, set widely, truth to say.
Easily on an ambling horse she sat
480 Well wimpled[65] up, and on her head a hat
As broad as is a buckler[66] or a shield;
She had a flowing mantle that concealed
Large hips, her heels spurred sharply under that.
In company she liked to laugh and chat
485 And knew the remedies for love's mischances,
An art in which she knew the oldest dances.
    A holy-minded man of good renown
There was, and poor, the *Parson* to a town,
Yet he was rich in holy thought and work.
490 He also was a learned man, a clerk,
Who truly knew Christ's gospel and would preach it
Devoutly to parishioners, and teach it.
Benign and wonderfully diligent,
And patient when adversity was sent
495 (For so he proved in great adversity)
He much disliked extorting tithe[67] or fee,
Nay rather he preferred beyond a doubt
Giving to poor parishioners round about
From his own goods and Easter offerings
500 He found sufficiency in little things.
Wide was his parish, with houses far asunder,
Yet he neglected not in rain or thunder,
In sickness or in grief, to pay a call
    On the remotest, whether great or small,
505 Upon his feet, and in his hand a stave.

61. Bath: English resort city.

62. Ypres (ē′ prə) **and of Ghent** (gent): Flemish cities known for wool making.

63. ground: Composite fabric.

64. Jerusalem . . . Rome . . . Boulogne . . . St. James of Compostella . . . Cologne: Famous pilgrimage sites at the time.
65. wimpled: Wearing a scarf covering the head, neck, and chin.
66. buckler: Small round shield.

67. tithe (ti*th*): One tenth of a person's income, paid as a tax to support the church.

This noble example to his sheep he gave,
First following the word before he taught it,
And it was from the gospel he had caught it.
This little proverb he would add thereto
510 That if gold rust, what then will iron do?
For if a priest be foul in whom we trust
No wonder that a common man should rust;
And shame it is to see—let priests take stock—
A soiled shepherd and a snowy flock.
515 The true example that a priest should give
Is one of cleanness, how the sheep should live.
He did not set his benefice to hire[68]
And leave his sheep encumbered in the mire
Or run to London to earn easy bread
520 By singing masses for the wealthy dead,
Or find some Brotherhood and get enrolled.
He stayed at home and watched over his fold
So that no wolf should make the sheep miscarry.
He was a shepherd and no mercenary.
525 Holy and virtuous he was, but then
Never contemptuous of sinful men,
Never disdainful, never too proud or fine,
But was discreet in teaching and benign.
His business was to show a fair behavior
530 And draw men thus to Heaven and their Savior,
Unless indeed a man were obstinate;
And such, whether of high or low estate,
He put to sharp rebuke to say the least.
I think there never was a better priest.
535 He sought no pomp or glory in his dealings,
No scrupulosity had spiced his feelings.
Christ and His Twelve Apostles and their lore
He taught, but followed it himself before.
   There was a *Plowman* with him there, his brother.
540 Many a load of dung one time or other
He must have carted through the morning dew.
He was an honest worker, good and true,
Living in peace and perfect charity,
And, as the gospel bade him, so did he,
545 Loving God best with all his heart and mind
And then his neighbor as himself, repined
At no misfortune, slacked for no content,
For steadily about his work he went
To thrash his corn, to dig or to manure
550 Or make a ditch; and he would help the poor
For love of Christ and never take a penny
If he could help it, and, as prompt as any,
He paid his tithes in full when they were due
On what he owned, and on his earnings too.
555 He wore a tabard[69] smock and rode a mare.
   There was a *Reeve*,[70] also a *Miller*, there,
A College *Manciple*[71] from the Inns of Court,

68. set . . . hire: Pay someone else to perform his parish duties.

69. tabard: Loose jacket.
70. *Reeve:* Estate manager.
71. *Manciple:* Buyer of provisions.

A papal *Pardoner*[72] and, in close consort,
A Church-Court *Summoner*,[73] riding at a trot,
560   And finally myself—that was the lot.
     The *Miller* was a chap of sixteen stone,[74]
A great stout fellow big in brawn and bone.
He did well out of them, for he could go
And win the ram at any wrestling show.
565   Broad, knotty and short-shouldered, he would boast
He could heave any door off hinge and post,
Or take a run and break it with his head.
His beard, like any sow or fox, was red
And broad as well, as though it were a spade;
570   And, at its very tip, his nose displayed
A wart on which there stood a tuft of hair.
Red as the bristles in an old sow's ear.
His nostrils were as black as they were wide.
He had a sword and buckler at his side,
575   His mighty mouth was like a furnace door.
A wrangler and buffoon, he had a store
Of tavern stories, filthy in the main.
His was a master-hand at stealing grain.
He felt it with his thumb and thus he knew
580   Its quality and took three times his due—
A thumb of gold, by God, to gauge an oat!
He wore a hood of blue and a white coat.
He liked to play his bagpipes up and down
And that was how he brought us out of town.
585   The *Manciple* came from the Inner Temple;
All caterers might follow his example
In buying victuals; he was never rash
Whether he bought on credit or paid cash.
He used to watch the market most precisely
590   And go in first, and so he did quite nicely.
Now isn't it a marvel of God's grace
That an illiterate fellow can outpace
The wisdom of a heap of learned men?
His masters—he had more than thirty then—
595   All versed in the abstrusest legal knowledge,
Could have produced a dozen from their College
Fit to be stewards in land and rents and game
To any Peer in England you could name,
And show him how to live on what he had
600   Debt-free (unless of course the Peer were mad)
Or be as frugal as he might desire,
And they were fit to help about the Shire
In any legal case there was to try;
And yet this Manciple could wipe their eye.
605   The *Reeve* was old and choleric and thin;
His beard was shaven closely to the skin,
His shorn hair came abruptly to a stop
Above his ears, and he was docked on top
Just like a priest in front; his legs were lean,

72. *Pardoner*: One who dispenses papal pardons.
73. *Summoner*: One who serves summonses to church courts.
74. sixteen stone: 224 pounds. A stone equals 14 pounds.

> ◆ **Reading Strategy**
> How is the Manciple better than his masters (lines 585–604)?

610 Like sticks they were, no calf was to be seen.
He kept his bins and garners[75] very trim;
No auditor could gain a point on him.
And he could judge by watching drought and rain
The yield he might expect from seed and grain.

615 His master's sheep, his animals and hens,
Pigs, horses, dairies, stores and cattle-pens
Were wholly trusted to his government.
And he was under contract to present
The accounts, right from his master's earliest years.

620 No one had ever caught him in arrears.
No bailiff, serf or herdsman dared to kick,
He knew their dodges, knew their every trick;
Feared like the plague he was, by those beneath.
He had a lovely dwelling on a heath,

625 Shadowed in green by trees above the sward.[76]
A better hand at bargains than his lord,
He had grown rich and had a store of treasure
Well tucked away, yet out it came to pleasure
His lord with subtle loans or gifts of goods,

630 To earn his thanks and even coats and hoods.
When young he'd learnt a useful trade and still
He was a carpenter of first-rate skill.
The stallion-cob he rode at a slow trot
Was dapple-gray and bore the name of Scot.

635 He wore an overcoat of bluish shade
And rather long; he had a rusty blade
Slung at his side. He came, as I heard tell,
From Norfolk, near a place called Baldeswell.
His coat was tucked under his belt and splayed.

640 He rode the hindmost of our cavalcade.

 There was a *Summoner* with us in the place
Who had a fire-red cherubinnish face,[77]
For he had carbuncles. His eyes were narrow,
He was as hot and lecherous as a sparrow.

645 Black, scabby brows he had, and a thin beard.
Children were afraid when he appeared.
No quicksilver, lead ointments, tartar creams,
Boracic, no, nor brimstone, so it seems,
Could make a salve that had the power to bite,

650 Clean up or curve his whelks of knobby white.
Or purge the pimples sitting on his cheeks.
Garlic he loved, and onions too, and leeks,
And drinking strong wine till all was hazy.
Then he would shout and jabber as if crazy,

655 And wouldn't speak a word except in Latin
When he was drunk, such tags as he was pat in;
He only had a few, say two or three,
That he had mugged up out of some decree;
No wonder, for he heard them every day.

660 And, as you know, a man can teach a jay
To call out "Walter" better than the Pope.

75. garners *n.*: Buildings for storing grain.

76. sward *n.*: Turf.

77. fire-red . . . face: In the art of the Middle Ages, the faces of cherubs, or angels, were often painted red.

But had you tried to test his wits and grope
For more, you'd have found nothing in the bag.
Then *"Questio quid juris"*[78] was his tag.

665 He was a gentle varlet and a kind one,
No better fellow if you went to find one.
He would allow—just for a quart of wine—
Any good lad to keep a concubine
A twelvemonth and dispense it altogether!

670 Yet he could pluck a finch to leave no feather:
And if he found some rascal with a maid
He would instruct him not to be afraid
In such a case of the Archdeacon's curse
(Unless the rascal's soul were in his purse)

675 For in his purse the punishment should be.
"Purse is the good Archdeacon's Hell," said he.
But well I know he lied in what he said;
A curse should put a guilty man in dread,
For curses kill, as shriving brings, salvation.

680 We should beware of excommunication.
Thus, as he pleased, the man could bring duress
On any young fellow in the diocese.
He knew their secrets, they did what he said.
He wore a garland set upon his head

685 Large as the holly-bush upon a stake
Outside an ale-house, and he had a cake,
A round one, which it was his joke to wield
As if it were intended for a shield.

He and a gentle *Pardoner* rode together,
690 A bird from Charing Cross of the same feather,
Just back from visiting the Court of Rome.
He loudly sang *"Come hither, love, come home!"*
The Summoner sang deep seconds to this song,
No trumpet ever sounded half so strong.

695 This Pardoner had hair as yellow as wax,
Hanging down smoothly like a hank of flax.
In driblets fell his locks behind his head
Down to his shoulder which they overspread;
Thinly they fell, like rat-tails, one by one.

700 He wore no hood upon his head, for fun;
The hood inside his wallet had been stowed,
He aimed at riding in the latest mode;
But for a little cap his head was bare
And he had bulging eyeballs, like a hare.

705 He'd sewed a holy relic on his cap;
His wallet lay before him on his lap,
Brimful of pardons come from Rome all hot.
He had the same small voice a goat has got.
His chin no beard had harbored, nor would harbor,

710 Smoother than ever chin was left by barber.
I judge he was a gelding, or a mare.
As to his trade, from Berwick down to Ware
There was no pardoner of equal grace,

78. *"Questio quid juris"*: "The question is, What is the point of the law?" (Latin)

The Pardoner
Arthur Szyk for *The Canterbury Tales*

▶ **Critical Viewing** How well does this picture of the Pardoner match Chaucer's description of him in lines 695–710? **[Assess]**

For in his trunk he had a pillowcase
715 Which he asserted was Our Lady's veil.
He said he had a gobbet[79] of the sail
Saint Peter had the time when he made bold
To walk the waves, till Jesu Christ took hold.
He had a cross of metal set with stones
720 And, in a glass, a rubble of pigs' bones.
And with these relics, any time he found
Some poor up-country parson to astound,
On one short day, in money down, he drew
More than the parson in a month or two,
725 And by his flatteries and prevarication
Made monkeys of the priest and congregation.
But still to do him justice first and last
In church he was a noble ecclesiast.
How well he read a lesson or told a story!
730 But best of all he sang an Offertory,[80]
For well he knew that when that song was sung
He'd have to preach and tune his honey-tongue

79. gobbet: Piece.

◆ **Reading Strategy**
How does the Pardoner get money (lines 712–726)?

80. Offertory: Song that accompanies the collection of the offering at a church service.

And (well he could) win silver from the crowd.
That's why he sang so merrily and loud.

735   Now I have told you shortly, in a clause,
The rank, the array, the number and the cause
Of our assembly in this company
In Southwark, at that high-class hostelry
Known as *The Tabard*, close beside *The Bell*.
740 And now the time has come for me to tell
How we behaved that evening; I'll begin
After we had alighted at the inn,
Then I'll report our journey, stage by stage,
All the remainder of our pilgrimage.
745 But first I beg of you, in courtesy,
Not to condemn me as unmannerly
If I speak plainly and with no concealings
And give account of all their words and dealings,
Using their very phrases as they fell.
750 For certainly, as you all know so well,
He who repeats a tale after a man
Is bound to say, as nearly as he can,
Each single word, if he remembers it,
However rudely spoken or unfit,
755 Or else the tale he tells will be untrue,
The things invented and the phrases new.
He may not flinch although it were his brother,
If he says one word he must say the other.
And Christ Himself spoke broad[81] in Holy Writ,
760 And as you know there's nothing there unfit,
And Plato[82] says, for those with power to read,
"The word should be as cousin to the deed."
Further I beg you to forgive it me
If I neglect the order and degree
765 And what is due to rank in what I've planned.
I'm short of wit as you will understand.

    Our *Host* gave us great welcome; everyone
Was given a place and supper was begun.
He served the finest victuals you could think,
770 The wine was strong and we were glad to drink.
A very striking man our Host withal,
And fit to be a marshal in a hall.
His eyes were bright, his girth a little wide;
There is no finer burgess in Cheapside.[83]
775 Bold in his speech, yet wise and full of tact,
There was no manly attribute he lacked,
What's more he was a merry-hearted man.
After our meal he jokingly began
To talk of sport, and, among other things
780 After we'd settled up our reckonings,
He said as follows: "Truly, gentlemen,
You're very welcome and I can't think when
—Upon my word I'm telling you no lie—
I've seen a gathering here that looked so spry,

81. **broad:** Bluntly.

82. **Plato:** Greek philosopher (427?– 347? B.C.)

83. **Cheapside:** District in London.

◆ **Build Vocabulary**

prevarication (pri var´ i kā´ shən) *n.*: Evasion of truth

785 No, not this year, as in this tavern now.
I'd think you up some fun if I knew how.
And, as it happens, a thought has just occurred
And it will cost you nothing, on my word.
You're off to Canterbury—well, God speed!
790 Blessed St. Thomas answer to your need!
And I don't doubt, before the journey's done
You mean to while the time in tales and fun.
Indeed, there's little pleasure for your bones
Riding along and all as dumb as stones.
795 So let me then propose for your enjoyment,
Just as I said, a suitable employment.
And if my notion suits and you agree
And promise to submit yourselves to me
Playing your parts exactly as I say
800 Tomorrow as you ride along the way,
Then by my father's soul (and he is dead)
If you don't like it you can have my head!
Hold up your hands, and not another word."
    Well, our consent of course was not deferred,
805 It seemed not worth a serious debate;
We all agreed to it at any rate
And bade him issue what commands he would.
"My lords," he said, "now listen for your good,
And please don't treat my notion with disdain.
810 This is the point. I'll make it short and plain.
Each one of you shall help to make things slip
By telling two stories on the outward trip
To Canterbury, that's what I intend,
And, on the homeward way to journey's end
815 Another two, tales from the days of old;
And then the man whose story is best told,
That is to say who gives the fullest measure
Of good morality and general pleasure,
He shall be given a supper, paid by all,
820 Here in this tavern, in this very hall,
When we come back again from Canterbury.
And in the hope to keep you bright and merry
I'll go along with you myself and ride
All at my own expense and serve as guide.
825 I'll be the judge, and those who won't obey
Shall pay for what we spend upon the way.
Now if you all agree to what you've heard
Tell me at once without another word,
And I will make arrangements early for it."
830   Of course we all agreed, in fact we swore it
Delightedly, and made entreaty too
That he should act as he proposed to do,
Become our Governor in short, and be
Judge of our tales and general referee,
835 And set the supper at a certain price.
We promised to be ruled by his advice

◆ Literature
and Your Life
When traveling
with friends or
family, what games
do you play?
What songs do
you sing?

Come high, come low; unanimously thus
We set him up in judgment over us.
More wine was fetched, the business being done;
840   We drank it off and up went everyone
To bed without a moment of delay.
    Early next morning at the spring of day
Up rose our Host and roused us like a cock,
Gathering us together in a flock,
845   And off we rode at slightly faster pace
Than walking to St. Thomas' watering-place;[84]
And there our Host drew up, began to ease
His horse, and said, "Now, listen if you please,
My lords! Remember what you promised me.
850   If evensong and matins will agree[85]
Let's see who shall be first to tell a tale.
And as I hope to drink good wine and ale
I'll be your judge. The rebel who disobeys,
However much the journey costs, he pays.
855   Now draw for cut[86] and then we can depart;
The man who draws the shortest cut shall start."

84. St. Thomas' water-ing-place: A brook two miles from the inn.

85. If evensong . . . agree: If what you said last night holds true this morning.

86. draw for cut: Draw lots, as when pulling straws from a bunch; the person who pulls the short straw is "it."

Guide for Responding

◆ Literature and Your Life

Reader's Response Which pilgrim would you most like to meet? Why?

Thematic Focus What modern character types can you match up with the characters in the Prologue? What types would Chaucer not have anticipated?

Casting Call Imagine that you are making a film of *The Canterbury Tales*, using a contemporary setting and characters. With a small group, create a list of characters for the pilgrimage taken from your own experiences and those of the other group members.

☑ Check Your Comprehension

1. What does Chaucer say that people long to do when spring comes?
2. (a) Where does the Prologue take place?
   (b) Why have people gathered at this place?
3. Briefly describe four of Chaucer's pilgrims.
4. What entertainment does the host propose for the journey?

◆ Critical Thinking

INTERPRET

1. Chaucer pokes gentle fun at some of the pilgrims. What is his opinion of the Nun's singing voice and of her French? **[Deduce]**
2. What are some of the ways in which two of the religious men—the Friar and the Parson—differ?
3. What does Chaucer seem to dislike about (a) the Skipper? (b) the Doctor? **[Infer]**
4. Judging from his pilgrims, do you think Chaucer believes people are basically good? Support your answer with details from the description of three pilgrims. **[Draw Conclusions]**

APPLY

5. If Chaucer were writing *The Canterbury Tales* today, what three kinds of pilgrims might he consider adding to the group? **[Hypothesize]**

EXTEND

6. Most of Chaucer's characters are named after a profession. What does Chaucer's emphasis on social roles suggest to you about medieval society? **[Social Studies Link]**

Guide for Responding (continued)

◆ Reading Strategy

ANALYZE DIFFICULT SENTENCES

Asking questions like *who, what, when, where, why,* and *how* as you read can help you **analyze difficult sentences.** For example, look again at lines 47–50.
1. *Who* is being described? 3. *When* did he do it?
2. *What* did this person do? 4. *Where* did he do it?

◆ Literary Focus

CHARACTERIZATION

In creating vivid portraits of his pilgrims, Chaucer uses both **direct characterization**—describing their personalities directly—and **indirect characterization**—revealing their personalities by describing their appearance, thoughts, or actions. In your notebook, answer the following:
1. Give three details that Chaucer uses to characterize the Doctor. For each detail, note whether the characterization is direct or indirect.
2. (a) Give one example of each of the following kinds of details in Chaucer's characterizations: direct statement, physical appearance, and action. (b) Explain how your examples of physical appearance and action indirectly characterize the pilgrim concerned.

◆ Build Vocabulary

USING THE LATIN SUFFIX *-tion*

Using your knowledge that a word ending in the suffix *-tion* refers to an action or process and its result, define these words in your notebook:
1. narration   3. elevation
2. accumulation   4. oration

USING THE WORD BANK: Synonyms

Match each numbered vocabulary word with its lettered synonym.
1. solicitous   a. asserts
2. garnished   b. authorization
3. sanguine   c. freeing from sin
4. avouches   d. confident
5. commission   e. caring
6. absolution   f. decorated
7. prevarication   g. lying

◆ Grammar and Style

PAST AND PAST PERFECT TENSES

Chaucer's use of the **past and past perfect tenses** makes clear to readers which events happened earlier than others.

Writing Application Rewrite these sentences, putting one of the verbs in the past tense and one in the past perfect tense to show a sequence of events.
1. The narrator of the Prologue *meets* the pilgrims the next morning. He *stays* the night at the Tabard Inn.
2. The Pardoner *tricks* a parson into buying a relic. He *tells* him it was part of Saint Peter's sail.
3. The Sergeant at Arms *makes* a success at law. His learning *earns* him many important positions.

 ## Idea Bank

Writing

1. **Modern Types** Chaucer's Prologue is full of rich characterizations. Write a brief description of a character from the modern world.

2. **Comparison and Contrast** Chaucer's Prologue contains three figures involved in religion— a friar, a monk, and a nun. Write a paper in which you compare and contrast their characters.

3. **Response to Criticism** The poet John Dryden referred to Chaucer as the "father of English poetry." Using examples from the Prologue, show why Chaucer deserves this title.

Speaking, Listening, and Viewing

4. **Monologue** Write a monologue in which you capture the character of one of Chaucer's pilgrims. Then present your monologue to the class. **[Performing Arts Link]**

Researching and Representing

5. **Portraits of the Pilgrims** Use Chaucer's verbal portrait of a pilgrim to paint, draw, or sculpt this character. **[Art Link]**

Online Activity www.phlit.phschool.com

The Nun's Priest's Tale

◆ Review and Anticipate

Each pilgrim from the Prologue agrees to tell a tale on the way to Canterbury. It's of interest that the teller of this tale, the Nun's Priest, is mentioned in the Prologue but not fully described. He reappears suddenly when the Host spots him at a crucial moment: The Knight has objected to the Monk's tragic tale, and it looks as if the storytelling game might end in bitterness.

The Nun's Priest is asked to save the game with a merry tale. Here's a brief description of the new storyteller: He's riding a "jade," an old, filthy cart-horse. Yet he vows to be "merry," and Chaucer describes him as both "sweet" and "goodly."

See if you can use this scanty description to predict the kind of story this character will tell. Then review your prediction when you've finished reading and see whether you were on target.

◆ Build Vocabulary

LATIN WORD ROOTS: -cap-

In "The Nun's Priest's Tale," Chaucer writes of the widow: "Little she had in capital or rent." *Capital* is formed on the Latin root *-cap-*, from *caput*, meaning "a head," and it refers to money or property that is the chief part of a person's fortune.

WORD BANK

Before you read, preview this list of words from "The Nun's Priest's Tale."

capital
timorous
derision
maxim
stringent
cant

◆ Grammar and Style

PRONOUN CASE

Most personal pronouns have different subject and object forms, or **cases,** which reflect how they are used in a sentence.

Subjective Case Pronouns: *I, he, she, we, they, who*
The subjective case is used for subjects and subject complements.

> subject
> *She* had a yard that was enclosed about . . .

Objective Case Pronouns: *me, him, her, us, them, whom*
The objective is used for direct and indirect objects and objects of prepositions.

> direct object
> . . . apoplexy struck *her* not . . .

◆ Literary Focus

MOCK-HEROIC STYLE

In the **mock-heroic style,** a writer uses a style of language usually used for describing heroes in order to describe ordinary characters. This results in a hilarious disparity between content and style.

In "The Nun's Priest's Tale," Chaucer uses heroic language to retell a popular tale about a charming rooster, Chanticleer, and a fox. By mismatching these noble words with barnyard doings, he shows the silly side of heroic tales and of the serious words that he loves. In the end, his affection for his characters rules the day, and Chanticleer triumphs by words alone.

◆ Reading Strategy

CONTEXT CLUES

When you encounter an unfamiliar word as you read, use **context clues** from the surrounding passage to determine its meaning. Such clues may include synonyms or antonyms of the new word, or examples that clarify its meaning.

In line 14, a phrase may be unfamiliar to you: "There was no *sauce piquante* to spice her veal." You can deduce that if "spice" is similar in meaning to *sauce piquante,* then the phrase must mean "a spicy or sharp-tasting sauce."

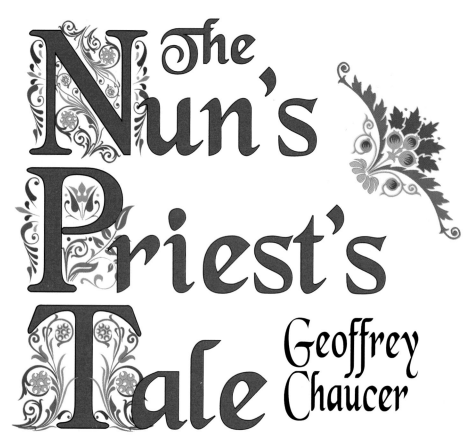

The Nun's Priest's Tale

Geoffrey Chaucer

Translated by Nevill Coghill

Once, long ago, there dwelt a poor old widow
In a small cottage, by a little meadow
Beside a grove and standing in a dale.
This widow-woman of whom I tell my tale
5 Since the sad day when last she was a wife
Had led a very patient, simple life.
Little she had in capital or rent,
But still, by making do with what God sent,
She kept herself and her two daughters going.
10 Three hefty sows—no more—were all her showing,
Three cows as well; there was a sheep called Molly.
    Sooty her hall, her kitchen melancholy,
And there she ate full many a slender meal;
There was no *sauce piquante*[1] to spice her veal,
15 No dainty morsel ever passed her throat,
According to her cloth she cut her coat.
Repletion[2] never left her in disquiet
And all her physic was a temperate diet,
Hard work for exercise and heart's content.

1. *sauce piquante*
(pē´ kənt): French for a
pleasantly sharp
sauce, used for fancy
and expensive meals.
2. **Repletion** (ri plē´
shən) *n.*: The state of
having eaten too
much.

◆ **Build Vocabulary**

capital (kap´ət 'l) *n.*: Wealth in money or
property

20 And rich man's gout did nothing to prevent
Her dancing, apoplexy[3] struck her not;
She drank no wine, nor white nor red had got.
Her board was mostly served with white and black,
Milk and brown bread, in which she found no lack;
25 Broiled bacon or an egg or two were common,
She was in fact a sort of dairy-woman.
      She had a yard that was enclosed about
By a stockade and a dry ditch without,
In which she kept a cock called Chanticleer.
30 In all the land for crowing he'd no peer;
His voice was jollier than the organ blowing
In church on Sundays, he was great at crowing.
Far, far more regular than any clock
Or abbey bell the crowing of this cock.
35 The equinoctial wheel and its position[4]
At each ascent he knew by intuition;
At every hour—fifteen degrees of movement—
He crowed so well there could be no improvement.
His comb was redder than fine coral, tall
40 And battlemented like a castle wall,
His bill was black and shone as bright as jet,
Like azure were his legs and they were set
On azure toes with nails of lily white,
Like burnished gold his feathers, flaming bright.
45   This gentlecock was master in some measure
Of seven hens, all there to do his pleasure.
They were his sisters and his paramours,
Colored like him in all particulars;
She with the loveliest dyes upon her throat
50 Was known as gracious Lady Pertelote.
Courteous she was, discreet and debonair,
Companionable too, and took such care
In her deportment, since she was seven days old
She held the heart of Chanticleer controlled,
55 Locked up securely in her every limb;
O such happiness his love to him!
And such a joy it was to hear them sing,
As when the glorious sun began to spring,
In sweet accord *My love is far from land*[5]
60 —For in those far off days I understand
All birds and animals could speak and sing.
      Now it befell, as dawn began to spring,
When Chanticleer and Pertelote and all
His wives were perched in this poor widow's hall
65 (Fair Pertelote was next him on the perch),
This Chanticleer began to groan and lurch
Like someone sorely troubled by a dream,
And Pertelote who heard him roar and scream
Was quite aghast and said, "O dearest heart,
70 What's ailing you? Why do you groan and start?
Fie, what a sleeper! What a noise to make!"

3. apoplexy: Old-fashioned term for a stroke.

4. equinoctial . . . position: Chaucer and his contemporaries accounted for changes in the positions of stars and planets by imagining that the heavens circled the Earth once a day, moving fifteen degrees each hour.

5. *My love is far from land:* Refrain of a popular song.

◆ **Reading Strategy**
What context clues might help you figure out the meaning of *aghast* in line 69?

English Travelers Setting Forth, From *The Canterbury Tales*, The British Library

▲ Critical Viewing How do you think these pilgrims would have reacted to "The Nun's Priest's Tale"? [Speculate]

"Madam," he said, "I beg you not to take
Offense, but by the Lord I had a dream
So terrible just now I had to scream;
75 I still can feel my heart racing from fear.
God turn my dream to good and guard all here.
And keep my body out of durance vile![6]
I dreamt that roaming up and down a while
Within our yard I saw a kind of beast,
80 A sort of hound that tried or seemed at least
To try and seize me. . . would have killed me dead!
His color was a blend of yellow and red,
His ears and tail were tipped with sable fur
Unlike the rest; he was a russet cur.
85 Small was his snout, his eyes were glowing bright.
It was enough to make one die of fright.
That was no doubt what made me groan and swoon."
    "For shame," she said, "you timorous poltroon![7]
Alas, what cowardice! By God above,
90 You've forfeited my heart and lost my love.
I cannot love a coward, come what may.
For certainly, whatever we may say,
All women long—and O that it might be!—
For husbands tough, dependable and free,
95 Secret, discreet, no niggard,[8] not a fool
That boasts and then will find his courage cool
At every trifling thing. By God above,
How dare you say for shame, and to your love,
That anything at all was to be feared?
100 Have you no manly heart to match your beard?
And can a dream reduce you to such terror?
Dreams are a vanity, God knows, pure error.
Dreams are engendered in the too-replete
From vapors in the belly, which compete
105 With others, too abundant, swollen tight.
    "No doubt the redness in your dream tonight
Comes from the superfluity and force
Of the red choler in your blood. Of course.
That is what puts a dreamer in the dread
110 Of crimsoned arrows, fires flaming red,
Of great red monsters making as to fight him,
And big red whelps and little ones to bite him;
Just so the black and melancholy vapors
Will set a sleeper shrieking, cutting capers
115 And swearing that black bears, black bulls as well,
Or blackest fiends are haling him to Hell.
And there are other vapors that I know
That on a sleeping man will work their woe,
But I'll pass on as lightly as I can.
120   "Take Cato[9] now, that was so wise a man,
Did he not say, 'Take no account of dreams'?
Now, sir," she said, "on flying from these beams,
For love of God do take some laxative;

6. **durance vile:** Long imprisonment.

◆ **Literary Focus**
How does Pertelote's reaction (lines 88–105) lend comedy to this passage?

7. **poltroon** (päl trōōn´) *n.*: Coward.

8. **niggard:** Stingy person.

9. **Cato:** Dionysius Cato, supposed author of a book of maxims used in elementary education.

◆ **Build Vocabulary**
timorous (tim´ ər əs) *adj.*: Timid

The Canterbury Tales: The Nun's Priest's Tale ◆ 115

Upon my soul that's the advice to give
125 For melancholy choler; let me urge
You free yourself from vapors with a purge.
And that you may have no excuse to tarry
By saying this town has no apothecary,
I shall myself instruct you and prescribe
130 Herbs that will cure all vapors of that tribe,
Herbs from our very farmyard! You will find
Their natural property is to unbind
And purge you well beneath and well above.
Now don't forget it, dear, for God's own love!
135 Your face is choleric and shows distension;
Be careful lest the sun in his ascension
Should catch you full of humors,[10] hot and many.
And if he does, my dear, I'll lay a penny
It means a bout of fever or a breath
140 Of tertian ague.[11] You may catch your death.
    "Worms for a day or two I'll have to give
As a digestive, then your laxative.
Centaury, fumitory, caper-spurge
And hellebore will make a splendid purge;
145 And then there's laurel or the blackthorn berry,
Ground-ivy too that makes our yard so merry;
Peck them right up, my dear, and swallow whole.
Be happy, husband, by your father's soul!
Don't be afraid of dreams. I'll say no more."
150   "Madam," he said, "I thank you for your lore,
But with regard to Cato all the same,
His wisdom has, no doubt, a certain fame,
But though he said that we should take no heed
Of dreams, by God in ancient books I read
155 Of many a man of more authority
Than ever Cato was, believe you me,
Who say the very opposite is true
And prove their theories by experience too.
Dreams have quite often been significations
160 As well of triumphs as of tribulations
That people undergo in this our life.
This needs no argument at all, dear wife,
The proof is all too manifest indeed.
    "One of the greatest authors one can read
165 Says thus: there were two comrades once who went
On pilgrimage, sincere in their intent.
And as it happened they had reached a town
Where such a throng was milling up and down
And yet so scanty the accommodation,
170 They could not find themselves a habitation,
No, not a cottage that could lodge them both.
And so they separated, very loath,
Under constraint of this necessity
And each went off to find some hostelry,
175 And lodge whatever way his luck might fall.

10. humors: People in Chaucer's time believed that bodily fluids, called humors, were responsible for one's health and disposition. An excess of the fluid called yellow bile resulted in a choleric, or quick-tempered, personality. In lines 108 and 125, Chaucer seems to use the word *choler* as a synonym for the term *humor.*

11. tertian ague (tʉr´ shən ā´ gyo͞o) Malarial fever.

"The first of them found refuge in a stall
Down in a yard with oxen and a plow.
His friend found lodging for himself somehow
Elsewhere, by accident or destiny,
180 Which governs all of us and equally.
     "Now it so happened, long ere it was day,
This fellow had a dream, and as he lay
In bed it seemed he heard his comrade call,
'Help! I am lying in an ox's stall
185 And shall tonight be murdered as I lie.
Help me, dear brother, help or I shall die!
Come in all haste!' Such were the words he spoke;
The dreamer, lost in terror, then awoke.
But once awake he paid it no attention,
190 Turned over and dismissed it as invention,
It was a dream, he thought, a fantasy.
And twice he dreamt this dream successively.
     "Yet a third time his comrade came again,
Or seemed to come, and said, 'I have been slain.
195 Look, look! my wounds are bleeding wide and deep,
Rise early in the morning, break your sleep

And go to the west gate. You there shall see
A cart all loaded up with dung,' said he,
'And in that dung my body has been hidden.
200 Boldly arrest that cart as you are bidden.
It was my money that they killed me for.'
    "He told him every detail, sighing sore,
And pitiful in feature, pale of hue.
This dream, believe me, Madam, turned out true;
205 For in the dawn, as soon as it was light,
He went to where his friend had spent the night
And when he came upon the cattle-stall
He looked about him and began to call.
    "The innkeeper, appearing thereupon,
210 Quickly gave answer, 'Sir, your friend has gone.
He left the town a little after dawn.'
The man began to feel suspicious, drawn
By memories of his dream—the western gate,
The dung-cart—off he went, he would not wait,
215 Towards the western entry. There he found,
Seemingly on its way to dung some ground,
A dung-cart loaded on the very plan
Described so closely by the murdered man.
So he began to shout courageously
220 For right and vengeance on the felony,
'My friend's been killed! There's been a foul attack,
He's in that cart and gaping on his back!
Fetch the authorities, get the sheriff down
—Whosever job it is to run the town—
225 Help! My companion's murdered, sent to glory!'
    "What need I add to finish off the story?
People ran out and cast the cart to ground,
And in the middle of the dung they found
The murdered man. The corpse was fresh and new.
230   "O blessed God, that art so just and true,
Thus thou revealest murder! As we say,
'Murder will out.' We see it day by day.
Murder's a foul, abominable treason,
So loathsome to God's justice, to God's reason,
235 He will not suffer its concealment. True,
Things may lie hidden for a year or two,
But still 'Murder will out,' that's my conclusion.
    "All the town officers in great confusion
Seized on the carter and they gave him hell,
240 And then they racked the innkeeper as well,
And both confessed. And then they took the wrecks
And there and then they hanged them by their necks.
    "By this we see that dreams are to be dreaded.
And in the self-same book I find embedded,
245 Right in the very chapter after this
(I'm not inventing, as I hope for bliss)
The story of two men who started out
To cross the sea—for merchandise no doubt—

But as the winds were contrary they waited.
250 It was a pleasant town, I should have stated,
Merrily grouped about the haven-side.
A few days later with the evening tide
The wind veered round so as to suit them best;
They were delighted and they went to rest
255 Meaning to sail next morning early. Well,
To one of them a miracle befell.
    "This man as he lay sleeping, it would seem,
Just before dawn had an astounding dream.
He thought a man was standing by his bed
260 Commanding him to wait, and thus he said:
'If you set sail tomorrow as you intend
You will be drowned. My tale is at an end.'
    "He woke and told his friend what had occurred
And begged him that the journey be deferred
265 At least a day, implored him not to start.
But his companion, lying there apart,
Began to laugh and treat him to <u>derision</u>.
'I'm not afraid,' he said, 'of any vision,
To let it interfere with my affairs;
270 A straw for all your dreamings and your scares.
Dreams are just empty nonsense, merest japes;[12]
Why, people dream all day of owls and apes,
All sorts of trash that can't be understood,
Things that have never happened and never could.
275 But as I see you mean to stay behind
And miss the tide for wilful sloth of mind,
God knows I'm sorry for it, but good day!'
And so he took his leave and went his way.
    "And yet, before they'd covered half the trip
280 —I don't know what went wrong—there was a rip
And by some accident the ship went down,
Her bottom rent,[13] all hands aboard to drown
In sight of all the vessels at her side,
That had put out upon the self-same tide.
285   "So, my dear Pertelote, if you discern
The force of these examples, you may learn
One never should be careless about dreams,
For, undeniably, I say it seems
That many are a sign of trouble breeding.
290   "Now, take St. Kenelm's life which I've been reading;
He was Kenulphus' son, the noble King
Of Mercia. Now, St. Kenelm dreamt a thing
Shortly before they murdered him one day.
He saw his murder in a dream, I say.
295 His nurse expounded it and gave her reasons
On every point and warned him against treasons
But as the saint was only seven years old
All that she said about it left him cold.
He was so holy how could visions hurt?
300   "By God, I willingly would give my shirt

12. japes: Jokes.

13. rent: Torn.

◆ **Build Vocabulary**

derision (di rizh´ ən) *n*.: Contempt or ridicule

To have you read his legend as I've read it;
And, Madam Pertelote, upon my credit,
Macrobius wrote of dreams and can explain us
The vision of young Scipio Africanus,[14]
305 And he affirms that dreams can give a due
Warnings of things that later on come true.
    "And then there's the Old Testament—a manual
Well worth your study; see the *Book of Daniel*.
Did Daniel think a dream was vanity?
310 Read about Joseph too and you will see
That many dreams—I do not say that all—
Give cognizance of what is to befall.
    "Look at Lord Pharaoh, king of Egypt! Look
At what befell his butler and his cook.
315 Did not their visions have a certain force?
But those who study history of course
Meet many dreams that set them wondering.
    "What about Croesus too, the Lydian king,
Who dreamt that he was sitting in a tree,
320 Meaning he would be hanged? It had to be.
    "Or take Andromache, great Hector's wife;[15]
The day on which he was to lose his life
She dreamt about, the very night before,
And realized that if Hector went to war
325 He would be lost that very day in battle.
She warned him; he dismissed it all as prattle
And sallied forth to fight, being self-willed,
And there he met Achilles and was killed.
The tale is long and somewhat overdrawn,
330 And anyhow it's very nearly dawn,
So let me say in very brief conclusion
My dream undoubtedly foretells confusion,
It bodes me ill, I say. And, furthermore,
Upon your laxatives I set no store,
335 For they are venomous. I've suffered by them
Often enough before and I defy them.
    "And now, let's talk of fun and stop all this.
Dear Madam, as I hope for Heaven's bliss.
Of one thing God has sent me plenteous grace,
340 For when I see the beauty of your face,
That scarlet loveliness about your eyes,
All thought of terror and confusion dies.
For it's as certain as the Creed, I know,
Mulier est hominis confusio
345 (A Latin tag, dear Madam, meaning this:
'Woman is man's delight and all his bliss').
For when at night I feel your feathery side,
Although perforce I cannot take a ride
Because, alas, our perch was made too narrow,
350 Delight and solace fill me to the marrow
And I defy all visions and all dreams!"
    And with that word he flew down from the beams,

14. **Scipio Africanus**
(sip´ē ō af´ ri kā´ nəs):
Famous Roman general (237–183 B.C.).

15. **Andromache**
(an dräm´ ə kē) . . .
wife: The wife of
Hector, the greatest
warrior in Troy at the
time of the Trojan War.

◆ **Literary Focus**
References to heroes
appear often in
epics. What effect do
the references in this
passage have?

For it was day, and down his hens flew all,
And with a chuck he gave the troupe a call
355 For he had found a seed upon the floor.
Royal he was, he was afraid no more.
He feathered Pertelote in wanton play
And trod her twenty times ere prime of day.
Grim as a lion's was his manly frown
360 As on his toes he sauntered up and down;
He scarcely deigned to set his foot to ground
And every time a seed of corn was found
He gave a chuck, and up his wives ran all.
Thus royal as a prince who strides his hall
365 Leave we this Chanticleer engaged on feeding
And pass to the adventure that was breeding.
    Now when the month in which the world began,
March, the first month, when God created man,
Was over, and the thirty-second day
370 Thereafter ended, on the third of May
It happened that Chanticleer in all his pride,
His seven wives attendant at his side,
Cast his eyes upward to the blazing sun,
Which in the sign of *Taurus* then had run
375 His twenty-one degrees and somewhat more,
And knew by nature and no other lore
That it was nine o'clock. With blissful voice
He crew triumphantly and said, "Rejoice,
Behold the sun! The sun is up, my seven.
380 Look, it has climbed forty degrees in heaven,
Forty degrees and one in fact, by this.
Dear Madam Pertelote, my earthly bliss,
Hark to those blissful birds and how they sing!
Look at those pretty flowers, how they spring!
385 Solace and revel fill my heart!" He laughed.
    But in that moment Fate let fly her shaft;
Ever the latter end of joy is woe,
God knows that worldly joy is swift to go.
A rhetorician[16] with a flair for style
390 Could chronicle this <u>maxim</u> in his file
Of Notable Remarks with safe conviction.
Then let the wise give ear; this is no fiction
My story is as true, I undertake,
As that of good Sir Lancelot du Lake[17]
395 Who held all women in such high esteem.
Let me return full circle to my theme.
    A coal-tipped fox of sly iniquity[18]
That had been lurking round the grove for three
Long years, that very night burst through and passed
400 Stockade and hedge, as Providence forecast,
Into the yard where Chanticleer the Fair
Was wont, with all his ladies, to repair.
Still, in a bed of cabbages, he lay
Until about the middle of the day

Chaucer Reciting Troilus and Cressida Before a Court Gathering (Frontispiece) Corpus Christi College

▲ **Critical Viewing** Judging from this scene, what was a storytelling event in Chaucer's time like? **[Interpret]**

16. **rhetorician** (ret´ ə rish´ ən) *n.:* Person skilled in public speaking or writing.

17. **Sir Lancelot du Lake:** The most celebrated of King Arthur's Knights of the Round Table.

18. **iniquity** (i nik´ wi tē) *n.:* Wickedness.

◆ **Build Vocabulary**

maxim (maks´ im) *n.:* Briefly expressed general truth or rule of conduct

405   Watching the cock and waiting for his cue,
      As all these homicides so gladly do
      That lie about in wait to murder men.
      O false assassin, lurking in thy den!
      O new Iscariot, new Ganelon!
410   And O Greek Sinon,[19] thou whose treachery won
      Troy town and brought it utterly to sorrow!
      O Chanticleer, accursed be that morrow
      That brought thee to the yard from thy high beams!
      Thou hadst been warned, and truly, by thy dreams
415   That this would be a perilous day for thee.
         But that which God's foreknowledge can foresee
      Must needs occur, as certain men of learning
      Have said. Ask any scholar of discerning;
      He'll say the Schools are filled with altercation
420   On this vexed matter of predestination[20]
      Long bandied by a hundred thousand men.
      How can I sift it to the bottom then?
      The Holy Doctor St. Augustine shines
      In this, and there is Bishop Bradwardine's
425   Authority, Boethius'[21] too, decreeing
      Whether the fact of God's divine foreseeing
      Constrains me to perform a certain act
      —And by "constraint" I mean the simple fact
      Of mere compulsion by necessity—
430   Or whether a free choice is granted me
      To do a given act or not to do it
      Though, ere it was accomplished, God foreknew it.

19. Iscariot . . . Ganeton . . . Sinon: Each of these men was famous for betrayal. Judas Iscariot betrayed Jesus Christ; Ganelon betrayed Charlemagne's greatest knight, Roland; and Sinon convinced King Priam to bring the Trojan horse, filled with Greek troops, into Troy.

20. predestination (prē des′ tə nā′ shən) n.: The idea that God arranges beforehand everything that will happen.

21. Bishop Bradwardine's . . . Boethius' (bō ē′ thē əs): Bishop Bradwardine was a well-known theologian of Chaucer's time. Boethius (A.D. 480–524) was a famous Roman philosopher.

The Nun's Priest, Detail from the Ellesmere Manuscript, The Huntington Library, San Marino, California

▶ **Critical Viewing** How do the position and facial expression of the subject of this painting suggest he is telling a story? **[Support]**

Or whether Providence is not so <u>stringent</u>
And merely makes necessity contingent.
435   But I decline discussion of the matter;
My tale is of a cock and of the clatter
That came of following his wife's advice
To walk about his yard on the precise
Morning after the dream of which I told.
440   O woman's counsel is so often cold!
A woman's counsel brought us first to woe.
Made Adam out of Paradise to go
Where he had been so merry, so well at ease.
But, for I know not whom it may displease
445 If I suggest that women are to blame,
Pass over that; I only speak in game.
Read the authorities to know about
What has been said of women; you'll find out
These are the cock's words, and not mine, I'm giving;
450 I think no harm of any woman living.
      Merrily in her dust-bath in the sand
Lay Pertelote. Her sisters were at hand
Basking in sunlight. Chanticleer sang free,
More merrily than a mermaid in the sea
455 (For *Physiologus*[22] reports the thing
And says how well and merrily they sing).
And so it happened as he cast his eye
Towards the cabbage at a butterfly
It fell upon the fox there, lying low.
460 Gone was all inclination then to crow.
"Cok cok," he cried, giving a sudden start,
As one who feels a terror at his heart,
For natural instinct teaches beasts to flee
The moment they perceive an enemy,
465 Though they had never met with it before.
      This Chanticleer was shaken to the core
And would have fled. The fox was quick to say
However, "Sir! Whither so fast away?
Are you afraid of me, that am your friend?
470 A fiend, or worse, I should be, to intend
You harm, or practice villainy upon you;
Dear sir, I was not even spying on you!
Truly I came to do no other thing
Than just to lie and listen to you sing.
475 You have as merry a voice as God has given
To any angel in the courts of Heaven;
To that you add a musical sense as strong
As had Boethius who was skilled in song.
My Lord your Father (God receive his soul!),
480 Your mother too—how courtly, what control!—
Have honored my poor house, to my great ease;
And you, sir, too, I should be glad to please.
For, when it comes to singing, I'll say this
(Else may these eyes of mine be barred from bliss),

◆ **Reading Strategy**
Explain what context clues could help you to decode the word *counsel* in line 441.

22. *Physiologus*:
Book on nature written in Latin meter.

◆ **Build Vocabulary**
stringent (strin′ jənt) *adj.*: Strict

485 There never was a singer I would rather
Have heard at dawn than your respected father.
All that he sang came welling from his soul
And how he put his voice under control!
The pains he took to keep his eyes tight shut
490 In concentration—then the tip-toe strut,
The slender neck stretched out, the delicate beak!
No singer could approach him in technique
Or rival him in song, still less surpass.
I've read the story in *Burnel the Ass*,[23]
495 Among some other verses, of a cock
Whose leg in youth was broken by a knock
A clergyman's son had given him, and for this
He made the father lose his benefice.
But certainly there's no comparison
500 Between the subtlety of such an one
And the discretion of your father's art
And wisdom. Oh, for charity of heart,
Can you not emulate your sire and sing?"
     This Chanticleer began to heat a wing
505 As one incapable of smelling treason,
So wholly had this flattery ravished reason.
Alas, my lords! there's many a sycophant[24]
And flatterer that fill your courts with <u>cant</u>
And give more pleasure with their zeal forsooth
510 Than he who speaks in soberness and truth.
Read what *Ecclesiasticus*[25] records
Of flatterers. 'Ware treachery, my lords!
     This Chanticleer stood high upon his toes,
He stretched his neck, his eyes began to close,
515 His beak to open; with his eyes shut tight
He then began to sing with all his might.

23. *Burnel the Ass:* Twelfth-century poem in which a rooster gains revenge after being mistreated by a priest's son.

24. sycophant (sik′ ə fənt) *n.*: Person who seeks favor by flattering influential people.

25. *Ecclesiasticus*: Not Ecclesiastes, but a book of proverbs included with the Apocrypha in the Authorized Version of the Bible.

▲ **Critical Viewing** Which elements in this etching seem realistic? Which elements seem mythic or fantastic? Why did the artist choose to combine these elements? **[Deduce]**

Sir Russel Fox then leapt to the attack,
Grabbing his gorge he flung him o'er his back
And off he bore him to the woods, the brute,
520 And for the moment there was no pursuit.
O Destiny that may not be evaded!
Alas that Chanticleer had so paraded!
Alas that he had flown down from the beams!
O that his wife took no account of dreams!
525 And on a Friday too to risk their necks!
O Venus, goddess of the joys of sex,
Since Chanticleer thy mysteries professed
And in thy service always did his best,
And more for pleasure than to multiply
530 His kind, on thine own day is he to die?
  O Geoffrey, thou my dear and sovereign master[26]
Who, when they brought King Richard to disaster
And shot him dead, lamented so his death,
Would that I had thy skill, thy gracious breath,
535 To chide a Friday half so well as you!
(For he was killed upon a Friday too.)
Then I could fashion you a rhapsody
For Chanticleer in dread and agony.
  Sure never such a cry or lamentation
540 Was made by ladies of high Trojan station,
When Ilium fell and Pyrrhus with his sword
Grabbed Priam by the beard, their king and lord,
And slew him there as the *Aeneid* tells,[27]
As what was uttered by those hens. Their yells
545 Surpassed them all in palpitating fear
When they beheld the rape of Chanticleer.
Dame Pertelote emitted sovereign shrieks
That echoed up in anguish to the peaks
Louder than those extorted from the wife
550 Of Hasdrubal,[28] when he had lost his life
And Carthage all in flame and ashes lay.
She was so full of torment and dismay
That in the very flames she chose her part
And burnt to ashes with a steadfast heart.
555 O woeful hens, louder your shrieks and higher
Than those of Roman matrons when the fire
Consumed their husbands, senators of Rome,
When Nero burnt their city and their home,
Beyond a doubt that Nero was their bale![29]
560   Now let me turn again to tell my tale;
This blessed widow and her daughters two
Heard all these hens in clamor and halloo
And, rushing to the door at all this shrieking,
They saw the fox towards the covert streaking
565 And, on his shoulder, Chanticleer stretched flat.
"Look, look!" they cried, "O mercy, look at that!
Ha! Ha! the fox!" and after him they ran,
And stick in hand ran many a serving man,

26. O Geoffrey . . . master: Geoffrey de Vinsauf, twelfth-century author of a book on rhetoric.

27. Sure never . . . Aeneid tells: Reference to the destruction of Troy as described in the Roman poet Virgil's *Aeneid*.

28. Hasdrubal (haz´ drōō bəl): Carthaginian general.

29. bale *n*.: Evil; harm.

◆ **Build Vocabulary**
cant (kant) *n*.: Insincere or meaningless talk

Ran Coll our dog, ran Talbot, Bran and Shaggy,
570 And with a distaff in her hand ran Maggie,
Ran cow and calf and ran the very hogs
In terror at the barking of the dogs;
The men and women shouted, ran and cursed,
They ran so hard they thought their hearts would burst,
575 They yelled like fiends in Hell, ducks left the water
Quacking and flapping as on point of slaughter,
Up flew the geese in terror over the trees,
Out of the hive came forth the swarm of bees;
So hideous was the noise—God bless us all,
580 Jack Straw and all his followers in their brawl[30]
Were never half so shrill, for all their noise,
When they were murdering those Flemish boys,
As that day's hue and cry upon the fox.
They grabbed up trumpets made of brass and box,
585 Of horn and bone, on which they blew and pooped,
And therewithal they shouted and they whooped
So that it seemed the very heavens would fall.
    And now, good people, pay attention all.
See how Dame Fortune quickly changes side
590 And robs her enemy of hope and pride!
This cock that lay upon the fox's back
In all his dread contrived to give a quack
And said, "Sir Fox, if I were you, as God's
My witness, I would round upon these clods
595 And shout, 'Turn back, you saucy bumpkins all!
A very pestilence upon you fall!
Now that I have in safety reached the wood
Do what you like, the cock is mine for good;
I'll eat him there in spite of every one.'"
600   The fox replying, "Faith, it shall be done!"
Opened his mouth and spoke. The nimble bird,
Breaking away upon the uttered word,
Flew high into the tree-tops on the spot.
And when the fox perceived where he had got,
605 "Alas," he cried, "alas, my Chanticleer,
I've done you grievous wrong, indeed I fear
I must have frightened you; I grabbed too hard
When I caught hold and took you from the yard.
But, sir, I meant no harm, don't be offended,
610 Come down and I'll explain what I intended;
So help me God I'll tell the truth—on oath!"
"No," said the cock, "and curses on us both,
And first on me if I were such a dunce
As let you fool me oftener than once.
615 Never again, for all your flattering lies,
You'll coax a song to make me blink my eyes;
And as for those who blink when they should look,
God blot them from his everlasting Book!"
"Nay, rather," said the fox, "his plagues be flung
620 On all who chatter that should hold their tongue."

30. Jack Straw . . . brawl: Jack Straw was one of the leaders of the Peasants' Revolt (1381).

Lo, such it is not to be on your guard
Against the flatterers of the world, or yard,
And if you think my story is absurd,
A foolish trifle of a beast and bird,
625   A fable of a fox, a cock, a hen,
Take hold upon the moral, gentlemen.
    St. Paul himself, a saint of great discerning,
Says that all things are written for our learning;
So take the grain and let the chaff be still.
630   And, gracious Father, if it be thy will
As saith my Savior, make us all good men,
And bring us to his heavenly bliss.
    Amen.

Guide for Responding

◆ Literature and Your Life

Reader's Response In what part of the tale did you find the mismatch between Chaucer's style and the events of the story the funniest? Why?

Thematic Focus In this tale, what members of society might Chaucer be mocking?

Role Play With a partner, role-play a conversation between Chanticleer and Pertelote about the day's events.

☑ Check Your Comprehension

1. Who are Chanticleer and Pertelote?
2. Why is Chanticleer disturbed at the beginning of the story?
3. What is Pertelote's advice to Chanticleer when he tells her his dream?
4. (a) How does the fox capture Chanticleer? (b) How does Chanticleer escape?

◆ Critical Thinking

INTERPRET

1. (a) Name three characteristics of Chanticleer that are realistic. (b) Name three characteristics of Chanticleer that it would be absurd to attribute to a rooster. **[Classify]**
2. Compare and contrast the methods of argument that Pertelote and Chanticleer use to defend their interpretations of dreams. **[Compare and Contrast]**
3. The first story that Chanticleer tells has the three-part structure typical of medieval tales: an exposition describing the characters and setting, a complication or problem, and a climax. Does "The Nun's Priest's Tale" as a whole follow this pattern? Why or why not? **[Analyze]**
4. (a) What is the moral of this fable? (b) How seriously do you think the narrator takes this moral? Explain. **[Interpret]**
5. What does this tale suggest about its teller, the nun's priest? **[Draw Conclusions]**

Guide for Responding (continued)

◆ Reading Strategy

CONTEXT CLUES

Synonyms, antonyms, or examples from the passage in which a word appears often provide **context clues** to its meaning. For instance, when Chaucer says of Chanticleer's feathers that they were "Like burnished gold . . . flaming bright," you can use his description of the effects of burnishing to figure out that *burnished* means "polished."

1. In lines 68–71, use context clues to figure out the meaning of *aghast*.
2. In lines 106–108, show how a synonym helps you figure out the meaning of *superfluity*.

◆ Grammar and Style

PRONOUN CASE

Pronoun case indicates whether a personal pronoun serves as the subject of a sentence or clause, or whether it is the object of a verb or preposition.

Practice In your notebook, identify the pronoun and its case in each passage.
1. "No," said the cock, "and curses on us both, . . ."
2. Alas that he had flown down from the beams!
3. They saw the fox towards the covert streaking . . .
4. God bless us all, . . .
5. They grabbed up trumpets made of brass and box, . . .

Writing Application In your notebook, write a pronoun in the proper case for each blank. Next to each sentence, write an *S* if you have chosen a subjective pronoun or an *O* if you have chosen an objective one.
1. Chanticleer and ____?____ roamed the barnyard like a king and queen.
2. I've told you that ____?____ was a common character in medieval literature.
3. We know the fox was wily because the clever Chanticleer was tricked by ____?____.
4. It was ____?____, Chanticleer, that the fox abducted.
5. After finishing the tale, he gave ____?____ a blessing.

◆ Literary Focus

MOCK-HEROIC STYLE

Chaucer uses the **mock-heroic style** in this description of a rooster, which makes him sound like the hero of an epic: "His comb was redder than fine coral, tall / And battlemented like a castle wall." The subject is only a barnyard animal, but the comparisons of his comb to "coral" and a "castle wall" give the rooster a nobility that is absurd.

1. Epic heroes are often boastful. (a) Give two examples of Chanticleer's boastfulness. (b) Why does this boastfulness seem humorous?
2. Which words and phrases in the description of Pertelote would be more suitable for a noble lady than for a hen?
3. Epics often depict the intervention of gods or goddesses in the affairs of humans. Where does Chaucer imitate this convention?

◆ Build Vocabulary

USING THE LATIN ROOT *-cap-*

The Latin root *-cap-* means "head." It also refers to the main, chief, or highest part of living and non-living things. Use your knowledge of this root to explain these phrases:
1. a capital city
2. a capital crime
3. per capita income
4. capital that is taxed
5. a captain of industry
6. to capitulate

USING THE WORD BANK: Definitions

Match each of the words with its definition in the right column.

1. timorous		a.	idle talk
2. derision		b.	principle guiding behavior
3. maxim		c.	fearful
4. stringent		d.	strict; severe
5. cant		e.	scorn; ridicule
6. capital		f.	money or property

Build Your Portfolio

Idea Bank

Writing

1. **Animals as Symbols** List three animals used to symbolize teams or products, and briefly describe the qualities they represent.

2. **Modern Beast Fable** Write your own beast fable, in which animals are characters, that has some sort of moral or lesson.

3. **Critical Response** Chaucer scholar Michael Hoy says of "The Nun's Priest's Tale": "This is a poem which raises searching questions about the nature of existence and man's response to the human predicament." Find examples from the poem that support or contradict his view.

Speaking, Listening, and Viewing

4. **Oral Interpretation of a Debate** Pertelote and Chanticleer debate the meaning of dreams in the passage beginning with line 89 and ending on line 337. With a partner, perform this debate for the class, using your tone of voice to convey humor. **[Performing Arts Link]**

5. **Mock-Heroic Scene** With a small group, improvise dialogue and actions to make small, everyday occurrences seem like events in a tragedy or a heroic tale. **[Performing Arts Link]**

Researching and Representing

6. **Mock-Heroic Comic Book** Using what you know of comic book heroes—their origins, powers, enemies—create a mock-heroic fully illustrated comic book. **[Art Link]**

7. **Pilgrim's Path** Do research on the traditions of pilgrims and pilgrimages in various cultures. Create a map that shows some of the important places pilgrims visit, such as Mecca in Saudi Arabia. **[Social Studies Link]**

Online Activity www.phlit.phschool.com

Guided Writing Lesson

Script for an Animated Fable

Chaucer does with words what an animated cartoon does with moving pictures and dialogue. In the spirit of "The Nun's Priest's Tale," write a script for your own animated fable. Besides the dialogue your animal characters will speak, include bracketed directions describing their appearance and actions. Remember to exaggerate their traits and problems to create humor.

Writing Skills Focus: Using Exaggeration

Comic writing of all kinds uses **exaggeration,** making little problems seem gigantic and therefore ridiculous. Notice, for example, Chaucer's use of exaggeration in describing a fox as if he were one of the greatest betrayers in history:

Model From Literature

O false assassin, lurking in thy den!
O new Iscariot, new Ganelon!

The following strategies will guide you as you draft your script.

Prewriting To help you add humor to your script, jot down the key events in the plot and how you can exaggerate each.

Drafting Follow your story outline, but allow yourself to invent exaggerated details and situations as you go. Create such details by picturing the actions you describe. Then you can exaggerate each situation.

Revising Check your script to make sure that you've described your characters' exaggerated actions as well as provided their words. If not, add bracketed directions where necessary.

CONNECTIONS TO TODAY'S WORLD

Elizabeth II: A New Queen

Thematic Connection

A NATIONAL SPIRIT

A thousand years ago, the bloody wars of kings and queens defined Britain's national identity in a decisive way. *The Anglo-Saxon Chronicle* tells how Alfred, ninth-century warrior-king of a small kingdom in southern England, fought off the invading Danes and united all of Britain's Anglo-Saxon kingdoms under his rule. The affairs of kings and queens—their births and deaths, marriages and friendships, rivalries and assassinations—continued to govern the nation's destiny for centuries after Alfred's time.

THE NEW ROYALTY

Since the 1640's, though, when the people revolted and executed their king, the real power to govern has shifted to the country's Parliament and prime minister. Modern kings and queens have little to do with running the country. Their official duties are ceremonial—handing out awards or receiving foreign dignitaries. The kings and queens of the twentieth century may seem like shadows compared with the monarchs of the past.

Yet government officials in Britain still act in the name of "Her Majesty." And even while the gossip columns dissect the private lives of the royal family, the appearance of Queen Elizabeth II in public, waving from a car or balcony, still has a thrilling effect on her subjects.

NATIONAL SYMBOLS

A national identity binds together diverse people, most of whom have never met and may have few things in common. To anchor that idea of a nation in their hearts as well as in their minds, people look to emotionally charged symbols of national identity. Britain's monarch remains the foremost symbol of the British nation.

NEWSPAPER ACCOUNTS OF BRITISH ROYALTY

Open any newspaper in Britain and you're bound to find an article about a member of the royal family. Whether opening Parliament, visiting a hospital, or yachting in the Caribbean, the royal family makes the news.

Following is an especially important article about the royal family that appeared in *The London Times* on February 7, 1952. It gives a brief biography of Elizabeth II, Britain's new queen. (The report of George VI's death appears in the same paper.)

Elizabeth II: A New Queen

The London Times 2/7/52

DEATH OF THE KING

THE NEW QUEEN EXPECTED IN LONDON TO-DAY

PUBLIC PROCLAMATION TO BE MADE TO-MORROW

It is with profound regret that we announce the death of the King at Sandringham early yesterday.

The following statement was issued from Buckingham Palace:

"It was announced from Sandringham at 10.45 a.m. to-day, February 6, 1952, that the King, who retired to rest last night in his usual health, passed peacefully away in his sleep early this morning."

The London Times 2/7/52

THE NEW QUEEN

AN OUTSTANDING REPRESENTATIVE OF HER GENERATION

Princess Elizabeth Alexandra Mary was born a little before three o'clock on the morning of April 21, 1926, at No. 17, Bruton Street, the London home of her grandparents, the late Lord and Lady Strathmore. At the age of five weeks she was baptized at Buckingham Palace by the late Lord Lang of Lambeth, then Dr. Cosmo Gordon Lang, Archbishop of York.

At that time the Prince of Wales, though unmarried, was not quite 32; and there was no expectation that the newly born Princess, especially as she might some day have a brother, would ever come very close to the succession. Even if there had been, it would probably not have been allowed to influence her early upbringing, which the Duke and Duchess of York deliberately kept as simple as possible. In infancy her time was divided between her parents' home in Piccadilly and the various country houses of her maternal grandparents in England and Scotland; and Lady Strathmore took charge of her when the Duke and Duchess went to Australia in 1927 to inaugurate the new capital.

King George V was devoted to his grandchild, and at his desire she was sent, at the age of two and a half, to keep him company at Bognor during his convalescence after his dangerous illness in 1928. The birth of her sister in August, 1930, brought her a playmate who was destined to be by far her closest friend until she was fully grown up. Her nursery days, spent mostly in the country and in constant association with horses, dogs, and other pets, may be said to have ended with the death of King George V in 1936 and the abdication of her uncle at the end of the same year. At this date the family moved from Piccadilly to Buckingham Palace, and the position of the Princess as Heiress-Presumptive took on new importance.

It was not, however, allowed to overshadow her education. She did not go to school but was taught, under the close personal direction of the Queen, by a governess, Miss Marion Crawford, who joined the household in 1933.

The outbreak of war found the Royal Family at Balmoral; but the Princesses were soon moved to Windsor, where the quiet routine of lessons continued through the darkest and most stirring days. Gradually, subjects specially appropriate to a future queen, notably constitutional history, were introduced into the curriculum; and the Provost of Eton took a large part in the Princess's instruction. She became a good musician and singer; and in regular participation in amateur theatricals she not only showed a marked talent for acting but overcame the tendency to shyness which at one time looked like becoming a handicap to her in the great position that lay ahead.

On her sixteenth birthday in 1942 the

Princess registered for national service, and soon after her eighteenth birthday—when special legislation was passed to qualify her to act as a Counsellor of State in the King's absence from the realm—she was gazetted to a commission in the A.T.S. This was at her own insistence, the King withdrawing his original ruling that her duties as heir precluded her entry to any of the services. She in fact became an efficient driver in the mechanical transport branch of the A.T.S.

PUBLIC CAREER

Her public career may be said to have begun with her broadcast to the children of the Empire during the Battle of Britain; but it was only when war ended that she began to emerge into full publicity as a leading figure in ceremonial and social life. Naturally most of her appearances were made under the wing of one or both of her parents. But she was accompanied only by members of her own staff—her first lady in waiting had been appointed in July—when she went to Greenock in November 1944, and launched the great battleship H.M.S. Vanguard. The commissioning of this ship was the principal event of her notable visit to Northern Ireland—again without her parents—in the summer of 1946; and it was in the Vanguard that she embarked with the rest of the Royal Family on February 1, 1947, for their tour of South Africa and Rhodesia.

This was the Princess's first journey outside the British Isles, and the beginning of her introduction to those dominions beyond the seas over which, equally with the United Kingdom, she will now reign.

Although she was content to remain somewhat in the background, especially in the early part of the tour, South Africans rapidly became conscious of her as a personality, and her character made a great and favourable impression. A speech at the opening of the graving dock, named after herself, at East London seemed to mark the emergence of a new representative of the younger generation; and at her coming of age, which she celebrated in Cape Town, she broadcast to the Empire, and especially to the young, in vigorous and vibrant terms which carried the impression farther.

She was already outstandingly qualified to be the representative figure among the girls who came to womanhood with her. She had absorbed an admirably balanced education and entered into the gaieties appropriate to her age, from the racecourse to the ballroom. But she already combined with a capacity for enjoyment a high seriousness which even at that time made her insist upon doing thoroughly everything that her hand found to do, and spare herself nothing that belonged to her preparation for the greater responsibilities that she knew lay ahead.

Soon after the return of the Royal Family from South Africa, the nation learnt with joy on July 9, 1947, that the King had gladly given his consent to the betrothal of the Heiress-Presumptive to Lieutenant Philip Mountbatten, R.N., son of the late Prince Andrew of Greece and Princess Andrew (Princess Alice of Battenberg). Messages of congratulation to the betrothed couple from the people of the Commonwealth and from all parts of the world showed clearly the affection in which Princess Elizabeth was held, and the four months of their engagement during which preparations for the royal wedding went forward were a period of intense and eager expectation for the nation. The feelings of the nation were expressed by the then Prime Minister, Mr. Attlee, when, on October 22, he moved a congratulatory Address to their Majesties on the occasion of the royal marriage, and said: "Her royal Highness has shown, in the public duties which she has undertaken, the same unerring graciousness and understanding, and the same human simplicity, which has endeared the Royal House to the people of this country," and by Mr. Churchill, who prophesied that millions would welcome the joyous event as a flash of colour on the hard road we had to travel.

On the eve of the wedding came the announcement that Lieutenant Mountbatten had been made Duke of Edinburgh.

MARRIAGE

The marriage was solemnized[1] in Westminster Abbey on November 20, when the royal processions were watched by countless thousands. The ceremony was per-

---

1. **solemnized:** Done according to ritual or tradition.

formed by the Archbishop of Canterbury in the presence of three generations of the Royal Family, and was followed by scenes of rich pageantry and of homely greetings from people gathered from all parts of the British Isles as the bride and bridegroom left for Winchester, on their journey to Broadlands, near Romsey, where they spent their honeymoon.

Early in the New Year they set out on their public life together, and in May paid an official visit to Paris, where they were greeted with a welcome of great warmth and spontaneity. Then early in June it was announced that the Princess would soon cancel all her engagements. On November 14 her son, Prince Charles, was born. In 1949 Princess Elizabeth resumed her busy public life and during that year the Duke of Edinburgh returned to sea. He was stationed at Malta and in November was joined there by his wife.

At the end of March, 1950, the Princess paid a second visit to Malta and while there it was announced that her Royal Highness was expecting a baby. Princess Anne was born in August. In November Princess Elizabeth joined the Duke of Edinburgh and together they visited Athens. In the spring of 1951 they went to Rome, where they were received by the Pope, and it was in Rome that her Royal Highness celebrated her twenty-fifth birthday.

Returning to England in time for the open-ing of the Festival of Britain, she embarked upon a programme of public duties more formidable[2] even than those of the years immediately before. It fell to her more than once on great state occasions to stand in the place of her father and to speak for him.

When, last September, the King underwent an operation, Princess Elizabeth and the Duke of Edinburgh deferred their departure for Canada, but the King's progress enabled them to leave by air on October 7. Their six weeks' tour, probably the most strenuous ever undertaken by royal personages, took them across Canada in a memorable series of visits and ceremonies. Not least successful was their visit to Washington, where they were welcomed by President Truman. Upon their return, a "brilliant mission" accomplished, they were ceremonially received in Liverpool on November 17, and given an official welcome at Guildhall two days later.

After spending Christmas with the Royal Family at Sandringham, the Princess and the Duke left London Airport last Thursday on the first stage of the journey which was to have taken them to Ceylon, Australia, and New Zealand, but which has been so untimely cut short only four days after they reached their hunting lodge at Nyeri, in Kenya.

---

2. **formidable:** Awe-inspiring in size.

Guide for Responding

◆ *Literature and Your Life*

Reader's Response Name three things that you would most enjoy about being a monarch.
Thematic Focus Describe the effect of the article's serious treatment of Elizabeth's life.

☑ Check Your Comprehension

1. What is Elizabeth's relation to the king whom she succeeded?
2. Name three public functions that Princess Elizabeth performed after World War II.

◆ Critical Thinking

INTERPRET

1. Name three details that show the new queen's virtues. **[Analyze]**
2. What overall impression of the new queen does the *Times* strive to create? **[Interpret]**

EVALUATE

3. At points, the reader of the *Times* article may suspect that royalty does not have a "real job." (a) Identify two passages that might encourage such suspicions. (b) Explain the implications of these passages. **[Evaluate]**

Thematic Connection

A NATIONAL SPIRIT

The continued presence through the centuries of a monarch on the British throne shows the importance of symbols in creating and nourishing a national identity.

1. Name two respects in which the British monarchy of today has a different relation to England than King Alfred the Great had.

2. The *Times* article implies that common sentiment—a people's ability to mourn their old king and to welcome proudly their new queen—helps to bind the nation of Britain together. Contrast this idea with the sources of Britain's national identity found in *The History of the English Church and People*, in *The Anglo-Saxon Chronicle*, and in Chaucer's *The Canterbury Tales*.

 Idea Bank

Writing

1. **Symbolic People** Monarchs symbolize the countries they rule. List people who symbolize things you or others value. Next to each name, write down the qualities the person seems to embody.

2. **Diary of an Unhappy Queen** If you feel unwell at four, it's on the news at six. However, they rarely ask for your opinion on really important matters. Also, for goodness' sake, don't forget to smile, however grumpy you may feel. Being a ceremonial royal ruler must certainly have its drawbacks. Write down the inner thoughts of a royal ruler in diary form.

3. **The Rhetoric of Royalty** Write an essay in which you compare and contrast newspaper or magazine profiles of celebrities in a particular field (professional sports, the movies, rock, politics, or some other field). What virtues (or vices) are commonly discussed in these articles?

Speaking, Listening, and Viewing

4. **Crowning Event** The coronation of a monarch in Great Britain is a ceremony of the highest order. Research the events surrounding the coronation of Queen Elizabeth in 1953, paying special attention to the visual elements of the ceremony. As you do your research, ask what impression the coronation is meant to make on viewers and how that effect is achieved. **[Social Studies Link]**

Researching and Representing

5. **The Royal Family Tree** Elizabeth II is the latest in a long line of England's Monarchs. Create an annotated family tree of the rulers of Britain—from Alfred the Great to the present. For each ruler, explain how they came to the throne—did they inherit it or fight for it? **[Social Studies Link; Art Link]**

Online Activity www.phlit.phschool.com

Writing Process Workshop

College-Application Essay

During the Anglo-Saxon period, writers such as Bede began producing vivid records of key historical events. As you grow older, you may be called on to develop written records of your own personal history. In a **college-application essay,** for instance, you'll be called on to describe key experiences that shaped you as a person and to explain what you gained from these experiences. This type of essay may also require you to outline your achievements and describe your personality.

The following skills, introduced in this section's Guided Writing Lessons, will help you write an effective college-application essay.

Writing Skills Focus

▶ **Use a clear organization plan** to ensure that your audience will be able to follow the events and absorb the information you present. Keep in mind that your organization plan should fit your topic.

▶ **Establish coherence** by making logical connections between sentences so that each idea clearly follows the one before it. (See p. 85.)

▶ **Use humor** where appropriate to grab your readers' attention and to reveal your personality.

These skills are evident in the following paragraph from a college-application essay.

WRITING MODEL

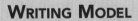

Can you imagine being angry with your third-grade teacher for offering you encouragement? ① It wasn't until I graduated from elementary school that I realized my teacher, Mrs. Allerton, had become one of the most important people in my life. ② As I waited in line for her to sign my graduation album, ③ I noticed that she seemed to be studying each entry in the albums of others ahead of me.

① The writer begins the application essay with a humorous question. It grabs the reader's attention and indicates that the writer is about to learn a valuable lesson.

② The writer constructs his introduction effectively by beginning with a question that draws the reader in and then follows up with a statement that reveals the focus of the essay.

③ This phrase connects this sentence to the previous one, making the passage coherent.

Applying Language Skills: Using Transitions

Use transitions to indicate relationships among ideas and tighten your organization.

• To indicate **chronological order** use transitions such as *before, as soon as, next, after, then,* and *at that point.*

• To indicate **order of importance** use transitions such as *first, best,* or *least of all.*

• To introduce an **example** use transitional words such as *namely, in other words,* or *such as.*

Writing Application Identify areas in your paper that indicate relationships in time, importance, or where examples are introduced. Add transitions to tie ideas together.

Writer's Solution Connection
Writing Lab

To help you organize details for your college-application essay, use the graphic organizers in the Writing Lab Tutorial on Practical Writing.

Prewriting

Consider Your Audience A college-application essay has a clearly defined audience: the members of the admissions committee. Before you even choose your topic, think carefully about the types of things that might impress this audience. Ask yourself:

• What achievements would catch their interest? What personal qualities would they like to see?

• What experiences have you had in which you exhibited these personal qualities?

Choose Your Topic Use your ideas about what will impress your audience to come up with a topic. You might choose to focus on a single event—such as your most powerful learning experience or your greatest personal experience—or you might focus on a series of events or a relationship with a special person.

Develop a Clear Organization Most likely, your topic will dictate how you organize your essay. For example, if you're describing a series of events, you'll probably want to use a chronological organization. On the other hand, if your essay is outlining your most important personal qualities, you may want to use an order-of-importance organization. Once you've chosen your organization, jot down some details you'll include in your essay and arrange them in the proper order.

Drafting

Maintain Coherence As you draft your paper, create coherence by using transitions to indicate how the ideas and events in your essay fit together. Also, be careful not to include any details that don't fit in with the main points you're making.

Incorporate Humor Using humor to reveal your personality is an excellent way to grab your readers' attention and help them evaluate you as a real person, not just an academic student. For example, you may use exaggeration to emphasize a reaction you had to an absurd or ridiculous situation. As you write, determine the best places in your essay to include humorous events.

Organize As you draft your paper, follow your organizational plan. Stop after each paragraph to double-check the direction in which your essay is headed. You may decide that another type of organization is more suitable.

Revising

Use the following checklist, which refers to the Writing Skills Focus on page 135, while revising your paper.

▶ Did you use transitions to maintain coherence?
Underline the transitions in your paper and the repetition of key ideas. If you have not used enough of either, add more.

▶ Have you kept to the organizational pattern you chose?
Review your essay and create an outline as you read. Then check the order of details in the outline to ensure that you've used a clear, consistent organization.

▶ Is your use of humor effective?
Read your essay to a friend or family member and ask for their opinions of your humorous descriptions.

REVISION MODEL

Ever since the seventh grade, I've been known as "Indiana Grimes."
① Although my real name is Lois, my friends recognize the
This thirst for excitement
longing I have for adventures. ② It stemmed from a tubing

mishap that left a friend and me stranded on the rocks in

the mighty Delaware River. ③ There I learned a great deal about
responsibility and a respect for nature.

① The writer adds this statement to begin her discussion of a serious occurrence with a light, humorous tone.
② She adds this phrase to make a clear connection to the previous sentence.
③ To establish the cause-and-effect format of the paper, the writer adds this statement summing up the effect of her adventure.

Publishing

▶ **Portfolio** Add your college-application essays to a personal portfolio of other essays you have written.

▶ **Classroom** Share your techniques and ideas for college applications with other students. Compile a list of the most effective techniques to help other students prepare their essays.

APPLYING LANGUAGE SKILLS: Using Pronouns Correctly

When using pronouns, avoid confusion by making sure that there is a clear antecedent—the word or group of words to which the pronoun refers. A vague reference will result if an antecedent is not clear.

Unclear: Move the plastic tab to a closed position. This prevents accidental erasure. (*This has no apparent antecedent.*)

Clear: Move the plastic tab to a closed position. This shift prevents accidental erasure. (The meaning is clarified by adding the noun *shift* to the sentence.)

Writing Application Underline the pronouns in your paper. Make sure that they all have clear antecedents.

Writer's Solution Connection Language Lab

For more practice with pronouns, complete the Pronouns and Antecedents lesson in the Sharpening Language Skills section.

Student Success Workshop

Real-World Reading Skills

Discriminate Between Connotative and Denotative Meanings

Strategies for Success

Words can have meanings beyond their dictionary definitions. The dictionary meaning of a word is its denotative meaning. The suggested, or implied, meaning of a word is its connotative meaning, which often evokes emotional associations. For instance, the words *observe* and *stare* both mean "to look at carefully," but their connotative meanings differ. The associations with the word *observe* will be positive or neutral. The connotative meaning of the word *stare* can be negative—staring is considered rude.

Use Systematic Word Study Using a dictionary, glossary, and thesaurus can help you sort out the connotative and denotative meanings of words so you can better understand the writer's intent. Suppose a character is described as *obliging*. You can use a dictionary to determine the denotative meaning: "ready to do favors; accommodating." A dictionary may also use the word in context, which helps determine its connotative meaning. A thesaurus may help you by providing synonyms: Synonyms for *obliging* are "affable," "agreeable," and "grateful," which are positive connotations. The thesaurus also lists antonyms, such as "irritating" and "obnoxious."

Use Connotation to Create Impact Writers often use connotation to intensify their writing. For example, if a writer states that "Ms. Trujillo drove to the party in a brown car," the writer is objectively using denotative meaning to describe the action and the vehicle. If the writer states that "Ms. Trujillo sped to the party in a muddy jalopy," you get a more powerful picture. *Sped, muddy,* and *jalopy* evoke stronger connotative associations than *drove, brown,* and *car.*

Be Aware of Denotation and Connotation

Writers sometimes avoid using words with powerful connotations. If you're reading a research paper or textbook, the facts are usually stated objectively, using words with precise denotative meanings. On the other hand, if you're reading a persuasive speech or an advertisement, be alert to the connotative meanings of words—words with strong emotional overtones. Look up synonyms in a thesaurus to discover the connotative meanings.

Apply the Strategies

Read the following paragraph, and answer the questions that follow:

Sam took a *trip* to China. His *trek* began in early January when he *hiked* along the Great Wall for two weeks. Then he *roamed* through the open-air markets in Beijing. The day he returned, he *dashed* to my house to tell me about his adventures. He's planning another *vacation* for next July.

1. What is the denotative meaning of *trip*?
2. What are the connotative meanings of *trek* and *dashed*?
3. Which word's connotative meaning implies difficulty: *hiked* or *roamed*?

✔ Here are some other situations in which your understanding of denotation and connotation might be useful:
  ▶ Understanding the message of an advertisement or billboard
  ▶ Thinking critically about a political speech
  ▶ Telling your friend a story

Part 4

Perils and Adventures

St. George and the Dragon,
c.1506, Raphael,
National Gallery of Art, Washington, D.C.

Guide for Interpreting

Legendary Knights

The feudal system of medieval Europe grew out of the tradition of warriors swearing an oath of loyalty to a chief who provided for their needs. Medieval nobles carried on this tradition by providing for knights, or mounted warriors, in exchange for their loyalty.

The Code of Chivalry Beginning in the eleventh century, feudal nobles developed a code of conduct called chivalry. This code combined Christian values and the virtues of being a warrior. A knight was expected to be brave, generous, and loyal; to right wrongs; and to defend the helpless without hope of reward.

King Arthur and His Knights The legendary King Arthur and his Knights of the Round Table served as models of chivalrous behavior in countless medieval tales. *Sir Gawain and the Green Knight,* for example, tells how Arthur's nephew Sir Gawain was put to the test. In meeting this test, Sir Gawain is admirable but not invulnerable, which lends psychological truth to this medieval story. As one critic puts it, the hero "gains in human credibility what he loses in ideal perfection."

Sir Thomas Malory
(1405?–1471)

The identity of Sir Thomas Malory is a mystery. Several crimes were attributed to him—such as looting, extorting money, setting an ambush with intent to murder, and raiding cattle. He was even charged with breaking out of jail and once escaped custody by swimming a moat! However, he denied any wrongdoing.

A Prisoner It is generally accepted that during the War of the Roses (the bloody conflict between the two factions of royalty that marred the latter half of the fifteenth century in England), Malory was imprisoned at least once. It is not certain to what extent the criminal charges were justified; nevertheless, Malory spent the greater portion of his later years in prison.

A Book From Behind Bars It is believed that Malory completed *Morte d'Arthur*, his account of King Arthur's life, in prison and may even have died there. His great prose work was given its name and published posthumously in 1485 by William Caxton, the man who established the first printing press in England.

◆ Background for Understanding

HISTORY: THE LEGENDS OF KING ARTHUR

Legends are anonymous traditional stories that reflect the attitudes and values of the society that created them. The heroes of legends, such as Sir Gawain or King Arthur, usually possess qualities that the society considers admirable.

The legend of King Arthur is probably based on the life of a Celtic warrior who fought the Germanic invaders of England in the late fifth and early sixth centuries. His role as a defender of England made him a hero to Britons and led people to invent stories about his miraculous deeds.

Although the legend of Arthur arose in England, it has appealed to people from many different countries. Everywhere, readers are stirred by the story of a wise and noble king who rules from the great castle of Camelot and wields the magical sword Excalibur. They are touched by his death, which seems more like a strange vanishing, and by the notion that he will return one day.

Journal Writing Think about a legend of today—someone who has accomplished difficult or important tasks. Identify this person and briefly describe his or her achievements.

from Sir Gawain and the Green Knight
◆ from Morte d'Arthur ◆

◆ Literature and Your Life

CONNECT YOUR EXPERIENCE

You may not slay many dragons on an average day. However, if you volunteer at a soup kitchen, defend someone weaker than you, or remain loyal to friends, you are living by a knightly code of behavior called chivalry.

In *Sir Gawain and the Green Knight* and *Morte d'Arthur,* you encounter the legendary men from chivalry's hall of fame: King Arthur and the Knights of the Round Table.

THEMATIC FOCUS: PERILS AND ADVENTURES

As you read these selections, ask yourself why a code of chivalry was especially important in the Middle Ages.

◆ Build Vocabulary

WORD ROOTS: *-droit-*

As you read these selections, you will come across the word *adroitly,* which means "with great skill." This word is built upon the root *-droit-,* meaning "right." The use of "right" to mean "skillful" reflects a historical bias for right-handedness.

WORD BANK

Before you read, preview this list of words.

assay
adjure
feigned
adroitly
largesse
righteous
entreated
peril
interred

◆ Grammar and Style

COMPARATIVE AND SUPERLATIVE FORMS

These selections, like many others, contain comparative and superlative forms of adjectives and adverbs. The **comparative form** compares one thing with another by adding *-er* to short modifiers and using *more* with most modifiers of two or more syllables. The **superlative form** compares more than two things by adding *-est* to one-syllable modifiers and using *most* with modifiers of two or more syllables.

Comparative Form: Grow green as the grass, and *greener* it seemed. Then green fused on gold *more glorious* by far.

Superlative Form: . . . thereupon sat King Arthur in the *richest* cloth of gold that might be made.

◆ Literary Focus

MEDIEVAL ROMANCE

Medieval romances are based on the ideal of chivalry, the code of behavior by which knights lived. Filled with adventure, love, and the supernatural, they featured kings, knights, and damsels in distress.

Of all the medieval romances, the best known are those about King Arthur, a legendary British king of the fifth or sixth century, and his knights. In reading these romances, you will see how they blend realistic elements with supernatural ones.

◆ Reading Strategy

SUMMARIZE

When you **summarize** a passage of a work, you express and keep track of its key ideas or events. As you read, capture key ideas and events in a summary like this:

From *Morte d'Arthur*

"Ah, traitor unto me and untrue," said King Arthur, "now hast thou betrayed me twice. Who would have weened that thou that has been to me so loved and dear, and thou art named a noble knight, and would betray me for the riches of this sword."

Summary: King Arthur's knight lies to him twice about Arthur's sword.

from *Sir Gawain and the Green Knight*

Translated by Marie Borroff

The scene begins at the start of a New Year's Eve feast at King Arthur's Court in Camelot. Before anyone has started eating, the festivities are interrupted by an immense green knight who suddenly appears at the hall door. The knight rides a green horse and is armed with a gigantic ax.

This horseman hurtles in, and the hall enters;
Riding to the high dais,[1] recked he no danger;
Not a greeting he gave as the guests he o'erlooked,
Nor wasted his words, but "Where is," he said,
5   "The captain of this crowd? Keenly I wish
To see that sire with sight, and to himself say my say."
    He swaggered all about
    To scan the host so gay;
    He halted, as if in doubt
10   Who in that hall held sway.

There were stares on all sides as the stranger spoke,
For much did they marvel what it might mean
That a horseman and a horse should have such a hue,
Grow green as the grass, and greener, it seemed.
15   Then green fused on gold more glorious by far.
All the onlookers eyed him, and edged nearer,
And awaited in wonder what he would do,
For many sights had they seen, but such a one never,
So that phantom and fairy the folk there deemed it,
20   Therefore chary[2] of answer was many a champion bold,
And stunned at his strong words stone-still they sat
In a swooning silence in the stately hall.
As all were slipped into sleep, so slackened their speech apace.
    Not all, I think, for dread,
25   But some of courteous grace
    Let him who was their head
    Be spokesman in that place.

1. **dais** (dā´ is) *n.*: Platform.

2. **chary** (cher´ ē) *adj.*: Not giving freely.

From *The Romance of King Arthur and His Knights of the Round Table,* Arthur Rackham

◀ Critical Viewing
Could this castle be a setting for the opening scene of this tale? Why or why not? [Interpret]

Then Arthur before the high dais that entrance beholds,
And hailed him, as behooved, for he had no fear.
30 And said "Fellow, in faith you have found fair welcome;
The head of this hostelry Arthur am I;
Leap lightly down, and linger, I pray,
And the tale of your intent you shall tell us after."
"Nay, so help me," said the other, "He that on high sits,
35 To tarry here any time, 'twas not mine errand;
But as the praise of you, prince, is puffed up so high,
And your court and your company are counted the best,
Stoutest under steel-gear on steeds to ride,
Worthiest of their works the wide world over,
40 And peerless to prove in passages of arms,
And courtesy here is carried to its height,
And so at this season I have sought you out.
You may be certain by the branch that I bear in hand
That I pass here in peace, and would part friends,
45 For had I come to this court on combat bent,
I have a hauberk³ at home, and a helm beside,
A shield and a sharp spear, shining bright,
And other weapons to wield, I ween well, to boot,
But as I willed no war, I wore no metal.
50 But if you be so bold as all men believe,
You will graciously grant the game that I ask by right."
     Arthur answer gave
     And said, "Sir courteous knight,
     If contest here you crave,
55   You shall not fail to fight."

◆ Literature
and Your Life
Which of the virtues in lines 36–41 do you find most admirable?

3. **hauberk** (hô´ bərk)
n.: Coat of armor.

from *Sir Gawain and the Green Knight* ◆ 143

"Nay, to fight, in good faith, is far from my thought;
There are about on these benches but beardless children,
Were I here in full arms on a haughty[4] steed,
For measured against mine, their might is puny.

60 And so I call in this court for a Christmas game,
For 'tis Yule, and New Year, and many young bloods about;
If any in this house such hardihood claims,
Be so bold in his blood, his brain so wild,
As stoutly to strike one stroke for another,

65 I shall give him as my gift this gisarme[5] noble,
This ax, that is heavy enough, to handle as he likes,
And I shall bide the first blow, as bare as I sit.
If there be one so wilful my words to assay,
Let him leap hither lightly, lay hold of this weapon;

70 I quitclaim it forever, keep it as his own,
And I shall stand him a stroke, steady on this floor,
So you grant me the guerdon to give him another, sans blame.[6]
    In a twelvemonth[7] and a day
    He shall have of me the same;

75   Now be it seen straightway
    Who dares take up the game."

If he astonished them at first, stiller were then
All that household in hall, the high and the low;
The stranger on his green steed stirred in the saddle,

80 And roisterously his red eyes he rolled all about,
Bent his bristling brows, that were bright green,
Wagged his beard as he watched who would arise.
When the court kept its counsel he coughed aloud,
And cleared his throat coolly, the clearer to speak:

85 "What, is this Arthur's house," said that horseman then,
"Whose fame is so fair in far realms and wide?
Where is now your arrogance and your awesome deeds,
Your valor and your victories and your vaunting words?
Now are the revel and renown of the Round Table

90 Overwhelmed with a word of one man's speech,
For all cower and quake, and no cut felt!"
With this he laughs so loud that the lord grieved;
The blood for sheer shame shot to his face, and pride.
    With rage his face flushed red,

95   And so did all beside.
    Then the king as bold man bred
    Toward the stranger took a stride.

And said, "Sir, now we see you will say but folly,
Which whoso has sought, it suits that he find.

100 No guest here is aghast of your great words.
Give to me your gisarme, in God's own name,

4. **haughty** (hôt´ ē)
adj.: Lofty.

5. **gisarme** (gi zärm´)
n.: Battle-ax.

6. **I . . . blame:** I will
stand firm while he
strikes me with the ax
provided that you
reward me with the
opportunity to do the
same to him without
being blamed for it.
7. **twelvemonth:** A
year.

◆ Literary Focus
How is this descrip-
tion of the Green
Knight (lines 79–86)
characteristic of a
medieval romance?

◆ **Build Vocabulary**
assay (as ā´) *v.*: Prove or test

And the boon you have begged shall straight be granted."
He leaps to him lightly, lays hold of his weapon;
The green fellow on foot fiercely alights.
105   Now has Arthur his ax, and the haft[8] grips,
And sternly stirs it about, on striking bent.
The stranger before him stood there erect,
Higher than any in the house by a head and more;
With stern look as he stood, he stroked his beard,
110   And with undaunted countenance drew down his coat,
No more moved nor dismayed for his mighty dints
Than any bold man on bench had brought him a drink of wine.

8. haft *n.:* Handle of a weapon or tool.

Three Knights Returning From a Tournament

▲ **Critical Viewing** From this picture, what can you infer about a knight's preparations for challenges of skill, such as tournaments and the Green Knight's challenge? **[Infer]**

from *Sir Gawain and the Green Knight* ◆ 145

Gawain by Guenevere
Toward the king doth now incline:
115   "I beseech, before all here,
That this melee may be mine."

"Would you grant me the grace," said Gawain to the king,
"To be gone from this bench and stand by you there,
If I without discourtesy might quit this board,
120 And if my liege lady[9] misliked it not,
I would come to your counsel before your court noble.
For I find it not fit, as in faith it is known,
When such a boon is begged before all these knights,
Though you be tempted thereto, to take it on yourself
125 While so bold men about upon benches sit,
That no host under heaven is hardier of will,
Nor better brothers-in-arms where battle is joined;
I am the weakest, well I know, and of wit feeblest;
And the loss of my life would be least of any;
130 That I have you for uncle is my only praise;
My body, but for your blood, is barren of worth;
And for that this folly befits not a king,
And 'tis I that have asked it, it ought to be mine,
And if my claim be not comely let all this court judge in sight."
135   The court assays the claim,
And in counsel all unite
To give Gawain the game
And release the king outright.

Then the king called the knight to come to his side,
140 And he rose up readily, and reached him with speed,
Bows low to his lord, lays hold of the weapon,
And he releases it lightly, and lifts up his hand,
And gives him God's blessing, and graciously prays
That his heart and his hand may be hardy both.
145 "Keep, cousin," said the king, "what you cut with this day,
And if you rule it aright, then readily, I know,
You shall stand the stroke it will strike after."
Gawain goes to the guest with gisarme in hand,
And boldly he bides there, abashed not a whit.
150 Then hails he Sir Gawain, the horseman in green:
"Recount we our contract, ere you come further.
First I ask and adjure you, how you are called
That you tell me true, so that trust it I may."
"In good faith," said the good knight, "Gawain am I
155 Whose buffet befalls you,[10] whate'er betide after,
And at this time twelvemonth take from you another
With what weapon you will, and with no man else alive."

9. **liege** (lēj) **lady:**
Guenevere, the wife of
the lord, Arthur, to
whom Gawain is
bound to give service
and allegiance.

◆ **Reading Strategy**
Summarize the key
points and conditions
of the challenge, as
described in lines
150–184.

10. **Whose . . . you:**
Whose blow you will
receive.

The other nods assent:
"Sir Gawain, as I may thrive,
160   I am wondrous well content
That you this dint[11] shall drive."

"Sir Gawain," said the Green Knight, "By God, I rejoice
That your fist shall fetch this favor I seek,
And you have readily rehearsed, and in right terms,
165   Each clause of my covenant with the king your lord,
Save that you shall assure me, sir, upon oath,
That you shall seek me yourself, wheresoever you deem
My lodgings may lie, and look for such wages[12]
As you have offered me here before all this host."
170   "What is the way there?" said Gawain, "Where do you dwell?
I heard never of your house, by Him that made me,
Nor I know you not, knight, your name nor your court.
But tell me truly thereof, and teach me your name,
And I shall fare forth to find you, so far as I may,
175   And this I say in good certain, and swear upon oath."
"That is enough in New Year, you need say no more,"
Said the knight in the green to Gawain the noble,
"If I tell you true, when I have taken your knock,
And if you handily have hit, you shall hear straightway
180   Of my house and my home and my own name;
Then follow in my footsteps by faithful accord.
And if I spend no speech, you shall speed the better:
You can feast with your friends, nor further trace my tracks.[13]
     Now hold your grim tool steady
185   And show us how it hacks."
     "Gladly, sir; all ready,"
     Says Gawain; he strokes the ax.

The Green Knight upon ground girds him with care:
Bows a bit with his head, and bares his flesh:
190   His long lovely locks he laid over his crown,
Let the naked nape for the need be shown
Gawain grips to his ax and gathers it aloft—
The left foot on the floor before him he set—
Brought it down deftly upon the bare neck,
195   That the shock of the sharp blow shivered the bones
And cut the flesh cleanly and clove it in twain,[14]
That the blade of bright steel bit into the ground.
The head was hewn off and fell to the floor;
Many found it at their feet, as forth it rolled;
200   The blood gushed from the body, bright on the green,
Yet fell not the fellow, nor faltered a whit,
But stoutly he starts forth upon stiff shanks,

11. dint *n.:* Blow.

12. wages *n.:* A blow.

13. If I tell you . . . tracks: (lines 178–183): The Green Knight tells Gawain that he will let him know where he lives after he has taken the blow. If he is unable to speak following the blow, there will be no need for Gawain to know.

14. clove it in twain: Split it in two.

♦ **Build Vocabulary**

adjure (ə joor′) *v.:* Appeal earnestly

And as all stood staring he stretched forth his hand,
Laid hold of his head and heaved it aloft,
205   Then goes to the green steed, grasps the bridle,
Steps into the stirrup, bestrides his mount,
And his head by the hair in his hand holds,
And as steady he sits in the stately saddle
As he had met with no mishap, nor missing were his head.
210   His bulk about he haled,
      That fearsome body that bled;
      There were many in the court that quailed
      Before all his say was said.

For the head in his hand he holds right up;
215   Toward the first on the dais directs he the face,
And it lifted up its lids, and looked with wide eyes,
And said as much with its mouth as now you may hear:
"Sir Gawain, forget not to go as agreed,
And cease not to seek till me, sir, you find,
220   As you promised in the presence of these proud knights.
To the Green Chapel come, I charge you, to take
Such a dint as you have dealt—you have well deserved
That your neck should have a knock on New Year's morn.
The Knight of the Green Chapel I am well-known to many,
225   Wherefore you cannot fail to find me at last;
Therefore come, or be counted a recreant[15] knight."
With a roisterous rush he flings round the reins,
Hurtles out at the hall door, his head in his hand,
That the flint fire flew from the flashing hooves.
230   Which way he went, not one of them knew
Nor whence he was come in the wide world so fair.
      The king and Gawain gay
      Make a game of the Green Knight there,
      Yet all who saw it say
235   'Twas a wonder past compare.

Though high-born Arthur at heart had wonder,
He let no sign be seen, but said aloud
To the comely queen, with courteous speech,
"Dear dame, on this day dismay you no whit;
240   Such crafts are becoming at Christmastide,
Laughing at interludes, light songs and mirth,
Amid dancing of damsels with doughty knights.
Nevertheless of my meat now let me partake,
For I have met with a marvel, I may not deny."
245   He glanced at Sir Gawain, and gaily he said,
"Now, sir, hang up your ax, that has hewn enough,"
And over the high dais it was hung on the wall
That men in amazement might on it look,
And tell in true terms the tale of the wonder.

◆ **Literary Focus**
How is the description in lines 219–229 characteristic of a medieval romance?

15. Recreant: *adj.*
Cowardly.

Sir Gawain and the Green Knight, The Bodleian Library, Oxford

▲ **Critical Viewing** Compare the depiction of Sir Gawain in the picture (center) and in the text. **[Compare and Contrast]**

250   Then they turned toward the table, those two together,
       The good king and Gawain, and made great feast,
       With all dainties double, dishes rare,
       With all manner of meat and minstrelsy both,
       Such happiness wholly had they that day in hold.
255   Now take care, Sir Gawain,
          That your courage wax not cold
          When you must turn again
          To your enterprise foretold.

🔱

The following November, Sir Gawain sets out to fulfill his promise to the Green Knight. For weeks he travels alone through the cold, threatening woods of North Wales. Then, after he prays for shelter, he comes upon a wondrous castle on Christmas Eve, where he is greeted warmly by the lord of the castle and his lady. Sir Gawain inquires about the location of the Green Chapel, and the lord assures him that it is nearby and promises to provide him with a guide to lead him there on New Year's Day. Before the lord and Sir Gawain retire for the night, they agree to exchange whatever they receive during the next three days. Sir Gawain keeps his pledge for the first two days, but on the third day he does not give the lord the magic green girdle that the lady gives him because she promises that the girdle will protect him from any harm. The next day, Gawain sets out for the Green Chapel. His guide urges him not to proceed, but Gawain refuses to take this advice. He feels that it would be dishonorable not to fulfill his pledge. He is determined to accept his fate; however, he does wear the magic green girdle that the lady had given him.

⚜

He puts his heels to his horse, and picks up the path;
260 Goes in beside a grove where the ground is steep,
Rides down the rough slope right to the valley;
And then he looked a little about him–the landscape was wild,
And not a soul to be seen, nor sign of a dwelling,
But high banks on either hand hemmed it about,
265 With many a ragged rock and rough-hewn crag;
The skies seemed scored by the scowling peaks.
Then he halted his horse, and hoved there a space,
And sought on every side for a sight of the Chapel,
But no such place appeared, which puzzled him sore,
270 Yet he saw some way off what seemed like a mound,
A hillock high and broad, hard by the water,
Where the stream fell in foam down the face of the steep
And bubbled as if it boiled on its bed below.
The knight urges his horse, and heads for the knoll;
275 Leaps lightly to earth; loops well the rein
Of his steed to a stout branch, and stations him there.
He strides straight to the mound, and strolls all about,
Much wondering what it was, but no whit the wiser;
It had a hole at one end, and on either side,
280 And was covered with coarse grass in clumps all without,
And hollow all within, like some old cave,
Or a crevice of an old crag—he could not discern aright.
　　"Can this be the Chapel Green?
　　Alack!" said the man, "Here might
285 　　The devil himself be seen
　　Saying matins[16] at black midnight!"

"Now by heaven," said he, "it is bleak hereabouts;
This prayer house is hideous, half covered with grass!
Well may the grim man mantled in green
290 Hold here his orisons,[17] in hell's own style!
Now I feel it is the Fiend, in my five wits,
That has tempted me to this tryst,[18] to take my life;
This is a Chapel of mischance, may the mischief take it!
As accursed a country church as I came upon ever!"
295 With his helm on his head, his lance in his hand,
He stalks toward the steep wall of that strange house.
Then he heard, on the hill, behind a hard rock,
Beyond the brook, from the bank, a most barbarous din:
Lord! it clattered in the cliff fit to cleave it in two,
300 As one upon a grindstone ground a great scythe!
Lord! it whirred like a mill-wheel whirling about!
Lord! it echoed loud and long, lamentable to hear!
Then "By heaven," said the bold knight, "That business up there
Is arranged for my arrival, or else I am much misled.

16. matins *n*.:
Morning prayers.

17. orisons *n*.: Prayers.

18. tryst (trist) *n*.:
Meeting.

305   Let God work! Ah me!
        All hope of help has fled!
        Forfeit my life may be
        But noise I do not dread."

        Then he listened no longer, but loudly he called,
310   "Who has power in this place, high parley to hold?
        For none greets Sir Gawain, or give him good day;
        If any would a word with him, let him walk forth
        And speak now or never, to speed his affairs."
        "Abide," said one on the bank above over his head,
315   "And what I promised you once shall straightway be given."
        Yet he stayed not his grindstone, nor stinted its noise,
        But worked awhile at his whetting before he would rest,
        And then he comes around a crag, from a cave in the rocks,
        Hurtling out of hiding with a hateful weapon,
320   A Danish ax[19] devised for that day's deed,
        With a broad blade and bright, bent in a curve,
        Filed to a fine edge—four feet it measured
        By the length of the lace that was looped round the haft.
        And in form as at first, the fellow all green,
325   His lordly face and his legs, his locks and his beard,
        Save that firm upon two feet forward he strides,
        Sets a hand on the ax-head, the haft to the earth;
        When he came to the cold stream, and cared not to wade,
        He vaults over on his ax, and advances amain
330   On a broad bank of snow, overbearing and brisk of mood.
            Little did the knight incline
            When face to face they stood;
            Said the other man, "Friend mine,
            It seems your word holds good!"

335   "God love you, Sir Gawain!" said the Green Knight then,
        "And well met this morning, man, at my place!
        And you have followed me faithfully and found me betimes,
        And on the business between us we both are agreed:
        Twelve months ago today you took what was yours,
340   And you at this New Year must yield me the same.
        And we have met in these mountains, remote from all eyes:
        There is none here to halt us or hinder our sport;
        Unhasp your high helm, and have here your wages;
        Make no more demur than I did myself
345   When you hacked off my head with one hard blow."
        "No, by God," said Sir Gawain, "that granted me life,
        I shall grudge not the guerdon [20] grim though it prove;
        And you may lay on as you like till the last of my part be paid."

♦ *Literature and Your Life*

Think of a time you may have been apprehensive about approaching a situation. Did you react in the same way as Sir Gawain? Explain.

19. **Danish ax:** Long-bladed ax.

20. **guerdon** *n.:* Reward.

He proffered, with good grace,
His bare neck to the blade,
And feigned a cheerful face:
He scorned to seem afraid.

Then the grim man in green gathers his strength,
Heaves high the heavy ax to hit him the blow.
With all the force in his frame he fetches it aloft,
With a grimace as grim as he would grind him to bits;
Had the blow he bestowed been as big as he threatened,
A good knight and gallant had gone to his grave.
But Gawain at the great ax glanced up aside
As down it descended with death-dealing force,
And his shoulders shrank a little from the sharp iron.
Abruptly the brawny man breaks off the stroke,
And then reproved with proud words that prince among knights.
"You are not Gawain the glorious," the green man said,
"That never fell back on field in the face of the foe,
And now you flee for fear, and have felt no harm:
Such news of that knight I never heard yet!
I moved not a muscle when you made to strike,
Nor caviled[21] at the cut in King Arthur's house;
My head fell to my feet, yet steadfast I stood,
And you, all unharmed, are wholly dismayed—
Wherefore the better man I, by all odds, must be."
    Said Gawain, "Strike once more;
    I shall neither flinch nor flee;
    But if my head falls to the floor
    There is no mending me!"

"But go on, man, in God's name, and get to the point!
Deliver me my destiny, and do it out of hand,
For I shall stand to the stroke and stir not an inch
Till your ax has hit home—on my honor I swear it!"
"Have at thee then!" said the other, and heaves it aloft,
And glares down as grimly as he had gone mad.
He made a mighty feint, but marred not his hide;
Withdrew the ax adroitly before it did damage.
Gawain gave no ground, nor glanced up aside,
But stood still as a stone, or else a stout stump
That is held in hard earth by a hundred roots.
Then merrily does he mock him, the man all in green:
"So now you have your nerve again, I needs must strike;
Uphold the high knighthood that Arthur bestowed,
And keep your neck-bone clear, if this cut allows!"
Then was Gawain gripped with rage, and grimly he said,
"Why, thrash away, tyrant, I tire of your threats;
You make such a scene, you must frighten yourself."

◆ **Reading Strategy**
Summarize Sir Gawain's actions in lines 359–363.

21. **caviled:** Raised trivial objections.

◆ **Build Vocabulary**
feigned (fānd) v.: Made a false show of; pretended

adroitly (ə droit´ lē) adv: Physically or mentally skillful

395   Said the green fellow, "In faith, so fiercely you speak
That I shall finish this affair, nor further grace allow."
      He stands prepared to strike
      And scowls with both lip and brow;
      No marvel if the man mislike
400   Who can hope no rescue now.

He gathered up the grim ax and guided it well:
Let the barb at the blade's end brush the bare throat;
He hammered down hard, yet harmed him no whit
Save a scratch on one side, that severed the skin;
405   The end of the hooked edge entered the flesh,
And a little blood lightly leapt to the earth.
And when the man beheld his own blood bright on the snow,
He sprang a spear's length with feet spread wide,
Seized his high helm, and set it on his head,
410   Shoved before his shoulders the shield at his back,
Bares his trusty blade, and boldly he speaks—
Not since he was a babe born of his mother
Was he once in this world one half so blithe—
"Have done with your hacking—harry me no more!
415   I have borne, as behooved, one blow in this place;
If you make another move I shall meet it midway
And promptly, I promise you, pay back each blow with brand.
      One stroke acquits me here;
      So did our covenant stand
420   In Arthur's court last year—
      Wherefore, sir, hold your hand!"

He lowers the long ax and leans on it there,
Sets his arms on the head, the haft on the earth,
And beholds the bold knight that bides there afoot,
425   How he faces him fearless, fierce in full arms,
And plies him with proud words—it pleases him well.
Then once again gaily to Gawain he calls,
And in a loud voice and lusty, delivers these words:
"Bold fellow, on this field your anger forbear!
430   No man has made demands here in manner uncouth,
Nor done, save as duly determined at court.
I owed you a hit and you have it; be happy therewith!
The rest of my rights here I freely resign.
Had I been a bit busier, a buffet, perhaps,
435   I could have dealt more directly; and done you some harm.
First I flourished with a feint, in frolicsome mood,
And left your hide unhurt—and here I did well
By the fair terms we fixed on the first night;
And fully and faithfully you followed accord:
440   Gave over all your gains as a good man should.

♦ *Literature
and Your Life*

Do you consider
Sir Gawain's behav-
ior heroic?

A second feint, sir, I assigned for the morning
You kissed my comely wife—each kiss you restored.
For both of these there behooved but two feigned blows by right.
    True men pay what they owe;
445   No danger then in sight.
    You failed at the third throw,
    So take my tap, sir knight.

"For that is my belt about you, that same braided girdle,
My wife it was that wore it; I know well the tale,
450   And the count of your kisses and your conduct too,
And the wooing of my wife—it was all my scheme!
She made trial of a man most faultless by far
Of all that ever walked over the wide earth;
As pearls to white peas, more precious and prized,
455   So is Gawain, in good faith, to other gay knights.
Yet you lacked, sir, a little in loyalty there,
But the cause was not cunning, nor courtship either,
But that you loved your own life; the less, then, to blame."
The other stout knight in a study stood a long while,
460   So gripped with grim rage that his great heart shook.
All the blood of his body burned in his face
As he shrank back in shame from the man's sharp speech.
The first words that fell from the fair knight's lips:
"Accursed be a cowardly and covetous heart!
465   In you is villainy and vice, and virtue laid low!"
Then he grasps the green girdle and lets go the knot,
Hands it over in haste, and hotly he says:
"Behold there my falsehood, ill hap betide it!
Your cut taught me cowardice, care for my life,
470   And coveting came after, contrary both
To largesse and loyalty belonging to knights.
Now am I faulty and false, that fearful was ever
Of disloyalty and lies, bad luck to them both! and
    greed.
    I confess, knight, in this place,
475   Most dire is my misdeed;
    Let me gain back your good grace,

◆ Reading Strategy
Summarize Sir Gawain's response to the Green Knight in lines 459–477.

▶ Critical Viewing Assess the effectiveness of a woodcut like this one in illustrating the poem, as opposed to a painted representation. [Assess]

Gawain Receiving the Green Girdle, Woodcut by Fritz Kredel from Gardner, *The Complete Works of the Gawain Poet,* 1965, The University of Chicago

And thereafter I shall take heed."

Then the other laughed aloud, and lightly he said,
"Such harm as I have had, I hold it quite healed.
480 You are so fully confessed, your failings made known,
And bear the plain penance of the point of my blade,
I hold you polished as a pearl, as pure and as bright
As you had lived free of fault since first you were born.
And I give you sir, this girdle that is gold-hemmed
485 And green as my garments, that, Gawain, you may
Be mindful of this meeting when you mingle in throng
With nobles of renown—and known by this token
How it chanced at the Green Chapel, to chivalrous knights.
And you shall in this New Year come yet again
490 And we shall finish out our feast in my fair hall with cheer."

◆ **Build Vocabulary**

largesse (lär jes´) *n.:* Nobility of spirit

Guide for Responding

◆ Literature and Your Life

Reader's Response If you were King Arthur, would you have allowed Sir Gawain to accept the Green Knight's challenge? Why or why not?

Thematic Focus How does Sir Gawain's concern for his own life lead him into greater danger?

Casting Ideas With a small group, cast the parts of King Arthur, Sir Gawain, the Green Knight, and the lady of the castle for a film version of this story.

☑ Check Your Comprehension

1. The Green Knight's challenge has two parts. (a) What is Sir Gawain to do immediately? (b) What is he to do a year later?
2. What does Sir Gawain get from the lady of the castle, and what is the purpose of this present?
3. What occurs when Sir Gawain and the Green Knight meet at the Chapel Green?
4. Summarize what the Green Knight tells Sir Gawain at the end of the story.

◆ Critical Thinking

INTERPRET
1. Why does the Green Knight laugh at the members of the Round Table in line 92? **[Analyze]**
2. When Sir Gawain sees the Green Chapel, who does he think the Green Knight might be? **[Deduce]**
3. In lines 464–477, why is Sir Gawain upset? **[Interpret]**
4. What do you think Sir Gawain has learned from his second encounter with the Green Knight? **[Draw Conclusions]**

EVALUATE
5. In your opinion, has Sir Gawain failed to live up to his knightly ideals? Explain. **[Make a Judgment]**

EXTEND
6. What modern occupation do you think comes closest to matching the duties and ideals of the Knights of the Round Table? Explain your answer. **[Career Link]**

from *Morte d'Arthur*

Sir Thomas Malory

This selection begins after King Arthur has traveled to France at the insistence of his nephew, Gawain, to besiege his former friend and knight, Lancelot, for his involvement with Queen Guenevere. However, the king's attempts to punish are halfhearted, and he is soon forced to abandon them altogether when he learns that his nephew, Mordred, has seized control of England. Arthur leads his forces back to England, and Mordred attacks them upon their landing. Gawain is killed in the fighting, but before he dies, he manages to send word to Lancelot that Arthur is in need of assistance.

So upon Trinity Sunday at night King Arthur dreamed a wonderful dream, and in his dream him seemed[1] that he saw upon a chafflet[2] a chair, and the chair was fast to a wheel, and thereupon sat King Arthur in the richest cloth of gold that might be made. And the King thought there was under him, far from him, an hideous deep black water, and therein was all manner of serpents, and worms, and wild beasts, foul and horrible. And suddenly the King thought that the wheel turned upside down, and he fell among the serpents, and every beast took him by a limb. And then the King cried as he lay in his bed, "Help, help!"

And then knights, squires, and yeomen awaked the King, and then he was so amazed that he wist[3] not where he was. And then so he awaked until it was nigh day, and then he fell on slumbering again, not sleeping nor thoroughly waking. So the King seemed[4] verily that there came Sir Gawain unto him with a number of fair ladies with him. So when King Arthur saw him, he said, "Welcome, my sister's son. I weened ye had been dead. And now I see thee on-live, much am I beholden unto Almighty Jesu. Ah, fair nephew and my sister's son, what been these ladies that hither be come with you?"

"Sir," said Sir Gawain, "all these be ladies for whom I have foughten for when I was man living. And all these are those that I did battle for in righteous quarrels, and God hath given them that grace, at their great prayer, because I did battle for them for their right, that they should bring me hither unto you. Thus much hath given me leave God, for to warn you of your death. For and ye fight as tomorn[5] with Sir Mordred, as ye both have assigned, doubt ye not ye must be slain, and the most party of your people on both parties. And for the great grace and goodness that Almighty Jesu hath unto you, and for pity of you and many more other good men there shall be slain, God hath sent me to you of his special grace to give you warning that in no wise ye do battle as tomorn, but that ye take a treaty for a month from today. And proffer you largely[6] you so that tomorn ye put in a delay. For within a month shall come Sir Lancelot with all his noble knights and rescue you worshipfully and slay Sir Mordred and all that ever will hold with him."

Then Sir Gawain and all the ladies vanished. And anon the King called upon his knights, squires, and yeomen, and charged them

1. **him seemed:** It seemed to him.
2. **chafflet:** Platform.
3. **wist:** Knew.
4. **the King seemed:** It seemed to the King.

5. **and . . . tomorn:** If you fight tomorrow.
6. **proffer you largely:** Make generous offers.

wightly[7] to fetch his noble lords and wise bishops unto him. And when they were come the King told them of his avision,[8] that Sir Gawain had told him and warned him that, and he fought on the morn, he should be slain. Then the King commanded Sir Lucan the Butler and his brother Sir Bedivere the Bold, with two bishops with them, and charged them in any wise to take a treaty for a month from today with Sir Mordred. "And spare not: proffer him lands and goods as much as ye think reasonable."

So then they departed and came to Sir Mordred where he had a grim host of an hundred thousand, and there they <u>entreated</u> Sir Mordred long time. And at the last Sir Mordred was agreed for to have Cornwall and Kent by King Arthur's days, and after that, all England, after the days of King Arthur.

Then were they condescended[9] that King Arthur and Sir Mordred should meet betwixt both their hosts, and each of them should bring fourteen persons. And so they came with this word unto Arthur. Then said he, "I am glad that this is done," and so he went into the field.

And when King Arthur should depart, he warned all his host that, and they see any sword drawn, "Look ye come on fiercely and slay that traitor Sir Mordred, for I in no wise

King Arthur's Round Table and the Holy Grail

▲ **Critical Viewing** Using your knowledge of chivalry, draw conclusions about King Arthur's decision to set his knights at a round table. **[Draw Conclusions]**

trust him." In like wise Sir Mordred warned his host that "And ye see any manner of sword drawn, look that ye come on fiercely, and so slay all that ever before you standeth, for in no wise I will not trust for this treaty." And in the same wise said Sir Mordred unto his host, "For I know well my father will be avenged upon me."

And so they met as their pointment[10] was and were agreed and accorded thoroughly. And wine was fetched and they drank together. Right so came an adder out of a little heathbush, and it stung a knight in the foot. And so when the knight felt him so stung, he looked down and saw the adder. And anon he drew his sword to slay the adder, and thought none other harm. And when the host on both parties saw that sword drawn, then they blew beams,[11] trumpets, horns, and shouted grimly. And so both hosts dressed them together. And King Arthur took his horse and said, "Alas, this unhappy day!" and so rode to his party, and Sir Mordred in like wise.

---

10. **pointment:** Arrangement.
11. **beams:** Type of trumpet.

◆ **Build Vocabulary**

righteous (rī′chəs) *adj.*: Acting in a just, upright manner; doing what is right

entreated (en trēt′ id) *v.*: Made an earnest appeal; pleaded

---

7. **wightly:** Quickly.
8. **avision:** Dream.
9. **condescended:** Agreed.

The Nine Heroes Tapestries: Christian Heroes: Arthur, Probably Nicolas Bataille, Paris; The Metropolitan Museum of Art

▲ Critical Viewing What can you deduce about King Arthur's heroic stature from his depiction in this tapestry? [Deduce]

And never since was there never seen a more dolefuller battle in no Christian land, for there was but rushing and riding, lunging and striking; and many a grim word was there spoken of either to other, and many a deadly stroke. But ever King Arthur rode throughout the battle[12] of Sir Mordred many times and did full nobly, as a noble king should do, and at all times he fainted never. And Sir Mordred did his devoir that day and put himself in great <u>peril</u>.

And thus they fought all the long day, and never stinted[13] till the noble knights were laid to the cold earth. And ever they fought still till it was near night, and by then was there an hundred thousand laid dead upon the down. Then was King Arthur wood-wroth[14] out of measure when he saw his people so slain from him. And so he looked about him and could see no more of all his host, and good knights left no more on-live, but two knights: the t'one was Sir Lucan the Butler and the other his brother Sir Bedivere. And yet they were full sore wounded.

"Jesu, mercy," said the King, "where are all my noble knights become? Alas that ever I should see this doleful day! For now," said King Arthur, "I am come to mine end. But would to God," said he, "that I wist now where were that traitor Sir Mordred that has caused all this mischief."

Then King Arthur looked about and was ware where stood Sir Mordred leaning upon his sword among a great heap of dead men.

12. **battle:** Battalion.
13. **stinted:** Stopped.

14. **wood-wroth:** Wild with rage.

"Now give me my spear," said King Arthur unto Sir Lucan, "for yonder I have espied the traitor that all this woe hath wrought."

"Sir, let him be," said Sir Lucan, "for he is unhappy. And if ye pass this unhappy day ye shall be right well revenged upon him. And, good lord, remember ye of your night's dream, and what the spirit of Sir Gawain told you tonight, and yet God of his great goodness hath preserved you hitherto. And for God's sake, my lord, leave off by this, for, blessed be God, ye have won the field: for yet we been here three on-live, and with Sir Mordred is not one on-live. And therefore if ye leave off now, this wicked day of destiny is past."

"Now, tide[15] me death, tide me life," said the King, "now I see him yonder alone, he shall never escape mine hands. For at a better avail shall I never have him."

"God speed you well!" said Sir Bedivere.

Then the King got his spear in both his hands and ran toward Sir Mordred, crying and saying, "Traitor, now is thy deathday come!"

And when Sir Mordred saw King Arthur he ran until him with his sword drawn in his hand, and there King Arthur smote Sir Mordred under the shield, with a thrust of his spear, throughout the body more than a fathom. And when Sir Mordred felt that he had his death's wound, he thrust himself with the might that he had up to the burr[16] of King Arthur's spear, and right so he smote his father King Arthur with his sword holden in both his hands, upon the side of the head, that the sword pierced the helmet and the casing of the brain. And therewith Sir Mordred dashed down stark dead to the earth.

And noble King Arthur fell in a swough to the earth, and there he swooned oftentimes, and Sir Lucan and Sir Bedivere ofttimes heaved him up. And so, weakly betwixt them, they led him to a little chapel not far from the seaside, and when the King was there, him

◆ **Reading Strategy**
Summarize the events leading to the death of Mordred and the mortal wounding of King Arthur.

thought him reasonably eased. Then heard they people cry in the field. "Now go thou, Sir Lucan," said the King, "and do me to wit[17] what betokens that noise in the field."

So Sir Lucan departed, for he was grievously wounded in many places. And so as he walked he saw and harkened by the moonlight how that pillagers and robbers were come into the field to pill and to rob many a full noble knight of brooches and bracelets and of many a good ring and many a rich jewel. And who that were not dead all out there they slew them for their harness and their riches. When Sir Lucan understood this work, he came to the King as soon as he might and told him all what he had heard and seen. "Therefore by my read,"[18] said Sir Lucan, "it is best that we bring you to some town."

"I would it were so," said the King, "but I may not stand, my head works so. Ah, Sir Lancelot," said King Arthur, "this day have I sore missed thee. And alas that ever I was against thee, for now have I my death, whereof Sir Gawain me warned in my dream."

Then Sir Lucan took up the King the t'one party[19] and Sir Bedivere the other party; and in the lifting up the King swooned and in the lifting Sir Lucan fell in a swoon that part of his guts fell out of his body, and therewith the noble knight's heart burst. And when the King awoke he beheld Sir Lucan how he lay foaming at the mouth and part of his guts lay at his feet.

"Alas," said the King, "this is to me a full heavy sight to see this noble duke so die for my sake, for he would have helped me that had more need of help than I. Alas that he would not complain him for his heart was so set to help me. Now Jesu have mercy upon his soul."

Then Sir Bedivere wept for the death of his brother.

"Now leave this mourning and weeping gentle knight," said the King, "for all this will not avail me. For wit thou well, and might I live myself, the death of Sir Lucan would grieve me evermore. But my time passeth on fast," said the King. "Therefore," said King Arthur unto Sir Bedivere, "take thou here Excalibur my good sword and go with it to yonder water's side;

---

15. **tide:** Befall.
16. **burr:** Hand guard.

◆ **Build Vocabulary**

peril (per´ əl) *n.*: Exposure to harm or injury

---

17. **me to wit:** Let me know.
18. **read:** Advice.
19. **party:** Side.

and when thou comest there I charge thee throw my sword in that water and come again and tell me what thou sawest there."

"My lord," said Sir Bedivere, "your commandment shall be done, and I shall lightly[20] bring you word again."

So Sir Bedivere departed. And by the way he beheld that noble sword, that the pommel and the haft[21] was all precious stones. And then he said to himself, "If I throw this rich sword in the water, thereof shall never come good, but harm and loss." And then Sir Bedivere hid Excalibur under a tree. And so, as soon as he might, he came again unto the King and said he had been at the water and had thrown the sword into the water.

"What saw thou there?" said the King.

"Sir," he said, "I saw nothing but waves and winds."

"That is untruly said of thee," said the King. "And therefore go thou lightly again and do my commandment; as thou art to me loved and dear, spare not, but throw it in."

Then Sir Bedivere returned again and took the sword in his hand. And yet him thought sin and shame to throw away that noble sword. And so eft[22] he hid the sword and returned again and told the King that he had been at the water and done his commandment.

"What sawest thou there?" said the King.

"Sir," he said, "I saw nothing but waters wap and waves wan."[23]

"Ah, traitor unto me and untrue," said King Arthur, "now hast thou betrayed me twice. Who would have weened that thou that has been to me so loved and dear, and thou art named a noble knight, and would betray me for the riches of this sword. But now go again lightly, for thy long tarrying putteth me in great jeopardy of my life, for I have taken cold. And but if thou do now as I bid thee, if ever I may see thee I shall slay thee mine own hands, for thou wouldest for my rich sword see me dead."

Then Sir Bedivere departed and went to the sword and lightly took it up, and so he went to the water's side; and there he bound the girdle about the hilts, and threw the sword as far into the water as he might. And there came an arm and an hand above the water and took it and clutched it, and shook it thrice and brandished; and then vanished away the hand with the sword into the water. So Sir Bedivere came again to the King and told him what he saw.

"Alas," said the King, "help me hence, for I dread me I have tarried overlong."

Then Sir Bedivere took the King upon his back and so went with him to that water's side. And when they were at the water's side, even fast[24] by the bank floated a little barge with many fair ladies in it; and among them all was a queen; and all they had black hoods, and all they wept and shrieked when they saw King Arthur.

"Now put me into that barge," said the King; and so he did softly. And there received him three ladies with great mourning, and so they set them down. And in one of their laps King Arthur laid his head, and then the queen said, "Ah, my dear brother, why have ye tarried so long from me? Alas, this wound on your head hath caught overmuch cold." And anon they rowed fromward the land, and Sir Bedivere beheld all tho ladies go froward him.

Then Sir Bedivere cried and said, "Ah, my lord Arthur, what shall become of me, now ye go from me and leave me here alone among mine enemies?"

"Comfort thyself," said the King, "and do as well as thou mayest, for in me is no trust for to trust in. For I must into the vale of Avilion[25] to heal me of my grievous wound. And if thou hear nevermore of me, pray for my soul."

But ever the queen and ladies wept and shrieked, that it was pity to hear. And as soon as Sir Bedivere had lost sight of the barge he wept and wailed, and so took the forest and went all that night.

And in the morning he was ware, betwixt two bare woods, of a chapel and an hermitage. Then was Sir Bedivere glad, and thither he went, and when he came into the chapel he saw where lay an hermit groveling on all fours, close thereby a tomb was new dug. When the hermit saw Sir Bedivere he knew him well, for he was but little tofore Bishop of Canterbury,

◆ **Literary Focus**
In what ways is the description of King Arthur's death characteristic of medieval romances?

---

20. **lightly:** Quickly.
21. **pommel . . . haft:** Hilt and hand guard.
22. **eft:** Again.
23. **waters . . . wan:** Waters lap and waves grow dark.

24. **fast:** Close.
25. **Avilion:** Legendary island.

that Sir Mordred put to flight.

"Sirs," said Sir Bedivere, "what man is there here interred that you pray so fast for?"

"Fair son," said the hermit. "I wot not verily but by guessing. But this same night, at midnight, here came a number of ladies and brought here a dead corpse and prayed me to inter him. And here they offered an hundred tapers, and gave me a thousand gold coins."

"Alas," said Sir Bedivere, "that was my lord King Arthur, which lieth here buried in this chapel."

Then Sir Bedivere swooned, and when he awoke he prayed the hermit that he might abide with him still, there to live with fasting and prayers:

"For from hence will I never go," said Sir Bedivere, "by my will, but all the days of my life here to pray for my lord Arthur."

"Sir, ye are welcome to me," said the hermit, "for I know you better than ye think that I do: for ye are Sir Bedivere the Bold, and the full noble duke Sir Lucan the Butler was your brother."

Then Sir Bedivere told the hermit all as you have heard tofore, and so he stayed with the hermit that was beforehand Bishop of Canterbury. And there Sir Bedivere put upon him poor clothes, and served the hermit full lowly in fasting and in prayers.

Thus of Arthur I find no more written in books that been authorized, neither more of the very certainty of his death heard I nor read, but thus was he led away in a ship wherein were three queens; that one was King Arthur's sister, Queen Morgan le Fay, the other was the Queen of North Galis, and the third was the Queen of the Waste Lands.

Now more of the death of King Arthur could I never find, but that these ladies brought him to his grave, and such one was interred there which the hermit bare witness that was once Bishop of Canterbury. But yet the hermit knew not in certain that he was verily the body of King Arthur; for this tale Sir Bedivere, a knight of the Table Round, made it to be written.

Yet some men say in many parts of England that King Arthur is not dead, but carried by the will of our Lord Jesu into another place; and men say that he shall come again, and he shall win the Holy Cross. Yet I will not say that it shall be so, but rather I would say: here in this world he changed his life. And many men say that there is written upon the tomb this:

> HIC IACET ARTHURUS, REX
> QUONDAM, REXQUE FUTURUS[26]

---

26. **Hic . . . futurus:** Here lies Arthur, who was once king and king will be again.

◆ Build Vocabulary

interred (in turd') v.: Buried

Guide for Responding

◆ Literature and Your Life

Reader's Response If King Arthur had asked you to throw his sword into the water, would you have hesitated as Sir Bedivere did? Why or why not?

Thematic Focus Would you classify this tale as one of peril or one of adventure? Explain.

Epitaph for Arthur Write an epitaph, or tomb inscription, that captures King Arthur's magical life.

☑ Check Your Comprehension

1. What warning does King Arthur receive in his dream?

2. (a) How does Arthur slay Mordred? (b) What does Mordred do just before he dies?

3. Summarize what happens when Arthur asks Sir Bedivere to throw Excalibur into the water.

Guide for Responding (continued)

◆ Critical Thinking

INTERPRET

1. How are Arthur and Mordred similar and how are they different? **[Compare and Contrast]**
2. What do you think are Sir Bedivere's reasons for twice failing to obey Arthur's request to throw Excalibur into the water? **[Interpret]**
3. How does the ending add to the mysterious, magical quality of the tale? **[Draw Conclusions]**

APPLY

4. Why do you think the legend of King Arthur has retained its popularity for so long? **[Generalize]**

◆ Reading Strategy

SUMMARIZE

As your read *Sir Gawain and the Green Knight* and *Morte d'Arthur*, you **summarized** passages so you could identify key ideas and events in the stories. Use your summaries to answer these questions:
1. If you were retelling *Sir Gawain and the Green Knight* for an audience of fifth graders, which key events would you emphasize?
2. As Sir Bevidere, summarize for a curious traveler who is visiting your hermitage the events leading up to King Arthur's death.

◆ Literary Focus

MEDIEVAL ROMANCES

Most **medieval romances** embody the ideals of chivalry, are set in a remote time or place, and combine supernatural events with realistic ones. They also feature a hero engaged in pure adventure and feature spontaneous, unmotivated fighting and include love as a major part of the story.
1. Which of these characteristics *is not* displayed in this excerpt from *Sir Gawain and the Green Knight?*
2. Does Sir Gawain fit the mold of a medieval hero? Explain.
3. In the excerpt from *Morte d'Arthur*, how do the supernatural events surrounding Arthur's death link the story to the future?
4. King Arthur was supposedly a Briton who fought against the invading Anglo-Saxons. Why do you think Britons kept his memory alive for centuries after their defeat by the Anglo-Saxons?

◆ Build Vocabulary

USING THE WORD ROOT -*droit*-

The word root -*droit*-, which means "right," reveals a historical bias toward right-handedness.
1. Knowing that the prefix *mal* means "bad," what might *maladroit* mean?
2. *Gauche* means the opposite of "socially adroit." Which of these two might it also mean—"left" or "right"?

USING THE WORD BANK: Definitions

On your paper, write the letter of the word that best expresses the meaning of the first word.
1. assay: (a) test, (b) deny, (c) ignore
2. adjure: (a) reject, (b) appeal, (c) ask
3. feigned: (a) revealed, (b) refused, (c) pretended
4. largesse: (a) nobility, (b) insignificance, (c) wisdom
5. interred: (a) included, (b) uncovered, (c) buried
6. righteousness: (a) awkwardness, (b) virtuousness, (c) dishonorableness
7. entreated: (a) pleaded, (b) requested, (c) refused
8. peril: (a) safety, (b) security, (c) danger

◆ Grammar and Style

COMPARATIVE AND SUPERLATIVE FORMS

The world of medieval romances is a world of **comparatives** and **superlatives**. Supernatural wonders are the *most* marvelous ever seen, and one knight is always *braver* or *more* skillful than another.
Practice Identify the comparative and superlative forms of modifiers in the following passages.

	One Syllable	Two Syllables
Comparative Form:	-er	more
Superlative Form:	-est	most

1. She made trial of a man most faultless by far / Of all that ever walked over the wide earth; / As pearls to white peas, more precious and prized,
2. [W]here battle is joined; / I am the weakest, well I know, and of wit feeblest; And the loss of my life would be least of any;

Writing Application In a brief paragraph, use comparative and superlative modifiers to compare and contrast characters from either story.

Build Your Portfolio

 Idea Bank

Writing

1. T-shirt Write a message for a T-shirt featuring a legendary character. Include the name and a brief description of his or her accomplishments.

2. Résumé Create a résumé that highlights Sir Gawain's skills. Be creative, but arrange the information clearly: name and address on top, job objective, work history, education, and special skills and talents. **[Career Link]**

3. Response to Criticism One critic views Sir Gawain and the Green Knight as: "... a rare combination: at once a comedy—even a satire—of manners and a profoundly Christian view of man's character and his destiny." Write a short essay agreeing or disagreeing with this view.

Speaking, Listening, and Viewing

4. Oral Report Explore methods of combat in the medieval era. Prepare a brief oral report with illustrations and present it to your class. **[Social Studies Link]**

5. Multimedia Presentation Use clips from movies, illustrations, reproductions of fine art, and computer games to give a multimedia presentation on the Arthurian legend. **[Media Link; Social Studies Link]**

Researching and Representing

6. Musical Presentation Find a piece of instrumental music that matches the tone or mood of *Sir Gawain and the Green Knight.* Play a recording of the music in class. **[Music Link]**

7. Illuminated Manuscript Create one page of an illuminated manuscript for either *Sir Gawain and the Green Knight* or *Morte d'Arthur.* You may choose to depict a certain scene or the entire piece. **[Art Link]**

Online Activity www.phlit.phschool.com

 Guided Writing Lesson

Valedictory Speech

The final paragraphs of the excerpt from *Morte d'Arthur* sum up the facts of Arthur's death and hint at future events. A valedictory speech at a high-school graduation performs a similar function, summing up the high-school experience and suggesting what the future holds.

Write such a valedictory speech for your own graduation, and follow these hints for using repetition effectively.

Writing Skills Focus: Effective Repetition

Repeated words or phrases can make any piece of writing more memorable. Notice how Malory uses repetition to suggest the return of Arthur:

Model From Literature

Yet some men say in many parts of England that King Arthur is not dead, . . . and *men say* that he shall come again, and he shall win the Holy Cross. . . .

Use the following strategies to guide you as you write.

Prewriting Outline your speech. Then scan your outline for a memorable word or group of words that sums up your whole message. Underline these words so you can refer to them as you write.

Drafting Using your outline, write a rough draft of your speech. Try repeating the word or words you underlined at varying intervals. Also, be sure to use your "refrain" in the final part of your speech.

Revising Read your speech aloud, emphasizing the repeated phrase. If you are overusing the word or words, eliminate some examples of repetition. If the words sound insincere, replace them with a phrase that sounds better.

Guide for Interpreting

Margaret Paston (1423–1484)

Brokering deals . . . defending the manor . . . fighting lawsuits . . . hiring staff . . . This description would fit today's top executives, but it could also apply to Margaret Paston, a woman who lived in fifteenth-century England. Margaret Paston, born a Mautby, married John Paston, the son of a well-to-do landowner educated in the law. Because of John Paston's profession, he was frequently called to London on business, leaving Margaret to run the estates, settle rent disputes, and defend their manors against takeovers—which she did admirably.

The Legacy of the Pastons The letters of the Paston family deal with everyday matters. They also deal with scandals, like one daughter's secret marriage to the family's bailiff and the other daughter's marriage to the son of her father's rival.

Sometimes these letters seem like a script for a medieval soap opera.

Numbering in the hundreds, they provide us with a glimpse into life as it really was in the fifteenth century.

Folk Ballads

Long before most people in Britain could read or write, they were familiar with the stories told in ballads. A ballad is a narrative poem meant to be sung.

Much like country western songs of today, these ballads tell stories about characters who face challenges in life and love. Some ballads are very gruesome, however, and show the dark side of love and life.

The Ballad's Origins No one knows when the first folk ballads appeared in England, but it was probably during the twelfth century. Because the ballads were unwritten, they were passed along orally for many centuries. The earliest written ballads we know date from about the fifteenth century, but no one can absolutely identify the original versions of many of them.

In 1765, ballad enthusiast Bishop Thomas Percy published *Reliques of Ancient English Poetry*, an extensive collection of ballads. People began to appreciate the ballads for their literary value as well as for their fascinating glimpses into history. Percy's collection of ballads was based on an old manuscript he rescued from a housemaid who was about to light a fire with it.

◆ Background for Understanding

HISTORY: POLITICAL UNCERTAINTY

The Hundred Years' War had just come to an end, with the English military suffering defeat. King Henry VI's inability and later senility caused the government to lapse into chaos. In the midst of this upheaval and uncertainty, many families were able to struggle out of poverty by seizing properties to which they had no legal claim.

The Paston family had recently emerged from the upper class of the peasantry and were eager to increase their landholdings and rise in society. Holding onto their estates was not easy: The Pastons were sued, threatened, and bullied over the years by those who wanted to profit from their holdings.

CULTURE: PERILS OF EVERYDAY LIFE

Life was half over by the age of eighteen for most people who lived during the Middle Ages. Living in an uncertain world, where death before the age of thirty-five was the norm, prompted an unsentimental, cynical outlook on life. This view of life was expressed in folk ballads that tell about everyday people and their adventures, loves, jealousies, and disasters.

Throughout the centuries, these ballads changed as the times and language changed. Luckily for us, some of these early ballads have survived the remaining centuries and still give pleasure and entertainment today.

The Letters of Margaret Paston
◆ Four Ballads ◆

◆ *Literature and Your Life*

CONNECT YOUR EXPERIENCE

Certain television shows and soap operas hook viewers into eagerly awaiting each episode because they depict the adventure and romance of everyday life.

This appeal of the drama of everyday life is not new. Margaret Paston's letters, written long ago, reveal incredible but true happenings at the Paston manors. Also, folk ballads that are centuries old contain riveting stories of doomed lovers and twisted fates.

Journal Writing Write about the qualities that make a popular song a classic.

THEMATIC FOCUS: PERILS AND ADVENTURES

As you read the following letters and ballads, ask yourself: What were the perils and challenges of medieval life?

◆ Literary Focus

LETTER; FOLK BALLAD

A **letter** is a form of communication that usually contains a date, greeting, body, and closing. Letters range from short news-bearing notes to action-packed narratives.

As you read Margaret Paston's letters, note what they reveal about medieval life.

A **folk ballad** is a narrative poem by an unknown author, which is meant to be sung. Most ballads have four-line stanzas, in which the second and fourth lines rhyme. Many have regularly repeated lines, called a refrain, and contain elements such as dialogue and repetition.

These ballads, from the rugged area near the Scottish-English border, are cynical or darkly humorous.

◆ Grammar and Style

DIRECT ADDRESS

The folk ballads that follow use **direct address,** which is the name, title, or descriptive phrase used when speaking directly to someone or something. For example: "Oh where ha'e ye been, *Lord Randall my son?*"

The person being addressed is Lord Randall. The words "my son" indicate that Lord Randall's mother is addressing him.

◆ Reading Strategy

UNDERSTAND DIALECT

A **dialect** is the form of a language spoken by people in a particular region or group. The ballads that follow are in Scottish-English dialect.

To understand the dialect, follow these strategies:

1. Read the lines aloud. The word sounds and context may lead you to the corresponding current English word. Look at this example:

   The wind *sae cauld* blew.

   The sound of *sae cauld* and the fact that these words describe the wind lead you to recognize their meaning as "so cold."

2. Use the footnotes to get definitions of words no longer in use. For example, you'll see that "twa corbies" are two ravens.

◆ Build Vocabulary

LATIN ROOTS: -cert-

Margaret Paston uses the phrase, "certify to him the names of. . . ." The root of *certify, -cert-,* comes from the Latin *certus,* which means "sure." *Certify* means "to make sure," or "to verify."

WORD BANK

Before you read, preview this list of words.

aldermen
enquiry
succor
certify
remnant
ransacked
asunder
assault

LETTERS OF
Margaret Paston

Margaret Paston

❧

Hellesdon, one of the Paston manors, was coveted by the Duke of Suffolk. The duke bribed the mayor of Norwich, which lies southeast of London, to assist him in launching a campaign of terror to force the Pastons to surrender their property. Although Margaret Paston, along with a garrison of sixty, successfully repelled the first attacks, Hellesdon eventually was seized and plundered by the duke. In this letter Margaret writes to her husband in London with the news.

⚜

Margaret Paston to John Paston
17 October 1465
Norwich

. . . The Duke came to Norwich on Tuesday at 10 o'clock with some 500 men. And he sent for the mayor and <u>aldermen</u> with the Sheriffs, desiring them in the King's name that they should make <u>enquiry</u> of the constables of every ward in the City as to what men had gone to help or <u>succor</u> your men at any time during these gatherings and, if they could find any, that they should take and arrest and correct them, and <u>certify</u> to him the names by 8 o'clock on Wednesday. Which the Mayor did and will do anything that he may for him and his men . . .

I am told that the old Lady [the Dowager Duchess] and the Duke are fiercely set against us on the information of Harleston, the bailiff of Costessey . . . and such other false shrews which would have this matter carried through for their own pleasure . . . And as for Sir John Heveningham, Sir John Wingfield and other worshipful men, they are but made their dogge-bolds [lackeys], which I suppose will cause their disworship hereafter. I spoke with Sir John Heveningham and informed him of the truth of the matter and of all our demeaning at Drayton, and he said he would that all things were well, and that he would inform my Lord what I told him, but that Harleston had all the influence with the Duke here, and at this time he was advised by him and Dr. Aleyn.

The lodge and the <u>remnant</u> of your place was beaten down on Tuesday and Wednesday and the Duke rode on Wednesday to Drayton and so forth to Costessey while the lodge at Hellesdon was being beaten down. And this night at midnight Thomas Slyforth . . . and others had a cart and fetched away featherbeds and all our stuff that was left at the parson's and Thomas Waters' house to be kept . . . I pray you send me word how I shall act—whether you wish that I abide at Caister or come to you at London . . .

◆ Build Vocabulary

aldermen (ôl´ dər mən) *n.*: Chief officers in a shire, or district

enquiry (en kwīr´ ē) *n.*: Question

succor (suk´ ər) *v.*: Help; aid; relieve

certify (sʉrt´ ə fī´) *v.*: Declare a thing true or accurate; verify; attest

remnant (rem´ nənt) *n.*: What is left over; remainder; residue

ransacked (ran´ sakt´) *v.*: Searched through for plunder; pillaged; robbed

asunder (ə sun´ dər) *adv.*: Into parts or pieces

Margaret Paston to John Paston
27 October 1465
Norwich

. . . Please you to know that I was at Hellesdon on Thursday last and saw the place there, and, in good faith, nobody would believe how foul and horrible it appears unless they saw it. There come many people daily to wonder at it, both from Norwich and many other places, and they speak of it with shame. The Duke would have been a £1000 better off if it had not happened, and you have the more good will of the people because it was so foully done. They made your tenants of Hellesdon and Drayton, with others, break down the walls of both the place and the lodge—God knows full much against their wills, but they dare not refuse for fear. I have spoken with your tenants of Hellesdon and Drayton and comforted them as well as I can. The Duke's men <u>ransacked</u> the church and bore away all the goods that were left there, both of ours and of the tenants, and even stood upon the high altar and ransacked the images and took away those that they could find, and put the parson out of the church till they had done, and ransacked every man's house in the town five or six times . . . As for lead, brass, pewter, iron, doors, gates and other stuff of the house, men from Costessey and Cawston have it, and what they might not carry away they have hewn <u>asunder</u> in the most spiteful manner . . .

At the reverence of god, if any worshipful and profitable settlement may be made in your matters, do not forsake it, to avoid our trouble and great costs and charges that we may have and that may grow hereafter . . .

◆ Literary Focus
How does the detail about the "high altar" show the desperation of the situation?

▼ **Critical Viewing** The Pastons' manors were often attacked by their enemies. Using clues from this photograph, what would have made this manor worth fighting over? **[Speculate]**

The following letter was sent to Sir John Paston, Margaret's knighted son. Caister, with many manors and estates, had been willed to the Paston family by Sir John Fastolf, for whom John Paston worked as financial adviser. There followed years of legal wrangles during which the Pastons faced numerous challenges to *the will. John Paston having died the year before, Margaret turned to her son Sir John for help defending Caister. Sir John sent his younger brother, also named John, to protect the castle. John failed, however, surrendering the castle after his protector, King Edward IV, was captured during the Wars of the Roses.*

Margaret Paston to Sir John Paston
11 July 1467
Norwich

. . . Also this day was brought me word from Caister that Rising of Fritton had heard in divers places in Suffolk that Fastolf of Cowhawe gathers all the strength he may and intends to <u>assault</u> Caister and to enter there if he may, insomuch that it is said that he has five score men ready and daily sends spies to know what men guard the place. By whose power or favour or support he will do this I know not, but you know well that I have been afraid there before this time, when I had other comfort than I had now: I cannot guide nor rule soldiers well and they set not by [do not respect] a woman as they should by a man. Therefore I would that you should send home your brothers or else Daubeney to take control and to bring in such men as are necessary

> ◆ *Literature and Your Life*
>
> Of what fictional tales does this true-life adventure remind you?

for the safeguard of the place . . . And I have been about my livelode to set a rule therein, as I have written to you, which is not yet all performed after my desire, and I would not go to Caister till I had done. I do not want to spend more days near thereabouts, if I can avoid it; so make sure that you send someone home to keep the place and when I have finished what I have begun I shall arrange to go there if it will do any good—otherwise I had rather not be there . . .

. . . I marvel greatly that you send me no word how you do, for your enemies begin to grow right bold and that puts your friends in fear and doubt. Therefore arrange that they may have some comfort, so that they be not discouraged, for if we lose our friends, it will be hard in this troublous world to get them again . . .

◆ **Build Vocabulary**
assault (ə sôlt´) *v.*: Violently attack

Beyond Literature

Cultural Connection

Land Rights Margaret Paston's letters provide insights into daily life in medieval England. One disturbing aspect of medieval life that she documents is the continual feudal warfare over land and power. Laws governing land ownership in England in the 1500's involved complex feudal rights and obligations. Feudal lords battled to acquire and retain control of property. Meanwhile, peasants, who comprised the majority of the populations, could work and live on the land but not own it.

Battles for land are as old as civilization. In North America, land grabbing occurred with disastrous effects. For thousands of years, Native Americans had lived in the plains and woodlands of North America. The people lived in harmony with nature, forming a strong connection with plants, animals, and the land. Then, in the 1600's, European settlers arrived and claimed the lands for themselves. In the process of taking and settling the land, they nearly destroyed Native American culture.

Activity Discuss the common elements in medieval England and colonial America that might have led to battles over land.

Guide for Responding

◆ Literature and Your Life

Reader's Response Would you have liked Margaret Paston? Why or why not?

Thematic Focus Do families still have to fight for their property as the Pastons did? Explain.

Continuation of the Adventure As Margaret Paston, write a letter to your husband requesting his aid in still another difficulty.

☑ Check Your Comprehension

1. What does the Duke want?
2. At the end of the second letter, what does Margaret urge John to do?
3. Who is planning to attack Caister? To whom does Margaret appeal for help?

◆ Critical Thinking

INTERPRET
1. Margaret Paston says, "The lodge and the remnant of your place was beaten down." Why do you think she refers to the lodge as John Paston's place and not *our* place? **[Infer]**
2. What attitude does Margaret Paston have toward the tenants of the Paston's lands? Explain. **[Analyze]**
3. What do these letters reveal about Margaret Paston? **[Draw Conclusions]**

APPLY
4. What do these letters suggest about the ease or difficulty of the landowner's life in the fifteenth century? **[Generalize]**

EXTEND
5. What modern careers might suit the abilities of a woman like Margaret Paston? Explain your response. **[Career Link]**

Lord Randall

"O where hae ye been, Lord Randall, my son?
O where hae ye been, my handsome young man?"
"I hae been to the wild wood; mother, make my bed soon,
For I'm weary wi' hunting, and fain[1] wald[2] lie down."

5   "Where gat ye your dinner, Lord Randall, my son?
Where gat ye your dinner, my handsome young man?"
"I dined wi' my true-love; mother, make my bed soon,
For I'm weary wi' hunting, and fain wald lie down."

"What gat ye to your dinner, Lord Randall, my son?
10   What gat ye to your dinner, my handsome young man?"
"I gat eels boil'd in broo;[3] mother, make my bed soon,
For I'm weary wi' hunting, and fain wald lie down."

---

1. **fain:** Gladly.
2. **wald:** Would.
3. **broo:** Broth.

Noble Hunting With a Falcon in May

◄ Critical Viewing Lord Randall tells his mother that he's tired from hunting. What does this painting reveal about the sport? **[Infer]**

"What became of your bloodhounds, Lord Randall, my son?
What became of your bloodhounds, my handsome young man?"
15 "O they swell'd and they died; mother, make my bed soon,
For I'm weary wi' hunting, and fain wald lie down."

"O I fear ye are poison'd, Lord Randall, my son!
O I fear ye are poison'd, my handsome young man!"
"O yes! I am poison'd; mother, make my bed soon,
20 For I'm sick at the heart, and I fain wald lie down."

Guide for Responding

◆ Literature and Your Life

Reader's Response Do you think that Lord Randall deserves his fate? Explain.

Thematic Focus In what way is falling in love perilous for Lord Randall?

Bill of Indictment Suppose Lord Randall's "true love" is arrested for her crime. Draw up the indictment by giving her name, address, and a brief description of the crime for which she is being charged.

☑ Check Your Comprehension

1. Who are the two speakers in the ballad?
2. What does Lord Randall say he wants to do?
3. What happens to Lord Randall?

◆ Critical Thinking

INTERPRET

1. What two clues in stanzas three and four foreshadow Lord Randall's fate? **[Infer]**
2. What two meanings can you derive from line 20? **[Infer]**
3. In the poem's fifth stanza, the wording of the repeated line, or refrain, varies. What emotional impact does this have on the reader? **[Interpret]**
4. What underlying message about love is implied in this ballad? Give details from the text to support your answer. **[Draw Conclusions]**

APPLY

5. To make this ballad into a modern rock song, what elements would you change? **[Modify]**

Get Up and Bar the Door

▶ **Critical Viewing** What does this painting tell you about domestic life in medieval times? **[Infer]**

It fell about the Martinmas time,[1]
    And a gay time it was then,
When our goodwife got puddings to make,
    She's boild them in the pan.

5   The wind sae cauld blew south and north,
    And blew into the floor;
Quoth our goodman to our goodwife,
    "Gae out and bar the door."

"My hand is in my hussyfskap,[2]
10   Goodman, as ye may see;
An it should nae be barrd this hundred year,
    It's no be barrd for me."[3]

They made a paction[4] tween them twa,
    They made it firm and sure,
15 That the first word whaeer shoud speak,
    Shoud rise and bar the door.

Then by there came two gentlemen,
    At twelve o'clock at night,
And they could neither see house nor hall,
20   Nor coal nor candlelight.

"Now whether is this a rich man's house,
    Or whether it is a poor?"
But neer a word wad ane o' them[5] speak,
    For barring of the door.

1. **Martinmas time:** November 11.

2. **hussyfskap:** Household duties.

3. **"An it should . . . me":** If it has to be barred by me, then it will not be barred in a hundred years.
4. **paction:** Agreement.

5. **them:** The man and his wife.

25 And first they[6] ate the white puddings,
    And then they ate the black:
    Tho muckle[7] thought the goodwife to hersel,
        Yet neer a word she spake.

    Then said the one unto the other,
30   "Here, man, take ye my knife;
    Do ye tak aff the auld man's beard,
        And I'll kiss the goodwife."

    "But there's nae water in the house,
        And what shall we do than?"
35   "What ails ye at the pudding broo,[8]
        That boils into[9] the pan?"

    O up then started our goodman,
        An angry man was he:
    "Will ye kiss my wife before my een,
40   And scad[10] me wi pudding bree?"[11]

    Then up and started our goodwife,
        Gied three skips on the floor:
    "Goodman, you've spoken the foremost word;
        Get up and bar the door."

6. **they:** The strangers.

7. **muckle:** Much.

8. **"What . . . broo":** What's the matter with pudding water?
9. **into:** In.

10. **scad:** Scald.
11. **bree:** Broth.

Guide for Responding

◆ Literature and Your Life

Reader's Response Whom do you like better—the goodman or the goodwife? Explain.

Thematic Focus This ballad tells of an ordinary adventure that takes place in the home of a bickering couple. What elements of this adventure could happen today?

Advice Column Acting as an advice columnist, help the goodman and goodwife communicate better. Use your own experience and knowledge to guide your advice.

☑ **Check Your Comprehension**

1. What does the goodman want the goodwife to do? What's the goodwife's reply?
2. How do the goodman and goodwife resolve their problem?
3. Who wins the battle of wills between goodman and goodwife? How?

◆ Critical Thinking

INTERPRET

1. Why does the goodman want the door barred? **[Analyze]**
2. In lines 25–29, the goodwife is thinking to herself. What might she be thinking? **[Infer]**
3. What does the stranger mean when he suggests taking "aff the auld man's beard"? **[Interpret]**
4. What serious point does this humorous ballad make? **[Interpret]**

EVALUATE

5. Which of the two characters in "Get Up and Bar the Door" is more foolish? Why? **[Make a Judgment]**

APPLY

6. Can people be hurt by stubbornness—their own or someone else's? Explain. **[Generalize]**

The Twa Corbies[1]

As I was walking all alane,
I heard twa corbies making a mane.[2]
The tane unto the tither did say,
"Whar sall we gang and dine the day?"

5   "In behint yon auld fail dyke,[3]
I wot[4] there lies a new-slain knight;
And naebody kens[5] that he lies there
But his hawk, his hound, and his lady fair.

"His hound is to the hunting gane,
10 His hawk to fetch the wild-fowl hame,
His lady's ta'en anither mate,
So we may mak our dinner sweet.

"Ye'll sit on his white hause-bane,[6]
And I'll pike out his bonny blue e'en;[7]
15 Wi' ae lock o' his gowden hair
We'll theek[8] our nest when it grows bare.

"Mony a one for him maks mane,
But nane sall ken whar he is gane.
O'er his white banes, when they are bare,
20 The wind sall blaw for evermair."

1. **Twa Corbies:** Two ravens.
2. **mane:** Moan.

3. **fail dyke:** Bank of earth.
4. **wot:** Know.
5. **kens:** Knows.

6. **hause-bane:** Neck-bone.
7. **e'en:** Eyes.

8. **theek:** Thatch.

▲ **Critical Viewing** In what ways do these ravens resemble the ones in the poem? **[Compare and Contrast]**

Guide for Responding

◆ *Literature and Your Life*

Reader's Response Do you find "The Twa Corbies" amusing or sad? Explain.

Thematic Focus In what ways does this ballad draw a connection between romance and danger? Explain.

Changing Perspectives Briefly retell this ballad from the point of view of the hawk and the hound.

☑ Check Your Comprehension

1. Who are the "twa corbies"?
2. Where is the knight lying?
3. In what condition is the knight?
4. Who knows that the knight lies there?

◆ Critical Thinking

INTERPRET

1. How would you describe the ravens' attitude toward the knight? Cite examples to support your answer. **[Analyze]**
2. What effect would be lost if the incident were described by a human speaker rather than by ravens? **[Infer]**
3. What does the ballad ultimately say about loyalty and love? **[Draw Conclusions]**

EXTEND

4. The hawk, the hound, and the lady seem to be given equal status in this ballad. Why were the hawk and hound so important to a man of the fifteenth century? **[Social Studies Link]**

Barbara Allan

It was in and about the Martinmas time,[1]
    When the green leaves were a-fallin';
That Sir John Graeme in the West Country
    Fell in love with Barbara Allan.

5   He sent his man down through the town
    To the place where she was dwellin':
"O haste and come to my master dear,
    Gin[2] ye be Barbara Allan."

O slowly, slowly rase[3] she up,
10   To the place where he was lyin',
And when she drew the curtain by:
    "Young man, I think you're dyin'."

"O it's I'm sick, and very, very sick,
    And 'tis a' for Barbara Allan."
15   "O the better for me ye sal[4] never be,
    Though your heart's blood were a-spillin'.

"O dinna ye mind,[5] young man," said she,
    "When ye the cups were fillin',
That ye made the healths gae round and round,
20   And slighted Barbara Allan?"

He turned his face unto the wall,
    And death with him was dealin':
"Adieu, adieu, my dear friends all,
    And be kind of Barbara Allan."

25   And slowly, slowly rase she up,
    And slowly, slowly left him;
And sighing said she could not stay,
    Since death of life had reft[6] him.

She had not gane a mile but twa,[7]
30   When she heard the dead-bell knellin',
And every jow[8] that the dead-bell ga'ed[9]
    It cried, "Woe to Barbara Allan!"

"O mother, mother, make my bed,
    O make it soft and narrow:
35 Since my love died for me today,
    I'll die for him tomorrow."

1. **Martinmas time:** November 11.

2. **Gin:** If.

3. **rase:** Rose.

4. **sal:** Shall.

5. **dinna ye mind:** Don't you remember.

6. **reft:** Deprived.

7. **not . . . twa:** Gone but two miles.

8. **jow:** Stroke.
9. **ga'ed:** Made.

Veronica Veronese, Dante Gabriel Rossetti, Delaware Art Museum

◀ **Critical Viewing** How does the artist's choice of color and the posture of the subject suit the description of the fictional Barbara Allan? **[Interpret]**

Guide for Responding

◆ Literature and Your Life

Reader's Response Which character—Sir John or Barbara Allan—do you find more sympathetic? Why?

Thematic Focus This ballad, like many others of its kind, makes a connection between love and death. Why do you think this theme is so predominant in literature and songs of the Middle Ages?

Extra Stanza Add a stanza at any point in this ballad giving more information about the characters, how they met, or the nature of Sir John's illness.

☑ Check Your Comprehension

1. Why does Sir John Graeme send his man to Barbara Allan?
2. What reason does Barbara Allan give for seeming unconcerned about his illness?
3. What does Barbara Allan do after Sir John dies?

◆ Critical Thinking

INTERPRET
1. Why is Sir John sick? **[Infer]**
2. Lines 25 and 26 describe Barbara Allan's reaction to the death of Sir John. What do those lines reveal about her emotional state? **[Analyze]**
3. When Barbara Allan asks her mother to "make my bed . . . soft and narrow" in lines 33 and 34, what kind of "bed" does she mean? **[Infer]**
4. What overall message about love and death is conveyed by "Barbara Allan"? **[Draw Conclusions]**

EVALUATE
5. Do the characters in "Barbara Allan" seem believable or romanticized? Give details from the text to support your ideas. **[Criticize]**

COMPARE LITERARY WORKS
6. In each poem, identify the central misunderstanding between the man and woman involved. Then characterize each conflict as either tragic or humorous. **[Distinguish]**

Guide for Responding (continued)

◆ Literary Focus

LETTER

The **letters** of Margaret Paston—personal messages to her husband and son—show her to be capable and observant.

1. Find a passage that shows Margaret in the role of an information gatherer and reporter, and explain your choice.
2. (a) In what passage does Margaret indicate her limitations as a battle-chief? (b) What does this passage suggest about the role of women in medieval times?

FOLK BALLAD

The **folk ballad** "Barbara Allan" contains many elements typical of ballads. Notice the use of the four-line stanza called a quatrain, the rhyme in the second and fourth lines, the repetition of the word *slowly*, and the use of dialogue in the last line:

O slowly, slowly rase she up,
　　To the place where he was lyin',
And when she drew the curtain by:
　　"Young man, I think you're dyin'."

1. Find examples of these elements in a stanza from one of the other ballads: quatrain, rhyme, repetition, and dialogue.
2. Choose one of the ballads and explain how repetition, refrain, and dialogue make it dramatic.
3. Choose one of these ballads and explain how it reflects the harsher elements of medieval times.

◆ Reading Strategy

UNDERSTAND DIALECT

The **dialect** in these ballads—specialized language of the English-Scots region—made use of variances in word pronunciations and vocabulary.

1. Give the modern English words whose pronunciation is similar to the italicized words:
　a. And *naebody* kens that he lies there ...
　b. But neer a word *wad ane* o' them speak, ...
　c. O where *ha'e* ye been, ...
2. Give three words from the ballads that are particular to the dialect of the time and place.

◆ Build Vocabulary

USING THE LATIN ROOT -cert-

Knowing that the root *-cert-* means "sure," choose the best definition for each word.

1. ascertain: (a) question, (b) sort through, (c) make certain
2. certificate: (a) written proof of qualifications, (b) form showing receipt of goods, (c) application form for a diploma
3. certitude: (a) vagueness, (b) sureness, (c) righteousness

USING THE WORD BANK: Definitions

Match each vocabulary word with its definition.

1. aldermen   **a.** looted
2. enquiry   **b.** attack
3. succor   **c.** officials
4. remnant   **d.** remainder
5. ransacked   **e.** to pieces
6. asunder   **f.** assist
7. assault   **g.** question

◆ Grammar and Style

DIRECT ADDRESS

Terms of **direct address** indicate to whom (or sometimes to what) the speaker or writer is talking. In writing, terms of direct address are set off by commas.

Practice In your notebook, identify each instance of direct address:

1. Here, man, take ye my knife; ...
2. O dinna ye mind, young man, said she, ...
3. O mother, mother, make my bed, ...

Writing Application In your notebook, rewrite the following as dialogue. Use at least three examples of direct address.

Clara called to her raven named Beak to come back home. Beak replied to Clara that his bones were old and cold and that it was time to leave her. Clara ran to her dear mother, crying that Beak was lost and hurt and gone for good. Clara's mother told her that Beak knew best and that when she got older, she'd begin to understand.

Build Your Portfolio

 Idea Bank

Writing

1. **Casting Call** Reread the letters of Margaret Paston, taking notes about Margaret's personality. Then cast an actress to play her life story. Give reasons for your choice. **[Performing Arts Link]**

2. **A Modern Ballad** Write a ballad about an everyday person, using language that reflects how he or she really speaks. **[Performing Arts Link]**

3. **Critical Response** Critic John Fenn writes of the Paston letters: "the distress of private life . . . will present a truer picture of that turbulent period than could be exhibited by the artful pen of a sedate historian." Support or disagree with this opinion in a brief essay.

Speaking, Listening, and Viewing

4. **Letter vs. Phone Call** Margaret Paston had no phone, fax, or e-mail system to send messages to her husband. With a classmate, improvise a phone conversation between Margaret and John. **[Social Studies Link; Performing Arts Link]**

5. **Song Translation** Choose one of the ballads in this series to translate into modern English. Perform your translation for the class.

Researching and Representing

6. **Holidays Chart** Research the origins of medieval holidays and festivals such as Martinmas. Make a poster listing each holiday or festival and describing its origins. **[Social Studies Link; Art Link]**

7. **An English Manor** With a small group, research fifteenth-century manors like those of the Pastons, and create a scale model of one that is typical of the period. **[Social Studies Link; Art Link]**

Online Activity www.phlit.phschool.com

 Guided Writing Lesson

Persuasive Letter

When Margaret Paston urges her husband to settle a dispute or her son to defend their property, she gives reasons to support her points. Write a persuasive letter in which you convince someone to do something. Like Margaret Paston, use elaboration to support your argument.

Writing Skills Focus: Elaboration to Support an Argument

When writing persuasively, support your argument with examples, anecdotes, statistics, or causes and effects. Notice, for example, how Margaret Paston uses causes and effects to show what will happen if the Pastons do not respond to their enemies' boldness:

Model From Literature

Your enemies begin to grow right bold and that puts your friends in fear and doubt. . . . [F]or if we lose our friends, it will be hard in this troublous world to get them again . . .

Prewriting Decide what you want the recipient of your persuasive letter to think or do. Write a statement expressing your desired outcome. Then list the points or reasons that will convince him or her to agree with you or do what you suggest. Make notes elaborating on each point, with the details you will use to support or explain it.

Drafting Use a standard letter format and write the heading, greeting, body, and closing of your letter. Refer to your prewriting notes as you develop your argument in the body of the letter.

Revising Evaluate the elaboration that you've used to support your arguments. If an argument seems to be weak, consider replacing one type of elaboration with another to strengthen your point. Proofread the heading of the letter carefully.

CONNECTIONS TO WORLD LITERATURE

from The Nibelungenlied: How Siegfried Was Slain
Translated by A. T. Hatto

Thematic Connection

THE THEME OF PERILS AND ADVENTURES

Medieval literature might remind you of a television adventure series: Deception and betrayal, power and triumph make for exciting stories—whether written hundreds of years ago or today. From Malory's King Arthur, who combated enemies while seeking to create a better world, to Margaret Paston, who battled real-life thugs to save the manors belonging to her family, perils and adventures seem to be part of medieval life.

Perils and adventures also occurred throughout medieval Europe. The literature of the period highlights the adventures of several warrior heroes: Spain's El Cid, a tremendous warrior, was exiled by King Alfonso VI because other nobles were jealous of his victories; France's Roland, from *The Song of Roland*, was based on an actual warrior who was ambushed by Basques while serving with Charlemagne; and Germany's Siegfried was a brave warrior who risked life and limb to please his king and claim a wife.

THE NIBELUNGENLIED

The epic poem *The Nibelungenlied* is one of the great works of German literature. Composed more than eight hundred years ago by an unknown author, its themes of betrayal, forgiveness, and salvation still ring true.

The Nibelungenlied tells the tale of Kriemhild and Siegfried, a doomed couple who suffer betrayal at the hands of their family. Siegfried falls in love with Kriemhild, a Burgundian princess, when he hears of her great beauty. In order to marry her, he must first help her brother, King Gunther, win the hand of Brunhild, a maiden warrior.

In the course of winning Brunhild's hand for the king, Siegfried steals Brunhild's belt and ring. His mission accomplished, Siegfried marries Kriemhild and suffers the wrath of the jealous Brunhild. When Brunhild accuses Kriemhild of acting like a powerful queen, Kriemhild shows her the tokens that suggest her dishonor. When Brunhild vows revenge, her loyal servant Hagen plots with King Gunther to murder Siegfried. Kriemhild foolishly reveals that Siegfried's vulnerable spot is between his shoulders.

from *The* Nibelungenlied: How Siegfried *Was* Slain

TRANSLATED BY A. T. HATTO

The fearless warriors Gunther and Hagen treacherously proclaimed a hunt in the forest where they wished to chase the boar, the bear, and the bison—and what could be more daring? Siegfried rode with their party in magnificent style. They took all manner of food with them; and it was while drinking from a cool stream that the hero was to lose his life at the instigation of Brunhild, King Gunther's queen.

Bold Siegfried went to Kriemhild while his and his companions' hunting-gear was being loaded onto the sumpters in readiness to cross the Rhine,[1] and she could not have been more afflicted. "God grant that I may see you well again, my lady," he said, kissing his dear wife, "and that your eyes may see me too. Pass the time pleasantly with your relations who are so kind to you, since I cannot stay with you at home."

Kriemhild thought of what she had told Hagen, but she dared not mention it and began to lament that she had ever been born. "I dreamt last night—and an ill-omened dream it was—"

said lord Siegfried's noble queen, weeping with unrestrained passion, "that two boars chased you over the heath and the flowers were dyed with blood! How can I help weeping so? I stand in great dread of some attempt against your life.—What if we have offended any men who have the power to vent their malice on us? Stay away, my lord, I urge you."

"I shall return in a few days time, my darling. I know of no people here who bear me any hatred. Your kinsmen without exception wish me well, nor have I deserved otherwise of them."

"It is not so, lord Siegfried. I fear you will come to grief. Last night I had a sinister dream of how two mountains fell upon you and hid you from my sight! I shall suffer cruelly if you go away and leave me." But he clasped the noble woman in his arms and after kissing and caressing her fair person very tenderly, took his leave and went forthwith. Alas, she was never to see him alive again.

They rode away deep into the forest in pursuit of their sport. Gunther and his men were accompanied by numbers of brave knights, but Gernot and Giselher stayed at home. Ahead of the hunt many horses had crossed the Rhine laden with their bread, wine, meat, fish, and

---

1. **sumpters . . . Rhine:** Sumpters are pack horses, and the Rhine River flows from eastern Switzerland north through Germany, then west through the Netherlands into the North Sea.

King Konrad "the Younger" of Germany, Hunting With Falcons

▲ **Critical Viewing** Like Siegfried, Gunther, and his men, the hunters in this picture seem to enjoy the sport as a group activity. What practical reason may they have had for hunting in a group? [Infer]

various other provisions such as a King of Gunther's wealth is bound to have with him.

The proud and intrepid hunters were told to set up their lodges on a spacious isle in the river on which they were to hunt, at the skirt of the greenwood over toward the spot where the game would have to break cover. Siegfried, too, had arrived there, and this was reported to the King. Thereupon the sportsmen everywhere manned their relays.[2]

"Who is going to guide us through the forest to our quarry, brave warriors?" asked mighty Siegfried.

"Shall we split up before we start hunting here?" asked Hagen. "Then my lords and I

could tell who are the best hunters on this foray into the woods. Let us share the huntsmen and hounds between us and each take the direction he likes—and then all honor to him that hunts best!" At this, the hunters quickly dispersed.

"I do not need any hounds," said lord Siegfried, "except for one tracker so well fleshed that he recognizes the tracks which the game leave through the wood: then we shall not fail to find our quarry."

An old huntsman took a good sleuth-hound and quickly led the lord to where there was game in abundance. The party chased everything that was roused from its lair, as good hunting-men still do today. Bold Siegfried of the Netherlands killed every beast that his hound started, for his hunter was so swift that nothing could elude him. Thus, versatile as he was, Siegfried outshone all the others in that hunt.

The very first kill was when he brought down a strong young tusker,[3] after which he soon chanced on an enormous lion. When his hound had roused it he laid a keen arrow to his bow and shot it so that it dropped in its tracks at the third bound. Siegfried's fellow-huntsmen acclaimed him for this shot. Next, in swift succession, he killed a wisent, an elk, four mighty aurochs,[4] and a fierce and monstrous buck—so well mounted was he that nothing, be it hart or hind, could evade him. His hound then came upon a great boar, and, as this turned to flee, the champion hunter at once blocked his path, bringing him to bay; and when in a trice the beast sprang at the hero in a fury, Siegfried slew him with his sword, a feat no other hunter could have performed with such ease. After the felling of this boar, the tracker was returned to his leash and Siegfried's splendid bag was made known to the Burgundians.

"If it is not asking too much, lord Siegfried," said his companions of the chase, "do leave some of the game alive for us. You are emptying the hills and woods for us today." At this the brave knight had to smile.

---

2. **relays:** Fresh horses to relieve tired ones.

3. **tusker** (tusk´ ər): Wild boar.
4. **wisent** (vē´ zant) . . . **aurochs** (ô´ räks´): European bison and wild oxen.

There now arose a great shouting of men and clamor of hounds on all sides, and the tumult grew so great that the hills and the forest re-echoed with it—the huntsmen had unleashed no fewer than four and twenty packs! Thus, many beasts had to lose their lives there, since each of these hunters was hoping to bring it about that *he* should be given the high honors of the chase. But when mighty Siegfried appeared beside the campfire there was no chance of that.

The hunt was over, yet not entirely so. Those who wished to go to the fire brought the hides of innumerable beasts, and game in plenty—what loads of it they carried back to the kitchen to the royal retainers! And now the noble King had it announced to those fine hunters that he wished to take his repast, and there was one great blast of the horn to tell them that he was back in camp.

At this, one of Siegfried's huntsmen said: "Sir, I have heard a horn-blast telling us to return to our lodges.—I shall answer it." There was much blowing to summon the companions.

"Let us quit the forest, too," said lord Siegfried. His mount carried him at an even pace, and the others hastened away with him but with the noise of their going they started a savage bear, a very fierce beast.

"I shall give our party some good entertainment," he said over his shoulder. "Loose the hound, for I can see a bear which will have to come back to our lodges with us. It will not be able to save itself unless it runs very fast." The hound was unleashed, and the bear made off at speed. Siegfried meant to ride it down but soon found that his way was blocked and his intention thwarted, while the mighty beast fancied it would escape from its pursuer. But the proud knight leapt from his horse and started to chase it on foot, and the animal, quite off its guard, failed to elude him. And so he quickly caught and bound it, without having wounded it at all—nor could the beast use either claws or teeth on the man. Siegfried tied it to his saddle, mounted his horse, and in his high-spirited fashion led it to the campfire in order to amuse the good knights.

And in what magnificent style Siegfried rode! He bore a great spear, stout of shaft and broad of head; his handsome sword reached down to his spurs; and the fine horn which this lord carried was of the reddest gold. Nor have I ever heard tell of a better hunting outfit: he wore a surcoat of costly black silk and a splendid hat of sable,[5] and you should have seen the gorgeous silken tassels on his quiver, which was covered in panther-skin for the sake of its fragrant odor![6] He also bore a bow so strong that apart from Siegfried any who wished to span it would have had to use a rack. His hunting suit was all of otter-skin, varied throughout its length with furs of other kinds from whose shining hair clasps of gold gleamed out on either side of this daring lord of the hunt. The handsome sword that he wore was Balmung, a weapon so keen and with such excellent edges that it never failed to bite when swung against a helmet. No wonder this splendid hunter was proud and gay. And (since I am bound to tell you all) know that his quiver was full of good arrows with gold mountings and heads a span[7] in width, so that any beast they pierced must inevitably soon die.

Thus the noble knight rode along, the very image of a hunting man. Gunther's attendants saw him coming and ran to meet him to take his horse—tied to whose saddle he led a mighty bear! On dismounting, he loosed the bonds from its muzzle and paws, whereupon all the hounds that saw it instantly gave tongue. The beast made for the forest and the people were seized with panic. Affrighted by the tumult, the bear strayed into the kitchen—and how the cooks scuttled from their fire at its approach! Many caldrons were sent flying and many fires were scattered, while heaps of good food lay among the ashes. Lords and retainers leapt from their seats, the bear

---

5. surcoat . . . sable (sa´ bəl): A surcoat is a loose, short cloak worn over armor, and sable is the costly fur of the marten.
6. panther-skin . . . odor: The odor of panther skin was supposed to lure other animals and therefore help with the hunt.
7. span: Nine inches.

became infuriated, and the King ordered all the hounds on their leashes to be loosed—and if all had ended well they would have had a jolly day! Bows and spears were no longer left idle, for the brave ones ran toward the bear, yet there were so many hounds in the way that none dared shoot. With the whole mountain thundering with people's cries the bear took to flight before the hounds and none could keep up with it but Siegfried, who ran it down and then dispatched it with his sword. The bear was later carried to the campfire, and all who had witnessed this feat declared that Siegfried was a very powerful man.

The proud companions were then summoned to table. There were a great many seated in that meadow. Piles of sumptuous dishes were set before the noble huntsmen, but the butlers who were to pour their wine were very slow to appear. Yet knights could not be better cared for than they and if only no treachery had been lurking in their minds those warriors would have been above reproach.

"Seeing that we are being treated to such a variety of dishes from the kitchen," said lord Siegfried, "I fail to understand why the butlers bring us no wine. Unless we hunters are better looked after, I'll not be a companion of the hunt. I thought I had deserved better attention."

"We shall be very glad to make amends to you for our present lack," answered the perfidious[8] King from his table. "This is Hagen's fault—he wants us to die of thirst."

"My very dear lord," replied Hagen of Troneck, "I thought the day's hunting would be away in the Spessart and so I sent the wine there. If we go without drink today I shall take good care that it does not happen again."

"Those fellows!" said lord Siegfried. "It was arranged that they were to bring along seven panniers of spiced wine and mead[9] for me. Since that proved impossible, we should have been placed nearer the Rhine."

---

8. **perfidious** (pər fid´ ē əs) adj.: Treacherous.
9. **panniers** (pan´ yərz) . . . **mead** (mēd): Panniers are baskets, and mead is an alcoholic liquor made of fermented honey and water.

"You brave and noble knights," said Hagen of Troneck, "I know a cool spring nearby—do not be offended!—let us go there."—A proposal which (as it turned out) was to bring many knights into jeopardy.

Siegfried was tormented by thirst and ordered the board to be removed all the sooner in his eagerness to go to that spring at the foot of the hills. And now the knights put their treacherous plot into execution.

Word was given for the game which Siegfried had killed to be conveyed back to Worms on wagons, and all who saw it gave him great credit for it.

Hagan of Troneck broke his faith with Siegfried most grievously, for as they were leaving to go to the spreading lime-tree he said: "I have often been told that no one can keep up with Lady Kriemhild's lord when he cares to show his speed. I wish he would show it us now."

"You can easily put it to the test by racing me to the brook," replied gallant Siegfried of the Netherlands. "Then those who see it shall declare the winner."

"I accept your challenge," said Hagen.

"Then I will lie down in the grass at your feet, as a handicap," replied brave Siegfried, much to Gunther's satisfaction. "And I will tell you what more I shall do. I will carry all my equipment with me, my spear and my shield and all my hunting clothes." And he quickly strapped on his quiver and sword. The two men took off their outer clothing and stood there in their white vests. Then they ran through the clover like a pair of wild panthers. Siegfried appeared first at the brook.

Gunther's magnificent guest who excelled so many men in all things quickly unstrapped his sword, took off his quiver, and after leaning his great spear against a branch of the lime, stood beside the rushing brook. Then he laid down his shield near the flowing water, and although he was very thirsty he most courteously refrained from drinking until the King had drunk. Gunther thanked him very ill for this.

The stream was cool, sweet, and clear. Gunther stooped to its running waters and after drinking stood up and stepped aside.

Siegfried in turn would have liked to do the same, but he paid for his good manners. For now Hagen carried Siegfried's sword and bow beyond his reach, ran back for the spear, and searched for the sign on the brave man's tunic. Then, as Siegfried bent over the brook and drank, Hagen hurled the spear at the cross, so that the hero's heart's blood leapt from the wound and splashed against Hagen's clothes. No warrior will ever do a darker deed. Leaving the spear fixed in Siegfried's heart, he fled in wild desperation, as he had never fled before from any man.

When lord Siegfried felt the great wound, maddened with rage he bounded back from the stream with the long shaft jutting from his heart. He was hoping to find either his bow or his sword, and, had he succeeded in doing so, Hagen would have had his pay. But finding no sword, the gravely wounded man had nothing but his shield. Snatching this from the bank he ran at Hagen, and King Gunther's vassal was unable to elude him. Siegfried was wounded to death, yet he struck so powerfully that he sent many precious stones whirling from the shield as it smashed to pieces. Gunther's noble guest would dearly have loved to avenge himself. Hagen fell reeling under the weight of the blow and the riverside echoed loudly. Had Siegfried had his sword in his hand it would have been the end of Hagen, so enraged was the wounded man, as indeed he had good cause to be.

The hero's face had lost its color and he was no longer able to stand. His strength had ebbed away, for in the field of his bright countenance he now displayed Death's token. Soon many fair ladies would be weeping for him.

The lady Kriemhild's lord fell among the flowers, where you could see the blood surg-

▲ **Critical Viewing** What aspects of the scene does the artist emphasize? What did he omit? What conclusion can you draw based on his choices? **[Draw Conclusions]**

ing from his wound. Then—and he had cause—he rebuked those who had plotted his foul murder. "You vile cowards," he said as he lay dying. "What good has my service done me now that you have slain me? I was always loyal to you, but now I have paid for it. Alas, you have wronged your kinsmen so that all who are born in days to come will be dishonored by your deed. You have cooled your anger on me beyond all measure. You will be held in contempt and stand apart from all good warriors."

The knights all ran to where he lay wounded to death. It was a sad day for many of them. Those who were at all loyal-hearted mourned for him, and this, as a gay and valiant knight, he had well deserved.

The King of Burgundy too lamented Siegfried's death.

"There is no need for the doer of the deed to weep when the damage is done," said the dying man. "He should be held up to scorn. It would have been better left undone."

"I do not know what you are grieving for," said Hagen fiercely. "All our cares and sorrows are over and done with. We shall not find many who will dare oppose us now. I am glad I have put an end to his supremacy."

"You may well exult," said Siegfried. "But had I known your murderous bent I should easily have guarded my life from you. I am sorry for none so much as my wife, the lady Kriemhild. May God have mercy on me for ever having got a son who in years to come will suffer the reproach that his kinsmen were murderers. If I had the strength I would have good reason to complain. But if you feel at all inclined to do a loyal deed for anyone, noble King," continued the mortally wounded man, "let me commend my dear sweetheart to your mercy. Let her profit from being your sister. By the virtue of all princes, stand by her loyally! No lady was ever more greatly wronged through her dear friend. As to my father and his vassals, they will have long to wait for me."

The flowers everywhere were drenched with blood. Siegfried was at grips with Death, yet not for long, since Death's sword ever was too sharp. And now the warrior who had been so brave and gay could speak no more.

When those lords saw that the hero was dead they laid him on a shield that shone red with gold, and they plotted ways and means of concealing the fact that Hagen had done the deed. "A disaster has befallen us," many of them said. "You must all hush it up and declare with one voice that Siegfried rode off hunting alone and was killed by robbers as he was passing through the forest."

"I shall take him home," said Hagen of Troneck. "It is all one to me if the woman who made Brunhild so unhappy should come to know of it. It will trouble me very little, however much she weeps."

Guide for Responding

◆ *Literature and Your Life*

Reader's Response How would you describe Siegfried?

Thematic Focus Which perils are brought on by Siegfried's character flaws?

Questions for Research Siegfried killed a wisent and four aurochs on his hunt. Do these unfamiliar animals still exist or are they extinct? Generate other questions about these animals for research.

☑ Check Your Comprehension

1. Why doesn't Kriemhild want Siegfried to go hunting?
2. Why does Siegfried become angry at dinner?
3. Why does Hagen challenge Siegfried to a race?

◆ Critical Thinking

INTERPRET

1. What might the two boars in Kriemhild's dream stand for? **[Interpret]**
2. What do you learn about Siegfried's character and judgment from the passage in which Siegfried chases and kills a bear? **[Connect]**
3. What causes Siegfried's downfall? **[Infer]**

APPLY

4. What message might this story send to people your age? **[Relate]**

EXTEND

5. Larger-than-life heroes, like Siegfried, are found throughout literature and across cultures. Name one with whom you're familiar and compare and contrast your choice with Siegfried. **[Literature Link]**

Thematic Connection

THE THEME OF PERILS AND ADVENTURES

During the Middle Ages, people faced upheavals and dangers from all sides. The struggles were many and varied: people against their neighbors, countries against invaders, king versus king. These struggles were very much a part of life and were explored in the songs and stories of the time. So, too, were more subtle but equally wrenching struggles, such as winning the love of another.

1. Whom do you find more courageous—Margaret Paston or Siegfried? Explain your choice.

2. In "How Siegfried Was Slain," love comes hand in hand with danger: Brunhild's love for Siegfried provokes her to instigate his murder; Siegfried, in turn, is too blinded by his love for Kriemhild and for adventure to foresee any danger. In medieval ballads, there is also a connection between love and danger. Choose a ballad to compare with "How Siegfried Was Slain." Explore the idea of love and danger in both works.

3. In what ways does Siegfried's stubbornness compare with that of the couple in "Get Up and Bar the Door"?

Idea Bank

Writing

1. **Finding Siegfried a Job** Imagine that Siegfried is looking for a job in contemporary America. Help him out by writing a résumé that lists his accomplishments and skills. **[Career Link]**

2. **A Modern Fable** Rewrite this story as a modern fable with modern dialogue and characters. Keep the theme and message of the original, but revise settings, symbols, and other details as much as you wish.

3. **Hunting the Hunter** In the medieval romance and epic, the hunter often becomes the hunted. In what ways does the hunt scene foreshadow what is to come in the story? How does Siegfried's death become part of the hunting ritual? Explore the answers to these questions in a written analysis. Support your ideas with examples from the story.

4. **Critical Response** The author Robert Service asserts, "Fate has written a tragedy; its name is 'The Human Heart.'" In a written response, explore how this quotation relates to Siegfried; then explain how it relates to life in general.

Speaking, Listening, and Viewing

5. **Dramatizing the Story** Imagine that a knight who was loyal to Siegfried returns to tell Kriemhild what has happened. What details would he give her of the hunt and the death of the hero? How would Kriemhild react? Write your version of the conversation between the knight and Kriemhild. With a classmate, perform the scene for the class. **[Performing Arts Link]**

6. **Telling the Story With Music** *The Nibelungenlied* was set to music by German composer Richard Wagner; it consists of four operas that are frequently performed and recorded. Obtain a recording of the opera *Siegfried* and listen to scenes corresponding with this passage from the story. Then write a review in which you explain how well the essence of the tragedy is captured through music. **[Art Link]**

Researching and Representing

7. **A Map of Medieval Heroes** Create a map of medieval Europe, labeling things like kingdoms, rivers, centers of religion. Indicate locations of fictional and real-life heroes like Siegfried. Display your map. **[Social Studies Link]**

Online Activity www.phlit.phschool.com

Persuasive Speech

Writing Process Workshop

Persuasive Speech

To convince her husband and family to take certain actions, Margaret Paston used persuasive techniques in her letters. You may encounter similar persuasive techniques when you hear news commentaries or campaign speeches. You probably use them yourself when you ask favors of friends. These modern examples are all forms of **persuasive speech**, in which the speaker tries to influence or change people's views on a topic.

The following skills, introduced in this section's Guided Writing Lessons, will help you write an effective persuasive speech.

Writing Skills Focus

▶ **Use effective repetition** to draw attention to the points in your speech that you want listeners to remember. (See p. 163.)

▶ **Maintain a consistent perspective** so your ideas are unified and your argument is solid. For example, you might discuss an issue from the standpoint of a consumer or from that of all the world's people. (See p. 179.)

▶ **Build an argument** by using an effective organizational plan, such as order of importance, cause and effect, or pro and con.

This excerpt from a speech by Britain's former prime minister Margaret Thatcher incorporates all these skills.

① Thatcher establishes a cause-and-effect relationship from which she will build her argument.

② She repeats the word weapons to emphasize the main idea of her speech: control of weapons.

③ Throughout the passage, Thatcher maintains a consistent perspective by observing the situation from a global standpoint.

MODEL FROM LITERATURE

from a speech given by Margaret Thatcher

The Soviet collapse has also aggravated the single most awesome threat of modern times: the proliferation of weapons of mass destruction. ① These weapons ② —and the ability to develop and deliver them—are today acquired by middle-income countries with modest populations such as Iraq, Iran, Libya, and Syria; acquired sometimes from other powers like China and North Korea; but most ominously from former Soviet arsenals or unemployed scientists or from organized criminal rings, all via a growing international black market ③.

Prewriting

Choose a Topic Focus on an issue or idea that you feel strongly about, or choose one of the following topic ideas.

> ## Topic Ideas
>
> - Take a side on an environmental issue
> - Compare and contrast going to college and going into the work force
> - Create a campaign speech
> - Defend an issue on which you feel strongly

Evaluate Information You may want to research information. If you do, consider the credibility and appropriateness of the source material.

Create an Outline Plan the most effective way of building your argument and organizing details—order of importance, pro and con (reasons to support and oppose your stand), and cause and effect (examine various causes of one effect). Create an outline that reflects your choice of organization.

List Key Ideas Before drafting, list the points you want to convey in your speech and different ways of phrasing them. Then list key words related to your points. You can later use these lists to incorporate repetition into your speech.

Drafting

Keep a Consistent Perspective Decide upon the point of view from which you will prepare your argument. For example, if you are upset about a company's lack of environmental concern, you may choose to present your speech from the perspective of a consumer who buys that company's products. Then try to match each point to that perspective.

Use Persuasive Language Your choice of wording and use of repetition can make your argument weak or strong. Use positive terms—such as *fine, superior, best*—to make your recommendations more appealing. Use negative terms—such as *bad, appalling, poor, terrible*—to sharpen your criticism.

Read Aloud Read your speech aloud as you draft. Pause at places you want to stress and decide on words you want to emphasize. You may find that you have too many key ideas in one place, detracting from their force.

APPLYING LANGUAGE SKILLS: Using Parallel Structure

Effective persuasion often uses parallel, or similar, grammatical structures to express similar ideas.

Not Parallel: Think of our store when you plan to hike, to bike, or go fishing.

Parallel: Think of our store when you plan to hike, to bike, or to fish.

Practice Rewrite the following sentences so all parts are parallel.

1. She has served on the library board, the school board, and is a town council member.

2. As state senator, she plans to reduce taxes, increase aid to education, and she is concerned about protecting the environment.

Writing Application Review your persuasive speech for constructions that are not parallel. Revise constructions so they are parallel.

Writer's Solution Connection Writing Lab

To help a peer review your paper, use the Peer Evaluation Checklist in the Writing Lab tutorial on Persuasion.

APPLYING LANGUAGE SKILLS: Eliminating Unnecessary Words

Clear, direct writing is more persuasive than writing weighed down with unnecessary words. Use the following tips while writing:

• Eliminate words and phrases that contribute no meaning, such as *due to the fact that.*

• Avoid expressions that repeat meanings unnecessarily, such as *past history.* (All history is past.)

• Replace wordy expressions with shorter words or phrases; for example, replace *at this point in time* with *now.*

Writing Application After you draft your speech, go through it sentence by sentence to find words or phrases that do not add meaning, and eliminate them.

Writer's Solution Connection Language Lab

To help you identify and eliminate unnecessary words in your persuasive speech, use the Language Lab lesson on Eliminating Unnecessary Words.

Revising

Use the following checklist, which refers to the Writing Skills Focus points on p. 188, while revising your speech.

▶ Have I kept a clear and consistent perspective?
Delete or revise areas in which you stray from your chosen perspective; they weaken your argument.

▶ Did I use repetition effectively?
Underline instances where you have repeated key ideas and phrases. Evaluate their effectiveness by reading your speech to a peer and getting his or her reaction.

▶ Have I built my argument effectively?
Go back through your speech and create an outline of the way you have presented details in your speech. Compare it with the outline you prepared before drafting. Make sure your organization is effective and coherent.

REVISION MODEL

Physical activity is not good for you ① *just* ; it is essential if you are to remain healthy. ~~As a student I~~

read ② studies that have shown that people who

regularly engaged in activities such as walking, climbing

stairs, or dancing have lived longer, ③ *healthier* lives.

① The writer added this information so she could begin with a clear cause-and-effect statement on which to build her argument.

② Deleting these words makes the perspective clearer. The writer presents herself as an authority on the subject.

③ By repeating forms of the word *healthy,* the writer focuses on the benefits of exercise.

Publishing

▶ **Presentation** Present your speech to your classmates.

▶ **Internet** Post your speech to a message board in a news group.

▶ **Media Presentation** Either audiotape or videotape yourself giving your speech. Then present it at a school club or town organization where your subject would be relevant.

Student Success Workshop

Vocabulary Development

Strategies for Success

An analogy compares the relationship between two words to the relationship between two other words. For example, the analogy "A yacht is to a boat as a biography is to a book" states that the relationship between a *yacht* and a *boat* is the same as that between a biography and a book: A yacht is a type of boat, and a biography is a type of book. Because many standardized tests include analogy questions, being able to understand the relationships between two words and to see a similar relationship between another pair of words can improve your test-taking ability. It also increases your overall understanding and comprehension by helping you to think logically and critically.

Analogies on Tests On standardized tests, an analogy is often expressed as a formula. Here's an example: FISH : SCHOOL :: ACTOR : CAST. Written as a sentence, this analogy reads, *Fish is to school as actor is to cast.* When you encounter an analogy on a test, usually one pair of words in the analogy is missing. Sometimes only one word is missing: *fish : school ::* ____?____ *: cast.* On a test, several possible choices will be listed to fill in the missing word or pair. For example,

FACULTY : TEACH ::

A DRIVER : CAR   **C** MAMMAL : WALK
B SKY : BLUE   **D** ORCHESTRA : PLAY

As you consider the choices, think about the meanings of the words in the first pair and how they are related. Use your critical thinking skills. Then look for the answer choice that best expresses that same relationship. Eliminate the answers that are clearly wrong. Then analyze the relationship of the remaining choices.

Types of Analogies The challenge in figuring out analogies is in recognizing the type of analogy you're reading. Some analogies show relationships of a part to the whole, such as *fish : school :: actor : cast.* Some analogies are synonyms—*teacher : instructor :: student : pupil*—or antonyms—*love : hate :: generous : parsimonious.* Analogies can also express relationships of purpose and function, such as *faculty : teach :: orchestra : play,* or location, such as *juror : courtroom :: skater : rink.* Another type is description, such as *fox : cunning :: dog : loyal.*

Apply the Strategies

Use your analogy skills to answer the questions below. Remember: Analyze the type of relationship between the first pair of words.

1. What word best completes this analogy:
   horns : bull :: ____?____ *: horse*
   A tail   **B** hay   **C** reins

2. Choose the pair that best completes this analogy: *keyboard : screen ::*
   A controls : television   **C** pen : paper
   B eraser : pencil

3. What type of analogy is this:
   tall : diminutive :: effortless : arduous

✔ *Here are some other situations in which analogies can be useful:*
▶ **Reading or writing a poem**
▶ **Understanding a product advertisement**
▶ **Telling a friend about an experience you had**

Speaking, Listening, and Viewing Workshop

In a persuasive speech, the speaker tries to convince listeners to think and, possibly, act in a certain way. When lawyers argue to persuade jurors and politicians speak to win votes, the content of their speeches and the drama of their delivery are meant to have an effect on the audience. Learning how to analyze and evaluate a persuasive speech can help you become a critical listener and a more competent speaker.

Analyze the Structure and Organization Effective persuasive speeches include a logical structure. As you evaluate the speaker's organization, ask yourself if the speech includes

- A clear introduction and conclusion
- A logical order of ideas and information
- Transitional words to signal connections
- Repetition of an idea in a variety of ways at the beginning, middle, and end

Analyze the Content To convince the audience to think or act in a certain way, a speaker uses persuasive strategies. When you analyze the speaker's message, listen for features like these:

- Claims backed up by facts, examples, or evidence
- Arguments supported by relevant and accurate information
- Strong, persuasive images
- Words with strong connotations, such as "unbearable situation"

These persuasive techniques are powerful tools for shaping the listener's opinion. You must decide which ones you consider valid. Although speakers don't rely heavily on all these strategies, they use them to some extent.

As you analyze content, watch for strategies that speakers use to mislead you, such as:

- Omission of pertinent information or inclusion of irrelevant information
- Catchy slogans that have little meaning
- Memorable statements that oversimplify complex issues and ideas

Evaluate the Delivery The clearest organization and most brilliant arguments may be ignored if the person making a speech does not hold the attention of the audience. *How* a speaker delivers a speech is as important as *what* is said. When you listen to a persuasive speech, evaluate how effectively the speaker:

- Establishes eye contact with the audience
- Uses a confident but courteous manner
- Varies the volume, pitch, and tone of voice to reflect the content of the speech
- Uses appropriate gestures for emphasis

Apply the Strategies

Work in small groups to find persuasive texts, such as letters to the editor, product advertisements, editorials, and political speeches. Each member should choose one to present to the group. Use the strategies you have learned to prepare your speech and to analyze and evaluate others' speeches. After each speech, discuss these points:

- Was the organization of the speech logical and sequential?
- Were the statements and arguments backed by facts and strong images? Or was information omitted and irrelevant facts included?
- Did the speaker seem confident? Was eye contact with the audience maintained?
- Did the speaker's gestures reinforce the persuasiveness of the speech?

Tips for Evaluating a Persuasive Speech

✔ *Identify the persuasive techniques used.*
✔ *Determine whether the claims are backed by evidence and examples.*
✔ *Decide whether the gestures, tone of voice, and eye contact are effective.*

Test Preparation Workshop

Reading Comprehension — Sequential Order; Complex Written Directions

Strategies for Success

The reading sections of standardized tests often require you to read a passage and answer questions on arranging events in sequential order. They also ask you to follow complex directions. Use the following strategies to help you answer test questions on these skills:

Follow Sequential Order Passages are not always written in chronological order. To understand the sequence of events, watch for key sequence words, such as *first, next, then,* and *finally.* Look at the following example of sequential order:

> To wash a car the correct way, start by hosing the car down to loosen and wash away the surface dirt and grime. Spray the hubcaps vigorously. Next, prepare a bucket of warm, soapy water, and grab at least two sponges. Starting with the hood, use a soapy sponge to rub the car's surface gently. Work from front to back, along each side, and end with the trunk lid. Wash and rinse small sections of the surface as you go. Ensure that yet-to-be-washed surfaces remain wet. When you have finished washing and rinsing the entire surface, buff the car with a chamois cloth.

I When should you rinse the soap from the car?
  A Before you wash the car
  B After you spray the tires
  C After you wash each section
  D Before you wash the car's hood

Answer **A** is clearly incorrect. **B** is incorrect because this step occurs before you soap the car. **D** is not correct because you soap the hood before rinsing it. **C** is the correct answer, because you should wash and rinse small sections of the car at a time.

Follow Complex Directions In order to follow complex directions, you must read carefully. Move slowly through the process in your mind. Notice what the most important steps are and which minor steps support those important steps.

Refer to the previous passage to answer this question:

2 How do you prepare the car for washing?
  A Hose it off to loosen surface dirt.
  B Start with the hood, and work your way back.
  C Prepare a bucket of warm, soapy water.
  D Buff it with a chamois cloth.

Answer **D** is clearly incorrect because it's the final direction. **B** is not correct because it explains how to wash, not how to prepare. **C** is incorrect because it's a step that comes after hosing the car. **A** is correct because it is the first direction for preparation.

Apply the Strategies

Answer the following questions based on the sample passage:

I When should you buff the car?
  A After you wash and rinse each section
  B After hosing off the surface dirt
  C After washing and rinsing the entire car
  D Before you wash the car's hood

2 What do you use to scrub the car's surface?
  A Chamois cloth
  B Sponges
  C Bucket of soapy water
  D Hose

Wedding Celebration at Bermondsey, England, Joris Hoefnagel

Celebrating Humanity:

The English Renaissance (1485–1625)

What a piece of work is man!
How noble in reason! how infinite in
faculty! in form, in moving, how
express and admirable! in action how
like an angel!

—William Shakespeare,
from *Hamlet*

Timeline
1485–1625

1485	1520	1550

British Events

- **c. 1500** *Everyman* first performed.
- **1512** First masque performed.
- **1516 Thomas More** publishes *Utopia*.
- **1520** Bowling becomes popular in London.

- **1534** Henry VIII issues Act of Supremacy. ▲
- **1534** Church of England established.
  - **1535 Thomas More** executed. ◀
  - **1541** John Knox leads Calvinist reformation in Scotland.
  - **1547** Henry VIII dies.
  - **1549** The *Book of Common Prayer* issued.

- **1558 Elizabeth I** becomes queen. ▶
- **1560** Thomas Tallis publishes English cathedral music.
- **1563** More than 20,000 Londoners die in plague.
- **1564 William Shakespeare** born. ▼

World Events

- **1492** Columbus lands in Western Hemisphere.
- **1497** North America: John Cabot explores northeastern coast.
- **1497** Africa: Vasco da Gama rounds Cape of Good Hope.
- **1503** Italy: Leonardo da Vinci paints *Mona Lisa*. ▲
- **1509** Italy: Michelangelo paints ceiling of Sistine Chapel.
- **1513** North America: Ponce de León explores Florida.
- **1518** Africa: Algiers and Tunisia founded.
- **1519–22** Magellan sails around the world.

- **1521** Italy: Pope Leo X excommunicates Martin Luther.
- **1530** Poland: Copernicus completes treatise on astronomy.
- **1532** Peru: Pizarro conquers Incas. ▶
- **1532** France: Rabelais publishes *Gargantua and Pantagruel*, Book 1.
- **1534** Spain: St. Ignatius Loyola founds Jesuit brotherhood.

- **1554** Italy: Cellini completes bronze statue of Perseus.
- **1556** India: Akbar the Great comes to power.
- **1565** Malta: Knights of St. John fight off Turkish invasion.
- **1566** Belgium: Bruegel paints *The Wedding Dance*.
- **1567** South America: 2 million Indians die of typhoid.
- **1567** Brazil: Rio de Janeiro founded by Portuguese.

| 1570 | 1600 | 1610 | 1625 |

- **1580** Francis Drake returns from circumnavigating the globe.
- **c. 1582 Sir Philip Sidney** writes *Astrophel and Stella*.
- **1587** Mary, Queen of Scots, executed.
- **1588** English navy defeats Spanish Armada. ▼

- **1590 Edmund Spenser** publishes *The Faerie Queene*, Part I.
- **1594 Shakespeare** writes *Romeo and Juliet*. ▶
- **1599** Globe theater opens.

- **1600** East India Company founded.
- **1603 Elizabeth I** dies; James I becomes king.
- **1605 Shakespeare's** *Macbeth* first performed.
- **1606** Guy Fawkes executed for gun powder plot.

Romeo and Juliet.

- **1611** King James Bible published. ▼

- **1620** Francis Bacon publishes *Novum Organum*.
- **1623** First patent laws passed.
- **1625** James I dies.

- **1580** France: Montaigne's *Essays* published.
- **1582** Italy: Pope Gregory XIII introduces new calendar. ▼
- **1595** South America: Sir Walter Raleigh explores Orinoco River.

- **1605** Spain: Cervantes publishes Part I of *Don Quixote*.
- **1607** North America: British colony established at Jamestown.
- **1608** North America: French colony of Quebec established.
- **1609** Italy: Galileo builds first telescope. ▶

- **1618** Germany: Kepler proposes laws of planetary motion.
- **1620** North America: Pilgrims land at Plymouth Rock. ▼

The Story of the Times
(1485–1625)

Historical Background

The ending of the Wars of the Roses and the founding of the Tudor dynasty in 1485 opened a new era in English life. Monarchs assured stability by increasing their own power and undercutting the strength of the nobles. At the same time, they dramatically changed England's religious practices and helped to transform England from a small nation into one of the world's great powers.

The Tudors The first Tudor monarch, Henry VII, inherited an England that had been depleted and exhausted by years of civil war. By the time he died in 1509, he had rebuilt the nation's treasury and established law and order. In doing so, he had restored the prestige of the monarchy and had set the stage for his successors.

Henry VII was succeeded by his handsome and athletic son, Henry VIII. Like his father, Henry VIII was a practicing Catholic. He even wrote a book against Martin Luther, for which a grateful Pope granted him the title "Defender of the Faith."

Henry VIII's good relationship with the Pope did not last, however. Because his marriage with Catherine of Aragon had not produced a son, Henry tried to obtain an annulment from the Pope so that he could marry Anne Boleyn. When the Pope refused, Henry remarried anyway. This defiance of papal authority led to an open break with the Roman Catholic Church. Henry seized the Catholic Church's English property and dissolved the powerful monasteries. He even had his former friend and leading advisor, Thomas More, executed because More had refused to renounce his faith.

Henry married six times in all. His first two marriages produced two daughters, Mary and Elizabeth. His third wife, Jane Seymour, bore a son, Edward, who was but a frail child when Henry died in 1547.

▲ **Infer** Hornbooks such as this one served the same purpose as today's textbooks. What can you infer from this hornbook about the curriculum taught during Shakespeare's time?

Religious Turmoil Henry VIII's son, Edward VI, became king at the age of nine and died at the age of fifteen. During his brief reign, a series of parliamentary acts dramatically changed the nation's religious practices. English replaced Latin in church ritual, and the Anglican prayer book, the *Book of Common Prayer*, became required in public worship. By Edward's death in 1553, England was well on its way to becoming a Protestant nation.

Roman Catholicism made a turbulent comeback, however, when Edward's half-sister Mary took the throne. Mary I was Catholic, and she restored Roman practices to the Church of England. She also restored the authority of the Pope over the English Church. Ordering the execution of nearly 300 Protestants, Mary I earned the nickname "Bloody Mary" and strengthened anti-Catholic sentiment within England.

Elizabeth I When Mary I died after a five-year reign, her half-sister, Elizabeth I, came to the throne. Strong and clever, Elizabeth was probably England's ablest monarch since William the Conqueror. She had received a Renaissance education and read widely in the Greek and Latin classics. Becoming a great patron of the arts, she gathered around her the best writers of her day.

Elizabeth also put an end to the religious turmoil that had existed during Mary I's reign. She reestablished the monarch's supremacy in the Church of England, restored the *Book of Common Prayer*, and instituted a policy of religious moderation that enjoyed great popular support, although it failed to please many devout Catholics and Protestants.

Elizabeth's one outstanding problem was her Catholic cousin Mary Stuart, queen of Scotland by birth and next in line for the throne of England. Because Catholics did not recognize Henry VIII's marriage to Elizabeth's mother, Anne Boleyn, they considered Mary Stuart the queen of England. Imprisoned by Elizabeth for nineteen years, Mary instigated numerous Catholic plots against Elizabeth. Following the advice of her advisors, Elizabeth stepped up punishment of the Catholics but let her royal cousin live. Finally, Parliament insisted on Mary's execution. Mary was beheaded in 1587, a Catholic martyr.

▲ **Draw Conclusions** This painting depicts a noble family at dinner. From this scene, what conclusions can you draw about family life during the Renaissance?

◄ **Hypothesize** These gold coins were minted during the reigns of Henry VIII and Elizabeth I. Hypothesize about the types of things an Elizabethan might have bought with these coins.

▲ **Infer** This armor belonged to King Henry VIII. Why do you think medieval ideals of chivalry—associated with such armor—inspired some Elizabethan poets?

▲ **Infer** This picture dates from the nineteenth century, but it portrays the type of pastoral scene that appealed to many Elizabethan poets. Why do you think the lives of shepherds and shepherdesses like these interested court poets?

Stuarts and Puritans The English Renaissance continued after Elizabeth died in 1603, although a new dynasty—the Stuarts—came to the throne of England. Determined to avoid a dispute over the throne and a return of civil strife, Elizabeth named King James VI of Scotland as her successor. James's claim to England's throne rested on his descent from King Henry VII through his mother, Mary Stuart, Elizabeth's old antagonist. Unlike Mary, however, James was a Protestant.

The years of James I's reign are sometimes described as the Jacobean era, from *Jacobus*, the Latin word for James. Like his predecessor, James I was a strong supporter of the arts. He also took measures to further England's position as a world power, sponsoring the establishment of England's first successful American colony—Jamestown, Virginia.

During his reign, however, James and Parliament struggled for power, a conflict that would later erupt into war. Guided by the idea of the "divine right of kings," James I often treated Parliament with contempt, and they quarreled over taxes and foreign wars. James I also persecuted the Puritans, who were strongly represented in the House of Commons. Prompted by James's religious intolerance, a group of Puritans migrated to America and established the Plymouth Colony in 1620.

Philosophy One of the most exciting periods in history, the Renaissance was both a worldly and a religious age. It blossomed first in the Italian city-states (1350–1550), where commerce and a wealthy middle class supported learning and the arts. Slowly, Renaissance ideas spread northward, making possible the English Renaissance (1485–1625). During the Renaissance, scholars reacted against what they saw as the "dark ages" of medieval Europe and revived the learning of ancient Greece and Rome. They thought they were bringing about a rebirth of civilization.

The Age of Exploration The Renaissance thirst for knowledge prompted a great burst of exploration by sea. Navigators ventured far and wide, aided by the development of the compass and by advances in astronomy, which freed them from the need to cling to the shores of the Atlantic.

Their explorations culminated in Columbus's arrival in the Western Hemisphere in 1492.

England's participation in the Age of Exploration began in 1497, when the Italian-born explorer John Cabot, sailing for an English company, reached Newfoundland (an island off the east coast of what is now Canada) and perhaps also the mainland. Cabot thus laid the basis for future English claims in North America.

Religion A growing sense of nationalism along with the Renaissance spirit led many Europeans to question the authority of the Roman Catholic Church. Many people had grievances against the Church. Some felt that Church officials were corrupt; others questioned Church teachings and hierarchy.

The great Dutch scholar Desiderius Erasmus's (1466–1536) edition of the New Testament raised serious questions about standard interpretations of the Bible. Through his friendship with such English writers as Thomas More (1478–1535), Erasmus focused attention on issues of morality and religion, which continued as central concerns of the English Renaissance.

Although Erasmus himself remained a Roman Catholic, he helped to pave the way for a split in the Church that began in 1517, when a German monk named Martin Luther (1483–1546) nailed a list of dissenting beliefs to the door of a German church. Luther's protest resulted in dividing the Church and introducing a new Christian denomination known as Lutheranism. The process that Luther started has come to be called the Protestant Reformation.

Literature of the Period

Like painting and sculpture, literature expressed the attitudes of the Renaissance. Narratives, poetry, dramas, and comedies reflected the ideas of the times. They also provided a forum for subtle and satirical criticisms of social institutions such as the monarchy and the Church.

Elizabethan Poetry During the reign of Elizabeth I, English literature came of age. The most significant literary developments came in the area of poetry. Favoring lyric poetry, rather than the narrative poems favored by their medieval predecessors, the Elizabethan poets perfected

▲ **Speculate** These portraits show Queen Elizabeth and Sir Walter Raleigh dressed in elaborate fashions. Speculate about the types of lives led by the people who could afford these clothes.

▲ **Speculate** Doctors could do little to stop epidemics of smallpox, measles, influenza, and yellow fever which regularly swept through cities and towns, killing thousands. Study this picture and speculate about the measures taken in epidemics: (a) Why has the door been padlocked? (b) Why is a fire burning before the house?

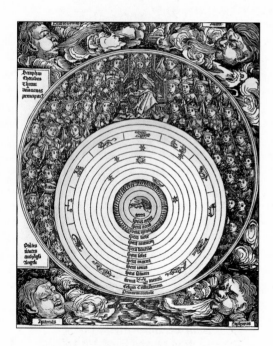

▲ **Compare and Contrast** Ptolemy was an astronomer and mathematician who lived in the second century A.D. Renaissance thinkers believed in his model of the universe with the Earth at the center. Compare and contrast this view of the universe with our view of the universe today.

the sonnet and began experimenting with other poetic forms.

One of the most popular literary forms during the Elizabethan Age was the sonnet cycle, a series of sonnets that fit loosely together to form a story. The first of the great Elizabethan sonnet cycles was *Astrophel and Stella* by Sir Philip Sidney. Sidney also helped to adapt classical verse forms to fit the English language.

Another major Elizabethan poet was Edmund Spenser, who wrote intricate verse filled with rich imagery. His sonnet cycle *Amoretti* is unique for being addressed to the poet's wife.

The brilliant lyric poet William Shakespeare brought the Elizabethan sonnet to new heights. Shakespeare changed the pattern and rhyme scheme of the Petrarchan, or Italian, sonnet, employing a form now known as the English, or Shakespearean, sonnet.

Elizabethan Drama During the Elizabethan Age, playwrights turned away from religious subjects and began writing more complex and sophisticated plays. Drawing upon the classical models of ancient Greece and Rome, playwrights reintroduced tragedies and dramas.

Also a leading poet, Christopher Marlowe became the first major Elizabethan dramatist in the 1580's, writing such plays as *Tamburlaine the Great* and *The Tragical History of Doctor Faustus.* Had Marlowe lived past the age of thirty, he might well have rivaled Shakespeare as England's greatest playwright.

Shakespeare began his involvement with the theater as an actor. By 1592, he was a popular playwright, his works having been performed even at Elizabeth I's court. Shakespeare wrote thirty-seven plays, among them many of the greatest dramas of all time. Filled with powerful and beautiful language, his works display his deep understanding of human nature. Because of their eloquent language and depth, Shakespeare's plays have retained their popularity for centuries. The seventeenth-century writer Ben Jonson said of Shakespeare, "He was not of an age but for all time."

Elizabethan and Jacobean Prose Prose took a back seat to poetry and drama in the English Renaissance. Scholars still preferred to write in Latin, and their English prose had a Latin flavor. Because they used long words and ornate sentences, their work is often difficult to read today.

Several Elizabethan poets also contributed major works of prose. Sir Philip Sidney's *Defence of Poesie* (about 1582) is one of the earliest works of English literary criticism. Thomas Nashe's *The Unfortunate Traveler* (1594), a fictional tale, was a forerunner of the novel. *History of the World*, another important work of prose, was written by Sir Walter Raleigh during his imprisonment in the Tower of London.

Perhaps the leading prose writer of the English Renaissance was Sir Francis Bacon, a high government official under James I. "I have taken all knowledge to be my province," Bacon wrote, and his literary output reflects his scholarship in many fields. *Novum Organum* (1620), his greatest work, made major contributions to natural science and philosophy.

The most monumental prose achievement of the entire English Renaissance is undoubtedly the English translation of the Bible commissioned by King James on the advice of Protestant clergymen. Fifty-four scholars labored for seven years to bring this magnificent work to fruition. The King James Bible, or Authorized Version, is among the most widely quoted and influential works in the English language.

The English Renaissance moved England out of its medieval past and into the modern world. No writers since have surpassed the literary achievements of Shakespeare or the majestic language of the King James Bible. They provide the standard against which all English literature has been judged right down to the present time.

▲ **Infer** The English navy gained supremacy of the sea after defeating the Spanish Armada. Examine this painting and infer the types of war tactics used by the English that may have contributed to their success.

▶ **Speculate** In 1577, Sir Francis Drake set out on a three-year journey, sailing around the world. This cup commemorates his feat. Speculate on the scientific ideas of the time, suggested by the cup.

The Changing English Language

"A MAN OF FIRE—NEW WORDS"

by Richard Lederer

The Ageless Bard

Shakespeare's plays, which he wrote in London between approximately 1590 and 1613, have been in almost constant production since their creation. Because the playwright dealt with universal truths and conflicts in human nature, his tragedies, comedies, and history plays continue to draw audiences from all walks of life, just as they did in their own day. Time has proved the truth of what Shakespeare's contemporary, Ben Jonson, said of him: "He was not of an age but for all time."

Word-Maker Supreme

William Shakespeare's words, as well as his works, were not just of an age, but for all time. He was, quite simply, the greatest word maker who ever lived—an often neglected aspect of his genius.

Of the 20,138 different words that Shakespeare employs in his plays, sonnets, and other poems, his is the first known use of more than 1,700 of them. The most verbally innovative of our authors, Shakespeare made up more than 8.5 percent of his written vocabulary. Reading his works is like witnessing the birth of language itself.

"I pitied thee,/Took pains to make thee speak," says Prospero to Caliban in *The Tempest*. "I endow'd thy purposes/With words that made them known." Shakespeare is our Prospero; he dressed our thoughts with words and set our tongue teeming with phrases.

Consider the following list of thirty representative words that, as far as we can tell, Shakespeare was the first to use in writing. So great is his influence on his native tongue that we find it hard to imagine a time when these words did not exist.

aerial	bedroom	critic	frugal
invulnerable	monumental	amazement	bump
dishearten	generous	lapse	perusal
assassination	castigate	dislocate	gloomy
laughable	pious	auspicious	countless
dwindle	hurry	lonely	sneak
baseless	courtship	exposure	impartial
majestic	useless		

The striking compound that Shakespeare fashioned to describe Don Adriano de Armando in *Love's Labour's Lost* is an important label for the playwright himself: "a man of fire—new words." No day goes by that we do not speak and hear, and read and write using his legacy.

Activity

Oscar Wilde once quipped, "Now we sit through Shakespeare in order to recognize the quotations." Unrivaled in his invention of words, William Shakespeare is unequaled as a phrasemaker. Complete the following expressions, each of which first saw the light in one of his plays:

1. Neither a ___?___ nor a ___?___ be
2. All the world's a ___?___
3. With bated ___?___
4. Break the ___?___
5. Come full ___?___
6. Eaten me out of house and ___?___
7. A foregone ___?___
8. Laugh yourselves into ___?___
9. Not ___?___ an inch
10. Too much of a good ___?___

Lovers and Their Lines

The Sonnet, William Mulready,
Victoria and Albert Museum

Guide for Interpreting

Edmund Spenser
(1552–1599)

Born into a working-class family, Edmund Spenser attended the Merchant Taylors' School on a scholarship and worked his way through Cambridge University. During his university years, Spenser published his first poems.

Pay for Poetry Unlike other poets, Spenser depended on the payment he received for his work. When the queen's treasurer balked at paying him, he sent this verse to the queen: "I was promised on a time/To have reason for my rhyme./From that time unto this season/I have received nor rhyme, nor reason." Spenser was immediately paid.

A Poet's Poet Spenser was an innovative poet. The Spenserian sonnet, which he created, contains a unique structure and rhyme scheme. Also, his sonnet sequence *Amoretti* is unique for being addressed to his own wife. In writing his long poem *The Faerie Queene*, Spenser created a new type of stanza, later named for him. It has nine lines, the first eight being in iambic pentameter and the ninth being two syllables longer. This poem dedicated to Queen Elizabeth I brought him a small pension, but he never received a position at court.

Sir Philip Sidney
(1554–1586)

A man of many accomplishments, Sir Philip Sidney was a courtier, scholar, poet, and soldier. He attended both Oxford and Cambridge, and furthered his knowledge by traveling extensively through Europe. He became a favorite in the court of Queen Elizabeth I.

A Brave Soldier In 1580, he fell out of favor with the queen for writing a letter urging her not to marry. Eventually he regained status with the queen and was knighted in 1583. In 1586, during a military engagement against the Spanish Catholics in Holland, Sidney was severely wounded. As he lay on the ground, Sidney bravely insisted that the water offered to him be given to another wounded soldier. Twenty-six days later he died, to the great grief of his country.

Pioneering Sonneteer Sir Philip wrote the first great sonnet sequence in English, *Astrophel and Stella*. Before Sidney, others had written excellent sonnets, but Sidney's were the first linked by subject matter and theme. This sonnet sequence had been inspired by Penelope Devereux—Stella—to whom Sir Philip—Astrophel—had been engaged. The engagement was later broken, and Penelope married Lord Rich.

◆ Background for Understanding

CULTURE: ELIZABETHAN IDEAS OF DESIGN AND ORDER

The English Renaissance, or "rebirth," was a time during which literary, artistic, and intellectual developments were celebrated. Philosophically, the Elizabethans viewed themselves as part of a grand universal design.

This idea of design was mirrored in many aspects of Elizabethan life. For example, people imagined that the heavens were so perfectly balanced that the planets and stars created a glorious music, which they called "music of the spheres." The movements in dances reflected this balance, as did the symmetrical and orderly design of gardens. It is hardly surprising that the sonnet, a perfectly designed little poem, became wildly popular, and most poets of the age explored this form. In many sonnets, lovers are idealized and compared to other "perfect" things, such as the sun, stars, waves, and rosebuds.

Spenser's Sonnet 1 ◆ Sonnet 35 ◆ Sonnet 75
Sidney's Sonnet 31 ◆ Sonnet 39

◆ *Literature and Your Life*

CONNECT YOUR EXPERIENCE

If you've ever written a love song or a valentine, you've had to convey a message of love in just a few memorable lines.

Spenser and Sidney faced this same challenge as they wrote their sonnets. Not only did they have to pour their hearts into fourteen lines, but they had to make sure that their feelings rhymed!

THEMATIC FOCUS: LOVERS AND THEIR LINES

As you read these sonnets, think about the attitudes toward love expressed by Spenser and Sidney. How are these attitudes like and unlike modern attitudes about love?

Journal Writing In your journal, write a valentine to a real or fictitious person.

◆ Build Vocabulary

RELATED WORDS: FORMS OF *LANGUISHED*

In Sonnet 31 the moon is described as being full of "languished grace." *Languished* is a past participle of the verb *languish*, which means "to become weak." Other forms of this word are *languid*, an adjective that means "drooping" or "weak," and the noun *languor*, meaning "weakness."

WORD BANK

Before you read, preview this list of words from the sonnets.

deign
assay
devise
wan
languished
balm

◆ Grammar and Style

CAPITALIZATION OF PROPER NOUNS

Both Spenser and Sidney capitalize some of the nouns they use. When a noun names someone or something, it is a **proper noun** and should be capitalized. An ordinary noun may also be treated like a proper noun if it is used in a direct address. Look at the following examples from Sidney's sonnets.

With how sad steps, O *Moon*, thou climb'st the skies!

Livelier than elsewhere, *Stella's* image see.

In reading these sonnets, notice other examples of proper nouns.

◆ Literary Focus

THE SONNET

A **sonnet** is a fourteen-line lyric poem with a single theme. Sonnets are usually written in iambic pentameter and take a definite form.

The **Petrarchan sonnet**, for example, is divided into an eight-line octave and a six-line sestet. The octave rhymes *abba abba* and the sestet generally rhymes *cdecde*. The octave raises a question or presents a situation, and the sestet gives a response.

The **Spenserian sonnet** rhymes *ababbcbc cdcdee*. Sometimes there is no break in a Spenserian sonnet between the octave and the sestet.

THE SONNET SEQUENCE

A **sonnet sequence** is a group of sonnets linked by theme or subject. Perfected by Petrarch, a fourteenth-century Italian poet, the sonnet sequence was imitated and refined by English poets.

The following sonnets contain elements that are expected in a sequence: The lady is beautiful and unreachable, and the lover remains ever true.

Reading for Success

Strategies for Reading Poetry

A poem, much like a song, differs from other forms of writing in its appearance, its use of language, and its musical qualities. Poets create the poetic experience through the imaginative use of language. Poems are visual—written in lines and stanzas. Poems are also musical—written to be recited or heard. To read poetry successfully, use the following strategies:

Identify the poem's speaker.

The voice "speaking" the poem is not necessarily that of the poet, although it can be. Decide who you think is telling the poem. Recognizing the speaker will give you insight into the dramatic situation of a poem.

Envision the imagery.

Because much poetry appeals to the senses, involve your senses in reading it. Then think about how the images contribute to the poem's meaning.

Follow sentence structure to understand meaning.

It's tempting to read poetry line by line. However, a thought may span several lines or an entire stanza. To understand complete thoughts, read in sentences. Follow the punctuation to see where sentences begin and end.

Paraphrase.

Restate passages in your own words.

Listen.

Read a poem aloud, or listen to it in your head. Hear the poem's sounds, and feel its rhythm. Also, listen for its tone and pace.

Respond.

Let yourself respond to what the poet is saying. How does the poem make you feel? What do you think about the sentiments it expresses?

Consider the historical context and characteristics of the time period.

Review the introduction to this unit, which provides background on the period. Read the selections with the historical context in mind.

As you read the poems that follow, notice the notes in the boxes. The notes demonstrate how to apply these strategies.

Edmund Spenser
Sonnet 1

Happy ye leaves when as those lily hands,
which hold my life in their dead doing[1] might,
Shall handle you and hold in love's soft bands,
Like captives trembling at the victor's sight,

5 And happy lines, on which with starry light,
Those lamping[2] eyes will <u>deign</u> sometimes to look
And read the sorrows of my dying spright,[3]
Written with tears in heart's close[4] bleeding book.
And happy rhymes bathed in the sacred brook

10 Of Helicon[5] whence she derived is,
When ye behold that angel's blessed look,
My soul's long lacked food, my heaven's bliss.
Leaves, lines, and rhymes, seek her to please alone,
Whom if ye please, I care for other none.

---

1. **doing:** Killing.
2. **lamping:** Flashing.
3. **spright:** Spirit.
4. **close:** Secret.
5. **sacred . . . Helicon:** From Greek mythology, the Hippocrene, the fountain from which the waters of poetic inspiration flowed.

◆ **Build Vocabulary**

deign (dān) *v.*: Condescend; lower oneself

A **paraphrase** of lines 1–3 might read: The pages of a book are happy when held in the beautiful, soft hands of my beloved, hands that also hold me in their power.

Read Sonnet 1 aloud and **listen** for the rhymes. Also listen for the tone, the author's feelings toward his subject.

Edmund Spenser
Sonnet 35

My hungry eyes through greedy covetize,
Still to behold the object of their pain,
With no contentment can themselves suffice:
But having pine and having not complain.

5   For lacking it they cannot life sustain,
And having it they gaze on it the more:
In their amazement like Narcissus[1] vain
Whose eyes him starved: so plenty makes me poor.
Yet are mine eyes so fillèd with the store

10   Of that fair sight, that nothing else they brook,
But loathe the things which they did like before,
And can no more endure on them to look.
All this world's glory seemeth vain to me,
And all their shows but shadows, saving she.

---

1. Narcissus: From Greek mythology, a youth who fell in
love with his own reflection in a spring and was changed into
the narcissus flower.

Follow the **sentence structure** through to the period at the end of line 4.

Respond to the speaker's fascination with the woman who is the subject of the poem. Do you think it is understandable?

Edmund Spenser
Sonnet 75

One day I wrote her name upon the strand,[1]
But came the waves and washèd it away:
Again I wrote it with a second hand,
But came the tide, and made my pains his prey.
5 "Vain man," said she, "that dost in vain assay,
A mortal thing so to immortalize,
For I myself shall like to this decay,
And eek[2] my name be wipèd out likewise."
"Not so," quod[3] I, "let baser things devise.
10 To die in dust, but you shall live by fame:
My verse your virtues rare shall eternize,
And in the heavens write your glorious name.
Where whenas death shall all the world subdue,
Our love shall live, and later life renew."

1. **strand:** Beach.
2. **eek:** Also.
3. **quod:** Said.

> Referring to himself as *I*, the **speaker** lets the reader know that the lines that follow recall a personal experience.

> When you **envision** the image of the beach, you can better understand the situation the poet describes. Use the picture on page 210 to help you.

◆ Build Vocabulary

assay (a sā´) *v.*: Try or attempt

devise (de vīz´) *v.*: Work out or create; plan

Guide for Responding

◆ Literature and Your Life

Reader's Response Which of Spenser's sonnets do you like the best? Why?

Thematic Focus Which of Spenser's sonnets would best convey modern feelings of love? Explain.

☑ Check Your Comprehension

1. (a) In Sonnet 1, what three listeners does the speaker address? (b) What are the listeners asked to do?
2. In Sonnet 35, what does the speaker want?
3. In Sonnet 35, to what does the speaker compare his eyes in their amazement?
4. (a) What occurs in the first four lines of Sonnet 75? (b) Who are the two speakers in the poem?

◆ Critical Thinking

INTERPRET

1. In Sonnet 1, what is the physical and emotional state of the speaker? **[Interpret]**
2. In line 2 of Sonnet 35, what is the "object of their pain" to which the speaker refers? **[Deduce]**
3. In Sonnet 75, what ideas does the man express about mortality and poetry? **[Analyze]**
4. Compare and contrast the relationship between the speaker and his love in each of the sonnets. **[Compare and Contrast]**

EVALUATE

5. In Sonnet 1, how effective is the speaker's comparison of his love to heavenly things such as stars and angels? **[Evaluate]**
6. In Sonnet 75, the lady calls the speaker "vain." Do you agree? **[Make a Judgment]**

Sonnet 31

Sir Philip Sidney

◄ **Critical Viewing**
How well does this photograph of the moon convey the mood of Sonnet 31? **[Evaluate]**

With how sad steps, O Moon, thou climb'st the skies!
  How silently, and with how <u>wan</u> a face!
  What, may it be that even in heavenly place
That busy archer[1] his sharp arrows tries?
5 Sure, if that long-with-love-acquainted eyes
  Can judge of love, thou feel'st a lover's case.
  I read it in thy looks, thy <u>languished</u> grace,
To me, that feel the like, thy <u>state descries.</u>[2]
  Then even of fellowship, O Moon, tell me
10 Is constant love deemed there but want of wit?[3]
Are beauties there as proud as here they be?
Do they above love to be loved, and yet
  Those lovers scorn whom that love doth possess?
  Do they call virtue there ungratefulness?

---

1. **busy archer:** Cupid, the Roman god of love.
2. **descries:** Reveals.
3. **wit:** Intelligence.

◆ Build Vocabulary

wan (wän) *adj.*: Sickly; pale

languished (laŋ´ gwisht) *adj.*: Weak or sickly looking

balm (bäm) *n.*: Anything healing or soothing

Sonnet 39

Sir Philip Sidney

Come sleep. O sleep, the certain knot of peace,
The baiting place[1] of wit, the balm of woe,
The poor man's wealth, the prisoner's release,
The indifferent judge between the high and low;
5   With shield of proof[2] shield me from out the prease[3]
Of those fierce darts Despair at me doth throw:
O make in me those civil wars to cease;
I will good tribute pay, if thou do so.
Take thou of me smooth pillows, sweetest bed,
10 A chamber deaf to noise, and blind to light,
A rose garland, and a weary head:
And if these things, as being thine by right,
Move not thy heavy grace, thou shalt in me,
Livelier than elsewhere, Stella's image see.

---

1. **baiting place:** Place for refreshment.
2. **proof:** Proven strength.
3. **prease:** Crowd.

Guide for Responding

◆ Literature and Your Life

Reader's Response Do you agree with the speakers' views of love and sleep in the sonnets?

Thematic Focus Do you think the speakers in the sonnets express timeless and universal moods that people in love experience? Why or why not?

☑ Check Your Comprehension

1. To whom is Sonnet 31 addressed?
2. (a) In Sonnet 31, how does the moon appear to the speaker? (b) What does the speaker think is the cause of the moon's sadness?
3. What six benefits does the speaker attribute to sleep in lines 1–4 of Sonnet 39?
4. In Sonnet 39, why does the speaker want to sleep?

◆ Critical Thinking

INTERPRET
1. In Sonnet 31, what is the connection between the appearance of the moon and the thoughts the speaker utters? **[Analyze]**
2. From what do you think the speaker is seeking to escape through sleep? **[Infer]**
3. Judging by what is said in each sonnet, what conclusion can you draw about each speaker's relationship with his lady? **[Draw Conclusions]**

APPLY
4. In Sonnet 39, what psychological truth about people's desire for sleep is the basis for the speaker's calling upon sleep? **[Speculate]**

COMPARE LITERARY WORKS
5. Compare the sonnets of Spenser—especially lines 10–14 of Sonnet 75—with those by Sidney. Which author appears more optimistic and which more pessimistic? **[Compare and Contrast]**

Guide for Responding (continued)

◆ Reading for Success

STRATEGIES FOR READING POETRY

Review the reading strategies and the notes for reading poetry effectively. Then apply them to answer these questions.

1. What do lines 5–8 tell you about the speaker in Edmund Spenser's Sonnet 1?
2. Review the structure of Edmund Spenser's Sonnet 75: three quatrains and a couplet. Then explain how this structure enhances the sonnet's meaning.
3. How would you respond to the series of questions ending Sir Philip Sidney's Sonnet 31?
4. Paraphrase lines 5–8 from Sir Philip Sidney's Sonnet 39.

◆ Grammar and Style

CAPITALIZATION OF PROPER NOUNS

Spenser and Sidney capitalize proper nouns and other common nouns they treat as if they were proper. This capitalization gives those nouns a human quality.

> A **proper noun** names a specific person or thing. It begins with a capital letter.

Practice In your notebook, identify the proper noun in each line.

1. "In their amazement like Narcissus vain"
2. "Of those fierce darts Despair at me doth throw"
3. "And happy rhymes bathed in the sacred brook/Of Helicon ..."

Writing Application Rewrite the following, capitalizing the proper nouns.

> After staring at the moon for a while, romeo the cat howled as though his heart were broken. The moon dimmed as though she too felt romeo's pain. Softly, luna's whispering tones floated down through the night air to cupid's wounded victim. "Hush, little one. Let morpheus take care of you, and when you awaken, all will be well."

◆ Literary Focus

THE SONNET AND THE SONNET SEQUENCE

The **sonnets** in this section come from **sonnet sequences**, a group of sonnets linked by subject matter or theme. Spenser's sonnets follow the structure and rhyme scheme he invented (*ababbcbc cdcdee*), while Sidney's follow the Petrarchan structure and rhyme scheme (*abbaabba cdcdee*).

1. The rhyme scheme of a Spenserian sonnet differs from that of the more familiar Petrarchan sonnet. If you were a poet, which rhyme scheme would you prefer to use? Explain.
2. Reread Sidney's Sonnet 39. Then indicate the elements that identify it as Petrarchan.
3. Compare and contrast one of Sidney's poems with one of Spenser's. Consider both subject matter and structure.
4. Review Sidney's two sonnets or Spenser's three. Then explain what poets can do in a group of sonnets that they can't do in individual poems. Consider such factors as mood, ideas about love, and characters.

◆ Build Vocabulary

USING FORMS OF LANGUISHED

Knowing that *languished* means "weak" or "sickly looking," choose from these related words to complete each sentence.

languor   languid

1. The cat's movements were ___?___ and graceful.
2. His ___?___ was caused by extreme exercise.

USING THE WORD BANK: Context

In your notebook, replace each italicized word or phrase using words or forms of words listed in the Word Bank.

The woman did not *condescend* to acknowledge the *pale* poet's feelings. No *healing ointment* on Earth could sooth his heartache, and his *attempts* at courtship were in vain, so he *created* a plan for winning her hand.

*B*uild *Y*our *P*ortfolio

 ## Idea Bank

Writing

1. **Analysis of a Love Song** Choose a love song that's a favorite of yours and write an analysis of its lyrics. Explain what is effective about its images and sound devices.

2. **Response to the Poem** In these sonnets, the moon, sleep, and the ocean are addressed as if they were human. Take on the voice of one of these things and write a poem in response.

3. **Spenser vs. Sidney** Compare the forms, content, and images used by the poets in these sonnets. Then write a paper in which you discuss each poet's technique and style.

Speaking, Listening, and Viewing

4. **Dialogue Between Man and Woman** Rewrite Sonnet 75 as a scene with dialogue between the two speakers. With a partner, perform the scene for the class. **[Performing Arts Link]**

5. **Poetry Reading** With a partner, take turns reading these sonnets aloud, emphasizing complete ideas rather than line breaks. After each reading, have your partner evaluate your oral interpretation. **[Performing Arts Link]**

Researching and Representing

6. **Visual Sonnet** Using art materials, create a visual sonnet. You can represent the physical objects mentioned in the sonnet or try to capture its mood or essence instead. **[Art Link]**

7. **Scientific Paper** In Sidney's Sonnet 31, he gives the moon human qualities: It climbs the skies and has a wan appearance. Describe the moon's appearance and movement in scientific terms. **[Science Link]**

Online Activity www.phlit.phschool.com

 ## Guided Writing Lesson

Paraphrase of a Sonnet

Poetry is condensed and compact: Words are used sparingly. It usually takes a few readings for a person to understand a poem's nuances. **Paraphrasing**—restating passages in your own words—can help you to unlock a poem's meaning.

Choose a sonnet to paraphrase. A paraphrase of a poem should state the poem's main ideas, but in your own language.

The following tips should help you to paraphrase successfully.

Writing Skills Focus: Clear Beginning, Middle, and End

Most types of writing contain a clear **beginning, middle,** and **end**. As you paraphrase, retain the original author's beginning, middle, and end.
- Break the sonnet into parts: Look for octaves, quatrains, sestets, and couplets.
- Paraphrase what is said in each unit of the sonnet.

Prewriting Identify the couplets, quatrains, octaves, or sestets. Also look for beginnings and endings of thoughts within the sonnet. Notice how these thoughts match up with the structure of the sonnet.

Drafting Refer to the original sonnet as you write. Restate the poet's words. You might think of your paraphrase as retelling the sonnet to a friend. Begin a new paragraph each time you paraphrase a specific section of the poem.

Revising Review the paragraphs in your written paraphrase, making sure that each paragraph contains the main ideas in a section. Also be sure that you've included in order the ideas from the beginning, middle, and ending of the sonnet.

PASTORAL POETRY

Pastoral poems are lyrics that celebrate the pleasures of a simple life in the country. Renaissance poets use a number of traditional conventions, such as making the speaker a shepherd who addresses or describes a shepherdess with whom he is in love and presenting an idealized world of nature.

Background for Understanding

Christopher Marlowe's "The Passionate Shepherd to His Love" is a well-known example of pastoral poetry. It has inspired a number of responses to the invitation issued by Marlowe's shepherd. The most famous, and—some have argued—the best response was written by Sir Walter Raleigh in 1600.

CHRISTOPHER MARLOWE
1564–1593

Killed before the age of thirty, Christopher Marlowe nonetheless managed to achieve renown as a brilliant playwright and poet. He spent his college days writing plays and serving as a government agent. *Tamburlaine*, his first drama, dazzled the public with its dynamic characterization of the tyrant-hero, and his tragedy *Doctor Faustus* is often performed even today.

A Life of Intrigue Marlowe has been described as a scoundrel, a ladies' man, and a hothead; however, it is clear that he was full of personal magnetism, for his numerous friends—and even his enemies—were drawn to him like moths to a flame. When the council of Queen Elizabeth I wrote a letter implying that Marlowe had performed important government services, rumors flew about that he was a spy. Marlowe was knifed to death in a tavern brawl in 1593. To this day, scholars question whether his death was really caused by his drunken refusal to pay his bill or whether he was murdered because of his undercover activities.

SIR WALTER RALEIGH
1554–1618

Sir Walter Raleigh is famed for being a courtier, a navigator, a poet, and a historian.

A Charmed yet Tragic Life A favorite of Queen Elizabeth I, Raleigh was given estates and many other favors. In 1584, he set up a colony on Roanoke Island, Virginia. Returning home, Raleigh introduced tobacco and potatoes into England and Ireland.

While away, Raleigh was replaced in the queen's affection by the Earl of Essex, and, when it was discovered that Raleigh had been secretly married to one of the queen's maids, he was banished from court for four years. Following the death of the queen in 1603, Raleigh was stripped of his favors and estates. He was accused of conspiring against James I and was sent to the Tower of London, where he lived for thirteen years. He was released to seek out gold along the Orinoco river in Guiana, but the expedition was plagued by ill luck and he lost his fleet and his son. Raleigh was beheaded at Whitehall under the old sentence of treason.

The Passionate Shepherd to His Love

CHRISTOPHER MARLOWE

Come live with me, and be my love,
And we will all the pleasures prove[1]
That valleys, groves, hills, and fields,
Woods, or steepy mountain yields.

5   And we will sit upon the rocks,
Seeing the shepherds feed their flocks,
By shallow rivers to whose falls
Melodious birds sing madrigals.

And I will make thee beds of roses,
10 And a thousand fragrant posies,
A cap of flowers, and a kirtle[2]
Embroidered all with leaves of myrtle;

A gown made of the finest wool,
Which from our pretty lambs we pull;
15 Fair lined slippers for the cold,
With buckles of the purest gold;

A belt of straw and ivy buds,
With coral clasps and amber studs;
And if these pleasures may thee move,
20 Come live with me, and be my love.

The shepherds' swains shall dance and sing
For thy delight each May morning;
If these delights thy mind may move,
Then live with me and be my love.

---

1. **prove:** Experience.
2. **kirtle:** Skirt.

The Nymph's Reply to the Shepherd

SIR WALTER RALEIGH

If all the world and love were young
and truth in every shepherd's tongue
These pretty pleasures might me move
To live with thee, and be thy love.

5   Time drives the flocks from field to fold,
When rivers rage and rocks grow cold,
and Philomel[1] becometh dumb,
the rest complains of cares to come.

The flowers do fade, and wanton fields
10 to wayward winter reckoning yields:
A honey tongue, a heart of gall,
Is fancy's spring, but sorrow's fall.

Thy gowns, thy shoes, thy beds of roses,
Thy cap, thy kirtle,[2] and thy posies
15 Soon break, soon wither, soon forgotten,
In folly ripe, in reason rotten.

Thy belt of straw and ivy buds,
Thy coral clasps and amber studs,
All these in me no means can move
20 To come to thee and be thy love.

But could youth last and love still breed,
Has joy no date[3] nor age no need,
Then these delights my mind might move,
To live with thee and be thy love.

---

1. **Philomel:** The nightingale.
2. **kirtle:** Skirt.
3. **date:** Ending.

Guide for Interpreting

William Shakespeare
(1564–1616)

Shakespeare may be the most admired author of all time. If this writing star lived today, the facts of his life would be widely known from magazine articles, books, Web pages, and chat lines. However, the few facts we know about him were painstakingly traced from legal and church records and from references in his work.

Bare-Bones Biography Shakespeare was born in the country town of Stratford-on-Avon and probably attended the town's free grammar school. When he was eighteen, he married twenty-six-year-old Anne Hathaway. They had a daughter, Susanna, and twins, Hamnet and Judith.

He acquired a public reputation as an actor and playwright. Also, he was part owner of a London theater called the Globe, where many of his plays were performed. (For more about Shakespeare and his work as a dramatist, see pages 268–269.)

The Sonnet In the years 1593–1594, London's theaters were closed because of an outbreak of the plague. This general misfortune had at least one benefit: It provided the time that Shakespeare needed to write his 154 sonnets.

In writing a long sequence of sonnets, Shakespeare was being fashionable. Elizabethan poets were sonnet-crazy, writing fourteen-line lyric poems to both real and imaginary lovers. The great Italian poet Petrarch (1304–1374) began the writing of sonnet sequences, and Henry Howard, Earl of Surrey, developed the English form of the sonnet that Shakespeare used.

Scholars have studied Shakespeare's sonnets for their masterly use of form and their variety of themes, including time, death, love, friendship, and the immortality of poetry. Because these brief lyrical poems are more personal than the plays, they have also appealed to readers eager to learn about Shakespeare's life.

◆ Background for Understanding

LITERATURE: THE STORY BEHIND SHAKESPEARE'S SONNETS

Shakespeare's 154 sonnets, like those of other sonnet sequences, are numbered and fit loosely together to form a story. Most of the sonnets are addressed to a handsome, talented young man, urging him to marry and have children. The speaker also warns the young man about the destructive powers of time, age, and moral weakness.

Midway through the sequence, the sonnets focus on a rival poet who has also addressed poems to the young man. Twenty-five of the later sonnets are addressed to a "dark lady," who is romantically involved with both the speaker and the young man. These later sonnets focus on the grief she causes the speaker by betraying him.

Scholars fiercely debate the identity of the young man ("Mr. W. H." in the dedication to the book), the "dark lady," and the rival poet. Leading candidates for the role of Mr. W. H. are Henry Wriothesley, third Earl of Southampton, to whom Shakespeare dedicated his narrative poems, and William Herbert, third Earl of Pembroke. Those favoring Southampton claim Mrs. John Davenant was the "dark lady," but the Pembroke side believes it was Mary Fitton, an attendant of the queen and a woman of doubtful reputation. The many nominees for the rival poet include Christopher Marlowe, George Chapman, Ben Jonson, and John Donne—all Shakespeare's contemporaries.

Sonnets 29, 106, 116, 130

◆ *Literature and Your Life*

CONNECT YOUR EXPERIENCE

Gossip columnists buzz with speculation about celebrities' private lives. Just imagine what people whispered in Elizabethan times about the young man, "dark lady," and rival poet of Shakespeare's sonnets.

Journal Writing As an Elizabethan gossip columnist, write a brief paragraph to interest your readers in the sonnets.

THEMATIC FOCUS: LOVERS AND THEIR LINES

Why do you think so many Elizabethan poets used the sonnet to express romantic love?

◆ Literary Focus

SHAKESPEAREAN SONNET

Shakespeare may have borrowed the sonnet from Francesco Petrarch and Henry Howard, but he used it so well that he gave it his name forever. A **Shakespearean sonnet** has these characteristics:

- fourteen rhymed lines
- a usual rhyme scheme of *abab cdcd efef gg*
- five iambic feet to the line, a foot being an unstressed syllable followed by a stressed syllable (sometimes this pattern varies)
- three quatrains (four-line stanzas) followed by a rhyming couplet

As you read, notice how artfully Shakespeare uses the first twelve lines to present a problem, idea, or situation and then resolves or emphasizes it in the final couplet.

◆ Grammar and Style

PARTICIPLES AS ADJECTIVES

Shakespeare uses **participles**—verb forms usually ending in *-ing* or *-ed* used as adjectives—to modify nouns or pronouns.

Sonnet 106: When in the chronicle of *wasted* time

And, for they look'd but with *divining* eyes

The italicized words, *wasted* and *divining*, are participles. As adjectives, they modify *time* and *eyes*.

◆ Reading Strategy

RELATE STRUCTURE TO THEME

As you read any literary work, you should **relate structure to theme** by thinking how the form of the work influences the contents. A sonnet, for example, is like a small but elegant gift box. It can contain something valuable, but that something has to fit in a small space.

Notice how Shakespeare deals with themes in the form of a sonnet. In the space allowed, he moves quickly from point to point, often rounding off thoughts to fit quatrains.

◆ Build Vocabulary

GREEK ROOTS: *-chron-*

In Sonnet 106 you'll encounter the word *chronicle,* whose root *-chron-* comes from the Greek *khronos,* meaning "time." Knowing the meaning of this word root, you can guess that *chronicle* is associated with time—it means "a record of events."

WORD BANK

As you read, you'll encounter the words on this list. Each word is defined on the page where it first appears. Preview the list before you read.

scope
sullen
chronicle
prefiguring
impediments
alters

▶ Critical Viewing What details suggest that the person in this painting could be the speaker of Sonnet 29? **[Analyze]**

Autumn, 1865, Frederick Walker, Victoria and Albert Museum

SONNET 29
WILLIAM SHAKESPEARE

When in disgrace with fortune and men's eyes,
I all alone beweep my outcast state,
And trouble deaf heaven with my bootless¹ cries,
And look upon myself and curse my fate,
5   Wishing me like to one more rich in hope,
Featured like him, like him with friends possessed,
Desiring this man's art, and that man's <u>scope</u>,
With what I most enjoy contented least.
Yet in these thoughts myself almost despising,
10   Haply I think on thee, and then my state,
Like to the lark at break of day arising
From <u>sullen</u> earth, sings hymns at heaven's gate;
     For thy sweet love remembered such wealth brings
     That then I scorn to change my state with kings.

1. bootless: Futile.

SONNET 106
WILLIAM SHAKESPEARE

When in the <u>chronicle</u> of wasted time
I see descriptions of the fairest wights,[1]
And beauty making beautiful old rhyme,
In praise of ladies dead and lovely knights,
5   Then in the blazon of sweet beauty's best
Of hand, of foot, of lip, of eye, of brow,
I see their antique pen would have express'd
Even such a beauty as you master now.
10 So all their praises are but prophecies
Of this our time, all you <u>prefiguring</u>;
And, for they look'd but with divining eyes,
They had not skill enough your worth to sing:
    For we, which now behold these present days,
    Have eyes to wonder, but lack tongues to praise.

1. **wights** (wīts) *n.*: Human beings; people.

◆ Build Vocabulary

scope (skōp) *n.*: Range of perception or understanding

sullen (sul´ ən) *adj.*: Gloomy; dismal

chronicle (krän´ i kəl) *n.*: Historical record of annals or facts

prefiguring (prē fig´ yer iŋ) *v.*: Suggesting beforehand

Guide for Responding

◆ Literature and Your Life

Reader's Response In Sonnet 29, Shakespeare feels consoled by the thought of a special person. When have you had a similar experience?

Thematic Focus Do you think Shakespeare is sincere in these sonnets? Explain.

☑ Check Your Comprehension

1. With whom or what is the speaker of Sonnet 29 in disfavor?
2. What brings "wealth" to the speaker of Sonnet 29?
3. Why did the ancient writers, mentioned in Sonnet 106, fail to describe the beauty of the person Shakespeare addresses?

◆ Critical Thinking

INTERPRET

1. How would you describe the shifting moods in Sonnet 29? **[Analyze]**
2. How do the last two lines summarize the theme of the sonnet? **[Draw Conclusions]**
3. In Sonnet 106, what is "the chronicle of wasted time"? **[Interpret]**
4. Explain how, in Sonnet 106, writers of the past and those of the present fail in different ways. **[Compare and Contrast]**

EVALUATE

5. Based on what he reveals about himself, assess the character of the speaker in each sonnet. **[Assess]**

Justa. Bartolome Esteban Murillo

▶ **Critical Viewing**
Which elements of this portrait seem idealized? Which seem realistic? **[Classify]**

SONNET 116
WILLIAM SHAKESPEARE

Let me not to the marriage of true minds
Admit impediments. Love is not love
Which alters when it alteration finds,
Or bends with the remover to remove.
5   O, no! It is an ever-fixèd mark
That looks on tempests and is never shaken;
It is the star to every wandering bark,[1]
Whose worth's unknown, although his height be taken.
Love's not Time's fool, though rosy lips and cheeks
10   Within his bending sickle's compass come;
Love alters not with his brief hours and weeks,
But bears it out even to the edge of doom.[2]
     If this be error, and upon me proved,
     I never writ, nor no man ever loved.

◆ **Build Vocabulary**

impediments (im ped´ə mənts) *n.*: Anything preventing the making of a legal contract

alters (ôl´ tərs) *v.*: Changes; becomes different

1. star . . . bark: The star that guides every wandering ship: the North Star.

2. doom: Judgment Day.

SONNET 130
WILLIAM SHAKESPEARE

My mistress' eyes are nothing like the sun,
Coral is far more red than her lips' red;
If snow be white, why then her breasts are dun;
If hairs be wires, black wires grow on her head.

5 I have seen roses damasked,[1] red and white,
But no such roses see I in her cheeks;
And in some perfumes is there more delight
Than in the breath that from my mistress reeks.[2]
I love to hear her speak. Yet well I know

10 That music hath a far more pleasing sound.
I grant I never saw a goddess go;[3]
My mistress, when she walks, treads on the ground.
 And yet, by heaven, I think my love as rare
 As any she belied with false compare.

1. **damasked:** Variegated.

2. **reeks:** Emanates.

3. **go:** Walk.

Guide for Responding

◆ Literature and Your Life

Reader's Response Which speaker's attitude toward love do you prefer? Explain.

Thematic Focus What do these poems suggest about Shakespeare's attitude toward love?

Group Discussion As a group, explore some of today's love poetry, especially that found in popular music. Try to find some with the distinctly realistic and unromantic tone of Shakespeare's Sonnet 130.

☑ Check Your Comprehension

1. To what is love compared in the second quatrain of Sonnet 116?
2. In Sonnet 116, what does the speaker say about the effect of time on love?
3. In Sonnet 130, what is less than perfect about the mistress's lips, cheeks, breath, and voice?
4. What does the speaker say about his mistress in the last two lines of Sonnet 130?

◆ Critical Thinking

INTERPRET

1. In Sonnet 116, what are the points of similarity between true love and the North Star? **[Compare and Contrast]**
2. In Sonnet 130, what point does the couplet make about the content of the rest of the sonnet? **[Draw Conclusions]**
3. What does the speaker of Sonnet 130 mean when he says his mistress "treads on the ground"? **[Interpret]**
4. In his sonnets, the Italian poet Petrarch placed his mistress on a pedestal and looked up to her. Why do you think Sonnet 130 has been called anti-Petrarchan? **[Draw Conclusions]**

APPLY

5. In which of these sonnets does the speaker's attitude toward love seem more typical of our times? Explain. **[Apply]**

Guide for Responding *(continued)*

◆ Reading Strategy

RELATE STRUCTURE TO THEME

You can **relate structure to theme** in these sonnets by noticing how Shakespeare fits his message to the quatrains and couplet of a Shakespearean sonnet. For example, in Sonnet 116, each self-contained quatrain offers additional "proof" of the timelessness of true love. The couplet is like Shakespeare's final oath that everything he has said is the truth.

1. For Sonnet 106, show how Shakespeare fits his message into the three-quatrain, one-couplet form.
2. If Shakespeare adapted one of these sonnets to the Petrarchan form (eight lines and six lines), how might it affect the presentation of his message?

◆ Build Vocabulary

USING THE GREEK ROOT *-chron-*

Keeping in mind that the root *-chron-* means "time," write a brief definition for each of the italicized words.

1. What is known about the *chronology* of Shakespeare's life?
2. List the Tudors in *chronological* order.
3. As *chronicles* of history, Shakespeare's plays are inaccurate.
4. Dramatists can be untrustworthy as *chroniclers*.
5. Was Shakespeare a *chronic* inventor of puns?

USING THE WORD BANK: Synonyms

On your paper, write the letter of the word closest in meaning to the term from the Word Bank.

1. scope: (a) shovel, (b) range, (c) exploration
2. sullen: (a) stained, (b) dull, (c) sulky
3. impediments: (a) obstacles, (b) utensils, (c) commands
4. alters: (a) argues, (b) sacrifices, (c) changes
5. chronicle: (a) record, (b) newspaper, (c) dates
6. prefiguring: (a) guessing, (b) foreshadowing, (c) introducing

◆ Literary Focus

SHAKESPEAREAN SONNET

These four sonnets on the theme of love, while different in their messages, are **Shakespearean sonnets**—consisting of three quatrains that present a problem or premise and a couplet that presents a solution, conclusion, or change of direction. They are written in iambic pentameter lines (a pattern of unstressed and stressed syllables repeated five times) and have a rhyme scheme of *abab cdcd efef gg*.

1. For any sonnet, (a) identify the three quatrains and the couplet; (b) show which rhyming words represent the *b's, e's,* and *g's* of the rhyme scheme.
2. How does the couplet in Sonnet 130 represent a sudden shift in attitude?
3. Why is the couplet in Sonnet 29 strongly linked to the last quatrain?

◆ Grammar and Style

PARTICIPLES AS ADJECTIVES

A **participle** is a verb form ending in *-ing* or *-ed* that acts as an adjective. It must always appear near the noun or pronoun that it modifies:

A poet is a *questing* soul.
The *yearning* young poet wrote a love sonnet.

Practice In your notebook, write for each sentence both the participle used as an adjective and the noun it modifies.

1. It is the star to every wandering bark
2. . . . rosy lips and cheeks/Within his bending sickle's compass come
3. Yet well I know/That music hath a far more pleasing sound
4. When in the chronicle of wasted time/I see descriptions of the fairest wights

Writing Application Write a brief review of your favorite sonnet, including three examples of participles.

Build Your Portfolio

Idea Bank

Writing

1. **Personal Response** Does love bring "wealth" to us as it seemed to do for Shakespeare (Sonnet 29)? Write a brief response to this question.

2. **Updating** Choose your favorite quatrain from any of these sonnets and rewrite it in contemporary language. However, don't lose Shakespeare's meaning in "translation."

3. **Shakespearean Sonnet** Write a Shakespearean sonnet on the theme of love or friendship. Use iambic pentameter lines and a rhyme scheme of *abab cdcd efef gg*. However, your language can be contemporary.

Speaking, Listening, and Viewing

4. **Recitation** The word *sonnet* comes from the Italian *sonetto*, meaning "little song." Keeping the rhythms of song in mind, recite one of these sonnets for your classmates. **[Performing Arts Link]**

5. **Debate** Do Shakespeare's sonnets express the ups and downs of love better than today's love songs? Divide into two teams and debate this question with classmates.

Researching and Representing

6. **Elizabethan Fashions** Mr. W. H., the "dark lady," and the rival poet dressed differently from the way we do. Research the fashions of Elizabethan times, and present your findings to the class. Illustrate your talk with your own drawings or with pictures from books. **[Social Studies Link; Art Link]**

7. **Elizabethan Music** What kind of music "hath a far more pleasing sound" than the voice of the mistress in Sonnet 130? Research Elizabethan music and play some for the class. **[Music Link]**

Online Activity www.phlit.phschool.com

Guided Writing Lesson

Introduction to Shakespeare's Sonnets

Write a brief introduction to a book of Shakespeare's sonnets for high-school students. In it, help teenagers appreciate his work. Besides explaining the form of the Shakespearean sonnet, tell about some of the clues to Shakespeare's life hidden in the sonnets. Give your readers any background they'll need to understand and appreciate these poems.

Writing Skills Focus: Necessary Background

Many types of writing—including introductions and comparative analyses—require you to provide **necessary background,** the information readers must know to understand your points. For example, review Shakespeare's biography and the Background for Understanding on p. 218. Notice that the information they provide helps you appreciate the Shakespearean sonnets in this book.

As you write your introduction, use the following strategies.

Prewriting What information helped you understand the sonnets? What additional information would have increased your appreciation? If necessary, do further research to uncover details that will entertain and inform your readers.

Drafting In your first paragraph, give an interesting fact or anecdote that will uncover your readers' attention. As you continue, speak to your readers in a direct, natural way. As you provide background information, you might relate it to specific sonnets or even to specific lines in sonnets.

Revising Have several classmates read your introduction and two of Shakespeare's sonnets. Then ask your readers whether you provided the background they needed to understand the poems. If not, work with the classmates to generate questions for further research that would help illuminate the sonnets.

CONNECTIONS TO WORLD LITERATURE

Sonnets 18, 28
Francesco Petrarch

Sonnets 69, 89
Pablo Neruda

Cultural Connection

A REBIRTH OF LOVE AND POETRY

The poets in this section were English, but they all owed a debt to the Italian Renaissance (the word *renaissance* means "rebirth"). This period of history—from 1350 to 1550—marked a rebirth of interest in the literature of ancient Greece and Rome. It also marked a rebirth of interest in all things human, including love. In particular, the Italian poet Francesco Petrarcha, called Petrarch (pe´ trärk) by the English, began to write about love in a new way and with a new type of poem.

THE INVENTION OF THE MODERN SONNET

That new type of poem was the sonnet, a fourteen-line lyric with an elaborate rhyme scheme. Petrarch perfected the sonnet, writing a sequence of 366 of them. Two of the sonnets from this sequence—numbers 18 and 28—are in this group of selections.

In his sonnet sequence, Petrarch invented many of the attitudes and conventions that would be imitated by all proper poet-lovers, including the poets of the English Renaissance. The key point about Petrarch's love is that it is never fulfilled. That would be a disaster—no more sonnets! Although Petrarch writes about Laura from afar, this distance gives him the opportunity to examine all his contradictory feelings about her.

THE PSYCHOLOGY OF LOVE

Armed with this new tool for self-exploration—the sonnet—Petrarch could disclose every aspect of love as he experienced it. In his sonnet sequence he could take his emotional temperature with every new sonnet and find a different reading. The woman herself was beautiful, unreachable, and almost beside the point.

THE IMMORTAL SONNET

The sonnet continues to be a widely read and appreciated form, as you will see when you read Sonnets 69 and 89 by Chilean poet Pablo Neruda. In these modern sonnets, however, Neruda seems to be writing about a real relationship—not just an imaginary one.

FRANCESCO PETRARCH
(1304–1374)

Petrarch was the greatest Italian poet of the fourteenth century. Born in Arezzo, Italy, he moved to Avignon, France when he was eight. In 1320, he returned to Italy to study law but began to write poetry.

Returning to Avignon in 1326, he first saw the famous Laura whom he celebrates in his love poetry. Who was this woman? Some scholars think she may have been Laura de Noyes, wife of Hugues de Sade. Whoever she was, Laura died in the Great Plague of 1348.

PABLO NERUDA
(1904–1973)

Pablo Neruda was born in Parral, Chile, the son of a railway worker. He was only twenty when his book *Twenty Love Poems and a Desperate Song* earned him recognition as one of Chile's best young poets.

Much of Neruda's work expresses political sentiments. However, he never lost his sense of poetry's irrational magic. In 1971, he received the Nobel Prize for Literature.

SONNET 18

❦ Francesco Petrarch ❦

Translated by Noti

Ashamed sometimes thy beauties should remain
As yet unsung, sweet lady, in my rhyme;
When first I saw thee I recall the time.
Pleasing as none shall ever please again.
5   But no fit polish can my verse attain,
Not mine is strength to try the task sublime:
My genius, measuring its power to climb,
From such attempt doth prudently refrain.
Full oft I oped my lips to chant thy name;
10 Then in mid utterance the lay was lost:
But say what muse can dare so bold a flight?
Full oft I strove in measure to indite;
But ah, the pen, the hand, the vein I boast,
At once were vanquish'd by the mighty theme!

Portrait of Laura,
Biblioteca Laurenziana, Firenze

SONNET 28

❦ Francesco Petrarch ❦

Anonymous Translator

Alone, and lost in thought, the desert glade
Measuring I roam with ling'ring steps and slow;
And still a watchful glance around me throw,
Anxious to shun the print of human tread:
5   No other means I find, no surer aid
From the world's prying eye to hide my woe:
So well my wild disorder'd gestures show,
And love lorn looks, the fire within me bred,
That well I deem each mountain, wood and plain,
10 And river knows, what I from man conceal,
What dreary hues my life's fond prospects dim.
Yet whate'er wild or savage paths I've ta'en,
Where'er I wander, love attends me still,
Soft whisp'ring to my soul, and I to him.

▲ **Critical Viewing** Petrarch invented
the idea of the "unattainable woman."
To what extent does this portrait
reflect such a woman? **[Apply]**

Man and Woman, 1981, Rufino Tamayo, Tate Gallery, London

▲ Critical Viewing In what ways does the painting echo Neruda's belief that he and his love are one? **[Analyze]**

Sonnet 69

Pablo Neruda
Translated by
Stephan Tapscott

Maybe nothingness is to be without your presence,
without you moving, slicing the noon
like a blue flower, without you walking
later through the fog and the cobbles,

5   without the light you carry in your hand,
golden, which maybe others will not see,
which maybe no one knew was growing
like the red beginnings of a rose.

In short, without your presence: without your coming
10   suddenly, incitingly,[1] to know my life,
gust of a rosebush, wheat of wind:

since then I am because you are,
since then you are, I am, we are,
and through love I will be, you will be, we'll be.

---

1. incitingly *adv.:* Set in motion; stimulated to action.

Sonnet 89

Pablo Neruda
Translated by Stephan Tapscott

When I die, I want your hands on my eyes:
I want the light and wheat of your beloved hands
to pass their freshness over me once more:
I want to feel the softness that changed my destiny.

5 I want you to live while I wait for you, asleep.
I want your ears still to hear the wind, I want you
to sniff the sea's aroma that we loved together,
to continue to walk on the sand we walk on.

I want what I love to continue to live,
10 and you whom I love and sang above everything else
to continue to flourish, full-flowered:

so that you can reach everything my love directs you to.
so that my shadow can travel along in your hair,
so that everything can learn the reason for my song.

Guide for Responding

◆ Literature and Your Life

Reader's Response Do the sonnets convince you that Petrarch and Neruda have experienced the depth of true love? Why or why not?

Thematic Focus Does love transcend time, place, and even death?

Valentine Create a Valentine that expresses your feelings about someone important to you.

☑ Check Your Comprehension

1. In Sonnet 28, what stays with the speaker wherever he goes?
2. In Sonnet 18, what does the speaker cite as the most pleasing event of his life?
3. In Sonnet 69, to what does Neruda compare being without his lover?
4. In Sonnet 89, what does the speaker want his love to do after his death?

◆ Critical Thinking

INTERPRET

1. In Sonnet 28, what settings does the speaker seek to find refuge from his feelings? Why would he choose these settings? **[Infer]**

2. What do you think Neruda means by the line "Maybe nothingness is to be without your presence," in Sonnet 69? **[Interpret]**

3. In Sonnet 89, how does Neruda use sensory imagery to convey his feelings of love? **[Analyze]**

4. Compare and contrast the depth of love expressed by Petrarch with that expressed by Neruda. **[Compare and Contrast]**

APPLY

5. Petrarch was a fourteenth-century writer. In what ways are the feelings he describes recognizable today?

6. Do you think that poets will continue to use the sonnet to express feelings of love? Why or why not? **[Speculate]**

Cultural Connection

LOVERS AND THEIR LINES

Surprising as it sounds, you can trace the current fascination with love—in songs, television shows, movies, and poems—back to the Renaissance. That's when writers like Petrarch, Sidney, Spenser, and Shakespeare began to examine carefully their own feelings of love. The instrument these writers used to examine love was the newly invented sonnet. Sonnet sequences, circulated in manuscript, may have prompted as much buzzing as gossip columns today: "Who is Laura, and why did she do Petrarch wrong?"

1. Of all the sonnets you read in the section "Lovers and Their Lines," which were your favorite and why?

2. Show how Sidney or Spenser adopts some of Petrarch's attitudes toward love. (a) Find a sonnet by Shakespeare in which he seems to make fun of Petrarch's attitudes. (b) Explain how Shakespeare is poking fun at his literary ancestor.

3. Compare and contrast the expressions of love in a sonnet by Petrarch or Neruda with those in a modern love song.

 Idea Bank

Writing

1. **Advice to the Lovelorn** Imagine that you are an advice columnist who has received a letter from Petrarch describing his love for Laura. Write a response in which you advise him how to deal with his problem.

2. **Essay on Love** Alfred, Lord Tennyson said, "'Tis better to have loved and lost, than never to have loved at all." Write an essay in which you agree or disagree with this statement. Use passages from the sonnets in "Lovers and Their Lines" to support your arguments.

3. **Sonnet** Choose one of the poets you have studied, and write a sonnet based on his style. Use the same rhyme scheme and rhythm, but modernize the language.

Speaking, Listening, and Viewing

4. **Role Play** With a partner, re-create a meeting between Petrarch and Laura. Have him express the sentiments found in his sonnets, and then have her respond. **[Performing Arts Link]**

Researching and Representing

5. **Collage** Create a collage in which you explore the theme of love at first sight in literature, nonfiction, and movies. Combine your own artwork and clippings from magazines and newspapers. **[Art Link]**

6. **History of Valentine's Day** Research how the traditions of Valentine's day came about and how they have changed. Summarize your findings in a short paper. **[Social Studies Link]**

Online Activity www.phlit.phschool.com

Writing Process Workshop

Comparative Analysis

A response to literature can take many forms. For example, it can be a poem written in response to another—like Sir Walter Raleigh's poem responding to Christopher Marlowe's poem—or it can be a **comparative analysis** that examines two or more literary works side by side and point for point. You might look at the similarities and differences between the messages that two works convey, or look for parallels in two writers' use of literary devices.

Choose two of the poems or poets in this section, and write a comparative analysis of them. The following skills will help you write your comparative analysis.

Writing Skills Focus

▶ Create a **clear beginning, middle,** and **end.** Introduce your main points in your introduction; develop and support your ideas in the body; and reinforce your points in your conclusion. (See p. 215.)

▶ Provide **context** and **background** information necessary for understanding your analysis. Information may include details about the authors' lives, the historical period, or the works themselves. (See p. 225.)

▶ Use **transitions** such as *both, also,* and *in contrast* to make clear comparisons.

WRITING MODEL

Two of the most famous sonnet sequences in English were written by Sir Philip Sidney and Edmund Spenser. Although the sequences contain many of the same conventions, the speakers are extremely different. ①

② The speaker in Spenser's *Amoretti* is more arrogant than the bewildered speaker of Sidney's *Astrophel and Stella*. ③ For example, in Spenser's Sonnet 35, the speaker gleefully anticipates his love's reaction to his verse, and in Sonnet 75, the speaker tells his love that through his verse, she will become immortal. The speaker's attitude may contain some of the poet's actual feelings: His humble background and his struggle for recognition may be reflected in the speaker's attitude.④

① The essay begins with this paragraph, introducing the main point.

② Each body paragraph contains a topic sentence, such as this one. The other sentences support or clarify the topic sentence.

③ Transitions, such as for example, show connections among ideas.

④ Details about the author and his work provide a context that gives depth to an analysis.

Applying Language Skills: Using Quotation Marks

Use quotation marks to mark direct quotations or passages from a work.

Example

In his poem, Yeats laments, "Things fall apart: the center cannot hold."

Practice On your paper, rewrite the following sentences, using quotation marks.

1. Eavan Boland writes, A poem or other work of literature is a little bit like a field that gets parched.
2. Herrick's rosebuds and Marvell's morning dew are images of youth.
3. The dull and mute lover in Suckling's poem is wasting his youthful years.

Writing Application When reviewing your response, be sure you have properly indicated quoted passages and that quotations are accurate.

Writer's Solution Connection Writing Lab

To help you find transitions to link your ideas, use the Transition Word Bin in the Drafting section of the Response to Literature tutorial.

Prewriting

Choose a Topic For a comparative analysis to be effective, choose two works to compare that have some similarities—either in content, structure, theme, or authorship. Consider these possibilities:

Topic Ideas

■ Analysis of structure of Petrarchan and Spenserian sonnets
■ Comparison of message, mood, and speaker's attitude in two of Sidney's sonnets
■ Comparative analysis of speakers in Sidney's and Spenser's sonnets

---

Locate Information As you read through the works you're comparing, jot down on note cards your thoughts. Include any passages you will cite in your analysis. If appropriate, use text and resources, such as the Internet and databases, to locate information on authors and historical periods. Sort and rearrange your note cards when you are drafting your response.

Drafting

Be Specific Refer to your prewriting notes as you draft. As you develop your comparative analysis, use transitional words and phrases to clarify relationships among your ideas. Use this chart to help you find appropriate transitions.

Comparison and Contrast: *some, a few, both, more, less, most, too, likewise*

Cause and Effect: *because, as a result, if, then, when, despite, although*

Pro and Con: *on the other hand, yet, however, therefore, if*

Order of Importance: *mainly, last, finally, better, best, more importantly*

Strive for Unity Structure your paper to have a clear beginning, or introduction, a middle, or body of information, and an end, or conclusion. Begin each paragraph with a main idea. Then use examples and details to develop each main idea. The final sentence of each paragraph should lead in to the paragraph that follows.

Cite Sources Use quotation marks around excerpted passages that you cite within the text of your analysis. For longer passages that are set off from the text, omit the quotation marks and set the quoted passage to a narrower margin.

Revising

Add Information Review your draft critically. Check to see that you have provided enough background information about the two works or authors, and look for places to insert passages from the works you're discussing to illustrate your points.

Add Transitional Words and Phrases Read your draft aloud as if you were reading to an audience. Whenever a passage is unclear or confusing, add transitions to make clear the connections among your ideas.

Proofread Your Work Reread your draft carefully, checking your response for errors in spelling, punctuation, and grammar. Take extra care when proofreading names, titles, and quoted material.

REVISION MODEL

Shakespeare writes of love in Sonnets 29 and 116. In the earlier sonnet, he writes of youthful love—Shakespeare himself was only eighteen when he married twenty-six-year-old Anne Hathaway—① and in the latter, of mature love. Most likely, The speaker's ideas about love that can be traced through the sonnets mirror Shakespeare's own recognition of the changing aspects of love.② Besides this progression of maturity, there is more evidence that Shakespeare's sonnets are somewhat autobiographical. ③

① Including background information on Shakespeare's life is key in this response.

② The transitional phrase connects Shakespeare's life to his works.

③ Adding this sentence, helps to clearly end one paragraph and set up the next.

Publishing

▶ **Response Collection** Work with a group of classmates to create an anthology of responses to selected literary works. Include a table of contents and illustrations.

▶ **Discussion Group** Gather a group of individuals to discuss and compare responses to the same work.

▶ **Classroom** Share your comparative analysis with your class. Hold a question-and-answer period following your reading.

APPLYING LANGUAGE SKILLS: Avoiding Ambiguous References

Pronouns allow writers to avoid repetition of words, phrases, and clauses. To avoid ambiguous references which confuse the reader, be sure there is a clear relationship between the pronoun and its antecedent— the word, phrase, or clause that the pronoun replaces.

Unclear Antecedent

two antecedents
Although James and Harry
pronoun
wrote well, his spelling was atrocious.

Revision

Although James and Harry wrote well, Harry's spelling was atrocious.

Writing Application Locate the pronouns in your response. If the pronoun-antecedent relationship is unclear, revise it.

Writer's Solution Connection Language Lab

For more help using correct pronouns and antecedents, complete the Pronoun and Antecedent lesson.

Student Success Workshop

Real-World Reading Skills

Analyzing Text Structures

Strategies for Success

Writers can express their ideas clearly by organizing them in some way. Books have chapters and paragraphs; news articles have headlines and subheads. The structure that a writer uses is influenced by the content and the writer's purpose. Newspaper articles and textbooks are often organized by main ideas with supporting facts and examples. Knowing how to analyze the structure of a text can help you become an active reader and make sense of what you're reading.

Chronological and Cause-and-Effect Structures Writers use different types of structures depending upon their stories. In a narrative story, a writer might choose a chronological or sequential structure, arranging the events in the order in which they occurred. For another story, a cause-and-effect structure might work well to explain why events occurred. If, for example, the arrival of a rare monkey species at the zoo increased the number of visitors and created traffic problems, a cause-and-effect structure could be used to tell the story.

Comparison-and-Contrast Structure A writer may use a comparison-and-contrast structure to illustrate how certain things are alike and different. Here's an example: Both the British and American novels are humorous stories set in England. *Both feature quirky main characters, but those in the British novel are more believable.*

Problems and Solutions Introducing problems and solutions is another common way that writers structure text. For example, if you're reading a letter to a newspaper editor discussing highway construction, look for the problem that the writer presents. As you read further, search for possible solutions that the writer may suggest.

Apply the Strategies

Identify the different text structures in the paragraph below. Then answer the questions that follow.

TWELVE ESCAPE BLAZE

When the fire broke out, the manager checked the lobby and the stairwell. Then he made his way along each floor of the hotel. As the flames advanced, twelve people found themselves trapped on the third floor. A 17-year-old girl managed to secure a rope to a bureau and pass it out the window to the ground. The twelve hotel guests lowered themselves down. Investigators determined that the blaze resulted from a broken vent in the boiler room.

1. Do any of these sentences show a problem-and-solution relationship? What is the problem? How is it solved?
2. Which of these sentences contains a cause-and-effect relationship? Which words helped you understand the relationship?
3. Write down the chronological order of the events.

✔ Here are situations in which you'll see text structured in different ways:
► Movie reviews
► Magazine articles
► Autobiographical works

PART *2*

The Influence of the Monarchy

King Henry VIII of England,
after Hans Holbein

Queen Elizabeth I of England,
Unknown Artist

King James I of England,
John De Critz the Elder,
Galleria Platina, Palazzo Pitti, Florence, Italy

After the Wars of the Roses ended, the Tudors and James I brought a new era to English life. These monarchs increased their own power while undercutting the strength of the nobles. They dramatically changed the country's religious practices and transformed England from a small, insular nation into a world power. As a result, the English people gained a new pride in what Shakespeare called "this earth, this realm, this England."

*G*uide *for Interpreting*

Sir Thomas More *(1478–1535)*

Devoted husband and father, passionate defender of the common citizen, sophisticated legal adviser, and deeply religious man—Sir Thomas More had the respect even of the king who put him to death.

Opposing the King More was an important advisor to King Henry VIII. At different times, however, More's stand on issues made him a friend and then a bitter enemy of the king. More certainly aroused the king's anger when he refused to support Henry's bid to divorce Catherine of Aragon. This divorce went against More's conscience as a Catholic. In the end, More's conscience cost him his life, because the king had him beheaded for his opposition.

An Ideal Kingdom More, however, had a kind of revenge. In his book *Utopia,* about an ideal kingdom (the title means "not a place"), he casts a disapproving eye on the injustices of his time.

Elizabeth I *(1533–1603)*

The only child of Henry VIII and Anne Boleyn, Elizabeth Tudor had a childhood filled with sadness and danger. Her mother was executed by her father when Elizabeth was not even three years old. Then Elizabeth was proclaimed illegitimate by Parliament when Henry's son by Jane Seymour was born. Finally, in 1558, after the death of her half sister, Mary, Elizabeth was crowned queen of England and Ireland.

The Elizabethan Age Today, Elizabeth is regarded as one of the finest monarchs ever to rule England. She was highly intelligent, and her colorful personality made her popular with her subjects. Moreover, her reign was a time of artistic achievement, military success, and expanding industry and trade. As a result of this success, the young girl who grew up in danger gave her name to an era of English history: the Elizabethan Age.

◆ Background for Understanding

HISTORY: MORE, ELIZABETH I, AND RELIGIOUS CONFLICT

The late sixteenth century was a period of religious conflict within England and between England and Spain. England was a Catholic country in 1516 when More wrote *Utopia*, about eleven years before Henry VIII divorced Catherine of Aragon. Henry's divorce led not only to More's execution but to England's permanent break with the Roman Catholic Church, as Henry declared himself the head of an independent Church of England.

Mary I, Henry's daughter and Elizabeth's half sister, brought Catholicism back. Then, when Elizabeth ascended to the throne in 1558, she reestablished the Church of England. During her reign, Roman Catholics tried on several occasions to oust her from the throne. As a result, Elizabeth I stepped up persecution of Catholics. The climax of this persecution came in 1587, when Elizabeth agreed to have her Catholic cousin, Mary, Queen of Scots, executed. This act gave Philip II, the Catholic king of Spain, an excuse to attack England with the Spanish Armada.

◆ from Utopia ◆
Speech Before Defeating the Spanish Armada

◆ Literature and Your Life

CONNECT YOUR EXPERIENCE

Just before the start of a big game, when nervous energy is at its greatest, a coach may gather a team together for a "pep talk." Such a talk is similar to Elizabeth's stirring speech to her subjects before the war with Spain. More's text is philosophical, but it is also designed to stir emotions and to promote cooperation.

THEMATIC FOCUS: THE INFLUENCE OF THE MONARCHY

As you read the passage from *Utopia* and Elizabeth's speech, consider what qualities a good ruler must have.

Journal Writing Jot down some ways in which the United States would be different if it were ruled by a monarch rather than governed by a president.

◆ Build Vocabulary

LATIN WORD ROOTS: -sequent-

In *Utopia,* Thomas More uses the adverb *subsequently*. Knowing that its Latin root *-sequent-* means "following in time or order," you can figure out that *subsequently* means "at a later time."

WORD BANK

Before you read, preview this list of words from *Utopia* and Elizabeth's speech.

confiscation
sloth
subsequently
abrogated
forfeited
fraudulent
treachery
stead

◆ Grammar and Style

COMPLEX SENTENCES

In **complex sentences**—sentences with a main clause and one or more subordinate clauses—the main clause can stand by itself as a sentence, and subordinate clauses are dependent on the main clause. Through its structure, a complex sentence expresses the relationship between a main and subordinate ideas.

The main clause can appear at the beginning, middle, or end of a sentence. In this example from *Utopia*, the main clause appears at the end.

Subordinate clauses: When a ruler enjoys wealth and pleasure while all about him are grieving and groaning,

Main clause: he acts as a jailer rather than as a king.

◆ Literary Focus

THEME: MONARCH AS HERO

The literature of the English Renaissance (1485–1625) contains many depictions of the **monarch as hero**, the ruler as a perfect or larger-than-life person.

Look for this **theme** in More's depiction of what a king should be and Elizabeth's presentation of herself as an ideal monarch.

◆ Reading Strategy

SUMMARIZE

To keep track of ideas in sentences, you can **summarize** them by restating the main idea.

In reading More's *Utopia* and Elizabeth's speech, identify the main idea of a long or difficult sentence. Then see how the other ideas qualify, explain, or support it.

More's Sentence

Let him curb crime, and by his wise conduct prevent it rather than allow it to increase, only to punish it subsequently.

Summary

The monarch should prevent crime.

from Utopia

SIR THOMAS MORE

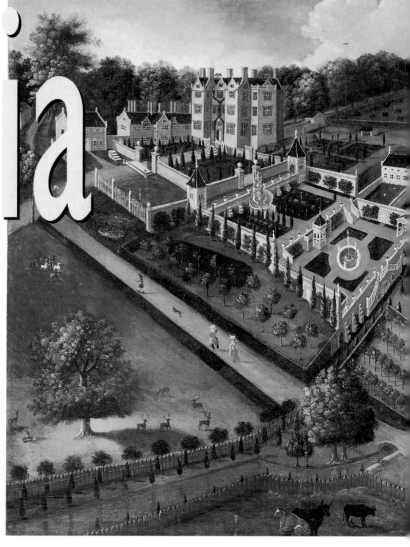

Suppose I should maintain that men choose a king not for his sake, but for theirs, that by his care and efforts they may live comfortably and safely. And that therefore a prince

◆ **Reading Strategy**
Summarize the first two sentences.

ought to take more care of his people's happiness than of his own, as a shepherd ought to take more care of his flock than of himself. Certainly it is wrong to think that the poverty of the people is a safeguard of public peace. Who quarrel more than beggars do? Who long for a change more earnestly than the dissatisfied? Or who rushes in to create disorders which such desperate boldness as the man who has nothing to lose and everything to gain? If a king is so hated and scorned by his subjects that he can rule them only by insults, ill-usage, confiscation, and impoverishment, it would certainly be better for him to quit his kingdom than to keep the name of authority when he has lost the majesty of kingship through his misrule. It is less befitting the dignity of a king to reign over beggars than over rich and happy subjects. Thus Fabricius, a man of noble and exalted spirit, said he would rather govern rich men than be rich himself. When a ruler enjoys wealth and pleasure while all about him are grieving and groaning, he acts as a jailor rather than as a king. He is a poor physician who cannot cure a disease except by throwing his patient into another. A king who can only rule his people by taking from them the pleasures of life shows that he does not know how to govern free men. He ought to shake off either his sloth or his pride, for the people's hatred and scorn arise from these faults in him. Let him live on his own income without wronging others, and limit his expenses to his revenue. Let him curb crime, and by his wise conduct prevent it rather than allow it to increase, only to punish it subsequently. Let him not rashly revive laws already abrogated by disuse, especially if they have been long forgotten and never wanted. And let him never seize any property on the ground that it is forfeited as a fine, when a judge would regard a subject as wicked and fraudulent for claiming it.

Gardens at Llancerch, Denbigshire, Yale Center for British Art, New Haven, Connecticut

▲ **Critical Viewing** How does this painting illustrate the order of the well-run kingdom More describes? **[Apply]**

◆ Build Vocabulary

confiscation (kän´ fis kā´ shən) *n.*: Act of seizing private property for the public treasury or for personal gain, usually as a penalty

sloth (slôth) *n.*: Laziness, idleness

subsequently (sub´ si kwənt lī) *adv.*: At a later time

abrogated (ab´rō gāt´ id) *v.*: Repealed; annulled

forfeited (fôr´ fit id) *v.*: Gave up, as a penalty

fraudulent (frô´ jə lənt) *adj.*: Characterized by deceit or trickery

Guide for Responding

◆ *Literature and Your Life*

Reader's Response Do you think Thomas More's ideas apply to leaders today?

Thematic Focus How much power should a monarch have? What limits should be set on powers of a monarch?

Questions for Research More was executed by King Henry over disputes concerning questions of political and religious authority. Generate one or more questions you could use to further explore the issues between More and the king.

☑ Check Your Comprehension

1. What reason does More give for poverty's becoming a threat to peace in a nation?
2. According to More, what is lacking in a king who can govern people only by taking their pleasures away?
3. How does More think a monarch should deal with the problem of crime?

◆ Critical Thinking

INTERPRET

1. How important does More think wealth is to a king? **[Analyze]**
2. From where do you think More draws his examples of a bad ruler? **[Infer]**
3. In general, what is the principle character trait that More thinks makes a good ruler? **[Draw Conclusions]**
4. Is More the kind of person who would say that the ends justify the means? Explain. **[Deduce]**
5. What universal lessons about good leadership are provided by this selection? **[Draw Conclusions]**

EVALUATE

6. How persuasive is More's argument? **[Make a Judgment]**

EXTEND

7. In what ways do More's views of good government resemble modern democratic ideals? **[Social Studies Link]**

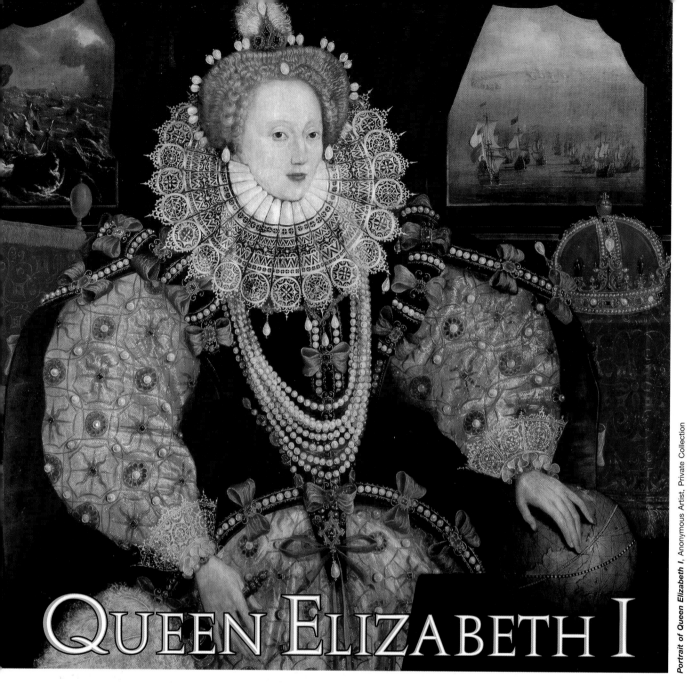

Portrait of Queen Elizabeth I, Anonymous Artist, Private Collection

QUEEN ELIZABETH I

Speech Before Defeating the Spanish Armada

▲ **Critical Viewing** How does this rendering of Elizabeth symbolize her great success? [Interpret]

My loving people, we have been persuaded by some, that are careful of our safety, to take heed how we commit ourselves to armed multitudes, for fear of treachery; but I assure you, I do not desire to live to distrust my faithful and loving people. Let tyrants fear; I have always so behaved myself that, under God, I have placed my chiefest strength and safeguard in the loyal hearts and good will of my subjects. And therefore I am come amongst you at this time, not as for my recreation or sport, but being resolved, in the midst and heat of the battle, to live or die amongst you all; to lay down, for my God, and for my kingdom, and for my people, my honor and my blood, even the dust. I know I have but the body of a weak and feeble woman; but I have the heart of a king, and of a king of England, too; and think foul scorn that Parma or Spain, or any prince of Europe, should dare to invade the borders of my realms: to which, rather than any dishonor should grow by me, I myself will take up arms; I myself will be your general, judge, and rewarder of every one of your virtues in the field. I know already, by your forwardness, that you have deserved rewards and crowns; and we do assure you, on the word of a prince, they shall be duly paid you. In the mean my lieutenant general shall be in my stead, than whom never prince commanded a more noble and worthy subject; not doubting by your obedience to my general, by your concord in the camp, and by your valor in the field, we shall shortly have a famous victory over the enemies of my God, of my kingdom, and of my people.

◆ **Literary Focus**

Make a list of words that Elizabeth uses that make her appear heroic.

◆ **Build Vocabulary**

treachery (trech´ ər ē) *n*.: Betrayal of trust, faith, or allegiance

stead (sted) *n*.: Position of a person as filled by a replacement or substitute

▶ **Critical Viewing** These *Dangers Averted* medals celebrated the defeat of the Spanish Armada. How do you think those who received this medal were treated by average British citizens? **[Hypothesize]**

Guide for Responding

◆ *Literature and Your Life*

Reader's Response Do you think Elizabeth really intended to reward her subjects in the way she promised? Why or why not?

Thematic Focus What words does Elizabeth use to present herself as a friend of the common man or woman?

☑ **Check Your Comprehension**

1. What does Queen Elizabeth I say she is willing to risk for her people when they go to war?

2. What does the queen say to assure her subjects that being a woman won't hinder her performance during wartime?

3. What prediction does Elizabeth make about the war's outcome?

◆ **Critical Thinking**

INTERPRET

1. (a) Name two concerns of her audience that Elizabeth addresses. (b) Indicate how she puts these concerns to rest. **[Interpret]**

2. Do Elizabeth's words mean that she will actually fight and die with her soldiers? Why or why not? **[Interpret]**

3. Name two ways in which Elizabeth appeals to her subjects' patriotism. **[Analyze]**

4. What effect do you think Elizabeth hoped her speech would have? **[Draw Conclusions]**

EVALUATE

5. How effective is Elizabeth's speech as a "pep talk"? **[Evaluate]**

COMPARE LITERARY WORKS

6. Describe how the different motives of Sir Thomas More and Queen Elizabeth affect the tone of these two writings. **[Compare and Contrast]**

Guide for Responding (continued)

◆ Reading Strategy

SUMMARIZE

Summarizing passages by restating their main ideas will help you better understand what you read. This sentence from More's *Utopia*, for example, can be boiled down to the statement in the main clause about what a good ruler should do:

> Let him not rashly revive laws already abrogated by disuse, especially if they have been long forgotten and never wanted.

1. Identify the main clause and summarize it in your own words.
2. As a reporter, take notes on the queen's speech. Jot down the key ideas she expresses.

◆ Literary Focus

THE MONARCH AS HERO

In *Utopia* and "Speech Before Defeating the Spanish Armada," the **monarch as hero** is a central idea. More is writing about an ideal ruler, and Elizabeth is talking about herself! However, both writers portray the monarch as a superior person, endowed with courage and generosity.

1. Indicate another way in which More expects a king to be generous.
2. What words does Elizabeth use to portray herself as generous and heroic? Explain.

◆ Build Vocabulary

USING THE LATIN ROOT -SEQUENT-

Knowing that the Latin root -*sequent*- means "following in time or order," match the number of the -*sequent*- words with the letter of the correct definitions:

1. consequence
2. sequential
3. non sequitur
4. sequel

a. something that doesn't follow
b. episode that follows
c. following in time or order
d. result of an action

USING THE WORD BANK: Context

Use all the words in the Word Bank to write a brief profile of an ideal monarch.

◆ Grammar and Style

COMPLEX SENTENCES

By using complex sentences, More and Queen Elizabeth I are able to create a tone that is persuasive and full of authority.

A **complex sentence** contains a main clause with the key idea and one or more subordinate clauses relating to that idea.

Practice On your paper, write the following complex sentences. Underline the main clause once and the subordinate clauses twice.

1. And let him never seize any property on the ground that it is forfeited as a fine, when a judge would regard a subject as wicked and fraudulent for claiming it.
2. He is a poor physician who cannot cure a disease except by throwing his patient into another.
3. . . . we have been persuaded by some, that are careful of our safety, to take heed how we commit ourselves to armed multitudes . . .
4. . . . my lieutenant general shall be in my stead, than whom never prince commanded a more noble and worthy subject . . .
5. . . . I know already, by your forwardness, that you have deserved rewards and crowns . . .

Writing Application On your paper, combine each pair of simple sentences into a complex sentence. (You may use connecting words like *because, although, when,* and *who.*)

1. Sir Thomas More was amazingly self-possessed. He was even able to make a joke at his own execution.
2. More knew what his king wanted him to do. He still insisted on opposing the king's wishes.
3. Elizabeth was a woman in a man's world. She showed the men what a "feeble woman" could do.
4. King Philip II was the ruler of Catholic Spain. He thought he could conquer England.
5. Elizabeth I restored the Church of England. The persecution of Catholics intensified.

Build Your Portfolio

 ## Idea Bank

Writing

1. **Help Wanted** Using Thomas More's ideas about a perfect monarch, write a Help Wanted ad for such a ruler.

2. **Letter of Support** As a loyal subject of Elizabeth I, write her a letter telling why you support her decision to fight the Spanish and pledging your aid. **[Social Studies Link]**

3. **Updated Utopia** Following More's lead, write a fantasy about an ideal place where all of America's problems have been corrected.
[Social Studies Link]

Speaking, Listening, and Viewing

4. **Debate** Form two groups and debate this question: Do Sir Thomas More's ideas about the qualities of a perfect king still apply to today's leaders? **[Social Studies Link]**

5. **Visual Research** Artists sometimes portray the world in Utopian ways, as in the painting found on pages 238 and 239. What does Utopia look like to you? Research art books to find an image that portrays your ideal and prepare a statement about what appeals most deeply to you in the art. **[Art Link]**

Researching and Representing

6. **Timeline of Elizabethan England** Research this era of English history. Then create a large, illustrated timeline of the period, indicating its major achievements. **[Art Link; Social Studies Link]**

7. **Movie Review** Robert Bolt wrote a play and filmscript about Sir Thomas More entitled *A Man for All Seasons*. Rent the video of the movie and review it for your class. (You can read an excerpt from the play on page 253.) **[Media Link; Social Studies Link]**

Online Activity www.phlit.phschool.com

 ## Guided Writing Lesson

Letter to an Editor

Sir Thomas More and Elizabeth I waste no time in revealing their opinions to readers and listeners. Reveal your own opinion in a letter to an editor about a political leader in the news. Respond to a particular story about this leader, giving your own perspective on the story and on the leader. Follow these tips to make your arguments convincing.

Writing Skills Focus: Persuasive Tone

In all types of persuasive writing—from letters to the editor to persuasive essays—it is important to maintain a **persuasive tone**. The word *tone* refers to the writer's attitude toward a subject, and a persuasive tone should reflect the writer's sense of conviction. It should also inspire readers to feel that their interests are the same as the writer's.

Notice how Elizabeth I signals her conviction with words like *strength* and *safeguard*, then links herself to listeners with words like *loyal* and *good will:*

> . . . I have always so behaved myself that, under God, I have placed my chiefest strength and safeguard in the loyal hearts and good will of my subjects.

Prewriting Outline your own point of view, and choose words and phrases that reflect it.

Drafting As you write, imagine yourself talking to someone you respect. Draw from your prewriting notes the words and phrases that will convince—not antagonize—this person. Develop the points you want to make by supporting them with specific examples.

Revising Add words and phrases that will bring you and your readers together in a community of concern. Whenever possible, use the pronoun *we* rather than *I*.

*G*uide for Interpreting

The King James Bible

(completed 1611)

When King James I ascended the throne, one of the issues he faced was the demand for a uniform English version of the Bible. He commissioned fifty-four scholars and clergymen in 1604 to compare all texts of the Bible and come up with a definitive English edition.

> *The King James version of the Bible has been called "the only classic ever created by a committee."*

Laboring for seven years, the group produced a translation that has been regarded as one of the great works of English literature.

Early Bibles The Bible, a collection of books developed over a period of more than 1,200 years, consists of two main parts—the Old Testament and the New Testament. The Old Testament was originally written in Hebrew; the New Testament, in Greek. In the fourth century A.D., St. Jerome began translating the Bible into Latin. This translation, the Vulgate, remained the standard Bible of the West for centuries.

The reformer John Wycliffe produced the first English translation from Latin in the late 1300's. The Protestant Reformation in the 1500's, and the growing use of Gutenberg's movable type, resulted in an increased demand for a Bible in the vernacular, or common language of the people. William Tyndale, a Protestant chaplain and tutor, decided to prepare such a Bible.

Tyndale's Legacy Faced with clerical opposition at home, Tyndale fled to what is now Germany and there published his English translation of the New Testament. He had translated only part of the Old Testament when he was arrested for heresy and executed near Brussels, Belgium, in 1536.

Ironically, Henry VIII two years before had broken with Rome and established the Church of England. As England became more Protestant, the nation viewed Tyndale not as a heretic but as a hero. Throughout the sixteenth century, many others translated all or part of the Bible into English. However, when the committee appointed by James I began work on what would be called the King James or Authorized Version of the Bible, the magnificent diction and rhythms of Tyndale's translation were followed most closely.

◆ Background for Understanding

HISTORY: THE IMPACT OF THE BIBLE

Up through the Middle Ages, Bibles were painstakingly copied by hand. The resulting manuscripts, though often beautiful to behold, were rare and costly. In 1456, the German inventor Johann Gutenberg used a portion of the Bible to illustrate his newly devised method of printing with movable type. The development of printing made the Bible far more accessible than it had ever been before and also helped spur the demand for vernacular translations.

Still, prior to its translation into English, the Bible could be read only by well-educated members of the upper class who understood Latin. With the publication of the King James Bible, however, the Bible became available to the masses. Generations of people in Great Britain and the United States have grown up reading the King James Bible and adding its wisdom to the common store of knowledge.

from The King James Bible

◆ *Literature and Your Life*

CONNECT YOUR EXPERIENCE

In today's world, it seems that almost every day there are new inventions or developments that make it easier to access information. Think how inventions such as the cellular phone and the personal computer have changed people's lives. Then try to imagine the impact of the publication of the King James Bible on a society where few people ever had access to the information in the Bible.

Journal Writing Jot down your thoughts about how reactions to new methods of communication might be similar to Renaissance reactions to the printing press or a new Bible translation.

THEMATIC FOCUS: INFLUENCE OF THE MONARCHY

The fact that the King James Bible was commissioned by the king played an important role in contributing to its impact. What does this suggest about the influence of the monarchy?

◆ Build Vocabulary

LATIN WORD ROOTS: *-stat-*

The excerpt from the Sermon on the Mount includes the word *stature*, which includes the Latin root *-stat-*, meaning "to stand." The root offers a clue to the word's meaning, "a person's height or standing." The root is also spelled *-stit-*, as in *substitute*.

| righteousness |
| stature |
| prodigal |
| entreated |
| transgressed |

WORD BANK

Preview the list before you read.

◆ Grammar and Style

INFINITIVE PHRASES

An **infinitive phrase** is a group of words consisting of an infinitive (the base form of a verb preceded by *to*) and its modifiers and complements. An infinitive phrase functions as a noun, adjective, or adverb. The following example from the Bible serves as an adverb modifying *sent*.

He sent him into his fields *to feed swine*.

◆ Literary Focus

PSALM, SERMON, AND PARABLE

A **psalm** is a sacred song or lyric poem in praise of God. The Old Testament's Book of Psalms contains 150 such pieces.

A **sermon** is a speech offering religious or moral instruction. Given by Jesus on a mountainside in Galilee, the Sermon on the Mount contains the basic teachings of Christianity.

A **parable** is a short, simple story from which a moral or religious lesson can be drawn. The most famous parables are those in the New Testament.

◆ Reading Strategy

INFERRING MEANING

Although some portions of the Bible are clear and direct, others require you to **draw inferences**, or conclusions, about the messages they convey. For example, Psalm 23 includes the line "The Lord is my shepherd."

To understand the psalm, you must infer the meaning of this comparison. By considering the role that a shepherd performs, you can infer that, like a shepherd, God watches over his flock and leads them toward a better place.

Psalm 23

from THE KING JAMES BIBLE

1 The Lord is my shepherd; I shall not want.

2 He maketh me to lie down in green pastures: he leadeth me beside the still waters.

3 He restoreth my soul: he leadeth me in the paths of <u>righteousness</u> for his name's sake.

4 Yea, though I walk through the valley of the shadow of death, I will fear no evil: for thou art with me; thy rod and thy staff they comfort me.

5 Thou preparest a table before me in the presence of mine enemies; thou anointest my head with oil; my cup runneth over.

6 Surely goodness and mercy shall follow me all the days of my life: and I will dwell in the house of the Lord forever.

▶ **Critical Viewing** What can you infer about the King James Bible from the style of the art on this title page? **[Infer]**

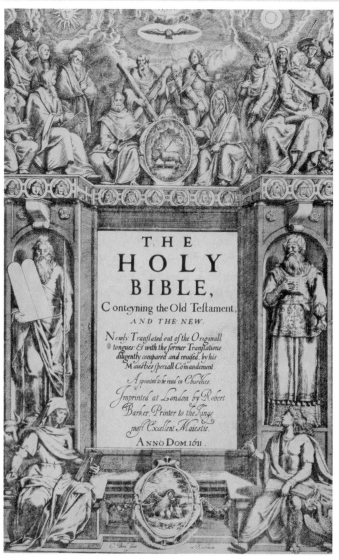

King James Bible, 1611, title page of the New Testament, The Folger Shakespeare Library, Washington, D.C.

from the Sermon on the Mount

from THE KING JAMES BIBLE

Matthew 6: 24–30

24 No man can serve two masters: for either he will hate the one, and love the other; or else he will hold to the one, and despise the other. Ye cannot serve God and mammon.[1]

25 Therefore I say unto you, Take no thought for your life, what ye shall eat, or what ye shall drink; nor yet for your body, what ye shall put on. Is not the life more than meat, and the body than raiment?[2]

26 Behold the fowls of the air: for they sow not, neither do they reap, nor gather into barns; yet your heavenly Father feedeth them. Are ye not much better than they?

27 Which of you by taking thought can add one cubit unto his stature?

28 And why take ye thought for raiment? Consider the lilies of the field, how they grow; they toil not, neither do they spin:

29 And yet I say unto you, That even Solomon[3] in all his glory was not arrayed like one of these.

30 Wherefore, if God so clothe the grass of the field, which to day is, and to morrow is cast into the oven, *shall he* not much more *clothe* you, O ye of little faith?

---

1. **mammon** (mam´ ən) *n.*: Money personified as a false god.
2. **raiment** (rā´ mənt) *n.*: Clothing; wearing apparel.
3. **Solomon** (säl´ ə mən) *n.*: Tenth-century B.C. king of Israel.

◆ Build Vocabulary

righteousness (rī´ chəs nis) *n.*: Doing what is fair and just

stature (stach´ ər) *n.*: Height of a person standing; development, growth, or level of achievement

---

Guide for Responding

◆ Literature and Your Life

Reader's Response Which words or phrases in Psalm 23 and the excerpt from the Sermon on the Mount are familiar to you?

Thematic Response How do you think the quality of this translation would have reflected on King James?

☑ Check Your Comprehension

1. In the first part of Psalm 23, what images convey the idea of the Lord as a shepherd?
2. What two masters does Jesus say you cannot serve at the same time?
3. What does he point out about the "lilies of the field"?

The Parable of the Prodigal Son

from THE KING JAMES BIBLE   Luke 15: 11–32

11 And he said, A certain man had two sons:

12 And the younger of them said to *his* father, Father, give me the portion of goods that falleth *to me*. And he divided unto them *his* living.

13 And not many days after the younger son gathered all together, and took his journey into a far country, and there wasted his substance with riotous living.

14 And when he had spent all, there arose a mighty famine in that land; and he began to be in want.

15 And he went and joined himself to a citizen of that country; and he sent him into his fields to feed swine.

16 And he would fain[1] have filled his belly with the husks that the swine did eat: and no man gave unto him.

17 And when he came to himself, he said, How many hired servants of my father's have bread enough and to spare, and I perish with hunger!

18 I will arise and go to my father, and will say unto him, Father, I have sinned against heaven, and before thee,

19 And am no more worthy to be called thy son: make me as one of thy hired servants.

20 And he arose, and came to his father. But when he was yet a great way off, his father saw him, and had compassion, and ran, and fell on his neck, and kissed him.

21 And the son said unto him, Father, I have sinned against heaven, and in thy sight, and am no more worthy to be called thy son.

22 But the father said to his servants, Bring forth the best robe, and put *it* on him; and put a ring on his hand, and shoes on *his* feet:

---

1. **fain** *adv.*: Gladly.

23 And bring hither the fatted calf, and kill *it*; and let us eat, and be merry:

24 For this my son was dead, and is alive again; he was lost, and is found. And they began to be merry.

25 Now his elder son was in the field: and as he came and drew nigh to the house, he heard music and dancing.

26 And he called one of the servants, and asked what these things meant.

27 And he said unto him, Thy brother is come; and thy father hath killed the fatted calf, because he hath received him safe and sound.

28 And he was angry, and would not go in: therefore came his father out, and <u>entreated</u> him.

29 And he answering said to *his* father, Lo, these many years do I serve thee, neither <u>transgressed</u> I at any time thy commandment: and yet thou never gavest me a kid, that I might make merry with my friends:

30 But as soon as this thy son was come, which hath devoured thy living with harlots, thou hast killed for him the fatted calf.

31 And he said unto him, Son, thou art ever with me, and all that I have is thine.

32 It was meet[2] that we should make merry, and be glad: for this thy brother was dead, and is alive again; and was lost, and is found.

---

2. **meet** *adj.*: Fitting.

◆ **Build Vocabulary**

prodigal (präd´ i gəl) *adj.*: Addicted to wasteful expenditure

entreated (in trēt´ id) *v.*: Begged; pleaded

transgressed (trans grest´) *v.*: Overstepped or broken (a law or commandment)

Guide for Responding

◆ *Literature and Your Life*

Reader's Response If you were the elder son, how would you have reacted to the father's response at the end? Why?

Research Translations of the Bible allow people around the world to read it. Do research to find out into how many languages the Bible has been translated.

☑ Check Your Comprehension

1. What causes the younger son to return home?
2. Summarize the father's reaction to his return.
3. (a) What complaint does the elder son make?
   (b) Summarize the father's response.

Guide for Responding (continued)

◆ Critical Thinking

INTERPRET

1. In Psalm 23, why is the speaker comforted by the Lord's (shepherd's) rod and staff? **[Analyze]**
2. What is the central message of Psalm 23? Support your answer. **[Draw Conclusions]**
3. On what central choice in life does the passage from the Sermon on the Mount focus? **[Connect]**
4. (a) With what specific human activities does Jesus contrast the fowls' and the lilies' behavior in the Sermon on the Mount? (b) What does he suggest the fowls and lilies have in common? **[Compare and Contrast]**
5. How would you describe the two sons in the Parable of the Prodigal Son? **[Compare and Contrast]**
6. What does the parable suggest about how we should treat others? **[Connect]**

EVALUATE

7. Which of these selections conveys its message most effectively? Why? **[Assess]**

EXTEND

8. What modern poems or songs can you think of that convey a message similar to that of one of these selections? **[Literature Link]**

◆ Grammar and Style

INFINITIVE PHRASES

An **infinitive phrase** consists of an infinitive (the base form of the verb preceded by *to*) and its modifiers and complements. It can function as an adjective, adverb, or noun.

Practice In your notebook, write the infinitive phrases that appear in the following sentences and identify whether they function as adjectives, adverbs, or nouns.

1. The younger son chose to take his inheritance.
2. He began to spend it on riotous living.
3. To avoid starvation he returned to his home.
4. His father made plans to feast his son lavishly.
5. His elder brother did not want to attend the feast.

◆ Reading Strategy

INFERRING MEANING

Use details from the selections, along with your prior knowledge, to **make inferences**, or draw conclusions, about the meaning of each of these lines. Explain each answer.

1. "dwell in the house of the Lord forever" (Psalm 23)
2. "my son was dead, and is alive again" (Parable of the Prodigal Son)

◆ Literary Focus

PSALM, SERMON, AND PARABLE

The three selections in this grouping illustrate three literary forms included in the Bible. A **psalm** is a sacred song or lyric poem in praise of God. A **sermon** is a speech giving religious or moral instruction. A **parable** is a short, simple story from which a moral or religious lesson can be drawn.

1. (a) Contrast the styles of the selections. (b) How is the style of each selection appropriate to its function or purpose?
2. What is the central message of this portion of the Sermon on the Mount? Support your answer.
3. (a) What is the chief moral lesson of the Parable of the Prodigal Son? (b) Is this lesson directed only at family members? Explain.

◆ Build Vocabulary

USING THE LATIN ROOT -stat-

The Latin root -stat-, sometimes spelled -stit-, means "to stand" or "to set up." Define each of the following words, incorporating the idea of standing or setting up.

1. statue   2. stationary   3. institute

USING THE WORD BANK: Synonyms

In your notebook, write the letter of the word that is the best synonym of the first word.

1. righteousness: (a) justness, (b) neatness, (c) error
2. stature: (a) depth, (b) status, (c) interference
3. prodigal: (a) brilliant, (b) wasteful, (c) awful
4. entreated: (a) agreed, (b) financed, (c) begged
5. transgressed: (a) sinned, (b) poached, (c) traveled

Build Your Portfolio

 ## Idea Bank

Writing

1. **Letters** Write a series of letters that the prodigal son might have written to a friend back home.

2. **Modern Update** Create an updated version of one of these selections by changing the language, setting, characters, and/or circumstances. Your psalm, sermon, or parable should focus on the same moral lesson as those in the originals.

3. **Allusion** English speakers often make allusions, or references, to the King James Bible. Write your own poem, story, or essay in which you allude at least once to each of the three Bible selections.

Speaking, Listening, and Viewing

4. **Oral Retelling** Prepare a retelling of the Parable of the Prodigal Son for an audience of young children. Deliver your modified version to your classmates or to such an audience.

5. **Sermon** Imagine that you are a member of the clergy and the class is your congregation. Compose and deliver a sermon built around one of the three Bible selections.

Researching and Representing

6. **Compare Translations** The King James version is only one of many English translations of the Bible. Working in a small group, compare two other translations of one of the selections. Share your impressions in a panel discussion. **[Literature Link]**

7. **Song** Set Psalm 23 to your own original music or to music composed by someone else. Performyour musical version of the psalm live, on audiocassette, or on videotape. **[Music Link]**

Online Activity www.phlit.phschool.com

 ## Guided Writing Lesson

Opening Argument of a Debate

Imagine that you are part of a team planning to debate the father's decision in the Parable of the Prodigal Son. One side will defend the father's decision; the other will argue against that decision. You are in charge of preparing a written opening argument for your side of the debate. The following tips on elaboration should help you develop your opening argument.

Writing Skills Focus: Elaboration

In your opening statement, you must do more than simply state your key points. Instead, use these techniques to **elaborate** on your points.
- Support your argument with examples, reasons, and other details.
- Clarify broad information by providing more specific details.
- Anticipate counterarguments and provide information to rebut them.
- Anticipate questions and provide information to answer them.
- Restate your main point in different words.

Use the following strategies to guide you as you write.

Prewriting Taking either side of the argument, write a clear, brief statement of your position and jot down details that support it. Also, anticipate the questions and counterarguments of others and jot down possible answers.

Drafting Organize details so they effectively support your position. Incorporate answers to possible questions and counterarguments. End with a restatement of your main argument.

Revising Practice presenting your opening statement to an audience, using a peer reviewer. Have the reviewer make suggestions about where you could add more support for your arguments.

CONNECTIONS TO TODAY'S WORLD

from A Man for All Seasons
Robert Bolt

Thematic Connection

ROYAL PROCLAMATIONS

Imagine waking up tomorrow and finding out that the president has decided that everyone in the country has to drive a station wagon. Although it seems impossible and absurd, for the people of the sixteenth century, living according to the whim of a ruler was a way of life. At that time, monarchs of Europe wielded absolute power. By simply issuing a royal proclamation, a monarch could radically change how people lived their lives.

BATTLE OF POWER

The authority and power of the Church during the Renaissance were also great and far-reaching. The Church was wealthy, and politically and socially powerful. When the Church and monarchy disagreed, the power of the Church usually prevailed, until the reign of Henry VIII. Henry VIII sought an annulment of his marriage to Catherine of Aragon. When his request was denied, King Henry asserted that royal power was greater than the power of the Church. He remarried and formed his own church, the Church of England, of which he was head.

DIMINISHING POWER

Through the centuries, parliamentary authority has grown while royal power has diminished. By the end of World War I, most Western monarchies had ceased to exist. Present-day monarchies are considered "constitutional monarchies," in which a royal figure exists for purposes of tradition and as a symbol of national unity but has no political authority.

Although the power of monarchies has diminished, the influence of the monarchies has had long-reaching effects, such as the present-day use of the King James Bible and fascination with the possibilities of absolute power. The monarchy is still a popular theme in today's literature and movies. For example, the screenplay *A Man for All Seasons* presents a historical struggle with the monarchy. In the following excerpt, King Henry VIII is trying to force Sir Thomas More to choose allegiance to the king over his religious beliefs. More chose to adhere to his personal belief. He was later tried and put to death.

ROBERT BOLT
(1924–1995)

Robert Bolt was a successful British playwright and writer of screenplays. He was born in Manchester and educated at Manchester University. He served three years in the army and air force before trying his hand as a playwright. He was teaching when his first play, *Flowing Cherry,* was produced in London. Its great success led Bolt to leave the classroom for the stage.

Bolt wrote the screenplay for *A Man for All Seasons,* as well as for other successful movies, including *Dr. Zhivago, Lawrence of Arabia,* and *Ryan's Daughter.*

from

A MAN *for* ALL SEASONS

Robert Bolt

In the following scene, Sir Thomas More, friend and colleague of King Henry VIII, is being forced to chose between his devotion to the Church and respect for its teaching, and his loyalty to his ruler. His strong religious principles prevent him from taking an oath of supremacy, an assertion that papal authority could not supersede the king's authority. This defiance cost him his life.

HENRY. I am a fool.

MORE. How so, Your Grace?

HENRY. [*A pause, during which the music fades to silence*] What else but a fool to live in a Court, in a licentious[1] mob—when I have friends, with gardens.

MORE. Your Grace—

HENRY. No courtship, no ceremony, Thomas. Be seated. You *are* my friend, are you not? [MORE *sits*]

MORE. Your Majesty.

HENRY. [*Eyes lighting on the chain on the table by* MORE] And thank God I have a friend for my Chancellor.[2] [*Laughingly,*

---

1. **licentious** (lī sen´ shəs) *adj.*: Disregarding accepted rules and standards.
2. **Chancellor** (chan´ sə lər) *n.*: More's position as an important advisor to the king.

but implacably, he takes up the chain and lowers it over MORE's *head]* Readier to be friends, I trust, than he was to be Chancellor.

MORE. My own knowledge of my poor abilities—

HENRY. I will judge of your abilities, Thomas . . . Did you know that Wolsey named you for Chancellor?

MORE. Wolsey!

HENRY. Aye, before he died. Wolsey named you and Wolsey was no fool.

MORE. He was a statesman of incomparable ability, Your Grace.

HENRY. Was he? Was he so? [*He rises*] Then why did he fail me? Be seated—it was villainy then! Yes, villainy. I was right to break him; he was all pride, Thomas; a proud man; pride right through. And he failed me! [MORE *opens his mouth*] He failed me in the one thing that mattered! The one thing that matters, Thomas, then or now. And why? He wanted to be Pope! Yes, he wanted to be the Bishop of Rome. I'll tell you something, Thomas, and you can check this for yourself—it was never merry in England while we had Cardinals amongst us. [*He nods significantly at* MORE, *who lowers his eyes*] But look now— [*Walking away*] —I shall forget the feel of that . . . great tiller[3] under my hands . . . I took her down to Dogget's Bank, went about and brought her up in Tilbury Roads. A man could sail clean round the world in that ship.

MORE. [*With affectionate admiration*] Some men could, Your Grace.

3. **tiller** (til′ ər) *n.*: Bar or handle for turning a boat's rudder.

Beyond Literature

Cultural Connection

Separation of Church and State Sir Thomas More was beheaded because he refused to accept King Henry VIII as the supreme ruler of the Church of England. The issue of separation of church and state is an old one.

Activity Discuss the theme of church and state in medieval England and in the United States today. How are the issues similar and different?

▲ **Critical Viewing** How does this movie still illustrate the conflict in this excerpt from *A Man for All Seasons*? **[Support]**

HENRY. [*Offhand*] Touching this matter of my divorce, Thomas; have you thought of it since we last talked?

MORE. Of little else.

HENRY. Then you see your way clear to me?

MORE. That you should put away Queen Catherine, Sire? Oh, alas [*He thumps the chair in distress*] as I think of it I see so clearly that I can *not* come with Your Grace that my endeavor is not to think of it at all.

HENRY. Then you have not thought enough! . . . [*With real appeal*] Great God, Thomas, why do you hold out against me in the desire of my heart—the very wick of my heart?

MORE. [*Draws up his sleeve, baring his arm*] There is my right arm. [*A practical proposition*] Take your dagger and saw it from my shoulder, and I will laugh and be thankful, if by that means I can come with Your Grace with a clear conscience.

HENRY. [*Uncomfortably pulls at the sleeve*] I know it, Thomas, I know . . .

MORE. [*Rises, formally*] I crave pardon if I offend.

HENRY. [*Suspiciously*] Speak then.

MORE. When I took the Great Seal your Majesty promised not to pursue me on this matter.

HENRY. Ha! So I break my word, Master More! No no, I'm joking . . . I joke roughly . . . [*He wanders away*] I often think I'm a rough fellow . . . Yes, a rough young fellow. [*He shakes his head indulgently*] Be seated

from *A Man for All Seasons* ◆ 255

. . . That's a rosebay.[4] We have one like it at Hampton—not so red as that though. Ha—I'm in an excellent frame of mind. [*Glances at the rosebay*] Beautiful. [*Reasonable, pleasant*] You must consider, Thomas, that I stand in peril of my soul. It was no marriage; she was my brother's widow. Leviticus: "Thou shalt not uncover the nakedness of thy brother's wife." Leviticus, Chapter eighteen, Verse sixteen.[5]

MORE. Yes, Your Grace. But Deuteronomy—[6]

HENRY. [*Triumphant*] Deuteronomy's ambiguous!

MORE. [*Bursting out*] Your Grace, I'm not fit to meddle in these matters—to me it seems a matter for the Holy See—

HENRY. [*Reprovingly*] Thomas, Thomas, does a man need a Pope to tell him when he's sinned? It was a sin, Thomas; I admit it; I repent. And God has punished me; I have no son . . . Son after son she's borne me, Thomas, all dead at birth, or dead within the month; I never saw the hand of God so clear in anything . . . I have a daughter, she's a good child, a well-set child— But I have no son. [*He flares up*] It is my bounden *duty* to put away the Queen, and all the Popes back to St. Peter shall not come between me and my duty! How is it that you cannot see? Everyone else does.

MORE. [*Eagerly*] Then why does Your Grace need my poor support?

HENRY. Because you are honest. What's more to the purpose, you're known to be honest . . . There are those like Norfolk who follow me because I wear the crown, and there are those like Master Cromwell who follow me because they are jackals with sharp teeth and I am their lion, and there is a mass that follows me because it follows anything that moves—and there is you.

MORE. I am sick to think how much I must displease Your Grace.

HENRY. No, Thomas, I respect your sincerity. Respect? Oh, man, it's water in the desert . . . How did you like our music? That air they played, it had a certain— well, tell me what you thought of it.

MORE. [*Relieved at this turn; smiling*] Could it have been Your Grace's own?

HENRY. [*Smiles back*] Discovered! Now I'll never know your true opinion. And that's irksome, Thomas, for we artists, though we love praise, yet we love truth better.

MORE. [*Mildly*] Then I will tell Your Grace truly what I thought of it.

HENRY. [*A little disconcerted*] Speak then.

MORE. To me it seemed—delightful.

HENRY. Thomas—I chose the right man for Chancellor.

MORE. I must in fairness add that my taste in music is reputedly deplorable.[7]

HENRY. Your taste in music is excellent. It exactly coincides with my own. Ah music! Music! Send them back without me, Thomas; I will live here in Chelsea and make music.

---

4. **rosebay** (rōz′ bā) *n*.: Any of the genus (rhododendron) of trees or shrubs with showy flowers of pink, white, or purple.

5. **Leviticus** (lə′ vit′ i kəs), **Chapter eighteen, Verse sixteen:** Reference to the third book of the Pentateuch in the Bible, containing the laws relating to priests and their assistants, the Levites.

6. **Deuteronomy** (do͞ot′ ər än′ ə mē): Fifth book of the Pentateuch in the Bible, in which the laws of Moses are set down.

---

7. **deplorable** (dē plôr′ə bəl) *adj*.: Regrettable or wretched.

MORE. My house is at Your Grace's disposal.

HENRY. Thomas, you understand me; we will stay here together and make music.

MORE. Will Your Grace honor my roof after dinner?

HENRY. [*Walking away, blowing moodily on his whistle*] Mm? Yes, I expect I'll bellow for you . . .

MORE. My wife will be more—

HENRY. Yes, yes. [*He turns, his face set*] Touching this other business, mark you, Thomas, I'll have no opposition.

MORE. [*Sadly*] Your Grace?

HENRY. No opposition, I say! No opposition! Your conscience is your own affair; but you are my Chancellor! There, you have my word—I'll leave you out of it. But I don't take it kindly, Thomas, and I'll have no opposition! I see how it will be; the bishops will oppose me. The full-fed, hypocritical, "Princes of the *Church*"! Ha! As for the Pope! Am I to burn in Hell because the Bishop of Rome, with the King of Spain's knife to his throat, mouths me Deuteronomy? Hypocrites! They're all hypocrites! Mind they do not take you in, Thomas! Lie low if you will, but I'll brook no opposition—no noise! No words, no signs, no letters, no pamphlets—Mind that, Thomas —no writings against me!

MORE. Your grace is unjust. I am Your Grace's loyal minister. If I cannot serve Your Grace in this great matter of the Queen—

HENRY. I have no Queen! Catherine is not my wife and no priest can make her so, and they that say she is my wife are not only liars . . . but traitors! Mind it, Thomas!

MORE. Am I a babbler, Your Grace? [*But his voice is unsteady*]

HENRY. You are stubborn . . . [*Wooingly*] If you could come with me, you are the man I would soonest raise—yes, with my own hand.

MORE. [*Covers his face*] Oh, Your Grace overwhelms me!

Guide for Responding

◆ *Literature and Your Life*

Reader's Response If you were Sir Thomas More, how would you have responded to the king? Explain.

Thematic Focus Aside from government, what other situations can you think of in which it is dangerous for one person to have absolute power? Explain.

☑ Check Your Comprehension

1. What position does More hold in Henry's court?
2. Why does Henry feel he has the right to divorce Queen Catherine?
3. How does More feel about Henry's decision to divorce the queen?

◆ Critical Thinking

INTERPRET

1. Why does Henry think Wolsey failed him? Why do you think the king brings this up to More? **[Interpret]**

2. Henry asked More to critique his music as well as his decision to divorce Catherine. What do his reactions reveal about how he feels about More's opinions? Support your answer. **[Infer]**

3. Judging by More's final gesture of covering his face and his words "Your Grace overwhelms me," what do you think his decision will be? **[Predict]**

4. How do the stage directions add to your understanding of the relationship between Henry and More? **[Explain]**

EXTEND

5. In which countries in today's world does a ruler have absolute power? **[Social Studies Link]**

Thematic Connection

THE INFLUENCE OF THE MONARCHY

Bolt's screenplay captures a time when the British monarchy had absolute power. Today, in contrast, the monarchy has little power and serves mostly as a symbol of the nation's unity.

1. Which of the monarchs represented in the selections in this section do you believe had the most power? Which used power for the good of the people? Which used it for selfish reasons? Support your answers.

2. How might the world be different if European monarchies still had absolute authority? Support your answer.

3. Being part of a democracy, we become part of the decision-making process at the age of eighteen. In many countries people are not given the privilege of voting and live by the will of a dictator. How do you feel about having the privilege to vote?

 Idea Bank

Writing

1. **Letter to a Monarch** Write a letter to Henry VIII explaining why you agree or disagree with the decision he has made. Provide reasons to support your position.

2. **Opening Argument** The defense lawyer for Sir Thomas More was eventually tried and sentenced to death for opposing Henry VIII. As More's lawyer, write an opening argument.

3. **Continuation** Write a continuation of this scene. Base your dialogue and your depiction of the characters on the portion of the screenplay you've just read.

Speaking, Listening, and Viewing

4. **Television Interview** Team up with fellow students to interview Henry VIII and Thomas More for the evening news. Prepare questions for each character, and write their responses based on what you learned from this excerpt. Stage your interview for the class.

Researching and Representing

5. **Visual History** Create a visual history of one of the monarchs of England. Using images from books and magazines, or your own drawings, create a timeline that covers the most important events that took place during the reign of that monarch.

Online Activity www.phlit.phschool.com

Writing Process Workshop

Persuasive Essay

The selections in this unit—a political statement, a rousing speech, and a sermon—all contain elements of persuasion. You can use persuasion yourself, whenever you try to get someone to see things your way. Put that skill to use in a persuasive essay in which you convince your readers of something. In a persuasive essay, you present an argument in favor of your point and support your argument with unbiased, accurate evidence.

The following skills, introduced in this section's Guided Writing Lessons, will help you write a persuasive essay.

Writing Skills Focus

▶ **Use a persuasive tone** to convince readers to adopt a point of view or to take a specific action. Your readers should feel that you have their interests in mind. (See p. 243.)

▶ **Support your argument** with logical reasons, examples, research, or anecdotal data. (See p. 251.)

▶ **Maintain coherence** by focusing the elements of the essay on your purpose. Close your essay by summarizing your central position.

MODEL FROM LITERATURE

from Queen Elizabeth I's *Speech Before Defeating the Spanish Armada*

I know I have but the body of a weak and feeble woman; but I have the heart of a king, and of a king of England, too: ① and think foul scorn that Parma or Spain, or any prince of Europe, should dare to invade the borders of my realms ② to which rather than dishonor should grow by me, I myself will take arms: I myself ③ will be your general, judge and rewarder of every one of your virtues in the field.

① The Queen begins with an appeal to emotions to set the persuasive tone.

② To support her appeal, the Queen gives a specific example of an invasion that is threatening England.

③ By repeating the pronoun *I*, she maintains coherence and reinforces the personal tone.

Applying Language Skills: Using Active Voice

The active voice, in which the subject of the sentence performs the action, is usually more effective than the passive voice, in which the subject of the sentence receives the action. As much as possible, use the active voice in your persuasive essay.

Passive Voice
Pollution was created by people.
[subject receives the action]

Active Voice
People create pollution.
[subject performs the action]

Practice Rewrite each sentence, changing the passive voice to the active voice.

1. Tuition at Levitt University has been raised by its trustees.
2. The fund drive was called off by school officials.
3. The scholarship fund was created by the Garden Club.

Writing Application As you draft your persuasive essay, change the passive voice to the active voice.

Writer's Solution Connection
Language Lab

For more practice using the active voice, complete the Active and Passive Voice lesson on the Language Lab CD-ROM.

Prewriting

Choose a Topic Consider issues that personally concern you, such as the cost of college tuition or the importance of sports. You may also want to consider as a topic global issues, such as pollution, world hunger, or military spending.

Keep these points in mind as you choose a topic:
1. **Scope** Choose a topic you can fully discuss within a short persuasive essay.
2. **Debate** Choose a topic that is subject to debate.
3. **Research** Choose a topic about which sufficient information is available.

Evaluate Information Make use of facts, statistics, reasons, and quotations to support your argument. Use a variety of current sources, such as articles, interviews, nonfiction books, databases, and the Internet. When gathering evidence, consider the credibility and appropriateness of your sources.

Organize Evidence Choose one of the following organizational strategies to present your argument effectively.

▶ **Main Idea and Details** Make key points, then support them with specific evidence.
▶ **Order of Importance** Arrange supporting details from weakest to strongest to build your argument.
▶ **Pro and Con** Present the opposition to your position, then refute the argument using your evidence.
▶ **Cause and Effect** Arrange key points to show how your audience's action or inaction could affect their lives.

Drafting

Write an Introduction, Body, and Conclusion In the introduction, state your argument in a way that will grab the attention of your audience. State your main points and support each with solid evidence in the body of your essay. In the conclusion, restate your argument and emphasize the action you want your audience to take.

Create a Persuasive Tone A persuasive tone is the manner (pleading, urgent, commanding) in which you get your message across. Decide on a tone that will suit your topic as well as appeal to your audience. Then, as you weave together the facts for your essay, choose words that create that persuasive tone.

Revising

Strengthen the Persuasive Tone Make your essay as appealing as possible by strengthening its persuasive tone. To do this, replace any weak, vague words with words that convey urgency, seriousness, or joy, depending on your tone. For example, if your tone is urgent, change the message "Register to vote" to "Don't waste your vote."

Check Support Review the details you use to support your topic. Do they support it strongly, or will they give your opponent an opportunity to point out weaknesses in your argument? Eliminate details that do not support your argument.

REVISION MODEL

It is ~~pretty important~~ crucial ① to practice the guitar every day. Many guitar players gain confidence by practicing daily. ② *I was given a guitar for my twelfth birthday. I took lessons and practiced faithfully every day after school.* As an adult, I have had many opportunities to play at large parties and gatherings.③ Many ~~musicians are able to earn a small income playing at local events.~~ Remember, you won't become an accomplished musician overnight, but if you keep practicing, you'll find that persistence pays off.

① This wording has been revised to reflect the persuasive tone of the essay, which is serious.

② A personal anecdote supports the persuasive argument.

③ To maintain coherence, the writer deleted a sentence that takes the reader away from the main purpose of the piece.

Publishing

▶ **Local Radio Station** Call a local radio talk show and make your persuasive argument before a live audience.

▶ **Local Newspaper** Submit your essay as a letter to the editor.

▶ **Community** Present a persuasive argument for a community improvement idea before your town or county council.

APPLYING LANGUAGE SKILLS: Using Persuasive Language

Use words that have positive or negative connotations—or associated meanings—to make your argument convincing. The following chart lists words with similar definitions according to their positive or negative connotations.

Positive Connotations	Negative Connotations
visionary	dreamer
challenge	problem
introverted	self-absorbed

Practice Replace the italicized words with ones that have strong positive or negative connotations.

1. The *health farm* was run by *athletes*.
2. Marv's *car* runs on diesel.
3. We had two of Rosa's *small cookies*.

Writing Application As you revise your essay, replace neutral terms with ones that have more positive connotations.

Writer's Solution Connection Writing Lab

To guide your revision, complete the Self-Evaluation Checklist in the Revising and Editing section of the Persuasion tutorial.

Student Success Workshop

Real-World Reading Skills

Strategies for Success

It's sometimes easier to understand text that presents a lot of facts, ideas, concepts, and relationships when you can see the information and the relationships arranged in a visual form. Learning to organize complex text material in graphic organizers can increase your overall comprehension. For example, if you were to compare Neruda's sonnet to a Shakespearean sonnet, a comparison chart with two columns might make your analysis more understandable.

Evaluate the Text Structure As you read, look at the structure of the text. The organization may be obvious from the heads and subheads. Or the text may be more complex and include several different structures. Decide which kind of graphic organizer is most appropriate for expressing the information. If you are reading a complex story or a text of historical events, you might draw a story map, flowchart, timeline, or sequence diagram.

Consider Connections and Relationships Among Ideas Nonfiction texts are frequently organized by main idea and supporting details. A simple diagram or outline can show relationships among these various parts. When you read a history text, look for cause-and-effect relationships. Note that there may be a number of causes that led to an event. To simplify the information, use arrows to create a cause-and-effect diagram.

Look for Comparisons To increase the readers' understanding, writers often discuss similarities and differences among items. You can diagram these comparisons in a number of ways. For instance, if a writer is comparing and contrasting three literary works, you might create a three-column chart. You'd then insert the data for each literary work so you could look at the works side by side. A Venn diagram is another useful graphic organizer that shows comparison-and-contrast relationships.

Sonnet — Ballad

Different: 14 lines, Set meter, Set rhyme pattern, Tells of one theme

Alike: Both are poems, Contain meter, Lines rhyme

Different: No set length, No set meter, No set rhyme pattern, Tells a story

Apply the Strategies

Examine a variety of texts. Using the strategies that you have learned, construct appropriate graphic organizers for the information in each.

1. Construct a sequence diagram, story map, or timeline that organizes events from a story you've read recently.

2. Look for text with comparison-and-contrast relationships, and create a Venn diagram.

3. Find an article that expresses a cause-and-effect relationship, and construct a graphic organizer that shows how the details relate to each other.

> ✔ Here are situations in which you might find it useful to organize your ideas graphically:
> ▶ Drawing up a savings and spending plan
> ▶ Time management—keeping track of your activities
> ▶ Comparing merchandise before making a purchase

PART 3 *Focus on Literary Forms:*
Drama

"All the world's a stage," exclaims one of Shakespeare's characters, and the audience agreed. Elizabethan England had a dramatic sense of itself as a new power, acting its part on the world's stage. That's why it loved the bold new dramas that playwrights like Marlowe and Shakespeare were creating. In open-air theaters with names like the Globe, these writers let the English language strut and swagger.

THE *Elizabethan Theater*

English drama came of age during the reign of Elizabeth I, developing into a sophisticated and very popular art form. Although playwrights like Shakespeare were mainly responsible for the great theatrical achievements of the time, the importance of actors, audiences, and theater buildings should not be underestimated.

Before the reign of Elizabeth I, theater companies traveled about the country putting on plays wherever they could find an audience, often performing in the open courtyards of inns. Spectators watched either from the ground or from balconies or galleries above.

England's First Playhouse

When Shakespeare was twelve years old, an actor named James Burbage built London's first theater, called simply The Theater, just beyond the city walls in Shoreditch. Actors—even prominent and well-to-do actors like Burbage—occupied a strange place in London society: They were frowned upon by the city fathers but were wildly popular with the common people, who clamored to see them perform in plays. Though actors were considered rogues and vagabonds by some, they were held in sufficient repute to be called on frequently to perform at court. A man like Burbage enjoyed a reputation somewhat like a rock star's today.

The Globe

In 1597, the city fathers closed down The Theater. In late 1598, Richard Burbage (James's son) and his men dismantled it and hauled it in pieces across the Thames to Southwark. It took them six months to rebuild it, and when they did they renamed it the Globe.

Scholars disagree about what the Globe actually looked like, since there are no surviving drawings from the time or detailed written descriptions. Shakespeare refers to the building in *Henry V* as "this wooden O," so we have a sense that it was round or octagonal. It is presumed that an important influence on the design of the theater was the bear-baiting and bull-baiting rings built in Southwark. These "sports" arenas were circular, open to the sky, and had galleries all around.

The building had to have been small enough to ensure that the actors would be heard, but we know that performances could draw audiences as large as 2,500 to 3,000 people. These truly packed houses must have been quite uncomfortable at times, especially when you consider that people didn't bathe or change their clothes very often! Those who paid an admission price of a penny (not an inconsiderable sum of money then) stood throughout the performance. Some of the audience even sat in a gallery behind the performers. Their seats were the second most expensive in the house, and though they saw only the actors' backs and probably couldn't hear very well, they were content to be seen by the other members of the audience.

Actors of the period had none of the elaborate technology that helps modern actors. There were no sets or lighting at the Globe. Plays were performed in the bright afternoon sunlight, and a playwright's words alone had to create moods like the one in the eerie first scene of *Macbeth*. Holding an audience spellbound was made even more difficult by the fact that most were eating and drinking throughout the performance.

▲ **Critical Viewing** Would you have preferred standing near the stage or sitting in the galleries to see Shakespeare's plays? Explain. **[Relate]**

The Globe Theatre, London

The first Globe met its demise in 1613, when a cannon fired as part of a performance of *Henry VIII* ignited the theater's thatched roof. Everyone escaped unharmed, but the Globe burned to the ground. Although the theater was rebuilt, the Puritans had it permanently closed in 1642.

The New Globe

Almost four centuries after the original Globe opened, an actor stood onstage in the replica of the Globe and recited these lines from Shakespeare's *Henry V*: "Can this cockpit hold/The vasty fields of France? Or may we cram/Within this wooden O the very casques/That did affright the air at Agincourt?"

Building a replica of Shakespeare's Globe was American actor Sam Wanamaker's dream. After long years of fund-raising and construction, the theater opened to its first full season on June 8, 1997, with a production of *Henry V*. Like the earlier Globe, this one is made of wood, with a thatched roof and lime plaster covering the walls. The stage and the galleries are covered, but the "bear pit," where the modern-day groundlings stand, is open to the skies, exposing the spectators to the weather.

Perhaps the most striking aspect of seeing Shakespeare's plays performed at the Globe is the immediacy of the action. "They are talking to you, asking you questions, involving you in their fears," wrote Benedict Nightingale of the performers in the *Times* of London. At the Globe you are part of the debate. Isn't that what theater is all about?

Macbeth on Stage

Actors have played Macbeth and Lady Macbeth in a variety of ways—as evil, sympathetic, noble—as these quotations illustrate.

Many Faces of Macbeth

Poetic Murderer John Gielgud portrayed Macbeth as "the most poetic of all murderers." For Gielgud, the key point about Macbeth is that he is able to describe how he feels and what he does in "poetic" language.

Lion-Hearted The director Glen Baym Shaw, who directed Laurence Olivier in the part of Macbeth, describes the role in these words: "A superb leader with the courage of a lion and the imagination of a poet . . . No one would ever dare to slap Macbeth on the back . . ."

Enthusiastic Warrior Following Shaw's direction, Olivier portrayed Macbeth so enthusiastically that one night, he injured the actor playing Macduff in their staged sword fight. On another occasion, with a substitute Macduff, Olivier fought the sword battle so vigorously that his sword broke and flew into the audience.

A Haitian Dictator In 1936 Orson Welles directed a version of *Macbeth* set in Haiti rather than Scotland. In this innovative production with an all black cast, Macbeth was modeled after a famous Haitian dictator.

Lady Macbeth:

Ambition Above All Sarah Siddons, who played the role of Lady Macbeth about 200 years ago, declared, "In this astonishing creature one sees a woman in whose bosom the passion of ambition has almost obliterated all the characteristics of human nature . . ."

Essentially Feminine The famous nineteenth-century actress Ellen Terry believed that "Shakespeare's Lady is essentially feminine, even in the urgency of her appeal to her husband, and one strong argument is the very feminine way in which, when all is over—the deed done . . . she faints."

Beauty and Evil Vivien Leigh played Lady Macbeth to bring out the mixture of beauty and evil in her personality. In a striking gesture, for example, Leigh's Lady Macbeth sent Duncan off to bed with a betraying kiss.

A Psychiatric Opinion Dame Judith Anderson consulted psychiatrists to find out why Lady Macbeth sleepwalks in Act V. "In all mental cases you can trace the trouble back to a moment when the disintegration commenced. With Lady Macbeth it was here."

Guide for Interpreting

Featured in
**AUTHORS
IN DEPTH**
Series

William Shakespeare
(1564–1616)

Because of his deep understanding of human nature, his compassion for all types of people, and the power and beauty of his language, William Shakespeare is regarded as the greatest writer in the English language. Nearly four hundred years after his death, Shakespeare's plays continue to be read widely and produced throughout the world. They have the same powerful impact on today's audiences as they had when they were first staged.

Timeline of Praise

No other English writer has won such universal and enthusiastic praise from critics and fellow writers. Here are just a few samples of that praise, shown on a timeline from Shakespeare's day to our own:

1600 — —Ben Jonson (1572–1637)
"He was not of an age, but for all time!"

—John Dryden (1631–1700)
"He was the man who of all modern, and perhaps ancient poets, had the largest and most comprehensive soul."

1700 — —Samuel Johnson (1709–1784)
"Shakespeare is, above all writers, at least above all modern writers, the poet of nature: the poet that holds up to his readers a faithful mirror of manners and life."

1800 — —Samuel Taylor Coleridge (1772–1834)
"The Englishman, who, without reverence, a proud and affectionate reverence, can utter the name of William Shakespeare, stands disqualified for the office of critic."

1900 — —A. C. Bradley (1851–1935)
"Where his power or art is fully exerted, it really does resemble that of nature."

—T. S. Eliot (1888–1965)
"About any one so great as Shakespeare, it is probable that we can never be right . . ."

The Playwright in His Own Time

It is a myth that we know absolutely nothing about Shakespeare's life. As critic Irving Ribner attests, "we know more about him than we do about virtually any other of his contemporary dramatists, with the exception of Ben Jonson." Shakespeare was born on April 23, 1564, in Stratford-on-Avon, northwest of London. (The date is based on a record of his baptism on April 26th.) Stratford, with a population of about 2,000 in Shakespeare's day, was the market town for a fertile agricultural region.

Shakespeare's father, John, was a successful glove maker and businessman who held a number of positions in the town government. His mother, whose maiden name was Mary Arden, was the daughter of his father's landlord. Their marriage, therefore, boosted the Shakespeare family's holdings. Nevertheless, there is evidence that in the late 1570's, John Shakespeare began to suffer financial reverses.

Shakespeare's Education

No written evidence of Shakespeare's boyhood exists—not even a name on a school attendance list. However, given his father's status, it is highly probable that he attended the Stratford Grammar School, where he acquired a knowledge of Latin.

Although Shakespeare did not go on to study at a university, his attendance at the grammar school from ages seven to sixteen would have provided him with a good education. Discipline at such a school was strict, and the school day lasted from 6:00 A.M. in the summer (7:00 in the winter) until 5:00 P.M. From 11:00 to 1:00, students were dismissed to eat lunch with their families. At 3:00, they were allowed to play for a quarter of an hour!

Shakespeare's Marriage and Family

Shakespeare's name enters the official records again in November 1582, when he receives a license to marry

The Tragedy of Macbeth

Anne Hathaway. The couple had a daughter, Susanna, in 1583, and twins, Judith and Hamnet, in 1585. Beyond names and years in which his children were born, we know little about his family life. Some writers have made much of the fact that Shakespeare left his wife and children behind when he went to London not long after his twins were born. However, he visited his family in Stratford regularly during his years as a playwright, and they may have lived with him for a time in London.

His Career as Actor and Playwright

It's uncertain how Shakespeare became connected with the theater in the late 1580's and early 1590's. By 1594, however, he had become a part owner and the principal playwright of the Lord Chamberlain's Men, one of the most successful theater companies in London.

In 1599, the company built the famous Globe theater on the south bank of the Thames river, in Southwork. This is where most of Shakespeare's plays were performed. When James I became king in 1603, following the death of Elizabeth I, he took control of the Lord Chamberlain's Men and renamed the company The King's Men.

Retirement In about 1610, Shakespeare retired to Stratford, though he continued to write plays. He was a prosperous middle-class man, having profited from his share in a successful theater company. Six years later, on April 23, 1616, he died and was buried in Holy Trinity Church in Stratford. Because it was common practice to move bodies after burial to make room for others, Shakespeare wrote the following as his epitaph:

> Good friends, for Jesus' sake forbear
> To dig the dust encloséd here!
> Blest be the man that spares these stones,
> And curst be he that moves my bones.

His Literary Record Shakespeare did not think of himself as a man of letters. He wrote his plays to be performed and did not bring out editions of them for the reading public. The first published edition of his work, called the First Folio, was issued in 1623 by two members of his theater company, John Heminges and Henry Condell, and contained thirty-six of the thirty-seven plays now attributed to him.

Shakespeare's varied output includes romantic comedies like *A Midsummer Night's Dream* and *As You Like It*; history plays like *Henry IV*, Parts 1 and 2; tragedies like *Romeo and Juliet*, *Hamlet*, *Othello*, *King Lear*, and *Macbeth*; and later romances like *The Tempest*. In addition to his plays, he wrote 154 sonnets and three longer poems.

"Speaking" Shakespeare

You may not realize the extent to which you already "speak" Shakespeare. For example, have you ever used or heard any of these common phrases?

He's full of *the milk of human kindness*. (I, v, 17)

She thinks she's *the be-all and the end-all*. (I, vii, 5)

What *a sorry sight that was*! (II, ii, 20)

Don't worry about it, *what's done is done*! (III, ii, 12)

That will last until *the crack of doom*. (IV, i, 117)

She finished the jobs in *one fell swoop*. (IV, iii, 219)

Shakespeare invented each of these now common phrases, which were unknown in English before their appearance in *Macbeth*. Look for them as you read—their place in the play is indicated in parentheses—and discover if their meanings have changed since Shakespeare's time.

Guide for Interpreting, Act I

◆ Background for Understanding

LITERATURE: SHAKESPEARE'S SOURCES

By Shakespeare's time, the story of the eleventh-century Scottish king Macbeth was a mixture of fact and legend. Shakespeare and his contemporaries, however, probably regarded the account of Macbeth in Raphael Holinshed's *Chronicles of England, Scotland, and Ireland* as completely factual. The playwright drew on the *Chronicles* as a source for the play. Yet he freely adapted the material for his own purposes, as this chart indicates:

Holinshed's Chronicles	Shakespeare's Macbeth
• Macbeth meets the witches.	• Shakespeare uses this account.
• Duncan is slain in an ambush set up by Macbeth and his friends, who are angry at the naming of Malcolm as Prince of Cumberland. Macbeth's claim to the throne has some basis.	• Duncan is slain while he is a guest at Macbeth's castle. Macbeth and his wife are the only conspirators, and Macbeth does not apparently have a legitimate claim to the throne.
• Banquo is Macbeth's accomplice in the slaying, and Lady Macbeth does not have a prominent role in the narrative.	• Banquo is not an accomplice. Using a different story in the Chronicles , in which a wife urges her husband to kill a friend and guest, Shakespeare creates Lady Macbeth.

Although Shakespeare may have consulted other Scottish histories, it is probable that he primarily relied on Holinshed's *Chronicles* for his "facts."

Some scholars have suggested that Shakespeare became aware of Holinshed's account of Macbeth in the summer of 1605. At that time he may have seen, at Oxford, an entertainment titled *Tres Sibyllae* staged for King James. In this pageant, three sibyls—the prophetesses named in the title—predict that the descendants of the Scottish king Banquo would reign over a great kingdom. This was meant to flatter King James because he regarded Banquo as his own mythical ancestor.

HISTORY: A TRIBUTE TO THE KING

Macbeth is set in eleventh-century Scotland. However, Shakespeare wrote the play with an eye on seventeenth-century current events. In November 1605, a group of Catholics seeking revenge for the severe anti-Catholic laws of James I plotted to blow up the king and Parliament. With the help of Guy Fawkes, a soldier of fortune, they rented a cellar directly beneath the House of Lords, in which to stockpile barrels of gunpowder. Incredibly, the conspirators succeeded in storing thirty-six barrels of gunpowder in that cellar. To appreciate the magnitude of the threat, imagine a group of terrorists today smuggling tons of high explosives into the Capitol building in Washington, D.C.

The plot was revealed when a lord, who happened to be a brother-in-law of one of the conspirators, was anonymously warned by letter not to attend the opening of Parliament. This warning helped the authorities to break the case, and they arrested Guy Fawkes as he entered the cellar. Fawkes and some of the other chief conspirators were executed. Although their numbers were few, their plan was so frightening that it led, for a time, to increased persecution of all English Catholics. In England, Guy Fawkes day is still commemorated on November 5th each year with fireworks and the burning of dummies representing Guy Fawkes.

In *Macbeth*, Shakespeare capitalized on the sympathy generated for the king by this incident. He chose the Scottish setting for his play, knowing that James's family, the Stuarts, first came to the Scottish throne in the eleventh century. One of the most virtuous characters in the play, Banquo, was thought to be the father of the first of the Stuart kings.

Shakespeare included witches in the play knowing that James I had written a book that argued for the existence of witches.

Journal Writing Think of a play, movie, or novel about a famous political figure. Was it flattering or not? Explain in your journal.

The Tragedy of Macbeth

◆ Literature and Your Life

CONNECT YOUR EXPERIENCE

If you've ever been elbowed aside by a team member eager for glory, you've experienced the effects of blind and driving ambition. An elbow in the ribs isn't usually fatal. In *Macbeth*, however, blind ambition causes a brave soldier to become an evil plotter who will stop at nothing to accomplish his goal.

THEMATIC FOCUS: THE INFLUENCE OF THE MONARCHY

If Shakespeare were alive today, do you think he would write plays flattering the royal family? Why or why not?

◆ Literary Focus

ELIZABETHAN DRAMA

During the late sixteenth century, **Elizabethan drama** came into full bloom. Playwrights turned away from religious subjects and began writing more sophisticated plays. Drawing on models from ancient Greece and Rome, writers reintroduced tragedies—plays in which disaster befalls a hero or heroine. Dramatists also began writing their plays in carefully crafted unrhymed verse, using rich language and vivid imagery.

Macbeth, like other Shakespearean plays, was performed at the Globe theater. This structure was circular, open to the sky, and lined with galleries. Because the Globe, like other Elizabethan theaters, had no lighting, the plays were performed in broad daylight. Also there were no sets, so the words of the play had to create the illusion of time and place for the audience.

As you read *Macbeth*, Act I, imagine what it would have been like to be watching the play at the Globe.

◆ Grammar and Style

ACTION VERBS AND LINKING VERBS

Shakespeare uses both action verbs and linking verbs. **Action verbs** express physical or mental action. **Linking verbs** connect subjects with a subject complement that either renames or modifies the subject.

Action Verb: "Shipwracking storms and direful thunders *break* . . ." (I, ii, 26)

Linking Verb: ". . . he *seems* rapt withal." (I, iii, 57)

◆ Reading Strategy

USE TEXT AIDS

Like all drama, Shakespeare's plays were meant to be performed, not read in a classroom. Playwrights provide directions for actors that can help readers as well. The stage directions that tell actors where and how to move can help you to picture what is happening on the stage. Pay attention to the stage directions, printed in italics in the text, to help you follow the stage action.

Elizabethan plays prepared for a modern reading audience provide another aid: Notes along the sides of the text lines explain the meanings of words and phrases that are no longer in use. Refer to these notes to clarify unfamiliar language.

◆ Build Vocabulary

WORDS ABOUT POWER

In *Macbeth*, Act I, Shakespeare uses words from the world of politics and power. Two of these words, *liege* and *sovereign*, refer to the role of the king as chief lord in a feudal system (*liege*) and to his supreme power over his subjects (*sovereign* power).

WORD BANK

Before you read, preview this list of words from Act I of *Macbeth*.

valor
treasons
imperial
liege
sovereign

THE TRAGEDY OF

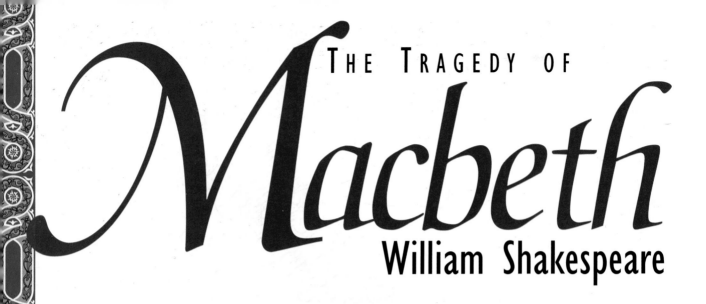

Macbeth

William Shakespeare

CHARACTERS	
Duncan, King of Scotland	**Seyton,** an officer attending on Macbeth
Malcolm ⎱ his sons **Donalbain** ⎰	**Son to Macduff** **An English Doctor**
Macbeth	**A Scottish Doctor**
Banquo	**A Porter**
Macduff	**An Old Man**
Lennox — noblemen of Scotland	**Three Murderers**
Ross	**Lady Macbeth**
Menteith	**Lady Macduff**
Angus	**A Gentlewoman attending** on Lady Macbeth
Caithness	**Hecate**
Fleance, son to Banquo	**Witches**
Siward, Earl of Northumberland, general of the English forces	**Apparitions** **Lords, Officers, Soldiers, Attendants,**
Young Siward, his son	**and Messengers**

Setting: Scotland; England

Act I

Scene i. *An open place.*
[*Thunder and lightning. Enter* THREE WITCHES.]

    FIRST WITCH. When shall we three meet again?
      In thunder, lightning, or in rain?

    SECOND WITCH. When the hurlyburly's done,
      When the battle's lost and won.

5   **THIRD WITCH.** That will be ere the set of sun.

> **A Critic's Response**
> "These were not ordinary witches or seeresses. They were great powers of destiny, great ministers of fate."
> —**George Lyman Kittredge**

▲ **Critical Viewing** Examine Fuseli's rendering of the witches. Explain how his depiction of the witches makes them appear other-worldly. [**Draw Conclusions**]

FIRST WITCH. Where the place?

SECOND WITCH.   Upon the heath.

THIRD WITCH. There to meet with Macbeth.

FIRST WITCH. I come, Graymalkin.[1]

SECOND WITCH. Paddock[2] calls.

THIRD WITCH.   Anon![3]

10 **ALL.** Fair is foul, and foul is fair.
     Hover through the fog and filthy air.   [*Exit.*]

1. **Graymalkin:** First witch's helper, a gray cat.
2. **Paddock:** Second witch's helper, a toad.

3. **Anon:** At once.

Scene ii. *A camp near Forres, a town in northeast Scotland.*
[*Alarum within.*[1] *Enter* KING DUNCAN, MALCOLM, DONALBAIN, LENNOX, *with* ATTENDANTS, *meeting a bleeding* CAPTAIN.]

KING. What bloody man is that? He can report,
As seemeth by his plight, of the revolt
The newest state.

MALCOLM.   This is the sergeant[2]
Who like a good and hardy soldier fought
5   'Gainst my captivity. Hail, brave friend!
Say to the king the knowledge of the broil[3]
As thou didst leave it.

CAPTAIN.   Doubtful it stood,
As two spent swimmers, that do cling together
And choke their art.[4] The merciless Macdonwald—
10   Worthy to be a rebel for to that
The multiplying villainies of nature
Do swarm upon him—from the Western Isles[5]
Of kerns and gallowglasses[6] is supplied;
And fortune, on his damnèd quarrel[7] smiling,
15   Showed like a rebel's whore:[8] but all's too weak:
For brave Macbeth—well he deserves that name—
Disdaining fortune, with his brandished steel,
Which smoked with bloody execution,
Like <u>valor</u>'s minion[9] carved out his passage
20   Till he faced the slave;
Which nev'r shook hands, nor bade farewell to him,
Till he unseamed him from the nave to th' chops,[10]
And fixed his head upon our battlements.

KING. O valiant cousin! Worthy gentleman!

25   CAPTAIN. As whence the sun 'gins his reflection[11]
Shipwracking storms and direful thunders break,
So from that spring whence comfort seemed to come
Discomfort swells. Mark, King of Scotland, mark:
No sooner justice had, with valor armed,
30   Compelled these skipping kerns to trust their heels
But the Norweyan lord,[12] surveying vantage,[13]
With furbished arms and new supplies of men,
Began a fresh assault.

KING.   Dismayed not this
Our captains, Macbeth and Banquo?

1. **Alarum within:** Trumpet call offstage.

2. **sergeant:** Officer.

3. **broil:** Battle.

4. **choke their art:** Prevent each other from swimming.

5. **Western Isles:** The Hebrides, off Scotland.

6. **Of kerns and gallowglasses:** With lightly armed Irish foot soldiers and heavily armed soldiers.

7. **damned quarrel:** Accursed cause.

8. **Showed . . . whore:** Falsely appeared to favor Macdonwald.

9. **minion:** Favorite.

10. **unseamed . . . chops:** Split him open from the navel to the jaws.

11. **'gins his reflection:** Rises.

12. **Norweyan lord:** King of Norway.
13. **surveying vantage:** Seeing an opportunity.

◆ **Build Vocabulary**

valor (val´ ər) *n*.: Marked courage or bravery

CAPTAIN.   Yes;

35   As sparrows eagles, or the hare the lion.
        If I say sooth,[14] I must report they were
        As cannons overcharged with double cracks;[15]
        So they doubly redoubled strokes upon the foe.
        Except[16] they meant to bathe in reeking wounds,
40   Or memorize another Golgotha,[17]
        I cannot tell—
        But I am faint; my gashes cry for help.

KING. So well thy words become thee as thy wounds;
        They smack of honor both. Go get him surgeons.

                                    [*Exit* CAPTAIN, *attended.*]

[*Enter* ROSS *and* ANGUS.]

        Who comes here?

45   **MALCOLM.**   The worthy Thane[18] of Ross.

     LENNOX. What a haste looks through his eyes! So should he look
        That seems to[19] speak things strange.

     ROSS.   God save the king!

     KING. Whence cam'st thou, worthy Thane?

     ROSS.   From Fife, great King;
        Where the Norweyan banners flout the sky
50   And fan our people cold.
        Norway[20] himself, with terrible numbers,
        Assisted by that most disloyal traitor
        The Thane of Cawdor, began a dismal[21] conflict;
        Till that Bellona's bridegroom, lapped in proof,[22]
55   Confronted him with self-comparisons,[23]
        Point against point, rebellious arm 'gainst arm,
        Curbing his lavish [24] spirit: and, to conclude,
        The victory fell on us.

        KING.   Great happiness!

        ROSS.   That now
        Sweno, the Norways' king, craves composition;[25]
60   Nor would we deign him burial of his men
        Till he disbursed, at Saint Colme's Inch,[26]
        Ten thousand dollars to our general use.

◆ **Literary Focus**
What background
does this conversa-
tion (ll. 1–43)
provide?

14. sooth: Truth.
15. cracks: Explo-
sives.
16. except: Unless.
**17. memorize . . .
Golgotha** (gôl′ gə thə):
Make the place as
memorable for slaugh-
ter as Golgotha, the
place where Christ
was crucified.

18. Thane: Scottish
title of nobility.

19. seems to: Seems
about to.

20. Norway: King of
Norway.
21. dismal: Threaten-
ing.
**22. Bellona's . . .
proof:** Macbeth is
called the mate of
Bellona, the goddess
of war, clad in tested
armor.
23. self-comparisons:
Counter movements.
24. lavish: Insolent.

25. composition:
Terms of peace.

26. St. Colme's Inch:
Island near Edinburgh,
Scotland.

KING. No more that Thane of Cawdor shall deceive
Our bosom interest:[27] go pronounce his present[28] death,
65   And with his former title greet Macbeth.

ROSS. I'll see it done.

KING. What he hath lost, noble Macbeth hath won.

[*Exit.*]

Scene iii. *A heath near Forres.*
[*Thunder. Enter the* THREE WITCHES.]

FIRST WITCH. Where hast thou been, sister?

SECOND WITCH. Killing swine.[1]

THIRD WITCH. Sister, where thou?

FIRST WITCH. A sailor's wife had chestnuts in her lap,
And mounched, and mounched, and mounched.
5   "Give me," quoth I.
"Aroint thee,[2] witch!" the rump-fed ronyon[3] cries.
Her husband's to Aleppo[4] gone, master o' th' Tiger:
But in a sieve[5] I'll thither sail,
And, like a rat without a tail,[6]
10   I'll do, I'll do, and I'll do.

SECOND WITCH. I'll give thee a wind.

FIRST WITCH. Th' art kind.

THIRD WITCH. And I another.

FIRST WITCH. I myself have all the other;
15   And the very ports they blow,[7]
All the quarters that they know
I' th' shipman's card.[8]
I'll drain him dry as hay:
Sleep shall neither night nor day
20   Hang upon his penthouse lid;[9]
He shall live a man forbid:[10]
Weary sev'nights[11] nine times nine
Shall he dwindle, peak,[12] and pine:
Though his bark cannot be lost,
25   Yet it shall be tempest-tossed.
Look what I have.

---

27. **our bosom interest:** My heart's trust.
28. **present:** Immediate.

1. **Killing swine:** It was commonly believed that witches killed domestic animals.

2. **Aroint thee:** Be off.
3. **rump-fed ronyon:** Fat-rumped, scabby creature.
4. **Aleppo:** Trading center in Syria.
5. **sieve:** It was commonly believed that witches often sailed in sieves.
6. **rat . . . tail:** According to popular belief, witches could assume the form of any animal, but the tail would always be missing.

7. **they blow:** To which the winds blow.
8. **card:** Compass.

9. **penthouse lid:** Eyelid.
10. **forbid:** Cursed.
11. **sev'nights:** Weeks.
12. **peak:** Waste away.

SECOND WITCH. Show me, show me.

FIRST WITCH. Here I have a pilot's thumb,
Wracked as homeward he did come.

                                    [*Drum within.*]

30   **THIRD WITCH.** A drum, a drum!
Macbeth doth come.

ALL. The weird[13] sisters, hand in hand,
Posters[14] of the sea and land,
Thus do go about, about:
35   Thrice to thine, and thrice to mine,
And thrice again, to make up nine.
Peace! The charm's wound up.

[*Enter* MACBETH *and* BANQUO.]

MACBETH. So foul and fair a day I have not seen.

BANQUO. How far is 't called to Forres? What are these

13. **weird:** Destiny-serving.
14. **Posters:** Swift travelers.

▼ Critical Viewing Which of the two soldiers on the right
do you think is Macbeth? Explain your reasoning. [**Deduce**]

Macbeth and the Witches, Clarkson Stanfield, Leicestershire Museums, Art Galleries and Records Service

40 So withered, and so wild in their attire,
That look not like th' inhabitants o' th' earth,
And yet are on 't? Live you, or are you aught
That man may question? You seem to understand me,
By each at once her choppy[15] finger laying
45 Upon her skinny lips. You should be women,
And yet your beards forbid me to interpret
That you are so.

15. **choppy:** Chapped.

MACBETH.   Speak, if you can: what are you?

FIRST WITCH. All hail, Macbeth! Hail to thee, Thane of Glamis!

SECOND WITCH. All hail, Macbeth! Hail to thee, Thane of Cawdor!

50 THIRD WITCH. All hail, Macbeth, that shalt be King hereafter!

BANQUO. Good sir, why do you start, and seem to fear
Things that do sound so fair? I' th' name of truth,
Are you fantastical,[16] or that indeed
Which outwardly ye show? My noble partner
55 You greet with present grace[17] and great prediction
Of noble having[18] and of royal hope,
That he seems rapt withal:[19] to me you speak not.
If you can look into the seeds of time,
And say which grain will grow and which will not,
60 Speak then to me, who neither beg nor fear
Your favors nor your hate.

16. **fantastical:** Imaginary.
17. **grace:** Honor.
18. **having:** Possession.
19. **rapt withal:** Entranced by it.

FIRST WITCH. Hail!

SECOND WITCH. Hail!

THIRD WITCH. Hail!

◆ **Literary Focus**
How could Elizabethan actors have made this scene mysterious without help from special lighting effects?

65 FIRST WITCH. Lesser than Macbeth, and greater.

SECOND WITCH. Not so happy,[20] yet much happier.

20. **happy:** Fortunate.

THIRD WITCH. Thou shalt get kings, though thou be none.
So all hail, Macbeth and Banquo!

FIRST WITCH. Banquo and Macbeth, all hail!

70 MACBETH. Stay, you imperfect[21] speakers, tell me more:
By Sinel's[22] death I know I am Thane of Glamis;

21. **imperfect:** Incomplete.
22. **Sinel's** (sī´ nəlz): Macbeth's father's.

But how of Cawdor? The Thane of Cawdor lives,
A prosperous gentleman; and to be King
Stands not within the prospect of belief,
75   No more than to be Cawdor. Say from whence
You owe[23] this strange intelligence?[24] Or why
Upon this blasted heath you stop our way
With such prophetic greeting? Speak, I charge you.
                         [WITCHES *vanish.*]

BANQUO. The earth hath bubbles as the water has,
80   And these are of them. Whither are they vanished?

MACBETH. Into the air, and what seemed corporal[25] melted
As breath into the wind. Would they had stayed!

BANQUO. Were such things here as we do speak about?
Or have we eaten on the insane root[26]
85   That takes the reason prisoner?

MACBETH. Your children shall be kings.

BANQUO.   You shall be King.

MACBETH. And Thane of Cawdor too. Went it not so?

BANQUO. To th' selfsame tune and words. Who's here?

[*Enter* ROSS *and* ANGUS.]

ROSS. The King hath happily received, Macbeth,
90   The news of thy success; and when he reads[27]
Thy personal venture in the rebels' fight,
His wonders and his praises do contend
Which should be thine or his.[28] Silenced with that,
In viewing o'er the rest o' th' selfsame day,
95   He finds thee in the stout Norweyan ranks,
Nothing afeard of what thyself didst make,
Strange images of death.[29] As thick as tale
Came post with post,[30] and every one did bear
Thy praises in his kingdom's great defense,
And poured them down before him.

100 **ANGUS.**   We are sent
To give thee, from our royal master, thanks;
Only to herald thee into his sight,
Not pay thee.

---

23. owe: Own.
24. intelligence: Information.

25. corporal: Real.

26. insane root: Henbane or hemlock, believed to cause insanity.

27. reads: Considers.

28. His wonders . . . his: His admiration contends with his desire to praise you.
29. Nothing . . . death: Killing, but not being afraid of being killed.
30. As thick . . . post: As fast as could be counted came messenger after messenger.

ROSS. And for an earnest[31] of a greater honor,
105   He bade me, from him, call thee Thane of Cawdor;
In which addition,[32] hail, most worthy Thane!
For it is thine.

BANQUO. [*Aside*] What, can the devil speak true?

MACBETH. The Thane of Cawdor lives: why do you dress me
In borrowed robes?

ANGUS.   Who was the thane lives yet,
110   But under heavy judgment bears that life
Which he deserves to lose. Whether he was combined[33]
With those of Norway, or did line[34] the rebel
With hidden help and vantage,[35] or that with both
He labored in his country's wrack,[36] I know not;
115   But <u>treasons</u> capital, confessed and proved,
Have overthrown him.

MACBETH.   [*Aside*] Glamis, and Thane of Cawdor:
The greatest is behind.[37] [*To* ROSS *and* ANGUS]
   Thanks for your pains.
[*Aside to* BANQUO] Do you not hope your children shall be kings,
When those that gave the Thane of Cawdor to me
Promised no less to them?

120 **BANQUO.** [*Aside to* MACBETH] That, trusted home,[38]
Might yet enkindle you unto[39] the crown,
Besides the Thane of Cawdor. But 'tis strange:
And oftentimes, to win us to our harm,
The instruments of darkness tell us truths,
125   Win us with honest trifles, to betray 's
In deepest consequence.
Cousins,[40] a word, I pray you.

MACBETH.   [*Aside*] Two truths are told,
As happy prologues to the swelling act
Of the <u>imperial</u> theme.[41]—I thank you, gentlemen.—
130   [*Aside*] This supernatural soliciting
Cannot be ill, cannot be good. If ill,
Why hath it given me earnest of success,
Commencing in a truth? I am Thane of Cawdor:
If good, why do I yield to that suggestion[42]
135   Whose horrid image doth unfix my hair
And make my seated[43] heart knock at my ribs,
Against the use of nature?[44] Present fears
Are less than horrible imaginings.
My thought, whose murder yet is but fantastical

31. earnest: Pledge.

32. In which addition: With this new title.

33. combined: Allied.
34. line: Support.
35. vantage: Assistance.
36. wrack: Ruin.

37. behind: Still to come.

38. home: Fully.
39. enkindle you unto: Encourage you to hope for.

40. Cousins: Often used as a term of courtesy between fellow noblemen.

41. swelling . . . theme: Stately idea that I will be King.

42. suggestion: Thought of murdering Duncan.
43. seated: Fixed.
44. Against . . . nature: In an unnatural way.

140   Shakes so my single[45] state of man that function
        Is smothered in surmise, and nothing is
        But what is not.

     BANQUO.   Look, how our partner's rapt.

     MACBETH. [*Aside*] If chance will have me King, why,
        chance may crown me,
        Without my stir.

     BANQUO.   New honors come upon him,
145   Like our strange[46] garments, cleave not to their mold
        But with the aid of use.

     MACBETH.   [*Aside*] Come what come may,
        Time and the hour runs through the roughest day.

     BANQUO. Worthy Macbeth, we stay upon your leisure.[47]

     MACBETH. Give me your favor.[48] My dull brain was wrought
150   With things forgotten. Kind gentlemen, your pains
        Are registered where every day I turn
        The leaf to read them. Let us toward the King.
        [*Aside to* BANQUO] Think upon what hath chanced,
        and at more time,
        The interim having weighed it,[49] let us speak
        Our free hearts[50] each to other.

155 BANQUO.   Very gladly.

     MACBETH. Till then, enough. Come, friends.   [*Exit.*]

Scene iv. *Forres. The palace.*
[*Flourish.*[1] *Enter* KING DUNCAN, LENNOX, MALCOLM, DONALBAIN, *and* ATTENDANTS.]

     KING. Is execution done on Cawdor? Are not
        Those in commission[2] yet returned?

     MALCOLM.   My liege,
        They are not yet come back. But I have spoke
        With one that saw him die, who did report
5   That very frankly he confessed his treasons,
        Implored your Highness' pardon and set forth
        A deep repentance: nothing in his life
        Became him like the leaving it. He died

45. single: Unaided, weak.

46. strange: New.

47. stay upon your leisure: Await your convenience.
48. favor: Pardon.

49. The interim . . . it: When we have had time to think about it.
50. Our free hearts: Our minds freely.

1. Flourish: Trumpet fanfare.
2. in commission: Commissioned to oversee the execution.

◆ **Build Vocabulary**

treasons (trē´ zenz) *n*.: Betrayals of one's country or oath of loyalty
imperial (im pir´ ē əl) *adj*.: Of an empire; having supreme authority
liege (lēj) *n*.: Lord or king

As one that had been studied[3] in his death,
10   To throw away the dearest thing he owed[4]
As 'twere a careless[5] trifle.

KING.   There's no art
To find the mind's construction[6] in the face:
He was a gentleman on whom I built
An absolute trust.

[*Enter* MACBETH, BANQUO. ROSS, *and* ANGUS.]

                   O worthiest cousin!
15   The sin of my ingratitude even now
Was heavy on me: thou art so far before,
That swiftest wing of recompense is slow
To overtake thee. Would thou hadst less deserved,
That the proportion both of thanks and payment
20   Might have been mine![7] Only I have left to say,
More is thy due than more than all can pay.

MACBETH.   The service and the loyalty I owe,
In doing it, pays itself.[8] Your Highness' part
Is to receive our duties: and our duties
25   Are to your throne and state children and servants;
Which do but what they should, by doing every thing
Safe toward[9] your love and honor.

KING.   Welcome hither.
I have begun to plant thee, and will labor
To make thee full of growing. Noble Banquo,
30   That hast no less deserved, nor must be known
No less to have done so, let me enfold thee
And hold thee to my heart.

BANQUO.   There if I grow,
The harvest is your own.

KING.   My plenteous joys,
Wanton[10] in fullness, seek to hide themselves
35   In drops of sorrow. Sons, kinsmen, thanes,
And you whose places are the nearest, know,
We will establish our estate upon
Our eldest, Malcolm,[11] whom we name hereafter
The Prince of Cumberland: which honor must
40   Not unaccompanied invest him only,
But signs of nobleness, like stars, shall shine
On all deservers. From hence to Inverness,[12]
And bind us further to you.

▲ Critical Viewing How does this Scottish
castle reflect the mood of the play? [Connect]

MACBETH. The rest is labor, which is not used for you.[13]
45   I'll be myself the harbinger,[14] and make joyful
The hearing of my wife with your approach;
So, humbly take my leave.

KING.   My worthy Cawdor!

MACBETH. [*Aside*] The Prince of Cumberland! That is a step
On which I must fall down, or else o'erleap,
50   For in my way it lies. Stars, hide your fires;
Let not light see my black and deep desires:
The eye wink at the hand;[15] yet let that be
Which the eye fears, when it is done, to see.   [*Exit.*]

KING. True, worthy Banquo; he is full so valiant,
55   And in his commendations I am fed;
It is a banquet to me. Let's after him,
Whose care is gone before to bid us welcome.
It is a peerless kinsman.   [*Flourish. Exit.*]

13. The rest . . . you:
Anything not done for
you is laborious.
14. harbinger:
Advance representative
of the army or royal
party who makes
arrangements for a
visit.

15. wink at the hand:
Be blind to the hand's
deed.

Scene v. *Inverness.* MACBETH'S *castle.*
[*Enter* MACBETH'S WIFE, *alone, with a letter.*]

    LADY MACBETH. [*Reads*] "They met me in the day of
    success; and I have learned by the perfect'st report
    they have more in them than mortal knowledge.
    When I burned in desire to question them further,
5   they made themselves air, into which they vanished.
    Whiles I stood rapt in the wonder of it, came
    missives[1] from the King, who all-hailed me 'Thane
    of Cawdor'; by which title, before, these weird sisters
    saluted me, and referred me to the coming on
10   of time, with 'Hail, King that shalt be!' This have I
    thought good to deliver thee,[2] my dearest partner of
    greatness, that thou mightst not lose the dues of
    rejoicing, by being ignorant of what greatness is
    promised thee. Lay it to thy heart, and farewell."

15   Glamis thou art, and Cawdor, and shalt be
    What thou art promised. Yet do I fear thy nature;
    It is too full o' th' milk of human kindness
    To catch the nearest[3] way. Thou wouldst be great,
    Art not without ambition, but without
20   The illness[4] should attend it. What thou wouldst highly,
    That wouldst thou holily; wouldst not play false,
    And yet wouldst wrongly win. Thou'dst have, great Glamis,
    That which cries "Thus thou must do" if thou have it;
    And that which rather thou dost fear to do
25   Than wishest should be undone.[5] Hie thee hither,
    That I may pour my spirits in thine ear,
    And chastise with the valor of my tongue
    All that impedes thee from the golden round[6]
    Which fate and metaphysical aid doth seem
    To have thee crowned withal.

[*Enter* MESSENGER.]
30   What is your tidings?

    MESSENGER. The King comes here tonight.

    LADY MACBETH.   Thou'rt mad to say it!
    Is not thy master with him, who, were't so,
    Would have informed for preparation?

    MESSENGER. So please you, it is true. Our thane is coming.
35   One of my fellows had the speed of him,[7]
    Who, almost dead for breath, had scarcely more
    Than would make up his message.

◆ **Reading Strategy**
Use the stage directions and the footnotes to make sense of Lady Macbeth's speech.

1. **missives:** Messengers.

2. **deliver thee:** Report to you.

3. **nearest:** Quickest.

4. **illness:** Wickedness.

5. **that which . . . undone:** What you are afraid of doing you would not wish undone once you have done it.
6. **round:** Crown.

7. **had . . . him:** Overtook him.

LADY MACBETH.   Give him tending;
He brings great news.   [*Exit* MESSENGER.]
                                   The raven himself is hoarse
That croaks the fatal entrance of Duncan
40 Under my battlements. Come, you spirits
That tend on mortal[8] thoughts, unsex me here,
And fill me, from the crown to the toe, top-full
Of direst cruelty! Make thick my blood,
Stop up th' access and passage to remorse[9]
45 That no compunctious visitings of nature[10]
Shake my fell[11] purpose, nor keep peace between
Th' effect[12] and it! Come to my woman's breasts,
And take my milk for gall,[13] you murd'ring ministers,[14]
Wherever in your sightless[15] substances
50 You wait on[16] nature's mischief! Come, thick night,
And pall[17] thee in the dunnest[18] smoke of hell,
That my keen knife see not the wound it makes,
Nor heaven peep through the blanket of the dark,
To cry "Hold, hold!"

[*Enter* MACBETH.]
                              Great Glamis! Worthy Cawdor!
Greater than both, by the all-hail hereafter!
55 Thy letters have transported me beyond
This ignorant[19] present, and I feel now
The future in the instant.[20]

MACBETH.   My dearest love,
Duncan comes here tonight.

LADY MACBETH.   And when goes hence?

MACBETH. Tomorrow, as he purposes.

LADY MACBETH.   O, never
60 Shall sun that morrow see!
Your face, my Thane, is as a book where men
May read strange matters. To beguile the time,[21]
Look like the time; bear welcome in your eye,
Your hand, your tongue: look like th' innocent flower,
65 But be the serpent under 't. He that's coming
Must be provided for: and you shall put
This night's great business into my dispatch;[22]
Which shall to all our nights and days to come
Give solely <u>sovereign</u> sway and masterdom.

MACBETH. We will speak further.

70 **LADY MACBETH.**   Only look up clear.[23]
To alter favor ever is to fear.[24]

8. **mortal:** Deadly.

9. **remorse:** Compassion.
10. **compunctious . . . nature:** Natural feelings of pity.
11. **fell:** Savage.
12. **effect:** Fulfillment.
13. **milk for gall:** Kindness in exchange for bitterness.
14. **ministers:** Agents.
15. **sightless:** Invisible.
16. **wait on:** Assist.
17. **pall:** Enshroud.
18. **dunnest:** Darkest.

19. **ignorant:** Unknowing.
20. **instant:** Present.

21. **beguile the time:** Deceive the people tonight.

22. **dispatch:** Management.
23. **look up clear:** Appear innocent.
24. **To alter . . . fear:** To show a disturbed face will arouse suspicion.

◆ **Build Vocabulary**

sovereign (säv´ rən) *adj.*: Supreme in power, rank, or authority

Leave all the rest to me.   [*Exit.*]

Scene vi. *Before* MACBETH'S *castle.*
[*Hautboys.*[1] *Torches. Enter* KING DUNCAN, MALCOLM, DONALBAIN,
BANQUO, LENNOX, MACDUFF, ROSS, ANGUS, *and* ATTENDANTS.]

KING. This castle hath a pleasant seat;[2] the air
Nimbly and sweetly recommends itself
Unto our gentle[3] senses.

BANQUO.   This guest of summer,
The temple-haunting martlet,[4] does approve[5]
5   By his loved mansionry[6] that the heaven's breath
Smells wooingly here. No jutty,[7] frieze,
Buttress, nor coign of vantage,[8] but this bird
Hath made his pendent bed and procreant cradle.[9]
Where they most breed and haunt,[10] I have observed
The air is delicate.

[*Enter* LADY MACBETH.]

10   **KING.**   See, see, our honored hostess!
The love that follows us sometime is our trouble,
Which still we thank as love. Herein I teach you
How you shall bid God 'ield us for your pains
And thank us for your trouble.[11]

LADY MACBETH.   All our service
15   In every point twice done, and then done double,
Were poor and single business[12] to contend
Against those honors deep and broad wherewith
Your Majesty loads our house: for those of old,
And the late dignities heaped up to them,
We rest your hermits.[13]

20   **KING.**   Where's the Thane of Cawdor?
We coursed[14] him at the heels, and had a purpose
To be his purveyor:[15] but he rides well,
And his great love, sharp as his spur, hath holp[16] him
To his home before us. Fair and noble hostess,
We are your guest tonight.

25   **LADY MACBETH.**   Your servants ever
Have theirs, themselves, and what is theirs, in compt,[17]
To make their audit at your Highness' pleasure,
Still[18] to return your own.

KING.   Give me your hand.
Conduct me to mine host: we love him highly,

---

1. **Hautboys:** Oboes announcing the arrival of royalty.
2. **seat:** Location.
3. **gentle:** Soothed.
4. **temple-haunting martlet:** Martin, a bird that usually nests in churches. In Shakespeare's time, *martin* was a slang term for a person who is easily deceived.
5. **approve:** Show.
6. **mansionry:** Nests.
7. **jutty:** Projection.
8. **coign of vantage:** Advantageous corner.
9. **procreant** (prō krē ənt) **cradle:** Nest where the young are hatched.
10. **haunt:** Visit.
11. **The love . . . trouble:** Though my visit inconveniences you, you should ask God to reward me for coming, because it was my love for you that prompted my visit.
12. **single business:** Feeble service.
13. **rest your hermits:** Remain your dependents bound to pray for you. Hermits were often paid to pray for another person's soul.
14. **coursed:** Chased.
15. **purveyor:** Advance supply officer.
16. **holp:** Helped.
17. **compt:** Trust.
18. **Still:** Always.

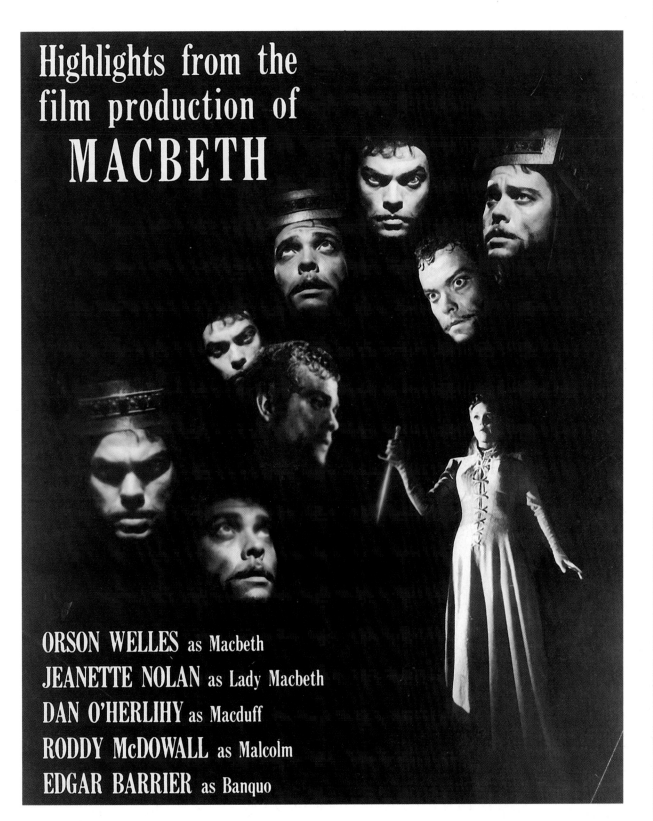

Highlights from the
film production of
MACBETH

ORSON WELLES as Macbeth
JEANETTE NOLAN as Lady Macbeth
DAN O'HERLIHY as Macduff
RODDY McDOWALL as Malcolm
EDGAR BARRIER as Banquo

▲ Critical Viewing How does this poster capture the
suspense created in Act I of *Macbeth*? [Connect]

30   And shall continue our graces towards him.
        By your leave, hostess.   [*Exit.*]

Scene vii. MACBETH'S *castle.*
[*Hautboys. Torches. Enter a* SEWER,[1] *and diverse* SERVANTS *with dishes and service over the stage. Then enter* MACBETH.]

      MACBETH. If it were done[2] when 'tis done, then 'twere well
        It were done quickly. If th' assassination
        Could trammel up the consequence, and catch,
        With his surcease, success;[3] that but this blow
5   Might be the be-all and the end-all—here,
        But here, upon this bank and shoal of time,
        We'd jump the life to come.[4] But in these cases
        We still have judgment here; that we but teach
        Bloody instructions, which, being taught, return
10   To plague th' inventor: this even-handed[5] justice
        Commends[6] th' ingredients of our poisoned chalice[7]
        To our own lips. He's here in double trust:
        First, as I am his kinsman and his subject,
        Strong both against the deed; then, as his host,
15   Who should against his murderer shut the door,
        Not bear the knife myself. Besides, this Duncan
        Hath borne his faculties[8] so meek, hath been
        So clear[9] in his great office, that his virtues
        Will plead like angels trumpet-tongued against
20   The deep damnation of his taking-off;
        And pity, like a naked newborn babe,
        Striding the blast, or heaven's cherubin[10] horsed
        Upon the sightless couriers[11] of the air,
        Shall blow the horrid deed in every eye,
25   That tears shall drown the wind. I have no spur
        To prick the sides of my intent, but only
        Vaulting ambition, which o'erleaps itself
        And falls on th' other—

[*Enter* LADY MACBETH.]
                    How now! What news?

      LADY MACBETH. He has almost supped. Why have you
        left the chamber?

      MACBETH. Hath he asked for me?

30 **LADY MACBETH.**   Know you not he has?

      MACBETH. We will proceed no further in this business:
        He hath honored me of late, and I have bought[12]
        Golden opinions from all sorts of people,

1. **sewer:** Chief butler.

2. **done:** Over and done with.

3. **If . . . success:** If the assassination could be done successfully and without consequence.
4. **We'd . . . come:** I would risk life in the world to come.
5. **even-handed:** Impartial.
6. **commends:** Offers.
7. **chalice:** Cup.

8. **faculties:** Powers.
9. **clear:** Blameless.

10. **cherubin:** Angels.
11. **sightless couriers:** Unseen messengers (the wind).

12. **bought:** Acquired.

Which would be worn now in their newest gloss,
Not cast aside so soon.

35 **LADY MACBETH.**   Was the hope drunk
  Wherein you dressed yourself? Hath it slept since?
  And wakes it now, to look so green and pale
  At what it did so freely? From this time
  Such I account thy love. Art thou afeard
40 To be the same in thine own act and valor
  As thou art in desire? Wouldst thou have that
  Which thou esteem'st the ornament of life,[13]
  And live a coward in thine own esteem,
  Letting "I dare not" wait upon[14] "I would,"
  Like the poor cat i' th' adage?[15]

45 **MACBETH.**   Prithee, peace!
  I dare do all that may become a man;
  Who dares do more is none.

  LADY MACBETH.   What beast was 't then
  That made you break[16] this enterprise to me?
  When you durst do it, then you were a man;
50 And to be more than what you were, you would

13. ornament of life:
The crown.
14. wait upon: Fol-
low.
15. poor . . . adage:
From an old proverb
about a cat who wants
to eat fish but is afraid
of getting its paws wet.

16. break: Reveal.

▲ Critical Viewing What sort of person would be worthy
of wearing a crown such as this one? [Generalize]

Be so much more the man. Nor time nor place
Did then adhere,[17] and yet you would make both.
They have made themselves, and that their[18] fitness now
Does unmake you. I have given suck, and know
55   How tender 'tis to love the babe that milks me:
I would, while it was smiling in my face,
Have plucked my nipple from his boneless gums,
And dashed the brains out, had I so sworn as you
Have done to this.

MACBETH.   If we should fail?

LADY MACBETH.   We fail?
60   But[19] screw your courage to the sticking-place[20]
And we'll not fail. When Duncan is asleep—
Whereto the rather shall his day's hard journey
Soundly invite him—his two chamberlains
Will I with wine and wassail[21] so convince,[22]
65   That memory, the warder of the brain,
Shall be a fume, and the receipt of reason
A limbeck only:[23] when in swinish sleep
Their drenchèd natures lies as in a death,
What cannot you and I perform upon
70   Th' unguarded Duncan, what not put upon
His spongy[24] officers, who shall bear the guilt
Of our great quell?[25]

MACBETH.   Bring forth men-children only;
For thy undaunted mettle[26] should compose
Nothing but males. Will it not be received,
75   When we have marked with blood those sleepy two
Of his own chamber, and used their very daggers,
That they have done 't?

LADY MACBETH.   Who dares receive it other,[27]
As we shall make our griefs and clamor roar
Upon his death?

MACBETH.   I am settled, and bend up
80   Each corporal agent to this terrible feat.
Away, and mock the time[28] with fairest show:
False face must hide what the false heart doth know.
                                                      [*Exit.*]

17. Did then adhere:
Was then suitable (for
the assassination).
18. that their: Their very.

◆ *Literature
and Your Life*
What is shocking
about the ambition
Lady Macbeth
expresses in
ll. 54–59?

19. But: Only.
20. sticking-place:
The notch that holds
the bowstring of a taut
crossbow.
21. wassail: Carousing.
22. convince: Over-
power.
23. That . . . only: That
memory, the guardian of
the brain, will be con-
fused by the fumes of
the drink, and the rea-
son become like a still,
distilling confused
thoughts.
24. spongy: Sodden.
25. quell: Murder.

26. mettle: Spirit.
27. other: Otherwise.

28. mock the time:
Mislead the world.

Beyond Literature

Guide for Responding

◆ Literature and Your Life

Reader's Response Do you find the developments in Macbeth's character believable? Why or why not?

Thematic Focus Which scene do you think would be most effective on stage? Why?

Questions for Research Shakespeare portrays Lady Macbeth as a driving force behind her husband's bloody acts. What was she really like? Generate research questions about her role as queen to the real Macbeth, who died in 1057.

☑ Check Your Comprehension

1. What do we learn about Macbeth's battlefield deeds and the activities of the Thane of Cawdor?
2. What reward does Macbeth receive from the king?
3. What do the three witches predict for Macbeth and Banquo?
4. (a) How does Lady Macbeth first learn of the witches' predictions? (b) What in Macbeth's personality does she fear will hold him back?
5. (a) What action does Lady Macbeth plan to take during the king's visit? (b) How does she intend to accomplish it?

◆ Critical Thinking

INTERPRET

1. Both the witches and Macbeth make statements about "foul and fair." (a) What are two possible meanings for the witches' words? (b) What does Macbeth mean by his remark? **[Interpret]**
2. Compare and contrast Banquo's and Macbeth's reactions to the witches. **[Compare and Contrast]**
3. Why is Macbeth indecisive about killing the king? **[Analyze Cause and Effect]**
4. How does Lady Macbeth's understanding of her husband's character help her to convince him that the murder plot should be carried out? **[Analyze]**

APPLY

5. How should Macbeth have answered Lady Macbeth when, speaking of the planned murder, she said, "What beast was't then / That made you break this enterprise to me?" **[Apply]**

EXTEND

6. Identify someone in history who is similar to a character in *Macbeth*. Explain your choice. **[Social Studies Link]**

Guide for Responding (continued)

◆ Reading Strategy

USE TEXT AIDS

Notes and stage directions help you to understand the action in *Macbeth*. For example, the directions at the beginning of I, ii, help you imagine the scene as the king and his followers encounter a bleeding captain. The side note tells you that a trumpet is sounding offstage.

1. Use the stage directions and side notes to describe the action in these scenes.
   a. I, i   **b.** Beginning of I, v
2. Use the side notes to explain the following terms:
   a. anon   **b.** Thane   **c.** cousins

◆ Literary Focus

ELIZABETHAN DRAMA

In **Elizabethan drama**, words did extra work. As in modern dramas, the characters' dialogue provided information on the story behind the play. However, words also created the illusion that elaborate sets and fancy lighting do in modern drama. For example, the dialogue between Banquo and the king helps the audience "see" Macbeth's castle: "This castle hath a pleasant seat . . . (I, vi, 1–10).

1. Use this dialogue to describe a set that would work for I, vi.
2. What "lighting effects" do the witches' words in I, i, 10–11 suggest? Explain.
3. What important background information do you learn from the speech in I, ii, 48–58?

◆ Grammar and Style

ACTION VERBS AND LINKING VERBS

Shakespeare uses **action verbs** to depict physical or mental actions that heighten the drama. He uses **linking verbs**—like *seem* and forms of the verb *to be*—to connect nouns and pronouns with vivid modifiers.

Practice Identify each verb in the following sentences from *Macbeth* as an action or a linking verb.
1. Fair is foul, and foul is fair. (I, i, 10)
2. But I am faint; my gashes cry for help. (I, ii, 42)
3. Speak then to me . . . (I, iii, 60)

◆ Build Vocabulary

USING WORDS ABOUT POWER

Shakespeare uses words relating to the themes of power, political loyalty, and political betrayal. Write these three themes in your notebook. Then, under each, list words from the play that relate to that theme. Use these three examples to begin your lists: Power—*sovereign*, *king*; political loyalty—*honor*; political betrayal—*assassination*.

USING THE WORD BANK

On your paper, write the letter of the word that is the antonym (opposite in meaning) of the first word.
1. valor: (a) courage, (b) bravery, (c) cowardice
2. treason: (a) loyalty, (b) betrayal, (c) treachery
3. imperial: (a) royal, (b) submissive, (c) powerful
4. liege: (a) authority, (b) king, (c) peasant
5. sovereign: (a) insignificant, (b) supreme, (c) solid

Idea Bank

Writing

1. **Speech of Welcome** Write the speech of welcome that Macbeth might have addressed to Duncan as Duncan entered Macbeth's castle. You can use prose or you can imitate Shakespeare's blank verse.

2. **Comparison and Contrast** Compare and contrast Macbeth and Lady Macbeth. Support your points with references to at least two passages from Act I. Consider such traits as courage, imagination, and ruthlessness.

Speaking, Listening, and Viewing

3. **Oral Interpretation** Reread Macbeth's speech in I, vii, 1–28. Practice reciting it, allowing the meaning of the passage to guide you, not the line endings. Decide where to quicken or slow your pace, and choose the words you want to emphasize. When you finish rehearsing, read the speech aloud for the class. **[Performing Arts Link]**

Guide for Interpreting, Act II

◆ Review and Anticipate

In Act I, we learn that Macbeth has distinguished himself in battle. Returning from the battlefield, he and Banquo meet three witches. These "weird sisters" predict that Macbeth will not only be rewarded by King Duncan but that he will become king himself. However, the witches also greet Banquo as a father of kings. Motivated by the witches' prophecy, Macbeth considers killing Duncan. The assassination becomes more likely when the king decides to visit Macbeth's castle. Lady Macbeth, on hearing about the witches' predictions and the king's visit, resolves that she and her husband will kill Duncan. When Macbeth hesitates, she urges him on.

As Act II begins, Macbeth and Lady Macbeth are about to commit this evil deed.

◆ Literary Focus

BLANK VERSE

Blank verse—unrhymed iambic pentameter—was invented during the English Renaissance to reflect natural speech rhythms. An *iamb* is a metrical foot consisting of an unstressed syllable followed by a stressed syllable, and the term *pentameter* means that there are five such feet to the line. *Macbeth* is written mainly in blank verse:

Me thought I heard a voice cry, "Sleep no more" (II, ii, 34)

(Unstressed syllables are represented by ˘ and stressed syllables by ´.) Unvaried blank verse would soon grow dull, however. That's why Shakespeare introduces variations, like a trochaic foot (´ ˘) at the beginning of a line: "List'ning their fear ... (II, ii, 28–29). As you hear the "melody" of Shakespeare's dialogue, listen for the rhythm too: a drumbeat iambic, with variations.

◆ Grammar and Style

COMMONLY CONFUSED WORDS: *LIE* AND *LAY*

Shakespeare correctly uses two easily confused words, *lie* and *lay*.

Lie (past: *lay*; past participle: *lain*) means "lie down or on":

"A heavy summons *lies* like lead upon me ..." (II, i, 6)

Lay (past and past participle: *laid*) means "to place":

"I *laid* their daggers ready...." (II, ii, 11)

◆ Reading Strategy

READ VERSE FOR MEANING

When you first learn about blank verse, you may find yourself beating out the rhythm of each line and stopping at the ends of lines. However, to **read blank verse for meaning**, you should focus on sentences and not lines.

To make sense of Shakespeare's sentences, you must follow them past the line endings. If you don't follow this sentence to the next line, you don't learn what the owl does. "It was the owl that shriek'd, the fatal bellman / Which gives the stern'st good-night ..." (II, ii, 3–4).

◆ Build Vocabulary

WORD ROOTS: -*voc*-

The word *equivocate* in Act II has the root -*voc*-, which means "voice." To equivocate is to speak in two equal "voices" so that two meanings can be given to what you say. Equivocation is a way of deceiving others without technically lying.

WORD BANK

Before you read, preview this list of words from Act II of *Macbeth*.

augment
palpable
stealthy
multitudinous
equivocate
predominance

Act II

Scene i. *Inverness. Court of* MACBETH'S *castle.*
[*Enter* BANQUO, *and* FLEANCE, *with a torch before him.*]

BANQUO. How goes the night, boy?

FLEANCE. The moon is down; I have not heard the clock.

BANQUO. And she goes down at twelve.

FLEANCE.   I take't, 'tis later, sir.

BANQUO. Hold, take my sword. There's husbandry[1] in heaven.
5   Their candles are all out. Take thee that[2] too.
        A heavy summons[3] lies like lead upon me,
        And yet I would not sleep. Merciful powers,
        Restrain in me the cursèd thoughts that nature
        Gives way to in repose!

[*Enter* MACBETH, *and a* SERVANT *with a torch.*]
                                        Give me my sword!
10   Who's there?

MACBETH. A friend.

BANQUO. What, sir, not yet at rest? The King's a-bed:
        He hath been in unusual pleasure, and
        Sent forth great largess to your offices:[4]
15   This diamond he greets your wife withal,
        By the name of most kind hostess; and shut up[5]
        In measureless content.

MACBETH.   Being unprepared,
        Our will became the servant to defect,
        Which else should free have wrought.[6]

BANQUO.   All's well.
20   I dreamt last night of the three weird sisters:
        To you they have showed some truth.

MACBETH.   I think not of them.
        Yet, when we can entreat an hour to serve,
        We would spend it in some words upon that business,
        If you would grant the time.

---

1. **husbandry:** Thrift.
2. **that:** Probably his sword belt.
3. **summons:** Weariness.

4. **largess . . . offices:** Gifts to your servants' quarters.
5. **shut up:** Retired.

6. **Being . . . wrought:** Because we did not have enough time to prepare, we were unable to entertain as lavishly as we wanted to.

◆ Build Vocabulary

augment (ôg ment´) *v*.: To make greater; enlarge

palpable (pal´ pə bəl) *adj*.: Capable of being touched or felt

stealthy (stel´ thē) *adj*.: Sly; furtive

BANQUO.   At your kind'st leisure.

25 **MACBETH.** If you shall cleave to my consent, when 'tis,[7]
        It shall make honor for you.

BANQUO.   So[8] I lose none
        In seeking to augment it, but still keep
        My bosom franchised[9] and allegiance clear,
        I shall be counseled.

MACBETH.   Good repose the while!

30 **BANQUO.** Thanks, sir. The like to you!

[*Exit* BANQUO *with* FLEANCE.]

MACBETH. Go bid thy mistress, when my drink is ready,
        She strike upon the bell. Get thee to bed.
                                    [*Exit* SERVANT.]
        Is this a dagger which I see before me,
        The handle toward my hand? Come, let me clutch thee.
35   I have thee not, and yet I see thee still.
        Art thou not, fatal vision, sensible[10]
        To feeling as to sight, or art thou but
        A dagger of the mind, a false creation,
        Proceeding from the heat-oppressèd brain?
40   I see thee yet, in form as palpable
        As this which now I draw.
        Thou marshal'st[11] me the way that I was going;
        And such an instrument I was to use.
        Mine eyes are made the fools o' th' other senses,
45   Or else worth all the rest. I see thee still;
        And on thy blade and dudgeon[12] gouts[13] of blood,
        Which was not so before. There's no such thing.
        It is the bloody business which informs[14]
        Thus to mine eyes. Now o'er the one half-world
50   Nature seems dead, and wicked dreams abuse[15]
        The curtained sleep; witchcraft celebrates
        Pale Hecate's offerings;[16] and withered murder,
        Alarumed by his sentinel, the wolf,
        Whose howl's his watch, thus with his stealthy pace,
55   With Tarquin's[17] ravishing strides, towards his design
        Moves like a ghost. Thou sure and firm-set earth,
        Hear not my steps, which way they walk, for fear
        Thy very stones prate of my whereabout,
        And take the present horror from the time,
60   Which now suits with it.[18] Whiles I threat, he lives:
        Words to the heat of deeds too cold breath gives.
[*A bell rings.*]

Reading Strategy
How many sentences are in lines 35–39?

7. **cleave . . . 'tis:** Join my cause when the time comes.

8. **So:** Provided that.

9. **bosom franchised:** Heart free (from guilt).

10. **sensible:** Able to be felt.

11. **marshal'st:** Leads.

12. **dudgeon:** Wooden hilt.
13. **gouts:** Large drops.
14. **informs:** Takes shape.
15. **abuse:** Deceive.
16. **Hecate's** (hek´ə tēz) **offerings:** Offerings to Hecate, the Greek goddess of witchcraft.
17. **Tarquin's:** Of Tarquin, a Roman tyrant.

18. **take . . . it:** Remove the horrible silence which suits this moment.

I go, and it is done: the bell invites me.
Hear it not, Duncan, for it is a knell
That summons thee to heaven, or to hell.   [*Exit.*]

Scene ii. *Macbeth's castle.*
[*Enter* LADY MACBETH.]

LADY MACBETH. That which hath made them drunk hath made me bold;
    What hath quenched them hath given me fire. Hark! Peace!
    It was the owl that shrieked, the fatal bellman,
    Which gives the stern'st good-night.[1] He is about it.
5   The doors are open, and the surfeited grooms[2]
    Do mock their charge with snores. I have drugged their possets,[3]
    That death and nature do contend about them,
    Whether they live or die.

MACBETH.   [*Within*] Who's there? What, ho?

LADY MACBETH. Alack, I am afraid they have awaked
10   And 'tis not done! Th' attempt and not the deed
    Confounds[4] us. Hark! I laid their daggers ready;
    He could not miss 'em. Had he not resembled
    My father as he slept, I had done 't.

[*Enter* MACBETH.]

My husband!

MACBETH. I have done the deed. Didst thou not hear a noise?

15 LADY MACBETH. I heard the owl scream and the crickets cry.
    Did not you speak?

MACBETH.   When?

LADY MACBETH.   Now.

MACBETH.   As I descended?

LADY MACBETH. Ay.

MACBETH. Hark!
    Who lies i' th' second chamber?

LADY MACBETH.   Donalbain.

1. **bellman . . . goodnight:** It was customary for a bell to be rung at midnight outside a condemned person's cell on the night before an execution.
2. **surfeited grooms:** Overfed servants.
3. **possets:** Warm bedtime drinks.

4. **Confounds:** Ruins.

Ellen Terry as Lady Macbeth, John Singer Sargent, Tate Gallery, on Loan to National Portrait Gallery, London

▶ **Critical Viewing** This is an artist's rendering of nineteenth-century actress Ellen Terry playing Lady Macbeth. Judging by the picture, how do you think Terry would have spoken lines 1–2 in II, ii? **[Deduce]**

20   **MACBETH.** This is a sorry[5] sight.

     LADY MACBETH. A foolish thought, to say a sorry sight.

     MACBETH. There's one did laugh in 's sleep, and one cried "Murder!"
       That they did wake each other. I stood and heard them.
       But they did say their prayers, and addressed them
       Again to sleep.

5. sorry: Miserable.

◆ **Literary Focus**
What is the pattern of accented and unaccented syllables in line 21?

Macbeth, Act II, Scene ii ◆ 297

25   **LADY MACBETH.** There are two[6] lodged together.

    MACBETH. One cried "God bless us!" and "Amen" the other,
    As they had seen me with these hangman's hands:
    List'ning their fear, I could not say "Amen,"
    When they did say "God bless us!"

    LADY MACBETH.   Consider it not so deeply.

    MACBETH. But wherefore could not I pronounce "Amen"?
30   I had most need of blessing, and "Amen"
    Stuck in my throat.

    LADY MACBETH.   These deeds must not be thought
    After these ways; so, it will make us mad.

    MACBETH. Methought I heard a voice cry "Sleep no more!
35   Macbeth does murder sleep"—the innocent sleep,
    Sleep that knits up the raveled sleave[7] of care,
    The death of each day's life, sore labor's bath,
    Balm of hurt minds, great nature's second course,[8]
    Chief nourisher in life's feast—

    LADY MACBETH.   What do you mean?

40   **MACBETH.** Still it cried "Sleep no more!" to all the house:
    "Glamis hath murdered sleep, and therefore Cawdor
    Shall sleep no more: Macbeth shall sleep no more."

    LADY MACBETH. Who was it that thus cried? Why, worthy Thane,
    You do unbend[9] your noble strength, to think
45   So brainsickly of things. Go get some water,
    And wash this filthy witness[10] from your hand.
    Why did you bring these daggers from the place?
    They must lie there: go carry them, and smear
    The sleepy grooms with blood.

    MACBETH.   I'll go no more.
50   I am afraid to think what I have done;
    Look on 't again I dare not.

    LADY MACBETH.   Infirm of purpose!
    Give me the daggers. The sleeping and the dead
    Are but as pictures. 'Tis the eye of childhood
    That fears a painted devil. If he do bleed,
55   I'll gild[11] the faces of the grooms withal,
    For it must seem their guilt. [*Exit. Knock within.*]

6. two: Malcolm and Donalbain, Duncan's sons.

7. knits . . . sleave: Straightens out the tangled threads.
8. second course: Main course; sleep.

9. unbend: Relax.

10. witness: Evidence.

11. gild: Paint.

◆ **Build Vocabulary**

multitudinous: (mul′ tə tōod′ 'n əs) *adj.*: Existing in great numbers

equivocate: (ē kwiv′ ə kāt) *v.*: To use terms that have two or more meanings to mislead purposely or deceive

MACBETH.   Whence is that knocking?
How is 't with me, when every noise appalls me?
What hands are here? Ha! They pluck out mine eyes!
Will all great Neptune's ocean wash this blood
60 Clean from my hand? No; this my hand will rather
The multitudinous seas incarnadine,[12]
Making the green one red.

[*Enter* LADY MACBETH.]

LADY MACBETH. My hands are of your color, but I shame
To wear a heart so white. [*Knock.*] I hear a knocking
65 At the south entry. Retire we to our chamber.
A little water clears us of this deed:
How easy is it then! Your constancy
Hath left you unattended.[13] [*Knock.*] Hark! more knocking.
Get on your nightgown, lest occasion call us
70 And show us to be watchers.[14] Be not lost
So poorly in your thoughts.

MACBETH. To know my deed, 'twere best not know myself. [*Knock.*]
Wake Duncan with thy knocking! I would thou couldst!
                                                              [*Exit.*]

Scene iii. Macbeth's castle.
[*Enter a* PORTER.[1] *Knocking within.*]

PORTER. Here's a knocking indeed! If a man were porter
of hell gate, he should have old[2] turning the key.
[*Knock.*] Knock, knock, knock! Who's there, i' th'
name of Beelzebub?[3] Here's a farmer, that
5 hanged himself on th' expectation of plenty.[4] Come
in time! Have napkins enow[5] about you; here you'll
sweat for 't. [*Knock*] Knock, knock! Who's there, in
th' other devil's name? Faith, here's an equivocator,
that could swear in both the scales against
10 either scale;[6] who committed treason enough for
God's sake, yet could not equivocate to heaven. O,
come in, equivocator. [*Knock.*] Knock, knock, knock!
Who's there? Faith, here's an English tailor come
hither for stealing out of a French hose:[7]
15 come in, tailor. Here you may roast your goose.[8]
[*Knock.*] Knock, knock; never at quiet! What are you?
But this place is too cold for hell. I'll devil-porter it no
further. I had thought to have let in some of all
professions that go the primrose way to th'
20 everlasting bonfire. [*Knock.*] Anon, anon!
[*Opens an entrance.*] I pray you, remember the porter.

12. **incarnadine** (in
kär′ nə din): Redden.

♦ *Literature
and Your Life*
What does Macbeth realize about
his ambition that
Lady Macbeth
does not?

13. **Your constancy . . .
unattended:** Your firmness of purpose has left
you.
14. **watchers:** Up late.

1. **porter:** Doorkeeper.

2. **should have old:**
Would have plenty of.

3. **Beelzebub** (bē el′ zə
bub): The chief devil.
4. **A farmer . . . plenty:**
A farmer who hoarded
grain, hoping that the
prices would come up as
a result of a bad harvest.
5. **enow:** Enough.
6. **an equivocator . . .
scale:** A liar who could
make two contradictory
statements and swear that
both were true.
7. **stealing . . . hose:**
Stealing some cloth from
the hose while making
them.
8. **goose:** Pressing iron.

[*Enter* MACDUFF *and* LENNOX.]

MACDUFF. Was it so late, friend, ere you went to bed,
That you do lie so late?

PORTER. Faith, sir, we were carousing till the second
25   cock:[9] and drink, sir, is a great provoker of three
things.

MACDUFF. What three things does drink especially
provoke?

PORTER. Marry, sir, nose-painting, sleep, and urine.
30   Lechery, sir, it provokes and unprovokes; it provokes
the desire, but it takes away the performance: therefore much drink may be said to be an equivocator
with lechery: it makes him and it mars him; it
sets him on and it takes him off; it persuades him
35   and disheartens him; makes him stand to and not
stand to; in conclusion equivocates him in a sleep, and
giving him the lie, leaves him.

MACDUFF. I believe drink gave thee the lie[10] last night.

PORTER. That it did, sir, i' the very throat on me: but I
40   requited him for his lie, and, I think, being too strong
for him, though he took up my legs sometime, yet I
make a shift to cast[11] him.

MACDUFF. Is thy master stirring?

[*Enter* MACBETH.]

Our knocking has awaked him; here he comes.

LENNOX. Good morrow, noble sir.

45   **MACBETH.**   Good morrow, both.

MACDUFF. Is the king stirring, worthy Thane?

MACBETH.   Not yet.

MACDUFF. He did command me to call timely[12] on him:
I have almost slipped the hour.

9. **second cock:**
3:00 A.M.

A Critic's Response
"Hence it is, that when the deed is done . . . the knocking at the gate is heard . . . and the re-establishment of the goings-on of the world in which we live, first makes us profoundly sensible of the awful [episode] that had suspended them."
—Thomas De Quincey

10. **gave thee the lie:**
Laid you out.

11. **cast:** Vomit.

12. **timely:** Early.

MACBETH.   I'll bring you to him.

MACDUFF.   I know this is a joyful trouble to you;
50   But yet 'tis one.

MACBETH.   The labor we delight in physics pain.[13]
     This is the door.

13. labor . . . pain:
Labor that we enjoy
cures discomfort.

MACDUFF.   I'll make so bold to call,
     For 'tis my limited service.[14]   [*Exit* MACDUFF.]

14. limited service:
Assigned duty.

LENNOX.   Goes the king hence today?

MACBETH.   He does: he did appoint so.

55   **LENNOX.**   The night has been unruly. Where we lay,
     Our chimneys were blown down, and, as they say,
     Lamentings heard i' th' air, strange screams of death,
     And prophesying with accents terrible
     Of dire combustion[15] and confused events
60   New hatched to th' woeful time: the obscure bird[16]
     Clamored the livelong night. Some say, the earth
     Was feverous and did shake.

> ◆ **Reading Strategy**
> Read lines 55–60,
> aloud. How many
> sentences are there?

15. combustion:
Confusion.
16. obscure bird:
Bird of darkness, the
owl.

MACBETH.   'Twas a rough night.

LENNOX.   My young remembrance cannot parallel
     A fellow to it.

[*Enter* MACDUFF.]

65   **MACDUFF.**   O horror, horror, horror! Tongue nor heart
     Cannot conceive nor name thee.

MACBETH AND LENNOX.   What's the matter?

MACDUFF.   Confusion[17] now hath made his masterpiece.
     Most sacrilegious murder hath broke ope
     The Lord's anointed temple,[18] and stole thence
     The life o' th' building.

17. Confusion:
Destruction.
**18. The Lord's
anointed temple:** The
King's body.

70   **MACBETH.**   What is 't you say? The life?

LENNOX. Mean you his Majesty?

MACDUFF. Approach the chamber, and destroy your sight
With a new Gorgon:[19] do not bid me speak;
See, and then speak yourselves. Awake, awake!

                                 [*Exit* MACBETH *and* LENNOX.]

75   Ring the alarum bell. Murder and Treason!
Banquo and Donalbain! Malcolm! Awake!
Shake off this downy sleep, death's counterfeit,
And look on death itself! Up, up, and see
The great doom's image![20] Malcolm! Banquo!
80   As from your graves rise up, and walk like sprites,[21]
To countenance[22] this horror. Ring the bell.

[*Bell rings. Enter* LADY MACBETH.]

LADY MACBETH. What's the business,
That such a hideous trumpet calls to parley[23]
The sleepers of the house? Speak, speak!

MACDUFF.   O gentle lady,
85   'Tis not for you to hear what I can speak:
The repetition, in a woman's ear,
Would murder as it fell.

[*Enter* BANQUO.]

                    O Banquo, Banquo!
Our royal master's murdered.

LADY MACBETH.   Woe, alas!
What, in our house?

BANQUO.   Too cruel anywhere.
90   Dear Duff, I prithee, contradict thyself,
And say it is not so.

[*Enter* MACBETH, LENNOX, *and* ROSS.]

MACBETH. Had I but died an hour before this chance,
I had lived a blessèd time; for from this instant
There's nothing serious in mortality:[24]
95   All is but toys.[25] Renown and grace is dead,
The wine of life is drawn, and the mere lees[26]
Is left this vault[27] to brag of.

[*Enter* MALCOLM *and* DONALBAIN.]

---

19. Gorgon: Medusa, a mythological monster whose appearance was so ghastly that those who looked at it turned to stone.

20. great doom's image: Likeness of Judgment Day.
21. sprites: Spirits.
22. countenance: Be in keeping with.

23. parley: War conference.

24. serious in mortality: Worthwhile in mortal life.
25. toys: Trifles.
26. lees: Dregs.
27. vault: World.

DONALBAIN. What is amiss?

MACBETH.   You are, and do not know 't.
    The spring, the head, the fountain of your blood
100   Is stopped; the very source of it is stopped.

MACDUFF. Your royal father's murdered.

MALCOLM.   O, by whom?

LENNOX. Those of his chamber, as it seemed, had done 't:
    Their hands and faces were all badged[28] with blood;
    So were their daggers, which unwiped we found
105   Upon their pillows. They stared, and were distracted.
    No man's life was to be trusted with them.

MACBETH. O, yet I do repent me of my fury,
    That I did kill them.

MACDUFF.   Wherefore did you so?

MACBETH. Who can be wise, amazed, temp'rate and furious,
110   Loyal and neutral, in a moment? No man.
    The expedition[29] of my violent love
    Outrun the pauser, reason. Here lay Duncan,
    His silver skin laced with his golden blood,
    And his gashed stabs looked like a breach in nature
115   For ruin's wasteful entrance: there, the murderers,
    Steeped in the colors of their trade, their daggers
    Unmannerly breeched with gore.[30] Who could refrain,
    That had a heart to love, and in that heart
    Courage to make 's love known?

LADY MACBETH.   Help me hence, ho!

MACDUFF. Look to the lady.

120 **MALCOLM.** [ASIDE TO DONALBAIN] WHY DO WE HOLD OUR TONGUES,
    That most may claim this argument for ours?[31]

DONALBAIN. [*Aside to* MALCOLM] What should be spoken here,
    Where our fate, hid in an auger-hole,[32]
    May rush, and seize us? Let's away:
    Our tears are not yet brewed.

125 **MALCOLM.** [*Aside to* DONALBAIN] Nor our strong sorrow
    Upon the foot of motion.[33]

◆ **Literary Focus**
Write out lines 99–100 of blank verse and mark syllables as unstressed and stressed. Where is there a pause in line 100? How does it reinforce the meaning?

28. **badged:** Marked.

29. **expedition:** Haste.

30. **breeched with gore:** Covered with blood.

31. **That most . . . ours:** Who are the most concerned with this topic.
32. **auger-hole:** Tiny hole, an unsuspected place because of its size.
33. **Our tears . . . motion:** We have not yet had time for tears nor to turn our sorrow into action.

BANQUO.   Look to the lady.

                    [LADY MACBETH *is carried out.*]

And when we have our naked frailties hid,[34]
That suffer in exposure, let us meet
And question[35] this most bloody piece of work,

130   To know it further. Fears and scruples[36] shake us.
In the great hand of God I stand, and thence
Against the undivulged pretense[37] I fight
Of treasonous malice.

MACDUFF.   And so do I.

ALL.   So all.

34. **when . . . hid:** When we have put on our clothes.
35. **question:** Investigate.
36. **scruples:** Doubts.
37. **undivulged pretense:** Hidden purpose.

Lady Macbeth Seizing the Daggers, Henry Fuseli, The Tate Gallery, London

▲ **Critical Viewing** This painting depicts the moment when Macbeth comes from murdering Duncan (II, ii, 14). However, it also captures the nature of the relationship between Macbeth and Lady Macbeth in the first part of the play. What do their facial expressions and body language suggest about that relationship? **[Interpret]**

MACBETH. Let's briefly[38] put on manly readiness,
And meet i' th' hall together.

135 **ALL.**   Well contented.
[*Exit all but* MALCOLM *and* DONALBAIN.]

MALCOLM. What will you do? Let's not consort with them.
To show an unfelt sorrow is an office[39]
Which the false man does easy. I'll to England.

DONALBAIN. To Ireland, I; our separated fortune
140 Shall keep us both the safer. Where we are
There's daggers in men's smiles; the near in blood,
The nearer bloody.[40]

MALCOLM.   This murderous shaft that's shot
Hath not yet lighted,[41] and our safest way
Is to avoid the aim. Therefore to horse;
145 And let us not be dainty of leave-taking,
But shift away. There's warrant [42] in that theft
Which steals itself[43] when there's no mercy left.
                                                    [*Exit.*]

Scene iv. *Outside Macbeth's castle.*
[*Enter* ROSS *with an* OLD MAN.]

OLD MAN. Threescore and ten I can remember well:
Within the volume of which time I have seen
Hours dreadful and things strange, but this sore[1] night
Hath trifled former knowings.

ROSS.   Ha, good father,
5 Thou seest the heavens, as troubled with man's act,
Threatens his bloody stage. By th' clock 'tis day,
And yet dark night strangles the traveling lamp:[2]
Is 't night's predominance, or the day's shame,
That darkness does the face of earth entomb,
When living light should kiss it?

10 **OLD MAN.**   'Tis unnatural,
Even like the deed that's done. On Tuesday last
A falcon, tow'ring in her pride of place,[3]
Was by a mousing owl hawked at and killed.

38. **briefly:** Quickly.

◆ **Reading Strategy**
How do the brief sentences in lines 136–138 reinforce the meaning?

39. **office:** Function.

40. **the near . . . bloody:** The closer we are in blood relationship to Duncan, the greater our chance of being murdered.
41. **lighted:** Reached its target.
42. **warrant:** Justification.
43. **that theft . . . itself:** Stealing away.

1. **sore:** Grievous.

2. **traveling lamp:** The sun.

3. **tow'ring . . . place:** Soaring at its summit.

◆ **Build Vocabulary**

predominance (pri däm´ ə nəns) *n.*: Superiority

ROSS. And Duncan's horses—a thing most strange
　　　and certain—
15　　Beauteous and swift, the minions of their race,
　　　Turned wild in nature, broke their stalls, flung out,
　　　Contending 'gainst obedience, as they would make
　　　War with mankind.

OLD MAN.　　　　　　　'Tis said they eat⁴ each other.

ROSS. They did so, to th' amazement of mine eyes,
　　　That looked upon 't.

[*Enter* MACDUFF.]

20　　　　　　　　　　Here comes the good Macduff.
　　　How goes the world, sir, now?

MACDUFF.　　　　　　　Why, see you not?

ROSS. Is 't known who did this more than bloody deed?

MACDUFF. Those that Macbeth hath slain.

ROSS.　　　　　　　　Alas, the day!
　　　What good could they pretend?⁵

MACDUFF.　　　　　They were suborned:⁶
25　　Malcolm and Donalbain, the king's two sons,
　　　Are stol'n away and fled, which puts upon them
　　　Suspicion of the deed.

ROSS.　　　　　　'Gainst nature still.
　　　Thriftless ambition, that will ravin up⁷
　　　Thine own life's means! Then 'tis most like
30　　The sovereignty will fall upon Macbeth.

MACDUFF. He is already named, and gone to Scone⁸
　　　To be invested.

ROSS.　　　Where is Duncan's body?

MACDUFF. Carried to Colmekill,
　　　The sacred storehouse of his predecessors
　　　And guardian of their bones.

4. **eat:** Ate.

◆ **Literary Focus**
What rhythmic variation in the blank verse do you find at the beginning of line 23?

5. **pretend:** Hope for.

6. **suborned:** Bribed.

7. **ravin up:** Devour greedily.

8. **Scone** (skōōn): Where Scottish kings were crowned.

35 **ROSS.**   Will you to Scone?

MACDUFF. No, cousin, I'll to Fife.[9]

9. **Fife:** Where Macduff's castle is located.

ROSS.   Well, I will thither.

MACDUFF. Well, may you see things well done there.
   Adieu,
Lest our old robes sit easier than our new!

ROSS. Farewell, father.

40 **OLD MAN.** God's benison[10] go with you, and with those
   That would make good of bad, and friends of foes!
                       [*Exit.*]

10. **benison:** Blessing.

Guide for Responding

◆ Literature and Your Life

Reader's Response Who do you think bears the greatest responsibility for the murder of King Duncan—Macbeth or Lady Macbeth? Explain.
Thematic Focus What conflicts will Macbeth experience as the play continues?

☑ Check Your Comprehension

1. Briefly summarize how Macbeth and Lady Macbeth conspire to murder Duncan.
2. What does the drunken porter imagine he is doing?
3. How is the murder discovered?
4. (a) What action does Macbeth take against the grooms? (b) Why do Malcolm and Donalbain leave the castle?
5. (a) Who does Macduff say has killed Duncan? (b) Why do Malcolm and Donalbain fall under suspicion, according to Macduff?

◆ Critical Thinking

INTERPRET

1. Compare and contrast Macbeth's reaction to the murder with Lady Macbeth's. **[Compare and Contrast]**
2. (a) Why do you think critics consider the porter's speech comic relief? (b) How do the porter's comments on the people arriving at "hell gate" mirror Macbeth's dilemma? **[Interpret]**
3. What causes Lady Macbeth to faint? **[Infer]**
4. Why does Ross have doubts about accepting the grooms as murderers? **[Draw Conclusions]**

APPLY

5. In his soliloquy in Scene i, Macbeth speaks of "vaulting ambition." (a) How can "vaulting ambition" result in great success? (b) How can it result in destruction? **[Speculate]**

EXTEND

6. Could an assassination like this happen in our times? Why or why not? **[Social Studies Link]**

Guide for Responding (continued)

◆ Reading Strategy

READ VERSE FOR MEANING

Read Shakespeare's verse for meaning by following the sentences past the line endings. In reading II, i, 62–64, for example, do not stop at line 63.

1. How many sentences are there in this passage?
2. Express the meaning of these sentences in your own words.

◆ Literary Focus

BLANK VERSE

Most of the lines in Shakespeare's plays are in **blank verse**—unrhymed iambic pentameter. Each line has ten syllables, with stress falling on every other syllable:

Ĭ hăve thĕe nŏt, ănd yĕt Ĭ sée thĕe stíll (II, i, 35)

To vary this rhythm, Shakespeare introduces pauses in lines, ends lines with unstressed syllables, and substitutes trochees (stress, unstressed) and anapests (unstressed, unstressed, stressed) for iambs. Here are some examples:

• Trochee (˘) begins a line:
  It is the bloody business which informs (II, i, 48)
• Anapest (˘˘´) replaces an iamb in final foot:
  Macbeth does murder sleep—the innocent sleep

1. Mark stressed and unstressed syllables in II, ii, 59–62.
2. Identify three metrical variations in these lines.

◆ Grammar and Style

COMMONLY CONFUSED WORDS: *LIE* AND *LAY*

Don't confuse *lie* with *lay*. *Lie* means "to lie down or on" and *lay* means "to place."

Practice In your notebook, write each of these sentences using *lie* or *lay* correctly.

1. Macbeth kills Duncan as the king is ____?____ in bed.
2. Lady Macbeth thought the daggers should ____?____ beside King Duncan, so she went to ____?____ them there.
3. Before the porter started knocking, Lady Macbeth intended to ____?____ down and pretend to have been asleep.

◆ Build Vocabulary

USING THE LATIN ROOT *-voc-*

Use the meaning of the Latin root *-voc-* ("voice or calling") to define each of the italicized words.

1. The *vocalist* stood near the piano.
2. The young woman was *vocal* about the rights to which she was entitled.
3. The minister spoke the *invocation* at the beginning of the dinner.

USING THE WORD BANK: Antonyms

In your notebook, write the letter of the word that is an antonym (opposite in meaning) to the first word.

1. augment: (a) add, (b) reduce, (c) move
2. palpable: (a) imperceptible, (b) impolite, (c) obvious
3. stealthy: (a) reputable, (b) sneaky, (c) open
4. multitudinous: (a) scarce, (b) agitated, (c) ample
5. equivocate: (a) falsify, (b) declare, (c) ruin
6. predominance: (a) equality, (b) superiority, (c) inferiority

Idea Bank

Writing

1. **Detective's Journal** As a medieval detective, keep a journal of the clues you find at the scene of Duncan's murder. Record each person's version of what happened.

2. **Response to Criticism** G. B. Harrison argues that Macbeth "is controlled by an overpowering imagination which makes him see not only . . . the results of an action . . . but also its essential meaning." Agree or disagree with this statement, citing specific passages from Act II.

Researching and Representing

3. **Costume Design** Using the pictures that accompany the play and your own imagination as guides, design costumes for Macbeth, Lady Macbeth, and Duncan. **[Art Link]**

Online Activity ▸ www.phlit.phschool.com

Guide for Interpreting, Act III

◆ Review and Anticipate

In Act II, Lady Macbeth drugs those who are guarding Duncan, enabling Macbeth to kill the king. Macbeth then kills the guards too so that he can more easily blame them for this murder. Duncan's sons, Malcolm and Donalbain, flee. They are afraid that they will be murdered by a kinsman eager to claim the throne. Because they run away, some people suspect them of killing their own father. As the act closes, it seems that Macbeth will be named king.

Act III begins with Macbeth on the throne, as the witches had predicted. All is going well for him—or is it? There's still Banquo to think of, whom the witches hailed as "Lesser than Macbeth, and greater."

◆ Literary Focus

CONFLICT

Conflict—the struggle between two forces—is what creates drama. This struggle can be an **external conflict** between two characters or groups or it can be an **internal conflict** within a character. The **climax** of a play is the point at which the internal and external conflicts are greatest. Usually the action rises to the climax—the moment of highest tension—and then falls as the conflicts are resolved.

In *Macbeth,* Act III, the rising action leads the new king to a state dinner and the sight of a guest—who should not be there!

◆ Grammar and Style

SUBJECT AND VERB AGREEMENT

In Shakespeare's writing, verbs agree with subjects in number (singular or plural). Notice that the verbs change form to agree with a singular or a plural subject.

Singular: After life's fitful fever *he sleeps* well.

Plural: Our *fears* in Banquo / *Stick* deep . . .

◆ Reading Strategy

READ BETWEEN THE LINES

When you read a play or any work of literature, you read it line by line to follow the action. However, you can also **read between the lines** by considering what the lines suggest and by connecting earlier passages with later ones. Reading line by line tells you *what* happens, but reading between the lines tells you *why* it happens.

In *Macbeth,* Act III, read between the lines by asking yourself why Macbeth is so concerned with Banquo's afternoon plans: "Is't far you ride?" Macbeth asks his friend.

◆ Build Vocabulary

LATIN PREFIXES: *mal-*

Act III contains the word *malevolence.* The Latin prefix *mal-,* meaning "bad," contributes to the definition of this word, which means "bad will toward others; evil influence."

WORD BANK

Before you read, preview this list of words from Act III of *Macbeth.*

indissoluble
dauntless
jocund
infirmity
malevolence

ACT III

Scene i. *Forres. The palace.*
[*Enter* BANQUO.]

BANQUO. Thou hast it now: King, Cawdor, Glamis, all,
As the weird women promised, and I fear
Thou play'dst most foully for 't. Yet it was said
It should not stand[1] in thy posterity,

5 But that myself should be the root and father
Of many kings. If there come truth from them—
As upon thee, Macbeth, their speeches shine—
Why, by the verities on thee made good,
May they not be my oracles as well

10 And set me up in hope? But hush, no more!

[*Sennet[2] sounded. Enter* MACBETH *as King*, LADY MACBETH,
LENNOX, ROSS, LORDS, *and* ATTENDANTS.]

MACBETH. Here's our chief guest.

LADY MACBETH.   If he had been forgotten,
It had been as a gap in our great feast,
And all-thing[3] unbecoming.

MACBETH. Tonight we hold a solemn[4] supper, sir,
And I'll request your presence.

15 **BANQUO.**   Let your Highness
Command upon me, to the which my duties
Are with a most indissoluble tie
For ever knit.

MACBETH. Ride you this afternoon?

BANQUO.   Ay, my good lord.

20 **MACBETH.** We should have else desired your good advice
(Which still hath been both grave and prosperous[5])
In this day's council; but we'll take tomorrow.
Is't far you ride?

BANQUO. As far, my lord, as will fill up the time
25 'Twixt this and supper. Go not my horse the better,[6]
I must become a borrower of the night
For a dark hour or twain.

1. **stand:** Continue.

2. **Sennet:** Trumpet call.

3. **all-thing:** Altogether.

4. **solemn:** Ceremonious.

5. **grave and prosperous:** Weighty and profitable.

6. **Go not . . . better:** Unless my horse goes faster than I expect.

◆ **Build Vocabulary**

indissoluble (in′di säl′ yoō bəl) *adj.*: Not able to be dissolved or undone

dauntless (dônt′ lis) *adj.*: Fearless; cannot be intimidated

MACBETH. Fail not our feast.

BANQUO. My lord, I will not.

MACBETH. We hear our bloody cousins are bestowed
30　In England and in Ireland, not confessing
　　Their cruel parricide, filling their hearers
　　With strange invention.[7] But of that tomorrow,
　　When therewithal we shall have cause of state
　　Craving us jointly.[8] Hie you to horse. Adieu,
35　Till you return at night. Goes Fleance with you?

BANQUO. Ay, my good lord: our time does call upon 's.

MACBETH. I wish your horses swift and sure of foot,
　　And so I do commend you to their backs.
　　Farewell.　　　　　　　　　　　　[*Exit* BANQUO.]
40　Let every man be master of his time
　　Till seven at night. To make society
　　The sweeter welcome, we will keep ourself
　　Till suppertime alone. While[9] then, God be with you!

　　　　　[*Exit* LORDS *and all but* MACBETH *and a* SERVANT.]

　　Sirrah,[10] a word with you: attend those men
45　Our pleasure?

ATTENDANT. They are, my lord, without the palace gate.

MACBETH. Bring them before us.　　　　[*Exit* SERVANT.]
　　To be thus[11] is nothing, but[12] to be safely thus—
　　Our fears in Banquo stick deep,
50　And in his royalty of nature reigns that
　　Which would be feared. 'Tis much he dares;
　　And, to[13] that dauntless temper of his mind,
　　He hath a wisdom that doth guide his valor
　　To act in safety. There is none but he
55　Whose being I do fear: and under him
　　My genius is rebuked,[14] as it is said
　　Mark Antony's was by Caesar. He chid[15] the sisters,
　　When first they put the name of King upon me,
　　And bade them speak to him; then prophetlike
60　They hailed him father to a line of kings.
　　Upon my head they placed a fruitless crown
　　And put a barren scepter in my gripe,[16]
　　Thence to be wrenched with an unlineal hand,
　　No son of mine succeeding. If 't be so,
65　For Banquo's issue have I filed[17] my mind;
　　For them the gracious Duncan have I murdered;
　　Put rancors in the vessel of my peace

7. **invention:** Lies.

8. **cause . . . jointly:** Matters of state demanding our joint attention.

9. **While:** Until.

10. **Sirrah:** Common address to an inferior.

11. **thus:** King.
12. **but:** Unless.

13. **to:** Added to.

14. **genius is rebuked:** Guardian spirit is cowed.
15. **chid:** Scolded.

16. **gripe:** Grip.

17. **filed:** Defiled.

Only for them, and mine eternal jewel[18]
Given to the common enemy of man,[19]
70   To make them kings, the seeds of Banquo kings!
Rather than so, come, fate, into the list,
And champion me to th' utterance![20] Who's there?

[*Enter* SERVANT *and* TWO MURDERERS.]

Now go to the door, and stay there till we call.

[*Exit* SERVANT.]

Was it not yesterday we spoke together?

MURDERERS. It was, so please your Highness.

75 MACBETH.   Well then, now
Have you considered of my speeches? Know
That it was he in the times past, which held you
So under fortune,[21] which you thought had been
Our innocent self: this I made good to you
80   In our last conference; passed in probation[22] with you,
How you were born in hand,[23] how crossed, the instruments,
Who wrought with them, and all things else that might
To half a soul[24] and to a notion[25] crazed
Say "Thus did Banquo."

FIRST MURDERER.   You made it known to us.

85 MACBETH. I did so; and went further, which is now
Our point of second meeting. Do you find
Your patience so predominant in your nature,
That you can let this go? Are you so gospeled,[26]
To pray for this good man and for his issue,
90   Whose heavy hand hath bowed you to the grave
And beggared yours for ever?

FIRST MURDERER.   We are men, my liege.

MACBETH. Ay, in the catalogue ye go for[27] men;
As hounds and greyhounds, mongrels, spaniels, curs,
Shoughs, water-rugs[28] and demi-wolves, are clept[29]
95   All by the name of dogs: the valued file[30]
Distinguishes the swift, the slow, the subtle,
The housekeeper, the hunter, every one
According to the gift which bounteous nature
Hath in him closed,[31] whereby he does receive
100 Particular addition,[32] from the bill
That writes them all alike: and so of men.
Now if you have a station in the file,[33]
Not i' th' worst rank of manhood, say 't,

---

18. **eternal jewel:** Soul.
19. **common . . . man:** The Devil.

20. **champion me to th' utterance:** Fight against me to the death.

21. **held . . . fortune:** Kept you from good fortune.
22. **passed in probation:** Reviewed the proofs.
23. **born in hand:** Deceived.
24. **half a soul:** Halfwit.
25. **notion:** Mind.

◆ **Reading Strategy**
What does the first murderer mean in line 91 when he answers Macbeth "We are men"?

26. **gospeled:** Ready to forgive.

27. **go for:** Pass as.
28. **Shoughs** (shuks), **water-rugs:** Shaggy dogs, long-haired dogs.
29. **clept:** Called.
30. **valued file:** Classification by valuable traits.
31. **closed:** Enclosed.
32. **addition:** Distinction (to set it apart from other dogs).
33. **file:** Ranks.

And I will put that business in your bosoms
105 Whose execution takes your enemy off,
Grapples you to the heart and love of us,
Who wear our health but sickly in his life,[34]
Which in his death were perfect.

34. **wear . . . life:** Are sick as long as he lives.

SECOND MURDERER.   I am one, my liege,
Whom the vile blows and buffets of the world
110 Hath so incensed that I am reckless what
I do to spite the world.

FIRST MURDERER.   And I another
So weary with disasters, tugged with fortune,
That I would set[35] my life on any chance,
To mend it or be rid on 't.

35. **set:** Risk.

MACBETH.   Both of you
Know Banquo was your enemy.

115 **BOTH MURDERERS.**   True, my lord.

MACBETH. So is he mine, and in such bloody distance[36]
That every minute of his being thrusts
Against my near'st of life:[37] and though I could
With barefaced power sweep him from my sight
120 And bid my will avouch[38] it, yet I must not,
For certain friends that are both his and mine,
Whose loves I may not drop, but wail his fall[39]
Who I myself struck down: and thence it is
That I to your assistance do make love,
125 Masking the business from the common eye
For sundry weighty reasons.

36. **distance:** Disagreement.
37. **near'st of life:** Most vital parts.
38. **avouch:** Justify.

39. **wail his fall:** (I must) bewail his death.

SECOND MURDERER.   We shall, my lord,
Perform what you command us.

FIRST MURDERER.   Though our lives—

MACBETH. Your spirits shine through you. Within this hour at most
I will advise you where to plant yourselves,
130 Acquaint you with the perfect spy o' th' time,
The moment on 't;[40] for 't must be done tonight,
And something[41] from the palace; always thought[42]
That I require a clearness:[43] and with him—
To leave no rubs[44] nor botches in the work—
135 Fleance his son, that keeps him company,
Whose absence is no less material to me

40. **the perfect . . . on't:** Exact information of the exact time.
41. **something:** Some distance.
42. **thought:** Remembered.
43. **clearness:** Freedom from suspicion.
44. **rubs:** Flaws.

Than is his father's, must embrace the fate
Of that dark hour. Resolve yourselves apart:[45]
I'll come to you anon.

MURDERERS.   We are resolved, my lord.

140 MACBETH I'll call upon you straight.[46] Abide within.
It is concluded: Banquo, thy soul's flight,
If it find heaven, must find it out tonight.   [Exit.]

Scene ii. *The palace.*
[*Enter* MACBETH'S LADY *and a* SERVANT.]

LADY MACBETH. Is Banquo gone from court?

SERVANT. Ay, madam, but returns again tonight.

LADY MACBETH. Say to the King, I would attend his leisure
For a few words.

SERVANT.   Madam, I will.   [*Exit.*]

LADY MACBETH.   Nought's had, all's spent,
5   Where our desire is got without content:
'Tis safer to be that which we destroy
Than by destruction dwell in doubtful joy.

[*Enter* MACBETH.]

How now, my lord! Why do you keep alone,
Of sorriest fancies your companions making,
10   Using those thoughts which should indeed have died
With them they think on? Things without all remedy
Should be without regard: what's done is done.

MACBETH. We have scotched[1] the snake, not killed it:
She'll close[2] and be herself, whilst our poor malice
15   Remains in danger of her former tooth.[3]
But let the frame of things disjoint,[4] both the worlds[5] suffer,
Ere we will eat our meal in fear, and sleep
In the affliction of these terrible dreams
That shake us nightly: better be with the dead,
20   Whom we, to gain our peace, have sent to peace,
Than on the torture of the mind to lie
In restless ecstasy.[6] Duncan is in his grave;
After life's fitful fever he sleeps well.
Treason has done his worst: nor steel, nor poison,
25   Malice domestic, foreign levy,[7] nothing,
Can touch him further.

**45. Resolve your-
selves apart:** Make
your own decision.

46. straight: Immedi-
ately.

◆ *Literature
and Your Life*

What has Lady
Macbeth realized
about her actions?

1. scotched:
Wounded.
2. close: Heal.
3. in . . . tooth: In
as much danger as
before.
**4. frame of things
disjoint:** Universe
collapse.
5. both the worlds:
Heaven and earth.
6. ecstasy: Frenzy.

7. Malice . . . levy:
Civil and foreign war.

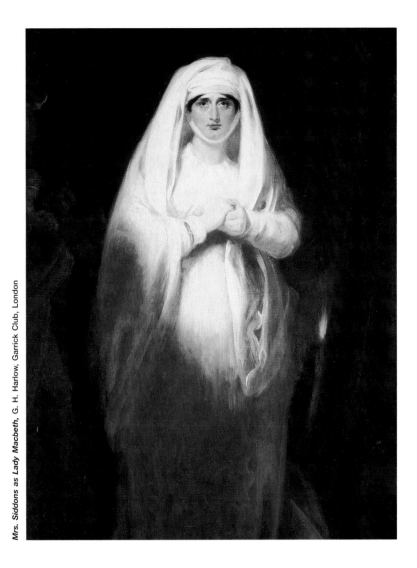

Mrs. Siddons as Lady Macbeth, G. H. Harlow, Garrick Club, London

◀ **Critical Viewing** This artist depicted actress Sarah Siddons (1755–1831) playing Lady Macbeth. How does Mrs. Siddons's body language suggest the same inner conflict as do lines 4–7 in Act III, ii? **[Connect]**

LADY MACBETH.   Come on.
  Gentle my lord, sleek o'er your rugged looks;
  Be bright and jovial among your guests tonight.

MACBETH. So shall I, love; and so, I pray, be you:
30 Let your remembrance apply to Banquo;
  Present him eminence,[8] both with eye and tongue:
  Unsafe the while, that we must lave[9]
  Our honors in these flattering streams
  And make our faces vizards[10] to our hearts,
  Disguising what they are.

35 **LADY MACBETH.**   You must leave this.

MACBETH. O, full of scorpions is my mind, dear wife!
  Thou know'st that Banquo, and his Fleance, lives.

LADY MACBETH. But in them nature's copy's not eterne.[11]

8. **Present him eminence:** Honor him.
9. **Unsafe . . . lave:** We are unsafe as long as we have to wash.
10. **vizards** (viz´ ərdz): Masks.

11. **nature's . . . eterne:** Nature's lease is not eternal.

MACBETH. There's comfort yet; they are assailable.
40 Then be thou jocund. Ere the bat hath flown
His cloistered flight, ere to black Hecate's summons
The shard-borne[12] beetle with his drowsy hums
Hath rung night's yawning peal, there shall be done
A deed of dreadful note.

LADY MACBETH.   What 's to be done?

45 **MACBETH.** Be innocent of the knowledge, dearest chuck,[13]
Till thou applaud the deed. Come, seeling[14] night,
Scarf up[15] the tender eye of pitiful day,
And with thy bloody and invisible hand
Cancel and tear to pieces that great bond[16]
50 Which keeps me pale! Light thickens, and the crow
Makes wing to th' rooky[17] wood.
Good things of day begin to droop and drowse,
Whiles night's black agents to their preys do rouse.
Thou marvel'st at my words: but hold thee still;
55 Things bad begun make strong themselves by ill:
So, prithee, go with me.   [*Exit.*]

Scene iii. *Near the palace.*
[*Enter* THREE MURDERERS.]

FIRST MURDERER. But who did bid thee join with us?

THIRD MURDERER.   Macbeth.

SECOND MURDERER. He needs not our mistrust; since he delivers
Our offices[1] and what we have to do
To the direction just.[2]

FIRST MURDERER.   Then stand with us.
5 The west yet glimmers with some streaks of day.
Now spurs the lated traveler apace
To gain the timely inn, and near approaches
The subject of our watch.

THIRD MURDERER.   Hark! I hear horses.

BANQUO. [*Within*] Give us a light there, ho!

SECOND MURDERER.   Then 'tis he. The rest
10 That are within the note of expectation[3]
Already are i' th' court.

12. **shard-borne:** Borne on scaly wings.

13. **chuck:** Term of endearment.
14. **seeling:** Eye-closing. Falconers sometimes sewed a hawk's eyes closed in order to train it.
15. **Scarf up:** Blind-fold.
16. **great bond:** Between Banquo and fate.
17. **rooky:** Full of rooks, or crows.

1. **offices:** Duties.
2. **direction just:** Exact detail.

3. **within . . . expectations:** On the list of expected guests.

FIRST MURDERER.   His horses go about.[4]

4. His . . . about: His horses have been taken to the stable.

THIRD MURDERER. Almost a mile: but he does usually—
So all men do—from hence to th' palace gate
Make it their walk.

[*Enter* BANQUO *and* FLEANCE, *with a torch.*]

SECOND MURDERER. A light, a light!

THIRD MURDERER.   'Tis he.

15 **FIRST MURDERER.**   Stand to 't

BANQUO. It will be rain tonight.

FIRST MURDERER.   Let it come down.

[*They set upon* BANQUO.]

BANQUO. O, treachery! Fly, good Fleance, fly, fly, fly!

[*Exit* FLEANCE.]

Thou mayst revenge. O slave! [*Dies.*]

THIRD MURDERER. Who did strike out the light?

FIRST MURDERER.   Was 't not the way?[5]

5. way: Thing to do.

◆ **Literary Focus**
Why does Fleance's escape create an external conflict for Macbeth?

20 **THIRD MURDERER.** There's but one down; the son is fled.

SECOND MURDERER. We have lost best half of our affair.

FIRST MURDERER. Well, let 's away and say how much is done.   [*Exit.*]

Scene iv. *The palace.*
[*Banquet prepared. Enter* MACBETH, LADY MACBETH, ROSS, LENNOX, LORDS, *and* ATTENDANTS.]

MACBETH. You know your own degrees;[1] sit down:
At first and last, the hearty welcome.

1. degrees: Ranks. At state banquets guests were seated according to rank.

◆ **Build Vocabulary**
jocund (jäk´ ənd) *adj.*: Cheerful; jovial

LORDS. Thanks to your Majesty.

MACBETH. Ourself will mingle with society[2]
5   And play the humble host.
      Our hostess keeps her state,[3] but in best time
      We will require[4] her welcome.

LADY MACBETH. Pronounce it for me, sir, to all our friends,
      For my heart speaks they are welcome.

[*Enter* FIRST MURDERER.]

10   **MACBETH.** See, they encounter thee with their hearts' thanks.
      Both sides are even: here I'll sit i' th' midst:
      Be large in mirth; anon we'll drink a measure[5]
      The table round. [*Goes to* MURDERER] There's blood upon thy face.

MURDERER. 'Tis Banquo's then.

15   **MACBETH.** 'Tis better thee without than he within.[6]
      Is he dispatched?

MURDERER. My lord, his throat is cut; that I did for him.

MACBETH. Thou art the best o' th' cutthroats.
      Yet he's good that did the like for Fleance;
20   If thou didst it, thou art the nonpareil.[7]

MURDERER. Most royal sir, Fleance is 'scaped.

MACBETH. [*Aside*] Then comes my fit again: I had else been perfect,
      Whole as the marble, founded as the rock,
      As broad and general as the casing[8] air:
25   But now I am cabined, cribbed, confined, bound in
      To saucy[9] doubts and fears.—But Banquo's safe?

MURDERER. Ay, my good lord: safe in a ditch he bides,
      With twenty trenchèd[10] gashes on his head,
      The least a death to nature.[11]

MACBETH.   Thanks for that.
30   [*Aside*] There the grown serpent lies; the worm that's fled
      Hath nature that in time will venom breed,
      No teeth for th' present. Get thee gone. Tomorrow
      We'll hear ourselves[12] again.   [*Exit* MURDERER.]

2. **society:** Company.

3. **keeps her state:** Remains seated on her throne.

4. **require:** Request.

5. **measure:** Toast.

6. **thee . . . within:** You outside than he inside.

7. **nonpareil:** Without equal.

8. **as . . . casing:** As unrestrained as the surrounding.

9. **saucy:** Insolent.

10. **trenchèd:** Trench-like.

11. **nature:** Natural life.

12. **hear ourselves:** Talk it over.

LADY MACBETH. My royal lord,
You do not give the cheer.[13] The feast is sold
35 That is not often vouched, while 'tis a-making,
'Tis given with welcome.[14] To feed were best at home;
From thence, the sauce to meat is ceremony;[15]
Meeting were bare without it.

[*Enter the* GHOST OF BANQUO *and sits in* MACBETH's *place.*]

MACBETH. Sweet remembrancer!
Now good digestion wait on appetite,
And health on both!

40 **LENNOX.** May't please your Highness sit.

MACBETH. Here had we now our country's honor roofed,[16]
Were the graced person of our Banquo present—
Who may I rather challenge for unkindness
Than pity for mischance![17]

ROSS. His absence, sir,
45 Lays blame upon his promise. Please 't your Highness
To grace us with your royal company?

MACBETH. The table's full.

LENNOX. Here is a place reserved, sir.

MACBETH. Where?

LENNOX. Here, my good lord. What is 't that moves your Highness?

MACBETH. Which of you have done this?

50 **LORDS.** What, my good lord?

MACBETH. Thou canst not say I did it. Never shake
Thy gory locks at me.

ROSS. Gentlemen, rise, his Highness is not well.

LADY MACBETH. Sit, worthy friends. My lord is often thus,
55 And hath been from his youth. Pray you, keep seat.
The fit is momentary; upon a thought[18]
He will again be well. If much you note him,
You shall offend him and extend his passion.[19]
Feed, and regard him not.—Are you a man?

13. **give the cheer:** Make the guests feel welcome.
14. **The feast . . . welcome:** The feast at which the host fails to make the guests feel welcome while the food is being prepared is no more than a bought dinner.
15. **From . . . ceremony:** Ceremony adds a pleasant flavor to the food.

16. **our . . . roofed:** The most honorable men in the country under one roof.
17. **Who . . . mischance:** Whom I hope I may reproach for being absent due to discourtesy rather than pity because he has had an accident.

◆ **Reading Strategy**
How might you connect Macbeth's agitation with his knowledge that Fleance has escaped?

An Actor's Response
"I cannot accept the idea . . . that in the banquet scene the ghost of Banquo, which appears to Macbeth, is seen at the same time by his wife . . . Lady Macbeth is no ghost-seer."
—Fanny Kemble

18. **upon a thought:** In a moment.
19. **passion:** Suffering.

60 **MACBETH.** Ay, and a bold one, that dare look on that
Which might appall the devil.

LADY MACBETH.   O proper stuff!
This is the very painting of your fear.
This is the air-drawn dagger which, you said,
Led you to Duncan. O, these flaws[20] and starts,
65 Impostors to true fear, would well become
A woman's story at a winter's fire,
Authorized[21] by her grandam. Shame itself!
Why do you make such faces? When all's done,
You look but on a stool.

MACBETH.   Prithee, see there!
70 Behold! Look! Lo! How say you?
Why, what care I? If thou canst nod, speak too.
If charnel houses[22] and our graves must send
Those that we bury back, our monuments
Shall be the maws of kites.[23]   [*Exit* GHOST.]

75 **LADY MACBETH.**   What, quite unmanned in folly?

MACBETH. If I stand here, I saw him.

LADY MACBETH.   Fie, for shame!

MACBETH. Blood hath been shed ere now, i' th' olden time,
Ere humane statute purged the gentle weal;[24]
Ay, and since too, murders have been performed
Too terrible for the ear. The times has been
80 That, when the brains were out, the man would die,
And there an end; but now they rise again,
With twenty mortal murders on their crowns,[25]
And push us from our stools. This is more strange
Than such a murder is.

LADY MACBETH.   My worthy lord,
Your noble friends do lack you.

85 **MACBETH.**   I do forget.
Do not muse at me, my most worthy friends;
I have a strange infirmity, which is nothing
To those that know me. Come, love and health to all!
Then I'll sit down. Give me some wine, fill full.

[*Enter* GHOST.]

90 I drink to th' general joy o' th' whole table,
And to our dear friend Banquo, whom we miss;

---

20. **flaws:** Gusts of wind; outbursts of emotion.

21. **Authorized:** Vouched for.

◆ **Literary Focus**
How does the incident with Banquo's ghost convey Macbeth's inner conflict?

22. **charnel houses:** Vaults containing human bones dug up in making new graves.
23. **our . . . kites:** Our tombs shall be the bellies of birds of prey.

24. **Ere . . . weal:** Before humane laws civilized the state and made it gentle.

25. **mortal . . . crowns:** Deadly wounds on their heads.

◆ **Build Vocabulary**
infirmity (in fur´ mə tē) *n*.: Physical or mental defect; illness

Scene from Macbeth, Cattermole, The Folger Shakespeare Library, Washington,D.C.

▲ **Critical Viewing** In what ways does the artist's use of light and shadow suggest the conflict in III, iv? **[Interpret]**

Would he were here! To all and him we thirst,[26]
And all to all.

26. **thirst:** Drink.

LORDS.   Our duties, and the pledge.

MACBETH. Avaunt![27] and quit my sight! Let the earth hide thee!

95 Thy bones are marrowless, thy blood is cold;
Thou hast no speculation[28] in those eyes
Which thou dost glare with.

27. **Avaunt:** Be gone!

28. **speculation:**
Sight.

LADY MACBETH.   Think of this, good peers,
But as a thing of custom, 'tis no other.
Only it spoils the pleasure of the time.

100 **MACBETH.** What man dare, I dare.
Approach thou like the rugged Russian bear,
The armed rhinoceros, or th' Hyrcan[29] tiger;
Take any shape but that,[30] and my firm nerves
Shall never tremble. Or be alive again,

105 And dare me to the desert[31] with thy sword.
If trembling I inhabit[32] then, protest me

29. **Hyrcan** (hər´ kən):
From Hyrcania, a
province of the ancient
Persian and Macedon-
ian empires south of
the Caspian Sea.
30. **that:** Banquo's
shape.
31. **desert:** Place
where neither of us
could escape.
32. **inhabit:** Remain
indoors.

The baby of a girl. Hence, horrible shadow!
Unreal mock'ry, hence!   [*Exit* GHOST.]
                  Why, so: being gone,
I am a man again. Pray you, sit still.

LADY MACBETH. You have displaced the mirth, broke the
110   good meeting,
    With most admired[33] disorder.

                    33. admired: Amazing.

MACBETH.   Can such things be,
And overcome us[34] like a summer's cloud,
Without our special wonder? You make me strange
Even to the disposition that I owe,[35]
115 When now I think you can behold such sights,
And keep the natural ruby of your cheeks,
When mine is blanched with fear.

34. overcome us:
Come over us.

**35. disposition. . .
owe:** My own nature.

ROSS.   What sights, my lord?

LADY MACBETH. I pray you, speak not: He grows worse and worse;
Question enrages him: at once, good night.
120 Stand not upon the order of your going,[36]
But go at once.

36. Stand . . . going:
Do not wait to depart
in order of rank.

LENNOX.   Good night; and better health
Attend his Majesty!

LADY MACBETH.   A kind good night to all!

                  [*Exit* LORDS.]

MACBETH. It will have blood, they say: blood will have blood.
Stones have been known to move and trees to speak;
125 Augures and understood relations[37] have
By maggot-pies and choughs[38] and rooks brought forth
The secret'st man of blood.[39] What is the night?

**37. Augures and
understood relations:**
Omens and the rela-
tionship between the
omens and what they
represent.
**38. maggot-pies and
choughs** (chufs)**:** Magpies and crows.
39. man of blood:
Murderer.
40. at odds: Disputing.

LADY MACBETH. Almost at odds[40] with morning, which is which.

MACBETH. How say'st thou, that Macduff denies his person
At our great bidding?

130 **LADY MACBETH.**   Did you send to him, sir?

MACBETH. I hear it by the way, but I will send:
There's not a one of them but in his house
I keep a servant fee'd.[41] I will tomorrow,

                  41. fee'd: Paid to spy.

And betimes[42] I will, to the weird sisters:
135 More shall they speak, for now I am bent[43] to know
By the worst means the worst. For mine own good
All causes shall give way. I am in blood
Stepped in so far that, should I wade no more,
Returning were as tedious as go o'er.
140 Strange things I have in head that will to hand,
Which must be acted ere they may be scanned.[44]

LADY MACBETH. You lack the season of all natures,[45] sleep.

MACBETH. Come, we'll to sleep. My strange and self-abuse[46]
Is the initiate fear that wants hard use.[47]
145 We are yet but young in deed.   [*Exit.*]

Scene v. *A witches' haunt.*
[*Thunder. Enter the* THREE WITCHES, *meeting* HECATE.]

FIRST WITCH. Why, how now, Hecate! you look angerly.

HECATE. Have I not reason, beldams[1] as you are,
Saucy and overbold? How did you dare
To trade and traffic with Macbeth
5 In riddles and affairs of death;
And I, the mistress of your charms,
The close contriver[2] of all harms,
Was never called to bear my part,
Or show the glory of our art?
10 And, which is worse, all you have done
Hath been but for a wayward son,
Spiteful and wrathful; who, as others do,
Loves for his own ends, not for you.
But make amends now: get you gone,
15 And at the pit of Acheron[3]
Meet me i' th' morning: thither he
Will come to know his destiny.
Your vessels and your spells provide,
Your charms and everything beside.
20 I am for th' air; this night I'll spend
Unto a dismal and a fatal end:
Great business must be wrought ere noon.
Upon the corner of the moon
There hangs a vap'rous drop profound;
25 I'll catch it ere it come to ground:
And that distilled by magic sleights[4]
Shall raise such artificial sprites[5]
As by the strength of their illusion
Shall draw him on to his confusion.[6]
30 He shall spurn fate, scorn death, and bear
His hopes 'bove wisdom, grace, and fear:

42. **betimes:** Quickly.
43. **bent:** Determined.

◆ **Literary Focus**
How do lines 137–139 mark a turning point in Macbeth's inner conflict?

44. **scanned:** Examined.

45. **season . . . natures:** Preservative of all living creatures.
46. **My . . . self-abuse:** My strange delusion.
47. **initiate . . . use:** Beginner's fear that will harden with experience.

1. **beldams:** Hags.

2. **close contriver:** Secret inventor.

3. **Acheron** (ak´ ər än´): Hell; in Greek mythology the river of Hades.

4. **sleights:** Devices.
5. **artificial sprites:** Spirits created by magic.
6. **confusion:** Ruin.

And you all know security[7]
Is mortals' chiefest enemy.

[*Music and a song.*]

35 Hark! I am called; my little spirit, see,
Sits in a foggy cloud and stays for me.   [*Exit.*]

[*Sing within,* "Come away, come away," *etc.*]

FIRST WITCH.   Come, let's make haste; she'll soon be back
again.   [*Exit.*]

Scene vi. *The palace.*
[*Enter* LENNOX *and another* LORD.]

LENNOX.   My former speeches have but hit[1] your thoughts,
Which can interpret farther.[2] Only I say
Things have been strangely borne.[3] The gracious Duncan
Was pitied of Macbeth: marry, he was dead.
5 And the right-valiant Banquo walked too late;
Whom, you may say, if 't please you, Fleance killed,
For Fleance fled. Men must not walk too late.
Who cannot want the thought,[4] how monstrous
It was for Malcolm and for Donalbain
10 To kill their gracious father? Damnèd fact![5]
How it did grieve Macbeth! Did he not straight,
In pious rage, the two delinquents tear,
That were the slaves of drink and thralls[6] of sleep?
Was not that nobly done? Ay, and wisely too;
15 For 'twould have angered any heart alive
To hear the men deny 't. So that I say
He has borne all things well: and I do think
That, had he Duncan's sons under his key—
As, an 't[7] please heaven, he shall not—they should find
20 What 'twere to kill a father. So should Fleance.
But, peace! for from broad[8] words, and 'cause he failed
His presence at the tyrant's feast, I hear,
Macduff lives in disgrace. Sir, can you tell
Where he bestows himself?

LORD.   The son of Duncan,
25 From whom this tyrant holds the due of birth,[9]
Lives in the English court, and is received
Of the most pious Edward[10] with such grace
That the <u>malevolence</u> of fortune nothing
Takes from his high respect.[11] Thither Macduff
30 Is gone to pray the holy King, upon his aid[12]
To wake Northumberland and warlike Siward;[13]
That by the help of these, with Him above
To ratify the work, we may again
Give to our tables meat, sleep to our nights,

7. **security:** Overconfidence.

1. **hit:** Coincided with.
2. **Which . . . farther:** From which you can draw your own conclusions.
3. **borne:** Managed.

4. **cannot . . . thought:** Can fail to think.
5. **fact:** Deed.

6. **thralls:** Slaves.

◆ **Reading Strategy**
In lines 1–24, what is Lennox really saying?

7. **an 't:** If it.

8. **broad:** Unguarded.

9. **due of birth:** Birthright; claim to the throne.
10. **Edward:** Edward the Confessor, king of England 1042–1066.
11. **with . . . respect:** Does not diminish the high respect he is given.
12. **upon his aid:** To aid Malcolm.
13. **To . . . Siward:** To call to arms the commander of the English forces, the Earl of Northumberland, and his son Siward.

35   Free from our feasts and banquets bloody knives,
     Do faithful homage and receive free honors:[14]
     All which we pine for now. And this report
     Hath so exasperate the King that he
     Prepares for some attempt of war.

LENNOX.   Sent he to Macduff?

40 **LORD.** He did: and with an absolute "Sir, not I,"
     The cloudy[15] messenger turns me his back,
     And hums, as who should say "You'll rue the time
     That clogs[16] me with this answer."

LENNOX.   And that well might
     Advise him to a caution, t' hold what distance
45   His wisdom can provide. Some holy angel
     Fly to the court of England and unfold
     His message ere he come, that a swift blessing
     May soon return to this our suffering country
     Under a hand accursed!

LORD.   I'll send my prayers with him.

                            [*Exit.*]

14. free honors:
Honors given to free-
men.

15. cloudy: Disturbed.

16. clogs: Burdens.

◆ **Build Vocabulary**

malevolence (mə lev′ ə
ləns) *n.*: Ill will; spitefulness

Guide for Responding

◆ *Literature and Your Life*

Reader's Response Did you find the banquet scene frightening, funny, or something else? Explain.

Thematic Focus Macbeth is making Scotland into an evil place. Who will lead the forces of good in a campaign against him?

☑ **Check Your Comprehension**

1. In III, i, what does Banquo say about the witches' prophecies?
2. What does Macbeth plan to do to Banquo and Fleance?
3. How does Macbeth's plot against Banquo and Fleance go wrong?
4. Briefly summarize what happens at the banquet.
5. What does the final scene reveal about the opposition to Macbeth?

◆ **Critical Thinking**

INTERPRET
1. Compare and contrast Macbeth's feelings about murdering Duncan with his feelings about murdering Banquo. **[Compare and Contrast]**
2. What is similar about Macbeth's arguments for murder in III, i, 92–108, and Lady Macbeth's arguments for murder in I, vii, 47–51? **[Connect]**
3. How has the relationship between Macbeth and Lady Macbeth changed? **[Analyze]**
4. Support the idea that Macbeth will not be satisfied with Banquo's death, but will go further into evil. **[Support]**

EVALUATE
5. Is the banquet scene an effective piece of dramatic action? Why or why not? **[Make a Judgment]**

APPLY
6. What does this act suggest about the effects of evil on an evil-doer? **[Generalize]**

Guide for Responding (continued)

◆ Reading Strategy

READ BETWEEN THE LINES

By **reading between the lines**—linking earlier and later passages and finding suggested meanings—you can enrich your understanding of the play. For example, you can figure out that one theme of the play is manhood. Macbeth tells the murderers that they aren't real men if they don't dare to kill Banquo. Later, when Macbeth is startled by Banquo's ghost, he asserts that he's as much of a man as anyone: "What man dares, I dare."

1. Use these and other passages to define manhood according to Macbeth and Lady Macbeth.
2. By reading between the lines, figure out what the presence of the third murderer suggests about Macbeth.

◆ Literary Focus

CONFLICT

The **conflicts** in Act III include an external struggle between Macbeth and Banquo and a struggle within Macbeth as he faces the ghost of Banquo.

1. Why does Macbeth view Banquo as his opponent?
2. In what way does Macbeth fail to resolve his conflict with Banquo?
3. How is Macbeth's behavior at the dinner an outward sign of an inner conflict?
4. How does Macbeth resolve his inner conflict, at least temporarily?

◆ Build Vocabulary

USING THE LATIN PREFIX *mal-*

Knowing that the Latin prefix *mal-* means "bad, ill, or poorly," define these words.

1. maladjusted   2. malady   3. malcontent

USING THE WORD BANK: Context

In your notebook, write a brief profile of Macbeth using all the words in the Word Bank.

◆ Grammar and Style

SUBJECT AND VERB AGREEMENT

Use the **verb form that agrees with its subject in number.** Do not be misled by other words that come between the subject and the verb.

Practice Write these sentences in your notebook, choosing the singular or plural form of the verb.

1. Macbeth, of all the Scottish kings, (is, are) most evil.
2. Scotland, country of stark contrasts, (is, are) the setting of *Macbeth*.
3. Malcolm, despite his worries, (does, do) what must be done.
4. Lady Macbeth, expressing some concerns, (begin, begins) to doubt what she has done.
5. Not everyone in this country of ghosts (support, supports) Macbeth.

 Idea Bank

Writing

1. **Diary Entry** As a lord returning from Macbeth's feast, write a diary entry about the strange events you have just witnessed.

2. **Critical Note** Some critics have argued that the third murderer is Macbeth himself. Write a brief critical note agreeing or disagreeing with this theory. Support your argument with specific passages.

Speaking, Listening, and Viewing

3. **Performance** With a group of classmates, perform the banquet scene (iv) for the class. Use stage directions and clues from the dialogue—for example, "Sit, worthy friends"—to map out the action in this scene. Also, remember to follow sentences, not line endings, in reading speeches.
[Performing Arts Link]

Guide for Interpreting, Act IV

◆ Review and Anticipate

Macbeth hires murderers to kill Banquo and Banquo's son, Fleance. The murderers botch the job, killing Banquo but letting Fleance escape. Then, at a state dinner, Macbeth is shocked to see the ghost of Banquo sitting in the king's chair. Macbeth decides to visit the witches again, determined to know "the worst." At the end of Act III, we learn that Malcolm is in England, preparing to invade Scotland, and that Macduff has gone to join him.

Act IV will be a turning point in the play. Macbeth seeks help from the witches to secure his power. The forces of good, however, are beginning to gather against him.

◆ Literary Focus

IMAGERY

Imagery is the language that writers use to re-create sensory experiences. It is what helps you see, hear, feel, smell, and taste, rather than just read words or listen to them spoken. In Elizabethan theater, imagery was especially important because there was no lighting or elaborate scenery to "paint" a scene for the audience. Words alone had to do the work.

Shakespeare was a master of imagery, packing sense experiences into every line: "Though bladed corn be lodged and trees blown down." Notice how this line appeals to the senses of touch and sight.

In addition, Shakespeare creates patterns of images that run through a whole play. In *Macbeth*, for instance, images relating to blood, ill-fitting clothes, and babies are just three of the patterns he uses to create a mood and enhance the play's meaning.

◆ Grammar and Style

POSSESSIVE FORMS: SINGULAR AND PLURAL

Most singular nouns form the **possessive** by adding an apostrophe and s. Plural nouns ending in s form the possessive by adding an apostrophe, and plural nouns not ending in s add an apostrophe and s.

Shakespeare uses both singular and plural possessives in this act:

Singular: adder's   traitor's   baboon's
Plural: witches'   warders'   men's

◆ Reading Strategy

USE YOUR SENSES

You will enjoy a literary work more if you use your senses to experience the imagery it contains.

In reading this passage from Act IV, for example, understand it with your mind but also experience it with your senses of sight, touch, and hearing:

Though you untie the winds and let them fight / Against the churches; though the yesty waves / Confound and swallow navigation up / Though bladed corn be lodged and trees blown down; / Though castles topple on their warders' heads . . .

◆ Build Vocabulary

LATIN ROOTS: -cred-

The word *credulous* in Act IV has the Latin root -cred-, which means "belief." To be credulous is "to believe something too readily."

WORD BANK

Before you read, preview this list of words from Act IV of *Macbeth*.

| pernicious |
| judicious |
| sundry |
| intemperance |
| avarice |
| credulous |

Act IV

Scene i. *A witches' haunt.*
[*Thunder. Enter the* THREE WITCHES.]

FIRST WITCH. Thrice the brinded[1] cat hath mewed.

SECOND WITCH. Thrice and once the hedge-pig[2] whined.

THIRD WITCH. Harpier[3] cries. 'Tis time, 'tis time.

FIRST WITCH. Round about the caldron go:
5   In the poisoned entrails throw.
    Toad, that under cold stone
    Days and nights has thirty-one
    Swelt'red venom sleeping got,[4]
    Boil thou first i' th' charmèd pot.

10 **ALL.** Double, double, toil and trouble;
    Fire burn and caldron bubble.

SECOND WITCH. Fillet of a fenny snake,
    In the caldron boil and bake;
    Eye of newt and toe of frog,
15   Wool of bat and tongue of dog,
    Adder's fork[5] and blindworm's[6] sting,
    Lizard's leg and howlet's[7] wing,
    For a charm of pow'rful trouble,
    Like a hell-broth boil and bubble.

20 **ALL.** Double, double, toil and trouble;
    Fire burn and caldron bubble.

THIRD WITCH. Scale of dragon, tooth of wolf,
    Witch's mummy, maw and gulf[8]
    Of the ravined[9] salt-sea shark,
25   Root of hemlock digged i' th' dark,
    Liver of blaspheming Jew,
    Gall of goat, and slips of yew
    Slivered in the moon's eclipse,
    Nose of Turk and Tartar's lips,[10]
30   Finger of birth-strangled babe
    Ditch-delivered by a drab,
    Make the gruel thick and slab:[11]
    Add thereto a tiger's chaudron,[12]
    For th' ingredience of our caldron.

1. **brinded:** Striped.

2. **hedge-pig:** Hedgehog.

3. **Harpier:** One of the spirits attending the witches.

4. **Swelt'red . . . got:** Venom sweated out while sleeping.

5. **fork:** Forked tongue.
6. **blindworm's:** Small, limbless lizards.
7. **howlet's:** Small owl's.

8. **maw and gulf:** Stomach and gullet.
9. **ravined:** Ravenous.

10. **blaspheming Jew . . . Tartar's lips:** For many in Shakespeare's audience, the words "Jew," "Turk," and "Tartar" evoked stereotypical enemies of Christianity.
11. **slab:** Sticky.
12. **chaudron** (shô′ drən): Entrails.

Poster for Macbeth, His Majesty's Theater, 1911, Edmund Dulac

▲ **Critical Viewing** Has this artist captured the spirit of the witches as it is portrayed in IV, i? Explain. **[Evaluate]**

35   **ALL.** Double, double, toil and trouble;
       Fire burn and caldron bubble.

    SECOND WITCH. Cool it with a baboon's blood,
       Then the charm is firm and good.

[*Enter* HECATE *and the other* THREE WITCHES.]

    HECATE. O, well done! I commend your pains;
40   And every one shall share i' th' gains:
       And now about the caldron sing,
       Like elves and fairies in a ring,
       Enchanting all that you put in.

[*Music and a song:* "Black Spirits," *etc. Exit* HECATE *and the other* THREE WITCHES.]

    SECOND WITCH. By the pricking of my thumbs,
45   Something wicked this way comes:
       Open, locks,
       Whoever knocks!

[*Enter* MACBETH.]

    MACBETH. How now, you secret, black, and midnight hags!
       What is 't you do?

    ALL.   A deed without a name.

50   **MACBETH.** I conjure you, by that which you profess,
       Howe'er you come to know it, answer me:
       Though you untie the winds and let them fight
       Against the churches; though the yesty[13] waves
       Confound[14] and swallow navigation up;
55   Though bladed corn be lodged[15] and trees blown down;
       Though castles topple on their warders' heads;
       Though palaces and pyramids do slope[16]
       Their heads to their foundations; though the treasure
       Of nature's germens[17] tumble all together,
60   Even till destruction sicken, answer me
       To what I ask you.

    FIRST WITCH.   Speak.

    SECOND WITCH.   Demand.

A Critic's Response
"The feeling of fear, horror, and pain is increased by the constant and recurring images of blood . . ."
—Carolyn F. E. Spurgeon

◆ **Reading Strategy**
Use your senses to imagine this scene from another world that Shakespeare depicts in IV, i.

13. **yesty:** Foamy.
14. **Confound:** Destroy.
15. **lodged:** Beaten down.
16. **slope:** Bend.

17. **nature's germens:** Seeds of all life.

THIRD WITCH.   We'll answer.

FIRST WITCH.   Say, if th' hadst rather hear it from our mouths,
Or from our masters?

MACBETH.   Call 'em, let me see 'em.

FIRST WITCH.   Pour in sow's blood, that hath eaten
65   Her nine farrow;[18] grease that's sweaten
From the murderer's gibbet[19] throw
Into the flame.

ALL.   Come, high or low,
Thyself and office[20] deftly show!

[*Thunder.* FIRST APPARITION: *an Armed Head.*[21]]

MACBETH.   Tell me, thou unknown power—

FIRST WITCH.   He knows thy thought:
70   Hear his speech, but say thou nought.

FIRST APPARITION.   Macbeth! Macbeth! Macbeth! Beware Macduff!
Beware the Thane of Fife. Dismiss me: enough.
                              [*He descends.*]

MACBETH.   Whate'er thou art, for thy good caution thanks:
Thou hast harped[22] my fear aright. But one word more—

75   **FIRST WITCH.**   He will not be commanded. Here's another,
More potent than the first.

[*Thunder.* SECOND APPARITION: *a Bloody Child.*[23]]

SECOND APPARITION.   Macbeth! Macbeth! Macbeth!

MACBETH.   Had I three ears, I'd hear thee.

SECOND APPARITION.   Be bloody, bold, and resolute! Laugh to scorn
80   The pow'r of man, for none of woman born
Shall harm Macbeth.   [*Descends.*]

MACBETH.   Then live, Macduff: what need I fear of thee?
But yet I'll make assurance double sure,
And take a bond of fate.[24] Thou shalt not live;

18. **farrow:** Young pigs.
19. **gibbet** (jib´ it): Gallows.

20. **office:** Function.

21. **an Armed Head:** Symbol of Macduff.

22. **harped:** Hit upon.

23. **a Bloody Child:** Symbol of Macduff at birth.

24. **take . . . fate:** Get a guarantee from fate (by killing Macduff).

85　That I may tell pale-hearted fear it lies,
　　And sleep in spite of thunder.

[*Thunder.* THIRD APPARITION: *a Child Crowned, with a tree in his hand.*[25]]

25. a Child . . . hand: Symbol of Malcolm.

　　　　　　　　　　　　What is this,
　　That rises like the issue of a king,
　　And wears upon his baby-brow the round
　　And top of sovereignty?[26]

26. top of sovereignty: Crown.

　　ALL.　　　　　　Listen, but speak not to 't.

90　**THIRD APPARITION.**　Be lion-mettled, proud, and take no care
　　Who chafes, who frets, or where conspirers are:
　　Macbeth shall never vanquished be until
　　Great Birnam Wood to high Dunsinane Hill
　　Shall come against him.　　　　　[*Descends.*]

　　MACBETH.　　　　　That will never be.
95　Who can impress[27] the forest, bid the tree
　　Unfix his earth-bound root? Sweet bodements,[28] good!
　　Rebellious dead, rise never, till the Wood
　　Of Birnam rise, and our high-placed Macbeth
　　Shall live the lease of nature,[29] pay his breath
100　To time and mortal custom.[30] Yet my heart
　　Throbs to know one thing. Tell me, if your art
　　Can tell so much: shall Banquo's issue ever
　　Reign in this kingdom?

27. impress: Force into service.
28. bodements: Prophecies.

29. lease of nature: Natural lifespan.
30. mortal custom: Natural death.

　　ALL.　　　　　　Seek to know no more.

　　MACBETH.　I will be satisfied. Deny me this,
105　And an eternal curse fall on you! Let me know.
　　Why sinks that caldron? And what noise is this?

[*Hautboys.*]

　　FIRST WITCH.　Show!

　　SECOND WITCH.　Show!

　　THIRD WITCH.　Show!

◆ Literary Focus
How do the apparitions that Macbeth sees at IV, i, 68, 75, and 86 connect with the patterns of imagery in the play?

110　ALL.　Show his eyes, and grieve his heart;
　　Come like shadows, so depart!

[*A show of eight* KINGS *and* BANQUO, *last* KING *with a glass*[31] *in his hand.*]

31. glass: Mirror.

MACBETH. Thou art too like the spirit of Banquo. Down!
Thy crown does sear mine eyelids. And thy hair,
Thou other gold-bound brow, is like the first.
115   A third is like the former. Filthy hags!
Why do you show me this? A fourth! Start, eyes!
What, will the line stretch out to th' crack of doom?
Another yet! A seventh! I'll see no more.
And yet the eighth appears, who bears a glass
120   Which shows me many more: and some I see
That twofold balls and treble scepters³² carry:
Horrible sight! Now I see 'tis true;
For the blood-boltered³³ Banquo smiles upon me,
And points at them for his.³⁴ What, is this so?

125   **FIRST WITCH.** Ay, sir, all this is so. But why
Stands Macbeth thus amazedly?
Come, sisters, cheer we up his sprites,
And show the best of our delights:
I'll charm the air to give a sound,
130   While you perform your antic round,³⁵
That this great king may kindly say
Our duties did his welcome pay.

[*Music.* THE WITCHES *dance, and vanish.*]

MACBETH. Where are they? Gone? Let this <u>pernicious</u> hour
Stand aye accursèd in the calendar!
Come in, without there!

[*Enter* LENNOX.]

135   **LENNOX.**   What's your Grace's will?

MACBETH. Saw you the weird sisters?

LENNOX.   No, my lord.

MACBETH. Came they not by you?

LENNOX.   No indeed, my lord.

MACBETH. Infected be the air whereon they ride,
And damned all those that trust them! I did hear
140   The galloping of horse. Who was 't came by?

LENNOX. 'Tis two or three, my lord, that bring you word
Macduff is fled to England.

◆ **Literary Focus**
What does Macbeth learn from the images of the kings?

32. twofold . . . scepters: Coronation emblems and insignia of the kingdoms of England. Scotland, and Ireland, united in 1603 when James VI of Scotland became James I of England.
33. blood-boltered: With his hair matted with blood.
34. his: His descendants.
35. antic round: Grotesque circular dance.

◆ **Build Vocabulary**
pernicious (pər nish′ əs) *adj.*: Fatal; deadly

MACBETH.   Fled to England?

LENNOX. Ay, my good lord.

MACBETH. [*Aside*] Time, thou anticipat'st[36] my dread exploits.
145   The flighty purpose never is o'ertook
Unless the deed go with it.[37] From this moment
The very firstlings of my heart[38] shall be
The firstlings of my hand. And even now,
To crown my thoughts with acts be it thought and done:
150   The castle of Macduff I will surprise;
Seize upon Fife; give to th' edge o' th' sword
His wife, his babes, and all unfortunate souls
That trace[39] him in his line. No boasting like a fool;
This deed I'll do before this purpose cool:
155   But no more sights!—Where are these gentlemen?
Come, bring me where they are.

                                              [*Exit.*]

Scene ii. *Macduff's castle.*
[*Enter* MACDUFF'S WIFE, *her* SON, *and* ROSS.]

LADY MACDUFF. What had he done, to make him fly the land?

ROSS. You must have patience, madam.

LADY MACDUFF.   He had none:
His flight was madness. When our actions do not,
Our fears do make us traitors.

ROSS.   You know not
5   Whether it was his wisdom or his fear.

LADY MACDUFF. Wisdom! To leave his wife, to leave his babes,
His mansion and his titles,[1] in a place
From whence himself does fly? He loves us not;
He wants the natural touch:[2] for the poor wren,
10   The most diminutive of birds, will fight,
Her young ones in her nest, against the owl.
All is the fear and nothing is the love;
As little is the wisdom, where the flight
So runs against all reason.

ROSS.   My dearest coz,[3]
15   I pray you, school[4] yourself. But, for your husband,
He is noble, wise, judicious, and best knows

36. anticipat'st:
Foretold.
37. The flighty . . . it:
The fleeting plan is
never fulfilled unless it
is carried out at once.
**38. firstlings . . .
heart:** First thoughts,
impulses.

39. trace: Succeed.

1. titles: Possessions.

2. wants . . . touch:
Lacks natural affection.

3. coz: Cousin.
4. school: Control.

◆ *Literature
and Your Life*
How does Macbeth
blindly interpret what
the witches show
him in IV, i? How are
the murders he is
planning worse than
the others?

The fits o' th' seasons,[5] I dare not speak much further:
But cruel are the times, when we are traitors
And do not know ourselves;[6] when we hold rumor
20 From what we fear,[7] yet know not what we fear,
But float upon a wild and violent sea
Each way and move. I take my leave of you.
Shall not be long but I'll be here again.
Things at the worst will cease, or else climb upward
25 To what they were before. My pretty cousin,
Blessing upon you!

LADY MACDUFF. Fathered he is, and yet he's fatherless.

ROSS. I am so much a fool, should I stay longer,
It would be my disgrace and your discomfort.[8]
I take my leave at once. [*Exit* ROSS.]

30 **LADY MACDUFF.** Sirrah, your father's dead;
And what will you do now? How will you live?

SON. As birds do, mother.

LADY MACDUFF. What, with worms and flies?

SON. With what I get, I mean; and so do they.

LADY MACDUFF. Poor bird! thou'dst never fear the net nor lime,[9]
35 The pitfall nor the gin.[10]

SON. Why should I, mother? Poor birds they are not set for.
My father is not dead, for all your saying.

LADY MACDUFF. Yes, he is dead: how wilt thou do for a father?

SON. Nay, how will you do for a husband?

40 **LADY MACDUFF.** Why, I can buy me twenty at any market.

SON. Then you'll buy 'em to sell[11] again.

LADY MACDUFF. Thou speak'st with all thy wit, and yet i' faith,
With wit enough for thee.[12]

SON. Was my father a traitor, mother?

5. fits o' th' season: Disorders of the time.
6. when . . . ourselves: When we are treated as traitors but do not know of any treason.
7. when . . . fear: Believe rumors based on our fears.

8. It . . . discomfort: I would disgrace myself and embarrass you by weeping.

◆ **Literary Focus**
What does the imagery in IV, ii, 34–35, suggest about what might happen?

9. lime: Birdlime, a sticky substance smeared on branches to catch birds.
10. gin: Trap.

11. sell: Betray.
12. for thee: For a child.

◆ **Build Vocabulary**
judicious (jōō dish′ əs) *adj*.: Showing good judgment

45   **LADY MACDUFF.** Ay, that he was.

SON. What is a traitor?

LADY MACDUFF. Why, one that swears and lies.[13]

SON. And be all traitors that do so?

LADY MACDUFF. Every one that does so is a traitor, and must be hanged.

50   **SON.** And must they all be hanged that swear and lie?

LADY MACDUFF. Every one.

SON. Who must hang them?

LADY MACDUFF. Why, the honest men.

SON. Then the liars and swearers are fools; for there are liars and
55   swearers enow[14] to beat the honest men and hang up them.

LADY MACDUFF. Now, God help thee, poor monkey! But how wilt thou
do for a father?

SON. If he were dead, you'd weep for him. If you would not, it were a
60   good sign that I should quickly have a new father.

LADY MACDUFF. Poor prattler, how thou talk'st!

[*Enter a* MESSENGER.]

MESSENGER. Bless you, fair dame! I am not to you known,
    Though in your state of honor I am perfect.[15]
65   I doubt[16] some danger does approach you nearly:
    If you will take a homely[17] man's advice,
    Be not found here; hence, with your little ones.
    To fright you thus, methinks I am too savage;
    To do worse to you were fell[18] cruelty,
70   Which is too nigh your person. Heaven preserve you!
    I dare abide no longer.   [*Exit* MESSENGER.]

LADY MACDUFF.   Whither should I fly?
    I have done no harm. But I remember now
    I am in this earthly world, where to do harm

13. swears and lies: Takes an oath and breaks it.

14. enow: Enough.

15. in . . . perfect: I am fully informed of your honorable rank.
16. doubt: Fear.
17. homely: Simple.

18. fell: Fierce.

Is often laudable, to do good sometime
75 Accounted dangerous folly. Why then, alas,
Do I put up that womanly defense,
To say I have done no harm?—What are these faces?

[*Enter* MURDERERS.]

MURDERER. Where is your husband?

LADY MACDUFF. I hope, in no place so unsanctified
Where such as thou mayst find him.

80 **MURDERER.**   He's a traitor.

SON. Thou li'st, thou shag-eared[19] villain!

19. **shag-eared:**
Hairy-eared.

▲ **Critical Viewing** This engraving shows the murderers menacing
Macduff's family. In what way does the artist capture the defiance
reflected in IV, ii, 81? [**Interpret**]

MURDERER.   What, you egg!
                              [*Stabbing him.*]
Young fry[20] of treachery!

SON.   He has killed me, mother:
Run away, I pray you!   [*Dies.*]

[*Exit* LADY MACDUFF *crying "Murder!" followed by* MURDERERS.]

Scene iii. *England. Before the King's palace.*
[*Enter* MALCOLM *and* MACDUFF.]

MALCOLM. Let us seek out some desolate shade, and there
Weep our sad bosoms empty.

MACDUFF.   Let us rather
Hold fast the mortal[1] sword, and like good men
Bestride our down-fall'n birthdom.[2] Each new morn
5 New widows howl, new orphans cry, new sorrows
Strike heaven on the face, that it resounds
As if it felt with Scotland and yelled out
Like syllable of dolor.[3]

MALCOLM.   What I believe, I'll wail;
What know, believe; and what I can redress,
10 As I shall find the time to friend,[4] I will.
What you have spoke, it may be so perchance.
This tyrant, whose sole[5] name blisters our tongues,
Was once thought honest:[6] you have loved him well;
He hath not touched you yet. I am young; but something
15 You may deserve of him through me;[7] and wisdom[8]
To offer up a weak, poor, innocent lamb
T' appease an angry god.

MACDUFF. I am not treacherous.

MALCOLM.   But Macbeth is.
A good and virtuous nature may recoil
20 In an imperial charge.[9] But I shall crave your pardon;
That which you are, my thoughts cannot transpose:[10]
Angels are bright still, though the brightest[11] fell:
Though all things foul would wear[12] the brows of grace,
Yet grace must still look so.[13]

MACDUFF.   I have lost my hopes.

20. **fry:** Offspring.

1. **mortal:** Deadly.
2. **Bestride . . . birthdom:** Protectively stand over our native land.

3. **Like . . . dolor:** Similar cry of anguish.

4. **to friend:** Be friendly.
5. **sole:** Very.
6. **honest:** Good.

7. **deserve . . . me:** Earn by betraying me to Macbeth.
8. **wisdom:** It is wise.

9. **recoil . . . charge:** Give way to a royal command.
10. **transpose:** Transform.
11. **the brightest:** Lucifer.
12. **would wear:** Desire to wear.
13. **so:** Like itself.

25 **MALCOLM.** Perchance even there where I did find my doubts.
　　 Why in that rawness[14] left you wife and child,
　　 Those precious motives, those strong knots of love,
　　 Without leave-taking? I pray you,
　　 Let not my jealousies[15] be your dishonors.
30 　But mine own safeties.[16] You may be rightly just
　　 Whatever I shall think.

MACDUFF.　　　　　　　　　　Bleed, bleed, poor country:
　　 Great tyranny, lay thou thy basis sure,
　　 For goodness dare not check thee: wear thou thy wrongs:
　　 The title is affeered.[17] Fare thee well, lord:
35 　I would not be the villain that thou think'st
　　 For the whole space that's in the tyrant's grasp
　　 And the rich East to boot.

MALCOLM.　　　　　　　　　Be not offended:
　　 I speak not as in absolute fear of you.
　　 I think our country sinks beneath the yoke;
40 　It weeps, it bleeds, and each new day a gash
　　 Is added to her wounds. I think withal
　　 There would be hands uplifted in my right;[18]
　　 And here from gracious England[19] have I offer
　　 Of goodly thousands: but, for all this,
45 　When I shall tread upon the tyrant's head,
　　 Or wear it on my sword, yet my poor country
　　 Shall have more vices than it had before,
　　 More suffer, and more <u>sundry</u> ways than ever,
　　 By him that shall succeed.

MACDUFF.　　　　　　　　　What should he be?

50 **MALCOLM.** It is myself I mean, in whom I know
　　 All the particulars of vice so grafted[20]
　　 That, when they shall be opened,[21] black Macbeth
　　 Will seem as pure as snow, and the poor state
　　 Esteem him as a lamb, being compared
　　 With my confineless harms.[22]

55 **MACDUFF.**　　　　　　　　　Not in the legions
　　 Of horrid hell can come a devil more damned
　　 In evils to top Macbeth.

MALCOLM.　　　　　　　　　I grant him bloody,
　　 Luxurious,[23] avaricious, false, deceitful,
　　 Sudden,[24] malicious, smacking of every sin
60 　That has a name: but there's no bottom, none,
　　 In my voluptuousness: your wives, your daughters,
　　 Your matrons and your maids, could not fill up

14. **rawness:** Unprotected state or condition.

15. **jealousies:** Suspicions.
16. **safeties:** Protections.

17. **affeered:** Legally confirmed.

◆ **Literary Focus**
Why are the images Malcolm uses to describe Scotland in lines 39–42 more effective than simply stating that the country is in trouble and getting worse?

18. **in my right:** On behalf of my claim.
19. **England:** King of England.

20. **grafted:** Implanted.
21. **opened:** In bloom.
22. **confineless harms:** Unbounded evils.

23. **luxurious:** Lecherous.
24. **Sudden:** Violent.

◆ **Build Vocabulary**
sundry (sun´ drē) *adj*.: Various; miscellaneous

The cistern of my lust, and my desire
All continent impediments[25] would o'erbear,
65   That did oppose my will. Better Macbeth
Than such an one to reign.

MACDUFF.   Boundless <u>intemperance</u>
In nature[26] is a tyranny; it hath been
Th' untimely emptying of the happy throne,
And fall of many kings. But fear not yet
70   To take upon you what is yours: you may
Convey[27] your pleasures in a spacious plenty,
And yet seem cold, the time you may so hoodwink.
We have willing dames enough. There cannot be
That vulture in you, to devour so many
75   As will to greatness dedicate themselves,
Finding it so inclined.

MALCOLM.   With this there grows
In my most ill-composed affection[28] such
A stanchless[29] <u>avarice</u> that, were I King,
I should cut off the nobles for their lands,
80   Desire his jewels and this other's house:
And my more-having would be as a sauce
To make me hunger more, that I should forge
Quarrels unjust against the good and loyal,
Destroying them for wealth.

MACDUFF.   This avarice
85   Sticks deeper, grows with more pernicious root
Than summer-seeming[30] lust, and it hath been
The sword of[31] our slain kings. Yet do not fear.
Scotland hath foisons[32] to fill up your will
Of your mere own.[33] All these are portable,[34]
90   With other graces weighed.

MALCOLM.   But I have none: the king-becoming graces,
As justice, verity, temp'rance, stableness,
Bounty, perseverance, mercy, lowliness,
Devotion, patience, courage, fortitude,
95   I have no relish of them, but abound
In the division of each several crime,[35]
Acting it many ways. Nay, had I pow'r, I should
Pour the sweet milk of concord into hell,
Uproar the universal peace, confound[36]
All unity on earth.

100   **MACDUFF.**   O Scotland, Scotland!

25. continent impediments: Restraints.

26. nature: Man's nature.

27. Convey: Secretly manage.

28. affection: Character.
29. stanchless: Never-ending.

30. summer-seeming: Summerlike.
31. of: That killed.
32. foisons (foi´ zənz): Plenty.
33. mere own: Own property.
34. portable: Bearable.

35. division . . . crime: Variations of each kind of crime.

36. confound: Destroy.

◆ **Literary Focus**
How does the image in IV, iii, 98, echo those in I, v, 47–48?

MALCOLM. If such a one be fit to govern, speak:
I am as I have spoken.

MACDUFF.   Fit to govern!
No, not to live. O nation miserable!
With an untitled[37] tyrant bloody-sceptered,
105 When shalt thou see thy wholesome days again,
Since that the truest issue of thy throne[38]
By his own interdiction[39] stands accursed,
And does blaspheme his breed?[40] Thy royal father
Was a most sainted king: the queen that bore thee,
110 Oft'ner upon her knees than on her feet,
Died[41] every day she lived. Fare thee well!
These evils thou repeat'st upon thyself
Hath banished me from Scotland. O my breast,
Thy hope ends here!

MALCOLM.   Macduff, this noble passion,
115 Child of integrity, hath from my soul
Wiped the black scruples, reconciled my thoughts
To thy good truth and honor. Devilish Macbeth
By many of these trains[42] hath sought to win me
Into his power; and modest wisdom[43] plucks me
120 From over-<u>credulous</u> haste: but God above
Deal between thee and me! For even now
I put myself to thy direction, and
Unspeak mine own detraction,[44] here abjure
The taints and blames I laid upon myself,
125 For[45] strangers to my nature. I am yet
Unknown to woman, never was forsworn,
Scarcely have coveted what was mine own,
At no time broke my faith, would not betray
The devil to his fellow, and delight
130 No less in truth than life. My first false speaking
Was this upon myself. What I am truly,
Is thine and my poor country's to command:
Whither indeed, before thy here-approach,
Old Siward, with ten thousand warlike men,
135 Already at a point,[46] was setting forth.
Now we'll together, and the chance of goodness
Be like our warranted quarrel![47] Why are you silent?

MACDUFF. Such welcome and unwelcome things at once
'Tis hard to reconcile.

[*Enter a* DOCTOR.]

140 **MALCOLM.** Well, more anon. Comes the King forth, I pray you?

37. **untitled:** Having no right to the throne.

38. **truest . . . throne:** Child of the true king.

39. **interdiction:** Exclusion.

40. **blaspheme his breed:** Slander his ancestry.

41. **Died:** Prepared for heaven.

42. **trains:** Enticements.

43. **modest wisdom:** Prudence.

44. **detraction:** Slander.

45. **For:** As.

46. **at a point:** Prepared.

47. **the chance . . . quarrel:** May our chance of success equal the justice of our cause.

◆ **Build Vocabulary**

intemperance (in tem´ pər əns) *n.*: Lack of restraint

avarice (av´ ər is) *n.*: Greed

credulous (krej´ ͡oo ləs) *adj.*: Tending to believe too readily

DOCTOR. Ay, sir. There are a crew of wretched souls
    That stay[48] his cure: their malady convinces
    The great assay of art;[49] but at his touch,
    Such sanctity hath heaven given his hand,
    They presently amend.[50]

145 **MALCOLM.**   I thank you, doctor.

                               [*Exit* DOCTOR.]

MACDUFF. What's the disease he means?

MALCOLM.   'Tis called the evil:[51]
    A most miraculous work in this good King,
    Which often since my here-remain in England
    I have seen him do. How he solicits heaven,
150   Himself best knows: but strangely-visited people,
    All swoll'n and ulcerous, pitiful to the eye,
    The mere[52] despair of surgery, he cures,
    Hanging a golden stamp[53] about their necks,
    Put on with holy prayers: and 'tis spoken,
155   To the succeeding royalty he leaves
    The healing benediction. With this strange virtue
    He hath a heavenly gift of prophecy,
    And sundry blessings hang about his throne
    That speak him full of grace.

[*Enter* ROSS.]

MACDUFF.   See, who comes here?

160 **MALCOLM.** My countryman; but yet I know him not.

MACDUFF. My ever gentle[54] cousin, welcome hither.

MALCOLM. I know him now: good God, betimes[55] remove
    The means that makes us strangers!

ROSS.   Sir, amen.

MACDUFF. Stands Scotland where it did?

ROSS.   Alas, poor country!
165   Almost afraid to know itself! It cannot
    Be called our mother but our grave, where nothing[56]
    But who knows nothing is once seen to smile;
    Where sighs and groans, and shrieks that rent the air,
    Are made, not marked, where violent sorrow seems

48. **stay:** Wait for.
49. **convinces . . . art:** Defies the efforts of medical science.
50. **presently amend:** Immediately recover.

51. **evil:** Scrofula (skräf′ yə lə), Skin disease called "the king's evil" because it was believed that it could be cured by the king's touch.
52. **mere:** Utter.
53. **stamp:** Coin.

54. **gentle:** Noble.

55. **betimes:** Quickly.

◆ **Reading Strategy**
To which senses does Ross's description of Scotland in lines 164–174 appeal? How does the description help you envision the state of Scotland?

56. **nothing:** No one.

170 A modern ecstasy.[57] The dead man's knell
　　Is there scarce asked for who,[58] and good men's lives
　　Expire before the flowers in their caps,
　　Dying or ere they sicken.

MACDUFF.　　　　　　　　　　　　O, relation
　　Too nice,[59] and yet too true!

MALCOLM.　　　　　　　　　What's the newest grief?

175 **ROSS.** That of an hour's age doth hiss the speaker;[60]
　　Each minute teems[61] a new one.

MACDUFF.　　　　　　　　　　　How does my wife?

ROSS. Why, well.

MACDUFF.　　　And all my children?

ROSS.　　　　　　　　　　　Well too.

MACDUFF. The tyrant has not battered at their peace?

ROSS. No; they were well at peace when I did leave 'em.

180 **MACDUFF.** Be not a niggard of your speech: how goes 't?

ROSS. When I came hither to transport the tidings,
　　Which I have heavily borne, there ran a rumor
　　Of many worthy fellows that were out; [62]
　　Which was to my belief witnessed[63] the rather,
185　For that I saw the tyrant's power[64] afoot.
　　Now is the time of help. Your eye in Scotland
　　Would create soldiers, make our women fight,
　　To doff[65] their dire distresses.

MALCOLM.　　　　　　　　　　Be 't their comfort
　　We are coming thither. Gracious England hath
190　Lent us good Siward and ten thousand men;
　　An older and a better soldier none
　　That Christendom gives out.

ROSS.　　　　　　　　　　Would I could answer
　　This comfort with the like! But I have words
　　That would be howled out in the desert air,
　　Where hearing should not latch[66] them.

57. modern ecstasy: Ordinary emotion.
58. The dead . . . who: People can no longer keep track of Macbeth's victims.

59. nice: Exact.

60. That . . . speaker: Report of the grief of an hour ago is hissed as stale news.
61. teems: Gives birth to.

62. out: In rebellion.
63. witnessed: Confirmed.
64. power: Army.

65. doff: Put off.

66. latch: Catch.

MACDUFF.   What concern they?

195   The general cause or is it a fee-grief[67]
     Due to some single breast?

ROSS.   No mind that's honest
     But in it shares some woe, though the main part
     Pertains to you alone.

MACDUFF.   If it be mine,
200   Keep it not from me, quickly let me have it.

ROSS.   Let not your ears despise my tongue for ever,
     Which shall possess them with the heaviest sound
     That ever yet they heard.

MACDUFF.   Humh! I guess at it.

ROSS.   Your castle is surprised; your wife and babes
205   Savagely slaughtered. To relate the manner,
     Were, on the quarry[68] of these murdered deer,
     To add the death of you.

MALCOLM.   Merciful heaven!
     What, man! Ne'er pull your hat upon your brows;
     Give sorrow words. The grief that does not speak
210   Whispers the o'er-fraught heart[69] and bids it break.

MACDUFF.   My children too?

ROSS.   Wife, children, servants, all
     That could be found.

MACDUFF.   And I must be from thence!
     My wife killed too?

ROSS.   I have said.

MALCOLM.   Be comforted.
     Let's make us med'cines of our great revenge,
215   To cure this deadly grief.

MACDUFF.   He has no children. All my pretty ones?
     Did you say all? O hell-kite![70] All?
     What, all my pretty chickens and their dam
     At one fell swoop?

67. fee-grief: Personal grief.

68. quarry: Heap of game slain in a hunt.

69. o'er-fraught: Overburdened.

70. hell-kite: Hellish bird of prey.

MALCOLM. Dispute it[71] like a man.

220 **MACDUFF.**   I shall do so;
But I must also feel it as a man.
I cannot but remember such things were,
That were most precious to me. Did heaven look on,
And would not take their part? Sinful Macduff,
225 They were all struck for thee! Naught[72] that I am,
Not for their own demerits but for mine
Fell slaughter on their souls. Heaven rest them now!

MALCOLM. Be this the whetstone of your sword. Let grief
Convert to anger; blunt not the heart, enrage it.

230 **MACDUFF.** O, I could play the woman with mine eyes,
And braggart with my tongue! But, gentle heavens,
Cut short all intermission; front to front[73]
Bring thou this fiend of Scotland and myself;
Within my sword's length set him. If he 'scape,
235 Heaven forgive him too!

MALCOLM.   This time goes manly.
Come, go we to the King. Our power is ready;
Our lack is nothing but our leave.[74] Macbeth
Is ripe for shaking, and the pow'rs above
Put on their instruments.[75] Receive what cheer you may.
240 The night is long that never finds the day.   [*Exit.*]

71. Dispute it:
Counter your grief.

72. Naught: Wicked.

73. front to front:
Face to face.

74. Our . . . leave:
We need only to take
our leave.
**75. Put . . . instru-
ments:** Urge us
onward as their
agents.

Guide for Responding

◆ *Literature and Your Life*

Reader's Response Do you blame Macduff for abandoning his family? Why or why not?
Thematic Focus In what way does the English monarch influence events in Scotland?

☑ Check Your Comprehension

1. Briefly summarize what each of the three apparitions tells Macbeth and what the final vision shows him.
2. What happens to Macduff's family?
3. How does Malcolm test Macduff?
4. What convinces Malcolm that Macduff is trustworthy?
5. What news does Ross bring from Scotland?

◆ Critical Thinking

INTERPRET
1. Why does Macbeth accept the predictions made by the second and third apparitions? **[Analyze]**
2. What does the murder of Macduff's family suggest about Macbeth's state of mind?
[Draw Conclusions]
3. What does the dialogue in IV, iii, reveal about Malcolm's character? **[Analyze]**
4. How would you characterize Macduff based on his reaction to the murder of his wife and son?
[Interpret]
APPLY
5. In staging Macbeth, some producers eliminate IV, ii. Indicate why they might make this cut, and state your reaction to it. **[Speculate]**

Guide for Responding (continued)

◆ Reading Strategy

USE YOUR SENSES

By **using your senses** as you read *Macbeth,* you experience the play more powerfully. For example, the descriptions of the cauldron in IV, i, address the senses of sight, sound, and touch. Many of these images are repellent, but they reveal in a powerful way the evil that Macbeth has chosen.

1. To which senses does Shakespeare appeal in Ross's description of Scotland (IV, iii, 164–173)?
2. Briefly describe the overall impression of Scotland that these images convey.

◆ Literary Focus

IMAGERY

The varied sensory descriptions in Shakespeare's **imagery** not only add liveliness to the play, but also contribute to its meaning. In Act IV, i, for example, the second and third apparitions are babies, "a Bloody Child" and a child "who wears upon his baby-brow the round / And top of sovereignty." These images reflect Macbeth's concern about who will inherit the throne.

1. (a) How does Macbeth's final speech in this scene indicate that he's making war on babies? (b) In what way is a war against babies a war against the future itself?
2. (a) Find two passages in Act IV with images of sickness. (b) Explain how these images relate to the conflict between Macbeth and Malcolm.

◆ Grammar and Style

POSSESSIVE FORMS

Most singular nouns and plural nouns not ending in s form the **possessive** by adding an apostrophe and s. Plural nouns ending in s just add an apostrophe. Do not use an apostrophe to make a word plural.

Practice Write possessives for the following nouns:

1. the Macbeths   3. the witches   5. Ross
2. Fleance   4. the women   6. Lennox

◆ Build Vocabulary

USING THE LATIN ROOT *-cred-*

The root *-cred-* means "belief." Use these word parts to build five *-cred-* words:

in-   -ulous   -ible   -ulity

Write the meanings of these words. Verify your definitions by referring to a dictionary.

USING THE WORD BANK: Denotations

In your notebook, answer each question.

1. Whose influence in this play is the most *pernicious*? Why?
2. Which character do you think is most *judicious*? Why?
3. If you were staging IV, i, what *sundry* items might you have lying around the witches' haunt?
4. Does *intemperance*, rather than ambition, cause Macbeth's downfall? Explain.
5. Is ambition a kind of *avarice*? Why or why not?
6. How would you refute someone claiming that Malcolm is too *credulous* to rule Scotland?

Idea Bank

Writing

1. **Malcolm Wants You!** As a consultant to Malcolm, write a flyer he could use to recruit soldiers. The flyer should motivate young working-class Englishmen to join the army that will be invading Scotland. **[Social Studies Link]**

2. **Plot Analysis** Often the fourth act in a five-act Shakespearean drama discloses a crucial shift, or turning point, in the play's action. Explain why this is or is not the case in *Macbeth.* Refer to specific passages in Act IV of the play to support your analysis.

Speaking, Listening, and Viewing

3. **Role Play** With a small group, role-play an interview between Malcolm's staff and a young Englishman who wants to join their cause. Have the staff test the young man's motivation and abilities. **[Performing Arts Link]**

Guide for Interpreting, Act V

◆ Review and Anticipate

In Act IV, Macbeth learns from the witches that he must "Beware Macduff" but that he need not fear any man "of woman born." He also learns that he will never be vanquished until the forest itself marches against him. However, he sees a vision indicating that Banquo will indeed father a long line of kings.

Armed with his new knowledge, Macbeth orders the murder of Macduff's wife and son. Macduff himself is in England to join forces with Malcolm and is overcome when he hears the news. Nevertheless, he and Malcolm will lead an army against Macbeth.

Act V will determine the outcome as Macbeth, grown reckless in evil, battles against Malcolm and his men.

◆ Literary Focus

SHAKESPEAREAN TRAGEDY

In **Shakespearean tragedy**, the central character is a person of high rank and personal quality. Through some fatal weakness—a **tragic flaw**—this person is enmeshed in events that lead to his or her downfall. As the audience views the destruction of this character, its members experience a mixture of pity, fear, and awe that lifts them out of their everyday lives.

At the beginning of this play, the hero, Macbeth, is pictured as courageous and loyal. By the end of the play, his ambition has driven him to commit a series of horrendous acts. Shakespeare, however, adds nobility to Macbeth's destruction by giving him a reckless bravery in Act V—even when everything is lost. This courage in the face of impossible odds reminds us of the man's stature and increases the awe that his downfall inspires.

◆ Grammar and Style

PRONOUNS AND ANTECEDENTS

Like other writers, Shakespeare uses **pronouns** to avoid the monotony of repeating names. The word or group of words to which a pronoun refers is its **antecedent**. Pronouns and their antecedents must agree in gender and number.

The English pow'r is near, led on by Malcolm,
His uncle Siward and the good Macduff.

The pronoun *His* agrees with its antecedent, *Malcolm*, in gender (masculine) and number (singular).

◆ Reading Strategy

INFER BELIEFS OF THE PERIOD

Great plays are timeless, but they are also historical documents. As products of a certain era, they reflect the **beliefs** and assumptions of those who lived during that period. You can **infer** those beliefs by looking carefully at the ideas the characters express and comparing them to modern ideas on the same subject.

In *Macbeth V, i,* for example, you have the opportunity to watch a doctor in action. Listen carefully to what he says about a case of mental disturbance, and compare his ideas with those that a modern psychologist might express.

◆ Build Vocabulary

LATIN ROOTS: *-turb-*

As you read Act V, you will encounter the word *perturbation.* The Latin root of this word, *-turb-*, means "to disturb." To experience perturbation is "to experience a great disturbance."

WORD BANK

Before you read, preview this list of words from Act V of *Macbeth.*

perturbation
pristine
clamorous
harbingers

Act V

Scene i. *Dunsinane. In the castle.*
[*Enter a* DOCTOR OF PHYSIC *and a* WAITING-GENTLEWOMAN.]

DOCTOR. I have two nights watched with you, but can perceive no truth in your report. When was it she last walked?

GENTLEWOMAN. Since his Majesty went into the field.[1] I have seen
5 her rise from her bed, throw her nightgown upon her, unlock her closet,[2] take forth paper, fold it, write upon 't, read it, afterwards seal it, and again return to bed; yet all this while in a most fast sleep.

DOCTOR. A great <u>perturbation</u> in nature, to receive at
10 once the benefit of sleep and do the effects of watching![3] In this slumb'ry agitation, besides her walking, and other actual performances, what, at any time, have you heard her say?

15 **GENTLEWOMAN.** That, sir, which I will not report after her.

DOCTOR. You may to me, and 'tis most meet[4] you should.

GENTLEWOMAN. Neither to you nor anyone, having no witness to confirm my speech.

[*Enter* LADY MACBETH, *with a taper.*]

Lo you, here she comes! This is her very guise,[5] and, upon my
20 life, fast asleep! Observe her; stand close.[6]

DOCTOR. How came she by that light?

GENTLEWOMAN. Why, it stood by her. She has light by her continually. 'Tis her command.

25 **DOCTOR.** You see, her eyes are open.

GENTLEWOMAN. Ay, but their sense[7] are shut.

DOCTOR. What is it she does now? Look, how she rubs her hands.

GENTLEWOMAN. It is an accustomed action with her,

---

1. **field:** Battlefield.

2. **closet:** Chest.

3. **effects of watching:** Deeds of one awake.

4. **meet:** Suitable.

5. **guise:** Custom.
6. **close:** Hidden.

7. **sense:** Powers of sight.

◆ **Build Vocabulary**
perturbation (pʉrˊ tər bāˊ shən) *n.*: Disturbance

Lady Macbeth Sleepwalking, Henry Fuseli, Louvre, Paris

▲ **Critical Viewing** What can you infer about Lady Macbeth's
state of mind from her facial expressions and gestures? **[Infer]**

30 to seem thus washing her hands: I have known her continue in this a quarter of an hour.

LADY MACBETH. Yet here's a spot.

DOCTOR. Hark! She speaks. I will set down what comes
35 from her, to satisfy[8] my remembrance the more strongly.

LADY MACBETH. Out, damned spot! Out, I say! One: two: why, then 'tis time to do 't. Hell is murky. Fie, my lord, fie! A soldier, and afeard? What need we fear who knows it, when none can call our pow'r to
40 accompt?[9] Yet who would have thought the old man to have had so much blood in him?

DOCTOR. Do you mark that?

LADY MACBETH. The Thane of Fife had a wife. Where is she now? What, will these hands ne'er be clean? No
45 more o' that, my lord, no more o' that! You mar all with this starting.

DOCTOR. Go to, go to! You have known what you should not.

GENTLEWOMAN. She has spoke what she should not, I am
50 sure of that. Heaven knows what she has known.

LADY MACBETH. Here's the smell of the blood still. All the perfumes of Arabia will not sweeten this little hand. Oh, oh, oh!

55 **DOCTOR.** What a sigh is there! The heart is sorely charged.[10]

GENTLEWOMAN. I would not have such a heart in my bosom for the dignity[11] of the whole body.

DOCTOR. Well, well, well—

GENTLEWOMAN. Pray God it be, sir.

60 **DOCTOR.** This disease is beyond my practice. Yet I have known those which have walked in their sleep who have died holily in their beds.

LADY MACBETH. Wash your hands; put on your nightgown; look not so pale! I tell you yet again, Banquo's

8. **satisfy:** Support.

9. **to accompt:** Into account.

10. **charged:** Burdened.
11. **dignity:** Worth.

> **An Actor's Response**
> "[Macbeth] . . . has been continually pouring out his miseries to his wife. His heart has therefore been eased, from time to time, by unloading its weight of woe; while she, on the contrary, has perseveringly endured in silence the uttermost anguish of a wounded spirit."
> —Sarah Siddons

65   buried. He cannot come out on 's[12] grave.

DOCTOR. Even so?

LADY MACBETH. To bed, to bed! There's knocking at
     the gate. Come, come, come, come, give me your hand!
70   What's done cannot be undone. To bed, to bed, to bed!
                 [*Exit* LADY MACBETH.]

DOCTOR. Will she go now to bed?

GENTLEWOMAN. Directly.

DOCTOR. Foul whisp'rings are abroad. Unnatural deeds
     Do breed unnatural troubles. Infected minds
     To their deaf pillows will discharge their secrets.
75   More needs she the divine than the physician.
     God, God forgive us all! Look after her;
     Remove from her the means of all annoyance,[13]
     And still keep eyes upon her. So good night.
     My mind she has mated[14] and amazed my sight:
80   I think, but dare not speak.

GENTLEWOMAN.   Good night, good doctor.
                 [*Exit.*]

Scene ii. *The country near Dunsinane.*
[*Drum and colors. Enter* MENTEITH, CAITHNESS, ANGUS, LENNOX, SOLDIERS.]

MENTEITH. The English pow'r[1] is near, led on by Malcolm,
     His uncle Siward and the good Macduff.
     Revenges burn in them; for their dear causes
     Would to the bleeding and the grim alarm
     Excite the mortified man.[2]

5 **ANGUS.**   Near Birnam Wood
     Shall we well meet them; that way are they coming.

CAITHNESS. Who knows if Donalbain be with his brother?

LENNOX. For certain, sir, he is not. I have a file[3]
     Of all the gentry: there is Siward's son,
10   And many unrough[4] youths that even now
     Protest[5] their first of manhood.

MENTEITH.   What does the tyrant?

---

12. **on 's:** Of his.

◆ **Reading Strategy**
What can you infer about medicine and disease during this time from the doctor's words in V, i, 72–80?

13. **annoyance:** Injury.

14. **mated:** Baffled.

1. **pow'r:** Army.

2. **Would . . . man:** Would incite a dead man to join the bloody, grim call to arms.

3. **file:** List.

4. **unrough:** Beardless.
5. **Protest:** Assert.

CAITHNESS. Great Dunsinane he strongly fortifies.
    Some say he's mad; others, that lesser hate him,
    Do call it valiant fury: but, for certain,
15   He cannot buckle his distempered cause
    Within the belt of rule.[6]

ANGUS.   Now does he feel
    His secret murders sticking on his hands;
    Now minutely revolts upbraid his faith-breach.[7]
    Those he commands move only in command,
20   Nothing in love. Now does he feel his title
    Hang loose about him, like a giant's robe
    Upon a dwarfish thief.

MENTEITH.   Who then shall blame
    His pestered[8] senses to recoil and start,
    When all that is within him does condemn
    Itself for being there?

25 **CAITHNESS.**   Well, march we on,
    To give obedience where 'tis truly owed.
    Meet we the med'cine of the sickly weal,[9]
    And with him pour we, in our country's purge,
    Each drop of us.[10]

LENNOX.   Or so much as it needs
30   To dew the sovereign flower and drown the weeds.[11]
    Make we our march towards Birnam.

                        [Exit, marching.]

Scene iii. *Dunsinane. In the castle.*
[Enter MACBETH, DOCTOR, *and* ATTENDANTS.]

MACBETH. Bring me no more reports; let them fly all![1]
    Till Birnam Wood remove to Dunsinane
    I cannot taint[2] with fear. What's the boy Malcolm?
    Was he not born of woman? The spirits that know
5   All mortal consequences[3] have pronounced me thus:
    "Fear not, Macbeth; no man that's born of woman
    Shall e'er have power upon thee." Then fly, false thanes,
    And mingle with the English epicures.[4]
    The mind I sway[5] by and the heart I bear
10   Shall never sag with doubt nor shake with fear.

[Enter SERVANT.]

◆ **Literary Focus**

Do you agree with those that Caithness quotes—Is Macbeth "mad"? Why or why not?

6. rule: Self-control.

7. minutely . . . faith-breach: Every minute revolts rebuke his disloyalty.

8. pestered: Tormented.

9. Med'cine . . . weal: Malcolm and his supporters are "the medicine" that will heal "the sickly" common-wealth.

10. Each . . . us: Every last drop of our blood.

11. dew . . . weeds: Water the royal flower (Malcolm) and drown the weeds (Macbeth).

1. let . . . all: Let them all desert me!

2. taint: Become infected.

3. mortal conse-quences: Future human events.

4. epicures: Gluttons.

5. sway: Move.

The devil damn thee black, thou cream-faced loon.[6]
Where got'st thou that goose look?

SERVANT. There is ten thousand—

MACBETH.   Geese, villain?

SERVANT.   Soldiers, sir.

MACBETH. Go prick thy face and over-red thy fear.
15 Thou lily-livered boy. What soldiers, patch?[7]
Death of thy soul! Those linen[8] cheeks of thine
Are counselors to fear. What soldiers, whey-face?

SERVANT. The English force, so please you.

MACBETH. Take thy face hence.   [*Exit* SERVANT.]
`   Seyton!—I am sick at heart.
20 When I behold—Seyton, I say!—This push[9]
Will cheer me ever, or disseat[10] me now.
I have lived long enough. My way of life
Is fall'n into the sear,[11] the yellow leaf,
And that which should accompany old age,
25 As honor, love, obedience, troops of friends,
I must not look to have; but, in their stead,
Curses not loud but deep, mouth-honor, breath,
Which the poor heart would fain deny, and dare not.
Seyton!

[*Enter* SEYTON.]

SEYTON. What's your gracious pleasure?

30 **MACBETH.**   What news more?

SEYTON. All is confirmed, my lord, which was reported.

MACBETH. I'll fight, till from my bones my flesh be hacked.
Give me my armor.

SEYTON.   'Tis not needed yet.

MACBETH. I'll put it on.
35 Send out moe[12] horses, skirr[13] the country round.
Hang those that talk of fear. Give me mine armor.
How does your patient, doctor?

6. **loon:** Fool.

7. **patch:** Fool.
8. **linen:** Pale as linen.

9. **push:** Effort.
10. **disseat:** Unthrone.

11. **the sear:** Withered state.

◆ **Literary Focus**
Does this passage, lines 20–28, evoke sympathy for Macbeth? Explain.

12. **moe:** More.
13. **skirr:** Scour.

DOCTOR. Not so sick, my lord,
   As she is troubled with thick-coming fancies
   That keep her from her rest.

MACBETH. Cure her of that.
40 Canst thou not minister to a mind diseased,
   Pluck from the memory a rooted sorrow,
   Raze out[14] the written troubles of the brain,
   And with some sweet oblivious antidote
   Cleanse the stuffed bosom of that perilous stuff
   Which weighs upon the heart?

45 **DOCTOR.** Therein the patient
   Must minister to himself.

MACBETH. Throw physic[15] to the dogs, I'll none of it.
   Come, put mine armor on. Give me my staff.
   Seyton, send out.—Doctor, the thanes fly from me.—
50 Come, sir, dispatch. If thou couldst, doctor, cast
   The water[16] of my land, find her disease
   And purge it to a sound and pristine health,
   I would applaud thee to the very echo,
   That should applaud again.—Pull 't off,[17] I say.—
55 What rhubarb, senna, or what purgative drug,
   Would scour these English hence? Hear'st thou of them?

DOCTOR. Ay, my good lord; your royal preparation
   Makes us hear something.

MACBETH. Bring it[18] after me.
   I will not be afraid of death and bane[19]
60 Till Birnam Forest come to Dunsinane.

DOCTOR. [*Aside*] Were I from Dunsinane away and clear,
   Profit again should hardly draw me here.   [*Exit.*]

Scene iv. *Country near Birnam Wood.*
[*Drum and colors. Enter* MALCOLM, SIWARD, MACDUFF, SIWARD'S SON,
MENTEITH, CAITHNESS, ANGUS, *and* SOLDIERS, *marching.*]

MALCOLM. Cousins, I hope the days are near at hand
   That chambers will be safe.[1]

MENTEITH. We doubt it nothing.

SIWARD. What wood is this before us?

---

14. **Raze out:** Erase.

◆ **Reading Strategy**
Would a modern psychologist answer as the doctor does in V, iii, 45–46?

15. **physic:** Medicine.

16. **cast the water** Diagnose the illness.
17. **Pull 't off:** Pull off a piece of armor which has been put on incorrectly in Macbeth's haste.

18. **it:** His armor.
19. **bane:** Destruction.

1. **That . . . safe:** That people will be safe in their own homes.

◆ **Build Vocabulary**
pristine (pris tēn´) *adj.*: Original; unspoiled

MENTEITH.   The Wood of Birnam.

MALCOLM. Let every soldier hew him down a bough
5   And bear 't before him. Thereby shall we shadow[2]
The numbers of our host, and make discovery[3]
Err in report of us.

SOLDIERS.   It shall be done.

SIWARD. We learn no other but the confident tyrant
Keeps still in Dunsinane, and will endure
Our setting down before 't.[4]

10 **MALCOLM.**   'Tis his main hope,
For where there is advantage to be given
Both more and less[5] have given him the revolt,
And none serve with him but constrained things
Whose hearts are absent too.

MACDUFF.   Let our just censures
15 Attend the true event,[6] and put we on
Industrious soldiership.

SIWARD.   The time approaches,
That will with due decision make us know
What we shall say we have and what we owe.[7]
Thoughts speculative their unsure hopes relate,
20 But certain issue strokes must arbitrate:[8]
Towards which advance the war.[9]   [*Exit, marching.*]

Scene v. Dunsinane. Within the castle.
[*Enter* MACBETH, SEYTON, *and* SOLDIERS, *with drum and colors.*]

MACBETH. Hang out our banners on the outward walls.
The cry is still "They come!" Our castle's strength
Will laugh a siege to scorn. Here let them lie
Till famine and the ague[1] eat them up.
5   Were they not forced[2] with those that should be ours,
We might have met them dareful,[3] beard to beard,
And beat them backward home.
            [*A cry within of women.*]
                          What is that noise?

SEYTON. It is the cry of women, my good lord.   [*Exit.*]

MACBETH. I have almost forgot the taste of fears:

Sidenotes:

2. **shadow:** Conceal.
3. **discovery:** Those who see us.

4. **setting down before 't:** Laying seige to it.

5. **more and less:** People of high and low rank.

6. **our . . . event:** True judgment awaits the actual outcome.

7. **owe:** Own.

8. **strokes . . . arbitrate:** Fighting must decide.
9. **war:** Army.

1. **ague:** Fever.
2. **forced:** Reinforced.
3. **dareful:** Boldly.

10 The time has been, my senses would have cooled
To hear a night-shriek, and my fell[4] of hair
Would at a dismal treatise[5] rouse and stir
As life were in 't. I have supped full with horrors.
Direness, familiar to my slaughterous thoughts,
Cannot once start[6] me.

[*Enter* SEYTON.]

15   Wherefore was that cry?

SEYTON. The queen, my lord, is dead.

MACBETH. She should[7] have died hereafter;
There would have been a time for such a word.[8]
Tomorrow, and tomorrow, and tomorrow
20 Creeps in this petty pace from day to day,
To the last syllable of recorded time;
And all our yesterdays have lighted fools
The way to dusty death. Out, out, brief candle!
Life's but a walking shadow, a poor player
25 That struts and frets his hour upon the stage
And then is heard no more. It is a tale
Told by an idiot, full of sound and fury
Signifying nothing.

[*Enter a* MESSENGER.]

Thou com'st to use thy tongue; thy story quickly!

30 **MESSENGER.** Gracious my lord,
I should report that which I say I saw,
But know not how to do 't.

MACBETH.   Well, say, sir.

MESSENGER. As I did stand my watch upon the hill,
I looked toward Birnam, and anon, methought,
The wood began to move.

35 **MACBETH.**   Liar and slave!

MESSENGER. Let me endure your wrath, if 't be not so.
Within this three mile may you see it coming;
I say a moving grove.

MACBETH.   If thou speak'st false,

4. **fell:** Scalp.
5. **treatise:** Story.

6. **start:** Startle.

7. **should:** Inevitably would.
8. **word:** Message.

◆ **Literary Focus**
This speech, lines 17-28, is a powerful expression of life's futility. Is Macbeth's story really "a tale/ Told by an idiot, full of sound and fury,/ Signifying nothing"? Why or why not?

40 Upon the next tree shalt thou hang alive,
Till famine cling[9] thee. If thy speech be sooth,[10]
I care not if thou dost for me as much.
I pull in resolution, and begin
To doubt th' equivocation of the fiend
45 That lies like truth: "Fear not, till Birnam Wood
Do come to Dunsinane!" And now a wood
Comes toward Dunsinane. Arm, arm, and out!
If this which he avouches[11] does appear,
There is nor flying hence nor tarrying here.
I 'gin to be aweary of the sun,
50 And wish th' estate o' th' world were now undone.
Ring the alarum bell! Blow wind, come wrack!
At least we'll die with harness[12] on our back.   [*Exit.*]

9. **cling:** Wither.
10. **sooth:** Truth.

11. **avouches:** Asserts.

12. **harness:** Armor.

Scene vi. *Dunsinane. Before the castle.*
[*Drum and colors. Enter* MALCOLM, SIWARD, MACDUFF, *and their army, with boughs.*]

MALCOLM. Now near enough. Your leavy[1] screens throw down,
And show like those you are. You, worthy uncle,
Shall, with my cousin, your right noble son,
Lead our first battle.[2] Worthy Macduff and we
5 Shall take upon 's what else remains to do,
According to our order.[3]

1. **leavy:** Leafy.

2. **battle:** Battalion.

3. **order:** Plan.

SIWARD.   Fare you well.
Do we find the tyrant's power[4] tonight,
Let us be beaten, if we cannot fight.

4. **power:** Forces.

MACDUFF. Make all our trumpets speak; give them all breath.
10 Those <u>clamorous</u> <u>harbingers</u> of blood and death.
                    [*Exit. Alarums continued.*]

Scene vii. *Another part of the field.*
[*Enter* MACBETH.]

MACBETH. They have tied me to a stake; I cannot fly,
But bearlike I must fight the course.[1] What's he
That was not born of woman? Such a one
Am I to fear, or none.

1. **bearlike . . .
course:** Like a bear
chained to a stake
being attacked by
dogs, I must fight until
the end.

[*Enter* YOUNG SIWARD.]

YOUNG SIWARD. What is thy name?

◆ **Build Vocabulary**

clamorous (klam′ ər əs) *adj.*: Noisy
harbingers (här′ bin jərs) *n.*: Forerunners

5   **MACBETH.**   Thou'lt be afraid to hear it.

  YOUNG SIWARD. No; though thou call'st thyself a hotter name
    Than any is in hell.

  MACBETH.   My name's Macbeth.

  YOUNG SIWARD. The devil himself could not pronounce a title
    More hateful to mine ear.

  MACBETH.   No, nor more fearful.

10   **YOUNG SIWARD.** Thou liest, abhorrèd tyrant; with my sword
    I'll prove the lie thou speak'st.
            [*Fight, and* YOUNG SIWARD *slain.*]

  MACBETH.   Thou wast born of woman.
    But swords I smile at, weapons laugh to scorn,
    Brandished by man that's of a woman born.   [*Exit.*]

[*Alarums. Enter* MACDUFF.]

  MACDUFF. That way the noise is. Tyrant, show thy face!
15   If thou be'st slain and with no stroke of mine,
    My wife and children's ghosts will haunt me still.
    I cannot strike at wretched kerns, whose arms
    Are hired to bear their staves.[2] Either thou, Macbeth,
    Or else my sword, with an unbattered edge,
20   I sheathe again undeeded.[3] There thou shouldst be;
    By this great clatter, one of greatest note
    Seems bruited.[4] Let me find him, Fortune!
    And more I beg not.   [*Exit. Alarums.*]

[*Enter* MALCOLM *and* SIWARD.]

  SIWARD. This way, my lord. The castle's gently rend'red:[5]
25   The tyrant's people on both sides do fight;
    The noble thanes do bravely in the war;
    The day almost itself professes yours,
    And little is to do.

  MALCOLM.   We have met with foes
    That strike beside us.[6]

  SIWARD.   Enter, sir, the castle.
                    [*Exit. Alarum.*]

2. **staves:** Spears.

3. **undeeded:** Unused.

4. **bruited:** Reported.

5. **gently rend'red:** Easily surrendered.

6. **strike . . . us:** Deliberately miss us.

Scene viii. *Another part of the field.*
[*Enter* MACBETH.]

MACBETH. Why should I play the Roman fool, and die
On mine own sword?[1] Whiles I see lives,[2] the gashes
Do better upon them.

[*Enter* MACDUFF.]

MACDUFF.   Turn, hell-hound, turn!

MACBETH. Of all men else I have avoided thee.
5   But get thee back! My soul is too much charged
With blood of thine already.

MACDUFF.   I have no words:
My voice is in my sword, thou bloodier villain
Than terms[3] can give thee out!
                              [*Fight. Alarum.*]

MACBETH.   Thou losest labor:
As easy mayst thou the intrenchant[4] air
10   With thy keen sword impress[5] as make me bleed:
Let fall thy blade on vulnerable crests;
I bear a charmèd life, which must not yield
To one of woman born.

MACDUFF.   Despair thy charm,
And let the angel[6] whom thou still hast served
15   Tell thee, Macduff was from his mother's womb
Untimely ripped.[7]

MACBETH. Accursèd be that tongue that tells me so,
For it hath cowed my better part of man![8]
And be these juggling fiends no more believed,
20   That palter[9] with us in a double sense;
That keep the word of promise to our ear,
And break it to our hope. I'll not fight with thee.

MACDUFF. Then yield thee, coward,
And live to be the show and gaze o' th' time:[10]
25   We'll have thee, as our rarer monsters[11] are,
Painted upon a pole,[12] and underwrit,
"Here may you see the tyrant."

MACBETH.   I will not yield,
To kiss the ground before young Malcolm's feet,

1. play . . . sword:
Die like Brutus or
Cassius, who killed
themselves with their
own swords in the
moment of defeat.
2. While . . . lives:
So long as I see living
men.

3. terms . . . out:
Words can describe
you.

4. intrenchant:
Incapable of being cut.
5. impress: Make a
dent in.

6. angel: Fallen
angel; fiend.
7. his . . . ripped:
Macduff's mother died
before giving birth to
him.
8. better. . . man:
Courage.
9. palter: Juggle.

10. gaze o' th' time:
Spectacle of the age.
11. monsters: Freaks.
12. Painted . . . pole:
Pictured on a banner
stuck on a pole by a
showman's booth.

And to be baited with the rabble's curse.
30 Though Birnam Wood be come to Dunsinane,
And thou opposed, being of no woman born,
Yet I will try the last. Before my body
I throw my warlike shield. Lay on, Macduff;
And damned be him that first cries "Hold, enough!"

[*Exit, fighting. Alarums.*]

[*Re-enter fighting, and* MACBETH *slain. Exit* MACDUFF, *with* MACBETH.
Retreat and flourish.[13] *Enter, with drum and colors,*
MALCOLM, SIWARD, ROSS, THANES, *and* SOLDIERS.]

13. Retreat and flourish: Trumpet call to withdraw and fanfare.

35 **MALCOLM.** I would the friends we miss were safe arrived.

SIWARD. Some must go off;[14] and yet, by these I see,
So great a day as this is cheaply bought.

14. go off: Die.

MALCOLM. Macduff is missing, and your noble son.

ROSS. Your son, my lord, has paid a soldier's debt:
40 He only lived but till he was a man;
The which no sooner had his prowess confirmed
In the unshrinking station[15] where he fought,
But like a man he died.

15. unshrinking station: Place where he stood firmly.

SIWARD.   Then he is dead?

ROSS. Ay, and brought off the field. Your cause of sorrow
45 Must not be measured by his worth, for then
It hath no end.

SIWARD.   Had he his hurts before?

ROSS. Ay, on the front.

SIWARD.   Why then, God's soldier be he!
Had I as many sons as I have hairs,
I would not wish them to a fairer death:
And so his knell is knolled.

50 **MALCOLM.**   He's worth more sorrow,
And that I'll spend for him.

SIWARD.   He's worth no more:
They say he parted well and paid his score:
And so God be with him! Here comes newer comfort.

> **★ A Critic's Response**
> "... the movement throughout is the most rapid of all Shakespeare's plays."
> —**Samuel Taylor Coleridge**

[*Enter* MACDUFF, *with* MACBETH'S *head.*]

MACDUFF. Hail, King! for so thou art: behold, where stands
55   Th' usurper's cursèd head. The time is free.[16]
       I see thee compassed with thy kingdom's pearl,[17]
       That speak my salutation in their minds,
       Whose voices I desire aloud with mine:
       Hail, King of Scotland!

ALL.   Hail, King of Scotland!

[*Flourish.*]

60   MALCOLM. We shall not spend a large expense of time
       Before we reckon with your several loves,[18]
       And make us even with you.[19] My thanes and kinsmen,
       Henceforth be earls, the first that ever Scotland
       In such an honor named. What's more to do,
65   Which would be planted newly with the time[20]—
       As calling home our exiled friends abroad
       That fled the snares of watchful tyranny,
       Producing forth the cruel ministers
       Of this dead butcher and his fiendlike queen,
70   Who, as 'tis thought, by self and violent hands
       Took off her life—this, and what needful else
       That calls upon us, by the grace of Grace
       We will perform in measure, time, and place:[21]
       So thanks to all at once and to each one,
       Whom we invite to see us crowned at Scone.

                              [*Flourish. Exit all.*]

16. **The . . . free:** Our country is liberated.
17. **compassed . . . pearl:** Surrounded by the noblest people in the kingdom.

18. **reckon . . . loves:** Reward each of you for your devotion.
19. **make . . . you:** Pay what we owe you.
20. **What's . . . time:** What remains to be done at the beginning of this new age.

21. **in measure . . . place:** Fittingly at the appropriate time and place.

Guide for Responding

◆ Literature and Your Life

Reader's Response Does the ending of the play satisfy you? Why or why not?

Thematic Focus Why do you think this drama continues to appeal to audiences after nearly four hundred years?

Research In many of his plays, Shakespeare dealt with the question of legitimate monarchy vs. usurpation. Do research to find the names of legitimate monarchs still active in cultures around the world.

☑ Check Your Comprehension

1. To what three previous events in the play does Lady Macbeth refer in her sleepwalking?
2. What happens to Lady Macbeth before the final battle?
3. What does Macbeth learn in V, v, that makes him doubt the apparitions' prophecies?
4. (a) In V, viii, why does Macbeth tell Macduff he doesn't wish to fight him? (b) What does Macduff tell Macbeth concerning the apparitions' second prophecy?
5. (a) What is Macbeth's fate in the battle? (b) At the end of the play, who is to be crowned king of Scotland?

Guide for Responding (continued)

◆ Critical Thinking

INTERPRET

1. (a) What causes Lady Macbeth to sleepwalk?
   (b) How have Macbeth and Lady Macbeth reversed roles by the end of the play? **[Infer]**
2. Judging by the way Macbeth behaves in V, iii and v, describe his state of mind. **[Interpret]**
3. On learning of his wife's death, why does Macbeth say, "She should have died hereafter"? **[Interpret]**
4. What admirable traits does Macbeth show at the end? **[Draw Conclusions]**

EVALUATE

5. Would this play be as effective if Macbeth's temptations came from within and not from the witches? Explain. **[Make a Judgment]**

EXTEND

6. How would the recently foiled Guy Fawkes plot have influenced the way Shakespeare's audience viewed *Macbeth* (p. 270)? **[Social Studies Link]**

◆ Reading Strategy

INFER BELIEFS OF THE PERIOD

You can **infer** early seventeenth-century **beliefs** about sleepwalking and mental disturbances by reading what the doctor says in V, i and iii.

1. Find two speeches by the doctor suggesting that he doesn't feel qualified to treat mental illness.
2. (a) What line indicates that the doctor knows the cause of Lady Macbeth's disturbance?
   (b) To whose care would he refer her? Why?

◆ Grammar and Style

PRONOUN AND ANTECEDENTS

Pronouns must agree in gender, number, and person with their **antecedents**—the words to which they refer.

Practice Identify the antecedents of the italicized pronouns, and explain the ways in which the pronouns and their antecedents agree.

1. Who knows if Donalbain be with *his* brother?
2. Make all our trumpets speak, give *them* all breath.
3. What does the tyrant? / Great Dunsinane *he* strongly fortifies.

◆ Literary Focus

SHAKESPEAREAN TRAGEDY

The last act of this **Shakespearean tragedy** depicts the downfall of Macbeth, the tragic hero. The road to Dunsinane and destruction begins for him in Act I, when he first meets the three witches. In response to their "supernatural soliciting," he is tempted to murder Duncan. His **tragic flaw**—a weakness in his nature—makes it possible for him to have these evil thoughts and then to turn them into evil deeds.

1. (a) In your own words, what is Macbeth's tragic flaw? (b) How does Banquo's response to the witches emphasize that flaw?
2. What role does Lady Macbeth play in Macbeth's choice of evil?
3. Once Macbeth kills Duncan, can he turn back? Why or why not?
4. Find three passages that show how the intensity of Macbeth's imagination adds to the tragedy. Support your choices.
5. Explain how the positive qualities that Macbeth demonstrates in V add to the sense of tragedy.

◆ Build Vocabulary

USING THE LATIN ROOT -*turb*-

Knowing that the root -*turb*- means "to disturb," define the italicized words.

1. The pilot said that they would encounter some *turbulence*.
2. The eleventh century must have been a *turbulent* time in Scotland.
3. Elizabethans believed that a *perturbation* in the heavens meant disorder in society too.

USING THE WORD BANK: Sentence Completions

Fill in each blank space with a word from the Word Bank, using each word only once.

The movement of Birnam Wood was a strange development. The first ____?____, rustling trees that approached Dunsinane were ____?____ of the army. Farmers who saw the ____?____ wood suddenly begin to move confessed to feeling a ____?____ in their hearts.

Build Your Portfolio

 ## Idea Bank

Writing

1. **Independence Day** Write a proclamation for King Malcolm establishing a yearly celebration on the day of Macbeth's downfall. Indicate the purpose of the day and how it will be celebrated.

2. **Dear Diary** As Lady Macbeth, write a series of diary entries that reveal your deteriorating relationship with your husband. Date the first entry sometime after the murder of Duncan.

3. **Response to Criticism** A. C. Bradley wrote about *Macbeth*: "Darkness, we may even say blackness, broods over this tragedy. . . . all the scenes which at once recur to memory take place either at night or in some dark spot." Agree or disagree with this statement, supporting your points with specific references to the play.

Speaking, Listening, and Viewing

4. **Performance** With a group of classmates, perform a scene from *Macbeth*. In rehearsing, focus on conveying the meaning and emotion of the dialogue. **[Performing Arts Link]**

5. **Battlefield Report** With a group, cover the battle described in Act V for television. Combining blow-by-blow descriptions with battlefield interviews, perform your coverage for the class. **[Media Link; Social Studies Link]**

Researching and Representing

6. **Set Design** With a partner, choose a scene from *Macbeth* and design a set that captures its mood. **[Art Link]**

7. **Macbeth, the Opera** Find a recording of Verdi's opera based on *Macbeth*. Play a portion of it for the class, explaining how Verdi adapted Shakespeare's drama. **[Music Link]**

Online Activity www.phlit.phschool.com

 ## Guided Writing Lesson

Macbeth: The Film Version?

Before directors decide whether to film a play, they might ask someone to analyze its screen potential. Write such an analysis of *Macbeth*. Considering elements like dialogue, setting, characters, and theme, advise the director whether to go ahead with filming the production. To make your analysis convincing, refer to precise details in the play.

Writing Skills Focus: Precise Details

Whether you write an analysis of a play or a play itself, use **precise details** to support arguments or depict characters. For example, to convince the director that special effects could play a role in the film, you can quote specific passages that invite such effects:

> Is this a dagger which I see before me,
> The handle toward my hand? Come, let me
>   clutch thee! (II, i, 33–34)

Then, having quoted the precise passage, you can describe how it might be filmed.

Even before you start to write, find precise details that will help you make your case.

Prewriting Identify elements of the play that will or won't work in a film; a universal theme is a plus but hard-to-understand dialogue might be a minus. Organize precise details from the play in parallel lists that illustrate these elements.

Drafting Refer to your notes as you write. Be sure to support each point you make with details or quotations from the play.

Revising Ask yourself whether you've helped the director envision the wonderful or disastrous film that the play could become. If not, use precise details to describe a scene from the potential movie. For example, you might want to show how the murder of Banquo or the final battle could make good action scenes.

CONNECTIONS TO WORLD LITERATURE

from Oedipus the King
Sophocles

Literary Connection

Shakespeare did not invent tragedy, although he wrote a number of great tragedies, including *Macbeth*. The honor of creating this literary form, and of creating drama itself, goes to the ancient Greeks. Drama and tragedy may have evolved from the religious festivals honoring the Greek god Dionysius, who exercised power over the grape harvest and the production of wine.

WHAT MAKES A TRAGEDY?

In this section, you will read an excerpt from *Oedipus the King*, an ancient Greek tragedy by Sophocles. Like *Macbeth*, Oedipus is high-born and comes to grief through his own choices. The destruction of a noble character is an essential ingredient of tragedy—whether Greek or Elizabethan.

The element of choice in tragedy is not so clear-cut, however. Macbeth obviously makes an evil choice or is coaxed into one by his wife. Oedipus, however, seems less evil than unaware. His own choices and acts lead him to destruction, but he isn't fully conscious of what he is doing. He may be overproud (the Greeks called this haughty spirit *hubris*), but he doesn't traffic with evil as Macbeth does.

THE MYSTERY OF TRAGEDY

The meaning of choice in tragedy brings us to an unsolvable mystery—one that may be related to the origins of tragedy in religion. The mystery of tragedy is that it presents two contradictory ideas: The central character is free to choose, and yet he or she also seems fated to be destroyed. When viewed rationally, these two possibilities could not exist at the same time. By uniting these opposite ideas, however, tragedy forces us to go beyond reason. In that realm beyond reason, we encounter the emotions of pity, fear, and awe that make us tremble.

SOPHOCLES
(496–406 B.C.)

Sophocles' life corresponded with the splendid rise and tragic fall of fifth-century B.C. Athens. As a young man, he performed in a public celebration of Athens's great naval victory over the Persians at Salamis. He died only two years before Athens surrendered to Sparta in the Peloponnesian War.

His life also coincided with the rise and fall of the Golden Age of Greek tragedy. His career as a dramatist began in 468 B.C., when he entered an annual theatrical competition and defeated the established and brilliant playwright Aeschylus. Over the next 62 years, Sophocles wrote more than 120 plays, twenty-four of which won first prize. Unfortunately, only seven of Sophocles' plays have survived, one of them being *Oedipus the King*.

Sophocles was an innovative dramatist who made many significant contributions to Greek tragedy. For example, Sophocles expanded the use of stage machinery and sets. He was the first to use the *mechane*, a crane that lowered the gods "miraculously" onto the stage at the end of the play.

from Oedipus THE KING

Sophocles
Translated by David Grene

It had been prophesied that the son of Jocasta and Laius would kill his father and marry his mother. When their son Oedipus was born, the infant was to be left to die of exposure, but the servant given the task pitied him. He was eventually given to Merope, wife of King Polybus. In a search for the truth about his identity, Oedipus learns of the prophecy and flees from his adoptive parents. During his journey, he gets in a conflict with a charioteer who pur- posely runs over Oedipus' foot, and the man in the chariot strikes Oedipus in the head. Furious, Oedipus kills both men; one of the men was his real father, King Laius. When he arrives at Thebes, he rescues the city from the Sphinx and marries Queen Jocasta, widow of Laius and his mother. At the beginning of the play, Oedipus' city is suffering from a blight, which he has caused by fulfilling the prophecy. At this point Oedipus is still unaware of what he has done.

PART I

[**Scene:** In front of the palace of Oedipus at Thebes. To the right of the stage near the altar stands the priest with a crowd of children. Oedipus emerges from the central door.]

    OEDIPUS. Children, young sons and daughters of old Cadmus,[1]
    why do you sit here with your suppliant crowns?[2]
    The town is heavy with a mingled burden
    of sounds and smells, of groans and hymns and incense;
5   I did not think it fit that I should hear
    of this from messengers but came myself,—
    I Oedipus whom all men call the Great.

                [He turns to the PRIEST.]

    You're old and they are young; come, speak for them.
    What do you fear or want, that you sit here

1. Cadmus (kad′ məs): Mythical founder and first king of Thebes, a city in central Greece where the play takes place.
2. suppliant (sup′ lē ənt) **crowns:** Wreaths worn by people who ask favors of the gods.

10　suppliant? Indeed I'm willing to give all
　　that you may need; I would be very hard
　　should I not pity suppliants like these.

　　PRIEST. O ruler of my country, Oedipus,
　　you see our company around the altar;
15　you see our ages; some of us, like these,
　　who cannot yet fly far, and some of us
　　heavy with age; these children are the chosen
　　among the young, and I the priest of Zeus.
　　Within the market place sit others crowned
20　with suppliant garlands,[3] at the double shrine
　　of Pallas[4] and the temple where Ismenus
　　gives oracles by fire.[5] King, you yourself
　　have seen our city reeling like a wreck
　　already; it can scarcely lift its prow
25　out of the depths, out of the bloody surf.
　　A blight is on the fruitful plants of the earth,
　　a blight is on the cattle in the fields,
　　a blight is on our women that no children
　　are born to them; a God that carries fire,
30　a deadly pestilence,[6] is on our town,
　　strikes us and spares not, and the house of Cadmus
　　is emptied of its people while black Death
　　grows rich in groaning and in lamentation.[7]
　　We have not come as suppliants to this altar
35　because we thought of you as of a God,
　　but rather judging you the first of men
　　in all the chances of this life and when
　　we mortals have to do with more than man.
　　You came and by your coming saved our city,
40　freed us from tribute which we paid of old
　　to the Sphinx,[8] cruel singer. This you did
　　in virtue of no knowledge we could give you,
　　in virtue of no teaching; it was God
　　that aided you, men say, and you are held
45　with God's assistance to have saved our lives.
　　Now Oedipus, Greatest in all men's eyes,
　　here falling at your feet we all entreat you,
　　find us some strength for rescue.
　　Perhaps you'll hear a wise word from some God
50　perhaps you will learn something from a man
　　(for I have seen that for the skilled of practice
　　the outcome of their counsels live the most).
　　Noblest of men, go, and raise up our city,
　　go,—and give heed. For now this land of ours
55　calls you its savior since you saved it once.
　　So, let us never speak about your reign
　　as of a time when first our feet were set
　　secure on high, but later fell to ruin.
　　Raise up our city, save it and raise it up.
60　Once you have brought us luck with happy omen;

3. suppliant garlands *n.*: Branches wound in wool, that were placed on the altar and left there until the suppliant's request was granted.
4. double shrine of Pallas: Two temples of Athena.
5. temple where Ismenus gives oracles by fire: Temple of Apollo, located by Ismenus, the Theban river, where the priests studied patterns in the ashes of sacrificial victims to foretell the future.
6. pestilence (pes´ tə ləns) *n.*: Fatal, contagious disease of epidemic proportions.
7. lamentation (lam ən tā´ shən) *n.*: Act of expressing deep sorrow and grief.

8. Sphinx (sfinks) *n.*: Winged female monster who ate Theban men who could not answer her riddle: "What is it that walks on four legs at dawn, two legs at midday, and three legs in the evening, and has only one voice, when it walks on most feet, it is weakest?" Creon, appointed ruler of Thebes, offered the kingdom and the hand of his sister, Jocasta, to anyone who could answer the riddle. Oedipus saved Thebes by answering correctly, "Man, who crawls in infancy, walks upright in his prime, and leans on a cane in old age." Outraged, the Sphinx destroyed herself, and Oedipus became King of Thebes.

▲ Critical Viewing In what ways is this costume appropriate for Oedipus? [Evaluate]

be no less now in fortune.
If you will rule this land, as now you rule it,
better to rule it full of men than empty.
For neither tower nor ship is anything
65   when empty, and none live in it together.

OEDIPUS. I pity you, children. You have come full of longing,
but I have known the story before you told it
only too well. I know you are all sick,
yet there is not one of you, sick though you are,
70   that is as sick as I myself.
Your several sorrows each have single scope
and touch but one of you. My spirit groans
for city and myself and you at once.
You have not roused me like a man from sleep;
75   know that I have given many tears to this,
gone many ways wandering in thought,
but as I thought I found only one remedy
and that I took. I sent Menoeceus' son
Creon, Jocasta's brother, to Apollo,
80   to his Pythian temple,[9]
that he might learn there by what act or word
I could save this city. As I count the days,
it vexes me what ails him; he is gone
far longer than he needed for the journey.
85   But when he comes, then, may I prove a villain,
if I shall not do all the God commands.

PRIEST. Thanks for your gracious words. Your servants here
signal that Creon is this moment coming.

9. Pythian (pith' ē ən) **temple:** Shrine of Apollo at Delphi, below Mount Parnassus in central Greece.

from *Oedipus the King* ◆ *367*

OEDIPUS. His face is bright. O holy Lord Apollo,
90 grant that his news too may be bright for us and bring us safety.

PRIEST. It is happy news,
I think, for else his head would not be crowned
with sprigs of fruitful laurel.[10]

OEDIPUS. We will know soon,
he's within hail. Lord Creon, my good brother,
95 what is the word you bring us from the God?

[CREON *enters.*]

10. sprigs of fruitful laurel: Laurel symbolized triumph; a crown of laurel signified good news.

CREON. A good word,—for things hard to bear themselves
if in the final issue all is well I count complete good fortune.

OEDIPUS. What do you mean?
What you have said so far
100 leaves me uncertain whether to trust or fear.

CREON. If you will hear my news before these others
I am ready to speak, or else to go within.

OEDIPUS. Speak it to all;
the grief I bear, I bear it more for these
105 than for my own heart.

CREON. I will tell you, then, what I heard from the God.
King Phoebus[11] in plain words commanded us
to drive out a pollution from our land,
pollution grown ingrained within the land;
110 drive it out, said the God, not cherish it, till it's past cure.

OEDIPUS. What is the rite
of purification? How shall it be done?

11. King Phoebus
(fē´ bəs): Apollo, god of sun.

▼ Critical Viewing Examine the pose of these two followers of Oedipus. What does their pose indicate about their feelings toward Oedipus? **[Speculate]**

CREON. By banishing a man, or expiation[12]
of blood by blood, since it is murder guilt
115 which holds our city in this destroying storm.

OEDIPUS. Who is this man whose fate the God pronounces?

CREON. My Lord, before you piloted[13] the state
we had a king called Laius.

OEDIPUS. I know of him by hearsay.[14] I have not seen him.

120 **CREON.** The God commanded clearly: let some one
punish with force this dead man's murderers.

OEDIPUS. Where are they in the world? Where would a trace
of this old crime be found? It would be hard to guess where.

CREON. The clue is in this land;
125 that which is sought is found;
the unheeded thing escapes:
so said the God.

OEDIPUS. Was it at home,
or in the country that death came upon him,
or in another country traveling?

130 **CREON.** He went, he said himself, upon an embassy,[15]
but never returned when he set out from home.

OEDIPUS. Was there no messenger, no fellow traveller
who knew what happened? Such a one might tell
something of use.

135 **CREON.** They were all killed save one. He fled in terror
and he could tell us nothing in clear terms
of what he knew, nothing, but one thing only.

OEDIPUS. What was it?
If we could even find a slim beginning
140 in which to hope, we might discover much.

CREON. This man said that the robbers they encountered
were many and the hands that did the murder
were many; it was no man's single power.

OEDIPUS. How could a robber dare a deed like this
145 were he not helped with money from the city,
money and treachery?[16]

CREON. That indeed was thought.
But Laius was dead and in our trouble
there was none to help.

12. expiation (eks´ pē
ā shən) *n.*: Act of
making amends for
wrongdoing.

13. piloted (pī´ lət əd)
v.: Led or guided
through difficulty.

14. hearsay (hir´ sā)
n.: Rumor; gossip.

15. embassy
(em´ bə sē) *n.*: Impor-
tant mission or errand.

16. treachery (trech´
ər ē) *n.*: Disloyalty or
treason.

OEDIPUS. What trouble was so great to hinder you
150 inquiring out the murder of your king?

CREON. The riddling Sphinx induced[17] us to neglect
mysterious crimes and rather seek solution
of troubles at our feet.

OEDIPUS. I will bring this to light again. King Phoebus
155 fittingly took this care about the dead,
and you too fittingly.
And justly you will see in me an ally,
a champion of my country and the God.
For when I drive pollution from the land
160 I will not serve a distant friend's advantage,
but act in my own interest. Whoever
he was that killed the king may readily
wish to dispatch me with his murderous hand;
so helping the dead king I help myself.
165 Come, children, take your suppliant boughs and go;
up from the altars now. Call the assembly
and let it meet upon the understanding
that I'll do everything. God will decide
whether we prosper or remain in sorrow.

170 **PRIEST.** Rise, children—it was this we came to seek,
which of himself the king now offers us.
May Phoebus who gave us the oracle
come to our rescue and stay the plague.

[*Exeunt all but the* CHORUS.]

17. induced
(in dō̄ost′) *v.*:
Persuaded; caused.

Guide for Responding

◆ *Literature and Your Life*

Reader's Response Do you think Oedipus is a good king? Why or why not?

Thematic Focus What key problems does Sophocles introduce at the start of the drama?

☑ Check Your Comprehension

1. From what is the city of Thebes suffering?
2. How does Oedipus respond to the pleas of his people?
3. Who is Creon, and what was his mission?
4. What news does Creon bring back?

◆ Critical Thinking

INTERPRET

1. Is there any evidence of Oedipus' *hubris*—excessive pride—in this scene? **[Infer]**

2. Oedipus has two main interests in locating Laius' murderer. One is to lift the plague from Thebes. (a) What is Oedipus' second reason for wanting to bring the murderer to justice? (b) What is strange about this reason? **[Interpret]**

3. What is ironic—contradictory or surprising—about the priest's appeal to Oedipus as savior of Thebes? **[Analyze]**

APPLY

4. What does this excerpt from *Oedipus the King* suggest about the religious beliefs of the ancient Greeks? **[Generalize]**

EXTEND

5. Compare and contrast the characters of Oedipus and Macbeth as they first appear in their respective plays. **[Literature Link]**

Literary Connection

DRAMA

Two thousand years separate Greek tragedy from Shakespearean tragedy. Despite this gap in time and differences between ancient Greece and Elizabethan England, some elements of tragedy remain constant: a central character who through a tragic flaw and the action of fate is led to destruction.

1. What is the earliest evidence of Macbeth's tragic flaw?

2. In this scene from *Oedipus the King,* is there any evidence as yet of the central character's tragic flaw? Explain.

3. Compare the role of the witches in Act I of *Macbeth* with that of Apollo in this scene from *Oedipus the King.*

 Idea Bank

Writing

1. **Greece's Most Wanted** Write the script for an episode of a crime-fighting television show that reenacts the murder of Laius and offers a reward for further information.

2. **Journal of a King** As Oedipus, write a journal entry that chronicles the events of the day. Describe your reactions to events and include a plan of action for saving Thebes.

3. **The Tragic Flaw** Both Oedipus and Macbeth are brave and honorable men, yet something makes these good men evil. Analyze the use of the tragic flaw in presenting both men's characters. Who do you think is more evil? Should both men be brought to justice? Are their circumstances different?

Speaking, Listening, and Viewing

4. **Visual Presentation** In the Greek city-states of the fifth century B.C., drama was a central public art form and theaters were among the great architectural accomplishments. With a partner, research the ancient Greek theaters, and make a visual presentation to classmates showing the essential forms of the theaters. **[Art Link]**

Researching and Representing

5. **Greek Mask** Research Greek masks. From your findings, choose a design that you would like to imitate. Then, using cardboard, papier-mâché, or some other suitable material, create a mask like those worn by actors in ancient Greece. **[Art Link]**

Online Activity www.phlit.phschool.com

Writing Process Workshop

Although Shakespeare wrote *The Tragedy of Macbeth* about four hundred years ago, the elements that contributed to its success are still used by dramatists today. Write a drama in which you tell a story through your characters' dialogue and action.

The following skills will help you write a dramatic piece.

Writing Skills Focus

▶ **Complete a storyline diagram** to build a plot that hinges on a conflict and that has a logical sequence of events.

▶ **Develop characters** that are interesting and believable. Identify their traits and flaws, and have their actions and motives make sense within the play.

▶ **Write realistic dialogue** that fits each character's personality and background.

▶ **Use precise details** in stage directions to describe the settings in which the drama takes place. (See p. 363.)

The Tragicall Historie of the Life and Death of Doctor Faustus.

With new Additions.

Written by Ch. Mar.

Printed at London for *Iohn Wright*, and are to be sold at his shop without Newgate. 1631.

① Precise details in stage directions reveal such things as entrances, exits, actors' gestures, and sound effects.

② Marlowe's dialogue is written in blank verse, which closely approximates the rhythms of everyday speech.

③ This passage of dialogue reveals Faustus's thirst for power.

④ The last two lines of dialogue develop the plot: We learn that Mephostophilis came to Faustus of his own free will.

MODEL FROM LITERATURE

from *The Tragical Life and Death of Doctor Faustus*, by Christopher Marlowe

[Enter **MEPHOSTOPHILIS.**] ①

MEPHOSTOPHILIS. Now, Faustus, what wouldst thou have me do?

FAUSTUS. I charge thee wait upon me whilst I live,
To do whatever Faustus shall command, ②
Be it to make the moon drop from her sphere,
Or the ocean to overwhelm the world. ③

MEPHOSTOPHILIS. I am a servant to great Lucifer,
And may not follow thee without his leave.
No more than he commands must we perform.

FAUSTUS. Did he not charge thee to appear to me?

MEPHOSTOPHILIS. No, I came hither of my own accord. ④

Prewriting

Choose a Subject for Your Drama You may want to base your play on a story you've read, or you could continue in dramatic form a story that already exists. Other options are to write a drama about a historical event, an event you've experienced or witnessed, or a totally imaginary incident.

Create a Story-Line Diagram Since a play tells a story, it should have a plot, or sequence of events, that develops around a conflict. Create a story-line diagram like this one in which you plan the exposition, rising action, climax, falling action, and resolution.

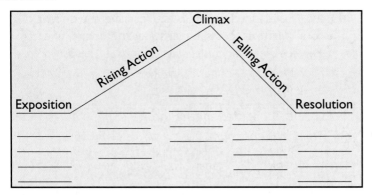

Jot Down Precise Details The setting, character descriptions, and notes about costumes, lighting, and sound effects all contribute to the effectiveness of a drama. Jot down some precise details about each of these aspects before you begin drafting.

Develop Interesting Characters Create a Character Trait chart in which you list characters' traits, habits, attitudes, and levels of intelligence. You might also jot down ideas about how each character might speak.

Drafting

Refer to Your Story-Line Diagram Review the plot events in your story-line diagram before you begin drafting. You may elect to write a scene involving the climax first, then write the surrounding scenes.

Let the Characters Take Over Put yourself in the place of each character, and, as you draft your drama, let the voice of each character "take over." Let each character's personality come through the words he or she speaks.

Use Precise Details Include concise stage directions that tell actors how to deliver their lines, what props to use, and what gestures to make. You may also include precise details about costumes, sets, lighting, and sound effects.

APPLYING LANGUAGE SKILLS: Formatting Drama

Although there is no single way to format a script the following tips will help you determine a style and follow it consistently.

(*Lights up.* **RONALD** *is revealed in the center of a sparsely furnished room.*) (1)

RONALD (2) Whew. It's a hot one. (3)

General Guidelines

1. Stage directions are usually italicized and appear in parentheses or brackets.

2. Dialogue is preceded by the character's name in boldfaced capital letters. A period or colon may separate it from the dialogue.

3. Following a character's name are lines of dialogue. These are the words that are actually spoken onstage.

Writing Application Review your draft and standardize the format of the script.

Writer's Solution Connection Writing Lab

For guidance, see the Proof-reading Checklist for Dramas in the Revising and Editing section of the Creative Writing tutorial.

Revising

Use a Checklist Use the writing skills listed on page 372 as a checklist to evaluate and revise your dramatic piece.

▶ Does one plot event follow logically from another?
  Review the events and rearrange those that are out of order.

▶ Does the dialogue develop interesting characters and further the action of the play?
  Reexamine your notes on each character and reveal his or her traits through dialogue. Cut out dialogue that isn't realistic, or that is unimportant to the action of the play.

▶ Have I used precise details to describe the setting, actors' gestures, costume, lighting, and sound effects?
  Replace vague or misleading details with precise details.

REVISION MODEL

(QUEEN ELIZABETH I *seated on the throne. She is surrounded by various writers of her court:* SIR WALTER RALEIGH, EDMUND SPENSER, and SIR PHILIP SIDNEY. *There is confusion, and voices are raised.* ①)

QUEEN. (*in a raised, aristocratic voice*) Silence!

SIR WALTER. ~~I'm sorry,~~ A thousand pardons, ② Your Majesty.

QUEEN Silence! ~~You will all be invited to the festival, but~~ ③ only one of you is to ~~go to the festival and~~ wear my favor. By tomorrow, submit your best verse to me, and I'll choose the victor then.

① These precise details were added to deepen the readers' understanding of the events.

② The phrase "I'm sorry" was changed to one more realistic for this era, situation, and character.

③ The writer changed the dialogue to add suspense to the plot.

Publishing

▶ **Internet** Post your writing on a message board for theater enthusiasts.

▶ **Drama Club** Have a local drama group act out your play.

▶ **School Literary Magazine** Publish your dramatic work for your peers to critique. Ask them to submit alternative endings to your play.

▶ **Classroom** With classmates playing roles, conduct a reading of your play.

Student Success Workshop

Real-World Reading Skills

Use Study Strategies for Reading Comprehension

Strategies for Success

When you are assigned texts to read in school, it's important to analyze and organize the information. By applying study strategies, you actively involve yourself with the material and will understand it better. Note taking, outlining, study-guide questions, mapping, and summarizing help you comprehend and remember what you've read. As you practice the following study strategies, note which ones work best for you.

Note-Taking Strategies As you read, summarize the most important text information, and where appropriate, include examples. You may use index cards to organize separate ideas and topics. Or you may organize your notes by using a mapping strategy, such as a diagram, to illustrate how complex ideas are related. Summarizing large sections of information in your own words using complete sentences will strengthen your note-taking skills.

Outlining Strategies An outline can also help you comprehend and remember reading assignments. Each idea in an outline is labeled with a roman numeral, capital letter, number, or lowercase letter to show the hierarchy of information. To make an outline, show topic areas with roman numerals, main ideas with capital letters, details that support the main ideas with numbers, and so on. (See sample outline.) Text heads and subheads may help you organize your outline.

Study-Guide Questions Many textbooks provide study-guide questions to help you focus your reading. Preview important points in the text by skimming these questions before you read. A study-guide question might ask you to explain a cause-and-effect relationship. To make

your own study-guide questions, skim the comprehension and critical thinking questions, look at heads, and note unfamiliar terms. Then write your own questions.

Apply the Strategies

Choose three different text samples—a newspaper article, work of fiction (short story or novel chapter), and textbook chapter.

1. For each sample, which study strategies would you choose to help you organize and remember the material? Why?

2. Apply the note-taking strategy to the textbook sample.

3. If you created an outline of the newspaper article, what would the first heading and subheading be?

4. Write a one-paragraph summary of the fiction piece.

✔ Here are situations in which using study strategies might help you:
▶ Preparing a book review
▶ Learning about new computer software
▶ Researching a term paper

Speaking, Listening, and Viewing Workshop

Any literary work—short story, poem, essay, or novel—can be read aloud or recited. Such oral performances of literature can enhance your understanding and appreciation of the work. Learning to evaluate and critique oral performances will help you become a better listener and will also aid you in giving an oral presentation.

Identify Artistic Elements To heighten the impact and mood of a work, writers use various artistic elements. A poet might use rhyme, rhythm, figures of speech, and sensory words. A writer of fiction might use dialogue, character development, or rising action building to a climax. An essayist might include persuasive or emotional language, well-organized text, and quoted source material.

If you were identifying the artistic elements in a poetry reading, for example, you would look carefully for elements like the following:

▶ Repeated sounds at the beginnings and ends of words
▶ The flow of the language
▶ Words and phrases that create vivid mental images
▶ Words or phrases that evoke one of the senses, such as taste or touch

Analyze Artistic Elements As you notice artistic elements, decide whether they are effective in conveying the meaning of the work. For instance, in listening to a poem, decide whether rhyme, or the lack of it, has an effect upon a poem. Is there a meter, or is the poem written in free verse? Determine whether the rhythm pattern of the poem enhances or detracts from the overall effect. If you notice figures of speech and sensory words, decide how these elements deepen the work's meaning. You can apply this same technique for analyzing and evaluating other literary works.

Evaluate the Performance When you listen to a literary work, you must apply valid criteria to evaluate the performance: Judge a work by reasonable standards. For example, if you are listening to a choral reading, you might notice volume, pauses and stops, and pitch. As you listen to a literary work performed, ask yourself these questions:

▶ Does the performer seem to have an understanding of the work?
▶ Does the performer help to clarify the work's meaning through intonation, gestures, and posture?
▶ Does the performance call attention to the work rather than to the performer?

Apply the Strategies

Work in small groups to choose a poem, essay, short story, or passage from a novel to read aloud. As a group, identify the artistic elements. Decide why the writer might have chosen them, and discuss how effective they are.

Each member should perform the work aloud for the group. After each has read aloud, others should critique the performance and offer suggestions for improving parts that seemed weak. Then each member should revise the performance based on the feedback given. Choose someone to give a final reading for the class.

Tips for Evaluating Oral Interpretations

✔ *Identify key artistic elements.*
✔ *Assess the performer's interpretation of the work.*

Test Preparation Workshop

Critical Reading | Forms of Propaganda; Fact and Opinion

Strategies for Success

The reading sections of certain standardized tests require you to recognize forms of propaganda and to distinguish between fact and opinion. Use the following strategies to help you answer test questions on these skills:

Be Aware of Propaganda Propaganda is a systematic promotion of certain ideas to promote a particular cause. It may appear in a number of forms, including advertising, political flyers, and editorials. Propaganda deliberately manipulates information to convince you of something. Look for exaggerated and unsupported statements that present a biased opinion. They do not tell you the whole truth. Look at the following example:

(1) More than 5,000 people voted last week in favor of building a new shopping center, but the opposition won out. (2) The margin of victory is irrelevant. (3) Those radical voters who opposed the center are obviously self-serving elitists who don't care about anyone but themselves. (4) This month's unemployment figures for Braden are 12 perdent, which represents an increase of some 3 percent over the figures for last year. (5) These figures mean that unemployment in Braden is worsening. (6) But the people who voted against the mall probably don't care about creating new jobs.

I Which of the statements can be labeled as propaganda?
A Statements 1, 2, 6   **C** Statements 2, 3, 6
B Statements 2, 5   **D** Statements 2, 4

Statements 1 and 4 state facts. Statement 5 is an interpretation, but it is supported by the facts in the selection. Statements 2, 3, and 6 are propaganda because they express opinions that are unsupported by facts. **C** is correct.

Distinguish Between Fact and Opinion

Facts—such as numbers, dates, and events can be verified independently by checking reliable resources. Opinions represent the way a writer feels and cannot be verified independently.

2 Which of the following statements in the passage represents an opinion?
A Statement 1   **C** Statement 4
B Statement 5   **D** Statement 3

Answers **A**, **B**, and **C** refer to statements that can be verified independently by checking reliable sources. **D** is correct because it expresses the writer's opinion.

Apply the Strategies

Read the following passage, and answer the questions that follow.

(1) The first new Tiger automobiles rolled off the assembly line at the Dearborn assembly plant on Monday. (2) The cars, which feature such luxury appointments as programmable destination mapping, retail at $48,000 each. (3) Nothing compares with the Tiger's luxury. (4) Tigers are available in 17 colors, ranging from Dark Midnight to Dazzle Red. (5) And they offer 37 percent better gas mileage over last year's model. (6) When you're behind the wheel of a Tiger, you're the envy of every driver on the road.

I Which statements might be considered propaganda?
A Statement 1   **C** Statements 2, 4
B Statements 4, 5 **D** Statement 3

2 Which statements represent facts?
A Statements 1, 6   **C** Statements 2, 5
B Statements 3, 4   **D** Statements 5, 6

King Charles I After the Battle of Naseby (June 14, 1645)

3

A Turbulent Time:

The Seventeenth and Eighteenth Centuries (1625–1798)

Methinks I see in my mind a noble . . . nation rousing herself like a strong man after sleep, and shaking her invincible locks.

—John Milton,
from Areopagitica

Timeline
1625–1798

1625   **1640**   **1655**

British Events

- **1627** Sir Francis Bacon's *The New Atlantis* is published. ▼
- **1628** William Harvey explains blood circulation.
- **1633 John Donne's** *Songs and Sonnets* published.
- **1633** George Herbert's *The Temple* published.
- **1635** Public mail service established.
- **1637 John Milton** publishes *Lycidas*.

- **1640** Charles I summons Long Parliament.
- **1642** English Civil War begins.
- **1646 John Suckling** publishes *Fragmenta Aurea*.
- **1647** George Fox founds Society of Friends (Quakers).
- **1648 Robert Herrick** publishes *Hesperides*.

- **1649** Charles I beheaded. ▲
- **1649** Puritans close theaters.
- **1649 Richard Lovelace** publishes *Lucasta*.
- **1649** Oliver Cromwell becomes Lord Protector.
- **c. 1650** Early newspaper ads appear.
- **c. 1650** Full-bottomed wigs come into fashion. ▶

- **1658** Oliver Cromwell dies.
- **1658** Puritan government collapses.
- **1660** Monarchy restored.
- **1660** Theaters reopened.
- **1660 Samuel Pepys** begins *Diary*.
- **1662** Royal Society chartered.
- **1663** Drury Lane Theater opens. ▲
- **1666** Great Fire of London.
- **1666** First cheddar cheese produced.
- **1667 John Milton's** *Paradise Lost* published. ▼
- **1668** John Dryden publishes *An Essay of Dramatic Poesy*.
- **1670** Covent Garden Market opens.

World Events

- **c. 1600** Japan: Kabuki theater developed. ▲
- **1614** North America: Dutch found New Amsterdam. ▼
- **1630** North America: William Bradford begins writing *Of Plymouth Plantation*.

- **1630** Boston founded by John Winthrop.
- **1635** Japan: All Europeans expelled.
- **1636** North America: Rhode Island founded by Roger Williams.

- **1640** India: English settlement established at Madras.
- **1640** North America: *Bay Psalm Book* published in Massachusetts.
- **1642** Holland: Rembrandt paints *Night Watch*.
- **1643** France: Louis XIV becomes king.
- **1644** China: Ming Dynasty ends. ▶
- **1650** North America: Anne Bradstreet's collection of poems *The Tenth Muse Lately Sprung Up in America* published.
- **1651** North America: William Bradford finishes *Of Plymouth Plantation*.

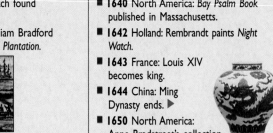

- **1661** Holland: Rembrandt paints *The Syndics*.

- **1662** France: Louis XIV begins building palace at Versailles. ▲
- **1664** North America: Britain seizes New Netherlands.
- **1664** France: Molière's *Tartuffe* first produced.
- **1666** Italy: Stradivari labels first violin.

British Events

- **1685** James II becomes king.
- **1687** Sir Isaac Newton publishes his *Principia*.
- **1688** Glorious Revolution.
- **1688** Bill of Rights becomes law.
- **1690** John Locke publishes his *Two Treatises of Government*. ▼
- **1702** First daily newspaper begins publication.
- **1707** Great Britain created by Act of Union.
- **1709** First Copyright Act.
- **1709** First literary magazine, *The Tatler*, begins publication.

- **1712 Alexander Pope** publishes *The Rape of the Lock*.
- **1714** George I becomes king.
- **1719** First organized cricket match takes place. ▼
- **1719 Daniel Defoe** publishes *Robinson Crusoe*.
- **1726 Jonathan Swift** publishes *Gulliver's Travels*.
- **1735** William Hogarth paints *The Rake's Progress*.
- **1745** Last Jacobite rebellion in Scotland.
- **1749** Henry Fielding publishes *Tom Jones*.
- **1751 Thomas Gray** publishes "Elegy in a Country Churchyard."

- **1755 Samuel Johnson** publishes *Dictionary of the English Language*.
- **1756** Britain enters Seven Years' War.
- **1766** Oliver Goldsmith publishes *The Vicar of Wakefield*.
- **1775** Actress Sarah Siddons debuts at Drury Lane Theater. ▼
- **1786 Robert Burns** publishes *Poems Chiefly in Scottish Dialect*.
- **1791 James Boswell** publishes *The Life of Samuel Johnson*.
- **1793** England goes to war with France.
- **1798** Admiral Nelson defeats the French off Alexandria, Egypt.

World Events

- **1680** Dodo becomes extinct.
- **1680** China: All ports open to foreign trade. ▲
- **1682** North America: La Salle claims Louisiana for France.
- **1690** India: Calcutta founded by British.
- **1703** Russia: Peter the Great begins building St. Petersburg.

- **1715** France: Louis XV succeeds to throne.
- **1721** Germany: Bach composes *Brandenburg Concertos*. ▶
- **1727** Brazil: First coffee planted.
- **1728** Pacific: Bering explores Alaskan waters.
- **1740** Prussia: Frederick the Great succeeds to the throne.
- **1748** France: Montesquieu publishes *The Spirit of the Laws*.
- **1752** North America: Benjamin Franklin invents lightning rod.

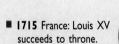

- **1759** Canada: British troops capture Quebec.
- **1773** North America: Boston Tea Party. ▲
- **1775** North America: American Revolution begins.
- **1784** France: First school for the blind established.
- **1789** France: Revolution begins with storming of the Bastille.

The Story of the Times
(1625–1798)

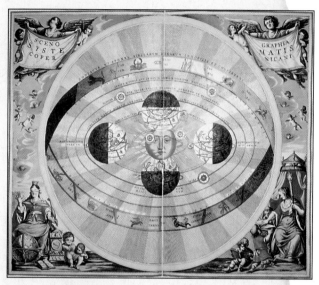

▲ **Analyze Primary Sources** By the seventeeth century the sun-centered solar system of Copernicus had gained greater acceptance. (a) What features of this Copernican map of the solar system reflect a scientific view of the universe? (b) What features tend to reinforce a reassuring "human-centric" perspective?

▲ **Interpret** (a) Describe the style in which Charles's execution is rendered in this picture. (b) How would the mood of the picture and your sense of the event be different if the picture were more realistic?

Historical Background

In 1649, the English shocked the world by beheading their king and abolishing the monarchy. Even in the decades before civil war tore England apart, revolutions in science and religion had unsettled people's world view. The new astronomy had exiled the Earth from the center of the universe to the vastness of infinite space: new religious creeds had brought down the traditions of centuries. John Donne wrote with his new found insecurity: "Tis all in pieces, all coherence gone." By the 1700's, though, a monarch was back on the throne, and a new, competitive society had sprung up, with a looser social structure and greater freedom in religion and politics.

Charles I and Parliament Charles I, crowned in 1625, clashed with Parliament frequently over a basic question: money. Charles needed money for his wars; Parliament refused to fund them. The king then extorted loans from his wealthy subjects and pressed the poor into service as soldiers and sailors. Parliament tried to prevent such abuses of power; Charles eventually dissolved Parliament, and would not call it into session for the next eleven years.

Charles I also turned up the flame under a simmering religious controversy. He insisted that clergymen "conform," or observe all the ceremonies of the Anglican Church. Puritans—Calvinists who wished to purify the Church of its Catholic traditions—were enraged by some of these requirements.

Radical Puritans believed that each group of worshipers, moved by the members' divinely granted consciences, had the right to choose its own minister—an idea dangerously close to democracy. For these and other ideas "dissenters" were persecuted and tortured as criminals.

The Civil War Charles's problems grew worse after he was forced to fight Scottish rebels outraged by his insistence on religious conformity. Desperate for money, he summoned a hostile Parliament, which passed wave upon wave of reforms. Angered when Charles tried to outmaneuver the reformers, Parliament condemned him as a tyrant in 1642. Civil war broke out. In 1645, Parliament's forces, led by Oliver Cromwell, defeated a royalist army and captured Charles. Radical Puritans, who by then dominated Parliament, tried the king and convicted him of treason. Charles I was beheaded on January 30, 1649.

Cromwell led the new government, called the English Commonwealth. Facing discontent at home and wars abroad, he dissolved Parliament in 1653 and named himself Lord Protector. Until his death in 1658, he ruled as a virtual dictator.

Civil war had not led to the free society for which many who fought against the king had hoped. Their idealistic hopes, coupled with economic hardships, led to social unrest. The Commonwealth also fueled popular discontent by outlawing gambling, horse racing, newspapers, fancy clothes, public dancing, and theater.

The Restoration By the time of Cromwell's death, England had had enough of taxation, violence, and disorder. In 1658, Parliament offered the crown to the exiled son of Charles I, who became Charles II in 1660. The monarchy was restored.

In sharp contrast to the drab Puritan leaders, Charles II's court copied the plush fashions of Paris. An avid patron of the arts and sciences, Charles invited Italian composers and Dutch painters to live and work in London. In 1662, he chartered the Royal Society, devoted to the study of natural science.

A Glorious Revolution Religious differences resurfaced with Charles II's successor, James II, a devout Catholic. Parliament eventually invited Mary, the Protestant daughter of James II, to rule England jointly with her husband, William of Orange. Rather than fight, James escaped to France. The people of England hailed the event as the "Glorious Revolution of 1688" since not a drop of blood had been shed.

In 1689, William and Mary agreed to respect a Bill of Rights passed by Parliament. The Bill guar-

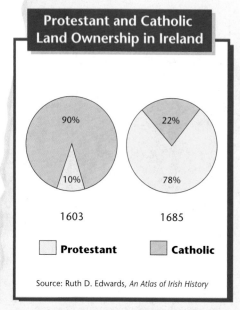

Protestant and Catholic Land Ownership in Ireland

90% · 10% — 1603
22% · 78% — 1685

☐ Protestant   ☐ Catholic

Source: Ruth D. Edwards, *An Atlas of Irish History*

▲ **Read a Chart** The religious differences that drove the Civil War also festered in Ireland, where English and Scottish Protestants took over Irish Catholic lands. Judging from the chart, what was the rate at which the native Irish were losing land to others?

▲ **Speculate** The *Encyclopedia* produced by the French writer Diderot (1772) aimed to be a compendium of all knowledge. Its emphasis on what could be known by reason, unassisted by faith, angered some religious thinkers. What sort of eighteenth-century reader would have referred to Diderot's massive work on human knowledge?

▲ **Infer** At the beginning of this era, the majority of people farmed the land. Judging from the painting, what was the role of women in farming during this period?

◀ **Draw Conclusions** After the mid-1700's, many people left farms and traveled to cities. What conclusion can you draw from this engraving about the conditions that met workers who came to the cities?

anteed Parliament the right to approve all taxes and forbade a king from suspending the law. England thus attained a limited, or constitutional, monarchy. In ensuing decades, two political factions crystallized in Parliament: the conservative, aristocratic Tories and the Whigs, drawn largely from Britain's growing merchant class. A cabinet of ministers drawn from Parliament, and eventually unified under the leadership of a prime minister, began to rule the country.

An Agricultural Revolution In 1660, the vast majority of the British people were farmers who rented their fields from a landlord or cultivated a patch of common land. By the late 1600's, new farm tools made it possible for farmers to plant and harvest a much bigger crop. Landlords began to fence in the land they had once rented out, hiring laborers to work the land for them. Bigger, more efficient estates replaced the small holdings of earlier times.

By the mid-1700's, British farms were producing much more food. With more food available, the population of the small island surged upward. Since fewer farmhands were needed, many people left the countryside. In the growing towns, they became the factory hands who ran the machines of the early Industrial Revolution.

The Industrial Age British inventions after 1750 made the spinning and weaving of cloth much more efficient. The steam engine was perfected and adapted to run a power loom. Factories were built to produce vast quantities of cotton cloth. Merchants sold the goods all over the world, adding more gold to the nation's coffers. As late as the 1790's, a majority of British people still earned their living as farmers. Yet the economic revolution of the 1700's increased Britain's wealth enormously.

The Enlightenment The scientific revolution that made industry possible stemmed from a larger development in thought known as the Enlightenment. Enlightenment thinkers in all fields believed that, through reason and observation of nature, human beings can discover the order underlying all things. In 1687, Sir Isaac Newton published one of the touchstone works of the Enlightenment, a monumental study of gravity and the movement of the planets.

By 1750, Britain was rapidly industrializing and the theories of the Enlightenment were eclipsed. Mills and factories belched smoke into the country air. Men, women, and children toiled at machines for twelve and fourteen hours a day. Poor people crowded into the towns and cities, unable to find regular work and barely able to survive. By the late 1700's, "progress" seemed to mean misery for millions. Writers and intellectuals began to lose faith in the ability of human reason to solve every problem.

Literature of the Period

The Schools of Jonson and Donne In his writing Ben Jonson (1572–1637) strove for the perfection and harmony he found in his beloved classical authors, turning away from the ornate style of Elizabethan times to create his own modern, strong voice. He wrote poems, plays, and masques (court entertainments). His critical opinion exercised a powerful influence on other poets of the time. Among the best-known "Sons of Ben" were Robert Herrick (1591–1674), Sir John Suckling (1609–1642), and Richard Lovelace (1618–1657).

John Donne (1572–1631) pioneered a new witty, cerebral style known as metaphysical poetry. Metaphysical poetry is characterized by the use of the intellect in the service of the imagination, drawing on science, philosophy, and legend for images. His poems are frequently structured like ingenious, subtle arguments. The most notable followers of John Donne were George Herbert (1593–1633) and Andrew Marvell (1621–1678). Herbert's best poems are the religious lyrics collected in *The Temple*. Marvell's best lyrics blend the metaphysical brilliance of Donne and the classical finish of Jonson.

The Puritan Writers Like Ben Jonson, John Milton (1608–1674) was a learned disciple of the Greek and Latin authors. He was also a profound Calvinist. In his later life, Milton set about composing an epic on Christian themes—a poetic act on an audacious scale. *Paradise Lost*, published in 1667, reflects Milton's humanistic love of poetry and his Puritan devotion to God.

John Bunyan (1628–1688) had little education beyond reading the Bible. A tinker by trade,

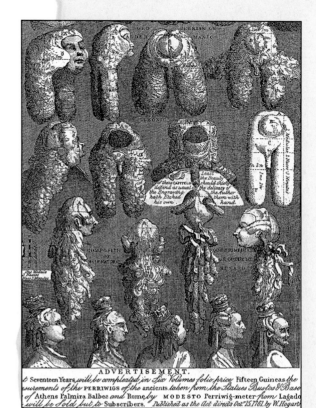

▲ **Speculate** After the Restoration in 1660, stark Puritan dress was replaced by new fashions. Middle-class men began wearing the wig that King Louis XVI of France had first popularized. What inconveniences might the wearers of wigs such as those in the picture suffer? Explain.

▲ **Speculate** By the end of the eighteenth century, England's middle classes had begun to come into their own. Newspapers sprang up to keep them informed; coffee houses like the one in the painting offered a place to read, meet, and socialize. Judging from this scene, what place do you suppose paintings had in the lives of middle-class people?

◄ Draw Conclusions
Alexander Pope's couplet attests to popular appreciation of Sir Isaac Newton's achievements: "Nature and Nature's laws lay hid in night: /God said, Let Newton be! and all was light." The artist depicts light rays in a distinctive manner. What ideas do they suggest about the spirit of science?

European Political Thinkers

Thinker	Major Ideas	Quotation
Thomas Hobbes *Leviathan* (1651) 	People are driven by selfishness and greed. To avoid chaos, they give up their freedom to a government that will ensure order. Such a government must be strong and able to suppress rebellion.	The condition of man [in the state of nature] . . . is a condition of war of everyone against everyone.
John Locke *Two Treatises of Government* (1690)	People have a natural right to life, liberty, and property. Rulers have a responsibility to protect those rights. People have the right to change a government that fails to do so.	Men being . . . by nature all free, equal, and independent, no one can be put out of this estate and subjected to the political power of another without his own consent.
Baron de Montesquieu *The Spirit of the Laws* (1748) 	The powers of government should be separated into executive, legislative, and judicial branches, to prevent any one group from gaining too much power.	In order to have . . . liberty, it is necessary that government be set up so that one man need not be afraid of another.

▲ Read a Chart Compare Locke's and Hobbes's notions of what drives human society.

Bunyan, like many others of the day, wandered from town to town in rural England, preaching wherever people would listen. After the restoration of Charles II, Bunyan was imprisoned, and it was there that he wrote *The Pilgrim's Progress*. The allegory tells the story of a man who flees sin to lead a holy life.

Literature of the Age of Reason Enlightenment writers discovered the qualities they admired most—harmony, restraint, and clarity—among the writers of ancient Greece and Rome, such as Homer, Virgil, and Horace. Neoclassical writers—English writers who imitated the styles of classical writers—often referred to the myths, gods, and heroes of ancient times. They favored generalities rather than the viewpoint of the individual, had a fondness for satires poking fun at society's follies, and often expressed their thoughts in aphorisms—short, quotable sentences—such as "The proper study of mankind is man."

From 1660 to 1700, a period known as the Restoration, John Dryden (1631–1700) dominated literature. Named poet laureate, England's official poet, by Charles II, he wrote celebratory poems, which hailed the achievements of humanity; plays; and satirical poems. His essays about drama and his other prose compositions represent the first modern prose.

Restoration Theater The Restoration was also noted for its plays, especially comedies. When Charles II became king, he reopened the London theaters. The Restoration theaters, fancier and more costly than those of Shakespeare's time, did a thriving business.

The Age of Pope and Swift The poetry of Alexander Pope (1688–1744), written in the early 1700's, is a shining example of neoclassical style, exhibiting wit, elegance, and moderation. All these qualities show forth in his most famous work, *The Rape of the Lock*, a satire on the war between the sexes. Pope also had enormous influence as a critic.

Jonathan Swift (1667–1745), a close friend of Pope's, was a scornful critic of the rising merchant class, whom he viewed as shameless money grubbers. In his great satires, *Gulliver's Travels* and *A Modest Proposal*, he presents human nature as deeply flawed, suggesting that moral progress must begin from a recognition of our intellectual and moral limitations.

The first English novel, *Robinson Crusoe* by Daniel Defoe (1660–1731), appeared in this period. This new form of fiction would, in the 1800's, become the favorite reading matter of the growing middle classes. England's first literary periodicals, *The Tatler and The Spectator*, also appeared in the early 1700's. Written by Joseph Addison (1672–1719) and Richard Steele (1672–1729), these one-page papers included crisply written reflective essays and news addressed to the middle classes.

The Age of Johnson Samuel Johnson (1709–1784) dominated his age not only by his writings but also by his conversation and acquaintanceships. A brilliant and inexhaustible talker, he was friendly with most of the writers, painters, and actors of his time. His wise advice helped nurture the careers of many younger talents. *The Dictionary of the English Language*, published in 1755, is his most important work. It is the first dictionary that could be considered a standard and authoritative reference work on English.

The Eclipse of the Enlightenment By 1750, Britain was launched on a course of rapid industrialization. Mills and factories began to belch smoke into the air of new towns. Inside, men, women, and children toiled at machines for over twelve hours a day. Every year more poor people crowded into the towns and cities, unable to find regular work and barely able to survive. By the late 1700's, the "progress" celebrated by Enlightenment thinkers seemed to be bringing misery to millions.

As they lost faith in the power of human reason, writers turned away from the standards of neoclassicism. Writing in the language of everyday life, writers such as Thomas Gray charged their poems with new emotion. The Age of Reason was coming to an end. Emerging new voices would make the 1800's a new literary age.

▲ **Draw Conclusions** In William Hogarth's *Signing the Marriage Contract*, one of a series of six paintings poking fun at British marriage customs, the fathers of the groom and the bride (both seated), and two lawyers discuss the bride's dowry—the property that she will give her new husband. Using the details of their dress, posture, and expression, draw conclusions about the characters' attitudes and Hogarth's opinion of them.

▲ **Speculate** Richard Wilson's (1714–1782) landscape paintings influenced the work of nineteenth-century Romantic painters such as John Constable and J.W.M. Turner. What feelings do the lighting and the view inspire in you?

The Changing English Language

NO HARMLESS DRUDGE, HE

by Richard Lederer

On April 15, 1755, Dr. Samuel Johnson—blind in one eye, impoverished, and incompletely educated—produced the first modern *Dictionary of the English Language*. "Languages are the pedigrees of nations," he proclaimed, and, in compiling his wordbook, Johnson conferred a pedigree on the English-speaking nations. In garnering the rich, exuberant vocabulary of eighteenth-century England, the *Dictionary of the English Language* marks a turning point in the history of our tongue.

Johnson's Firsts

Johnson set himself the task of making a different kind of dictionary, one of the first that would include all the words in the English language, not just the difficult ones. In addition, he would show how to divide words into syllables and where words came from. He would establish a consistent system of defining words and draw from his own gigantic learning to provide, for the first time in any dictionary, illustrative quotations from famous writers. Johnson's lexicon, like its modern descendants, is a report on the way writers actually used the English language.

Underfunded and working almost alone in a Fleet Street garret room, Johnson defined

some 43,000 words and illuminated their meanings with more than 114,000 supporting quotations drawn from every area of literature. Laboring for almost nine years, he captured the majesty of the English language and gave it a dignity that was long overdue.

Johnson defined a lexicographer as "a writer of dictionaries, a harmless drudge that busies himself in tracing the original and detailing the signification of words." However, he was obviously far more than a harmless drudge, and his two-volume dictionary was by far the most comprehensive and readable that had appeared. The reputation of the *Dictionary of the English Language* was so great that it dominated the field until the turn of this century.

dedication. A servile address to a patron

excise. A hateful tax levied upon commodities, and adjudged not by the common judges of property, but wretches hired by those to whom excise is paid.

gambler. (A cant word, I suppose, for game, or gamster.) A knave whose practice it is to invite the unwary to game and cheat them.

opera. An exotic and irrational entertainment.

parasite. One that frequents rich tables, and earns his welcome by flattery.

patron. One who supports with insolence, and is paid with flattery.

pensioner. A slave of state hired by a stipend to obey his master. In England it is generally understood to mean pay given to a state hireling for treason to his country.

Tory. One who adheres to the ancient constitution of the state, and the apostolical hierarchy of the church of England, opposed to a whig.

whig. The name of a faction.

Activities

1. How do these definitions (above) differ from those you would find in current dictionaries? For example, what can you tell about Johnson's political loyalties from his definition of Tory and Whig?

2. Reviewing Johnson's definitions, (above) write three definitions in his style.

3. Secure a copy from your school or local library of *Johnson's Dictionary: A Modern Selection*, edited by E. L. McAdam, Jr., and George Milne (Pantheon Books). Browse through it and report any interesting and unusual definitions to the class.

PART 1 *The War Against Time*

A Musical Garden Party (detail)
Metropolitan Museum of Art

Guide for Interpreting

John Donne
(1572?–1631)

Donne's life and poetry seem to fall neatly into two contradictory parts. Wild young "Jack" Donne wrote clever love poems read by sophisticated aristocrats. In later life, sober Dr. John Donne, Dean of St. Paul's and England's most popular preacher, published widely read meditations and sermons.

> *Contradiction and conflict were the stuff of Donne's life; they are also at the heart of his poetic style.*

As Jack or as John, in his writings Donne excelled at dramatizing—and wittily resolving—the contradictions of life.

Religious Conflict Donne, a distant relative of Sir Thomas More, was raised Catholic. In Queen Elizabeth's England, Catholics faced prejudice and restrictive laws. Though Donne studied law, he never obtained his degree, probably because of religious issues. Later, he abandoned Catholicism and joined the official church of England, the Anglican Church. To this day, scholars debate whether Donne experienced a genuine conversion or made a shrewd move to try to gain advancement in court society.

A Secret Marriage A highly educated young man, Donne served as private secretary to one of the queen's highest-ranking officials. Bright, clever, and charming, he secretly wed Anne More, his employer's niece, in 1602. Donne's marriage ruined his chances for social advancement.

The devoted couple lived for sixteen years plagued by poverty and illness, during which Donne managed to write widely read, influential poetry. He finally attained a secure position in 1615 when, at King James's insistence, he entered the clergy, becoming first a royal chaplain and then, in 1621, dean of St. Paul's Cathedral in London, where he served until his death.

A Modern Individual John Donne's reputation has changed over time. He was very popular during his own lifetime, but his writings soon went out of favor. At the beginning of the twentieth century, interest in Donne's poetry was rekindled. Perhaps this is because the conflicts Donne faced have a distinctively modern flavor. His family's faith and his secret marriage pitted the private man against the demands of the world. Society was no longer ready with clear answers to the question, Where do I fit in? Donne, in his contradictory life and complex poetry, had to invent answers on his own.

◆ Background for Understanding

HISTORY: DONNE AND THE SYSTEM OF PATRONAGE

There were no bestsellers, movie deals, or syndicated columns in Donne's time. Before the eighteenth century, a writer trying to make a living had to attract the patronage—money and other support—of a well-born person. In return, the writer might write on subjects chosen by or pleasing to the patron. The young Donne did not publish his poems (most were printed only after his death). Instead, they circulated among a select literary audience, which included patrons like the Countess of Bedford.

After Donne was dismissed from his position with Sir Thomas Egerton as a result of his secret marriage, he and his family depended in part on patrons for financial support. Eventually, Donne gained the patronage of Sir Robert Drury by writing an elegy on his fourteen-year-old daughter, who had died in December 1610.

◆ *Literature and Your Life*

CONNECT YOUR EXPERIENCE

When night falls in a strange and lonely place, solitary travelers become uneasy. By calling up a cheerful memory, repeating a parent's advice, or even by whistling a tune, many can keep their spirits up despite the night.

Donne is perhaps our greatest whistler in the dark. His poems confront the uncertainties of parting and death. Nimble-witted, he improvises extravagantly to fill the silence, inventing fresh answers to old doubts. Perhaps he shows, too, that the imagination is the only source of certainties.

Journal Writing Describe two ways in which people use their imagination to keep up their courage.

THEMATIC FOCUS: THE WAR AGAINST TIME

As you read, notice how Donne uses wit to turn the tables on separation and death, two of time's destructive effects.

◆ Build Vocabulary

LATIN PREFIXES: *inter-*

In "Meditation 17," Donne writes of the bell that, having rung, "intermits." The Latin prefix *inter-* means "between," "among," or "with each other," and *intermit* means "to put between," or "to pause."

WORD BANK

As you read, preview this list of words from the selections.

contention
piety
intermit
covetousness
profanation
laity
trepidation
breach

◆ Grammar and Style

ACTIVE AND PASSIVE VOICE

A verb expressing an action performed by the subject of a sentence is in the **active voice.** To express an action received by the subject, the verb is in the **passive voice,** which uses a form of *to be* with a past participle. In the following passage, Donne uses both active and passive voice:

Active Voice: God *employs* several translators;

Passive Voice: . . . some pieces *are translated* by age, . . .

◆ Literary Focus

METAPHYSICAL POETRY

Metaphysical poetry is characterized by the use of metaphysical conceits and of paradoxes. Metaphysical conceits are extended comparisons that link objects or ideas not commonly associated, often mixing abstract ideas and emotional matters. A paradox is an image or description that appears to contradict itself but that reveals a truth. Metaphysical poetry is also known for carrying the rhythms of conversational English into verse.

Donne's detailed comparison of two lovers to the two legs of a drawing compass in "A Valediction: Forbidding Mourning" is a metaphysical conceit. Donne uses paradox in "Holy Sonnet 10" when he writes "Death, thou shalt die." (How can the power of death die?) Whatever the conceits and paradoxes he expresses, Donne voices them in a forceful, conversational English that makes a poem into a dramatic speech.

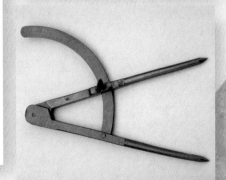

Reading for Success

Strategies for Constructing Meaning

As soon as you begin reading a work of literature, you are already constructing meaning. Is it a poem or a piece of nonfiction? Why did the author write it? What ideas are at work in it? What does it mean to you? As you read, you naturally ask and answer such questions to understand what you are reading. Here are a few strategies to help you sharpen these skills:

Recognize the speaker's voice and motivation.

The words of a literary work do not always directly represent the thoughts of the author. A work's speaker is often a special voice used by the author. The speaker can even be a fictional character, with motives that color what he or she says. Ask yourself about the speaker's motives for speaking, and identify the situation that gives rise to the speech.

Hypothesize.

As you read, ask yourself who the speaker is and what the situation is. Test possible answers as you read further.

Draw inferences.

Writers don't always tell you everything directly, but they often provide details from which you can infer their message. You need to "read between the lines" to uncover the ideas writers suggest but don't spell out.

Draw conclusions.

A conclusion is a general statement about a work that is supported by details in the text. A series of inferences can lead you to a conclusion. Drawing conclusions about a text helps you to understand the work as a whole and recognize its purpose.

Interpret the text.

Explain to yourself the meaning or the significance of what the author is saying. Figure out the author's perspective on the subject or on life.

Use your knowledge of the historical context.

The political climate and the intellectual trends of a specific time period are reflected in the writing that comes out of it. Apply the information from the introduction to this unit as you read the selections.

As you read "Meditation 17," look at the notes along the sides. The notes demonstrate how to apply these strategies to a work of literature.

Meditation 17

John Donne

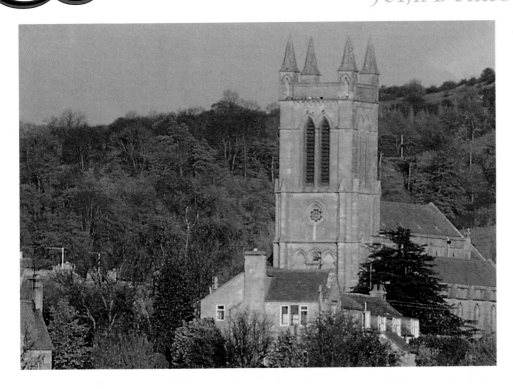

◀ **Critical Viewing**
The bells in this tower would ring on the occasion of someone's death, as Donne notes. On what other occasions might they ring? **[Deduce]**

Nunc lento sonitu dicunt, Morieris.
(Now, this bell tolling softly for another,
says to me, Thou must die.)

Perchance he for whom this bell tolls may be so ill as that he knows not it tolls for him; and perchance I may think myself so much better than I am as that they who are about me and see my state may have caused it to toll for me, and I know not that. The church is catholic,[1] universal, so are all her actions; all that she does belongs to all. When she baptizes a child, that action concerns me; for that child is thereby connected to that head

---

1. **catholic:** Applying to humanity generally.

Knowing the **histori-
cal context** enables
you to appreciate
how influential the
Christian church was
in Donne's time.

which is my head too, and ingrafted into that
body[2] whereof I am a member. And when she
buries a man, that action concerns me: all
mankind is of one author and is one volume;
when one man dies, one chapter is not torn out of
the book, but translated[3] into a better language;
and every chapter must be so translated. God employs several translators; some pieces are translated by age,
some by sickness, some by war, some by justice; but God's
hand is in every translation, and his hand shall bind up all
our scattered leaves again for that library where every book
shall lie open to one another. As therefore the bell that rings
to a sermon calls not upon the preacher only, but upon the
congregation to come, so this bell calls us all; but how much
more me, who am brought so near the door by this sickness.
There was a contention as far as a suit[4] (in which both piety
and dignity, religion and estimation,[5] were mingled) which of the religious orders should ring to
prayers first in the morning; and it was determined that they should ring first that rose earliest. If we understand aright the dignity of this bell
that tolls for our evening prayer, we would be glad
to make it ours by rising early, in that application, that it might be ours as well as his whose indeed it is. The bell doth toll for him that thinks it
doth; and though it intermit again, yet from that
minute that that occasion wrought upon him, he
is united to God. Who casts not up his eye to the
sun when it rises? but who takes off his eye from
a comet when that breaks out? Who bends not
his ear to any bell which upon any occasion
rings? but who can remove it from that bell which
is passing a piece of himself out of this world? No
man is an island, entire of itself; every man is a
piece of the continent, a part of the main.[6] If a
clod be washed away by the sea, Europe is the
less, as well as if a promontory were, as well as if
a manor of thy friend's or of thine own were. Any man's
death diminishes me because I am involved in mankind, and
therefore never send to know for whom the bell tolls; it tolls
for thee. Neither can we call this a begging of misery or a
borrowing of misery, as though we were not miserable
enough of ourselves but must fetch in more from the next
house, in taking upon us the misery of our neighbors. Truly
it were an excusable covetousness if we did; for affliction is a

When Donne writes
that the bell tolls for
"him that thinks it
doth" you might
interpret his meaning
this way: The antici-
pation of one's own
death is itself a spiri-
tual step towards
death and union with
God.

Donne's purpose in
using rhetorical ques-
tions is to achieve
the agreement and
engage the passions
of his audience.

---

2. head . . . body: The Church is both a head (a
spiritual leader) and a body (a group of the faithful).
3. translated: Carried across on a spiritual level
from one sphere to another.
4. suit: Lawsuit.
5. estimation: Self-esteem.
6. main: Mainland.

From Donne's explanation of how we can learn from another's suffering, you can **draw the conclusion** that Donne places such importance on the awareness of death because it helps detach us from this world, causing us to turn to God for security.

treasure, and scarce any man hath enough of it. No man hath affliction enough that is not matured and ripened by it, and made fit for God by that affliction. If a man carry treasure in bullion, or in a wedge of gold, and have none coined into current money, his treasure will not defray him as he travels. Tribulation is treasure in the nature of it, but it is not current money in the use of it, except we get nearer and nearer our home, heaven, by it. Another man may be sick too, and sick to death, and this affliction may lie in his bowels as gold in a mine and be of no use to him; but this bell that tells me of his affliction digs out and applies that gold to me, if by this consideration of another's danger, I take mine own into contemplation and so secure myself by making my recourse to my God, who is our only security.

Guide for Responding

◆ Literature and Your Life

Reader's Response Is suffering ever a good thing for people? Explain why you agree or disagree with Donne's idea that "affliction is a treasure."

Thematic Focus According to Donne, how does knowing that the bell tolls for you help you conquer time and suffering?

☑ Check Your Comprehension

1. On what occasions does the bell toll?
2. Why might someone not realize that the bell tolls for him or her?
3. According to Donne, what happens when a person dies?
4. Donne uses several conceits—extended comparisons—in "Meditation 17." In one conceit, he compares people to chapters in a book. Describe two other conceits he uses.

◆ Critical Thinking

INTERPRET

1. Why does Donne say the tolling bell applies to him as well as to others? **[Analyze]**
2. What does Donne mean by "No man is an island entire of itself; every man is a piece of the continent"? **[Interpret]**
3. (a) What is the difference between treasure, such as gold, and "current money"? (b) In Donne's metaphor, when does the "treasure" of affliction turn into "current money"? **[Analyze]**
4. Why does Donne say that contemplation of the tolling bell brings one closer to God? **[Interpret]**

APPLY

5. During World War II, Donne's phrase "No man is an island" was widely used as a slogan to justify Britain's joining the fight against Nazi Germany. How does this use of the phrase compare with Donne's intended meaning? **[Synthesize]**

Song

John Donne

Sweetest love, I do not go,
    For weariness of thee,
Nor in hope the world can show
    A fitter love for me;
5   But since that I
Must die at last, 'tis best
To use[1] myself in jest,
    Thus by feigned[2] deaths to die.

1. **use**: Condition.
2. **feigned** (fānd) *v.*: Imagined.

Yesternight the sun went hence,
10 And yet is here today;
He hath no desire nor sense,
    Nor half so short a way;
    Then fear not me,
But believe that I shall make
15 Speedier journeys, since I take
    More wings and spurs than he.

O how feeble is man's power,
    That if good fortune fall,
Cannot add another hour,
20 Nor a lost hour recall!
    But come bad chance,
And we join to it our strength,
And we teach it art and length,
    Itself o'er us to advance.

25 When thou sigh'st, thou sigh'st not wind,
    But sigh'st my soul away;
When thou weep'st, unkindly kind,
    My life's blood doth decay.
    It cannot be
30 That thou lovest me as thou say'st,
If in thine my life thou waste,
    That art the best of me.

◀ **Critical Viewing** How does the relationship of the man and woman in this painting compare with the relationship described in the poem? **[Compare and Contrast]**

Let not thy divining heart
    Forethink me any ill,
35   Destiny may take thy part,
    And may thy fears fulfill;
      But think that we
Are but turned aside to sleep.
They who one another keep
40   Alive, ne'r parted be.

Guide for Responding

◆ Literature and Your Life

Reader's Response Do you agree with the speaker when, in lines 17–24, he says we contribute to our own misfortunes? Why or why not?

Thematic Focus What assessment of time's power does Donne give in lines 17–20?

☑ Check Your Comprehension

1. What does the speaker say is his reason for leaving his beloved?
2. What does the speaker say happens when "bad chance" comes (lines 21–24)?
3. What does the speaker say may happen if his beloved worries about him (lines 33–36)?
4. How does the speaker suggest that his beloved view their parting (lines 37–40)?

◆ Critical Thinking

INTERPRET

1. To what remark of the speaker's beloved could this poem be a response? **[Infer]**
2. To what is the sun compared in stanza 2? **[Interpret]**
3. (a) Of what is the speaker trying to convince his beloved? (b) How would you outline the speaker's argument? **[Analyze]**
4. Why might the speaker have chosen to present his ideas in the form of an argument? **[Draw Conclusions]**

APPLY

5. The speaker in this poem uses exaggeration as a means of persuasion. Do you think that exaggerating in order to win an argument is a valid technique? Explain. **[Generalize]**

A Valediction: Forbidding Mourning[1]

John Donne

As virtuous men pass mildly away,
   And whisper to their souls to go,
Whilst some of their sad friends do say
   The breath goes now, and some say, No;

5   So let us melt, and make no noise,
   No tear-floods, nor sigh-tempests move,
'Twere profanation of our joys
   To tell the laity our love.

Moving of th'earth brings harms and fears,
10   Men reckon what it did and meant;
But trepidation of the spheres,[2]
   Though greater far, is innocent.

Dull sublunary[3] lovers' love
   (Whose soul is sense) cannot admit
15   Absence, because it doth remove
   Those things which elemented it.[4]

But we by a love, so much refined,
   That our selves know not what it is,
Inter-assurèd of the mind,[5]
20   Care less, eyes, lips, and hands to miss.

Our two souls therefore, which are one,
   Though I must go, endure not yet
A breach, but an expansion,
   Like gold to airy thinness beat.

1. valediction: Farewell speech.

2. trepidation of the spheres: Movements of the stars and planets that are inconsistent with a perfect circular orbit.

3. sublunary (sub´ lōō nər´ ē): Referring to the region below the moon, considered in early astronomy the domain of changeable and perishable things.

4. Those things . . . elemented it: The basic materials or parts of their love.

5. Inter-assurèd of the mind: Mutually confident of each other's thoughts.

25   If they be two, they are two so
    As stiff twin compasses[6] are two;
Thy soul the fixed foot, makes no show
    To move, but doth, if th'other do.

    And though it in the center sit,
30   Yet when the other far doth roam,
It leans, and hearkens after it,
    And grows erect, as that comes home.

    Such wilt thou be to me, who must
    Like th'other foot, obliquely[7] run;
35   Thy firmness makes my circle just,[8]
    And makes me end where I begun.

6. twin compasses:
The two legs of a
drawing compass.

7. obliquely: At an
angle; not straight.
8. just: True; perfect.

◆ Build Vocabulary

profanation (präf´ ə nā´ shən) *n.*: Action showing
disrespect for something sacred

laity (lā´ ət ē) *n.*: Those not initiated into the priesthood or other profession

trepidation (trep´ ə dā´ shən) *n.*: Trembling

breach (brēch) *n.*: Breaking open; the opening
created by a break

▶ **Critical Viewing**
The mapmaker
in the painting
holds a compass
like the one to
which Donne refers
in the poem. Using
the painted com-
pass as a clue,
describe the
picture "painted"
by Donne's meta-
physical conceit.
[Connect]

A Geographer, Johannes Vermeer

Holy Sonnet 10

John Donne

Death be not proud, though some have called thee
Mighty and dreadful, for thou art not so;
For those whom thou think'st thou dost overthrow,
Die not, poor death, nor yet canst thou kill me.
5 From rest and sleep, which but thy pictures[1] be,
Much pleasure; then from thee much more must flow,
And soonest our best men with thee do go,
Rest of their bones, and soul's delivery[2]
Thou art slave to fate, chance, kings, and desperate men,
10 And dost with poison, war, and sickness dwell,
And poppy,[3] or charms can make us sleep as well
And better than thy stroke; why swell'st[4] thou then?
One short sleep past, we wake eternally,
And death shall be no more; Death, thou shalt die.

---

1. **pictures:** Images.
2. **And . . . delivery:** Our best men go with you to rest their bones and find freedom for their souls.
3. **poppy:** Opium.
4. **swell'st:** Swell with pride.

◀ **Critical Viewing** The painting shows Lady Aston both when she is alive and when she is dead. Compare the relationship between death and life implied by the painting with that developed in "Holy Sonnet 10." **[Compare and Contrast]**

Guide for Responding

◆ *Literature and Your Life*

Reader's Response If you were the woman addressed by the speaker in "Valediction," how persuasive would you find his reassurances? Explain.

Thematic Focus From these two poems, what do you think were Donne's views on mortality—humans' time on Earth?

☑ Check Your Comprehension

1. In what manner does the poem's speaker in "Valediction" suggest that he and his beloved should part?
2. In what way does the speaker's relationship with his lover differ from relationships of other couples?
3. Whom or what is the speaker addressing in "Holy Sonnet 10"?
4. In what sense does the speaker in "Holy Sonnet 10" claim that death shall be no more?

◆ Critical Thinking

INTERPRET

1. Why might the speaker of "Valediction" be unwilling to announce their love to the general population (lines 7–8)? **[Infer]**
2. In the final stanza, the speaker in "Valediction" compares himself to the moveable foot of a compass and his love to the fixed foot. What might this comparison indicate about their relationship? **[Draw Conclusions]**
3. In "Holy Sonnet 10," how are lines 3–4 reinforced by lines 13–14? **[Analyze]**
4. (a) What does the statement "Death, thou shalt die" mean? (b) What makes it paradoxical? **[Interpret]**

COMPARE LITERARY WORKS

5. Compare and contrast the compass conceit in "A Valediction" with the imagery in lines 35–40 of "Song." Are they both examples of metaphysical imagery? **[Compare and Contrast]**

Guide for Responding (continued)

◆ Reading for Success

STRATEGIES FOR CONSTRUCTING MEANING

A Donne lyric is often like a speech from a little drama. You can better understand the poem by figuring out what is going on in the "play."

1. What can you infer about the speaker in this poem? (a) Who is he, to whom is he speaking, and what is the occasion? (b) What is his purpose in speaking?

2. What conclusions can you draw about the relationship between the speaker and the person he is addressing?

◆ Literary Focus

METAPHYSICAL POETRY

Metaphysical poetry challenges your intellect through paradoxes (contradictory statements) and conceits (unusual comparisons).

Donne's "A Valediction: Forbidding Mourning" contains a famous conceit. Donne compares two lovers who are temporarily parting to the two feet of a compass. The comparison is strange, but it is also strangely accurate. Picture a compass with the point fixed and the extension, with the pencil, circling around it. The "fixed foot" of the compass, as it leans, does seem to "hearken" after the moving one, just as the speaker's love will yearn after him when he is gone.

1. (a) Give one example of a metaphysical conceit from each of the following: "Meditation 17," "Holy Sonnet 10," and "Song." (b) For each conceit, explain how, despite the differences between the things being compared, the comparison "works."

2. (a) Give one example of a paradox from each of the following: "Song" and "A Valediction: Forbidding Mourning." (b) In each case, explain the sense behind the apparent contradiction.

3. The eighteenth-century writer Samuel Johnson complained that in metaphysical poetry, "The most heterogeneous [different] ideas are yoked by violence together." (a) Explain how Johnson's criticism applies to the conceit of the compass in "A Valediction: Forbidding Mourning." (b) What, if anything, is Johnson missing?

◆ Build Vocabulary

USING THE LATIN PREFIX *inter-*

Knowing that the Latin prefix *inter-* means "among," "between," or "with each other," define these words in your notebook:

1. intermingle   3. interact   5. interrupt

2. intertwine   4. interwoven

USING THE WORD BANK: Synonyms

Choose the lettered word or words closest in meaning to the first word:

1. contention: (a) gathering, (b) campsite, (c) dispute
2. piety: (a) devotion, (b) partiality, (c) roundness
3. intermit: (a) interfere, (b) pause, (c) deny
4. covetousness: (a) greed, (b) agreement, (c) sloth
5. profanation: (a) violation, (b) arson, (c) prediction
6. laity: (a) the uninitiated, (b) those who stand, (c) professionals
7. trepidation: (a) hunger, (b) fear, (c) calm
8. breach: (a) birth, (b) pants, (c) break

◆ Grammar and Style

ACTIVE AND PASSIVE VOICE

In the **active voice,** the verb expresses an action performed by the subject. In the **passive voice,** which uses a form of *to be* with the past participle, the subject receives the action of the verb.

Practice In your notebook, rewrite the following sentences in the active voice.

1. Their love is expanded by separation.
2. His soul is sighed away by her sighs.
3. His life's blood is weakened by her weeping.
4. It has been said that Death is mighty.
5. Life is not conquered by death.

Writing Application The passive voice tends to hide who did what to whom. That's why it is often used in press releases. As a public relations consultant for John Donne, write a statement about his recent dismissal from the service of Sir Thomas Egerton. Use five examples of the passive voice to disguise exactly what happened. For example, you might begin, "It was agreed that . . ." (Check Donne's biography on p. 390 for details.)

Build Your Portfolio

 ## Idea Bank

Writing

1. **Journal Entry** When parting, some draw out their goodbyes. Others may say as little as possible. Write a journal entry exploring the best way to say goodbye.

2. **The Lady's Turn** Write a poem in which the speaker's beloved in "Song" or "Valediction" answers his attempts to reassure her.

3. **Critical Response** The modern poet T. S. Eliot celebrated Donne as one of the best (and last) poets to integrate mind and heart: "A thought to Donne was an experience; it modified his sensibility [feeling and perception]." Evaluate Eliot's idea using examples from Donne's work.

Speaking, Listening, and Viewing

4. **Oral Interpretation** With a partner, rehearse reading two of Donne's poems. Practice reading the poems as dramatic speeches, and perform your reading for the class. **[Performing Arts Link]**

5. **Presentation of a Conceit** Analyze the movements of a common device, like a blender. Diagram a comparison of the device with human relations or feelings, and present your diagrammed conceit to the class. **[Art Link]**

Researching and Representing

6. **Sculpture of a Conceit** Make a sculpture of a metaphysical conceit by yoking together two things that seem to be different but really do belong together in some way. **[Art Link]**

7. **Map of the Universe** Create an annotated map that illustrates Donne's "trepidations of the spheres." **[Art Link; Science Link]**

Online Activity www.phlit.phschool.com

 ## Guided Writing Lesson

Speech

Many of Donne's poems are like little speeches for specific occasions. Graduation from school can be a very important occasion and is usually marked by speeches. Write a speech that you would like to give (or to hear) at your graduation ceremony. Use the following skill to give your speech unity.

Writing Skills Focus: Unity

A good speech, like most writing, has an introduction with a strong statement of the theme, a body, and a conclusion. Each part of an effective speech—one that can move or please an audience—is connected to the others in clear ways. Such a speech has **unity.**

To keep your speech unified, make sure that

- the introduction clearly introduces a main theme.
- the ideas in the body relate to the main theme.
- the conclusion sums up the development of the main theme in the body.

Prewriting Jot down memories from your school career and your hopes for the future. Draw on the connections between memories and hopes to identify your main theme.

Drafting Introduce your theme using humor or a story. Develop the theme in the body of the speech, supporting your ideas with examples. Use only those examples that relate to your theme. Leave out other details. Then write a conclusion summing up your insights.

Revising Verify that your introduction states your theme, that each paragraph in the body supports the theme, and that sentences within each paragraph support the topic sentence. Finally, be sure that your conclusion sums up your development of the main theme.

Guide for Interpreting

Ben Jonson *(1572(?)–1637)*

Not only did Ben Jonson's life have mythic proportions, but his physique did too. He was a large man with boundless energy and enormous courage. Coming from a working-class background, Ben Jonson became a friend as well as chief rival of Shakespeare and Donne.

> *From bricklayer to poet laureate, Ben Jonson's life story is a true "rags to riches" tale.*

Brilliant in his poetry and dangerous in a duel, a classical scholar and a veteran soldier, an astute critic and a brassy talker, Jonson's colorful, sometimes violent, career culminated with his being recognized as the most influential judge of literature, setting literary taste for a generation of poets.

A Poet at War Adopted in infancy, Jonson worked for his stepfather, a bricklayer, while attending the equivalent of high school under a private tutor. Too poor to study at a university, Jonson joined the army and fought in the wars for Dutch independence from Spain. A large, energetic man, Jonson at one point met an enemy champion in single combat before the massed armies of Holland and Spain. Jonson won.

Scandal and Success After returning to England, Jonson went on the stage as an actor. Despite his turbulent life—jailed for his part in a "slanderous" play, almost hanged for killing a fellow actor in a duel, and even suspected of plotting against the king— Jonson became a major dramatist. William Shakespeare acted in his first play, and noted acting companies performed his later plays.

Jonson was so successful that he was granted a handsome pension by King James I and treated as if he were poet laureate of England. Over the years he wrote masques—elaborate entertainments—for the royal court, where he was a favorite writer. He was also extremely influential, functioning as a virtual dictator over the literary efforts of the day.

A Lasting Influence Jonson's influence on writers is still felt today, and his plays, such as *Volpone* and *The Alchemist,* continue to be produced. What Jonson said of Shakespeare can be said of Jonson as well: "He was not of an age, but for all time."

◆ Background for Understanding

LITERATURE: THE SONS OF BEN

Historic accounts help us picture Jonson at the Mermaid Tavern, surrounded by admirers and engaged in duels of wit with Shakespeare. The best of the young court writers, including Robert Herrick and Sir John Suckling, flocked about Jonson, calling themselves the "Sons of Ben" or "Tribe of Ben."

Jonson's emphasis on graceful, balanced expression in verse shaped their work, offering an alternative to Donne's "rough" lines. Critic Douglas Bush writes, "Jonson demanded, and unceasingly strove for, the ageless classical virtues of clarity, unity, symmetry, and proportion." Jonson was the first English poet with a "school"; he was also the first to insist that poetry was in itself an important vocation. Shakespeare, who did not publish his plays, regarded himself as a working dramatist, a tradesman in words. Jonson, however, risked controversy by publishing his verse in the form of a "Collected Works"—a format previously reserved for theological or historical works.

As you read, note the examples of superb craftsmanship that inspired so many other poets to admire and imitate Jonson.

On My First Son ◆ Song: To Celia
◆ Still to Be Neat ◆

◆ *Literature and Your Life*

CONNECT YOUR EXPERIENCE

Memorable sayings are all around you—inscribed in rings and on mugs, emblazoned on T-shirts and bumper stickers, and printed on plaques and posters.

Ben Jonson probably would have understood this desire to preserve witty and profound sayings. He wanted his poems to contain truths that could be engraved in metal or carved in stone.

Journal Writing Jot down your favorite sayings, slogans, or words to live by.

THEMATIC FOCUS: THE WAR AGAINST TIME

One way to win the war against time is to create an image or make an observation that will hold true for all time. As you read these poems, think about how Jonson's unique and profound observations remain timeless.

◆ Build Vocabulary

ARCHAIC WORDS

Ben Jonson's poetry contains **archaic words**—words that are no longer in general use. Because these words appear frequently in classic English literature, it is useful to become familiar with them.

Pairs of Archaic and Modern Words: wast-was; wert-were; hast-have; hath-has; dost-do; doth-does; thou-you; thy-your; thine-yours

Before reading the poems, become familiar with these words.

◆ Grammar and Style

THE PLACEMENT OF *ONLY*

In crafting the line, "Drink to me only with thine eyes," Jonson carefully **placed the modifier *only*** to ensure that the meaning of the line was clear. For clarity, modifiers such as *only* should always be placed as close as possible to the words that they modify.

Example: Drink only to me with thine eyes (Gaze upon the speaker and upon no one else.)

Example: Only drink to me with thine eyes (Only gaze at the speaker, do nothing else.)

◆ Literary Focus

EPIGRAMS

An **epigram** is a short poem in which brevity, clarity, and permanence are emphasized. (*Epigram* is derived from the Greek word meaning "inscription," words preserved on a monument.)

Jonson sometimes uses statements that seem to go against common sense in order to give his work the little "twist" that makes it memorable. One such statement is "Drink to me only with thine eyes." How could the woman drink to the poet with her eyes but not with her mouth? The answer is, she can give him a loving look.

◆ Reading Strategy

HYPOTHESIZE

As you read, you can **hypothesize**—make informed guesses—based on the information that is given. Reading further, you encounter more information that either proves or disproves your hypothesis.

For example, when you read Jonson's line, "Farewell, thou child of my right hand," you might guess that the speaker is a father. When you reach the line, "here doth lie Ben Jonson his best piece of poetry," you realize that the speaker is also the poet.

On My First Son

Ben Jonson

Farewell, thou child of my right hand,[1] and joy;
    My sin was too much hope of thee, loved boy,
Seven years thou wert lent to me, and I thee pay,
    Exacted by thy fate, on the just[2] day.

5   O, could I lose all father,[3] now. For why
    Will man lament the state he should envy?
To have so soon scaped world's, and flesh's rage,
    And, if no other misery, yet age?
Rest in soft peace, and, asked, say here doth lie

10   Ben Jonson his best piece of poetry.
For whose sake, henceforth, all his vows be such,
    As what he loves may never like too much.

---

1. child. . . hand: Literal translation of the Hebrew name
Benjamin. Jonson's son was born in 1596 and died in 1603.
2. just: Exact.
3. lose. . . father: Give up all thoughts of being a father.

Ben Jonson

Song: To Celia

Drink to me only with thine eyes,
And I will pledge with mine:
Or leave a kiss but in the cup,
And I'll not look for wine.
5   The thirst that from the soul doth rise,
Doth ask a drink divine:
But might I of Jove's[1] nectar sup,
I would not change for thine.

I sent thee late[2] a rosy wreath,
10 Not so much honoring thee,
As giving it a hope, that there
It could not withered be.
But thou thereon did'st only breathe,
And sent'st it back to me;
15 Since when it grows and smells, I swear,
Not of itself, but thee.

---

1. **Jove's:** Jupiter's. In Roman mythology, Jupiter is the ruler of the gods.
2. **late:** Recently.

Guide for Responding

◆ Literature and Your Life

Reader's Response Do you think the speaker in "On My First Son" is wise in not wanting to love anything so strongly again? Explain.

Thematic Focus What attitude toward time and loss is suggested by lines 3–4 of "On My First Son"?

☑ Check Your Comprehension

1. In line 5 of "On My First Son," how does the speaker wish he could respond to his son's death?
2. To what does "Ben Jonson his best piece of poetry" refer?
3. What vow does the speaker make as part of his son's epitaph?
4. (a) In lines 5–8 of "Song: To Celia," what does the speaker say the soul requires? (b) What does he choose to fill this need?
5. (a) Why does the speaker send a wreath to Celia? (b) What happens to the wreath?

◆ Critical Thinking

INTERPRET

1. How would you explain the "sin" the speaker of "On My First Son" attributes to himself in line 2? **[Interpret]**
2. Why does the speaker say in lines 6–8 that an early death is enviable? **[Infer]**
3. In line 5 of "Song: To Celia," what is "the thirst that from the soul doth rise"? **[Interpret]**
4. (a) What do the images of love in the poem—eyes, drinks, and the wreath—have in common? (b) What does this suggest about love? **[Draw Conclusions]**

EVALUATE

5. In "On My First Son," is Jonson's way of presenting the speaker's grief effective? Why or why not? **[Criticize]**
6. (a) How much do you know about the speaker of "Song: To Celia" or his beloved? (b) How would more information affect your appreciation of his poem? **[Make a Judgment]**

Still to Be Neat

Ben Jonson

Still[1] to be neat, still to be dressed,
As you were going to a feast;
Still to be powdered, still perfumed;
Lady, it is to be presumed,
5   Though art's hid causes[2] are not found,
All is not sweet, all is not sound.

Give me a look, give me a face,
That makes simplicity a grace;
Robes loosely flowing, hair as free;
10 Such sweet neglect more taketh me
        Than all th'adulteries[3] of art,
They strike mine eyes, but not my heart.

---

1. **still:** Always.
2. **causes:** Reasons.
3. **adulteries:** Adulterations; corruptions.

Guide for Responding

◆ Literature and Your Life

Reader's Response Do you agree with the speaker about the attractiveness of a "spontaneous" look? Why or why not?

Thematic Focus In what ways do beauty regimes and fashion wage a war against time?

Questions for Research "Still to Be Neat" suggests that Ben Jonson found fault in some of the luxurious fashions of his day. Generate questions that could guide research on the subject.

☑ Check Your Comprehension

1. Does the speaker approve of the woman's fashion sense?
2. What sort of look does the speaker prefer?

◆ Critical Thinking

INTERPRET
1. What hidden causes might the speaker have in mind in line 6? **[Interpret]**
2. (a) How does Jonson use the repetition of words and word patterns in the first stanza to support his meaning? (b) How does Jonson adapt this structure in the second stanza? **[Analyze]**

APPLY
3. What trends in modern advertising can you connect with the attitude expressed in Jonson's poem? **[Relate]**

The Interrupted Sleep, François Boucher, The Metropolitan Museum of Art

▲ **Critical Viewing** Compare what the painting suggests about the attractiveness of artifice and disarray with the speaker's opinion in the poem. **[Compare and Contrast]**

Beyond ◆ Literature

History Connection

Ben Jonson and Renaissance Warfare

War was all too common in sixteenth- and seventeenth-century Europe, and Ben Jonson was not the only poet of the time with military as well as literary talents. The one story that survives of his battlefield adventures—his triumph over an enemy soldier in single combat—suggests that warfare was still governed by the laws of chivalry. However, by Jonson's time, the knights of the Middle Ages had been replaced by soldiers-for-hire and other professionals.

Victory increasingly depended on foot-soldiers. The knight's lance had met its match in the pike, a spear long enough to give a foot-soldier the advantage over a horseman. A knight's armor was also vulnerable to the long-

bows wielded by trained archers, to the cross-bows given to less experienced recruits, and to the latest innovation of violence, the musket.

The Spanish style of fighting dominated the battlefield. Disciplined columns of pikemen with musket-men at the corners would advance against the enemy. War in Jonson's time was less and less a matter of honor and skill, and more and more a question of discipline and sheer firepower. While Jonson the man was understandably proud of his wartime exploits, Jonson the poet devoted his pen to more peaceful subjects.

From the fact that Jonson's poetry was rarely preoccupied with battle, what conclusions can you draw about his attitude toward his own military exploits?

Guide for Responding (continued)

◆ Reading Strategy

HYPOTHESIZE

As you read Ben Jonson's poems, you **hypothe-sized** by forming and testing ideas about the situation and the speaker.

Reenact this process for "On My First Son" by answering these questions.

1. Using only lines 1–4, make a hypothesis about the situation and the speaker's relationship with his son.
2. Do lines 5–8 require you to modify your hypothesis about the speaker's feelings for his son? Why or why not?
3. Basing your answer on lines 11–12, what final hypothesis can you make about the speaker's feelings for his son?

◆ Grammar and Style

THE PLACEMENT OF *ONLY*

As you can see in the first line of "Song: To Celia," it's important to **place the modifier *only*** as close as possible to the word that it modifies. When *only* is misplaced, it can confuse or mislead the reader.

Practice In your notebook, add the word *only* to the following sentences to reflect the meaning indicated in parentheses.

1. Drink to me with thine eyes. (just to me, no one else)
2. Drink to me with thine eyes. (use your eyes, no one else's)
3. Drink to me with thine eyes. (drink to me using just your eyes)
4. They strike mine eyes. (they, and no others)
5. They strike mine eyes. (only my eyes, not my heart)

Writing Application Write a paragraph about Ben Jonson, using biographical information from page 404. In your paragraph, use the modifier *only* at least twice.

◆ Literary Focus

EPIGRAMS

Jonson's poems are **epigrams** because they are brief and witty, expressing truths in a memorable fashion. In "Still to Be Neat," for example, Jonson uses parallel phrases ("Still to be neat, still to be dressed") that are elegant and easy to remember. In addition, phrases like "sweet neglect" grab your attention and linger in your mind because they seem to be contradictory. Yet when you puzzle them out, they contain a hidden truth.

1. Find two additional examples of parallelism in the first stanza of "Still to Be Neat."
2. Explain how the phrase "sweet neglect" appears to violate common sense but really doesn't.
3. What gives the first stanza of "Song: To Celia" an epigrammatic quality?
4. Identify and explain the paradoxical sentiment expressed in the final line of "On My First Son."
5. (a) Would "On My First Son" be suitable for putting on the subject's gravestone? Explain. (b) Why do some epigrams make good epitaphs?

◆ Build Vocabulary

USING ARCHAIC WORDS

Use your knowledge of **archaic words** to "translate" the following passage from Jonson's "To the Memory of My Beloved Master, William Shakespeare" into modern English. Remember that *hast* and *hath* are present tenses of *have, dost* and *doth* are present tenses of *do,* and *wast* and *wert* are past tenses of *be.* Thy and *thine* indicate possession, and *thou* and *thee* are subjective and objective pronouns.

> For, if I thought my judgment were of years,
> I should commit thee surely with thy peers,
> And tell, how far thou didst our Lyly
>   outshine,
> Or sporting Kyd, or Marlowe's mighty line.
> And though thou hadst small Latin, and less
>   Greek,
> From thence to honor thee, I would not seek
> For names; but call forth thund'ring
>   Aeschylus . . .

Build Your Portfolio

 ## Idea Bank

Writing

1. **T-shirt Saying** These days, epigrammatic statements are found on T-shirts as well as on monuments. Jot down two or three brief, insightful statements that would be worthy of capturing on a T-shirt.

2. **Fashion Essay** In "Still to Be Neat," Jonson reveals his views on fashion. What would Jonson have to say about fashion in today's world? Capture his views in a brief essay.

3. **Literary Analysis** Reread "On My First Son" carefully. Analyze the poem's structure, rhyme scheme, and imagery, and evaluate how these elements help convey heart-wrenching emotion.

Speaking, Listening, and Viewing

4. **Love Song** With a group, write a modern version of "Song: To Celia," set it to music, and perform it for your class. **[Music Link; Performing Arts Link]**

5. **Fashion Debate** Form a small group, and collect images of "natural" styles (grunge, afros) versus artificial styles (punk, permed hair) to present to your class. Then debate the merits of each style with classmates. **[Social Studies Link]**

Researching and Representing

6. **Sons of Ben** Obtain pictures of the writers who called themselves the "Sons of Ben." Then draw a scene depicting all the writers sitting together, discussing their art. **[Art Link]**

7. **Biographical Report** Research and write a biographical report on Jonson's colorful life and career. Using several sources, reconstruct his personality as well as the events of his life. **[Social Studies Link]**

Online Activity www.phlit.phschool.com

 ## Guided Writing Lesson

Persuasive Letter

In "Still to Be Neat," Jonson delivers strong opinions about artificial styles that have gotten out of hand. Write a letter to your school newspaper in which you reveal your opinions on a similar subject.

As Jonson does in his poem, use elaboration to support your opinions. Gather evidence through research.

Writing Skills Focus: Elaboration to Support an Argument

An argument—in a courtroom, in a newspaper column, or in a professional journal—will not be persuasive unless the writer uses **elaboration** to support it. Elaboration may include:

• Evidence in the form of facts, statistics, experiences, and quotations
• Answers to counterarguments
• Freshly and succinctly stated ideas

Prewriting Jot down your opinions about contemporary fashion. Also jot down some counterarguments. Do research in various resources, including the Internet, to find statistics and other evidence to support your argument. You may also take a poll and use the results as supporting data.

Drafting Begin your letter with the date and the salutation "To the Editor." Weave together your argument using the evidence you collected. Include evidence intended to destroy the counterargument. Close the letter with your name and signature.

Revising Make sure you have followed the proper format for a letter. Use elaboration to strengthen arguments that you haven't supported. Reword any phrases that sound stale, and delete examples of wordiness. Proofread your letter carefully before sending it to your school newspaper.

Guide for Interpreting

Andrew Marvell (1621–1678)

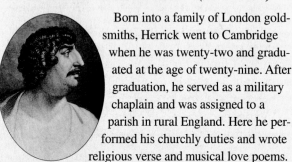

Marvell showed an extraordinary ability to adjust to the realities of his turbulent time. Although he was the son of a Puritan minister and frowned on the abuses of the monarch, he enjoyed close friendships with supporters of Charles I in the king's dispute with the largely Puritan Parliament.

Several years later, however, he worked for Lord Fairfax, the commanding general of the antiroyalist Parliamentary army. Still later, Marvell tutored the ward of Oliver Cromwell, leader of the Puritan rebellion and ruler of England. Obviously capable, Marvell gained the attention and sponsorship of the great English poet John Milton. Eventually he served as Milton's assistant.

In 1659, after Cromwell's death and shortly before Charles II was restored, Marvell was elected the Member of Parliament from Hull. He served in that position until his death, almost twenty years later.

Robert Herrick (1591–1674)

Born into a family of London goldsmiths, Herrick went to Cambridge when he was twenty-two and graduated at the age of twenty-nine. After graduation, he served as a military chaplain and was assigned to a parish in rural England. Here he performed his churchly duties and wrote religious verse and musical love poems.

Though not politically active, Herrick was evicted from his parish by the Puritans and allowed back only with the Restoration of Charles II. While barred from his church, Herrick returned to his native and much-loved London and published his poetry—his religious verse in *Noble Numbers* and his other poems in *Hesperides*, an ancient Greek name for a garden at the edge of the world.

Published during a turbulent time, Herrick's light verses were ignored by his contemporaries; however, these verses are highly regarded today.

Sir John Suckling (1609–1642)

In some ways, Sir John Suckling lived a life more romantic than those of Marvell and Herrick. A privileged young courtier, Suckling inherited his vast estates when he was only eighteen, and he later served as a gentleman in the privy chamber of Charles I. Praised as the cleverest of conversationalists, Suckling was said to be able to compose a poem at a moment's notice. He incorporated some of his best lyrics, including the poem "Song," into plays that he lavishly produced at his own expense.

Suckling's military exploits proved less successful than his poems, however. The cavalry troop he raised and lavishly uniformed for the king was defeated in Scotland, and Suckling was mocked for caring more about his men's uniforms than about their military performance. After joining a failed Cavalier plot to rescue a royal minister from prison, he fled to France, where he died in despair at the age of thirty-three.

◆ Background for Understanding

LANGUAGE: WORD PLAY AND WIT

By the seventeenth century, English had become a fluid combination of Anglo-Saxon, Gaelic, Latin, and French. As such, English was far more than a language of basic communication. Through it, one could express philosophical ideas, convey abstract theories, and create humorous word play.

Shakespeare excelled in brilliant word-play, sometimes losing himself in a labyrinth of puns. Following Shakespeare's lead, seventeenth-century poets took up the witty "*sword*play" of humor.

As you read these poems, look for examples of witty word play: puns, putdowns, and clowning.

◆ *Literature and Your Life*

CONNECT YOUR EXPERIENCE

It's easy for students to feel that, with studying for tests and preparing for graduation, life is one, big, totally booked schedule. If there's no time anymore for enjoyment, maybe it's time to add enjoyment to the schedule.

That's exactly the message that these poets convey as they urge you to hurry up and—have fun!

Journal Writing Note some things you enjoy doing—like having a long talk with a friend—but haven't had time for lately.

THEMATIC FOCUS: THE WAR AGAINST TIME

These poems were written during a troubled era of English history. Look for evidence of that trouble in the urgency with which these writers plead for fun and happiness.

◆ Build Vocabulary

RELATED WORDS: FORMS OF *PRIME*

When Herrick refers to a person's "prime," he means both the first and the most important years. (The word comes from a Latin word meaning "first in importance" or "first in time.") Similarly, the noun *primer* refers to "a first or earliest textbook," and the adjective *primary* can mean "most important" or "earliest."

WORD BANK

Before you read, preview this list of words from the poems.

coyness
amorous
languish
prime
wan

◆ Grammar and Style

IRREGULAR FORMS OF ADJECTIVES

Herrick's poem contains adjectives whose comparative and superlative forms are **irregular**—they do not add *-er* or *-est* and are not preceded by *more* or *most*. Following are common examples:

Positive Form	Comparative	Superlative
good	better	best
bad	worse	worst

This line from the poem contains the superlative form of the adjective *good*: "That age is *best* which is the first . . ."

◆ Literary Focus

CARPE DIEM THEME

The imperative "Gather ye rosebuds while ye may" from Robert Herrick's "To the Virgins" best expresses the **carpe diem theme** (kär´ pē dē´ em). This theme—*carpe diem* is Latin for "seize the day"—permeates world literature and has come to mean "Time is fleeting, so enjoy life."

In reading these poets, look for the playful imperatives that are a sign of this theme: "Let us . . . tear our pleasures" (Marvell); "use your time . . ." (Herrick); "Quit, quit, for shame . . ." (Suckling).

◆ Reading Strategy

INFER SPEAKERS' ATTITUDES

A poem's **speaker**, who may or may not be the poet, usually expresses a certain **attitude** toward the subject or toward the person he or she is addressing. You can infer this attitude, and better understand the poem, by focusing on the words, images, and rhythms the speaker uses.

In "Song," for example, words like "Nothing" and "The devil" signal the speaker's impatience with his friend's love-sickness:

> If of herself she will not love,/Nothing can make her:/The devil take her!

Notice, too, how the clipped rhythms of the last two lines suggest the speaker's exasperation with the whole business.

To His Coy Mistress

Andrew Marvell

Had we but world enough, and time,
This coyness lady were no crime.
We would sit down, and think which way
To walk, and pass our long love's day.
5   Thou by the Indian Ganges' side
Should'st rubies find; I by the tide
Of Humber[1] would complain. I would
Love you ten years before the Flood,
And you should if you please refuse
10   Till the conversion of the Jews.[2]
My vegetable love should grow
Vaster than empires, and more slow;
An hundred years should go to praise
Thine eyes, and on thy forehead gaze;
15   Two hundred to adore each breast,
But thirty thousand to the rest;
An age at least to every part,
And the last age should show your heart.
For, lady, you deserve this state,[3]
20   Nor would I love at lower rate.
    But at my back I always hear
Time's wingèd chariot hurrying near:
And yonder all before us lie
Deserts of vast eternity.
25   Thy beauty shall no more be found,
Nor, in thy marble vault, shall sound
My echoing songs; then worms shall try
That long-preserved virginity,
And your quaint honor turn to dust,
30   And into ashes all my lust:
The grave's a fine and private place,
But none I think do there embrace.

1. **Humber:** River flowing through Hull, Marvell's home town.

2. **conversion of the Jews:** According to Christian tradition, the Jews were to be converted immediately before the Last Judgment.

3. **state:** Dignity.

Now therefore, while the youthful hew
Sits on thy skin like morning dew,
35 And while thy willing soul transpires[4]
At every pore with instant fires,
Now let us sport us while we may,
And now, like <u>amorous</u> birds of prey,
Rather at once our time devour
40 Than <u>languish</u> in his slow-chapped[5] power.
Let us roll all our strength, and all
Our sweetness, up into one ball,
And tear our pleasures with rough strife
Thorough[6] the iron gates of life:
45 Thus, though we cannot make our sun
Stand still, yet we will make him run.

4. **transpires:**
Breathes out.

5. **slow-chapped:**
Slow-jawed.

6. **thorough:**
Through.

◆ **Build Vocabulary**

coyness (koi′ nis) *n.*: Reluctance to make
a commitment

amorous (am′ ə res) *adj.*: Full of love

languish (laŋ′ gwish) *v.*: To become weak; droop

Guide for Responding

◆ *Literature and Your Life*

Reader's Response What is your impression
of the speaker in this poem? How would you
respond to him?

Thematic Response Explain how the message
of Marvell's poem is suited to the turbulent time
in which it was written.

☑ Check Your Comprehension

1. Under what conditions would the lady's coyness
not be a crime?
2. What would the speaker do if time weren't
an issue?
3. Why is the speaker anxious?
4. What does the speaker conclude that he and
his coy mistress should do?

◆ **Critical Thinking**

INTERPRET

1. How would you define the speaker's attitude
toward time? **[Interpret]**
2. Point to the word pictures and to the comparisons that convey the slow or rapid passage
of time. **[Analyze]**
3. Explain the role that each of the poem's sections
(lines 1–20, 21–32, and 33–46) plays in the
poem's "argument." **[Draw Conclusions]**

COMPARE LITERARY WORKS

4. Compare the attitude toward love found in
Marvell's "To His Coy Mistress" with that found
in Ben Jonson's "Song: To Celia." Characterize
each in terms of their realism and idealism.
[Compare and Contrast]

To the Virgins, to Make to Much of Time

Robert Herrick

Three Ladies Adorning a Term of Hymen, Sir Joshua Reynolds
The Tate Gallery, London

◀ **Critical Viewing**
In what ways do the women in this painting, created more than a century after Herrick's poem was written, express the carpe diem theme? **[Infer]**

Gather ye rosebuds while ye may,
    Old time is still a-flying;
And this same flower that smiles today
    Tomorrow will be dying.

5   The glorious lamp of heaven, the sun,
    The higher he's a-getting,
The sooner will his race be run,
    And nearer he's to setting.

That age is best which is the first,
10   When youth and blood are warmer:
But being spent, the worse, and worst
    Times still succeed the former.

Then be not coy, but use your time,
    And, while ye may, go marry;
15 For, having lost but once your <u>prime</u>,
    You may forever tarry.[1]

---

1. tarry (tar´ē) *v.*: Delay.

◆ **Build Vocabulary**

prime (prīm) *n.*: Best stage of time

Song

Sir John Suckling

Why so pale and <u>wan</u>, fond lover?
    Prithee, why so pale?
Will, when looking well can't move her,
    Looking ill prevail?
5   Prithee, why so pale?

Why so dull and mute, young sinner?
    Prithee, why so mute?
Will, when speaking well can't win her,
    Saying nothing do't?
10   Prithee, why so mute?

Quit, quit, for shame; this will not move,
    This cannot take her.
If of herself she will not love,
    Nothing can make her:
15   The devil take her!

◆ **Build Vocabulary**

wan (wän) *adj.*: Sickly pale; faint or weak

Guide for Responding

◆ Literature and Your Life

Reader's Response What experiences, past, present, or future, do these poems call to mind?

Thematic Focus Why might finding love become more important in times of war and uncertainty?

Group Activity In a small group, identify songs you know that express the *carpe diem* theme.

Journal Writing Describe a situation in which you might give advice to a friend similar to the advice given by the speaker of "Song."

☑ Check Your Comprehension

1. What advice does the speaker in Herrick's poem give the young women in lines 1–4?
2. What warning does this speaker issue in lines 13–16?
3. In "Song," whom is the speaker addressing?
4. How is the lover described in the first stanza of "Song"? In the second stanza?
5. What advice does the speaker in "Song" give in the final stanza?

Guide for Responding *(continued)*

◆ Critical Thinking

INTERPRET

1. How does Herrick use images in lines 1–4 to convey the idea of passing time? **[Interpret]**
2. What attitude toward age does the speaker in Herrick's poem reveal in lines 9–12? **[Analyze]**
3. In "Song," what has caused the lover's pale, wan appearance and dull, mute behavior? **[Infer]**
4. What attitude toward love does the third stanza of "Song" reflect? **[Draw Conclusions]**

EXTEND

5. How does "Song" differ from other poems about unrequited, unreturned love? **[Literature Link]**

◆ Reading Strategy

INFER SPEAKERS' ATTITUDES

To **infer the speaker's attitude** toward the subject of the poem or the person being addressed, make educated guesses based on imagery, word choice, and rhythm. For example, the ridiculous images in lines 1–20 of "To His Coy Mistress" suggest that the speaker is humorously exaggerating his lover's delay.

1. (a) Find three vivid verbs that convey the speaker's attitude toward love in lines 37–46 of "To His Coy Mistress." (b) Explain this attitude.
2. Explain where and in what way the speaker's attitude in Suckling's "Song" undergoes a change.
3. Choose two of these poems, and compare the speakers' attitudes toward love.

◆ Literary Focus

CARPE DIEM THEME

"To His Coy Mistress" and "To the Virgins, to Make Much of Time" are probably the best-known English poems expressing the **carpe diem theme**, which urges people to enjoy life while they can.

1. Which line or lines in each poem most memorably express the *carpe diem* theme? Explain.
2. Of the two poems, which do you find more persuasive in its *carpe diem* message? Why?
3. Suckling's "Song" has a different take on this theme. Explain how it conforms with yet deviates from the traditional meaning of the theme.

◆ Build Vocabulary

USING RELATED FORMS OF *PRIME*

Knowing that the root of *prime* means "first in importance" or "first in time," define the italicized forms of the word in these sentences.

1. The Democrats will hold a *primary* election.
2. Marvell wrote the poem while still in his *prime*.
3. Who is the *prime* minister of Great Britain?
4. Every television star wants a *prime*-time show.
5. In earlier years, schoolchildren used *primers*.

USING THE WORD BANK: True or False?

In your notebook, indicate whether each statement is true or false.

1. When a person turns purple with rage, his or her cheeks are quite <u>wan</u>.
2. *The <u>Prime</u> of Miss Jean Brodie* is probably about a woman on her deathbed.
3. A plant without water may <u>languish</u>.
4. An <u>amorous</u> couple will probably hug and kiss.
5. A person's <u>coyness</u> indicates that he or she is one-hundred percent committed.

◆ Grammar and Style

IRREGULAR FORMS OF ADJECTIVES

By using a few common **irregular forms of adjectives,** the speaker in Herrick's poem demonstrates a knowing assurance. Irregular comparative and superlative forms of adjectives do not end in -er or -est and are not preceded by *more* or *most*.

Practice Identify the comparative or superlative form of each irregular adjective.

> That age is best which is the first / When youth and blood are warmer; / But being spent, the worse, and worst / Times still succeed the former.

Writing Application In your notebook, correct errors in irregular forms of adjectives.

1. Herrick's speaker feels that the most best time to marry is in one's prime.
2. He says that old age is worser than youth.
3. In "Song," the speaker suggests that the bestest thing to do is to find someone else.
4. All three poems imply that one of the baddest things you can do is to waste time.

Build Your Portfolio

 Idea Bank

Writing

1. **Persuasive Essay** Write a brief persuasive essay for your school yearbook, convincing readers to "seize the day."

2. **Advice Column** Rewrite one of these poems as an advice columnist's letter. Change the language as appropriate, but continue to express the poem's basic ideas.

3. **Comparison-and-Contrast Essay** Compare and contrast "Song" with "To the Virgins" or "To His Coy Mistress." Citing specific examples from the poems, discuss theme, rhythm, imagery, and speakers' attitudes.

Speaking, Listening, and Viewing

4. **Phone Conversation** Using modern language, express the ideas of "Song" in a simulated phone conversation that you perform in class with another student. **[Performing Arts Link]**

5. **Oral Interpretation** Perform one of these poems for the class, capturing the speaker's attitude in your tone of voice. Follow sentences, not lines, as you read. **[Performing Arts Link]**

Researching and Representing

6. **Wedding Plan** Plan a wedding for the lovers from one of these poems. Be sure the theme of the wedding is in keeping with the poem's message as you provide for the clothing, the ceremony, the wedding feast, and the entertainment. **[Social Studies Link]**

7. **Song** Set one of the poems to music that you compose or to an existing tune that suits it. Perform your song version on audiocassette or on videotape. **[Music Link]**

Online Activity **www.phlit.phschool.com**

 Guided Writing Lesson

Witty Poem

The speakers in these poems display cleverness and wit as they attempt to persuade their listeners to "seize the day." Write a poem in which you use humor and word play to make a point or to win an argument.

Use the following skill to make your poem persuasive as well as witty.

Writing Skills Focus: Persuasive Tone

Create a **persuasive tone** by doing the following:
- Sounding confident about your arguments.
- Using words that create a sense of urgency about the action you recommend.
- Choosing details and creating images that will capture the imagination of your audience.

Marvell uses all these techniques in this passage from "To His Coy Mistress":

> But at my back I always hear
> Time's wingèd chariot hurrying near:
> And yonder all before us lie
> Deserts of vast eternity.

Prewriting Identify the speaker of your poem and its audience, and decide on the type of humor that will work with this audience. List some key words that will add urgency to your argument.

Drafting Keep the dramatic situation in mind as you draft. If you "discover" appealing words and images as you write, see where they will take you. Go with the flow rather than trying to control it.

Revising Read your draft as if you were the person the speaker is trying to convince. If the speaker doesn't win you over, delete words like *maybe* and *perhaps,* and replace neutral terms with those that convey a sense of urgency—for example, use *hurrying* not *moving.*

CONNECTIONS TO WORLD LITERATURE

Freeze Tag
Suzanne Vega

New Beginning
Tracy Chapman

Thematic Connection

THE WAR AGAINST TIME

The poets in this section wrote during one of the most turbulent periods of English history, the years leading up to and including the Civil War. Religious persecution and political strife created a new awareness of the limited time one has on earth. Against this backdrop of conflict, poets like Marvell and Herrick remind us that time is fleeting and advise us to seize each moment and fill it with pleasure. The elusiveness of time, central to the works of these seventeenth-century poets, is still a popular theme in today's literature, movies, and songs.

SONGS THAT REFLECT ON TIME

The lyrics of popular songwriters Suzanne Vega and Tracy Chapman also reflect anxieties about time. Vega's "Freeze Tag" presents a moment frozen in time due to inaction. The song speaks of how indecision can prevent us from making the best of what we have. The central message of the song echoes the *carpe diem* ("seize the day") theme of Marvell and Herrick. Chapman's "New Beginning" describes a world in turmoil. Her socially conscious lyrics encourage people to stop time, erase the past, and re-create the world.

"SEIZE THE DAY"

The fast pace of today's world often robs us of the opportunity to make the most of our time. The advice given by the seventeenth-century poets to "seize the day" and make the most of life is still valid today.

SUZANNE VEGA

(1959–) Songwriter Suzanne Vega grew up in New York's Spanish Harlem. She began writing music by age fourteen and was performing in

coffeehouses by the time she was sixteen. Her simple folk style and relevant themes appeal to a diverse audience. Vega won nominations for the Grammy Awards for record of the year, song of the year, and best female pop performance in 1987.

TRACY CHAPMAN

(1964–) Tracy Chapman grew up in a working-class neighborhood in

Cleveland, Ohio. At an early age, she taught herself to play guitar and began to write music. Chapman's love of music and knowledge motivated her to seek the best education possible. After attaining a scholarship to a prestigious prep school, she observed that her wealthy classmates were often ignorant of the harshness of poverty. Chapman uses her music to combat that ignorance and raise social awareness of issues from spirituality to racism.

Freeze Tag

Suzanne Vega

We go to the playground
in the wintertime
the sun is fading fast
upon the slides into the past
upon the swings of indecision
in the winter time

in the dimming diamonds
scattering in the park
in the tickling
and the trembling
of freeze tag
in the dark

We play that we're actors
on a movie screen
I will be Dietrich
and you can be Dean

you stand
with your hand
in your pocket
and lean against the wall
You will be Bogart
and I will be
Bacall

And we can only say yes now
to the sky, to the street, to the night

Slow fade now to black
Play me one more game
of chivalry
you and me
do you see
where I've been hiding
in this hide-and-seek?

We go to the playground
in the wintertime
the sun is fading fast
upon the slides into the past
upon the swings of indecision
in the wintertime
wintertime
wintertime

We can only say yes now,
to the sky, to the street, to the night
We can only say yes now
to the sky, to the street, to the night

New Beginning

Tracy Chapman

The whole world's broke and it ain't worth fixing
It's time to start all over, make a new beginning
There's too much pain, too much suffering
Let's resolve to start all over make a new beginning
Now don't get me wrong—I love life and living
But when you wake up and look around at everything
        that's going down—
All wrong
You see we need to change it now, this world with too
        few happy endings
We can resolve to start all over make a new beginning

Refrain:
Start all over
Start all over
Start all over
Start all over

The world is broken into fragments and pieces
That once were joined together in a unified whole
But now too many stand alone—There's too much
        separation
We can resolve to come together in the new beginning

(Refrain)

We can break the cycle—We can break the chain
We can start all over—In the new beginning
We can learn, we can teach
We can share the myths the dream the prayer
The notion that we can do better
Change our lives and paths
Create a new world and

(Refrain)

The whole world's broke and it ain't worth fixing
It's time to start all over, make a new beginning
There's too much fighting, too little understanding
It's time to stop and start all over
Make a new beginning

(Refrain)

We need to make new symbols
Make new signs
Make a new language
With these we'll define the world

(Refrain)

Guide for Responding

◆ Literature and Your Life

Reader's Response Do you believe we can control time by freezing a moment or starting all over again? Explain.

Thematic Focus In what ways do these songs tell us to "seize the day"?

Advertisement As the owner of a futuristic time-travel company, create an advertisement that invites people to use your time-travel machine. Include the *carpe diem* theme in your message.

☑ Check Your Comprehension

1. (a) What is the setting for "Freeze Tag"? (b) What words and images does Vega use to describe the setting?
2. What games do the characters in "Freeze Tag" play?
3. In Chapman's "New Beginning" what are some of the problems the songwriter identifies?
4. What does Chapman suggest should be done about these problems?

◆ Critical Thinking

INTERPRET
1. How do the images in Vega's song explain the title "Freeze Tag"? **[Connect]**
2. Speculate about the type of situation Vega may be writing in her song. **[Speculate]**
3. Explain what Chapman means by "We can break the cycle." In what ways is this method of dealing with time effective? **[Interpret]**

EVALUATE
4. (a) Compare and contrast Vega's and Chapman's attitudes toward time. (b) Which treatment do you find more effective? Why? **[Evaluate]**

APPLY
5. Chapman speaks about making "new symbols" and a "new language." Suggest what such a language might be like. **[Speculate]**

EXTEND
6. How do these modern treatments of time compare to those in seventeenth-century poems? **[Literature Link]**

Thematic Connection

THE WAR AGAINST TIME

The lyrics of songwriters Suzanne Vega and Tracy Chapman, like the poems of this section, express the elusiveness of time. They show how time flows by almost too quickly to be seized, captures us in a frozen moment, or needs the blessing of a new start.

1. What attitudes toward time expressed by these writers do you share? Why? Support your answer with specific passages from the poems or songs.
2. How can the words of songs and poems help people experience life more deeply?
3. Write a refrain—a repeated phrase—for your own song about time. If you like, borrow words from any of the poems or songs you have read.

 Idea Bank

Writing

1. **Time Log** Create a time journal in which you log how you spend all of your time for one week. Did you waste time? Do you feel you used it wisely? Conclude your journal with a brief passage evaluating your use of time.

2. **Song** Write a song expressing your ideas about the value of time. Include a refrain, a repeated phrase or verse placed between stanzas, that sums up your central idea about time. You may want to set your song to the tune of a popular song or write your own music.

3. **Editorial for Teenagers** As a senior, write an editorial for the yearbook in which you provide advice for younger students on making the most of their high school years.

Speaking, Listening, and Viewing

4. **Talk-Show Host** As a talk-show host, prepare interview questions that will help your guests elaborate on how they manage their time. Ask several classmates to act as guests and then conduct your "show" for your class. **[Performing Arts Link]**

Researching and Representing

5. **Time Experiment** Do an experiment to compare subjective impressions of time with actual clock time. Have classmates focus on a pleasant memory with their eyes closed. Stop them after three minutes and then ask them how much time they *think* has passed. After performing the experiment with several classmates, write your conclusions and share them with the class. **[Science Link]**

Online Activity www.phlit.phschool.com

Writing Process Workshop

In many seventeenth-century poems, the speaker tries to persuade his audience to believe or do something. Those who write or broadcast editorials today have the same task. Their messages may not be rhymed, but the destination of their words is still the heart and mind of the reader or listener.

Write a radio, television, or newspaper editorial, taking a clear position on a current issue. In the brief space or time allowed to you, defend your opinion with statistics, examples, reasons, or other details.

These skills, introduced in the Guided Writing Lessons, will help you write an effective editorial.

Writing Skills Focus

▶ Create **unity** by relating your argument and supporting details to the main topic. (See p. 403.)

▶ **Research and write down information** to support your argument. Provide statistics, facts, examples, and quotations. (See p. 411.)

▶ **Elaborate on your opinion.** List ideas and reasons based on your own experience. (See p. 411.)

▶ Set a **persuasive tone** by using language that expresses confidence, carries positive associations, and dramatizes your argument. (See p. 419.)

WORKPLACE WRITING MODEL

from an editorial in *The Oakland* (Michigan) *Press*

A generation ago our parents could earn a good living without a college education. Well-paying jobs were open to high school graduates. . . . Now, high tech manufacturing processes demand ① sophisticated abilities at all levels of employment ② . . . where do we hone these abilities? ③ In college . . . while a year or two of college may do for entry-level jobs, advancement and career development often depend on a four-year degree—at least. . . .

① A forceful word, *demand*, dramatizes the author's argument.

② The author elaborates on the argument by demonstrating how a change in jobs has caused a change in conditions.

③ The author's question helps to unify the editorial by leading back to the central topic—college education—that was introduced at first.

APPLYING LANGUAGE SKILLS: Avoiding Logical Fallacies

Following are some common types of faulty logic and ways to correct them:

- **Circular reasoning:** You expect readers to assume that the conclusion is true in order to prove it.
  Example: *It is essential to be stylish because it is important to be fashionably dressed.*

- **Faulty generalization:** You make a sweeping statement based on little or no evidence.
  Example: *Studies prove that Americans dislike cereal.*

- **Either/or arguments:** You allow for only two possibilities.
  Example: *Either I get the lead role or I might as well forget about an acting career.*

Writing Application Check your paper for examples of faulty logic. Then delete or revise them.

Writer's Solution Connection
Writing Lab

For help with the Pro-and-Con chart, review the Organizing Evidence section of the Persuasion tutorial.

Prewriting

Choose a Topic As you watch the news, look for a current issue on which you can take a stand. Develop a Pro-and-Con chart to consider the arguments for and against your opinion.

Topic: The "V" Chip	
Pros	**Cons**
Helps working parents control which TV programs children watch	Results in more government regulations
	Increases cost to consumers

Consider the following topic ideas for your editorial:

Topic Ideas

- Enacting mandatory sentencing laws
- Supporting or attacking a particular politician
- Repealing mandatory school attendance
- Raising the minimum wage

Research Your Topic Find supporting information by using a variety of resources, including databases and the Internet.

List Persuasive Words List commonly used persuasive words to set the tone. Next to each, put a more urgent or dramatic synonym. For example, use *imperative* instead of *important* or use *sluggish* instead of *slow*.

Drafting

Maintain Unity by Orienting Yourself As you write, be alert to where you are in your editorial—introduction, body, or conclusion—and write appropriately. For example, use the conclusion to restate or summarize arguments. Include words or phrases from the introduction, without mechanically repeating your points, to give readers or listeners a sense of unity.

Support Your Arguments For every argument you make, include supporting facts, statistics, examples, or quotations. Refer to your Prewriting chart to identify these details.

Revising

Consult a Peer Reviewer Get specific suggestions for strengthening your argument from someone who is neutral towards it or opposes it.

Use a Revision Checklist Ask yourself questions based on the writing skills focus:

▶ Have I created unity by relating each argument to the central topic?

▶ Have I supported each point with details that relate to it?

▶ Have I used vivid words that convey confidence and dramatize my argument?

Add Visuals While reviewing your editorial, note places where a chart or graph will support your argument. Revise your editorial to introduce and incorporate such effective visual support.

REVISION MODEL

Because the prom is the ~~most fun~~ *crowning* ① event of the year, the seniors deserve a live band. The absence of the live band makes our prom merely a dance with a disc jockey. *Having live music will give us an experience to reminisce over at* ~~As we all know, our school is closing next year.~~ ② *reunions. We must fight to preserve the live band tradition at our Senior Prom.* ③

① The writer replaces a weak phrase with a vivid word to enhance the persuasive tone.

② The writer eliminates an irrelevant statement and adds a strong supporting detail.

③ This sentence helps unify the paragraph by restating the main topic.

Publishing

▶ **Internet** Send your editorial to a friend or chat group concerned about the topic.

▶ **Local Newspaper** Send your editorial to a local newspaper for publication on the op ed or letters page.

▶ **Videotape** Record your editorial on videotape, using charts, props, and other visual aids to enhance your presentation. Then play your tape for the class.

APPLYING LANGUAGE SKILLS: Fixing Misplaced Modifiers

A misplaced modifier can cause writing to be unclear and ineffective. Place modifiers as close as possible to the words they modify.

Example:
Misplaced Modifier:
The rose, who finds it too demanding, is avoided by many weekend gardeners.

The gardeners not the rose find the flower too demanding. The modifier should be placed after gardeners.

Practice Correct any misplaced modifiers in the following passage.

Designing a garden begins with an inspection of the site where the garden will be located for most people. All gardeners will nearly benefit from taking the time to determine the uses to which the garden will be put. Some plants cannot survive the winters in areas where the temperatures drop below freezing, such as dahlias.

Writer's Solution Connection Language Lab

For more help identifying and fixing misplaced modifiers, see the lesson on misplaced modifiers on the Language Lab CD-ROM.

Student Success Workshop

Real-World Reading Skills

Recognizing Modes of Persuasion

Strategies for Success

Every day, you are bombarded by various modes of persuasion. Persuasion occurs anytime someone uses words or images to attempt to influence your opinions, thoughts, or preferences. Knowing how to analyze and interpret the persuasive techniques you encounter will enable you to make independent, thoughtful judgments about the validity of the message:

Examine the Logical Examine the logic of persuasive writing. Do relevant, accurate facts support the conclusion? Is the information complete? For instance, in a newspaper editorial that advocates raising the driving age to twenty, the writer might include accident statistics showing that teens have more accidents than other age groups, without providing data indicating that the majority of teens drive safely. The information, as presented, is incomplete.

Be Alert to Deception Be alert to deceptive persuasive strategies, such as leaving out information or providing partial or irrelevant information. For example, in a television commercial, an attractive woman might tell you about a fantastic bargain but fail to mention the conditions for the offer. Ask yourself if you are being swayed by emotionally charged language, such as "Jan's Jeans will make you popular!"

Be Aware of Faulty Logic To persuade you, some writers and speakers use faulty logic, including erroneous generalizations, inaccurate conclusions, and oversimplification. A political candidate, for example, may attack her opponent by drawing the faulty conclusion that because he voted twice to raise taxes, voting for him would lead to a lower standard of living for you.

Apply the Strategies

Read the sample paragraph, and answer the questions that follow:

It's Time for a Teen Curfew

Intelligent citizens throughout the city know that it is time that the local police department forced the city's teenagers off the streets by 8 P.M. Police records show that teenagers are responsible for 60 percent of the vandalism that destroys citizens' shops. Most teenagers who spend time on the streets after 8 P.M. are not good students and will probably end up committing crimes. In our survey, 75 percent of the citizens agree that it's time for a curfew.

---

1. What are the writer's main arguments? What facts, expert opinions, and examples are given to support the arguments? Are they valid?

2. What evidence can you find of deceptive persuasion through emotional language?

3. What faulty generalizations and conclusions can you find?

✔ Here are situations in which it's important to recognize modes of persuasion:

▶ Listening to a sales pitch
▶ Reading a movie, book, or play review
▶ Listening to a discussion of a proposed policy at a student council meeting

PART **2**   *A Nation Divided*

Whitehall, January 30th, 1649, (Execution of Charles I)
Ernest Crofts, Forbes Magazine

In 1651, Thomas Hobbes asserted that without laws, "the life of man" is "solitary, poor, nasty, brutish, and short." This philosopher wasn't merely spinning ideas. The English had just beheaded their king after a bloody civil war between Calvinist Puritans and Cavalier supporters of the monarchy. That war still echoes in the contrast between the mighty words of Milton, "God's poet," and the verbal flourishes of the Cavalier Lovelace.

Guide for Interpreting

John Milton *(1608–1674)*

Never lacking self-confidence, Milton clearly and loudly voiced his opinions on the political, religious, and moral issues of his time. He spent the major part of his life studying literature and writing political pamphlets, but the few poems he managed to complete, especially the epic *Paradise Lost,* firmly establish him along with Chaucer and Shakespeare as one of the greatest English poets ever to live.

A Privileged Childhood

Milton was born in London to a middle-class family and grew up in a highly cultured environment. His father, a notary and money-lender, was a composer of considerable ability. Milton's father was also deeply religious and devoted to the Protestant cause. Milton, educated at first by tutors, started his formal education in the equivalent of high school before the age of thirteen. There he mastered Greek, Latin, and Hebrew as well as several modern European languages.

God's Poet

After Milton entered Cambridge University, he decided to prepare himself for a career as a great poet in the service of God. From this point until the English Civil War broke out, he devoted himself to a life of study. After earning his degrees from Cambridge, he withdrew to his father's house for nearly six years, reading everything that was written in the ancient and modern languages that he knew. During this time he wrote one of his best-known poems, "Lycidas." That work, together with poems he had written during his college career, would have earned him lasting fame as a major poet, even if he had never written *Paradise Lost.*

A Man of Ideals

Following his studies, Milton went to Europe for a two-year "Grand Tour." While he was away, Parliament rebelled against King Charles I. Learning of the revolt, Milton cut short his trip and returned to England. He began writing political pamphlets during the English Revolution and the Civil War that followed. As a result of his brilliant writings, Oliver Cromwell, the new head of England, made Milton Secretary for Foreign Tongues. This position required him to translate documents into Latin and to defend the government against royalist attacks.

Milton was imprisoned when the monarchy was restored. His friend, the poet Andrew Marvell, may have been instrumental in gaining his release. Having lost most of his property, Milton withdrew into his blindness and poverty to write *Paradise Lost*, the greatest epic of the English language.

◆ Background for Understanding

HISTORY: MILTON'S EPIC RESPONSE TO CONFLICT

Paradise Lost was written as the dust was settling after years of war and turmoil. From 1642 to 1660, England went from being a monarchy (Charles I) to a commonwealth (Oliver Cromwell) to a protectorate (Lord Protector Cromwell) to a restored monarchy (Charles II). No matter which side of the civil war you were on or how you regarded Cromwell and his politics, at some point during this two-decade period, you experienced both defeat and triumph.

Perhaps Milton wrote *Paradise Lost* because he sensed that the nation needed an anchor, a work of literature that would once again help define and unite a culture. In his epic, Milton seems to have the nation's strife in mind as he offers a poetic explanation for God's allowing suffering and unhappiness in the world. He also seems to have recent conflicts in mind when he describes the fierce "civil war" in heaven between God and Lucifer!

◆ *Literature and Your Life*

CONNECT YOUR EXPERIENCE

Throughout life, you will reach milestones that mark the stages of your growth. In the sonnets that follow, you can trace two milestones in Milton's life: his twenty-fourth birthday and—a sadder event—the onset of his blindness.

Journal Writing Jot down three positive goals that you hope to achieve in the next five years.

THEMATIC FOCUS: A NATION DIVIDED

What specific evidence of the conflict between Royalists and Puritans do you see in the excerpt from *Paradise Lost?*

◆ Literary Focus

THE ITALIAN SONNET; EPIC POETRY

The **Italian sonnet** is a fourteen-line lyric poem divided into an octave of eight lines and a sestet of six. The octave, which rhymes *abbaabba*, presents a problem, and the sestet, whose rhyme scheme can vary, offers a response. In Milton's Italian sonnets, the sestet flows easily and naturally from the octave.

The **epic** is a long narrative poem written in a lofty style. It tells the story of a cultural hero and reflects the values of the society in which it was produced. However, it also deals with universal themes, like the struggle between good and evil.

In *Paradise Lost*, Milton follows classical epic traditions by beginning in the middle of the story and by calling on the muse for aid. However, he also says he will justify "the ways of God to men."

◆ Reading Strategy

BREAK DOWN SENTENCES

When you encounter complex sentences like those in *Paradise Lost*, **break them down** to find the main clause, which can stand by itself, and supporting clauses, which can't. In this passage from *Paradise Lost*, the main clause is underlined.

Of man's first disobedience and the fruit/Of that forbidden tree, whose mortal taste/Brought death into the world, and all our woe,/With loss of Eden, till one greater Man/Restore us, and regain the blissful seat,/Sing Heavenly Muse . . .

To clarify the sentence, place the main clause at the beginning.

◆ Build Vocabulary

LATIN WORD ROOTS: -lum-

As you read *Paradise Lost*, you'll find the word *illumine*, which means "to light up." The root of this word, *-lum-*, is from a Latin word meaning "light" or "lamp."

semblance
illumine
transgress
guile
obdurate
tempestuous
transcendent
suppliant
ignominy

WORD BANK

Before you read, preview this list of words from the poems.

◆ Grammar and Style

CORRECT USE OF *WHO* AND *WHOM*

Milton uses both **who** and **whom** in these poems. He uses *who* as the subject of a verb and *whom* as the object of a verb or preposition.

Subjective case
who best/Bear his mild yoke . . .

Objective case
if he whom mutual league/ . . . / Joined with me . . .

In the first example, *who* is the subject of the verb *bear*, and in the second example, *whom* is the object of the verb *joined*.

Sonnet VII ("How soon hath Time")

John Milton

How soon hath Time, the subtle thief of youth,
    Stolen on his wing my three and twentieth year!
    My hasting days fly on with full career,[1]
    But my late spring no bud or blossom showeth.
5   Perhaps my <u>semblance</u> might deceive[2] the truth,
    That I to manhood am arrived so near,
    And inward ripeness doth much less appear,
    That some more timely-happy spirits[3] endueth.[4]
    Yet be it less or more, or soon or slow,
10   It shall be still[5] in strictest measure even
    To that same lot,[6] however mean or high,
    Toward which Time leads me, and the will of Heaven;
    All is, if I have grace to use it so,
    As ever in my great Taskmaster's eye.

---

1. **career:** Speed.
2. **deceive:** Prove false.
3. **timely-happy spirits:** Others who seem to be more accomplished poets at the age of twenty-three.
4. **endueth:** Endoweth.
5. **still:** Always.
6. **lot:** Fate.

◆ **Build Vocabulary**

semblance (sem´ bləns) *n.*: Appearance; image

Guide for Responding

◆ Literature and Your Life

Reader's Response Do you usually judge people by how much they've accomplished by a certain age? Why or why not?

Thematic Focus Explain how this poem reveals Milton's unrest and dissatisfaction.

✓ Check Your Comprehension

1. What occasion causes Milton to express these thoughts?
2. What is the contrast between Milton's outward appearance and his inward sense of himself?
3. To what does Milton trust himself and his life in lines 9–14?

◆ Critical Thinking

INTERPRET
1. (a) Overall, what are Milton's concerns in the first eight lines? (b) What does he mean by his "late spring"? **[Infer]**
2. How do the last six lines answer the concern expressed in the first eight? **[Draw Conclusions]**

EVALUATE
3. Does Milton deal well with the process of growing older? Explain. **[Evaluate]**

EXTEND
4. What other poems have you read that express alarm about the passage of time? **[Literature Link]**

Sonnet XIX
("When I consider how my light is spent")
John Milton

When I consider how my light is spent
    Ere half my days, in this dark world and wide,
    And that one talent[1] which is death to hide,
    Lodged with me useless, though my soul more
        bent
5   To serve therewith my Maker, and present
    My true account, lest he returning chide;
    "Doth God exact day labor, light denied?"
    I fondly[2] ask; but Patience to prevent
    That murmur, soon replies, "God doth not need
10   Either man's work or his own gifts; who best
    Bear his mild yoke, they serve him best. His
        state
    Is kingly. Thousands[3] at his bidding speed
    And post[4] o'er land and ocean without rest:
    They also serve who only stand and wait."

---

1. **talent:** Allusion to the parable of the talents (Matthew 25: 14–30).
2. **fondly:** Foolishly.
3. **thousands:** Thousands of angels.
4. **post:** Travel.

▲ **Critical Viewing** How does Milton's pose in this portrait reflect the theme of the poem? **[Speculate]**

Guide for Responding

◆ Literature and Your Life

Reader's Response Milton is facing the physical challenge of blindness. What is a challenge that you have successfully met?

Thematic Focus What words indicate that Milton feels he still has a mission to perform?

☑ Check Your Comprehension

1. According to the poem, at what point in the speaker's life did his eyesight fail?
2. When the speaker thinks about serving God, he voices a complaint. What is this complaint?
3. What qualities does the second speaker attribute to God?
4. What image of God and his angels does the speaker paint in the last three lines?

◆ Critical Thinking

INTERPRET
1. Why do you think Milton feels that blindness has made his "talent . . . / . . . useless . . ."? **[Infer]**
2. What is the meaning of the question, "Doth God exact day labor, light denied?" **[Interpret]**
3. The sestet in this poem is the answer to the question in line 7. Explain that answer, paying special attention to line 14. **[Interpret]**

EVALUATE
4. Does Milton's use of dialogue make the sonnet more effective? Why or why not? **[Criticize]**

APPLY
5. Do you think this poem could inspire someone today who is facing a physical challenge? Explain. **[Hypothesize]**

John Milton

from

Paradise Lost

Of man's first disobedience, and the fruit
   Of that forbidden tree, whose mortal[1] taste
   Brought death into the world, and all our woe,
With loss of Eden, till one greater Man[2]
5 Restore us, and regain the blissful seat,
   Sing Heavenly Muse,[3] that on the secret top
   Of Oreb, or of Sinai,[4] didst inspire
   That shepherd, who first taught the chosen seed,
   In the beginning how the Heavens and Earth
10 Rose out of Chaos: or if Sion hill[5]
   Delight thee more, and Siloa's brook[6] that flowed
   Fast[7] by the oracle of God, I thence
   Invoke thy aid to my adventurous song,
   That with no middle flight intends to soar

1. **mortal:** Deadly.
2. **one . . . Man:** Christ.
3. **Heavenly Muse:** Urania, the muse of astronomy and sacred poetry in Greek mythology. Here, Milton associates Urania with the holy spirit that inspired Moses ("That shepherd") to receive and interpret the word of God for the Jews ("the chosen seed"). To convey the message of God to his people, Moses wrote the first five books of the Bible, including Genesis. Genesis is the book on which *Paradise Lost* is based.
4. **Oreb** (ôr´ eb) **. . . Sinai** (sī´ nī): Alternate names for the mountain where God communicated the laws to Moses.
5. **Sion** (sī´ ən) **hill:** Hill near Jerusalem on which the temple ("the oracle of God") stood.
6. **Siloa's** (sī lō´ ez) **brook:** Stream near Sion hill.
7. **fast:** Close.

15　Above the Aonian mount,[8] while it pursues
　　Things unattempted yet in prose or rhyme.
　　And chiefly thou O Spirit,[9] that dost prefer
　　Before all temples the upright heart and pure,
　　Instruct me, for thou know'st; thou from the first
20　Wast present, and with mighty wings outspread
　　Dovelike sat'st brooding on the vast abyss
　　And mad'st it pregnant: what in me is dark
　　<u>Illumine</u>, what is low raise and support;
　　That to the height of this great argument[10]
25　I may assert Eternal Providence,
　　And justify the ways of God to men.
　　　　Say first, for Heaven hides nothing from thy view
　　Nor the deep tract of Hell, say first what cause
　　Moved our grand[11] parents in that happy state,
30　Favored of Heaven so highly, to fall off
　　From their Creator, and <u>transgress</u> his will
　　For[12] one restraint,[13] lords of the world besides?[14]
　　Who first seduced them to that foul revolt?
　　The infernal Serpent; he it was, whose <u>guile</u>
35　Stirred up with envy and revenge, deceived
　　The mother of mankind, what time his pride
　　Had cast him out from Heaven, with all his host
　　Of rebel angels, by whose aid aspiring
　　To set himself in glory above his peers,
40　He trusted to have equaled the Most High,
　　If he opposed; and with ambitious aim
　　Against the throne and monarchy of God
　　Raised impious war in Heaven and battle proud
　　With vain attempt. Him the Almighty Power
45　Hurled headlong flaming from the ethereal sky
　　With hideous ruin and combustion down
　　To bottomless perdition, there to dwell
　　In adamantine[15] chains and penal fire,
　　Who durst defy the Omnipotent to arms.
50　Nine times the space that measures day and night
　　To mortal men, he with his horrid crew
　　Lay vanquished, rolling in the fiery gulf,
　　Confounded though immortal. But his doom
　　Reserved him to more wrath; for now the thought
55　Both of lost happiness and lasting pain
　　Torments him; round he throws his baleful eyes
　　That witnessed[16] huge affliction and dismay,
　　Mixed with <u>obdurate</u> pride and steadfast hate.
　　At once as far as angels' ken,[17] he views

8. Aonian (ā ō′ nē ən) **Mount:** Mount Helicon in Greek mythology, home of the Muses. Milton is drawing a comparison between the epic he is now presenting and the epics written by the classical poets, Homer and Virgil.

9. Spirit: The Holy Spirit, the voice that provided inspiration for the Hebrew prophets.

10. argument: Theme.

11. grand: First in importance and in time.

12. For: Because of.

13. one restraint: That Adam and Eve should not eat of the fruit of the tree of knowledge.

14. besides: In every other respect.

◆ Reading Strategy

On a sheet of paper reorder the words of line 34 to make the meaning clearer.

---

15. adamantine (ad′ ə man′ tēn) *adj.*: Unbreakable.

16. witnessed: Gave evidence of.

17. ken: Can see.

◆ Build Vocabulary

illumine (i lōō′ mən) *v.*: Light up

transgress (trans gres′) *v.*: Violate a law or command

guile (gīl) *n.*: Artful trickery; cunning

obdurate (äb′ door it) *adj.*: Stubborn; unyielding

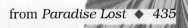

60　The dismal situation waste and wild:
　　A dungeon horrible, on all sides round,
　　As one great furnace flamed, yet from those flames
　　No light, but rather darkness visible
　　Served only to discover sights of woe,
65　Regions of sorrow, doleful shades, where peace
　　And rest can never dwell, hope never comes
　　That comes to all; but torture without end
　　Still urges,[18] and a fiery deluge, fed
　　With ever-burning sulfur unconsumed:
70　Such place eternal justice had prepared
　　For these rebellious, here their prison ordained
　　In utter darkness, and their portion set
　　As far removed from God and light of Heaven
　　As from the center thrice to the utmost pole.[19]
75　O how unlike the place from whence they fell!
　　There the companions of his fall, o'erwhelmed
　　With floods and whirlwinds of tempestuous fire,
　　He soon discerns, and weltering by his side
　　One next himself in power, and next in crime,
80　Long after known in Palestine, and named
　　Beelzebub.[20] To whom the archenemy,
　　And thence in Heaven called Satan, with bold words
　　Breaking the horrid silence thus began:
　　　　"If thou beest he; but O how fallen! how changed
85　From him, who in the happy realms of light
　　Clothed with transcendent brightness didst outshine
　　Myriads though bright: if he whom mutual league,
　　United thoughts and counsels, equal hope
　　And hazard in the glorious enterprise,
90　Joined with me once, now misery hath joined
　　In equal ruin: into what pit thou seest
　　From what height fallen, so much the stronger proved
　　He with his thunder:[21] and till then who knew
　　The force of those dire arms? Yet not for those,
95　Nor what the potent Victor in his rage
　　Can else inflict, do I repent or change,
　　Though changed in outward luster, that fixed mind
　　And high disdain, from sense of injured merit,
　　That with the Mightiest raised me to contend,
100　And to the fierce contention brought along
　　Innumerable force of spirits armed
　　That durst dislike his reign, and me preferring,
　　His utmost power with adverse power opposed
　　In dubious battle on the plains of Heaven,
105　And shook his throne. What though the field be lost?
　　All is not lost; the unconquerable will,
　　And study[22] of revenge, immortal hate,
　　And courage never to submit or yield:
　　And what is else not to be overcome?
110　That glory never shall his wrath or might
　　Extort from me. To bow and sue for grace

18.　urges: Afflicts.

19.　center . . . pole: Three times the distance from the center of the universe (Earth) to the outermost sphere of the universe.

20.　Beelzebub (bē el′ zə bub′): Traditionally, the chief devil, or Satan. In this poem, Satan's chief lieutenant among the fallen angels.

21.　He . . . thunder: God.

◆ **Literary Focus**
Is Satan a typical epic character?

22.　study: Pursuit.

◄ **Critical Viewing** Is this illustration an accurate visual representation of Milton's text? Explain. [Evaluate]

Paradise Lost, 1688, From the British Library

◆ Build Vocabulary

tempestuous (tem pes´ choo wəs) *adj.*: Turbulent; violently stormy

transcendent (tran sen´ dənt) *adj.*: Surpassing; exceeding beyond all limits

With suppliant knee, and deify his power
Who from the terror of this arm so late
Doubted[23] his empire, that were low indeed,
115 That were an ignominy and shame beneath
This downfall; since by fate the strength of gods
And this empyreal[24] substance cannot fail,
Since through experience of this great event,
In arms not worse, in foresight much advanced,
120 We may with more successful hope resolve
To wage by force or guile eternal war
Irreconcilable, to our grand Foe,
Who now triumphs, and in the excess of joy
Sole reigning holds the tyranny of Heaven."
125   So spake the apostate angel, though in pain,
Vaunting aloud, but racked with deep despair;
And him thus answered soon his bold compeer.[25]
      "O prince, O chief of many thronèd Powers,
That led the embattled Seraphim[26] to war
130 Under thy conduct, and in dreadful deeds
Fearless, endangered Heaven's perpetual King,
And put to proof his high supremacy,
Whether upheld by strength, or chance, or fate!
Too well I see and rue the dire event[27]
135 That with sad overthrow and foul defeat
Hath lost us Heaven, and all this mighty host
In horrible destruction laid thus low,
As far as gods and heavenly essences
Can perish: for the mind and spirit remains
140 Invincible, and vigor soon returns,
Though all our glory extinct, and happy state
Here swallowed up in endless misery.
But what if he our conqueror (whom I now
Of force[28] believe almighty, since no less
145 Than such could have o'erpowered such force as ours)
Have left us this our spirit and strength entire
Strongly to suffer and support our pains,
That we may so suffice[29] his vengeful ire,
Or do him mightier service as his thralls
150 By right of war, whate'er his business be
Here in the heart of Hell to work in fire,
Or do his errands in the gloomy deep?
What can it then avail though yet we feel
Strength undiminished, or eternal being
155 To undergo eternal punishment?"
Whereto with speedy words the Archfiend replied:
      "Fallen cherub, to be weak is miserable,
Doing or suffering:[30] but of this be sure,
To do aught[31] good never will be our task,
160 But ever to do ill our sole delight,
As being the contrary to his high will
Whom we resist. If then his providence
Out of our evil seek to bring forth good,

23. Doubted: Feared for.

24. empyreal (em pir´ ē əl) **substance:** The indestructible substance of which Heaven, or the empyrean, is composed.

25. compeer: Comrade, equal.

26. Seraphim (ser´ ə fim): The highest order of angels.

27. event: Outcome.

28. Of force: Necessarily.

29. suffice: Satisfy.

◆ **Reading Strategy**
Rewrite lines 153–155, reordering the words. Why do you think Milton used the word order he did?

30. doing or suffering: Whether one is active or passive.
31. aught: Anything.

Our labor must be to pervert that end,
And out of good still[32] to find means of evil;
Which oft times may succeed, so as perhaps
Shall grieve him, if I fail not,[33] and disturb
His inmost counsels from their destined aim.
But see the angry Victor[34] hath recalled
His ministers of vengeance and pursuit
Back to the gates of Heaven: the sulfurous hail
Shot after us in storm, o'erblown hath laid
The fiery surge, that from the precipice
Of Heaven received us falling, and the thunder,
Winged with red lightning and impetuous rage,
Perhaps hath spent his shafts, and ceases now
To bellow through the vast and boundless deep.
Let us not slip[35] the occasion, whether scorn,
Or satiate[36] fury yield it from our Foe.
Seest thou yon dreary plain, forlorn and wild,
The seat of desolation, void of light,
Save what the glimmering of these livid flames
Casts pale and dreadful? Thither let us tend
From off the tossing of these fiery waves,
There rest, if any rest can harbor there,
And reassembling our afflicted powers,[37]
Consult how we may henceforth most offend
Our Enemy, our own loss how repair,
How overcome this dire calamity,
What reinforcement we may gain from hope,
If not what resolution from despair."

    Thus Satan talking to his nearest mate,
With head uplift above the wave, and eyes
That sparkling blazed; his other parts besides
Prone on the flood, extended long and large,
Lay floating many a rood,[38] in bulk as huge
As whom the fables name of monstrous size,
Titanian, or Earthborn, that warred on Jove,
Briareos or Typhon,[39] whom the den
By ancient Tarsus[40] held, or that sea beast
Leviathan,[41] which God of all his works
Created hugest that swim the ocean stream:
Him haply slumbering on the Norway foam
The pilot of some small night-foundered skiff,
Deeming some island, oft, as seamen tell,
With fixed anchor in his scaly rind
Moors by his side under the lee, while night
Invests[42] the sea, and wished morn delays:
So stretched out huge in length the Archfiend lay

Line numbers:
165, 170, 175, 180, 185, 190, 195, 200, 205

◆ Build Vocabulary

suppliant (sup´ lē ənt) *adj.*: Beseeching prayerfully; imploring

ignominy (ig´ nə min´ ē) *n.*: Humiliation; dishonor; disgrace

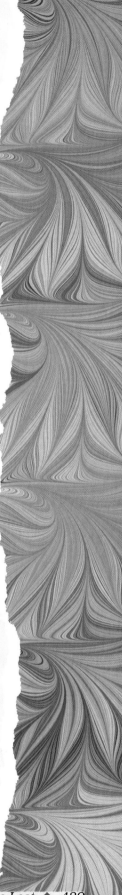

32. **still:** Always.

33. **if . . . not:** Unless I am mistaken.

34. **angry Victor:** God.

35. **slip:** Fail to take advantage of.
36. **satiate:** (sā´ shē it´) Satisfied.

◆ *Literature and Your Life*
Satan and Beelzebub disagree about what to do now that they have been cast from Heaven. (lines 128–191) With whose point of view do you agree?

37. **afflicted powers:** Overthrown armies.

38. **rood:** Old unit of measure equal to seven or eight yards.
39. **Titanian** (tī tā´ nē ən) . . . **Earthborn** . . . **Briareos** (brī ar´ ē əs) . . . **Typhon** (tī´ fən): In classical mythology, both the Titans, led by Briareos, who had a hundred hands, and the Giants (Earthborn), led by Typhon, a hundred-headed serpent monster, fought with Jove. As punishment for their rebellion, both Briareos and Typhon were thrown into the underworld.
40. **Tarsus** (tär´ səs): Capital of Cilicia (sə lish´ə). Typhon is said to have lived in Cilicia near Tarsus.
41. **Leviathan** (lə vī´ ə thən): Great sea monster.
42. **Invests:** Covers.

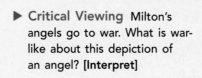

▶ **Critical Viewing** Milton's angels go to war. What is war-like about this depiction of an angel? **[Interpret]**

Paradise Lost, 1688, (detail) John Milton British Library

210 Chained on the burning lake, nor
          ever thence
      Had risen or heaved his head, but
          that the will
      And high permission of all-ruling Heaven
      Left him at large to his own dark designs,
      That with reiterated crimes he might
215 Heap on himself damnation, while he sought
      Evil to others, and enraged might see
      How all his malice served but to bring forth
      Infinite goodness, grace and mercy shown
      On man by him seduced, but on himself
220 Treble confusion, wrath and vengeance poured.
      Forthwith upright he rears from off the pool
      His mighty stature; on each hand the flames
      Driven backward, slope their pointing spires, and
          rolled
      In billows leave in the midst a horrid vale.
225 Then with expanded wings he steers his flight
      Aloft, incumbent⁴³ on the dusky air
      That felt unusual weight, till on dry land
      He lights, if it were land that ever burned
      With solid, as the lake with liquid fire;
230 And such appeared in hue, as when the force
      Of subterranean wind transports a hill
      Torn from Pelorus, or the shattered side
      Of thundering Etna,⁴⁴ whose combustible
      And fueled entrails thence conceiving fire,
235 Sublimed⁴⁵ with mineral fury, aid the winds,
      And leave a singèd bottom all involved⁴⁶
      With stench and smoke: such resting found the sole
      Of unblessed feet. Him followed his next mate,
      Both glorying to have scaped the Stygian⁴⁷ flood
240 As gods, and by their own recovered strength,
      Not by the sufferance⁴⁸ of supernal⁴⁹ power.
      "Is this the region, this the soil, the clime,"
      Said then the lost Archangel, "this the seat
      That we must change⁵⁰ for Heaven, this mournful
          gloom
245 For that celestial light? Be it so, since he
      Who now is sovereign can dispose and bid
      What shall be right: farthest from him is best,
      Whom reason hath equaled, force hath made supreme
      Above his equals. Farewell happy fields,

43. **incumbent:** Lying.

44. **Pelorus** (pə lôr´əs) . . . **Etna:** Volcanic mountains in Sicily.
45. **Sublimed:** Vaporized.
46. **involved:** Enveloped.
47. **Stygian** (stij´ ē ən): Of the river Styx, which, in Greek mythology, encircled Hades, (hā´ dēz´): the home of the dead.

48. **sufferance:** Permission.
49. **supernal:** (sə pʉrn´ əl): Heavenly.
50. **change:** Exchange.

250   Where joy forever dwells. Hail horrors! Hail
        Infernal world! and thou, profoundest Hell
        Receive thy new possessor, one who brings
        A mind not to be changed by place or time.
        The mind is its own place, and in itself
255   Can make a Heaven of Hell, a Hell of Heaven.
        What matter where, if I be still the same,
        And what I should be, all but less than he
        Whom thunder hath made greater? Here at least
        We shall be free; the Almighty hath not built
260   Here for his envy, will not drive us hence:
        Here we may reign secure, and in my choice
        To reign is worth ambition though in Hell:
        Better to reign in Hell than serve in Heaven.
        But wherefore[51] let we then our faithful friends,
265   The associates and copartners of our loss
        Lie thus astonished[52] on the oblivious[53] pool,
        And call them not to share with us their part
        In this unhappy mansion, or once more
        With rallied arms to try what may be yet
270   Regained in Heaven, or what more lost in Hell?"

> ◆ **Literary Focus**
> Is there anything heroic about Satan's speech? Explain.

51. wherefore: Why.

52. astonished: Stunned.
53. oblivious: Causing forgetfulness.

Guide for Responding

◆ *Literature and Your Life*

Reader's Response What in Milton's description of Hell do you find the most vivid? Explain.

Thematic Focus How does the war in heaven, as described by Satan, mirror events that had recently occurred in England?

☑ Check Your Comprehension

1. Summarize the story of Adam and Eve, as Milton tells it in lines 29–36.
2. Lines 36–53 tell of another, earlier fall from grace. Who fell that earlier time and what caused the fall?
3. Lines 59–74 describe Hell. What are its main features?
4. (a) When Satan and Beelzebub have a conversation, what does Satan vow to do? (b) What is Beelzebub's advice?
5. To what creatures is Satan compared in lines 193–209?

◆ Critical Thinking

1. What effect does Milton create in lines 1–26 by mixing Hebrew allusions and references to classical mythology? **[Interpret]**
2. How is the Fall of Adam and Eve paralleled by the Fall of Satan and his cohorts? **[Connect]**
3. In lines 242–270, identify words and phrases that show Satan's despair and those that demonstrate his resolve. **[Analyze]**
4. Is Satan petty, mean, grand, self-pitying, stubborn, heroic, weak, rebellious, or some combination of these? Support your answer with specific references. **[Draw Conclusions]**

EVALUATE

5. Will Satan's efforts ever bring him satisfaction? Explain. **[Make a Judgment]**
6. In your opinion, how well has Milton "justified the ways of God to men"? Explain. **[Assess]**

Guide for Responding (continued)

◆ Literary Focus

ITALIAN SONNET

In his **Italian sonnets**, Milton is famous for closely linking the first eight lines—the octave, rhymed *abbaabba*—and the following six lines—the sestet. In Sonnet VII for example, the sestet answers a concern about his achievements that he voices in the octave.

1. In which sonnet does Milton slightly break the pattern of octave and sestet to link the problem and solution even more closely? Explain.
2. (a) Which sonnet has the more regular pattern of rhymes in the sestet? (b) What effect does this regular pattern have on the "solution" or "answer" in the sestet?

EPIC POETRY

Epic poems express cultural values and universal themes. A timeless theme in *Paradise Lost* is the conflict between good and evil. In expressing this theme, however, Milton had a problem. God, champion of the good, is all-powerful, according to Christian doctrine. The battle between God and Satan is therefore no contest. However, Milton dramatizes the conflict by giving you glimpses into the mind of Satan.

1. What causes Satan the greatest anguish? Why?
2. (a) What does Satan mean by saying, "The mind . . . / Can make a Heaven of Hell, a Hell of Heaven"? (b) How does this remark reflect his own inner conflict?
3. (a) What plans does Satan have for the future? (b) How do these plans create suspense?

◆ Grammar and Style

CORRECT USE OF *WHO* AND *WHOM*

Who is used as the subject of a verb, and *whom* can be the object of a verb or preposition.

Practice In your notebook, write *who* or *whom*.

1. With____?____ did the Serpent quarrel?
2. ____?____ lay chained on the burning lake?
3. To ____?____ did Eve offer the apple?
4. The pair was condemned to eternal punishment by ____?____
5. ____?____ did Adam and Eve blame for their suffering?

◆ Reading Strategy

BREAK DOWN SENTENCES

Because Milton's sentences tend to be complicated, it helps to **break them down** into the clause expressing the main idea and the supporting clauses. Often you'll find that Milton places the main clause in the middle or at the end of a sentence for a special effect. By holding back the main clause of the epic's first sentence—"Sing Heavenly Muse"—Milton piles up supporting clauses that impress readers with the weightiness of his theme.

1. In Sonnet XIX ("When I consider . . ."), lines 1–8 are a single sentence. (a) Identify the main clause and the idea it expresses. (b) Identify the supporting clauses and the ideas they express.
2. (a) Find the main clause in the sentence in lines 27–32 of *Paradise Lost*. (b) Restate the sentence in a paraphrase that makes its meaning clear.
3. Read lines 50–53 of *Paradise Lost*. (a) Find the main clause of this sentence. (b) How does the position of this clause in the sentence suggest the position of Satan and his men in "the fiery gulf"?

◆ Build Vocabulary

USING THE LATIN ROOT *-lum-*

Knowing that the word root *-lum-* means "light" or "lamp," match each numbered *-lum-* word with its lettered definition.

1. luminary   **a.** shining
2. luminous   **b.** person who enlightens mankind
3. illumine   **c.** to light up

USING THE WORD BANK: Synonyms

In your notebook, match each word with its synonym.

1. transcendent   **a.** appearance
2. ignominy   **b.** stubborn
3. tempestuous   **c.** sin
4. suppliant   **d.** trickery
5. transgress   **e.** stormy
6. obdurate   **f.** beyond
7. semblance   **g.** begging
8. guile   **h.** light
9. illumine   **i.** disgrace

Build Your Portfolio

Idea Bank

Writing

1. **Description of a Place** Milton's description of Hell in *Paradise Lost* has captured the imagination of many readers. In your own words, describe the strange world into which Satan has fallen.

2. **Poem** Take stock of your life up to this point, and write a poem about a milestone you've reached. If you wish, write your poem using the Italian sonnet form.

3. **Response to Criticism** Douglas Bush writes of *Paradise Lost*, "Its characterization of Satan is one of the supreme achievements of world literature." Support or refute this view in an essay.

Speaking, Listening, and Viewing

4. **Dramatic Readings** With a small group, take turns reading Milton's sonnets as if they were dramatic monologues. Remember to follow sentences past line endings, stopping only where punctuation indicates a pause. **[Performing Arts Link]**

5. **Visual Presentation** Research various cultures' images of beings that tempt or torment humans, like Milton's "infernal Serpent." Create a visual presentation of the images used by some cultures to represent such beings.

Researching and Representing

6. **Illustration for *Paradise Lost*** Translate one of Milton's vivid word pictures into a drawing or painting. **[Art Link]**

7. **Blindness and Creativity** Milton's blindness did not deter him from creating his masterpiece, *Paradise Lost*. Research a well-known, creative person who is blind, like Stevie Wonder, and prepare a report on his or her life. Present your report to the class. **[Career Link]**

Online Activity www.phlit.phschool.com

Guided Writing Lesson

Retelling a Story

In *Paradise Lost*, Milton vividly retells the story of Satan's fall from Heaven. Choose a well-known story that you can retell. Keep the same plot, but add a few new details to give the story your signature. Whatever twist you give to the story, be consistent in the point of view from which you retell it.

Writing Skills Focus: Consistent Point of View

There are a few different points of view from which to tell a story. Whichever one you choose, keep a **consistent point of view** so that readers do not become confused. Milton, for example, writes from an omniscient point of view that enables him to tell you the thoughts of any character: "So spake the apostate angel, though in pain, /Vaunting aloud, but racked with deep despair."

You can also use the first-person point of view, allowing a character to tell the story. Another choice is the third-person limited point of view, in which someone outside the events tells the story knowing only the thoughts of a single character.

Prewriting Decide on the point of view you will use in your retelling. A first-person narrator, who refers to himself or herself as "I," will give your story a greater sense of immediacy. However, an omniscient narrator will be able to give readers a sense of everyone's thoughts.

Drafting As you draft your retellings, keep your point of view in mind. Don't have an omniscient narrator say "I" or don't assume that a third-person limited narrator knows the thoughts of several characters.

Revising Review your retelling critically, making sure that the characters and plot events are true to the original. Also have several classmates read your retelling and double-check that the point of view from which the story is told is consistent.

Guide for Interpreting

Amelia Lanier (1569–1645)

Amelia Lanier saw the need for women's rights three hundred years before any Western woman had even won the right to vote. She was a writer who saw beyond her times and dared to question the unfair treatment of women.

From Court Life to Working Woman

Throughout her life, Lanier had ties to the royal court, where her father, Baptista Bassano, was musician to Queen Elizabeth I. Lanier's husband, Alphonso, and her son, Nicholas, were also court musicians. Despite her court connections, however, Lanier and her husband were not wealthy. When her husband died in 1613, Lanier opened a school outside London in order to make a living.

A Radical Work

In 1611, Lanier published a volume of poetry called *Salve Deus Rex Judaeorum* (Hail, God, King of the Jews) in which she questioned class privilege and called for women's social and religious equality with men. Today she is considered a visionary feminist who spoke out when few realized the need to do so.

Richard Lovelace (1618–1657)

Born to an extremely wealthy family, Richard Lovelace was the handsome favorite of Charles I and a firm supporter of those traditional values that the king symbolized.

Looks and Talent

A rumor from the time has it that Lovelace was so handsome that the king and queen ordered that he be granted a master's degree before he completed his studies at Oxford! Lovelace was, however, also talented. While at Oxford he wrote a play, painted pictures, and played several instruments.

An Exciting Life

Lovelace was chosen by the Royalists to demand of Parliament the restoration of the king's authority. He was immediately arrested. After his release from prison, he rejoined Charles's forces and spent most of his fortune equipping the king's army. Upon Charles's defeat in 1645, Lovelace went to France and fought against Holland. Returning to England years later, Lovelace was again imprisoned by the Puritans. No one knows for certain how his life ended, but it is believed that he died in discouragement and poverty.

◆ Background for Understanding

HISTORY: AFTERMATH OF THE CIVIL WAR

During the reign of Charles I, tensions between Catholics and Puritans rose to a dangerous level. To make matters worse, wars against Spain and France had led to a money shortage, and the king was pressuring the nobles for money and forcing commoners to fight in England's armies.

Charles I's handling of his increasingly turbulent country eventually cost him his life. He was beheaded by anti-Royalists, and England became a Commonwealth. However, during the years of the Commonwealth, Oliver Cromwell enforced order with an iron hand and new tensions arose. The sternest and most radical Puritans controlled the country, and they had little tolerance for Royalists, Catholics, or more moderate Puritans.

Richard Lovelace, a Royalist, was imprisoned twice during these turbulent years. During his incarceration, he wrote some of his finest poetry, including "To Althea, from Prison" and "To Lucasta, on Going to the Wars."

from Eve's Apology in Defense of Women
To Lucasta, on Going to the Wars ◆ To Althea, from Prison

◆ *Literature and Your Life*

CONNECT YOUR EXPERIENCE

Throughout history, people dissatisfied with our country's laws and values have campaigned for various causes—equal rights, environmental protection, and campaign reforms, to name a few. Sometimes their efforts have won the support of the majority, but in other cases their efforts have failed because the opposing forces were too strong.

Lanier was like some of today's campaigners for reform. Lovelace, however, was a passionate supporter of things-as-they-are at a time when things were changing.

Journal Writing Jot down some "reforms" that you'd like to see made in your community or in the country as a whole.

THEMATIC FOCUS: A NATION DIVIDED

Why do you think that strongly clashing points of view emerge during certain periods of history?

◆ Build Vocabulary

TERMS WITH *BREACH*

In the excerpt from "Eve's Apology," you will encounter the word *breach,* meaning "breaking." This word appears in many phrases, especially those related to the law. An example is *breach of the peace,* which means "creating a public disturbance."

WORD BANK

Before you read, preview this list of words from the selections.

| breach |
| discretion |
| inconstancy |

◆ Grammar and Style

CORRELATIVE CONJUNCTIONS

Lanier and Lovelace use **correlative conjunctions,** paired coordinating conjunctions that connect two equal words or groups of words. Such conjunctions enable them to express ideas briefly and clearly, as in this example:

For he was Lord and King of all the earth,
Before poor Eve had *either* life *or* breath. (Lanier, "Eve's Apology")

Correlative conjunctions are especially useful in poems, where space is tight and every word must count.

◆ Literary Focus

TRADITION AND REFORM

Tradition and reform go hand in hand. Few reformers propose ideas that come out of thin air. Even when their proposals are radical, reformers base them on traditional ideas and beliefs familiar to everyone in the culture.

For example, Lanier bases her ideas on a reinterpretation of the Bible. She reinterprets the story of Adam and Eve to give Adam more responsibility for the Fall.

◆ Reading Strategy

USE HISTORICAL CONTEXT

As you read a work, place it in a **historical context** by asking whether its ideas and assumptions are typical of its era. Also ask how its ideas, whether typical or not, are a response to events of the period.

Before reading these authors, for instance, remind yourself of the turbulent events to which they were responding. (You'll find historical information in the Introduction on p. 382 and in the biographies and Background on p. 444.) Then look for evidence of the conflicts and beliefs of the time in the works themselves. Such evidence might take the form of direct statements or images.

from
Eve's Apology in Defense of Women

Amelia Lanier

Dorothy Seton—A Daughter of Eve
1903, James McNeil Whistler, University of Glasgow, Scotland

◀ **Critical Viewing** In this poem, Lanier argues that Eve has been judged too harshly. Does the way in which the artist portrays his subject, called "A daughter of Eve," support Lanier's arguments? Why or why not? **[Connect]**

But surely Adam cannot be excused;
Her fault though great, yet he was most to blame.
What weakness offered, strength might have refused;
Being lord of all, the greater was his shame;
5 Although the serpent's craft had her abused,
God's holy word ought all his actions frame;
    For he was lord and king of all the earth,
    Before poor Eve had either life or breath,

Who being framed by God's eternal hand
10 The perfectest man that ever breathed on earth,
And from God's mouth received that strait command,

The <u>breach</u> whereof he knew was present death;
Yea, having power to rule both sea and land,
Yet with one apple won to lose that breath
15   Which God had breathéd in his beauteous face,
        Bringing us all in danger and disgrace;

And then to lay the fault on patience's back,
That we (poor women) must endure it all;
We know right well he did <u>discretion</u> lack,
20   Being not persuaded thereunto at all.
If Eve did err, it was for knowledge sake;
The fruit being fair persuaded him to fall.
        No subtle serpent's falsehood did betray him;
        If he would eat it, who had power to stay him?

25   Not Eve, whose fault was only too much love,
Which made her give this present to her dear,
That what she tasted he likewise might prove,
Whereby his knowledge might become more clear;
He never sought her weakness to reprove
30   With those sharp words which he of God did hear;
        Yet men will boast of knowledge, which he took
        From Eve's fair hand, as from a learned book.

◆ Build Vocabulary

breach (brēch) *n.*: Breaking or being broken; failure to observe terms

discretion (di skresh´ ən) *n.*: Freedom or authority to make decisions and choices

Guide for Responding

◆ Literature and Your Life

Reader's Response Is Lanier's argument convincing? Why or why not?

Thematic Focus Lanier's poem appeared in 1611, while King James I was experiencing increasing conflicts with the Puritans. How do you think it was received by the public when it was published?

☑ Check Your Comprehension

1. Whom does Lanier blame more for the Fall, Adam or Eve? Why?
2. According to Lanier, why did Eve taste of the tree of knowledge?
3. According to Lanier, what was Eve's real fault?

◆ Critical Thinking

INTERPRET

1. (a) What can you infer about Eve's character from this poem? (b) What can you infer about Adam's character? **[Infer]**
2. To whom does Lanier give most of the responsibility for what happened in the Garden of Eden? Why has she done this? **[Draw Conclusions]**
3. According to this poem, in what way do men apply a double standard to the story of Adam and Eve? **[Interpret]**

EVALUATE

4. Does this poem place women in a good light in terms of today's standards? Explain. **[Evaluate]**

To Lucasta, on Going to the Wars

Richard Lovelace

Going to the Battle, Edward Burne-Jones, Fitzwilliam Museum, Cambridge

▲ **Critical Viewing** Like the speaker in "To Lucasta," the knight in the background is going to war. Do the knight and the poem's speaker seem to be leaving in the same spirit? Explain. **[Compare and Contrast]**

Tell me not, Sweet, I am unkind,
    That from the nunnery
Of thy chaste breast, and quiet mind,
    To war and arms I fly.

5 True, a new mistress now I chase,
    The first foe in the field;
And with a stronger faith embrace
    A sword, a horse, a shield.

Yet this <u>inconstancy</u> is such,
10   As <u>you too shall</u> adore;
I could not love thee, Dear, so much,
    Loved I not honor more.

◆ **Build Vocabulary**

inconstancy (in kän´ stən sē) *n.*: Fickleness; change-ableness

To Althea, from Prison
Richard Lovelace

When love with unconfined wings
   Hovers within my gates,
And my divine Althea brings
   To whisper at the grates;
5 When I lie tangled in her hair
   And fettered to her eye,
The gods[1] that wanton[2] in the air
   Know no such liberty.

When flowing cups run swiftly round,
10   With no allaying Thames,[3]
Our careless heads with roses bound,
   Our hearts with loyal flames;
When thirsty grief in wine we steep,
   When healths[4] and drafts[5] go free,
15 Fishes that tipple in the deep,
   Know no such liberty.

When, like committed linnets,[6] I
   With shriller throat shall sing
The sweetness, mercy, majesty,
20   And glories of my King;
When I shall voice aloud how good
   He is, how great should be,
     Enlarged[7] winds that curl the flood,
   Know no such liberty.

25 Stone walls do not a prison make,
   Nor iron bars a cage;
Minds innocent and quiet take
   That for an hermitage;
If I have freedom in my love,
30   And in my soul am free,
Angels alone that soar above,
   Enjoy such liberty.

---

1. **gods:** The word *gods* is replaced by *birds* in some versions of this poem.
2. **wanton:** Play.
3. **cups . . . Thames** (temz): Wine that has not been diluted by water (from the river Thames).
4. **healths:** Toasts.
5. **drafts:** Drinks.
6. **committed linnets:** Caged finches.
7. **enlarged:** Released.

Guide for Responding

◆ Literature and Your Life

Reader's Response Were you persuaded by Lovelace's arguments in these poems? Why or why not?

Thematic Focus In times of crisis we are likely to interpret traumatic events in ways that keep us hopeful. How do these poems serve such a purpose?

Definition of Honor Lovelace was concerned with honor above all. Write your own definition of *honor* and give examples of honorable behavior.

☑ Check Your Comprehension

1. What do lines 1–4 of "To Lucasta" indicate that the poet is doing?
2. According to lines 9–12 of "To Lucasta," why will the abandoned lady "adore" the speaker's "inconstancy"?
3. In "To Althea," what are three things the poet does in prison?
4. Why does the poet say in lines 25–32 of "To Althea" that he is really "free"?

Guide for Responding (continued)

◆ Critical Thinking

INTERPRET

1. What is Lovelace's relationship to Lucasta, and what is the purpose of his speech to her in "To Lucasta"? **[Hypothesize]**
2. What is the "stronger faith" Lovelace refers to in line 7 of "To Lucasta"? **[Interpret]**
3. Summarize Lovelace's conception of freedom in "To Althea." **[Interpret]**

EXTEND

4. What attitudes expressed in these poems mark Lovelace as a Royalist? **[Social Studies Link]**

◆ Reading Strategy

USE HISTORICAL CONTEXT

In reading about the **historical context** of Lovelace's poems, you learned that the poet came from the upper classes and was a favorite of Charles I at a time when the Royalist supporters of the king were in conflict with the Puritans. This information helps you appreciate that Lovelace's poem "To Althea, from Prison" is as much a political poem as it is a love poem.

1. Given the historical context, why do you think Lovelace was writing his poem from prison?
2. Which stanza of "To Althea" is a defiant expression of the poet's politics? Explain.
3. (a) What have you learned about the role of women in seventeenth-century English society? (b) How does that information add to your understanding of Lanier's poem "Eve's Apology"?

◆ Literary Focus

TRADITION AND REFORM

Amelia Lanier was a radical in her day, but she drew on the widely known **tradition** of biblical stories and beliefs to support her ideas.

1. Read the story of Adam and Eve in Genesis. (a) What elements of the story remain the same in her poem? (b) How does Lanier reinterpret the story in order to make her point?
2. How does Lanier's use of a Bible story make it easier for her to communicate with readers, even if they disagree with her arguments?

◆ Build Vocabulary

USING TERMS WITH *BREACH*

Use your knowledge of the word *breach* to define each of the italicized terms:

1. The woman sued her fiancé for a *breach of promise.*
2. The policewoman arrested the girls for a *breach of the peace.*

USING THE WORD BANK: Synonyms

In your notebook, write the lettered word closest in meaning to the first word.

1. discretion: (a) prudence, (b) falseness, (c) speed
2. inconstancy: (a) faithlessness, (b) doubt, (c) anger
3. breach: (a) promise, (b) help, (c) violation

◆ Grammar and Style

CORRELATIVE CONJUNCTIONS

These writers use **correlative conjunctions,** pairs of conjunctions that link two words or groups of words both elegantly and economically. The words *both . . . and* in the previous sentence are correlative conjunctions. Other examples are *neither . . . nor, either . . . or, not so . . . as,* and *not only . . . but also.*

Practice In your notebook, copy these sentences and underline the correlative conjunctions in each.

1. Lanier put neither woman nor man before God.
2. Whether Lovelace was in prison or spending time with friends, he was able to feel free.
3. Both Lanier and Lovelace had strong opinions about politics.
4. Either you agree with Lovelace or you agree with Lanier.
5. Lovelace was not only a poet but also a soldier.

Writing Application Use correlative conjunctions to combine these sentences.

1. Lanier believed that men had to take some of the responsibility for sin. She believed that women had to take some of the responsibility for sin.
2. Richard Lovelace wasn't only fighting for the King. He was fighting for honor.
3. Lanier was traditional in her poem. Lanier was radical in her poem.

Build Your Portfolio

Idea Bank

Writing

1. **Editorial** Lanier's defense of women was, in a sense, an editorial. With your school or local newspaper in mind, write your own editorial about a current issue.

2. **Declaration of Parliament** As a member of the English Parliament, respond to the demands of Lovelace to reinstate absolute power to the King. **[Social Studies Link]**

3. **Response to Criticism** The critic Douglas Bush says that in Lovelace's best poems, he displays the Royalist values of "beauty, love, and loyal honor." Agree or disagree with this observation, citing specific passages from the poems.

Speaking, Listening, and Viewing

4. **Ballad** For several centuries, people have written ballads designed to express points of view about social issues or current events. Write a simple rhymed song about a cause you want to support, and perform it for the class. **[Music Link]**

5. **Role Play** With a partner, perform a scene in which Lovelace departs from Lucasta to go to the wars. Have him express the sentiments he voices in "To Lucasta," and have her respond. **[Performing Arts Link]**

Researching and Representing

6. **Poster** As a seventeenth-century artist, design a poster that promotes the political beliefs of Lovelace or Lanier. **[Art Link]**

7. **Civil War** Research and report on the English Civil War of the seventeenth century. **[Social Studies Link]**

Online Activity www.phlit.phschool.com

Guided Writing Lesson

College Application

To capture their readers' interest and emphasize important points, these writers make bold and dramatic statements. They also link their ideas to traditions with which their audience is familiar. Use both these devices in writing a college application essay on how you would change the world. These tips will help you turn a ho-hum essay into a dramatic one.

Writing Skills Focus: Using Dramatic Effects

Speeches, poems, editorials, and many types of essays use dramatic effects to engage readers. For example, Amelia Lanier begins with a startlingly new take on an time-honored story:

Model From the Poem

But surely Adam cannot be excused;
Her fault though great, yet he was most to blame.
What weakness offered, strength might have refused;
Being lord of all, the greater was his shame; . . .

This beginning must have startled readers, but it probably kept them reading as well.

Prewriting Think of a traditional idea or saying that you can slant in a surprising way. For example, if you want log-rolling included in the Olympics, you might say, "log-rolling is as American as apple pie, but it's also a sport that the whole world can enjoy."

Drafting Dramatize your subject with an unusual comparison. If you are proposing ways to change schools, for example, you might compare schools to something unusual, like circuses. However, be sure you can show that the comparison makes sense.

Revising Have classmates read your essay. In passages where their interest flags, try using an unusual comparison or a surprising take on a familiar saying.

CONNECTIONS TO TODAY'S WORLD

from Light Shining in Buckinghamshire
Caryl Churchill

Thematic Connection

A NATION DIVIDED

The writers in this section comment upon the political, social, and religious issues that divided England before, during, and after the Civil War. Milton's *Paradise Lost* includes passages that criticize the monarchy and express his religious values and beliefs. Lanier calls the public's attention to the unfair treatment of women, and Lovelace defiantly asserts his support for Charles I even from prison.

Amid all this conflict, splinter groups like the Diggers were formed to call attention to the plight of the oppressed. The Diggers believed that the English Civil Wars had been fought against the king and the great landowners. Now that Charles I had been executed, they demanded that land be made available for the very poor to cultivate and live on.

INJUSTICE TODAY

Caryl Churchill's play *Light Shining in Buckinghamshire* is about the plight of the Diggers in the seventeenth century. She uses their plight to draw attention to oppression that continued after the Civil War. In this scene, Gerrard Winstanley, a founder of the Diggers, proclaims the group's right to freedom. Churchill uses the scene to expose the injustices suffered by the group and leaves a vivid impression of the hardships endured by the poor during the turbulent seventeenth century. Churchill wants to demonstrate how the inequities in seventeenth-century society resemble the injustices of our own time.

CARYL CHURCHILL
(1938–   )

English dramatist and scriptwriter Caryl Churchill is one of the most successful female playwrights in British theater. Churchill's plays are known for their treatment of controversial issues, for their innovative use of casting and characters, and for their groundbreaking dramatic structure.

Among Churchill's most famous plays are *Cloud Nine* (1978), *Top Girls* (1980–82), and *Serious Money* (1987). In addition to stage plays, Churchill has also written several television and radio plays.

from Light Shining in Buckinghamshire

Caryl Churchill

ACT TWO   DIGGERS

ONE OF THE ACTORS [*announces*]: Information of Henry Sanders, Walton-upon-Thames, April the sixteenth, sixteen hundred and forty-nine.

One Everard, Gerrard Winstanley, and three more, all living at Cobham, came to St. George's Hill in Surrey and began to dig, and sowed the ground with parsnips and carrots and beans. By Friday last they were increased in number to twenty or thirty. They invite all to come in and help them, and promise them meat, drink and clothes.

WINSTANLEY [*announces*]: The true Levellers' standard advanced, sixteen hundred and forty-nine:

A declaration to the powers of England and to all the powers of the world, showing the cause why the common people of England have begun to dig up, manure and sow corn upon George Hill in Surrey. Take notice that England is not a free people till the poor that have no land have a free allowance to dig and labor the commons. It is the sword that brought in property and holds it up, and everyone upon recovery of the conquest ought to return into freedom again, or what benefit have the common people got by the victory over the king?

All men have stood for freedom; and now the common enemy has gone you are all like men in a mist, seeking for freedom, and know not where it is: and those of the richer sort of you that see it are afraid to own it. For freedom is the man that will turn the world upside down, therefore no wonder he hath enemies.

True freedom lies where a man receives his nourishment and that is in the use of the earth. A man had better have no body than have no food for it. True freedom lies in the true enjoyment of the earth. True religion and undefiled is to let every one quietly have earth to manure. There can be no universal liberty till this universal community be established.

1ST ACTOR [*announces*]: A Bill of Account of the most remarkable sufferings that the Diggers have met with since they began to dig the commons for the poor on George Hill in Surrey.

2ND ACTOR: We were fetched by above a hundred people who took away our spades, and some of them we never had again and taken to prison at Walton.

3RD ACTOR: The dragonly enemy pulled down a house we had built and cut our spades to pieces.

4TH ACTOR: One of us had his head sore wounded, and a boy beaten. Some of us were beaten by the gentlemen, the sherriff looking on, and afterwards five were taken to White Lion prison and kept there about five weeks.

5TH ACTOR: We had all our corn spoilt, for the enemy was so mad that they tumbled the earth up and down and would suffer no corn to grow.

6TH ACTOR: Next day two soldiers and two or three men sent by the parson pulled down another house and turned an old man and his wife out of doors to lie in the field on a cold night.

1ST ACTOR: It is understood the General gave his consent that the soldiers should come to help beat off the Diggers, and it is true the soldiers came with the gentlemen and caused others to pull down our houses; but I think the soldiers were sorry to see what was done.

Guide for Responding

◆ Literature and Your Life

Reader's Response Were the Diggers entitled to freely cultivate the land of England? Explain.

Thematic Focus How have the problems of England's poor changed since the seventeenth century?

☑ Check Your Comprehension

1. What were people doing at St. George's Hill?
2. What injustices were suffered by the Diggers?

◆ Critical Thinking

INTERPRET

1. What is meant by "For freedom is the man that will turn the world upside down, therefore no wonder he hath enemies"? **[Interpret]**
2. How does this support the belief of the Diggers that all people are entitled to the land? **[Support]**
3. Compare and contrast Winstanley's ideas of freedom with those of the common people. **[Compare and Contrast]**

Thematic Connection

A NATION DIVIDED

The authors of the selections in this section have opposing viewpoints. For example, while Milton supported the Commonwealth, Royalists like Lovelace supported the monarchy. In countries that treasure freedom, people still have opposing views on many different issues. Although these viewpoints may not divide the nation, they often upset communities and greatly change people's relationships and outlook.

1. (a) How do the authors in this section treat the subject of equality and freedom? (b) Compare and contrast your definition of freedom with the definitions given or suggested by these authors.
2. The former colonies of England—such as India, Trinidad, the West Indies, and Jamaica—now find themselves free from England's rule. What do you think a country should do in reestablishing itself as a "free" country?

Idea Bank

Writing

1. **Newspaper Article** As a seventeenth-century reporter, write a brief newspaper article based on the scene from *Light Shining in Buckinghamshire*.

2. **Press Release** As a politician, prepare a press release that addresses the issues involving the Diggers that are depicted in Churchill's play. The release should be an attempt to calm temperaments not incite more trouble.

3. **Retelling** Rewrite this scene so it is based on a current-day controversial issue. Define the viewpoint of your characters, and use dialogue to reveal any injustices suffered.

Speaking, Listening, and Viewing

4. **Panel Discussion** Create a panel of historical freedom fighters. Each member should research the person he or she is to portray. Have your classmates ask each panel member questions that pertain to his or her historical struggles. **[Social Studies Link]**

Researching and Representing

5. **Collage** Create a collage that illustrates your own personal definition of freedom. You may choose poems or songs that also present your ideas on freedom to accompany the collage. **[Art Link]**

Online Activity ▸ www.phlit.phschool.com

Writing Process Workshop

The writers in this section express feelings, thoughts, and insights about their personal experiences. Invite readers to learn more about you by writing an autobiographical incident—a real-life story of something you experienced.

When writing an **autobiographical incident**, tell your story using the first-person point of view and refer to yourself using the pronouns *I* and *me*. The following skills will help you write about an autobiographical incident:

Writing Skills Focus

▶ **Maintain a consistent point of view** by presenting events from one perspective. Being consistent will help readers follow the events in your incident. (See p. 443.)

▶ **Use dramatic effects,** such as startling facts or unusual perspectives, to capture your audience's attention and emphasize important points. (See p. 451.)

▶ A **personal tone** will help you express feelings, thoughts, and insights about your experiences.

These skills are evident in the passage from Fanny Burney's *Diary,* which is excerpted below. In the excerpt, Burney relates an autobiographical incident, in which the author observed Dr. Samuel Johnson, who wrote *A Dictionary of the English Language,* reacting violently to criticism of his writings.

Fanny Burney (1752–1840)

MODEL FROM LITERATURE

from The Diary of Fanny Burney

I ① was quite frightened to hear my own name mentioned in a debate which began so seriously; but Dr. Johnson made not this any answer: he repeated his attack and his challenge, and a violent disputation ensued, in which this great but mortal man did, to own the truth, appear unreasonably furious and grossly severe ②. I never saw him so before, and I heartily hope I never shall again ③.

① Burney consistently uses the pronoun *I* to indicate the first-person viewpoint from which the story is told.

② This vivid description of Johnson's temper emphasizes the dramatic effect of the situation.

③ By revealing her innermost feelings, Burney gives this incident a personal tone.

APPLYING LANGUAGE SKILLS: Agreement With Indefinite Pronouns

Because indefinite pronouns vary in number, they can cause problems in agreement.

Always Singular:

another, either, neither, other, anybody, no one, everyone, anything, each, someone, everybody

Always Plural:

both, few, many, several

Can be Singular or Plural:

all, some, any, most, none, enough, more, plenty

Practice Complete the following sentences with the correct verb.

1. All the athletes (is/are) varsity.
2. Few of these people (has/have) acrophobia.
3. Each of the actors (was/were) talented.

Writing Application Check your paper for possible errors in agreement.

Writer's Solution Connection

Writing Lab

For help in organizing your writing, review the audio-annotated writing models of types of organization in the Drafting section of the Narration tutorial.

Prewriting

Choose a Topic If you keep a diary, look through it to find a writing idea. If you do not keep a diary, recall humorous, unexpected, interesting, or strange situations in which you've found yourself. Consider the following topics for your autobiographical incident:

> ### Topic Ideas
> - Your most recent birthday
> - A lesson learned
> - A time of hardship

Create a Personal Tone Jot down some details about the incident that uniquely reveal your personal thoughts and insights. For example, take notes about what you saw, heard, thought, and felt during the incident you're describing.

Plan Dramatic Effects Identify the high point of your autobiographical incident. Then jot down interesting comparisons, vivid images, or startling details that spring to mind when you relive it.

Drafting

Maintain a Consistent Point of View As you draft, maintain a consistent perspective. Keep in mind that you, as the narrator, are participating in the action. Refer only to incidents as you see, feel, hear, or participate in them.

Create a Personal Tone Review the notes you took during prewriting, and create a personal tone as you draft. Avoid clichés and neutral observations, and let your unique standpoint shine through. To do this, use personal pronouns such as *I, me, my, mine,* and include dialogue where appropriate. Also give information that makes the story uniquely yours.

> **Neutral Tone:** Aunt Sophia opened the door and let me in.
>
> **Personal Tone:** My dearest Auntie Sophie greeted me with an excited "Hiya!"

Build Dramatic Effects As you write your autobiographical incident, use dramatic effects to lead up to, and describe, the high point of your story.

> **No Dramatic Effects:** I scored the winning touchdown.
>
> **Dramatic Effects:** As the audience roared, I sprinted past the goal posts, scoring the winning touchdown!

Revising

Look Critically at What You Have Written Ask yourself, "If this wasn't my own story, would I find it interesting?" Be sure you have included details that create a personal tone and capture your readers' attention.

Ask a Peer Reviewer Ask a peer to read your autobiographical incident and mark places where the point of view was inconsistent or events were confusing. Then revise your incident so it flows smoothly.

REVISION MODEL

Seeing pictures of the ocean reminds me of a family vacation

① We

my family took when I was eleven years old. They went

② , during a sweltering, record-breaking summer

during the summer; right after Independence Day. We spent

several days sitting on the beach and splashing in the

③ Indulging our passion for ice cream, we went each evening
to Coneheads, an ice cream parlor on the boardwalk.

surprisingly cool ocean. ~~We walked down the boardwalk for~~

~~ice cream every night.~~

① The writer changed *they* to *we* to maintain a consistent point of view.

② The writer added this detail to create a dramatic effect.

③ The writer revised an impersonal sentence to give it a more personal tone.

Publishing

▶ **Home** Compile a scrapbook focusing on a specific time in your life. Start with your autobiographical incident, and include pictures and other memorabilia.

▶ **School** Organize a storytelling festival at your school. Select a theme, for example: *Taking the Driver's Exam.* Have several classmates relate their own experience. Videotape the festival.

▶ **Classroom Collection** Collect and bind together autobiographical incidents of your classmates. You may sort them according to theme, time period, or another organizational method.

Applying Language Skills: Appositive Phrases

An appositive phrase is a noun or pronoun with modifiers that is placed next to a noun or pronoun to add information or detail.

Examples:
Virginia Trask, my mother's aunt, voted in every national election from 1921 to 1994.

Practice Identify the appositive phrase in each sentence.

1. Jackie and Philippa, Jackie's best friend, sang together.
2. The house, an architectural marvel, was built in the last century.
3. We saw Tough Jackets, the nation's best-selling rock band.
4. Our guests, Eric and Trudy, left early.

Writing Application Check your autobiographical incident for places where appositive phrases may provide more information.

Writer's Solution Connection Writing Lab

For help in making your writing more interesting, review the Sensory Details Word Bins in the Revising and Editing section of the Narration tutorial.

Student Success Workshop

Real-World Reading Skills

Evaluating a Writer's Motivation

Strategies for Success

We tend to think that newspaper and magazine articles report the facts. However, writers may word facts to create a bias in favor of one point of view. Certain signs can help you recognize the writer's motivation:

Identify the Writer's Point of View Many subjects, especially controversial ones, can be approached from different angles. Decide whether the writer's subject is one about which people hold different opinions. Check to see if one side seems to be favored.

Look at the Writer's Motivation Identify ways that the writer's stance affects the credibility of the article. A writer may present one group of people as more normal or acceptable, in hopes that you'll identify with their point of view. Look for descriptions that portray people on one side of an issue more sympathetically than people on the other side.

Look at the Writer's Language Look for words or phrases that spark an emotional response, such as "horrible conditions" or "as innocent as a child," especially when such charged words replace objective evidence.

✔ Here are other forms of writing that often call for evaluating a writer's motivation:

► Campaign literature
► Editorials
► Textbooks

Apply the Strategies

Use your reading skills to detect the writer's motivation:

NEWS CHRONICLE

NEWS CHRONICLES   Section II   February 19, 1984

SCHOOL BOARD CONDEMNS HOUSES

Knuckling under to a few misguided state legislators, the school board revealed that it plans to condemn private property and homes worth $10 million for expansion of school facilities. One homeowner affected by this sudden measure declared, "We never had a chance to state our case." The condemnation would be part of a $25 million school bond issue going before voters this November.

1. (a) What is the topic at issue? (b) Which point of view does the writer favor? Explain. (c) How does the writer's position affect the credibility of the news story?

2. (a) Which group of people does the writer present more favorably? (b) Which words or images contribute to this impression? Explain.

3. Rewrite this paragraph, keeping the same facts but introducing a bias in the opposite direction.

PART **3** 𝒯*he Ties That Bind*

Illustration From *Gulliver's Travels*

*G*uide for Interpreting

Samuel Pepys *(1633–1703)*

Samuel Pepys (pēps) is an unusual literary celebrity. Not only does his fame rest on a single work but that work was never intended for publication! The work in question is Pepys's diary, which he wrote in shorthand and in his own private code. Undeciphered until the nineteenth century, the Diary provides a fascinating glimpse of London from 1660 to 1669, when Pepys's failing eyesight forced him to abandon the project.

An Ideal Observer Pepys was in a good position to report on the era. The son of a London tailor, he attended Cambridge University and after graduation became the secretary of his influential cousin, the Earl of Sandwich. In 1660, the year the monarchy was restored, he got his first government post as a clerk for the navy. From there, his rise to fame and fortune was rapid, though not always smooth. Twice his political connections made him a prisoner in the Tower of London, once on charges of treason. Despite these setbacks, Pepys earned a lasting reputation as a man of intelligence and a keen observer.

Daniel Defoe *(1660–1731)*

"A false, shuffling, prevaricating rascal"— that was how fellow author Joseph Addison described Daniel Defoe. In many ways, Addison was not far wrong. Constantly in debt, Defoe often engaged in shady business deals and declared bankruptcy in 1692, owing a small fortune to his creditors. He was also a sometime government spy and propagandist who even upgraded his own name, originally Foe, by adding an aristocratic De.

An Innovative Novelist Despite all these flaws, we remember Defoe for an important literary achievement. He practically invented the modern realistic novel. He did so with a handful of works published around his sixtieth birthday: *Robinson Crusoe* (1719), his almost documentary narrative of a man marooned on a desert island; *Moll Flanders* (1722), a satirical tale of a lowborn woman seeking respectability; and *A Journal of the Plague Year* (1722), his fictional journal of the great plague that devastated England in 1664–1665, "the plague year."

◆ Background for Understanding

HISTORY: TWIN DISASTERS

In the 1660's, following years of upheaval and a short period of peace, London was struck by twin disasters. The first of these was a plague that began in 1664 and by the next year killed nearly 70,000 Londoners—in a population of about 460,000.

A usually fatal infectious disease, bubonic plague is spread by fleas from an infected host, such as the black rat. Then, in 1666, just as the city was beginning to recover, the Great Fire of London broke out, destroying more than 13,000 buildings.

Like the plague, the Great Fire of London also had a devastating effect on London.

You will read about these disasters in two unusual literary works, a novel about the plague that is written in journal form, and an actual diary that contains an account of the plague and the Great Fire of London.

The Great Fire of London, 1666

◆ *from* The Diary ◆
from A Journal of the Plague Year

◆ *Literature and Your Life*

CONNECT YOUR EXPERIENCE

Despite the best efforts of scientists and doctors, disasters and diseases still threaten us. Although, on average, we may live longer than our ancestors, we're not yet germproof or fireproof. As you read this diary and journal, you will become familiar with two disasters that threatened seventeenth-century England, the bubonic plague and the Great Fire of London.

Journal Writing Jot down in your journal any unfortunate events that you've experienced or seen reported on television.

THEMATIC FOCUS: THE TIES THAT BIND

Although misfortunes strike at human relationships, they may strengthen emotional ties. As you read, look for evidence of compassion on the part of Pepys and the narrator of Defoe's *Journal*.

◆ Literary Focus

DIARY OR JOURNAL

A **diary** or **journal** is a daily account of a writer's experiences and reactions. The words *diary* and *journal* are from the Latin (*dies*) and French (*jour*) words for "day" respectively. Most diaries or journals record the small details of a life, but diaries that become literature provide insights into important historical events or periods.

Pepys's *Diary* describes not only his personal life but also historical events that he witnessed, like the bubonic plague and the Great Fire of London. Defoe's *Journal of the Plague Year* is actually a well-researched novel posing as a journal to make it seem more realistic.

◆ Grammar and Style

GERUNDS

In Pepys's *Diary* and Defoe's *Journal*, you'll find many examples of **gerunds,** verb forms that end in -*ing* and function as nouns. Gerunds can be preceded by articles, as nouns are.

Church being done, my Lord Bruncker, Sir J. Minnes, and I up to the vestry ... in order to the *doing* something for the *keeping* of the plague from *growing*.

As you read, note the different ways gerunds are used.

◆ Reading Strategy

DRAW CONCLUSIONS

You can learn more about a person or a period by using given details to **draw conclusions.** As you read, keep a chart of details from the selections and conclusions that you draw from them.

The Diary	Conclusions
"I had appointed a boat to attend me...."	Pepys was probably fairly rich since he could hire his own boat.

◆ Build Vocabulary

PREFIXES: *dis-*

In *A Journal of the Plague Year* you'll see the word *distemper*, a term for an infectious disease. Its prefix *dis-*, which means "apart," combines with *temper*, meaning "balance," to suggest the imbalance of the disease.

WORD BANK

Before you read, preview this list of words from the selections.

apprehensions
abated
lamentable
combustible
malicious
discoursing
distemper
importuning
prodigious

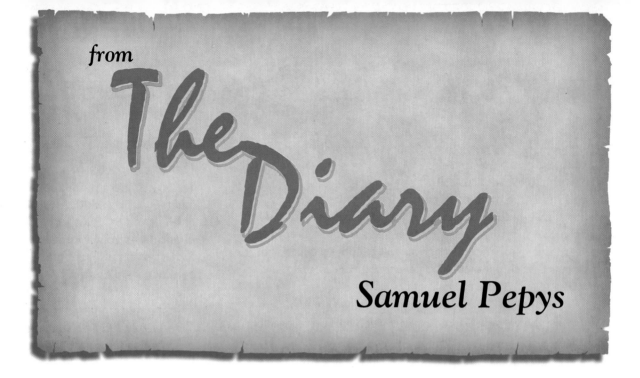

from

The Diary

Samuel Pepys

The Plague

Sept. 3, 1665. (Lord's Day.) Church being done, my Lord Bruncker, Sir J. Minnes, and I up to the vestry[1] at the desire of the Justices of the Peace, Sir Theo. Biddulph and Sir W. Boreman and Alderman Hooker, in order to the doing something for the keeping of the plague from growing; but Lord! to consider the madness of the people of the town, who will (because they are forbid) come in crowds along with the dead corps[2] to see them buried; but we agreed on some orders for the prevention thereof.[3] Among other stories, one was very passionate, methought of a complaint brought against a man in the town for taking a child from London from an infected house. Alderman Hooker told us it was the child of a very able citizen in Gracious Street, a saddler,[4] who had buried all the rest of his children of the plague, and himself and wife now being shut up and in despair of escaping, did desire only to save the life of this little child; and so prevailed to have it received stark-naked into the arms of a friend, who brought it (having put it into new fresh clothes) to Greenwich; where upon hearing the story, we did agree it should be permitted to be received and kept in the town. Thence with my Lord Bruncker to Captain Cocke's, where we mighty merry and supped, and very late I by water to Woolwich, in great apprehensions of an ague . . . .

Sept. 14, 1665. When I come home I spent some thoughts upon the occurrences of this day, giving matter for as much content on one hand and melancholy on another, as any day in all my life. For the first; the finding of my money and plate,[5] and all safe at London, and speeding in my business of money this day. The hearing of this good news to such excess, after so great a despair of my Lord's doing anything this year; adding to that, the decrease of 500 and more, which is the first decrease we have yet had in the sickness since it begun: and great hopes that the next week it will be greater. Then, on the other side, my finding that though the bill[6] in general is abated, yet the city within the walls is increased, and likely to continue so, and is close to our house there. My meeting dead corpses of the plague, carried to be buried close to me at noonday through the city in Fanchurch Street. To see a person

---

1. **vestry** (ves´ trē) _n._: Church meeting-room.
2. **corps:** Corpses.
3. **but we . . . thereof:** Funeral processions were forbidden in London during the plague. However, the law was often ignored.
4. **saddler** _n._: Person who makes, sells, and repairs saddles.

---

5. **plate:** Valuable serving dishes and flatware.
6. **bill:** Weekly list of burials.

▶ Critical Viewing
What line from Pepys's account of the fire would be an appropriate caption for this painting? Why? [Connect]

The Great Fire of London, 1666

sick of the sores, carried close by me by Grace church in a hackney coach.[7] My finding the Angell Tavern at the lower end of Tower Hill, shut up, and more than that, the alehouse at the Tower Stairs, and more than that, the person was then dying of the plague when I was last there, a little while ago, at night, to write a short letter there, and I overheard the mistress of the house sadly saying to her husband somebody was very ill, but did not think it was of the plague. To hear that poor Payne, my waiter, hath buried a child, and is dying himself. To hear that a laborer I sent but the other day to Dagenhams, to know how they did there, is dead of the plague; and that one of my own watermen, that carried me daily, fell sick as soon as he had landed me on Friday morning last, when I had been all night upon the water (and I believe he did get his infection that day at Brainford), and is now dead of the plague. To hear that Captain Lambert and Cuttle are killed in the taking these ships; and that Mr. Sidney Montague is sick of a desperate fever at my Lady Carteret's, at Scott's Hall. To hear that Mr. Lewes hath another daughter sick. And,

◆ Literary Focus
What abbreviated language in this passage is evidence of Pepys's own personal shorthand?

lastly, that both my servants, W. Hewer and Tom Edwards, have lost their fathers, both in St. Sepulcher's parish, of the plague this week, do put me into great apprehensions of melancholy, and with good reason. But I put off the thoughts of sadness as much as I can, and the rather to keep my wife in good heart and family also. After supper (having eat nothing all this day) upon a fine tench[8] of Mr. Shelden's taking, we to bed.

The Fire of London

Sept. 2, 1666. (Lord's day.) Some of our maids sitting up late last night to get things ready against our feast today, Jane called us up about three in the morning, to tell us of a great fire they saw in the city. So I rose and slipped on my night-gown, and went to her window, and thought it to be on the back side of Mark Lane at the farthest; but, being unused to such fires as followed, I thought it far enough off; and so went to bed again and to sleep. About seven rose again to dress myself, and there looked out at the window, and saw the fire not so much as it was and farther off.

---

7. **hackney coach:** Carriage for hire.

8. **tench** *n.*: Type of fish.

◆ **Build Vocabulary**

apprehensions (ap′ rē hen′ shəns) *n.*: Fears; concerns

abated (ə bāt′ id) *v.*: Lessened

So to my closet to set things to rights after yesterday's cleaning. By and by Jane comes and tells me that she hears that above 300 houses have been burned down tonight by the fire we saw, and that it is now burning down all Fish Street, by London Bridge. So I made myself ready presently, and walked to the Tower,[9] and there got up upon one of the high places, Sir J. Robinson's little son going up with me; and there I did see the houses at that end of the bridge all on fire, and an infinite great fire on this and the other side the end of the bridge; which, among other people, did trouble me for poor little Michell and our Sarah on the bridge. So down, with my heart full of trouble, to the Lieutenant of the Tower, who tells me that it begun this morning in the King's baker's house in Pudding Lane, and that it hath burned St. Magnus's Church and most part of Fish Street already. So I down to the waterside, and there got a boat and through bridge, and there saw a lamentable fire. Poor Michell's house, as far as the Old Swan, already burned that way, and the fire running farther, that in a very little time it got as far as the steel yard, while I was there. Everybody endeavoring to remove their goods, and flinging into the river or bringing them into lighters that lay off; poor people staying in their houses as long as till the very fire touched them, and then running into boats, or clambering from one pair of stairs by the waterside to another. And among other things, the poor pigeons, I perceive, were loth to leave their houses, but hovered about the windows and balconies till they were, some of them burned, their wings, and fell down. Having stayed, and in an hour's time seen the fire rage every way, and nobody, to my sight, endeavoring to quench it, but to remove their goods, and leave all to the fire, and having seen it get as far as the steel yard, and the wind mighty high and driving it into the city; and everything, after so long a drought, proving combustible, even the very stones of churches,

---

9. **Tower:** Tower of London.

and among other things the poor steeple by which pretty Mrs.—lives, and whereof my old schoolfellow Elborough is parson, taken fire in the very top, and there burned till it fell down. I to Whitehall (with a gentleman with me who desired to go off from the Tower, to see the fire, in my boat), and there up to the King's closet in the chapel, where people come about me, and I did give them an account dismayed them all, and word was carried in to the King. So I was called for, and did tell the King and Duke of York what I saw, and that unless his Majesty did command houses to be pulled down nothing could stop the fire. They seemed much troubled, and the King commanded me to go to my Lord Mayor from him, and command him to spare no houses, but to pull down before the fire every way. The Duke of York bid me tell him that if he would have any more soldiers he shall; and so did my Lord Arlington afterwards, as a great secret. Here meeting with Captain Cocke, I in his coach, which he lent me, and Creed with me to Paul's,[10] and there walked along Watling Street, as well as I could, every creature coming away loaden with goods to save, and here and there sick people carried away in beds. Extraordinary good goods carried in carts and on backs. At last met my Lord Mayor in Canning Street, like a man spent, with a handkerchief about his neck. To the King's message he cried, like a fainting woman, "Lord! what can I do? I am spent: people will not obey me. I have been pulling down houses; but the fire overtakes us faster than we can do it." That he needed no more soldiers; and that, for himself, he must go and refresh himself, having been up all night. So he left me, and I him, and walked home, seeing people all almost distracted, and no manner of means used to quench the fire. The houses, too, so very thick thereabouts, and full of matter for burning, as pitch and tar, in Thames Street; and warehouses of oil, and wines, and brandy, and other things. Here I saw Mr. Isaake Houblon, the handsome man, prettily dressed and dirty, at his door at Dowgate, receiving some of his brothers' things, whose houses were on fire; and, as he says, have been removed twice already; and he doubts (as it soon proved) that they must be in a little time removed from his house also, which was a sad consideration. And to see the churches all filling with goods by people who themselves should have been quietly there at this time. By this time it was about twelve o'clock; and so home. Soon as dined, and walked through the city, the streets full of nothing but people and horses and carts loaden with goods, ready to run over one another, and removing goods from one burned house to another. They now removing out of Canning Street (which received goods in the morning) into Lumbard Street, and farther; and among others I now saw my little goldsmith, Stokes, receiving some friend's goods, whose house itself was burned the day after. I to Paul's Wharf, where I had appointed a boat to attend me, and took in Mr. Carcasse and his brother, whom I met in the street, and carried them below and above bridge to and again to see the fire, which was now got farther, both below and above, and no likelihood of stopping it. Met with the King and Duke of York in their barge, and with them to Queen-hithe, and there called Sir Richard Browne to them. Their order was only to pull down houses apace, and so below bridge at the waterside; but little was or could be done, the fire coming upon them so fast. Good hopes there was of stopping it at the Three Cranes above, and at Buttolph's Wharf below bridge, if care be used; but the wind carries it into the city, so as we know not by the waterside what it do there. River full of lighters and boats taking in goods, and good goods swimming in the water, and only I observed that hardly one lighter or boat in three that had the goods of a house in, but there was a pair of virginals[11] in it. Having seen as much as I could now, I away to Whitehall by appointment, and there walked to St. James's Park,

◆ Literature and Your Life

In what ways is Pepys's account similar to an account you may have heard on television or radio news or read in the newspaper?

---

10. **Paul's:** St. Paul's Cathedral.

11. **virginals** *n.*: Small, legless harpsichords.

◆ Build Vocabulary

lamentable (lam´ mən tə bəl) *adj.*: Distressing

combustible (kəm bus´ tə bəl) *adj.*: Capable of igniting and burning; flammable

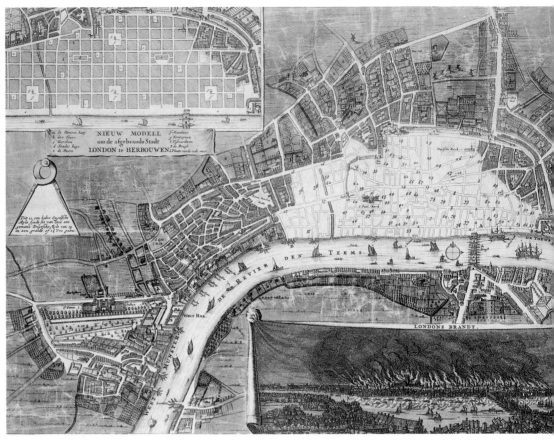

► **Critical Viewing**
This map of London includes an inset depicting the area destroyed by the Great Fire. Does this image enhance Pepys's eyewitness description? Explain. [Make a Judgment]

and there met my wife and Creed and Wood and his wife, and walked to my boat; and there upon the water again, and to the fire up and down, it still increasing, and the wind great. So near the fire as we could for smoke; and all over the Thames, with one's face in the wind, you were almost burned with a shower of fire-drops. This is very true; so as houses were burned by these drops and flakes of fire, three or four, nay, five or six houses, one from another. When we could endure no more upon the water, we to a little alehouse on the Bank-side, over against the Three Cranes, and there stayed till it was dark almost, and saw the fire grow; and, as it grew darker, appeared more and more, and in corners and upon steeples, and between churches and houses, as far as we could see up the hill of the city, in a most horrid malicious bloody flame, not like the fine flame of an ordinary fire. Barbary and her husband away before us. We stayed till, it being darkish, we saw the fire as only one entire arch of fire from this to the other side the bridge, and in a bow up the hill for an arch of above a mile long: it made me weep to see it. The

churches, houses, and all on fire and flaming at once; and a horrid noise the flames made, and the cracking of houses at their ruin. So home with a sad heart, and there find everybody discoursing and lamenting the fire; and poor Tom Hater come with some of his few goods saved out of his house, which is burned upon Fish Street Hill. I invited him to lie at my house, and did receive his goods, but was deceived in his lying there, the news coming every moment of the growth of the fire; so as we were forced to begin to pack up our own goods, and prepare for their removal; and did by moon-shine (it being brave dry, and moonshine, and warm weather) carry much of my goods into the garden, and Mr. Hater and I did remove my money and iron chests into my cellar, as thinking that the safest place. And got my bags of

◆ **Build Vocabulary**

malicious (mə lish´ əs) *adj.*: Deliberately harmful; destructive

discoursing (dis kôrs´ iŋ) *v.*: Talking about; discussing

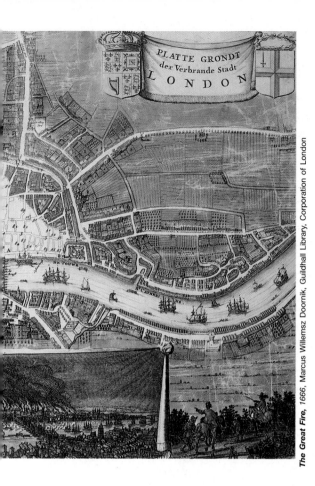

The Great Fire, 1666, Marcus Willemsz Doornik, Guildhall Library, Corporation of London

gold into my office, ready to carry away, and my chief papers of accounts also there, and my tallies into a box by themselves. So great was our fear, as Sir W. Batten hath carts come out of the country to fetch away his goods this night. We did put Mr. Haters, poor man, to bed a little; but he got but very little rest, so much noise being in my house, taking down of goods.

3rd. About four o'clock in the morning, my Lady Batten sent me a cart to carry away all my money, and plate, and best things, to Sir W. Rider's at Bednall Green. Which I did, riding myself in my nightgown in the cart; and, Lord! to see how the streets and the highways are crowded with people running and riding, and getting of carts at any rate to fetch away things. I find Sir W. Rider tired with being called up all night, and receiving things from several friends. His house full of goods, and much of Sir W. Batten's and Sir W. Pen's. I am eased at my heart to have my treasure so well secured. Then home, with much ado to find a way, nor any sleep all this night to me nor my poor wife.

> ◆ **Reading Strategy**
> What conclusions can you draw about Pepys from the last two sentences?

Guide for Responding

◆ *Literature and Your Life*

Reader's Response Does Pepys's *Diary* make the plague and fire seem real to you? Why or why not?

Thematic Focus What does the excerpt reveal about Pepys's ties to family, friends, and colleagues?

Questions for Research According to Pepys, during the fire people acted to save their own goods, not to put out the blaze. Generate questions that would help you research whether ordinary people were responsible for such firefighting.

☑ Check Your Comprehension

1. According to the entry for September 3, 1665, what happened to the saddler's family?
2. When does Pepys first learn of the Great Fire?
3. (a) What does Pepys recommend to the King and the Duke of York? (b) What is the reply?
4. Summarize Pepys's actions on Sept. 3, 1666.

◆ Critical Thinking

INTERPRET

1. What does the entry for September 3, 1665, reveal about Pepys? Explain. **[Infer]**
2. (a) What seems to be Pepys's attitude toward business? (b) What seems to be his attitude toward pleasure? **[Infer]**
3. From the evidence of these diary entries, how would you describe Pepys's character and personality? **[Draw Conclusions]**

APPLY

4. (a) In Pepys's London, which do you think was a greater disaster—the plague in 1665 or the Great Fire in 1666? Explain. (b) What disasters in modern times do you think compare with these unfortunate events? **[Relate]**

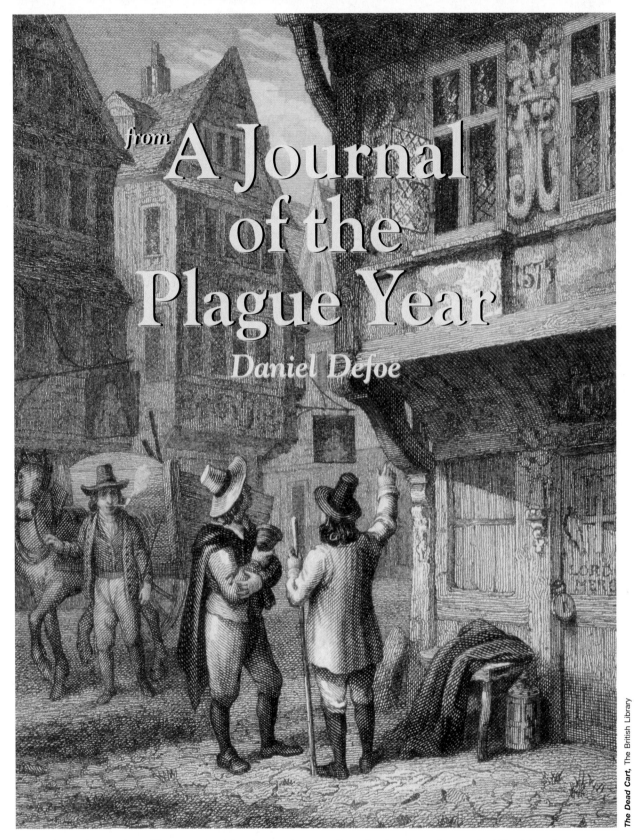

from # A Journal of the Plague Year

Daniel Defoe

The Dead Cart, The British Library

▶ **Critical Viewing** The cart in this picture is carrrying the bodies of people killed by the plague. What can you infer about the plague's impact on daily life from the number of people on the street and from the gestures of the men in conversation? **[Infer]**

The face of London was now indeed strangely altered, I mean the whole mass of buildings, city, liberties, suburbs, Westminster, Southwark, and altogether; for as to the particular part called the city, or within the walls, that was not yet much infected. But in the whole the face of things, I say, was much altered; sorrow and sadness sat upon every face; and though some parts were not yet overwhelmed, yet all looked deeply concerned; and as we saw it apparently coming on, so everyone looked on himself and his family as in the utmost danger. Were it possible to represent those times exactly to those that did not see them, and give the reader due ideas of the horror that everywhere presented itself, it must make just impressions upon their minds and fill them with surprise. London might well be said to be all in tears; the mourners did not go about the streets indeed, for nobody put on black or made a formal dress of mourning for their nearest friends; but the voice of mourning was truly heard in the streets. The shrieks of women and children at the windows and doors of their houses, where their dearest relations were perhaps dying, or just dead, were so frequent to be heard as we passed the streets, that it was enough to pierce the stoutest heart in the world to hear them. Tears and lamentations were seen almost in every house, especially in the first part of the visitation; for toward the latter end men's hearts were hardened, and death was so always before their eyes, that they did not so much concern themselves for the loss of their friends, expecting that themselves should be summoned the next hour . . . .

I went all the first part of the time freely about the streets, though not so freely as to run myself into apparent danger, except when they dug the great pit in the churchyard of our parish of Aldgate. A terrible pit it was, and I could not resist my curiosity to go and see it. As near as I may judge, it was about forty feet in length, and about fifteen or sixteen feet broad, and, at the time I first looked at it, about nine feet deep; but it was said they dug it near twenty feet

deep afterwards in one part of it, till they could go no deeper for the water; for they had, it seems, dug several large pits before this. For though the plague was long a-coming to our parish, yet, when it did come, there was no parish in or about London where it raged with such violence as in the two parishes of Aldgate and Whitechapel.

I saw they had dug several pits in another ground, when the distemper began to spread in our parish, and especially when the dead carts began to go about, which was not, in our parish, till the beginning of August. Into these pits they had put perhaps fifty or sixty bodies each; then they made larger holes, wherein they buried all that the cart brought in a week, which, by the middle to the end of August, came to from 200 to 400 a week; and they could not well dig them larger, because of the order of the magistrates confining them to leave no bodies within six feet of the surface; and the water coming on at about seventeen or eighteen feet, they could not well, I say, put more in one pit. But now, at the beginning of September, the plague raging in a dreadful manner, and the number of burials in our parish increasing to more than was ever buried in any parish about London of no larger extent, they ordered this dreadful gulf to be dug, for such it was rather than a pit.

They had supposed this pit would have supplied them for a month or more when they dug it, and some blamed the churchwardens for suffering[1] such a frightful thing, telling them they were making preparations to bury the whole parish, and the like; but time made it appear the churchwardens knew the condition of the parish better than they did, for the pit being finished the 4th of September, I think, they began to bury in it the 6th, and by the 20th, which was just two weeks, they had thrown into it 1114 bodies, when they were obliged to fill it up, the bodies being then come to lie within six feet of the surface. I doubt not

---

1. **suffering:** Allowing.

◆ **Build Vocabulary**

distemper (dis tem´ pər) *n*.: Infectious disease such as the plague

but there may be some ancient persons alive in the parish who can justify the fact of this, and are able to show even in what place of the churchyard the pit lay better than I can. The mark of it also was many years to be seen in the churchyard on the surface, lying in length parallel with the passage which goes by the west wall of the churchyard out of Hounds-ditch, and turns east again into Whitechapel, coming out near the Three Nuns' Inn.

It was about the 10th of September that my curiosity led, or rather drove, me to go and see this pit again, when there had been near 400 people buried in it; and I was not content to see it in the daytime, as I had done before, for then there would have been nothing to have been seen but the loose earth; for all the bodies that were thrown in were immediately covered with earth by those they called the buriers, which at other times were called bearers; but I resolved to go in the night and see some of them thrown in.

◆ **Reading Strategy**
From the information in this paragraph, what do you conclude about the narrator's motives?

There was a strict order to prevent people coming to those pits, and that was only to prevent infection. But after some time that order was more necessary, for people that were infected and near their end, and delirious also, would run to those pits, wrapped in blankets or rugs, and throw themselves in, and, as they said, bury themselves. I cannot say that the officers suffered any willingly to lie there; but I have heard that in a great pit in Finsbury, in the parish of Cripplegate, it lying open then to the fields, for it was not then walled about, [some] came and threw themselves in, and expired there, before they threw any earth upon them; and that when they came to bury others, and found them there, they were quite dead, though not cold.

This may serve a little to describe the dreadful condition of that day, though it is impossible to say anything that is able to give a true idea of it to those who did not see it, other than this, that it was indeed very, very, very dreadful, and such as no tongue can express.

I got admittance into the churchyard by being acquainted with the sexton who attended, who, though he did not refuse me at all, yet earnestly persuaded me not to go, telling me very seriously, for he was a good, religious, and sensible man, that it was indeed their business and duty to venture, and to run all hazards, and that in it they might hope to be preserved; but that I had no apparent call to it but my own curiosity, which, he said, he believed I would not pretend was sufficient to justify my running that hazard. I told him I had been pressed in my mind to go, and that perhaps it might be an instructing sight, that might not be without its uses. "Nay," says the good man, "if you will venture upon that score, name of God go in; for, depend upon it, 't will be a sermon to you, it may be, the best that ever you heard in your life. 'T is a speaking sight," says he, "and has a voice with it, and a loud one, to call us all to repentance"; and with that he opened the door and said, "Go, if you will."

His discourse had shocked my resolution a little, and I stood wavering for a good while, but just at that interval I saw two links[2] come over from the end of the Minories, and heard the bellman, and then appeared a dead cart, as they called it, coming over the streets; so I could no longer resist my desire of seeing it, and went in. There was nobody, as I could perceive at first, in the churchyard, or going into it, but the buriers and the fellow that drove the cart, or rather led the horse and cart; but when they came up to the pit they saw a man go to and again,[3] muffled up in a brown cloak, and making motions with his hands under his cloak, as if he was in a great agony, and the buriers immediately gathered about him, supposing he was one of those poor delirious or desperate creatures that used to pretend, as I have said, to bury themselves. He said nothing as he walked about, but two or three times groaned very deeply and loud, and sighed as he would break his heart.

When the buriers came up to him they soon found he was neither a person infected and desperate, as I have observed above, or a person distempered in mind, but one oppressed with a dreadful weight of grief indeed, having his wife and several of his children all in the cart that was just come in with him, and he followed in an agony and excess of sorrow. He mourned heartily, as it was easy to see, but

---

2. **links:** Torches.
3. **to and again:** To and fro.

with a kind of masculine grief that could not give itself vent by tears; and calmly defying the buriers to let him alone, said he would only see the bodies thrown in and go away, so they left importuning him. But no sooner was the cart turned round and the bodies shot into the pit promiscuously,[4] which was a surprise to him, for he at least expected they would have been decently laid in, though indeed he was afterwards convinced that was impracticable; I say, no sooner did he see the sight but he cried out aloud, unable to contain himself. I could not hear what he said, but he went backward two or three steps and fell down in a swoon. The buriers ran to him and took him up, and in a little while he came to himself, and they led him away to the Pie Tavern over against the end of Houndsditch, where, it seems, the man was known, and where they took care of him. He looked into the pit again as he went away, but the buriers had covered the bodies so immediately with throwing in earth, that though there was light enough, for there were lanterns, and candles in them, placed all night round

the sides of the pit, upon heaps of earth, seven or eight, or perhaps more, yet nothing could be seen.

This was a mournful scene indeed, and affected me almost as much as the rest; but the other was awful and full of terror. The cart had in it sixteen or seventeen bodies: some were wrapped up in linen sheets, some in rags, some little other than naked, or so loose that what covering they had fell from them in the shooting out of the cart, and they fell quite naked among the rest; but the matter was not much to them, or the indecency much to anyone else, seeing they were all dead, and were to be huddled together into the common grave of mankind, as we may call it, for here was no difference made, but poor and rich went together; there was no other way of burials, neither was it possible there should, for coffins were not to be had for the prodigious numbers that fell in such a calamity as this.

---

4. **promiscuously:** Without care or thought.

◆ **Build Vocabulary**

importuning (im´ pôr toon´ iŋ) *v.*: Pleading
prodigious (prō´dij´ əs) *adj.*: Enormous; huge

Guide for Responding

◆ *Literature and Your Life*

Reader's Response Which passages in *A Journal of the Plague Year* seem especially vivid to you? Why?
Thematic Focus What does the selection reveal about family and community feelings during a time of crisis?

☑ Check Your Comprehension

1. What was the purpose of the great pit dug in Aldgate?
2. (a) What prompts the narrator to visit the pit? (b) Why does he go at night?
3. Summarize the incident concerning the man in the brown cloak.

◆ Critical Thinking

INTERPRET

1. Why do you think the narrator describes the pit in such a specific way? **[Infer]**
2. What does the sexton mean when he says that visiting the pit will "be a sermon" to the narrator? **[Interpret]**
3. Judging by the tone of this excerpt and the narrator's actions, what kind of person do you think the narrator is? **[Classify]**

COMPARE LITERARY WORKS

4. Compare the way Pepys briefly handles the subject of burial of the dead in his diary with Defoe's fictional treatment beginning with the second paragraph on page 469. **[Compare and Contrast]**

Guide for Responding (continued)

◆ Reading Strategy

DRAW CONCLUSIONS

Reading a diary such as Pepys's, you can **draw conclusions** about its author's personality, attitude, or situation. In the case of a fictional journal like Defoe's, your conclusions will apply to the fictional narrator. For example, when Defoe's narrator says "I went all the first part of the time freely about the streets, though not so freely as to run myself into apparent danger . . ." you can conclude that the narrator is bold, but not reckless.

1. What does the entry dated Sept. 14, 1665, in Pepys's *Diary* reveal about his position in society? Support your conclusion with details.
2. (a) Which narrator—Pepys or Defoe's fictional narrator—seemed more observant to you? (b) On what details do you base your conclusion?

◆ Build Vocabulary

USING THE PREFIX *dis-*

Knowing that the prefix *dis-* can mean "apart," "not," or "do the opposite of," define the following words.

1. disease   3. disable   5. dishonest
2. dismiss   4. disobey

USING THE WORD BANK: Sentence Completions

In your notebook, write the word from the Word Bank that best completes each sentence.

1. London's wooden buildings were highly ____?____.
2. The flames of the fire seemed ____?____, as if they wanted to devour all in their path.
3. People trying to escape the flames began ____?____ boatmen to take them aboard.
4. The fire did a ____?____ amount of damage.
5. When the fire at last ____?____, 13,000 buildings had been destroyed.
6. Worried people were ____?____ about raising money to rebuild their homes.
7. For years afterward, many Londoners had ____?____ that another fire would destroy the city.
8. Others just wished to forget the ____?____ episode.

◆ Literary Focus

DIARY OR JOURNAL

As day-to-day accounts of writers' personal experiences and reactions, **diaries** and **journals** offer fresh and immediate descriptions of people, places, and events. The descriptions are often so engaging because the author was on the scene and refers to himself or herself as "I." This personal pronoun gives you a personal stake in events.

In reading Pepys's entry of Sept. 2, 1666, for example, you experience both daily concerns (planning a feast) and historic events (a catastrophic fire) through Pepys's "I." With Pepys as guide and companion, you get a firsthand look at the ordinary and extraordinary events of London life.

1. (a) Find a passage in *The Diary* that conveys the flavor and freshness of real life. (b) Explain what makes the passage so immediate.
2. In what ways does Defoe's novel *A Journal of the Plague Year* resemble a real journal?
3. How do the accounts by Pepys and Defoe differ from typical news reports of a disaster?

◆ Grammar and Style

GERUNDS

Both Pepys and Defoe extend the range of nouns in their writing by using **gerunds,** verbs with an *-ing* ending that serve as nouns.

Because gerunds end in *-ing*, it is easy to mistake them for present participles, verbs with *-ing* endings. Keep in mind that gerunds serve as nouns, while present participles function as verbs or as adjectives modifying nouns and pronouns.

Practice In your notebook, identify the gerund in the sentence or write *none* if there is no gerund.

1. The plague was a time for deep mourning.
2. Human suffering was all around.
3. Wailing people were fleeing London.
4. The ranks of the dead and dying were swelling every day.
5. Still shuddering from the tragedy, the city had barely finished burying its dead when the Great Fire broke out.

Build Your Portfolio

 Idea Bank

Writing

1. Poster Sometimes, simple precautions can help prevent fires and illnesses. Create a warning poster about fire safety or disease prevention.

2. News Report Write an article about the plague or fire as it might have been reported in an English newspaper of the day. Incorporate factual information from the selections.

3. Response to Criticism Brian Fitzgerald says of Defoe, "He used literature to express his views on social and other questions and only secondarily as a craftsman and artist." Use the excerpt from Defoe's *A Journal of the Plague Year* to refute or support Fitzgerald's comment.

Speaking, Listening, and Viewing

4. Town Crier Many seventeenth-century Londoners got their news orally from a town crier, who called it out. As a town crier, call out news and warnings at the time of the plague or fire. **[Performing Arts Link]**

5. Oral Report Using library resources, learn the causes and history of bubonic plague. Present your findings in an oral report. **[Science Link; Social Studies Link]**

Researching and Representing

6. Map With a partner, research and create a map of the London area at the time of the plague and fire. Include major streets and landmarks mentioned in the selections. **[Social Studies Link]**

7. Timeline of Plagues Europe experienced several devastating epidemics of plague. Construct a timeline showing when those epidemics struck, how long they lasted, and the casualties they caused. **[Social Studies Link; Science Link]**

Online Activity www.phlit.phschool.com

 Guided Writing Lesson

Diary Entry

Samuel Pepys captured what life was like for an upper-class Londoner living in an extraordinary time. Like Samuel Pepys, bring to life in a diary entry an incident you witnessed today. It might be an event of significance to your area or simply something important to you. A diary entry should be descriptive, honest, and accurate.

Writing Skills Focus: Accuracy

In all types of writing, it is important to be precise and **accurate.** Since diaries are kept to capture fleeting events and impressions, the more accurate diary entries are, the more fully you can relive your experiences later on.

Here are some tips to ensure accuracy:

- Choose vivid and precise words to describe the people or events you see.
- Include correct names, dates, times, and locations, when appropriate.
- Truthfully record your observations and reactions. Your ideas and feelings *count*.

The following strategies will help you maintain accuracy as you write your diary entry.

Prewriting Jot down the event you plan to describe. Also list the people you saw, the time of day it occurred, and the main impression you wish to convey.

Drafting Put yourself back in the moment and capture on paper the event as it really happened. When you are uncertain about a name or fact, put a question mark beside it.

Revising Reread your diary entry, and verify names or facts about which you were uncertain. Make sure that you've described the event from your personal point of view. Date the diary entry if you have not already done so.

Guide for Interpreting

Jonathan Swift
(1667–1745)

While Swift was writing *Gulliver's Travels*, he had already started to suffer from the inner ear disease that eventually disabled him. "I always expect tomorrow to be worse," he wrote in a letter, "but I enjoy today as well as I can." The result of the author's determination to keep up his spirits was that rarest of books: a literary masterpiece that is loved by children and adults alike.

Finding His Way Swift was born in Dublin, Ireland, to English parents. His father died before he was born. With the assistance of relatives, he received a good education and then obtained an appointment in the household of Sir William Temple, a wealthy kinsman who lived on an estate in Surrey, England. Swift hoped for a career in politics, but receiving no support from Sir William, he decided on a career in the church. After Temple's death in 1699, he was given a small parish near London.

The satirical writing Swift had done while in the Temple household was out of character for a clergyman, but its brilliance was widely acknowledged when it appeared as two separate books in 1704. Published anonymously, *A Tale of a Tub* satirizes excesses in religion and learning, while *The Battle of the Books* describes a comic encounter between ancient and modern literature.

Ambition and Achievement In Swift's day, religion was interwoven with politics. A staunch Anglican, Swift changed his allegiance in 1710 from the Whig party to the Tory party favored by Queen Anne. He benefited immediately from the switch. As the leading party writer for the government, he wrote many pamphlets and wielded considerable political influence.

The Story Behind the Novel The concept of writing a series of imaginary journeys probably originated in 1714 at the meetings of the Scriblerus Club, a group of Swift's literary friends. Apparently, the group assigned this project to Swift because they knew he enjoyed reading travel books. When *Gulliver's Travels* was published in 1726, it was an instant triumph: Ten thousand copies were sold in the first three weeks.

Later Years Embittered by his failure to be named a bishop, Swift served for more than thirty years as dean of St. Patrick's Cathedral in Dublin. He continued to write satires, including *Drapier's Letters* (1724) and *A Modest Proposal* (1729).

Swift's death in 1745 deprived the world of a generous and learned man who despised the fanaticism, selfishness, and pride of people in general but admired individual human beings.

◆ Background for Understanding

HISTORY: SWIFT'S TARGETS FOR SATIRE

Swift's lifetime was a turbulent era in England due to religious strife and the struggles of political factions. These conflicts inspired Swift to ridicule in satire those whose intolerance and pride overcome their reason.

Swift satirizes the conflicts between the established Anglican Church and Roman Catholicism in "A Voyage to Lilliput," where the followers of each denomination are portrayed as Little-Endians and Big-Endians, respectively. Swift also ridicules the wars between officially Protestant England and heavily Catholic France, under the guise of conflict between Lilliput and Blefuscu.

In "A Voyage to Brobdingnag," Swift attacks the political institutions of England, though he can see some "half erased" value in their foundations. He suggests that the politicians leading the country are guilty of "ignorance, idleness, and vice."

from Gulliver's Travels

◆ *Literature and Your Life*

CONNECT YOUR EXPERIENCE

Have you ever caught sight of your reflection without realizing that it was you? Funhouses use distorted mirrors to create this effect.

Literature has its own funhouse mirror—the satire, which exposes human weaknesses. By stretching and shrinking our image, satire gives us a new perspective on ourselves, just as Gulliver discovers on his visits with the tiny Lilliputians and giant Brobdingnagians.

Journal Writing List examples of modern-day satire. Then jot down two reasons why people enjoy satirical humor.

THEMATIC FOCUS: THE TIES THAT BIND

Swift aimed his satire at the conflicts of his age. What is his opinion of the bonds that connect people in society?

◆ Literary Focus

SATIRE

Satire is writing that uses wit and humor to expose and ridicule human vice and folly. Satire can be light and good-humored, or it can be bitter and unsparing. It can take the form of a story, a novel, or a song.

This type of writing may have grown from ancient harvest celebrations, where the entertainment included mocking wisecracks. Roman poets developed satire still further, using it as a way to get people to recognize their faults.

Gulliver's Travels extends this tradition by using realistic details to create a vivid fantasy world. He uses this world to mirror and criticize the follies of his time.

◆ Grammar and Style

CORRECT USE OF *BETWEEN* AND *AMONG*

Swift correctly uses the prepositions *between* and *among*. He uses *between* when referring to two items: "a bloody war hath been carried on *between* the two empires. . . ."

He uses *among* when referring to more than two items: "I kept *among* other little necessaries a pair of spectacles in a private pocket. . . ."

As you read the story, look for other examples of Swift's use of these prepositions in their proper places.

◆ Reading Strategy

INTERPRET

Satirists don't always state their opinions or name their targets directly. **Interpreting** clues to determine who is the object of the satire and why is part of the fun of reading satire.

For example, Swift's reference in "A Voyage to Lilliput" to "schism in religion" and to an (imaginary) sacred book help you interpret the Lilliputian wars as a satire on religious conflict. The fact that the fuss is about which end of the egg to break—not a very meaningful question—is an indication of Swift's opinion on the importance of some of the religious differences of the time.

◆ Build Vocabulary

LATIN ROOTS: *-jec-*

In this selection, you will find the words *conjecture* and *project*. Both contain the Latin root *-jec-*, which means "throw." To *conjecture* is to guess by "throwing" facts or inferences together. A *project* is literally a "throw forward"—"a plan or scheme for the future."

WORD BANK

Before you read, preview this list of words from the selection.

conjecture
expostulate
schism
expedient
habituate
odious

from GULLIVER'S TRAVELS

Jonathan Swift

In Gulliver's Travels, *Swift exposes the corruption and defects in England's political, social, and economic institutions. The work centers on the four imaginary voyages of Lemuel Gulliver, the narrator, a well-educated but unimaginative ship's surgeon. Each of these voyages takes Gulliver to a different remarkable and bizarre world. During his stays in these imaginary lands, Gulliver is led toward realizations about the flawed nature of the society from which he had come, and he returns to England filled with disillusionment.*

from A VOYAGE TO LILLIPUT

After being shipwrecked, Gulliver swims to shore and drifts off to sleep. When he awakens, he finds that he has been tied down by the Lilliputians (lil′ ə py͞oo′ shənz), a race of people who are only six inches tall. Though he is held captive and his sword and pistols are taken from him, Gulliver gradually begins to win the Lilliputians' favor because of his mild disposition, and he is eventually granted his freedom. Through Gulliver's exposure to Lilliputian politics and court life, the reader becomes increasingly aware of the remarkable similarities between the English and Lilliputian affairs of state. The following excerpt begins during a discussion between the Lilliputian Principal Secretary of Private Affairs and Gulliver concerning the affairs of the Lilliputian empire.

We are threatened with an invasion from the island of Blefuscu,[1] which is the other great empire of the universe, almost as large and powerful as this of his Majesty. For as to what we have heard you affirm, that there are other kingdoms and states in the world, inhabited by human creatures as large as yourself, our philosophers are in much doubt, and would rather conjecture that you dropped from the moon, or one of the stars; because it is certain, that an hundred mortals of your bulk would, in a short time, destroy all the fruits and cattle of his Majesty's dominions. Besides, our histories of six thousand moons make no mention of any other regions, than the two great empires of Lilliput and Blefuscu. Which two mighty powers have, as I was going to tell you, been engaged in a most obstinate war for six and thirty moons past. It began upon the following occasion. It is allowed on all hands, that the primitive way of breaking eggs before we eat them, was upon the larger end; but his present Majesty's grandfather, while he was a boy, going to eat an egg, and breaking it according to the ancient practice, happened to cut one of his fingers. Where-

---

1. **Blefuscu:** Represents France.

◄ **Critical Viewing** Judging from this picture, what situation does Gulliver find himself in? [Infer]

for refuge to that empire. It is computed that eleven thousand persons have, at several times, suffered death rather than submit to break their eggs at the smaller end. Many hundred large volumes have been published upon this controversy; but the books of the Big-Endians have been long forbidden, and the whole party rendered incapable by law of holding employments.[3] During the course of these troubles, the emperors of Blefuscu did frequently expostulate by their ambassadors, accusing us of making a schism in religion, by offending against a fundamental doctrine of our great prophet Lustrog, in the fifty-fourth chapter of the *Brundecral* (which is their Alcoran).[4] This, however, is thought to be a mere strain upon the text, for the words are these: That all true believers shall break their eggs at the convenient end; and which is the convenient end, seems, in my humble opinion, to be left to every man's conscience, or at least in the power of the chief magistrate[5] to determine. Now the Big-Endian

upon the Emperor, his father, published an edict, commanding all his subjects, upon great penalties, to break the smaller end of their eggs. The people so highly resented this law that our histories tell us there have been six rebellions raised on that account; wherein one emperor lost his life, and another his crown.[2] These civil commotions were constantly fomented by the monarchs of Blefuscu; and when they were quelled, the exiles always fled

---

3. **the whole party . . . employments:** The Test Act (1673) prevented Catholics from holding office.
4. **Alcoran:** Koran, the sacred book of the Moslems.
5. **chief magistrate:** Ruler.

---

2. **It is allowed . . . crown:** Here, Swift satirizes the dispute in England between the Catholics (Big-Endians) and Protestants (Little-Endians). King Henry VIII who "broke" with the Catholic church, King Charles I, who "lost his life," and King James, who lost his "crown," are each referred to in the passage.

◆ Build Vocabulary

conjecture (kən jek´ chər) *v*.: Guess

expostulate (ik späs´ chə lāt´) *v*.: Reason earnestly with

schism (siz´ əm) *n*.: Division into groups or factions

exiles have found so much credit in the Emperor of Blefuscu's court, and so much private assistance and encouragement from their party here at home, that a bloody war hath been carried on between the two empires for six and thirty moons with various success; during which time we have lost forty capital ships, and a much greater number of smaller vessels, together with thirty thousand of our best seamen and soldiers; and the damage received by the enemy is reckoned to be somewhat greater than ours. However, they have now equipped a numerous fleet, and are just preparing to make a descent upon us; and his Imperial Majesty, placing great confidence in your valor and strength, hath commanded me to lay this account of his affairs before you.

I desired the Secretary to present my humble duty to the Emperor, and to let him know, that I thought it would not become me, who was a foreigner, to interfere with parties; but I was ready, with the hazard of my life, to defend his person and state against all invaders.

The empire of Blefuscu is an island situated to the north-northeast side of Lilliput, from whence it is parted only by a channel of eight hundred yards wide. I had not yet seen it, and upon this notice of an intended invasion, I avoided appearing on that side of the coast,

◆ Reading Strategy
How might the mention of a narrow channel suggest England and France?

for fear of being discovered by some of the enemy's ships, who had received no intelligence of me, all intercourse between the two empires having been strictly forbidden during the war, upon pain of death, and an embargo laid by our Emperor upon all vessels whatsoever. I communicated to his Majesty a project I had formed of seizing the enemy's whole fleet; which, as our scouts assured us, lay at anchor

in the harbor ready to sail with the first fair wind. I consulted the most experienced seamen upon the depth of the channel, which they had often plumbed, who told me, that in the middle at high water it was seventy *glumgluffs* deep (which is about six feet of European measure), and the rest of it fifty *glumgluffs* at most. I

▼ Critical Viewing How well has the artist conveyed Gulliver's extreme patience when dealing with the Lilliputians? [Assess]

A Voyage to Lilliput, Illustration from a nineteenth-century edition of *Gulliver's Travels*

walked to the northeast coast over against Blefuscu, where, lying down behind a hillock, I took out my small pocket perspective-glass, and viewed the enemy's fleet at anchor, consisting of about fifty men of war, and a great number of transports. I then came back to my house and gave order (for which I had a warrant) for a great quantity of the strongest cable and bars of iron. The cable was about as thick as packthread, and the bars of the length and size of a knitting-needle. I trebled the cable to make it stronger, and for the same reason I twisted three of the iron bars together, bending the extremities into a hook. Having thus fixed fifty hooks to as many cables, I went back to the northeast coast and, putting off my coat, shoes, and stockings, walked into the sea in my leathern jerkin, about half an hour before high water. I waded with what haste I could, and swam in the middle about thirty yards until I felt ground; I arrived at the fleet in less than half an hour. The enemy was so frightened when they saw me, that they leaped out of their ships, and swam to shore, where there could not be fewer than thirty thousand souls. I then took my tackling, and, fastening a hook to the hole at the prow of each, I tied all the cords together at the end. While I was thus employed, the enemy discharged several thousand arrows, many of which struck in my hands and face and, besides the excessive smart, gave me much disturbance in my work. My greatest apprehension was for my eyes, which I should have infallibly lost, if I had not suddenly thought of an <u>expedient</u>. I kept among other little necessaries a pair of spectacles in a private pocket, which, as I observed before, had escaped the Emperor's searchers. These I took out and fastened as strongly as I could upon my nose and thus armed went on boldly with my work in spite of the enemy's arrows, many of which struck against the glasses of my spectacles, but without any other effect further than a little to discompose them. I had now fastened all the hooks and, taking the knot in my hand, began to pull, but not a ship would stir, for they were all too fast held by their anchors, so that the boldest part of my enterprise remained. I therefore let go the cord, and, leaving the hooks fixed to the ships, I resolutely cut with my knife the cables that fastened the anchors, receiving above two hundred shots in

my face and hands; then I took up the knotted end of the cables to which my hooks were tied and, with great ease, drew fifty of the enemy's largest men-of-war after me.

The Blefuscudians, who had not the least imagination of what I intended, were at first confounded with astonishment. They had seen me cut the cables and thought my design was only to let the ships run adrift or fall foul on each other; but when they perceived the whole fleet, moving in order, and saw me pulling at the end, they set up such a scream of grief and despair that it is almost impossible to describe or conceive. When I had got out of danger, I stopped a while to pick out the arrows that stuck in my hands and face, and rubbed on some of the same ointment that was given me at my first arrival, as I have formerly mentioned. I then took off my spectacles, and, waiting about an hour until the tide was a little fallen, I waded through the middle with my cargo and arrived safe at the royal port of Lilliput.

The Emperor and his whole court stood on the shore expecting the issue of this great adventure. They saw the ships move forward in a large half-moon but could not discern me, who was up to my breast in water. When I advanced to the middle of the channel, they were yet more in pain, because I was under water to my neck. The Emperor concluded me to be drowned, and that the enemy's fleet was approaching in a hostile manner; but he was soon eased of his fears; for, the channel growing shallower every step I made, I came in a short time within hearing, and holding up the end of the cable by which the fleet was fastened, I cried in a loud voice, Long live the most puissant[6] Emperor of Lilliput! This great prince received me at my landing with all possible encomiums and created me a *Nardac* upon the spot, which is the highest title of honor among them.

His Majesty desired I would take some other opportunity of bringing all the rest of his enemy's ships into his ports. And so unmea-

---

6. **puissant** (pyo͞o´ i sənt): Powerful.

◆ **Build Vocabulary**

expedient (ik spē´ dē ənt) *n*.: Device used in an emergency

surable is the ambition of princes, that he seemed to think of nothing less than reducing the whole empire of Blefuscu into a province and governing it by a viceroy; of destroying the Big-Endian exiles and compelling that people to break the smaller end of their eggs, by which he would remain sole monarch of the whole world. But I endeavored to divert him from this design by many arguments drawn from the topics of policy as well as justice, and I plainly protested that I would never be an instrument of bringing a free and brave people into slavery. And when the matter was debated in council, the wisest part of the ministry were of my opinion.

This open bold declaration of mine was so opposite to the schemes and politics of his Imperial Majesty that he could never forgive me; he mentioned it in a very artful manner at council, where I was told that some of the wisest appeared, at least, by their silence, to be of my opinion; but others, who were my secret enemies, could not forbear some expressions, which by a sidewind reflected on me. And from this time began an intrigue between his Majesty and a junta of ministers maliciously bent against me, which broke out in less than two months and had like to have ended in my utter destruction. Of so little weight are the greatest services to princes when put into the balance with a refusal to gratify their passions.

from A VOYAGE TO BROBDINGNAG

Gulliver's second voyage leads him to Brobdingnag (bräb´ diŋ nag´), an island located near Alaska that is inhabited by giants twelve times as tall as Gulliver. After being sold to the Queen of Brobdingnag, Gulliver describes the English social and political institutions to the King, who reacts to his description with contempt and disgust.

It is the custom that every Wednesday (which, as I have before observed, was their Sabbath) the King and Queen, with the royal issue of both sexes, dine together in the apartment of his Majesty, to whom I was now become a favorite; and at these times my little chair and table were placed at his left hand before one of the saltcellars. This prince took a

pleasure in conversing with me, inquiring into the manners, religion, laws, government, and learning of Europe, wherein I gave him the best account I was able. His apprehension was so clear, and his judgment so exact, that he made very wise reflections and observations upon all I said. But I confess, that after I had been a little too copious in talking of my own beloved country, of our trade, and wars by sea and land, of our schisms in religion, and parties in the state, the prejudices of his education prevailed so far, that he could not forbear taking me up in his right hand, and stroking me gently with the other, after an hearty fit of laughing, asked me whether I were a Whig or a Tory.[7] Then turning to his first minister, who waited behind him with a white staff, near as tall as the mainmast of the *Royal Sovereign*,[8] he observed how contemptible a thing was human grandeur, which could be mimicked by such diminutive insects as I. And yet, said he, I dare engage, those creatures have their titles and distinctions of honor, they contrive little nests and burrows, that they call houses and cities; they make a figure in dress and equipage;[9] they love, they fight, they dispute, they cheat, they betray. And thus he continued on, while my color came and went several times, with indignation to hear our noble country, the mistress of arts and arms, the scourge of France, the arbitress of Europe, the seat of virtue, piety, honor and truth, the pride and envy of the world, so contemptuously treated. . . .

He laughed at my odd kind of arithmetic (as he was pleased to call it) in reckoning the numbers of our people by a computation drawn from the several sects among us in religion and politics. He said he knew no reason why those who entertain opinions prejudicial to the public should be obliged to change or should not be obliged to conceal them. And, as it was tyranny in any government to require

> ◆ Literary Focus
> What details in this paragraph show Swift's satire to be directed against English affairs? Which details suggest a more general mockery of humanity?

---

7. **Whig . . . Tory:** British political parties.
8. *Royal Sovereign*: One of the largest ships in the British Navy.
9. **equipage** (ek´ wi pij´): Horses and carriages.

the first, so it was weakness not to enforce the second; for, a man may be allowed to keep poisons in his closets, but not to vend them about as cordials.

He observed, that among the diversions of our nobility and gentry[10] I had mentioned gaming.[11] He desired to know at what age this entertainment was usually taken up, and when it was laid down. How much of their time it employed; whether it ever went so high as to affect their fortunes. Whether mean vicious people by their dexterity in that art might not arrive at great riches, and sometimes keep our very nobles in dependence, as well as habituate them to vile companions, wholly take them from the improvement of their minds, and force them, by the losses they received, to learn and practice that infamous dexterity upon others.

He was perfectly astonished with the historical account I gave him of our affairs during the last century, protesting it was only an heap of conspiracies, rebellions, murders, massacres, revolutions, banishments, the very worst effects that avarice, faction, hypocrisy, perfidiousness, cruelty, rage, madness, hatred, envy, lust, malice, and ambition could produce.

His Majesty in another audience was at the pains to recapitulate the sum of all I had spoken; compared the questions he made with the answers I had given; then taking me into his hands, and stroking me gently, delivered himself in these words, which I shall never forget, nor the manner he spoke them in. "My little

A Voyage to Brobdingnag, Illustration from a nineteenth-century edition of *Gulliver's Travels*

---

10. **gentry:** The class of landowning people ranking just below the nobility.
11. **gaming:** Gambling.

◆ **Build Vocabulary**

habituate (hə bich´ ơ āt´) v.: Make used to

friend Grildrig, you have made a most admirable panegyric upon your country. You have clearly proved that ignorance, idleness, and vice are the proper ingredients for qualifying a legislator. That laws are best explained, interpreted, and applied by those whose interest and abilities lie in perverting, confounding, and eluding them. I observe among you some lines of an institution, which in its original might have been tolerable, but these half erased, and the rest wholly blurred and blotted by corruptions. It doth not appear from all you have said how any one perfection is required toward the procurement of any one station among you, much less that men are ennobled on account of their virtue, that priests are advanced for their piety or learning, soldiers for their conduct or valor, judges for their integrity, senators for the love of their country, or counselors for their wisdom. As for yourself," continued the King, "who have spent the greatest part of your life in traveling, I am well disposed to hope you may hitherto have escaped many vices of your country. But, by what I have gathered from your own relation, and the answers I have with much pains wringed and extorted from you, I cannot but conclude the bulk of your natives to be the most pernicious race of little odious vermin that nature ever suffered to crawl upon the surface of the earth."

Nothing but an extreme love of truth could have hindered me from concealing this part of my story. It was in vain to discover my resentments, which were always turned into ridicule; and I was forced to rest with patience while my noble and most beloved country was so injuriously treated. I am heartily sorry as any of my readers can possibly be that such an occasion was given, but this prince happened to be so curious and inquisitive upon every particular that it could not consist either with gratitude or good manners to refuse giving him what satisfaction I was able. Yet thus much I may be allowed to say in my own vindication that I artfully eluded many of his questions and gave to every point a more favorable turn by many

degrees than the strictness of truth would allow. For I have always borne that laudable partiality to my own country, which Dionysius Halicarnassensis[12] with so much justice recommends to an historian. I would hide the frailties and deformities of my political mother and place her virtues and beauties in the most advantageous light. This was my sincere endeavor in those many discourses I had with that mighty monarch, although it unfortunately failed of success.

But great allowances should be given to a king who lives wholly secluded from the rest of the world, and must therefore be altogether unacquainted with the manners and customs that most prevail in other nations: the want of which knowledge will ever produce many prejudices, and a certain narrowness of thinking, from which we and the politer countries of Europe are wholly exempted. And it would be hard indeed, if so remote a prince's notions of virtue and vice were to be offered as a standard for all mankind.

To confirm what I have now said, and further to show the miserable effects of a confined education, I shall here insert a passage which will hardly obtain belief. In hopes to ingratiate myself farther into his Majesty's favor, I told him of an invention discovered between three and four hundred years ago, to make a certain powder, into an heap of which the smallest spark of fire falling, would kindle the whole in a moment, although it were as big as a mountain, and make it all fly up in the air together, with a noise and agitation greater than thunder. That a proper quantity of this powder rammed into an hollow tube of brass or iron, according to its bigness, would drive a ball of iron or lead with such violence and speed as nothing was able to sustain its force. That the largest balls, thus discharged, would not only destroy whole ranks of an army at once, but batter the strongest

◆ **Build Vocabulary**
odious (ō′ dē əs) *adj.*: Hateful; disgusting

12. **Dionysius** (dī′ ə nīsh′ əs) **Halicarnassensis** (hal′ ə kär na sen′ sis): Greek writer who lived in Rome and attempted to persuade the Greeks to submit to their Roman conquerors.

walls to the ground, sink down ships, with a thousand men in each, to the bottom of the sea; and when linked together by a chain, would cut through masts and rigging, divide hundreds of bodies in the middle, and lay all waste before them. That we often put this powder into large hollow balls of iron, and discharged them by an engine into some city we were besieging, which would rip up the pavement, tear the houses to pieces, burst and throw splinters on every side, dashing out the brains of all who came near. That I knew the ingredients very well, which were cheap, and common; I understood the manner of compounding them, and could direct his workmen how to make those tubes of a size proportionable to all other things in his Majesty's kingdom, and the largest need not be above two hundred foot long; twenty or thirty of which tubes, charged with the proper quantity of powder and balls, would batter down the walls of the strongest town in his dominions in a few hours, or destroy the whole metropolis, if ever it should pretend to dispute his absolute commands. This I humbly offered to his Majesty as a small tribute of acknowledgment in return of so many marks that I had received of his royal favor and protection.

The King was struck with horror at the description I had given of those terrible engines and the proposal I had made. He was amazed how so impotent and groveling an insect as I (these were his expressions) could entertain such inhuman ideas, and in so familiar a manner as to appear wholly unmoved at all the scenes of blood and desolation which I had painted as the common effects of those destructive machines; whereof he said some evil genius, enemy to mankind, must have been the first contriver. As for himself, he protested that although few things delighted him so much as new discoveries in art or in nature, yet he would rather lose half his kingdom than be privy to such a secret, which he commanded me, as I valued my life, never to mention any more.

Guide for Responding

◆ Literature and Your Life

Reader's Response Explain why you would or would not like to travel with Gulliver.

Thematic Focus What might Swift find to satirize in today's society?

Questions for Research Swift was inspired to write *Gulliver's Travels* by the travel stories current at the time. Generate research questions that will help you find out more about those stories.

☑ Check Your Comprehension

1. Describe the conflict between Lilliput and Blefuscu over the breaking of eggs.
2. How does Gulliver aid the King of Lilliput?
3. What are the consequences of Gulliver's refusal to destroy the King of Lilliput's enemies?
4. How does the King of Brobdingnag view English history of the preceding hundred years?
5. What is the King of Brobdingnag's reaction to Gulliver's proposal that he use gunpowder?

◆ Critical Thinking

INTERPRET

1. What does Swift's attitude seem to be toward the dispute between English Catholics and Protestants? Explain your answer. **[Infer]**
2. Swift gives a realistic account of how Gulliver captures the Blefuscudian fleet. Explain how this episode adds to or detracts from his satirical points. **[Analyze]**
3. (a) How is Gulliver's perspective on the Lilliputians different from his perspective on the Brobdingnagians? (b) How is the Brobdingnagians' view of Gulliver similar to Gulliver's view of the Lilliputians? **[Compare and Contrast]**
4. Find a passage suggesting that Swift thinks there is hope for human beings. **[Support]**

EVALUATE

5. In this excerpt, Gulliver visits one tiny race and one huge one. (a) Why does Swift use this device? (b) Explain how effective it is. **[Assess]**

Guide for Responding (continued)

◆ Reading Strategy

INTERPRET

To appreciate satire, readers must **interpret** authors' attitudes and their references to historical facts. For example, before the King of Brobdingnag asks Gulliver which political party he belongs to, he laughs and picks Gulliver up. His laughter, and the fact that he treats Gulliver like a pet or child, are clues to Swift's meaning. You can interpret them as a reflection of how small and insignificant human politics can appear.

1. Before telling how the King of Brobdingnag reacts to the idea of gunpowder, Gulliver requests the reader to make "great allowances" for the King of Brobdingnag's "narrowness of thinking." (a) Does Swift think the King is narrow-minded? Explain. (b) Show how Gulliver's inability to see the King's point of view makes the satire more effective.
2. To what actual historical facts does Swift refer when he says that thousands have "suffered death rather than submit to break their eggs at the smaller end"?

◆ Build Vocabulary

USING THE LATIN ROOT -*jec*-

Knowing that the Latin root -*jec*- means "throw," write definitions for the following words.

1. projection
2. eject
3. trajectory
4. inject
5. reject

USING THE WORD BANK: Antonyms

For each word in Column A, write on your paper the letter of the term in Column B whose meaning is its opposite.

1. conjecture	a. fusion
2. expostulate	b. unworkable device
3. schism	c. certainty
4. expedient	d. pleasant
5. habituate	e. surprise
6. odious	f. demand

◆ Literary Focus

SATIRE

Satire uses wit, humor, and sharp contrasts to expose human vice and folly. One such contrast in *Gulliver's Travels* is Gulliver's pride in gunpowder and the king's horror at its uses. The contrast creates effective satire—Swift lets us look at gunpowder through the eyes of the "ignorant" king, forcing us to see the evil of what we might otherwise accept unquestioningly.

1. Describe the method Swift uses to satirize disputes between Catholics and Protestants.
2. (a) Find a passage that emphasizes the difference in size between Gulliver and the King of Brobdingnag. (b) Explain how the difference helps Swift make a satirical point.
3. Compare Gulliver's perceptions of Lilliput with the King of Brobdingnag's perceptions of Gulliver and the English. Which picture leaves you with more hope for humanity? Why?

◆ Grammar and Style

CORRECT USE OF *BETWEEN* AND *AMONG*

Use **between** when referring to only two items or groups of items. Use **among** when referring to more than two items.

Practice In your notebook, fill in each blank with the correct preposition: *between* or *among*.

1. I learned about the war ____?____ Lilliput and Blefuscu from the Principal Secretary of the Lilliputians.
2. A channel eight hundred yards wide lies ____?____ the two countries.
3. ____?____ the Lilliputians, a Big-Endian faction refused to accept the emperor's edict.
4. Wednesday is the Sabbath ____?____ the Brobdingnagians.
5. The difference in size ____?____ Gulliver and the Lilliputians was remarkable.
6. The king noticed gambling was ____?____ the upper-class pastimes mentioned by Gulliver.
7. The Lilliputians did not agree ____?____ themselves whether Gulliver should destroy Blefuscu.

Build Your Portfolio

Idea Bank

Writing

1. **Imaginary Language** Invent five imaginary words like the ones used in Lilliput that would be useful in Brobdingnag. Then write a dictionary entry for each, giving the pronunciation, part of speech, and meaning.

2. **Spy's Report** A (small) spy for Brobdingnag is among us! Write the letter such a spy might send the King, emphasizing features of today's world that would surprise or horrify His Majesty.

3. **News Story** Write a news article for Lilliputian readers, reporting on Gulliver's achievements against the Blefuscudians and summarizing the reactions of the Emperor and his ministers. **[Media Link]**

Speaking, Listening, and Viewing

4. **Film Conference** With a small group, plan the special effects for a filmed version of *Gulliver's Travels*. Discuss where in the story you will use them and how you will carry them out. **[Media Link]**

5. **Readers Theatre** With a small group, design and present a Readers Theatre production of either selection, converting Swift's reported dialogue into direct speech. **[Performing Arts Link]**

Researching and Representing

6. **A New Adventure** Write and illustrate a story in which Gulliver visits another land. Decide on its inhabitants, and focus your satire on one aspect of human folly. **[Social Studies Link]**

7. **Gunpowder Report** Write a research report on how the invention of gunpowder changed the rules of war. Include reactions of people of the time to its invention. **[Social Studies Link]**

Online Activity www.phlit.phschool.com

Guided Writing Lesson

Satirical Essay

In his novel, Swift uses outlandish settings and situations to ridicule human vices and follies. You can write a satirical essay that describes, exaggerates, and mocks a foolish behavior or trend in today's world. Also, you can design your essay for print, radio, or television, whichever medium will help you reach the audience you want.

Writing Skills Focus: Appropriateness for Medium

In writing your satire, take into account the **medium** in which it will appear. Because people can reread a newspaper essay, you can use longer sentences than you could for a radio or television piece. Radio and television require punchier writing. For television, you will probably also want to come up with a visual or visuals that will accompany the reading of the essay.

Prewriting Target your satire. Choose a particular behavior, trend, or attitude to attack. Then consider how you can exaggerate or describe it to make it seem even more foolish. Sometimes an unusual point of view—like that of a visiting Brobdingnagian—can give you a satiric "angle" on your subject. Also, decide whether your essay will appear in a newspaper or on the radio or television.

Drafting Write a punchy lead to capture readers' or listeners' attention. For example, ask a provocative question or tell an anecdote that illustrates the foolishness of what you are mocking. For the electronic media, be briefer than you would be in print. If you're writing for television, think of a dramatic picture or film clip to help you make your point.

Revising Have classmates read your print essay or respond to a "broadcast" of your radio or television piece. Ask them to suggest ways of using the medium to better advantage, and use their suggestions to revise your satire.

Guide for Interpreting

Alexander Pope *(1688–1744)*

Despite a crippling childhood disease and persistent ill health, Alexander Pope triumphantly achieved his boyhood ambition of becoming a great poet. By the time he was twenty-four, he had captured the attention of the leading literary figures of England with *An Essay on Criticism* and *The Rape of the Lock*. A brilliant satirist in verse, Pope gave his name to the literary era (the Age of Pope and Swift) in which he lived and wrote.

A Struggle for Position Born into the Roman Catholic family of a London linen merchant, Pope had to struggle for a position or place in society. After the expulsion of King James II, English Catholics could not legally vote, hold office, attend a university, or live within ten miles of London. To comply with the rule of residency, his family moved to Binfield, a rural setting where Pope spent his formative years writing poetry, studying the classics, and becoming broadly self-educated. Pope's physical problems were as severe as his religious ones. Deformed by tuberculosis of the spine, Pope stood only about four and a half feet tall. He also suffered from nervousness and excruciating headaches. In 1718

Pope moved to an estate at Twickenham (twit´ nəm), a village on the Thames, where he lived until his death.

A Satiric Circle Although Pope, "the Wasp of Twickenham," is more often remembered for his quarrels than for his cordiality, he became friends, and remained so for life, with members of a Tory group that included Jonathan Swift, John Gay, and Lord Bolingbroke. Pope instigated the formation of the Scriblerus Club, whose purpose was to ridicule what its members regarded as "false tastes in learning." The club's satiric emphasis probably inspired Swift's *Gulliver's Travels* and Pope's *The Dunciad*—an attack on his literary enemies.

A Turn to Philosophy In the 1730's Pope's writing became increasingly philosophical. He embarked on a massive work concerning morality and government, but completed only *An Essay on Man* and *Moral Essays*. Nevertheless, the entire body of his work is sufficient for critics today to accord him exceptionally high praise. The twentieth-century poet Edith Sitwell calls Pope "perhaps the most flawless artist our race has yet produced."

◆ Background for Understanding

LITERATURE: THE STORY BEHIND THE POEM

Pope's mock-epic *The Rape of the Lock*, a tale about the theft of a lock of hair, is based on a real incident. Two families, the Petres and the Fermors, became involved in a dispute when Robert Petre flirtatiously cut a lock of hair from the head of beautiful Arabella Fermor.

Pope wrote about this incident, in the hopes that a humorous poem would bring the families together. The result was an early two-part version of the five-part poem we know as *The Rape of the Lock*. In the longer version, published two years later, he added among other things the passage on

the parlor game, which is presented here.

A silly feud therefore inspired Pope's affectionate mockery of high society and its displays. Those displays were so elaborate that a gentleman would not venture out without wearing a freshly powdered wig and a gilt, diamond-hilted sword. He would probably be scented with flower water, and would have been groomed with tweezers and brushes. Be ready for such pretense, and Pope's mockery of it, as you read a poem inspired by a petty theft.

◆ *Literature and Your Life*

CONNECT YOUR EXPERIENCE

When you attend the prom, your attire, mode of transportation, and pre- and post-prom activities are determined by certain "unwritten rules." Whether you care about such "rules" or not, violating them can cause some people to disapprove of you.

In upper-class English society of Pope's time, the "unwritten" rules were so elaborate, and the pretension so great, that Pope made fun of them in *The Rape of the Lock*.

Journal Writing Jot down social customs associated with your prom. Which are worthwhile and which are absurd?

THEMATIC FOCUS: THE TIES THAT BIND

How does Pope's mockery of false values call attention to the true values that bind society together?

◆ Literary Focus

MOCK EPIC

A **mock epic** is a long, humorous narrative poem that treats a trivial subject in the grand, elevated style of a true epic such as the *Odyssey* or *Paradise Lost*. It applies to petty matters the standard elements of an epic: descriptions of heroic actions and the participation of gods and goddesses in human affairs.

In *The Rape of the Lock*, Pope applies the mighty style of Homer and Milton to the theft of a lock of hair. He describes a high society parlor game, for instance, with terms more appropriate for a bloody battle: "And particolored troops, a shining train, Draw forth to combat on the velvet plain."

◆ Grammar and Style

INVERTED WORD ORDER

In *The Rape of the Lock*, Pope uses **inverted word order**, a change in the normal English word order of subject-verb-complement. He does this to achieve regular rhythm, emphasize key words, and place strong rhyme words at the end of a line.

                            s   v   c

Normal Order: The hungry judges soon sign the sentence.

                            s   c   v

Inverted Order: The hungry judges soon the sentence sign.

◆ Reading Strategy

AUTHOR'S PURPOSE

Understanding an **author's purpose**, the reason for writing, gives you insight into a work of literature. Knowing the author's intention, you can understand why he or she includes certain details or descriptions.

For example, Pope's exaggerated descriptions of a parlor game called *omber* can be puzzling: "Belinda now, whom thirst of fame invites,/Burns to encounter two adventurous knights,/ At *omber* singly to decide their doom." When you know that Pope's purpose was to make fun of petty social pursuits, the heroic language becomes understandable.

◆ Build Vocabulary

RELATED WORDS: WORDS ABOUT SOCIETY

In a poem mocking high society and its pursuits, it isn't surprising that Pope uses words relating to social classes and attitudes, such as *plebeian*, which refers to common people, and *haughty*, which means "proud" or "arrogant."

WORD BANK

Before you read, preview this list of words from the poems.

obliquely
plebeian
destitute
assignations
stoic
disabused

from

The Rape of the Lock

Alexander Pope

The Rape of the Lock, *a mock epic, or a humorous poem written in the style of and recalling situations from the famous epic poems of Homer, Virgil, and Milton, is based on an actual incident. Filled with allusions to the great literary works of the past, the poem is a poignant appraisal of the social manners and human behavior of the time.*

The first of the poem's five cantos opens with a formal statement of theme and an invocation to the Muse for poetic inspiration. Then Belinda, the poem's heroine, receives a warning from the sylph Ariel that a dreadful event will take place in her immediate future. In Canto II, during a boat ride on the Thames, an adventurous baron admires Belinda's hair and is determined to cut two bright locks from her head and keep them as a prize. Aware of the baron's desires, Ariel urges the spirits to protect Belinda.

Canto III

Close by those meads, forever crowned with flowers,
Where Thames with pride surveys his rising towers,
There stands a structure of majestic frame,[1]
Which from the neighboring Hampton takes its name.

5   Here Britain's statesmen oft the fall foredoom
Of foreign tyrants, and of nymphs at home;
Here thou, great Anna![2] whom three realms obey,
Dost sometimes counsel take—and sometimes tea.
    Hither the heroes and the nymphs resort,

10   To taste awhile the pleasures of a court;
In various talk th' instructive hours they passed,
Who gave the ball, or paid the visit last;
One speaks the glory of the British Queen,
And one describes a charming Indian screen;

15   A third interprets motions, looks, and eyes;
At every word a reputation dies.

---

1. **structure . . . frame:** Hampton Court, a royal palace near London.
2. **Anna:** Queen Anne, who ruled England, Ireland, and Scotland from 1702 through 1714.

Snuff, or the fan,[3] supply each pause of chat,
With singing, laughing, ogling, and all that.
⠀⠀⠀Meanwhile, declining from the noon of day,
20⠀The sun obliquely shoots his burning ray;
The hungry judges soon the sentence sign,
And wretches hang that jurymen may dine;
The merchant from th' Exchange[4] returns in peace,
And the long labors of the toilet[5] cease.

The Barge, 1895–96 Aubrey Beardsley

◀ **Critical Viewing** Has the artist approached the drawing of Belinda sincerely or mockingly? Explain. **[Speculate]**

25⠀Belinda now, whom thirst of fame invites,
Burns to encounter two adventurous knights,
At omber[6] singly to decide their doom;
And swells her breast with conquests yet to come.
Straight the three bands prepare in arms to join,
30⠀Each band the number of the sacred nine.[7]
Soon as she spreads her hand, th' aerial guard
Descend, and sit on each important card:
First Ariel perched upon a Matadore,[8]

⠀3. **snuff . . . fan:** At the time, gentlemen commonly took snuff and ladies usually carried a fan.
⠀4. **Exchange:** London financial center where merchants, bankers, and brokers conducted business.
⠀5. **toilet:** Dressing tables.
⠀6. **omber:** Popular card game.
⠀7. **sacred nine:** Reference to the nine Muses of Greek mythology.
⠀8. **Matadore:** Powerful card that could take a trick.

◆ **Build Vocabulary**

obliquely (ə blēk′ lē) *adv.*: At a slant; indirect

Then each, according to the rank they bore;
35 For sylphs, yet mindful of their ancient race,
Are, as when women, wondrous fond of place.
        Behold, four kings in majesty revered,
With hoary whiskers and a forky beard;
And four fair queens whose hands sustain a flower,
40 Th' expressive emblem of their softer power;
Four knaves in garbs succinct,[9] a trusty band,
Caps on their heads, and halberts[10] in their hand;
And particolored troops, a shining train,
Draw forth to combat on the velvet plain.
45   The skilful nymph reviews her force with care:
Let spades be trumps! she said, and trumps they were.
        Now move to war her sable Matadores,
In show like leaders of the swarthy Moors.
Spadillio[11] first, unconquerable Lord!
50 Led off two captive trumps, and swept the board.
As many more Manillio[12] forced to yield,
And marched a victor from the verdant field.[13]
Him Basto[14] followed, but his fate more hard
Gained but one trump and one plebeian card.
55 With his broad saber next, a chief in years,
The hoary majesty of spades appears,
Puts forth one manly leg, to sight revealed,
The rest, his many-colored robe concealed.
The rebel knave, who dares his prince engage,
60 Proves the just victim of his royal rage.
Even mighty Pam,[15] that kings and queens o'erthrew
And mowed down armies in the fights of loo,
Sad chance of war! now destitute of aid,
Falls undistinguished by the victor spade!
65   Thus far both armies to Belinda yield;
Now to the baron fate inclines the field.
His warlike Amazon her host invades,
Th' imperial consort of the crown of spades.
The club's black tyrant first her victim died,
70 Spite of his haughty mien, and barbarous pride.
What boots[16] the regal circle on his head,
His giant limbs, in state unwieldy spread;
That long behind he trails his pompous robe,
And, of all monarchs, only grasps the globe?
75   The baron now his diamonds pours apace;
Th' embroidered king who shows but half his face,
And his refulgent queen, with powers combined

◆ Literary Focus
What elements of the mock epic does Pope employ by comparing the card game to a battle in lines 60–75?

---

  9. **succinct** (sək siŋkt´): Belted.
 10. **halberts:** Long-handled weapons.
 11. **Spadillio:** Ace of spades.
 12. **Manillio:** Two of spades.
 13. **Verdant field:** The card table, covered with a green cloth.
 14. **Basto:** Ace of clubs.
 15. **Pam:** Knave of clubs, the highest card in the game called "loo."
 16. **what boots:** Of what benefit is.

Of broken troops an easy conquest find.
Clubs, diamonds, hearts, in wild disorder seen,
80 With throngs promiscuous strew the level green.
Thus when dispersed a routed army runs,
Of Asia's troops, and Afric's sable sons,
    With like confusion different nations fly,
Of various habit, and of various dye,
85 The pierced battalions disunited fall,
In heaps on heaps; one fate o'erwhelms them all.
    The knave of diamonds tries his wily arts,
And wins (oh shameful chance!) the queen of hearts.
At this, the blood the virgin's cheek forsook,

The Rape of the Lock, 1895–96, Aubrey Beardsley

◀ **Critical Viewing** In this poem, Pope glorifies a trivial event. In what manner does this artist do the same? Explain. **[Analyze]**

90 A livid paleness spreads o'er all her look;
She sees, and trembles at th' approaching ill,
Just in the jaws of ruin, and codille.[17]
And now (as oft in some distempered state)
On one nice trick depends the general fate.
95 An ace of hearts steps forth; the king unseen
Lurked in her hand, and mourned his captive queen.
He springs to vengeance with an eager pace,
And falls like thunder on the prostrate ace.
The nymph exulting fills with shouts the sky;

---

17. **codille:** Term meaning the defeat of a hand of cards.

◆ **Build Vocabulary**

plebeian (pli bē′ ən) *adj*.: Common; ordinary

destitute (des′ tə toot) *adj*.: Lacking

100   The walls, the woods, and long canals reply.
        Oh thoughtless mortals! ever blind to fate,
    Too soon dejected, and too soon elate.
    Sudden, these honors shall be snatched away,
    And cursed forever this victorious day.
105   For lo! the board with cups and spoons is
        crowned,
    The berries crackle, and the mill turns round;[18]
    On shining altars of Japan[19] they raise
    The silver lamp; the fiery spirits blaze;
    From silver spouts the grateful liquors glide,
110   While China's earth[20] receives the smoking tide.
    At once they gratify their scent and taste,
    And frequent cups prolong the rich repast.
    Straight hover round the fair her airy band;
    Some, as she sipped, the fuming liquor fanned,
115   Some o'er her lap their careful plumes displayed,
    Trembling, and conscious of the rich brocade.
    Coffee (which makes the politician wise,
    And see through all things with his half-shut eyes)
    Sent up in vapors to the baron's brain
120   New stratagems, the radiant lock to gain.
    Ah cease, rash youth! desist ere 'tis too late,
    Fear the just gods, and think of Scylla's fate![21]
    Changed to a bird, and sent to flit in air,
    She dearly pays for Nisus' injured hair!
125   But when to mischief mortals bend their will,
    How soon they find fit instruments of ill!
    Just then, Clarissa drew with tempting grace
    A two-edged weapon from her shining case:
    So ladies in romance assist their knight,
130   Present the spear, and arm him for the fight.
    He takes the gift with reverence, and extends
    The little engine[22] on his fingers' ends;
    This just behind Belinda's neck he spread,
    As o'er the fragrant steams she bends her head.
135   Swift to the lock a thousand sprites repair,
    A thousand wings, by turns, blow back the hair;
    And thrice they twitched the diamond in her ear;
    Thrice she looked back, and thrice the foe drew
       near.
    Just in that instant, anxious Ariel sought
140   The close recesses of the virgin's thought;
    As on the nosegay in her breast reclined,
    He watched th' ideas rising in her mind,

---

18. **the berries . . . round:** Coffee beans are ground in a hand mill at the table.
19. **altars of Japan:** Small imported lacquer tables.
20. **China's earth:** Earthenware cups imported from China.
21. **Scylla's** (sil′ əz) **fate:** Scylla, the daughter of King Nisus, was turned into a sea bird because she cut off the lock of her father's hair on which his safety depended and sent it to his enemy.
22. **engine:** Instrument.

Beyond Literature

Cultural Connection

Fashion of the Times The obsession with fashion satirized by Alexander Pope was a phenomenon of the upper classes in the 1700's. The world's first fashion magazine dates from 1785, and although it was French, fashion had become an international affair, reflecting the culture of European aristocracy. Queen Marie Antoinette's hairdresser, Leonard, had stunned the world when he rolled her hair over pads of horse hair, then added accessories, such as gauze and feathers, to create elegant "hair statues," some of which were four feet tall!

Clothing fashions of the European upper class were just as frivolous as hair styles. Women's dresses were made of luxurious fabrics, decorated lavishly with lace and ribbons. High fashion also dictated that women wear hooped skirts and boned corsets that cinched their waists.

Wealthier American colonists bought the fashionable clothes imported from England, but that trade stopped abruptly with the outbreak of the Revolutionary War.

The Industrial Revolution brought dramatic cultural change for both England and the United States. Mass production of goods made stylish clothes available to the middle class.

Activity Clothing worn in different periods of history reflects the culture of the time and place. How are fashions today similar to and different from those in England and New England in the 1700's?

The Battle of the Beaux and Belles
Aubrey Beardsley

▲ **Critical Viewing** In what ways is the elaborate decorative style
of the drawing similar to the language of the poem? **[Evaluate]**

Sudden he viewed, in spite of all her art,
An earthly lover lurking at her heart.[23]
145 Amazed, confused, he found his power expired,
Resigned to fate, and with a sigh retired.
     The peer now spreads the glittering forfex[24] wide,
T' enclose the lock; now joins it, to divide.
Even then, before the fatal engine closed,
150 A wretched sylph too fondly interposed;
Fate urged the shears, and cut the sylph in twain,
(But airy substance soon unites again).
The meeting points the sacred hair dissever
From the fair head, forever, and forever!
155   Then flashed the living lightning from her eyes,
And screams of horror rend th' affrighted skies.
Not louder shrieks to pitying heaven are cast,
When husbands, or when lap dogs breathe their last;
Or when rich China vessels fallen from high,
160 In glittering dust, and painted fragments lie!
     "Let wreaths of triumph now my temples twine,"
The victor cried, "the glorious prize is mine!"
While fish in streams, or birds delight in air,
Or in a coach and six the British Fair,
165 As long as *Atalantis*[25] shall be read,
Or the small pillow grace a lady's bed,
While visits shall be paid on solemn days,
When numerous wax lights in bright order blaze,
While nymphs take treats, or assignations give,
170 So long my honor, name, and praise shall live!
What time would spare, from steel receives its date,[26]
And monuments, like men, submit to fate!
Steel could the labor of the gods destroy,
And strike to dust th' imperial towers of Troy;
175 Steel could the works of mortal pride confound,
And hew triumphal arches to the ground.
What wonder then, fair nymph! thy hairs should feel,
The conquering force of unresisted steel?

from **Canto V**

   *In Canto IV, after Umbriel, "a dusky, melancholy sprite,"
empties a bag filled with "the force of female lungs, sighs,
sobs, and passions, and the war of tongues" onto Belinda's head, the lady erupts over the loss of her lock. Then
she "bids her beau," Sir Plume, to "demand the precious
hairs," but Plume is unable to persuade the baron to return
the hair.*

◆ **Reading Strategy**
Why does the author
describe the scene in
lines 145-160 in such
an elevated manner?

---

23. earthly lover . . . heart: If in her heart Belinda wants
the baron to succeed, they cannot protect her.
24. forfex: Scissors.
25. *Atalantis:* Popular book of scandalous gossip.
26. receives its date: Is destroyed.

In the beginning of Canto V, Clarissa, a level-headed nymph, tries to bring an end to the commotion, but rather than being greeted with applause, her speech is followed by a battle cry.

"To arms, to arms!" the fierce virago[27] cries,
And swift as lightning to the combat flies.
All side in parties, and begin th' attack;
Fans clap, silks rustle, and tough whalebones crack;
5   Heroes' and heroines' shouts confusedly rise,
And bass and treble voices strike the skies.
No common weapons in their hands are found,
Like gods they fight, nor dread a mortal wound.
     So when bold Homer makes the gods engage,
10 And heavenly breasts with human passions rage;
'Gainst Pallas, Mars, Latona, Hermes[28] arms;
And all Olympus[29] rings with loud alarms:
Jove's[30] thunder roars, heaven trembles all around,
Blue Neptune[31] storms, the bellowing deeps resound;
15 Earth shakes her nodding towers, the ground gives way,
And the pale ghosts start at the flash of day!
     Triumphant Umbriel on a sconce's height[32]
Clapped his glad wings, and sat to view the fight;
Propped on their bodkin spears,[33] the sprites survey
20 The growing combat, or assist the fray.
     While through the press enraged Thalestris[34] flies,
And scatters death around from both her eyes,
A beau and witling[35] perished in the throng,
One died in metaphor, and one in song.
25 "O cruel nymph! a living death I bear,"
Cried Dapperwit, and sunk beside his chair.
A mournful glance Sir Fopling[36] upwards cast,
"Those eyes are made so killing"—was his last.
Thus on Maeander's[37] flowery margin lies

◆ **Literary Focus**
In what ways does the preparation for battle in lines 1–20 fit the mock heroic?

---

27. virago (vi rā′ gō): Scolding woman.
28. Pallas . . . Hermes: Gods who directed the Trojan War. Pallas and Hermes supported the Greeks, while Mars and Latona sided with the Trojans.
29. Olympus: Mountain which was supposed to be the home of the gods.
30. Jove's: Referring to Jupiter, the ruler of the Gods in Roman mythology: identified with Zeus in Greek mythology.
31. Neptune: Roman god of the sea; identified with Poseidon in Greek mythology.
32. sconce's height: Candleholder attached to the wall.
33. bodkin spears: Large needles.
34. Thalestris (thə lēs′ tris): An Amazon (a race of female warriors supposed to have lived in Scythia) who played a role in the medieval tales of Alexander the Great.
35. witling: Person who fancies himself or herself a wit.
36. Dapperwit, Sir Fopling: Names of amusing characters in comedies of the time.
37. Maeander's: Referring to a river in Asia.

◆ **Build Vocabulary**

assignations (as′ ig nā′ shənz) *n.:* Appointments to meet

from *The Rape of the Lock* ◆ 495

30　Th' expiring swan, and as he sings he dies.
　　　　When bold Sir Plume had drawn Clarissa down,
　　Chloe[38] stepped in, and killed him with a frown;
　　She smiled to see the doughty hero slain,
　　But, at her smile, the beau revived again.
35　　　　Now Jove suspends his golden scales in air,
　　Weighs the men's wits against the lady's hair;
　　The doubtful beam long nods from side to side;
　　At length the wits mount up, the hairs subside.
　　　　See, fierce Belinda on the baron flies,
40　With more than usual lightning in her eyes;
　　Nor feared the chief th' unequal fight to try,
　　Who sought no more than on his foe to die.
　　But this bold lord with manly strength endued,
　　She with one finger and a thumb subdued:
45　Just where the breath of life his nostrils drew,
　　A charge of snuff the wily virgin threw;
　　The gnomes direct, to every atom just,
　　The pungent grains of titillating dust.
　　Sudden with starting tears each eye o'erflows,
50　And the high dome re-echoes to his nose.
　　　　"Now meet thy fate," incensed Belinda cried,
　　And drew a deadly bodkin[39] from her side . . .
　　　　"Boast not my fall," he cried, "insulting foe!
　　Thou by some other shalt be laid as low.
55　Nor think, to die dejects my lofty mind;
　　All that I dread is leaving you behind!
　　Rather than so, ah let me still survive,
　　And burn in Cupid's flames—but burn alive."
　　　　"Restore the lock!" she cries; and all around
60　"Restore the lock!" the vaulted roofs rebound.
　　Not fierce Othello in so loud a strain
　　Roared for the handkerchief that caused his pain.[40]
　　But see how oft ambitious aims are crossed,
　　And chiefs contend till all the prize is lost!
65　The lock, obtained with guilt, and kept with pain,
　　In every place is sought, but sought in vain.
　　With such a prize no mortal must be blessed,
　　So Heaven decrees! with Heaven who can contest?
　　　　Some thought it mounted to the lunar sphere,
70　Since all things lost on earth are treasured there.
　　There heroes' wits are kept in ponderous vases,
　　And beaux' in snuffboxes and tweezer cases.
　　There broken vows and deathbed alms are found,

◆ *Literature*
and Your Life

Hair has always
been an important
aspect of fashion.
In what ways is
it an important
part of today's
fashions?

---

38. Chloe (klō′ ē)**:** Heroine of the ancient Greek pastoral romance,
Daphnis and Chloe.
39. bodkin: Ornamental pin shaped like a dagger.
40. not . . . pain: In Shakespeare's *Othello*, the hero is convinced
that his wife is being unfaithful to him when she cannot find the
handkerchief that he had given her. Actually, the handkerchief had
been taken by the villain, Iago, who uses it as part of his evil plot.

And lovers' hearts with ends of riband bound . . .
75   But trust the Muse—she saw it upward rise,
Though marked by none but quick, poetic eyes . . .
A sudden star, it shot through liquid[41] air
And drew behind a radiant trail of hair . . .[42]
          Then cease, bright Nymph! to mourn thy ravished hair,
80   Which adds new glory to the shining sphere!
Not all the tresses that fair head can boast,
Shall draw such envy as the lock you lost.
For, after all the murders of your eye,[43]
When, after millions slain, yourself shall die;
85   When those fair suns shall set, as set they must,
And all those tresses shall be laid in dust,
This lock, the Muse shall consecrate to fame,
And midst the stars inscribe Belinda's name.

---

41. liquid: Clear.
42. trail of hair: The word *comet* comes from a Greek word meaning long-haired.
43. murders . . . eye: Lovers struck down by her glances.

Guide for Responding

◆ Literature and Your Life

Reader's Response Do you think Pope effectively satirizes his subject? Explain.

Thematic Focus Is there any evidence in the poem of the true values that should bind a people together? Explain.

Group Discussion What social conventions would Pope have written about if he were writing now? Form a group and, using your own knowledge and experience, choose several contemporary targets for Pope's wit.

☑ Check Your Comprehension

1. (a) In what activity is Belinda engaged during the first half of Canto III? (b) What is the outcome?
2. (a) What is the "two-edged weapon" that Clarissa gives the baron? (b) How many times does the baron fail to get the lock of hair?
3. (a) How does Belinda respond when the baron manages to get the lock of hair? (b) How does the baron react?
4. What has happened to the lock of hair at the end of Canto V?

◆ Critical Thinking

INTERPRET

1. Why do you think Pope precedes the trivial episodes in Canto III with such a grisly image as "wretches hang that jurymen may dine"? **[Analyze]**
2. What similarity is there between Pope's description of the omber game and his description of the events following the theft of the lock? **[Compare and Contrast]**
3. Lines 79–88 in Canto V are "elegant spoofing," according to one critic. Yet, in a sense, Pope made the poem's extravagant claim come true. How did he do it? **[Interpret]**

APPLY

4. Pope based *The Rape of the Lock* on an actual incident. What incident in the news today might provide the basis for a similar mock epic? **[Apply]**

EXTEND

5. (a) How would you compare *The Rape of the Lock* with Swift's *Gulliver's Travels*? (b) How are they similar in their treatment of social manners? How do they differ? **[Literature Link]**

from

An Essay on Man

Alexander Pope

An Essay on Man *is an examination of human nature, society, and morals. In the following passage, Pope cautions against intellectual pride by vividly describing the uncertain "middle state" in which humans have been placed.*

Know then thyself, presume not God to scan;
The proper study of mankind is man.
Placed on this isthmus of a middle state,
A being darkly wise, and rudely great:
5 With too much knowledge for the skeptic side,
With too much weakness for the <u>stoic</u>'s pride,
He hangs between; in doubt to act, or rest;
In doubt to deem himself a god, or beast;
In doubt his mind or body to prefer;
10 Born but to die, and reasoning but to err;
Alike in ignorance, his reason such,
Whether he thinks too little, or too much:
Chaos of thought and passion, all confused;
Still by himself abused, or <u>disabused</u>;
15 Created half to rise, and half to fall;
Great lord of all things, yet a prey to all;
Sole judge of truth, in endless error hurled:
The glory, jest, and riddle of the world!

◆ Build Vocabulary

stoic (stō´ ik) *n.*: Person indifferent to joy, grief, pleasure, or pain

disabused (dis´ ə byo͞ozd´) *adj.*: Freed from false ideas

Guide for Responding

◆ Literature and Your Life

Reader's Response How does your understanding of human nature compare with Pope's? Explain.

Thematic Focus Judging by Pope's description of human nature, do you think he believed that people needed rules to restrain them? Explain.

☑ Check Your Comprehension

1. What does Pope say should be the object of man's study?
2. According to Pope, what prevents man from being a skeptic or a stoic?

◆ Critical Thinking

INTERPRET

1. Pope writes that man stands on an "isthmus of a middle state." In a single word, what is (a) at one end of the isthmus? (b) at the other end? **[Analyze]**
2. What do you think Pope means by the line "In doubt his mind or body to prefer"? **[Interpret]**
3. Is Pope's view of human nature original? Why or why not? **[Make a Judgment]**

APPLY

4. Most writers today reject the idea that literature should present an obvious moral. Pope believed that poetry has a didactic, or instructional, role to play. What do you think? **[Generalize]**

Guide for Responding (continued)

◆ Reading Strategy

AUTHOR'S PURPOSE

Once you know that the **author's purpose** in *The Rape of the Lock* is to poke affectionate fun at the pretensions of high society, many details in the poem become more understandable. Explain how each of these lines or devices accomplishes Pope's purpose:

1. "Oh thoughtless mortals ever blind to fate, Too soon dejected, and too soon elate." (Canto III, lines 101–102)
2. Heroic description of the pouring of coffee (Canto III, lines 105–110)
3. Elaborate description of a pair of scissors (Canto III, lines 125–132)
4. Use of fantastic characters like Ariel, sprites, and sylphs (Canto III, lines 135–154)
5. "But see how often ambitious aims are crossed, And chiefs contend till all the prize is lost!" (Canto V, lines 63–64)

◆ Build Vocabulary

USING RELATED WORDS ABOUT SOCIETY

Knowing Pope's words about society and social attitudes, tell who would be *haughty* in the following encounters and why:

1. a baron and a king
2. a baron and a plebeian person
3. a baron acting in a plebeian way and a lady

USING THE WORD BANK: Synonyms

In your notebook, write down the letter of the word or phrase in Column B that is closest in meaning to the word in Column A.

Column A	Column B
1. plebeian	a. lacking
2. obliquely	b. arrogant
3. assignations	c. impassive person
4. stoic	d. cease
5. haughty	e. undeceived
6. desist	f. indirectly
7. destitute	g. meetings
8. disabused	h. common

◆ Literary Focus

MOCK EPIC

Pope's **mock epic** is a humorous narrative poem that treats a petty incident—the theft of a lock of hair—in the grand manner of epics like the *Odyssey*. That grand manner includes descriptions of heroic deeds, references to mythology, and supernatural beings who help or hinder human actions.

Notice how in Canto III, lines 105–115, for example, Pope describes the pouring of coffee as if it were a sacred, heroic ritual. He also refers to the supernatural "airy band" who "hover round" Belinda. These supernatural creatures help her not to achieve heroic deeds but to drink a cup of coffee!

As you can see, the contrast between the grand manner of description and the trivial activities described produces a humorous contrast.

1. (a) Find two trivial incidents in *The Rape of the Lock* that Pope presents in a heroic manner. (b) Show how in each case the description humorously contrasts with the action.
2. (a) What are some of the mythical creatures, including deities and muses, mentioned in the poem? Find at least five. (b) Would the poem be less humorous without them? Why or why not?

◆ Grammar and Style

INVERTED WORD ORDER

To achieve a certain rhythm or to emphasize ideas, Pope uses **inverted word order**—a change in the normal English word order of subject-verb-complement.

Practice After labeling the subject, verb, and complement in each of these lines, rewrite the lines in normal English word order.

1. Here Britain's statesmen oft the fall foredoom.... (III, 5)
2. His warlike Amazon her host invades.... (III, 67)
3. The baron now his diamonds pours apace.... (III, 75)

Build Your Portfolio

 ## Idea Bank

Writing

1. **Paraphrase** Review the main points of the passage from *An Essay on Man*. Then write a prose version of the selection, expressing Pope's ideas in your own words.

2. **Reply** As one of the characters in *The Rape of the Lock*, write a letter to Pope letting him know how you feel about his portrayal of you.

3. **Comparison and Contrast** *An Essay on Man* and *The Rape of the Lock* are works that differ in purpose and attitude. Write a comparison-and-contrast paper pointing out differences and similarities, if any, between the two works.

Speaking, Listening, and Viewing

4. **Reading and Pantomime** Present a dramatic reading of *The Rape of the Lock*. Assign passages to readers and have actors pantomime the actions being described. **[Performing Arts Link]**

5. **Graduation Speech** Present your ideas on humankind in a speech to be given at your high-school graduation. If you like, quote words and phrases from Pope's *An Essay on Man*. **[Performing Arts Link]**

Researching and Representing

6. **High Society in Pope's Day** Using books like Maynard Mack's biography of Pope, do further research on the high society that Pope makes fun of in *The Rape of the Lock*. Present your findings in a written report. **[Social Studies Link]**

7. **Classical Glossary** List terms from ancient Greek and Roman literature and mythology in *The Rape of the Lock*. Use encyclopedias, dictionaries, and other reference sources to help you define the terms listed. **[Literature Link]**

Online Activity www.phlit.phschool.com

 ## Guided Writing Lesson

Imitating an Author's Style

In *The Rape of the Lock*, Pope's use of rhyming couplets and his serious treatment of silly matters contribute to a distinctive style. Choose an author—Pope or someone else—whose style is unmistakable, and write an imitation of it.

These hints will help you keep the author's style in focus as you imitate it.

Writing Skills Focus: Maintain Consistent Style

Whether you write an imitation of an author's style or a piece of your own, it's important to maintain a consistent style:

- Use the same level of formal or informal language throughout
- Be consistent in your use of imagery, meter, or inverted word order
- Keep the same attitude toward your subject and the same mood.

You can deal with these style issues at every stage of the writing process.

Prewriting Choose the author you will imitate and carefully analyze his or her style. Consider such factors as average sentence length, word choice and vocabulary level, literary devices, and attitude toward the subject.

Drafting Approach the drafting like an acting assignment. After studying the author's stylistic mannerisms and rereading a passage from his or her work, write as if you were the author. It may help you keep samples of the author's writing at hand for easy reference.

Revising Read your draft critically, and look for places where you slipped into your own style. Rewrite them by taking on an attitude typical of your author or using a literary device that he or she uses.

Guide for Interpreting

Samuel Johnson *(1709–1784)*

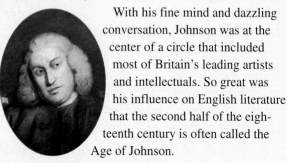

With his fine mind and dazzling conversation, Johnson was at the center of a circle that included most of Britain's leading artists and intellectuals. So great was his influence on English literature that the second half of the eighteenth century is often called the Age of Johnson.

A Life of Hardship Samuel Johnson overcame severe physical and economic hardships to become one of England's most outstanding figures. The son of a bookseller in Lichfield, England, Johnson suffered a series of childhood illnesses that left him weak and disfigured. Bright enough to read Shakespeare at the age of eight, he was too poor to attend the schools of the aristocracy and instead pursued his education largely by reading books in his father's shop. Even when he was able to enter Oxford in 1728, lack of funds forced him to leave early.

A Great Work In 1737 Johnson moved to London to try to earn his living as a writer; a decade later he began work on his *Dictionary of the English Language.* This landmark effort took eight years to complete—eight difficult years in which Johnson lost his wife and continued to be dogged by poverty. When at last the dictionary was published, however, it ensured Johnson's place in literary history.

James Boswell *(1740–1795)*

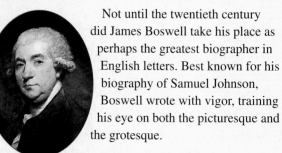

Not until the twentieth century did James Boswell take his place as perhaps the greatest biographer in English letters. Best known for his biography of Samuel Johnson, Boswell wrote with vigor, training his eye on both the picturesque and the grotesque.

Celebrity Chaser The son of a prominent and demanding Scottish judge, James Boswell was made to study law when he would have preferred literature. Riddled with insecurities, he became something of a celebrity chaser, introducing himself to famous figures like the French philosophers Voltaire and Rousseau. In Samuel Johnson he found not only a friendly celebrity but also the father figure he apparently sought. Deciding to become Johnson's biographer, he devoted thirty years to compiling detailed records of Johnson's life.

A Brilliant Biographer Though Boswell's *Life of Samuel Johnson* (1791) was a popular book, for decades its subject far outshone its author, and Boswell was viewed much as a ghost writer is today. In recent years it has been affirmed that Boswell had a genius of his own, which is evident from studying the trove of his personal papers discovered in the twentieth century. His powers of listening, observation, and recall enabled him to bring the subject of a biography to life as no one had done before.

◆ Background for Understanding

CULTURE: SYSTEMATIZING KNOWLEDGE

Eighteenth-century thinkers seemed to sense that a "summit of knowledge" had been reached, and they set down in writing scientific, philosophical, and historical facts and ideas.

Among the intellectual "mountaineers" were Samuel Johnson and James Boswell, whose dictionary and biography, respectively, set the standard for nonfiction works of their type. The eighteenth century also saw the birth of the first Encyclopedia Britannica (1768–1771), and Adam Smith's *Wealth of Nations* (1776), which revolutionized economics.

As you read the following selections, notice how Boswell is "setting down" Samuel Johnson even as Johnson "sets down" the English language!

from The Preface to A Dictionary of the English Language
◆ from A Dictionary of the English Language ◆
from The Life of Samuel Johnson

◆ Literature and Your Life

CONNECT YOUR EXPERIENCE

Think about some of the new words that have entered your vocabulary recently that describe things as varied as fashion trends and scientific discoveries. Johnson's *Dictionary* was one man's heroic attempt to master a changing language by setting down all the English words in existence and defining them!

Journal Writing Jot down three slang words that have entered your language within the past year.

THEMATIC FOCUS: THE TIES THAT BIND

How do Johnson's *Dictionary* and Boswell's biography strengthen social bonds by sharing language and experience?

◆ Literary Focus

DICTIONARY; BIOGRAPHY

A **dictionary** lists and defines words and usually provides information about their pronunciation, history, and usage. The achievement of Samuel Johnson, who created the first standard dictionary, is remarkable. Not only did he think up the idea of such a dictionary, but he executed it so well that its format is still used today!

A **biography** presents the life story of someone other than the writer. A good biography presents an accurate and complete picture of the subject against the backdrop of the times in which he or she lived. Some biographies are written by people who've never met the subject. Others, like Boswell's *Life of Samuel Johnson*, are written after intense, personal interviews with the subject.

◆ Grammar and Style

COMMAS WITH PARENTHETICAL EXPRESSIONS

In *The Life of Samuel Johnson*, you'll encounter several **parenthetical expressions**, which interrupt the main part of a sentence to comment on it or to give additional information. Boswell sets these expressions off with commas, to avoid confusion.

The character of Samuel Johnson has, *I trust*, been so developed in the course of this work . . .

Man is, *in general*, made up of contradictory qualities . . .

◆ Reading Strategy

ESTABLISH A PURPOSE

Establish a purpose before you read to identify the type of information for which you're looking. By giving yourself a goal, you'll get something specific from your reading and avoid being overwhelmed by facts.

For example, you might read Johnson's *Preface* to learn about Johnson's writing style, about the process of creating a dictionary, about Johnson's attitudes, or some combination of these. Once you've decided on your purpose, set up a KWL chart showing what you Know of the subject, what you Want to know, and what you Learn from your reading. Then fill in the chart as you read.

K	W	L

◆ Build Vocabulary

LATIN ROOTS: -dict-

In this unit, you'll read a portion of the earliest standard dictionary of English. *Dictionary,* a listing of words, contains the root -dict-, from the Latin word for "to say."

WORD BANK

Before you read, preview these words.

recompense
caprices
adulterations
propagators
risible
abasement
credulity
malignity
pernicious
inculcated

A

DICTIONARY

OF THE

ENGLISH LANGUAGE:

IN WHICH

The WORDS are deduced from their ORIGINALS,

AND

ILLUSTRATED in their DIFFERENT SIGNIFICATIONS

BY

EXAMPLES from the beſt WRITERS.

TO WHICH ARE PREFIXED,

A HISTORY of the LANGUAGE,

AND

AN ENGLISH GRAMMAR.

BY SAMUEL JOHNSON, A. M.

IN TWO VOLUMES

VOL. I.

Cum tabulis animum cenſoris ſumet honeſti:
Audebit quæcunque parum ſplendoris habebunt,
Et ſine pondere erunt, et honore indigna ferentur,
Verba movere loco; quamvis invita recedant,
Et verſentur adhuc intra penetralia Veſtæ:
Obſcurata diu populo bonus eruet, atque
Proferet in lucem ſpecioſa vocabula rerum,
Quæ priſcis memorata Catonibus atque Cethegis,
Nunc ſitus informis premit et deſerta vetuſtas.   HOR.

LONDON.
Printed by W. STRAHAN,
For J. and P. KNAPTON; T. and T. LONGMAN; C. HITCH and L. HAWES;
A. MILLAR; and R. and J. DODSLEY.
MDCCLV.

Critical Viewing What does this title page of Johnson's *Dictionary* tell you about the contents? [Infer]

from

The Preface to A Dictionary of the English Language

SAMUEL JOHNSON

It is the fate of those who toil at the lower employments of life, to be rather driven by the fear of evil, than attracted by the prospect of good; to be exposed to censure, without hope of praise; to be disgraced by miscarriage, or punished for neglect, where success would have been without applause, and diligence without reward.

Among these unhappy mortals is the writer of dictionaries; whom mankind have considered, not as the pupil, but the slave of science, the pioneer of literature, doomed only to remove rubbish and clear obstructions from the paths through which learning and genius press forward to conquest and glory, without bestowing a smile on the humble drudge that facilitates their progress. Every other author may aspire to praise; the lexicographer can only hope to escape reproach, and even this negative recompense has been yet granted to very few.

I have, notwithstanding this discouragement, attempted a dictionary of the English language, which, while it was employed in the cultivation of every species of literature, has itself been hitherto neglected; suffered to spread under the direction of chance, into wild exuberance; resigned to the tyranny of time and fashion: and exposed to the corruptions of ignorance and caprices of innovation.

When I took the first survey of my undertaking, I found our speech copious without order and energetic without rule: wherever I turned my view, there was perplexity to be disentangled and confusion to be regulated; choice was to be made out of boundless variety, without any established principle of selection; adulterations were to be detected, without a settled test of purity; and modes of expression to be rejected or received, without the suffrages of any writers of classical reputation or acknowledged authority.

Having therefore no assistance but from general grammar, I applied myself to the perusal of our writers; and noting whatever

◆ Build Vocabulary

recompense (rek´əm pens´) *n*.: Reward; payment

caprices (kə prē sis´) *n*.: Whims

adulterations (ə dul´tər ā´ shənz) *n*.: Impurities; added ingredients that are improper or inferior

might be of use to ascertain or illustrate any word or phrase, accumulated in time the materials of a dictionary, which, by degrees, I reduced to method, establishing to myself, in the progress of the work, such rules as experience and analogy suggested to me; experience, which practice and observation were continually increasing; and analogy, which, though in some other words obscure, was evident in others . . .

In hope of giving longevity to that which its own nature forbids to be immortal, I have devoted this book, the labor of years, to the honor of my country, that we may no longer yield the palm of philology, without a contest to the nations of the continent. The chief glory of every people arises from its authors. Whether I shall add anything by my own writings to the reputation of English literature, must be left to time. Much of my life has been lost under the pressures of disease; much has been trifled away; and much has always been spent in provision for the day that was passing over me; but I shall not think my employment useless or ignoble, if by my assistance foreign nations and distant ages gain access to the propagators of knowledge, and understand the teachers of truth; if my labors afford light to the repositories of science, and add celebrity to Bacon, to Hooker, to Milton, and to Boyle.[1]

When I am animated by this wish, I look with pleasure on my book, however defective, and deliver it to the world with the spirit of a man that has endeavored well. That it will immediately become popular, I have not promised to myself. A few wild blunders, and risible absurdities, from which no work of such multiplicity was ever free, may for a time furnish folly with laughter, and harden ignorance into contempt; but useful diligence will at last prevail, and there never can be wanting some who distinguish desert; who will

consider that no dictionary of a living tongue ever can be perfect, since, while it is hastening to publication, some words are budding, and some falling away; that a whole life cannot be spent upon syntax and etymology, and that even a whole life would not be sufficient; that he, whose design includes whatever language can express, must often speak of what he does not understand; that a writer will sometimes be hurried by eagerness to the end, and sometimes faint with weariness under a task which Scaliger[2] compares to the labors of the anvil and the mine; that what is obvious is not always known, and what is known is not always present; that sudden fits of inadvertency will surprise vigilance, slight avocations[3] will seduce attention, and casual eclipses of the mind will darken learning; and that the writer shall often in vain trace his memory at the moment of need, for that which yesterday he knew with intuitive readiness, and which will come uncalled into his thoughts tomorrow.

In this work, when it shall be found that much is omitted, let it not be forgotten that much likewise is performed; and though no book was ever spared out of tenderness to the author, and the world is little solicitous to know whence proceed the faults of that which it condemns; yet it may gratify curiosity to inform it, that the *English Dictionary* was written with little assistance of the learned, and without any patronage of the great; not in the

soft obscurities of retirement, or under the shelter of academic bowers, but amidst inconvenience and distraction, in sickness and in sorrow. It may repress the triumph of malignant criticism to observe that if our language is not here fully displayed, I have only failed

---

1. **Bacon . . . Boyle:** Writers quoted by Johnson in the *Dictionary*.

2. **Scaliger:** Joseph Justus Scaliger (1540–1609), a scholar who suggested that criminals should be condemned to writing dictionaries.
3. **avocation:** Something that calls one away or distracts one from something.

in an attempt which no human powers have hitherto completed. If the lexicons of ancient tongues, now immutably fixed and comprised in a few volumes, be yet, after the toil of successive ages, inadequate and delusive; if the aggregated knowledge and cooperating diligence of the Italian academicians did not secure them from the censure of Beni;[4] if the embodied critics of France, when fifty years had been spent upon their work, were obliged to change its economy[5] and give their second edition another form, I may surely be contented without the praise of perfection, which,

---

4. **Beni:** Paolo Beni severely criticized the first Italian dictionary.
5. **economy:** Organization.

if I could obtain, in this gloom of solitude, what would it avail me? I have protracted my work till most of those whom I wished to please have sunk into the grave,[6] and success and miscarriage are empty sounds: I therefore dismiss it with frigid tranquility, having little to fear or hope from censure or from praise.

---

6. **sunk . . . grave:** Johnson's wife had died three years earlier.

◆ Build Vocabulary

propagators (präp´ ə gā´ tərz) *n.*: Those who cause something to happen or to spread

risible (riz´ə bəl) *adj.*: Prompting laughter

Guide for Responding

◆ Literature and Your Life

Reader's Response Based on this preface, what do you expect the body of Johnson's dictionary to be like? Why?

Thematic Focus Would you guess that Johnson's ties to literature and reading were important to him? Explain.

Questions for Research What were some of the predecessors of Johnson's dictionary? Generate questions you could use to explore the origin of dictionaries in ancient civilizations and other cultures.

☑ Check Your Comprehension

1. Among what class of workers does Johnson place writers of dictionaries?
2. (a) What was English lacking when Johnson "took the first survey"? (b) What gave him his only assistance in compiling his dictionary?
3. Why, according to the preface, can "no dictionary of the living tongue ever be perfect"?

◆ Critical Thinking

INTERPRET
1. What is Johnson's chief reason for undertaking the creation of a dictionary? **[Interpret]**
2. Do you think Johnson is hopeful or pessimistic (or perhaps both) about the fate of his dictionary? Explain.

EVALUATE
3. Johnson devotes his dictionary to the "honor of my country." In what ways, if any, do you think his dictionary honors England? **[Assess]**

APPLY
4. What opinion do you think Johnson would have of today's unabridged dictionaries? **[Hypothesize]**

EXTEND
5. How have computers changed the task of making dictionaries? **[Science Link]**

from

A

Dictionary of the
English Language

SAMUEL JOHNSON

athle´ tick. Strong of body; vigorous; lusty; robust.

> Science distinguishes a man of honor from one of those *athletick* brutes, whom undeservedly we call heroes. Dryden.

bang. A blow; a thump; a stroke: a low word.

> I am a bachelor. That's to say, they are fools that marry; you'll bear me a *bang* for that. Shakespeare, *Julius Caesar.*

to ba´rbecue. A term used in the West Indies for dressing a hog whole; which, being split to the backbone, is laid flat upon a large gridiron, raised about two foot above a charcoal fire, with which it is surrounded.

> Oldfield, with more than harpy throat endu'd,
> Cries, send me, gods, a whole hog *barbecu'd.* Pope.

bu´ffleheaded. A man with a large head, like a buffalo; dull; stupid; foolish.

cream. The unctuous or oily part of milk, which, when it is cold, floats on the top, and is changed by the agitation of the churn into butter; the flower of milk.

electri´city. A property in some bodies, whereby, when rubbed so as to grow warm, they draw little bits of paper, or such like substances, to them. Quincy.

> Such was the account given a few years ago of electricity; but the industry of the present age, first excited by the experiments of Gray, has discovered in electricity a multitude of philosophical wonders. Bodies electrified by a sphere of glass, turned nimbly round, not only emit flame, but may be fitted with such a quantity of the electrical vapor as, if discharged at once upon a human body, would endanger life. The force of this vapor has hitherto appeared instantaneous, persons at both ends of a long chain seeming to be struck at once. The philosophers are now endeavoring to intercept the strokes of lightning.

to fu´rnace. To throw out as sparks from a furnace. A bad word.

> He *furnaces*
> The thick sighs from him. Shakespeare's *Cymbeline.*

gang. A number herding together; a troop; a company; a tribe; a herd. It is seldom used but in contempt or abhorrence.

ha´tchet-face. An ugly face; such, I suppose, as might be hewn out of a block by a hatchet.

> An ape his own dear image will embrace;
> An ugly beau adores a *hatchet-face*. Dryden.

lifegua´rd. The guard of a king's person.

mo´dern. In Shakespeare, vulgar; mean; common.

> We have our philosophical persons to make *modern* and familiar things supernatural and causeless. Shakespeare.

pa´tron. One who countenances, supports or protects. Commonly a wretch who supports with insolence, and is paid with flattery.

pi´ckle. Condition; state. A word of contempt and ridicule.

> How cam'st though in this *pickle*? Shakespeare.

plu´mper. Something worn in the mouth to swell out the cheeks.

> She dex'trously her *plumpers* draws,
> That serve to fill her hollow jaws. *Swift's Miscellanies.*

shill-I-shall-I. A corrupt reduplication of *shall I*? The question of a man hesitating. To stand *shill-I-shall-I*, is to continue hesitating and procrastinating.

> I am somewhat dainty in making a resolution, because when I make it, I keep it; I don't stand shill-I-shall-I then; if I say't, I'll do't. Congreve's *Way of the World.*

to sneeze. To emit wind audibly by the nose.

wi´llow. A tree worn by forlorn lovers.

to wipe. To cheat; to defraud.

> The next bordering lords commonly encroach one upon another, as one is stronger, or lie still in wait to *wipe* them out of their lands. Spenser, *On Ireland.*

you´ngster, you´nker. A young person. In contempt.

youth. The part of life succeeding to childhood and adolescence; the time from fourteen to twenty-eight.

> ◆ **Literary Focus**
> In addition to definitions, what information does Johnson supply about entry words?

Guide for Responding

◆ *Literature and Your Life*

Reader's Response Do you find Johnson's definitions fair? funny? prejudiced? Explain.

Thematic Focus Johnson cites examples from great works of literature in some of his dictionary entries. How do these works serve to bridge centuries and cultures?

Paraphrase Rewrite one of the dictionary entries in your own words.

☑ Check Your Comprehension

1. What is Johnson's definition of *modern*?
2. According to Johnson, what is "a tree worn by forlorn lovers"?
3. What years does Johnson assign to youth?

◆ **Critical Thinking**

INTERPRET
1. How does Johnson indicate that a word is a verb? **[Infer]**
2. Which definitions are most like those in a modern dictionary? Explain. **[Compare and Contrast]**
3. Why do you think the word *electricity* receives such a long definition? **[Speculate]**
4. (a) Which definitions are the most revealing about Johnson's character and situation? (b) What are some of the things they reveal? **[Analyze]**

EVALUATE
5. Do you find Johnson's definitions more or less useful than those in modern dictionaries? Explain. **[Assess]**

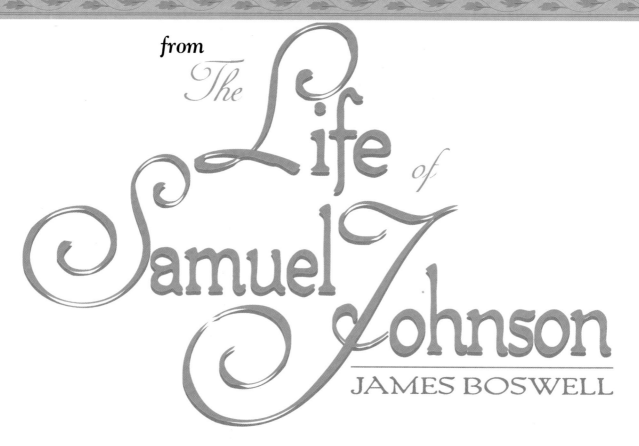

from
The Life of Samuel Johnson
JAMES BOSWELL

BOSWELL MEETS JOHNSON
1763

This is to me a memorable year; for in it I had the happiness to obtain the acquaintance of that extraordinary man whose memoirs I am now writing; an acquaintance which I shall ever esteem as one of the most fortunate circumstances in my life. Though then but two-and-twenty, I had for several years read his works with delight and instruction, and had the highest reverence for their author, which had grown up in my fancy into a kind of mysterious veneration, by figuring to myself a state of solemn elevated abstraction, in which I supposed him to live in the immense metropolis of London . . . .

Mr. Thomas Davies[1] the actor, who then kept a bookseller's shop in Russel Street, Covent Garden, told me that Johnson was very much his friend, and came frequently to his house, where he more than once invited me to meet him; but by some unlucky accident or other he was prevented from coming to us.

At last, on Monday the 16th day of May, when I was sitting in Mr. Davies's back parlor, after having drunk tea with him and Mrs. Davies, Johnson unexpectedly came into the shop; and Mr. Davies having perceived him through the glass door in the room in which we were sitting, advancing towards us—he announced his aweful[2] approach to me, somewhat in the manner of an actor in the part of Horatio, when he addresses Hamlet on the appearance of his father's ghost, "Look, my Lord, it comes,"[3] I found that I had a very perfect idea of Johnson's figure, from the portrait of him painted by Sir Joshua Reynolds[4] soon after he had published his *Dictionary*, in the attitude

---

1. Thomas Davies: English bookseller and unsuccessful actor (1712–1785).

2. aweful: Awe-inspiring.

3. Horatio ". . . it comes": From Shakespeare's *Hamlet* (Act I, Scene iv).

4. Sir Joshua Reynolds: Celebrated portrait painter at the time (1723–1792).

of sitting in his easy chair in deep meditation, which was the first picture his friend did for him, which Sir Joshua very kindly presented to me, and from which an engraving has been made for this work. Mr. Davies mentioned my name, and respectfully introduced me to him. I was much agitated; and recollecting his prejudice against the Scotch, of which I had heard much, I said to Davies, "Don't tell where I come from." "From Scotland," cried Davies roguishly. "Mr. Johnson," said I, "I do indeed come from Scotland, but I cannot help it." I am willing to flatter myself that I meant this as light pleasantry to sooth and conciliate him, and not as an humiliating <u>abasement</u> at the expense of my country. But however that might be, this speech was somewhat unlucky; for with that quickness of wit for which he was so remarkable, he seized the expression "come from Scotland," which I used in the sense of being of that country; and, as if I had said that I had come away from it, or left, retorted, "That, Sir, I find, is what a very great many of your countrymen cannot help." This stroke stunned me a good deal; and when we had sat down, I felt myself not a little embarrassed, and apprehensive of what might come next. He then addressed himself to Davies: "What do you think of Garrick?[5] He has refused me an order for the play for Miss Williams, because he knows the house will be full, and that an order would be worth three shillings." Eager to take any opening to get into conversation with him, I ventured to say, "O, Sir, I cannot think Mr. Garrick would grudge such a trifle to you." "Sir," said he, with a stern look, "I have known David Garrick longer than you have done: and I know no right you have to talk to me on the subject." Perhaps I deserved this check; for it was rather presumptuous in me, an entire stranger, to express any doubt of the justice of his animadversion upon his old acquaintance and pupil. I now felt myself much mortified, and began to think that the hope which I had long indulged of obtaining his acquaintance

was blasted. And, in truth, had not my ardor been uncommonly strong, and my resolution uncommonly persevering, so rough a reception might have deterred me forever from making any further attempts. Fortunately, however, I remained upon the field not wholly discomfited; and was soon rewarded by hearing some of his conversation, of which I preserved the following short minute,[6] without marking the questions and observations by which it was produced.

"People," he remarked, "may be taken in once, who imagine that an author is greater in private life than other men. Uncommon parts require uncommon opportunities for their exertion."

"In barbarous society, superiority of parts is of real consequence. Great strength or great wisdom is of much value to an individual. But in more polished times there are people to do everything for money; and then there are a number of other superiorities, such as those of birth and fortune, and rank, that dissipate men's attention, and leave no extraordinary share of respect for personal and intellectual superiority. This is wisely ordered by Providence, to preserve some equality among mankind."

"Sir, this book (*The Elements of Criticism*,[7] which he had taken up) is a pretty essay, and deserves to be held in some estimation, though much of it is chimerical."

Speaking of one[8] who with more than ordinary boldness attacked public measures and the royal family, he said, "I think he is safe

---

6. **minute:** Note.
7. ***Elements of Criticism:*** One of the works of Scottish philosophical writer Henry Home (1696–1782).
8. **one:** John Wilkes (1727–1797), an English political agitator.

◆ **Build Vocabulary**

abasement (ə bās′mənt) *n*.: Condition of being put down or humbled

---

5. **Garrick:** David Garrick (1717–1779), a famous actor who had been educated by Johnson. Garrick was also one of the managing partners of the Drury Lane Theater in London.

from the law, but he is an abusive scoundrel; and instead of applying to my Lord Chief Justice to punish him, I would send half a dozen footmen and have him well ducked."[9]

"The notion of liberty amuses the people of England, and helps to keep off the *taedium vitae*.[10] When a butcher tells you that his heart bleeds for his country, he has, in fact, no uneasy feeling."

"Sheridan[11] will not succeed at Bath with his oratory. Ridicule has gone down before him, and, I doubt,[12] Derrick[13] is his enemy."

"Derrick may do very well, as long as he can outrun his character; but the moment his character gets up with him, it is all over."

It is, however, but just to record, that some years afterwards, when I reminded him of this sarcasm, he said, "Well, but Derrick has now got a character that he need not run away from."

I was highly pleased with the extraordinary vigor of his conversation, and regretted that I was drawn away from it by an engagement at another place. I had, for a part of the evening, been left alone with him, and had ventured to make an observation now and then, which he received very civilly; so that I was satisfied that though there was a roughness in his manner, there was no ill nature in his disposition. Davies followed me to the door, and when I complained to him a little of the hard blows which the great man had given me he kindly took upon him to console me by saying, "Don't be uneasy. I can see he likes you very well."

◆ **Literary Focus**
Do you think Boswell has sufficiently supported his statement about the "extraordinary vigor" of Johnson's conversation? Why or why not?

JOHNSON'S CHARACTER

The character of Samuel Johnson has, I trust, been so developed in the course of this work, that they who have honored it with a perusal, may be considered as well acquainted with him. As, however, it may be expected that I should collect into one view the capital and distinguishing features of this extraordinary man, I shall endeavor to acquit myself of that part of my biographical undertaking, however difficult it may be to do that which many of my readers will do better for themselves.

His figure was large and well formed, and his countenance of the cast of an ancient statue; yet his appearance was rendered strange and somewhat uncouth by convulsive cramps, by the scars of that distemper[14] which it was once imagined the royal touch could cure,[15] and by a slovenly mode of dress. He had the use only of one eye; yet so much does mind govern and even supply the deficiency of organs, that his visual perceptions, as far as they extended, were uncommonly quick and accurate. So morbid was his temperament, that he never knew the natural joy of a free and vigorous use of his limbs: when he walked, it was like the struggling gait of one in fetters; when he rode, he had no command or direction of his horse, but was carried as if in a balloon. That with his constitution and habits of life he should have lived seventy-five years, is a proof that an inherent *vivida vis*[16] is a powerful preservative of the human frame.

Man is, in general, made up of contradictory qualities; and these will ever show themselves in strange succession, where a consistency in appearance at least, if not in reality, has not been attained by long habits of philosophical discipline. In proportion to the native vigor of the mind, the contradictory qualities will be the more prominent, and more difficult to be adjusted; and, therefore, we are not to wonder that Johnson exhibited an eminent example of this remark which I have made upon human nature. At different times, he seemed

---

9. ducked: Tied to a chair at the end of a plank and plunged into water.
10. *taedium vitae* (tī′ dē əm vē′ tī): Boredom.
11. Sheridan: Thomas Sheridan (1719–1788), an Irish actor and author. At the time, Sheridan was reading lectures at the Oratory at Bath.
12. doubt: Fear.
13. Derrick: The Master of Ceremonies of the Oratory at Bath.

---

14. distemper: Scrofula, a type of tuberculosis that causes swelling and scarring of the neck.
15. royal touch . . . cure: It was at one time believed that the touch of an English monarch had the power to heal. As a child Johnson was taken to Queen Anne to receive her touch in the hope that it would cure him.
16. *vivida vis:* Lively force.

◀ **Critical Viewing** This engraving shows the ghost of Samuel Johnson haunting Boswell. What does this suggest about the relationship between Johnson and Boswell? **[Interpret]**

a different man, in some respects; not, however, in any great or essential article, upon which he had fully employed his mind, and settled certain principles of duty, but only in his manners and in the display of argument and fancy in his talk. He was prone to superstition, but not to credulity. Though his imagination might incline him to a belief of the marvelous and the mysterious, his vigorous reason examined the evidence with jealousy.[17] He was a sincere and zealous Christian, of high Church of England and monarchical principles, which he would not tamely suffer to be questioned; and had, perhaps, at an early period, narrowed his mind somewhat too much, both as to religion and politics. His being impressed with the danger of extreme latitude in either, though he was of a

---

17. **jealousy:** Suspicion.

◆ **Build Vocabulary**

credulity (krə doo′ lə tē) *n.*: Tendency to believe too readily

very independent spirit, occasioned his appearing somewhat unfavorable to the prevalence of that noble freedom of sentiment which is the best possession of man. Nor can it be denied, that he had many prejudices; which, however, frequently suggested many of his pointed sayings that rather show a playfulness of fancy than any settled malignity. He was steady and inflexible in maintaining the obligations of religion and morality; both from a regard for the order of society, and from a veneration for the Great Source of all order; correct, nay, stern in his taste; hard to please, and easily offended; impetuous and irritable in his temper, but of a most humane and benevolent heart, which showed itself not only in a most liberal charity, as far as his circumstances would allow, but in a thousand instances of active benevolence. He was afflicted with a bodily disease, which made him often restless and fretful; and with a constitutional melancholy, the clouds of which darkened the brightness of his fancy, and gave a gloomy cast to his whole course of thinking: we, therefore, ought not to wonder at his sallies of impatience and passion at any time; especially when provoked by obtrusive ignorance, or presuming petulance; and allowance must be made for his uttering hasty and satirical sallies even against his best friends. And, surely, when it is considered, that, "amidst sickness and sorrow," he exerted his faculties in so many works for the benefit of mankind, and particularly that he achieved the great and admirable Dictionary of our language, we must be astonished at his resolution. The solemn text, "of him to whom much is given, much will be required," seems to have been ever present to his mind, in a rigorous sense, and to have made him dissatisfied with his labors and acts of goodness, however comparatively great; so that the unavoidable consciousness of his superiority was, in that respect, a cause of disquiet. He suffered so much from this, and from the gloom which perpetually haunted him and made solitude frightful, that it may be said of him, "If in this life only he had hope, he was of all men most miserable."[18] He loved praise, when it was brought to him; but was too proud to seek for it. He was somewhat susceptible of flattery. As he was general and unconfined in his studies, he cannot be considered as master of any one particular science; but he had accumulated a vast and various collection of learning and knowledge, which was so arranged in his mind, as to be ever in readiness to be brought forth. But his superiority over other learned men consisted chiefly in what may be called the art of thinking, the art of using his mind; a certain continual power of seizing the useful substance of all that he knew and exhibiting it in a clear and forcible manner; so that knowledge, which we often see to be no better than lumber[19] in men of dull understanding, was, in him, true, evident, and actual wisdom. His moral precepts are practical; for they are drawn from an intimate acquaintance with human nature. His maxims carry conviction; for they are founded on the basis of common sense, and a very attentive and minute survey of real life. His mind was so full of imagery, that he might have been perpetually a poet; yet it is remarkable, that, however rich his prose is in this respect, his poetical pieces, in general, have not much of that splendor, but are rather distinguished by strong sentiment and acute observation, conveyed in harmonious and energetic verse, particularly in heroic couplets. Though usually grave, and even aweful, in his deportment, he possessed uncommon and peculiar powers of wit and humor; he frequently indulged himself in colloquial pleasantry; and the heartiest merriment was often enjoyed in his company; with this great advantage, that as it was entirely free from any poisonous tincture of vice or impiety, it was salutary to those who shared in it. He had accustomed himself to such accuracy in his common conversation, that he at all times expressed his thoughts with great force, and an elegant choice of language, the effect of which was aided by his having a loud voice, and a slow deliberate utterance. In him were united a most logical head with a most fertile imagination, which gave him an extraordinary advantage

---

18. **"If . . . miserable":** From I Corinthians 15:19.

19. **lumber:** Rubbish.

in arguing: for he could reason close or wide, as he saw best for the moment. Exulting in his intellectual strength and dexterity, he could, when he pleased, be the greatest sophist[20] that ever contended in the lists of declamation; and, from a spirit of contradiction and a delight in showing his powers, he would often maintain the wrong side with equal warmth and ingenuity; so that, when there was an audience, his real opinions could seldom be gathered from his talk; though when he was in company with a single friend, he would discuss a subject with genuine fairness: but he was too conscientious to make error permanent and pernicious, by deliberately writing it; and, in all his numerous works, he earnestly inculcated what appeared to him to be the truth; his piety being constant, and the ruling principle of all his conduct.

Such was Samuel Johnson, a man whose talents, acquirements, and virtues, were so extraordinary, that the more his character is considered the more he will be regarded by the present age, and by posterity, with admiration and reverence.

---

20. sophist (säf´ ist) *n.*: One who makes misleading arguments.

◆ **Build Vocabulary**

malignity (mə lig´ nə tē) *n.*: Strong desire to harm others

pernicious (pər nish´ əs) *adj.*: Causing serious injury; deadly

inculcated (in kul´ kāt id) *v.*: Impressed upon the mind by frequent repetition

---

Guide for Responding

◆ *Literature and Your Life*

Reader's Response Based on this selection, do you think you would have liked Samuel Johnson? Why or why not?

Thematic Focus What ties seemed to bind Boswell to Johnson and Johnson to his admirers?

Personality Profile Capture the personality of someone you admire in a brief paragraph.

☑ **Check Your Comprehension**

1. Why was 1763 such a memorable year for Boswell?
2. How did Boswell meet Johnson?
3. What aspects of Johnson's appearance prompt Boswell to describe him as "strange and somewhat uncouth"?
4. According to the selection, what was Johnson's position on (a) superstition? (b) religion? (c) praise? (d) flattery?

◆ **Critical Thinking**

INTERPRET

1. What are Samuel Johnson's chief qualities? **[Connect]**
2. What details of Johnson's personality explain (a) his sarcastic remark about Scotland? (b) his desire to claim a free theater ticket for a friend? (c) his harsh reply to Boswell's comment on Garrick? **[Connect]**
3. What do you learn about Boswell himself from this selection? Explain. **[Infer]**

EVALUATE

4. Do you think Boswell paints a fairly objective portrait of Johnson? Why or why not? **[Assess]**

APPLY

5. What similarities and differences do you detect between the lifestyles and habits of eighteenth-century celebrities and those in our own age? **[Relate]**

Guide for Responding (continued)

◆ Reading Strategy

SET A PURPOSE

By reading with a **purpose** in mind, you're able to locate and absorb the information you need. For example, if your purpose in reading Johnson's *Dictionary* was to learn how to pronounce a word, you'd turn immediately to the pronunciation re-spellings. If your purpose was to verify a word's meaning, you'd skim the listing of definitions until you found what you were looking for.

1. Read the second and third paragraphs of the excerpt from *The Life of Samuel Johnson* with these two purposes: (a) to learn about Johnson's sense of humor and (b) to learn more about Boswell's character. Then list the details that suit each purpose.
2. Explain the differences between the lists you made for the questions above.

◆ Literary Focus

DICTIONARY

Like **dictionaries** today, Johnson's *Dictionary* lists words alphabetically and includes definitions, pronunciations, word histories, and parts of speech. It is unusual in that Johnson allowed his personal attitudes about the entries to color the definitions!

1. How is the listing for *patron* in Johnson's *Dictionary* similar to and different from one in a modern dictionary?
2. What is the value, if any, of a dictionary?

BIOGRAPHY

Boswell's **biography** of Johnson is an account of the life of a writer written by a close personal friend. Besides offering factual information like names, dates, and conversations, Boswell weaves in his personal opinions and observations, as when he says that a comment of Johnson's "stunned him." This combination of fact and opinion gives this literary portrait an especially personal feeling.

1. Reread the section entitled "Johnson's Character." Find three examples of facts and three examples of opinions.
2. Which do you find more revealing about the character of Johnson: Boswell's facts or his opinions? Why?

◆ Build Vocabulary

USING THE LATIN ROOT -dict-

Words that contain the Latin root *-dict-* convey the idea of something said or spoken. For example, *diction* refers to the words people choose to say things, and a *dictionary* is a book that provides information about spoken words. Explain how these words convey the idea of saying or speaking:

1. dictate   2. dictator   3. predict

USING THE WORD BANK: Sentence Completions

Complete these sentences with the words from the Word Bank. Use each word only once.

1. One of Boswell's ___?___ led to his meeting Johnson.
2. Johnson expressed joking disaffection for the Scots, but he felt no ___?___ toward them.
3. Because of misuses and ___?___ of the English language, Johnson created a dictionary.
4. Johnson took advantage of Boswell's ___?___ .
5. ___?___ of badly spoken English annoyed Johnson.
6. A ___?___ illness left Johnson's face disfigured.
7. Johnson received little monetary ___?___ for his *Dictionary*.
8. Although Boswell's celebrity-chasing was ___?___ , he was an excellent biographer.
9. Boswell's ___?___ resulted from Johnson's scolding him.

◆ Grammar and Style

COMMAS WITH PARENTHETICAL EXPRESSIONS

Boswell gives his biography the flavor of speech by setting off in **parenthetical expressions** his comments on the main ideas. He uses commas to separate these opinions and observations.

Practice Identify each parenthetical expression, and add commas where necessary.

1. Boswell I have heard was a young man when he first met Johnson.
2. Johnson on the other hand was much older.
3. Many in Johnson's circle were contemptuous of Boswell by the way.
4. Sad to say the poet Thomas Gray made scathing remarks about Boswell.
5. Johnson in contrast was kind to Boswell.

Build Your Portfolio

 ## Idea Bank

Writing

1. Book Ad Write an ad that the publishers of Johnson's *Dictionary* or Boswell's biography might have used to lure readers. You might also use quotations from the work that will generate interest in the book. **[Career Link]**

2. Revised Preface Rewrite Johnson's preface for a modern audience. Express the same ideas, but use vocabulary suited for modern readers.

3. Response to Criticism Edmund Wilson writes: "Boswell, in spite of his great respect . . . could not help making Johnson a character in an eighteenth-century comedy . . . " Using examples from the text, explain what Wilson means.

Speaking, Listening, and Viewing

4. Reenactment Working with another student, reenact the meeting between Johnson and Boswell, as Boswell describes it. **[Performing Arts Link]**

5. Interpretation of Attitudes Read aloud Johnson's dictionary definitions, using your voice to express the different attitudes Johnson's definitions convey. **[Performing Arts Link]**

Researching and Representing

6. First-Person Biography Like James Boswell, create a biography of someone you know well. Include anecdotes, pictures, and quotations. **[Social Studies Link]**

7. The School of Johnson Create a diagram showing the writers on whom Samuel Johnson had a direct influence. If possible, include pictures or drawings of each writer, along with a list of his or her major works. **[Art Link]**

Online Activity www.phlit.phschool.com

 ## Guided Writing Lesson

Dictionary of New Words

Samuel Johnson created a dictionary of English that was so thorough and well thought out that it set the standard for years to come. Like Johnson, create a dictionary of your own. In it, define words that have recently entered the language. As you compile your dictionary, decide on a format and maintain it throughout.

Writing Skills Focus: Keeping to a Format

To be clear and well organized, informational writing should maintain a **consistent format.** Dictionaries, in particular, should be formatted consistently from entry to entry. Follow these rules:

- List entries alphabetically.
- Use capitalization, punctuation, boldface, italics, and underscoring consistently.
- List the elements of each entry—pronunciation, part of speech, definitions, word history—in the same order from entry to entry.

The following strategies will help you keep to your format at every stage of the writing process.

Prewriting List the words that you plan to define. Work out each word's pronunciation, spelling, part of speech, and definition. Also jot down context sentences or examples, if you like.

Drafting Alphabetize the entries, and decide on the order in which to present the elements of the entries. Copy out the words and definitions, along with all the examples and illustrations you plan to include.

Revising Check spellings, pronunciation guides, and definitions for accuracy. Check the format for consistency, making sure the entries are listed in alphabetical order and that the elements within each entry are arranged in the same order.

Guide for Interpreting

Thomas Gray (1716–1771)

Life's uncertainty was something that Thomas Gray understood all too well. The only one of twelve Gray children to survive infancy, he himself barely made it out of boyhood. Remarkably, he managed to withstand the primitive medical treatment for his childhood convulsions. Lavishing her affections on this one surviving son, Gray's mother, a London shopkeeper, saved up her pennies to pay for his schooling at prestigious Eton and Cambridge.

A Quiet Life   After making the Grand Tour of Europe with his friend Horace Walpole, Gray lived with his mother and aunts in the village of Stoke Poges, whose church and graveyard probably inspired his best-known poem, "Elegy Written in a Country Churchyard." After age thirty, Gray returned to Cambridge and busied himself with private studies of classical literature and Celtic and Norse mythology. Never in the best of health, he died of an extremely painful attack of gout. Though his literary output was rather small, he is today remembered as one of England's finest poets.

Anne Finch, Countess of Winchilsea (1661–1720)

Anne Kingsmill Finch, Countess of Winchilsea, lived in an era in which women intellectuals were looked on with scornful amusement. Even her friend Alexander Pope poked fun of her as the character Phoebe Clinket in the play *Three Hours After Marriage*. Despite this mockery, Finch pursued her interest in poetry, publishing a volume of verse in 1713 and leaving behind additional manuscripts at her death.

A Poet and Countess   Anne Kingsmill met her husband, Heneage Finch, when he was serving as a royal attendant and she was a maid of honor to the wife of the Duke of York, later James II. The Finches' fortunes soured when James II was driven from power in 1688, but after a period of poverty, Heneage inherited from a distant cousin the title Earl of Winchilsea and a lovely estate at Eastwell in rural Kent. It was here that Anne Finch wrote most of her poems, many of which applaud the rural pleasures of Eastwell.

◆ Background for Understanding

LITERATURE: DAYLIGHT OF REASON, NIGHTTIME OF FEELING

In the eighteenth century, many writers placed a high value on reason, clarity, and logic, qualities that they found in ancient Greek and Roman poetry. In a sense, these are "daylight" qualities, associated with the brightness of sunlight. Alexander Pope compared Sir Isaac Newton, the greatest scientist of the age, to the sun itself: "God said, Let Newton be! And there was light."

Pope's own bright couplets, Johnson's all-explaining dictionary, Addison's popular essays—these works communicate in the light of day. They address readers not as isolated individuals but as members of society and fellow reasoners. They are witty, brisk, and businesslike.

By contrast, Gray's "Elegy Written in a Country Churchyard" and Anne Finch's "A Nocturnal Reverie" are set in twilight or nighttime. The authors present themselves as isolated, feeling individuals, reaching out to others like themselves. These works represent the "nighttime" side of eighteenth-century literature. In stressing what other works neglect—emotion, the worth of the individual—they anticipate the artistic movement we call Romanticism.

Elegy Written in a Country Churchyard
◆ A Nocturnal Reverie ◆

◆ *Literature and Your Life*

CONNECT YOUR EXPERIENCE

What situations prompt your thoughts to turn inward? Sometimes nighttime walks bring on such thoughts; sometimes, simply being alone makes people introspective.

In the poems that follow, the speakers share their innermost thoughts and personal feelings during solitary evening walks.

Journal Writing Briefly describe a place or a situation that prompted you to think more deeply about life.

THEMATIC FOCUS: THE TIES THAT BIND

How do these poems suggest that even our quiet thoughts when alone can join us with other people?

◆ Literary Focus

PRE-ROMANTIC POETRY

Pre-Romantic poetry has the polish of formal eighteenth-century poetry, but it also anticipates the Romantic emphasis on mystery, emotion, and individual expression.

In simple terms, the difference between poetry like Pope's and pre-Romantic poetry is the difference between the head and the heart. Pope's brilliant lines—"The proper study of mankind is man"—speak to your mind. However, Gray's lonely musings stir your emotions: "...all the air a solemn stillness holds."

Even the types of poems that Gray and Finch write are linked to emotion and mystery. Gray's poem is an **elegy**, a solemn work that mourns someone's death or reflects on a serious theme. Finch's is a **reverie**, which is a fanciful, dreamlike poem.

◆ Grammar and Style

PRONOUN-ANTECEDENT AGREEMENT

In the poems that follow, you'll find several examples of **pronouns** and **antecedents**, the words to which pronouns refer. A pronoun must agree with its antecedent in gender and number, as in these examples from Gray's "Elegy":

Examples: The *plowman* homeward plods *his* weary way ...
No *children* run to lisp *their* sire's return ...

◆ Reading Strategy

PARAPHRASE

To ensure understanding, **paraphrase** passages by identifying key ideas and expressing them in your own words. Paraphrasing poetry is an especially useful strategy for unlocking the meaning of lines that contain difficult words or sentence structures.

Use a chart like the following when paraphrasing difficult lines in poetry.

Original	Paraphrase
Now fades the glimmering landscape on the sight ...	Nightfall is making it difficult to see the landscape.

◆ Build Vocabulary

LATIN PREFIXES: *circum-*

From *circus*, Latin for "circle," comes the prefix *circum-*, which means "around." When combined with the root *scribe*, as in the word *circumscribed*, it creates a word meaning "limit the activity of" or "draw a line around."

WORD BANK

Before you read, preview this list of words from the poems.

penury
circumscribed
ingenuous
ignoble
nocturnal
temperate
venerable
forage

Elegy Written in a Country Churchyard

Thomas Gray

The curfew tolls the knell of parting day,
    The lowing herd winds slowly o'er the lea,[1]
The plowman homeward plods his weary way,
    And leaves the world to darkness and to me.

5   Now fades the glimmering landscape on the sight,
    And all the air a solemn stillness holds,
Save where the beetle wheels his droning flight,
    And drowsy tinklings lull the distant folds;

Save that from yonder ivy-mantled tower,
10   The moping owl does to the moon complain
Of such as, wandering near her secret bower,
    Molest her ancient solitary reign.

Beneath those rugged elms, that yew tree's shade,
    Where heaves the turf in many a moldering heap,
15   Each in his narrow cell forever laid,
    The rude[2] forefathers of the hamlet sleep.

---

1. **lea:** Meadow.
2. **rude:** Uneducated.

▲ **Critical Viewing** The churchyard in this photograph looks untended and forgotten. How does the photograph reflect the meaning of Gray's poem? **[Deduce]**

The breezy call of incense-breathing morn,
　　The swallow twittering from the straw-built shed,
The cock's shrill clarion, or the echoing horn,[3]
20　　　No more shall rouse them from their lowly bed.

For them no more the blazing hearth shall burn,
　　Or busy housewife ply her evening care;
No children run to lisp their sire's return,
　　Or climb his knees the envied kiss to share.

25　Oft did the harvest to their sickle yield,
　　Their furrow oft the stubborn glebe[4] has broke;
How jocund[5] did they drive their team afield!
　　How bowed the woods beneath their sturdy stroke!

Let not Ambition mock their useful toil,
30　　Their homely joys, and destiny obscure;
Nor Grandeur hear with a disdainful smile
　　The short and simple annals of the poor.

The boast of heraldry,[6] the pomp of power,
　　And all that beauty, all that wealth e'er gave,
35　Awaits alike the inevitable hour.
　　The paths of glory lead but to the grave.

Nor you, ye proud, impute to these the fault,
　　If memory o'er their tomb no trophies[7] raise,
Where through the long-drawn aisle and fretted vault[8]
40　　The pealing anthem swells the note of praise.

Can storied urn,[9] or animated[10] bust,
　　Back to its mansion call the fleeting breath?
Can honor's voice provoke[11] the silent dust,
　　Or Flattery soothe the dull cold ear of Death?

45　Perhaps in this neglected spot is laid
　　Some heart once pregnant with celestial fire;
Hands, that the rod of empire might have swayed,
　　Or waked to ecstasy the living lyre.

---

3. **horn:** Hunter's horn.
4. **glebe:** Soil.
5. **jocund:** Cheerful.
6. **heraldry:** Noble descent.
7. **trophies:** Symbolic figures or pictures depicting the achievements of the dead man.
8. **fretted vault:** Church ceiling decorated with intersecting lines.
9. **storied urn:** Funeral urn with an epitaph inscribed on it.
10. **animated:** Lifelike.
11. **provoke:** Call forth.

But Knowledge to their eyes her ample page
    Rich with the spoils of time did ne'er unroll;
50 Chill Penury repressed their noble rage,
    And froze the genial current of the soul.

Full many a gem of purest ray serene
    The dark unfathomed caves of ocean bear:
55 Full many a flower is born to blush unseen,
    And waste its sweetness on the desert air.

Some village Hampden,[12] that, with dauntless breast,
    The little tyrant of his fields withstood,
Some mute inglorious Milton[13] here may rest,
60   Some Cromwell[14] guiltless of his country's blood.

The applause of listening senates to command,
    The threats of pain and ruin to despise,
To scatter plenty o'er a smiling land,
    And read their history in a nation's eyes,

65 Their lot forbade: nor circumscribed alone
    Their growing virtues, but their crimes confined
Forbade to wade through slaughter to a throne,
    And shut the gates of mercy on mankind,

The struggling pangs of conscious truth to hide,
70   To quench the blushes of ingenuous shame,
Or heap the shrine of Luxury and Pride
    With incense kindled at the Muse's flame.

Far from the madding[15] crowd's ignoble strife,
    Their sober wishes never learned to stray;
75 Along the cool sequestered vale of life
    They kept the noiseless tenor[16] of their way.

Yet even these bones from insult to protect
    Some frail memorial still erected nigh,
With uncouth rhymes and shapeless sculpture decked,[17]
80   Implores the passing tribute of a sigh.

---

12. Hampden: John Hampden (1594–1643), an English statesman who defied King Charles I by resisting the king's efforts to revive an obsolete tax without the authority of Parliament.
13. Milton: English poet, John Milton (1608–1674).
14. Cromwell: Oliver Cromwell (1599–1658), English revolutionary leader and Lord Protector of the Commonwealth from 1653 to 1658.
15. madding: Frenzied.
16. tenor: General tendency or course.
17. Some . . . decked: Contrasts with "the storied urn[s] or animated bust[s]" (line 41) inside the church.

◆ Build Vocabulary

penury (pen´ yoo rē) *n*.: Poverty

circumscribed (sʉr´ kəm skrībd) *v*.: Limited; confined

ingenuous (in jen´ yoo əs) *adj*.: Naive; simple

ignoble (ig nō´ bəl) *adj*.: Not noble; common

Elegy Written in a Country Churchyard ◆ 523

Their name, their years, spelt by the unlettered Muse,[18]
    The place of fame and elegy supply:
And many a holy text around she strews,
    That teach the rustic moralist to die.

85 For who, to dumb Forgetfulness a prey,
    This pleasing anxious being e'er resigned,
Left the warm precincts of the cheerful day,
    Nor cast one longing lingering look behind?

On some fond breast the parting soul relies,
90   Some pious drops[19] the closing eye requires;
Even from the tomb the voice of Nature cries,
    Even in our ashes live their wonted fires.

For thee,[20] who, mindful of the unhonored dead,
    Dost in these lines their artless tale relate;
95 If chance, by lonely contemplation led,
    Some kindred spirit shall enquire thy fate,

Haply[21] some hoary-headed[22] swain may say,
    "Oft have we seen him at the peep of dawn
Brushing with hasty steps the dews away,
100   To meet the sun upon the upland lawn.

"There at the foot of yonder nodding beech,
    That wreathes its old fantastic roots so high,
His listless length at noontide would he stretch,
    And pore upon the brook that babbles by.

105 "Hard by yon wood, now smiling as in scorn,
    Muttering his wayward fancies he would rove;
Now drooping, woeful wan, like one forlorn,
    Or crazed with care, or crossed in hopeless love.

"One morn I missed him on the customed hill,
110   Along the heath, and near his favorite tree;
Another came; nor yet beside the rill,[23]
    Nor up the lawn, nor at the wood was he;

"The next, with dirges due in sad array
    Slow through the churchway path we saw him borne.
115 Approach and read (for thou canst read) the lay
    Graved on the stone beneath yon aged thorn."[24]

---

18. **the unlettered Muse:** Uneducated gravestone carver.
19. **drops:** Tears.
20. **thee:** Gray himself.
21. **haply:** Perhaps.
22. **hoary-headed:** White-haired.
23. **rill:** Brook.
24. **thorn:** Hawthorn tree.

The Epitaph

Here rests his head upon the lap of Earth
  A youth, to Fortune and to Fame unknown.
Fair Science[25] frowned not on his humble birth,
120   And melancholy marked him for her own.

Large was his bounty, and his soul sincere,
  Heaven did a recompense as largely send:
He gave to misery (all he had) a tear,
  He gained from Heaven ('twas all he wished) a friend.

125 No farther seek his merits to disclose,
  Or draw his frailties from their dread abode
(There they alike in trembling hope repose),
  The bosom of his Father and his God.

---

25. Science: Learning.

Guide for Responding

◆ Literature and Your Life

Reader's Response Did you share the speaker's sense of loss? Why or why not?

Thematic Focus What does the poem suggest about the ties that bind all human beings, regardless of status in society?

Added Stanza Continue Gray's elegy by writing a stanza praising an everyday person who was un-appreciated in life. Your person could be modern and actual or from the past and fictional.

☑ Check Your Comprehension

1. At what time of day does the speaker find himself in the country churchyard?
2. (a) Who are the forefathers referred to by the speaker? (b) Of what will those forefathers no longer partake, according to lines 21–25?
3. In lines 57–60, what does the speaker say about the lives these people *might* have led?
4. To whom is "The Epitaph" in the last three stanzas dedicated?

◆ Critical Thinking

INTERPRET

1. (a) What is meant by "the inevitable hour" in line 35? (b) by "its mansion" in line 42? **[Interpret]**
2. To what is Gray comparing the "gem" and the "flower" in lines 53–56? **[Interpret]**
3. How would you explore the sentiment in lines 77–92? **[Interpret]**
4. Does the speaker come to accept his loss by the end of the poem? Explain your answer. **[Draw Conclusions]**

EVALUATE

5. Gray's "Elegy" is often quoted. Which lines do you find the most memorable? Why? **[Assess]**

EXTEND

6. Thomas Hardy wrote a famous novel called *Far from the Madding Crowd*, whose title comes from line 73 of Gray's poem. What sort of life would you guess this book celebrates? Explain. **[Literature Link]**

A Nocturnal Reverie

**Anne Finch,
Countess of Winchilsea**

In such a night, when every louder wind
Is to its distant cavern safe confined;
And only gentle Zephyr[1] fans his wings,
And lonely Philomel,[2] still waking, sings;
5   Or from some tree, famed for the owl's delight,
She, hollowing clear, directs the wanderer right:
In such a night, when passing clouds give place,
Or thinly veil the heavens' mysterious face;
When in some river, overhung with green,
10   The waving moon and trembling leaves are seen;
When freshened grass now bears itself upright,
And makes cool banks to pleasing rest invite,
Whence springs the woodbind, and the bramble-rose,
And where the sleepy cowslip sheltered grows;
15   Whilst now a paler hue the foxglove takes,
Yet checkers still with red the dusky brakes:[3]
When scattered glow-worms, but in twilight fine,
Show trivial beauties watch their hour to shine;

---

1. **Zephyr** (zefʹ ər): West Wind; a breeze.
2. **Philomel** (filʹ ə melʹ): Nightingale from mythology.
3. **brakes:** Overgrown areas; thickets.

Whilst Salisbury[4] stands the test of every light,
20 In perfect charms, and perfect virtue bright:
When odors, which declined repelling day,
Through temperate air uninterrupted stray;
When darkened groves their softest shadows wear,
And falling waters we distinctly hear;
25 When through the gloom more venerable shows
Some ancient fabric,[5] awful in repose,
While sunburnt hills their swarthy looks conceal,
And swelling haycocks thicken up the vale:
When the loosed horse now, as his pasture leads,
30 Comes slowly grazing through the adjoining meads,[6]

---

4. Salisbury: This may refer to a Lady Salisbury, daughter of a
friend, not to the town of Salisbury.
5. ancient fabric: Edifice or large, imposing building.
6. meads: Archaic term for "meadows."

◆ Build Vocabulary

nocturnal (näk tʉr′ nəl): *adj.*: Occurring at night

temperate (tem′ pər it) *adj.*: Mild

venerable (ven′ ər ə bəl) *adj.*: Commanding respect by
virtue of age, character, or social rank

Cottage and Pond, Moonlight, Thomas Gainsborough, Victoria and Albert Museum, London

▲ **Critical Viewing** What visual elements in this picture help create a mood like that of the poem? **[Analyze]**

Whose stealing pace, and lengthened shade we fear,
Till torn-up <u>forage</u> in his teeth we hear:
When nibbling sheep at large pursue their food,
And unmolested kine[7] rechew the cud;
35   When curlews cry beneath the village walls,
And to her straggling brood the partridge calls;
Their shortlived jubilee the creatures keep,
Which but endures, whilst tyrant man does sleep;
When a sedate content the spirit feels,
40   And no fierce light disturbs, whilst it reveals;
But silent musings urge the mind to seek
Something, too high for syllables to speak;

---

7. kine: Archaic plural of "cow"; cattle.

Till the free soul to a composedness charmed,
Finding the elements of rage disarmed,
45 O'er all below a solemn quiet grown,
Joys in the inferior world, and thinks it like her own:
In such a night let me abroad remain,
Till morning breaks, and all's confused again;
Our cares, our toils, our clamors are renewed,
50 Or pleasures, seldom reached, again pursued.

◆ **Build Vocabulary**

forage (fôr´ ij) *n.*: Food for farm animals, especially
any food found by grazing outdoors

Guide for Responding

◆ Literature and Your Life

Reader's Response Could you share the speaker's mood? Why or why not?

Thematic Focus What does the poem suggest about the ties that bind nature together and the ties that bind us to nature?

Nocturnal Reverie List some of the details that you would put in your own "nocturnal reverie."

☑ Check Your Comprehension

1. (a) Describe the setting of the poem. (b) List specific images from the poem that support your description of the setting.
2. Where does the speaker want to remain on such a night?
3. According to the speaker, what happens when morning breaks again?

◆ Critical Thinking

INTERPRET
1. What is the mood of the poem? **[Classify]**
2. According to lines 9–12, is the night fresh, dull, or chaotic? Explain. **[Analyze]**
3. This poem is one sentence containing many thoughts. How does the poem's structure affect its meaning? **[Interpret]**

APPLY
4. If the speaker were taking a nocturnal walk in modern times, would her observations be the same? Explain. **[Hypothesize]**

EXTEND
5. In Act V, Scene i, of *The Merchant of Venice* by William Shakespeare, the lovers Lorenzo and Jessica speak of famous lovers, using the phrase "in such a night" seven times. Why do you think Finch opened her poem with the phrase made famous in this scene? **[Literature Link]**

Guide for Responding *(continued)*

◆ Reading Strategy

PARAPHRASE

Paraphrasing, or restating in your own words a writer's key ideas, helps you understand and enjoy literature. Once you've paraphrased an author's words, you are better able to understand the author's message. Here, for example, is a paraphrase of two lines from Gray's "Elegy":

Original: Let not Ambition mock their useful toil, / Their homely joys, and destiny obscure . . .

Paraphrase: Those who are ambitious shouldn't make fun of their useful work, simple pleasures, and unknown lives.

I. (a) Paraphrase lines 53–56 of Thomas Gray's "Elegy." (b) What key ideas do these lines express?

2. Lines 47–50 of "A Nocturnal Reverie" reveal the speaker's wishes. Express these wishes in your own words.

◆ Build Vocabulary

USING THE LATIN PREFIX *circum-*

Explain how the Latin prefix *circum-*, which means "around" or "surrounding," contributes to the meaning of the italicized words.

I. Magellan is known for *circumnavigating* the globe.

2. She *circumvented* the rules by sneaking into line.

3. When people don't want to say something outright, they use *circumlocutions.*

4. *Circumspect,* he always thought before acting.

5. Have you learned how to measure a circle's radius and *circumference?*

USING THE WORD BANK: Synonyms or Antonyms?

Copy these word pairs into your notebook and indicate whether they are synonyms or antonyms.

I. penury, wealth
2. ingenuous, sophisticated
3. ignoble, lowly
4. nocturnal, daytime
5. temperate, moderate
6. venerable, respected
7. forage, fodder

◆ Literary Focus

PRE-ROMANTIC POETRY

Poems like Gray's "Elegy" and Finch's "Reverie" are **pre-Romantic** in their emphasis on the worth of the common person, the mystery of life, and the importance of emotions. The **elegy** that Gray writes, for example, mourns for an ordinary person, rather than for a well-known figure: "A youth, to Fortune and to Fame unknown." This "youth" is mysterious for the very fact that he is unknown, and the poem expresses sadness concerning his fate.

Finch's dreamlike **reverie** shares the quiet of Gray's poem, a quiet in which deep thought flows into feeling.

I. Explain how lines 39–50 of Finch's "A Nocturnal Reverie" stress mystery and emotion rather than achievement and intellectual striving.

2. (a) What is similar about Gray's concern for the unknown dead of a village graveyard and Finch's loving attention to humble "creatures"? (b) What is pre-Romantic about this type of subject?

3. Both poets choose a nighttime setting. How is this choice itself a reflection of pre-Romantic ideals?

◆ Grammar and Style

PRONOUN-ANTECEDENT AGREEMENT

Pronouns agree with their **antecedents,** the words to which they refer, in number and gender. When an antecedent is a compound linked by *and*, the number is plural. If a compound is linked by *or*, the number may be singular.

Practice Copy these sentences and correct errors in pronoun-antecedent agreement. If a sentence is correct as is, write *correct.*

I. Everything in the woods had their beauties.
2. The nightingale or the owl sang their song.
3. Some of the flowers opened their petals.
4. The woodbine and the bramble-rose wafted its scent into the nighttime air.
5. Each of the farm animals had their habits.

Build Your Portfolio

 Idea Bank

Writing

1. Diary Entry Imagine that you are the speaker of Gray's "Elegy" or Finch's "Reverie." Write a diary entry describing the experience behind your poem.

2. Epitaphs Drawing on biographical information as well as on the poems, write epitaphs for the graves of Gray and Finch. Each epitaph should say something important about the writer.

3. Response to Criticism Dr. Johnson wrote of Gray's elegy, "The Churchyard abounds with images which find a mirror in every mind, and with sentiments to which every bosom returns an echo." Agree or disagree with this statement, citing specific references from the poem.

Speaking, Listening, and Viewing

4. Choral Reading Working in a group, prepare and perform a choral reading of either poem. **[Performing Arts Link]**

5. Visual Presentation Is there an old, unused building near you? With a partner, prepare a report for your classmates that shows the building today and a re-creation of how it would have looked when new. **[History Link]**

Researching and Representing

6. Nighttime Walk The thoughts of the speakers in Gray's and Finch's poems are inspired by the nighttime. Design a park that would allow people to take safe nighttime walks. **[Social Studies Link]**

7. Brain Study Use science magazines to research brain waves and their effects on dreams and daydreams. Present your findings to the class, explaining the scientific basis for Finch's reverie. **[Science Link]**

Online Activity www.phlit.phschool.com

 Guided Writing Lesson

Reflective Essay

In both Gray's "Elegy" and Finch's "Reverie," a particular time and place inspire a reflective journey. Take a journey of your own by writing a reflective essay. In it, re-create a special time and place, together with your personal response to the setting.

These tips will help you give your essay a distinctive, personal flavor.

Writing Skills Focus: Elaboration to Make Writing Personal

Some types of writing are more powerful if they express the personal thoughts and feelings of the writer. In a reflective essay, for example, a writer reveals a personal experience and his or her reactions to it.

Here are some ways to reveal yourself in an essay:
- Base the essay on a setting that inspired you.
- Describe the time and place vividly, just as you experienced it.
- Trace any changes in your thoughts and feelings that may have taken place over time.

Prewriting Begin to gather details that will effectively convey your reflective journey. You may want to use a two-column chart to list details describing the source of inspiration (col. 1) and the thoughts and feelings inspired in you (col. 2).

Drafting As you draft, refer to the details you've gathered in order to relive your original experience. If you remember additional thoughts and feelings inspired by that experience, add them to your essay.

Revising Have a friend read your essay, and ask if he or she senses your personality in it. If a passage seems distant and purely descriptive, add your thoughts and feelings about what you're describing. Also, be sure that you've noted any changes in your thoughts and feelings that have been inspired by the original experience.

CONNECTIONS TO WORLD LITERATURE

from The Analects   *from* The Declaration of Independence
Confucius   Thomas Jefferson

Cultural Connection

THE TIES THAT BIND

The pieces in this section and the ones you are about to read illustrate the shared experiences and beliefs that bind people together. You have had such experiences in your own school. As you study and participate in activities with others, you begin to feel like a member of a community.

A country is obviously larger than a school. However, the citizens of a country can face challenges and threats that bring them together. The two disasters documented by Pepys and Defoe, a fire and a plague, were national tragedies. Yet the English experienced them as communal misfortunes.

In a more positive way, Johnson's *Dictionary* also contributed to a national identity. With its publication, the English language became touchable and portable. It moved from the breath and tongue to the page. Now people could carry around and study the words that united them as a nation.

Like Johnson's *Dictionary*, the collected sayings of the Chinese philosopher Confucius, *The Analects*, and Thomas Jefferson's *Declaration of Independence* serve to link people together. *The Analects* states the beliefs of Confucianism, which was for centuries the dominant political, ethical, and social philosophy of China. Jefferson's *Declaration* delineates the bond that united Americans in their struggle to become a nation.

CONFUCIUS (551–479 B.C.)

Confucius was a Chinese philosopher and reformer who lived during a time of conflict and corruption. In this dark period of Chinese history, he wandered the land and instructed any young men who appeared to have a talent for learning. In all his teachings, Confucius emphasized the importance of right conduct. He taught his students to be morally and spiritually superior men.

As compiled in *The Analects*, Confucian beliefs have deeply influenced the Chinese way of life. These beliefs were the official state doctrine of China until the overthrow of the imperial system in 1911. Even under communism, Confucian thinking still exerts a strong, underground influence.

THOMAS JEFFERSON (1743–1826)

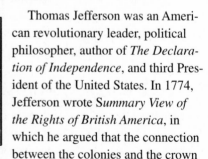

Thomas Jefferson was an American revolutionary leader, political philosopher, author of *The Declaration of Independence*, and third President of the United States. In 1774, Jefferson wrote *Summary View of the Rights of British America*, in which he argued that the connection between the colonies and the crown was voluntary and that England therefore had no power over American communities. The eloquence and power of this document made Jefferson the obvious choice as writer of the *Declaration*. Jefferson succeeded in his assignment beyond anyone's dreams, giving voice to the American goal of independence and liberty.

from The Analects

Confucius
Translated by Arthur Waley

The Master said, He who rules by moral force is like the pole-star, which remains in its place while all the lesser stars do homage[1] to it.

The Master said, Govern the people by regulations, keep order among them by chastisements,[2] and they will flee from you, and lose all self-respect. Govern them by moral force, keep order among them by ritual, and they will keep their self-respect and come to you of their own accord.

---

1. **homage** (häm´ ij) *n.*: Anything given or done to show honor or respect.
2. **chastisements** (chas tīz´ mənts) *n*: Acts of scolding or condemning.

▼ **Critical Viewing** How does this painting of thirteen emperors illustrate the elements of leadership that Confucius promotes? **[Connect]**

The Thirteen Emperors, Yan Liben, Museum of Fine Arts, Boston

The Master said, High office filled by men of narrow views, ritual performed without reverence,[3] the forms of mourning observed without grief— these are things I cannot bear to see!

Chi K'ang-tzu asked Master K'ung about government, saying, Suppose I were to slay those who have not the Way in order to help on those who have the Way, what would you think of it? Master K'ung replied saying, You are there to rule, not to slay. If you desire what is good, the people will at once be good. The essence of the gentleman is that of wind; the essence of small people is that of grass. And when a wind passes over the grass, it cannot choose but bend.

Tzu-kung asked about government. The Master said, sufficient food, sufficient weapons, and the confidence of the common people. Tzu-kung said, Suppose you had no choice but to dispense with one of these three, which would you forgo? The Master said, Weapons. Tzu-kung said, Suppose you were forced to dispense with one of the two that were left, which would you forgo? The Master said, Food. For from of old death has been the lot of all men; but a people that no longer trusts its rulers is lost indeed.

Master Yu said, Those who in private life behave well towards their parents and elder brothers, in public life seldom show a disposition to resist the authority of their superiors. And as for such men starting a revolution, no instance of it has ever occurred. It is upon the trunk that a gentleman works. When that is firmly set up, the Way grows. And surely proper behavior towards parents and elder brothers is the trunk of Goodness?

---

3. reverence (rev´ ər əns) *n*.: Feeling or attitude of deep respect, love, and awe.

from *The*

DECLARATION
of
INDEPENDENCE

When in the course of human events, it becomes necessary for one people to dissolve the political bands which have connected them with another, and to assume among the powers of the earth, the separate and equal station to which the laws of nature and of nature's God entitle them, a decent respect to the opinions of mankind requires that they should declare the causes which impel them to the separation.

Thomas Jefferson, Gilbert Stuart, National Portrait Gallery, Smithsonian Institution

We hold these truths to be self-evident: that all men are created equal; that they are endowed by their Creator with certain unalienable[1] rights; that among these are life, liberty and the pursuit of happiness; that to secure these rights, governments are instituted among men, deriving their just powers from the consent of the governed; that whenever any form of government becomes destructive of these ends, it is the right of the people to alter or to abolish it, and to institute new government, laying its foundation on such principles and organizing its powers in such form, as to them shall seem most likely to effect their safety and happiness. Prudence, indeed, will dictate that governments long established should not be changed for light and transient causes; and accordingly all experience hath shown, that mankind are more disposed to suffer while evils are sufferable than to right themselves by abolishing the forms to which they are accustomed. But when a long train of abuses and usurpations,[2] pursuing invariably the same object, evinces a design to reduce them under absolute despotism,[3] it is their right, it is their duty, to throw off such government, and to provide new guards for their future security. Such has been the patient sufferance of these colonies; and such is now the necessity which constrains them to alter their former systems of government. The history of the present king of Great Britain is a history of repeated injuries and usurpations, all having in direct object the establishment of an absolute tyranny over these states.

---

1. **unalienable** (ən āl´ yən ə bəl) *adj.*: That which may not be taken away or transferred.
2. **usurpations** (yo̅o̅´ zər pā´ shənz) *n.*: Unlawful or violent seizure of a throne.
3. **despotism** (des´ pət iz´ əm) *n.*: Methods or acts of a tyrant.

◀ **Critical Viewing** How does Gilbert Stuart's rendering of Jefferson reveal some of the attributes that made Jefferson a great leader? **[Evaluate]**

Guide for Responding

◆ Literature and Your Life

Reader's Response Would you define yourself as a Confucian or a Jeffersonian? Explain.

Thematic Focus Could Jefferson have been a Confucian? Why or why not? Would Confucius have endorsed the American Revolution, as justified by Jefferson? Explain.

☑ Check Your Comprehension

1. How does Confucius suggest that people be governed?
2. (a) According to Confucius, what are the three most important aspects of government? (b) Which of these is the most crucial?
3. What reason does Jefferson give for writing the Declaration?
4. What are the unalienable rights that Jefferson mentions?

◆ Critical Thinking

INTERPRET

1. For Confucius, what is the relationship between behavior in a family and behavior in a nation? **[Interpret]**

2. Does Jefferson imply that there is a law above the laws that nations make? Explain. **[Infer]**

3. Compare and contrast effective and ineffective leadership as described by Confucius and Jefferson. **[Compare and Contrast]**

EVALUATE

4. How well does the language of *The Declaration* motivate people to unite in opposition to England? **[Assess]**

EXTEND

5. Judging by this passage from *The Analects*, what would Confucius say about the "unwritten rules" of athletic competitions? **[Physical Education Link]**

Thematic Connection

THE TIES THAT BIND

Pepys and Defoe write as witnesses to tragedies that brought a nation together in grief. Samuel Johnson, Confucius, and Jefferson all used words to bring people together—Johnson as a compiler of words that everyone spoke; Confucius as the speaker of words that almost everyone followed; and Jefferson as the shaper of words that moved people's hearts.

1. (a) In the past few years, what national triumphs or tragedies have brought Americans together? Explain. (b) Are these events similar to the ones that Pepys and Defoe describe? Why or why not?

2. (a) How can the words of songs lift and unite an audience or a people? (b) Name some songs that serve this purpose.

 ## Idea Bank

Writing

1. **Yearbook Entry** In a brief paragraph that will accompany your yearbook photo, describe the experiences that have united you and your schoolmates.

2. **Analects for Today** Write three brief passages in the style of *The Analects* that teach moral lessons by using current-day situations.

3. **Imaginary Correspondence** Suppose that Samuel Johnson and Thomas Jefferson could have written to each other about American independence. Create a letter for each of them. **[Social Studies Link]**

Speaking, Listening, and Viewing

4. **Ask Confucius** With a group, do a call-in radio show called "Ask Confucius." Have people call in daily problems for Confucius to solve—callers can even be historical figures like Pepys or Jefferson. Be sure that the person playing Confucius answers in the spirit of *The Analects*. **[Media Link; Performing Arts Link]**

Researching and Representing

5. **Charter or Constitution** Write a charter or constitution setting up a new organization, whether a study group or an athletic team. Be sure you specify the ties that bind the members together. **[Social Studies Link]**

Online Activity www.phlit.phschool.com

Writing Process Workshop

Multimedia Presentation

The writers in this section present their ideas through one medium: written text. If you want to present ideas and information in a lively and engaging way, do a multimedia presentation. A multimedia presentation supplies information through a variety of media: slide shows, videos, audio recordings, graphs, charts, and fine art, as well as written materials.

Whether written or oral, your presentation is built on solid research and supported with a variety of media. The following skills, introduced in this section's Guided Writing Lessons, will help make your multimedia presentation effective.

Writing Skills Focus

▶ **Accuracy** in a factual report creates a strong and effective presentation. It gives the viewer confidence in the conclusions you draw from your research. (See p. 473.)

▶ **Choosing sources that are appropriate for the medium** will allow you to create an effective presentation. (See p. 485.)

▶ **Elaborating to add a personal dimension** enables the viewer to make the connection between the media and the written or spoken part of your presentation. (See p. 531.)

A

DICTIONARY

OF THE

ENGLISH LANGUAGE:

IN WHICH

The WORDS are deduced from their ORIGINALS,

AND

ILLUSTRATED in their DIFFERENT SIGNIFICATIONS

BY

EXAMPLES from the best WRITERS.

TO WHICH ARE PREFIXED,

A HISTORY of the LANGUAGE,

AND

AN ENGLISH GRAMMAR.

BY SAMUEL JOHNSON, A.M.

IN TWO VOLUMES

VOL. I.

Cum tabulis animum censoris sumet honesti;
Audebit quaecunque parum splendoris habebunt,
Et sine pondere erunt, et honore indigna ferentur,
Verba movere loco; quamvis invita recedant,
Et versentur adhuc intra penetralia Vestæ:
Obscurata diu populo bonus eruet, atque
Proferet in lucem speciosa vocabula rerum,
Quæ priscis memorata Catonibus atque Cethegis,
Nunc situs informis premit et deserta vetustas.   Hor.

LONDON,
Printed by W. STRAHAN,
For J. and P. KNAPTON; T. and T. LONGMAN; C. HITCH and L. HAWES;
A. MILLAR; and R. and J. DODSLEY.
MDCCLV.

WRITING MODEL

A Multimedia Presentation of
Samuel Johnson's *Dictionary*

Samuel Johnson's *Dictionary of the English Language* was published in 1755 and provided the first record of the English language. ①
The following are examples from his *Dictionary*:

patron: One who countenances, supports or protects. Commonly a wretch who supports with insolence, and is paid with flattery. ②
As shown in this image of a current-day patron, a patron is still someone who supports but is not necessarily a "wretch." ③

① By providing the exact year of publication, the writer shows that the presentation includes accurate, factual details.

② The writer uses appropriate sources, such as Johnson's *Dictionary*.

③ By explaining why she includes the photo, the writer adds a personal dimension.

APPLYING LANGUAGE SKILLS: Using Documentation

Through the following methods of documentation, you give credit to the sources used in your presentation.

Parenthetical Documentation: Include the source information in parentheses immediately after quoted passages.

Footnotes: Place a number at the end of the cited passage. Place the same number at the bottom of the page followed by source information. A subsequent citation from a book would include the note number, author's last name, and page number.

Endnotes: Place a number at the end of each cited passage. Create a separate page at the end for all of your source notes.

Writing Application Review your paper for quoted material or another person's ideas and make sure you have used appropriate documentation.

Writer's Solution Connection Writing Lab

For more help in formatting citations, see the Drafting section in the Writing Lab tutorial on Research Writing.

Prewriting

Choose a Topic Do you have a strong interest in the literature or culture of another country? Do you have a unique hobby or skill? Do you want to pursue a high-tech profession? One of these interests may lead you to an idea for a multimedia presentation. You can also choose one of the topic ideas listed here.

Topic Ideas

- Poking fun at eighteenth-century high society
- Famous baseball players and statistics
- Great musicians
- Dictionary of British writers

Locate Appropriate Text and Technical Resources Use an encyclopedia as a springboard for finding other sources; do not base your research on encyclopedia entries. Look for nonfiction books, CD-ROMs, and magazine or newspaper articles. The Internet is a great source of information, but sites may not be appropriate for a factual report if they are based on the creator's views. Evaluate them carefully before incorporating information from them in your report.

Find Media Sources Choose media carefully. Just because a piece of media may be related to your topic and purpose does not mean that it will reinforce the points you want to make. Look for pieces that directly support your topic and purpose. If audio, video, slide shows, illustrations, charts, or graphs require too much explanation, then they should not be included.

Drafting

Elaborate to Add a Personal Dimension As you put your multimedia presentation together, include details that make your presentation personal. Letting readers know your purpose can provide a personal element.

Document Accurately As you incorporate quotations and media into your report, make sure that you document them correctly in the written version of your report. Follow your teacher's requirements for footnotes or parenthetical documentation. Also make sure you copy all quotations exactly as they appear in the original text. If you only present orally, complete a Works Cited page that lists all your sources.

Revising

Use the following checklist to help you evaluate and revise your presentation.

▶ **Have I used elaboration to add a personal dimension?**
Look for places where adding personal details or explanation will clarify why you used certain information or media.

▶ **Are my facts and citations accurate?**
Double-check dates, quotations, and page numbers to make sure your information is accurate. Look for statements that are not definitive, or use terms such as probably and I assume. Revise statements in which you draw conclusions but present them as fact.

▶ **Did I use sources appropriate for the medium?**
Present your work to a peer and ask him or her to evaluate whether your presentation of media and fact are appropriate for a multimedia presentation based on research. If anything seems inappropriate, eliminate it.

REVISION MODEL

Multimedia Report on Samuel Johnson's *Dictionary*

① *a well-known writer*
Although Johnson's *Dictionary* made him ~~really famous~~ it did

② *(Show picture of The Dictionary)*
not make him financially secure. ~~(Show cover of The~~

③ *Who would have thought that this modest-looking*
Dictionary would be such a great contribution to literature.
~~Rambler.)~~

① *Changing really famous, which implies that Johnson received world-wide fame for his publication, to a well-known writer, which implies he was popular only among a certain group of people, is more accurate.*
② *Showing a picture of The Rambler is inappropriate because it is not directly related to the Dictionary.*
③ *This final detail adds a personal dimension to the piece.*

Publishing

▶ **Internet** Publish your work on a site devoted to your topic.

▶ **Presentation to the Public** Show your multimedia presentation to an organization where your topic would be of particular interest. For example, if it's on basketball, present it to the high school basketball team.

APPLYING LANGUAGE SKILLS: Incorporating Media

When preparing your multimedia presentation, work your media smoothly into your presentation. Include statements of introduction or explanations of inclusion.

For example:
When touring the homes of the literary figures of England, I saw Charles Dickens's home. As you can see from the photo, he worked in a comfortable setting.

Practice Rewrite the following paragraph, adding introductory statements for the media being presented.

Samuel Johnson was born September 18, 1709 in Lichfield, England. He was a scholar, but not an ideal student. Johnson did much of his learning on his own from books at his parents' home. He is best known for his creation of *A Dictionary of the English Language.*

Writer's Solution Connection Writing Lab

For more help in incorporating media into your presentation, see instruction on creating maps, charts, and graphs in the Drafting section of the tutorial on Research Writing.

Student Success Workshop

Real-World Reading Skills

Strategies for Success

As your reading assignments and your personal reading choices become longer and more advanced, you will benefit by using strategies for sustained silent reading. Maintaining comprehension when you read for long time periods will increase your enjoyment and retention of the material.

Prepare to Read Before you begin a long reading assignment, look over the material. Scan the table of contents. If the work is nonfiction, preview chapter headings, photos and illustrations, charts, and maps, which may give you an overview of the book. Keep in mind your purpose for reading. If you're reading a novel, pay close attention to characters and setting in the early chapters of the book. Remembering this information as you read will contribute to your understanding.

Pace Yourself Set realistic goals for yourself when you read silently for a sustained period of time. Don't expect to read and comprehend a full novel in one night. Break the reading down, and set time or chapter limits for yourself. Pause after chapters or sections to summarize, recall, and restate some of the key information and ideas. Pacing yourself will help you to remember critical points more easily.

Question Yourself To improve your comprehension, quiz yourself about what you've read. Review the main points or plot of your reading. Go over names or characters mentioned. Test yourself by jotting down a quick summary of what you've read or draw a diagram of the information you've read so far. Try to predict what might happen next, based on what you've

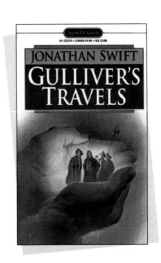

read so far. Glance ahead to upcoming chapter headings to focus your attention.

Apply the Strategies

Choose a nonfiction or fiction selection to read silently to yourself for a sustained period of time. Follow the suggestions just given, and answer the questions that follow.

1. How did you pace yourself during sustained reading of the fiction selection?

2. What strategies did you use to read the nonfiction selection?

3. What corrective strategies did you use to help you understand text that you had trouble understanding?

✔ Here are situations in which you might apply sustained silent reading:
► Romance novel
► Biography of a historical figure
► Full text of an important trial

PART 4

Focus on Literary Forms:
The Essay

Girl Writing by Lamplight
William Henry Hunt, The Mass Gallery, London

The titles of the new eighteenth-century periodicals—*The Rambler, The Spectator, The Tatler*—expressed the fun of getting out into the world, looking, listening, and telling. In the pages of these periodicals, the informal essay was also getting around. Like a friendly companion and guide, it was whispering into the public's ear, advising it what to think and telling it that it *was* a public!

Guide for Interpreting

Samuel Johnson *(1709–1784)*

Writing was never a promising way of making a living, but Samuel Johnson was determined to try. After a few unsuccessful projects, Johnson finally decided to move to London in 1737.

He got a break in the big city.

Success When he arrived, he bombarded *The Gentleman's Magazine*—the most successful magazine of the day—with his ideas and became an influential contributor. From 1750 to 1752, Johnson published his own magazine, *The Rambler*, twice a week. The essays and moral tales in the journal became popular after they were reprinted in book form.

Classics and Commerce Johnson's style is meticulously balanced, yet much of his work was done to meet the needs of the moment. Even the classic essays in *Lives of the Poets* were written for the market—a publisher, facing tough competition, commissioned them to dress up a new edition of English poetry. (For more on Johnson's life and his *Dictionary*, see p. 502.)

Joseph Addison *(1672–1719)*

In 1709, Joseph Addison, an Oxford-educated government official, eagerly read an article in *The Tatler*, an entertaining new literary magazine that had become all the rage in the coffee-houses of London. The article was signed "Isaac Bickerstaff," but Addison immediately recognized the style of Sir Richard Steele, an old college friend.

A Lifetime Partnership After Addison began submitting articles, notes, and suggestions to *The Tatler*, the two formed a lifetime partnership. Addison and Steele became the most celebrated journalists in England. Their essays in Steele's papers, *The Tatler* and *The Spectator*, earned them a permanent place in English literature.

A Stellar Career Addison's rapid rise as a journalist was one more step in a prospering literary career. Now, Addison's literary works, such as *The Campaign*, are remembered only by specialists. However, almost every magazine you can buy today uses the informal, popular style that he invented.

◆ Background for Understanding

CULTURE: NEWSPAPERS AND MAGAZINES

The first daily newspapers began appearing in England in 1702, the result of increased literacy, more efficient printing, and the fact that some people had more money to spend. The growing middle class was clamoring for information about the world. They also wanted a cheap source of written entertainment. Newspapers provided both.

As the market for words grew more sophisticated, magazines began to come into their own in the mid-1700's. The first periodical to take the name *magazine* (meaning "a storehouse") was *The Gentleman's Magazine*, founded in 1731. Originally, it reprinted selected articles from other journals. With Johnson's help, it expanded to include original writing, including criticism and poetry.

Johnson's, Addison's, and Steele's magazines helped create a new popular taste for sophisticated writing about books, ideas, and fashions. They popularized the brief, informal essay, which discussed issues in a relaxed, conversational manner. This tradition continues—*The New Yorker*, *The Atlantic*, and *Harper's* are, in spirit, the great-grandchildren of *The Tatler*.

◆ On Spring ◆
from The Aims of the Spectator

◆ *Literature and Your Life*

CONNECT YOUR EXPERIENCE

Kids bubble over with questions about what's out there and how it all fits together. As you grow older, you begin to ask questions about yourself: Who am I? What's important to me? These are not questions about facts but about your viewpoint and values.

Essays are a way of asking this kind of question. When Johnson writes on spring, he does not just give you facts. Using humor and argument, he lets you watch his mind work out a view of the world.

Journal Writing Compare some questions you asked as a kid with an important question you have about life now.

THEMATIC FOCUS: A NATION DIVIDED

How do these essays show that, with turbulent times behind them, eighteenth-century authors could address life playfully?

◆ Literary Focus

ESSAY

An **essay** is a short prose piece that explores a topic as if the author were letting you overhear his or her thoughts. The word *essay* means an "attempt" or a "test." It was first applied to writing by Montaigne (1533–1592), a Frenchman whose essays questioned life without always finding answers. Although he wrote on many subjects, he said that his aim was always to learn about himself.

Johnson's and Addison's essays are each in their own way "tests"—experiments to discover the connections the mind can make as it reviews experience. In reading them, be aware of the observations they contain *and* of the mind that is doing the observing.

◆ Grammar and Style

ADJECTIVE CLAUSES

Both Johnson and Addison use **adjective clauses**—subordinate clauses beginning with the relative pronouns *who, whom, which, that,* and *whose*. These clauses qualify or describe nouns or pronouns that precede them, as in this example from Addison's essay:

. . . the mind *that lies fallow but a single day*

◆ Reading Strategy

DRAW INFERENCES

To appreciate a writer's attitudes, you need to **draw inferences**—reach logical conclusions about what the writer leaves unstated.

In the second paragraph of "On Spring," Johnson describes how even after disappointments, we still find things to anticipate "with equal eagerness." Johnson implies that we do not learn from our setbacks. Because he seems easygoing about this fact, you can infer that his attitude toward this human weakness is one of mild amusement.

◆ Build Vocabulary

LATIN ROOTS: *-spec-*

Johnson calls his essay a speculation, meaning "reflections on a subject"—what the mind can "see," beyond what is there. *-Spec-*, the root in *speculation*, is from a Latin word meaning "to look."

WORD BANK

Before you read, preview this list of words from the selections.

procured
divert
speculation
transient
affluence
contentious
trifles
embellishments

On Spring

Samuel Johnson

Tuesday, April 3, 1750

Et nunc omnis ager, nunc omnis parturit arbos,
Nunc frondent silvae, nunc formosissimus annus.

Now ev'ry field, now ev'ry tree is green;
Now genial nature's fairest face is seen.

Virgil, *Eclogues III*, v. 56; Translator, Elphinston

Every man is sufficiently discontented with some circumstances of his present state, to suffer his imagination to range more or less in quest of future happiness, and to fix upon some point of time, in which, by the removal of the inconvenience which now perplexes him, or acquisition of the advantage which he at present wants, he shall find the condition of his life very much improved.

When this time, which is too often expected with great impatience, at last arrives, it generally comes without the blessing for which it was desired; but we solace ourselves with some new prospect,[1] and press forward again with equal eagerness.

It is lucky for a man, in whom this temper prevails, when he turns his hopes upon things wholly out of his own power; since he forbears then to precipitate his affairs,[2] for the sake of the great event that is to complete his felicity, and waits for the blissful hour, with less ne-glect of the measures necessary to be taken in the mean time.

I have long known a person of this temper, who indulged his dream of happiness with less hurt to himself than such chimerical[3] wishes commonly produce, and adjusted his scheme with such address, that his hopes were in full bloom three parts of the year, and in the other part never wholly blasted. Many, perhaps, would be desirous of learning by what means he procured to himself such a cheap and lasting satisfaction. It was gained by a constant practice of referring the removal of all his uneasiness to the coming of the next spring; if his health was impaired, the spring would restore it; if what he wanted was at a high price, it would fall in value in the spring.

The spring, indeed, did often come without any of these effects, but he was always certain that the next would be more propitious; nor was ever convinced that the present spring would fail him before the middle of summer; for he always talked of the spring as coming till it was past, and when it was once past, everyone agreed with him that it was coming.

By long converse with this man, I am, perhaps, brought to feel immoderate pleasure in the contemplation of this delightful season; but I have the satisfaction of finding many, whom it can be no shame to resemble, infected with the same enthusiasm; for there is, I believe, scarce any poet of eminence, who has not left some

---

1. **solace ourselves with some new prospect:** Comfort ourselves with something new to look forward to.
2. **forbears then to precipitate his affairs:** Refrains from rushing his affairs.
3. **chimerical:** Unrealistic; fantastic.

testimony of his fondness for the flowers, the zephyrs, and the warblers of the spring. Nor

◆ Literary Focus
Johnson tests the value of his own pleasure in spring. What tests does he use?

has the most luxuriant imagination been able to describe the serenity and happiness of the golden age,[4] otherwise than by giving a perpetual spring, as the highest reward of uncorrupted innocence.

There is, indeed, something inexpressibly pleasing, in the annual renovation of the world, and the new display of the treasures of nature. The cold and darkness of winter, with the naked deformity of every object on which we turn our eyes, make us rejoice at the succeeding season, as well for what we have escaped, as for what we may enjoy; and every budding flower, which a warm situation brings early to our view, is considered by us as a messenger to notify the approach of more joyous days.

The spring affords to a mind, so free from the disturbance of cares or passions as to be vacant to calm amusements, almost every thing that our present state makes us capable of enjoying. The variegated verdure[5] of the

fields and woods, the succession of grateful odors, the voice of pleasure pouring out its notes on every side, with the gladness apparently conceived by every animal, from the growth of his food, and the clemency of the weather, throw over the whole earth an air of gaiety, significantly expressed by the smile of nature.

Yet there are men to whom these scenes are able to give no delight, and who hurry away from all the varieties of rural beauty, to lose their hours, and <u>divert</u> their thoughts by cards, or assemblies, a tavern dinner, or the prattle of the day.

It may be laid down as a position which will seldom deceive, that when a man cannot bear his own company there is something wrong. He must fly from himself, either because he feels a tediousness in life from the equipoise[6] of an empty mind, which, having no tendency to one motion more than another but as it is impelled by some external power, must always have

---

6. **equipoise:** Balanced state.

---

4. **golden age:** In mythology, the time in the past when the world was free from suffering and evil.
5. **variegated verdure:** Varied greenery, striped or spotted with different colors.

◆ **Build Vocabulary**

procured (prō kyōord´) v.: Obtained; found
divert (də vʉrt´) v.: Amuse; entertain; distract

▲ **Critical Viewing** How does this image illustrate "the annual renovation of the world"? [Interpret]

recourse to foreign objects; or he must be afraid of the intrusion of some unpleasing ideas, and, perhaps, is struggling to escape from the remembrance of a loss, the fear of a calamity, or some other thought of greater horror.

Those whom sorrow incapacitates to enjoy the pleasures of contemplation, may properly apply to such diversions, provided they are innocent, as lay strong hold on the attention; and those, whom fear of any future affliction chains down to misery, must endeavor to obviate the danger.

My considerations shall, on this occasion, be turned on such as are burthensome to themselves merely because they want subjects for reflection, and to whom the volume of nature is thrown open, without affording them pleasure or instruction, because they never learned to read the characters.[7]

A French author has advanced this seeming paradox, that *very few men know how to take a walk*; and, indeed, it is true, that few know how to take a walk with a prospect of any other pleasure, than the same company would have afforded them at home.

There are animals that borrow their color from the neighboring body, and, consequently, vary their hue as they happen to change their place. In like manner it ought to be the endeavor of every man to derive his reflections from the objects about him; for it is to no purpose that he alters his position, if his attention continues fixed to the same point. The mind should be kept open to the access of every new idea, and so far disengaged[8] from the predominance of particular thoughts, as easily to accommodate itself to occasional entertainment.

A man that has formed this habit of turning every new object to his entertainment, finds in the productions of nature an inexhaustible stock of materials upon which he can employ himself, without any temptations to envy or malevolence; faults, perhaps, seldom totally avoided by those, whose judgment is much exercised upon the works of art. He has always a certain prospect of discovering new reasons for adoring the sovereign author of the universe, and probable hopes of making some discovery

---

7. **the characters:** Nature's signs.

8. **disengaged:** Free.

▼ Critical Viewing Relate the qualities of the flowers in the photograph to Johnson's description of spring. **[Relate]**

Crocus
Corel [1730843]

of benefit to others, or of profit to himself. There is no doubt but many vegetables and animals have qualities that might be of great use, to the knowledge of which there is not required much force of penetration, or fatigue of study, but only frequent experiments, and close attention. What is said by the chemists of their darling mercury, is, perhaps, true of everybody through the whole creation, that if a thousand lives should be spent upon it, all its properties would not be found out.

Mankind must necessarily be diversified by various tastes, since life affords and requires such multiplicity of employments, and a nation of naturalists is neither to be hoped, or desired; but it is surely not improper to point out a fresh amusement to those who languish in health, and repine in plenty, for want of some source of diversion that may be less easily exhausted, and to inform the multitudes of both sexes, who are burthened with every new day, that there are many shows which they have not seen.

He that enlarges his curiosity after the works of nature, demonstrably multiplies the inlets to happiness; and, therefore, the younger part of my readers, to whom I dedicate this vernal[9] speculation, must excuse me for calling upon them, to make use at once of the spring of the year, and the spring of life; to acquire, while their minds may be yet impressed with new images, a love of innocent pleasures, and an ardor for useful knowledge; and to remember, that a blighted spring makes a barren year, and that the vernal flowers, however beautiful and gay, are only intended by nature as preparatives to autumnal fruits.

---

9. **vernal:** Concerning spring

◆ **Build Vocabulary**

speculation (spek´ yōō lā´ shən) *n.*: Train of thought on a subject, especially one using hypotheses or guesses

Guide for Responding

◆ *Literature and Your Life*

Reader's Response What is your reaction to the coming of spring? How in tune is it with Johnson's feelings about the season?

Thematic Focus How does Johnson's idea of time compare with those of Donne or Marvell?

☑ Check Your Comprehension

1. According to Johnson, how do people take their minds off their present unhappiness?
2. What does the man who always fixes his thoughts on the coming spring do when spring turns out to be a disappointment?
3. According to Johnson, who is not heartened by the coming of spring?
4. What does Johnson think about science as a hobby?
5. What does nature offer the man who pays attention to the objects around him?

◆ **Critical Thinking**

INTERPRET

1. What is Johnson's opinion of people who are afraid to be alone with themselves? **[Interpret]**
2. What is the difference between Johnson's idea of happiness and the idea of those who are always looking forward to something? **[Compare and Contrast]**
3. Does Johnson claim that the person who is open to the wonders of nature will be a moral person? Explain your answer. **[Analyze]**
4. This essay is itself like a wandering walk. (a) List three of the points made along the way. (b) For each, show how it connects (or does not connect) to the others. **[Draw Conclusions]**

APPLY

5. Are you in the "spring of your life"? Explain. **[Relate]**

from **The Aims** *of the* **Spectator**

The Spectator, No. 10,
Monday, March 12, 1711

It is with much satisfaction that I hear this great city inquiring day by day after these my papers, and receiving my morning lectures with a becoming seriousness and attention. My publisher tells me that there are already three thousand of them distributed every day. So that if I allow twenty readers to every paper, which I look upon as a modest computation, I may reckon about three-score thousand[1] disciples in London and Westminster, who I hope will take care to distinguish themselves from the thoughtless herd of their ignorant and unattentive brethren. Since I have raised to myself so great an audience, I shall spare no pains to make their instruction agreeable, and their diversion useful. For which reasons I shall endeavor to enliven morality with wit, and to temper wit with morality, that my readers may, if possible, both ways find their account in the speculation of the day. And to the end that their virtue and discretion may not be short, transient, intermitting[2] starts of thought, I have resolved to refresh their memories from day to day, till I have recovered them out of that desperate state of vice and folly into which the age is fallen. The mind that lies fallow[3] but a single day sprouts up in follies that are only to be killed by a constant and assiduous culture. It was said of Socrates[4] that he brought philosophy down from heaven, to inhabit among men; and I shall be ambitious to have it said of me that I have brought philosophy out of closets and libraries, schools and colleges, to dwell in clubs and assemblies, at tea tables and in coffeehouses.

I would therefore in a very particular manner recommend these my speculations to all well-regulated families that set apart an hour in every morning for tea and bread and butter; and would earnestly advise them for their good to order this paper to be punctually served up, and to be looked upon as part of the tea equipage. . . .

In the next place, I would recommend this paper to the daily perusal of those gentlemen whom I cannot but consider as my good brothers and allies, I mean the fraternity of spectators, who live in the world without having anything to do in it; and either by the affluence of their fortunes or laziness of their dispositions have no other business with the rest of mankind but to look upon them. Under this class of men are comprehended all contemplative tradesmen, titular physicians, fellows of the Royal Society, Templars[5] that are not given to be contentious, and statesmen that are out of business; in short, everyone that considers the world as a theater, and desires to form a right judgment of those who are the actors on it.

There is another set of men that I must likewise lay a claim to, whom I have lately called the blanks of society, as being altogether unfurnished with ideas, till the business and conversation of the day has supplied them. I have often considered these poor souls with an eye of great commiseration, when I have heard them asking the first man they have met with, whether there was any news stirring? and by that means gathering together materials for thinking. These needy persons do not know what to talk of till about twelve o'clock in the morning; for by that time they are pretty good judges of the weather, know which way the wind sits, and whether the Dutch mail[6] be come in. As they lie at the mercy of the first man they meet, and are grave or impertinent all the day long, according to the notions which they have imbibed in the morning, I would earnestly entreat them not to stir out of their chambers till they have read this paper, and do promise them that I will daily instil into them such sound and wholesome sentiments as shall have a good effect on their conversation for the ensuing twelve hours.

> ◆ **Reading Strategy**
> From what Addison says about his "good brothers and allies," what inferences can you make about his attitude toward his paper and his readers?

---

1. **three-score thousand:** Sixty thousand.
2. **intermitting:** Pausing at times; not constant.
3. **fallow:** Unused; unproductive.
4. **Socrates:** Ancient Greek philosopher (470?–399 B.C.), immortalized as a character in Plato's dialogues, who cross-examined ancient Athenians about their lives and values.

5. **titular physicians, fellows of the Royal Society, Templars:** Physicians in title only; members of a group dedicated to scientific research; lawyers or law students with offices in the Inner or Middle Temple.
6. **Dutch mail:** Mail from Europe bearing news of the war.

But there are none to whom this paper will be more useful than to the female world. I have often thought there has not been sufficient pains taken in finding out proper employments and diversions for the fair ones. Their amusements seem contrived for them, rather as they are women, than as they are reasonable creatures; and are more adapted to the sex than to the species. The toilet is their great sense of business, and the right adjusting of their hair the principal employment of their lives. The sorting of a suit of ribbons is reckoned a very good morning's work; and if they make an excursion to a mercer's or a toyshop,[7] so great a fatigue makes them unfit for anything else all the day after. Their more serious occupations are sewing and embroidery, and their greatest drudgery the preparation of jellies and sweetmeats. This, I say, is the state of ordinary women; though I know there are multitudes of those of a more elevated life and conversation, that move in an exalted sphere of knowledge and virtue, that join all the beauties of the mind to the ornaments of dress, and inspire a kind of awe and respect, as well as love, into their male beholders. I hope to increase the number of these by publishing this daily paper, which I shall always endeavor to make an innocent if not an improving entertainment, and by that means at least divert the minds of my female readers from greater <u>trifles</u>. At the same time, as I would fain give some finishing touches to those which are already the most beautiful pieces in human nature, I shall endeavor to point all those imperfections that are the blemishes, as well as those virtues which are the <u>embellishments</u>, of the sex.

---

7. **suit of ribbons . . . mercer's or a toyshop:** A suit of ribbons was a set of matching ribbons; a mercer's store sold fabrics, ribbons, and so on; a toyshop sold small items of little value.

◆ Build Vocabulary

speculation (spek´ yoo lā´ shən) *n.*: Train of thought on a subject, especially one using hypotheses or guesses

transient (tran´ shənt) *adj.*: Temporary; passing

affluence (af´ loo əns) *n.*: Abundant wealth

contentious (kən ten´ shus) *adj.*: Quarrelsome

trifles (trī´ fəlz) *n.*: Things of little value or importance; trivial matters

embellishments (em bel´ ish məntz) *n.*: Decorative touches; ornamentation

---

Guide for Responding

◆ Literature and Your Life

Reader's Response Did you identify with any of the readers to whom Addison is recommending *The Spectator?* Why or why not?

Thematic Focus What kinds of things would Addison change about English society?

☑ Check Your Comprehension

1. What reason does Addison give for making the instruction of his readers agreeable?
2. What does Addison think of the age in which he is living?
3. How does Addison define a "spectator"?
4. Aside from spectators, to what two groups of people does Addison recommend his paper?

◆ Critical Thinking

INTERPRET

1. Addison felt that *The Spectator* would set a high standard for the common reader. What proof of this attitude can you find in this selection? **[Support]**
2. Addison uses a sympathetic tone to discuss the "blanks of society." Do you believe his tone, or is he being funny? Explain your answer. **[Analyze]**
3. Explain Addison's attitude toward women. **[Interpret]**
4. What is Addison's attitude toward his own aims and towards his audience? Explain, using three examples. **[Draw Conclusions]**

EVALUATE

5. What's your opinion of Addison's introduction of his paper to the public? Will people want to read it? **[Assess]**

Guide for Responding (continued)

◆ Reading Strategy

DRAW INFERENCES

You can **draw inferences** from what writers state directly to figure out their underlying attitudes. For example, when Addison compares himself to the legendary Greek thinker Socrates, common sense tells you that he intends the comparison as an exaggeration. You can infer that Addison is gently poking fun at his own aims.

Draw inferences about the author's attitude toward his subject in the following passages:
1. Johnson's description of the man who is always looking forward to spring
2. Johnson's description of men who do not delight in the scenes of spring
3. Johnson's description of the man who makes all new objects his entertainment
4. Addison's descriptions of his readers
5. Addison's description of his age as "a desperate state of vice and folly"

◆ Build Vocabulary

USING THE LATIN ROOT *-spec-*

Now that you know that the Latin root *-spec-* means "to look," write definitions for these words:

1. inspection
2. respect
3. spectacle
4. aspect
5. spectacular

USING THE WORD BANK: Synonyms

On your paper, write the letter of the word whose meaning is the closest to that of the first word.
1. embellishment: (a) food, (b) decoration, (c) remark
2. divert: (a) distract, (b) horrify, (c) inform
3. trifles: (a) trivia, (b) wonders, (c) dangers
4. contentious: (a) mild, (b) argumentative, (c) proud
5. procured: (a) obtained, (b) killed, (c) borrowed
6. affluence: (a) speed, (b) poverty, (c) wealth
7. transient: (a) powerful, (b) passing, (c) near
8. speculation: (a) reflection, (b) fear, (c) belief

◆ Literary Focus

ESSAY

Essays are informal discussions of a topic, in which writers test out ideas and attitudes. You can sense this informality when Johnson tells you, "I have long known a person of this temper…" and proceeds to make gentle fun of his friend. You feel that he is chatting with you.
1. (a) Give two other examples from Johnson's essay that show an informal, personal tone. (b) Explain your choices.
2. (a) Where does Johnson's discussion turn from hopes for the future to happiness? (b) Is this transition "logical"? Explain.
3. (a) Give two examples of Addison's not-so-serious attitude toward himself or his readers. (b) Does Addison identify himself with a particular group, or does his attitude set him above the society he observes? Explain.

◆ Grammar and Style

ADJECTIVE CLAUSES

Adjective clauses provide further information about nouns and pronouns. You can use them to combine ideas in a single sentence.

> **Adjective clauses** are clauses beginning with the relative pronouns *who, whom, which, that,* and *whose*. These clauses describe nouns or pronouns that precede them.

Practice On your paper, identify the adjective clauses in these sentences:
1. When this time, which is too often expected with great impatience, at last arrives. . . .
2. Every budding flower, which a warm situation brings early to our view, is considered by us as a messenger. . . .
3. I . . . recommend these my speculations to all well-regulated families that set apart an hour in every morning for tea and bread and butter. . . .
4. . . . they . . . are grave or impertinent all the day long, according to the notions which they have imbibed in the morning. . . .
5. . . . I allow twenty readers to every paper, which I look upon as a modest computation. . . .

Build Your Portfolio

 Idea Bank

Writing

1. **Advertisement** Using the information from Addison's essay, make up an advertisement to promote the sale of *The Spectator*.

2. **Seasonal Essay** Write an informal essay on a season besides spring. Just as Johnson moves from the subject of spring to that of happiness and nature, tie your essay to larger themes.

3. **Letter to the Editor** Choose an article from a newspaper or magazine that interests you. Write a response to it and mail it to the editor.

Speaking, Listening, and Viewing

4. **Monologue** Practice reading aloud part of an essay to capture its tone—sarcastic, generous, or serious. Read your selection to the class. **[Performing Arts Link]**

5. **Satiric Monologue** Who are the "blanks" of today's society? Write and perform a brief monologue in which you poke fun at a contemporary "blank"—the surfer, perhaps, or the slacker. **[Performing Arts Link]**

Researching and Representing

6. **Satirical Cartoons** Magazines entertain their readers or express their opinions with cartoons. Create your own cartoons that comment on issues or trends, then display them in class. **[Art Link]**

7. **Press Wars** Magazines often compete with each other for readers. Divide into teams to produce two or more magazines about events and trends in school during the last couple of months. **[Career Link]**

Online Activity www.phlit.phschool.com

 Guided Writing Lesson

Essay on Human Behavior

These essays offer sharp insights into human behavior and character. Write an essay about an aspect of human behavior that interests you. For example, you might describe the behavior of people at the beach. To convey your subject and your attitude toward it, choose precise details.

Writing Skills Focus: Precise Details

Your essay on human behavior will seem vital and relevant if you are able to furnish vivid, **precise details**—as Addison does when he describes the lounging lifestyle of some women:

Model From the Essay

The sorting of a suit of ribbons is reckoned a very good morning's work; and if they make an excursion to a mercer's or a toyshop, so great a fatigue makes them unfit for anything else all the day after.

By using precise details like these, you can create a perspective on your subject.

Prewriting Before you write, organize and record your thoughts by writing them down in outline form. Include sensory details and adjectives describing behaviors and attitudes.

Drafting Develop your notes as you draft. Focus your essay on a single scene or on several examples of a specific type of behavior. Choose specific details that highlight your attitude toward your subject.

Revising Ask a classmate to look over your draft and sum up the behavior you describe. Discuss where you could clarify your descriptions. Check your spelling, grammar, and punctuation. Finally, consider using adjective clauses to link your precise details to the nouns they concern. (For more on adjective clauses, see pp. 545 and 552.)

CONNECTIONS TO WORLD LITERATURE

Homeless
Anna Quindlen

Literary Connection

THE ESSAY

The French writer Montaigne (män tän´) invented the **essay** in the sixteenth century as a brief prose work for exploring ideas, and the word *essay* itself means "an attempt or trial." In other words, you don't have to get things *right* in an essay. You just have to get them down, honestly following your thoughts wherever they lead.

In the eighteenth century—with works like Johnson's "On Spring" and Addison's "Aims of the Spectator"—the essay found a new home. It took up residence in the pages of the periodicals created by men like Addison and Steele. From those pages, it became a means of entertaining and informing a wider readership.

Anna Quindlen's column "Homeless" is a direct descendant of these periodical essays. It also appeared in a "periodical," although one with a slightly larger circulation than Steele's *Tatler: The New York Times*. Quindlen's column may be briefer and more politically oriented than those earlier essays but, like them, it speaks directly with readers about their world. Quindlen's whole effort is to make readers see with fresh eyes what is everywhere around them in the city—not "the homeless," but people without homes.

ANNA QUINDLEN
(1953–   )

Anna Quindlen is currently a best-selling novelist. However, she first won recognition as a columnist for the *New York Times*. She provided a fresh voice in the editorial pages of that paper, addressing controversial issues like homelessness in a sensitive and caring manner. Her commentary won her the highest award in journalism, the Pulitzer Prize.

HOMELESS
ANNA QUINDLEN

Her name was Ann, and we met in the Port Authority Bus Terminal[1] several Januarys ago. I was doing a story on homeless people. She said I was wasting my time talking to her; she was just passing through, although she'd been passing through for more than two weeks. To prove to me that this was true, she rummaged through a tote bag and a manila envelope and finally unfolded a sheet of typing paper and brought out her photographs.

They were not pictures of family, or friends, or even a dog or cat, its eyes brown-red in the flashbulb's light. They were pictures of a house. It was like a thousand houses in a hundred towns, not suburb, not city, but somewhere in between, with aluminum siding and a chain-link fence, a narrow driveway running up to a one-car garage and a patch of backyard. The house was yellow. I looked on the back for a date or a name, but neither was there. There was no need for discussion. I knew what she was trying to tell me, for it was something I had often felt. She was not adrift, alone, anonymous, although her bags and her raincoat with the grime shadowing its creases had made me believe she was. She had a house, or at least once upon a time had had one. Inside were curtains, a couch, a stove, potholders. You are where you live. She was somebody.

I've never been very good at looking at the big picture, taking the global view, and I've always been a person with an overactive sense of place, the legacy of an Irish grandfather. So it is natural that the thing that seems most wrong with the world to me right now is that there are so many people with no homes. I'm not simply talking about shelter from the elements, or three square meals a day or a mailing address to which the welfare people can send the check—although I know that all these are important for survival. I'm talking about a home, about precisely those kinds of feelings that have wound up in cross-stitch and French knots on samplers over the years.

Home is where the heart is. There's no place like it. I love my home with a ferocity totally out of proportion to its appearance or location. I love dumb things about it: the hot-water heater, the plastic rack you drain dishes in, the roof over my head, which occasionally leaks. And yet it is precisely those dumb things that make it what it is—a place of certainty, stability, predictability, privacy, for me and for my family. It is where I live. What more can you say about a place than that? That is everything.

Yet it is something that we have been edging away from gradually during my lifetime and the lifetimes of my parents and grandparents. There was a time when where you lived often was where you worked and where you grew the food you ate and even where you were buried. When that era passed,

---

1. **Port Authority Bus Terminal:** Bus terminal located in New York City.

where you lived at least was where your parents had lived and where you would live with your children when you became enfeebled. Then, suddenly, where you lived was where you lived for three years, until you could move on to something else and something else again.

And so we have come to something else again, to children who do not understand what it means to go to their rooms because they have never had a room, to men and women whose fantasy is a wall they can paint a color of their own choosing, to old people reduced to sitting on molded plastic chairs, their skin blue-white in the lights of a bus station, who pull pictures of houses out of their bags. Homes have stopped being homes. Now they are real estate.

People find it curious that those without homes would rather sleep sitting up on benches or huddled in doorways than go to shelters. Certainly some prefer to do so because they are emotionally ill, because they have been locked in before and they are [darned] if they will be locked in again. Others are afraid of the violence and trouble they may find there. But some seem to want something that is not available in shelters, and they will not compromise, not for a cot, or

▲ Critical Viewing What details in this photograph show the conditions of this woman's situation? [Infer]

oatmeal, or a shower with special soap that kills the bugs. "One room," a woman with a baby who was sleeping on her sister's floor, once told me, "painted blue." That was the crux of it; not size or location, but pride of owner-ship. Painted blue.

This is a difficult problem, and some wise and compassionate people are working hard at it. But in the main I think we work around it, just as we walk around it when it is lying on the sidewalk or sitting in the bus terminal—the problem, that is. It has been customary to take people's pain and lessen our own participation in it by turning it into an issue, not a collection of human beings. We turn an adjective into a noun: the poor, not poor people; the homeless, not Ann or the man who lives in the box or the woman who sleeps on the subway grate.

Sometimes I think we would be better off if we forgot about the broad strokes and concentrated on the details. Here is a woman without a bureau. There is a man with no mirror, no wall to hang it on. They are not the homeless. They are people who have no homes. No drawer that holds the spoons. No window to look out upon the world. My [word]. That is everything.

Guide for Responding

◆ Literature and Your Life

Reader's Response In what ways did this essay change how you think about homeless people?

Thematic Focus How is the problem of home-lessness a threat to society as a whole?

Check Your Comprehension

1. (a) Describe Ann. (b) Where does the author meet her, and what is Ann doing there?
2. Summarize Quindlen's description of how the definition of a home has changed.
3. According to Quindlen, how do most people deal with homelessness?

◆ Critical Thinking

INTERPRET

1. What did Ann always carry with her at all times? Why is this possession so important to her? **[Interpret]**

2. Explain what Quindlen means when she says "Homes have stopped being homes. Now they are real estate." **[Interpret]**

3. (a) Why does Quindlen make a distinction between *the homeless* and *homeless people*? (b) What is the purpose of her essay? **[Draw Conclusions]**

EVALUATE

4. Is Quindlen's essay effective in getting you to see the homeless as real people? Why or why not? **[Criticize]**

APPLY

5. What do you think individuals and communities should do to help homeless people? **[Resolve]**

Connections to World Literature

THE ESSAY

The essay was invented as a means of exploring thoughts and feelings in a personal way. Whether the writer is Samuel Johnson or Anna Quindlen, you are always aware of the writer's presence. Writers use their personality on the page—and this is especially true in periodical and newspaper essays—to get you to see the social or political world in a fresh way.

1. Give two examples of Quindlen's use of an informal, personal tone. Explain your choices.

2. In what ways does Quindlen guide you to experiences you may not be able or willing to have on your own?

3. Compare and contrast Quindlen's essay with Johnson's or Addison's. Focus on differences of style—sentence and paragraph length, for example—and on differences in themes or concerns.

4. Will the essay find a new home and new life on the Internet? Why or why not?

 Idea Bank

Writing

1. **Public-Service Advertisement** Design a public-service advertisement—for print, radio, television, or the Internet—in which you urge people to help the homeless.

2. **Newspaper Column** Select a social issue about which you have strong opinions. Express your ideas in a newspaper column like Quindlen's.

3. **Response to Criticism** After receiving the Pulitzer Prize for Commentary, Anna Quindlen remarked, "I think of a column as having a conversation with a person it just so happens I can't see." In an essay, discuss whether Quindlen's essay seems like such a "conversation."

Speaking, Listening, and Viewing

4. **Photo Essay** What photographs would you use to illustrate Anna Quindlen's essay? Using old magazines, choose several pictures to accompany the text. Prepare captions for each. **[Social Studies Link]**

Researching and Representing

5. **Newsletter** Have your classmates write informal essays on a variety of subjects or on one particular theme. Then combine them into a newsletter that you distribute in your school. **[Social Studies Link]**

Online Activity www.phlit.phschool.com

Writing Process Workshop

In Samuel Johnson's reflective essay "On Spring," he shares his thoughts about the nature of happiness and relates an anecdote about a friend of his. Write a reflective essay in which you describe an important personal event, experience, or observation. Bring your essay to life by providing vivid and precise details that convey your insights and emotional responses.

The following skills will help you write an effective reflective essay.

Writing Skills Focus

▶ **Keep a consistent point of view.** Write from the first-person point of view as you share your thoughts and emotional responses.

▶ **Set the mood** for readers by using colors, sounds, and other sensory details to capture an emotion.

▶ **Use precise details** to create pictures and capture sensations that convey the richness of your experience. (To learn more about this skill, see p. 553.)

Samuel Johnson used all these skills in his essay, "On Spring."

MODEL FROM LITERATURE

from "On Spring" by Samuel Johnson

① Johnson establishes a mood of joy through his word choice.

② Johnson writes from a first-person plural point of view, using the pronouns us, we, and our.

③ Here, the first flower of spring is compared to a messenger bearing good news. Precise comparisons like this bring essays to life for readers.

There is, indeed, something inexpressibly pleasing in the annual renovation of the world, and the new display of the treasures of nature. ① The cold and darkness of winter, with the naked deformity of every object on which we turn our eyes, make us rejoice at the succeeding season, as well for what we have escaped, as for what we may enjoy; and every budding flower, which a warm situation brings early to our view, is considered by us ② as a messenger to notify the approach of more joyous days. ③

Prewriting

Choose a Topic Since reflective essays revolve around personal experience, you may find a topic by recalling holidays, neighborhood adventures, schooltime experiences, or outings with friends. You can also use one of the topic ideas listed here.

Topic Ideas
■ Your first day of high school
■ A favorite place
■ A memorable family celebration
■ A remarkable friend

Develop a List of "Mood" Details Colors, sounds, and other sensory details will create a mood for your writing. To set the tone for your reflective writing, begin with a list of sensory details that support the mood you want to create.

Take Notes as You Recall the Experience Cast your thoughts back to the experience you're writing about. Jot down precise details that capture the events and your emotional response to them.

Drafting

Use a Consistent Point of View Use the first-person point of view as you draft your reflective essay. To make the experience immediate and interesting, give your personal reactions to these events, people, or circumstances.

Create a Mood Through Word Choice Establish a mood as you draft by using details that create a mood or atmosphere. Use comparisons, images, or words that have positive or negative associations to help you create a mood.

Use Precise Details Choose vivid verbs, precise nouns, and accurate comparisons to share with readers your personal experience.

▶ Neutral Mood
I saw that she was happy with my news.

▶ Mood of Happiness
Her face lit up like a ray of sunshine when I gave her the news.

APPLYING LANGUAGE SKILLS: Using Vivid Verbs

Use vivid verbs to bring your essay to life. A vivid verb describes a precise action and needs no modifier.

Weak Verb With Modifiers:
Louise walked slowly and painfully around the track.

Vivid Verb:
Louise limped around the track.

Practice Write the following sentences in your notebook, replacing the underlined words with one precise verb.

1. The children at the playground shrilly yelled.
2. The band slowly ended the last song.
3. In Italy, we drove slowly through the wine country.
4. The students in the cafeteria quickly ate the ice cream.

Writing Application When drafting your essay, don't spend too much time thinking up vivid verbs. Mark the place and continue writing. When your draft is finished, use a thesaurus to help you find vivid verbs.

Writer's Solution Connection Writing Lab

For tips on organizing, see the Writing Models in the Organizing Details section of the tutorial on Description.

APPLYING LANGUAGE SKILLS: Using Troublesome Modifiers Correctly

These commonly used modifiers are often used incorrectly.

1. **good/well:** Use *good* as an adjective, *well* as an adverb.
2. **bad/badly:** Use *bad* after linking verbs such as *feel*, *look*, and *seem*. Use *badly* as an adverb.
3. **this (these)/that (those):** Use *this* to distinguish the thing that is nearer in comparison.

Practice Rewrite each sentence, choosing the correct term.

1. That birthday cake looks (good, well).
2. They were (bad, badly) injured in the skiing accident.
3. (These, Those) students in this room went to Washington.
4. The summer session is only for students who earned a C or a D in (this, that) class.

Writer's Solution Connection Language Lab

For help in using Modifiers, see the lesson on Problems with Modifiers in the Modifiers unit.

Revising

Read Your Reflective Essay Aloud Make an audiotape of your reflective essay. Listen and ask yourself the following questions:

▶ What language and details should I add or change to give my reflective essay a mood?
▶ What examples of elaboration can I add to give my writing a more personal feel?
▶ Does my reflective essay have a consistent point of view?

Proofread Read your paper beginning with the last paragraph searching for grammatical and spelling errors.

REVISION MODEL

① The students stared at me as I entered the classroom.
~~The students studied the new kid.~~ Red with embarrassment,

② The clock on the wall seemed to be abnormally loud as the students silently pronounced a judgment on me.

I felt myself shrinking within my stiff new school uniform. ∧

③ saying in his thin reedy voice, "Meet Jim Harte, who has recently moved here from Scranton."

Mr. Kelso broke the silence by introducing me. ∧

① This sentence was changed to make the first-person point of view more consistent.
② To enhance the mood of the essay, this detail about the sound of the clock was added.
③ Using precise details—sharing the teacher's exact words—gives the essay a more personal appeal.

Publishing

▶ **Classroom** Read your essay aloud to a small group of students.
▶ **School Magazine** Submit your reflective essay to your school literary magazine.
▶ **Writing Contest** Ask your teacher or librarian for information on student writing contests.
▶ **Anthology** Collect and organize the essays written by your class into a single volume. Consider organizing essays according to mood or time period.

Student Success Workshop

Real-World Reading Skills

Strategies for Success

Imagine being able to join an expedition to climb Mount Everest with Sherpa mountaineers, participate in a cultural exchange program to live with an Ecuadorian family, or travel on a voyage sailing to Pacific islands. Although these adventures may seem beyond reach, you can experience them vicariously by reading articles, essays, and books.

Enlarge Your Experience For the space of time it takes to read an article, you can become someone else, increase your knowledge of another culture, or immerse yourself in a different historical period.

TRIP TO IRELAND

I traveled to Ireland during spring break this year. I had saved a great deal of money by working, so I thought I deserved to take a trip to Ireland to celebrate St. Patrick's Day. This trip opened my eyes in many ways. For example, I discovered that the Irish, like people in Savannah, Georgia, dye the water green. Also, I discovered that being an American, I was treated almost as a celebrity and was even asked to join the parade. I had never been in a foreign country where I felt so much at home.

Relate Your Experience to That of Others

Perhaps your experience compares in some way to what you are reading. In that case, you can have a dialogue with the author as you might with a friend, comparing or possibly contrasting your emotions and behaviors.

Gain Understanding By reading about someone else's experiences, you can begin to understand his or her ideas, beliefs, and interests. Understanding other people's perspectives will help you become more tolerant and accepting. It may also inspire you to reach out to others in new ways.

Apply the Strategies

Reading through a college newsletter, you come across a student's description of how she spent spring break. Read about the student's trip to Ireland (in the left column). Answer the following questions to show how you might use the piece to increase your understanding of another culture.

1. What experiences have you had that are similar to the one the writer describes?

2. How does Irish culture seem similar to and different from that of the United States?

3. How does this article give you a new understanding of other people? Explain.

> ✔ Here are other forms of writing that can increase your cross-cultural understanding:
> ▶ Novels
> ▶ Short stories
> ▶ Memoirs
> ▶ Humorous essays

Speaking, Listening, and Viewing Workshop

Giving a Visual Presentation

Visuals like maps, videotapes, overhead projections, graphs, and charts can make a speech or other oral presentation more effective. If you don't have sophisticated visual displays and equipment, drawing or writing on a board or pad as you talk can help convey key ideas.

Plan Your Visual Presentation You may have sat through presentations where the speaker has fumbled with a VCR that wasn't hooked up correctly or has displayed maps showing the wrong country. Careful planning, organizing, checking equipment, and practice can help you avoid these mishaps and smoothly combine what you say and what you show.

Apply the Strategies

With a partner, take turns role-playing one of these situations. Work out an integrated verbal and visual presentation that will inform your audience in an entertaining way. Have your partner critique your presentation when you are done.

1. You're an exchange student just back from six months in another country. Use a map of the city where you lived to talk about places you saw.

2. You're a member of a hiking club involved in a trail reclamation project. Use photographs of overgrown areas of the trail to demonstrate the work that needs to be done.

3. You're a camp counselor teaching a class in life-saving techniques. Use drawings to teach the Heimlich maneuver to your campers.

Tips for Giving a Visual Presentation

🖋 Follow these strategies to use visuals effectively:

▶ Include only visuals that illustrate your points. Otherwise, they will distract from your presentation.

▶ Be sure that any equipment you are using is in working order. If you will need to dim the lights, have a partner work with you. Be sure that you agree on signals and timing.

▶ Rehearse your presentation several times. If possible, have a dress rehearsal in front of someone who can critique your presentation.

▶ In general, make your point orally first, and then show the visual to illustrate it. Gesture toward the visual as you explain the key points.

Test Preparation Workshop

Reading Comprehension — Writer's Purpose and Point of View

Strategies for Success

The reading sections of standardized tests often require you to read a passage to understand the writer's purpose and point of view. Use the following strategies to help you answer test questions on these skills:

Establish the Writer's Point of View Point of view refers to the writer's attitude toward the subject. Look for a sentence that establishes the topic. Then consider the writer's tone. Is it positive, negative, humorous, or serious? Read the following sample passage, and answer the question on the writer's point of view.

> The nine African Americans who were the first to integrate Little Rock Central High School are usually mentioned among the greatest heroes of the civil rights movement. On their first day at school, they were turned away by a violent mob. Only after President Eisenhower sent troops to protect the courageous "Little Rock Nine" were they able to attend classes.

I What is the writer's point of view toward the nine students?

A envy   **C** distaste
B admiration **D** fear

The tone of the passage is positive, so answers **A** and **C** are incorrect. At no time does the writer express fear of the students, so **D** is not correct. **B** is correct because the author uses words such as "heroes" and "courageous" to describe the students' actions.

Determine the Writer's Purpose and Intended Meaning Writers can write for one or more purposes. As you read, note whether the author's purpose is to inform by presenting information objectively, to persuade by arguing one side of an issue or urging you to act, or to entertain by writing humorously.

2 In the sample passage, what is the writer's main purpose?

A to entertain   **C** to persuade
B to express an opinion **D** to inform

Answer **A** is incorrect because the passage is serious. **B** and **C** are incorrect because the writer's opinion is not expressed and because there's no call to action. Since the ideas and details of the passage inform you of the students' accomplishments, **D** is correct.

Apply the Strategies

Read the passage, and answer the questions.

> A blaze caused by an unattended campfire destroyed 3,500 acres of Balsam Forest. This is more data to support banning fires at Balsam. Since 1984, more than 300 fires have burned there, causing one death and the destruction of acres of prime forest. Camp fires are simply impossible to control, especially in dry months. Tell your legislator today to vote for a ban on fires at Balsam Forest.

I What is the writer's point of view?

A Fires can be managed.
B Fires are too dangerous to be allowed.
C Only adults should light fires.
D Fires are not a big worry.

2 What is the writer's main purpose?

A to inform you   **C** to entertain
B to provide statistics **D** to persuade

Two Men Observing the Moon, Caspar David Friedrich, Staatl,
Kunstsammlungen, Neue Meister, Dresden, Germany

Rebels and Dreamers:

The Romantic Period (1798–1832)

Come forth into the light of things,
Let Nature be your teacher.

—William Wordsworth,
from "The Tables Turned"

Timeline
1798–1832

British Events

- **1798 William Wordsworth** and **Samuel Taylor Coleridge** publish *Lyrical Ballads*.
- **1798** Wolfe Tone Rebellion in Ireland.
- **1801** Act of Union creates United Kingdom of Great Britain and Ireland.
- **1801** Union Jack becomes official flag. ▼

- **1802** J.M.W. Turner's *Calais Pier* exhibited in London.
- **1803** Henry Shrapnel invents exploding shell.

- **1805** Battle of Trafalgar. ▼
- **1807** Thomas Moore writes *Irish Melodies*.

- **1811** King George III declared permanently insane.
- **1812 Byron** publishes *Childe Harold's Pilgrimage*.
- **1813 Jane Austen** publishes *Pride and Prejudice*. ▶
- **1814** George Stephenson constructs first successful steam locomotive. ▼
- **1814** Walter Scott publishes *Waverley*.

- **1815** John MacAdam constructs roads of crushed stone.

World Events

- **1799** France: Napoleon becomes head of revolutionary government. ▶
- **1799** Egypt: Rosetta Stone, key to deciphering hieroglyphics, discovered.
- **1800** Italy: Volta builds first electric battery.
- **1800** Spain: Goya paints *The Two Majas*.
- **1802** Haiti: Toussaint L'Ouverture leads rebellion against French rule. ▶
- **1803** United States: Louisiana Territory purchased from France.

- **1804** Germany: Beethoven composes *Symphony No. 3*.
- **1804** France: Napoleon crowns himself emperor.
- **1805** Eastern Europe: Napoleon defeats allies at Austerlitz.
- **1807** United States: Fulton's steamboat navigates Hudson River. ▲
- **1808** Italy: Excavation of Pompeii begins.
- **1808** Germany: Goethe publishes *Faust*, Part I.
- **1809** United States: Washington Irving writes "Rip Van Winkle."

- **1810** South America: Simón Bolívar leads rebellions against Spanish rule.
- **1812** Russia: Napoleon loses hundreds of thousands of troops in retreat from Moscow.
- **1812** United States: War with Britain declared.
- **1813** Mexico: Independence declared.
- **1814** France: Napoleon abdicates and is exiled to Elba.
- **1815** France: Napoleon returns for "Hundred Days."
- **1815** Belgium: Napoleon defeated at Waterloo.

1816	**1822**	**1828**	**1832**

- **1817** William Hazlitt writes *Characters of Shakespeare's Plays.*
- **1818 Mary Wollstonecraft Shelley** publishes *Frankenstein or the Modern Prometheus.* ▶
- **1819** Peterloo Massacre in Manchester.
- **1819 Percy Bysshe Shelley** writes "Ode to the West Wind"
- **1820 John Keats** publishes "Ode on a Grecian Urn."
- **1821** *Manchester Guardian* begins publication.
- **1821** John Constable paints *The Hay-Wain*

- **1825** Horse-drawn buses begin operating in London.
- **1825** John Nash completes rebuilding of Buckingham Palace.
- **1827** System for purifying London water installed.

- **1829** Catholic Emancipation Act passed.
- **1829** Robert Peel establishes Metropolitan Police in London.
- **1830** Liverpool-Manchester railway opens. ▼

- **1831** Michael Faraday demonstrates electromagnetic induction. ▼
- **1832** First Reform Act extends voting rights.

- **1817** United States: William Cullen Bryant publishes "Thanatopsis."
- **1818** First steamship crosses Atlantic.
- **1819** France: René Läennec invents stethescope. ▶
- **1821** Greece: War with Turkey begins.
- **1821** Germany: Heinrich Heine publishes *Poems.*

- **1822** Russia: Aleksandr Pushkin publishes *Eugene Onegin.*
- **1823** United States: Monroe Doctrine closes Americas to further Euro pean colonization.
- **1825** Russia: Bolshoi Ballet founded. ▶
- **1826** Germany: Mendelssohn composes *Overture to A Midsummer Night's Dream.*
- **1826** United States: James Fenimore Cooper publishes *The Last of the Mohicans.*

- **1830** France: Stendhal publishes *The Red and the Black.*
- **1831** United States: Edgar Allan Poe publishes *Poems.*
- **1831** France: Victor Hugo publishes *The Hunchback of Notre Dame.*

Declaration of the Rights of Man, 1793, with Robespierre's modifications of the 1789 document

▲ **Interpret** Featured in this presentation of the French Revolution's Declaration of the Rights of Man is a *fasces* (a bundle of rods surrounding an ax)—an ancient Roman symbol of the government's power. Explain why the revolutionaries included classical references in this document.

The Battle of Trafalgar, October 21, 1805, J.M.W. Turner, The Granger Collection, Ltd.

▲ **Speculate** The British fleet under Lord Nelson defeated Napoleon's fleet at the Battle of Trafalgar, off Spain. Using the details in this painting, describe the experience of participating in a sea battle.

The Story of the Times
(1798–1832)

Historical Background

After nearly a century of progress in science and industry, the faith of poets in reason had been eroded. Where eighteenth-century poets had celebrated the power of human understanding—their most bitter satire could say no more than, "humanity is unreasonable"—Wordsworth marked the end of the century with the warning "Our meddling intellect/Misshapes the beauteous forms of things—/We murder to dissect."

In the ensuing period, which was named the Romantic Age by historians during the late 1800's, nearly all the attitudes and tendencies of eighteenth-century classicism and rationalism were redefined or changed dramatically. To understand how these changes occurred, it is necessary to examine not only the impact of events in Britain, but also the effects of the social and political upheaval that began taking place in other parts of the world.

Revolution and Reaction Some of the defining events for British thought and politics at the end of the eighteenth century took place, not in England, but in France. The French Revolution began on July 14, 1789, when a group of French citizens stormed the Bastille, a Paris prison for political prisoners. The revolutionaries placed limits on the powers of King Louis XVI, established a new government, and approved a document called the Declaration of the Rights of Man, affirming the principles of "liberty, equality, and fraternity." France became a constitutional monarchy.

In England, the ruling class felt threatened by the events in France, which seemed to strike at the roots of social order. Most intellectuals, including the most important and influential writers of the Romantic Age, such as William Wordsworth, enthusiastically supported the revolution and the democratic ideals on which it was grounded.

The Reign of Terror As royalists, moderates, and radicals jockeyed for power, the French Revolution became more and more chaotic. In 1792, France declared war on Austria, touching off an invasion by Austrian and Prussian troops. Fuming with patriotic indignation, a radical group called the Jacobins gained control of the French legislative assembly, abolished the monarchy, and declared the nation a republic. Mobs attacked and killed many prisoners—including former aristocrats and priests—in the bloody "September massacres."

Within weeks the revolutionaries had tried and convicted Louis XVI on a charge of treason, then sent him to the guillotine early in 1793. The Jacobins, under the leadership of Maximilien Robespierre, then began what is called the Reign of Terror. Over the next year, they sent some 17,000 royalists, moderates, and even radicals—including finally Robespierre himself—to the guillotine.

At the same time, France's new "citizen army" was making war across Europe in the name of liberty. In 1793, France declared war on Britain. Thus began a series of wars that would drag on for twenty-two years, ending only when Britain and its allies defeated Napoleon in 1815. Lord Nelson, who broke the French navy at the Battle of Trafalgar, and the Duke of Wellington, who led the British forces in the final showdown with Napoleon, were two of Britain's great military heroes from the time.

British Reaction The September massacres and the Reign of Terror were so shocking that even Britons who had sympathized with the French Revolution now turned against it. Conservative Britons demanded a crackdown on reformers, whom they denounced as dangerous Jacobins. Adding to British alarm was the success of France's new "citizen army," which expelled the Austrian and Russian invaders and then set out to "liberate" other European nations from despotic rule. British leaders did not want France or any other nation to win dominance on the European continent. In 1793, France took the initiative by declaring war on Britain. Thus began a series of

▲ **Compare and Contrast** In the years of turmoil following the Revolution, Napoleon rose to lead France to victory. By 1807, France ruled Europe as far east as Russia. Contrast Napoleon with the other figures in the painting.

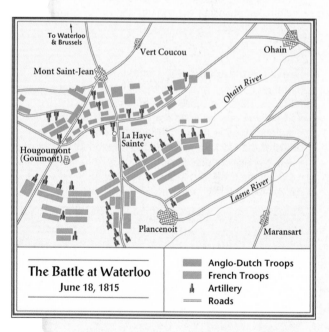

The Battle at Waterloo
June 18, 1815

- Anglo-Dutch Troops
- French Troops
- Artillery
- Roads

▲ **Read a Map** A crucial moment in the Battle of Waterloo came when one of Napoleon's officers, Marshall Ney, captured the farmhouse of La Haye-Sainte. (a) Describe the location of this farmhouse in relation to the British troops. (b) Why would its capture by the French give them an advantage?

Tea Time, David Emil

▲ **Interpret** By the early 1800's, tea was truly a national drink, popular with all classes.
a) Does the painting represent a formal tea, or a "tea break"? (b) What techniques does the artist use to emphasize how relaxing the act of drinking tea can be?

▼ **Draw Conclusions** Early cotton mills employed mostly women and children. The first factories were not thoroughly automatized. Factory workers retained some self-directedness and pride in their craft. (a) What does the dress of the workers in this picture suggest about factory conditions of the time? (b) Describe the tasks that you see being performed.

Power Loom, Anonymous, 18th Century

wars that would drag on for twenty-two years, creating fear and rigidity, and squelching all hope of reform within British society. The Tory government led by William Pitt (the Younger) outlawed all talk of parliamentary reform outside the halls of Parliament, banned public meetings, and suspended certain basic rights.

Liberal-minded Britons had no political outlet for their hopes and dreams. Many turned to literature and art instead.

Coping With Society's Problems Throughout the long wars with France, Britain's government kept a tight lid on domestic dissent. It ignored the problems caused by the Industrial Revolution—overcrowded factory towns, unpleasant and unsafe working conditions in the factories, and long working hours and low pay. The working class grew steadily larger and more restless. In the factory towns of northern England, workers protested the loss of jobs to new machinery in the violent Luddite Riots (1811–1813). Some attempted to organize in unions.

Britain's government claimed to be following a hands-off policy, but in fact it sided openly with factory owners against workers, even helping to crush the workers' attempts to form unions. In Manchester, mounted soldiers charged a peaceful mass meeting of cotton workers and killed several of them in what came to be known as the Peterloo Massacre (1819). To many, it seemed that British society was splitting into two angry camps—the working classes, who demanded reform, and the ruling classes, who resisted fiercely.

A new generation of Tories emerged in the 1820's, and a trickle of reforms began. A law was passed in 1824 permitting Britain's first labor unions to organize, and in 1829 the Catholic Emancipation Act restored economic and religious freedoms to Roman Catholics.

The trickle grew into a stream following a Whig victory in the election of 1830. The Reform Bill of 1832 brought sweeping changes to British political life. By extending voting rights to the small but important middle class (males only), this law threatened the traditional dominance of land-owning aristocrats in Parliament. Moreover, in 1833 Parliament passed the first law governing factory safety. In that same year, it also abolished slavery.

Literature of the Period

The Beginnings of Romanticism The British Romantic writers responded to the climate of their times. Their new interest in the trials and dreams of common people and their desire for radical change developed out of the democratic idealism that characterized the early part of the French Revolution. Their deep attachment to nature and to a pure, simple past was a response to the misery and ugliness born of industrialization. For the Romantics, the faith in science and reason, so characteristic of eighteenth-century thought and literature, no longer applied in a world of tyranny and factories.

Many of the ideas that influenced the British Romantics, though, originally arose on continental Europe well before the turn of the century. Swiss-born writer Jean-Jacques Rousseau (1712–1778), a leading philosopher of eighteenth-century France, saw society as a force that, through history, deformed and imprisoned an originally free human nature. "Man is born free," he wrote, "and everywhere he is in chains." His ideas influenced both American and French revolutionaries.

A group of late-eighteenth-century writers and artists living in German-speaking Europe began incorporating Rousseau's ideas into poetry, fiction, and drama. The most famous of this group, Johann Wolfgang von Goethe (1749–1832) found a primitive simplicity much in keeping with Rousseau's ideas and values in the German literature of the Middle Ages, works filled with myth, adventure and passion, not unlike the Anglo-Saxon *Beowulf*. The Romantic movement takes its name from this interest in medieval romances. Goethe's own works show a new attention to feelings and express an ideal of self-fulfillment and growth through experience.

The Romantic Age in British Poetry In music, Romanticism produced such brilliant European

Rush Hour at Whitehall, in the 1820's
The Granger Collection, Ltd.

▲ **Relate** With roughly one million inhabitants, London in 1800 was the biggest city in the West and probably in the world. (a) Name three details that the scene in the picture shares with a modern city. (b) Name three characteristics of a modern city that do not appear in the picture.

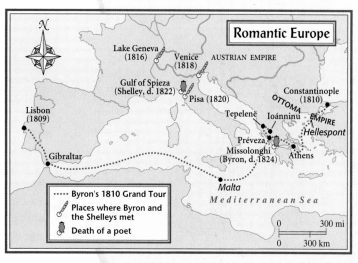

▲ **Read a Map** When peace with France came in 1815, the British discovered a passion for travel. At least one celebrity had already paved the way: Lord Byron went on an extensive tour of Europe in 1809. (a) How many years passed between Byron's Grand Tour of Europe and his move to Pisa? (b) Where in Europe and when did Shelley and Byron die?

▲ **Draw Conclusions** In 1825, the Stockton and Darlington Railway became the first to carry passengers as well as freight. Sixteen years later, 1,300 miles of railroad track covered Britain. (a) What details in the picture suggest changes the railroad made in British life and the British landscape? (b) What details suggest ways in which life stayed the same?

▲ **Compare and Contrast** In 1812, well before the invention of the microprocessor, the English inventor Charles Babbage thought up the idea of a "Difference Engine"—a machine that would compute tables of logarithms and other mathematical values. Name three differences between the Difference Engine depicted here and one of today's computers.

composers as Germany's Ludwig van Beethoven (1770–1827) and Austria's Franz Schubert (1797–1828). In painting, it influenced the intensely personal and warmly spontaneous rural landscapes of Britain's John Constable (1776–1837) and J. M. W. Turner (1775–1851). However, it is for literature, and especially for poetry, that Britain's Romantic Age is most famous. William Wordsworth provided an early statement of the goals of Romantic poetry in his preface to *Lyrical Ballads* (1798), his early collaboration with his friend Samuel Taylor Coleridge. The preface defined poetry as "the spontaneous overflow of powerful feelings" and explained that poetry "takes its origin from emotion recollected in tranquility." An emphasis on the emotions, then, was central to the new Romantic poetry.

Equally important was subject matter. The new poetry dealt with "incidents and situations from common life" over which the poet throws "a certain coloring of imagination, whereby ordinary things should be presented . . . in an unusual way."

Finally, Wordsworth's preface spoke about incorporating human passions with "the beautiful and permanent forms of nature." An emphasis on nature would become another important characteristic of British Romantic verse.

The Romantic view of nature was quite different from that of most eighteenth-century literature. Nature was not a force to be tamed and analyzed scientifically; rather, it was a wild, free force that could inspire poets to instinctive spiritual understanding.

Wordsworth and Coleridge blazed the way for a new generation of British Romantic poets—the so-called "second generation" of poets, which included George Gordon, Lord Byron; Percy Bysshe Shelley; and John Keats. These younger poets rebelled even more strongly than Wordsworth and Coleridge against the British conservatism of the time. All three died abroad after tragically short lives, and their viewpoints were those of disillusioned outsiders.

The Romantic Age in British Prose British readers of the Romantic Age could find brilliant literary criticism and topical essays in a variety of new periodicals. *The London Magazine,* although it appeared only from 1820 to 1829, attracted major contributions from the three greatest essayists of the era: Charles Lamb (1775–1834), William Hazlitt (1778–1830), and Thomas De Quincey (1785–1859). Lamb, in particular, transformed the informal essay of the eighteenth century into a more personal, more introspective Romantic composition.

Unlike the Romantic poets, the novelists of the Romantic Age did not make a sharp break with the past. The Gothic novel first appeared in the middle of the eighteenth century. It featured a number of standard ingredients, including brave heroes and heroines, threatening scoundrels, vast eerie castles, and ghosts. The Romantic fascination with mystery and the supernatural made such novels quite popular during the Romantic Age. One of the most successful was *Frankenstein, or the Modern Prometheus* (1818), written by Shelley's wife, Mary Wollstonecraft Shelley (1797–1851).

The Romantic novel of manners carried on in the tradition of earlier writers by turning a satirical eye on British customs. The most highly regarded writer of novels of manners was Jane Austen (1775–1817), whose works include *Sense and Sensibility* (1811) and *Pride and Prejudice* (1813). Her incisive portrayals of character are more reflective of the classical sensibility of the eighteenth century than the Romantic notions of the new age.

Historical romances—imaginative works of fiction built around a real person or historical event—had appeared long before the Romantic Age, but they attained their peak of popularity in the work of Sir Walter Scott (1771–1832). Passionately devoted to his native Scotland, Scott wrote about the days of knights and chivalry.

The close of Britain's Romantic Age is usually set in 1832, the year of the passage of the First Reform Bill. However, the ideas of Romanticism remained a strong influence on many writers from following generations. In fact, even today we can detect elements of Romanticism in many major works of contemporary fiction and poetry as well as in television dramas, movies, and popular songs.

Calais Pier: An English Packet Arriving, J. M. W. Turner

▲ **Interpret** The Romantic movement in literature found echoes in the other arts. The landscapes of J. M. W. Turner (1775–1851) shared the Romantics' new attention to and respect for nature. (a) Describe the relation between light and dark in the painting. (b) What does the interaction of light and dark in the painting suggest about the nature of life?

Sketch for Hadleigh Castle, John Constable

▲ **Interpret** Another painter linked with the Romantics is John Constable (1776–1837). (a) What mood do you think Constable wanted to create with this scene? (b) How do the clouds add to this mood?

The Changing English Language

THE ROMANTIC AGE

by Richard Lederer

The Sun Never Set on the British Empire

During the Romantic Age, Britannia ruled the waves and English ruled much of the land. Great Britain's smashing conquests in the Napoleonic Wars at the beginning of the nineteenth century—culminating in Nelson's famous victory at Trafalgar in 1805—established an undisputed naval supremacy. This, in turn, gave Great Britain control over most of the world's commerce. As British ships traveled throughout the world, they left the language of the mother country in their wake but also came home from foreign ports laden with cargoes of words from other languages freighted with new meanings for English speakers.

Words, Words, Words

The biggest and fattest unabridged English dictionaries hold more than 600,000 words, compared to German in second place with 185,000 words, and then Russian and French at 130,000 and 100,000. One reason we have accumulated the world's largest and most varied vocabulary is that English continues to be the most hospitable and democratic language that has ever existed, unique in the number and variety of its borrowed words. Although Anglo-Saxon is the

The following are words that became part of the English language as a result of England's great economic expansion.

Country	Borrowed Words
India	*bandanna, bungalow, calico, cashmere, china, cot, curry, juggernaut, jungle, loot, nirvana, polo, punch* (beverage), *thug,* and *verandah*
Asia	*gingham, indigo, mango,* and *typhoon*
New Zealand	*kiwi*
Australia	*boomerang* and *kangaroo*
Africa	*banana, boorish, chimpanzee, gorilla, gumbo,* and *zebra*

foundation of the English language, more than seventy percent of our words have been imported from other lands, ancient and modern, far and near. No wonder Ralph Waldo Emerson waxed ecstatic about "English speech, the sea which receives tributaries from every region under heaven" and Dorothy Thompson, employing a more prosaic metaphor, referred to "that glorious and imperial mongrel, the English language."

Activities

1. Open your dictionary at random and examine the etymology of the words listed at the top of fifteen pages. Record the earliest source for each word. Words noted as *AS* or *OE* are native; the rest are borrowed. What is the ratio of native versus borrowed words? Among the borrowed words, what percentage are derived from Latin? from Greek? from French? from other languages? Compare your results with those of your classmates and discuss the implications.

2. Now choose a passage from a newspaper or magazine. Analyze the first thirty words of that passage in the manner described above. Do you notice a different ratio of native to borrowed words? Discuss your conclusions regarding random dictionary entries versus the words in actual sentences.

PART 1 *Fantasy and Reality*

Hummingbird Hunters, 1884, James Farrington Gookins, Shelden Swope Art Museum, Terre Haute, Indiana

Guide for Interpreting

Mary Wollstonecraft Shelley

(1797–1851)

Perhaps you've sat around on a rainy day with your friends exchanging thrilling "tales of terror." The classic Gothic novel *Frankenstein* was born in a similar way. One day in 1816 Mary Shelley and her husband (the poet Percy Bysshe Shelley), the poet Lord Byron, and another friend challenged one another to write ghost stories.

> *The product of a challenge, Mary Shelley's horrific tale of the creation of a monster eventually became the full-length classic horror novel, Frankenstein.*

Since its publication in 1818, *Frankenstein* has thrilled countless readers and has been interpreted and reinterpreted by generations of filmmakers.

Literary and Political Legacy Literature and politics were in Mary Shelley's blood: her mother, Mary Wollstonecraft Godwin (who died at Mary's birth), wrote one of the first feminist books ever published, *A Vindication of the Rights of Woman* (1792). Her father, William Godwin, was an author and political philosopher. Amid this atmosphere of literary and political consciousness, Mary Godwin met her future husband, Percy Bysshe Shelley, a radically-minded young poet who had become William Godwin's admirer after reading his book *Political Justice*. Mary Godwin and Percy Bysshe Shelley fell in love and later married.

A Career of Her Own Married to one of the most famous poets of the nineteenth century, Mary Shelley had an active literary career of her own. After *Frankenstein*, she produced five more novels: *Valperga* (1823) and *The Fortunes of Perkin Warbeck* (1830), which are historical works; the autobiographical *Lodore* (1835); *Falkner* (1837), a complicated mystery tale; and *The Last Man* (1826). *Frankenstein* was the first of many works to explore the potential dangers of technology used for the wrong purposes—still an important theme today.

◆ Background for Understanding

LITERATURE: SHELLEY, FRANKENSTEIN, AND THE PROMETHEUS MYTH

During the Romantic era, when Mary Shelley wrote *Frankenstein*, the Greek mythological figure Prometheus was drawing renewed attention. Prometheus was one of the Titans—a race of giants; later myths say that Prometheus created man. He was the subject of part of a trilogy by the classic Greek writer Aeschylus, *Prometheus Bound*, and later of a lyric drama by Percy Shelley, *Prometheus Unbound*. Society's interest in this Titan was not far from Mary Shelley's mind when she wrote *Frankenstein*, about a doctor who attempts to create a man. In fact, the complete title of her famous work is *Frankenstein, or the Modern Prometheus*.

Journal Writing Jot down the title and plot of another myth or story you know that explains the origin of humans.

◆ *Literature and Your Life*

CONNECT YOUR EXPERIENCE

Looking back on your achievements during your high school years, you'll probably discover that you were greatly influenced by encouragement from or competition with your friends. Similarly, Mary Shelley's greatest accomplishment, the novel *Frankenstein,* was the result of a competition among friends. Just nineteen at the time, Shelley created a book that inspired dozens of movies—some of which you've probably seen. You may not realize, however, that Frankenstein is not the name of the soulless man-monster who eventually destroys his creator. Frankenstein is the creator himself—the infamous Dr. Frankenstein.

THEMATIC FOCUS: FANTASY AND REALITY

At the movies today, we're more likely to see space aliens than monsters (composites of animals and humans). Why are the fantastic creatures we envision now different from those envisioned in Shelley's time?

◆ Literary Focus

THE GOTHIC TRADITION

Mary Shelley's *Frankenstein* is a classic example of **gothic literature,** a form of literature in which the reader passes from the reasoned order of the everyday world into the dark and dreadful world of the supernatural. Gothic literature emerged in the eighteenth century as part of Romanticism, a movement that rejected the Age of Reason's claim that everything could be explained scientifically.

Gothic literature is characteristically set in castles, monasteries with underground passages, dark towers, and torture chambers—all featuring the Gothic architectural style of the period.

◆ Build Vocabulary

RELATED WORDS: *PHANTASM* AND *FANTASY*

Shelley uses the word *phantasm,* meaning "supernatural form or shape; figment of the imagination," to describe the monster she creates. The word is related to one with which you're probably quite familiar: *fantasy.*

WORD BANK

Preview the words on this list before you read the selection.

appendage
ungenial
acceded
platitude
phantasm
incitement

◆ Grammar and Style

PAST PARTICIPIAL PHRASES

Shelley frequently uses **past participial phrases**, which include a past participle—the past tense of a verb, usually ending in *-ed*, that functions as an adjective—and its modifiers and complements. The entire phrase functions as an adjective.

> . . . he would hope that, *left to itself,* the slight spark of light . . .

In this example, the participial phrase beginning with the irregular past participle *left* modifies the noun *spark.*

Reading for Success

Interactive Reading Strategies

When you read critically, you're interacting with a literary work. You're using your inner voice to probe, recall bits of your own experience, and question. Use these strategies for interactive reading:

Draw upon your prior background knowledge.

Special facts or incidents that you remember can help you connect with a given literary work. For example, if you know from Jewish folklore that a golem is an artificially created human being, you'll have a point of reference for Frankenstein's monster. As you read, trust your memory; it can annotate a literary work with useful references.

Question.

One role of your critical "voice" is to ask questions. In works of non-fiction, such as the "Introduction to *Frankenstein*," it's important to ask: What evidence supports these statements? What point of view influenced the author to draw this conclusion (or form this opinion)?

Predict.

Making predictions about what will happen in a literary work keeps you involved in your reading. Base your predictions on clues that the writer provides, along with what you learn about the characters and the pattern in which the work is organized. As you read, check your predictions, and revise them as necessary.

Clarify details and information.

When you're unclear about a detail in a selection, try rephrasing the detail to yourself. Review what you've read, or read ahead to see if you can find the information you need. In some cases, the information may not be included in the text, and you may want to look up the information later.

Use your knowledge of the historical context.

If you know that one distinguishing feature of the period was the growth in scientific thought, you'll be better prepared to understand the "Introduction to *Frankenstein*." Using your knowledge of historical periods helps you connect a literary work to the society that gave birth to it.

Respond to the work.

Even solitary reflection on a literary work is a way of interacting with it. You may finish "Introduction to *Frankenstein*," and two days later an event in your own life will call forth an aspect of the work. Remain open to the ideas in a literary work, and you'll see them echoed in the world around you.

As you read Mary Shelley's "Introduction to *Frankenstein*," look at the notes along the sides. These notes demonstrate how to apply these strategies to a work of literature.

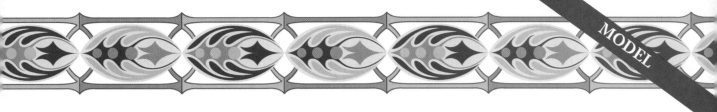

Introduction to
FRANKENSTEIN
MARY WOLLSTONECRAFT SHELLEY

In this introduction to the third edition of Frankenstein, *published in 1831, Mary Shelley recalls the circumstances that led her to write the novel during the summer of 1816.*

The Publishers of the Standard Novels, in selecting *Frankenstein* for one of their series, expressed a wish that I should furnish them with some account of the origin of the story. I am the more willing to comply, because I shall thus give a general answer to the question, so very frequently asked me: "How I, then a young girl, came to think of, and to dilate upon, so very hideous an idea?" It is true that I am very averse to bringing myself forward in print; but as my account will only appear as an appendage to a former production, and as it will be confined to such topics as have connection with my authorship alone, I can scarcely accuse myself of a personal intrusion. . . .

In the summer of 1816, we[1] visited Switzerland, and became the neighbors of Lord Byron. At first we spent our pleasant hours on the lake or wandering on its shores; and Lord Byron, who was writing the third canto of *Childe*

> Using your **prior background knowledge** of the Romantic period and the expectations of women at that time will help you understand the shock people felt about a young lady creating such a hideous tale.

Harold, was the only one among us who put his thoughts upon paper. These, as he brought them successively to us, clothed in all the light and harmony of poetry, seemed to stamp as divine the glories of heaven and earth, whose influences we partook with him.

But it proved a wet, <u>ungenial</u> summer, and incessant rain often confined us for days to the house. Some volumes of ghost stories, translated from the German into French,[2] fell into our hands. There was "The History of the Inconstant Lover,"[3] who, when he thought to clasp the bride to whom he had pledged his vows, found himself in the arms of the pale ghost of her whom he had deserted. There was the tale of the sinful founder of his race,[4]

---

2. volumes . . . French: *Fantasmagoriana,* or *Collected Stories of Apparitions of Specters, Ghosts, Phantoms, Etc.,* published anonymously in 1812.
3. "The History . . . Lover": The true name of the story is "The Dead Fiancée."
4. the tale . . . race: "Family Portraits."

◆ **Build Vocabulary**

appendage (ə pen′ dij) *n.*: Something added on
ungenial (un jēn′ yəl) *adj.*: Unfriendly; characterized by bad weather

---

1. we: Mary Shelley, her husband Percy Bysshe Shelley, and their two children.

whose miserable doom it was to bestow the kiss of death on all the younger sons of his fated house, just when they reached the age of promise. His gigantic, shadowy form, clothed like the ghost in Hamlet, in complete armor but with the beaver[5] up, was seen at midnight, by the moon's fitful beams, to advance slowly along the gloomy avenue. The shape was lost beneath the shadow of the castle walls; but soon a gate swung back, a step was heard, the door of the chamber opened, and he advanced to the couch of the blooming youths, cradled in healthy sleep. Eternal sorrow sat upon his face as he bent down and kissed the foreheads of the boys, who from that hour withered like flowers snapped upon the stalk. I have not seen these stories since then, but their incidents are as fresh in my mind as if I had read them yesterday.

"We will each write a ghost story," said Lord Byron; and his proposition was <u>acceded</u> to. There were four of us.[6] The noble author began a tale, a fragment of which he printed at the end of his poem of Mazeppa. Shelley, more apt to embody ideas and sentiments in the radiance of brilliant imagery, and in the music of the most melodious verse that adorns our language, than to invent the machinery of a story, commenced one founded on the experiences of his early life. Poor Polidori had some terrible idea about a skull-headed lady, who was so punished for peeping through a keyhole—what to see I forget—something very shocking and wrong of course; but when she was reduced to a worse condition than the renowned Tom of Coventry,[7] he did not know what to do with her, and was obliged to despatch her to the tomb of the Capulets,[8] the only place for which she was fitted. The illustrious poets also, annoyed by

Although this opinion of Percy Shelley's work was shared by others, it is worthwhile to **question** Mary Shelley's objectivity here; she was, after all, married to Shelley.

---

5. **beaver:** Hinged piece of armor that covers the face.
6. **four of us:** Byron, the two Shelleys, and John William Polidori, Byron's physician.
7. **Tom of Coventry:** "Peeping Tom" who, according to legend, was struck blind for looking at Lady Godiva as she rode naked through Coventry.
8. **tomb of the Capulets:** Where Romeo and Juliet died.

◆ **Build Vocabulary**

acceded (ak sēd´ id) *v.*: Yielded to; agreed upon

the platitude of prose, speedily relinquished their uncongenial task.

I busied myself to *think of a story*—a story to rival those which had excited us to this task. One which would speak to the mysterious fears of our nature and awaken thrilling horror—one to make the reader dread to look round, to curdle the blood, and quicken the beatings of the heart. If I did not accomplish these things, my ghost story would be unworthy of its name. I thought and pondered—vainly. I felt that blank incapability of invention which is the greatest misery of authorship, when dull Nothing replies to our anxious invocations.

> You might **predict** from this statement that if Shelley succeeded in her task of writing a horror story, she would do so splendidly.

Have you thought of a story? I was asked each morning, and each morning I was forced to reply with a mortifying negative. . . .

Many and long were the conversations between Lord Byron and Shelley, to which I was a devout but nearly silent listener. During one of these, various philosophical doctrines were discussed, and among others the nature of the principle of life and whether there was any probability of its ever being discovered and communicated. They talked of the experiments of Dr. Darwin[9] (I speak not of what the Doctor really did or said that he did, but, as more to my purpose, of what was then spoken of as having been done by him), who preserved a piece of vermicelli in a glass case till by some extraordinary means it began to move with voluntary motion. Not thus, after all, would life be given. Perhaps a corpse would be reanimated: galvanism[10] had given token of such things. Perhaps the component

> If you want to know more about reanimation, jot down a note to look up and **clarify** the concept later.

parts of a creature might be manufactured, brought together, and endued with vital warmth.

Night waned upon this talk, and even the witching hour had gone by, before we retired to rest. When I placed my head on my pillow, I did not sleep, nor could I be said to think. My imagination, unbidden, possessed and guided me, gifting the successive images that arose in my mind with a vividness far beyond the usual bounds of reverie. I saw—with shut eyes but acute mental vision—I saw the pale student of unhallowed arts kneeling beside the thing he had put together. I saw the hideous phantasm of a man stretched out, and then, on the working of some powerful engine, show signs of life and stir with an uneasy, half vital motion. Frightful must it be, for supremely frightful would be the effect of any human endeavor to mock the stupendous mechanism of the Creator of the world. His success would terrify the artist; he would rush away from his odious handiwork, horror-stricken. He would hope that, left to itself, the slight spark of life which he had communicated would fade; that this thing, which had received such imperfect animation, would subside into dead matter; and he might sleep in the belief that the silence of the grave would quench forever the transient existence of the hideous corpse which he had looked upon as the cradle of life. He sleeps; but he is awakened; he opens his eyes; behold the horrid thing stands at his bedside, opening his curtains, and looking on him with yellow, watery, but speculative eyes.

I opened mine in terror. The idea so possessed my mind, that a thrill of fear ran through me, and I wished to exchange the ghastly image of my fancy for the realities around. I see them still: the very room, the dark parquet,[11] the closed shutters, with the moonlight struggling through, and the sense I had that the glassy lake and white high Alps were beyond. I could not so easily get rid of my

---

9. Dr. Darwin: Erasmus Darwin (1731–1802), physician, natural scientist, and poet.
10. galvanism: Use of electric current to induce twitching in dead muscles.

---

11. parquet (pär kā´): Flooring made of wooden pieces arranged in a pattern.

hideous phantom: still it haunted me. I must try to think of something else. I recurred to my ghost story—my tiresome unlucky ghost story! O! if I could only contrive one which would frighten my reader as I myself had been frightened that night!

Swift as light and as cheering was the idea that broke in upon me. "I have found it! What terrified me will terrify others, and I need only describe the specter which had haunted my midnight pillow." On the morrow I announced that I had *thought of a story.* I began that day with the words, *It was on a dreary night of November,* making only a transcript of the grim terrors of my waking dream.

At first I thought but of a few pages—of a short tale—but Shelley urged me to develop the idea at greater length. I certainly did not owe the suggestion of one incident, nor scarcely of one train of feeling, to my husband, and yet but for his incitement, it would never have taken the form in which it was presented to the world. From this declaration I must except the preface. As far as I can recollect, it was entirely written by him.

And now, once again, I bid my hideous progeny go forth and prosper. I have an affection for it, for it was the offspring of happy days, when death and grief were but words, which found no true echo in my heart. Its several pages speak of many a walk, many a drive, and many a conversation, when I was not alone; and my companion was one who, in this world, I shall never see more. But this is for myself: my readers have nothing to do with these associations.

◆ Build Vocabulary

platitude (plat´ ə tōōd´) *n.*: Statement lacking originality

phantasm (fan´ taz´m) *n.*: Supernatural form or shape; ghost; figment of the mind

incitement (in sīt´ mənt) *n.*: Cause to perform; encouragement

Guide for Responding

◆ Literature and Your Life

Reader's Response Did you find Shelley's account interesting? Why or why not?

Thematic Focus Why do you think horror stories appeal to people?

☑ Check Your Comprehension

1. What is Shelley referring to when she says, "I have not seen these stories since then, but their incidents are as fresh in my mind . . ."?
2. Why did the "illustrious poets . . . relinquish their ungenial task"?
3. What provided the author with her inspiration for *Frankenstein?*
4. What did Shelley think she needed to do in order to write a successful ghost story?

◆ Critical Thinking

INTERPRET

1. Find the passage that supports Shelley's implication that her husband would fail at the ghost story assignment. Explain. **[Interpret]**
2. What effect does Mary Shelley's inability to think of a story have on her? **[Analyze]**
3. What do you think Shelley's attitude is toward Darwin's experiments? Explain. **[Draw Conclusions]**

APPLY

4. What does the "Introduction to *Frankenstein*" suggest about how writers get ideas? **[Generalize]**
5. What does this selection reveal to you about the relationship between Mary Shelley and her husband? **[Synthesize]**

EXTEND

6. What kinds of scientific experimentation today are comparable to Darwin's in the eighteenth century? Explain. **[Science Link]**

Guide for Responding (continued)

◆ Reading for Success

INTERACTIVE READING STRATEGIES

Review the reading strategies and the notes showing how to read interactively. Then apply them to answer the following:

1. (a) Give an example of a detail from the selection you'd like clarified. (b) In what specific ways will this clarification help you to understand "Introduction to *Frankenstein*"?
2. Explain how knowing that Percy Shelley died of drowning before the age of thirty will help you understand the last paragraph of the "Introduction to *Frankenstein*."

◆ Grammar and Style

PAST PARTICIPIAL PHRASES

Participial phrases are groups of words that serve as adjectives; the entire phrase modifies a noun or pronoun. "Introduction to *Frankenstein*" has several participial phrases that include past participles, verb forms ending in *-ed*.

Practice In the following passages, past participial phrases modify nouns and pronouns, including relative pronouns. Write each passage in your notebook. Underline the participial phrase, circle the word it modifies, and, after each item, identify the part of speech of the modified word.

1. . . . as he brought them successively to us, clothed in all the light and harmony of poetry, seemed. . . .
2. Some volumes of ghost stories, translated from the German into French, fell into. . . .
3. His gigantic shadowy form, clothed like the ghost in *Hamlet*, in complete armor . . . was seen. . . .
4. . . . and he advanced to the couch of the blooming youths, cradled in healthy sleep.
5. The illustrious poets also, annoyed by the platitude of prose, speedily relinquished their uncongenial task.

Writing Application Write a paragraph or two summarizing the key details in this selection. Include at least two past participial phrases.

◆ Literary Focus

THE GOTHIC TRADITION

The **Gothic novel** was a late-eighteenth-century revival of the tale of terror, which has its roots in antiquity. Gothic novels and stories are often set in sinister medieval times, with Gothic architecture as their backdrop. Mixing everyday events with supernatural ones, as Shelley does in *Frankenstein*, is another important trademark of Gothic tales.

1. What characteristics of Gothic literature do the ghost stories described in the third paragraph of the introduction share? Explain.
2. Explain why Mary Shelley's idea for *Frankenstein* fits within the defining parameters of the Gothic tradition.
3. Based on your reading of the introduction, what most likely is the theme of *Frankenstein*?
4. Compare and contrast the ingredients of Gothic tales that you learn about here with those used in current-day horror movies and books.

◆ Build Vocabulary

USING RELATED WORDS

Knowing that the word *phantasm* means "supernatural form or shape," define the following terms. If necessary, use a dictionary to help you.

1. phantom   2. phantasmagoric

How do these words relate to the word *fantasy*?

USING THE WORD BANK: Synonyms

In your notebook, write the letter of the word that is closest in meaning to the first word.

1. appendage: (a) accessory, (b) part, (c) addition
2. ungenial: (a) friendly, (b) mean, (c) unhappy
3. acceded: (a) defied, (b) broken, (c) agreed
4. platitude: (a) innovation, (b) cliché, (c) statement
5. phantasm: (a) reality, (b) illusion, (c) creation
6. incitement: (a) deterrent, (b) apparition, (c) motivation

Build **Y**our **P**ortfolio

 ## Idea Bank

Writing

1. **Journal Entry** In a journal entry, explain why "Introduction to *Frankenstein*" does or does not inspire you to read the novel.

2. **Physical Description** What would a monster created by Dr. Frankenstein look like today? Write a page-long description, using sensory images and precise details.

3. **Gothic Tale** Write a Gothic tale (at least two pages long) in which the familiar becomes sinister. Include shocking events and details that will horrify your audience. You might use horror movies you've seen to help you come up with ideas.

Speaking, Listening, and Viewing

4. **Radio Narration** Only a few decades ago, large audiences listened eagerly to tales of horror presented on radio. Think of a horror story you know, and re-create it as a radio drama. **[Performing Arts Link; Media Link]**

5. **Movie Review** View a movie based on *Frankenstein*. Then present a television-style review of the movie to the class. If possible, show segments to support your points. **[Media Link]**

Researching and Representing

6. **Set Design** Research Gothic architecture and create a set for a movie or play in the tradition of Gothic horror stories. The play or movie can be based on a story with which you're familiar, or it can be one you make up. **[Art Link; Social Studies Link]**

7. **Scientific Research** Biogenesis is the doctrine that living organisms develop only from other living organisms. Research biogenesis, and present your findings to the class. **[Science Link]**

Online Activity www.phlit.phschool.com

 ## Guided Writing Lesson

Comparison-and-Contrast Essay

Before reading Shelley's introduction, you probably knew about *Frankenstein* even though you might not have had direct exposure to the story. Write an essay in which you compare and contrast the impressions you had of *Frankenstein* before you read Shelley's "Introduction" with your impressions after reading it. Follow this tip as you develop and draft your essay:

Writing Skills Focus: Organization

A piece of writing should be **organized** in a way that fits the form and purpose of the writing. For example, when you write a comparison-and-contrast essay, you'll want to organize your details by points of comparison. You can either present all the similarities in one section and present the differences in another section or you can focus each paragraph on an aspect of your subject and point out both similarities and differences.

Prewriting To help gather details, use a chart like this one. In one column, list what you thought before you read Shelley's "Introduction." In the other column, list what you thought after reading it.

Before Reading	After Reading

Drafting Using the information in your chart, draft your comparison. Use terms that emphasize comparing and contrasting, such as *similar to* and *contrary to*, to show the relationships among ideas.

Revising Give your paper to a writing partner for feedback on whether your comparisons are clear and well organized.

Guide for Interpreting

Robert Burns *(1759–1796)*

Robert Burns wrote his first verse when he was fifteen. It was a love poem for a girl named Nellie, who was helping the Burns family with the harvest on their farm in Scotland. "Thus with me," Burns later wrote, "began Love and Poesy."

A Poor But Learned Life

Burns was born at Alloway, in Ayrshire. Although his family's poverty prevented him from receiving a formal education, with his father's encouragement he read widely, studying the Bible, Shakespeare, and Alexander Pope on his own. His mother, though herself illiterate, instilled in him a love of Scottish folk songs, legends, and proverbs.

Literary Triumph In 1786, Burns published his first collection of poems through a small local press.

Although the collection, which included "To a Mouse," was successful, Burns didn't come to the attention of the general public until the following year, when *Poems, Chiefly in the Scottish Dialect* was published at Edinburgh. He was invited to the Scottish capital, where he was swept into the social scene and hailed as the "heaven-taught plowman."

A Lasting Contribution Although Burns died prematurely in his thirties, having suffered for years from a weak heart, his brief career resulted in a lasting contribution to literature. Burns's poems are among the most natural and spontaneous ever produced in the English language. Written for the most part in dialect, they are characterized by innocence, simplicity, and honesty. Though some of the poet's work had its origins in folk tunes, "it is not," as James Douglas writes, "easy to tell where the vernacular ends and the personal magic begins."

Joanna Baillie *(1762–1851)*

When Joanna Baillie (bā´ lē) achieved literary fame in 1800 with the publication of a volume of plays, Sir Walter Scott hailed her as "the immortal Joanna." Born in Lanarkshire, Scotland, Baillie moved to London in her early twenties, and spent the rest of her life there.

A Successful Dramatist Baillie is best-known for her plays, including *De Montfort* (1800) and *The Family Legend* (1810). However, she was also a successful poet and essayist who foreshadowed the Romantics by arguing that poetry should focus on naturalness in language and subject matter. Like Robert Burns, she wrote poems in the dialect of her homeland, many of them on nature and rustic manners.

◆ Background for Understanding

CULTURE: ROBERT BURNS'S USE OF LANGUAGE

Before Robert Burns published his poetry, works of literature were almost always modeled on the classics in which structure, grammar, and vocabulary were polished and complex.

Robert Burns ignored these conventions and boldly put poetry in the hands of the people, writing in their language, Scottish dialect, and using

them as subject matter. This use of regional dialect had several effects: It flouted the idea that poems should deal with heroic topics and be written in heroic language, and it celebrated Scottish rural life. Writing in regional language also made the poetry accessible to the ordinary Scottish citizen, not just to scholars.

To a Mouse ♦ To a Louse
♦ Woo'd and Married and A' ♦

♦ *Literature and Your Life*

CONNECT YOUR EXPERIENCE

Your manner of speaking may reveal where you were brought up, your interests, or your education level. As you read the following poems, written in Scottish dialect, think about what the language of the speakers reveals about them.

Journal Writing Jot down in your journal three or four words or phrases that you often use in everyday speech. What, if anything, do they reveal about you?

THEMATIC FOCUS: FANTASY AND REALITY

If language can reveal a person's background, what does the theme of fantasy and reality in Burns's and Baillie's poems reveal about the poets and their culture?

♦ Literary Focus

DIALECT

Dialect is the language, and particularly the speech habits, of a particular social class, region, or group. A dialect may vary from the standard form of a language in grammar, in pronunciation, and in the use of certain expressions.

In literature, dialect helps establish character, mood, and setting. The use of dialect can also give warmth and familiarity to a piece of literature. As you read, think about the ways in which use of dialect enhances the poems' meaning and effect.

♦ Reading Strategy

TRANSLATE DIALECT

The poems in this section are written in Scottish dialect. As you read, **translate dialect** using these strategies.
1. Read footnotes to get definitions of dialect words.
2. Guess the meanings of other words by using the context. (*Cow'rin'* and *tim'rous* help you deduce that *wee* means "small".)
3. Speak words aloud and listen for similarities to standard English words. (Thou need *na* start *awa sae* hasty)
4. Look for similarities between the dialect words and standard English words. (*beastie = beast*)
5. Pay attention to apostrophes, which signal that a letter has been omitted. (*an' = and*; *lea'e = leave*)

♦ Build Vocabulary

WORDS RELATED TO CLOTHING

Both poets help you picture settings and people by using a number of words related to clothing, such as *bonnet* (a woman's hat) and *bodice* (the upper part of a woman's dress). As you read, look for other examples of words related to clothing.

WORD BANK

Before you read, preview this list of words from the poems.

dominion
impudence
winsome
discretion
inconstantly

♦ Grammar and Style

INTERJECTIONS

The speakers in these poems vividly convey feelings by the use of **interjections**, words or phrases used to express emotion. A comma separates a mild interjection from the rest of the sentence, and an exclamation mark follows a stronger interjection. Look at these examples from the poems you're about to read.

O, what a panic's in thy breastie!

But, *och!* I backward cast my e'e

To a Mouse

On Turning Her up in Her Nest with the Plow, November, 1785

Robert Burns

Wee, sleekit,[1] cow'rin', tim'rous beastie,
O, what a panic's in thy breastie!
Thou need na start awa sae hasty,
    Wi' bickering brattle![2]
5 I wad be laith[3] to rin an' chase thee
    Wi' murd'ring pattle![4]

I'm truly sorry man's dominion
Has broken Nature's social union,
An' justifies that ill opinion,
10   Which makes thee startle,
At me, thy poor, earth-born companion,
    An' fellow-mortal!

I doubt na, whyles,[5] but thou may thieve;
What then? poor beastie, thou maun[6] live!
15 A daimen icker in a thrave[7]
    'S a sma' request:
I'll get a blessin' wi' the lave,[8]
    And never miss't!

Thy wee bit housie, too, in ruin!
20 Its silly wa's[9] the win's are strewin'!
An' naething, now, to big[10] a new ane,
    O' foggage[11] green!
An' bleak December's winds ensuin',
    Baith snell[12] an' keen!

25 Thou saw the fields laid bare and waste,
An' weary winter comin' fast,

1. **sleekit:** Sleek.

2. **Wi' . . . brattle:** With a quick pattering sound.
3. **wad be laith:** Would be loath.
4. **pattle:** Paddle for cleaning a plow.

5. **whyles:** At times.
6. **maun:** Must.
7. **A . . . thrave:** An occasional ear of grain in a bundle.
8. **lave:** Rest.

9. **silly wa's:** Feeble walls.
10. **big:** Build.
11. **foggage:** Rough grass.
12. **snell:** Sharp.

An' cozie here, beneath the blast,
　　Thou thought to dwell,
Till crash! the cruel coulter[13] past
30　　Out through thy cell.

That wee bit heap o' leaves an' stibble,
Has cost thee mony a weary nibble!
Now thou's turned out, for a' thy trouble,
　　But[14] house or hald,[15]
35　To thole[16] the winter's sleety dribble,
　　An' cranreuch[17] cauld!

But, Mousie, thou art no thy lane,[18]
In proving foresight may be vain:
The best laid schemes o' mice an' men
40　　Gang aft a-gley,[19]
An' lea'e us nought but grief an' pain,
　　For promised joy.

Still thou art blest, compared wi' me!
The present only toucheth thee:
45　But, och! I backward cast my e'e
　　On prospects drear!
An' forward, though I canna see,
　　I guess an' fear!

13. coulter: Plow blade.

14. But: Without.
15. hald: Property.
16. thole: Withstand.
17. cranreuch (krən´ rəkh): Frost.
18. no thy lane: Not alone.

19. Gang aft a-gley: Go often awry.

◆ **Build Vocabulary**

dominion (də min´ yən) *n*.: Rule; authority

Guide for Responding

◆ *Literature and Your Life*

Reader's Response How would you have reacted to the plight of the mouse? Explain.

Thematic Focus Burns uses fantasy to imagine how the mouse must have felt. How does the speaker balance fantasy with reality in this poem?

☑ **Check Your Comprehension**

1. For what reason does the speaker apologize to the mouse?
2. Why does the speaker say that, compared with him, the mouse is blessed?

◆ **Critical Thinking**

INTERPRET

1. What does the sentiment in lines 13–14 suggest about the speaker's own social code? **[Infer]**
2. (a) What famous line in the poem carries the poem's theme about human life? (b) How would you state this theme in your own words? **[Synthesize]**

APPLY

3. What value do you place on foresight? Explain your answer. **[Evaluate]**

▲ **Critical Viewing** Does this lady's pose and costume link her to the lady in the poem? Explain. **[Connect]**

To a LOUSE

On Seeing One on a Lady's Bonnet at Church

Robert Burns

Ha! whare ye gaun, ye crowlin' ferlie![1]
Your impudence protects you sairly:[2]
I canna say but ye strunt[3] rarely,
    Owre gauze and lace;
5 Though faith! I fear ye dine but sparely
    On sic a place.

Ye ugly, creepin', blastit wonner,[4]
Detested, shunned by saunt an' sinner,
How dare ye set your fit[5] upon her,
10   Sae fine a lady?
Gae somewhere else, and seek your dinner
    On some poor body.

Swith![6] in some beggar's haffet[7] squattle;[8]
There ye may creep, and sprawl, and sprattle[9]
15 Wi' ither kindred, jumping cattle,
    In shoals and nations:
Whare horn nor bane[10] ne'er dare unsettle
    Your thick plantations.

Now haud[11] ye there, ye're out o' sight,
20 Below the fatt'rels,[12] snug an' tight;
Na, faith ye yet![13] ye'll no be right
    Till ye've got on it,
The vera tapmost, tow'ring height
    O' Miss's bonnet.

1. **crowlin' ferlie:** Crawling wonder.
2. **sairly:** Sorely.
3. **strunt:** Strut.

4. **blastit wonner:** Blasted wonder.
5. **fit:** Foot.

6. **swith:** Swift.
7. **haffet:** Locks.
8. **squattle:** Sprawl.
9. **sprattle:** Struggle.

10. **horn nor bane:** Comb made of horn or bone.

11. **haud:** Hold.
12. **fatt'rels:** Ribbon ends.
13. **Na faith ye yet!:** Confound you!

My sooth! right bauld ye set your nose out,
    As plump and gray as onie grozet;[14]
O for some rank, mercurial rozet,[15]
        Or fell,[16] red smeddum,[17]
I'd gie you sic a hearty dose o't,
        Wad dress your droddum![18]

I wad na been surprised to spy
You on an auld wife's flannen toy;[19]
Or aiblins some bit duddie boy,[20]
        On's wyliecoat;[21]
But Miss's fine Lunardi![22] fie,
        How daur ye do't?

O, Jenny, dinna toss your head,
An' set your beauties a' abread![23]
Ye little ken what cursèd speed
        The blastie's[24] makin'!
Thae[25] winks and finger-ends, I dread,
        Are notice takin'!

O wad some Pow'r the giftie gie us
To see oursels as ithers see us!
It wad frae monie a blunder free us
        And foolish notion:
What airs in dress an' gait wad lea'e us,
        And ev'n devotion!

14. **onie grozet** (gräz´ it): Any gooseberry.
15. **rozet** (räz´ it): Rosin.
16. **fell:** Sharp.
17. **smeddum:** Powder.
18. **Wad . . . droddum:** Would put an end to you.
19. **flannen toy:** Flannel cap.
20. **Or . . . boy:** Or perhaps on some little ragged boy.
21. **wyliecoat** (wī´ lē kōt´): Undershirt.
22. **Lunardi:** Balloon-shaped bonnet, named for Vincenzo Lunardi, a balloonist of the late 1700's.
23. **abread:** Abroad.
24. **blastie's:** Creature's.
25. **Thae:** Those.

◆ **Build Vocabulary**

impudence (im´ pyo͞o dəns) *n.*: Lack of shame; rudeness

Guide for Responding

◆ Literature and Your Life

Reader's Response What do you think of a louse (singular of lice) as a subject for a poem?

Thematic Focus What elements of fantasy does this poem contain? What elements of reality?

Questions for Research Generate questions that would help you research the Scottish traditions that shaped Burns and his poetry.

☑ Check Your Comprehension

1. (a) What is the louse doing? (b) What does the speaker command it to do instead?
2. (a) Whom does the speaker address in the seventh stanza? (b) Against what does he warn her?

◆ Critical Thinking

INTERPRET

1. (a) What is the louse's crime? (b) What does the speaker have in common with those he seems to associate with the louse? **[Analyze]**
2. (a) What conclusions can you draw about Jenny's character? (b) What evidence supports these conclusions? **[Draw Conclusions]**

EVALUATE

3. In "To a Louse," Burns pokes fun at vanity in society. Do you agree with his standpoint? Explain. **[Make a Judgment]**

Woo'd and Married and A'

Joanna Baillie

The bride she is <u>winsome</u> and bonny,
  Her hair it is snooded[1] sae sleek,
And faithfu' and kind is her Johnny,
  Yet fast fa' the tears on her cheek.
5 New pearlins[2] are cause of her sorrow,
    New pearlins and plenishing[3] too;
The bride that has a' to borrow
    Has e'en right mickle[4] ado.
      Woo'd and married and a'!
10   Woo'd and married and a'!
  Is na' she very weel aff
      To be woo'd and married at a'?

Her mither then hastily spak,
  "The Lassie is glaikit[5] wi' pride;
15 In my pouch I had never a plack[6]
  On the day when I was a bride.
E'en tak to your wheel and be clever,
  And draw out your thread in the sun;
The gear[7] that is gifted it never
20 Will last like the gear that is won.
      Woo'd and married and a'!
      Wi' havins and toucher[8] sae sma'!
  I think ye are very weel aff
      To be woo'd and married at a'."

25 "Toot, toot," quo' her gray-headed faither,
  "She's less o' a bride than a bairn,[9]
She's ta'en like a cout[10] frae the heather,
  Wi' sense and <u>discretion</u> to learn.
Half husband, I trow, and half daddy,
30 As humor <u>inconstantly</u> leans,
The chiel maun be patient and steady[11]

1. **snooded:** Bound up with a ribbon.

2. **pearlins:** Lace trimmings.
3. **plenishing:** Furnishings.
4. **mickle:** Much.

5. **glaikit:** Foolish.
6. **plack:** Farthing; a small coin equal to one fourth of a penny.

7. **gear:** Wealth or goods.

8. **havins and toucher:** Possessions and dowry.

9. **bairn:** Child.
10. **cout:** Colt.

11. **The chiel maun . . . steady:** The man must be patient and steady.

▲ Critical Viewing
Compare and contrast the setting and costumes in this painting with the scene described in Joanna Baillie's poem.
[Compare and Contrast]

That yokes wi' a mate in her teens.
    A kerchief sae douce[12] and sae neat
    O'er her locks that the wind used to blaw!
35 I'm baith like to laugh and to greet[13]
    When I think of her married at a'!"

Then out spak the wily bridegroom,
    Weel waled[14] were his wordies, I ween,
"I'm rich, though my coffer be toom,[15]
40   Wi' the blinks o' your bonny blue e'en.[16]
I'm prouder o' thee by my side,
    Though thy ruffles or ribbons be few,
Than if Kate o' the Croft were my bride
    Wi' purfles[17] and pearlins enow.
45   Dear and dearest of ony!
    Ye're woo'd and buikit[18] and a'!
And do ye think scorn o' your Johnny,
And grieve to be married at a'?"

She turn'd, and she blush'd, and she smiled,
50   And she looked sae bashfully down;
The pride o' her heart was beguiled,
    And she played wi' the sleeves o' her gown.
She twirled the tag o' her lace,
    And she nipped her boddice sae blue,
55 Syne blinkit sae sweet in his face,
    And aff like a maukin[19] she flew.
    Woo'd and married and a'!
Wi' Johnny to roose[20] her and a'!
She thinks hersel very weel aff
60   To be woo'd and married at a'!

12. **douce:** Respectable.
13. **greet:** Weep.

14. **waled:** Chosen.
15. **toom:** Empty.
16. **e'en:** Eyes.

17. **purfles:** Embroidered trimmings.
18. **buikit:** "Booked"; entered as married in the official registry.

19. **maukin:** Hare.

20. **roose:** Praise.

◆ **Build Vocabulary**

winsome
(win´ səm) adj.:
Having a charming, attractive appearance or manner

discretion
(di skresh´ ən) n.:
Good judgment; prudence

inconstantly
(in kän´ stənt lē) adv.: Changeably; in a fickle way

Guide for Responding

◆ Literature and Your Life

Reader's Response What advice might you offer the bride before her wedding? Explain.

Thematic Focus The characters all combine fantasy and reality in different ways. Which character is your favorite, and why?

☑ Check Your Comprehension

1. Why is the bride unhappy at the beginning of the poem?
2. Which speaker succeeds in changing the bride's outlook?

◆ Critical Thinking

INTERPRET
1. How would you describe the personality of the bridegroom? Support your answer with evidence from the fourth stanza. **[Support]**
2. Judging from the final stanza, do you think the marriage will be a happy one? Explain. **[Draw Conclusions]**

APPLY
3. If the bridegroom had remained silent, what do you think the outcome would have been? Explain. **[Hypothesize]**

Guide for Responding (continued)

◆ Literary Focus

DIALECT

Dialect, the speech habits and patterns of a specific group, class, or region, contributes to the character, tone, and setting of a literary work. Robert Burns and Joanna Baillie were two of the first poets to write using the Scottish dialect of English, incorporating its own unique grammar, pronunciation, and vocabulary. By doing so, they invested their poems with a warmth and familiarity that was lacking in poems of classical style.

1. (a) What does the use of dialect in the poems by Burns suggest about the speaker's social station? (b) What does dialect contribute to the setting of Joanna Baillie's "Woo'd and Married and A' "?

2. Like standard language, dialects of a language follow patterns. Find at least two examples in "To a Mouse" of the following pronunciation rules for Scottish English: (a) Final consonants are dropped. (b) The letter *o* is replaced by either *ae* or *a*.

3. How would the effect of these poems have been different if they had been written in standard English?

◆ Reading Strategy

TRANSLATE DIALECT

The regional dialect in which these poems were written may seem very foreign to non-Scots readers. **Translating dialect** allows you to understand the meaning and appreciate the unique flavor of poems such as these. Strategies such as using context clues, looking for similarities in spelling and sound, and reading footnotes help in the translation process. For example, using these strategies, you may translate the line "Wee, sleekit, cow'rin', tim'rous beastie" as "small, sleek, crouching, timid beast."

1. Choose one stanza from a Burns or Baillie poem and translate the stanza into standard English.

2. List words in dialect that appear in both poems and their equivalents in standard English.

◆ Build Vocabulary

USING WORDS RELATED TO CLOTHING

"To a Louse" and "Woo'd and Married and A' " contain several references to clothing and accessories, some of which are familiar to modern readers, some of which are not. For example, *bonnet* is still in use today, but *fatt'rels*, ribbon ends, is not. Explain the meaning of each word below, and tell whether it is still in use today.

1. wyliecoat
2. kerchief
3. boddice (bodice)
4. Lunardi
5. gown

USING THE WORD BANK: Synonyms

In your notebook, write the letter of the term that is the best synonym of the first word.

1. dominion: (a) ability, (b) rule, (c) pride
2. impudence: (a) rudeness, (b) shyness, (c) test
3. winsome: (a) competitive, (b) bold, (c) attractive
4. discretion: (a) disappointment, (b) good judgment, (c) gratitude
5. inconstantly: (a) changeably, (b) emptily, (c) sadly

◆ Grammar and Style

INTERJECTIONS

The speakers in "To a Mouse" and "To a Louse" use **interjections**, words or phrases expressing emotion, that give the poems a conversational feel. A comma separates a mild interjection from the rest of the sentence. An exclamation mark follows a stronger interjection.

Practice Identify the interjection in each line and punctuate the sentence correctly on your paper.
1. But och I backward cast my e'e
2. What then poor beastie thou maun live!
3. My sooth right bauld yet set your nose out,
4. O Jenny dinna toss your head,
5. Though faith I fear ye dine but sparely

Writing Application Write a short paragraph about a funny incident. In it, use at least two interjections, punctuated correctly.

Build Your Portfolio

Idea Bank

Writing

1. **Advice to the Newlyweds** Write a brief letter to the couple in "Woo'd and Married and A'," giving them advice on married life.

2. **Comparison and Contrast** Reread "To a Mouse" and "To a Louse." Write a short paper, comparing and contrasting the poems' messages and tones.

3. **Response to Criticism** William Hazlitt wrote, "Life is the art of being well deceived." How do you think Burns would respond to this statement? Write an essay in which you present your views. Support your points with details from the poems.

Speaking, Listening, and Viewing

4. **Oral Interpretation** With a partner, choose one of these poems and practice reading it aloud. When you are comfortable with the poem, read it aloud to the class. **[Performing Arts Link]**

5. **Lecture** Give an academic lecture on the life and poetry of Robert Burns. Research and write up your lecture in note form. Then present your lecture to the class.

Researching and Representing

6. **Comic Strip** Using the situation in "To a Mouse" as a springboard, create a comic strip in which the mouse has a dialogue with the human who has disturbed its nest. **[Art Link]**

7. **Multimedia Presentation** Although united with England since 1707, Scots have always been proud of their distinctive land, history, language, and culture. Assemble a multimedia presentation about Scotland that includes photographs, recordings, and maps. **[Social Studies Link]**

Online Activity www.phlit.phschool.com

Guided Writing Lesson

Scene With Dialogue

Although perfectly understandable to a native of Scotland, poems in Scottish dialect, like the ones in this section, are difficult for others to understand. Write a scene with dialogue between two people who are having a communication problem due to specialized language, slang, or dialect. At the end of your dialogue, add a glossary in which you list and define all the specialized or unfamiliar words or phrases.

Writing Skills Focus: Clear Beginning, Middle, and End

Although organizational structures vary from work to work, all types of literature contain a basic structure: **a beginning, middle,** and **end**.

As you write your scene with dialogue, create a beginning, in which the audience meets the characters; a middle, in which the conflict or problem develops; and an end, in which the scene is concluded and loose ends tied up.

Use the following strategies as you write your scene.

Prewriting Before you begin to write, plan how the scene will begin, proceed, and end. Think up two characters, and list and define at least five jargon terms that one character will speak in dialogue. Later, these terms will become glossary entries.

Drafting Draft your scene, showing how the characters meet, what happens as they speak, and how the meeting ends. Use the list of slang or jargon words in the dialogue of one character, and create a glossary defining those terms.

Revising With a partner, read your scene through. Be sure that your scene has a clear beginning, middle, and end. Check the glossary of slang or jargon terms for errors in definition and mistakes in spelling.

Guide for Interpreting

William Blake (1757–1827)

"I must create a system or be enslaved by another man's." So spoke William Blake, an artist and poet whose work defied all the conventions of the time.

Blake was a truly original thinker, claiming to find his inspiration from mystical visions.

Blake's visions began early, when, at the age of four, he suddenly began to scream because he thought he saw God at his window. Four years later, while working in the fields, Blake said he saw a tree filled with angels. Blake's parents, who were followers of the mystical teachings of Emanuel Swedenborg, a Swedish philosopher, inventor, and spiritualist, believed that their son had a "gift of vision" and did all they could to nurture this gift.

Finding His Way Blake's father was a poor Londoner, with a small hosiery shop. He did not send his son to school, choosing instead to educate him at home. By the age of twelve, the boy was already highly educated and wrote some of the simple, eloquent poems that became part of a collection entitled *Poetical Sketches* (1783). Because he also showed artistic talent, Blake became an engraver's apprentice and then went on to study at the Royal Academy.

Formal study did not last long, however. Rebelling against all the artistic conventions of the Academy, Blake left and set up his own print shop. He was to live most of his life eking out a poor living as an engraver, barely making enough to support his writing and his artistic pursuits.

Innocence and Experience

When Blake was thirty-two, he published *Songs of Innocence*, a series of poems expressing deep spiritual and philosophical insights that he illustrated himself. Five years later, having grown disillusioned and no longer believing in the possibility of easy human perfection, he wrote *Songs of Experience*, which explored the darker side of life. Taken together, these two collections seem to be saying that true purity and innocence is impossible without experience and that all opposites depend upon each other to exist.

An Unrecognized Genius

Unfortunately, Blake's talent was never recognized by his peers or by the public during his lifetime. Yet, while living only slightly above the poverty level, Blake spent his seventy years in constant creative activity. Many years after his death, his work finally achieved recognition and Blake came to be regarded as one of the most important poets of his time.

◆ Background for Understanding

HUMANITIES: BLAKE AS AN ARTIST

Blake illustrated his poems with striking, integrated designs. These illustrations seemed to swirl through the words and become part of their meaning. No one fully understands Blake's method of creating illustrated pages. It is thought that he drew words and pictures on a copper plate, using a liquid that could not be eaten away by acid. Then he applied acid that would eat away the areas of uncovered copper. The raised surfaces that were left could be inked. Finally, he hand-colored the page using water colors. Blake claimed that many of the images he drew as illustrations were likenesses of his inner visions. They had a childlike feeling and were very different from the strict classical styles of the time.

Journal Writing Note the expression on the tiger's face on p. 599. Why do you think Blake made the face look the way it does?

The Lamb ◆ The Tyger
The Chimney Sweeper ◆ Infant Sorrow

◆ *Literature and Your Life*

CONNECT YOUR EXPERIENCE

When childhood beliefs, such as the existence of the tooth fairy, are proved untrue, the former believer can become mistrustful or even sad. However, the learning experience may lead to a deeper understanding of how the world works. In "The Tyger," William Blake re-explores from a more mature stance a subject he explored in an earlier poem, "The Lamb."

THEMATIC FOCUS: FANTASY AND REALITY

The eighteenth century into which Blake was born valued reason and classical forms. Blake, on the other hand, valued imagination, intuition, and spirituality. As you read, notice how Blake invests ordinary subjects, such as a lamb and tiger, with elements of fantasy.

◆ Reading Strategy

USE VISUALS AS A KEY TO MEANING

When you read any literature that is accompanied by illustrations, you can **use the visuals as a key to meaning** by looking closely at the details of the illustrations and thinking about how they support or add to the author's words. For example, illustrations accompanying a novel might help you picture the characters or fill in details about the characters' personalities.

William Blake intended his illustrations to help convey the underlying meaning of his poems. Look at Blake's illustrations. What do they add to the details in the poems?

◆ Grammar and Style

COMMONLY CONFUSED WORDS: *RISE* AND *RAISE*

In "The Chimney Sweeper," you'll encounter the verb *rise*, which means "to get up." It is sometimes confused with the verb *raise*, which means "to lift or elevate." Notice how these two words are used in the following examples:

Present: They *rise* upon clouds, and sport in the wind.
Past: And so Tom awoke and we *rose* in the dark.
Past Participle: We had *risen* together yesterday.
Present: I *raise* my hand when I'm ready.
Past: They *raised* the flag on the pole.
Past Participle: We had *raised* a strong family.

◆ Literary Focus

SYMBOLS

Throughout literature, you'll encounter **symbols,** which are words, images, or ideas that stand for something else. Often, a symbol is something tangible, or solid, that stands for and helps readers to understand something intangible, like an emotion. Look at this line from "The Chimney Sweeper."

> And wash in a river, and
> shine in the Sun.

This line contains two actions that are religious symbols. To wash in the river symbolizes baptism, in which one is cleansed of sin; to "shine in the Sun" is to bask in the glory of God.

As you read, look for other symbols and analyze their meaning.

◆ Build Vocabulary

LATIN WORD ROOTS: *-spir-*

In "The Tyger," you'll encounter the word *aspire,* meaning "to yearn or seek after." *Aspire* contains the Latin root *-spir-*, meaning "breath" or "life." When you aspire to something, you live to reach it.

WORD BANK

Before you read, preview this list of words from the poems.

| vales |
| symmetry |
| aspire |

The Lamb

WILLIAM BLAKE

Little Lamb who made thee
Dost thou know who made thee
Gave thee life & bid thee feed.
By the stream & o'er the mead;
5 Gave thee clothing of delight,
Softest clothing wooly bright;
Gave thee such a tender voice,
Making all the <u>vales</u> rejoice!
Little Lamb who made thee
10 Dost thou know who made thee

Little Lamb I'll tell thee,
Little Lamb I'll tell thee!
He is called by thy name,
For he calls himself a Lamb:
15 He is meek & he is mild,
He became a little child:
I a child & thou a lamb,
We are called by his name.
Little Lamb God bless thee.
20 Little Lamb God bless thee.

From a manuscript of "The Lamb" by William Blake, Lessing J. Rosenwald Collection, Library of Congress, Washington, D.C.

◆ **Build Vocabulary**

vales (vāls) *n*.: Hollows or depressions in the ground

symmetry (sim′ə trē) *n*.: Beauty resulting from balance of forms

aspire (ə spīr′) *v*.: Rise high, yearn or seek after

▲ Critical Viewing What view of nature is expressed by the style of Blake's drawing? [Infer]

Guide for Responding

◆ Literature and Your Life

Reader's Response Is your response to the lamb similar to Blake's response?

☑ Check Your Comprehension

1. What questions does the speaker ask in the first stanza of "The Lamb"?
2. Who is the speaker in this poem?

◆ Critical Thinking

INTERPRET
1. How would you sum up the characteristics of the lamb? [Interpret]
2. What are the characteristics of the creator of the lamb? [Draw Conclusions]

APPLY
3. What kind of images would you use to represent the words? [Modify]

The TYGER

WILLIAM BLAKE

From a manuscript of "The Tyger" by William Blake, The Metropolitan Museum of Art

▲ **Critical Viewing** Compare and contrast the tiger's expression with the poem's image of the animal. **[Compare and Contrast]**

Tyger Tyger, burning bright,
In the forests of the night;
What immortal hand or eye,
Could frame thy fearful <u>symmetry</u>?

5   In what distant deeps or skies
Burnt the fire of thine eyes!
On what wings dare he <u>aspire</u>?
What the hand, dare seize the fire?

And what shoulder, & what art,
10 Could twist the sinews of thy heart?
And when thy heart began to beat,
What dread hand? & what dread feet?

What the hammer? what the chain,
In what furnace was thy brain?
15 What the anvil? what dread grasp,
Dare its deadly terrors clasp?

When the stars threw down their spears
And water'd heaven with their tears:
Did he smile his work to see?
20 Did he who made the Lamb make thee?

Tyger, Tyger burning bright,
In the forests of the night:
What immortal hand or eye,
Dare frame thy fearful symmetry?

Guide for Responding

◆ *Literature and Your Life*

Reader's Response How does this poem set you thinking about life's mysteries? Explain.

☑ Check Your Comprehension

1. What question is asked in the first stanza of "The Tyger"?
2. Is this question ever answered?

◆ Critical Thinking

INTERPRET
1. What kind of creature does Blake portray the tiger to be? **[Interpret]**
2. Explain lines 15 and 16. **[Infer]**

EVALUATE
3. Do "The Lamb" and "The Tyger" cover the extremes of the human spirit effectively? **[Assess]**

The Chimney Sweeper

WILLIAM BLAKE

▲ **Critical Viewing** Does Blake portray children's working conditions in nineteenth-century England as this artist does? Explain. **[Compare and Contrast]**

When my mother died I was very young,
And my father sold me while yet my tongue,
Could scarcely cry weep weep weep weep.
So your chimneys I sweep & in soot I sleep.

5 There's little Tom Dacre, who cried when his head
That curl'd like a lambs back, was shav'd, so I said.
Hush Tom never mind it, for when your head's bare,
You know that the soot cannot spoil your white hair.

And so he was quiet, & that very night,
10 As Tom was a sleeping he had such a sight,
That thousands of sweepers Dick, Joe, Ned & Jack
Were all of them lock'd up in coffins of black

And by came an Angel who had a bright key,
And he open'd the coffins & set them all free.
15 Then down a green plain leaping laughing they run
And wash in a river and shine in the Sun.

Then naked & white, all their bags left behind,
They rise upon clouds, and sport in the wind.
And the Angel told Tom if he'd be a good boy,
20 He'd have God for his father & never want joy.

And so Tom awoke and we rose in the dark
And got with our bags & our brushes to work.
Tho' the morning was cold, Tom was happy & warm,
So if all do their duty, they need not fear harm.

Infant

WILLIAM BLAKE

Sorrow

My mother groand![1] my father wept.
Into the dangerous world I leapt,
Helpless, naked, piping loud;
Like a fiend hid in a cloud.

5 Struggling in my father's hands,
Striving against my swaddling bands;
Bound and weary, I thought best
To sulk upon my mother's breast.

---

1. **groand:** groaned; an example of Blake's often
eccentric spelling.

Guide for Responding

◆ *Literature and Your Life*

Reader's Response Which poem's portrayal
of life do you agree with more? Why?

Thematic Focus Do these poems come closer
to "fantasy" or "reality"? Explain.

☑ Check Your Comprehension

1. How does the child in the first stanza of "The
   Chimney Sweeper" become a chimney sweep?
2. What is the dream that gives the chimney
   sweeper hope to go on?
3. In "Infant Sorrow," what are the reactions of the
   parents to the birth of the child?
4. How does the child react upon first being born,
   and how does this reaction change?

◆ Critical Thinking

INTERPRET

1. What social commentary do you find in
   "The Chimney Sweeper"? **[Interpret]**
2. In "Infant Sorrow," aside from tight "swaddling
   bands," in what larger sense is the speaker
   "bound"? **[Interpret]**
3. What conclusions about Blake's ideas on the
   meaning of life can you draw from these poems?
   [Draw Conclusions]

COMPARE LITERARY WORKS

4. How does each poem inspire readers to
   rethink assumptions about life and death?
   [Compare and Contrast]

Guide for Responding (continued)

◆ Literary Focus

SYMBOLS

Blake's poems are filled with **symbols**—words, images, or ideas that have an underlying meaning. In "The Chimney Sweeper," for example, Tom Dacre's hair, which was like a "lamb's back," symbolizes, or represents, youthful innocence. When it is shaved, it is a symbolic loss of his innocence and youth.

1. What two things does the lamb symbolize?
2. In "The Tyger," there are several images that pertain to fire: "burning bright," "fire of thine eyes," "seize the fire." Taken together, what might these images symbolize?
3. "Infant Sorrow" contains allusions to the Christian belief that as a result of Adam and Eve's sin, life is painful and full of struggles. How does this knowledge deepen your understanding of the work?

◆ Grammar and Style

COMMONLY CONFUSED WORDS: *RISE* AND *RAISE*

The verbs *rise* and *raise* are often confused. The forms of the verb *rise*, which means "to get up," are *rise, rose,* and *risen.* The forms of the verb *raise,* which means "to lift or elevate," are *raise, raised,* and *raised.*

Practice On your paper, write the present tense of each of the verbs used in these sentences.
1. Most mornings I rose early.
2. Hearing a sound, the bird raised its head.
3. Ever since the sun came out, the mist has risen from the lake.

Writing Application In your notebook, rewrite these sentences, correcting each improperly used verb form.

> The chimney sweepers raised early. They rose their brooms to their shoulders and went out to the street. It was still early, and the sun had not raised.

◆ Reading Strategy

USE VISUALS AS A KEY TO MEANING

Look at the illustrations accompanying "The Lamb" and "The Tyger," and consider how or whether they add to the poems' meanings.

1. How would you describe the mood of the illustration accompanying "The Lamb"? How does it relate to the poem's mood?
2. How does the tiger in Blake's illustration compare to the tiger described in the poem?

◆ Build Vocabulary

USING THE LATIN ROOT *-spir-*

The following words contain the Latin root *-spir-,* which means "breath" or "life." Define each word, incorporating the meaning of the root into your definition.
1. respiration 2. expire 3. inspire 4. spirit

USING THE WORD BANK: Context

Use words from the Word Bank to replace italicized words in the following sentences.
1. They traveled through *valleys* and over hills.
2. The *balanced forms* of the animal's body made it look graceful and powerful.
3. The student *desired* to attend a top college.

Beyond Literature

Cultural Connection

Blake and His Time Although Blake was a poet and painter absorbed in his own visions, he was not oblivious to the events of his time. His portrayal of Tom Dacre in "The Chimney Sweeper" indicates his concern for working conditions in Britain. The Industrial Revolution slowly but steadily transformed the daily lives of the people from a rural agrarian society, in which farmers used simple tools and made their own food and clothing, to an urban industrial society, in which workers operated complex machines for long hours and little pay, lived in crowded conditions, and bought goods.

Activity How was daily life in industrial Britain similar to and different from life today?

Build Your Portfolio

 ## Idea Bank

Writing

1. **Journal Entry** Write a journal entry about the wonders of childhood. Discuss the kinds of innocence that you value and hope will never be lost.

2. **Research Report** Blake's poem "The Chimney Sweeper" deals with a serious problem of the time—child labor. Do research on child labor in the nineteenth century and prepare a written report. **[Social Studies Link]**

3. **Response to Criticism** Northrop Frye has written of Blake's poetry: "Much of Blake's poetry is for the common reader, and will not mislead him. The lyrics speak for themselves . . ." Write a short paper agreeing or disagreeing with this statement. Support your argument with details from the poems.

Speaking, Listening, and Viewing

4. **Blake Reading** Hold a poetry reading in which you and classmates read aloud several of Blake's poems. **[Performing Arts Link]**

5. **Setting Blake to Music** Several composers and song writers have set Blake's simple poems to music. Choose one or two of his shorter poems and do the same. **[Performing Arts Link]**

Researching and Representing

6. **Advertisement** Even as far back as Blake's time, advertisers used symbols to lend a certain aura or to build associations with their products. Choose a product and create an advertisement for it centered on a single symbol. **[Career Link]**

7. **Illuminated Poem** Like Blake, write a poem and create an illustration that captures its meaning. As an alternative, you may want to create an illustration for one of Blake's poems. **[Art Link]**

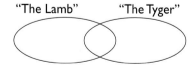

 ## Guided Writing Lesson

Comparative Analysis

"The Lamb," which is from *Songs of Innocence* and "The Tyger," which is from *Songs of Experience*, explore the same subject from different points of view. Write a comparative analysis in which you explore the similarities and differences between the two poems and analyze how the view presented in each poem relates to the period of Blake's life in which it was written. Keep in mind the following tip as you develop your essay.

Writing Skills Focus: Placement for Emphasis

Emphasize your main point by placing a clear, concise statement of your thesis both at the beginning and at the end of your essay. By starting with your thesis statement, you'll make your point clear to readers from the beginning. By ending with a restatement of your thesis, you'll leave a lasting impression on your readers' minds.

Prewriting Start by reviewing the information about Blake and his work in the Guide for Interpreting on page 596. Then review the two poems. Use a Venn diagram like this one to record similarities and differences in the views the two poems present. Jot down details and passages from the poems that illustrate the views presented.

"The Lamb"   "The Tyger"

Drafting After stating your thesis in your opening paragraph, present evidence to back up your position. Cite passages and details from both poems.

Revising Carefully review your essay. Check to see that you've organized your ideas in a way that makes sense and that you've thoroughly supported your thesis.

CONNECTIONS TO WORLD LITERATURE
The Oval Portrait

Thematic Connection

FANTASY AND REALITY

Although the Romantic movement led the writers in this section to focus on the realities of the common man, it also inspired them to explore more fantastic realms. For example, William Blake wrote visionary poetry like "The Tyger," in which he seems to travel to the ends of the universe seeking answers to his questions: "In what distant deep skies/Burnt the fire of thine eyes!" Mary Shelley goes on an even stranger journey in her novel *Frankenstein,* in which she shows what goes wrong when a scientist attempts to create life itself.

Her novel has its roots in the Gothic tradition, which combined supernatural events with historical settings. The popularity of Gothic stories like *Frankenstein* reached beyond England into other cultures and countries. American writer Edgar Allan Poe, for example, is considered a master of Gothic writing.

THE MASTER OF HORROR

In stories like "The Oval Portrait," Poe begins with what seems to be realistic description. However, he soon crosses the border between reality and fantasy so that you become disoriented and subject to feelings of anxiety and fear.

THE LURE OF THE UNKNOWN

Stories and movies that echo the Gothic tradition of mystery and the supernatural are still popular today. A great part of their fascination lies in their plausibility. This fine line between fantasy and reality keeps us in suspense and wondering, "Could this have really happened?" As you read "The Oval Portrait," try to identify where the author crosses from reality to fantasy.

EDGAR ALLAN POE
(1809–1849)

Poe's real-life troubles must have inspired his dark imaginings. An orphan before he was three years old, he was taken in by the Allans, a prosperous family in Richmond, Virginia. However, Poe quarreled with his foster father, John Allan, and was disowned. When Poe was expelled by the University of Virginia, he enrolled at West Point, where he was court-martialed while still a cadet.

Poe's writing career was a mixture of literary success and financial failure. He won recognition as a poet, critic, and short story writer while earning a meager living as a magazine editor in Richmond, Philadelphia, and New York. His earnings were hardly enough to support his young wife, Virginia Clemm, and his mother-in-law.

Virginia's early death from tuberculosis was a blow from which Poe never recovered. He himself died two years afterward.

The Oval Portrait

EDGAR ALLAN POE

The chateau into which my valet had ventured to make forcible entrance, rather than permit me, in my desperately wounded condition, to pass a night in the open air, was one of those piles of commingled gloom and grandeur which have so long frowned among the Apennines,[1] not less in fact than in the fancy of Mrs. Radcliffe.[2] To all appearance it had been temporarily and very lately abandoned. We established ourselves in one of the smallest and least sumptuously furnished apartments. It lay in a remote turret of the building. Its decorations were rich, yet tattered and antique. Its walls were hung with tapestry and bedecked with manifold and multiform armorial trophies, together with an unusually great number of very spirited modern paintings in frames of rich golden arabesque.[3] In these paintings, which depended from the walls not only in their main surfaces, but in very many nooks which the bizarre architecture of the chateau rendered necessary—in these paintings my incipient delirium, perhaps, had caused me to take deep interest; so that I bade Pedro to close the heavy shutters of the room—since it was already night—to light the tongues[4] of a tall candelabrum which stood by the head of my bed—and to throw open far and wide the fringed curtains of black velvet which enveloped the bed itself. I wished all this done that I might resign myself, if not to sleep, at least alternately to the contemplation of these

▲ **Critical Viewing** Does this portrait, like the one in the story, capture "Life" itself? Explain. **[Connect]**

Elizabeth Beale Bordley, Gilbert Stuart, Courtesy of the Museum of American Art of the Pennsylvania Academy of the Fine Arts, Philadelphia, Bequest of Elizabeth Mifflin

---

1. **Appennines** (ap´ ə nīnz): Mountain range located in Italy.
2. **Mrs. Radcliffe:** Ann Radcliffe (1764–1823), English novelist.

3. **arabesque** (ar´ ə besk´): Complex and elaborate design.
4. **tongues** (tuŋz): Candles.

pictures, and the perusal of a small volume which had been found upon the pillow, and which purported to criticize and describe them.

Long—long I read—and devoutly, devotedly I gazed. Rapidly and gloriously the hours flew by, and the deep midnight came. The position of the candelabrum displeased me, and outreaching my hand with difficulty, rather than disturb my slumbering valet, I placed it so as to throw its rays more fully upon the book.

But the action produced an effect altogether unanticipated. The rays of the numerous candles (for there were many) now fell within a niche of the room which had hitherto been thrown into deep shade by one of the bedposts. I thus saw in vivid light a picture all unnoticed before. It was the portrait of a young girl just ripening into womanhood. I glanced at the painting hurriedly, and then closed my eyes. Why I did this was not at first apparent even to my own perception. But while my lids remained thus shut, I ran over in mind my reason for so shutting them. It was an impulsive movement to gain time for thought—to make sure that my vision had not deceived me—to calm and subdue my fancy for a more sober and more certain gaze. In a very few moments I again looked fixedly at the painting.

That I now saw aright I could not and would not doubt; for the first flashing of the candles upon that canvas had seemed to dissipate the dreamy stupor which was stealing over my senses, and to startle me at once into waking life.

The portrait, I have already said, was that of a young girl. It was a mere head and shoulders, done in what is technically termed a *vignette*[5] manner; much in the style of the favorite heads of Sully.[6] The arms, the bosom and even the ends of the radiant hair, melted imperceptibly into the vague yet deep shadow which formed the background of the whole. The frame was oval, richly gilded and filigreed

in *Moresque*.[7] As a thing of art nothing could be more admirable than the painting itself. But it could have been neither the execution of the work, nor the immortal beauty of the countenance, which had so suddenly and so vehemently moved me. Least of all, could it have been that my fancy, shaken from its half slumber, had mistaken the head for that of a living person. I saw at once that the peculiarities of the design, of the *vignetting*, and of the frame, must have instantly dispelled such idea—must have prevented even its momentary entertainment. Thinking earnestly upon these points, I remained, for an hour perhaps, half sitting, half reclining, with my vision riveted upon the portrait. At length, satisfied with the true secret of its effect, I fell back within the bed. I had found the spell of the picture in an absolute *life-likeliness* of expression, which at first startled, finally confounded, subdued and appalled me. With deep and reverent awe I replaced the candelabrum in its former position. The cause of my deep agitation being thus shut from view, I sought eagerly the volume which discussed the paintings and their histories. Turning to the number which designated the oval portrait, I there read the vague and quaint words which follow:

'She was a maiden of rarest beauty, and not more lovely than full of glee. And evil was the hour when she saw, and loved, and wedded the painter. He, passionate, studious, austere, and having already a bride in his Art; she a maiden of rarest beauty, and not more lovely than full of glee: all light and smiles, and frolicksome as the young fawn: loving and cherishing all things: hating only the Art which was her rival: dreading only the pallet and brushes and other untoward instruments which deprived her of the countenance of her lover. It was thus a terrible thing for this lady to hear the painter speak of his desire to portray even his young bride. But she was humble and obedient, and sat meekly for many weeks in the dark high turret-chamber where the light dripped upon the pale canvas only from overhead. But he, the painter, took glory in his work, which

---

5. *vignette* (vin yet´) *n.*: Picture or photograph with no definite border.
6. *Sully:* Thomas Sully (1783–1872), American painter born in England.

---

7. *Moresque* (mô resk´): Decoration characterized by intricate tracery and bright colors.

went on from hour to hour and from day to day. And he was a passionate, and wild and moody man, who became lost in reveries; so that he *would* not see that the light which fell so ghastlily in that lone turret withered the health and the spirits of his bride, who pined visibly to all but him. Yet she smiled on and still on, uncomplainingly, because she saw that the painter, (who had high renown,) took a fervid and burning pleasure in his task, and wrought day and night to depict her who so loved him, yet who grew daily more dispirited and weak. And in sooth[8] some who beheld the portrait spoke of its resemblance in low words, as of a mighty marvel, and a proof not less of the power of the painter than of his deep love for her whom he depicted so surpassingly well. But at length, as the labor drew nearer to its conclusion, there were admitted none into the turret; for the painter had grown wild with the ardor of his work, and turned his eyes from the canvas rarely, even to regard the countenance of his wife. And he *would* not see that the tints which he spread upon the canvas were drawn from the cheeks of her who sat beside him. And when many weeks had passed, and but little remained to do, save one brush upon the mouth and one tint upon the eye, the spirit of the lady again flickered up as the flame within the socket of the lamp. And then the brush was given, and then the tint was placed; and, for one moment, the painter stood entranced before the work which he had wrought; but in the next, while he yet gazed, he grew tremulous and very pallid, and aghast, and crying with a loud voice, "This is indeed *Life* itself!" turned suddenly to regard his beloved:—*She was dead!*'

---

8. **sooth** (sōōth): Truth; fact.

Guide for Responding

◆ *Literature and Your Life*

Reader's Response Were you surprised by the ending of this story? Why or why not?

Thematic Focus In what way did the artist who painted the portrait go too far?

Reading Across Cultures If you like highly imaginative tales like "The Oval Portrait," you might want to read some works by Latin American author Gabriel García Marquez.

☑ Check Your Comprehension

1. Why does the narrator's valet break into the chateau?
2. Briefly describe the chateau's appearance.
3. (a) What is the narrator's first reaction to the portrait of the young girl? (b) What causes this reaction?
4. What is the relationship between the subject of the painting and the artist?
5. What happens to the subject when the artist finally finishes the painting?

◆ Critical Thinking

INTERPRET

1. (a) In what way does "The Oval Portrait" contain two stories? (b) How does the first story serve as an introduction to the second? **[Analyze]**
2. What is surprising about the artist's remark in the final sentence? **[Interpret]**
3. This story was originally called "Life in Death." Do you prefer this title to "The Oval Portrait"? Explain. **[Support]**
4. What statement is Poe making about the relationship between reality and fantasy, life and art? **[Draw Conclusions]**

APPLY

5. Jacques Barzun has written, "Art distills sensation and embodies it with enhanced meaning in memorable form—or else it is not art." How do Barzun's words relate to the painting in the story and to the story itself? **[Apply]**

Thematic Connections

FANTASY AND REALITY

The writers of the Romantic period deal with the realities of existence as well as the possibilities of the imagination. Poe, like Mary Shelley and William Blake, begins from realistic experiences and then moves into realms of imagination. In blurring the line between reality and fantasy, these writers open the reader's mind to a world of possibilities.

1. (a) Of Poe's, Mary Shelley's, or Blake's works, which selection is most rooted in reality? Explain. (b) Which is the most fantastic? Why?
2. Is Blake's depiction of a tiger lifelike in the same way Poe's oval portrait is? Give reasons for your answer.
3. Choose a modern tale of horror and explain how it is similar to or different from Poe's.

 Idea Bank

Writing

1. **Description of a Gothic Setting** Write a description of a setting for a modern Gothic tale like Poe's.

2. **Literary Analysis** Write an analysis of Poe's story in which you identify the point or points at which reality crosses into fantasy.

3. **Response to Criticism** G. R. Thompson has suggested that "The Oval Portrait" can be read as "the dream of a man delirious from pain and lack of sleep." Write an essay in which you agree or disagree with this statement.

Speaking, Listening, and Viewing

4. **Visual Presentation** Look at some paintings from Poe's time to learn what he meant by "very spirited modern paintings." Select examples and use them in an oral report for your classmates. **[Visual Arts Link]**

Researching and Representing

5. **Poe on Film** Several of Poe's works or combinations of them have been made into films. View one of these films and report on it to the class. Evaluate the camera work, the mood, and the balance between fantasy and reality. **[Media Link]**

Online Activity www.phlit.phschool.com

Writing Process Workshop

Comparison-and-Contrast Paper

Comparing and contrasting can be part of almost any type of writing, including poetry. William Blake, for example, uses two series of poems to contrast innocence and experience. In a **comparison-and-contrast paper**, you show how two or more subjects are similar and how they are different. The introduction states what you will be comparing; the body of the paper provides details and examples; and the conclusion sums up your main points. These tips will help you:

Writing Skills Focus

▶ To make your comparison-and-contrast paper easy to follow, **choose an organizational strategy**. (See p. 585.)

▶ Provide a clear **beginning, middle and end** for your paper. (See p. 595.)

▶ **Place your ideas for emphasis** by putting key points at the beginning or the end. (See p. 603.)

Two Farmers, Kasimir Malevich

MODEL FROM LITERATURE

Excerpt from *An Essay of Dramatic Poesy* by John Dryden

Those who accuse [Shakespeare] to have wanted [lacked] ① learning give him the greater commendation: he was naturally learned; he needed not the spectacles of books to read nature;. . . . He is many times flat, insipid; his comic wit degenerating into clenches [clichés], ② his serious swelling into bombast. But he is always great when some great occasion is presented to him.

As for Jonson, ... I think him the most learned and judicious writer. . . . One cannot say he wanted wit, but rather that he was frugal of it. . . . If there was any fault in his language, 'twas that he weaved it too closely and laboriously . . . . If I would compare him with Shakespeare, I must acknowledge him the more correct poet, but Shakespeare the greater wit. . . . I admire him, but I love Shakespeare. ③

① Dryden used subject-by-subject organization, discussing first Shakespeare, then Jonson.

② Dryden's audience was familiar with the works of Jonson and Shakespeare and comfortable with this style of language.

③ The placement of this statement gives it emphasis and impact.

Applying LANGUAGE SKILLS: Using Comparative and Superlative Modifiers

Most modifiers have a comparative form for comparing two items and a superlative form for comparing more than two items. Almost all one-syllable modifiers and some two-syllable modifiers use -er to form the comparative and -est to form the superlative. For most modifiers that are two syllables and longer, use *more* to form the comparative and *most* to form the superlative.

Practice Choose the correct modifier in these sentences.

1. Emmett Kelly had a (sadder, saddest) face than the average clown did.
2. Of Hurricane Paula and Hurricane Fran, Paula was the (more, most) recent storm.
3. Mary Shelley's *Frankenstein* is the (more scary, scariest) book ever written.

Writer's Solution Connection Writing Lab

For help narrowing your topic, review the Venn Diagram in the Narrowing Your Topic section of the tutorial on Exposition.

Prewriting

Choose a Topic If you need a topic for a comparison-and-contrast paper, consider using one listed below. Whatever your topic, be sure that there are enough similarities and differences between the subjects to make the examination worthwhile.

Know Your Audience Gauge what your readers know about your subject, as well as their level of interest in it. As you gather

---

Topic Ideas

- U.S. Congress and British Parliament
- Nuclear fission and nuclear fusion
- Scots dialect and British English
- The novel *Frankenstein* and a movie version

---

details, keep your readers in mind, choosing details that will help them understand your topic and hold their interest.

Organize Details As you gather details, sort them into categories or groups: subject by subject or point by point.

Topic: Spiders and Insects

Subject by Subject	Point by Point
A. Spiders	A. Body
a. 2 part body	a. Spiders: 2 part
b. 8 legs	b. Insects: 3 part

Drafting

Use Placement for Emphasis As you draft, place your details for the greatest impact. For example, if you have an intriguing fact that will interest your readers, you may present it in the introduction to whet their interest in reading further.

Consider Your Audience Keep your readers in mind as you draft your paper. Use a style of language and degree of formality that will appeal to them. Compare these examples:

▶ **Audience: School Children** Mars is the fourth planet from the sun. It is most like the Earth in climate, but its surface features—mountains, valleys, rocky soil—would make it almost impossible for humans to live there.

▶ **Audience: Scientists** Although Martian atmospheric conditions are close to Earth's, its topography alone would make it virtually impossible to colonize.

Revising

Use a Checklist Use the following questions, or develop your own, as you read your draft:

1. Could my writing be made more suitable for my readers?
2. How can I improve the organization to clarify comparison-and-contrast relationships?
3. Are any important or interesting details lost because of where they're placed?

REVISION MODEL

The Carolina wren is small, only about 5 inches at maturity. Its distinctive call, "TEA-kettle, TEA-kettle" ~~as opposed to the *chug-chug-chug* of the Cactus wren~~ ① can be heard throughout the southeastern United States at all times of the year. ② Habitats for this wren ~~Places the Carolina wren lives include~~ include dense thickets in ravines and woodlands. Nesting spots include tree stumps, stone walls, and even mailboxes. ③ ¶ The larger cousin to the Carolina wren is the Cactus wren, measuring up to 8 inches. . . .

① This statement is confusing and out of place in the subject-by-subject organization used in this paper.

② More sophisticated language reflects the high level of the audience.

③ A new paragraph should begin here. This will help emphasize the differences between the two wrens.

Publishing

▶ **Multimedia Presentation** Use a page layout program to format your work and to add media.

▶ **Literary Magazine** Send your paper to a publication devoted to your subject.

▶ **On-line Publishing** Find a site or bulletin board that is appropriate for your topic. Post your paper there.

APPLYING LANGUAGE SKILLS: Using Past Participial Phrases

A past participial phrase contains a past participle of a verb and any modifiers that go with it. The entire phrase acts as an adjective and should be placed close to the word it modifies.

Examples:

Held together with only a bit of glue, the equipment was unsafe for the climb.

The pianist, prepared from weeks of practice, gave an out-standing recital.

Practice Identify each past participial phrase and the word it modifies.

1. Supported by several million dollars, the Governor was ready for the race.

2. Buried under tons of lava, the treasures of Pompeii were preserved forever.

3. I was eager to read Poe's short story, "The Oval Portrait," reputed to be very mysterious.

Writer's Solution Connection Language Lab

For help in avoiding the use of double comparisons, see the Problems with Modifiers lesson.

Student Success Workshop

Real-World Reading Skills

Strategies for Success

Reading a review can help you decide whether you want to read a book, see a movie, or attend a performance. Reading a review after you have had the experience can help you interpret the work and may provide insight into the work. You may not agree with the reviewer's opinion, but you can analyze the writer's arguments to test their validity. Analyzing a review also prompts you to explore your own opinion and the reasons for it.

Analyze the Review To analyze a review, read it carefully. Identify the reviewer's arguments and conclusion, and evaluate the supporting facts and reasons. If you are familiar with the literature, film, or performance being reviewed, consider whether you have the same or a different response from the writer's. On which points do you agree or disagree?

Evaluate the Arguments An important part of analyzing a review is examining the strengths and weaknesses in the reviewer's argument. Check the reviewer's reasoning. Are the arguments logically supported? Is the opinion based on accurate and sufficient evidence? Are concrete examples, quotations from reliable authorities, and solid facts supplied? It can be difficult to evaluate a reviewer's opinion if you haven't read the book or seen the performance in question, but strong, credible reasons in support of an opinion will help you decide if the reviewer's opinion is valid.

Evaluate the Reviewer's Objectivity You should consider the reliability of the reviewer when you're analyzing a review. Is the reviewer unbiased? Is the reviewer someone you can trust? Look for reviews by experienced writers, recognized experts in their field, or seasoned reviewers for reputable newspapers, such as the *Los Angeles Times, The Houston Chronicle, The Washington Post.* Ask yourself whether the reviewer will profit in any way from your buying the book or purchasing a ticket to the performance.

Apply the Strategies

Collect written reviews of books you've read, films you have seen, or performances you've attended. Analyze one of the reviews.

1. What is the main argument or conclusion that the reviewer makes? Do you agree with that argument? Why or why not?
2. Are the reviewer's arguments valid and logical?
3. How objective do you think the reviewer is? Why do you think so?
4. Write your own brief review of a book, film, or performance. Use sound arguments backed by logical supporting information. How do your responses compare with those in the published reviews?

✔ Here are situations in which to analyze a written review:
► Deciding what film to watch
► Choosing a book to give as a present
► Getting another opinion of a performance you've seen

PART 2 *Focus on Literary Forms:* Lyric Poetry

The Wanderer over the Sea of Clouds, Caspar David Friedrich, Kunsthalle, Hamburg

Lyric poems express a writer's thoughts and feelings. The ancient Greeks, who set this type of poem to lyre music, gave the lyric its name. Romantic poets of the nineteenth century devoted themselves to lyric poetry, "singing" about nature and society's injustices. Today, songwriters are still influenced by the Romantic lyric as they bare their souls to driving rock rhythms.

Guide for Interpreting

William Wordsworth
(1770–1850)

One of England's greatest poets, William Wordsworth was a visionary who grew more conservative as his work became accepted. Today he is known as the pioneer of the Romantic movement, which took literature in a dramatic new direction.

The Lake District Born in the beautiful Lake District of England, Wordsworth spent his youth roaming the countryside. In later years, too, he found peace and reassurance in the gentle hills and serene lakes of this district. It is this region of northwestern England that is the cradle of the Romantic movement.

Revolution and Love By the time Wordsworth was a young teenager, both his parents had died. However, his education was provided for, and in 1787, he entered Cambridge University. After graduating from Cambridge, he traveled through Europe, spending considerable time in France. There he embraced the ideals of the newly born French Revolution, ideals that stressed social justice and individual rights. He also found time to fall in love with a young woman named Annette Vallon.

Disillusionment and Crisis Wordsworth's involvement with the revolution and with Annette Vallon ended abruptly in 1793 when England declared war on France, and Wordsworth had to return home. As the French Revolution became increasingly violent, Wordsworth lapsed into a depression. Two people who saw him through this crisis were his beloved sister Dorothy and fellow poet Samuel Taylor Coleridge.

Revolution in Art It is as if Wordsworth translated his revolutionary hopes from politics to literature. With Coleridge, he composed a collection of poems called *Lyrical Ballads* (1798). These poems were revolutionary in their use of the language of ordinary people rather than specialized "poetic" words. Also, these "ballads" showed how the lives and experiences of ordinary people, when properly viewed, were really *extra*ordinary. In both language and subject matter, these poems broke sharply with the past.

Poetry and Autobiography Critics agree that Wordsworth's greatest work is his autobiography in poetry, *The Prelude*. Wordsworth completed an early version of this poem in 1799. By 1805, he had expanded the poem considerably. As he wrote to a friend, *The Prelude* told the story of "the growth of my own mind." It is not always factually accurate but in its combination of —in Stephen Gill's words—"satire and narrative, description and meditation, the visionary and the deliberately banal," it was unique. Wordsworth grew more conservative in his politics as his revolutionary poetry gained acceptance. However, as time went on, his place as the father of English Romanticism was assured.

◆ Background for Understanding

HISTORY: WORDSWORTH, THE FRENCH REVOLUTION, AND ROMANTICISM

When Wordsworth traveled to France in 1790, the French Revolution was under way. On July 14, 1789, a Parisian mob had stormed the Bastille prison. Wordsworth was caught up in the revolutionary fervor and saw "France standing on the top of golden hours." In 1791, when he returned to France, the country was more chaotic, and hopes for peaceful social reform seemed unrealistic. The declared war between England and France (1793) and the violent turn taken by the French Revolution (1793–1794) dashed Wordsworth's hopes.

The crisis he experienced when his political hopes failed led Wordsworth to his revolution in literature: Romanticism. This movement embodied the same faith in ordinary people that had inspired his politics.

Poetry of William Wordsworth

◆ *Literature and Your Life*

CONNECT YOUR EXPERIENCE

Most people would list rock music and the ecology movement as products of twentieth-century America. Actually, both these cultural developments are the intellectual "grandchildren" of Romanticism, which began about two hundred years ago.

William Wordsworth's poems may not sound like rock music, but his ideas can still be found in our music and our politics.

Journal Writing Jot down your thoughts about freedom and nature, and then compare them to Wordsworth's.

THEMATIC FOCUS: FANTASY AND REALITY

Notice how Wordsworth considers the growth of his own mind an important element of reality.

◆ Literary Focus

ROMANTICISM AND THE LYRIC

Romanticism was a late-eighteenth-century literary movement that reacted against the Neoclassical style of the previous generation. The Neoclassicists favored rationalism, wit, and outward elegance. The Romantics wrote not from the head but from the heart and often used **lyric poems** to express personal emotions.

English Romanticism began with a great-hearted poet, William Wordsworth. Calling himself a "worshipper of Nature," he saw behind the things of nature a "motion and a spirit" that "rolls through all things." These words come from the lyric "Tintern Abbey," but you can sense this same depth of feeling in everything he wrote.

◆ Reading Strategy

USE LITERARY CONTEXT

Literary context refers to the whole climate of practices and assumptions that influence a writer. Sometimes that climate changes, as when the artificial verse of Neoclassicism yielded to the sincere poetry of Romanticism.

Wordsworth is one of those rare writers who actually brings about a change in literary context. You will understand him better if you realize that the qualities you find in his work—sincerity, spontaneity, a deep feeling for nature—were revolutionary at the time.

◆ Build Vocabulary

RELATED WORDS: FORMS OF *ANATOMIZE*

Although the noun *anatomy* and the related verb and adjective *anatomize* and *anatomical* pertain to "the study of the structure of animals or plants," they can also be applied to society. In *The Prelude*, for example, Wordsworth tries to *anatomize* society; that is, he tries "to study or dissect" it.

WORD BANK

Before you read, preview this list of words from the poems.

recompense
roused
presumption
anatomize
confounded
sordid
stagnant

◆ Grammar and Style

PRESENT PARTICIPIAL PHRASES

Wordsworth's long, easily flowing sentences contain many **present participial phrases**—phrases containing a present participle with its modifiers and complements. Such phrases function as adjectives. In the following example from "The World Is Too Much with Us," the present participial phrase modifies the pronoun "I":

So might I, standing on this pleasant lea.

Lines Composed a Few Miles Above Tintern Abbey

William Wordsworth

This poem was written in 1798 during Wordsworth's second visit to the valley of the River Wye and the ruins of Tintern Abbey, once a great medieval church, in Wales. Wordsworth had passed through the region alone five years earlier; this time he brought his sister with him to share the experience. Of this visit and the poem it inspired, Wordsworth wrote, "No poem of mine was composed under circumstances more pleasant for one to remember than this."

Five years have past; five summers, with the length
Of five long winters! and again I hear
These waters, rolling from their mountain springs
With a soft inland murmur. Once again
5   Do I behold these steep and lofty cliffs,
That on a wild secluded scene impress
Thoughts of more deep seclusion; and connect
The landscape with the quiet of the sky.
The day is come when I again repose
10   Here, under this dark sycamore, and view
These plots of cottage ground, these orchard tufts,
Which at this season, with their unripe fruits,
Are clad in one green hue, and lose themselves
'Mid groves and copses. Once again I see
15   These hedgerows, hardly hedgerows, little lines
Of sportive wood run wild: these pastoral farms,
Green to the very door; and wreaths of smoke
Sent up, in silence, from among the trees!
With some uncertain notice, as might seem
20   Of vagrant dwellers in the houseless woods,
Or of some hermit's cave, where by his fire
The hermit sits alone.

◆ **Literary Focus**
How do the sensory observations Wordsworth includes reflect what you know about Romanticism?

These beauteous forms,
Through a long absence, have not been to me
As is a landscape to a blind man's eye:
25 But oft, in lonely rooms, and 'mid the din
Of towns and cities, I have owed to them
In hours of weariness, sensations sweet,
Felt in the blood, and felt along the heart;
And passing even into my purer mind,
30 With tranquil restoration—feelings too
Of unremembered pleasure: such, perhaps,
As have no slight or trivial influence
On that best portion of a good man's life.
His little, nameless, unremembered, acts
35 Of kindness and of love. Nor less, I trust,
To them I may have owed another gift,
Of aspect more sublime; that blessed mood,
In which the burthen[1] of the mystery,
In which the heavy and the weary weight
40 Of all this unintelligible world
Is lightened—that serene and blessed mood,
In which the affections gently lead us on—
Until, the breath of this corporeal frame[2]
And even the motion of our human blood
45 Almost suspended, we are laid asleep
In body, and become a living soul;
While with an eye made quiet by the power
Of harmony, and the deep power of joy,
We see into the life of things.

If this
50 Be but a vain belief, yet, oh! how oft—
In darkness and amid the many shapes
Of joyless daylight; when the fretful stir
Unprofitable, and the fever of the world,
Have hung upon the beatings of my heart—
55 How oft, in spirit, have I turned to thee,
O sylvan[3] Wye! thou wanderer through the woods,
How often has my spirit turned to thee!

And now, with gleams of half-extinguished thought,
With many recognitions dim and faint,
60 And somewhat of a sad perplexity,
The picture of the mind revives again;
While here I stand, not only with the sense
Of present pleasure, but with pleasing thoughts
That in this moment there is life and food
65 For future years. And so I dare to hope,
Though changed, no doubt, from what I was when first
I came among these hills; when like a roe[4]

---

1. **burthen:** Burden.
2. **corporeal** (kôr pôr´ ē əl) **frame:** Body.
3. **sylvan** (sil´ vən): Wooded.
4. **roe:** Type of deer.

► Critical
Viewing
Romantic
writers liked
to immerse
themselves in
fantasies
about the
mysterious
past. How is
this painting
appropriate
to such an
attitude?
[Infer]

Tintern Abbey, J. M. W. Turner, British Museum

I bounded o'er the mountains, by the sides
Of the deep rivers, and the lonely streams,
70 Wherever nature led: more like a man
Flying from something that he dreads, than one
Who sought the thing he loved. For nature then
(The coarser pleasures of my boyish days,
And their glad animal movements all gone by)
75 To me was all in all—I cannot paint
What then I was. The sounding cataract
Haunted me like a passion; the tall rock,
The mountain, and the deep and gloomy wood,
Their colors and their forms, were then to me
80 An appetite; a feeling and a love,
That had no need of a remoter charm,
By thought supplied, nor any interest
Unborrowed from the eye. That time is past,
And all its aching joys are now no more,
85 And all its dizzy raptures. Not for this
Faint[5] I, nor mourn nor murmur; other gifts
Have followed; for such loss, I would believe,

---

5. **faint:** Lose heart.

Abundant recompense. For I have learned
To look on nature, not as in the hour
90 Of thoughtless youth; but hearing oftentimes
The still, sad music of humanity,
Nor harsh nor grating, though of ample power
To chasten and subdue. And I have felt
A presence that disturbs me with the joy
95 Of elevated thoughts; a sense sublime
Of something far more deeply interfused,
Whose dwelling is the light of setting suns,
And the round ocean and the living air,
And the blue sky, and in the mind of man;
100 A motion and a spirit, that impels
All thinking things, all objects of all thought,
And rolls through all things. Therefore am I still
A lover of the meadows and the woods
And mountains; and of all that we behold
105 From this green earth; of all the mighty world
Of eye, and ear—both what they half create,
And what perceive; well pleased to recognize
In nature and the language of the sense,
The anchor of my purest thoughts, the nurse,
110 The guide, the guardian of my heart, and soul
Of all my moral being.

                            Nor perchance,
If I were not thus taught, should I the more
Suffer[6] my genial spirits[7] to decay;
For thou art with me here upon the banks
115 Of this fair river; thou my dearest Friend,[8]
My dear, dear Friend, and in thy voice I catch
The language of my former heart, and read
My former pleasures in the shooting lights
Of thy wild eyes. Oh! yet a little while
120 May I behold in thee what I was once,
My dear, dear Sister! and this prayer I make
Knowing that Nature never did betray
The heart that loved her; 'tis her privilege,
Through all the years of this our life, to lead
125 From joy to joy; for she can so inform
The mind that is within us, so impress
With quietness and beauty, and so feed
With lofty thoughts, that neither evil tongues,
Rash judgments, nor the sneers of selfish men,
130 Nor greetings where no kindness is, nor all
The dreary intercourse of daily life,
Shall e'er prevail against us, or disturb
Our cheerful faith, that all which we behold

---

6. **suffer:** Allow.
7. **genial spirits:** Creative powers.
8. **Friend:** His sister Dorothy.

◆ **Literature and Your Life**

Has the way that you react to nature changed since you were younger? How?

◆ **Build Vocabulary**

recompense (rek´ əm pens´) *n.:* Payment in return

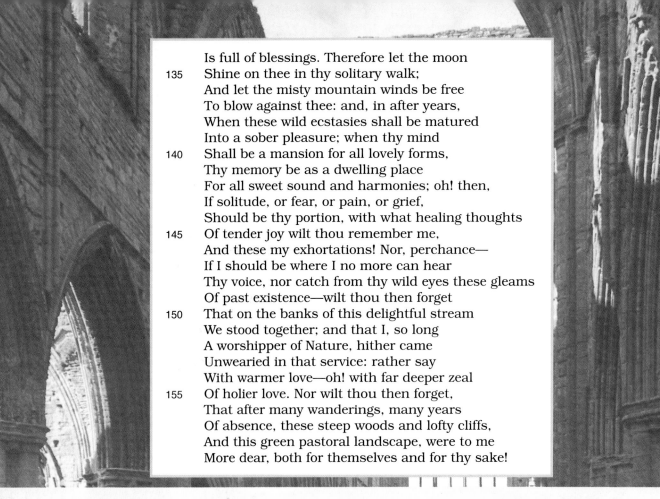

Is full of blessings. Therefore let the moon
135   Shine on thee in thy solitary walk;
And let the misty mountain winds be free
To blow against thee: and, in after years,
When these wild ecstasies shall be matured
Into a sober pleasure; when thy mind
140   Shall be a mansion for all lovely forms,
Thy memory be as a dwelling place
For all sweet sound and harmonies; oh! then,
If solitude, or fear, or pain, or grief,
Should be thy portion, with what healing thoughts
145   Of tender joy wilt thou remember me,
And these my exhortations! Nor, perchance—
If I should be where I no more can hear
Thy voice, nor catch from thy wild eyes these gleams
Of past existence—wilt thou then forget
150   That on the banks of this delightful stream
We stood together; and that I, so long
A worshipper of Nature, hither came
Unwearied in that service: rather say
With warmer love—oh! with far deeper zeal
155   Of holier love. Nor wilt thou then forget,
That after many wanderings, many years
Of absence, these steep woods and lofty cliffs,
And this green pastoral landscape, were to me
More dear, both for themselves and for thy sake!

Guide for Responding

◆ Literature and Your Life

Reader's Response When have you returned to a special place after an absence? What was your reaction?

Thematic Focus What does Wordsworth say about the growth of his mind that makes it seem as real as the things he sees around him?

☑ Check Your Comprehension

1. How long has it been since the poet visited Tintern Abbey?
2. How have the poet's memories of his first visit to the Wye Valley affected him?
3. (a) Apart from his pleasure in the moment, what does the poet hope to gain from his second visit? (b) What does he hope his sister will gain?

◆ Critical Thinking

INTERPRET

1. (a) At what time of year does the poet make his second visit to the area near Tintern Abbey? (b) Find evidence in the poem that supports your answer. **[Support]**
2. In line 36 of the poem, the poet mentions "another gift" that his contact with this rural scene has bestowed upon him. Briefly describe this gift. **[Interpret]**
3. Compare and contrast the differences in the poet's behavior and thoughts during each trip. **[Compare and Contrast]**

EVALUATE

4. Does Wordsworth succeed in expressing his feelings toward his sister? Explain. **[Evaluate]**

APPLY

5. What can you infer from this poem about the Romantic attitude toward cities? **[Generalize]**

from

The Prelude

William Wordsworth

O pleasant exercise of hope and joy!
For mighty were the auxiliars which then stood
Upon our side, us who were strong in love!
Bliss was it in that dawn to be alive,
5   But to be young was very Heaven! O times,
In which the meager, stale, forbidding ways
Of custom, law, and statute, took at once
The attraction of a country in romance!
When Reason seemed the most to assert her rights
10 When most intent on making of herself
A prime enchantress—to assist the work,
Which then was going forward in her name!
Not favored spots alone, but the whole Earth,
The beauty wore of promise—that which sets
15 (As at some moments might not be unfelt
Among the bowers of Paradise itself)
The budding rose above the rose full blown.
What temper at the prospect did not wake
To happiness unthought of? The inert
20 Were <u>roused</u>, and lively natures rapt away!
They who had fed their childhood upon dreams,
The play-fellows of fancy, who had made
All powers of swiftness, subtlety, and strength
Their ministers,—who in lordly wise had stirred
25 Among the grandest objects of the sense,
And dealt with whatsoever they found there
As if they had within some lurking right
To wield it;—they, too, who of gentle mood
Had watched all gentle motions, and to these
30 Had fitted their own thoughts, schemers more mild,
And in the region of their peaceful selves;—
Now was it that *both* found, the meek and lofty
Did both find helpers to their hearts' desire,
And stuff at hand, plastic as they could wish,—
35 Were called upon to exercise their skill,
Not in Utopia,—subterranean fields,—
Or some secreted island, Heaven knows where!
But in the very world, which is the world
Of all of us,—the place where, in the end,
40 We find our happiness, or not at all!

                       .   .   .

But now, become oppressors in their turn,
Frenchmen had changed a war of self-defense
For one of conquest, losing sight of all
Which they had struggled for: now mounted up,
45 Openly in the eye of earth and heaven,
The scale of liberty. I read her doom,

◆ Build Vocabulary

roused (rouzd) *v.*: Stirred up; risen from cover

With anger vexed, with disappointment sore,
But not dismayed, nor taking to the shame
Of a false prophet. While resentment rose
50 Striving to hide, what nought could heal, the wounds
Of mortified presumption, I adhered
More firmly to old tenets, and, to prove
Their temper, strained them more; and thus, in heat
Of contest, did opinions every day
55 Grow into consequence, till round my mind
They clung, as if they were its life, nay more,
The very being of the immortal soul.

.   .   .   .

I summoned my best skill, and toiled, intent
To anatomize the frame of social life,
60 Yea, the whole body of society
Searched to its heart. Share with me, Friend! the wish
That some dramatic tale, endued with shapes
Livelier, and flinging out less guarded words
Than suit the work we fashion, might set forth
65 What then I learned, or think I learned, of truth,
And the errors into which I fell, betrayed
By present objects, and by reasonings false
From their beginnings, inasmuch as drawn
Out of a heart that had been turned aside
70 From Nature's way by outward accidents,
And which are thus confounded, more and more
Misguided, and misguiding. So I fared,
Dragging all precepts, judgments, maxims, creeds,
Like culprits to the bar; calling the mind,

▶ Critical Viewing
Compare and contrast
the view of the French
Revolution presented in
this poem to the one
portrayed in this picture.
[Compare and Contrast]

Storming of the Bastille, 14 July 1789, , Anonymous, Chateau, Versailles, France

Execution of King Louis XVI on January 21, 1793, Musée de la Ville de Paris, Musée Carnavalet, Paris, France

◆ **Build Vocabulary**

presumption (prē zump´ shən) *n.*: Audacity, tending to assume certain things

anatomize (ə nat´ ə mīz´) *v.*: To dissect in order to examine structure

confounded (kən found´ id) *adj.*: Confused; bewildered

75 Suspiciously, to establish in plain day
    Her titles and her honors; now believing,
    Now disbelieving; endlessly perplexed
    With impulse, motive, right and wrong, the ground
    Of obligation, what the rule and whence
80 The sanction; till, demanding formal *proof,*
    And seeking it in every thing, I lost
    All feeling of conviction, and, in fine,
    Sick, wearied out with contrarieties,
    Yielded up moral questions in despair.

Guide for Responding

◆ Literature and Your Life

Reader's Response What emotions come through most clearly in this excerpt? Explain.

Thematic Focus According to this poem, in what way does society repeat its mistakes?

✓ Check Your Comprehension

1. How does the poet describe his first reaction to the French Revolution?
2. According to the poet, in what important way did the French change?

◆ Critical Thinking

INTERPRET

1. (a) What turn of events causes an inner conflict in Wordsworth? (b) Describe this conflict. (c) Is it resolved? Explain. **[Interpret]**
2. Would it be accurate to describe this episode in Wordsworth's life as one of soul-searching? Why or why not? **[Draw Conclusions]**

COMPARE LITERARY WORKS

3. In what way is the Romantic dismissal of neoclassical reason present in the final fifteen lines of both "The Prelude" and "Lines Composed a Few Miles Above Tintern Abbey"? **[Evaluate]**

The World Is Too Much with Us

William Wordsworth

▲ **Critical Viewing** Do you agree with Wordsworth that the moon-lit sea, such as the one pictured here, "moves us not"? Explain. **[Make a Judgment]**

The world is too much with us; late and soon,
Getting and spending, we lay waste our powers:
Little we see in Nature that is ours;
We have given our hearts away, a <u>sordid</u> boon!¹
5 This Sea that bares her bosom to the moon;
The winds that will be howling at all hours,
And are upgathered now like sleeping flowers;
For this, for everything, we are out of tune;
It moves us not.—Great God! I'd rather be
10 A Pagan suckled in a creed outworn;
So might I, standing on this pleasant lea,²
Have glimpses that would make me less forlorn;
Have sight of Proteus³ rising from the sea;
Or hear old Triton⁴ blow his wreathèd horn.

---

1. **boon:** Favor.
2. **lea:** Meadow.
3. **Proteus** (prō´ tē əs): In Greek mythology, a sea god who could change his appearance at will.
4. **Triton:** In Greek mythology, a sea god with the head and upper body of a man and the tail of a fish.

◆ **Build Vocabulary**

sordid (sôr´ did) *adj.*: Unclean, dirty

London, 1802

William Wordsworth

Milton![1] thou should'st be living at this hour:
England hath need of thee: she is a fen[2]
Of stagnant waters: altar, sword, and pen,
Fireside, the heroic wealth of hall and bower,
5 Have forfeited their ancient English dower
Of inward happiness. We are selfish men;
Oh! raise us up, return to us again;
And give us manners, virtue, freedom, power.
Thy soul was like a Star, and dwelt apart:
10 Thou hadst a voice whose sound was like the sea:
Pure as the naked heavens, majestic, free,
So didst thou travel on life's common way,
In cheerful godliness; and yet thy heart
The lowliest duties on herself did lay.

---

1. **Milton:** Seventeenth-century English poet John Milton.
2. **fen** (fen) *n.*: Area of low, flat, marshy land.

◆ **Build Vocabulary**

stagnant (stag′ nənt) *adj.*: Motionless, stale

Guide for Responding

◆ Literature and Your Life

Reader's Response When have you felt that "the world is too much with us"?

Thematic Focus How are these poems similar in describing the realities of Wordsworth's time?

✓ Check Your Comprehension

1. In "The World Is Too Much with Us," what activities cause people to give up their "powers"?
2. Why does England "need" the person Wordsworth addresses in "London, 1802"?

◆ Critical Thinking

INTERPRET

1. (a) In "The World Is Too Much with Us," what does Wordsworth mean by "The World"? (b) Why is he so "forlorn"? **[Interpret]**
2. What does Wordsworth feel England is lacking in "London, 1802"? **[Interpret]**
3. Do both of these poems address the same problem? Explain. **[Compare and Contrast]**

APPLY

4. Does Wordsworth's criticism of England also apply to modern America? Explain. **[Relate]**

Guide for Responding (continued)

◆ Reading Strategy

USE LITERARY CONTEXT

The **literary context** of a work is the climate of literary opinions and practices in which it was written. Most writers follow the assumptions and practices of the time in which they write. A few, like Wordsworth, challenge these assumptions and change the literary context for writers who come after them.

Suppose you are a Neoclassical writer, a sociable city-dweller committed to writing verse that is polished, witty, and rational. Now you are reading the work of this poet from the Lake District, William Wordsworth. Tell how you might react to each of these passages:

1. . . . The sounding cataract
   Haunted me like a passion; the tall rock,
   The mountain, and the deep and gloomy wood,
   Their colors and their forms, were then to me
   An appetite; a feeling and a love . . .
   ("Tintern Abbey," lines 76–80)
2. The world is too much with us; late and soon,
   Getting and spending, we lay waste our powers:
   Little we see in Nature that is ours;
   We have given our hearts away, a sordid boon!
   ("The World Is Too Much with Us," lines 1–4)

◆ Grammar and Style

PRESENT PARTICIPIAL PHRASES

Present participial phrases consist of a verb form ending in *-ing* and its complements and modifiers. The entire phrase functions as an adjective. Wordsworth, who writes in long, flowing sentences, uses such phrases to add information about nouns and pronouns.

Writing Application In your notebook, combine the following sentences using present participial phrases.
1. Today's world is still full of Romantics.
   They call for social change and praise nature.
2. Sometimes I stand on the shore. I wish
   I could travel to distant lands.

◆ Literary Focus

ROMANTICISM AND THE LYRIC

Wordsworth was one of the inventors of English Romanticism. For him, **Romanticism** arose from several personal passions: his deep feeling for nature, in which he saw a "spirit" that united all things; his sense of the dignity and importance of ordinary people and their language, especially in a rural setting; and his concern with his own personal development. This last concern was not a selfish one. Wordsworth viewed his own changing perceptions with amazement, as if they were a natural phenomenon, and in **lyric poems** he offers them to readers as an aid in their own development.

1. Find a passage from the poems to illustrate two of these Wordsworthian passions.
2. For each passage you find, explain how it illustrates an aspect of Wordsworth's Romanticism.

◆ Build Vocabulary

USING FORMS OF *ANATOMIZE*

Use your knowledge of the related forms of *anatomize* to explain the meanings of these book titles:
1. *An Anatomy of Melancholy*
2. *Anatomical Guide to the Human Body*
3. *The Life of Claude Lévi-Strauss, Anatomist of Societies*

USING THE WORD BANK: Synonyms

In your notebook, write the letter of the word or phrase in Column B that is closest in meaning to each word in Column A.

Column A	Column B
1. roused	a. audacity
2. sordid	b. dissect
3. stagnant	c. shameful
4. confounded	d. perplexed
5. anatomize	e. stirred
6. presumption	f. reward
7. recompense	g. stale

Build Your Portfolio

 Idea Bank

Writing

1. **Literary Analysis** Review the beginnings of Wordsworth's two sonnets, "The World Is Too Much with Us" and "London, 1802." Then explain how he immediately captures readers' interest.

2. **Romantic Travel Brochure** As Wordsworth, write a travel brochure for a scenic natural area. Describe the sights as he might describe them.

3. **Response to Criticism** Thomas Wolfe defined the true Romantic feeling as "not the desire to escape life, but to prevent life from escaping you." In an essay, explain whether or not Wordsworth exhibits this "feeling."

Speaking, Listening, and Viewing

4. **Debate** With a group of classmates, debate the point that Wordsworth makes in "The World Is Too Much with Us": that people put too much emphasis on acquiring material goods. **[Social Studies Link]**

5. **Photo Essay** The Romantic movement affected arts other than literature. With a partner, research Romanticism in either painting or sculpture and create a photo essay, complete with captions or text explaining the illustrations. **[Art Link]**

Researching and Representing

6. **Ecology and Romanticism** Read material published by an ecological group. Then using what you know about Romanticism, look for any Romantic influences in the group's statements. **[Science Link; Social Studies Link]**

7. **History of Gardening** Compare the different approaches to gardening taken by Neoclassicists and Romanticists. Present your findings, using the photos and illustrations from a history of gardening to make your points. **[Art Link]**

Online Activity www.phlit.phschool.com

 Guided Writing Lesson

Public-Service Announcement

In "The World Is Too Much with Us," Wordsworth warns readers that pursuing material possessions may cost them their souls. Turn his message into an effective public-service advertisement for print, radio, or television. Using words alone or a combination of words and images, convince your audience to find more time for family, friends, and personal interests. Adapt your message to the requirements of the medium you choose.

Writing Focus: Adapting the Message to the Medium

Whether you write for print, radio, or television, you must consider the best way to **adapt your message to the medium** in which it will appear. Knowing the different requirements of these media will help you achieve this goal. In print, for example, you may be able to use longer sentences than you could in other media. Briefer, punchier statements work better for radio and television. Also, because television is a visual medium, it requires a coordination between words and images.

Prewriting Note contrasts that will help you get your message across—for example, the contrast between a mindless rush to acquire goods and a mindful attitude of concern for others. Then come up with phrases and images that convey these contrasts. Also, think about the medium you will use and whether it requires you to create images.

Drafting Know whether you're writing a print ad, a radio spot, or a television commercial. Grab the attention of your audience with a powerful image and supporting words (television), image-creating phrases (radio), or words and design (print).

Revising To evaluate the suitability of your message for the medium, do a rough layout of words and design (print), read your script aloud (radio), or create a storyboard of words and images (television).

Guide for Interpreting

Samuel Taylor Coleridge
(1772–1834)

The poetry of Samuel Taylor Coleridge stands at the place where real life slips into dreams, where facts are reborn as fantasies. More than any other Romantic poet, he dared to journey inward—into the world of the imagination. However, in many ways, the imaginary life that fed his poetry was an escape from some very serious problems, including poor health and self-doubt.

Early Fantasies Coleridge was born in Ottery St. Mary on the Devon coast of England, the last of ten children, only four of whom survived. At an early age, he developed the habit of retreating into a world of books and fantasy. When he was nine, his father died, and Coleridge was sent to school in London. There, he became a riveting public speaker, who held his audience's attention with his originality and intelligence.

At Cambridge University, Coleridge's hunger for new ideas led him into radical politics. He became friends with an idealistic poet named Robert Southey. Together, they planned to form a settlement in Pennsylvania based on their utopian political ideas. The plan collapsed, however, when Southey's aunt refused to fund their project.

A Literary Breakthrough In 1795, Coleridge and his wife, Sara Fricker, moved to Somerset, where he became friends with poet William Wordsworth. In 1798, the two turned out *Lyrical Ballads*, a joint collection of their work. The four poems that make up Coleridge's contribution to the volume deal with spiritual matters and include his masterpiece, "The Rime of the Ancient Mariner." The collection of poems slowly gained critical attention and caused a revolution in poetic style and thought, firmly establishing the movement known as Romanticism.

Failing Health Coleridge's fame grew, but his marriage, his health, and his friendship with Wordsworth all crumbled. He suffered increasingly from asthma and rheumatism and began to rely heavily on painkillers. He moved to Germany, and despite his downward spiral, he kept writing on many subjects, and lectured on Shakespeare and Milton.

A Romantic Legacy Perhaps Coleridge's greatest legacy is the insight he affords readers on the role of imagination in literature. His belief that literature is a magical blend of thought and emotion is at the very heart of his great works, in which the unreal is often made to seem real.

◆ Background for Understanding

LITERATURE: COLERIDGE'S DREAMSCAPES

Coleridge used dreams as inspiration for many of his great poems. For example, Coleridge claimed to have dreamed his poem "Kubla Khan" line for line, after falling asleep while reading a passage from a work about the founder of the great Mongol dynasty. Upon awakening, he transcribed the lines as fast as he could. When interrupted by a visitor, however, the lines in his head disappeared, never to be remembered. As a result, he was unable to complete the poem.

Coleridge's "The Rime of the Ancient Mariner" was based on a dream reported by his friend John Cruikshank. Starting with the dream as raw material, Coleridge and William Wordsworth began to elaborate upon it. Wordsworth suggested that the act that would drive the entire poem was a crime committed at sea. Using this material and his own peculiar imagination, Coleridge wrote "The Rime of the Ancient Mariner," which has chilled and enthralled audiences to this day.

◆ Literature and Your Life

CONNECT YOUR EXPERIENCE

In your dreams or in childhood fantasies, you may have sailed the oceans, ventured deep into space, or journeyed back in time. Like those vivid dreams, these poems will sweep you away into imaginary worlds and stretch the boundaries of your experience.

Journal Writing Examine how dreams can be a positive incentive for real-life actions.

THEMATIC FOCUS: FANTASY AND REALITY

Coleridge relied upon fantasy and dreams as a creative tool. As you read his poems, look for elements of fantasy.

◆ Literary Focus

POETIC SOUND DEVICES

Romantic poetry like Coleridge's achieves some of its emotional effect and beauty through **poetic sound devices**. Chief among these is **alliteration**, the repetition of a consonant sound at the beginnings of words. **Consonance**, another sound device, is the repetition of similar final consonant sounds in stressed syllables with dissimilar vowel sounds, and **assonance** is the repetition of a vowel sound in stressed syllables with dissimilar consonant sounds. **Internal rhyme**, in which rhymes occur within a poetic line, can make a line of poetry more compelling and memorable.

Alliteration: The fair breeze blew, the white foam flew,

Consonance: a frightful fiend / Doth close behind . . .

Assonance: The western wave was all aflame.

Internal Rhyme: With heavy thump, a lifeless lump. . .

◆ Build Vocabulary

LATIN WORD ROOTS: -journ-

In the prose sidenotes accompanying "The Rime of the Ancient Mariner," Coleridge uses the verb *sojourn*, which means "to visit for a short while." This word contains the root *-journ-*, which is derived from French and Latin words meaning "day." How does the root contribute to the meaning of the word *sojourn*?

| averred |
| sojourn |
| expiated |
| reverence |
| sinuous |
| tumult |

WORD BANK

Before you read, preview this list of words from the poems.

◆ Reading Strategy

POETIC EFFECTS

Recognizing **poetic effects**, such as sound devices, will help you to appreciate poetry. For example, the internal rhyme in the following lines emphasizes the quickness and abruptness of the actions. The assonance in *loud* and *southward* stresses a sound that seems to howl with the wind:

> The ship drove fast, loud roared the blast, / And southward aye we fled.

Keep track of poetic effects in a chart such as this one:

Sound Device	Image	Reference

◆ Grammar and Style

INVERTED WORD ORDER

Inverted word order is a change in the normal English word order of subject-verb-complement. In his poems, Coleridge often inverts word order to achieve a particular rhythm, rhyme scheme, or poetic sound effect.

Inverted Order: . . . what evil looks / Had I from old and young!

Standard Order: I had evil looks from old and young!

The RIME of the ANCIENT MARINER

SAMUEL TAYLOR COLERIDGE

Argument

How a Ship having passed the Line[1] was driven by storms to the cold Country towards the South Pole: and how from thence she made her course to the tropical Latitude of the Great Pacific Ocean; and of the strange things that befell: and in what manner the Ancyent Marinere came back to his own Country.

Part I

An ancient Mariner meeteth three Gallants bidden to a wedding feast and detaineth one.

It is an ancient Mariner,
And he stoppeth one of three.
"By thy long gray beard and glittering eye,
Now wherefore stopp'st thou me?

"The Bridegroom's doors are opened wide,   5
And I am next of kin;
The guests are met, the feast is set:
May'st hear the merry din."

The Wedding Guest is spellbound by the eye of the old seafaring man and constrained to hear his tale.

He holds him with his skinny hand,
"There was a ship," quoth he.   10
"Hold off! unhand me, graybeard loon!"
Eftsoons[2] his hand dropped he.

◆ **Reading Strategy**
Can you find any internal rhymes and assonance in lines 5–8?

He holds him with his glittering eye—
The Wedding Guest stood still,
And listens like a three years' child: 15
The Mariner hath his will.

The Wedding Guest sat on a stone:
He cannot choose but hear;
And thus spake on that ancient man,
The bright-eyed Mariner.   20

---

1. **Line:** Equator.
2. **eftsoons:** Immediately.

630 ◆ Rebels and Dreamers (1798–1832)

"The ship was cheered, the harbor cleared,
Merrily did we drop
Below the kirk,[3] below the hill,
Below the lighthouse top.

"The Sun came up upon the left,   25
Out of the sea came he!
And he shone bright, and on the right
Went down into the sea.

"Higher and higher every day,
Till over the mast at noon[4]—"   30
The Wedding Guest here beat his breast,
For he heard the loud bassoon.

The bride hath paced into the hall.
Red as a rose is she;
Nodding their heads before her goes   35
The merry minstrelsy.

The Wedding Guest he beat his breast,
Yet he cannot choose but hear;
And thus spake on that ancient man
The bright-eyed Mariner.   40

"And now the Storm blast came, and he
Was tyrannous and strong:
He struck with his o'ertaking wings,
And chased us south along.

"With sloping masts and dipping prow,   45
As who pursued with yell and blow
Still treads the shadow of his foe,
And forward bends his head,
The ship drove fast, loud roared the blast,
And southward aye[5] we fled.   50

"And now there came both mist and snow.
And it grew wondrous cold;
And ice, mast-high, came floating by,
As green as emerald.

"And through the drifts the snowy clifts[6]   55
Did send a dismal sheen;
Nor shapes of men nor beasts we ken[7]—
The ice was all between.

---

3. **kirk:** Church.
4. **over . . . noon:** The ship has reached the equator.
5. **aye:** Ever.
6. **clifts:** Icebergs.
7. **ken:** Knew.

"The ice was here, the ice was there,
The ice was all around;   60
It cracked and growled, and roared and howled,
Like noises in a swound![8]

"At length did cross an Albatross,
Thorough[9] the fog it came;
As if it had been a Christian soul,   65
We hailed it in God's name.

"It ate the food it ne'er had eat,[10]
And round and round it flew.
The ice did split with a thunder-fit;
The helmsman steered us through!   70

"And a good south wind sprung up behind;
The Albatross did follow,
And every day, for food or play,
Came to the mariner's hollo!

"In mist or cloud, on mast or shroud,[11]   75
It perched for vespers[12] nine;
Whiles all the night, through fog-smoke white,
Glimmered the white Moonshine."

"God save thee, ancient Mariner!
From the fiends, that plague thee thus!—   80
Why look'st thou so?"[13] "With my crossbow
I shot the Albatross."

Part II

"The Sun now rose upon the right:[14]
Out of the sea came he,
Still hid in mist, and on the left   85
Went down into the sea.

"And the good south wind still blew behind,
But no sweet bird did follow.
Nor any day for food or play
Came to the mariners' hollo!   90

"And I had done a hellish thing,
And it would work 'em woe:
For all averred, I had killed the bird
That made the breeze to blow.

---

8. swound: Swoon.
9. thorough: Through.
10. eat (et): Old form of *eaten*.
11. shroud *n.*: Ropes stretching from the ship's side
to the masthead.
12. vespers: Evenings.
13. God . . . so: Spoken by the Wedding Guest.
14. The Sun . . . right: The ship is now headed north.

*Till a great sea bird,
called the Albatross, came
through the snowfog, and
was received with great
joy and hospitality.*

*And lo! the Albatross
proveth a bird of good
omen, and followeth the
ship as it returned northward through fog and
floating ice.*

*The ancient Mariner
inhospitably killeth the
pious bird of good omen.*

◆ **Reading Strategy**
How does the use
of alliteration, asso-
nance, and internal
rhyme in lines 91–94
give a fatal feeling to
the Mariner's curse?

*His shipmates cry out
against the ancient
Mariner for killing
the bird of good luck.*

◆ **Build Vocabulary**

averred (ə vurd´) *v.*: Stated
to be true

Engraving by Gustave Doré for "The Rime of the Ancient Mariner" by Samuel Taylor Coleridge

▲ **Critical Viewing** From the expression on the wedding guest's face (figure on far left), what can you infer about his reaction to the Ancient Mariner? **[Infer]**

Ah wretch! said they, the bird to slay,   95
That made the breeze to blow!

*But when the fog cleared
off, they justify the same,
and thus make themselves
accomplices in the crime.*

"Nor dim nor red, like God's own head,
The glorious Sun uprist;[15]
Then all averred, I had killed the bird
That brought the fog and mist.   100
'Twas right, said they, such birds to slay,
That bring the fog and mist.

*The fair breeze continues;
the ship enters the Pacific
Ocean, and sails north-
ward, even till it reaches
the Line.*

"The fair breeze blew, the white foam flew,
The furrow[16] followed free;
We were the first that ever burst   105
Into that silent sea.

*The ship hath been sud-
denly becalmed.*

"Down dropped the breeze, the sails dropped down,
'Twas sad as sad could be;
And we did speak only to break
The silence of the sea!   110

"All in a hot and copper sky,
The bloody Sun, at noon,
Right up above the mast did stand,
No bigger than the Moon.

"Day after day, day after day,   115
We stuck, nor breath nor motion;
As idle as a painted ship
Upon a painted ocean.

*And the Albatross
begins to be avenged.*

"Water, water, everywhere,
And all the boards did shrink;   120
Water, water, everywhere,
Nor any drop to drink.

"The very deep did rot: O Christ!
That ever this should be!
Yea, slimy things did crawl with legs   125
Upon the slimy sea.

"About, about, in reel and rout[17]
The death fires[18] danced at night;
The water, like a witch's oils,
Burned green, and blue and white.   130

---

15. uprist: Arose.
16. furrow: Ship's wake.
17. rout: Disorderly crowd.
18. death fires: St. Elmo's fire, a visible electrical discharge
from a ship's mast, believed by sailors to be an omen of disaster.

Engraving by Gustave Doré for "The Rime of the Ancient Mariner" by Samuel Taylor Coleridge

▲ **Critical Viewing** Locate the arrow in this picture. Speculate how the artist's capturing it in flight adds to the drama of the situation depicted. **[Speculate]**

Engraving by Gustave Doré for "The Rime of the Ancient Mariner" by Samuel Taylor Coleridge

▶ **Critical Viewing** If you had seen this illustration before reading the poem, how would you have interpreted it? **[Hypothesize]**

A Spirit had followed them; one of the invisible inhabitants of this planet, neither departed souls nor angels. They are very numerous, and there is no climate or element without one or more.

"And some in dreams assurèd were
Of the Spirit that plagued us so;
Nine fathom deep he had followed us
From the land of mist and snow.

"And every tongue, through utter drought,   135
Was withered at the root;
We could not speak, no more than if
We had been choked with soot.

The shipmates, in their sore distress, would fain throw the whole guilt on the ancient Mariner: in sign whereof they hang the dead sea bird round his neck.

"Ah! well a-day! what evil looks
Had I from old and young!   140
Instead of the cross, the Albatross
About my neck was hung.

Part III
"There passed a weary time. Each throat
Was parched, and glazed each eye.
A weary time! a weary time!   145
How glazed each weary eye,
When looking westward, I beheld
A something in the sky.

The ancient Mariner beholdeth a sign in the element afar off.

"At first it seemed a little speck,
And then it seemed a mist;   150
It moved and moved, and took at last
A certain shape, I wist.[19]

"A speck, a mist, a shape, I wist!
And still it neared and neared:
As if it dodged a water sprite,   155
It plunged and tacked and veered.

*At its nearer approach, it
seemeth him to be a ship;
and at a dear ransom he
freeth his speech from the
bonds of thirst.*

"With throats unslaked, with black lips baked,
We could nor laugh nor wail;
Through utter drought all dumb we stood!
I bit my arm, I sucked the blood,   160
And cried, A sail! a sail!

A flash of joy;

"With throats unslaked, with black lips baked,
Agape they heard me call:
Gramercy![20] for joy did grin,
And all at once their breath drew in,   165
As they were drinking all.

*And horror follows.
For can it be a ship that
comes onward without
wind or tide?*

"See! see! (I cried) she tacks no more!
Hither to work us weal;[21]
Without a breeze, without a tide,
She steadies with upright keel!   170

◆ **Reading Strategy**
Lines 167–170 use
the repetition of
vowel sounds as well
as the repetition of
whole words. What
effect do you think
this achieves?

"The western wave was all aflame.
The day was well nigh done!
Almost upon the western wave
Rested the broad bright Sun;
When that strange shape drove suddenly   175
Betwixt us and the Sun.

*It seemeth him but
the skeleton of a ship.*

"And straight the Sun was flecked with bars,
(Heaven's Mother send us grace!)
As if through a dungeon grate he peered
With broad and burning face.   180

*And its ribs are seen as
bars on the face of the
setting Sun.*

"Alas! (thought I, and my heart beat loud)
How fast she nears and nears!
Are those *her* sails that glance in the Sun,
Like restless gossameres?[22]

*The Specter Woman and
her Death- mate, and no
other on board the skele-
ton ship.*

"Are those *her* ribs through which the Sun   185
Did peer, as through a grate?
And is that Woman all her crew?
Is that a Death? and are there two?
Is Death that woman's mate?

---

19. wist: Knew.
20. Gramercy (grə mur′ sē): Great thanks.
21. work us weal: Assist us.
22. gossameres: Floating cobwebs.

"*Her* lips were red, *her* looks were free,   190
Her locks were yellow as gold;
Her skin was as white as leprosy,
The Nightmare Life-in-Death was she,
Who thicks man's blood with cold.

"The naked hulk alongside came,   195
And the twain were casting dice;
'The game is done! I've won! I've won!'
Quoth she, and whistles thrice.

"The Sun's rim dips; the stars rush out:
At one stride comes the dark;   200
With far-heard whisper, o'er the sea,
Off shot the specter bark.

"We listened and looked sideways up!
Fear at my heart, as at a cup,
My lifeblood seemed to sip!   205
The stars were dim, and thick the night,
The steersman's face by his lamp gleamed white;
From the sails the dew did drip—
Till clomb[23] above the eastern bar
The hornèd[24] Moon, with one bright star   210
Within the nether tip.

"One after one, by the star-dogged Moon,[25]
Too quick for groan or sigh,
Each turned his face with a ghastly pang,
And cursed me with his eye.   215

"Four times fifty living men,
(And I heard nor sigh nor groan)
With heavy thump, a lifeless lump,
They dropped down one by one.

"The souls did from their bodies fly—   220
They fled to bliss or woe!
And every soul, it passed me by,
Like the whizz of my crossbow!"

---

23. **clomb:** Climbed.
24. **hornèd:** Crescent.
25. **star-dogged Moon:** Omen of impending evil to sailors.

◆ *Literature
and Your Life*

Does the dice
game in lines
195–198 remind
you of a night-
mare? Have you
ever had a similar
nightmare?

Part IV

*The Wedding Guest
feareth that a Spirit is
talking to him;*

"I fear thee, ancient Mariner!
I fear thy skinny hand!   225
And thou art long, and lank, and brown,
As is the ribbed sea sand.

"I fear thee and thy glittering eye,
And thy skinny hand, so brown."

*But the ancient Mariner
assureth him of his bodily
life, and proceedeth to relate his horrible penance.*

"Fear not, fear not, thou Wedding Guest!   230
This body dropped not down.

"Alone, alone, all, all alone,
Alone on a wide wide sea!
And never a saint took pity on
My soul in agony.   235

*He despiseth the creatures
of the calm,*

"The many men, so beautiful!
And they all dead did lie:
And a thousand thousand slimy things
Lived on; and so did I.

*And envieth that they
should live, and so many
lie dead.*

"I looked upon the rotting sea,   240
And drew my eyes away;
I looked upon the rotting deck,
And there the dead men lay.

> **♦ Reading Strategy**
> What creates the
> strong emotional
> effect in lines
> 236–239?

"I looked to heaven, and tried to pray;
But or[26] ever a prayer had gushed,   245
A wicked whisper came, and made
My heart as dry as dust.

"I closed my lids, and kept them close,
And the balls like pulses beat;
For the sky and the sea and the sea and the sky   250
Lay like a load on my weary eye,
And the dead were at my feet.

*But the curse liveth for him
in the eye of the dead men.*

"The cold sweat melted from their limbs,
Nor rot nor reek did they;
The look with which they looked on me   255
Had never passed away.

"An orphan's curse would drag to hell
A spirit from on high;
But oh! more horrible than that
Is the curse in a dead man's eye!   260
Seven days, seven nights, I saw that curse,
And yet I could not die.

---

26. or: Before.

In his loneliness and fixed-
ness he yearneth towards
the journeying Moon, and
the stars that still sojourn,
yet still move onward; and
everywhere the blue sky
belongs to them, and is
their appointed rest, and
their native country and
their own natural homes,
which they enter unan-
nounced, as lords that are
certainly expected and yet
there is a silent joy at their
arrival.
By the light of the Moon he
beholdeth God's creatures
of the great calm.

"The moving Moon went up the sky,
And nowhere did abide:
Softly she was going up,   265
And a star or two beside—

"Her beams bemocked the sultry main,[27]
Like April hoarfrost spread;
But where the ship's huge shadow lay,
The charmèd water burned alway   270
A still and awful red.

"Beyond the shadow of the ship,
I watched the water snakes:
They moved in tracks of shining white,
And when they reared, the elfish light   275
Fell off in in hoary flakes.

"Within the shadow of the ship
I watched their rich attire:
Blue, glossy green, and velvet black,
They coiled and swam; and every track   280
Was a flash of golden fire.

*Their beauty and their
happiness.*

"O happy living things! no tongue
Their beauty might declare:
A spring of love gushed from my heart,
And I blessed them unaware;   285
Sure my kind saint took pity on me,
And I blessed them unaware.

*He blesseth them in his
heart.*

The spell begins to break.

"The selfsame moment I could pray;
And from my neck so free
The Albatross fell off, and sank   290
Like lead into the sea.

Part V

"Oh sleep! it is a gentle thing,
Beloved from pole to pole!
To Mary Queen the praise be given!
She sent the gentle sleep from Heaven,   295
That slid into my soul.

*By grace of the holy
Mother, the ancient Mariner
is refreshed with rain.*

"The silly[28] buckets on the deck.
That had so long remained,
I dreamed that they were filled with dew;
And when I awoke, it rained.   300

◆ **Literary Focus**
What repeated con-
sonant sound in
lines 303–304 above
creates alliteration?

"My lips were wet, my throat was cold,
My garments all were dank;
Sure I had drunken in my dreams,
And still my body drank.

---

27. **main:** Open sea.
28. **silly:** Empty.

"I moved, and could not feel my limbs: 305
I was so light—almost
I thought that I had died in sleep,
And was a blessèd ghost.

*He heareth sounds and
seeth strange sights and
commotions in the sky
and the element.*

"And soon I heard a roaring wind:
It did not come anear;   310
But with its sound it shook the sails,
That were so thin and sere.[29]

"The upper air burst into life!
And a hundred fire flags sheen,[30]
To and fro they were hurried about!   315
And to and fro, and in and out,
The wan stars danced between.

"And the coming wind did roar more loud,
And the sails did sigh like sedge;[31]
And the rain poured down from one black cloud;   320
The Moon was at its edge.

"The thick black cloud was cleft, and still
The Moon was at its side:
Like waters shot from some high crag,
The lightning fell with never a jag,   325
A river steep and wide.

*The bodies of the ship's
crew are inspired[32] and
the ship moves on;*

"The loud wind never reached the ship,
Yet now the ship moved on!
Beneath the lightning and the Moon
The dead men gave a groan.   330

"They groaned, they stirred, they all uprose,
Nor spake, nor moved their eyes;
It had been strange, even in a dream,
To have seen those dead men rise.

"The helmsman steered, the ship moved on: 335
Yet never a breeze up-blew;
The mariners all 'gan work the ropes,
Where they were wont[33] to do;
They raised their limbs like lifeless tools—
We were a ghastly crew.   340

*◆ Literature
and Your Life*

How does the
image of the body
of the speaker's
brother's son make
you feel?

"The body of my brother's son
Stood by me, knee to knee;
The body and I pulled at one rope,
But he said nought to me."

◆ **Build Vocabulary**

sojourn (sō´ jǝrn) *v.:* Stay
for a while

---

29. sere: Dried up.
30. fire flags sheen: The aurora australis, or southern
lights, shone.
31. sedge *n.:* Rushlike plant that grows in wet soil.
32. inspired: Inspirited.
33. wont: Accustomed.

Engraving by Gustave Doré for "The Rime of the Ancient Mariner" by Samuel Taylor Coleridge

▶ **Critical Viewing** What details support the mood
of hopelessness in this illustration? **[Support]**

But not by the souls of
the men, nor by demons
of earth or middle air,
but by a blessed troop of
angelic spirits, sent down
by the invocation of the
guardian saint.

"I fear thee, ancient Mariner!" 345
"Be calm, thou Wedding Guest!
'Twas not those souls that fled in pain,
Which to their corses[34] came again,
But a troop of spirits blessed:

"For when it dawned—they dropped their arms, 350
And clustered round the mast;
Sweet sounds rose slowly through their mouths,
And from their bodies passed.

"Around, around, flew each sweet sound,
Then darted to the Sun; 355
Slowly the sounds came back again,
Now mixed, now one by one.

"Sometimes a-dropping from the sky
I heard the skylark sing;
Sometimes all little birds that are, 360
How they seemed to fill the sea and air
With their sweet jargoning![35]

"And now 'twas like all instruments,
Now like a lonely flute;
And now it is an angel's song, 365
That makes the heavens be mute.

"It ceased; yet still the sails made on
A pleasant noise till noon,
A noise like of a hidden brook
In the leafy month of June, 370
That to the sleeping woods all night
Singeth a quiet tune.

"Till noon we quietly sailed on,
Yet never a breeze did breathe;
Slowly and smoothly went the ship, 375
Moved onward from beneath.

The lonesome Spirit from
the South Pole carries on
the ship as far as the Line,
in obedience to the angelic
troop, but still requireth
vengeance.

"Under the keel nine fathom deep,
From the land of mist and snow,
The spirit slid; and it was he
That made the ship to go. 380
The sails at noon left off their tune,
And the ship stood still also.

---

34. **corses:** Corpses.
35. **jargoning:** Singing.

"The Sun, right up above the mast,
Had fixed her to the ocean:
But in a minute she 'gan stir,   385
With a short uneasy motion—
Backwards and forwards half her length
With a short uneasy motion.

"Then like a pawing horse let go,
She made a sudden bound: 390
It flung the blood into my head,
And I fell down in a swound.

"How long in that same fit I lay,
I have not to declare;
But ere my living life returned,   395
I heard and in my soul discerned
Two voices in the air.

"'Is it he?' quoth one, 'Is this the man?
By him who died on cross,
With his cruel bow he laid full low   400
The harmless Albatross.

"'The spirit who bideth by himself
In the land of mist and snow,
He loved the bird that loved the man
Who shot him with his bow.'   405

"The other was a softer voice,
As soft as honeydew:
Quoth he, 'The man hath penance done,
And penance more will do.'

Part VI

FIRST VOICE

"'But tell me, tell me! speak again,   410
Thy soft response renewing—
What makes that ship drive on so fast?
What is the ocean doing?'

SECOND VOICE

"'Still as a slave before his lord,
The ocean hath no blast;   415
His great bright eye most silently
Up to the Moon is cast—

"'If he may know which way to go;
For she guides him smooth or grim.
See, brother, see! how graciously   420
She looketh down on him.'

The Polar Spirit's fellow demons, the invisible inhabitants of the element, take part in his wrong; and two of them relate, one to the other, that penance long and heavy for the ancient Mariner hath been accorded to the Polar Spirit, who returneth southward.

"'But why drives on that ship so fast,
Without or wave or wind?'

SECOND VOICE

"'The air is cut away before,
And closes from behind.   425

"'Fly, brother, fly! more high, more high!
Or we shall be belated:
For slow and slow that ship will go,
When the Mariner's trance is abated.'

The Mariner hath been cast into a trance; for the angelic power causeth the vessel to drive northward faster than human life could endure.

"I woke, and we were sailing on   430
As in a gentle weather:
'Twas night, calm night, the moon was high;
The dead men stood together.

The super-natural motion is retarded; the Mariner awakes, and his penance begins anew.

"All stood together on the deck,
For a charnel dungeon[36] litter;   435
All fixed on me their stony eyes,
That in the Moon did glitter.

"The pang, the curse, with which they died,
Had never passed away;
I could not draw my eyes from theirs,   440
Nor turn them up to pray.

The curse is finally expiated.

"And now this spell was snapped: once more
I viewed the ocean green,
And looked far forth, yet little saw
Of what had else been seen—   445

"Like one, that on a lonesome road
Doth walk in fear and dread,
And having once turned round walks on,
And turns no more his head;
Because he knows, a frightful fiend   450
Doth close behind him tread.

"But soon there breathed a wind on me,
Nor sound nor motion made:
Its path was not upon the sea,
In ripple or in shade.   455

"It raised my hair, it fanned my cheek
Like a meadow-gale of spring—
It mingled strangely with my fears,
Yet it felt like a welcoming.

◆ Build Vocabulary

expiated (ēkˊ spē ātˊ əd)
v.: Forgiven; absolved

---

36. charnel dungeon: Vault where corpses or bones are
deposited.

Engraving by Gustave Doré for "The Rime of the Ancient Mariner" by Samuel Taylor Coleridge

◀ **Critical Viewing** How closely can you connect this illustration to the events in the poem? Is the image being portrayed from the Ancient Mariner's point of view? Why or why not? **[Connect]**

"Swiftly, swiftly flew the ship,   460
Yet she sailed softly too:
Sweetly, sweetly blew the breeze—
On me alone it blew.

And the ancient Mariner
beholdeth his native country.

"Oh! dream of joy! is this indeed
The lighthouse top I see?   465
Is this the hill? is this the kirk?
Is this mine own countree?

"We drifted o'er the harbor bar,
And I with sobs did pray—
O let me be awake, my God!   470
Or let me sleep alway.

"The harbor bay was clear as glass,
So smoothly it was strewn![37]
And on the bay the moonlight lay,
And the shadow of the Moon.   475

"The rock shone bright, the kirk no less,
That stands above the rock;
The moonlight steeped in silentness
The steady weathercock.

"And the bay was white with silent light,   480
Till rising from the same,
Full many shapes, that shadows were,
In crimson colors came.

"A little distance from the prow
Those crimson shadows were;   485
I turned my eyes upon the deck—
Oh, Christ! what saw I there!

"Each corse lay flat, lifeless and flat,
And, by the holy rood![38]
A man all light, a seraph[39] man,   490
On every corse there stood.

"This seraph band, each waved his hand:
It was a heavenly sight!
They stood as signals to the land,
Each one a lovely light;   495

"This seraph band, each waved his hand,
No voice did they impart—
No voice; but oh! the silence sank
Like music on my heart.

"But soon I heard the dash of oars,   500
I heard the Pilot's cheer;
My head was turned perforce away
And I saw a boat appear.

"The Pilot and the Pilot's boy,
I heard them coming fast: 505
Dear Lord in Heaven! it was a joy
The dead men could not blast.

◆ Literary Focus
Find the internal
rhyme in lines
472–475.

*The angelic spirits leave
the dead bodies,*

*And appear in their own
forms of light.*

---

37. strewn: Spread.
38. rood: Cross.
39. seraph: Angel.

The Rime of the Ancient Mariner ◆ 647

"I saw a third—I heard his voice:
It is the Hermit good!
He singeth loud his godly hymns   510
That he makes in the wood.
He'll shrieve[40] my soul, he'll wash away
The Albatross's blood.

Part VII

The Hermit of the Wood,

"This Hermit good lives in that wood
Which slopes down to the sea.   515
How loudly his sweet voice he rears!
He loves to talk with mariners
That come from a far countree.

"He kneels at morn, and noon, and eve—
He hath a cushion plump: 520
It is the moss that wholly hides
The rotted old oak-stump.

"The skiff boat neared; I heard them talk.
'Why, this is strange, I trow![41]
Where are those lights so many and fair,   525
That signal made but now?'

Approacheth the ship
with wonder.

"'Strange, by my faith!' the Hermit said—
'And they answered not our cheer!
The planks looked warped! and see those sails,
How thin they are and sere!   530
I never saw aught like to them,
Unless perchance it were

"'Brown skeletons of leaves that lag
My forest brook along;
When the ivy tod[42] is heavy with snow,   535
And the owlet whoops to the wolf below,
That eats the she-wolf's young.'

"'Dear Lord! it hath a fiendish look'
(The Pilot made reply)
'I am a-feared'—'Push on, push on!'   540
Said the Hermit cheerily.

"The boat came closer to the ship,
But I nor spake nor stirred;
The boat came close beneath the ship,
And straight[43] a sound was heard.   545

---

40. **shrieve** (shrēv): Absolve from sin.
41. **trow:** Believe.
42. **tod:** Bush.
43. **straight:** Immediately.

Engraving by Gustave Doré for "The Rime of the Ancient Mariner" by Samuel Taylor Coleridge

▶ **Critical Viewing** In what way does this illustration help you predict how the albatross will first be treated by the sailors? **[Predict]**

The ship suddenly sinketh.

"Under the water it rumbled on,
Still louder and more dread;
It reached the ship, it split the bay;
The ship went down like lead.

The ancient Mariner is saved in the Pilot's boat.

"Stunned by that loud and dreadful sound,   550
Which sky and ocean smote,
Like one that hath been seven days drowned
My body lay afloat;
But swift as dreams, myself I found
Within the Pilot's boat.   555

"Upon the whirl, where sank the ship,
The boat spun round and round;
And all was still, save that the hill
Was telling of the sound.

"I moved my lips—the Pilot shrieked   560
And fell down in a fit;
The holy Hermit raised his eyes,
And prayed where he did sit.

"I took the oars; the Pilot's boy,
Who now doth crazy go,   565
Laughed loud and long, and all the while
His eyes went to and fro.
'Ha! ha!' quoth he, 'full plain I see,
The Devil knows how to row.'

"And now, all in my own countree,   570
I stood on the firm land!
The Hermit stepped forth from the boat,
And scarcely he could stand.

The ancient Mariner
earnestly entreateth the
Hermit to shrieve him;
and the penance of life
falls on him.

"'O shrieve me, shrieve me, holy man!'
The Hermit crossed his brow.[44]   575
'Say, quick,' quoth he, 'I bid thee say—
What manner of man art thou?'

"Forthwith this frame of mine was wrenched
With a woeful agony,
Which forced me to begin my tale;   580
And then it left me free.

And ever and anon
through out his future life
an agony constraineth him
to travel from land to land;

"Since then, at an uncertain hour,
That agony returns;
And till my ghastly tale is told,
This heart within me burns.   585

"I pass, like night, from land to land;
I have strange power of speech;
That moment that his face I see,
I know the man that must hear me:
To him my tale I teach.   590

"What loud uproar bursts from that door!
The wedding guests are there;
But in the garden bower the bride
And bridemaids singing are;
And hark the little vesper bell,   595
Which biddeth me to prayer!

"O Wedding Guest! this soul hath been
Alone on a wide wide sea:
So lonely 'twas, that God himself
Scarce seemed there to be.   600

"O sweeter than the marriage feast,
'Tis sweeter far to me,
To walk together to the kirk
With a goodly company!—

---

44. crossed his brow: Made the sign of the cross on his forehead.

"To walk together to the kirk,   605
And all together pray,
While each to his great Father bends,
Old men, and babes, and loving friends
And youths and maidens gay!

"Farewell, farewell! but this I tell   610
To thee, thou Wedding Guest!
He prayeth well, who loveth well
Both man and bird and beast.

"He prayeth best, who loveth best
All things both great and small: 615
For the dear God who loveth us,
He made and loveth all."

The Mariner, whose eye is bright,
Whose beard with age is hoar,
Is gone; and now the Wedding Guest   620
Turned from the bridegroom's door.

He went like one that hath been stunned
And is of sense forlorn;
A sadder and a wiser man,
He rose the morrow morn.   625

And to teach, by his own example, love and reverence to all things that God made and loveth.

◆ **Build Vocabulary**

reverence (rēv′ ər əns)
n.: Respect

Guide for Responding

◆ *Literature and Your Life*

Reader's Response What was your reaction to the Ancient Mariner's story? Explain.

Thematic Focus In what ways is this poem a blend of the real and the fantastic?

Questions for Research Generate research questions to explore the influences that shaped Coleridge's poetry and philosophy.

☑ Check Your Comprehension

1. What "hellish thing" does the Mariner do, and how do the other sailors react to it?
2. What happens to the Mariner's shipmates soon after the appearance of the Specter Woman and her Death-mate in Part III?
3. What does the Mariner hope the hermit will do for him?
4. What is the Mariner's lifelong penance?

◆ **Critical Thinking**

INTERPRET

1. Why do you think Coleridge chose a wedding as the destination of the Mariner's listener? **[Interpret]**
2. What do you think the Albatross symbolizes? Find evidence to support your answer. **[Interpret]**
3. As soon as the Mariner feels love, the albatross falls off his neck. Why do you think this happens? **[Infer]**
4. In what ways might the journey of the Mariner be seen as spiritual as well as actual? **[Analyze]**

EVALUATE

5. Coleridge includes both realistic and supernatural descriptions. Why do you think he includes both kinds in this poem? **[Evaluate]**

Kubla Khan

SAMUEL TAYLOR COLERIDGE

In Xanadu[1] did Kubla Khan
A stately pleasure dome decree:
Where Alph,[2] the sacred river, ran
Through caverns measureless to man
5   Down to a sunless sea.
So twice five miles of fertile ground
With walls and towers were girdled round;
And there were gardens bright with <u>sinuous</u> rills,[3]
Where blossomed many an incense-bearing tree;
10 And here were forests ancient as the hills,
Enfolding sunny spots of greenery.

But oh! that deep romantic chasm which slanted
Down the green hill athwart[4] a cedarn cover![5]
A savage place! as holy and enchanted
15 As e'er beneath a waning moon was haunted
By woman wailing for her demon lover!
And from this chasm, with ceaseless turmoil seething,
As if this earth in fast thick pants were breathing.
A mighty fountain momently was forced;
20 Amid whose swift half-intermitted burst
Huge fragments vaulted like rebounding hail,
Or chaffy grain beneath the thresher's flail;

▲ **Critical Viewing**
Coleridge's images of the pleasure dome seem based partly on what he knew about ancient Chinese culture. How do they compare with the details on this sixteenth-century box cover? **[Compare and Contrast]**

---

1. **Xanadu** (zan´ ə dōō): Indefinite area in China.
2. **Alph:** Probably derived from the Greek river Alpheus, the waters of which, it was believed in Greek mythology, joined with a stream to form a fountain in Sicily.
3. **rills:** Brooks.
4. **athwart:** Across.
5. **cedarn cover:** Covering of cedar trees.

And 'mid these dancing rocks at once and ever
It flung up momently the sacred river.
25 Five miles meandering with a mazy motion
Through wood and dale the sacred river ran,
Then reached the caverns measureless to man,
And sank in tumult to a lifeless ocean:
And 'mid this tumult Kubla heard from far
30 Ancestral voices prophesying war!
        The shadow of the dome of pleasure
        Floated midway on the waves;
        Where was heard the mingled measure
        From the fountain and the caves.
35 It was a miracle of rare device.[6]
A sunny pleasure dome with caves of ice!

        A damsel with a dulcimer[7]
        In a vision once I saw:
        It was an Abyssinian[8] maid,
40   And on her dulcimer she played,
        Singing of Mount Abora.[9]
        Could I revive within me
        Her symphony and song,
        To such a deep delight 'twould win me,
45 That with music loud and long,
I would build that dome in air,
That sunny dome! those caves of ice!
And all who heard should see them there,
And all should cry, Beware! Beware!
50 His flashing eyes, his floating hair!
Weave a circle round him thrice,
And close your eyes with holy dread,
For he on honeydew hath fed,
And drunk the milk of Paradise.

---

6. **device:** Design.
7. **dulcimer:** (dul´ sə mer) n.; Musical instrument with metal strings which produce sounds when struck by two small hammers.
8. **Abyssinian** (ab ə sin´ ē ən): Ethiopian.
9. **Mount Abora:** Probably Mount Amara in Abyssinia.

◆ **Build Vocabulary**

sinuous (sin´ yōō əs) adj.: Bending, winding, or curving in and out

tumult (tōō´ mult´) n.: Noisy commotion

Guide for Responding

◆ **Literature and Your Life**

Reader's Response Were you drawn to the description of Kubla Khan's pleasure dome? Did it remind you of any place you know?

Thematic Focus Do you think the world of this poem was an escape from the real world for Coleridge? How does Xanadu resemble a fantasy?

☑ **Check Your Comprehension**

1. What was the size of the palatial estate ordered to be built by Kubla Khan?

2. What did Kubla Khan hear over the noise made by the river emptying into the ocean?

3. According to the last stanza, what did the speaker once see in a vision?

◆ **Critical Thinking**

INTERPRET

1. Using your own words, explain what the speaker says would happen to him and "all who heard" if he were able to revive his vision. **[Interpret]**

2. Kubla Khan's pleasure dome seems both like a paradise on earth and like something sinister. Which elements make it beautiful? What is sinister about it? **[Analyze]**

3. What statement do you think Coleridge is making about the power of the imagination? **[Draw Conclusions]**

EVALUATE

4. Do you feel that Coleridge's imagination and "music" combine to make his vision real to the reader? Support your answer. **[Criticize]**

Guide for Responding (continued)

◆ Literary Focus

POETIC SOUND DEVICES

Coleridge skillfully uses **poetic sound devices** such as alliteration, consonance, assonance, and internal rhyme within his poetry. These sound devices, in addition to pleasing the ear, create vivid imagery, help to establish mood, and make the poetic lines interesting and memorable.

1. Find an example of alliteration in lines 9–12 of "The Rime of the Ancient Mariner."
2. What two sound devices does Coleridge use in the line: "It cracked and growled and roared and howled"?
3. Which words in this line create assonance? "Whiles all the night through fog-smoke white . . ."
4. What sound device is evident in this line from "Kubla Khan": "But oh! that deep romantic chasm which slanted"?
5. In what way do the sound devices in lines 45–54 enhance the mood and meaning of what is being described?

◆ Reading Strategy

POETIC EFFECTS

In these poems by Coleridge, **poetic effects** are created by sound devices such as alliteration, consonance, assonance, and rhyme. These sound devices please the ear, reinforce meaning, and create mood. In lines 41–44 of "The Rime of the Ancient Mariner," for example, the use of alliteration and consonance enables you almost to hear the hissing of the sea foam as the ship is tossed about.

1. Reread lines 472–483 of "The Rime of the Ancient Mariner." State the feeling you think Coleridge was trying to establish. Tell whether, in your opinion, his use of sound devices helps, and give your reasons.
2. What sound devices does Coleridge use in the first stanza of "Kubla Khan"? Explain how the sound devices enhance the poem's mood, imagery, and appeal or "catchiness."

◆ Grammar and Style

INVERTED WORD ORDER

When poets create certain rhymes, rhythms, or word pictures, they sometimes **invert word order**, or change the normal English word order of subject-verb-complement. For example, to rhyme *drowned* and *found*, Coleridge inverted the standard word order "I found myself."

> Like one that hath been seven days *drowned*
> My body lay afloat
> But swift as dreams, myself I *found*

Practice In your notebook, rewrite these lines in standard word order.
1. That moment that his face I see.
2. Red as a rose is she.
3. At length did cross an Albatross . . .
4. Nodding their heads before her goes/ The merry minstrelsy.
5. Whiles all the night . . ./Glimmered the white Moonshine.

Writing Application Write poetic lines in which you invert normal word order. You may find it helpful to begin with standard word order, then invert subject, verb, and object to achieve rhyme or rhythm.

◆ Build Vocabulary

USING THE LATIN ROOT *-journ-*

The Latin root *-journ-* means "day." Explain how the root contributes to the meaning of each of these words. If necessary, use a dictionary.

1. journey   2. adjourn   3. journalism

USING THE WORD BANK: Antonyms

Write the word or phrase whose meaning is most opposite to that of the first word.
1. sinuous: (a) narrow, (b) straight, (c) dark
2. expiated: (a) sold, (b) atoned, (c) sinned
3. averred: (a) denied, (b) claimed, (c) wished
4. reverence: (a) respect, (b) contempt, (c) hope
5. tumult: (a) peace, (b) pleasure, (c) wealth
6. sojourn: (a) leave, (b) visit, (c) rest

Build Your Portfolio

 ## Idea Bank

Writing

1. **Utopia** Coleridge was deeply interested in forming a Utopian, or perfect, community. Write a short paper describing what a Utopia of your own might be like.

2. **Response to the Poem** Write a short paper explaining why you would or would not want to visit Xanadu.

3. **Response to the Poet** Coleridge wrote that poetry should arouse "the sympathy of the reader by a faithful adherence to the truth of nature" while "giving the interest of novelty by modifying colors of the imagination." Write an essay in which you explain whether he has done that in "The Rime of the Ancient Mariner."

Speaking, Listening, and Viewing

4. **Dramatic Reading** With a group of class-mates, present a dramatic reading of a section of "The Rime of the Ancient Mariner." Assign parts and rehearse your reading, striving to evoke the atmosphere in the poem. **[Performing Arts Link]**

5. **Panel Discussion** With a small group of class-mates, hold a panel discussion on what you think people can learn from their dreams. **[Science Link]**

Researching and Representing

6. **Research Project** Wordsworth and Coleridge were successful poetic collaborators. Research portraits, letters, and other primary sources that give information about their friendship and writ-ing. Present your findings to the class. **[Literature Link]**

7. **Illustrated Journey** Create a poster-sized collage that illustrates the Ancient Mariner's journey. Represent major events from the story realistically or symbolically. **[Art Link]**

Online Activity www.phlit.phschool.com

 ## Guided Writing Lesson

Poem With Sound Effects

Coleridge and many other poets use sound devices to add music and beauty to their poems. Write a poem describing an imaginary world like the one in "Kubla Khan." In your poem, use a variety of sound devices such as rhyme, alliteration, assonance, and consonance.

Writing Skills Focus: Dramatic Effects Through Sound

Use **sound devices** to help establish the mood of your poem and to create a dramatic effect that will engage your readers. For example, notice how the sound devices in this stanza from "The Rime of the Ancient Mariner" reinforce the actions that Coleridge is describing and draw the reader into these actions.

Model From Literature

"The ice was here, the ice was there, / The ice was all around; / It cracked and growled, and roared and howled, / Like noises in a swound!"

Use the following strategies as you draft your poem.

Prewriting Use your imagination to come up with a fantastic setting that you can bring to life in your poem. Jot down details that capture how this setting looks, sounds, smells, and feels. Brainstorm for rhyming words, alliterative phrases, and other effective sound devices to use in creating your setting.

Drafting Using the details you've gathered, draft your poem. Then use a variety of sound devices to reinforce meaning and draw readers into the world you're describing.

Revising Read your poem aloud, first to yourself and then to some classmates. Use their suggestions to revise and strengthen your poem.

Guide for Interpreting

George Gordon, Lord Byron *(1788–1824)*

As famous for the life he led as for the things he wrote, George Gordon, Lord Byron, came from a long line of handsome but irresponsible aristocrats. Byron lived life in the "fast lane," and was looked on with disapproval by his contemporaries.

From Rags to Riches Byron was born in London, poor, but a member of the aristocracy. His father, a handsome ladies' man, died when Byron was just three years old. At the age of ten, while living in Aberdeen with his mother, Byron inherited his great-uncle's title, Baron, along with an estate at Newstead. Byron lived there until he was seventeen, when he left home to attend Trinity College at Cambridge.

A Zest for Life While at Cambridge Byron made lots of friends, played lots of sports, and spent lots of money. He even kept a pet bear. He also published a volume of verse, *Hours of Idleness* (1807), that received harsh criticism in Scotland's *Edinburgh Review*. In response he wrote his first major work, the satirical poem *English Bards and Scotch Reviewers* (1809), in which he pokes fun at the magazine that gave him a terrible review.

On graduating, Byron traveled to out-of-the-way corners of Europe and the Middle East. When he came home he brought with him two sections of a book-length poem entitled *Childe Harold's Pilgrimage,* which depicted a young hero not unlike himself—moody, reckless, sensitive, and adventuresome. The work was very well received, and Byron became very popular.

"I awoke one morning and found myself famous," Byron observed.

For a time Byron was the darling of London society. Hostesses vied to lure him to parties; women flocked to his side. But his lifestyle soon brought scandal, and in 1816 he left England, never to return.

Italy and Tragedy Eventually Byron settled in Italy, and worked on his masterful mock epic, *Don Juan* (pronounced jōō´ en). While there, however, tragedy struck: one of Byron's daughters died, and his good friend, the poet Percy Bysshe Shelley, drowned in a sailing accident in rough seas.

A Budding Revolutionary A champion of liberty, in 1823 Byron joined a group of revolutionaries seeking to free Greece from Turkish rule. Tragically, Byron died of a rheumatic fever soon after, while training troops to fight for Greek independence. To this day he is revered in Greece as a national hero.

◆ Background for Understanding

LITERATURE: THE BYRONIC HERO

Lord Byron was a true celebrity, a public figure of literary genius who in turn thrilled and scandalized his contemporaries. "Mad, bad, and dangerous to know"—that was Lady Caroline Lamb's famous description of Lord Byron.

Though Byron actually could be quite charming and friendly, his readers insisted on associating him with the dark, brooding hero, passionate about causes, whom he so often described. Such a figure—a staple of Romanticism—is known as the Byronic hero.

Because of this persona, or adopted personality, readers throughout the nineteenth century saw Byron as the quintessential Romantic poet.

◆ *Literature and Your Life*

CONNECT YOUR EXPERIENCE

Many musicians, writers, and other creative people are known for their artistic temperament and rebellious tendencies. Two centuries ago, Lord Byron, a creative and romantic person, exhibited the same kind of restless and rebellious nature.

THEMATIC FOCUS: THE REACTION TO SOCIETY'S ILLS

Byron flouted social convention and dreamed of liberating oppressed people. As you read, determine to which of society's ills Byron is reacting.

Journal Writing In your journal, describe a modern writer or celebrity who is also a social activist.

◆ Literary Focus

FIGURATIVE LANGUAGE

Poetry usually contains **figurative language**, language not meant to be taken literally. The most common figures of speech are **simile,** which makes a direct comparison using the word *like* or *as*; **metaphor,** which implies a comparison between two apparently unlike things; and **personification,** in which human qualities are attributed to nonhuman subjects. The following lines, addressed to the ocean, contain these three types of figurative language.

These are thy toys, and, as the snowy flake, / They melt into thy yeast of waves, . . .

◆ Grammar and Style

SUBJECT AND VERB AGREEMENT

Even in creative writing like Byron's poetry, it's important for the **verb to agree with its subject** in number. Don't be misled when other words intervene between the subject and the verb:

The *monsters* of the deep *are* made.

Also be careful when the subject comes after the verb, as in this sentence:

There *is* a *pleasure* in the pathless woods.

◆ Reading Strategy

QUESTION

Questioning as you read leads to a better comprehension of literature. Begin with *who, what, where, when,* and *why* questions. For example:

She walks in beauty, like the night / Of cloudless climes and starry skies; / And all that's best of dark and bright / Meet in her aspect and her eyes . . .

From these lines, you might ask: Who is *she*? What is her relationship with the speaker? To what does the speaker compare her? Why is she special?

Use this questioning strategy as you read Byron's poems.

◆ Build Vocabulary

LATIN SUFFIXES: *-ous*

In line 29 of *Don Juan,* the speaker uses the phrase "credulous hope of mutual minds." The suffix of the word *credulous, -ous,* means "full of," and its root -*cred*- means "belief." Therefore, *credulous* means "full of belief" or "too willing to believe."

WORD BANK

Before you read, preview this list of words from the poems.

arbiter
tempests
torrid
fathomless
retort
insensible
credulous
copious
avarice

She Walks in Beauty

**George Gordon,
Lord Byron**

*This poem, written to be set to music, was
inspired by Byron's first meeting with Lady
Wilmot Horton, his cousin by marriage, who
wore a black mourning gown with spangles.*

She walks in beauty, like the night
   Of cloudless climes and starry skies;
And all that's best of dark and bright
   Meet in her aspect and her eyes:
5 Thus mellowed to that tender light
   Which heaven to gaudy day denies.

One shade the more, one ray the less,
   Had half impaired the nameless grace
Which waves in every raven tress,
10   Or softly lightens o'er her face;
Where thoughts serenely sweet express
   How pure, how dear their dwelling place.

And on that cheek, and o'er that brow,
   So soft, so calm, yet eloquent,
15 The smiles that win, the tints that glow,
   But tell of days in goodness spent,
A mind at peace with all below,
   A heart whose love is innocent!

In The Garden, (detail) Thomas Wilmer Dewing, National Museum of American Art, Washington, D.C.

◀ **Critical Viewing**
How does the rendering of this woman suggest that, like Byron's cousin, she is intriguing? **[Analyze]**

Guide for Responding

◆ *Literature and Your Life*

Reader's Response Do you think the speaker idealizes the subject of this poem? Explain.

Thematic Response How does the poem's speaker remove the woman he describes from all of society's ills?

Sensory Switch This poem is full of visual imagery of dark and light. Rewrite the poem in your journal, describing the woman's beauty in terms of sound, scent, and touch.

☑ Check Your Comprehension

1. To what does the speaker compare the lady's beauty?
2. What does the speaker say about the lady's mind and heart?

◆ Critical Thinking

INTERPRET

1. What might "that tender light" in line 5 be? **[Interpret]**
2. What does the speaker suggest that the woman's appearance reveals about her character? **[Connect]**
3. Does Byron's picture emphasize the spiritual or physical aspect of the lady? Explain. **[Draw Conclusions]**

EVALUATE

4. Do you agree that goodness is part of beauty? Explain. **[Evaluate]**

APPLY

5. Do you think people today put too much emphasis on physical beauty? Explain. **[Relate]**

She Walks in Beauty ◆ 659

from

Childe Harold's Pilgrimage

Apostrophe to the Ocean

*George Gordon,
Lord Byron*

There is a pleasure in the pathless woods,
There is a rapture on the lonely shore,
There is society, where none intrudes,
By the deep sea, and music in its roar;
5   I love not man the less, but nature more,
From these our interviews, in which I steal
From all I may be, or have been before,
To mingle with the universe, and feel
What I can ne'er express, yet cannot all conceal.

10   Roll on, thou deep and dark blue ocean—roll!
Ten thousand fleets sweep over thee in vain;
Man marks the earth with ruin—his control
Stops with the shore; upon the watery plain
The wrecks are all thy deed, nor doth remain
15   A shadow of man's ravage, save[1] his own,
When, for a moment, like a drop of rain,
He sinks into thy depths with bubbling groan,
Without a grave, unknelled, uncoffined, and unknown.

His steps are not upon thy paths—thy fields
20   Are not a spoil for him—thou dost arise
And shake him from thee; the vile strength he wields
For earth's destruction thou dost all despise,
Spurning him from thy bosom to the skies,

▲ **Critical Viewing** Byron speaks of the sea with "music in its roar." Does this artist succeed in visually communicating the sound of the ocean? **[Assess]**

1. **save:** Except.

◆ **Build Vocabulary**
arbiter (är′ bət ər) *n.*: Judge; umpire

And send'st him, shivering in thy playful spray
25 And howling, to his gods, where haply[2] lies
His petty hope in some near port or bay,
And dashest him again to earth—there let him lay.[3]

The armaments which thunderstrike the walls
Of rock-built cities, bidding nations quake,
30 And monarchs tremble in their capitals,
The oak leviathans,[4] whose huge ribs make
Their clay creator[5] the vain title take
Of lord of thee, and <u>arbiter</u> of war—
These are thy toys, and, as the snowy flake,
35 They melt into thy yeast of waves, which mar
Alike the Armada's[6] pride or spoils of Trafalgar.[7]

Thy shores are empires, changed in all save thee—
Assyria, Greece, Rome, Carthage, what are they?
Thy waters washed them power while they were free,
40 And many a tyrant since; their shores obey
The stranger, slave, or savage: their decay
Has dried up realms to deserts—not so thou,

2. **haply:** Perhaps.
3. **lay:** A note on Byron's proof suggests that he intentionally made this grammatical error for the sake of the rhyme.
4. **leviathans** (lə vī´ ə thənz): Monstrous sea creatures, described in the Old Testament. Here the word means giant ships.
5. **clay creator:** Human beings.
6. **Armada's:** Refers to the Spanish Armada, defeated by the English in 1588.
7. **Trafalgar:** Battle in 1805 during which the French and Spanish fleets were defeated by the British fleet led by Lord Nelson.

Unchangeable, save to thy wild waves' play.
Time writes no wrinkle on thine azure brow;
45   Such as creation's dawn beheld, thou rollest now.

Thou glorious mirror, where the Almighty's form
Glasses[8] itself in tempests: in all time,
Calm or convulsed—in breeze, or gale, or storm,
Icing the pole, or in the torrid clime
50   Dark-heaving—boundless, endless, and sublime;
The image of eternity, the throne
Of the Invisible; even from out thy slime
The monsters of the deep are made: each zone
Obeys thee; thou goest forth, dread, fathomless, alone.

55   And I have loved thee, ocean! and my joy
Of youthful sports was on thy breast to be
Borne, like thy bubbles, onward; from a boy
I wantoned with thy breakers—they to me
Were a delight: and if the freshening sea
60   Made them a terror—'twas a pleasing fear,
For I was as it were a child of thee,
And trusted to thy billows far and near,
And laid my hand upon thy mane—as I do here.

8. **Glasses:** Mirrors.

◆ **Build Vocabulary**

tempests (tem′ pists) *n.*: Storms

torrid (tôr′ id) *adj.*: Very hot; scorching

fathomless (fath′ əm lis) *adj.*: Too deep to be measured or understood

Guide for Responding

◆ Literature and Your Life

Reader's Response What images from the poem linger in your mind? What thoughts and feelings do you associate with the ocean?

Thematic Focus What do you think the speaker means when he says "Man marks the earth with ruin"?

Journal Writing Write your own apostrophe, in verse or prose, directly addressing something in nature that evokes a strong reaction in you.

✓ Check Your Comprehension

1. What is the speaker's attitude toward nature?
2. An apostrophe is a figure of speech in which a speaker directly addresses an absent person or a personified quality or idea. Whom or what is the speaker addressing from stanza 2 on?
3. How does the ocean treat such things as warships and sea monsters?
4. What are the speaker's childhood memories of the ocean?

◆ Critical Thinking

INTERPRET
1. In line 11, the speaker describes the movement of ships over the ocean as "in vain." What might he mean by this? **[Interpret]**
2. What quality of the ocean does the speaker admire in the fifth stanza? **[Infer]**
3. When referring to the ocean as a "glorious mirror" in line 46, what does the speaker mean? **[Analyze]**
4. Whom does the speaker admire more—human beings or the ocean? **[Draw Conclusions]**

EVALUATE
5. The poem uses the Spenserian stanza, a nine-line stanza rhymed *ababbcbcc,* in which the ninth line is iambic hexameter (six beats to a line). What effect do the longer, last lines give the poem? **[Assess]**

EXTEND
6. Is the sea still as mysterious and powerful today as it was in Byron's day? Explain. **[Science Link]**

from

Don Juan

George Gordon, Lord Byron

Though it is unfinished, Don Juan *is generally regarded as Byron's finest work. A mock epic described by Shelley as "something wholly new and relative to the age," it satirizes the political and social problems of Byron's time.*

Traditionally Don Juan, the poem's hero, had been portrayed as a wicked and immoral character driven solely by his obsession with beautiful women. In Byron's work Don Juan is depicted as an innocent young man whose physical beauty, charm, and spirit prove to be extremely alluring to ladies. As a result, he finds himself in many difficult situations.

Many people feel that Don Juan *would not be a great poem without the periodic pauses in the story during which the narrator drifts away from the subject. In these digressions the narrator comments on the issues of the time and on life in general. In this excerpt the narrator sets aside the adventures of his hero to reflect on old age and death.*

But now at thirty years my hair is gray
   (I wonder what it will be like at forty?
I thought of a peruke[1] the other day)—
   My heart is not much greener; and in short, I
5 Have squandered my whole summer while 'twas May,
   And feel no more the spirit to <u>retort</u>; I
Have spent my life, both interest and principal,
And deem not, what I deemed, my soul invincible.

No more—no more—Oh! never more on me
10   The freshness of the heart can fall like dew,
Which out of all the lovely things we see
   Extracts emotions beautiful and new,
Hived in our bosoms like the bag o' the bee:
   Think'st thou the honey with those objects grew?
15 Alas! 'twas not in them, but in thy power
To double even the sweetness of a flower.

1. peruke (pə rōōk´): Wig.

◆ Build Vocabulary

retort (ri tôrt´) *v.:* Respond with a clever answer or wisecrack

No more—no more—Oh! never more, my heart,
    Canst thou be my sole world, my universe!
Once all in all, but now a thing apart,
20   Thou canst not be my blessing or my curse:
The illusion's gone forever, and thou art
    <u>Insensible</u>, I trust, but none the worse,
And in thy stead I've got a deal of judgment,
Though heaven knows how it ever found a lodgment.

25 My days of love are over; me no more
        The charms of maid, wife, and still less of widow
Can make the fool of which they made before—
    In short, I must not lead the life I did do;
The <u>credulous</u> hope of mutual minds is o'er,
30   The <u>copious</u> use of claret is forbid too,
So for a good old-gentlemanly vice,
I think I must take up with <u>avarice</u>.

Ambition was my idol, which was broken
    Before the shrines of Sorrow and of Pleasure;
35 And the two last have left me many a token
    O'er which reflection may be made at leisure:
Now, like Friar Bacon's brazen head, I've spoken,
    "Time is, Time was, Time's past,"[2] a chymic[3] treasure
Is glittering youth, which I have spent betimes—
40 My heart in passion, and my head on rhymes.

What is the end of fame? 'tis but to fill
    A certain portion of uncertain paper:
Some liken it to climbing up a hill,
    Whose summit, like all hills, is lost in vapor;
45 For this men write, speak, preach, and heroes kill,
    And bards burn what they call their "midnight taper,"
To have, when the original is dust,
A name, a wretched picture, and worse bust.

What are the hopes of man? Old Egypt's King
50   Cheops erected the first pyramid
And largest, thinking it was just the thing
    To keep his memory whole, and mummy hid:
But somebody or other rummaging
    Burglariously broke his coffin's lid:
55 Let not a monument give you or me hopes,
Since not a pinch of dust remains of Cheops.

But I, being fond of true philosophy,
    Say very often to myself, "Alas!
All things that have been born were born to die,
60   And flesh (which Death mows down to hay) is grass;
You've passed your youth not so unpleasantly,
    And if you had it o'er again—'twould pass—
So thank your stars that matters are no worse,
And read your Bible, sir, and mind your purse."

2. **Friar Bacon . . .
Time's past:** In Robert
Greene's comedy
*Friar Bacon and Friar
Burgandy* (1594), these
words are spoken by
a bronze bust, made
by Friar Bacon.
3. **chymic** (kim´ ik):
Alchemic: counterfeit.

65   But for the present, gentle reader! and
        Still gentler purchaser! the bard—that's I—
     Must, with permission, shake you by the hand,
        And so your humble servant, and good-bye!
     We meet again, if we should understand
70   Each other; and if not, I shall not try
     Your patience further than by this short sample—
     'Twere well if others followed my example.

     "Go, little book, from this my solitude!
        I cast thee on the waters—go thy ways!
75   And if, as I believe, thy vein be good,
        The world will find thee after many days."[4]
     When Southey's read, and Wordsworth understood,
        I can't help putting in my claim to praise—
     The four first rhymes are Southey's, every line:
80   For God's sake, reader! take them not for mine!

4. Go . . . days:
Lines from the last
stanza of Robert
Southey's (1774–1843)
*Epilogue to The Lay of
the Laureate.*

◆ **Build Vocabulary**

insensible (in sen´sə bəl) *adj.:* Unable to feel or
sense anything; numb

credulous (krej´ ōō ləs) *adj.:* Willing to believe; naive

copious (kō´ pē əs) *adj.:* Abundant; plentiful

avarice (av´ə ris) *n.:* Greed

Guide for Responding

◆ *Literature and Your Life*

Reader's Response Did you find the narrator
amusing? Why or why not?

Thematic Response In examining his life, the
narrator states that his illusions are gone forever.
Explain what he means by this statement.

Cast *Don Juan* With a small group, come
up with casting suggestions for *Don Juan.*

☑ Check Your Comprehension

1. (a) What is the narrator's age? (b) In what
   condition does he find himself?
2. (a) What, according to lines 17 and 18, has
   been the narrator's "sole world" and "universe"?
   (b) According to the fourth stanza, with what
   "old gentlemanly vice" will he replace it?
3. What is the narrator's attitude toward death?

◆ Critical Thinking

INTERPRET

1. In the fifth stanza, the narrator notes that "glittering youth" is "chymic," or counterfeit treasure.
   What do you think he means by this? **[Interpret]**
2. What point does stanza 7 make about fame?
   [Infer]
3. What might the narrator mean when he says,
   in stanza 8, "flesh is grass"? **[Interpret]**
4. In line 72, whom is the narrator poking fun at?
   [Infer]

EVALUATE

5. Do you share the narrator's attitude toward
   ambition? Why or why not? **[Make a Judgment]**

COMPARE LITERARY WORKS

6. Compare the tone of *Don Juan* with that
   of Byron's other poems. Does it seem to fit
   with the Romanticism elsewhere in his work?
   [Connect]

Guide for Responding (continued)

◆ Literary Focus

FIGURATIVE LANGUAGE

Figurative language—not to be taken literally—makes descriptions vivid and abstract ideas concrete. For example, when Byron says "She walks in beauty like the night / Of cloudless climes and starry skies," he is using a simile that provides a concrete image of the woman's beauty.

1. In *Don Juan*, the speaker says he "squandered [his] whole summer while 'twas May." (a) What type of figurative language is in this line? (b) What meaning does the comparison convey?
2. (a) Identify the simile in the second stanza of "Apostrophe to the Ocean." (b) What does the comparison suggest about the drowning man?
3. Throughout "Apostrophe to the Ocean," the speaker addresses the ocean and personifies it. What effect does this use of figurative language have on the poem as a whole?
4. Identify the types of figurative language in the following lines: (a) "Thou glorious mirror, where the Almighty's form/Glasses itself. . ." (b) "The freshness of the heart can fall like dew. . ."

◆ Build Vocabulary

USING THE LATIN SUFFIX -OUS

Knowing that the suffix -ous, as in *credulous,* means "full of" or "possessing," define the following words.

1. glorious   3. porous
2. marvelous   4. plenteous

USING THE WORD BANK: Antonyms

In your notebook, write the letter of the word that is most nearly the opposite in meaning to the first word.

1. arbiter: (a) plaintiff, (b) jury, (c) award
2. torrid: (a) angry, (b) obedient, (c) freezing
3. fathomless: (a) deep, (b) measurable, (c) dry
4. retort: (a) ask, (b) a dessert, (c) rescue
5. insensible: (a) sensitive, (b) nonsensical, (c) furious
6. copious: (a) anxious, (b) typed, (c) scarce
7. avarice: (a) earthbound, (b) sin, (c) generosity

◆ Reading Strategy

QUESTION

If you **question** as you read, you'll better understand the details and the larger meaning of a work. For instance, after reading the introduction to "She Walks in Beauty" and the poem itself, you might ask and answer these questions:

- *Question*: Who is *she*?
  Answer: Lady Wilmot Horton
- *Question*: What is her relationship to the speaker or poet? *Answer*: Byron's cousin by marriage
- *Question*: What does she look like? *Answer*: beautiful; serene; dressed in black with spangles
- *Question*: To what does the speaker compare her? *Answer*: the night; the stars

1. (a) What questions did you ask prior to reading Byron's poems? (b) What answers did you find?
2. Did questioning make your reading process more active or focused? Explain.

◆ Grammar and Style

SUBJECT AND VERB AGREEMENT

In all types of writing, from reports to poetry, **verbs must agree in number** with their subjects. Following are examples from poems of Lord Byron.
    Singular: There *is* a *rapture* on the lonely shore.
    Plural: My *days* of love *are* over.

Practice In your notebook, write the form of the verb that agrees with the subject.

1. The joys of the narrator of *Don Juan* (has, have) shrunk.
2. There (is, are) many gray hairs on his head.
3. The charms of romance no longer (seems, seem) possible.
4. The fame of writers (escapes, escape) him.
5. Over the waters (goes, go) his book of verse.

Writing Application Rewrite this paragraph, correcting errors in agreement.

The works of Byron reflects his romantic attitudes. Each of his poems illustrate his talent for writing. His audience of enthusiastic readers also admires him for his deep sympathy for the downtrodden.

Build Your Portfolio

Idea Bank

Writing

1. **Health Regimen** At the age of thirty, Don Juan seems washed up. Create a health regimen detailing the lifestyle changes he should make to revive himself, including information on exercise and diet. **[Health Link]**

2. **Ocean's Response** Write a brief poem in which the ocean responds to the musing of the speaker in "Apostrophe to the Ocean."

3. **Response to Criticism** "For all its bursts of cynicism, savagery, and melancholy, there is a fundamental good humor in *Don Juan*," wrote literary scholar Helen Gardner. React to her comment in a critical essay.

Speaking, Listening, and Viewing

4. **Oral Reading** Read aloud "Apostrophe to the Ocean," recording your performance on audio-cassette or videotape. Include background music and sounds. **[Performing Arts Link]**

5. **Eulogy** Write a eulogy, or farewell speech, to mourn the passing of Don Juan. Use details from the poem in your speech to make its subject vivid and interesting. Deliver the eulogy to the class. **[Performing Arts Link]**

Researching and Representing

6. **Portrait** Bring one of Byron's poems to life visually. You can create a seascape based on "Apostrophe to the Ocean," a portrait of the woman in "She Walks in Beauty," or a sketch of the narrator of *Don Juan*. **[Art Link]**

7. **Music** "She Walks in Beauty" was originally intended to be set to music. Do as Byron intended, and write music to accompany the poem. Then perform your song for classmates. **[Music Link; Performing Arts Link]**

Online Activity www.phlit.phschool.com

Guided Writing Lesson

Dramatic Monologue

The speaker in *Don Juan* reveals his innermost thoughts and emotions through poetry, just as dramatic characters reveal their thoughts and emotions through a **monologue**. Write a monologue—a dramatic speech—for a modern Byronic hero. Make it sound authentic by using realistic speech.

Writing Skills Focus: Realistic Speech

Realistic dialogue appears in many types of creative writing, from television scripts to dramatic poems. To make your modern-day character come alive, use speech that captures the flavor of contemporary life. Your monologue might even include sentence fragments and slang where appropriate.

Too formal and poetic: I have squandered my whole summer while 'twas May.

More realistic and contemporary: I burned my candle at both ends when I was young, and now I'm paying for it.

Prewriting Jot down things a Byronic hero like Childe Harold or Don Juan would have to say today. Identify both the central message and attitude that your hero would express. Then list words and phrases that convey the message and the attitude.

Drafting Take on the persona of your Byronic speaker and begin drafting the monologue. As you draft, use words and an attitude that are appropriate for your character.

Revising Review your word choice to make sure your monologue is as realistic as possible. Also check to be sure your writing is free from grammar, spelling, and other errors. (Sentence fragments are acceptable.) Check especially that your verbs agree with their subjects. For more on subject and verb agreement, see pp. 657 and 666.

Guide for Interpreting

Percy Bysshe Shelley
(1792–1822)

A poet of rare gifts, Percy Bysshe (bish) Shelley was also a self-appointed reformer who believed that humankind was capable of attaining a nearly perfect society.

A Loner and Rebel Born into the British upper class, Shelley was raised on a country estate in Sussex. He attended the finest schools, including the prestigious boarding school Eton, but spent most of his time wandering the countryside and performing private scientific experiments. At Oxford University, he published the radical tract *The Necessity of Atheism*. As a result of this incident, he was expelled and became estranged from his father.

Love and Tragedy Instead of going home, Shelley headed for London. There he met Harriet Westbrook, an unhappy schoolgirl who persuaded him to elope. Their marriage was a failure, and the two eventually separated. Continuing his travels in radical intellectual circles, Shelley fell in love with Mary Wollstonecraft Godwin, daughter of the radical philosopher William Godwin and the late Mary Wollstonecraft. After Harriet's tragic death in 1816, Shelley and Mary Godwin married.

A Poet and Outcast The radical politics, the elopement and separation, the tract about atheism—all helped make Shelley an outcast from his homeland. He and Mary settled in Italy, where he became close friends with Lord Byron, another famous exile. In fact, it was during a storytelling session with Shelley, Byron, and another friend that Mary Shelley was inspired to begin work on her famous novel *Frankenstein*.

Italy was a place of inspiration for Shelley as well. There he wrote many of his finest works, including "Ode to the West Wind," "To a Skylark," and his verse drama *Prometheus Unbound* (1820). This drama predicts that someday humanity will be free of tyranny.

An Early Death Shelley never lived to see his dreams for humanity come true. He was only thirty when he died in a boating accident. Grief-stricken, Lord Byron eulogized his friend as "without exception the best and least selfish man I ever knew."

◆ Background for Understanding

HUMANITIES: NATURE IN ROMANTIC POETRY AND ART

Romanticism influenced not just literature but all the arts. Reacting to this new movement, the visual arts became more personal. Perhaps the most important sign of Romanticism in painting was a new interest in the world of nature. As the eighteenth century ended, British art turned increasingly from portraits to landscapes, which blossomed in the hands of two of England's finest artists, J. M. W. Turner (1775–1851) and John Constable (1776–1837).

Turner's Subjective Landscapes Working in both water colors and oils, Turner produced highly subjective landscapes and seascapes that pioneered the use of light and color to capture atmosphere.

Getting Nature Right John Constable is often called the father of modern landscape painting. Not only did he express strong feelings in his work, but he also stressed the need to get nature right. Like Shelley, Constable loved science, and the accuracy of his cloud studies testifies to that love.

Journal Writing Observe the paintings by Constable on pp. 673 and 676. Jot down your impressions or any thoughts they evoke in you.

Ozymandias ◆ Ode to the West Wind ◆ To a Skylark

◆ *Literature and Your Life*

CONNECT YOUR EXPERIENCE

It could be a pet you've raised, a flower you've planted, or a tree you've learned to notice—once you develop a special interest in an animal or plant, it takes on an identity. It isn't just an *it* anymore, but a living being with which you have a relationship.

No wonder romantic authors like Shelley wrote poems in which they addressed natural forces and beings. In two of the poems that follow, Shelley "speaks" to the west wind and to a skylark.

THEMATIC FOCUS: THE REACTION TO SOCIETY'S ILLS

In what ways are Shelley's poems about nature also poems about society and its problems? How can the west wind and the skylark help us to live better?

◆ Build Vocabulary

LATIN WORD ROOTS: -puls-

Romantic poetry, especially Shelley's, often portrays movement. It's not surprising, therefore, to encounter the word *impulse* in "Ode to the West Wind." The Latin root of this word is *-puls-,* which means "push or drive" and appears in many words that express motion of one kind or another.

visage
verge
sepulcher
impulse
blithe
profuse
vernal
satiety

WORD BANK

Before you read, preview this list of words from the poems.

◆ Grammar and Style

SUBJUNCTIVE MOOD

Shelley uses verbs in the **subjunctive mood**, which expresses a wish or a condition contrary to fact. The subjunctive form of the verb *be* is *were* (it does not matter whether the subject is singular or plural):

If I *were* (not *was*) a swift cloud to fly with thee . . .

If we *were* things born / Not to shed a tear. . .

◆ Literary Focus

IMAGERY

Imagery is the descriptive language that poets and other writers use to re-create sensory experience. Poets often create patterns of images that support the theme of a poem. By recognizing and interpreting these patterns, you can understand the poem's meaning.

Notice, for example, how wind images—which appeal to the senses of sight, sound, and touch—appear throughout "Ode to the West Wind." Think about how your sensory experience of the wind, through imagery, helps you understand Shelley's prophetic message in the poem.

◆ Reading Strategy

RESPOND TO IMAGERY

You will enrich your reading of a poem by **responding to imagery**—experiencing a poem through your senses. Often it's possible to enjoy a poem this way before you fully understand it with your mind.

Before approaching "Ozymandias" as a puzzle to be figured out, respond to its visual imagery as if it were a scene in a music video. Picture the strange and marvelous sight that the "traveler" describes:

Two vast and trunkless legs of stone / Stand in the desert.

OZYMANDIAS[1]

PERCY BYSSHE SHELLEY

I met a traveler from an antique land
Who said: Two vast and trunkless legs of stone
Stand in the desert. Near them, on the sand,
Half sunk, a shattered visage lies, whose frown,
5   And wrinkled lip, and sneer of cold command,
Tell that its sculptor well those passions read
Which yet survive, stamped on these lifeless things,
The hand that mocked them and the heart that fed:
And on the pedestal these words appear:
10 "My name is Ozymandias, king of kings:
Look on my works, ye Mighty, and despair!"
Nothing beside remains. Round the decay
Of that colossal wreck, boundless and bare,
The lone and level sands stretch far away.

▶ **Critical Viewing** How is this Egyptian statue like and unlike the one in the poem? **[Compare and Contrast]**

---

1. Ozymandias (ōz´ i män´ dē əs): The Greek name for Ramses II, the king referred to in the poem, a pharaoh who ruled Egypt during the thirteenth century B.C. and built many great palaces and statues. One statue was inscribed with the words: "I am Ozymandias, king of kings, if anyone wishes to know what I am and where I lie, let him surpass me in some of my exploits."

◆ **Build Vocabulary**

visage (viz´ ij) *n*.: Person's face or facial expression

Guide for Responding

◆ Literature and Your Life

Reader's Response Do you think that the message of this poem is pertinent to today's world? Explain.

Thematic Focus How does Shelley use Ozymandias to comment on political power?

☑ **Check Your Comprehension**

1. Whom does the speaker meet?
2. What sight does this person describe?

◆ Critical Thinking

INTERPRET

1. Think of the words on the pedestal. (a) Why is it ironic that the statue crumbled? (b) Why is it ironic that it is surrounded by desert? **[Interpret]**
2. What is the theme of the poem? **[Interpret]**

APPLY

3. (a) What is your definition of *power?* (b) What is your definition of *pride?* (c) In what way do the two complement each other? **[Define]**

Ode to the West Wind

PERCY BYSSHE SHELLEY

Shelley composed this poem in the woods near Florence, Italy. He described the day of its composition as one "when that tempestuous wind, whose temperature is at once mild and animating, was collecting the vapors which pour down the autumnal rains."

I

O wild West Wind, thou breath of Autumn's being,
Thou, from whose unseen presence the leaves dead
Are driven, like ghosts from an enchanter fleeing,

Yellow, and black, and pale, and hectic red,
5   Pestilence-stricken multitudes: O thou,
Who chariotest to their dark and wintry bed

The wingèd seeds, where they lie cold and low,
Each like a corpse within its grave, until
Thine azure sister of the Spring[1] shall blow

10   Her clarion[2] o'er the dreaming earth, and fill
(Driving sweet buds like flocks to feed in air)
With living hues and odors plain and hill:

Wild Spirit, which art moving everywhere;
Destroyer and preserver; hear, oh, hear!

---

1. sister of the Spring: South wind.
2. clarion *n.*: Trumpet producing clear, sharp, shrill tones.

▲ **Critical Viewing** Would you say that Constable captured the spirit of Shelley's west wind? Why or why not? **[Evaluate]**

II

15 Thou on whose stream, 'mid the steep sky's commotion,
Loose clouds like earth's decaying leaves are shed,
Shook from the tangled boughs of Heaven and Ocean,

Angels³ of rain and lightning: there are spread
On the blue surface of thine aery surge,
20 Like the bright hair uplifted from the head

Of some fierce Maenad,⁴ even from the dim <u>verge</u>
Of the horizon to the zenith's height,
The locks of the approaching storm. Thou dirge

Of the dying year, to which this closing night
25 Will be the dome of a vast <u>sepulcher</u>,
Vaulted with all thy congregated might

Of vapors, from whose solid atmosphere
Black rain, and fire, and hail will burst: oh, hear!

---

3. angels: Messengers.
4. Maenad (mē´ nad): A priestess of Bacchus, the Greek and Roman god of wine and revelry.

◆ **Build Vocabulary**
verge (vʉrj) *n.*: Edge; rim
sepulcher (sep´ əl kər) *n.*: Tomb

III

Thou who didst waken from his summer dreams
30 The blue Mediterranean, where he lay,
Lulled by the coil of his crystalline streams,

Beside a pumice[5] aisle in Baiae's bay,[6]
And saw in sleep old palaces and towers
Quivering within the wave's intenser day,

35 All overgrown with azure moss and flowers
So sweet, the sense faints picturing them! Thou
For whose path the Atlantic's level powers

Cleave themselves into chasms, while far below
The sea-blooms and the oozy woods which wear
40 The sapless foliage of the ocean, know

Thy voice, and suddenly grow gray with fear,
And tremble and despoil themselves: oh, hear!

IV

If I were a dead leaf thou mightest bear;
If I were a swift cloud to fly with thee;
45 A wave to pant beneath thy power, and share

The impulse of thy strength, only less free
Than thou, O uncontrollable! If even
I were as in my boyhood, and could be

The comrade of thy wanderings over Heaven,
50 As then, when to outstrip thy skyey speed
Scarce seemed a vision; I would ne'er have striven

As thus with thee in prayer in my sore need.
Oh, lift me as a wave, a leaf, a cloud!
I fall upon the thorns of life! I bleed!

55 A heavy weight of hours has chained and bowed
One too like thee: tameless, and swift, and proud.

---

5. **pumice** (pum´ is) *n.*: Volcanic rock.
6. **Baiae's** (bā´ yēz) **bay:** Ancient Roman resort near Naples.

V

Make me thy lyre,[7] even as the forest is:
What if my leaves are falling like its own!
The tumult of thy mighty harmonies

60 Will take from both a deep, autumnal tone,
Sweet though in sadness. Be thou, Spirit fierce,
My spirit! Be thou me, impetuous one!

Drive my dead thought over the universe
Like withered leaves to quicken a new birth!
65 And, by the incantation of this verse,

Scatter, as from an extinguished hearth
Ashes and sparks, my words among mankind!
Be through my lips to unawakened earth

The trumpet of a prophecy! O Wind,
70 If Winter comes, can Spring be far behind?

---

7. lyre: Aeolian (ē ō´ lē ən) lute, or wind harp, a
stringed instrument which produces musical sounds
when the wind passes over it.

◆ **Build Vocabulary**

impulse (im´ puls´) *n.:* Driving
force forward

Guide for Responding

◆ *Literature and Your Life*

Reader's Response What natural force or
creature would you choose to express the ideas
of renewal and freedom?

Thematic Focus Could the poem's message
be interpreted politically? Explain.

☑ Check Your Comprehension

1. What season does the poem associate with
   the west wind?
2. What does the wind do to (a) the leaves
   and seeds, (b) the clouds, and (c) the ocean?
3. What does the speaker ask of the wind in
   section V of the poem?

◆ Critical Thinking

INTERPRET

1. In what sense is the wind both a "destroyer and
   preserver"? **[Interpret]**
2. (a) How, according to section IV, has the speaker
   changed? (b) What caused the change? **[Infer]**
3. What is the "new birth" the speaker wants
   to bring about? **[Infer]**
4. (a) What is the meaning of the famous last line?
   (b) How does this line tie the poem together?
   [Draw Conclusions]

EVALUATE

5. Is the poem successful in conveying a sense
   of breathless excitement? Explain. **[Evaluate]**

APPLY

6. How are the last five lines of the poem related
   to Shelley's lifelong mission? **[Generalize]**

Cloud Study, 1821, John Constable, Yale Center for British Art

To a Skylark

PERCY BYSSHE SHELLEY

▲ **Critical Viewing** Which lines from Shelley's poem does this painting by Constable best illustrate? **[Connect]**

Hail to thee, <u>blithe</u> spirit!
   Bird thou never wert,
That from heaven, or near it,
   Pourest thy full heart
5 In <u>profuse</u> strains of unpremeditated art.

Higher still and higher,
   From the earth thou springest
Like a cloud of fire;
   The blue deep thou wingest,
10 And singing still dost soar, and soaring ever singest.

In the golden lightning
   Of the sunken sun,
O'er which clouds are brightening,
   Thou dost float and run;
15 Like an unbodied joy whose race is just begun.

The pale purple even[1]
   Melts around thy flight;
Like a star of heaven,
   In the broad daylight
20 Thou art unseen, but yet I hear thy shrill delight,

Keen as are the arrows
   Of that silver sphere,[2]
Whose intense lamp narrows
   In the white dawn clear,
25 Until we hardly see—we feel that it is there.

All the earth and air
   With thy voice is loud,
As, when night is bare,
   From one lonely cloud
30 The moon rains out her beams, and Heaven is overflowed.

What thou art we know not;
   What is most like thee?
From rainbow clouds there flow not
   Drops so bright to see,
35 As from thy presence showers a rain of melody.

Like a poet hidden
   In the light of thought,
Singing hymns unbidden,
   Till the world is wrought
40 To sympathy with hopes and fears it heeded not:

Like a highborn maiden
   In a palace tower,
Soothing her love-laden
   Soul in secret hour
45 With music sweet as love, which overflows her bower:

---

1. **even:** Evening.
2. **silver sphere:** Morning star.

Like a glowworm golden
    In a dell of dew,
Scattering unbeholden
    Its aerial hue
50   Among the flowers and grass, which screen it from the view!

Like a rose embowered
    In its own green leaves,
By warm winds deflowered,[3]
    Till the scent it gives
55   Makes faint with too much sweet those heavy-wingèd thieves.[4]

Sound of vernal showers
    On the twinkling grass,
Rain-awakened flowers,
    All that ever was
60   Joyous, and clear, and fresh, thy music doth surpass:

Teach us, sprite or bird,
    What sweet thoughts are thine:
I have never heard
    Praise of love or wine
65   That panted forth a flood of rapture so divine.

Chorus Hymeneal,[5]
    Or triumphal chant,
Matched with thine would be all
    But an empty vaunt,
70   A thing wherein we feel there is some hidden want.

What objects are the fountains[6]
    Of thy happy strain?
What fields, or waves, or mountains?
    What shapes of sky or plain?
75   What love of thine own kind? what ignorance of pain?

With thy clear keen joyance
    Languor cannot be;
Shadow of annoyance
    Never came near thee;
80   Thou lovest—but ne'er knew love's sad satiety.

Waking or asleep,
    Thou of death must deem[7]
Things more true and deep
    Than we mortals dream,
85   Or how could thy notes flow in such a crystal stream?

---

3. **deflowered:** Fully open.
4. **thieves:** The "warm winds."
5. **Chorus Hymeneal** (hī′ mə nē′ əl): Marriage song, named after Hymen, the Greek god of marriage.
6. **fountains:** Sources, inspiration.
7. **deem:** Know.

◆ **Build Vocabulary**

vernal (vûrn′ əl) *adj*.: Relating to spring

satiety (sə tī′ ə tē) *n*.: State of being filled to excess

We look before and after,
      And pine for what is not;
   Our sincerest laughter
      With some pain is fraught;
90 Our sweetest songs are those that tell of saddest thought.

      Yet if[8] we could scorn
      Hate, and pride, and fear;
   If we were things born
      Not to shed a tear,
95 I know not how thy joy we ever should come near.

      Better than all measures
      Of delightful sound,
   Better than all treasures
      That in books are found,
100 Thy skill to poet were,[9] thou scorner of the ground!

      Teach me half the gladness
      That thy brain must know,
   Such harmonious madness
      From my lips would flow,
105 The world should listen then, as I am listening now.

---

8. **if:** Even if.
9. **were:** Would be.

Guide for Responding

◆ Literature and Your Life

Reader's Response Do you think that the pure joy of the skylark, as Shelley describes it, is possible for human beings? Why or why not?

Thematic Focus Does the last stanza of the poem hold out a promise for curing society's ills? Explain.

Choosing Symbols Make a list of five animals that symbolize joy and freedom for you, as the skylark did for Shelley.

☑ Check Your Comprehension

1. What does the speaker say the skylark pours from its heart?
2. To what four things does Shelley compare the lark in lines 36–55?
3. In the end, what does the speaker ask the bird to teach him?

◆ Critical Thinking

INTERPRET
1. Why do you think the poet avoids a precise physical description of the bird, calling it a "blithe spirit" and "an unbodied joy"? **[Infer]**
2. How is the skylark different from the poet and from other humans? **[Compare and Contrast]**
3. What changes could the skylark help the poet make in his own life and in the lives of others? **[Draw Conclusions]**

EVALUATE
4. Is the long line at the end of each stanza an effective device? Why or why not? **[Criticize]**

APPLY
5. Do you agree with the speaker's views of humanity in lines 76–95? Explain. **[Generalize]**

Guide for Responding (continued)

◆ Reading Strategy

RESPOND TO IMAGERY

By **responding to imagery**, you can experience Shelley's poems with your senses, and you can enter a world as vivid as that of a music video. "Ozymandias," for example, begins with a long shot that reveals "Two vast and trunkless legs of stone" standing in a desert. Then the camera zooms down for a closeup: "a shattered visage lies" next to the legs.

1. (a) Describe lines 4–5 and 9–11 of "Ozymandias" in terms of camera shots. (b) What is the long shot that ends the poem?
2. (a) Describe two vivid camera shots suggested by the visual imagery of "Ode to the West Wind." (b) Now describe two noises, suggested by the imagery, that could be used for the sound track of a "West Wind" video.

◆ Build Vocabulary

USING THE LATIN ROOT -puls-

Show how the Latin root -puls-, meaning "push or drive," contributes to the definition of each italicized word.

1. Shelley's *expulsion* from Oxford University disappointed his father.
2. This poet often acted on *impulse*, without thinking things through.
3. He rebelled against all forms of *compulsion* and tyranny.
4. The only drum to which Shelley marched was the beating of his own *pulse*.
5. Shelley did not think of nature as dead matter but as a *pulsating* force.

USING THE WORD BANK: Antonyms

On a separate sheet, write the lettered word from Column B that is opposite in meaning to the numbered word in Column A.

Column A	Column B
1. visage	a. careworn
2. vernal	b. scarce
3. blithe	c. hunger
4. sepulcher	d. center
5. profuse	e. back
6. verge	f. cradle
7. satiety	g. wintry

◆ Literary Focus

IMAGERY

Shelley uses **imagery**—sensory language—that gives you clues to the meaning of his poems. You can interpret these clues by relating one image to another and seeing the patterns they make.

In "Ode to a Skylark," for example, you probably noticed that many images relate to sound: "singing still dost soar," "shrill delight," "music sweet as love," and others. You can figure out that Shelley uses these sound images to suggest the mysterious "unbodied joy" of a bird he can hear but not see.

1. (a) Find another sound image that Shelley uses to suggest the bird's perfect delight. (b) What sound image in lines 86–90 suggests the imperfectness of human joy?
2. (a) In "Ode to the West Wind," find images of sight, sound, and touch that indicate the wind's power. (b) How does this sensory experience of the wind support Shelley's message of renewal?

◆ Grammar and Style

SUBJUNCTIVE MOOD

Romantic poets like Shelley, who were disappointed with things as they were, often used the subjunctive mood. In their hands, this grammatical tool became a means of expressing their hopes for a more just society and a more harmonious world.

> The **subjunctive mood** expresses a wish or a condition contrary to fact. The subjunctive form of the verb *be* is *were*.

Practice Rewrite the following sentences in your notebook, correcting the verbs that require the subjunctive mood. If a sentence is correct as is, write *correct.*

1. The speaker was addressing the skylark.
2. He wishes he was more like the bird.
3. He thinks that if he was a skylark, he would not know pain.
4. "If I was like you," he was saying, "I would know true gladness."
5. He said he was sure that the skylark was happy.

Build Your Portfolio

Idea Bank

Writing

1. **Direct Address** Write a poem or a paragraph that directly addresses something in nature, such as the west wind or a skylark. Focus on the thoughts and feelings it inspires.

2. **Comparison and Contrast** "Ozymandias" is about a tyrant, and "Ode to the West Wind" predicts a new birth of freedom. Compare and contrast the political themes in these two poems.

3. **Response to Criticism** In "A Defense of Poetry," Shelley writes, "Poets are the unacknowledged legislators of the world." Use passages from these poems to illustrate what he means.

Speaking, Listening, and Viewing

4. **Role Play** With a partner, role-play the incident in which the speaker of "Ozymandias" meets the traveler and hears about the Egyptian king or the incident in which Ozymandias posed for the sculptor centuries ago. **[Performing Arts Link]**

5. **Weather Report** Give a series of radio or television weather reports that capture the same conditions as those described in "Ode to the West Wind." **[Science Link; Media Link]**

Researching and Representing

6. **Observation Journal** Both Shelley and the artist John Constable were very interested in the science of weather. Write a journal in which you record your observations of the weather. **[Science Link]**

7. **Art Presentation** Research the landscape paintings of John Constable. Present your findings to the class, showing reproductions and pointing out similarities between Constable and the romantic poets. **[Art Link]**

Online Activity www.phlit.phschool.com

Guided Writing Lesson

Research Report

Shelley's poems suggest many topics that it would be fun to study further. Choose such a topic—anything from the real-life Ozymandias, Ramses II, to ideas about weather that Shelley used in "Ode to the West Wind"—and write a research paper on it. Whichever topic you select, provide readers with the background they'll need to understand it.

> #### Writing Skills Focus: Necessary Background
>
> Many different types of writing—from video scripts to research papers—require you to provide **necessary background** for readers. If you choose to write about scientific concepts that influenced Shelley, readers may want you to answer questions like these:
>
> - What scientific concepts influenced Shelley?
> - How did scientists of the time develop these concepts?
> - In what ways do these concepts differ from ours?
> - What evidence is there that Shelley knew about these ideas and used them in his poems?

Prewriting Choose a topic related to Shelley's poetry, and make a list of relevant questions about it. These questions will help point you toward the background information that readers will need. As you research these questions in biographies of Shelley and in books and articles about him, use note cards to record key details and ideas.

Drafting Begin by formulating a working thesis that will guide your writing and that you can modify as you draft your paper. Refer to your note cards as you write so that you can introduce facts and examples to support your arguments.

Revising Ask several classmates to read your paper and suggest where you could provide more information. Then evaluate their suggestions, giving special consideration to points on which they agree.

*G*uide for Interpreting

John Keats *(1795–1821)*

Every now and then, someone comes along who leaves a lasting imprint on the world in a life that is tragically cut short. John Keats was one of those people. Although he lived just twenty-five years, Keats left an indelible mark on the world of literature.

A Defender of Worthy Causes

Unlike his contemporaries Byron and Shelley, John Keats was not a well-born aristocrat. Instead, he was born in London of working-class parents. As a child, he earned attention for his striking good looks and his restless spirit. Keats developed a reputation for fighting, not as a bully but as a defender of worthy causes. It was not until he became friends with the schoolmaster's son that Keats became interested in poetry and reading.

From Medicine to Poetry

In 1815, Keats began studying medicine at a London hospital and earned a pharmacist's license before abandoning medicine for poetry. In 1818, he published his first major work, *Endymion,* a long poem that critics panned, in part because of Keats's association with the radical writer and publisher, Leigh Hunt. Despite the negative reviews, Keats did not swerve from his new career.

A Year of Sorrow and Joy

The year 1818 was significant to Keats in other ways. He lost his brother Tom to tuberculosis, but he also met the light of his life, Fanny Brawne, to whom he became engaged. A year later he wrote many of the poems for which he is famous, including "The Eve of St. Agnes" and his odes. The engagement and burst of creativity might have been the prelude to a happy, productive life, but Keats's own health soon deteriorated.

An Early Death

Recognizing that he suffered from the same illness as his brother, he moved to Italy in the hopes that the warmer climate would reverse the disease. Sadly, those hopes proved false, and, in 1821, his own battle with tuberculosis also ended in death. Keats wrote his own epitaph, which stresses the brevity of his life: "Here lies one whose name was writ in water."

A Legacy of Beauty

Despite his early death and the fact that the most important of his works were composed in the space of two years, John Keats remains one of the major influences of English poetry. Known as a pure artist, Keats saw the appreciation of beauty as an end in itself and made the pursuit of beauty the goal of his poetry. As Keats himself so eloquently put it, "Beauty is truth, truth beauty."

◆ Background for Understanding

HISTORY: THE INFLUENCE OF ANCIENT GREECE ON KEATS'S POETRY

Romantic poets such as Byron, Shelley, and Keats admired the culture of ancient Greece, deriving inspiration from its art and literature. Keats, in particular, was inspired by its art, and this admiration is reflected in his poetry.

Keats's friend Charles Cowden Clarke introduced him to Elizabethan poet George Chapman's translation of Homer's ancient Greek epics. They spent an evening reading the translations, and early the next morning Keats produced his famous sonnet "On First Looking into Chapman's Homer."

Keats often associated his ideas about beauty with Greek antiquities. This tendency is exhibited in his poem "Ode on a Grecian Urn," which was inspired by an urn such as this one.

The Orchard Vase (Column Krater), Side A: Gathering Apples, The Metropolitan Museum of Art

Journal Writing Describe some paintings, sculptures, or buildings you've admired.

Poetry of John Keats

◆ *Literature and Your Life*

CONNECT YOUR EXPERIENCE

Think about all the experiences in your life that have made strong impressions on you. If you could freeze just one moment, what would it be, and why? In many of Keats's poems, such as the ones presented here, the poet explores fleeting moments in time.

THEMATIC FOCUS: FANTASY AND REALITY

During flights of fancy it's sometimes possible to arrive at a truth that otherwise eludes you. For example, during a daydream, you may come to a realization about yourself. As you read, notice how flights of fancy lead the speakers of the poems to realizations of truths.

◆ Literary Focus

ODE

An **ode** is a lyric poem on a single, usually serious subject. Often it honors someone or something that the speaker addresses directly. The **Pindaric ode** (after the ancient Greek poet Pindar) was originally meant to be performed by a chorus of people onstage; it has three types of stanzas. In contrast, Rome's homostrophic or **Horatian odes** contain only one type of stanza, which is repeated throughout the poem. A third type of ode, the **irregular ode**, contains no set pattern.

Keats created ten-line stanzas of iambic pentameter (lines containing ten beats with a pattern of weak-strong) for his odes. The rhyme scheme of the stanzas varied from poem to poem. As you read Keats's odes, focus on their content as well as their form.

◆ Reading Strategy

PARAPHRASE

You'll come to a greater understanding of virtually any literary work if you **paraphrase**, or restate the text in your own words. Since poems use unusual language and word order, paraphrasing is especially helpful. For example:

Original: Forlorn! The very word is like a bell / To toll me back from thee to my sole self!

Paraphrase: The word *forlorn* is like a bell bringing me to my senses.

◆ Build Vocabulary

LATIN SUFFIXES: *-age*

In "Ode to a Nightingale," the speaker says "O, for a draft of vintage!" *Vintage* contains the Latin suffix *-age*, which means "state or quality of, amount of, cost of, place of, or collection of." Combined with the root *-vint-*, meaning "wine," the word *vintage* means "wine collected at a certain time."

WORD BANK

Before you read, preview this list of words from the poems.

ken
surmise
gleaned
teeming
vintage
requiem

◆ Grammar and Style

DIRECT ADDRESS

Throughout Keats's poetry you'll find terms of **direct address**, in which a person or thing is addressed by name or by a descriptive phrase. Commas set off terms of direct address. For example:

Bold lover, never, never canst thou kiss . . .

And, *little town*, thy streets forevermore will silent be . . .

Thou wast not born for death, *immortal Bird*!

Notice how Keats's use of direct address gives his poems an intimate, personal tone.

On First Looking into Chapman's HOMER

John Keats

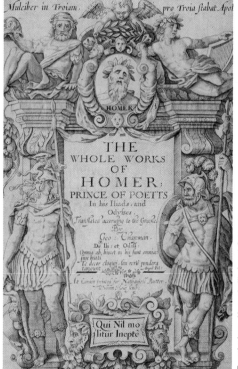

Frontispiece, Homer's Iliad and Odyssey,
1612, William Hole, The British Library

▲ **Critical Viewing**
From the design of the engraving, what would you predict about the content of the book? **[Predict]**

When Keats was twenty-one, his former teacher, Charles Cowden Clarke, introduced him to a translation of Homer by Elizabethan poet George Chapman. The two men spent the evening reading this book, and early the next morning Keats presented this sonnet to Clarke.

Much have I traveled in the realms of gold,
    And many goodly states and kingdoms seen;
    Round many western islands have I been
Which bards in fealty to Apollo[1] hold.
5 Oft of one wide expanse had I been told
    That deep-browed Homer ruled as his demesne;[2]
    Yet did I never breathe its pure serene[3]
Till I heard Chapman speak out loud and bold:
Then felt I like some watcher of the skies
10   When a new planet swims into his <u>ken</u>;
Or like stout Cortez[4] when with eagle eyes
    He stared at the Pacific—and all his men
Looked at each other with a wild <u>surmise</u>—
    Silent, upon a peak in Darien.[5]

---

1. Apollo: In Greek and Roman mythology, the god of music, poetry, and medicine.
2. demesne (di mān´): Realm.
3. serene: Clear air.
4. Cortez: Here, Keats was mistaken. The Pacific was discovered in 1513 by Balboa, not Cortez.
5. Darien (der´ ē ən): The Isthmus of Panama.

◆ **Build Vocabulary**

ken (ken) *n.*: Range of sight or knowledge

surmise (sər mīz´) *n.*: Guess; assumption

When I Have Fears That I May Cease to Be

John Keats

John Keats, 1821, Joseph Severn,
By courtesy of the National Portrait Gallery, London

▲ Critical Viewing From this rendering of Keats, how would you characterize him? **[Infer]**

When I have fears that I may cease to be
    Before my pen has <u>gleaned</u> my <u>teeming</u> brain,
Before high-piled books, in charactery,[1]
    Hold like rich garners[2] the full ripened grain;
5 When I behold, upon the night's starred face,
    Huge cloudy symbols of a high romance,
And think that I may never live to trace
    Their shadows, with the magic hand of chance;[3]
And when I feel, fair creature of an hour,
10   That I shall never look upon thee more,
Never have relish in the fairy power
    Of unreflecting love—then on the shore
Of the wide world I stand alone, and think
Till love and fame to nothingness do sink.

---

1. **charactery:** Written or printed letters of the alphabet.
2. **garners:** Storehouses for grain.
3. **chance:** Inspiration.

◆ **Build Vocabulary**

gleaned (glēnd) *v.*: Picked or gathered, as one does with fruit or crops

teeming (tēm′ iŋ) *adj.*: Filled to overflowing

Guide for Responding

◆ *Literature and Your Life*

Reader's Response Do you find the speakers' observations in these poems believable or moving?

Thematic Response Would you describe these poems as fantastic, realistic, or both? Explain.

☑ Check Your Comprehension

1. To what two things does the speaker in "Chapman's Homer" liken himself after reading it?
2. Of what is the speaker in "When I Have Fears" fearful?
3. How does the speaker resolve his fears?

◆ Critical Thinking

INTERPRET
1. What feelings about Chapman's Homer do the similes in lines 9–14 convey? **[Connect]**
2. What is meant by "cloudy symbols of a high romance" in "When I Have Fears"? **[Interpret]**
3. What does the speaker mean by "unreflecting love" in line 12? **[Interpret]**

APPLY
4. Can books change people's lives, as is suggested in "Chapman's Homer"? Explain. **[Generalize]**
5. What does "When I Have Fears" suggest about Keats's views on death? **[Apply]**

Ode to a Nightingale

John Keats

Keats composed the following ode in 1819, while living in Hampstead with his friend Charles Brown. Brown wrote the following description about how the ode was composed: "In the spring of 1819 a nightingale had built her nest near my house. Keats felt a tranquil and continued joy in her song; and one morning he took his chair from the breakfast table to the grass plot under the plum tree, where he sat for two or three hours. When he came into the house, I perceived he had some scraps of paper in his hand, and these he was quietly thrusting behind the books. On inquiry, I found those scraps, four or five in number, contained his poetic feeling on the song of our nightingale."

I

My heart aches, and drowsy numbness pains
    My sense, as though of hemlock[1] I had drunk,
Or emptied some dull opiate to the drains
    One minute past, and Lethe-wards[2] had sunk:
5 'Tis not through envy of thy happy lot,
    But being too happy in thine happiness,—
      That thou, light-winged Dryad[3] of the trees,
       In some melodious plot
    Of beechen green, and shadows numberless,
10   Singest of summer in full-throated ease.

II

O, for a draft[4] of vintage! that hath been
    Cooled a long age in the deep-delved earth,
Tasting of Flora[5] and the country green,
    Dance, and Provençal[6] song, and sunburnt mirth!

---

1. **hemlock:** Poisonous herb.
2. **Lethe-wards:** Toward Lethe, the river of forgetfulness in Hades, the underworld, in classical mythology.
3. **Dryad** (drī´ əd): In classical mythology, a wood nymph.
4. **draft:** Drink.
5. **Flora:** In classical mythology, the goddess of flowers, or the flowers themselves.
6. **Provençal** (prō´ vən säl´): Pertaining to Provence, a region in southern France, renowned in the late Middle Ages for its troubadours, who composed and sang love songs.

◆ **Build Vocabulary**

vintage (vin´ tij) *n*.: Wine of fine quality

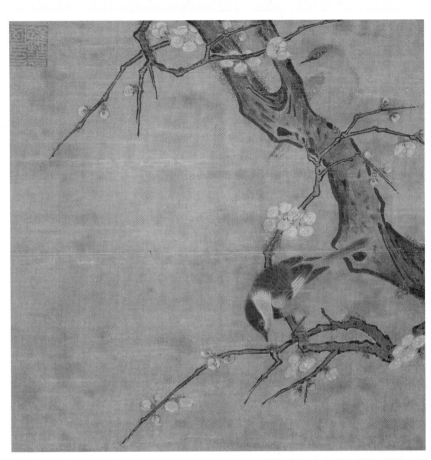

Small Bird on a Flowering Plum Branch
Attributed to Ma Lin, The Gotoh Museum

▲ Critical Viewing
Compare the mood of
this painting with that
of stanza III. [Compare
and Contrast]

15 O for a beaker full of the warm South,
    Full of the true, the blushful Hippocrene,[7]
      With beaded bubbles winking at the brim,
        And purple-stained mouth;
    That I might drink, and leave the world unseen,
20   And with thee fade away into the forest dim:

III

Fade far away, dissolve, and quite forget
    What thou among the leaves hast never known,
The weariness, the fever, and the fret
    Here, where men sit and hear each other groan;
25 Where palsy shakes a few, sad, last gray hairs,
    Where youth grows pale, and specter-thin, and dies;[8]
      Where but to think is to be full of sorrow
        And leaden-eyed despairs,
      Where Beauty cannot keep her lustrous eyes,
30   Or new Love pine at them beyond tomorrow.

---

7. Hippocrene (hip´ ə krēn´): In classical mythology, the fountain of the Muses on Mt. Helicon. From this fountain flowed
the waters of inspiration.
8. youth . . . dies: Keats is referring to his brother, Tom,
who had died from tuberculosis the previous winter.

IV

Away! away! for I will fly to thee,
    Not charioted by Bacchus[9] and his pards,
But on the viewless[10] wings of Poesy,[11]
    Though the dull brain perplexes and retards:
35 Already with thee! tender is the night,
    And haply[12] the Queen-Moon is on her throne,
      Clustered around by all her starry Fays;[13]
      But here there is no light,
    Save what from heaven is with the breezes blown
40   Through verdurous[14] glooms and winding mossy
    ways.

V

I cannot see what flowers are at my feet,
    Nor what soft incense hangs upon the boughs,
But, in embalmed[15] darkness, guess each sweet
    Wherewith the seasonable month endows
45 The grass, the thicket, and the fruit-tree wild;
    White hawthorn, and the pastoral eglantine;[16]
      Fast fading violets covered up in leaves;
      And mid-May's eldest child,
    The coming musk-rose, full of dewy wine,
50   The murmurous haunt of flies on summer eves.

VI

Darkling[17] I listen; and, for many a time
    I have been half in love with easeful Death,
Called him soft names in many a mused[18] rhyme,
    To take into the air my quiet breath;
55 Now more than ever seems it rich to die,
    To cease upon the midnight with no pain,
      While thou art pouring forth thy soul abroad
      In such an ecstasy!
    Still wouldst thou sing, and I have ears in vain—
60   To thy high requiem become a sod.

---

9. Bacchus (bak´ əs): In classical mythology, the god
of wine, who was often represented in a chariot drawn
by leopards ("pards").
10. viewless: Invisible.
11. Poesy: Poetic fancy.
12. haply: Perhaps.
13. Fays: Fairies.
14. verdurous: Green-foliaged.
15. embalmed: Perfumed.
16. eglantine (eg´ lən tīn´): Sweetbrier or honeysuckle.
17. Darkling: In the dark.
18. mused: Meditated.

◆ **Build Vocabulary**

requiem (rek´ wē əm) *n.*: Musical composition honoring the dead

VII

    Thou wast not born for death, immortal Bird!
        No hungry generations tread thee down;
    The voice I hear this passing night was heard
        In ancient days by emperor and clown:
65   Perhaps the selfsame song that found a path
        Through the sad heart of Ruth,[19] when, sick for home,
          She stood in tears amid the alien corn;
            The same that ofttimes hath
        Charmed magic casements, opening on the foam
70   Of perilous seas, in fairylands forlorn.

VIII

    Forlorn! the very word is like a bell
        To toll me back from thee to my sole self!
    Adieu! the fancy cannot cheat so well
        As she is famed[20] to do, deceiving elf.
75   Adieu! adieu! thy plaintive anthem[21] fades
        Past the near meadows, over the still stream,
        Up the hillside; and now 'tis buried deep
        In the next valley-glades:
    Was it a vision, or a waking dream?
80   Fled is that music:—Do I wake or sleep?

---

19. Ruth: In the Bible (Ruth 2:1–23), a widow who left her home and went to Judah to work in the corn (wheat) fields.
20. famed: Reported.
21. anthem: Hymn.

Guide for Responding

◆ Literature and Your Life

Reader's Response Have you ever experienced a mood similar to the speaker's while you were in natural surroundings? Explain.

Thematic Response Is the nightingale real or a figment of the poet's imagination? Explain.

☑ Check Your Comprehension

1. What wish does the speaker express in lines 19–20 and again in lines 31–35?
2. For what was the nightingale not born, according to line 61?
3. (a) What does hearing the word *forlorn* do to the speaker? (b) With what question does he conclude the poem?

◆ Critical Thinking

INTERPRET
1. What causes the speaker's emotional state in stanza I? **[Infer]**
2. (a) What differences between the speaker's world and the bird's are described in stanza IV? (b) What is meant in line 38 by "here there is no light"? **[Interpret]**
3. (a) What does the speaker find tempting in stanza VI? (b) In what ways does the poem shift focus in stanza VII? **[Interpret]**

APPLY
4. This poem ends with a question. What is its relevance, both to the poem and to the spirit of the Romantic movement? **[Apply]**

Ode on a Grecian Urn

John Keats

I

Thou still unravished bride of quietness
    Thou foster child of silence and slow time,
Sylvan[1] historian, who canst thus express
    A flowery tale more sweetly than our rhyme:
5   What leaf-fringed legend haunts about thy shape
        Of deities or mortals, or of both,
          In Tempe[2] or the dales of Arcady?[3]
      What men or gods are these? What maidens loath?[4]
What mad pursuit? What struggle to escape?
10   What pipes and timbrels?[5] What wild ecstasy?

II

Heard melodies are sweet, but those unheard
    Are sweeter; therefore, ye soft pipes, play on;
Not to the sensual[6] ear, but, more endeared,
    Pipe to the spirit ditties of no tone:
15 Fair youth, beneath the trees, thou canst not leave
      Thy song, nor ever can those trees be bare;
        Bold Lover, never, never canst thou kiss,
Though winning near the goal—yet, do not grieve;
      She cannot fade, though thou hast not thy bliss,
20   Forever wilt thou love, and she be fair!

III

Ah, happy, happy boughs! that cannot shed
    Your leaves, nor ever bid the Spring adieu;
And, happy melodist, unwearied,
    Forever piping songs forever new;
25 More happy love! more happy, happy love!
      Forever warm and still to be enjoyed,
        Forever panting, and forever young;
All breathing human passion far above,
      That leaves a heart high-sorrowful and cloyed,
30   A burning forehead, and a parching tongue.

---

1. **Sylvan:** Rustic, representing the woods or forest.
2. **Tempe** (tem´ pē)**:** Beautiful valley in Greece that has become a symbol of supreme rural beauty.
3. **Arcady** (är´ kə dē)**:** Region in Greece that has come to represent supreme pastoral contentment.
4. **loath:** Unwilling.
5. **timbrels:** Tambourines.
6. **sensual:** Involving the physical sense of hearing.

The Orchard Vase (Column Krater),
Side A: Gathering Apples,
The Metropolitan Museum of Art

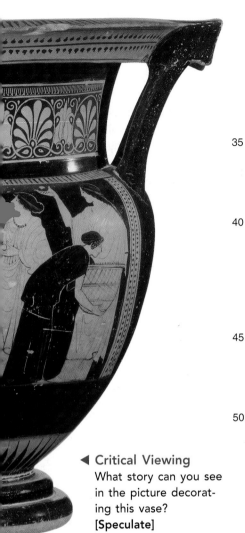

IV

Who are these coming to the sacrifice?
    To what green altar, O mysterious priest,
Lead'st thou that heifer lowing at the skies,
    And all her silken flanks with garlands dressed?
35 What little town by river or seashore,
        Or mountain-built with peaceful citadel,
            Is emptied of this folk, this pious morn?
And, little town, thy streets forevermore
        Will silent be; and not a soul to tell
40   Why thou art desolate, can e'er return.

V

O Attic[7] shape! Fair attitude! with brede[8]
    Of marble men and maidens overwrought,[9]
With forest branches and the trodden weed;
    Thou, silent form, dost tease us out of thought
45 As doth eternity: Cold[10] Pastoral!
        When old age shall this generation waste,
            Thou shalt remain, in midst of other woe
Than ours, a friend to man, to whom thou say'st,
        "Beauty is truth, truth beauty,"—that is all
50   Ye know on earth, and all ye need to know.

◀ **Critical Viewing**
What story can you see in the picture decorating this vase? **[Speculate]**

---

7. **Attic:** Attica was the region of Greece in which Athens was located; a region characterized by grace and simplicity.
8. **brede:** Interwoven pattern.
9. **overwrought:** All over.
10. **Cold:** Unchanging.

Guide for Responding

◆ Literature and Your Life

Reader's Response For Keats, great art embodies the ideas of unchanging beauty, love, and truth. What values do you place on art?

Thematic Response To what reality, or realization, does the speaker arrive at the end of this poem?

☑ Check Your Comprehension

1. Whom or what does this poem address in stanza II? in stanza III?
2. Summarize the two scenes that the urn depicts.
3. What message does the urn convey in line 49?

◆ Critical Thinking

INTERPRET
1. How can the urn tell its "flowery tale more sweetly than our rhyme"? **[Analyze]**
2. What does the speaker feel the leaves, the melodist, and the lovers on the urn all have in common? **[Infer]**
3. (a) Why might the lover in stanza II grieve? (b) Why does the speaker advise him not to grieve? **[Interpret]**

EVALUATE
4. What do you think of the urn's message in line 49? Support your answer. **[Assess]**

Guide for Responding (continued)

◆ Reading Strategy

PARAPHRASE

When you **paraphrase**, restating an author's ideas in your own words, it helps you understand complex or poetic language such as you'll find in Keats's poetry. For example, the line "When I have fears that I may cease to be" is poetically elegant, but its meaning may elude readers. When paraphrased, the line's meaning becomes more evident: "When I'm scared that I'll die." Paraphrase the following:

1. "Then felt I like some watcher of the skies / When a new planet swims into his ken"
2. Stanza VII of "Ode to a Nightingale"
3. First seven lines of "On First Looking into Chapman's Homer"
4. Lines 10–14 of "When I Have Fears That I May Cease to Be"

How did paraphrasing these passages aid your understanding?

◆ Build Vocabulary

USING THE LATIN SUFFIX *-age*

Knowing that the suffix *-age*, as in *vintage*, means "state or quality of, cost of , place of, or collection of," define the following words.

1. wattage   2. shortage   3. patronage
4. leverage   5. storage   6. wastage

USING THE WORD BANK: Sentence Completions

Complete these sentences with the best word from the Word Bank. Write the words in your notebook, and use each word only once.

1. At the funeral, the organist played a ____?____.
2. At harvest time, all the farmer's children ____?____ grain from the reaped fields.
3. Despite the evidence, nothing could sway his initial ____?____.
4. There are many mysteries beyond our ____?____.
5. The bird's breast was ____?____ with song.
6. The wine collector carefully labeled and stored each ____?____.

◆ Literary Focus

ODE

Two of Keats's poems, "Ode on a Grecian Urn" and "Ode to a Nightingale," are powerful **odes**—lyric poems that focus on a single, usually serious subject, often honoring that subject and addressing it directly. There are three basic types of odes. The **Pindaric ode** contains three different types of stanzas, and the **Horatian ode** contains one type of stanza that is repeated. A third type of ode, the **irregular ode**, follows no pattern.

1. (a) What do Keats's two odes honor? (b) Would you say he treats his subjects seriously? Why or why not?
2. Classify Keats's two odes as regular or Pindaric, Horatian, or irregular. Explain.

◆ Grammar and Style

DIRECT ADDRESS

Terms of **direct address**, in which a person or thing is addressed by name or by a phrase, appear frequently in Keats's poetry, investing the poems with an intimate tone. Commas are used to set off terms of direct address from the rest of a clause or sentence. In the following example, note how the inclusion of a term of direct address personalizes the poem, giving it immediacy and warmth.

> And when I feel, *fair creature of an hour,*
> That I shall never look upon thee more,

Practice In your notebook, identify the words of direct address within each passage.

1. "That thou, light-winged Dryad of the trees, / In some melodious plot . . ."
2. "Ah, happy, happy boughs! that cannot shed / Your leaves . . ."
3. "To what green altar, O mysterious priest, / Lead'st thou . . ."

Writing Application Rewrite this paragraph in your notebook, inserting two terms of direct address and punctuating them correctly.

I wandered through Athens thinking of you. Your memory burns bright in my mind. All others fade to nothingness when you're near. Please stay true.

Build Your Portfolio

 ## Idea Bank

Writing

1. **Prose Tribute** Write a prose tribute to the nightingale or the Grecian urn. Express ideas and attitudes similar to those of Keats, but in less lofty, more informal language.

2. **Irregular Ode** Write an irregular ode, or ode with no fixed stanza pattern, that pays tribute to someone or something you admire.

3. **Response to Criticism** Scholar Douglas Bush writes of Keats: "The romantic elements in him remained . . . central, sane, normal—in everything but their intensity—and did not run into transcendental . . . excesses. . . ." Write an essay in which you use passages from Keats's poetry to support this statement.

Speaking, Listening, and Viewing

4. **Informal Retelling** Perform for the class an informal retelling of either "When I Have Fears" or "Chapman's Homer" in contemporary English. **[Performing Arts Link]**

5. **Oral Report** Some of Keats's poems were inspired by the Elgin Marbles in the British Museum. Give an oral report on these works of art, which sparked much controversy. **[Science Link]**

Researching and Representing

6. **Museum Catalog** Working in a small group, create a catalog of ancient Greek pieces found in the British Museum or another museum housing Greek antiquities. You might obtain your information from books or tourist pamphlets. **[Art Link]**

7. **Science Display** Research the nightingale's call, appearance, habits, and habitat. Present your findings in a display that includes photos or other illustrations. **[Science Link]**

Online Activity www.phlit.phschool.com

 ## Guided Writing Lesson

Description of a Moment in Time

In many of his poems, Keats explores significant moments in his life, such as discovering the magic of Homer through Chapman's words, or finding the essence of beauty while gazing at a Grecian urn. Write a description that captures an important moment in your life. Use precise details to convey a main impression of the moment you're re-creating.

Writing Skills Focus: Precise Details

Your description will be more effective if you choose **precise details** to create a main impression. Precise details include these features:
- Vivid verbs and precise nouns
- Interesting and apt comparisons

Model From Literature

Then felt I like some watcher of the skies
   When a new planet swims into his ken;

In these two lines, Keats creates a strong impression of the moment of discovery. The precise details include a comparison of the poet to an astronomer and the vivid verb *swims*.

Prewriting Determine the main impression you wish to convey. Then gather precise details that will help you convey this impression.

Drafting Weave together the precise details you've gathered in an order your readers can follow. For example, if you are describing a scene, you might use a spatial order—for example, presenting details from left to right.

Revising Be sure your details convey a strong, single impression and make clear the significance of the moment you've tried to capture. Delete details that detract from the impression you're making and add details that will more clearly convey the significance of the moment.

CONNECTIONS TO WORLD LITERATURE

The Lorelei
Heinrich Heine

Haiku
Matsuo Bashō Yosa Buson Kobayashi Issa

Literary Connection

LYRIC POETRY

In ancient Greece, lyric poetry was verse recited or sung to the accompaniment of the stringed instrument called the lyre. Today, lyric poems provide their own verbal "music" as they express the personal thoughts and emotions of the poet.

THE ROMANTIC LYRIC POEM

Although lyric poems have been written for thousands of years, the Romantic era put its special stamp on the lyric. The preference of Romantic poets for brief, expressive poems isn't surprising, given their commitment to personal emotion. Wordsworth and Coleridge, writing in the Preface to *Lyrical Ballads* (1800), defined poetry itself as "the spontaneous overflow of powerful feelings."

A second generation of poets—Shelley, Byron, and Keats—contributed their own melodies and perspectives to the Romantic lyric. In "Ode to the West Wind," Shelley gives a political meaning to images from nature as the wind heralds a new era in history. Byron expresses awe at nature's power, and disdain for human pride, in his lyrical "Apostrophe to the Ocean" from *Childe Harold's Pilgrimage*. This poet's brooding pose as a mysterious, despairing hero, at home in nature and scornful of society, influenced Romantic poetry throughout Europe.

LYRIC POETRY AROUND THE WORLD

One European contemporary of Byron's was the German poet Heinrich Heine (hīn'rih hī nə). This talented lyric poet gave the time-honored subject of love a bittersweet flavor in his work, as you will see in "The Lorelei." His lyrics weren't written for music, as ancient Greek verse was, but they were later set to music by such famous composers as Robert Schumann and Franz Schubert.

Writing earlier than the English Romantics, Japanese poets like Bashō (ba' shō), Buson (bōō' sän), and Issa (ē' sä') anticipated the Romantics' love of nature. These writers conveyed suggestive images in the miniature poetic form of the haiku, which consists of three lines of five, seven, and five syllables each. Precise and simple, haiku always contain a reference to a particular season.

HEINRICH HEINE (1797–1856)

The German poet Heinrich Heine was a brilliant love poet and a gifted satirist and political writer whose fierce attacks on repression made him a controversial figure.

MATSUO BASHŌ (1644–1694)

Matsuo Bashō traveled widely through Japan, recording his observations and insights in poems and travel diaries.

YOSA BUSON (1716–1783)

Yosa Buson presents a romantic view of the Japanese landscape, vividly capturing the wonder and mystery of nature.

KOBAYASHI ISSA (1763–1827)

The poetry of Kobayashi Issa captures the essence of daily life in Japan, as experienced by common people, and conveys his compassion for the less fortunate.

The Lorelei

Heinrich Heine

Translated by

Aaron Kramer

I cannot explain the sadness
That's fallen on my breast.
An old, old fable haunts me,
And will not let me rest.

5   The air grows cool in the twilight,
And softly the Rhine[1] flows on;
The peak of a mountain sparkles
Beneath the setting sun.

More lovely than a vision,
10   A girl sits high up there;
Her golden jewelry glistens,
She combs her golden hair.

With a comb of gold she combs it,
And sings an evensong;
15   The wonderful melody reaches
A boat, as it sails along.

The boatman hears, with an anguish
More wild than was ever known;
He's blind to the rocks around him;
20   His eyes are for her alone.

—At last the waves devoured
The boat, and the boatman's cry;
And this she did with her singing,
The golden Lorelei.

---

1. **Rhine** (rīn): River in western Europe.

HAIKU
Bashō

Translated by

Harold G. Henderson (first 3)
and Geoffrey Bownas (last 3)

The sun's way:
Hollyhocks turn toward it
Through all the rain of May.

Poverty's child—
He starts to grind the rice,
And gazes at the moon.

Clouds come from time to time—
And bring to men a chance to rest
From looking at the moon.

The cuckoo—
Its call stretching
Over the water.

Seven sights were veiled
In mist—then I heard
Mii Temple's bell.[1]

Summer grasses—
All that remains
Of soldiers' visions.

---

1. Mii (mē´ ē´) **Temple's bell:**
The bell at Mii Temple is known
for its extremely beautiful sound.
The temple is located near Otsu,
a city in southern Japan.

Crows Taking Flight Through Spring Haze,
(1782–1846) Hanging scroll, Edo period,
dated 1841: Toyama Kinenkan Okada,
Foundation Toyama Memorial Museum

► **Critical Viewing** How
does this painting reflect
the changing of seasons
in the first haiku? **[Interpret]**

HAIKU
Yosa Buson

Translated by

Geoffrey Bownas

Scampering over saucers—
The sound of a rat.
Cold, cold.

Spring rain:
Telling a tale as they go,
Straw cape, umbrella.

Spring rain:
In our sedan
Your soft whispers.

Spring rain:
A man lives here—
Smoke through the wall.

Spring rain:
Soaking on the roof
A child's rag ball.

Fuji[1] alone
Left unburied
By young green leaves.

---

1. Fuji (foo´ jē): Mount Fuji is the
highest peak in Japan (12,388 ft).

HAIKU
Kobayashi Issa

Translated by

Geoffrey Bownas

Melting snow:
And on the village
Fall the children.

Beautiful, seen through holes
Made in a paper screen:
The Milky Way.

Far-off mountain peaks
Reflected in its eyes:
The dragonfly.

A world of dew:
Yet within the dewdrops—
Quarrels.

Viewing the cherry-blossom:
Even as they walk,
Grumbling.

With bland serenity
Gazing at the far hills:
A tiny frog.

Guide for Responding

◆ Literature and Your Life

Reader's Response Did you prefer the short, direct form of haiku or the longer lyric poem "The Lorelei"? Explain.

Thematic Focus Which poem best combines fantasy with reality? Why?

Lyric Subjects List experiences from your own life that might make suitable subjects for a lyric poem. Jot down some details and images you might use in a poem about these subjects.

☑ Check Your Comprehension

1. Describe the woman who entrances the boatman in "The Lorelei."
2. Name three images from nature captured in the poems of Bashō.
3. What season dominates Buson's haiku?
4. Which two haiku by Issa combine far things with near ones?

◆ Critical Thinking

INTERPRET

1. According to German legend, the Lorelei was a sea nymph whose singing on a rock in the Rhine River lured sailors to shipwrecks. (a) What impression of the Lorelei does Heine convey in his poem? (b) Which images contribute to this impression? **[Infer]**
2. Buson establishes the setting in the first line of each of his haiku. How does the setting shape your impression of the image in the final lines of each of these poems? **[Analyze]**
3. Do any of these haiku reflect the bittersweet attitude of Heine's "The Lorelei"? Explain. **[Compare and Contrast]**

EVALUATE

4. Which poet is most effective at conveying images of nature? Why? **[Make a Judgment]**

Literary Connection

LYRIC POETRY

Today, we expect lyric poetry to express a writer's deepest personal feelings, and that expectation is based on the practice of the British Romantic poets. Heine, a European poet influenced by Romanticism, also reveals personal emotion in his work. However, the Japanese haiku, which predate Romanticism and come from a non-European culture, express emotion more indirectly. At first, all the haiku seem to come from the same cookie-cutter. The more you compare them, however, the more you will see the feeling and personality hidden between the lines.

1. What conflict about love does Heine disclose in "The Lorelei"?

2. Which of the haiku writers reveals the best sense of humor? Use specific passages to prove your case.

3. (a) Choose a modern song that, like a Romantic lyric, expresses the writer's deepest emotions. (b) Cite passages from the song to explain what those emotions are.

 Idea Bank

Writing

1. **Japanese "Lorelei"** Rewrite Heine's "The Lorelei" as a haiku without losing the essence of the poem.

2. **Personality Profile** Write a profile of one of these poets based on the thoughts and feelings he expresses in his work. Imagine that this profile will appear on the back cover of his book.

3. **Response to Criticism** Robert Hass has written:

> The spirit of haiku required that the language be kept plain.... It also demanded accurate and original images, drawn mostly from common life.

In an essay, verify or contradict this observation by citing passages from the work of Bashō, Buson, or Issa.

Speaking, Listening, and Viewing

4. **Landscapes and Painting** Natural images play an important part in these haiku and also in Japanese painting. Research the subject of landscape painting in Japan to find visual images that match the images in these haiku. **[Art Link]**

Researching and Representing

5. **Personalities of Poets** Research the life of Heinrich Heine or one of the haiku poets, and present your findings to the class. For information on the Japanese poets, look at books like *The Essential Haiku* by Robert Hass. **[Literature Link]**

Online Activity **www.phlit.phschool.com**

Writing Process Workshop

Video Script

Wordsworth, Coleridge, Byron, Shelley, and Keats—the poets of the Romantic Age—pioneered a new kind of lyric poetry to express their observations, thoughts, and feelings. In our time, many people use film or video as new ways to express observations and ideas. Join them by writing a **video script**—a drama written for video production. A video script is different from a play, since, in addition to dialogue and stage directions, it includes detailed camera directions.

Use the following skills to help you write a video script.

Writing Skills Focus

▶ Your script should contain **details appropriate to the medium.** Such details include lighting directions, camera angles, and dialogue. (See p. 627.)

▶ **Dramatic sound effects** will add excitement and energy to your script. (See p. 655.)

▶ **Realistic speech** will lend authenticity to your work. The style of language and word choice should suit your setting and characters. (See p. 667.)

▶ Your script should **convey one main impression** by carefully focusing on one main topic or character. The details of setting, lighting, costumes, and sound effects should contribute to the one impression. (See p. 693.)

The following video script is adapted from Jane Austen's *Sense and Sensibility.*

MODEL FROM LITERATURE

from *The Sense and Sensibility Screenplay and Diaries*
by Emma Thompson

2. INT. NORLAND PARK. MR. DASHWOOD'S BEDROOM. NIGHT.

In the dim light shed by candles we see a bed in which a MAN *(*MR. DASHWOOD, *52) lies—his skin waxy, his breathing labored.* ① *Around him two silhouettes move and murmur, their clothing susurrating* ② *in the deathly hush.* DOCTORS. *A* WOMAN *(*MRS. DASHWOOD, *50) sits by his side, holding his hand, her eyes never leaving his face.* ③

        MR. DASHWOOD *(urgent)*
Is John not yet arrived? ④

① This description gives the main impression of a deathwatch.

② The use of sound adds tension and creates drama.

③ Extensive use of visual and auditory details makes this story appropriate for film or video.

④ The formality and word choice in this line of dialogue is realistic for an English gentleman of the 1800's.

APPLYING LANGUAGE SKILLS: Special Problems With Agreement

As you write dialogue or voice-over narration for your video script, avoid making errors in subject-verb agreement.

A verb should agree with its subject in number. If you are unsure about whether certain nouns, like *data*, are singular or plural, look them up in a dictionary.

Practice Rewrite the following paragraph, selecting the correct form of the verb from the choices given.

Two hours a day here (is, are) more than most people can endure. Inside, grunts and groans (fill, fills) the air. Large machines (creak, creaks) as devoted athletes build strength. Cheers (is, are) heard infrequently. Still, crowds (stand, stands) in line to join health clubs.

Writer's Solution Connection Language Lab

For more help with agreement, see the Agreement in Number and Special Problems in Agreement lessons in the Subject-Verb unit.

Prewriting

Choose a Topic To find a topic for your video script, look at an art book, visit a museum, or simply take a walk and observe the people and places you see. Following are more topic ideas.

Topic Ideas

- A chapter from a favorite novel
- An episode for a television series

Selection-Related Topic Ideas

- A biography of Lord Byron
- A dramatization of Coleridge's and Wordsworth's friendship and parting of the ways
- A tour of Grecian art and antiques

Select Appropriate Details Select details that will bring your topic to life through visuals and sounds. Jot down sound effects and settings that you would like to capture on film. Also note camera angles, lighting effects, and other special effects that will enhance your video.

Organize the Action If you're telling a story, whether fictional or true, create a plot diagram listing events in order. Show how conflict arises, builds, and reaches a resolution. If your video script is more experimental in nature, plan the order of your camera shots and sound effects.

Drafting

Establish a Main Impression As you draft your video script, focus on creating a main impression—a dominant atmosphere or mood. Use lighting, sound, costumes, setting, and dialogue to create this mood.

Create Effects Through Sound and Voice Sounds alone can establish a setting. For example, the chirping of crickets may indicate to an audience that a scene takes place on a summer night in the country. As you draft your video script, include notes about sound effects.

Use Realistic Speech Have your characters use a level of formality and word choice that is right for the time and place. You wouldn't have an early nineteenth-century aristocrat like Lord Byron speak like a twentieth-century gangster.

Revising

Turn the Script into a Mental Video Ask friends to read your video script aloud while you listen. View the video in your mind, noting where you can change details to support your main impression, revise dialogue to make it realistic, and add sound or camera effects to enhance drama or suspense. Jot down your ideas so that you can use them later as you revise the script.

REVISION MODEL

a video script based on
Percy Bysshe Shelley's "Ozymandias"

(Exterior. Temple Ruins. Mid Afternoon. Camera shows ①
The traveler, an old man whose features are shrouded in a
black cape.)

      NARRATOR *(speaks slowly,*
                  almost reverently) ②

I met a traveler from an antique land

Who said:
(camera pans up the monument.) ③
      TRAVELER *(solemn)*

"Two vast and trunkless legs of stone

Stand in the Desert. Near them on the sand . . ."

① Adding details of setting and a camera direction makes the script more appropriate for this medium.

② Speech directions like these help create a main impression.

③ A timely camera direction helps coordinate words and images.

Publishing

▶ **Storyboards** Illustrate each scene as you envision it would be filmed. Display these "storyboards" for classmates.

▶ **Reading** Cast the roles in your video script and hold a reading. If you like, invite your classmates to watch.

▶ **Rough Footage** Film your video script using a home video recorder. Show your footage to a group of friends.

APPLYING LANGUAGE SKILLS: Formatting Scripts

Video scripts contain many types of information. To avoid confusion, establish and adhere to a standard format in scripts.

In the following example, notice how the character names, technical directions, dialogue, and directions for actors have been formatted.

[Exterior. Lake in morning sunlight. Camera shows WORDSWORTH and COLERIDGE strolling along path]

NARRATOR: It's morning in Somerset, 1797, and Wordsworth and Coleridge are discussing ideas for poetry.

WORDSWORTH: *(with excitement)* Samuel! You've got to listen to this dream of my friend John!

Writing Application Write dialogue first, then go back and add technical and stage directions as necessary.

Writer's Solution Connection
Writing Lab

For help with camera and stage directions, see the Writing Models for Drama in the Drafting section of the tutorial on Creative Writing.

Student Success Workshop

Real-World Reading Skills

Comparing and Contrasting Themes Across Texts

Strategies for Success

As you broaden your reading experience, you will notice certain recurring themes in some of the works you read. For example, you may be reading a novel and recall another literary work that is similar in theme but entirely different in its literary style. Recognizing connections and relationships among different reading materials can be entertaining and enriching, as well as helpful in increasing your understanding.

Identify Themes One way to see connections within and among texts is to identify themes and then compare them. Some themes are universal, such as *love, friendship,* and *change.* Others are more specific, such as *spring.* As you read, look for themes that are ideas, such as *truth;* themes of purpose, such as *achievement;* or themes of concern, such as *environmental pollution;* and so on. Analyze the use of the theme within the book, and compare and contrast it with the same theme in other works.

Analyze Conflicts Another way to compare and contrast literary elements in different works is to identify and analyze conflicts or problems presented in the works. Figure out the central problem, and then ask yourself:

▶ Is the conflict personal, interpersonal, people against nature, people against technology, or some other kind of conflict?

▶ Does the problem involve social, class, political, religious, or racial conflict? How is this conflict similar to and different from those in other texts?

▶ How are the conflicts resolved? How do these resolutions compare and contrast with the resolutions in other texts?

Explore Literary Elements Analyze the text for literary elements, such as characterization, plot, figurative language, symbolism, foreshadowing, mood, and so on. Be alert to allusions, such as classical or biblical references. Compare and contrast these elements within the text, and then consider the use of similar literary elements in other texts.

Apply the Strategies

Choose two literary works that you have read. Use the strategies that you've learned to compare and contrast them. Identify and analyze the themes, conflicts, and literary elements before answering these questions:

1. What is the central theme of each text? What other themes are important? How are the themes alike and different?

2. Identify the main conflicts in each work. In what ways are they similar? How are the solutions similar and different?

3. In what ways do literary elements—such as mood, figurative language, and symbolism—compare and contrast?

✔ *Here are situations in which you might compare themes in different works:*

▶ Writing a term paper
▶ Recommending a book to a friend
▶ Searching the Internet for information on a topic

PART **3**

The Reaction to Society's Ills

Forging the Anchor, 1831, William James Muller, City of Bristol Museum and Art Gallery

The Industrial Revolution, while increasing the national
wealth, also created sharper divisions between rich and poor,
ruling aristocrats and disenfranchised workers. Poets and
historians knew better than politicians that England could not
continue as a divided nation. Writers took the lead in the
battle for reform.

Guide for Interpreting

George Gordon, Lord Byron
(1788–1824)

Though less of a firebrand than his friend Shelley, Lord Byron was in his day a far more prominent supporter of radical reform and political liberty. In Britain, he made his first speech in the House of Lords defending workers who sabotaged factory equipment that had caused them to lose their jobs. (You can read a portion of that speech in the following pages.) Overseas he was closely associated with the Italian freedom fighters known as the Carbonari and lost his life in the cause of independence for Greece. (For more on Byron, see p. 656.)

Percy Bysshe Shelley
(1792–1822)

Of the major romantic poets, Percy Bysshe Shelley was probably the most politically radical. Some of his poems are rallying cries encouraging the British working class to rebel. In 1820 Shelley wanted to publish a collection of these poems, including "A Song: 'Men of England.'" He asked a friend if he knew of "any bookseller who would like to publish a little volume of popular songs wholly political & destined to awaken & direct the imagination of the reformers." (For more on Shelley, see p. 668.)

Thomas Babington Macaulay
(1800–1859)

Before making his mark on history and politics, Thomas Babington Macaulay won fame as a literary critic with essays published in the *Edinburgh Review*. Trained as a lawyer, he then entered the House of Commons, where his eloquence helped ensure passage of the Reform Bill of 1832. This measure helped extend the vote to shopkeepers and other middle-class men. When his party was out of power, Macaulay devoted himself to his writing, producing among other things a famous history of seventeenth-century England.

◆ Background for Understanding

HISTORY: REFORM IN BRITAIN

From the outbreak of the French Revolution in 1789 until Napoleon's defeat at the Battle of Waterloo in 1815, Britain focused on foreign affairs at the expense of much-needed domestic reform. In fact, those demanding reform were often branded as French-inspired revolutionaries. Even after Waterloo, reform was delayed by a dangerous cycle of protests and government crackdowns. These protests, sometimes violent, were caused by postwar depression, high unemployment, and an 1815 Corn Law protecting landowners' high grain prices.

In the Luddite riots from 1811 to 1817, unemployed workers in the industrial north, claiming as their leader the mythical working-class hero General (or King) Ludd, wrecked factory equipment that they felt had taken their jobs. In the "Peterloo Massacre" of 1819, mockingly named after Waterloo, local officials ordered the cavalry to charge a crowd assembled in St. Peter's Field, Manchester, to hear reformer Henry Hunt.

Not until the 1820's did the reform movement begin to see some successes. In 1823, Tory politician Sir Robert Peel reformed Britain's harsh penal code. In 1828 and 1829, Parliament passed laws giving political rights to non-Anglicans. Finally, the Whig party came to power and, in 1832, passed the Reform Bill, extending the vote and ending many unfair election practices.

Speech to Parliament: In Defense of the Lower Classes
◆ A Song: "Men of England" ◆
On the Passing of the Reform Bill

◆ *Literature and Your Life*

CONNECT YOUR EXPERIENCE

The struggle for greater justice in society is evident today in protest marches, editorials, and civil-rights laws that are meant to right wrongs. Shelley, Byron, and Macaulay also worked to make nineteenth-century England a more just society.

Journal Writing Write a bumper sticker or a T-shirt slogan for a cause in which you believe.

THEMATIC FOCUS: THE REACTION TO SOCIETY'S ILLS

As you read the three selections, consider which author would probably be the most effective in remedying society's ills.

◆ Literary Focus

POLITICAL COMMENTARY

Political commentary is speech or writing that provides opinions on political issues. Today, a great deal of political commentary appears on electronic media. In the nineteenth century, such commentary appeared in print or was passed on by word of mouth.

These selections demonstrate three different forms of political commentary in early-nineteenth-century England. Shelley's poem is meant as a rallying cry for working-class people and reformers. Byron's speech is a defense, in Parliament, of textile workers who had destroyed their looms out of desperation. Macaulay's letter is a private communication on a major political event in which he played a role—the passage of the Reform Bill of 1832.

◆ Reading Strategy

ESTABLISH A PURPOSE FOR READING

You'll often get more from your reading if you **establish a purpose** and then read to fulfill it. You might read political commentary from another era to find out more about the writers, to learn about the issues that prompted them to write, or to compare those issues with problems that we face today.

In reading Byron's defense of impoverished workers, for example, your purpose might be to compare the issue of job losses because of technological advances in Byron's time and today.

◆ Build Vocabulary

LATIN ROOTS: -dec-

The word *decimation,* from Byron's speech, contains the Latin root -dec-, meaning "ten." *Decimation* originally referred to punishment for mutiny in the Roman army—killing every tenth person. Today it means "any large-scale killing or destruction."

WORD BANK

Before you read, preview this list of words from the selections.

impediments
decimation
efficacious
emancipate
balm
inauspicious

◆ Grammar and Style

CORRELATIVE CONJUNCTIONS

Macaulay and Byron use **correlative conjunctions**, conjunctions that work in pairs to link grammatically equal words or groups of words:

It is clear that the Reform Bill must pass, *either* in this *or* in another Parliament. (Macaulay)

Correlative conjunctions include *either ... or; not only ... but (also); both ... and;* and *neither ... nor.*

Speech to Parliament:
In Defense of the Lower Classes

— George Gordon, Lord Byron —

"As a person in some degree connected with the suffering county, though a stranger not only to this House in general but to almost every individual whose attention I presume to solicit, I must claim some portion of your Lordships' indulgence, . . .

"When we are told that these men are leagued together, not only for the destruction of their own comfort, but of their very means of subsistence, can we forget that it is the bitter policy, the destructive warfare, of the last eighteen years which has destroyed their comfort, your comfort, all men's comfort—that policy which, originating with 'great statesmen now no more,' has survived the dead to become a curse on the living, unto the third and fourth generation! These men never destroyed their looms till they were become useless—worse than useless; till they were become actual impediments to their exertions in obtaining their daily bread.

Can you then wonder that in times like these, when bankruptcy, convicted fraud, and imputed felony are found in a station not far beneath that of your Lordships, the lowest, though once most useful, portion of the people should forget their duty in their distresses, and become only less guilty than one of their representatives? But while the exalted[1] offender can find means to baffle the law, new capital punishments must be devised, new snares of death must be spread for the wretched mechanic who is famished[2] into guilt. These men were willing to dig, but the spade was in other hands: they were not ashamed to beg, but there was none to relieve them. Their own means of subsistence were cut off; all other employments preoccupied; and their excesses, however to be deplored or condemned, can hardly be the subject of surprise.

"I have traversed the seat of war in the Peninsula;[3] I have been in some of the most oppressed provinces of Turkey; but never, under the most despotic of infidel[4] governments, did I behold such squalid wretchedness as I have seen since my return, in the very heart of a Christian country. And what are your remedies? After months of inaction, and months of action worse than inactivity, at length comes forth the grand specific, the never-failing nostrum of all state physicians from the days of Draco[5] to the present time. After feeling the pulse and shaking the head over the patient, prescribing the usual course of warm water and bleeding[6]—the warm water of your mawkish police, and the lancets of your military— these convulsions must terminate in death, the sure consummation of the prescriptions of all political Sangrados.[7] Setting aside the palpable injustice and the certain inefficiency of the bill, are there not capital punishments sufficient on your statutes? Is there not blood enough upon

◆ **Literary Focus**
What political comments about the upper classes does Byron imply here?

---

1. **exalted:** Well-born; of high rank.
2. **famished:** Forced by hunger.
3. **the Peninsula:** Iberian Peninsula (Spain and Portugal).
4. **infidel** (in´ fə del) *n*.: Non-Christian.
5. **Draco** (drā´ kō): Ancient Greek politician famous for his very severe code of laws.
6. **bleeding:** In Byron's day, doctors often bled patients as a remedy for fever, convulsions, and so on.
7. **Sangrados:** Doctors who bled patients.

your penal code, that more must be poured forth to ascend to heaven and testify against you? How will you carry this bill into effect? Can you commit a whole country to their own prisons? Will you erect a gibbet[8] in every field, and hang up men like scarecrows? Or will you proceed (as you must, to bring this measure into effect) by decimation; place the country under martial law; depopulate and lay waste all around you, and restore Sherwood Forest as an acceptable gift to the crown in its former condition of a royal chase, and an asylum for outlaws?[9] Are these the remedies for a starving and desperate populace? Will the famished wretch who has braved your bayonets be appalled by your gibbets? When death is a relief, and the only relief it appears that you will afford him, will he be dragooned[10] into tranquillity? Will that which could not be effected by your grenadiers,[11] be accomplished by your executioners? If you proceed by the forms of law, where is your evidence? Those who refused to impeach their accomplices when transportation[12] only was the punishment will hardly be tempted to witness against them when death is the penalty.

With all due deference to the noble lords opposite, I think a little investigation, some previous inquiry, would induce even them to change their purpose. That most favorite state measure, so marvelously efficacious in many and recent instances, *temporizing*, would not be without its advantage in this. When a proposal is made to emancipate or relieve, you hesitate, you deliberate for years, you temporize and tamper with the minds of men; but a deathbill must be passed offhand, without a thought of the consequences."

---

12. **transportation:** Practice of sending people convicted of crimes to overseas penal colonies.

---

8. **gibbet** (jib' it): Device used for a hanging a person.
9. **Sherwood Forest . . . outlaws:** Sherwood Forest, near Nottingham, was famous as the refuge of Robin Hood and his band of outlaws.
10. **dragooned** (drə go͞ond'): Compelled by violence, especially as exerted by military troops.
11. **grenadiers** (gren' ə dirz'): Members of Britain's royal infantry.

◆ Build Vocabulary

impediments (im ped'ə mənts) *n*.: Hindrances; obstructions

decimation (des' ə mā' shun) *n*.: Destruction or killing of one in ten, or of any large group

efficacious (ef' i kā' shəs) *adj*.: Producing the desired result; effective

emancipate (ē man' sə pāt) *v*.: To free from slavery or oppression

---

Guide for Responding

◆ *Literature and Your Life*

Reader's Response Did you find this speech persuasive? Why or why not?

Thematic Response Do you think this speech made legislators more willing to remedy society's ills? Explain.

Questions for Research Generate research questions about the social and economic changes Britain was going through at the time Lord Byron made his speech.

✓ Check Your Comprehension

1. (a) According to Byron, why did the men wreck the looms? (b) How do they contrast with upper-class lawbreakers?
2. What does Byron predict will happen if those who destroy machinery are executed?

◆ Critical Thinking

INTERPRET
1. How would you describe Byron's attitude in the opening paragraph? **[Infer]**
2. In the third paragraph, what is Byron comparing to a doctor's patient? **[Analyze]**
3. To what extent is this address an appeal to emotion and to what extent is it an appeal to reason? Explain. **[Draw Conclusions]**

EVALUATE
4. Note an example of exaggeration in the speech and evaluate its effectiveness. **[Evaluate]**

EXTEND
5. Are there any laws today whose punishments you consider too strong or too weak? Explain. **[Social Studies Link]**

Song: "Men of England"

Percy Bysshe Shelley

Men of England, wherefore[1] plough
For the lords who lay ye low?
Wherefore weave with toil and care
The rich robes your tyrants wear?

5   Wherefore feed and clothe and save
From the cradle to the grave
Those ungrateful drones[2] who would
Drain your sweat—nay, drink your blood?

Wherefore, Bees of England, forge
10   Many a weapon, chain, and scourge,[3]
That these stingless drones may spoil
The forced produce of your toil?

Have ye leisure, comfort, calm,
Shelter, food, love's gentle <u>balm</u>?
15   Or what is it ye buy so dear
With your pain and with your fear?

The seed ye sow, another reaps;
The wealth ye find, another keeps;
The robes ye weave, another wears;
20   The arms ye forge, another bears.

Sow seed—but let no tyrant reap:
Find wealth—let no impostor heap:
Weave robes—let not the idle wear:
Forge arms—in your defense to bear.

25   Shrink to your cellars, holes, and cells—
In halls ye deck another dwells.
Why shake the chains ye wrought? Ye see
The steel ye tempered[4] glance on ye.

With plough and spade and hoe and loom
30   Trace your grave and build your tomb
And weave your winding-sheet[5]—till fair
England be your Sepulchre.

1. wherefore: For what purpose? Why?

2. drones: Male bees who perform no work and whose only function is to mate with the Queen Bee.

3. scourge (skʉrj): Whip used to inflict punishment.

4. tempered: Made hard by alternately heating and cooling.

5. winding-sheet (wīn′diŋ shēt): Sheet for wrapping a corpse; shroud.

◆ Build Vocabulary

balm *n*.: Anything healing or soothing

The Workshops at the Gobelins, 1840, Jean-Charles Develly, Musée Carnavalet, Paris

◀ Critical Viewing
In what ways is
this painting an
appropriate
accompaniment
to Shelley's song
for working men?
[Support]

Guide for Responding

◆ Literature and Your Life

Reader's Response How do you think the men of England reacted to this poem?

Thematic Response What advice does the speaker give to "the men of England" about responding to society's ills?

Group Activity Identify contemporary song-writers whose songs convey a message similar to that of Shelley's poem.

☑ Check Your Comprehension

1. What questions does the speaker ask of his audience?
2. What does the speaker ask his audience to do?

◆ Critical Thinking

INTERPRET
1. Sum up all the speaker's questions in a single ironic question to the men of England. **[Connect]**
2. Explain in your own words the comparison of workers to bees. **[Analyze]**
3. Is this a poem that advocates reform or revolution? Support your answer with specific passages from the poem. **[Draw Conclusions]**

EVALUATE
4. Would this poem make a good anthem for radical groups? Why or why not? **[Assess]**

EXTEND
5. Which is more radical, Byron's speech or Shelley's poem? Explain. **[Literature Link]**

On the Passing of the Reform Bill

Thomas Babington Macaulay

Caricature showing those for and against the 1832 Reform Bill, British Museum

◀ **Critical Viewing** How does this cartoon interpret the struggle over the reform bill that Macaulay describes? **[Interpret]**

Dear Ellis,

I have little news for you, except what you will learn from the papers as well as from me. It is clear that the Reform Bill must pass, either in this or in another Parliament. The majority of one does not appear to me, as it does to you, by any means inauspicious. We should perhaps have had a better plea for a dissolution[1] if the majority had been the other way. But surely a dissolution under such circumstances would have been a most alarming thing. If there should be a dissolution now there will not be that ferocity in the public mind which there would have been if the House of Commons had refused to entertain the Bill at all.—I confess that, till we had a majority, I was half inclined to tremble at the storm which we had raised. At present I think that we are absolutely certain of victory, and of victory without commotion.

Such a scene as the division of last Tuesday I never saw, and never expect to see again. If I should live fifty years the impression of it will be as fresh and sharp in my mind as if it had just

> ◆ **Reading Strategy**
> What would you like to learn about the Reform Bill from this letter?

taken place. It was like seeing Caesar stabbed in the Senate House,[2] or seeing Oliver taking the mace from the table,[3] a sight to be seen only once and never to be forgotten. The crowd overflowed the House in every part. When the strangers were cleared out and the doors locked we had six hundred and eight members present, more by fifty five than ever were at a division before. The Ayes and Noes were like two vollies of cannon from opposite sides of a field of battle. When the opposition went out into the lobby,—an operation by the by which took up twenty minutes or more,—we spread ourselves over the benches on both sides of the House. For there were many of us who had not been able to find a seat during the evening. When the doors were shut we began to speculate on our numbers. Every body was desponding. 'We have lost it. We are only two hundred and eighty at most. I do not think we are two hundred and fifty. They are three hundred. Alderman Thompson has counted them. He says they are two hundred and ninety-nine.' This was the talk on our benches. I wonder that men who have been long in parliament do not acquire a better coup d'œil[4] for numbers. The House when only the Ayes were in it looked to me a very fair house,—much fuller than it generally is even on debates of considerable interest. I had no hope however of three hundred. As the tellers[5] passed along our lowest row on the left hand side the interest was insupportable,—two hundred and ninety-one:—two hundred and ninety-two:—we were all standing up and stretching forward, telling with the tellers. At three hundred there was a short

---

1. **dissolution** (dis′ ə lo͞o′ shən): Dismissal of Parliament in order to hold a new election of members of the House of Commons.

2. **Caesar** (sē′zər) **stabbed in the Senate House:** Emperor Julius Caesar, assassinated in the legislative council of ancient Rome.
3. **Oliver taking the mace from the table:** Puritan leader Oliver Cromwell overriding Parliamentary authority by demanding removal of the mace, traditional symbol of the Speaker's authority in the House of Commons.
4. **coup d'œil** (ko͞o dë′ y′): Glance.
5. **tellers:** Those appointed to count votes.

cry of joy, at three hundred and two another—suppressed however in a moment. For we did not yet know what the hostile force might be. We knew however that we could not be severely beaten. The doors were thrown open and in they came. Each of them as he entered brought some different report of their numbers. It must have been impossible, as you may conceive, in the lobby, crowded as they must have been, to form any exact estimate. First we heard that they were three hundred and three—then the number rose to three hundred and ten, then went down to three hundred and seven. Alexander Baring told me that he had counted and that they were three hundred and four. We were all breathless with anxiety, when Charles Wood who stood near the door jumped on a bench and cried out, 'They are only three hundred and one.' We set up a shout that you might have heard to Charing Cross[6]—waving our hats—stamping against the floor and clapping our hands. The tellers scarcely got through the crowd:—for the house was thronged up to the table, and all the floor was fluctuating with heads like the pit of a theatre. But you might

have heard a pin drop as Duncannon read the numbers. Then again the shouts broke out—and many of us shed tears—I could scarcely refrain. And the jaw of Peel[7] fell; and the face of Twiss[8] was as the face of a damned soul; and Herries[9] looked like Judas taking his neck-cloth off for the last operation. We shook hands and clapped each other on the back, and went out laughing, crying, and huzzaing into the lobby. And no sooner were the outer doors opened than another shout answered that within the house. All the passages and the stairs into the waiting rooms were thronged by people who had waited till four in the morning to know the issue. We passed through a narrow lane between two thick masses of them; and all the way down they were shouting and waving their hats; till we got into the open air. I called a cabriolet—and the first thing the driver asked was, 'Is the Bill carried?'—'Yes, by one.' 'Thank God for it, Sir.' And away I rode to Grey's Inn—and so ended a scene which will probably never be equalled till the reformed Parliament wants reforming; and that I hope will not be till the days of our grandchildren—till that truly orthodox and apostolical person Dr Francis Ellis[10] is an archbishop of eighty.

---

6. **Charing Cross:** London neighborhood some distance from the Houses of Parliament.

◆ Build Vocabulary

inauspicious (in´ ô spish´əs) adj.: Not promising a good outcome; unfavorable

---

7. **Peel:** Sir Robert Peel (1788–1850), a leading member of the Tory party, which opposed the bill.
8. **Twiss:** Horace Twiss, another Tory who opposed the bill.
9. **Herries:** J. C. Herries, another Tory who opposed the bill.
10. **Francis Ellis:** Six-year-old son of Thomas Ellis.

Guide for Responding

◆ Literature and Your Life

Reader's Response Were you swept up in the excitement of Macaulay's account? Explain.

Thematic Response To what extent is Macaulay a rebel, a dreamer, a reformer, or a combination of these? Why?

☑ Check Your Comprehension

1. (a) What does Macaulay's friend Ellis find inauspicious? (b) What is Macaulay's argument against Ellis's view?
2. Summarize the events leading up to the passage of the Reform Bill of 1832.

◆ Critical Thinking

INTERPRET

1. In what ways does Macaulay add suspense to his account? **[Analyze]**
2. Give three details that help you picture the events that Macaulay describes. **[Distinguish]**
3. How does Macaulay's final statement convey the importance of the occasion? **[Draw Conclusions]**

COMPARE LITERARY WORKS

4. Compare Macaulay's letter and Lord Byron's Speech to Parliament in terms of their purpose and the effect each author tried to make on the audience. **[Compare and Contrast]**

Guide for Responding (continued)

◆ Build Vocabulary

USING THE LATIN ROOT -dec-

Match the lettered word with the Latin root
-dec- in Column B with its definition in Column A.

Column A	Column B
1. ten years	a. decimals
2. fractions in tenths	b. deciliter
3. contest with ten events	c. decahedron
4. ten-sided figure	d. decade
5. tenth of a liter	e. decathlon

USING THE WORD BANK: Synonyms

Replace each italicized word with a synonym
from the Word Bank.

Both Byron and Shelley saw the practices of
the English upper class as *hindrances* to their efforts
to *free* people and transform them into *effective*
individuals. These poets thought of poetry not as a
salve, but as a force that would *slaughter* outmoded
ideas. In their minds, the most *unfavorable* political
sign was the reluctance of the upper classes to yield
any power.

◆ Grammar and Style

CORRELATIVE CONJUNCTIONS

Correlative conjunctions work in pairs to link
grammatically equal words or groups of words.

Practice Use the following correlative conjunctions to combine each pair of sentences into a
single sentence. Make any other changes needed.

not only ... but (also)   neither ... nor
both ... and   just as ... so (too)
either ... or

1. a. Byron did not write "A Song: 'Men of
England.'"
   b. Macaulay did not write "A Song: 'Men
of England.'"
2. a. Byron supported workers' rights.
   b. Shelley supported workers' rights.
3. a. Shelley compares English workers to bees.
   b. He compares England to the workers' tomb.
4. a. The Tories would win the crucial vote.
   b. The Whigs would win the crucial vote.
5. a. The Whigs celebrate the passage of the bill.
   b. Macaulay celebrates the passage of the bill.

◆ Literary Focus

POLITICAL COMMENTARY

These works of **political commentary** agree
on the need for greater justice in early-nineteenth-
century England, but each writer has a different
goal, audience, and attitude.

1. Compare and contrast Macaulay's goal, audience,
and attitude to those of Shelley or Byron.
2. How do the forms these writers use (poem,
speech, letter) influence (a) the formality of their
language? (b) the inclusion of personal details?
3. Which of these pieces do you think was probably
most effective in achieving its goal? Why?

◆ Reading Strategy

SET A PURPOSE FOR READING

When you set a purpose for reading—determining beforehand what you want to learn—you can
read a work more effectively and efficiently.

1. Which passages of Byron's speech reveal his
purpose for making the speech?
2. Find three passages on which you could focus if
you wanted to learn about workers' grievances.
3. (a) Find a paragraph or stanza you like in one
of the other pieces. (b) Show how reading it
with two different purposes helps you uncover
different facts and ideas.

Beyond Literature

Technology Connection

The Luddites Between 1811 and 1816,
bands of stocking weavers destroyed the new,
more efficient weaving frames that had put
tens of thousands of skilled workers out of
work. The rebellious weavers said they were
acting on the authority of "King Ludd,"
"General Ludd," or "Captain Ludd"—hence
their name, the Luddites. The original Ned
Ludd was a legendary character who, in a fit
of madness, destroyed several weaving frames.
Do you see any parallel between the increasing reliance on computers in business today
and the problems of the Luddites?

Build Your Portfolio

 Idea Bank

Writing

1. **Casting Memo** Reread the biographies of Byron on pp. 656 and 704. Then choose an actor to play him in a movie, and write a memo to the director explaining your choice.

2. **Letter to the Editor** Imagine you are living in England during the early 1800's. Write a letter to the editor of a London newspaper, expressing your opinion of Byron's speech or Shelley's poem.

3. **Response to Criticism** Harold Bloom says, "Ideologically Shelley is of the permanent Left . . . he is nothing short of an extremist, and knew it." Using evidence from "A Song: 'Men of England,'" support or refute this statement.

Speaking, Listening, and Viewing

4. **Political Speech** Rehearse and give Byron's speech as he might have given it. Use your voice, pitch, tone, and volume to deliver your speech emphatically. **[Performing Arts Link]**

5. **Panel Discussion** What might Byron, Shelley, and Macaulay have said to each other in a panel discussion of the issues they address in these selections? Working with a group, role-play such discussion for a television appearance. **[Social Studies Link]**

Researching and Representing

6. **Political Cartoon** Research a controversial issue from history, like the Luddite riots, the 1815 Corn Law, or the Peterloo Massacre. Then create a political cartoon expressing an opinion on it. **[Social Studies Link; Visual Arts Link]**

7. **Song** Working alone or with a partner, set Shelley's poem to music. Then perform it live, on audiotape, or on videotape. **[Music Link]**

Online Activity www.phlit.phschool.com

 Guided Writing Lesson

News Article on a Political Issue

The authors of these selections were deeply involved with the political issues of their time. Imagine that you are a news reporter, and write a news article about a political issue of today.

The following pointers will help you decide what details to include.

Writing Skills Focus: Elaboration to Give Information

In writing articles, you will have to **elaborate to give information**. In writing a news article, answer the questions *who, what, where, when, why,* and *how* to generate the information you need. Here's how you might answer those questions if you were writing a news article about Byron's speech.

- *who*—Lord Byron, poet and Whig
- *what*—speech against frame-breaking bill to make destroying factory machinery a capital offense
- *where*—House of Lords
- *when*—February 27, 1812
- *why*—sympathy for lower classes based on his own sense of being an outsider
- *how*—by appealing to both reason and emotion

Prewriting After choosing a political event or issue to write about, jot down answers to the questions listed above. Include as much detail as you know in response to each question.

Drafting Use a pyramid structure in which the most important information comes first. Add further elaborating details as you develop your article. Make sure to present both sides of the issue and to support general statements with specific details.

Revising Have a classmate read your news article and find the answers to the questions. If he or she cannot easily do so, provide any missing information. Carefully proofread your work for errors in grammar, punctuation, and spelling.

Guide for Interpreting

Jane Austen (1775–1817)

Modest about her own genius, Jane Austen lived a quiet life, one devoted to her family. Never married, she nonetheless explored ideas about love, beauty, and marriage in her novels.

A Reserved Life Jane Austen was born in Steventon, Hampshire, England, the daughter of a clergyman. The seventh of eight children, Jane was educated at home by her father. In her teens Austen began writing parodies and skits primarily to amuse her family.

An Anonymous Novelist Austen's keen sense of awareness and observation helped her to become a successful novelist who captured the absurdities and injustices of society of the time. Like most women writers in her day, Austen published her work anonymously.

After her identity became known, she was honored by the Prince Regent a few years before her death. Her novel *Emma* is dedicated to him.

Hollywood Tributes Jane Austen's sharp satirical eye and brilliant use of dialogue have made her enormously popular in our own day. For example, Hollywood has "discovered" Austen and many of her works have been made into feature films, television films, and mini-series.

Mary Wollstonecraft (1759–1797)

Mary Wollstonecraft is recognized as one of the first major feminists. Despite growing up in poverty, Mary Wollstonecraft was given an education, and after a brief fiasco as a lady's companion, she, her sisters, and a friend established a girls' school near London. In 1787, she wrote *Thoughts on the Education of Daughters*, criticizing the poor education given to most females of her day.

A Voice for Women In 1790, when Edmund Burke attacked the French Revolution, Wollstonecraft defended it in *A Vindication of the Rights of Men.* Two years later she produced *A Vindication of the Rights of Woman,* a landmark work on women's rights. After a brief stay in Paris in which she witnessed the revolution, Wollstonecraft returned home and wed radical thinker William Godwin. A year later she died giving birth to their daughter Mary, who later became the author of *Frankenstein.*

◆ Background for Understanding

CULTURE: THE ROLE OF WOMEN

British women in the early nineteenth century had few economic or legal rights. In most cases a woman's property was legally her father's until she married, after which the property became her husband's. If a woman never wed, her property often remained in the hands of male relatives.

Abused women had little protection under the law, and divorces were almost impossible to obtain. Jobs, too, were limited: Whereas lower-class women might work as household help or in factories, more "genteel" females had to live on the charity of relatives, find posts as governesses or perhaps teach at a girls' school.

Women's education focused mainly on "ladylike" accomplishments such as embroidery, singing, and playing a musical instrument. Women who showed an interest in things beyond marriage and the home were generally regarded as unfeminine.

◆ On Making an Agreeable Marriage ◆
from A Vindication of the Rights of Woman

◆ *Literature and Your Life*

CONNECT YOUR EXPERIENCE

Gender sometimes unfairly influences people's judgment of a person. Think about an assumption you've made about someone based on his or her gender, only to be proved wrong. Notice what these selections reveal about bias and gender roles in nineteenth-century England.

Journal Writing Jot down three assumptions someone might make about you because of your gender. Then write three facts that disprove those assumptions.

THEMATIC FOCUS: THE REACTION TO SOCIETY'S ILLS

As you read the following, think about how ideas about marriage and the role of women might be classified as "society's ills."

◆ Build Vocabulary

LATIN WORD ROOTS: *-fort-*

From the Latin word *fortis*, which means "strong," comes the English root *-fort-*, which means "strength." The word *fortitude,* used by Mary Wollstonecraft in *Vindication,* means "strength of mind that allows one to endure pain or misfortune courageously."

WORD BANK

Before you read, preview the words on this list from the selections.

scruple
amiable
vindication
solicitude
fastidious
specious
fortitude
preponderates
gravity

◆ Reading Strategy

DETERMINE THE WRITER'S PURPOSE

When reading any work of literature, it's important to **determine the writer's purpose**. Knowing what the writer wants to accomplish enables you to read with the appropriate attitude. These techniques help you determine a writer's purpose.

- Look for clues in the work's title and opening paragraph.
- Identify the writer's tone, or attitude, toward the subject, and observe how it affects your opinion of the topic.
- Consider why the writer chose to include particular details and examples.

◆ Literary Focus

SOCIAL COMMENTARY

Social commentary is writing or speech that offers insights about society and its customs. Some social commentary is unconscious, reflecting social attitudes of its period without intentionally discussing them. Other social commentary is purposefully written to criticize society or record its customs.

As you read Jane Austen's letter and the passage from Mary Wollstonecraft's *A Vindication of the Rights of Woman,* use a chart like this to record social commentary that is conscious or unconscious.

Conscious	**Unconscious**

◆ Grammar and Style

COMMAS IN A SERIES

Austen and Wollstonecraft use **commas in a series**; they separate the items in a list with commas. Although it is common to include a comma before the conjunction, it is also acceptable to omit the final comma.

Example: His situation in life, family, friends, & above all his Character—

On Making an Agreeable Marriage

Jane Austen

To Fanny Knight[1]
Friday 18–Sunday 20 November 1814
Chawton Nov: 18.—Friday

I feel quite as doubtful as you could be my dearest Fanny as to *when* my Letter may be finished, for I can command very little quiet time at present, but yet I must begin, for I know you will be glad to hear as soon as possible, & I really am impatient myself to be writing something on so very interesting a subject, though I have no hope of writing anything to the purpose.—I shall do very little more I dare say than say over again, what you have said before.—I was certainly a good deal surprised *at first*—as I had no suspicion of any change in your feelings, and I have no scruple in saying that you cannot be in Love. My dear Fanny, I am ready to laugh at the idea—and yet it is no laughing matter to have had you so mistaken as to your own feelings—And with all my heart I wish I had cautioned you on that point when first you spoke to me;—but tho' I did not think you then so *much*

---

1. **Fanny Knight:** Fanny Austen Knight was the daughter of Austen's brother Edward, who had been made the heir of wealthy cousins on the understanding that he would adopt their surname, *Knight*. The practice was not unusual in Austen's day.

◆ **Build Vocabulary**

scruple (skrōō′ pəl) *n.*: Hesitation caused by one's conscience or principles; uneasy feeling; qualm

Marriage à la Mode: *The Marriage Contract*, 1743, William Hogarth, National Gallery of Art, London

▲ **Critical Viewing:** In what ways does Hogarth's satirical depiction of the signing of a wedding contract echo attitudes toward marriage that are present in Austen's letter? **[Evaluate]**

in love as you thought yourself, I did consider you as being attached in a degree—quite sufficiently for happiness, as I had no doubt it would increase with opportunity.—And from the time of our being in London together, I thought you really very much in love.—But you certainly are not at all—there is no concealing it.—What strange creatures we are!—It seems as if your being secure of him (as you say yourself) had made you Indifferent.—There was a little disgust I suspect, at the Races—& I do not wonder at it. His expressions then would not do for one who had rather more Acuteness, Penetration & Taste, than Love, which was your case. And yet, after all, I *am* surprised that the change in your feelings should be so great.—He is, just what he ever was, only more evidently & uniformly devoted to *you*. This is all the difference.—How shall we account for it?—My dearest Fanny, I am writing what will not be of the smallest use to you. I am feeling differently every moment, & shall not be able to suggest a single thing that can assist your Mind.—I could lament in one sentence & laugh in the next, but as to Opinion or Counsel I am sure none will [be *omitted*] extracted worth having from this Letter.—I read yours through the very even[2] I received it—getting away by myself—I could not bear to leave off, when I had once begun.—I was full of curiosity & concern. Luckily Your Aunt C. dined at the other house, therefore I had not to maneuver away from *her*;—& as to anybody else, I do not care.—Poor dear Mr J. P.![3]—Oh! dear Fanny, Your mistake has been one that thousands of women fall into. He was the *first* young Man who attached himself to you. That was the charm, & most powerful it is.—Among the multitudes however that make the same mistake with Yourself, there can be few indeed who have so little reason to regret it;—his Character & *his* attachment leave you nothing to be ashamed of.—Upon the whole, what is to be done? You certainly *have* encouraged him to such a point as to make him feel almost secure of you—you have no inclination for any other person —His situation in life, family, friends, & above all his Character— his uncommonly <u>amiable</u> mind, strict principles, just notions, good habits—*all* that *you* know so well how to value, *All* that really is of the first importance—everything of this nature pleads his cause most strongly.—You have no doubt of his having superior Abilities—he has proved it at the University—he is I dare say such a Scholar as your agreeable, idle Brothers would ill bear a comparison with.—Oh! my dear Fanny, the more I write about him, the warmer my feelings become, the more strongly I feel the sterling worth of such a young Man & the desirableness of your growing in love with him again. I recommend this most thoroughly.—There *are* such beings in the World perhaps, one in a Thousand, as the Creature You & I should think perfection, where Grace & Spirit are united to Worth, where the Manners are equal to the Heart & Understanding, but such a person may not come in your way, or if he does, he may not be the eldest son of a Man of Fortune,[4] the Brother of your particular friend, & belonging to your own County.—Think of all this Fanny. Mr J. P.- has advantages which do not often meet in one person. His only fault indeed seems Modesty. If he were less modest, he would be more agreeable, speak louder & look Impudenter;—and is not it a fine Character, of which Modesty is the only defect?—I have no doubt that he will get more lively & more like yourselves as he is more with you;—he will catch your ways if he belongs to you. And as to there being any objection from his *Goodness*, from the danger of his becoming even Evangelical,[5] I cannot admit *that*. I am by no means convinced that we ought not all to be Evangelicals, & am at least persuaded that they who are so from Reason & Feeling, must be happiest & safest.—Do not be frightened from the connection by your Brothers having most wit. Wisdom is better than Wit, & in the long run

◆ **Reading Strategy**
Why, if she believes that she has "no hope of writing anything to the purpose," do you think Austen writes anyway?

◆ **Literary Focus**
What do these details reveal about the criteria for judging a suitor in Austen's day?

---

2. **even:** Evening.
3. **Mr J. P.:** Fanny's suitor.

4. **eldest son of a Man of Fortune:** In Austen's day, the bulk of a British family's lands and wealth usually passed to the eldest son.
5. **Evangelical:** Of or relating to a group of earnest Church of England members active in social reform movements at the time of the letter.

will certainly have the laugh on her side; & don't be frightened by the idea of his acting more strictly up to the precepts of the New Testament than others.—And now, my dear Fanny, having written so much on one side of the question, I shall turn round & entreat you not to commit yourself farther, & not to think of accepting him unless you really do like him. Anything is to be preferred or endured rather than marrying without Affection; and if his deficiencies of Manner &c &c[6] strike you more than all his good qualities, if you continue to think strongly of them, give him up at once.— Things are now in such a state, that you must resolve upon one or the other, either to allow him to go on as he has done, or whenever you are together behave with a coldness which may convince him that he has been deceiving himself.—I have no doubt of his suffering a good deal for a time, a great deal, when he feels that he must give you up;—but it is no creed of mine, as you must be well aware, that such sort of Disappointments kill anybody.—Your sending the Music was an admirable device,[7] it made everything easy, & I do not know how I could have accounted for the parcel otherwise;

for tho' your dear Papa most conscientiously hunted about till he found me alone in the Din^g-parlor,[8] Your Aunt C. had seen that he *had* a parcel to deliver.—As it was however, I do not think anything was suspected.—We have heard nothing fresh from Anna. I trust she is very comfortable in her new home. Her Letters have been very sensible & satisfactory, with no *parade* of happiness, which I liked them the better for.—I have often known young married Women write in a way I did not like, in that respect.

You will be glad to hear that the first Edit: of M.P.[9] is all sold.—Your Uncle Henry is rather wanting me to come to Town, to settle about a 2^d Edit:—but as I could not very conveniently leave home now, I have written him my Will & pleasure, & unless he still urges it, shall not go.—I am very greedy & want to make the most of it;—but as you are much above caring about money, I shall not plague you with any particulars.—The pleasures of Vanity are more within your comprehension, & you will enter into mine, at receiving the *praise* which every now & then comes to me, through some channel or other.—

---

6. **&c &c:** Et cetera (the & symbol, called an ampersand, stands for et, Latin for "and").
7. **device:** Trick; ruse; ploy.

8. **Din^g-parlor:** Dining room.
9. **M.P.:** Austen's novel *Mansfield Park*.

◆ **Build Vocabulary**

amiable (āʹ mē ə bəl) *adj.*: Friendly; agreeable

Guide for Responding

◆ *Literature and Your Life*

Reader's Response How would you have reacted to this letter if you were Fanny? Explain.

Thematic Response Do you think Austen viewed marriage as one of society's ills? Explain.

☑ Check Your Comprehension

1. What is the "very interesting" subject of this letter?
2. (a) What virtues in Mr. J. P. does Austen ask Fanny to consider? (b) What does Austen think about marrying without affection?

◆ Critical Thinking

INTERPRET

1. What prompts Austen to write "What strange creatures we are"? **[Interpret]**
2. According to Austen, what good points about Mr. J. P. recommend him as a suitor? **[Support]**
3. What does Austen mean when she says that "Wisdom is better than Wit"? **[Interpret]**

EVALUATE

4. Based on this letter, would you say Austen is a good judge of human nature? Why or why not? **[Make a Judgment]**

from A Vindication of the Rights of Woman

Mary Wollstonecraft

After considering the historic page,[1] and viewing the living world with anxious <u>solicitude</u>, the most melancholy emotions of sorrowful indignation have depressed my spirits, and I have sighed when obliged to confess that either Nature has made a great difference between man and man,[2] or that the civilization which has hitherto taken place in the world has been very partial. I have turned over various books written on the subject of education, and patiently observed the conduct of parents and the management of schools; but what has been the result?—a profound conviction that the neglected education of my fellow creatures is the grand source of the misery I deplore, and that women, in particular, are rendered weak and wretched by a variety of concurring causes, originating from one hasty conclusion. The conduct and manners of women, in fact, evidently prove that their minds are not in a healthy state; for, like the flowers which are planted in too rich a soil, strength and usefulness are sacrificed to beauty; and the flaunting leaves, after having pleased a <u>fastidious</u> eye, fade, disregarded on the stalk, long before the season when they ought to have arrived at maturity. One cause of this barren blooming I attribute to a false system of education, gathered from the books written on this subject by men who, considering females rather as women than human creatures, have been more anxious to make them alluring . . . than affectionate wives and rational mothers; and the

understanding of the sex has been so bubbled by this <u>specious</u> homage, that the civilized women of the present century, with a few exceptions, are only anxious to inspire love, when they ought to cherish a nobler ambition, and by their abilities and virtues exact respect. . . .

The education of women has of late been more attended to than formerly; yet they are still reckoned a frivolous sex, and ridiculed or pitied by the writers who endeavor by satire or instruction to improve them. It is acknowledged that they spend many of the first years of their lives in acquiring a smattering of accomplishments; meanwhile strength of body and mind are sacrificed to libertine[3] notions of beauty, to the desire of establishing themselves—the only way women can rise in the world—by marriage. And this desire making mere animals of them, when they marry they act as such children may be expected to act—they dress, they paint, and nickname God's creatures. . . . Can they be expected to govern a family with judgment, or take care of the poor babes whom they bring into the world?

If, then, it can be fairly deduced from the present conduct of the sex, from the prevalent fondness for pleasure which takes place of ambition and those nobler passions that open and enlarge the soul, that the instruction which women have hitherto received has only tended,

---

3. **libertine:** Wasteful.

◆ **Build Vocabulary**

vindication (vin´ də kā´ shən) *n*.: Act of providing justification or support for

solicitude (sə lis´ ə tōōd) *n*.: Care; concern

fastidious (fas tid´ ē əs) *adj*.: Difficult to please

specious (spē´ shəs) *adj*.: Deceptively attractive; seeming valid but actually illogical or untrue

---

1. **the historic page:** The page of history.
2. **man and man:** Used here in the generic sense to mean human being and human being.

with the constitution of civil society, to render them insignificant objects of desire—mere propagators of fools!—if it can be proved that in aiming to accomplish them, without cultivating their understandings, they are taken out of their sphere of duties, and made ridiculous and useless when the short-lived bloom of beauty is over, I presume that *rational* men will excuse me for endeavoring to persuade them to become more masculine and respectable.

◆ **Reading Strategy**
What basic advice does the author want women to accept?

Indeed the word masculine is only a bugbear;[4] there is little reason to fear that women will acquire too much courage or fortitude, for their apparent inferiority with respect to bodily strength must render them in some degree dependent on men in the various relations of life; but why should it be increased by prejudices that give a sex to virtue, and confound simple truths with sensual reveries?

Women are, in fact, so much degraded by mistaken notions of female excellence, that I do not mean to add a paradox when I assert that this artificial weakness produces a propensity to tyrannize, and gives birth to cunning, the natural opponent of strength, which leads them to play off those contemptible infantine[5] airs that undermine esteem that undermine esteem even whilst they excite desire. Let me become more chaste and modest, and if women do not grow wiser in the same ratio it will be clear that they have weaker understandings. It seems scarcely necessary to say that I now speak of the sex in general. Many individuals have more sense than their male relatives; and, as nothing preponderates where there is a constant struggle for an equilibrium without it has[6] naturally more gravity, some women govern their husbands without degrading themselves, because intellect will always govern.

---

4. **bugbear:** Frightening imaginary creature, especially one that frightens children.
5. **infantine:** Infantile; childish.
6. **without it has:** Without having.

◆ **Build Vocabulary**

fortitude (fôrt′ ə tōōd) *n.*: Strength of mind that allows one to endure courageously

preponderates (prē pän′ də rāts′) *v.*: Becomes larger or heavier than something else

gravity (grav′ i tē) *n.*: Seriousness

Guide for Responding

◆ *Literature and Your Life*

Reader's Response Do you agree that, for a woman, respect may be more important than admiration? Why or why not?

Thematic Focus Which specific social ills does this selection address?

Research With a Partner With a partner, research the status of women's rights in any other culture at the time Wollstonecraft wrote her "Vindication." Generate questions you would most like to research about the subject.

☑ **Check Your Comprehension**

1. What does Wollstonecraft say is the direct cause of the difference between men and women of the time?
2. What, according to Wollstonecraft, is the result of women being poorly educated?

◆ **Critical Thinking**

INTERPRET

1. Judging from the first paragraph, what is the author's attitude toward the subject? **[Analyze]**
2. What does Wollstonecraft mean by the phrase "barren blooming" in the first paragraph? **[Interpret]**
3. According to Wollstonecraft, what role do "notions of beauty" play in most women's lives? **[Infer]**
4. Wollstonecraft, in paragraph three, says "I presume that *rational* men will excuse me …" Why do you think she emphasized *rational*? **[Infer]**

EVALUATE

5. Which elements of Wollstonecraft's argument do you find effective? Which elements are not? Explain. **[Assess]**

APPLY

6. Do you think there is still inequality in male-female education? Cite examples to support your opinion. **[Relate]**

Guide for Responding (continued)

◆ Literary Focus

SOCIAL COMMENTARY

Social commentaries, such as Austen's letter and Wollstonecraft's *Vindication,* offer insights into the customs and values of the time in which they were written. Some social commentary is unconscious, reflecting social attitudes of its period without intentionally discussing them. Other social commentary is intentionally written to criticize society or record its customs. To answer the following questions, use the chart you created while reading.

1. In what ways is Jane Austen's "On Making an Agreeable Marriage" a commentary on society?
2. Do you think *A Vindication of the Rights of Woman* was meant to be a social commentary? Why or why not?
3. Which of the two works do you find more effective as a social commentary? Why?

◆ Grammar and Style

COMMAS IN A SERIES

Writers use commas in a series to separate items for clarity. The usual practice is to include a comma before the conjunction, but it is also acceptable to omit the final comma.

Practice Copy the following sentences into your notebook and punctuate them with serial commas.

1. *Pride and Prejudice* is filled with grace wit and satire.
2. Characters include Jane Elizabeth Mary Kitty and Lydia Bennet.
3. Their amusements include balls visits and letter writing.
4. The Bennets meet Mr. Darcy Mr. Bingley and two of Mr. Bingley's sisters at a ball.
5. Jane falls ill at the Bingleys' home is put to bed and is visited by Elizabeth.

Writing Application Write a paragraph in response to Wollstonecraft's *Vindication.* In it, list reasons you agree or disagree with her ideas. Use serial commas to separate the reasons you list.

◆ Build Vocabulary

USING THE LATIN ROOT -*fort*-

The Latin root -*fort*- means "strong." Explain how its meaning is conveyed in the following words.

1. fortress   **2.** comfort   **3.** fortify   **4.** forte

USING THE WORD BANK: Synonyms or Antonyms?

Indicate in your notebook whether the word pairs are synonyms or antonyms.

1. preponderates, dwindles
2. specious, false
3. vindication, justification
4. amiable, hostile
5. gravity, frivolity
6. solicitude, thoughtlessness
7. scruple, qualm
8. fastidious, sloppy
9. fortitude, weakness

◆ Reading Strategy

DETERMINE THE WRITER'S PURPOSE

Once you determine the **writer's purpose**—the writer's goal—by observing clues as you read, you'll read more effectively. In *Vindication,* Wollstonecraft's sad tone helps her achieve her purpose, which is to persuade. "After...viewing the living world with anxious solicitude, the most melancholy emotions of sorrowful indignation have depressed my spirits ..."

Identifying a writer's purpose is not an exact science. Different readers may identify different purposes in the same material, and sometimes, a writer may have more than one purpose in a piece of writing.

1. (a) Identify Austen's main purpose in writing "On Making an Agreeable Marriage." What clues point you toward this purpose? (b) Might Austen have had any other purpose in writing to her niece? Explain.
2. (a) Mary Wollstonecraft's purpose in *Vindication* is to persuade. By what means did she convey this purpose? (b) Were you persuaded by her argument? Explain.
3. In what ways does identifying a writer's purpose focus your reading?

Build Your Portfolio

Idea Bank

Writing

1. Letter Write Fanny Knight's response to her Aunt Jane. Present her thoughts and feelings.

2. Comparison and Contrast Did Wollstonecraft and Austen have similar views about the role of women in society? Write a brief essay in which you compare and contrast their views.

3. Response to Criticism Author Virginia Woolf once spoke of "the high-handed and hot-blooded manner" in which Mary Wollstonecraft "cut her way to the quick of life." Write a response to this quotation, using excerpts from the work to support your ideas.

Speaking, Listening, and Viewing

4. Conversation In Austen's day, conversations between people separated by distance took place by letter. Update this "conversation" by role-playing a phone call between Jane Austen and her niece Fanny. **[Performing Arts Link]**

5. Persuasive Speech Deliver a portion of Wollstonecraft's *Vindication* to the class as a persuasive speech. Change the wording as necessary to fit an oral presentation. **[Performing Arts Link]**

Researching and Representing

6. Portrait Create a portrait of Fanny Knight's suitor, Mr. J. P., based on the details provided in Austen's letter. **[Art Link]**

7. Timeline of Women's Rights Research important dates in the history of English women and create a timeline for display. For example, note when women won the right to hold property and when they won the right to vote.
[Art Link; Social Studies Link]

Online Activity www.phlit.phschool.com

Guided Writing Lesson

Letter to an Author

Write a letter to Jane Austen or Mary Wollstonecraft in which you express your agreement or disagreement with the ideas she presents in the corresponding selection. For example, you might agree with Austen's views on love and marriage yet disagree with her interference in her niece's life. To be convincing, use language that will help you achieve your purpose.

Writing Skills Focus: Appropriate Language for a Purpose

In writing a letter expressing an opinion, you'll want to be as persuasive as possible. To do this, choose words that will help you to achieve your goal. In the following passage, Wollstonecraft uses strong words to help her accomplish her purpose, to persuade:

Model From the Selection

. . . a *profound conviction* that the *neglected* education of my fellow-creatures is the *grand* source of the *misery* I *deplore* . . .

Prewriting Decide to which author you will respond. Jot down your reactions to the work and the author's opinions. Find specific passages within the work with which you agree or disagree.

Drafting State your opinion and then support it with details. As you do so, carefully choose words that express your feelings.

Revising Add details, if necessary, to give your argument more weight. Review your word choice to determine if your words accomplish your purpose. Change words as necessary to get the effect you want. Be sure that you have used the correct format for a business letter, and check to see that your writing is free from grammar, spelling, and punctuation errors.

CONNECTIONS TO TODAY'S WORLD

from The *Sense and Sensibility* Screenplay and Diaries
Emma Thompson

Thematic Connection

THE REACTION TO SOCIETY'S ILLS

The pieces in this section serve as political and social commentary on the problems of early-nineteenth-century England. Shelley urges workers to fight for fair treatment, Byron defends the common worker from the tyranny of aristocrats, and Macaulay joyfully describes the passage of an important reform measure. In the field of women's rights, Wollstonecraft powerfully states the need for reform. Austen, in her private correspondence, offers not a political program but a playful commentary on social conditions.

SOCIAL AWARENESS TODAY

Contemporary writers also use their work to make people aware of social injustice. In her screenplay for the movie version of Jane Austen's *Sense and Sensibility,* Emma Thompson deals with issues relevant to both Austen's time and ours. These issues concern differences in the opportunities available to men and women, and to people of various backgrounds.

Thompson skillfully explores these issues in what appears to be an innocent conversation between two friends. Notice how Thompson uses the directions in italics to explain the emotional atmosphere in which this revealing discussion takes place.

As you read, note the CAM abbreviation that indicates camera direction. EXT stands for exterior or outside shot, and the numbers indicate the scene or shot.

EMMA THOMPSON
(1959–)

London-born Emma Thompson is one of England's most talented and successful actors. She studied literature at Cambridge, originally planning on becoming a writer. She then pursued a career in stand-up comedy and gained notoriety in a television comedy series in which she starred with her mother and sister. Thompson went on to achieve success in films; she has received an Academy Award for her performance in *Howard's End* and two other nominations for performances in *The Remains of the Day* and *In the Name of the Father.* Her writing career began with her script for an adaptation of Jane Austen's *Sense and Sensibility,* for which she won an Academy Award.

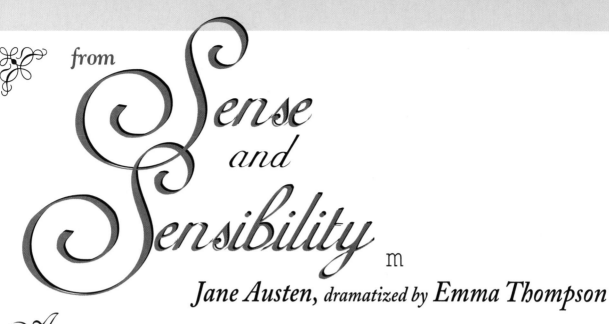

from

Sense and Sensibility

Jane Austen, dramatized by *Emma Thompson*

After the recent death of Mr. Dashwood, his daughters Elinor, Marianne, and Margaret are trying to overcome their grief. Mr. Dashwood's eldest son and his wife, Fanny, have taken possession of the family home. Edward Ferrars, Fanny's brother, makes a great effort to comfort Margaret, the youngest, and in doing so begins to win the love of the eldest daughter, Elinor.

27 INT. NORLAND PARK. VELVET ROOM. ANOTHER DAY. EDWARD *comes into the doorway and sees ELINOR who is listening to MARIANNE playing a concerto. ELINOR stands in a graceful, rather sad attitude, her back to us. Suddenly she senses EDWARD behind her and turns. He is about to turn away, embarrassed to have been caught admiring her, when he sees she has been weeping. Hastily she tries to dry her eyes. He comes forward and offers her a handkerchief, which she takes with a grateful smile. We notice his monogram in the corner: ECF.*

ELINOR *(apologetic)*
That was my father's favorite.

EDWARD *nods kindly.*

ELINOR
Thank you so much for your help with Margaret, Mr. Ferrars. She is a changed girl since your arrival.

EDWARD
Not at all. I enjoy her company.

ELINOR
Has she shown you her tree-house?

EDWARD
Not yet. Would you do me the honor, Miss Dashwood? It is very fine out.

ELINOR
With pleasure.

They start to walk out of shot, still talking.

ELINOR
Margaret has always wanted to travel.

EDWARD
I know. She is heading an expedition to China shortly. I am to go as her servant but only on the understanding that I will be very badly treated.

ELINOR
What will your duties be?

EDWARD
Sword-fighting, administering rum and swabbing.

ELINOR
Ah.

CAM *tilts up to find* MRS. DASHWOOD *on the middle landing of the staircase, smiling down at them.* CAM *tilts up*

yet further to find FANNY *on the landing above, watching* EDWARD *and* ELINOR *with a face like a prune.*
28 EXT. NORLAND PARK. GARDENS. DAY.
EDWARD *and* ELINOR *are still talking as they walk arm in arm in the late-afternoon sun.*

EDWARD
All I want—all I have ever wanted—is the quiet of a private life but my mother is determined to see me distinguished.

▲ **Critical Viewing** What can you tell from this movie still about the type of conversation Edward and Elinor are having? **[Interpret]**

ELINOR
As?

EDWARD
She hardly knows. Any fine figure will suit—a great orator, a leading politician, even a barrister would serve, but only on the condition that I drive my own barouche[1] and dine in the first circles.

His tone is light but there is an under-lying bitterness to it.

ELINOR
And what do you wish for?

EDWARD
I always preferred the church, but that is not smart enough for my mother—she prefers the army, but that is a great deal too smart for me.

ELINOR
Would you stay in London?

EDWARD
I hate London. No peace. A country living is my ideal—a small parish where I might do some good, keep chickens and give short sermons.

30 EXT. FIELDS NEAR NORLAND. DAY. EDWARD *and* ELINOR *are on horseback. The atmosphere is intimate, the quality of the conversation rooted now in their affections.*

ELINOR
You talk of feeling idle and useless— imagine how that is compounded when one has no choice and no hope whatso- ever of any occupation.

---

1. barouche (bə rōōsh´) *n.*: Four-wheeled carriage with a collapsible hood and two seats on each side.

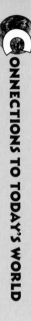
EDWARD *nods and smiles at the irony of it.*

EDWARD
Our circumstances are therefore precisely the same.

ELINOR
Except that you will inherit your fortune.

He looks at her slightly shocked but enjoying her boldness.

ELINOR (*cont.*)
We cannot even earn ours.

EDWARD
Perhaps Margaret is right.

ELINOR
Right?

EDWARD
Piracy is our only option.

They ride on in silence for a moment.

EDWARD (*cont.*)
What *is* swabbing exactly?

Guide for Responding

◆ *Literature and Your Life*

Reader's Response Do you feel sorry for either Edward or Elinor? Explain.

Thematic Connection What problems in society do the problems of Edward and Elinor reflect?

Journal Writing What problem in current-day society would you change? How would you go about achieving this goal?

☑ Check Your Comprehension

1. (a) What does Edward's mother want him to do? (b) What does Edward want to do?
2. (a) Why does Edward believe his and Elinor's situations are the same? (b) What is the major difference that Elinor points out?

◆ Critical Thinking

INTERPRET

1. Edward's mother seems to have set ideas about what he should do with his life. How might this be a reflection of the restrictions placed on women at this time? **[Infer]**
2. In response to Edward's comment about their similarities, Elinor replies, "Except that you will inherit your fortune. We cannot even earn ours." (a) What does Elinor mean by this? (b) How does her comment relate to the issues of the day? **[Interpret]**
3. How does this excerpt from the screenplay reflect the attitudes of Austen's letter and Wollstonecraft's essay? Explain. **[Compare and Contrast]**

EXTEND

4. In what ways can a screenplay be effective in making people socially aware? **[Media Link]**

Thematic Connection

THE REACTION TO SOCIETY'S ILLS

The writers in this section react to the oppressive roles that society defines for women and those belonging to certain social classes. For example, in the screenplay of *Sense and Sensibility*, Elinor and Edward are limited by their gender and social class. Even in a democratic society, barriers still exist based on social class, gender, and race.

1. What limitations in requesting reform might Shelley and Byron have experienced as a result of being men and belonging to upper-class society?
2. Which selections in this section convey themes of injustice that are still relevant today?
3. What successes has society had in improving social conditions for all people?

 Idea Bank

Writing

1. **Letter to the President** If there was one social issue that you believed needed more attention, what would it be? Write a letter to the President in which you describe the issue and offer solutions for it.

2. **Prediction** Looking back on the problems of the early part of the nineteenth century, you can probably see that many have been solved. Write a list of predictions that describe how some social problems that exist now may be solved in the future.

3. **Social Criticism** Write a scene from a play in which you use the dialogue and action to make people socially aware.

Speaking, Listening, and Viewing

4. **Interview** Interview someone from an older generation or different culture. Ask the person how societal norms and expectations shaped his or her life decisions, such as career or marriage. Ask what he or she might have done differently given today's opportunities. Ask permission to publish the interview in your school paper. **[Social Studies Link]**

Researching and Representing

5. **Historical Account** Research a moment in history that especially interests you. Then write a first-person account of the event as if you were present. Share your account with your classmates. **[Social Studies Link]**

Online Activity www.phlit.phschool.com

Writing Process Workshop

In the commentaries in this section the writers "sell" their ideas by supporting them with factual details. If these writers were selling their qualifications to a potential employer, they would use the same basic strategies. Promote yourself by creating a job portfolio that includes a cover letter and résumé. In your cover letter, briefly introduce yourself. In your résumé, give a brief summary of your work experience, educational history, and special skills.

Use the following skills as you develop a job portfolio.

Writing Skills Focus

▶ **Elaborate to give information.** Give prospective employers details about your education, skills, talents, and participation in clubs and organizations. (See p. 713.)

▶ **Use appropriate language for your purpose.** Persuade a prospective employer to hire you by using language that is clear, confident, enthusiastic, and correct. (See p. 723.)

▶ **Structure your résumé and letter** according to standard formats.

WRITING MODEL: COVER LETTER

Anna Turpin
874 Farley Road
Cornwells Heights, PA 19020
June 3, 2000 ①

Ms. Leslie Throckmorton
Village Bookery
Clinton, NY 13323

Dear Ms. Throckmorton: ②

I'm interested in obtaining a sales position at your bookstore. ③ This fall I'll be attending Hartsdale College, where I plan to study literature. I feel that my deep interest in literature would work to our mutual advantage.

Enclosed please find my résumé.

Sincerely, ④

Anna Turpin

① Your name, address, and the date appear at the top. The name and address of your potential employer should appear next.

② This standard greeting followed by a colon opens the letter.

③ It's advisable to state your objective at the outset.

④ The cover letter should end with a closing such as this one.

WRITING MODEL: RÉSUMÉ

Anna Turpin
874 Farley Road
Cornwells Heights, PA 19020
(215) 649-0086 ①

EMPLOYMENT: ②
<u>Summer 1999 to Fall 1999</u>: ③ Cornwells Public Library
Job Title: Assistant to Librarian
Responsibilities: Read stories to children; helped at check-out desk ④
<u>Summer 1998 to Fall 1998</u>: Mindy's Ice Cream
Job Title: Counter clerk
Responsibilities: Filled orders; operated cash register
EDUCATION:
June 2000: Graduated from Cornwells High
SKILLS AND ABILITIES: Driver's license; Scuba certified

① This information should appear prominently.

② Details should appear under headings like this one.

③ List work experience in reverse chronological order.

④ Entries should be brief, yet clear. Omit the pronoun "I."

Prewriting

Choose a Topic and Select Details To find a position for which you'd like to apply, look through the want ads in your local newspaper. After choosing a position, plan your cover letter and résumé. Jot down relevant details from your employment history, school activities, and education that might help you win the job.

Drafting

Be Sure Your Language Is Appropriate Your purpose is to persuade someone to offer you a job. To do this, use clear and specific details, an enthusiastic and confident tone, and language that is formal and sincere. For example, change "I'd get a kick out of working for you" to "I'm eager to work for you."

Use a Consistent Résumé Format In writing your résumé, keep to a consistent format. For example, use words with capital letters to head each section, use bold typeface for words such as *job title* and *responsibilities*, and underline dates.

Use Proper Format for a Cover Letter Use the standard business-letter format that you see in the model on the previous page.

APPLYING LANGUAGE SKILLS: Using Positive Language

Emphasize your skills with words and phrases that have positive, rather than neutral or negative, associations. Following are some examples:

Neutral Examples:
This is an interesting book.

I <u>learned</u> AutoCAD last summer.

Positive Examples:
This is an <u>incomparable</u> book.

My <u>internship gave me first-rate experience</u> with AutoCAD.

Practice Rewrite the following sentences, using positive language.

1. I would like this job.
2. Your firm has a decent reputation.
3. Having had four years of experience as a day-care aide, I would make a satisfactory teacher.
4. I trained some of my co-workers.

Writer's Solution Connection Language Lab

For more help organizing your cover letter, see the lessons on Unity and Coherence in Paragraphs and Composition.

APPLYING LANGUAGE SKILLS: Using Concise Language

Because space on a résumé is limited, it's important to be brief and concise in describing your job qualifications and work history.

Wordy:

Overseer of the collection of garbage

Typed letters; filed letters

Concise:

Sanitation Chief

Clerical duties

Practice Rewrite this portion of a résumé, making the language as brief and concise as possible.

Job Title: Administrative helper of principal

Job Responsibilities: standing in the hallways of a busy school, making sure that traffic flows smoothly and that no one is cutting class

Writing Application Review your résumé and cover letter, and delete instances of wordiness.

Writer's Solution Connection Writing Lab

For more help in revising, see the interactive Self-Evaluation checklists in the Revising and Editing section of the Practical and Technical Writing tutorial.

Revising

Revision Checklist As you review your cover letter and résumé, ask yourself the following:

1. Have I included all relevant work experience, education, and activities?
2. Have I conveyed confidence and enthusiasm through positive language?
3. Is the format of the résumé and cover letter proper and consistent?

REVISION MODEL

Julia Rose
143 Summer Walk Avenue
Boca Raton, FL 33268
November 17, 1999

Mr. James Evans
2000 Bayview Parkway
Tampa, FL 35987

Dear Mr. Evans, ①:

I am interested in a job ~~in your office~~. ② summer internship at your law firm. As valedictorian of

③ I volunteer for legal aid two hours a week.

my class, I have a strong academic background. My goal is

to pursue a career in law. . . .

① The comma was replaced with a colon, which is standard in business letters

② The writer replaces a vague statement with specific, positive information.

③ This sentence adds relevant information about the job seeker's experience and enthusiasm for the profession.

Publishing

▶ **Personal Portfolio** Add your job portfolio to your collection of other writing you've kept over the years.

▶ **Job Fair** Hold a job fair with other interested classmates. Invite prospective employers to meet your classmates and discuss career options with them. Ask them also to review your job portfolio.

▶ **Real-life Job Applications** Send your completed portfolio to potential employers.

Student Success Workshop

Analyze the Effects of Word Choice and Organization

Strategies for Success

An effective reader develops the habit of reading critically. By analyzing your response to an author's word choice and organization, you will increase your comprehension and enhance your understanding of the writer's purpose. Word choice and organization will differ, depending on the type of material you are reading: descriptive, informative, or persuasive.

Notice the Organization of the Text The organization of the material will affect the way the audience considers the subject. Informative text may be developed with a clear opening statement, detailed facts, and a strong conclusion. For certain subjects, the writer may make his or her points through a comparison-and-contrast pattern of organization. A novelist may tell a tale out of chronological order using flashbacks, to involve readers in unraveling a mystery. A science experiment, however, should be written in chronological order to explain the steps. An advertisement may rely on a cause-and-effect pattern to persuade.

Evaluate the Words Evaluate how a writer's language is intended to influence an audience. For instance, a scientist writing on a recent medical breakthrough for a group of doctors may use language that is formal and technical to express ideas precisely. A college recruiter writing for high-school seniors may use informal language, including slang and popular phrases, to attract students to the school. Writers also choose words to evoke emotion—anger, fear, laughter, or empathy—in the audience.

Determine the Purpose and Desired Effect As you read, ask yourself whether the writer is trying to inform you, entertain you, or persuade you. Often, the writer has more than one purpose for writing. For example, a magazine story may be written to inform as well as to entertain. Once you understand the writer's purpose, analyze the writer's organization and word choices to determine their effect on you, the audience.

Apply the Strategies

Read one example each of an informative, a descriptive, and a persuasive text. Determine how word choice and organization are used to affect the audience. Answer the following questions:

1. In the informative passage, how is the content organized?

2. In the descriptive passage, what tone does the author establish through language? How does the writer's language affect you?

3. In the persuasive passage, who is the target audience? What words has the writer chosen to persuade you?

✔ *Here are some other situations in which to evaluate texts for organization and word choice:*
▶ *Reading a political speech*
▶ *Studying a medical journal*
▶ *Choosing resource materials*

Speaking, Listening, and Viewing Workshop

Evaluating a Dramatic Performance

Learning how to evaluate dramatic performances can help you become a thoughtful critic. You'll be able to back up your opinions with specific reasons. To make a sound evaluation of a presentation, be an active listener and viewer and keep some specific criteria for drama analysis in mind as you watch.

Analyze a Dramatic Performance A dramatist combines many literary elements to create a successful play, movie, or television performance. These elements are similar in many ways to those used by a fiction writer. The dramatist, however, usually includes stage directions for the performers, props, lighting, and setting. As you analyze the artistic elements in the performance, ask yourself these questions:

▶ What is the plot of the drama? Is it interesting? How does the story build to a climax? What is the resolution? Does the story make sense?

▶ Who are the characters? Are they well developed and interesting or one dimensional and flat?

▶ What is the setting? How do the time and place affect the mood and characters?

▶ What costumes and props are used? Do they enhance the story?

▶ What, if any, special effects are used? Do they help—or hurt—the presentation?

Evaluate a Performance When you evaluate a dramatic performance, the oral and visual presentation is as important as the artistic elements. The speaking, acting, set design, and music are all important. In your evaluation, consider the following questions:

▶ How effective are the performers in portraying the characters? Are they believable? Are their actions appropriate?

▶ How well do they project their voices? Can you hear and understand their lines? Do the tone, pitch, and tempo match the action of the plot?

▶ Do the gestures of the performers help express what they are saying?

Critique a Performance When you are involved in a dramatic performance, you may be asked to critique the performances of others—to encourage them with praise and to give them concrete, positive criticism. When you critique others, consider each performer's interpretation of the artistic elements in the play: movements, voice, facial expressions, posture, gestures, and interactions with other performers. Tactfully point out his or her strengths and weaknesses, and give specific, constructive suggestions for improvement.

Apply the Strategies

Work with a group to plan and present a performance of a one-act play. As a group, figure out how the plot develops and how the characters should behave in each scene. Study the stage directions. Have a rehearsal, and evaluate and critique the performance of each member. Consider movements, actions, expressions, and gestures. Explain what was good about each performance, and give specific suggestions for improvement. Use the suggestions to revise and strengthen the performance.

Tips for evaluating a dramatic performance:

▶ Review the plot. Decide whether the story is being enacted in the most meaningful way.

▶ Determine whether the set design and music relate well to the story.

▶ Concentrate on the interactions of all the main characters.

Test Preparation Workshop

Critical Reading | Critical Reasoning

Strategies for Success

The reading sections of certain standardized tests require you to use your critical reasoning skills to evaluate written materials. Use the following strategies to help you answer test questions on these skills:

Evaluate a Writer's Assumptions A writer's work may be based on stated or implied assumptions. Use critical reasoning to determine the validity of the writer's assumptions. Ask: What does the writer take for granted? Look at the following example:

> The serious accident at the Three Mile Island nuclear facility began with a simple mechanical error. The plant, located on an island in the Susquehanna River, is near Harrisburg, Pennsylvania. Radiation leaked into the control room. Radioactive water discharged into the Susquehanna. A hydrogen bubble formed in the reactor, increasing the potential of a deadly explosion. People around the world were shocked by the news. Engineers prevented the core from melting down, but the facility was damaged beyond repair. The accident caused widespread fear in the nuclear industry. The lessons learned at Three Mile Island will prevent such accidents in the future.

I What potentially invalid assumption does the writer make?

A The accident began as a mechanical error.
B A hydrogen bubble can cause an explosion.
C The mechanics at the site were incompetent.
D Fear can prevent accidents.

Answers **A** and **B** are stated directly as facts, so they are not assumptions. **C** is incorrect because no assumption is made about the mechanics. **D** is correct. There are no supporting facts to validate this assumption.

Judge the Relevance of Facts Writers often use facts, examples, or experts' opinions to support their arguments. After identifying the support for an idea, decide whether or not it is relevant. Does it have a direct bearing on the argument?

2 In the sample passage, which fact is irrelevant to the main idea?

A Engineers prevented a meltdown.
B Mechanical error caused the accident.
C The plant is located near Harrisburg.
D Radiation leaked into the control room.

Remember the main idea of the passage—that there was a serious accident at Three Mile Island. Answers **A, B,** and **D** are relevant because they support this main idea. **C** is irrelevant, so it is the correct choice. The location of the plant does not support the idea of a serious accident.

Apply the Strategies

Refer to the sample passage to answer the following questions:

I What invalid assumption does the writer make?

A Hydrogen is explosive and should be banned.
B Radioactive gases escaped.
C Engineers at other reactors will avoid mechanical errors.
D Other nuclear power plants have better engineers.

2 Which fact is irrelevant?

A Radiation leaked into the control room.
B The plant is located on an island in the Susquehanna River.
C The facility was damaged beyond repair.
D Radioactive water emptied into the Susquehanna River.

The Railway Station, 1862, William Powell Frith, Royal Holloway and Bedford New College, Surrey

Progress and Decline:

The Victorian Period (1833–1901)

In order that people may be happy
in their work, these three things are
needed: They must be fit for it. They
must not do too much of it. And they
must have a sense of success in it.

—John Ruskin,
from *Pre-Raphaelitism*

Timeline
1833–1901

1833	1845	1855

British Events

- **1833** Slavery abolished in British empire.
- **1837** Victoria becomes queen. ▼
- **1837 Charles Dickens** writes *Oliver Twist.*
- **1837** Thomas Carlyle publishes *The French Revolution.*
- **1840** Michael Faraday experiments with electric currents.
- **1843 William Wordsworth** becomes poet laureate.
- **1844** George Williams founds YMCA.

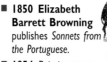

- **1845** Irish Potato Famine begins. ▼
- **1847** Factory Act passed.
- **1847 Charlotte Brontë** publishes *Jane Eyre.*
- **1847 Emily Brontë** publishes *Wuthering Heights.*
- **1848** Women begin attending University of London.
- **1850 Elizabeth Barrett Browning** publishes *Sonnets from the Portuguese.*
- **1854** Britain enters Crimean War.

- **1859** Charles Darwin publishes *On the Origin of Species.*
- **1860** Florence Nightingale founds school for nurses. ▼

- **1863** Construction of London Underground begins.
- **1868** Robert Browning publishes *The Ring and the Book.*

World Events

- **1836** United States: Ralph Waldo Emerson publishes *Nature.*
- **1841** South Pacific: New Zealand becomes a British colony.
- **1842** Asia: Hong Kong becomes a British Colony.
- **1842** France: Honoré de Balzac publishes *The Human Comedy.*
- **1844** United States: Samuel F. B. Morse patents telegraph. ▶

- **1848** France: Revolution establishes new republic under Louis Napoleon.
- **1848** Belgium: Marx and Engels publish the *Communist Manifesto.*
- **1850** France: Life insurance introduced.
- **1850** Germany: Wagner's opera *Lohengrin* first performed.
- **1851** Australia: Gold discovered in New South Wales.
- **1853** Eastern Europe: Crimean War begins.
- **1854** Japan: Trade with West reopened.
- **1854** United States: Henry David Thoreau publishes *Walden.* ▲

- **1856** France: Gustave Flaubert publishes *Madame Bovary.*
- **1857** India: Sepoy Mutiny against British.
- **1858** India: Political power of East India Company abolished.
- **1861** United States: Civil War begins. ▶

British Events

- **1865** London Fire Department established.
- **1865** Lewis Carroll publishes *Alice's Adventures in Wonderland*. ▼
- **1869** Debtors' prisons abolished.

- **1878** Salvation Army established.
- **1880** Joseph Swan installs first electric lighting. ▶
- **1883** Robert Louis Stevenson publishes *Treasure Island*.
- **1884** First edition of *Oxford English Dictionary* published.

- **1887** First Sherlock Holmes tale published.
- **1888** English Lawn Tennis Association founded at Wimbledon. ▼

- **1888** Jack the Ripper stalks London's East End.
- **1891 Thomas Hardy** publishes *Tess of the d'Urbervilles*.
- **1892 Rudyard Kipling** publishes *Barrack-room Ballads*.
- **1895** Oscar Wilde publishes *The Importance of Being Earnest*.
- **1896 A.E. Housman** publishes *A Shropshire Lad*.
- **1901** Queen Victoria dies.

World Events

- **1865** Russia: **Leo Tolstoy** publishes *War and Peace*.
- **1865** Austria: Gregor Mendel proposes laws of heredity. ▼
- **1866** Europe: Seven Weeks' War leads to unification of modern Germany.
- **1869** Egypt: Suez Canal completed.
- **1873** France: Jules Verne publishes *Around the World in Eighty Days*.

- **1876** United States: Alexander Graham Bell patents telephone. ▶
- **1877** United States: Thomas Edison patents phonograph.
- **1879** South Africa: Zulu War against British.
- **1880** Russia: Feodor Dostoevsky publishes *The Brothers Karamazov*.
- **1882** Egypt: Britain conquers nation.
- **1884** United States: Mark Twain publishes *The Adventures of Huckleberry Finn*.

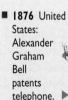

- **1894** Asia: Sino-Japanese War begins.
- **1896** Greece: First modern Olympics held.
- **1897** Russia: Anton Chekhov publishes *Uncle Vanya*.
- **1898** China: Boxer Rebellion against foreign influence.
- **1898** France: Marie and Pierre Curie discover radium. ▶

The Story of the Times
(1833–1901)

Plate
Presented by
the Ladies of Derby to
Queen Victoria on Her
1887 Golden Jubilee

▲ **Infer** This plate honors Queen Victoria.
(a) What signs can you find in it of the
pride the British took in their overseas
Empire? (b) The motto around the rim
of the plate refers to humanity's "great
and sacred mission" to discover the laws
of nature in order to "conquer nature."
What inferences can you make about
the Victorian faith in progress?

Historical Background

Living in the Victorian Age During Queen Victoria's
sixty-four–year reign, from 1837 to 1901, Britain's
booming economy and rapid expansion encouraged great optimism. Factory towns grew into
large cities as Britain became the world
leader in manufacturing. Banks, retail
shops, and other businesses expanded.
These changes in turn spurred the
growth of two important classes—an industrial working class and a modern
middle class, able to live a better life because of the low cost and large variety of
mass-produced factory goods.

Economic and military power—especially naval power—helped Britain to
acquire new colonies in far-flung parts
of the globe. Echoing the ringing confidence of the Victorian Age, Robert Browning exclaimed of morning in spring, "God's
in his heaven—/All's right with the world!"

A Reforming Age All was not really "right with
the world" of industrial England, though. Writers exposed a dark underside of a manufacturing
economy—brutal factory conditions and stinking
slums. Nonetheless, Victorian reformers had
great faith that their hard work could indeed
make all right in the future. Goaded by reformers
and radicals of many sorts, Victorian leaders did
indeed take steps to expand democracy and better the lot of the poor.

Two key issues—trade policy and electoral reform—dominated domestic politics during the
first half of the Victorian era. The trade controversy centered on the Corn Laws, which had long
slapped high tariffs on "corn" (grain). These laws
discouraged food imports and helped British landlords and farmers keep food prices high, which
angered the poorer classes. Popular organizations

sprang up to fight the Corn Laws. Reform came in 1846 when Parliament, confronting a massive famine in Ireland, sought to increase the food supply by suspending the Corn Laws. Over the following decade, it established a policy of free trade beneficial to rising British industries.

The other burning issue of the day involved strengthening democracy. In 1838, a working-class group drew up a "People's Charter" demanding, among other things, universal suffrage for all males, not just the wealthy and middle-class. Renewed demands for electoral change led to the Second Reform Bill of 1867. The Bill doubled the electorate by granting voting rights to tenant farmers and to better-paid male workers. In 1885, Britain established almost complete male suffrage.

Reform affected many areas. Women were allowed to attend universities. Parliament passed laws to reduce the working day for women and children, to establish a system of free grammar schools, and to legalize trade unions. It voted to provide public sanitation and to regulate factories and housing. Agitation continued, however, for further reform.

The Imperialist Urge Britons who supported a policy of imperialism could cite a long list of arguments: Colonies would provide raw materials and markets for British industry; they would offer a home for British settlers; Britain had no choice—if it didn't seize a territory, one of its European rivals would. Many Victorians tended to believe that Western civilization—commonly perceived as white, Christian, and progressive—was superior to all other cultures. This attitude led many Victorians to look condescendingly on non-Westerners as people in need of assistance. While such an attitude seems outrageous by today's standards, many people of the time sincerely believed it.

The Crimean War The Victorian years were generally peaceful. Britain fought only one major European war—the Crimean War (1853–1856), so called because it took place on the Crimean peninsula in southern Russia. Britain, France, and Turkey teamed up to thwart Russian expansion, but the battles were largely inconclusive. Today we remember the war mainly for the brave but disastrous charge of Britain's light brigade. This was commemorated in a famous

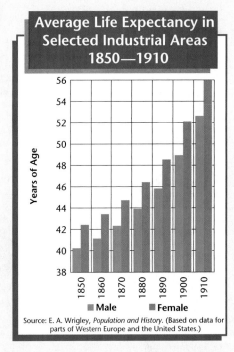

Average Life Expectancy in Selected Industrial Areas 1850—1910

Source: E. A. Wrigley, *Population and History*. (Based on data for parts of Western Europe and the United States.)

▲ **Read a Chart** (a) What was the difference between a man's average life expectancy in 1850 and 1890? (b) During which decade did women's life expectancy increase the most?

▲ **Speculate** The Crystal Palace, built for a trade show in 1851, was made of iron rods and glass; it became a symbol of the idea of progress. (a) Name two reasons why the Palace would have been built out of glass. (b) Why does the use of glass as a building material suggest progress or the future?

Children Paying Innkeeper

Suffragist medal with portrait of Pankhurst

poem by Alfred, Lord Tennyson, some lines of which follow:

> Theirs not to make reply,
> Theirs not to reason why,
> Theirs but to do and die.

Britain as a World Power Though the Liberals (formerly the Whigs) advocated limits to British rule, the Empire continued to grow. Britain acquired Hong Kong from China in 1842. After a rebellion in 1857 by sepoys (Indian troops under British command), Britain shouldered aside the British East India Company and took direct control of India.

In the last three decades of Victoria's rule Britain expanded its influence in Africa. It gained control of the new Suez Canal in Egypt and acquired such territories as Kenya, Uganda, Nigeria, and Rhodesia (Zimbabwe). Britain also consolidated its control over what is now South Africa, defeating Dutch settlers there in the Boer War of 1899–1902.

Victorian Thought Victorian thinkers often disagreed on the crucial issues of their times but they shared a deep confidence in humanity's ability to better itself. The changes brought about by the Industrial Revolution stirred conflicting feelings among Victorian thinkers. On the one hand, they admired the material benefits industrialization had brought. On the other, they deplored the brutality of factory life and of industrial slums. Much debate concerned whether business should be allowed free rein or whether, for the welfare of people, the government should take a strong role in the economy.

The Victorians grappled with the religious and philosophical as well as the social implications of modern life. The theory of evolution proposed by Charles Darwin (1809–1882) in *On the Origin of Species* (1859), for instance, stirred bitter controversy. Darwin believed that a process he called "natural selection" explained how different forms of life evolved from previous forms. His account is quite different from the Creation story found in the Bible. Some Victorian thinkers took Darwin's theory as a direct challenge to Biblical truth and traditional religious faith. Some accepted both Darwin and religion, striving to reconcile scientific and religious insights.

Literature of the Period

Romanticism and Realism Romanticism continued to influence Victorian writers, but it had by now become part of mainstream culture. When Victorian writers confronted the rapid technological and social change amidst which they lived, the Realist literary movement was born. Realist literature focused on ordinary people facing the day-to-day problems of life, an emphasis that reflected the trend toward democracy and the growing middle-class audience for literature.

Naturalism A related movement, known as Naturalism, sought to put the spirit of scientific observation to literary use. Naturalists crammed their novels with details—the sour smells of poverty, the harsh sounds of factory life—often with the aim of promoting social reform. They directly contradicted the Romantic idea that nature mirrored human feelings and portrayed nature instead as harsh and indifferent to the human suffering it caused.

The Anti-Realists Rather than embracing "real" life as the Realists did, two groups of artists attempted to refine art. The poets and painters of the Pre-Raphaelite Brotherhood (formed about 1848) rejected the ugliness of industrial life. They turned for inspiration to the spiritual intensity of medieval Italian art—art before the time of the painter Raphael (1483–1520). Toward the end of the Victorian Age, aesthetes like the writer Oscar Wilde (1854–1900) turned away from the everyday world and sought to create "art for art's sake"—works whose sole reason for being was their perfection or beauty.

Victorian Poetry The Victorian Age produced a large and diverse body of poetry. The most popular poet of the era—Alfred, Lord Tennyson (1809–1892)—was influenced by earlier Romantic poets. His verse displays a keen sense of the music of language. By contrast, Robert Browning's (1812–1889) dramatic monologues—long speeches in which a character reveals his or her inward thoughts—explore human personality in all its un-Romantic details. Browning's wife, Elizabeth Barrett (1806–1861), was the more famous poet at the time of their marriage. Today she is remembered mostly for the beautiful love poems she wrote her husband.

"The Old Rotten Tree," jug, 1832

▲ **Relate** Not the least effect of the Industrial Revolution was the widespread availability of cheap, mass-produced goods, such as Staffordshire chinaware. The jug bears a cartoon criticizing corrupt electoral policies. (a) On what household items do cartoons appear today? (b) Are they generally political?

Bayswater Omnibus, G. W. Joy

▲ **Speculate** Originally French, the first horse-drawn omnibuses came to London in 1829. How do you suppose the development of public spaces such as the inside of a bus may have influenced later fashion? Explain.

Edwardian London, 1901, Eugene Joseph McSwiney

▲ **Speculate** Public gas lighting was one of the innovations of Victorian England. Without this lighting, would so many people be on the street? Explain.

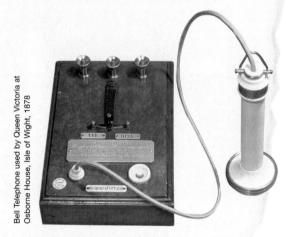

Bell Telephone used by Queen Victoria at Osborne House, Isle of Wight, 1878

▲ **Infer** What does the absence of a rotary dial or touch-tone pad suggest about the extent of the telephone system—and the number of people using telephones—in 1878? Explain.

Matthew Arnold (1822–1888) was probably the first Victorian poet to focus on "the bewildering confusion" of the industrial age—the loss of individuals' close ties to nature and with each other. Arnold was a forerunner of the more pessimistic Naturalist writers, such as Thomas Hardy (1840–1928) and A. E. Housman (1859–1936), for whom life's disappointments and the erosion of rural society were frequent subjects.

The poetry of Rudyard Kipling (1865–1936) spoke to the expansive spirit of the age, ranging across the breadth of the Empire with action-packed narratives like "Gunga Din" and poems written in the colorful speech of working-class soldiers in *Barrack-room Ballads.*

While Tennyson's and Kipling's well-known lyrics turned up occasionally as popular songs, Gerard Manley Hopkins (1844–1889) remained unpublished during his own century. His innovative rhythms and Romantic-inspired religious verse would later inspire twentieth-century poets.

Victorian Drama Playhouses in the Victorian Age were few in number and hemmed in by government restrictions. Only toward the end of the century did the theater begin to show some sparkle, with serious dramas like Sir Arthur Wing Pinero's *The Second Mrs. Tanqueray* (1893) and satirical ones like Oscar Wilde's *The Importance of Being Earnest* (1895).

Victorian Fiction Members of the new middle class were avid readers, and they loved novels—especially novels that reflected the main social issues of the day. Responding to the demand, weekly and monthly magazines published novels chapter by chapter, in serial form.

Emily Brontë's (1818–1848) classic *Wuthering Heights* (1847) tells the tale of the doomed passion of Catherine Earnshaw and Heathcliff, one of English fiction's outstanding Romantic heroes. Her sister Charlotte (1816–1855) wrote *Jane Eyre* (1847), a novel recounting the adventures of a governess who falls in love with her mysterious employer, Mr. Rochester.

The Realist elements of *Jane Eyre* probably owe much to the influence of Charles Dickens (1812–1870), who surpassed all other Victorian novelists in popularity. Dickens filled his novels with poignant, realistic details that dramatized the problems of a grimy industrial England. To his eye for injustice he married a marvelous sense of humor. His novels abound in deliciously eccentric characters, whose every peculiarity of speech and gesture affirms how individual people are.

Other, less sentimental Victorian Realists included William Makepeace Thackeray (1811–1863), Anthony Trollope (1815–1882), Elizabeth Gaskell (1810–1865), and Samuel Butler (1835–1902). George Meredith produced careful psychological studies of his characters in novels such as *The Egoist* (1879). Mary Ann Evans, writing as George Eliot (1819–1880), examined social issues and personal relationships in novels such as *Adam Bede* (1859).

As the century drew to a close, British novelists such as Thomas Hardy leaned more and more to Naturalism. Late Victorian readers shied away from Naturalism's dark outlook, though, preferring instead the adventure stories of writers like Robert Louis Stevenson (1850–1894) and Rudyard Kipling or the Sherlock Holmes mysteries of Sir Arthur Conan Doyle (1859–1930).

Nonfiction Prose All the great Victorian thinkers produced influential prose works. Matthew Arnold, for example, attacked the British class system in *Culture and Anarchy* (1869), his most famous work of social criticism. Other influential works included *Modern Painters* (1843) by John Ruskin (1819–1900), *On Liberty* (1859) by John Stuart Mill (1806–1873), *The Idea of a University Defined* (1873) by John Henry Newman (1801–1890), and *Studies in the History of the Renaissance* (1873) by Walter Pater (1839–1894). Greatest of the Victorian historians were Thomas Carlyle (1795–1881) and Thomas Babington Macaulay (1800–1859).

All in all, the Victorian Age produced a diverse body of literature—entertaining, scholarly, humorous, profound. Because the era is so close to our own times—and because in it we see the beginnings of our own problems, many of them still unresolved, Victorian literature has a special relevance to readers today. In addition, the Victorian writers were brilliant storytellers, and we read their works not only for literary appreciation and historical understanding but for pure reading pleasure.

Princess Sabra ou la Fille de Roi, 1865–66
Sir Edward Burne-Jones

▲ **Connect** In 1848, a group of young painters, led by Dante Gabriel Rosetti, formed the Pre-Raphaelite Brotherhood. They sought to recapture the direct, sincere communication of feeling they found in medieval art. Which elements in this painting seem to achieve that goal?

Granville, Wallpaper, Designed by John Henry Dearle (1860–1932) for Morris and Company, 1896

▲ **Assess** William Morris, a close associate of the Pre-Raphaelites and, like them, a lover of medieval art, single-handedly revolutionized Victorian decorative taste. How successful do you think this pattern, designed for his company, would be on wallpaper? Is it too "busy" or does it soothe the eye? Explain.

The Changing English Language

THE VICTORIAN AGE

by Richard Lederer

Euphemisms: The Fig Leaves of Language

Prudishness reached its golden age in the straitlaced Victorian era. Take the widely read *Lady Gough's Book of Etiquette.* Among Lady Gough's social pronouncements was that under no circumstances should books written by male authors be placed on shelves next to books written by "authoresses." Married writers, however, such as Robert and Elizabeth Barrett Browning, could be shelved together without impropriety.

So delicate were Victorian sensibilities that members of polite society would blush at the mention of anything physical. Instead of being *pregnant,* women were *in a delicate condition, in a family way,* or *expectant.* Women did not give birth; they experienced a *blessed event.* Their children were not born; rather, they were *brought by the stork,* or *came into the world.*

Such words and expressions are called *euphemisms* (from two Greek roots that mean "pleasant speech," "words of good omen"). A euphemism is a mild, indirect word or phrase used in place of one that is more direct or that may have an unpleasant connotation for some people. Using a euphemism is "calling a spade a heart" . . . or "telling it like it isn't."

Children were not born but rather brought by the stork.

In the Victorian Age, prudery extended even to animals and things. *Bull* was considered an indecent word, and the proper substitute was *he cow, male cow,* or (gasp!) *gentleman cow.* Victorian standards were so exacting that Victorians couldn't refer to something as vulgar as legs. They had to call them *limbs,* even when talking about the legs on a chicken or a piano. Instead of asking for a leg of chicken, they would ask for dark meat, and they went so far as to cover up piano legs with little skirts!

Activities

1. Shakespeare's Juliet sighs, "What's in a name? A rose by any other name would smell as sweet." Would it? Write an essay in which you defend or rebut Juliet's opinion of the relationship between words and things.

2. Many occupations have taken on glorified, euphemistic titles. Nowadays, a garbage collector is called a sanitation engineer and a dogcatcher an animal control warden. Collect other examples and share them with classmates.

Relationships

Faustine, 1904
Maxwell Armfield, Museé d'Orsay, Paris, France

Guide for Interpreting

Alfred, Lord Tennyson
(1809–1892)

You may think of Tennyson—or any male Victorian poet—as a bearded old man whose picture you see in a book. Think again. Here's the author Carlyle's description of the tall and handsome (if moody) young Tennyson: "One of the finest looking men in the world. A great shock of rough dusty-dark hair; bright-laughing hazel eyes . . . of sallow-brown complexion, almost Indian-looking." This is the young Alfred who in middle age became the most famous and celebrated poet of Victorian England: Alfred, Lord Tennyson.

An Unhappy Childhood Tennyson was born in the rural town of Somersby in Lincolnshire, the fourth of twelve children. He was a sensitive boy who, even before he could read, was charmed by the magical words "far, far away." His father, a clergyman, had a large library and personally supervised Tennyson's early education. He even predicted that his son would be "the greatest Poet of the Time." However, this well-educated clergyman was also extremely bitter, enraged at being disinherited by his own father. His anger poisoned the atmosphere of the Tennyson household, and as a teenager, Alfred was probably eager to escape to Cambridge University.

The Power of Friendship At first, Tennyson was disappointed by Cambridge. He wrote about his studies: "None but dry-headed, calculating, angular little gentlemen can take much delight in them." Then he met the young man who became his closest friend, Arthur Henry Hallam. They were often together, and Hallam intended to marry Tennyson's sister Emily.

Tragedy In 1833, however, Hallam died suddenly while traveling. Grief-stricken, Tennyson considered questions of death, religious faith, and immortality in a series of short poems that eventually became an elegy for his friend, "In Memoriam, A.H.H." (1850). The elegy so impressed Prince Albert that he encouraged Queen Victoria to appoint Tennyson the Poet Laureate of England when Wordsworth died in 1850. In 1884, the Queen made Tennyson a baron, the first English writer to be so titled.

Land, Literature, Long Life When royalties from "In Memoriam, A.H.H." began to flow in, Tennyson was able to buy the "acre" of land he'd always longed for, a farm on the Isle of Wight. There he and his wife Emily Sellwood raised two children. Tennyson remained alert to the end of his life, publishing poems when he was past eighty.

◆ Background for Understanding

LITERATURE: TENNYSON'S SOURCES OF INSPIRATION

The boy who was charmed by the words "far, far away" became a poet whose mind traveled far to find sources of inspiration: ancient Greece and medieval Italy and England.

In "Ulysses" (Latin for *Odysseus*) Tennyson continues the story of the *Odyssey*, describing life on the isle of Ithaca following the Greek hero's return home. To do this, Tennyson built upon hints about the final voyage found in the original epic by the ancient Greek poet Homer. Tennyson also drew upon Dante's *Inferno,* in which the hero Odysseus describes the final voyage home in his own words.

In the tragic "Lady of Shalott," Tennyson uses as his source Arthurian legend—medieval tales that describe the deeds of King Arthur and his knights of the Round Table.

Knowing Tennyson's sources, you can take a greater interest in his poetic "relay race."

from In Memoriam, A.H.H.
◆ The Lady of Shalott ◆
Ulysses ◆ Tears, Idle Tears

◆ *Literature and Your Life*

CONNECT YOUR EXPERIENCE

You write a song praising the virtues of someone special in your life. You lay a wreath of dried flowers at a relative's grave. These are two of many ways to pay tribute—to mark your respect or affection for someone.

Tennyson's poem "In Memoriam, A.H.H." is a personal tribute to a beloved friend who died too young. His poems "The Lady of Shalott" and "Ulysses" are literary tributes to the timeless works that inspired them: medieval romances, Homer's *Odyssey*, and Dante's *Inferno*.

THEMATIC FOCUS: RELATIONSHIPS

As you read "In Memoriam," notice how Tennyson's tribute to his friend transforms an ordinary person into a hero.

Journal Writing Describe some ways in which you honor your own friends and relatives.

◆ Build Vocabulary

RELATED WORDS: MEDIEVAL WORDS

Tennyson uses medieval words such as *churls*, meaning "farmers or peasants," to add atmosphere to his poems. In the poem "The Lady of Shalott," his choice of a medieval word helps create setting and atmosphere.

WORD BANK

Before you read, preview this list of words from the poems.

diffusive
churls
waning
furrows

◆ Grammar and Style

PARALLEL STRUCTURE

Tennyson uses **parallel structure**—similar grammatical form for similar ideas—to give rhythm and unity to his poems and to emphasize underlying meanings.

In lines 11–12 of "In Memoriam," for example, he uses three parallel infinitive phrases to lend his grief a haunting rhythm and to stress the importance of giving in to grief:

Ah, sweeter *to be drunk with loss,*

To dance with death, to beat the ground . . .

◆ Literary Focus

THE SPEAKER IN POETRY

The **speaker** in a poem—the person who "says" its words—is not necessarily the poet. It can also be a fictional character. If the speaker is fictional, however, the chances are that his or her situation relates to that of the poet. By knowing the identity of the speaker and the conflicts he or she faces, you can better understand the poet's purpose and meaning.

Tennyson himself is the speaker of "In Memoriam, A.H.H.," a tribute to his friend Arthur Hallam. In these excerpts from the poem, be aware of the passages in which Tennyson faces, and tries to make meaning of, his friend's early death.

In "The Lady of Shalott" and "Ulysses," however, Tennyson wears the mask of fictional characters: a woman hiding from life in medieval England and an aging Greek hero, respectively. Think about the conflicts that these characters face and why Tennyson might find these conflicts especially meaningful. Consider, for example, how the medieval lady, weaving her "magic web" on a "silent isle," is like an artist or poet.

Reading for Success

Strategies for Reading Critically

Reading critically requires you to examine and evaluate an author's ideas, whether the ideas are presented in prose or poetry. When you read critically, you identify the writer's purpose and you examine the ideas the writer includes (or doesn't include) in support of that purpose. Then you form a judgment about the validity of the work.

These strategies will help you read critically.

Draw inferences.

Writers don't always say everything they mean. Often they only suggest ideas, which you must infer from the details and evidence they provide. For example, knowing that Tennyson's best friend died, you can infer that Tennyson wrote "In Memoriam, A.H.H." from a deep personal grief.

Recognize an author's purpose or bias.

▶ An author's purpose influences what he or she includes and how he or she chooses to present material. When you recognize an author's purpose, you can examine his or her ideas in light of that purpose.

▶ Be alert also for an author's *bias*, a preference for one person, thing, or idea above another.

Discriminate between denotative and connotative language.

Language with strong connotations—"Let love clasp Grief lest both be drowned"—can excite strong emotions. Denotative language—"On either side the river lie / long fields of barley and of rye"—is without color or emotion. Writers use connotative language to engage your feelings; denotative language describes a situation more objectively.

Evaluate the writer's points or statements.

To evaluate a writer's assertions, weigh the evidence the writer brings to bear on a subject. Consider whether the examples, reasons, or illustrations used to support points are sound and effective.

Consider the historical and biographical context.

In evaluating a writer's work, think about the prevailing social attitudes of the time and place in which a writer lived.

Judge the writer's work.

Apply your critical judgment to the work as a whole. As you look at a work in its totality, consider questions like these: Do the statements or points follow logically? Is the writer's evidence appropriate and relevant? Are the characters and situations true to life?

As you read "In Memoriam, A.H.H.," look at the side notes. These notes demonstrate how to apply these strategies to your reading.

from

In Memoriam, A. H. H.

Alfred, Lord Tennyson

The Stages of Life, Caspar David Friedrich, Museum der Bildenden Kunst, Leipzig

1

I held it truth, with him who sings
   To one clear harp in divers[1] tones,
   That men may rise on stepping stones
Of their dead selves to higher things.

---

1. divers (dī´ vərz) *adj.*: Varied; having many parts.

▲ **Critical Viewing** In what ways does this painting reflect ideas expressed in Tennyson's poem? **[Evaluate]**

5   But who shall so forecast the years
      And find in loss a gain to match?
      Or reach a hand through time to catch
   The far-off interest of tears?

   Let Love clasp Grief lest both be drowned,
10   Let darkness keep her raven gloss.
      Ah, sweeter to be drunk with loss,
   To dance with death, to beat the ground,

   Than that the victor Hours should scorn
      The long result of love, and boast,
15   "Behold the man that loved and lost,
   But all he was is overworn."

> The poet clearly establishes that his **purpose** in writing is to express grief.

7

   Dark house, by which once more I stand
      Here in the long unlovely street,
      Doors, where my heart was used to beat
20   So quickly, waiting for a hand,

   A hand that can be clasped no more—
      Behold me, for I cannot sleep,
      And like a guilty thing I creep
   At earliest morning to the door.

25   He is not here; but far away
      The noise of life begins again,
      And ghastly through the drizzling rain
   On the bald street breaks the blank day.

> From what you've read so far, you can **infer** that this is the house where the speaker's friend had lived.

82

   I wage not any feud with Death
30   For changes wrought on form and face;
      No lower life that earth's embrace
   May breed with him, can fright my faith.

   Eternal process moving on,
      From state to state the spirit walks;
35   And these are but the shattered stalks,
   Or ruined chrysalis of one.

   Nor blame I Death, because he bare
      The use of virtue out of earth;
      I know transplanted human worth
40   Will bloom to profit, otherwhere.

   For this alone on Death I wreak
      The wrath that garners in my heart;
      He put our lives so far apart
   We cannot hear each other speak.

> This use of **connotative language**—words and phrases that can excite the emotions—helps you to feel the depth of the speaker's grief.

130

45 Thy voice is on the rolling air;
  I hear thee where the waters run;
  Thou standest in the rising sun,
And in the setting thou art fair.

What art thou then? I cannot guess;
50 But though I seem in star and flower
  To feel thee some <u>diffusive</u> power,
I do not therefore love thee less.

My love involves the love before;
  My love is vaster passion now;
55 Though mixed with God and Nature thou,
I seem to love thee more and more.

Far off thou art, but ever nigh;
  I have thee still, and I rejoice;
  I prosper, circled with thy voice;
60 I shall not lose thee though I die.

> To judge this poem, **question** whether this conclusion is powerful and convincing, and if so, why.

◆ Build Vocabulary

diffusive (di fyoo′siv) *adj.*: Spread out

Guide for Responding

◆ Literature and Your Life

Reader's Response Were you moved by Tennyson's lament for his friend? Why or why not?
Thematic Focus What does Tennyson reveal about his friendship by writing such a tribute?

☑ Check Your Comprehension

1. In Part 1, what truth does the speaker say he once held but now doubts?
2. Where is the speaker standing in Part 7?
3. In Part 82, what is the one reason the speaker gives for being angry with Death?
4. In Part 130, what does the speaker say has happened to his love for his friend?

◆ Critical Thinking

INTERPRET
1. (a) In what way is the poet's friend lost forever? (b) What part of his friend will live forever? **[Interpret]**
2. Explain the paradox in line 57: "Far off thou art, but ever nigh." **[Interpret]**
3. How does a comparison of the first two parts with the last two show that the poet's feelings have changed? **[Draw Conclusions]**

EVALUATE
4. How would you assess the speaker's adjustment to the death of his friend? **[Assess]**

APPLY
5. Judging from Tennyson's poem, what are the qualities of a good elegy? **[Define]**

The Lady of Shalott

Alfred, Lord Tennyson

Part I

On either side the river lie
Long fields of barley and of rye,
That clothe the wold[1] and meet the sky;
And through the field the road runs by
5   To many-towered Camelot,[2]
And up and down the people go,
Gazing where the lilies blow[3]
Round an island there below,
   The island of Shalott.

10   Willows whiten, aspens quiver,
Little breezes dusk and shiver
Through the wave that runs forever
By the island in the river
   Flowing down to Camelot.
15   Four gray walls, and four gray towers,
Overlook a space of flowers,
And the silent isle imbowers
   The Lady of Shalott.

By the margin, willow-veiled,
20   Slide the heavy barges trailed
By slow horses; and unhailed
The shallop[4] flitteth silken-sailed
   Skimming down to Camelot:
But who hath seen her wave her hand?
25   Or at the casement seen her stand?
Or is she known in all the land,
   The Lady of Shalott?

Only reapers, reaping early
In among the bearded barley,
30   Hear a song that echoes cheerly,
From the river winding clearly,
   Down to towered Camelot:
And by the moon the reaper weary,
Piling sheaves in uplands airy,
35   Listening, whispers, " 'Tis the fairy
   Lady of Shalott."

1. **wold:** Rolling plains.

2. **Camelot:** Legendary English town where King Arthur had his court and Round Table.

3. **blow:** Bloom.

4. **shallop:** Light, open boat.

◆ Build Vocabulary

churls (chʉrlz) *n.:* Farm laborers; peasants

▲ **Critical Viewing** What symbols of the fate of the Lady of Shalott are in this painting? Explain why they are significant. **[Interpret]**

Part II

There she weaves by night and day
A magic web with colors gay.
She has heard a whisper say,
40   A curse is on her if she stay
      To look down to Camelot.
She knows not what the curse may be,
And so she weaveth steadily,
And little other care hath she,
45   The Lady of Shalott.

And moving through a mirror[5] clear
That hangs before her all the year,
Shadows of the world appear.
There she sees the highway near
50   Winding down to Camelot:
There the river eddy whirls,
And there the surly village <u>churls</u>,
And the red cloaks of market girls,
      Pass onward from Shalott.

55   Sometimes a troop of damsels glad,
An abbot on an ambling pad,[6]
Sometimes a curly shepherd lad,

5. mirror: Weavers placed mirrors in front of their looms, so that they could view the progress of their work.

6. pad: Easy-paced horse.

Or long-haired page in crimson clad,
   Goes by to towered Camelot;
60 And sometimes through the mirror blue
The knights come riding two and two:
She hath no loyal knight and true,
   The Lady of Shalott.

But in her web she still delights
65 To weave the mirror's magic sights,
For often through the silent nights
A funeral, with plumes and lights
   And music, went to Camelot:
Or when the moon was overhead,
70 Came two young lovers lately wed;
"I am half sick of shadows," said
   The Lady of Shalott.

Part III

A bow-shot from her bower eaves,
He rode between the barley sheaves,
75 The sun came dazzling through the leaves,
And flamed upon the brazen greaves[7]
   Of bold Sir Lancelot.
A red-cross knight[8] forever kneeled
To a lady in his shield,
80 That sparkled on the yellow field,
   Beside remote Shalott.

The gemmy[9] bridle glittered free,
Like to some branch of stars we see
Hung in the golden Galaxy.[10]
85 The bridle bells rang merrily
   As he rode down to Camelot:
And from his blazoned baldric[11] slung
A mighty silver bugle hung,
And as he rode his armor rung,
90   Beside remote Shalott.

All in the blue unclouded weather
Thick-jeweled shone the saddle leather,
The helmet and the helmet feather
Burned like one burning flame together,
95   As he rode down to Camelot.
As often through the purple night,
Below the starry clusters bright,
Some bearded meteor, trailing light,
   Moves over still Shalott.

100 His broad clear brow in sunlight glowed;
On burnish'd hooves his war horse trode;
From underneath his helmet flowed
His coal-black curls as on he rode,

7. greaves: Armor that protects the legs below the kneecaps.
8. red-cross knight: Refers to the Redcrosse Knight from *The Faerie Queene* by Edmund Spenser. In Spenser's work, the knight represents St. George, the patron saint of England, in addition to being a symbol of holiness.
9. gemmy: Jeweled.
10. Galaxy: The Milky Way.
11. blazoned baldric: Decorated sash worn diagonally across the chest.

    As he rode down to Camelot.
105 From the bank and from the river
    He flashed into the crystal mirror,
    "Tirra lirra," by the river
        Sang Sir Lancelot.

    She left the web, she left the loom,
110 She made three paces through the room,
    She saw the waterlily bloom,
    She saw the helmet and the plume,
        She looked down to Camelot.
    Out flew the web and floated wide;
115 The mirror cracked from side to side;
    "The curse is come upon me," cried
        The Lady of Shalott.

Part IV

    In the stormy east wind straining,
    The pale yellow woods were waning,
120 The broad stream in his banks complaining,
    Heavily the low sky raining
        Over towered Camelot;
    Down she came and found a boat
    Beneath a willow left afloat,
125 And round about the prow she wrote
        The Lady of Shalott.

    And down the river's dim expanse
    Like some bold seër in a trance,
    Seeing all his own mischance—
130 With a glassy countenance
        Did she look to Camelot.
    And at the closing of the day
    She loosed the chain, and down she lay;
    The broad stream bore her far away,
135   The Lady of Shalott.

    Lying, robed in snowy white
    That loosely flew to left and right—
    The leaves upon her falling light—
    Through the noises of the night
140   She floated down to Camelot:
    And as the boathead wound along
    The willowy hills and fields among,
    They heard her singing her last song,
        The Lady of Shalott.

145 Heard a carol, mournful, holy,
    Chanted loudly, chanted lowly,
    Till her blood was frozen slowly,
    And her eyes were darkened wholly,

◆ **Build Vocabulary**

waning (wān´ iŋ) *v.*:
Gradually becoming
dimmer

<pre>
                Turned to towered Camelot.
150   For ere she reached upon the tide
            The first house by the waterside,
            Singing in her song she died,
                The Lady of Shalott.

            Under tower and balcony,
155   By garden wall and gallery,
            A gleaming shape she floated by,
            Dead-pale between the houses high,
                Silent into Camelot.
            Out upon the wharfs they came,
160   Knight and burgher, lord and dame,
            And round the prow they read her name,
                The Lady of Shalott.

            Who is this? and what is here?
            And in the lighted palace near
165   Died the sound of royal cheer;
            And they crossed themselves for fear,
                All the knights at Camelot:
            But Lancelot mused a little space;
            He said, "She has a lovely face;
170   God in his mercy lend her grace,
                The Lady of Shalott."
</pre>

Guide for Responding

◆ Literature and Your Life

Reader's Response Do you think the Lady was wise or unwise in deciding to sail for Camelot? Explain.

Thematic Focus Why do you think the Lady of Shallot has decided to live on an island, cut off from all relationships?

Questions for Research Generate a series of research questions that would help you explore what modern scholars know about Camelot, Lancelot, and the legendary King Arthur.

☑ Check Your Comprehension

1. What does the Lady spend all her time doing, and why?
2. Where does the Lady glimpse "shadows of the world"?
3. What does the Lady do after seeing Sir Lancelot in the mirror?
4. What happens to her as a result of the action she takes?

◆ Critical Thinking

INTERPRET

1. In line 42 the speaker says the Lady "knows not what the curse may be." Explain the curse in your own words. **[Infer]**
2. Critics have seen this poem as a commentary on the plight of the artist. Keeping this interpretation in mind, what do you think is meant by the Lady's complaint in lines 71–72? **[Interpret]**
3. (a) Why do you think the author devotes so much space to his description of Sir Lancelot? (b) How does this description relate to the Lady's action and to the overall meaning of the poem? **[Draw Conclusions]**

APPLY

4. What do you think might have happened if the Lady had actually met Sir Lancelot? Why? **[Apply]**

Ulysses

Alfred, Lord Tennyson

In this poem Tennyson extends the story of Ulysses (yoo lis′ ēz), the hero of the Odyssey, *beyond the narrative in Homer's epic. Here we learn that he has grown restless in the years since returning to his home in Ithaca. Although he had been away for twenty long years—ten fighting in the Trojan War and another ten making the long and adventure-filled voyage back—Ulysses finds that he is contemplating making another, final journey.*

It little profits that an idle king,
By this still hearth, among these barren crags,
Matched with an aged wife, I mete and dole[1]
Unequal[2] laws unto a savage race,
5   That hoard, and sleep, and feed, and know not me.
I cannot rest from travel; I will drink
Life to the lees.[3] All times I have enjoyed
Greatly, have suffered greatly, both with those
That loved me, and alone; on shore, and when
10   Through scudding drifts the rainy Hyades[4]
Vexed the dim sea. I am become a name;
For always roaming with a hungry heart
Much have I seen and known—cities of men
And manners, climates, councils, governments,
15   Myself not least, but honored of them all—
And drunk delight of battle with my peers,
Far on the ringing plains of windy Troy.
I am a part of all that I have met;
Yet all experience is an arch wherethrough

1. **mete and dole:** Measure and give out.
2. **unequal:** Unfair.

3. **lees:** Sediment.

4. **Hyades** (hī′ ə dēz′): Group of stars whose rising was assumed to be followed by rain.

Ulysses Mourning for Home, Staatliche Museen zu Berlin

▲ **Critical Viewing** What qualities of Ulysses revealed in the poem are depicted in this rendering? **[Compare and Contrast]**

20   Gleams that untraveled world, whose margin fades
     Forever and forever when I move.
     How dull it is to pause, to make an end,
     To rust unburnished, not to shine in use!
     As though to breathe were life. Life piled on life
25   Were all too little, and of one to me
     Little remains; but every hour is saved
     From that eternal silence, something more,
     A bringer of new things; and vile it were
     For some three suns to store and hoard myself,

30 And this gray spirit yearning in desire
    To follow knowledge like a sinking star,
    Beyond the utmost bound of human thought.
        This is my son, mine own Telemachus,
    To whom I leave the scepter and the isle[5]
35 Well-loved of me, discerning to fulfill
    This labor, by slow prudence to make mild
    A rugged people, and through soft degrees
    Subdue them to the useful and the good.
    Most blameless is he, centered in the sphere
40 Of common duties, decent not to fail
    In offices of tenderness, and pay
    Meet[6] adoration to my household gods,
    When I am gone. He works his work, I mine.
        There lies the port; the vessel puffs her sail;
45 There gloom the dark broad seas. My mariners,
    Souls that have toiled and wrought, and thought with
            me—
    That ever with a frolic welcome took
    The thunder and the sunshine, and opposed
    Free hearts, free foreheads—you and I are old;
50 Old age hath yet his honor and his toil;
    Death closes all; but something ere the end,
    Some work of noble note, may yet be done,
    Not unbecoming men that strove with Gods.
    The lights begin to twinkle from the rocks;
55 The long day wanes; the slow moon climbs; the deep
    Moans round with many voices. Come, my friends,
    'Tis not too late to seek a newer world.
    Push off, and sitting well in order smite
    The sounding <u>furrows</u>; for my purpose holds
60 To sail beyond the sunset, and the baths
    Of all the western stars, until I die.
    It may be that the gulfs will wash us down;
    It may be we shall touch the Happy Isles,[7]
    And see the great Achilles,[8] whom we knew.
65 Though much is taken, much abides; and though
    We are not now that strength which in old days
    Moved earth and heaven, that which we are, we are—
    One equal temper of heroic hearts,
    Made weak by time and fate, but strong in will
70 To strive, to seek, to find, and not to yield.

5. **isle:** Ithaca, an island off the coast of Greece.

6. **meet:** Appropriate.

7. **Happy Isles:** Elysium, or the Islands of the Blessed: in classical mythology, the place heroes went after death.
8. **Achilles** (ə´ kil´ ēz´): Greek hero of the Trojan War.

◆ **Build Vocabulary**

furrows (fʉr´ ōz) *n.*: Narrow grooves made in the ground by a plow

Beach at Heist (Belgium), 1892, Georges Lemmen, Musée d'Orsay, Paris, France

▲ **Critical Viewing** How does this painting evoke the feelings of sadness and longing for the past that "Tears, Idle Tears" expresses? [**Apply**]

The Princess (1847) is a long narrative poem that contains a number of songs. Some of these songs, including the one that follows, are considered to be among the finest of Tennyson's lyrics.

---

from

The Princess

Alfred, Lord Tennyson

Tears, Idle Tears

Tears, idle tears, I know not what they mean,
Tears from the depth of some divine despair
Rise in the heart, and gather to the eyes,
In looking on the happy autumn fields,
And thinking of the days that are no more.

5

Fresh as the first beam glittering on a sail,
That brings our friends up from the underworld,
Sad as the last which reddens over one
That sinks with all we love below the verge;
So sad, so fresh, the days that are no more.

Ah, sad and strange as in dark summer dawns
The earliest pipe of half-awakened birds
To dying ears, when unto dying eyes
The casement slowly grows a glimmering square;
So sad, so strange, the days that are no more.

Dear as remembered kisses after death,
And sweet as those by hopeless fancy feigned
On lips that are for others; deep as love,
Deep as first love, and wild with all regret;
O Death in Life, the days that are no more.

10

15

20

Guide for Responding

◆ *Literature and Your Life*

Reader's Response Which of these poems seems more hopeful to you? Why?

Thematic Focus Compare and contrast Ulysses' relationship to the past with that of the speaker in "Tears, Idle Tears."

Research Many authors and poets have returned to the theme of the original *Odyssey,* composed around 800 B.C. Use a reference book to review the story line of this epic.

☑ Check Your Comprehension

1. (a) How does Ulysses describe his current situation? (b) What past experiences does he mention?
2. What work is Ulysses leaving to his son?
3. According to lines 58–61, what is Ulysses' purpose?
4. According to the first stanza of "Tears, Idle Tears," what causes the tears to rise?
5. What three comparisons in "Tears, Idle Tears" describe "the days that are no more"?

◆ Critical Thinking

INTERPRET
1. How does Ulysses' current situation contrast with his previous experiences? **[Compare and Contrast]**
2. (a) What is Ulysses' attitude toward his experiences and accomplishments? (b) What are his feelings about aging? (c) What is his attitude toward life in general? **[Draw Conclusions]**
3. (a) What is the refrain—repeated line or phrase—in "Tears, Idle Tears"? (b) What feeling do you think Tennyson wanted it to evoke in readers? **[Interpret]**

APPLY
4. In what way is the nostalgia expressed in "Tears, Idle Tears" a bittersweet emotion? **[Synthesize]**

EXTEND
5. In Dante's *Inferno,* Ulysses explains how he and his crew drowned soon after setting forth. Does knowing that the voyage will end in disaster lead you to question Ulysses' judgment? Why or why not? **[Literature Link]**

Guide for Responding (continued)

◆ Reading for Success

STRATEGIES FOR READING CRITICALLY

The skill of critical reading is useful, whether you're reading poetry, legal documents, or science-fiction. Review the strategies for reading critically on page 750 and apply them to answer the following questions.

1. Are lines 25–28 of "In Memoriam" examples of connotative or denotative language? Explain.
2. Reread lines 33–36 of "In Memoriam." What can you infer from these lines about the speaker's beliefs? Explain.
3. Evaluate what Tennyson says in line 47 of the poem: "Thou standest in the rising sun." (a) Does he mean this statement in an objective or in an emotional sense? (b) Do you think it is true in the sense that he means it? Explain.
4. Do you think "In Memoriam" conveys Tennyson's personal grief and expresses timeless concerns? Why or why not?

◆ Build Vocabulary

USING MEDIEVAL WORDS

Words such as *churls* in Tennyson's "The Lady of Shalott" contribute to the poem's medieval atmosphere. Using the context of "The Lady of Shalott," define the following words.

1. knight	3. baldric	5. burgher
2. reapers	4. plume	6. mischance

USING THE WORD BANK: Word Choice

In your notebook, write the Work Bank word that is closest in meaning to each italicized word or phrase.

From the old dirt road leading to the medieval village, the *long ridges* made by the plows were clearly visible. Off in the distance, you could hear the *farm laborers* on their long journey home after a hard day's work. The *spreading* scent of newly turned earth pervaded the air as the moon was *growing dim.*

◆ Literary Focus

THE SPEAKER IN POETRY

The **speakers** in these poems may be Tennyson himself or a character he creates. Even when he puts on the mask of a character, however, Tennyson may be expressing conflicts that relate to his own situation or experiences.

One speaker, the Lady of Shalott, must choose between a secret existence in which she weaves a "magic web" and the life of action that passes by her window. This poem could mirror Tennyson's own conflict about hiding from or facing life.

1. Tennyson wrote "In Memoriam" in direct response to Arthur Hallam's death. How does the speaker's conflict in this poem reflect one that Tennyson might have been feeling?
2. What is similar about the choices made by the speakers in "Ulysses" and "The Lady of Shalott"?

◆ Grammar and Style

PARALLEL STRUCTURE

Tennyson, whose verse is so musical, uses the equal grammatical forms of **parallel structure** to achieve balanced rhythms and memorable phrases. The forms he uses include, among others, single words, phrases beginning with infinitives (*to* + a verb), phrases beginning with prepositions like *from,* and clauses with subjects, verbs, and objects.

Practice On your paper, identify the examples of parallel structure in these passages from Tennyson's poems. Then tell whether they involve single words, infinitive phrases, prepositional phrases, or clauses.

1. "How dull it is to pause, to make an end, / To rest unburnished, not to shine in use!"
2. "My love involves the love before; / My love is vaster passion now …"
3. "One equal temper of heroic hearts, / Made weak by time and fate, but strong in will / To strive, to seek, to find, and not to yield."
4. "So sad, so fresh, the days that are no more."
5. "From the bank and from the river …"

Writing Application Write an additional stanza for any of Tennyson's poems. Use at least one example of parallel structure.

Build Your Portfolio

Idea Bank

Writing

1. Song "Tears, Idle Tears" meditates upon the past. Write a song expressing your ideas about the past. Include a strong refrain (a verse recurring at intervals).

2. Literary Analysis Write a literary analysis in which you draw conclusions about the speaker of "In Memoriam." Explain how the poem reveals the speaker's beliefs and disposition.

3. Critical Response Christopher Ricks says of the last line in "Ulysses": "Does not the last line poignantly convey a sense that "Tis far too late to seek a newer world'?" Do you agree with this critic's reading of the line? Why or why not?

Speaking, Listening, and Viewing

4. Oral Interpretation Practice reading "Ulysses" aloud, varying your tone of voice to capture the discontent and final determination of the speaker. Then perform the poem for your class. **[Performing Arts Link]**

5. Camelot Late-Night News As the anchor for this news show, report on the discovery of the Lady of Shalott's body. In spot interviews, get reactions from Lancelot, King Arthur, and an ordinary citizen of Camelot. **[Media Link]**

Researching and Representing

6. Set Design Sketch a set for a play based on "The Lady of Shalott." Include her room, with the loom and mirror. **[Art Link; Performing Arts Link]**

7. Tennyson on Tape Tennyson may have been the first major English poet to be recorded. Ask a librarian to help you find that recording and play it for the class. Find material to explain how the recording was made. **[Media Link]**

Online Activity www.phlit.phschool.com

Guided Writing Lesson

Essay of Tribute

"In Memoriam" pays tribute to Arthur Hallam, who died too young. You can write your own tribute —an essay expressing praise and gratitude—for a living person who has contributed to your school this year. Write this essay as a piece to be included in your school's yearbook.

Writing Skills Focus: Clear Explanation of Cause and Effect

In a yearbook tribute, it's important to give clear **explanations of cause and effect**. For example, you might show step by step how the qualities or actions of your subject (causes) helped create a desirable outcome for the school (effect).

Prewriting To help you focus on your subject's accomplishments, fill in a cause-and-effect chart like this one:

Cause	Effect
I. poor math scores in middle school	After D. tutored five students, all scored in upper 85 percentile
2.	

Drafting In your draft, piece together the causes and effects that illustrate your subject's special qualities. Include transitional words that signal a relationship between thoses causes and effects, such as *therefore, because, as a result, consequently,* and *due to.*

Revising Read your tribute aloud to a friend and ask if it expresses gratitude or esteem. Also ask if your friend understands exactly what the subject did to earn this tribute. If not, clarify how the subject's actions led to his or her position of respect or esteem.

Guide for Interpreting

Robert Browning (1812–1889)

Young Robert Browning's best teacher may have been . . . not a person, but his father's 6,000-book library! He devoured those books, hungry for knowledge about history, art, and literature. By the time he was a teenager, he had decided to make poetry his life's goal. That decision, however, did not ensure immediate success. His first book, the long poem *Pauline*, modeled after Shelley's work, sold no copies!

Like *Pauline*, his other early volumes of poetry attracted little public notice, and his literary reputation was eclipsed by that of his wife, the poet Elizabeth Barrett Browning. However, the 1869 publication of *The Ring and the Book* marked a turning point in Browning's career. A long poem that tells the story of a murder in dramatic monologues (speeches by characters), *The Ring and the Book* achieved wide recognition for its author. It led readers to see how much Browning had given to nineteenth-century poetry: a more down-to-earth, less "poetic" language and the dramatic monologue itself, a form ideally suited to reveal character.

Today Browning ranks with Tennyson as one of the greatest Victorian poets. His shorter dramatic monologues, such as "My Last Duchess," remain favorites of many readers.

Elizabeth Barrett Browning (1806–1861)

Like her future husband, Elizabeth Barrett had no formal education. However, her zest for knowledge spurred her to learn eight languages on her own. By the time she was ten, she had read some Shakespeare plays, passages from *Paradise Lost*, and the histories of England, Greece, and Rome. She began writing poetry as a child, and by the time she reached adulthood she had published four popular volumes of verse.

Elizabeth Barrett's frail health made her something of a recluse, yet she met and fell in love with Robert Browning. After a secret romance, she eloped with him to Florence, Italy, in 1846. They had a son, whom they nicknamed Pen, and the family lived in happy Italian exile until Elizabeth Barrett's death in 1861.

It's hard for us to believe today, when Robert Browning's reputation is so great, that his wife was the better-known poet during her lifetime. Her love story in verse, *Aurora Leigh* (1857), was so popular that the income from it helped support the Brownings. Also popular was her *Sonnets from the Portuguese*, a sequence of forty-four love poems written to her husband. Sonnet 43, which comes from this collection, has appeared in countless anthologies.

◆ Background for Understanding

LITERATURE: THE BROWNING LEGEND

When Elizabeth Barrett met Robert Browning in 1845, she was a well-known poet of thirty-nine. However, she was extremely isolated due to her frail health and possessive father. She saw only family members and a few close friends.

One of those friends arranged for Elizabeth to meet Robert Browning, a great admirer of Barrett's poems. That meeting marks the beginning of one of the most famous courtships in literature. The two poets fell deeply in love, but Elizabeth's father disapproved, and they had to conduct a secret courtship, exchanging love letters every day. In September 1846, they were secretly wed.

A week after their marriage, they moved to Italy, where many of their poems are set. Mr. Barrett disinherited his daughter and never forgave her for having made the romantic match that has since become legendary.

My Last Duchess ◆ Love Among the Ruins
Life in a Love ◆ Sonnet 43

◆ *Literature and Your Life*

CONNECT YOUR EXPERIENCE

How do people find true love? Maybe you think that finding the right person takes work and patience. Perhaps you believe that two people are meant for each other. Robert Browning and Elizabeth Barrett Browning felt that they had been destined to meet. They not only wrote about true love—in poems like "Love Among the Ruins," "Life in a Love," and Sonnet 43—but they lived it!

THEMATIC FOCUS: RELATIONSHIPS

What do the Brownings say or suggest about the importance of love between two people?

Journal Writing Jot down the title of your favorite poem, story, or movie dealing with romantic love. Then briefly explain why you like it so much.

◆ Literary Focus

DRAMATIC MONOLOGUE

Both Shakespeare and Chaucer gave us versions of the form we call the **dramatic monologue**, in which a single character delivers a speech. However, Browning perfected the form and made it his own. In his hands, and at its best, it contains these elements: a speaker who reveals his or her soul, knowingly or not; and a silent listener who interacts with the speaker.

"My Last Duchess," contains both these elements. Notice how Browning turns the page into a little stage, allowing the Duke to reveal his soul in apparently casual remarks to a silent listener.

◆ Reading Strategy

DRAW INFERENCES ABOUT THE SPEAKER

You draw **inferences,** educated guesses, about people who speak to you every day. Similarly, in a poem you can infer a speaker's thoughts or feelings from his or her words and actions. Often, as in life, words and actions carry a double message. They reveal something that the speaker doesn't even realize.

Look carefully behind the words of the speakers in these poems. What, for example, do the comments of the Duke in "My Last Duchess" reveal about his relationship with his first wife?

◆ Build Vocabulary

LATIN SUFFIXES: *-ence*

The Latin suffix *-ence* means "quality, or state of being." When you add *-ence* to an adjective, you create a noun suggesting a state of being. The adjective *munificent* from "My Last Duchess," for example, means "very generous." By dropping the final *-ent* and adding *-ence,* you create the noun *munificence,* meaning "the state of being very generous."

WORD BANK

Before you read, preview this list of words from the poems.

countenance
officious
munificence
dowry
eludes
vestige
sublime
minions

◆ Grammar and Style

THE USE OF *LIKE* AND *AS*

The Brownings frequently use the words *like* and *as* to make comparisons. These words, however, are not interchangeable. *Like,* meaning "similar to," is used to compare nouns or pronouns. It is the preposition in a prepositional phrase. *As,* a subordinating conjunction, is used to compare actions. It introduces a clause with a noun and verb.

Strangers *like* <u>you</u> . . .

I love thee freely, *as* <u>men strive for Right</u>.

My Last Duchess

Robert Browning

This poem, set in the sixteenth century in a castle in northern Italy, is based on events from the life of the Duke of Ferrara, an Italian nobleman, whose first wife died after only three years of marriage. Following his wife's death, the Duke began making arrangements to remarry. In Browning's poem, the Duke is showing a painting of his first wife to an agent who represents the father of the woman he hopes to marry.

▶ **Critical Viewing**
What do you think is the artist's attitude toward the subject of this painting? How does it compare with the Duke's attitude toward his "Last Duchess"? **[Infer]**

That's my last Duchess painted on the wall,
Looking as if she were alive. I call
That piece a wonder, now: Frà Pandolf's[1] hands
Worked busily a day, and there she stands.
5 Will't please you sit and look at her? I said
"Frà Pandolf" by design, for never read
Strangers like you that pictured <u>countenance</u>,
The depth and passion of its earnest glance,
But to myself they turned (since none puts by
10 The curtain I have drawn for you, but I)
And seemed as they would ask me, if they durst,[2]
How such a glance came there; so, not the first
Are you to turn and ask thus. Sir, 'twas not

1. **Frà Pandolf's:** Work of Brother Pandolf, an imaginary painter.
2. **durst:** Dared.

Her husband's presence only, called that spot
15 Of joy into the Duchess' cheek: perhaps
Frà Pandolf chanced to say "Her mantle laps
Over my lady's wrist too much," or "Paint
Must never hope to reproduce the faint
Half-flush that dies along her throat"; such stuff
20 Was courtesy, she thought, and cause enough
For calling up that spot of joy. She had
A heart—how shall I say?—too soon made glad,

◆ **Build Vocabulary**

countenance (koun′tə nəns) *n.*: Face

Antea (Portrait of a Lady), Parmigianino, Museo Nazionale di Capodimonte, Naples

Too easily impressed; she liked whate'er
She looked on, and her looks went everywhere.
25 Sir, 'twas all one! My favor at her breast,
The dropping of the daylight in the West,
The bough of cherries some <u>officious</u> fool
Broke in the orchard for her, the white mule
She rode with round the terrace—all and each
30 Would draw from her alike the approving speech,
Or blush, at least. She thanked men—good! but
 thanked
Somehow—I know not how—as if she ranked
My gift of a nine-hundred-years-old name
With anybody's gift. Who'd stoop to blame
35 This sort of trifling? Even had you skill
In speech—(which I have not)—to make your will
Quite clear to such an one, and say, "Just this
Or that in you disgusts me; here you miss,
Or there exceed the mark"—and if she let
40 Herself be lessoned so, nor plainly set
Her wits to yours, forsooth,[3] and made excuse,
—E'en then would be some stooping; and I choose
Never to stoop. Oh sir, she smiled, no doubt,
Whene'er I passed her; but who passed without
45 Much the same smile? This grew; I gave commands;
Then all smiles stopped together. There she stands
As if alive. Will 't please you rise? We'll meet
The company below, then. I repeat,
The Count your master's known <u>munificence</u>
50 Is ample warrant that no one just pretense
Of mine for <u>dowry</u> will be disallowed;
Though his fair daughter's self, as I avowed
At starting, is my object. Nay, we'll go
Together down, sir! Notice Neptune,[4] though,
55 Taming a sea horse, thought a rarity,
Which Claus of Innsbruck[5] cast in bronze for me!

---

3. **forsooth:** In truth.
4. **Neptune:** In Roman mythology, the god of the sea.
5. **Claus of Innsbruck:** Imaginary Austrian sculptor.

◆ Build Vocabulary

officious (ə fish´ əs) *adj.*: Overly eager to please

munificence (myo͞o nif´ə səns) *n.*: State of being very generous in giving; lavish

dowry (dou´ rē) *n.*: Property that a woman brings to her husband at marriage

Life in a Love

Robert Browning

Escape me?
  Never—
  Beloved!
While I am I, and you are you,
5   So long as the world contains us both,
    Me the loving and you the loth,
While the one eludes, must the other pursue.
My life is a fault at last, I fear:
It seems too much like a fate, indeed!
10   Though I do my best I shall scarce succeed.
But what if I fail of my purpose here?
It is but to keep the nerves at strain,
To dry one's eyes and laugh at a fall,
And, baffled, get up and begin again,—
15   So the chase takes up one's life, that's all.
While, look but once from your farthest bound
At me so deep in the dust and dark,
No sooner the old hope goes to ground
Than a new one, straight to the self-same mark,
20   I shape me—
  Ever
  Removed!

◆ Build Vocabulary

eludes (ē lōōdz´) *v.:* Avoids or escapes

Guide for Responding

◆ Literature and Your Life

Reader's Response In what ways are these poems alike? How do they differ?

Thematic Focus What ideas about romantic relationships do the speakers in these two poems have?

Songwriting With a small group, discuss changes you could make to either of these poems so that it would work as a contemporary rock song.

☑ Check Your Comprehension

1. In "My Last Duchess" what are the speaker and his companion looking at?
2. What was the Duke's "gift" to his wife?
3. What does the Duke say in his final remark to the agent?
4. What does the speaker of "Life in a Love" do as his beloved eludes him?

◆ Critical Thinking

INTERPRET

1. In "My Last Duchess," what initial question do you think the speaker's companion asked him? **[Infer]**
2. (a) What has happened to the last Duchess? (b) Where in the poem is this revealed? **[Interpret]**
3. What does the final remark in "My Last Duchess" reveal about the speaker and his attitudes toward marriage and life? **[Draw Conclusions]**
4. To what does the speaker of "Life in a Love" refer when he mentions "the chase" that "takes up one's life"? **[Infer]**

EVALUATE

5. If you had to choose one of these speakers as a spouse or a friend, which one would you prefer? **[Make a Judgment]**

Italian Ruins, John Claude Nattes, Victoria and Albert Museum

▲ **Critical Viewing** Which phrase in the first line of Browning's poem could describe this painting? Explain. **[Support]**

Love Among the Ruins
Robert Browning

Where the quiet-colored end of evening smiles,
    Miles and miles
On the solitary pastures where our sheep
    Halt asleep
5 Tinkle homeward through the twilight, stray or stop
    As they crop—
Was the site once of a city great and gay
    (So they say),
Of our country's very capital, its prince
10   Ages since
Held his court in, gathered councils, wielding far
    Peace or war.

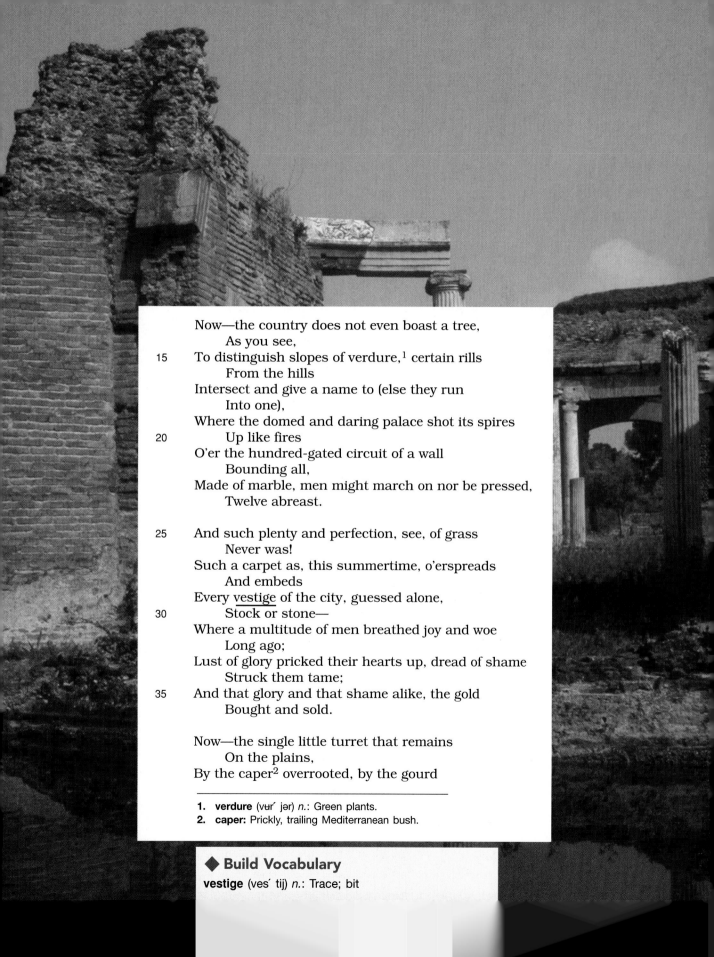

Now—the country does not even boast a tree,
    As you see,
15   To distinguish slopes of verdure,[1] certain rills
      From the hills
Intersect and give a name to (else they run
      Into one),
Where the domed and daring palace shot its spires
20   Up like fires
O'er the hundred-gated circuit of a wall
      Bounding all,
Made of marble, men might march on nor be pressed,
      Twelve abreast.

25   And such plenty and perfection, see, of grass
      Never was!
Such a carpet as, this summertime, o'erspreads
      And embeds
Every vestige of the city, guessed alone,
30   Stock or stone—
Where a multitude of men breathed joy and woe
      Long ago;
Lust of glory pricked their hearts up, dread of shame
      Struck them tame;
35   And that glory and that shame alike, the gold
      Bought and sold.

Now—the single little turret that remains
      On the plains,
By the caper[2] overrooted, by the gourd

---

1. **verdure** (vʉr´ jər) *n.*: Green plants.
2. **caper:** Prickly, trailing Mediterranean bush.

◆ **Build Vocabulary**
vestige (ves´ tij) *n.*: Trace; bit

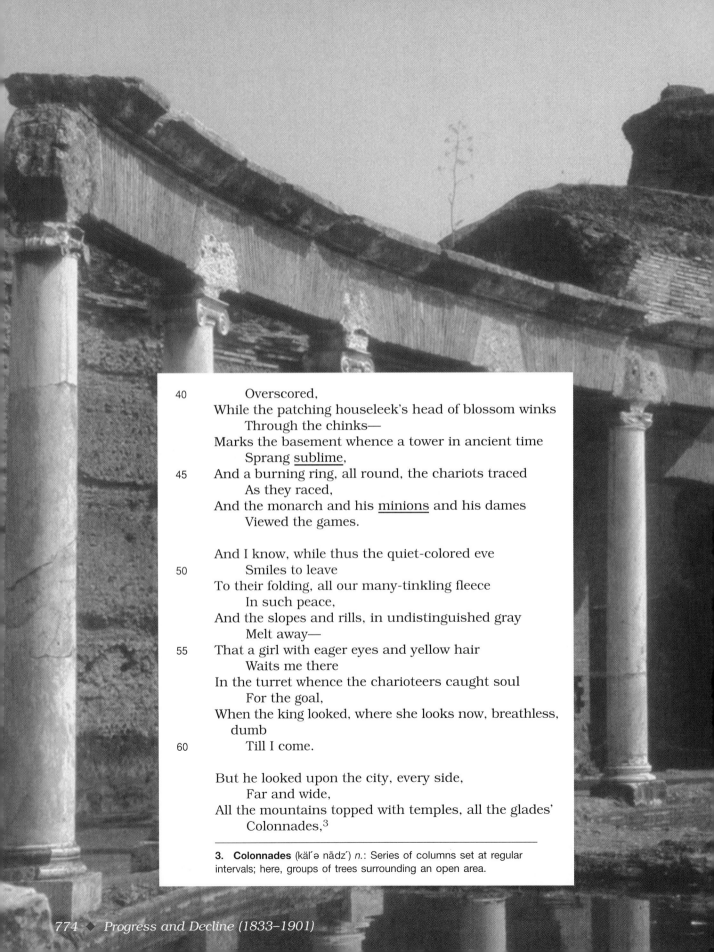

40   Overscored,
While the patching houseleek's head of blossom winks
  Through the chinks—
Marks the basement whence a tower in ancient time
  Sprang <u>sublime</u>,
45 And a burning ring, all round, the chariots traced
  As they raced,
And the monarch and his <u>minions</u> and his dames
  Viewed the games.

And I know, while thus the quiet-colored eve
50 Smiles to leave
To their folding, all our many-tinkling fleece
  In such peace,
And the slopes and rills, in undistinguished gray
  Melt away—
55 That a girl with eager eyes and yellow hair
  Waits me there
In the turret whence the charioteers caught soul
  For the goal,
When the king looked, where she looks now, breathless, dumb
60 Till I come.

But he looked upon the city, every side,
  Far and wide,
All the mountains topped with temples, all the glades'
  Colonnades,[3]

---

3. Colonnades (käl´ə nādz´) *n.*: Series of columns set at regular intervals; here, groups of trees surrounding an open area.

65   All the causeys,[4] bridges, aqueducts—and then,
        All the men!
    When I do come, she will speak not, she will stand,
        Either hand
    On my shoulder, give her eyes the first embrace
70   Of my face,
    Ere we rush, ere we extinguish sight and speech
        Each on each.

    In one year they sent a million fighters forth
        South and North,
75   And they built their gods a brazen pillar[5] high
        As the sky,
    Yet reserved a thousand chariots in full force—
        Gold, of course.
    Oh heart! oh blood that freezes, blood that burns!
80   Earth's returns
    For whole centuries of folly, noise and sin!
        Shut them in,
    With their triumphs and their glories and the rest!
    Love is best.

---

4. causeys: Causeways or raised roads.
5. brazen pillar: Built from the brass of captured chariots.

◆ Build Vocabulary

sublime (sə blīm´) *adj.*: Inspiring admiration through greatness or beauty

minions (min´ yənz) *n.*: Attendants or agents

Guide for Responding

◆ Literature and Your Life

Reader's Response Do you agree with the speaker's conclusion that present love is worth more than past glories? Explain.

Thematic Focus Would you rather read about a romance or a conflict between empires? Why?

Sketch Briefly sketch a view of the ruins described by the speaker.

☑ Check Your Comprehension

1. What once stood where the speaker's sheep now head homeward?
2. Compare and contrast the way the city once looked with the way it looks now.
3. Who waits in the old turret for the speaker?

◆ Critical Thinking

INTERPRET

1. Explain the speaker's feelings toward the civilization he describes. **[Interpret]**
2. (a) In what way is the whole poem based on a contrast between past and present? (b) How do the alternating long and short lines help to emphasize this contrast? **[Analyze]**
3. In your own words, express the conclusion at which the poem arrives. **[Draw Conclusions]**

EVALUATE

4. Is "Love Among the Ruins" a good title for this poem? Explain your answer. **[Assess]**

COMPARE LITERARY WORKS

5. Compare the message of this poem with that of Shelley's "Ozymandias," on p. 670. **[Distinguish]**

Sonnet 43

Elizabeth Barrett Browning

◀ **Critical Viewing**
Does this image capture for you the depth of love des cribed in the poem? Explain. **[Assess]**

How do I love thee? Let me count the ways.
I love thee to the depth and breadth and height
My soul can reach, when feeling out of sight
For the ends of Being and ideal Grace.
5   I love thee to the level of every day's
Most quiet need, by sun and candlelight.
I love thee freely, as men strive for Right;
I love thee purely, as they turn from Praise.
I love thee with the passion put to use
10   In my old griefs, and with my childhood's faith.
I love thee with a love I seemed to lose
With my lost saints—I love thee with the breath,
Smiles, tears, of all my life!—and, if God choose,
I shall but love thee better after death.

Beyond Literature

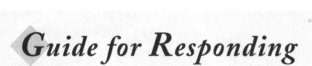
Guide for Responding

◆ Literature and Your Life

Reader's Response Do you find the speaker's description of the depth of her love effective or moving? Explain.

Thematic Focus How would you describe the speaker's relationship with her love?

☑ Check Your Comprehension

1. In Sonnet 43, what question does the speaker ask?
2. Briefly summarize the speaker's answers to her own questions.

◆ Critical Thinking

INTERPRET

1. What does the speaker of Sonnet 43 mean in lines 9–10 by the words "...with the passion put to use / In my old griefs..."? **[Interpret]**
2. Describe the kind of love expressed by the speaker in Sonnet 43. **[Draw Conclusions]**

APPLY

3. Give two ways in which you might complete the line "I love thee...." **[Apply]**
4. Cite a popular song that praises love, and compare its language, attitude, and images to those of Sonnet 43. **[Relate]**

Guide for Responding (continued)

◆ Reading Strategy

DRAW INFERENCES ABOUT THE SPEAKER

Although Browning does not directly describe the speakers in these poems, by examining their speech and actions, you were probably able to draw **inferences** that enabled you to know them. When the speaker of "My Last Duchess" says, "She had /a heart—how shall I say?—too soon made glad," he's telling you that his wife was too easily pleased by any act of kindness. Yet he's also revealing that he is an extremely proud and bitterly jealous man.

1. Why does the Duke in "My Last Duchess" show the Count's agent the portrait of his dead wife?
2. In "Love Among the Ruins," what can you infer about the speaker's attitude (a) toward the ruined civilization? (b) toward the woman he is going to meet?
3. What inferences can you make about the speaker in "Life in a Love" from lines 18–20?

◆ Build Vocabulary

USING THE LATIN SUFFIX -*ence*

Knowing that the Latin suffix -*ence* means "quality, or state of being," add -*ence* to the following adjectives to make nouns. Write the definition for each noun.

1. innocent   2. prominent   3. permanent

USING THE WORD BANK: Analogies

On your paper, complete the following analogies using the words from the Word Bank.

1. *Chases* is to *pursuer* as _____?_____ is to *escapee.*
2. *Cruelty* is to *tormentor* as _____?_____ is to *benefactor.*
3. *Toe* is to *foot* as _____?_____ is to *head.*
4. *Salary* is to *employee* as _____?_____ is to *husband.*
5. *Troops* are to *general* as _____?_____ are to *king.*
6. *Plain* is to *stick figure* as _____?_____ is to *masterpiece.*
7. *Totality* is to *whole* as _____?_____ is to *part.*
8. *Patient* is to *teacher* as _____?_____ is to *helper.*

◆ Literary Focus

DRAMATIC MONOLOGUE

Reading a **dramatic monologue** by Browning is like going to a mini-play: In a speech (sometimes to a silent listener), a character indicates a setting and a dramatic conflict. More important, this character reveals his or her inmost feelings, sometimes without knowing it.

In "My Last Duchess," the setting is the private gallery of a Duke living in sixteenth-century Italy. He is speaking to a messenger from the Count whose daughter he wants to marry.

1. (a) What conflict relating to his first wife does the Duke reveal? (b) How did he solve that conflict? (c) What will his next marriage be like, assuming the negotiation is successful?
2. (a) What is the dramatic situation in "Love Among the Ruins"? (b) Is the conflict in the poem between two people or between two different ideas about life? Explain.
3. What are the setting and conflict in "Life in a Love"?

◆ Grammar and Style

THE USE OF *LIKE* AND *AS*

In making comparisons, do not confuse **like,** a preposition used to compare nouns and pronouns, with **as,** a conjunction used to compare actions.

Practice Write these sentences in your journal, replacing the blanks with the correct word, *like* or *as.* Remember that *as* can introduce a clause in which the verb is implied or understood.

1. No interpretation of Robert Browning's *The Ring and the Book* is exactly _____?_____ another.
2. The Duke depicted his last duchess _____?_____ he chose.
3. When Robert Browning and Elizabeth Barrett were married, his poems were not as famous _____?_____ hers.
4. Do you think Elizabeth Barrett Browning's sonnets are _____?_____ contemporary love songs?

Writing Application Write a paragraph comparing Sonnet 43 to "Life in a Love." Use *like* and *as* at least once each.

Build Your Portfolio

Idea Bank

Writing

1. **Profile** Write a profile of any speaker in the four poems. Use the speaker's words to speculate on various aspects of his or her personality.

2. **Messenger's Report** As the agent who listens to the Duke in "My Last Duchess," report on your meeting to the Count. Tell simply and clearly what the Duke wants.

3. **Response to Criticism** Philip Langbaum says, "Most successful dramatic monologues deal with speakers who are in some way reprehensible" (deserving of blame). Agree or disagree with him, using evidence from the poems in this group.

Speaking, Listening, and Viewing

4. **Oral Interpretation** Perform one of Browning's dramatic monologues for the class. Vary the tone of your voice and the words you emphasize to capture the speaker's personality. **[Performing Arts Link]**

5. **Visual Presentation** The ruins Browning writes about are Roman. With a partner, prepare a visual presentation of architecture in the city of Rome that dates back to the Classical era. **[Art Link]**

Researching and Representing

6. **The Brownings in the Media** View movies that depict the Brownings, like *The Barretts of Wimpole Street*. Then report to the class on the way in which these films portray the famous couple. **[Media Link]**

7. **The Brownings in Italy** Using biographies of the Brownings, research their life in Italy. Present your results to the class, indicating on a map exactly where they lived. **[Social Studies Link]**

Online Activity www.phlit.phschool.com

Guided Writing Lesson

Written Recommendation

Imagine that you are the count's agent. After having just heard the Duke's account of his relationship with his previous wife, what recommendation would you present to the father of the woman the Duke hopes to marry? State your opinion in a formal written recommendation to present to the father upon your return from visiting the Duke. Keep the following tip in mind as you develop your paper.

Writing Skills Focus: Cause-and-Effect Transitions

As you build your argument, use **transitions to show cause-and-effect relationships.** Following are just a few of the transitions you'll want to consider: *the reason for, as a result, because, therefore,* and *consequently.*

Prewriting Start by reviewing the poem and noting what it reveals about the Duke's personality and his relationship with his first wife. Review these details and decide on your position regarding the proposed marriage.

Drafting Start with a paragraph in which you present your position clearly and succinctly. Then follow with a series of paragraphs in which you explain the reasons for your recommendation. Use details from the poem to back up your argument. Wherever appropriate use cause-and-effect transitions to show how your details fit together.

Revising Have a classmate assume the role of the woman's father and read your recommendation. Have you presented your case clearly? Have you backed up your argument? Have you written in a respectful tone? Use your classmate's answers to these questions to help you revise.

CONNECTIONS TO WORLD LITERATURE

You Know the Place: Then
Sappho

Invitation to the Voyage
Charles Baudelaire

Cultural Connection

RELATIONSHIPS

Most of the poems in this section arise from and describe close relationships between friends or lovers. For example, Alfred, Lord Tennyson's "In Memoriam" expresses grief at the death of his good friend Arthur Henry Hallam. Elizabeth Barrett Browning counts up the uncountable ways she loves her husband in a poem that could sum up every lover's devotion.

The poems of the ancient Greek poet Sappho (saf´ ō) and the nineteenth-century French poet Charles Baudelaire (shàrl bōd ler´) also express wholehearted devotion to a loved one. For Sappho, the loved one is Aphrodite herself, the Greek goddess of love. For Baudelaire, the beloved is a mortal woman whom he addresses endearingly as "child" and "sister."

INVITATIONS TO LOVE

Both Sappho and Baudelaire write their poems in the form of invitations. Sappho urges Aphrodite to come from Crete and take up residence on the poet's own island. She wants Aphrodite to accept her devotions and bless her loves. Baudelaire paints for his beloved the image of a magical world of "Richness, quietness, and pleasure" where they can "live together" at peace.

You, too, can accept the invitations these poets offer and journey to distant lands of love.

SAPPHO
(c. 610 B.C.–570 B.C.)

Sappho was an ancient Greek lyricist whose works were known for a personal expression of love and loss. Sappho was one of the first poets to write in the first person rather than from the viewpoint of gods and muses. Although Sappho wrote nearly five hundred poems, only a small fraction of these survive, either intact or in fragments.

CHARLES BAUDELAIRE
(1821–1867)

Known as much for his unconventional life style as his poetry, Baudelaire was one of the most startling and innovative poets of the nineteenth century. Attempting to break away from the Romantic tradition, Baudelaire created poems that are objective rather than sentimental and celebrate the city and the artificial rather than nature. Yet his work still exhibits many of the imaginative and mystical qualities associated with Romanticism.

Sappho, L. Alma Tadema, The Walters Art Gallery, Baltimore, Maryland

▲ **Critical Viewing** This poem describes a place of beauty and peace. What details in this picture reflect the place described in the poem? **[Connect]**

You Know the Place: Then

Sappho
Translated by Mary Barnard

You know the place: then

Leave Crete and come to us
waiting where the grove is
pleasantest, by precincts

5   sacred to you; incense
smokes on the altar, cold
streams murmur through the

apple branches, a young
rose thicket shades the ground
10   and quivering leaves pour

down deep sleep; in meadows
where horses have grown sleek
among spring flowers, dill

scents the air. Queen! Cyprian![1]
15   Fill our gold cups with love
stirred into clear nectar

---

1. Cyprian (sī′ prē ən) *n.:* Name Sappho uses to address the goddess Aphrodite.

Invitation to the Voyage

Charles Baudelaire

Translated by Richard Wilbur

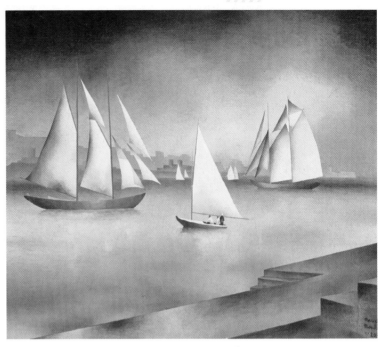

Marine. Marcel Mouillot, Galleria d'arte Moderna, Nancy

▲ **Critical Viewing** Where, according to the speaker in this poem, might these "drowsy ships" be sailing? **[Interpret]**

My child, my sister, dream
How sweet all things would seem
Were we in that kind land to live together
And there love slow and long,
5   There love and die among
Those scenes that image you, that sumptuous[1]
  weather.
Drowned suns that glimmer there
Through cloud-disheveled[2] air
Move me with such a mystery as appears
10   Within those other skies
Of your treacherous eyes
When I behold them shining through their tears.

There, there is nothing else but grace and
  measure,
Richness, quietness, and pleasure.

15   Furniture that wears
The luster of the years
Softly would glow within our glowing chamber,
Flowers of rarest bloom
Proffering their perfume
20 Mixed with the vague fragrances of amber;
Gold ceilings would there be,
Mirrors deep as the sea,

---

1. sumptuous (sump´ chŏŏ əs) *adj.*: Magnificent or
splendid.
2. disheveled (di shev´ əld) *adj.*: Disarranged and untidy.

The walls all in an Eastern splendor hung—
   Nothing but should address
25   The soul's loneliness,
Speaking her sweet and secret native tongue.

There, there is nothing else but grace and
   measure,
Richness, quietness, and pleasure.

      See, sheltered from the swells
30   There in the still canals
Those drowsy ships that dream of sailing forth;
      It is to satisfy
      Your least desire, they ply
Hither through all the waters of the earth.
35   The sun at close of day
      Clothes the fields of hay,
Then the canals, at last the town entire
      In hyacinth and gold:
      Slowly the land is rolled
40 Sleepward under a sea of gentle fire.

There, there is nothing else but grace and
   measure,
Richness, quietness, and pleasure.

Guide for Responding

◆ Literature and Your Life

Reader's Response Are the invitations issued by these poets persuasive? Why or why not?

Thematic Focus Could either of these poems have been written in today's world? Explain.

Journal Writing Briefly describe an ideal place to which you'd like to journey.

☑ Check Your Comprehension

1. What two requests does the speaker of "You Know the Place: Then" make of Aphrodite?
2. For what is the speaker of "You Know the Place: Then" waiting?
3. How does Baudelaire describe the "kind land"?

◆ Critical Thinking

INTERPRET

1. How does Sappho present love as being imposed by external forces? **[Infer]**
2. What impression of love does Baudelaire convey by linking it to the notion of escaping to an ideal, dreamlike world? **[Infer]**
3. How does Baudelaire suggest a sense of longing for the place he describes? **[Interpret]**

COMPARE LITERARY WORKS

4. Compare and contrast the places in which Sappho and Baudelaire believe they will find love. **[Compare and Contrast]**

Cultural Connection

RELATIONSHIPS

Like Tennyson and the Brownings, Sappho and Baudelaire capture the essence of a relationship in the rhythms and imagery of their poetry. For these two poets, the love that inspires their work becomes inseparable from the magical place where their love will be fulfilled. That place, in turn, becomes an enticement to the god or person they are inviting.

1. Show how both Sappho and Baudelaire use the same techniques in their poetic invitations that you would use to invite a friend on a date.
2. Compare and contrast the relationship Elizabeth Barrett Browning describes in Sonnet 43 with the one Baudelaire describes in the poem "Invitation to the Voyage."
3. (a) Identify a contemporary song that, like the poems of Sappho and Baudelaire, is also an invitation to love. (b) What devices does the songwriter use to make the invitation seem attractive?

Idea Bank

Writing

1. **Invitation** Use poetry or prose to invite a friend on a date or to a special occasion.

2. **Literary Analysis** Choose one of the poems in this section, and analyze its use of imagery. Show how the images in the poem contribute to its meaning.

3. **Response to Criticism** Geoffrey Brereton writes that "Baudelaire's choice of words and images. . . gave his verse its original force and has now raised him . . . to the status of 'classic.'" Use passages from "Invitation to the Voyage" to analyze Baudelaire's "words and images." Then support or refute this critic's claim.

Speaking, Listening, and Viewing

4. **Eastern Splendor** Baudelaire uses the phrase "Eastern splendor" to echo the "richness" and "luster" he speaks of earlier in the poem. Form a small group to collect a series of images that suggest Eastern splendor to you, and present them to your class in an oral report. **[Art Link]**

Researching and Representing

5. **Poetry Reading** Find other translations of the work of Sappho and Baudelaire, and read them aloud to your class. If possible, find recordings of the same poems in their original language as well, so that your classmates can have the sounds of the original poems in their ears. **[Performing Arts Link]**

Online Activity www.phlit.phschool.com

Writing Process Workshop

Cause-and-Effect Essay

Life is an ongoing series of cause-and-effect relationships. In a cause-and-effect essay, you examine relationships in greater detail. You focus on the results of a particular event or situation (effects) or the factors giving rise to a particular event or situation (causes). Even the poets in this section speculate about the causes of past events. Browning, for example, writes of the emotions that motivated an ancient people: ". . . dread of shame/Struck them tame. . . ."

Use the following skills as you prepare your cause-and-effect essay:

Writing Skills Focus

▶ **Research and write down information** about situations, events, and actions that clearly illustrate cause-and-effect relationships.

▶ Organize your details to **show connections among causes and effects.** (See p. 765.)

▶ **Use cause-and-effect transitions** such as *because, since, then, as a result,* to indicate relationships. (See p. 779.)

▶ **Give specific examples** of causes and effects.

In the following passage, two writers explore cause-and-effect relationships between animals and their habitats.

MODEL FROM LITERATURE

from *Last Chance to See* by Douglas Adams and Mark Carwardine

① An island, on the other hand, is small. There are far fewer species, and the competition for survival has never reached anything like the pitch that it does on the mainland. Species are only as tough as they need to be. . . . This is why you find on Madagascar, for instance, species like the lemurs that were overwhelmed eons ago on the mainland. ② Islands are fragile time capsules.

So what happens on Mauritius, or indeed any island, is that when the endemic vegetation or animals are destroyed for any reason, the exotic forms leap into the breach ③.

① The writers use these two paragraphs to examine the effects of island life on the survival of species.

② The reference to lemurs is a specific example of the effect of less competition.

③ The transition *when* links cause (destruction of endemic species) to effect (exotic forms take over).

APPLYING LANGUAGE SKILLS:
Revising Stringy Sentences

Stringy sentences result when a writer runs together a long series of clauses connected by conjunctions. Avoid stringy sentences as you draft your cause-and-effect essay.

Practice Rewrite the following stringy sentence. Make it into a series of related sentences in a paragraph.

Most infants have little control over their bodies at first, and then they develop from the head down and from the torso out, and as a result, they generally will have control of their heads and necks before their bodies and of their arms and legs before their fingers and hands, so that it takes several months for a baby to move its fingers or toes voluntarily.

Writing Application As you write scientific cause-and-effect essays, consider creating bulleted lists of details to avoid stringy sentences.

Writer's Solution Connection
Writing Lab

For help in narrowing your topic, see the activities in the Narrowing Your Topic section of the tutorial on Exposition.

Prewriting

Choose a Topic To find a topic, think about cause-and-effect relationships that you discussed in a history or science class. You might also use the topic ideas below:

Topic Ideas
- Causes and effects of "brown tide"
- An unexpected effect of an action

Selection-Related Topic Ideas
- Events and situations that led to Tennyson's writing of "In Memoriam—"
- Real-life inspirations for the poetry of the Brownings

Research Appropriate Information Use a variety of texts and technical resources, including databases and the Internet.

Limit Your Topic If you limit your focus to a few causes and effects, you'll be able to write a clearer and more thoughtful explanation. For example, instead of covering a broad topic like "The Causes of World War II," choose a narrower topic, like "The Events That Brought Churchill to Power."

Create a Cause-and-Effect Chain or Cluster Diagram Gather details for your cause and effect essay, and list them in a chain like the one below. If there is more than one effect per cause, you may want to use a cluster diagram.

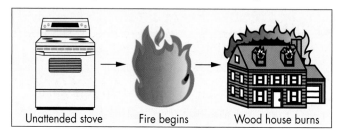

Unattended stove   Fire begins   Wood house burns

Drafting

Create a Logical Organization If the organization of your paper is clear, readers will readily understand the links between causes and effects. Within each paragraph, you might want to examine just one cause-and-effect relationship.

Use Cause-and-Effect Transitions Use transitions—such as *following, after, because, since, as a result,* and *then*—to help clarify the links between causes and effects.

Revising

Add Transitions Where Necessary Mark transitions as you proofread to avoid repeating the same words. Check to see that each transition provides a clear link between your ideas.

Revision Checklist As you revise, answer the following questions:

1. Does my essay's organization make cause-and-effect relationships clear?

2. What transitions might I add or revise to strengthen the relationships between ideas?

3. Have I included examples of specific causes and effects?

REVISION MODEL

from *A Retirement Speech*

① I am often asked, "Why specialize in cancer?" and I am reminded of a quotation by Robert Henri in *The Art of the Spirit*: "No knowledge is so easily found as when it is needed."

~~I am a cancer specialist.~~

② My decision to specialize in oncology was made the day my own cancer was diagnosed.

~~I chose to pursue a career in medicine.~~ For me medicine

③ As a result
was not only the obvious, but the only choice. I was able

to apply not only my intellect, but my heart to my studies,

and later to my patients.

① By rewriting the opening sentence, the author makes it clear that the essay will focus on a cause-and-effect relationship.

② The author replaces a general sentence with a specific detail to clarify a causal relationship.

③ The author adds a transition to link his illness with his success as a student and as a physician.

Publishing

▶ **Internet** Post your essay on an appropriate site or bulletin board.

▶ **Science Magazine** Collect scientific cause-and-effect essays from your classmates and publish them in a science magazine.

▶ **Oral Presentation** Have a group of classmates read their essays aloud for an audience. Then invite questions from the audience about the topics.

APPLYING LANGUAGE SKILLS: Using Precise Language

Cause-and-effect essays are more effective when you use precise language to describe events and situations. These techniques will help you make your language precise.

- To make nouns and verbs more exact, narrow their focus as much as possible.

General: food
Specific: broccoli

- Use specific nouns or verbs.

General: pull it through the hole
Specific: thread

- Use specific adjectives.

Vague: The result will be a nice sweater.
Specific: The result will be a bright blue angora sweater.

Practice Rewrite these sentences, making the italicized words more precise.

1. The Spaniards brought *animals* to America.

2. That runner *moves* down the track very fast.

Writer's Solution Connection Language Lab

For help in writing unified and coherent paragraphs, work through the Topic Sentence and Support lesson and the Unity in Paragraphs lesson.

Student Success Workshop

Real-World Reading Skills

Analyzing the Characteristics of Clear Text

Strategies for Success

A critical reader evaluates written information for conciseness, accuracy, and completeness, to assess the validity of the writing. The genre often determines the standards by which a text should be judged. A medical journal, for example, should use concise, accurate language. A persuasive message, on the other hand, should be truthful and forceful.

Examine a Text for Accuracy You cannot assume that facts, data, examples, or even quotations that you read are accurate. The author's motivation for writing will influence the accuracy of the information. The author of a textbook, for example, should provide you with correct information. A biographer, on the other hand, may dramatize a scene to enhance the story. As you read, ask yourself whether there are questionable data, misleading statements, or opinions stated as facts. Refer to resources, such as almanacs and encyclopedias, to confirm the validity of the information.

Analyze a Text for Conciseness Written materials that are unnecessarily long and complex are often confusing. Look for text that is precise and to the point. Ask yourself: Are the details appropriate and relevant? Are arguments supported by reliable facts and data? Are all the issues related to the main topic? Is the logic clear and concise?

Evaluate a Text for Completeness Analyze a text to determine whether the writer's presentation is complete. Are some facts obviously missing? If the topic is controversial, do the arguments appear balanced or one-sided? A writer who selectively presents only one side of an argument does not give you a clear picture of an issue. You may want to consult other resources to discover other arguments.

Apply the Strategies

Read and analyze the passage that follows. Apply the strategies to analyze the characteristics of clear text.

> We have come to the conclusion that it is unnecessary to raise taxes to pay for new books in the public-school system. Our research shows that the books the students currently have are adequate. If anyone is to blame for the deplorable condition of the books, it is the students who abuse them. Also, we don't believe that the funds would be used to acquire new books. We suspect the money would be squandered. Since students have read only 80% of the books on the shelves, there is no need to waste tax money on new books. People who vote in favor of this tax are confused in their thinking.

1. Which statements contain inaccurate facts and opinions presented as facts? Why are they inaccurate?

2. Which statements are irrelevant or inappropriate? Why?

3. In what ways is this passage incomplete and unbalanced? What information is missing?

✔ Here are situations in which you should analyze text for clarity:
▶ Report from a special-interest group
▶ Advertisements
▶ Historical accounts

PART 2

The Empire and Its Discontents

Miniature photographic portraits commemorative 1897 Jubilee Victoria (adult and child) Alexandra and George V

In one sense, the Victorian Age was a time of optimism and progress. Abroad, the British Empire was expanding. At home, new goods and gadgets were improving the quality of life. Yet beneath the blare of self-congratulation, the poet Matthew Arnold heard "an eternal note of sadness." One troubling foreign policy issue, Irish independence, was all too close to home. Also, those foreigners in their own country, Britain's urban poor, were not sharing in the general prosperity.

Guide for Interpreting

Matthew Arnold
(1822–1888)

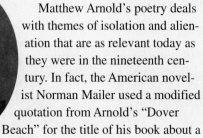

Matthew Arnold's poetry deals with themes of isolation and alienation that are as relevant today as they were in the nineteenth century. In fact, the American novelist Norman Mailer used a modified quotation from Arnold's "Dover Beach" for the title of his book about a major Vietnam War protest, *Armies of the Night*.

A Social Conscience While attending Oxford University, Arnold developed the social conscience that was to guide his career as a public servant, poet, and literary critic. In 1851, he accepted the post of Inspector of Schools. In this job he did much to improve education in Great Britain. All the while, he remained a poet at heart, though his first two books, published in 1849 and 1852, met with little success.

Literary Achievement Arnold's literary fortunes changed in 1853 with the publication of *Poems,* which included a long preface that established the author as a major critic. *New Poems*, published in 1867, contained Arnold's celebrated "Dover Beach." After completing this collection, Arnold believed that he had expressed everything he had to say in poetry. From that point on he wrote literary criticism, like the essays in *Culture and Anarchy* (1869). There, he argues that literature should train us to open our minds to what is true and valuable in life.

Rudyard Kipling *(1865–1936)*

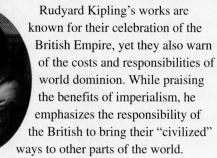

Rudyard Kipling's works are known for their celebration of the British Empire, yet they also warn of the costs and responsibilities of world dominion. While praising the benefits of imperialism, he emphasizes the responsibility of the British to bring their "civilized" ways to other parts of the world.

Early Success Kipling was born to British parents in India, one of Britain's largest colonies. At the age of five, he was placed in a foster home in England, due to the belief that British children should be educated in England. However, he returned to India in 1882 to work as a journalist. During the next seven years, he published a number of witty poems and stories, and by the time he visited London in 1890, he was a celebrity.

Kipling's Achievements Kipling is known as a Victorian author because he produced his best work before the death of Queen Victoria in 1901. In its great variety, that work includes children's classics—*The Jungle Book* (1895), *Second Jungle Book* (1896), *Captains Courageous* (1897), and *Kim* (1901) in addition to well-known poems like "Recessional," and his autobiography, *The Best of Me*. For many years Kipling was the most popular English poet and in 1907 he became the first English writer to be awarded the Nobel Prize for Literature.

◆ Background for Understanding

HISTORY: ARNOLD, KIPLING, AND IMPERIALISM

In 1857, Britain took direct control of all India, and in the 1880's and 1890's, seized the African colonies of Kenya and the Sudan. Even as the Empire expanded, however, writers expressed doubts about life in the world's most powerful nation.

In "Dover Beach," for example, Matthew Arnold laments the decline of religious faith and depicts the world as a place where "ignorant armies clash by night."

Even Kipling, who supported British imperialism, uses "Recessional" to warn against the perils of pride. Written for the sixtieth anniversary of Queen Victoria's reign, the poem was a warning to those who boasted of Britain's world domination.

Dover Beach ◆ Recessional
◆ The Widow at Windsor ◆

◆ *Literature and Your Life*

CONNECT YOUR EXPERIENCE

The photo of Earth taken from the moon shows a blue jewel of a planet, alone in the darkness of outer space, giving us a Big Picture of where we stand in the universe.

About a century before space travel, poets took flights of inspiration through Inner Space, allowing them to see another kind of Big Picture, a vision of things as a whole. Works like "Dover Beach" and "Recessional" convey this vision.

Journal Writing Briefly list some major trends that will influence life on this planet in the next century.

THEMATIC FOCUS: THE EMPIRE AND ITS DISCONTENTS

What are some problems that Arnold and Kipling see when they view things as a whole?

◆ Literary Focus

MOOD AS A KEY TO THEME

Poems contain emotional thoughts and thoughtful emotions. With thought and emotion so closely linked in a poem, the **mood** or feeling it calls up in you is bound to be related to its central idea or **theme**. By reading a poem with your feelings—responding to emotionally charged words and images—you'll gradually find your way to its ideas.

In "Dover Beach," the crash of waves brings "The eternal note of sadness in." This mood of sadness leads you to the poem's theme, which concerns a world that has "neither joy, nor love, nor light."

◆ Grammar and Style

PRESENT TENSE

In "Dover Beach," Matthew Arnold uses **present tense** verbs like *lies* and *gleams* to convey both the immediacy of an experience and the truth revealed by that experience:

Experience: ". . . the light / *Gleams* and *is* gone . . . "

Truth: "And we *are* here as on a darkling plain / Swept with confused alarms of struggle and flight, / Where ignorant armies *clash* by night."

◆ Build Vocabulary

LATIN ROOTS: *-domi-*

In "Recessional," Kipling uses the word *dominion* when referring to the power of the British empire. This word contains the Latin root *-domi-*, which means "lord" or "master." To have *dominion* means "to be master of; to rule."

WORD BANK

Before you read, preview this list of words from the poems.

tranquil
cadence
turbid
dominion
contrite

◆ Reading Strategy

DRAW CONCLUSIONS

By **drawing conclusions** about what you read—making generalizations based on evidence—you can link elements that at first seem unrelated.

In "The Widow at Windsor," for example, it may not be clear at first why a "widow" has a "gold crown" and "ships on the foam." However, when you see the reference to "Missis Victorier's sons," you can conclude that the widow is Queen Victoria herself. Using this information, you can draw further conclusions about who the speaker is and why the poem is written in dialect.

Read the other poems in the same way, drawing conclusions about the connections between details.

Dover Beach

Matthew Arnold

The sea is calm tonight.
The tide is full, the moon lies fair
Upon the straits:[1] on the French coast the light
Gleams and is gone; the cliffs of England stand,
5   Glimmering and vast, out in the tranquil bay.
Come to the window, sweet is the night air!
Only, from the long line of spray

Where the sea meets the moon-blanched land,
Listen! you hear the grating roar
10   Of pebbles which the waves draw back, and fling,
At their return, up the high strand,[2]
Begin, and cease, and then again begin,
With tremulous cadence slow, and bring
The eternal note of sadness in.

---

1. **straits:** Straits of Dover, between England and France.
2. **strand:** Shore.

▼ Critical Viewing
Does this photograph capture the "eternal note of sadness" Arnold describes? Explain. **[Support]**

15   Sophocles[3] long ago
      Heard it on the Aegaean,[4] and it brought
      Into his mind the <u>turbid</u> ebb and flow
      Of human misery; we
      Find also in the sound a thought,
20   Hearing it by this distant northern sea.

      The Sea of Faith
      Was once, too, at the full, and round earth's shore
      Lay like the folds of a bright girdle furled.
      But now I only hear
25   Its melancholy, long, withdrawing roar,
      Retreating, to the breath
      Of the night wind, down the vast edges drear
      And naked shingles[5] of the world.

      Ah, love, let us be true
30   To one another! for the world, which seems
      To lie before us like a land of dreams,
      So various, so beautiful, so new,
      Hath really neither joy, nor love, nor light,
      Nor certitude, nor peace, nor help for pain;
35   And we are here as on a darkling[6] plain
      Swept with confused alarms of struggle and flight,
      Where ignorant armies clash by night.

◆ Build
Vocabulary

tranquil
(tran´kwil) *adj.*:
Calm; serene;
peaceful

cadence
(kād´ əns) *n.*:
Measured
movement

turbid (tʉr´
bid) *adj.*: Con-
fused; per-
plexed

3. **Sophocles** (säf´ ə klēz´): Greek tragic dramatist
(496?-406 B.C.).
4. **Aegaean** (ē jē´ ən): Arm of the Mediterranean Sea
between Greece and Turkey.
5. **shingles** *n.*: Beaches covered with large, coarse, water-
worn gravel.
6. **darkling** *adj.*: In the dark.

Guide for Responding

◆ *Literature and Your Life*

Reader's Response Do you agree with the
speaker's view of the world? Why or why not?
Thematic Focus How does the final image of
the poem challenge the Victorian idea of progress?

☑ Check Your Comprehension

1. What does the speaker see from his window?
2. Who else does the speaker say "long ago"
   heard the "tremulous cadence slow"?
3. What does the speaker urge his beloved to do?
4. What sad reality does the speaker describe for
   his companion in lines 30-34?

◆ Critical Thinking

INTERPRET

1. A symbol is a thing, person, or place that stands
   for something beyond itself. Explain the symbolism of the "cliffs of England" (line 4) and "night"
   (line 37). **[Interpret]**
2. State the message of lines 35-37 in your own
   words. **[Draw Conclusions]**

EVALUATE

3. To what extent does Arnold's plea to "be true /
   To one another" in lines 29-30 provide a satisfac-
   tory answer to the problem "Of human misery"?
   [Make a Judgment]

Recessional[1] Rudyard Kipling

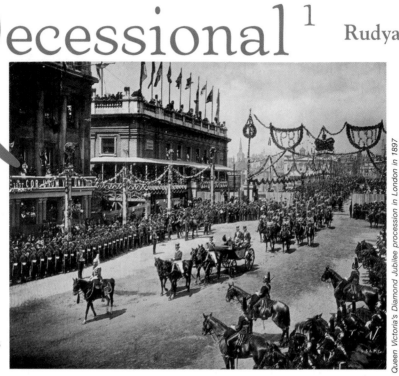

Queen Victoria's Diamond Jubilee procession in London in 1897

▶ **Critical Viewing**
Although the parade shown here took place in 1897, what elements are common to parades of today? [**Relate**]

In 1897 a national celebration called the "Diamond Jubilee" was held in honor of the sixtieth anniversary of Queen Victoria's reign. The occasion prompted a great deal of boasting about the strength and greatness of the empire. Kipling responded to the celebration by writing this poem, reminding the people of England that the British empire might not last forever.

God of our fathers, known of old—
    Lord of our far-flung battle-line—
Beneath whose awful Hand we hold
    <u>Dominion</u> over palm and pine—
5 Lord God of Hosts, be with us yet
Lest we forget—lest we forget!

The tumult and the shouting dies—
    The Captains and the Kings depart—
Still stands Thine ancient Sacrifice,
10   An humble and a <u>contrite</u> heart.[2]
Lord God of Hosts, be with us yet,
Lest we forget—lest we forget!

---

1. Recessional *n.*: Hymn sung at the end of a religious service.
2. An . . . heart: Allusion to the Bible (Psalms 51:17): "The sacrifices of God are a broken spirit: a broken and contrite heart, O God, thou wilt not despise."

Far-called, our navies melt away—
        On dune and headland sinks the fire[3]—
15 Lo, all our pomp of yesterday
        Is one with Nineveh[4] and Tyre![5]
Judge of the Nations, spare us yet,
Lest we forget—lest we forget!

    If, drunk with sight of power, we loose
20   Wild tongues that have not Thee in awe—
Such boasting as the Gentiles use
        Or lesser breeds without the Law—[6]
Lord God of Hosts, be with us yet,
Lest we forget—lest we forget!

25 For heathen heart that puts her trust
        In reeking tube[7] and iron shard[8]—
All valiant dust that builds on dust,
        And guarding calls not Thee to guard—
For frantic boast and foolish word,
30 Thy mercy on Thy People, Lord!

---

3. **On . . . fire:** Bonfires were lit on high ground all over Britain as part of the opening ceremonies of the Jubilee celebration.
4. **Nineveh** (nin´ ə və): Ancient capital of the Assyrian Empire, the ruins of which were discovered buried in desert sands in the 1850's.
5. **Tyre** (tīr): Once a great port and the center of ancient Phoenician culture, now a small town in Lebanon.
6. **Such boasting . . . Law:** Allusion to the Bible (Romans 2:14): "For when the Gentiles, which have not the law, do by nature the things contained in the law, these, having not the law, are a law unto themselves."
7. **tube:** Barrel of a gun.
8. **shard:** Fragment of a bombshell.

◆ **Build Vocabulary**

dominion (də min´yen) *n.*: Place of rule; home territory

contrite (kən trīt´) *adj.*: Willing to repent or atone

Guide for Responding

◆ *Literature and Your Life*

Reader's Response Do you think this poem is relevant to contemporary society? Explain.

Thematic Focus What warning does Kipling give in this poem?

☑ **Check Your Comprehension**

1. To whom is this poem addressed?
2. In lines 15–16, what does the speaker suggest happens to "our pomp of yesterday"?
3. What does the speaker beg for in the last line?

◆ **Critical Thinking**

INTERPRET
1. To whom is this poem really addressed? **[Interpret]**
2. What qualities and actions does the poem condemn? Support your answer. **[Infer]**
3. (a) What double meaning is contained in the poem's title? (b) How is this ambiguity appropriate to the overall mood? **[Interpret]**
4. What is the poem's theme? **[Draw Conclusions]**

APPLY
5. Does anyone today issue warnings similar to Kipling's? Explain. **[Relate]**

The Widow at Windsor

Rudyard Kipling

'Ave you 'eard o' the Widow at Windsor
    With a hairy gold crown on 'er 'ead?
She 'as ships on the foam—she 'as millions at 'ome,
    An' she pays us poor beggars in red.
5   (Ow, poor beggars in red!)
There's 'er nick on the cavalry 'orses,
    There's 'er mark on the medical stores—
An' 'er troopers you'll find with a fair wind be'ind
    That takes us to various wars.
10   (Poor beggars!—barbarious wars!)
    Then 'ere's to the Widow at Windsor,
        An' 'ere's to the stores an' the guns,
    The men an' the 'orses what makes up the forces
        O' Missis Victorier's sons.
15   (Poor beggars! Victorier's sons!)

Walk wide o' the Widow at Windsor,
    For 'alf o' Creation she owns:
We'ave bought 'er the same with the sword an' the flame,
    An' we've salted it down with our bones.

◄ Critical Viewing How well do these two visuals capture the familial relationship between Queen Victoria and her soldiers? [Criticize]

BRITISH INFANTRY IN BARRACKS, AT GALLIPOLI.

20   (Poor beggars!—it's blue with our bones!)
      Hands off o' the sons o' the widow,
          Hands off o' the goods in 'er shop.
      For the kings must come down an' the emperors frown
          When the Widow at Windsor says "Stop!"
25   (Poor beggars!—we're sent to say "Stop!")
          Then 'ere's to the Lodge o' the Widow,
              From the Pole to the Tropics it runs—
          To the Lodge that we tile with the rank an' the file,
              An' open in form with the guns.
30   (Poor beggars!—it's always they guns!)

      We 'ave 'eard o' the Widow at Windsor,
          It's safest to leave 'er alone:
      For 'er sentries we stand by the sea an' the land
          Wherever the bugles are blown.
35   (Poor beggars!—an' don't we get blown!)
          Take 'old o' the Wings o' the Mornin',
              An' flop round the earth till you're dead;
      But you won't get away from the tune that they play
          To the bloomin' old rag over'ead.
40   (Poor beggars!—it's 'ot over'ead!)
          Then 'ere's to the sons o' the Widow,
              Wherever, 'owever they roam.
          'Ere's all they desire, an' if they require
              A speedy return to their 'ome.
45   (Poor beggars!—they'll never see 'ome!)

Guide for Responding

◆ Literature and Your Life

Reader's Response What images, ideas, or lines in this poem do you find most striking? Explain.

Thematic Focus Does the speaker reveal any problems in the British empire? Why or why not?

☑ Check Your Comprehension

1. (a) Who is the Widow at Windsor? (b) According to line 17, what does she own?
2. (a) Who is the poem's speaker? (b) What does he do for the Widow at Windsor?
3. According to the last line of the poem, what fate lies in store for the soldiers?

◆ Critical Thinking

INTERPRET

1. What is surprising about the speaker's description of Queen Victoria as the Widow of Windsor? **[Infer]**
2. Would you describe the speaker's tone as disloyal or disrespectful? Explain. **[Analyze]**
3. Why does Kipling describe the empire from the perspective of a common soldier? **[Draw Conclusions]**

EVALUATE

4. Is Kipling's use of a cockney accent an effective way to convey that the speaker is a common man? Explain. **[Evaluate]**

Guide for Responding (continued)

◆ Reading Strategy

DRAW CONCLUSIONS

Drawing conclusions about what you read is a process by which you link different parts of a text to create meaningful patterns. For example, you may notice that "Dover Beach" is set at night and that the words *tonight* or *night* appear several times. In fact, the last word of the poem is *night*. You might conclude from this pattern that night, and what is associated with it, is important to the mood and theme of the poem.

1. What does the imagery of night contribute to the meaning and mood of "Dover Beach"?
2. (a) In "Recessional," what pattern do you notice with regard to the ends of the stanzas? (b) What does this pattern suggest about Kipling's message in the poem?
3. (a) Identify repeated words and phrases in "The Widow at Windsor." (b) Basing your answer on these repetitions, what conclusions can you draw about the poem's message?

◆ Build Vocabulary

USING THE LATIN ROOT -*domi*-

Use your knowledge of the Latin root -*domi*- to explain the meaning of each italicized word:

1. a *domineering* person
2. the *predominant* reason for doing something
3. a *domain* of knowledge
4. the *dominion* a country has over its territory
5. *domination* of one nation by another

USING THE WORD BANK: Antonyms

On your paper, match the words in Column A with the words in Column B that are most nearly opposite in meaning to them.

Column A	Column B
1. tranquil	a. clear
2. cadence	b. unrepentant
3. dominion	c. agitated
4. turbid	d. powerlessness
5. contrite	e. noise

◆ Literary Focus

MOOD AS A KEY TO THEME

In poetry, feeling and thought are so closely linked that **mood is a key to theme**. If you respond to elements that create mood—imagery, rhythm, and word associations—your feelings will lead you to a poem's meaning.

1. Explain how the mood of solemn scolding is related to the message about empire that Kipling wants to convey.
2. In "The Widow at Windsor," show how these elements contribute to the mood: (a) a rollicking rhythm, (b) emotionally charged words like *sword, flame,* and *bones,* and (c) imagery that compares an empire to a widow's possessions and shop.
3. Basing your answer on the mood of "The Widow at Windsor," explain which of these sentences best describes the poem's theme: (a) Maintaining an empire is ridiculous. (b) Maintaining an empire is a deadly serious game.

◆ Grammar and Style

PRESENT TENSE

The **present tense** of a verb expresses an action or state of being that is occurring now. However, both Arnold and Kipling know that the present tense is also effective in expressing a timeless truth.

Practice On your paper, identify the present-tense verb in each of these passages from the poems.

1. The sea is calm tonight.
2. Listen! You hear the grating roar / Of pebbles ...
3. The tumult and the shouting dies ...
4. The Captains and the Kings depart ...
5. Still stands Thine ancient Sacrifice ...

Writing Application In your notebook, make each statement into a timeless truth by using a present-tense verb. If necessary, add or delete words.

1. The winning of empires required great sacrifices.
2. For me, the ebb and flow of the tide represented the cycle of human life.

Build Your Portfolio

Idea Bank

Writing

1. **Letter to the Editor** As a Victorian, write a letter to the editor of a newspaper expressing your feelings about the queen and the empire.

2. **Proposal** As an advisor to Queen Victoria, write a proposal for celebrating the sixtieth anniversary of her reign. Include details on location, speakers, and appropriate music.

3. **Literary Analysis** Write a brief analysis of Arnold's poetic devices—varied line length and irregular rhythm—and how they relate to the overall theme of "Dover Beach."

Speaking, Listening, and Viewing

4. **Address to England** Create and present an address that Queen Victoria may have given to her empire on the day of her Diamond Jubilee. **[Performing Arts Link]**

5. **Visual Presentation** With a partner, prepare and present to your class a map of the world color-coded to show the extent of the British Empire at the time Kipling wrote "Recessional." **[Social Studies Link]**

Researching and Representing

6. **Film Review** View one of the films based on Kipling's works, such as *Kim, Captains Courageous,* and *The Jungle Book*. Read the work as well so you can evaluate the film adaptation of it. Then present your analysis to the class. **[Media Link]**

7. **Tour of a Castle** Windsor Castle has long been the chief residence of British monarchs. It also houses much of the royal art collection. Research the history and architecture of Windsor. Then present your findings to the class in an oral report. **[Art Link; Social Studies Link]**

Online Activity www.phlit.phschool.com

Guided Writing Lesson

World Responsibility Speech

In "Recessional," Kipling warns his fellow Britons against an unthinking pride. You, too, can issue a warning. As a presidential advisor, write a television speech for the president that deals with an urgent global issue, like safeguarding human rights or protecting the environment. Have the president use statistics to support key points.

Writing Skills Focus: Statistics as a Form of Support

When you write a persuasive speech, you may want to include **statistics**, numerical data, as evidence or support for your position. The responsible use of statistics adds an objective, authoritative note to a report or speech. Here are a few points to keep in mind when using statistics:

- Be sure your numbers come from reliable sources.
- Use statistics that can serve as a basis for generalization and don't just represent a small number of cases.
- Present statistics in a form that your audience can easily understand, like a chart, table, or graph.

Prewriting After choosing a topic, research statistics that will support your position. As you collect data, evaluate the credibility of all your information sources and their value to your project.

Drafting As you draft, incorporate statistics, examples, and reasons to support your position. However, avoid turning your audience off by bombarding them with numbers.

Revising Read the speech to a friend who isn't good with numbers, and see whether he or she "gets" your point. If not, eliminate statistics that are confusing or include additional explanations.

Guide for Interpreting

Newspapers and Progress

The British empire in the nineteenth century measured itself with a yardstick called *progress*. People wondered whether things were better in the present than they had been in the past or whether present trends would lead to a more reasonable future. These two articles from Victorian newspapers give two very different answers to these questions—one a cry of outrage, the other an exclamation of pride.

A Picture of the World The idea of progress was perhaps born with the modern newspaper. To even ask whether progress has been made, the mind must view the world as a collection of measurable facts—the number of people fed, of miles traveled, of diseases cured. By bringing together news from near and far, Victorian newspapers assemble an image of such a world. The reader cannot directly influence or experience this larger, public world but is nevertheless called on as its witness, critic, even judge. This is the world of progress—a world that belongs to no one but which is everyone's business, a world that can be judged in terms of efficiency, fairness, and common sense.

Ideals of Reform The Victorians who measured the world with these values often found it wanting. The "Condition of Ireland," an essay from a Victorian newspaper, criticizes England's policies towards the Irish Famine—policies built on the most up-to-date economic ideas. Progress in economic theory meant disaster in Ireland. The article judges this disaster, though, in terms that are themselves part of the ideal of progress—efficiency and the reasonable use of resources.

The "Conveniences" We Share Other Victorians used the yardstick of progress with more cheering results. Sydney Smith's nineteenth-century letter to the editor takes a rosy view of the progress in personal comfort—the innovations, some large, some small, that seem to have come out of nowhere but which ended up feeling indispensable: street-lighting, railways, umbrellas. Like the statistics in the *London News* editorial, Smith's conveniences belong to an anonymous, common world—the world of newspaper ads, say.

Both gloomy doomsayers and cheerleaders for progress judge the common world imagined by the newspaper. From the trivia of daily life to weighty political questions, the two newspaper articles span the extremes of this vast, new world.

◆ Background for Understanding

SCIENCE: PROGRESS AND POTATOES

At the center of the scenes of suffering and despair painted by the essay "Condition of Ireland" is the lowly Irish potato. The potato was the product of progress—of the improved navigational technology used by early European explorers to reach the New World. In the sixteenth century, Spanish explorers brought potatoes back to Europe from Peru.

By the mid-nineteenth century, the potato had become woven into the fabric of Irish life—one-third of the Irish ate potatoes almost exclusively. When disease ruined the potato crop of 1845, the Irish began to starve. More than a million people died of starvation and disease from 1846 to 1851. More than a million and a half emigrated, many to the United States.

The British government's disastrous attempts to deal with the famine were based on accepted economic theory, which favored large, efficient farms that hired wage-laborers and sold crops for trade. To promote such farms, the British government took land away from poor small farmers and heavily taxed Irish landowners to pay for aid to those starving in their own districts. In a sense, the British government acted in the name of progress—its measures were designed to promote general economic health, rather than merely to alleviate suffering.

◆ Condition of Ireland ◆
Progress in Personal Comfort

◆ *Literature and Your Life*

CONNECT YOUR EXPERIENCE

Do you remember life before personal computers and fax machines? In your lifetime, you may already have witnessed progress.

In the nineteenth century, a flood of technological changes began to alter daily life. As you read Sydney Smith's "Progress in Personal Comfort," you may chuckle over the "improvements" he finds exciting. As you read the *News* article, though, you may shake your head when you consider how much suffering the world still contains.

Journal Writing Jot down a few of the ways in which the world has progressed since you were a kid.

THEMATIC FOCUS: THE EMPIRE AND ITS DISCONTENTS

To what discontents did progress give rise? What satisfactions did it create?

◆ Literary Focus

JOURNALISTIC ESSAY

Journalistic essays are short prose pieces providing perspectives on current events or trends. These essays confront a world larger than any one individual's experience. Unlike essayists who explore the world to learn about themselves, journalistic essayists build unified stories out of the day's jumble of news. Their pieces may be written in the voice of an all-knowing witness, as in the *London News* editorial. They may also use the voice of an isolated individual, as in Mr. Smith's letter. Essay topics range from the weighty, the *News*'s protest against injustice, to the trivial, Smith's celebration of comfort.

◆ Reading Strategy

DISTINGUISH CONNOTATIVE AND DENOTATIVE LANGUAGE

The first sentence of the *London News* article mixes **connotative** and **denotative language**. Connotative language uses words, phrases, and examples for emotional effect. Denotative language conveys facts. To identify connotative language, look for words that express the author's attitude. For instance, the adjectives "ignorant and vicious" in the first sentence of "Condition of Ireland" tell us about the writer's feelings, not about the Poor-Laws.

◆ Build Vocabulary

THE HUMORS

The *London News* article uses the word *melancholy,* meaning "sad," to describe the plight of the Irish. The word originally meant "black bile," one of the four humors, or liquids, that people from ancient Greece to the Renaissance believed governed human health and personality. We still use words from this theory, such as *choleric* (from the humor *choler*), meaning ill-tempered, to describe people.

WORD BANK

Before you read, preview this list of words from the selections.

requisites
sanction
exonerate
melancholy
indolence
depredation

◆ Grammar and Style

COORDINATING CONJUNCTIONS

A **coordinating conjunction** links two sentence parts of the same grammatical kind. There are seven coordinating conjunctions: *and, but, or, nor, yet, so,* and *for.*

They were little used, and very dear.

As you read, recognize the writers' use of coordinating conjunctions to connect similar parts of speech or grammatical units.

CONDITION OF IRELAND:

Illustrations of the New Poor-Law

The Illustrated London News, December 15, 1849

During the Great Famine, progressive economic theories clashed with the realities of starvation. Guided by new ideas of economic health, British policy toward the poor changed in the early nineteenth century. To promote year-round employment and larger, more productive farms, the new Poor-Laws made unemployment as unattractive as possible. Rather than giving hand-outs to workers suffering from low wages and periodic unemployment, the new laws emphasized confining the poor in oppressive workhouses.

Whatever the merits of the theory, it could not accommodate a catastrophe of the magnitude of the Great Famine. Irish landowners were frequently bankrupted by the requirement that they pay for all aid in their district (some theorists believed that high taxes would encourage them to make their farms more productive, hire more workers, and so end poverty). The Irish Poor-Laws required that any Irishman farming a quarter acre or less give up his land before he could receive government aid—in effect, forbidding the poor from trying to grow their own food. In the meantime, export wheat continued to be shipped out of the country while millions starved or emigrated.

The following article was one of a series in which The Illustrated London News *presented, in words and pictures, the plight of the Irish.*

Woman Begging at Clonakilty, James Mahony,
The Illustrated London News, 1847

WOMAN BEGGING AT CLONAKILTY.

▲ **Critical Viewing**
Compare the portrayal of the Irish in this picture with the portrayal of the Irish in the article. [**Compare and Contrast**]

The present condition of the Irish, we have no hesitation in saying, has been mainly brought on by ignorant and vicious legislation. The destruction of the potato for one season, though a great calamity, would not have doomed them, fed as they were by the taxes of the state and the charity of the world, to immediate decay; but a false theory, assuming the name of political economy,[1] with which it has no more to do than with the slaughter of the Hungarians by General Haynau,[2] led the landlords and the legislature to believe that it was a favorable opportunity for changing the occupation of the land and the cultivation of the soil from potatoes to corn.[3] When more food, more cultivation, more employment, were the requisites for maintaining the Irish in existence, the Legislature and the landlords went about introducing a species of cultivation that could only be successful by requiring fewer hands, and turning potato gardens, that nourished the maximum of human beings, into pasture grounds for bullocks,[4] that nourished only the minimum. The Poor-Law, said to be for the relief of the people and the means of their salvation, was the instrument of their destruction. In their terrible distress, from that temporary calamity with which they were visited, they were to have no relief unless they gave up their holdings.[5] That law, too, laid down a form for evicting the people, and thus gave the sanction and encouragement of legislation to exterminate them. Calmly and quietly, but very ignorantly—though we cheerfully exonerate the parties from any malevolence; they only committed a great mistake, a terrible blunder, which in legislation is worse than a crime—but calmly and quietly from Westminster itself, which is the center of civilization, did the decree go forth which has made the temporary but terrible visitation[6] of a potato rot the means of exterminating, through the slow process of disease and houseless starvation, nearly the half of the Irish.

The land is still there, in all its natural beauty and fertility. The sparkling Shannon, teeming with fish, still flows by their doors, and might bear to them, as the Hudson and Thames bear to the people of New York and of London, fleets of ships laden with wealth. The low grounds or *Corcasses* of Clare are celebrated for their productiveness. The country abounds in limestone: coal, iron, and lead have been found. It has an area of 827,994 acres, 372,237 of which are uncultivated, or occupied by woods or water. It is estimated that there are 296,000 acres of unoccupied land; and that of these 160,000 are capable of cultivation and improvement. Why are they not cultivated and improved, as the wilds of America are cultivated and improved by the brethren of the Irish? Why are these starving people not allowed and encouraged to plant their potato-gardens on the wastes? Why are they not married to the unoccupied soil, as a humane politician proposes to provide for the starving needlewomen of the metropolis by marrying them to the *Currency Lads* of New South Wales?[7] A more important question cannot be asked. There is about Kilrush, and in Clare, and throughout Ireland, the doubly melancholy spectacle of a strong man asking for work as the means of getting food; and of the fertile earth wooing his labors, in order to yield up to him its rich but latent[8] stores: yet it lies idle and unfruitful. Why is not this doubly melan-

◆ **Literary Focus**
Does the "we" in this sentence participate in Westminster's decisions or in the suffering of the Irish, or neither? What is the role of "we" in a journalistic essay?

---

1. **political economy:** Theory of economics and society.
2. **General Haynau:** Julius Jacob; an Austrian general notorious for the brutality with which he suppressed uprisings by the Hungarians and other peoples who revolted against the Austrian empire in the 1840's. When Haynau visited London in 1850, he was attacked by outraged mobs.
3. **corn:** (Brit.) Grain.
4. **bullocks:** Oxen.
5. **The Poor-Law . . . gave up their holdings:** The Poor-Law determined how aid was to be given to the poor. During the famine, farmers with small farms ("holdings") were required to give them up before they would be given aid.

---

6. **visitation:** Divine punishment or reward.
7. **needlewomen . . . New South Wales:** Probably referring to a scheme encouraging emigration to Australia. The "New Currency Lads" are native-born Australians.
8. **latent:** Potential; not yet actual.

◆ **Build Vocabulary**

requisites (rek´wə zits) *n.*: Things necessary for a given purpose

sanction (saŋk´ shən) *n.*: Authorized approval or permission

exonerate (eg zän´ ər āt´) *v.*: Free from a charge of guilt; declare or prove blameless

melancholy (mel´ ən käl´ ē) *adj.*: Sad and depressed

choly spectacle destroyed by their union, and converted into life and happiness, as oxygen and hydrogen, each in itself destructive, become, when united as water, the pabulum[9] of existence? We shall fully consider that question before we quit the subject, but we shall now only say that the whole of this land, cultivated and uncultivated, is owned by a few proprietors—that many of them are absentees[10]—that almost all are in embarrassed circumstances—and that, from ignorance, or false theory, or indolence, they prefer seeing the land covered with such misery as we have described, to either bringing the land under cultivation themselves, or allowing the people to cultivate it. Their greatest ambition, apparently, is to get rid of the people.

---

9. **pabulum:** Nourishing substance.
10. **absentees:** Many landowners who rented to small Irish farmers lived in England and were thought to lack sufficient motivation to make the best use of their lands.

◆ **Build Vocabulary**

indolence (in´ də lens) *n.*: Idleness; laziness

Cultural Connection

The Irish Potato Famine of 1845–49

The Irish potato famine that *The Illustrated London News* blamed on "ignorant and vicious legislation" drastically changed the demographic characteristics of Ireland. More than one million people—one eighth of Ireland's population—died of starvation or diseases caused by famine. Another 1.5 million were forced to emigrate to countries like Britain and the United States. Despite the devastating decline in population that continued over the next fifty years, the Irish people rallied to preserve the Irish language and their cultural heritage. A rebirth in traditional Irish music, musical instruments, and dance, as well as literature and drama, followed. The Irish folk dances, such as those performed in *Riverdance,* have their roots in ancient Irish culture.

Activity Describe ways that various ethnic groups in this country preserve their cultures.

Guide for Responding

◆ *Literature and Your Life*

Reader's Response Does this article move you to feel outrage on behalf of the Irish, or does it leave you cold? Explain why.

Thematic Focus What responsibility should the British government have taken for Ireland during the famine?

☑ Check Your Comprehension

1. What is the "current condition" of the Irish?
2. According to the article, what is mainly responsible for this condition?
3. What kind of wealth does Ireland have?
4. According to the article, what is the obvious solution to Ireland's difficulties?

◆ Critical Thinking

INTERPRET

1. What measures, according to the article, would have kept the famine from becoming a crisis? **[Interpret]**
2. What were the objectives, according to the article, of Britain's response to the famine? **[Infer]**
3. The article poses a solution in a series of questions. Why is this more effective than making a simple statement? **[Analyze]**

EXTEND

4. Think of a firsthand memoir of suffering you have read, such as *Anne Frank: Diary of a Young Girl.* Which did you find more affecting, this editorial or the first-person account? Explain. **[Literature Link]**

Progress
in Personal Comfort

Sydney Smith

MODERN LOCOMOTIVE.

▲ **Critical Viewing** Describe what features (shapes, lines) give this "modern locomotive"—and this drawing—an "old-fashioned" look. How might such a locomotive appear through the eyes of Mr. Smith? **[Analyze]**

It is of some importance at what period a man is born. A young man, alive at this period, hardly knows to what improvements of human life he has been introduced; and I would bring before his notice the following eighteen changes which have taken place in England since I first began to breathe in it the breath of life—a period amounting now to nearly seventy-three years.

Gas[1] was unknown: I groped about the streets of London in all but the utter darkness of a twinkling oil lamp, under the protection of watchmen in their grand climacteric,[2] and exposed to every species of depredation and insult.

◆ **Build Vocabulary**

depredation (dep´ rə dā´ shən) *n.*: Act or instance of robbing, plundering or laying waste

1. **gas:** Coal gas, piped under the streets of London and used in street lamps after 1814.
2. **climacteric:** Old age; a period of great change associated in some theories with the age of 63.

MY WIFE AND I BOTH ARE DRY WITH OUR

140

UMBRELLA

AND ITS

HERCULES FRAME.

For Sale Everywhere.

◀ **Critical Viewing** To what values does this advertisement appeal? Why was the idea of advertising a particular brand of umbrella not silly in Mr. Smith's day, though it seems so in our own? **[Relate]**

I have been nine hours in sailing from Dover to Calais before the invention of steam. It took me nine hours to go from Taunton to Bath, before the invention of railroads, and I now go in six hours from Taunton to London! In going from Taunton to Bath, I suffered between 10,000 and 12,000 severe contusions,[3] before stone-breaking Macadam[4] was born.

I paid £15 in a single year for repairs of carriage-springs on the pavement of London; and I now glide without noise or fracture, on wooden pavements.

I can walk, by the assistance of the police, from one end of London to the other, without molestation; or, if tired, get into a cheap and active cab, instead of those cottages on wheels, which the hackney coaches[5] were at the beginning of my life.

I had no umbrella! They were little used, and very dear. There were no waterproof hats, and *my* hat has often been reduced by rains into its primitive pulp.

I could not keep my smallclothes in their proper place, for braces were unknown.[6] If I had the gout, there was no colchicum. If I was bilious, there was no calomel. If I was attacked by ague, there was no quinine.[7] There were filthy coffee houses instead of elegant clubs. Game could not be bought. Quarrels about uncommuted tithes[8] were endless. The corruption

3. **contusions:** Bruises.
4. **Macadam:** Road-surfacing made of small stones bound with adhesive.

5. **cheap and active cab . . . hackney coaches:** Hackney coaches were used, four-wheeled carriages for hire. The faster two-wheeled hansom cabs appeared in London in the 1830's.
6. **smallclothes . . . braces:** There were no suspenders to support his trousers.
7. **If I had the gout . . . there was no quinine:** Gout, bilious conditions, and ague are afflictions. Colchicum, calomel, and quinine are remedies.
8. **uncommuted tithes:** Taxes paid to the Church in the form of produce, "commuted" (changed to) an equivalent payment in money in 1840.

of Parliament, before Reform, infamous.[9] There were no banks to receive the savings of the poor. The Poor Laws were gradually sapping the vitals of the country; and whatever miseries I suffered, I had no post to whisk my complaints for a single penny[10] to the remotest corners of the empire; and yet, in spite of all these privations, I lived on quietly, and am now ashamed that I was not more discontented, and utterly surprised that all these changes and inventions did not occur two centuries ago.

I forgot to add, that as the basket of stage coaches, in which luggage was then carried, had no springs, your clothes were rubbed all to pieces. . . .

---

9. **The corruption of Parliament . . . infamous:** Before the reforms of the 1800's, the House of Commons was dominated by a few corrupt, wealthy landowners.

10. **I had no post . . . single penny:** Penny postage, in the form of an adhesive stamp, was first introduced in England in 1840.

◆ *Literature and Your Life*

What "comforts" do you consider vital to your life? Do you know where they came from or why they spread?

Guide for Responding

◆ *Literature and Your Life*

Reader's Response Name one kind of change seen by Mr. Smith in his own lifetime that you found impressive. Name one that did not impress you. Explain.

Thematic Focus How important is the kind of progress that Mr. Smith describes? Explain.

Brainstorm for Progress In a group, come up with a list of areas in which you think the modern world most needs to make progress.

☑ Check Your Comprehension

1. Over what period of time did the changes Smith reports take place?
2. What two improvements in public safety were noted in the article?
3. According to Smith, what two improvements in public transportation have occurred?
4. How does Smith view his own acceptance of life before it was "improved"?

◆ Critical Thinking

INTERPRET

1. How would the "young man" whom Smith addresses view the improvements he describes? **[Speculate]**
2. Judging from the details Smith reports, how "uncomfortable" was life before "improvements" were made? Explain. **[Infer]**
3. Give a definition of "personal comfort" that might cover all of the improvements Smith lists. **[Draw Conclusions]**

EVALUATE

4. Smith does not consider the possibility that people in the future might find *his* world fairly uncomfortable. Does his pride in his own time strike you as naïve? Explain. **[Make a Judgment]**

EXTEND

5. Smith's essay reflects a wider modern experience—the present is quickly outdated. Discuss a development in entertainment, sports, or fashion that demonstrates this trend. **[Social Studies Link]**

Guide for Responding (continued)

◆ Reading Strategy

DISTINGUISH BETWEEN CONNOTATIVE AND DENOTATIVE LANGUAGE

To form a reasonable opinion when you read, you must distinguish between **connotative language** (words that can excite your feelings) and **denotative language** (words that give you facts). Even language that sounds informative may be connotative. For instance, Sydney Smith's statement that "I suffered between 10,000 and 12,000 severe contusions," uses numbers for emotive effect (it is unlikely that he counted each bruise).

In the passages cited below, identify one example each of connotative language and denotative language:

1. Smith's description of life before gas
2. his description of the benefits of the penny post
3. the description in the *London News* of Ireland's natural resources
4. the sentence in the *London News* comparing Ireland's situation to hydrogen and oxygen

◆ Build Vocabulary

USING THE HUMORS

The word *melancholy,* used by the *London News,* comes from a word for black bile, a humor believed to make a person sad. Other modern words originate from the theory that humors control people's emotions and characters. In your notebook, write a definition for each "humor" word italicized below:

1. Despite the setbacks, she remained *sanguine.*
2. Some people are sunny through the day; is he always this *bilious* first thing in the morning?
3. Yelling "fire" just might get him going, but he's a pretty *phlegmatic* fellow.

USING THE WORD BANK: Antonyms

Match each Word Bank word in Column A with its antonym, or opposite, in Column B.

Column A	Column B
1. requisites	a. construction
2. sanction	b. disapprove
3. exonerate	c. industry
4. melancholy	d. joy
5. indolence	e. luxuries
6. depredation	f. convict

◆ Literary Focus

JOURNALISTIC ESSAY

Journalistic essays are short prose pieces on current events or trends. Their authors focus their attention on what would concern "anyone," rarely reflecting on themselves. For instance, when the *London News* essayist writes, "we cheerfully exonerate the parties from any malevolence; they only committed a great mistake," he does not write as someone involved in the action he describes but as a witness and judge.

1. Find another passage in which the *London News* writer shows his relation to his subject. What relations are they?
2. What does Sydney Smith mean by "personal comfort"? What other kinds of concerns might he be leaving out of his memoir?
3. Sydney Smith is "ashamed" that he did not miss modern conveniences before they were invented. According to what standards would he judge the quality of someone's life? Explain.

◆ Grammar and Style

COORDINATING CONJUNCTIONS

Each **coordinating conjunction** names a different kind of connection between things or ideas. A coordinating conjunction links two sentence parts of the same grammatical kind.

> **The coordinating conjunctions are** *and, but, yet, so, for, or, nor*

Practice In your notebook, fill in the blank with a suitable coordinating conjunction from the list above:

1. He could not keep his smallclothes in their proper place, ____?____ braces were unknown.
2. He now glides without noise ____?____ fracture, on wooden pavements.
3. Calmly and quietly, ____?____ very ignorantly, did the decree go forth, according to the *Times.*
4. In those days, he could walk without being bothered, ____?____ he could take a cab.
5. The *News* thought that their greatest ambition was to get rid of the people, ____?____ they would not allow the people to cultivate the land.

Build Your Portfolio

 ## Idea Bank

Writing

1. **Compare Opinions** Find editorials in two different newspapers commenting on the same event in the news. Compare the opinions that are presented.

2. **Fictional Memoir** Write a memoir in which Sydney Smith explains how his life would have been changed if progress had occurred earlier—what crime might have been prevented, or love saved, if only there had been a train to Taunton.

3. **Journalistic Essay** Write a journalistic essay on an event in the news. Research the facts, then connect the facts with a dramatic theme—for instance, success, courage, or neglect. **[Career Link]**

Speaking, Listening, and Viewing

4. **Comic Monologue** Computers are more convenient than typewriters—until they crash. Present a comic monologue about how inconvenient "conveniences" can be. **[Performing Arts Link]**

5. **Television Editorial** Present a television opinion-piece set in the future, looking back at today. Comment on how daily life in the future has changed from the present and why the change represents progress. **[Media Link]**

Researching and Representing

6. **History of the Newspaper** Write a research paper on the rise of the *London News* or another English newspaper. **[Social Studies Link]**

7. **Contemporary Famine** Find a magazine article documenting starvation. Compare this situation with the Great Famine described in the *London News* article. **[Social Studies Link]**

Online Activity www.phlit.phschool.com

 ## Guided Writing Lesson

Written Evaluation

In "Progress in Personal Comfort," Sydney Smith makes no bones about it—technology leads to a better life. Sometimes, though, technology that seems "reasonable," a faster or safer means to an end, has unintended bad results. Write an evaluation of a recent piece of technology in which you show whether it makes life better or not. To support your evaluation, present evidence.

Writing Skills Focus: Supporting Details

An evaluation, like other nonfiction pieces that present a point of view, must back up its conclusions with **supporting details**. Here are a few different kinds of evidence:

- eyewitness accounts
- logical analysis (examining statements for contradictions or self-consistency)
- scientific experiment
- statistics
- expert opinion
- examples
- analogies

Prewriting Browse through newspapers and magazines to find a technological innovation to evaluate. Look for precise, factual details that will support your opinions.

Drafting Discuss each aspect of your subject, giving evidence for each of your conclusions. Do not merely present your evidence. Show how it supports your conclusions, using transition words such as *therefore, because*, and *by comparison*.

Revising Reread your paper carefully to make sure that you clearly link your evidence to your conclusions. If links are weak, add sentences that explain the connection or transition words like the ones above to connect your ideas.

CONNECTIONS TO TODAY'S WORLD

Opening Statement for the Inaugural Session of the Forum for Peace and Reconciliation
Judge Catherine McGuinness

Thematic Connection

THE EMPIRE AND ITS DISCONTENTS

During the Victorian period, Great Britain saw rapid advances in science and technology and exercised great imperial power. The writers in this section focus on the positive and negative aspects of empire. Sydney Smith, for example, notes the progress in personal comfort that made life easier, at least for the privileged. In sharp contrast, the article from *The Illustrated London News* reveals the harsh treatment of the Irish by the British during the potato famine. Arnold and Kipling are not as specific in their criticisms of the empire. Arnold conveys a general sense of sadness and alienation, while Kipling offers a solemn warning against imperial pride and overconfidence.

DISCONTENTS THAT SURVIVE AN EMPIRE

In "Recessional," Kipling cautions against believing that the empire will last forever. History has proved him right. Countries once under England's rule, like India, are now independent. Southern Ireland is also a free nation. Yet Britain still retains control of Northern Ireland, where Protestants loyal to Britain battle with Catholics who want a united Ireland. In this last surviving corner of British imperial rule, the discontents have outlived the empire.

Many people of goodwill, like Judge Catherine McGuinness, are trying to solve these remaining discontents. This selection is a speech by Judge McGuinness to the Forum for Peace and Reconciliation (1995), which attempted to bring together Protestants and Catholics in Northern Ireland.

In her opening address to this group, McGuinness shares her hopes that the past can be overcome and peace established.

JUDGE CATHERINE MCGUINNESS
(1934–)

Judge Catherine McGuinness is the Chairperson of the Forum for Peace and Reconciliation and Judge of the High Court of Ireland. McGuinness, of British and Irish ancestry, spent her childhood in Belfast and adult years in Dublin. Her strong Protestant background and fierce pride in her Irish citizenship provide her with a unique perspective on the conflict in Northern Ireland. Active in Irish politics, she has dedicated her career to seeking a lasting peace and improved quality of life for all of Ireland's citizens.

Opening Statement for the Inaugural Session of the Forum for Peace and Reconciliation

Judge Catherine McGuinness

I am happy to welcome all who are here today in Dublin Castle, participants in the Forum, observers and distinguished guests.

The Forum for Peace and Reconciliation has been established by the Government in Accordance with the intentions expressed in the Joint Declaration, to consult on, and examine, ways in which lasting peace, stability and reconciliation can be established by agreement among all the people of Ireland, and on the steps required to remove barriers of distrust, on the basis of promoting respect for the equal rights and validity of both traditions and identities. In accordance with its terms of reference it will also explore ways in which new approaches can be developed to serve economic interests common to both parts of Ireland.

It will be a fundamental principle of the Forum that all differences [in] relation to the exercise of the right to self-determination of the people of Ireland, and to all other matters, will be resolved exclusively [by] peaceful and democratic means. The purpose of the Forum will be to provide an opportunity to both major traditions, as well as to others, to assist in identifying and clarifying issues which could most contribute to creating a new era of trust and cooperation. Participation in the Forum will be entirely without prejudice to the position on constitutional issues held by any Party.

It is clear that major negotiations regarding Ireland's future, North and South, are now taking place and will continue to take place elsewhere. This Forum is a consultative and advisory body, which I hope will create a background of mutual understanding against which those other negotiations may more readily move forward.

The Forum is inclusive in its nature; already it contains members from all of the island of Ireland. I very much hope that in the future other Parties and other individuals will feel able to join in our deliberations. The forum does not represent a threat to any section of the people of Ireland. As I have already said, participation in it is entirely without prejudice to the position on constitutional issues held by any Party. The only entry test is a commitment to "peaceful and democratic means."

This Forum is about people rather than about territory. It is about people's right to live peacefully on this island "which we love and for whose welfare we pray," as that courageous Presbyterian minister, James Armour of Ballymoney, once said. All who live in Ireland must be made [to] feel that their right to be here is unquestioned and that they and their traditions are valued, whether they arrived here a few years ago or whether their ancestors came here four thousand years or four hundred years ago. People's rights and freedoms should not be affected by their religion, by their political or social outlook, by their economic standing, by their race, or by the country of origin of their ancestors. "Ireland, as distinct from her people, is nothing to me" said James Connolly, in a ringing denunciation of mindless so-called patriotism. James Connolly, who established Ireland's first republican and socialist party, and who was executed following the 1916 Ris-

▲ **Critical Viewing** What elements in this photograph point to the solemnity of the occasion? **[Deduce]**

Judge Catherine McGuinness at podium, Forum for Peace and Reconciliation, Dublin Castle, October 28, 1994

ing, was born in Scotland of Ulster parents, and first arrived in Ireland as a British soldier in the Royal Scots Regiment.

The people of this country have many origins; these strands are woven together to make us what we are. My own personal background is, perhaps, an illustration. My great great grandfather, William Ellis, was twice Lord Mayor of York in England in 1799 and 1807. My great grandfather arrived in this country as a soldier in the 93rd Sutherland Highlanders regiment in 1803. He married a Clare woman whose mother's name was Morony. Their son settled in Spanish Point in County Clare, my own father's place of origin. My mother, whose family had both Irish and Scottish ancestors, came from Tullamore in County Offaly. My parents spent virtually all

their adult life in Dunmurry, near Belfast. I was born into the Belfast Protestant community, a "Child of the Rectory," and spent my childhood there. I in my turn have spent my adult life in Dublin. My love for Ulster is deep-rooted and my Protestant background is strong, but I am nonetheless proud to be a citizen of Ireland.

To say that this country faces many problems is to understate the position. In each jurisdiction the level of unemployment and under-employment is far too high; some of those in paid work or working in the home are exploited. There is poverty and deprivation in Dublin and in Belfast, in Leitrim and in Tyrone. Poverty and hardship dominate the lives of far too many people in Ireland, Protestant and Catholic, whether their government is in

Dublin or in London. Of this we must not lose sight; it is part and parcel of the Irish situation and cannot be ignored. The economic aspects of the work of this Forum are vitally important.

We cannot pretend that the armed conflict of the past twenty five years did not happen; nor can we say that it left no legacy. We mourn all those who died; we think of all who were wounded, some of whom will suffer from their injuries all their lives; we grieve for bereaved and broken families; we are conscious of homes where there are empty chairs; we know that all wars are cruel, bloody, harsh and merciless. We rejoice at the ending of violence. We salute all those who have worked for peace and who ultimately brought about the silence of the guns. Some of those are now members of this Forum; others are unsung, and wish to remain so; they each have earned the thanks and respect of us all.

This Forum is described as a Forum for Peace and Reconciliation. I would almost rather reverse the wording of the title and call it a forum for reconciliation and peace. At present we have a cessation of violence and the continuing peace process, but reconciliation is truly a prerequisite for a real and lasting peace. If we are to be reconciled we must be able to admit the errors and mistakes of the past; we must be able to express regret for past wrongs. Yet each of us must be able to retain pride and confidence in our history and in our traditions. Reconciliation can grow where there is both honesty and confidence, and where the old fears of each other are put behind us.

Unionist, socialist, republican, nationalist, liberal, conservative, feminist and all other views have legitimate rights and should be heard. There is no political test here; there is no censorship; there is openness. No party or group or tradition has a monopoly of wisdom. We hope to help banish hatred, incitement to hatred and intolerance from the politics of Ireland, and to lead through reconciliation to a true and lasting peace.

Guide for Responding

◆ Literature and Your Life

Reader's Response Do you find this an inspiring speech? Explain.

Thematic Focus How does this speech reveal discontents that have continued from Victorian times and even earlier?

Journal Writing Pay attention to the news, and describe in your journal any cases around the world where long-lived conflicts seem to be coming to an end.

☑ Check Your Comprehension

1. What does McGuinness see as the job of the Forum for Peace and Reconciliation?
2. What are some of the problems faced by the Irish people?
3. According to McGuinness, what is the key to achieving lasting peace?

◆ Critical Thinking

INTERPRET

1. (a) Explain the significance of James Connolly's statement that "Ireland, as distinct from her people, is nothing to me." (b) Why is it relevant in the context of this speech? **[Connect]**
2. (a) Why does McGuinness spend so much time discussing her ancestry? (b) How does this add to the significance of her speech? **[Analyze]**
3. What would you say is the overall aim of this forum? **[Draw Conclusions]**

EVALUATE

4. Does the tone of the speech add to or detract from its effectiveness? **[Criticize]**

EXTEND

5. What trouble spot in the world today would benefit from a forum like this one? Explain. **[Social Studies Link]**

Thematic Connection

THE EMPIRE AND ITS DISCONTENTS

When you read Arnold's "Dover Beach" and Kipling's "Recessional," you may think of them as part of a vanished historical era. The British Empire, which they comment on indirectly or directly, ceased to exist after World War II. However, conflict between Protestants and Catholics in Northern Ireland still continues, an unwelcome legacy of empire.

Judge McGuinness attempts to deal with this legacy in her speech to a Northern Ireland peace conference. She urges the participants in the conference to put aside their differences and recognize the rights of all those living in Ireland. This step, she hopes, will create an atmosphere in which the different parties can resolve conflicts peacefully.

1. According to McGuinness's speech, what are the major issues dividing Northern Ireland?
2. Are these issues discussed in any of the other works in this section? Explain.
3. McGuinness states that "Each of us must be able to retain pride and confidence in our history and traditions." What conflicts in the United States could be resolved more easily if people followed this advice?
4. Why does the establishment and decay of empires create problems that last for hundreds of years?

 Idea Bank

Writing

1. **Reporter's Questions** As a reporter covering the Forum for Peace and Reconciliation, formulate three or four questions you can ask Judge McGuinness about her speech.

2. **Personal Profile** Judge McGuinness discusses her own heritage as a way of illustrating the varied backgrounds of the participants. Profile your own background to show why you are the right person to do a job or solve a problem.

3. **Guidelines for Conflict Resolution** Establish common-sense procedures for any group trying to resolve conflicts. Then arrange these procedures in their order of importance.

Speaking, Listening, and Viewing

4. **Press Conference** With several classmates, role-play a press conference at which reporters question Judge McGuinness about the Forum for Peace and Reconciliation. **[Social Studies Link; Media Link]**

Researching and Representing

5. **Teens Caught up in Conflicts** Teens around the world have had to live with conflicts in their homelands. Research teenagers' views on these conflicts and their ways of coping with them. Then give a multimedia presentation on your findings, using films, recordings, and photographs. **[Social Studies Link]**

Online Activity www.phlit.phschool.com

Writing Process Workshop

During Victorian times, statistics became an increasingly important way of recording and evaluating dramatic advances in technology and equally dramatic changes in society. Write a statistical report about a social, historical, or scientific issue that can be understood through numbers. In a statistical report you use numerical data to support a thesis statement. Interpret and draw conclusions from your data to support your thesis. Consider including tables, charts, and graphs as visual displays to clarify your statistics.

Use the following skills to research and write a statistical report:

Writing Skills Focus

▶ **Locate statistical information** in a variety of appropriate text and technical resources, such as the Internet and databases. Choose reliable sources.

▶ **Build a thesis based on statistical information.** (See p. 799.)

▶ **Support statistical data with details,** such as expert opinions, experiment results, eyewitness accounts, and analogies. (See p. 809.)

▶ **Accuracy** in your data is critical to drawing valid conclusions.

MODEL FROM LITERATURE

from *A Review of Southey's Colloquies*
by Thomas Babington Macaulay

. . . the amount of parochial relief required by the laborers . . . is almost exactly in inverse proportion to the degree in which the manufacturing system has been introduced into those counties. ① The returns for the years ending in March, 1825, and in March, 1828, are now before us. In the former year we find the poor rate highest in Sussex, about twenty shillings to every inhabitant. . . . and when we come to Lancashire, ② we find it at four shillings, one-fifth of what it is in Sussex. ③

① The author states a thesis: The need for relief varies inversely with the presence of manufacturing.

② The author provides details on where (Sussex and Lancashire) and when (years ending March, 1825, and March, 1828).

③ Macaulay's thesis is supported by the data.

APPLYING LANGUAGE SKILLS: Introducing Statistical Information

Introducing data is much like introducing quotations. Just as you wouldn't introduce a quotation without explaining who said it, you should explain to readers the source of the numerical data you are presenting. You can introduce your data in a variety of ways. Notice the following examples: They also identify for readers the source of, or method for, obtaining the information.

- According to *The Times*, "Seventeen percent . . ."
- A thorough analysis of census figures indicates that infant mortality has steadily decreased . . .
- Students polled by the newspaper staff gave the following responses:

Writing Application As you introduce your data, be sure to note clearly the source or collection method.

Writer's Solution Connection Writing Lab

For guidelines on making inferences and drawing conclusions, review the writing tips in the Drafting section of the tutorial on Research Writing.

Prewriting

Choose a Topic In selecting a topic, you may want to consider numbers that are important in your life—for example, what you spend or earn or data on an exercise routine. You can also choose from among these topics.

> ### Topic Ideas
>
> - The cost of a trip to London
> - Success of movies based on novels
> - Hurricanes of the Atlantic
>
> ### Selection-Related Topic Ideas
>
> - Analysis of Queen Victoria's popularity
> - Importance of potato crop to Ireland's economy in the mid-nineteenth century

Research Information Identify sources, including the Internet, that would be most helpful for gathering statistical data. Use the following chart to help you locate appropriate sources.

Topic:	Resources:
Rainfall in Edinburgh	atlas, travel guide, almanacs
British economy, before and after repeal of the Corn Laws	history text, encyclopedia on-line, nonfiction books
Herb gardening for profit	vertical files, nonfiction books

Formulate a Working Thesis Use the preliminary data you collect to formulate a working thesis—the point you are going to prove—that will guide further research. Then revise your working thesis as you find data.

Check Your Data Review the data you've collected for accuracy and completeness. Avoid drawing conclusions based on insufficient or incomplete data.

Drafting

Write a Thesis Statement After reviewing all your data, revise your working thesis into a formal thesis statement.

Begin Where It Feels Comfortable Once you formulate your thesis, you may find that it's easier to start at the end and work backward. The order in which you write is not important, as long as you end up with an introduction that states your thesis, a body that supports it, and a conclusion that restates it.

Revising

Use a Revision Checklist Use the following questions, based on this lesson's focus points, to help you revise your statistical analysis:

1. Do all the statistics in my report support my thesis?
2. Have I clearly explained my data by answering relevant *who*, *what*, *where*, *when*, and *how* questions?
3. Are my statistics complete, accurate, and clearly presented?

REVISION MODEL

A Statistical Report on the Reading Habits of High School Students

What are seniors reading? At Lake Shore High School, the word is MYSTERY. ① *A whopping 58%* ~~Over half~~ of the students surveyed ② *Surveys asking students to identify the genre of the most recent book they had read revealed that* reported having read a mystery within the past month. ③ *229* 137 of the ~~237~~ students surveyed were reading mysteries:

everything from Arthur Conan Doyle to Patricia Cornwell.

Other categories were reported as follows: *10% identified*

biography, 12% historical fiction, and 20% science fiction.

① A statistic supporting the thesis replaces a vague detail.
② The author adds details that explain how the survey was conducted.
③ This statistic was not accurate, so it was revised.

Proofread Proofread your report, eliminating errors in grammar, punctuation, capitalization, and spelling. Also, proofread your statistics to make sure they are accurate.

Publishing

▶ **Illustrations** Use a computer program to illustrate and add media to your report.

▶ **Presentation** Invite an interested audience to a presentation of your statistical report. Add charts and graphs to support your presentation.

▶ **Internet** Publish your paper on an electronic bulletin board.

APPLYING LANGUAGE SKILLS: Interpreting Statistics

In your statistical analyses, don't stretch the facts to prove a particular point. Avoid sweeping generalizations based on small samples.

Misleading:
Ninety percent of poets prefer rhyming verse.

Accurate:
Of the ten poets surveyed, nine preferred rhyming verse.

Whether you conduct your own research or draw on others', describe for readers the data collection methods and the sample sizes. This information will allow readers to determine whether or not the data support your generalizations.

Writing Application When reporting data in percentage form, be sure to explain situations in which numbers may not add up to exactly 100%.

Writer's Solution Connection Language Lab

To help you review your report for subject-verb agreement, see the lesson on Agreement in Number.

Student Success Workshop

Real-World Reading Skills
Apply Modes of Reasoning

Strategies for Success

Every day, you make inferences and draw conclusions. Sometimes, your conclusions are accurate and sensible. Other times, your reasoning may be faulty—perhaps you drew a conclusion without considering all the facts. To analyze and understand what you read, it's crucial that you use sound reasoning.

Inductive Reasoning You use inductive reasoning when you start with specific information, such as facts and examples, and then use that information to draw a conclusion. For example:

Fact: Thirty patients participated in a medical study on the effects of pet ownership on high blood pressure.

Fact: Every patient in the study showed a reduction in his or her blood pressure after caring for a pet for three months.

Conclusion: Pet ownership is an effective method for treating high blood pressure.

In this case, the conclusion may or may not be valid. The more facts you know, the more likely you are to draw a sound conclusion. Be careful not to jump to conclusions!

Deductive Reasoning You use deductive reasoning when you start with a general statement, follow it with more specific statements, and end by drawing a specific conclusion. For example:

General statement: The blood pressure of every patient in the study was lower at the end of the three months of pet ownership.

Specific statement: Archie participated in the study.

Conclusion: Therefore, Archie had lower blood pressure at the end of the study.

If the premises that the author uses are true, the conclusion is also true. Be careful: One false premise will lead to a faulty conclusion.

Apply the Strategies

Read the passage, and answer the questions using inductive and deductive reasoning:

By the 1930's, there were no wolves in the American West. In the 1800's, the government had paid hunters a bounty for every wolf they killed. Without wolves, the number of coyotes increased greatly. Coyotes ate the same food as foxes, grizzly bears, and small rodents. These animals had difficulty finding food. Grizzly bears damaged trees while foraging for nuts and leaves. To restore the ecological balance, parks "imported" gray wolves. In two years, wolves thinned the coyote population, and the other animals had enough food.

1. *After the wolves were removed, other animals didn't have enough food to eat. Is this a valid conclusion? Explain your response.*

2. *Grizzly bears do not eat any plant life if they have access to meat. Is this a valid conclusion deduced from the facts? Explain your response.*

3. *Wolves are a natural enemy of coyotes. Is this conclusion based on sound reasoning? Explain your response.*

> ✔ *Here are other situations in which you can apply inductive and deductive reasoning:*
> ► *Analyzing a science experiment*
> ► *Evaluating a newspaper editorial*
> ► *Proving a geometry theorem*

PART 3

Focus on Literary Forms:
The Novel

Music and Literature, 1878
William M. Harnett, Albright-Knox Art Gallery Buffalo, New York

In an era before mass media, the new middle class looked to the novel for entertainment, ideas, and a fictional world they could share and discuss. Dickens, the premier British novelist, pioneered the publication of novels in magazines, episode by episode. In this way, the hungry public got its big fictions in bite-size tidbits. Britain still has its bestsellers today, but they have to compete with television and the movies.

$\mathcal{G}$uide for Interpreting

Charles Dickens *(1812–1870)*

No writer since Shakespeare has occupied as important a place in popular culture as Charles Dickens. His novels have held a special appeal for scholars and the public alike and have been dramatized time and again in plays and films.

A Childhood of Hardship

Born in Portsmouth on England's southern coast, Dickens had a generally unhappy childhood. His father was sent to debtor's prison, and the boy was sent to a "prison" of his own—a factory in which he worked long hours pasting labels. Such experiences, dramatizing the ills of the newly industrialized society, were to figure prominently in Dickens's novels.

The Birth of a Writer After becoming a court stenographer at the age of seventeen, Dickens became a court reporter. At twenty-one, he began to apply his keen powers of observation in humorous literary sketches of everyday life in London. A collection of these, *Sketches by Boz* (1836), earned him a small following, which he built up considerably with his first novel, *The Pickwick Papers,* published in 1837. Next came such favorites as *Oliver Twist* (1838) and *Nicholas Nickleby* (1839).

A Serious Novelist A turn toward more serious planning and characterization of greater psychological depth are evident in *Dombey and Son* (1848) and *David Copperfield* (1850). These novels emphasize social criticism, as do later masterpieces like *Bleak House* (1853) and *Hard Times* (1854).

Featured in **AUTHORS IN DEPTH** *Series*

Charlotte Brontë *(1816–1855)*

Charlotte Brontë came from one of the most famous literary families ever. Educated at home, siblings Charlotte, Emily, Anne, and Branwell had a rich fantasy life that nurtured their artistic development.

Early Failure, Then Success

In 1846, the three sisters published a volume of poems under the pseudonyms Currer, Ellis, and Acton Bell, but the book found little success. Charlotte's first novel, *The Professor,* failed to find a publisher, but she persevered, and when *Jane Eyre* was published in 1847 it became very popular.

Personal Struggle The final years of Charlotte Brontë's life were clouded by tragedy. Her brother died in 1848, and Emily and Anne died soon after. Despite her loneliness, Charlotte found the strength to complete the novels *Shirley* (1849) and *Villette* (1853). She married Arthur Bell Nicholls, her father's curate, a few months before she died.

◆ Background for Understanding

HISTORY: DICKENS AND UTILITARIANISM

Much as Spock in *Star Trek* irritates the crew of the *Enterprise* with his coldly logical view of life, Jeremy Bentham (1748–1831) irritated Dickens with a philosophy called Utilitarianism. Bentham used statistics and logic to bring about useful (which is the meaning of *utilitarian*) changes in law and government. He believed, however, that humans are selfish and that this selfishness is a positive trait.

Dickens felt that Utilitarianism did away with the qualities of sympathy and imagination. In *Hard Times,* Thomas Gradgrind is a relentless utilitarian, and Dickens uses him to show that this philosophy is deadening and destructive. The novel begins with Gradgrind's humorless praise of "Facts."

◆ *Literature and Your Life*

CONNECT YOUR EXPERIENCE

Your image of a crusader may come from the movies: a dynamic but downtrodden figure who stands up to corrupt officials.

Many nineteenth-century crusaders were novelists like Dickens and Brontë, armed only with their pens. By writing about characters who experience social injustices, they won the sympathy of their readers for the disadvantaged and misunderstood.

Journal Writing Jot down some possible subjects for a crusading novelist of today.

THEMATIC FOCUS: RELATIONSHIPS

How do the educational institutions depicted by these novelists prove harmful to human relationships?

◆ Literary Focus

THE NOVEL AND SOCIAL CRITICISM

A **novel** is a long work of fiction, which usually has a complex plot, major and minor characters, a significant theme, and several settings. The novel became popular during the nineteenth century, a period of disturbing social and economic change. It isn't surprising, therefore, that many novelists of the time include **social criticism** in their works, calling attention to society's injustices.

In this passage from *Hard Times,* for example, Dickens strongly condemns the mind-numbing system of education inflicted on the poor. Similarly, Brontë devotes an episode from *Jane Eyre* to painting a terrifying picture of a boarding school for poor girls.

◆ Reading Strategy

RECOGNIZE THE WRITER'S PURPOSE

A **writer's purpose** for creating a novel might be to redress a wrong, to satirize an institution, to amuse readers, or a combination of these. You can find clues to a writer's purpose in details like the writer's ideas, the outcome of events, the writer's attitudes toward characters, and the writer's choice of character names.

In *Hard Times*, for example, Dickens names a teacher M'Choakumchild, indicating his disgust with certain educational ideas and methods. These clues suggest that Dickens's purpose is to satirize the educational system of Victorian England.

◆ Build Vocabulary

GREEK ROOTS: -mono-

In *Hard Times,* Dickens describes a schoolroom as *monotonous*. The Greek root -mono-, which means "single" or "alone," contributes to the meaning of *monotonous*: "having a single 'tone' and therefore dull and unvarying." A *monotonous* room is boring in its sameness.

WORD BANK

Before you read, preview this list of words from the novels.

monotonous
obstinate
adversary
indignant
approbation
obscure
comprised
sundry

◆ Grammar and Style

PUNCTUATION OF DIALOGUE

Whenever dialogue appears in literature, the speaker's words are enclosed in quotation marks to distinguish them from the surrounding text.

In the following passage from *Hard Times,* the words spoken by Gradgrind appear in quotation marks.

"Girl number twenty," said Mr. Gradgrind, squarely pointing with his square forefinger, "I don't know that girl. Who is that girl?"

from HARD Times

Charles Dickens

Chapter 1
The One Thing Needful

"Now, what I want is, Facts. Teach these boys and girls nothing but Facts. Facts alone are wanted in life. Plant nothing else, and root out everything else. You can only form the minds of reasoning animals upon Facts: nothing else will ever be of any service to them. This is the principle on which I bring up my own children, and this is the principle on which I bring up these children. Stick to Facts, sir!"

The scene was a plain, bare, monotonous vault of a schoolroom, and the speaker's square forefinger emphasized his observations by underscoring every sentence with a line on the schoolmaster's sleeve. The emphasis was helped by the speaker's square wall of a forehead, which had his eyebrows for its base, while his eyes found commodious cellarage in two dark caves, overshadowed by the wall. The emphasis was helped by the speaker's mouth, which was wide, thin, and hard set. The emphasis was helped by the speaker's voice, which was inflexible, dry, and dictatorial. The emphasis was helped by the speaker's hair, which bristled on the skirts of his bald head, a plantation of firs to keep the wind from its shining surface, all covered with knobs, like the crust of a plum pie, as if the head had scarcely warehouse-room for the hard facts stored inside. The speaker's obstinate carriage, square coat, square legs, square shoulders—nay, his very neckcloth, trained to take him by the throat with an unaccommodating grasp, like a stubborn fact, as it was—all helped the emphasis.

"In this life, we want nothing but Facts, sir; nothing but Facts!"

The speaker, and the schoolmaster, and the third grown person present, all backed a little, and swept with their eyes the inclined plane of little vessels, then and there arranged in order, ready to have imperial gallons of facts poured into them until they were full to the brim.

Chapter 2
Murdering the Innocents

Thomas Gradgrind, sir. A man of realities. A man of fact and calculations. A man who proceeds upon the principle that two and two are four, and nothing over, and who is not to be talked into allowing for anything over. Thomas Gradgrind, sir—peremptorily Thomas—Thomas Gradgrind. With a rule and a pair of scales, and the multiplication table always in his pocket, sir, ready to weigh and measure any parcel of

◆ Build Vocabulary

monotonous (mə nät´ ən əs) *adj.*: Having little or no variation or variety

obstinate (äb´stə nət) *adj.*: Stubborn; dogged; mulish

London School for Orphan Boys, Wood engraving, 1870

▲ **Critical Viewing** Judging from the details in this engraving, what was school like in London of the 1870s? **[Speculate]**

human nature, and tell you exactly what it comes to. It is a mere question of figures, a case of simple arithmetic. You might hope to get some other nonsensical belief into the head of George Gradgrind, or Augustus Gradgrind, or John Gradgrind, or Joseph Gradgrind (all suppositious, non-existent persons), but into the head of Thomas Gradgrind—no, sir!

In such terms Mr. Gradgrind always mentally introduced himself, whether to his private circle of acquaintance, or to the public in general. In such terms, no doubt, substituting the words "boys and girls," for "sir," Thomas Gradgrind now presented Thomas Gradgrind to the little pitchers before him, who were to be filled so full of facts.

Indeed, as he eagerly sparkled at them from the cellarage before mentioned, he seemed a kind of cannon loaded to the muzzle with facts, and prepared to blow them clean out of the regions of childhood at one discharge. He seemed a galvanizing apparatus, too, charged with a grim mechanical substitute for the tender young imaginations that were to be stormed away.

"Girl number twenty," said Mr. Gradgrind, squarely pointing with his square forefinger, "I don't know that girl. Who is that girl?"

"Sissy Jupe, sir," explained number twenty, blushing, standing up, and curtseying.

"Sissy is not a name," said Mr. Gradgrind. "Don't call yourself Sissy. Call yourself Cecilia."

"It's father as calls me Sissy, sir," returned the young girl in a trembling voice, and with another curtsey.

"Then he has no business to do it," said Mr. Gradgrind. "Tell him he mustn't. Cecilia Jupe. Let me see. What is your father?"

"He belongs to the horse-riding, if you please, sir."

◆ **Literary Focus**
What outlook is Dickens criticizing by having Gradgrind use a number to call on Sissy Jupe?

Mr. Gradgrind frowned, and waved off the objectionable calling with his hand.

"We don't want to know anything about that, here. You mustn't tell us about that, here. Your father breaks horses, don't he?"

"If you please, sir, when they can get any to break, they do break horses in the ring, sir."

"You mustn't tell us about the ring, here. Very well, then. Describe your father as a horsebreaker. He doctors sick horses, I dare say?"

"Oh yes, sir."

"Very well, then. He is a veterinary surgeon, a farrier and horsebreaker. Give me your definition of a horse."

(Sissy Jupe thrown into the greatest alarm by this demand.)

"Girl number twenty unable to define a horse!" said Mr. Gradgrind, for the general behoof of all the little pitchers. "Girl number twenty possessed of no facts, in reference to one of the commonest of animals! Some boy's definition of a horse. Bitzer, yours."

The square finger, moving here and there, lighted suddenly on Bitzer, perhaps because he chanced to sit in the same ray of sunlight which, darting in at one of the bare windows of the intensely whitewashed room, irradiated Sissy. For, the boys and girls sat on the face of the inclined plane in two compact bodies, divided up the center by a narrow interval; and Sissy, being at the corner of a row on the sunny side, came in for the beginning of a sunbeam, of which Bitzer, being at the corner of a row on the other side, a few rows in advance, caught the end. But, whereas the girl was so dark-eyed and dark-haired, that she seemed to receive a deeper and more lustrous color from the sun when it shone upon her, the boy was so light-eyed and light-haired that the self-same rays appeared to draw out of him what little color he ever possessed. His cold eyes would hardly have been eyes, but for the short ends of lashes which, by bringing them into immediate contrast with something paler than themselves, expressed their form. His short-cropped hair might have been a mere continuation of the sandy freckles on his forehead and face. His skin was so unwholesomely deficient in the natural tinge, that he looked as though, if he were cut, he would bleed white.

"Bitzer," said Thomas Gradgrind. "Your definition of a horse."

"Quadruped. Graminivorous. Forty teeth, namely twenty-four grinders, four eye-teeth, and twelve incisive. Sheds coat in the spring; in marshy countries, sheds hoofs, too. Hoofs hard, but requiring to be shod with iron. Age known by marks in mouth." Thus (and much more) Bitzer.

"Now girl number twenty," said Mr. Gradgrind. "You know what a horse is."

She curtseyed again, and would have blushed deeper, if she could have blushed deeper than she had blushed all this time. Bitzer, after rapidly blinking at Thomas Gradgrind with both eyes at once, and so catching the light upon his quivering ends of lashes that they looked like the antennae of busy insects, put his knuckles to his freckled forehead, and sat down again.

The third gentleman now stepped forth. A mighty man at cutting and drying, he was; a government officer; in his way (and in most other people's too), a professed pugilist; always in training, always with a system to force down the general throat like a bolus,[1] always to be heard of at the bar of his little Public-office, ready to fight all England. To continue in fistic phraseology, he had a genius for coming up to the scratch, wherever and whatever it was, and proving himself an ugly customer. He would go in and damage any subject whatever with his right, follow up with his left, stop, exchange, counter, bore his opponent (he always fought All England[2]) to the ropes, and fall upon him neatly. He was certain to knock the wind out of common sense, and render that unlucky adversary deaf to the call of time. And he had it in charge from high authority to bring about the great public-office Millennium, when Commissioners should reign upon earth.

---

1. **bolus:** Small, round mass, often of chewed food.
2. **fought All England:** Fought according to the official rules of boxing.

◆ Build Vocabulary

adversary (ad´vər ser´ē) *n.*: Opponent; enemy

◀ Critical Viewing According to the selection, what would Mr. Gradgrind think of this wallpaper design? [Connect]

"Very well," said this gentleman, briskly smiling, and folding his arms. "That's a horse. Now, let me ask you girls and boys, Would you paper a room with representations of horses?"

After a pause, one half of the children cried in chorus, "Yes, sir!" Upon which the other half, seeing in the gentleman's face that Yes was wrong, cried out in chorus, "No, sir!"—as the custom is, in these examinations.

"Of course, No. Why wouldn't you?"

A pause. One corpulent slow boy, with a wheezy manner of breathing, ventured the answer, Because he wouldn't paper a room at all, but would paint it.

◆ **Reading Strategy**
What does Gradgrind's insistence hint about Dickens's purpose in this scene?

"You *must* paper it," said Thomas Gradgrind, "whether you like it or not. Don't tell *us* you wouldn't paper it. What do you mean, boy?"

"I'll explain to you, then," said the gentleman, after another and a dismal pause, "why you wouldn't paper a room with representations of horses. Do you ever see horses walking up and down the sides of rooms in reality—in fact? Do you?"

"Yes, sir!" from one half. "No, sir!" from the other.

"Of course no," said the gentleman, with an indignant look at the wrong half. "Why, then, you are not to see anywhere, what you don't see in fact; you are not to have anywhere, what you don't have in fact. What is called Taste, is only another name for Fact."

Thomas Gradgrind nodded his approbation.

"This is a new principle, a discovery, a great discovery," said the gentleman. "Now, I'll try you again. Suppose you were going to carpet a room. Would you use a carpet having a representation of flowers upon it?"

There being a general conviction by this time that "No, sir!" was always the right answer to this gentleman, the chorus of No was very strong. Only a few feeble stragglers said Yes; among them Sissy Jupe.

◆ Build Vocabulary

indignant (in dig′nənt) *adj.*: Be displeased about

approbation (ap′rə bā′shən) *n.*: Official approval, sanction or commendation

"Girl number twenty," said the gentleman, smiling in the calm strength of knowledge.

Sissy blushed, and stood up.

"So you would carpet your room—or your husband's room, if you were a grown woman, and had a husband—with representations of flowers, would you," said the gentleman. "Why would you?"

"If you please, sir, I am very fond of flowers," returned the girl.

"And is that why you would put tables and chairs upon them, and have people walking over them with heavy boots?"

"It wouldn't hurt them, sir. They wouldn't crush and wither if you please, sir. They would be the pictures of what was very pretty and pleasant, and I would fancy—"

"Ay, ay, ay! but you mustn't fancy," cried the gentleman, quite elated by coming so happily to his point. "That's it! You are never to fancy."

"You are not, Cecilia Jupe," Thomas Gradgrind solemnly repeated, "to do anything of that kind."

"Fact, fact, fact!" said the gentleman. And "Fact, fact, fact!" repeated Thomas Gradgrind.

"You are to be in all things regulated and governed," said the gentleman, "by fact. We hope to have, before long, a board of fact, composed of commissioners of fact, who will force the people to be a people of fact, and of nothing but fact. You must discard the word Fancy altogether. You have nothing to do with it. You are not to have, in any object of use or ornament, what would be a contradiction in fact. You don't walk upon flowers in fact; you cannot be allowed to walk upon flowers in carpets. You don't find that foreign birds and butterflies come and perch upon your crockery. You never meet with quadrupeds going up and down walls; you must not have quadrupeds represented upon walls. You must use," said the gentleman, "for all these purposes, combinations and modifications (in primary colors) of mathematical figures which are susceptible of proof and demonstration. This is the new discovery. This is fact. This is taste."

The girl curtseyed, and sat down. She was very young, and she looked as if she were frightened by the matter of fact prospect the world afforded.

"Now, if Mr. M'Choakumchild," said the gentleman, "will proceed to give his first lesson here, Mr. Gradgrind, I shall be happy, at your request, to observe his mode of procedure."

Mr. Gradgrind was much obliged. "Mr. M'Choakumchild, we only wait for you."

So, Mr. M'Choakumchild began in his best manner. He and some one hundred and forty other schoolmasters, had been lately turned at the same time, in the same factory, on the same principles, like so many pianoforte legs. He had been put through an immense variety of paces, and had answered volumes of head-breaking questions. Orthography, etymology, syntax, and prosody, biography, astronomy, geography, and general cosmography, the sciences of compound proportion, algebra, land-surveying and leveling, vocal music, and drawing from models, were all at the ends of his ten chilled fingers. He had worked his stony way into Her Majesty's most Honorable Privy Council's Schedule B, and had taken the bloom off the higher branches of mathematics and physical science, French, German, Latin, and Greek. He knew all about all the Water Sheds of all the world (whatever they are), and all the histories of all the peoples, and all the names of all the rivers and mountains, and all the productions, manners, and customs of all the countries, and all their boundaries and bearings on the two-and-thirty points of the compass. Ah, rather overdone, M'Choakumchild. If he had only learnt a little less, how infinitely better he might have taught much more!

He went to work in this preparatory lesson, not unlike Morgiana in the Forty Thieves:[3] looking into all the vessels ranged before him, one after another, to see what they contained. Say, good M'Choakumchild. When from thy boiling store, thou shalt fill each jar brim full by and by, dost thou think that thou wilt always kill outright the robber Fancy lurking within— or sometimes only maim him and distort him!

---

3. **Morgiana in the Forty Thieves:** In the tale "Ali Baba and the Forty Thieves," Ali Baba's clever servant, Morgiana, saves him from the thieves.

Guide for Responding

◆ Literature and Your Life

Reader's Response How did you feel about Mr. Thomas Gradgrind, Mr. M'Choakumchild, and their theory of education?

Thematic Focus What kind of people will students like Bitzer grow up to be? Explain.

Defining the Horse In a small group, discuss Bitzer's definition of a horse. Then use your own experience and knowledge to come up with a better one.

✓ Check Your Comprehension

1. What does Thomas Gradgrind believe to be the key to all learning?
2. Summarize the exchange between Gradgrind and Sissy Jupe.
3. How does Bitzer define a horse?
4. According to the government officer, what are the students never to do?

◆ Critical Thinking

INTERPRET

1. (a) Who are the "little pitchers" referred to at the beginning of Chapter 2? (b) Why is this an appropriate image? **[Interpret]**
2. What does Bitzer's definition of a horse reveal about his character? **[Connect]**
3. In his description of Gradgrind, Dickens compares him to "a kind of cannon." How is this simile appropriate? **[Analyze]**
4. What conclusion does Dickens want the reader to draw about the three adults in the schoolroom? Explain. **[Draw Conclusions]**

APPLY

5. Dickens hints at some important elements of education that are neglected by Gradgrind and his colleagues. Do modern schools address these elements? Explain. **[Apply]**

from

Jane Eyre

Charlotte Brontë

C H A P T E R   6

The next day commenced as before, getting up and dressing by rushlight; but this morning we were obliged to dispense with the ceremony of washing: the water in the pitchers was frozen. A change had taken place in the weather the preceding evening, and a keen northeast wind, whistling through the crevices of our bedroom windows all night long, had made us shiver in our beds, and turned the contents of the ewers to ice.

Before the long hour and a half of prayers and Bible reading was over, I felt ready to perish with cold. Breakfast time came at last, and this morning the porridge was not burnt; the quality was eatable, the quantity small; how small my portion seemed! I wished it had been doubled.

In the course of the day I was enrolled a member of the fourth class, and regular tasks and occupations were assigned to me: hitherto, I had only been a spectator of the proceedings at Lowood, I was now to become an actor therein. At first, being little accustomed to learn by heart, the lessons appeared to me both long and difficult: the frequent change from task to task, too, bewildered me; and I was glad, when, about three o'clock in the afternoon, Miss Smith put into my hands a border of muslin two yards long, together with

needle, thimble, etc., and sent me to sit in a quiet corner of the school room, with directions to hem the same. At that hour most of the others were sewing likewise; but one class still stood round Miss Scatcherd's chair reading, and as all was quiet, the subject of their lessons could be heard, together with the manner in which each girl acquitted herself, and the animadversions or commendations of Miss Scatcherd on the performance. It was English history; among the readers, I observed my acquaintance of the verandah; at the commencement of the lesson, her place had been at the top of the class, but for some error of pronunciation or some inattention to stops, she was suddenly sent to the very bottom. Even in that obscure position, Miss Scatcherd continued to make her an object of constant notice: she was continually addressing to her such phrases as the following:—

"Burns" (such it seems was her name: the girls here, were all called by their surnames, as boys are elsewhere), "Burns, you are standing on the side of your shoe, turn your toes out immediately." "Burns, you poke your chin most unpleasantly, draw it in." "Burns, I insist on your holding your head up: I will not have you before me in that attitude," etc. etc.

A chapter having been read through twice, the books were closed and the girls examined. The lesson had comprised part of the reign of

Charles I, and there were sundry questions about tonnage and poundage, and ship-money, which most of them appeared unable to answer; still, every little difficulty was solved instantly when it reached Burns: her memory seemed to have retained the substance of the whole lesson, and she was ready with answers on every point. I kept expecting that Miss Scatcherd would praise her attention; but, instead of that, she suddenly cried out:—

◆ **Reading Strategy**
What does Miss Scatcherd's reaction suggest about the writer's purpose in this scene?

"You dirty, disagreeable girl! you have never cleaned your nails this morning!"

Burns made no answer: I wondered at her silence.

"Why," thought I, "does she not explain that she could neither clean her nails nor wash her face, as the water was frozen?"

My attention was now called off by Miss Smith, desiring me to hold a skein of thread: while she was winding it, she talked to me from time to time, asking whether I had ever been at school before, whether I could mark, stitch, knit, etc.; till she dismissed me, I could not pursue my observations on Miss Scatcherd's movements. When I returned to my seat, that lady was just delivering an order, of which I did not catch the import; but Burns immediately left the class, and going into the small inner room where the books were kept, returned in half a minute, carrying in her hand a bundle of twigs tied together at one end. This ominous tool she presented to Miss Scatcherd with a respectful courtesy; then she quietly, and without being told, unloosed her pinafore, and the teacher instantly and sharply inflicted on her

neck a dozen strokes with the bunch of twigs. Not a tear rose to Burns's eye; and, while I paused from my sewing, because my fingers quivered at this spectacle with a sentiment of unavailing and impotent anger, not a feature of her pensive face altered its ordinary expression.

"Hardened girl!" exclaimed Miss Scatcherd, "nothing can correct you of your slatternly habits: carry the rod away."

Burns obeyed: I looked at her narrowly as she emerged from the book closet; she was just putting back her handkerchief into her pocket, and the trace of a tear glistened on her thin cheek.

The play-hour in the evening I thought the pleasantest fraction of the day at Lowood: the bit of bread, the draught of coffee swallowed at five o'clock had revived vitality, if it had not satisfied hunger; the long restraint of the day was slackened; the school room felt warmer than in the morning: its fires being allowed to burn a little more brightly to supply, in some measure, the place of candles, not yet introduced; the ruddy gloaming,[1] the licensed uproar, the confusion of many voices gave one a welcome sense of liberty.

On the evening of the day on which I had seen Miss Scatcherd flog her pupil, Burns, I wandered as usual among the forms and tables and laughing groups without a companion, yet not feeling lonely: when I passed the windows, I now and then lifted a blind and looked out; it snowed fast, a drift was already forming against the lower panes; putting my ear close to the window, I could distinguish from the gleeful tumult within, the disconsolate moan of the wind outside.

Probably, if I had lately left a good home and kind parents, this would have been the hour when I should most keenly have regretted the separation: that wind would then have saddened my heart; this obscure chaos would have disturbed my peace: as it was I derived from both a strange excitement, and reckless and feverish, I wished the wind to howl more

◆ **Build Vocabulary**

obscure (əb skyoor´) *adj.*: Not easily understood, vague or undefined

comprised (kəm prīz´ d) *v.*: Consisted of; to include, contain

sundry (sun´drē) *adj.*: Various, miscellaneous

---

1. **ruddy gloaming:** Glowing twilight; the sunset.

wildly, the gloom to deepen to darkness, and the confusion to rise to clamor.

Jumping over forms, and creeping under tables, I made my way to one of the fire-places: there, kneeling by the high wire fender, I found Burns, absorbed, silent, abstracted from all round her by the companionship of a book, which she read by the dim glare of the embers.

"Is it still 'Rasselas'?"[2] I asked, coming behind her.

"Yes," she said, "and I have just finished it."

And in five minutes more she shut it up. I was glad of this.

"Now," thought I, "I can perhaps get her to talk." I sat down by her on the floor.

"What is your name besides Burns?"

"Helen."

"Do you come a long way from here?"

"I come from a place further north; quite on the borders of Scotland."

"Will you ever go back?"

"I hope so; but nobody can be sure of the future."

"You must wish to leave Lowood?"

"No: why should I? I was sent to Lowood to get an education; and it would be of no use going away until I have attained that object."

♦ *Literature and Your Life*

What is the main point of Brontë's social criticism in the following paragraphs?

"But that teacher, Miss Scatcherd, is so cruel to you?"

"Cruel? Not at all! She is severe: she dislikes my faults."

"And if I were in your place I should dislike her: I should resist her; if she struck me with that rod, I should get it from her hand; I should break it under her nose."

"Probably you would do nothing of the sort: but if you did, Mr. Brocklehurst would expel you from the school; that would be a great grief to your relations. It is far better to endure patiently a smart which nobody feels but yourself, than to commit a hasty action whose evil consequences will extend to all connected with you— and, besides, the Bible bids us return good for evil."

"But then it seems disgraceful to be flogged, and to be sent to stand in the middle of a room full of people; and you are such a great girl: I am far younger than you, and I could not bear it."

"Yet it would be your duty to bear it, if you could not avoid it: it is weak and silly to say you *cannot bear* what it is your fate to be required to bear."

I heard her with wonder: I could not comprehend this doctrine of endurance; and still less could I understand or sympathize with the forbearance she expressed for her chastiser. Still I felt that Helen Burns considered things by a light invisible to my eyes. I suspected she might be right and I wrong; but I would not ponder the matter deeply: like Felix,[3] I put it off to a more convenient season.

"You say you have faults, Helen: what are they? To me you seem very good."

"Then learn from me, not to judge by appearances: I am, as Miss Scatcherd said, slatternly; I seldom put, and never keep, things in order; I am careless; I forget rules; I read when I should learn my lessons; I have no method; and sometimes I say, like you, I cannot *bear* to be subjected to systematic arrangements. This is all very provoking to Miss Scatcherd, who is naturally neat, punctual, and particular."

"And cross and cruel," I added; but Helen Burns would not admit my addition: she kept silence.

"Is Miss Temple as severe to you as Miss Scatcherd?"

At the utterance of Miss Temple's name, a soft smile flitted over her grave face.

"Miss Temple is full of goodness; it pains her to be severe to anyone, even the worst in the school: she sees my errors, and tells me of them gently; and, if I do anything worthy of praise, she gives me my meed liberally. One strong proof of my wretchedly defective nature

---

2. **Rasselas:** *The History of Rasselas, Prince of Abyssinia,* a moralizing novel by Samuel Johnson.

3. **Felix:** In the Bible, governor of Judea who released Paul from prison and deferred his trial until a more "convenient season" (Acts 24:25).

▶ **Critical Viewing** How well do the actresses in this still from a movie version of *Jane Eyre* match your vision of the story's characters Jane and Helen? **[Evaluate]**

is that even her expostulations, so mild, so rational, have not influence to cure me of my faults; and even her praise, though I value it most highly, cannot stimulate me to continued care and foresight."

"That is curious," said I: "it is so easy to be careful."

"For *you* I have no doubt it is. I observed you in your class this morning, and saw you were closely attentive: your thoughts never seemed to wander while Miss Miller explained the lesson and questioned you. Now, mine continually rove away: when I should be listening to Miss Scatcherd, and collecting all she says with assiduity,[4] often I lose the very sound of her voice; I fall into a sort of dream. Sometimes I think I am in Northumberland, and that the noises I hear round me are the bubbling of a little brook which runs through Deepden, near our house;— then, when it comes to my turn to reply, I have to be wakened; and, having heard nothing of what was read for listening to the visionary brook, I have no answer ready."

"Yet how well you replied this afternoon."

"It was mere chance: the subject on which we had been reading had interested me. This afternoon, instead of dreaming of Deepden, I was wondering how a man who wished to do right could act so unjustly and unwisely as Charles the First sometimes did; and I thought what a pity it was that, with his integrity and conscientiousness, he could see no farther than the prerogatives of the crown. If he had but been able to look to a distance, and see how what they call the spirit of the age was tending! Still, I like Charles— I respect him— I pity him, poor murdered king! Yes, his enemies were the worst: they shed blood they had no right to shed. How dared they kill him!"

Helen was talking to herself now: she had forgotten I could not very well understand her— that I was ignorant, or nearly so, of the subject she discussed. I recalled her to my level.

"And when Miss Temple teaches you, do your thoughts wander then?"

"No, certainly, not often; because Miss Temple has generally something to say which is newer to me than my own reflections: her language is singularly agreeable to me, and the information she communicates is often just what I wished to gain."

"Well, then, with Miss Temple you are good?"

"Yes, in a passive way: I make no effort; I follow as inclination guides me. There is no merit in such goodness."

"A great deal: you are good to those who are good to you. It is all I ever desire to be. If people were always kind and obedient to those who are cruel and unjust, the wicked people would have it all their own way: they would never feel afraid, and so they would never alter, but would grow worse and worse. When we are struck at without a reason, we should strike back again very hard; I am sure we should—so hard as to teach the person who struck us never to do it again."

"You will change your mind, I hope, when you grow older: as yet you are but a little untaught girl."

"But I feel this, Helen: I must dislike those who, whatever I do to please them, persist in disliking me; I must resist those who punish me unjustly. It is as natural as that I should love those who show me affection, or submit to punishment when I feel it is deserved."

". . . Love your enemies; bless them that curse you; do good to them that hate you and despitefully use you."

"Then I should love Mrs. Reed, which I cannot do; I should bless her son John, which is impossible."

In her turn, Helen Burns asked me to explain; and I proceeded forthwith to pour out, in my way, the tale of my sufferings and resentments. Bitter and truculent when excited, I spoke as I felt, without reserve or softening.

Helen heard me patiently to the end: I expected she would then make a remark, but she said nothing.

"Well," I asked impatiently, "is not Mrs. Reed a hard-hearted, bad woman?"

"She has been unkind to you, no doubt; because, you see, she dislikes your cast of char-

---

4. **assiduity** (as´ə dyo͞o´ə tē) *n.*: Constant care and attention; diligence.

acter, as Miss Scatcherd does mine: but how minutely you remember all she has done and said to you! What a singularly deep impression her injustice seems to have made on your heart! No ill usage so brands its record on my feelings. Would you not be happier if you tried to forget her severity, together with the passionate emotions it excited? Life appears to me too short to be spent in nursing animosity or registering wrongs. We are, and must be, one and all, burdened with faults in this world: but the time will soon come when, I trust, we shall put them off in putting off our corruptible bodies; when debasement and sin will fall from us with this cumbrous frame of flesh, and only the spark of the spirit will remain,—the impalpable principle of life and thought, pure as when it left the Creator to inspire the creature: whence[5] it came it will return; perhaps again to be communicated to some being higher than man—perhaps to pass through gradations of glory, from the pale human soul to brighten to the seraph![6] Surely it will never, on the contrary, be suffered to degenerate from man to fiend? No; I cannot believe that: I hold another creed; which no one ever taught me, and which I seldom mention; but in which I delight, and to which I cling: for it extends hope to all: it makes Eternity a rest—a mighty home, not a terror and abyss. Besides, with this creed, I can so clearly distinguish between the criminal and his crime; I can so sincerely forgive the first while I abhor the last: with this creed revenge never worries my heart, degradation never too deeply disgusts me, injustice never crushes me too low: I live in calm, looking to the end."

Helen's head, always drooping, sank a little lower as she finished this sentence. I saw by her look she wished no longer to talk to me, but rather to converse with her own thoughts. She was not allowed much time for meditation: a monitor, a great rough girl, presently came up, exclaiming in a strong Cumberland accent—

"Helen Burns, if you don't go and put your drawer in order, and fold up your work this minute, I'll tell Miss Scatcherd to come and look at it!"

Helen sighed as her reverie fled, and getting up, obeyed the monitor without reply as without delay.

---

5. **whence:** Place from which.
6. **seraph:** Angel of the highest order.

Guide for Responding

◆ *Literature and Your Life*

Reader's Response Do you relate more to Helen's or to Jane's attitude toward life? Explain.

Thematic Focus How does the relationship between Jane and Helen bring to light differences in philosophies of life?

☑ Check Your Comprehension

1. (a) For what offense does Miss Scatcherd punish Helen Burns? (b) What is the punishment?
2. Why does Helen Burns admire Miss Temple?
3. When Jane confesses her dislike of the Reed family, what advice does Helen give her?

◆ Critical Thinking

INTERPRET

1. When punished, why does Helen make every effort to hold back tears? **[Infer]**
2. Why might Jane wish "the wind to howl more wildly, the gloom to deepen to darkness"? **[Infer]**
3. Compare and contrast Jane's and Helen's views on how to treat those who mistreat them. **[Compare and Contrast]**

COMPARE LITERARY WORKS

4. Compare Charlotte Brontë's treatment of Miss Scatcherd with Dickens's treatment of Mr. Gradgrind, noting each author's use of realism and parody. **[Distinguish]**

Guide for Responding (continued)

◆ Reading Strategy

RECOGNIZE THE WRITER'S PURPOSE

Writers can reveal their **purpose**, their reason for writing a book, in several ways. Often their attitudes toward characters, events, and ideas are a clue to their purpose. In the excerpt from *Hard Times*, notice how Dickens's attitude toward M'Choakumchild comes out in this description of his education:

> He and some one hundred and forty other schoolmasters, had been lately turned at the same time, in the same factory, on the same principles, like so many pianoforte legs.

Dickens obviously thinks that this man is less than fully human, the mechanical product of a mechanical process. This attitude, in turn, suggests that one of Dickens's purposes in writing may have been to attack a coldly logical approach to education.

Using either the excerpt from *Hard Times* or the excerpt from *Jane Eyre*, show how each of the following elements is a clue to the author's attitude and purpose.

1. the name of a place or character
2. the description of a place or character
3. dialogue
4. an event or incident

◆ Build Vocabulary

USING THE GREEK ROOT -mono-

Use your knowledge of the Greek root -mono- ("single" or "alone") to define these words:

1. monopoly 3. monarch 5. monocle
2. monorail 4. monologue

USING THE WORD BANK: Antonyms

In your notebook, write the letter of the word that is opposite in meaning to the first word.

1. monotonous: (a) lengthy, (b) varied, (c) loud
2. obstinate: (a) still, (b) cooperative, (c) taciturn
3. adversary: (a) turncoat, (b) friend, (c) enemy
4. indignant: (a) worthy, (b) pleased, (c) wrathful
5. approbation: (a) freedom, (b) disapproval, (c) sin
6. obscure: (a) prominent, (b) sad, (c) realistic
7. comprised: (a) counted, (b) agreed, (c) excluded
8. sundry: (a) mixed, (b) tedious, (c) homogeneous

◆ Literary Focus

THE NOVEL AND SOCIAL CRITICISM

The **novels** of Dickens and Brontë are fictional worlds, with invented plots, characters, and settings. However, these fictional worlds mirrored nineteenth-century English society. In this way, made-up characters or places gave authors the chance to comment on real types of people and social institutions. This use of fiction to comment on fact is called **social criticism**.

For example, in *Jane Eyre*, Lowood is a fictional version of real institutions designed for young women without title or money. Jane's relationships at Lowood give Brontë the opportunity to criticize this type of institution.

1. (a) What does the relationship between Jane and Helen in *Jane Eyre* reveal about their characters? (b) What does it also reveal about the school?
2. (a) In *Hard Times*, what details make the setting vivid? (b) How do these details contribute to Dickens's social criticism?

◆ Grammar and Style

PUNCTUATION OF DIALOGUE

Following are rules for using other punctuation with quotation marks as you **punctuate dialogue:**

- Commas and periods fall within the close-quotation marks.
- Question marks and exclamation marks fall within the close-quotation marks when they end quotations, and outside them when they belong to a sentence that includes a quotation.

  Example: "Sissy Jupe, give me the Facts!"

Practice Copy these passages in your notebook, correctly punctuating the dialogue.

1. Sissy is not a name, said Mr. Gradgrind.
2. Girl number twenty unable to define a horse! said Mr. Gradgrind . . .
3. Bitzer, said Thomas Gradgrind. Your definition of a horse.
4. Well, I asked impatiently, is not Mrs. Reed a hard-hearted, bad woman?
5. Well, then, with Miss Temple you are good?

Build Your Portfolio

 ## Idea Bank

Writing

1. **Diary Entry** Write a diary entry from the point of view of Helen Burns in *Jane Eyre*. In your diary, record story events as well as Helen's own feelings and reactions to those events.

2. **Comparison and Contrast** Write a paper in which you compare and contrast the characters of Jane and Helen in *Jane Eyre*. Also, speculate as to what further adventures Jane will have.

3. **Response to Criticism** George Bernard Shaw wrote that, in *Hard Times*, Dickens "casts off, and casts off for ever, all restraint on his wild sense of humor." Is there evidence for this assertion in the section of the novel you have read? Explain.

Speaking, Listening, and Viewing

4. **Oral Presentation** View the film version of *Jane Eyre* starring Orson Welles as Rochester. Then present a critical film review to your class, explaining your recommendation. **[Media Link]**

5. **Dialogue** Imagine that, after school on the day of Mr. Gradgrind's visit, Sissy Jupe and Bitzer talk over what has happened. Keeping in mind Dickens's descriptions of these characters, role-play their dialogue with a partner. **[Performing Arts Link]**

Researching and Representing

6. **Caricature** A caricature is an exaggerated portrayal intended to make a person seem comic or ridiculous. Draw a caricature of one of the characters in *Hard Times*. **[Art Link]**

7. **Exploring Historical Background** Find out more about the educational system in Victorian times, and reveal your results in a report. **[Social Studies Link]**

Online Activity www.phlit.phschool.com

 ## Guided Writing Lesson

Observation of a Person

Both Dickens and Brontë used their powers of observation to create memorable characters. Follow their lead and observe people with a novelist's eye. Then write a vivid observation of a person you have watched. To make this person come alive for readers, show him or her in action.

Writing Skills Focus: Using an Incident to Reveal Character

When you write an observation of a person, you can show his or her character by describing a revealing **incident.** Dickens isn't writing an observation in *Hard Times*, but he does use an incident to characterize Gradgrind at the start of the book—the brief conversation with Sissy Jupe. Gradgrind addresses Sissy as "Girl number twenty" and tells her that Sissy is not a name. The incident shows how cold and unfeeling he is.

Prewriting Before you write a formal observation, jot down notes about the person you have observed. Your notes might include such information as age, gender, physical appearance, clothing, style of speaking, gestures, beliefs, and values. Then identify a revealing incident that vividly shows this person's character.

Drafting As you narrate an incident, remember to tell events in chronological order. Also, bring the incident you describe to life by using dialogue, precise details, and even a few striking figures of speech, like metaphors or similes.

Revising Delete any descriptions that don't reveal your subject's character. Also, glance back at your notes to see whether you have left out any revealing details that you can weave back in. If your observation seems too ordinary, write it from an unusual vantage point—for example, looking at your subject in a car's rear-view mirror.

CONNECTIONS TO WORLD LITERATURE

from War and Peace
Leo Tolstoy

Literary Connection

THE NOVEL

Charles Dickens's *Hard Times* and Charlotte Brontë's *Jane Eyre* are representative of the growing popularity of the novel during the nineteenth century. A novel is a long work of fiction with a complicated plot, many major and minor characters, a significant theme, and various settings. In the nineteenth century, The Realists made daily life a subject of literature and explored the scope of human experience in the novel. Their approach and the growing literacy rate made novels appealing to a large group of people. For the same reasons, the novel was also popular in France, the United States, and Russia.

THE RUSSIAN NOVEL

Russian novelist Leo Tolstoy was considered the greatest of the nineteenth-century Russian writers. In 1869, *War and Peace*, his masterful historical novel about Napoleon's invasion of Russia in 1812, was published. In this novel Tolstoy weaves together numerous plots and settings and includes more than 1,000 characters. The novel was immediately recognized as a masterpiece for its graphic depiction of war, insights into Russian life, and exploration into the meaning of life.

In the following excerpt from *War and Peace,* Tolstoy defends Kutuzov, a military general, when his tactics are criticized. Tolstoy presents the general as noble and true to himself—not as a man who is simply out for fame. As you read, note the ways in which Tolstoy brings Kutuzov to life as a character.

LEO TOLSTOY
(1828–1910)

Leo Tolstoy was a nineteenth-century Russian writer as well known for his radical life style and personal beliefs as for his writing. After briefly attending law school, Tolstoy joined the army in 1851. While serving as an artillery officer, he spent most of his free time writing, and in 1852 he published his first novel, *A History of My Childhood.*

He married Sonya Bers at age thirty-four. She was so supportive of his literary career that she would re-copy Tolstoy's manuscripts to make them legible for his publisher. *War and Peace* (1869), and *Anna Karenina* (1876), a portrait of the lives of the Russian upper classes, were among the most popular of Tolstoy's works.

from **WAR** *and* *Peace*

Leo Tolstoy

Chapter V

In 1812 and 1813[1] Kutuzov[2] was openly accused of blunders. The Tsar[3] was dissatisfied with him. And in a recent history inspired by promptings from the highest quarters, Kutuzov is spoken of as a designing, intriguing schemer, who was panic-stricken at the name of Napoleon, and guilty through his blunders at Krasnoe and Berezina of robbing the Russian army of the glory of complete victory over the French. Such is the lot of men not recognized by Russian intelligence as "great men," *grands hommes*; such is the destiny of those rare and always solitary men who divining the will of Providence submit their personal will to it. The hatred and contempt of the crowd is the punishment of such men for their comprehension of higher laws.

Strange and terrible to say, Napoleon, the most insignificant tool of history, who never even in exile displayed one trait of human dignity, is the subject of the admiration and enthusiasm of the Russian historians; in their eyes he is a *grand homme*.

Kutuzov, the man who from the beginning to the end of his command in 1812, from Borodino to Vilna, was never in one word or deed false to himself, presents an example exceptional in history of self-sacrifice and recognition in the present of the relative value of events in the future. Kutuzov is conceived of by historians as a nondescript, pitiful sort of creature, and whenever they speak of him in the year 1812, they seem a little ashamed of him.

And yet it is difficult to conceive of an historical character whose energy could be more invariably directed to the same unchanging aim. It is difficult to imagine an aim more noble and more in harmony with the will of a whole people. Still more difficult would it be to find an example in history where the aim of any historical personage has been so completely attained as the aim towards which all Kutuzov's efforts were devoted in 1812.

Kutuzov never talked of "forty centuries looking down from the Pyramids," of the sacrifices he was making for the fatherland, of what he meant to do or had done. He did not as a rule talk about himself, played no sort of part, always seemed the plainest and most ordinary man, and said the plainest and most ordinary things. He wrote letters to his daughters and to Madame de Staël,[4] read novels, liked the company of pretty women, made jokes with the generals, the officers, and the soldiers, and never contradicted the people, who tried to prove anything to him. When Count Rastoptchin galloped up to him at Yautsky bridge, and reproached him personally with being responsible for the loss of Moscow, and said: "Didn't you promise not to abandon

1. In 1812 and 1813: In June 1812, Napoleon and his troops invaded Russia. The French retreat from Russia began in October 1812.
2. Kutuzov: Mikhail Illarionovich Kutuzov (1745–1813); commander in chief of all Russian forces during Napoleon's invasion.
3. Tsar: Czar Alexander I, emperor of Russia, 1801–1825.

4. Madame de Staël: Anne-Louise-Germaine de Staël (1766–1817) French-Swiss woman of letters; regarded as personal enemy of Napoleon and banished from Paris.

Moscow without a battle?" Kutuzov answered: "And I am not abandoning Moscow without a battle," although Moscow was in fact already abandoned. When Araktcheev came to him from the Tsar to say that Yermolov was to be appointed to the command of the artillery, Kutuzov said: "Yes, I was just saying so myself," though he had said just the opposite a moment before. What had he, the one man who grasped at the time all the vast issues of events, to do in the midst of that dull-witted crowd? What did he care whether Count Rastoptchin put down the disasters of the capital to him or to himself? Still less could he be concerned by the question which man was appointed to the command of the artillery.

This old man, who through experience of life had reached the conviction that the thoughts and words that serve as its expression are never the motive force of men, frequently uttered words, which were quite meaningless—the first words that occurred to his mind.

But heedless as he was of his words, he never once throughout all his career uttered a single word which was inconsistent with the sole aim for the attainment of which he was working all through the war. With obvious unwillingness, with bitter conviction that he would not be understood, he more than once, under the most difficult circumstances, gave expression to his real thought. His first differed from all about him after the battle of Borodino,[5] which he alone persisted in calling a victory, and this view he continued to assert verbally and in reports and to his dying day. He alone said that *the loss of Moscow is not the loss of Russia*. In answer to the overtures for peace, his reply to Lauriston was: *There can be no peace, for such is the people's will*. He alone during the retreat of the French said that *all our maneuvers are unnecessary; that everything is being done of itself better than we could desire; that we must give the enemy a "golden bridge"; that the battles of Tarutino, of Vyazma, and of Krasnoe, were none of them*

Portrait of Koutouzov, Prince of Smolensk, George Dawe, Hermitage, St. Petersburg, Russia

▲ **Critical Viewing** Compare and contrast this rendering of Kutuzov with the description of him in the story. **[Compare and Contrast]**

necessary; that we must keep some men to reach the frontier with; that he wouldn't give one Russian for ten Frenchmen. And he, this intriguing courtier, as we are told, who lied to Araktcheev to propitiate[6] the Tsar, he alone dared to face the Tsar's displeasure by telling him at Vilna that *to carry the war beyond the*

---

5. battle of Borodino: Kutuzov was pressured into fighting this battle against his better judgment. Although the outcome was inconclusive, Kutuzov lost half his troops.

6. propitiate (prō pish´ ē āt´) v.: To cause to become favorably inclined.

frontier would be mischievous and useless.

But words alone would be no proof that he grasped the significance of events at the time. His actions—all without the slightest deviation—were directed toward the one threefold aim: first, to concentrate all his forces to strike a blow at the French; secondly, to defeat them; and thirdly, to drive them out of Russia, alleviating as far as was possible the sufferings of the people and the soldiers in doing so.

He, the lingerer Kutuzov, whose motto was always "Time and Patience," the sworn opponent of precipitate action, he fought the battle of Borodino, and made all his preparations for it with unwonted solemnity. Before the battle of Austerlitz he foretold that it would be lost, but at Borodino, in spite of the conviction of the generals that the battle was a defeat, in spite of the fact, unprecedented in history, of his army being forced to retreat after the victory, he alone declared in opposition to all that it was a victory, and persisted in that opinion to his dying day. He was alone during the whole latter part of the campaign in insisting that there was no need of fighting now, that it was a mistake to cross the Russian frontier and to begin a new war. It is easy enough now that all the events with their consequences lie before us to grasp their significance, if only we refrain from attributing to the multitude the aims that only existed in the brains of some dozen or so of men.

But how came that old man, alone in opposition to the opinion of all, to gauge so truly the importance of events from the national standard, so that he never once was false to the best interests of his country?

The source of this extraordinary intuition into the significance of contemporary events lay in the purity and fervor of patriotic feeling in his heart.

It was their recognition of this feeling in him that led the people in such a strange manner to pick him out, an old man out of favor, as the chosen leader of the national war, against the will of the Tsar. And this feeling alone it was to which he owed his exalted position, and there he exerted all his powers as commander-in-chief not to kill and maim men, but to save them and have mercy on them.

This simple, modest, and therefore truly great figure, could not be cast into the false mold of the European hero, the supposed leader of men, that history has invented.

To the flunky no man can be great, because the flunky has his own flunky conception of greatness.

Guide for Responding

Literature and Your Life

Reader's Response What is your opinion of Kutuzov? Explain.

Thematic Focus How does this excerpt show the gloom and glory of being a public figure?

Class Discussion As a class, discuss what Tolstoy meant when he mocked the "false mold of the European hero" and how that hero contrasted with Kutuzov.

✓ Check Your Comprehension

1. Was Kutuzov more popular with the Russian people or with the Russian military?
2. (a) What were Kutuzov's achievements? (b) What did others point out as his failings?
3. What was Kutuzov's threefold aim in the war with France?

◆ Critical Thinking

INTERPRET
1. What does Tolstoy mean when he states that Kutuzov "could not be cast into the false mold of the European hero . . ."? **[Interpret]**
2. What evidence is given that Kutuzov was "never once false to the interests of his country"? **[Support]**
3. (a) Compare and contrast the two opposing views of Kutuzov. (b) With which view do you agree? Explain. **[Compare and Contrast]**
4. Explain the meaning of the following statement in relation to Kutuzov: "To the flunky no man can be great, because the flunky has his own flunky conception of greatness." **[Interpret]**

EVALUATE
5. How does Tolstoy's attitude toward Kutuzov affect your opinion of the general? **[Evaluate]**

Literary Connection

THE NOVEL

"The art of novels," wrote Thackeray, "is to represent nature: to convey as strongly as possible the sentiment of reality." The nineteenth century saw the flowering of the novel, not only in England but all across Europe. Novels explored all aspects of human life and experience. Tolstoy's picture of Russian life in *War and Peace*, set against a background of Napoleon's invasion, is one of the great novels of world literature. In its great length and complexity, it explores sociological, psychological, historical, and political issues. The popularity of novels as a vehicle for exploring human thought and interaction continues to this day.

1. What literary elements—plot, setting, characterization—predominate in the works of Dickens, Brontë, and Tolstoy? Explain.
2. Compare and contrast the methods by which Dickens, Brontë, and Tolstoy develop their main characters. Which author do you think is the most effective? Explain.
3. What criteria do you use to evaluate a novel? Explain how your criteria affect your decision to read a novel.

Idea Bank

Writing

1. **Character Description** Make a list of character traits of Kutuzov. Then write a character description in which you include your own opinions of the general.

2. **Scene From Everyday Life** Novels sometimes explore the details of everyday life. Write a one-page description of a scene from everyday life that might be part of a novel. Your scene should develop an interaction between two or more characters and may be a part of a larger plot.

3. **Essay on Leadership** Tolstoy presents Kutuzov as a significant military leader. Write a brief essay in which you describe the qualities you believe modern leaders need in order to address the world's problems effectively. **[Social Studies Link]**

Speaking, Listening, and Viewing

4. **Music as the Messenger** Much Russian music and literature from the nineteenth century focused on the many military battles in Russian history. Find musical pieces from the period that depict themes of battle. Present the musical compositions to your class with an explanation of how they depict war and peace. **[Music Link]**

Researching and Representing

5. **Novel Study** Choose a favorite novelist and study his or her technique. Read one or more novels by this author, then write an analysis of the author's literary style and themes. Analyze the use of character, setting, and plot, and give your opinion on whether the author employs them successfully. **[Literature Link]**

Online Activity **www.phlit.phschool.com**

Writing Process Workshop

Character Sketch

Oliver Twist and Fagin, Miss Havisham and Pip—these characters sprang to life under the pen of Charles Dickens. Dickens was a master at characterization, using a character's words, physical appearance, actions, and thoughts to bring him or her to life.

Taking your cue from Dickens, write a character sketch describing a real person you know, a famous figure, or a fictional character. Make readers feel they have actually met the subject by describing his or her physical appearance and personality. Also, provide insights into the subject's behavior and motivation. If appropriate, include other people's responses to the subject and directly quote remarks made to, about, or by the subject. These tips will help you:

Writing Skills Focus

▶ **Relate an incident** that offers background information on and insight into the subject. (See p. 835.)

▶ **Use precise language** to give readers details about the subject's physical and mental traits.

▶ **Set a personal tone** by using intimate, familiar descriptions that help readers feel that they have met the subject.

Charles Dickens's famous character Ebenezer Scrooge, portrayed here, would make an excellent subject for a character sketch.

MODEL FROM LITERATURE

from *A Description of Bruce Chatwin* by Paul Theroux

When I think of Bruce Chatwin, who was my friend, ① I am always reminded of a particular night, a dinner at the royal Geographical Society, hearing him speak animatedly about various high mountains he had climbed. . . . ②

He spoke in his usual way, very rapidly and insistently, stuttering and interrupting and laughing. . . . ③ This talking was the most striking thing about him, yet there were so many other aspects of him that made an immediate impression, He was handsome; he had piercing eyes; he was very quick—full of nervous gestures, a rapid walker . . . ④

① The author sets a personal tone by identifying his relationship with the subject.

② Theroux describes an incident that gives background information on Chatwin's lifestyle, and insight into his personality.

③ With a dramatic, "rapid-fire" series of words, Theroux "shows" the reader Chatwin's style of speech.

④ The author gives a precise description of Chatwin's physical appearance.

APPLYING LANGUAGE SKILLS: Using Figurative Language

Spice up your character sketch with figurative language. Here are some tips:

- Use a simile to compare your subject's appearance to that of someone or something else.
- Use a metaphor to describe a person's emotional state.
- Exaggerate a person's behavior or personality with hyperbole.
- Avoid clichés.

Simile: His gestures, sudden and angular, were like those of a marionette.

Metaphor: Jim set off to work, a walking time bomb.

Hyperbole: Her smile outshone the spotlight.

Cliché: . . . as strong as an ox

Writing Application Use figurative language, but use it sparingly so readers don't lose sight of the real person or situation.

Writer's Solution Connection Writing Lab

To learn more about tone, see the audio-annotated models in the Drafting section of the tutorial on Description.

Prewriting

Choose a Topic Choose a person you find interesting to be the subject of your character sketch. If you prefer, choose a character from fiction, or create a character of your own. If you need help choosing a subject, use one of the following ideas.

Topic Ideas

- An older person whom you admire
- Joan of Arc
- An interesting extraterrestrial

Selection-Related Topic Ideas

- Charlotte Brontë
- Jeremy Bentham
- A Dickensian hero

Develop the Character Create a chart in which you list various details of your subject's physical appearance and personality, and refer to this chart as you draft your sketch. Here's an example:

Appearance: 5'10"; brunette, neatly dressed
Habits: chewing gum, pointing toes
Hopes: to be a dancer
Talents: dancing, crocheting, gymnastics

Identify a Revealing Incident Select an incident that will give your readers insight into your subject's thoughts and feelings. Sometimes it's more effective to reveal personality through action rather than describing it directly.

Drafting

Use Descriptive Words Help readers "see" your subject by writing clear and precise descriptions. Instead of describing a teen as being tall and thin, use words like *lanky*, *rangy*, or *gangly*.

Create a Personal Tone As you draft your character sketch, use words and phrases that give readers a sense of "knowing" your subject. Notice how the word choice in the second example below conveys a personal tone.

▶ **Neutral Tone:** *She was a kind, loving woman.*
▶ **Personal Tone:** *Her warm, cinnamon-colored eyes hugged you even before she reached out with soft, round arms.*

Revising

Clarify Vague Descriptions Reread your draft and replace vague, imprecise words with ones that create a stronger impression of your subject.

>   **Draft:** He was full because he ate too much.

>   **Revision:** He felt stuffed to bursting because he ate dozens of the spicy and delicious empanadas.

Use a Revision Checklist Answer the following questions as you revise your character sketch.

1. Does the incident described provide background about the subject and offer insight into his or her personality?

2. Do the physical descriptions create a clear and accurate picture of the subject?

3. Will the tone make readers feel as if they have actually met the subject?

REVISION MODEL

① my bouncing, bubbly niece, a bundle of energy who embraces each day as if it were an adventure more exciting than a walk in space.

② At thirty-three pounds, and three feet, three inches tall,

She is a happy child. She loves to throw tea parties.

③ was determined that I would attend a gala tea party in the nursery.

① The writer replaced this bland description with a warmer, more personal one.

② The writer added a concise physical description to help readers picture the child.

③ By describing a specific event, the writer revealed his niece's personality.

Publishing

▶ **Contest** Submit your character sketch to an appropriate writing contest.

▶ **Anthology** Collect character sketches from your classmates and bind them together. Organize them according to three categories: Fictional Characters, Historical Figures, and Actual People.

APPLYING LANGUAGE SKILLS: Dangling Modifiers

Avoid dangling modifiers, words or phrases that do not modify other elements of the sentence. Often dangling modifiers create ridiculous images:

Dangling Modifier

Laughing heartily, tears rolled down Joshua's cheeks.

Revised Sentence

Joshua laughed so heartily that tears rolled down his cheeks.

Practice Identify and correct the dangling modifiers in these sentences. If necessary, add words or change the word order.

1. Skating down the ramp, his new wheel fell off.

2. To understand the man's character, examination of his life is our first task.

3. Watching her perform, the quickness of her hands astonished me.

Writing Application In proofreading, review your sketch to make sure you haven't used any dangling modifiers.

Writer's Solution Connection Language Lab

For help in revising your sketch, see the Strengthening Sentences lesson in the Writing Style section.

Student Success Workshop

Real-World Reading Skills

Reading for Varying Purposes

Strategies for Success

You read a variety of materials every day besides school textbooks—newspapers, magazines, song lyrics, instructions to video games, recipes, college catalogs, and many others. Your purpose for reading varies according to the subject matter. Before you begin reading, think about one or more reasons for your reading.

Read for Entertainment Reading can provide great pleasure—whether it's through novels, biographies, science fiction, or magazines. When you read to be entertained, you'll find that you read faster and probably pay less attention to details, but you still need to note important information about plot, characters, themes, and text organization.

Analyze the Writer's Craft No matter what text you're reading, you can learn to appreciate a writer's style and craft by reading critically and intensively. Analyze the writer's use of language and detail. In reading poetry, pay special attention to figurative language, mood, rhyme, and rhythm. In fiction, note how the writer uses plot and portrays characters. Study an author's craft for the purpose of modeling the literary techniques in your own writing.

Read to Take a Position Read carefully and critically when you are reading to understand complex issues, problems, and questions. Consult a variety of sources, and research various points of view. Critical reading on different sides of an issue will enable you to take an intelligent stand, defend a position, or take an action. As you read, note information that can help you construct arguments and form opinions.

Apply the Strategies

1 Assemble a variety of reading materials, and identify your purpose for reading each.

2 Choose one text or part of a text that interests you, and use it as a model for your own writing. Think about the purpose for your own writing, and decide which literary elements in the text you will model.

> ✔ Here are examples of texts that you might read to be entertained, to be informed, or to study an author's craft:
> ▶ Nonfiction magazines
> ▶ Statistical data in a consumer report
> ▶ Collected poems by one poet

PART **4** *Gloom and Glory*

Past and Present (no. 2)
Augustus Leopold Egg, Tate Gallery, London

Guide for Interpreting

Emily Brontë
(1818–1848)

Although some literary critics attacked her for the violent passions of her writing, Emily Brontë's dark romanticism now is regarded as the focus of her genius.

A Writer's Beginnings

Emily Brontë was born in Yorkshire, a barren wasteland in the north of England dominated by fog, hedges, and scruffy grasses. As a child, Emily and her sisters, Charlotte and Anne, created fantasy stories about a magical kingdom, using their wooden soldiers as characters. They wrote their stories in tiny handwriting in dozens of little notebooks.

Recognition and Fame
As adults, the three sisters first wrote poetry. Then each began work on a novel. Emily's ever-popular novel *Wuthering Heights* was published in 1847. It tells the story of a tragic love affair played out against the turbulent and mysterious landscape of the moors. A year after *Wuthering Heights* was published, Emily suffered her own tragedy: She caught cold at her brother's funeral and a short time later, she died.

Thomas Hardy   *(1840–1928)*

Thomas Hardy, known as "the last of the great Victorians," was born in Dorset, a region of southwest England, on which he based his fictional setting of Wessex.

The Novelist
Fascinated by the fates of his neighbors in his native Dorset, Hardy used his writing to elaborate his own pessimistic view of life. His tragic novels, which include *Far from the Madding Crowd* (1874), *Tess of the D'Urbervilles* (1891), and *Jude the Obscure* (1895), all sought to show what happens when human beings rebel against their circumstances. Using vivid imagery to describe the changing seasons, weather, and landscape of his region, Hardy matched it to the psychological states of his characters.

The Poet
The bleakness of his fiction was disturbing to readers, and the response to *Jude the Obscure* was so hostile that Hardy abandoned fiction and turned to writing poetry. He earned immense public acclaim with *The Dynasts*, an epic verse drama about the Napoleonic Wars. With each book of verse he produced, Hardy's reputation as a poet grew.

A Poetic Legacy
Hardy's poetry marks a transition from the Victorian Age to the Modernist movement of the twentieth century. In his use of strict meter and stanza structure, Hardy was unmistakably Victorian, but his "nonpoetic" language and odd rhymes, coupled with a fatalistic outlook, inspired numerous twentieth-century writers.

◆ Background for Understanding

LITERATURE: BRONTË'S ROMANTICISM; HARDY'S NATURALISM

Victorian poets wrote in many voices and styles. Some writers, like Emily Brontë, are classified as Romantic because they explore and celebrate the human soul, nature's wildness, and the powers of the imagination. Thomas Hardy, however, embraced Naturalism, which focused on the victimization of ordinary people by social and natural forces.

The poems that follow call to mind both Romanticism and Naturalism. For example, although Brontë lived before the start of Naturalism, her poem contains an attitude that is more usual in Naturalist poets, and Hardy's poems contain instances of Romanticism, Brontë's specialty.

◆ *Literature and Your Life*

As time passes, we all experience losses of some kind: loss of youth, love, friendship. Human responses to loss can vary widely, from anger to intense sorrow. Think about a time in which you and a friend reacted differently to a loss of some kind.

Brontë's "Remembrance" and Hardy's "Ah, Are You Digging . . . ?" both deal with loss through death, but in very different ways.

THEMATIC FOCUS: GLOOM AND GLORY

As you read these poems by Brontë and Hardy, look for ways in which they express a gloomy outlook on life.

◆ Literary Focus

STANZA STRUCTURE AND IRONY

Many poets use elements of both predictability and surprise in their works. For example, **stanza structure** helps poets to establish expectations for their poems, whereas **irony** allows them to upset those expectations to amuse or surprise. A stanza usually consists of a certain number of lines arranged in a recurring pattern, rhythmic structure, and rhyme. Irony, on the other hand, is a deliberate contradiction between expectation and reality.

One interesting feature of the following poems is that they contain a consistent stanza structure, but the attitude toward their subjects changes, which ultimately creates irony. For example, the wildly dark, romantic mood in "Remembrance" is contradicted by the speaker's final resolution and outlook.

◆ Grammar and Style

PRONOUN CASE FOLLOWING *THAN* OR *AS*

In actual speech as well as in poetry, you find incomplete constructions, instances in which words are omitted because they are understood. When a **pronoun** occurs in an incomplete construction, especially following the words *than* or *as*, its **case** is what it would be if the construction were complete.

The following example contains an incomplete construction with the pronoun *I* following the word *as*. The word in brackets is the unspoken word that completes the sentence.

And every spirit upon earth / Seemed fervorless as *I* [was]

◆ Reading Strategy

READ STANZAS AS UNITS OF MEANING

Stanzas in poetry are not arbitrary chunks of poetry. Stanzas usually convey **a unit of meaning** or a main idea, as paragraphs do in prose. Some stanzas contain no complete sentences and serve instead to create a mood or single idea. Other stanzas may contain several complex ideas that together convey a larger idea or theme. By observing how the meaning of a poem's stanzas progress or build, you build an understanding of the poem as a whole.

As you read, look for the main idea, image, or thought within each stanza.

Journal Writing Jot down the main idea of each stanza as you read.

◆ Build Vocabulary

LATIN ROOTS: *-terr(a)-*

In "The Darkling Thrush," the word *terrestrial*, meaning "of the earth," contains the word root *terr(a)-*, which is derived from the Latin word for "land."

WORD BANK

Before you read, preview this list of words from the poems.

languish
rapturous
gaunt
terrestrial

My Sweet Rose, John William Waterhouse, Roy Miles Gallery, London

Emily Brontë

Remembrance

Cold in the earth, and the deep snow piled above thee!
Far, far removed, cold in the dreary grave!
Have I forgot, my Only Love, to love thee,
Severed at last by Time's all-wearing wave?

5   Now, when alone, do my thoughts no longer hover
Over the mountains, on that northern shore;
Resting their wings where heath and fern-leaves cover
Thy noble heart for ever, ever more?

10 Cold in the earth, and fifteen wild Decembers
From those brown hills have melted into spring—
Faithful indeed is the spirit that remembers
After such years of change and suffering!

Sweet Love of youth, forgive if I forget thee
15 While the World's tide is bearing me along:
Other desires and other hopes beset me,
Hopes which obscure but cannot do thee wrong.

No later light has lightened up my heaven,
No second morn has ever shone for me:
All my life's bliss from thy dear life was given—
20 All my life's bliss is in the grave with thee.

But when the days of golden dreams had perished
And even Despair was powerless to destroy,
Then did I learn how existence could be cherished,
Strengthened and fed without the aid of joy;

25 Then did I check the tears of useless passion,
Weaned my young soul from yearning after thine;
Sternly denied its burning wish to hasten
Down to that tomb already more than mine!

And even yet, I dare not let it languish,
30 Dare not indulge in Memory's rapturous pain;
Once drinking deep of that divinest anguish,
How could I seek the empty world again?

◆ **Build Vocabulary**

languish (laŋ′gwish) *v.*: Become weak; depressed

rapturous (rap′chər us) *adj.*: Ecstatic

Guide for Responding

◆ Literature and Your Life

Reader's Response Do you approve of the speaker's plan to forget her love and loss? Explain.

Thematic Focus In what ways is the speaker's outlook a gloomy one?

☑ Check Your Comprehension

1. Where and when is the poem set?
2. How long ago did the speaker's love die?
3. What does the speaker plan to do? Why is she planning this action?

◆ Critical Thinking

INTERPRET
1. Why has the speaker decided to forget her love? **[Infer]**
2. What does the speaker mean by "no later light has lightened up my heaven"? **[Interpret]**
3. Why is the speaker afraid to give in to her old feelings? **[Draw Conclusions]**
4. What do you consider the basic conflict of the speaker of this poem? **[Draw Conclusions]**

APPLY
5. What might an existence fed "without . . . joy" be like? **[Relate]**

The Darkling[1] Thrush

Thomas Hardy

I leant upon a coppice gate[2]
    When Frost was specter-gray,
And Winter's dregs made desolate
    The weakening eye of day.
5   The tangled bine-stems[3] scored the sky
    Like strings of broken lyres,
And all mankind that haunted nigh
    Had sought their household fires.

The land's sharp features seemed to be
10   The Century's corpse[4] outleant,
His crypt the cloudy canopy,
    The wind his death-lament.
The ancient pulse of germ[5] and birth

1. darkling *adj.*: In the dark.
2. coppice (kop′ is) **gate:** Gate leading to a thicket, or small wood.
3. bine-stems: Twining stems.

4. Century's corpse: This poem was written on December 31, 1900, the last day of the nineteenth century.
5. germ: Seed or bud.

15

20

25

30

Was shrunken hard and dry,
And every spirit upon earth
Seemed fervorless as I.

At once a voice arose among
The bleak twigs overhead
In a full-hearted evensong
Of joy illimited;
An aged thrush, frail, gaunt, and small,
In blast-beruffled plume,
Had chosen thus to fling his soul
Upon the growing gloom.

So little cause for carolings
Of such ecstatic sound
Was written on terrestrial things
Afar or nigh around,
That I could think there trembled through
His happy good-night air
Some blessed Hope, whereof he knew
And I was unaware.

◆ **Build Vocabulary**

gaunt (gônt) *adj.*: Very thin and angular

terrestrial (tə res´ trē əl) *adj.*: Relating to the earth

◀ **Critical Viewing** Why might Hardy have chosen a thrush like the one pictured to symbolize hope? **[Speculate]**

Guide for Responding

◆ Literature and Your Life

Reader's Response Does the ending of this poem surprise you? Why or why not?

Thematic Focus In what ways is this poem gloomy? Does it convey any hope for the future? Explain.

Questions for Research Develop research questions that you might use to find out whether other authors wrote about the end of the nineteenth century.

☑ **Check Your Comprehension**

1. In what season and time of year is "The Darkling Thrush" set?
2. What does the speaker suddenly hear in the third stanza?
3. Of what is the speaker unaware?

◆ Critical Thinking

INTERPRET

1. (a) What mood does the poet establish in the first two stanzas of "The Darkling Thrush"? (b) How does the mood change in the last two stanzas? **[Classify]**
2. To what are the land's "sharp features" compared? Why is this comparison appropriate for the time and place of the poem? **[Analyze]**
3. (a) Why do you think the poet characterizes the thrush as he does in lines 21–22? (b) What might the thrush symbolize? **[Interpret]**

COMPARE LITERARY WORKS

4. Compare "A Darkling Thrush" with Keats's "Ode to a Nightingale," looking for differences between the two in their use of the songbird as a symbol of hope. **[Compare and Contrast]**

"Ah, Are You Digging on My Grave?"

Thomas Hardy

"Ah, are you digging on my grave
    My loved one?—planting rue?"
—"No: yesterday he went to wed
One of the brightest wealth has bred.
5   'It cannot hurt her now,' he said,
    'That I should not be true.'"

"Then who is digging on my grave?
    My nearest dearest kin?"
—"Ah, no: they sit and think, 'What use!
10   What good will planting flowers produce?
No tendance of her mound can loose
    Her spirit from Death's gin.'"[1]

"But some one digs upon my grave?
    My enemy?—prodding sly?"
15   —"Nay: when she heard you had passed the Gate
That shuts on all flesh soon or late,
She thought you no more worth her hate,
    And cares not where you lie."

"Then, who is digging on my grave?
20   Say—since I have not guessed!"

---

1. **gin** *n.*: Trap.

—"O it is I, my mistress dear,
Your little dog, who still lives near,
And much I hope my movements here
　　Have not disturbed your rest?"

25　　"Ah, yes! *You* dig upon my grave . . .
　　Why flashed it not on me
That one true heart was left behind!
What feeling do we ever find
To equal among human kind
30　　A dog's fidelity!"

"Mistress, I dug upon your grave
　　To bury a bone, in case
I should be hungry near this spot
When passing on my daily trot.
35　I am sorry, but I quite forgot
　　It was your resting-place."

Guide for Responding

◆ *Literature and Your Life*

Reader's Response Do you feel sorry for the speaker in this poem? Why or why not?

Thematic Focus Is this poem gloomy or humorous or both? Explain.

Diary Write a diary entry that the speaker might have written while alive. Use clues from the poem about the people in the speaker's life to help you.

☑ Check Your Comprehension

1. (a) In the first stanza, who does the speaker suspect is digging on her grave? (b) In the second stanza? (c) In the third stanza?
2. (a) Who is actually digging on the speaker's grave? (b) What reason does the digger give for disturbing the grave?

◆ Critical Thinking

INTERPRET

1. (a) At what point do you begin to suspect the identity of the voice responding to the woman's questions? (b) What effect does Hardy achieve by withholding this information? **[Analyze]**
2. What mood does Hardy create by having a dead person speak? (b) How does this mood change once the digger is identified? **[Interpret]**
3. What point about human vanity and self-esteem is Hardy making in this poem? **[Draw Conclusions]**

EVALUATE

4. Do you find the message of this poem overly pessimistic? Explain. **[Assess]**

Guide for Responding (continued)

◆ Literary Focus

STANZA FORMS AND IRONY

Each of these poems has a different type of **stanza form**, containing a set number of lines, rhythmic pattern, and rhyme scheme. However, each poem contains only one type of stanza, which sets up expectations in the reader and helps to give the poem balance. When this balance is upset by the introduction of a surprising idea or outcome, it creates an interesting contradiction or **irony**.

For example, in "The Darkling Thrush" the stanzas are octets and each line contains eight alternating weak-strong beats. The singsong quality of the stanzas combined with the bleak descriptions and gloomy outlook of the speaker creates an interesting contrast, making the poem memorable.

1. (a) Describe the type of stanza—number of lines, type of meter, if any, and rhyme scheme—used in "Remembrance." (b) Explain how the surprising thoughts of the speaker in "Remembrance" help to create a sense of irony.
2. (a) Explain how the consistent stanza form in "Ah, Are You Digging on My Grave?" helps you understand the poem's meaning. (b) In which stanza does the pattern change? How does this change create irony?

◆ Build Vocabulary

USING THE LATIN ROOT -terr(a)-

Now that you are aware that the word root *-terr(a)-* is derived from a Latin word for "land," explain how these words relate to the meaning of the root.

1. terrain   2. terrestrial   3. subterranean

USING THE WORD BANK: Word Choice

Replace the italicized word or phrase with the correct word from the Word Bank. You will need to use an alternate form of one of the Word Bank words.

Although Brontë's hero, Heathcliff, is an *earthly* being, he has an almost supernatural aura. When parted from his beloved Cathy, he becomes *very thin* and he *weakens* in ill health. After his reunion with Cathy, Heathcliff is *extremely happy*.

◆ Reading Strategy

READ STANZAS AS UNITS OF MEANING

Once you discover **units of meaning** within stanzas of poems such as these, you'll be able to see the poem as a whole. For example, string together the main idea of each stanza and see if there's a progression of thoughts, sequence of events, or building argument within the poem.

1. (a) What is the overall meaning of the first stanza of "Remembrance"? (b) Given the title "Remembrance," what surprising attitude toward memory does the poem's speaker express in line 30?
2. Stanza one of "The Darkling Thrush" serves to create a setting and mood. Find details within the stanza that work together to do this.
3. Review the stanzas in "Ah, Are You Digging on My Grave?" Explain how the main ideas within the stanzas build to create a darkly humorous story.

◆ Grammar and Style

PRONOUN CASE FOLLOWING *THAN* OR *AS*

Sentences sometimes contain incomplete constructions, which contain omitted words whose meaning is understood. Incomplete constructions occur in real speech and in dialogue in poetry and prose. In an incomplete construction introduced by the words *than* or *as*, it's especially important to choose the correct **pronoun case** to complete the construction (*I, me, he, him, she, her, they, them*). To do this, mentally complete the sentence and it will become clear which pronoun to use.

Practice In your notebook, write the correct pronoun for each incomplete construction.
1. Charlotte Brontë was as talented as (she, her).
2. Brontë's *Jane Eyre* pleased me more than (he, him).
3. The bird had more hope than (he, him).
4. The dog was as forgetful as (I, me).
5. No group wrote more poetry than (they, them).

Writing Application Write a comparison involving two people or a person and a thing. Whenever you end a sentence with a pronoun that follows *than* or *as*, mentally complete the sentence to be sure you've chosen the correct pronoun.

Build Your Portfolio

 Idea Bank

Writing

1. **Remembrance** Write a remembrance of something past, like a winning football season, a friendship, or a summer long ago.

2. **Comparison and Contrast** Write an essay in which you compare and contrast Brontë's and Hardy's views of the passing of loved ones.

3. **Critical Essay** Hardy once said, "A sense of the truth of poetry, of its supreme place in literature, had awakened itself in me." Write an essay in which you agree or disagree with the idea that poetry has a "supreme place in literature." Use these poems to support your argument.

Speaking, Listening, and Viewing

4. **Dramatic Reading** Cast the parts of "Ah, Are You Digging on My Grave?" Then perform the poem for the class. **[Performing Arts Link]**

5. **Role Play** The speaker of "Remembrance" is eager to embrace a world without love or pain. With a friend, role-play a scene in which a counselor gives advice to the speaker. **[Performing Arts Link]**

Researching and Representing

6. **Biography** Emily, Charlotte, and Anne Brontë were part of a remarkable family of writers. Learn more about the Brontës, and write a brief biography of their lives and accomplishments. **[Literature Link]**

7. **Timeline of the Century** In "The Darkling Thrush" Hardy tells of a bird's song of hope on the brink of the twentieth century. Show Hardy what has indeed happened this century by creating a timeline of significant events. **[Social Studies Link]**

Online Activity www.phlit.phschool.com

 Guided Writing Lesson

Remembrance

Brontë's "Remembrance" is a sensitive, extremely personal memorial to a deceased love. Write your own memorial or remembrance of someone or something that is now absent from your life. For example, your remembrance could be about a favorite glove that got lost, a childhood pet, or a film star who passed away. An effective remembrance should convey the writer's personal views and attitudes about the subject.

Writing Skills Focus: Elaboration to Make Writing Personal

Put your own personal stamp on your writing to make it more believable and interesting. To do this, give specific details that reveal your responses to people, places, things, and ideas. Including candid details about your subject will draw your readers into your remembrance.

Prewriting Jot down those physical descriptions, remarks, or incidents that will help you bring the subject of your remembrance to life. Include details that reveal your personal ideas about the subject. Plan how you will fit these details together into a complete portrait.

Drafting Since you want to take your reader with you as you journey back in time, begin your draft with an interesting detail, quotation, or incident. Then weave together the details to create a full picture of the person, place, thing, or event you're describing.

Revising Ask some classmates to read your remembrance and respond to the following: Is the remembrance interesting? Does the writing contain enough personal details? Are any crucial details missing? Incorporate your classmates' suggestions into your final draft and proofread carefully.

Guide for Interpreting

Gerard Manley Hopkins
(1844–1889)

The most innovative poet of the Victorian period, Hopkins did not publish a collection of his work during his lifetime. It was not until 1918 that a generation of poets could read, and be influenced by, his startling poetry.

Fearless Youth This quietly rebellious poet was born just outside of London, the oldest of eight children in a prosperous middle-class family. While in grammar school, he began to write poetry and also showed artistic talent. Although physically slight, he was fearless and would perch at the top of a tree for hours, swaying in the wind and observing the landscape.

A Life of Devotion After entering Oxford University, Hopkins decided to become a Catholic priest in the Jesuit order. His parents, who were devout Anglican Protestants, were dismayed. The discipline of Hopkins's religious vocation was sometimes at odds with his writing of verse. However, he found in the fourteenth-century theologian Duns Scotus a verification of his own ideas about the individuality of all things, from a pebble to a leaf to a person. Hopkins called this precious individuality *inscape*, and he tried to capture it in highly original poems like "God's Grandeur" and "Spring and Fall."

Meanwhile, he worked tirelessly among the poor, dying of typhoid fever a month before his forty-fifth birthday.

A. E. Housman   *(1859–1936)*

A man of solitary habits and harsh self-discipline, Housman was also capable of creating delicately crafted poems, full of gentle regret.

Challenges of Youth He grew up in Worcestershire, a region northwest of London. His childhood came to an end on his twelfth birthday, when his mother died. Later, at Oxford University, his despair over unrequited love darkened his life still further. Perhaps because of this double grief, his poetry has bitter undertones.

Upon leaving Oxford, Housman went to work in the Patent Office. Determined to prove himself in the classics, he studied Greek and Latin at night and wrote scholarly articles. In 1892, his hard work paid off when he won a position as professor of Latin at University College in London.

Literary Success Though Housman spent most of his life engaged in teaching and scholarly pursuits, he is most remembered for three slender volumes of poetry that are as romantic and melancholy as any ever written. His first and most famous collection of verse, *A Shropshire Lad* (1896), has as its fictitious narrator a homesick farm boy living in the city.

Housman's image is that of an emotionless intellectual, but his poems display deep feelings. He himself maintained that a good poem should affect readers like a shiver down the spine or a punch in the stomach.

◆ Background for Understanding

LITERATURE: GERARD MANLEY HOPKINS, FROM OBSCURITY TO FAME

It is a surprising fact that when Gerard Manley Hopkins died, none of his obituaries mentioned that he was a poet! Only a few close friends knew that he was the author of highly original poems.

Chief among these friends was Oxford classmate Robert Bridges who was later to become the British Poet Laureate. Bridges was interested in the subject of rhythm in poetry and took an interest in Hopkins's experiments with sprung rhythm.

It was through Bridges's efforts that the first collection of Hopkins's poetry was published in 1918. Today Robert Bridges is little known, but his once-obscure friend Gerard Manley Hopkins is a famous Victorian poet!

God's Grandeur ◆ Spring and Fall: To a Young Child
To an Athlete Dying Young ◆ When I Was One-and-Twenty

◆ *Literature and Your Life*

CONNECT YOUR EXPERIENCE

As you enter each new period of your life, your views change. Certainly the games you played as a small child might bore you now, just as the fears you had then may seem petty today. In several of these poems, Hopkins and Housman examine how the passing of time colors emotions and changes priorities.

Journal Writing Briefly explain how your understanding of a word like *work* has deepened as you have grown.

THEMATIC FOCUS: GLOOM AND GLORY

How do these poets express, sometimes in the same poem, the pain and triumph of living and growing?

◆ Literary Focus

RHYTHM AND METER

Rhythm refers to the flow and movement of words in a poem, and poetry without a regular rhythm is called **free verse**. However, before the twentieth century, most poets wrote **metrical verse**, with set patterns of stressed and unstressed syllables.

The unit of metrical poetry is the **foot**, a combination of stressed and unstressed syllables. Common feet in English are the **iamb** (ī′am)—unstressed, stressed (˘ ′)—and the **trochee** (trō′kē)—stressed, unstressed (′ ˘). Number of feet per line is indicated by terms like **trimeter**, **tetrameter**, and **pentameter**—three, four, and five feet per line, respectively. Iambic tetrameter would be verse with four iambic feet per line.

Housman uses such regular meters as iambic and trochaic tetrameter. Hopkins, however, anticipates twentieth-century, free-verse poets by trying to develop rhythms more natural to speech. One experiment is **counterpoint rhythm** ("God's Grandeur"), in which two opposing rhythms appear together. Two trochaic feet, for example, can pop up in the middle of an iambic line:

> The wórld ĭs chárged wĭth thĕ grándeŭr ŏf Gód.

Another, more famous, Hopkins experiment is **sprung rhythm** ("Spring and Fall"), in which all feet begin with a stressed syllable and contain a varying number of unstressed syllables. In sprung rhythm, Hopkins often joins lines to form a rhythmic unit and marks stressed syllables with accents:

> Márgarét, áre you gríeving…

◆ Reading Strategy

APPLY BIOGRAPHY

You can often get more from your reading by applying what you know about an author's life to his or her work.

Reread the authors' biographies on p. 856 to find evidence of Housman's self-restraint and bitterness, and Hopkins's religious beliefs and love of nature.

◆ Build Vocabulary

COINED WORDS

Gerard Manley Hopkins sometimes combines old words to make new ones. In "Spring and Fall," Hopkins coins the words *wanwood* and *leafmeal,* which mean "pale trees" and "ground-up, mealy leaves," respectively.

WORD BANK

Preview these words before you read.

> grandeur
> blight
> rue

◆ Grammar and Style

CAPITALIZATION: COMPASS POINTS

In "God's Grandeur," words referring to specific regions are capitalized. Words that merely indicate direction are not: "last lights off the black *West* went . . . /. . . morning . . . *eastward*, springs—"

God's Grandeur

Gerard Manley Hopkins

Bird's Nest, Ros. W. Jenkins, Warrington Museum and Art Gallery

◀ **Critical Viewing** How does this painting reflect Hopkins's ideas in "God's Grandeur"? **[Apply]**

The world is charged with the grandeur of God.
It will flame out, like shining from shook foil;[1]
It gathers to a greatness, like the ooze of oil
Crushed.[2] Why do men then now not reck his rod?[3]
5 Generations have trod, have trod, have trod;
    And all is seared with trade; bleared, smeared with toil;
    And wears man's smudge and shares man's smell: the soil
Is bare now, nor can foot feel, being shod.

And for all this, nature is never spent;
10   There lives the dearest freshness deep down things;
And though the last lights off the black West went
    Oh, morning, at the brown brink eastward, springs—
Because the Holy Ghost over the bent
    World broods with warm breast and with ah! bright wings.

---

1. **foil** *n.*: Tinsel.
2. **crushed:** Squeezed from olives.
3. **reck his rod:** Heed God's authority.

Spring and Fall: To a Young Child

Gerard Manley Hopkins

Márgarét, áre you gríeving
Over Goldengrove unleaving?
Leáves, líke the things of man, you
With your fresh thoughts care for, can you?
5   Áh! ás the heart grows older
It will come to such sights colder
By and by, nor spare a sigh
Though worlds of wanwood[1] leafmeal[2] lie;
And yet you will weep and know why.
10   Now no matter, child, the name:
Sórrow's spríngs áre the same.
Nor mouth had, no nor mind, expressed
What heart heard of, ghost[3] guessed:
15   It ís the blight man was born for,
It is Margaret you mourn for.

---

1. **wanwood** (wän´ wood): Pale wood.
2. **leafmeal:** Ground-up decomposed leaves.
3. **ghost:** Spirit.

◆ Build Vocabulary

grandeur (grän´ jər) *n*.: Splendor, magnificence

blight (blīt) *n*.: Condition of withering

Guide for Responding

◆ *Literature and Your Life*

Reader's Response In which of these two poems do you find the more meaningful sentiment? Explain.

Thematic Focus What aspects of life, according to these poems, seem to make Hopkins feel gloomy?

☑ Check Your Comprehension

1. According to lines 5–8 of "God's Grandeur," what has humanity done to God's grandeur?
2. What has been the effect on the nature of humankind's behavior? Explain.
3. (a) To what is the Holy Ghost compared in lines 13-14? (b) What verb describes its action?
4. What is making Margaret unhappy in "Spring and Fall"?
5. According to the speaker, in what way will Margaret change as she grows older?

◆ Critical Thinking

INTERPRET

1. What opposition is present in lines 1–8 of "God's Grandeur"? **[Analyze]**
2. How does Hopkins resolve that opposition? **[Draw Conclusions]**
3. Explain how the speaker in "Spring and Fall" suggests Margaret will outgrow and not outgrow this sadness. **[Interpret]**
4. In what way is this a poem about death? **[Support]**
5. What lesson does the speaker offer to Margaret in this poem? **[Draw Conclusions]**

EVALUATE

6. Would you consider Hopkins's general outlook in "God's Grandeur" optimistic or pessimistic? Explain. **[Classify]**
7. Is the lesson in "Spring and Fall" a good one for a child to learn? Why or why not? **[Criticize]**

To an Athlete Dying Young

A. E. Housman

The time you won your town the race
We chaired you through the marketplace;
Man and boy stood cheering by,
And home we brought you shoulder-high.

5 Today, the road all runners come,
Shoulder-high we bring you home,
And set you at your threshold down,
Townsman of a stiller town.

Smart lad, to slip betimes away
10 From fields where glory does not stay
And early though the laurel[1] grows
It withers quicker than the rose.

Eyes the shady night has shut
Cannot see the record cut,

15 And silence sounds no worse than cheers
After earth has stopped the ears:

Now you will not swell the rout
Of lads that wore their honors out,
Runners whom renown outran
20 And the name died before the man.

So set, before its echoes fade,
The fleet foot on the sill of shade.
And hold to the low lintel up
The still-defended challenge cup.

25 And round that early-laureled head
Will flock to gaze the strengthless dead,
And find unwithered on its curls
The garland briefer than a girl's.

---

1. **laurel:** Symbol of victory.

When I Was One-and-Twenty

A. E. Housman

When I was one-and-twenty
    I heard a wise man say,
"Give crowns and pounds and guineas[1]
    But not your heart away;
5   Give pearls away and rubies
    But keep your fancy free."
But I was one-and-twenty,
    No use to talk to me.

When I was one-and-twenty
10   I heard him say again,
"The heart out of the bosom
    Was never given in vain;
'Tis paid with sighs a plenty
    And sold for endless <u>rue</u>."
15 And I am two-and-twenty,
    And oh, 'tis true, 'tis true.

---

1. **crowns . . . guineas:** Denominations of money.

◆ Build Vocabulary

rue (rōō) *n.*: Sorrow

Reader's Response If you were the young athlete Housman is addressing and could respond from beyond the grave, what would you say to the poet?

Thematic Focus Which of these two poems is the more gloomy? Why?

☑ Check Your Comprehension

1. In "To an Athlete Dying Young," in what sport did the athlete excel?
2. How did the townspeople show their admiration for the athlete?
3. In "When I Was One-and-Twenty," what advice did the speaker receive and how did he react?
4. (a) What is the second piece of advice the speaker receives?

◆ Critical Thinking

INTERPRET

1. (a) What visual image appears in each of the first two stanzas of "To an Athlete"? (b) How is the meaning of the image different in the second stanza? **[Interpret]**
2. (a) Summarize the speaker's comments in lines 9–20 of "To an Athlete." (b) What is meant by "the name died before the man"? **[Interpret]**
3. Does Housman believe completely that the young athlete was "smart" to die? Explain. **[Draw Conclusions]**
4. What clues are there in "When I Was One-and-Twenty" that Housman is mocking his speaker? **[Interpret]**

APPLY

5. Suppose you were to take a different position on the death of the young athlete. How would you modify the poem? **[Modify]**

COMPARE LITERARY WORKS

6. Compare and contrast the attitude toward youth in both these poems. **[Compare and Contrast]**

Guide for Responding (continued)

◆ Reading Strategy

APPLY BIOGRAPHY

Knowing about these poets' lives can give you greater insight into their work. Hopkins's biography, for example, suggests that he was deeply religious, loved nature, and looked for the uniqueness in things, their *inscape.* The first two lines of "God's Grandeur" reflect his religious nature—he senses the magnificence of God everywhere in the world. They also suggest his eye for the uniqueness of "shook foil" and the way in which it shines out.

1. (a) Find an image or phrase in "God's Grandeur" that reflects Hopkins's love of nature and explain your choice. (b) In "Spring and Fall," how does the coined word *leafmeal* show Hopkins's eye for the uniqueness of fallen leaves?
2. (a) List three traits or qualities of Housman suggested by his biography. (b) Explain how each of these is reflected in a specific word, phrase, or idea from a poem.

◆ Build Vocabulary

USING COINED WORDS

Hopkins combines *wan,* meaning "pale," and *wood* to make a new word, *wanwood,* that describes pale-looking trees in autumn. He also coins *leafmeal* to describe dead leaves ground into a kind of meal.

Imitate Hopkins and replace each italicized phrase in the following sentence with a new, understandable combination-word:

> At the *end of summer* a few *chilly mornings* remind us that the *snow-covered lawns* of winter can't be far away.

USING THE WORD BANK: Analogies

On your paper, complete the following analogies using the words from the Word Bank.

1. *Pride* is to *accomplishment* as _____?_____ is to *loss.*
2. *Shabbiness* is to *shack* as _____?_____ is to *palace.*
3. *Studying* is to *knowledge* as _____?_____ is to *death.*

◆ Literary Focus

RHYTHM AND METER

As you read the work of these two poets, you probably sensed the **rhythmic** flow of stressed and unstressed syllables. Hopkins and Housman differ sharply, however, in their approach to **meter**, the regular pattern of stressed and unstressed syllables.

Housman is more traditional, although he does use variations in meter. In lines 1–8 of "To an Athlete," for example, he varies the iambic tetrameter with three lines of trochaic tetrameter (lines 3, 6, and 8). The trochee (stressed, unstressed) is a "slower" foot and enables Housman to show how death "slows up" the runner.

Hopkins reinforces his meanings with daring experiments like the two opposing **counterpoint rhythms** in line 5 of "God's Grandeur": The first two feet are trochaic and the last three iambic. Still more daring is the **sprung rhythm** of "Spring and Fall," with stresses that pile up like fallen leaves (as in line 11, where a single stress can be a foot).

1. (a) Identify the meter in the first two lines of "One-and-Twenty." (b) In what way does the meter make the speaker seem a bit silly?
2. (a) How does the counterpoint rhythm in line 5 of "God's Grandeur" reinforce the line's meaning? (b) In line 11 of "Spring and Fall," how does the rhythm help Hopkins emphasize his point?

◆ Grammar and Style

CAPITALIZATION: COMPASS POINTS

Compass points referring to places are capitalized, but those indicating direction are not.

Practice On your paper, choose a capital or lower-case letter for each compass point.

1. Housman's Shropshire is located <u>n/N</u>orthwest of London.
2. The Shropshire lad would have traveled <u>s/S</u>outheast to get to London.
3. Hopkins traveled <u>n/N</u>orthwest from London to attend Oxford University.
4. Worcestershire, Housman's birthplace, is in the <u>w/W</u>est of England, near the Severn river.
5. Ireland, where Hopkins served as a priest, is an island <u>w/W</u>est of England.

Build Your Portfolio

 Idea Bank

Writing

1. **Tribute** Hopkins writes a poetic tribute to an athlete who died young. Write a tribute in prose to a professional athlete who is still living.

2. **Comparative Analysis** Write a comparative analysis of the work of Hopkins and Housman. Consider such elements as meter, attitude of the poets toward their subjects, and theme.

3. **Response to Criticism** W. H. Gardner writes, "Of all poets who have revered Shakespeare, Hopkins has learnt most from the master's skill in utilizing the full resources of the English language." Agree or disagree, citing specific passages.

Speaking, Listening, and Viewing

4. **Victorian Poetry Contest** Have a Hopkins team and a Housman team alternate in giving readings of their poet's work. Measure audience reaction to the readings and declare a winner. **[Performing Arts Link]**

5. **Newspaper Interview** With a partner, role-play a newspaper interview with Robert Bridges in 1918, just after he has published Hopkins's work. Remember that few readers will have heard of Hopkins. **[Media Link]**

Researching and Representing

6. **Biographical Report** Read a biography of one of these poets, such as Robert Bernard Martin's *Gerard Manley Hopkins: A Very Private Life*, and report on it to the class.

7. **Multimedia Presentation** Both of these poets attended Oxford University. Use readings, photographs, film clips, and artifacts to give a presentation on Oxford today. **[Social Studies Link]**

Online Activity www.phlit.phschool.com

 Guided Writing Lesson

Literary Analysis

Choose one of the four poems in this group. Then write an essay in which you analyze the poem's theme, or central message. Explain how the various elements of the poem—the images, the speaker, the tone, the main character, and so on—work together to convey the theme. Keep the following tip in mind as you develop your analysis.

Writing Skills Focus: Presenting a Thesis

Like many other types of writing, a literary analysis should be built around a thesis—a main point or general conclusion about the topic. All of the details presented should support the thesis. In a literary analysis the most effective support for a thesis usually consists of passages and details from the work.

Prewriting Start by reviewing the poem you've chosen. Read it over several times, considering the following questions: What is the poem about? Who is the poem's speaker? What is the speaker's attitude toward the subject? Which images stand out? Why? Use your answers to these questions to help you reach a conclusion about the poem's theme.

Drafting Start with an introduction in which you state your thesis in a sentence or two. Follow with a series of paragraphs in which you develop and support your thesis. Each of your body paragraphs should focus on a single subpoint of your thesis. In each paragraph cite details and passages from the poem for support. End your paper with a conclusion in which you restate your thesis.

Revising As you revise, look for places where you can add support for your thesis. In addition, eliminate any sections of your paper that do not directly relate to your thesis.

CONNECTIONS TO WORLD LITERATURE

Eternity
Arthur Rimbaud

Thematic Connection

GLOOM AND GLORY

The Victorian period marks a time of great progress for the British Empire. It also marks the beginning of its decline. The poems in this section reflect the passing of glory as part of a cyclical process of growth and decline. For example, in Gerard Manley Hopkins's poem "Spring and Fall: To a Young Child" he provides a contrast between birth and the decay that follows later in life. Thomas Hardy and A. E. Housman reinforce the contrast by juxtaposing the glory of life with the gloom of death. In "Ah, Are You Digging on My Grave?" Hardy offers the disturbing truth that we are never as important as we think we are. The poets examine their place in life and its cycles. While celebrating life, the poets also warn of assuming too much importance, for all must come to an end, just as the empire came to an end.

ETERNITY

While the poets in this section concentrate on the cycles of life, Arthur Rimbaud (ram bō´) focuses on the possibility of eternal life. Like other Victorian writers, he romanticizes a mundane concept and adds an air of mystery to its presentation. His poem "Eternity" contrasts the reality of life and the anguish of the ordinary with the freedom that a glimpse of eternity provides him. As you read "Eternity," note what is temporary and what is truly eternal.

ARTHUR RIMBAUD (1854–1891)

A poet of rare genius, French native Arthur Rimbaud first earned recognition for his poetry at age eight and was published when he was only fifteen. He stopped writing poetry at the age of nineteen and embarked on a life of adventure that has inspired scores of writers, musicians, and artists during the last one hundred years. Rimbaud spent the remainder of his life traveling throughout Africa and the Middle East. By the time of his death, his poetry had begun to influence other writers. His bohemian lifestyle became a model for such vagabond writers, musicians, and artists as Jack Kerouac and Bob Dylan.

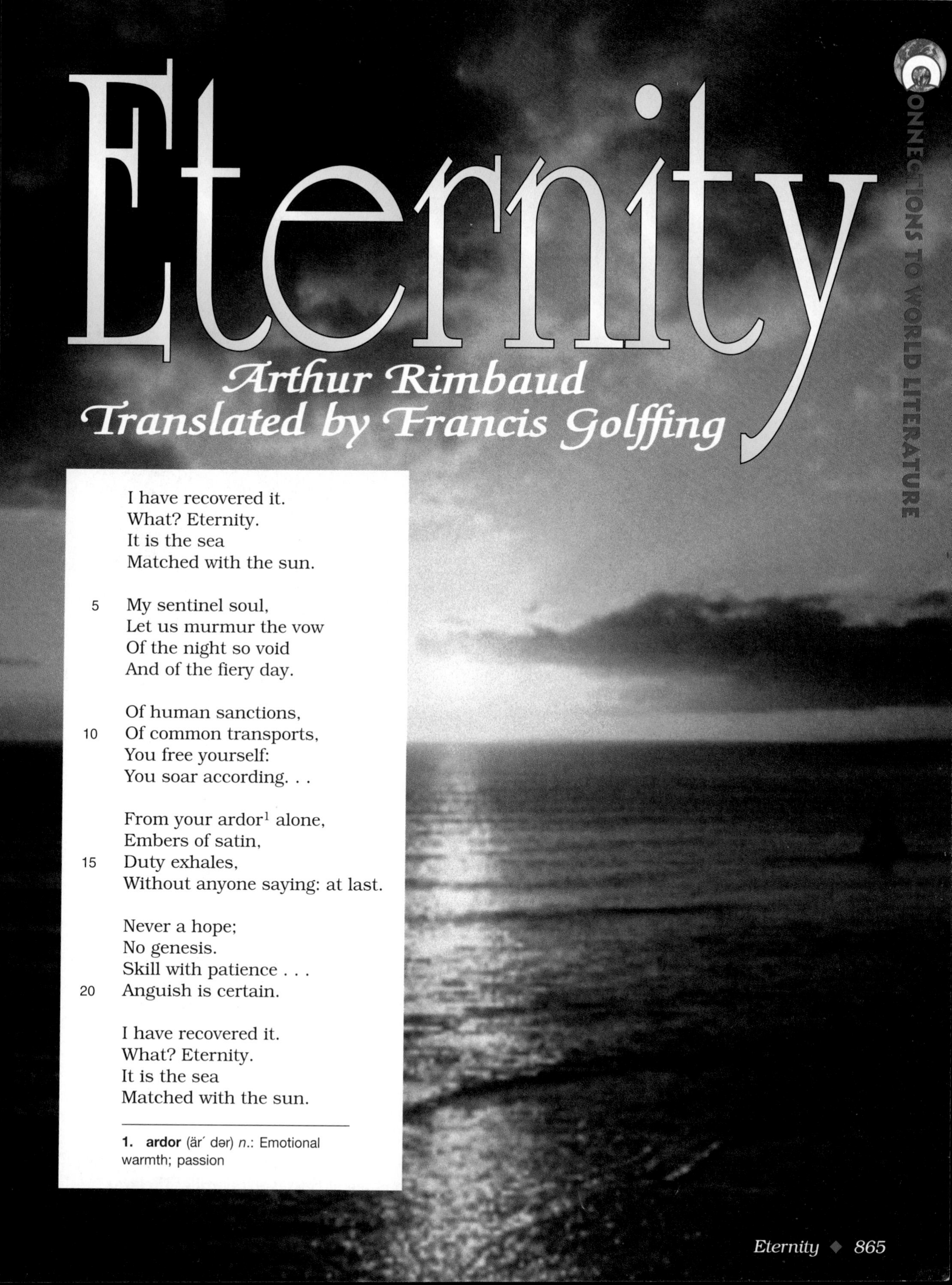

Eternity

Arthur Rimbaud
Translated by Francis Golffing

I have recovered it.
What? Eternity.
It is the sea
Matched with the sun.

5   My sentinel soul,
Let us murmur the vow
Of the night so void
And of the fiery day.

Of human sanctions,
10   Of common transports,
You free yourself:
You soar according. . .

From your ardor[1] alone,
Embers of satin,
15   Duty exhales,
Without anyone saying: at last.

Never a hope;
No genesis.
Skill with patience . . .
20   Anguish is certain.

I have recovered it.
What? Eternity.
It is the sea
Matched with the sun.

---

1. ardor (är´ dər) *n.*: Emotional warmth; passion

▲ **Critical Viewing** How does the "sea / Matched with the sun" suggest eternity? **[Interpret]**

Guide for Responding

◆ *Literature and Your Life*

Reader's Response What images come to mind as you read this poem? Explain.

Thematic Connection In your opinion, is this an optimistic or pessimistic poem? Why?

Journal Writing In your journal, list ways a person is immortalized, for example through fame, writing, painting, etc.

☑ Check Your Comprehension

1. What does the poet suggest is required to acquire eternity?
2. What images of nature does the poet use to engage the reader in thinking about immortality?

◆ Critical Thinking

INTERPRET

1. In this poem Rimbaud expresses the desire to escape from "human sanctions" and "common transports." How do the first and last stanzas relate to this desire? **[Infer]**
2. (a) What does Rimbaud mean when he refers to the sea "matching" the sun? (b) How is Rimbaud's juxtaposition of the sea and the sun similar to his juxtaposition of night and day (lines 7–8)? **[Interpret]**
3. How does Rimbaud's statement that "anguish is certain" (line 20) relate to the rest of the poem? **[Analyze]**

APPLY

4. What does eternity represent to you and how do you think it relates to your life? **[Relate]**

Thematic Connection

GLOOM AND GLORY

Some of the writers of this period explored the dichotomy—two contradictory parts—of life as we experience it. Birth and death, present and eternal, man and nature, gloom and glory are common themes in the literature as these writers observe the cycles of life and its passing.

1. Compare and contrast the various ways the writers in this section and Rimbaud treat the cycles of life in their poetry.
2. Which poet's view of the gloom and glory of life do you think is most realistic? Explain why.
3. Without opposing emotions, such as happiness and sadness, we would not truly be able to experience either emotion because we wouldn't have a basis for comparison. Do you agree or disagree with this statement? Explain.

 Idea Bank

Writing

1. **Perfect Place** In "Eternity," Rimbaud describes an ideal place where he could escape from anguish and the duties of ordinary life. What place provides you with the same feelings? Write a description of a perfect place to spend time.

2. **Dictionary of Abstract Words** Rimbaud uses a number of abstract words, words that express qualities that exist apart from any particular object. However, he links most of these words to concrete images. Make a list of abstract words in his poem. Then define them using concrete images in the poem.

3. **Response to Criticism** Some readers do not understand Rimbaud's poetry but are moved by his struggle to express an inner truth entirely his own. One critic states the point this way:

   > To those who read poetry for the sake of its accomplished beauty there is little promise in his outpourings, though dictated by a most genuine, impatient need to vent the burning truth within.   —L. Cazamian

   Write an essay in which you either agree or disagree that the poems are lacking in "accomplished beauty."

Speaking, Listening, and Viewing

4. **Ask the Poet** Choose one of the poets in this section or Rimbaud to be the guest on a radio interview program. Have one student play the part of the poet, one the interviewer, and three others as callers. The callers' questions can range from the style and theme of the poetry to the poet's opinion on modern issues. **[Media Link]**

Researching and Representing

5. **Past Glory** Choose a subject, such as sports, or theater, and research amazing people in that field. Find a lesser-known person, who once enjoyed fame and is now forgotten. Write a paper explaining the person's fame, disappearance from the news, and your opinion on why he or she did not achieve lasting fame.

6. **Multimedia Presentation** Using pictures, video, and drawings, prepare a visual description of a perfect place to spend time. Then present your multimedia report to your class. If you described the place in writing according to writing activity 1 on this page, you can combine your multimedia presentation with your writing.

Online Activity www.phlit.phschool.com

Writing Process Workshop

Newspaper writers, who are assigned articles that they must complete each day, face constant deadlines. When you take a timed essay test, you are under similar pressure. On the test, you should follow the test format exactly; draft your ideas quickly and efficiently; write your essay with logical reasoning and clear, concise language; and make revisions in just a few minutes.

The following skills, introduced in this section's Guided Writing Lessons, will help you write an effective test essay within a certain time limit.

Writing Skills Focus

▶ **Elaborate to make your writing personal.** Identify the point you want to make in your essay. Elaborate on the subject by choosing supporting facts and details from your knowledge and experience. (See p. 855.)

▶ **Present a "thesis"** in which you state your position on a subject. Support the thesis with details. (See p. 863.)

▶ **Be brief and concise,** since your time is limited. Choose words that are direct and precise in meaning. Eliminate unnecessary words or details.

Examine the following model:

WRITING MODEL

① The writer begins by stating a position.

② The writer elaborates to support the position by giving examples of ways that wearing seat belts saves lives.

③ The writer's conclusion is brief and to the point.

The new seat-belt law will save lives. ① Seat belts restrain passengers in the event of a collision and prevent the occupants of the car from crashing through the windshield. Seat belts can also minimize the injuries a driver could suffer on impact with the steering wheel. ② These advantages are a small price to pay for what some consider the inconvenience of buckling up. ③

Prewriting

Consider Your Purpose and Your Audience Usually in a timed essay test, you will be given a topic. Make sure that you completely understand the assignment. In this workshop, you will practice writing a persuasive essay. In a persuasive essay on a standardized test, your response will be formal and your purpose will be to convince an objective and impartial audience. Your writing approach, choice of words, style, and content all will influence your audience.

Practice writing a timed essay by responding to a question you think you might be asked on a test or by using one of the following prompts.

Topic Ideas

1. Your school board is considering a new policy that would require all participating school athletes to maintain a B average. State your opinion in a letter to your local newspaper.

2. A bill before the state legislature would limit licensed drivers under age 18 to driving between the hours of 6:00 A.M. and 6:00 P.M. Write your representative stating your position on this bill.

Plan Your Time Note the amount of time that you have to write your essay. Use the first few minutes to organize your thinking and to determine the thesis that you will present in your essay. Allot the most time to drafting your essay, but be sure to leave a few minutes at the end to revise.

Elaborate on Your Thesis Quickly brainstorm for facts and details that will support your thesis and will persuade your audience that your reasoning is sound. Then order your ideas logically. A rough outline will keep you organized and focused.

Drafting

Formulate and Support a Position Time is of the essence for this kind of test, so formulate your thesis and state it clearly in the introduction. Whether you take a pro or con position is your decision. In the body of the text, include supporting reasons that are complete, convincing, and logical. Strengthen your essay with transitional words and a strong conclusion that restates your position.

APPLYING LANGUAGE SKILLS: Use Formal English

In writing a timed-test essay, you should use formal English, which means using an objective tone, correct grammar and usage, no slang or contractions, and varied sentence lengths and structures.

Informal English:
Big business was totally crazed about the Y2K computer problem.

Formal English:
Corporations were concerned about the effects of the millennium on computers.

Practice On your paper, rewrite the following passage in formal English.

"Chill out, dude, the North High Panthers will crush South's wimpy Tigers."

Writing Application Check your essay to be sure that you have used formal English, as suggested above.

Writer's Solution Connection Language Lab

For additional practice, see the lessons on Formal and Informal English in the Language Lab unit on Usage.

APPLYING LANGUAGE SKILLS: Avoid Redundancy

Eliminate instances of redundancy, the unnecessary use of words that repeat ideas and don't contribute to the meaning. Redundancy makes all types of writing heavy and dull.

Examples of Redundant Phrases:

free gift; past history; completely finished; end result; advance warning

First Draft:

When in August the rain showers fall down . . .

Revision:

When in August it rains . . .

Writing Application Eliminate instances of redundancy in your essay.

Writer's Solution Connection Writing Lab

For help in drafting a persuasive essay, see the lesson on Persuasion in the Writing Lab.

Revising

Revise Quickly You'll have only a few minutes to revise your writing. Consider these tips:

▶ Review the essay question to be sure that you have responded completely to the assigned topic.

▶ Check your introduction, main ideas, and conclusion to make sure you remained focused on your position.

▶ Review your persuasive points to be sure your reasoning is logical and well organized. Delete information that is irrelevant, and strengthen supporting information where it is needed.

▶ Be sure you've used formal English in your essay. Check your spelling and grammar, and be sure you've used words that are clear, direct, and concise.

REVISION MODEL

In order to educate leaders of the twenty-first century, we need to equip our schools with the technology of the new millennium. Our school's computer lab is filled with ① *obsolete* out-of-date equipment. Many computers are too wrecked to ② use. Others don't have the capacity to hook up to the ③ *connect* Internet. Without more memory, these computers can't run the latest ④ new software programs our teachers want us to use. Please don't deprive our students of the computer lab equipment necessary for them to deal with future technology.

① The writer replaces imprecise wording with an accurate, concise word.
② The writer deletes tangential information.
③ The writer replaces jargon with formal English.
④ The writer eliminates redundancy.

Publishing

Expand Your Essay After getting feedback from your classmates and the teacher on ways to improve your writing, expand the essay to write a research paper.

Student Success Workshop

Real-World Reading Skills

Strategies for Success

How fast do you read? The answer should depend on what you're reading. Learning to monitor your reading strategies will help you get the most out of what you read. Whether it's a comic novel or a science textbook, determine your purpose for reading and adjust your reading rate accordingly.

Monitor Your Reading Strategies If you want to give a poem, a novel, or a textbook careful consideration, read slowly. Take time to pause and reflect as well as to go back and reread. If you want an overview of a magazine article, read through it quickly and focus on its main ideas, as reflected in topic sentences.

Slow Down for Details You can also adjust your reading rate while reading different parts of one work. You may need to slow down if you come to a section containing many specific details or visuals like charts, graphs, and tables. You may want to read more quickly if you come to a section that isn't closely related to your interest or to your reading goal.

Scan to Plan When reading nonfiction, you may find it helpful to scan the article or book first, looking for sections or chapters that you will want to study closely. You might even mark these sections with bookmarks or stick-on notes. When you go back and start reading, you'll remember to slow down when you see your reminders.

Apply the Strategies

Imagine that you're using the English history textbook in which the page at the left appears. Answer these questions about monitoring your reading strategies.

1. Describe a purpose for reading that would require only a quick scan of the details on this page.
2. What elements on this page would help you quickly grasp the key ideas? Explain.
3. Describe a purpose for reading that would require a careful study of the text on this page.
4. If you looked at this page quickly, what information might you miss? Why?

✔ Here are some other situations in which you may need to monitor your reading strategies:
► Poetry excerpted in criticism
► Statistics reported in news reports
► Descriptive images used in letters

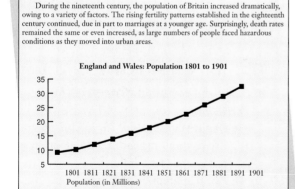

Population Trends: Urbanization

During the nineteenth century, the population of Britain increased dramatically, owing to a variety of factors. The rising fertility patterns established in the eighteenth century continued, due in part to marriages at a younger age. Surprisingly, death rates remained the same or even increased, as large numbers of people faced hazardous conditions as they moved into urban areas.

England and Wales: Population 1801 to 1901

Population (in Millions)

Indeed, urbanization, the movement of populations into large cities, was the dominant migratory trend during this period. This trend began during the eighteenth century, but continued aggressively as industrial manufacturing drew people to cities throughout the nineteenth century. In 1700, about sixteen percent of the English population lived in urban regions; by 1800 this percentage increased to twenty-seven. By 1900, almost eighty percent of the population was urbanized.

Living in Cities The rapid increase in urban populations led to difficult living conditions in most English cities. Overcrowded urban areas offered poor sanitation, paving, and water supply. As conditions worsened, wealthier families moved to outer regions, leaving cities with less financial support for necessary improvements.

Learning to give constructive criticism—and to receive it—are skills everyone needs. Negative statements about an oral presentation, such as "I didn't like it" or "It was a waste of time," have little value, but positive suggestions can be helpful. By listening to the viewpoints of others, exchanging ideas, and identifying problems, you can improve your presentations and performances.

Be an Engaged Listener and Viewer It's difficult for people to evaluate their own performance since they cannot see themselves. They need to hear the opinions of objective observers. You can help others by critiquing their performance. As you watch, ask yourself these questions:

▶ What is the content or subject matter? Does it sustain my interest? What would help to engage the audience?

▶ In what ways does the performance aid my understanding of the content? Is there an additional way that the speaker can reinforce the content?

▶ Does the performer's delivery contribute to the meaning of the work? How could the delivery be improved?

Offer Positive and Constructive Criticism When you give a critique of someone's performance, begin with a positive statement. Remember that the speaker deserves credit for having the courage to perform in front of an audience. The performer wants to hear praise for elements that were successful. In giving criticism, be tactful and constructive; avoid using negative wording. Instead, offer concrete suggestions on how to strengthen elements that you think need to be improved. Learning to give and take constructive criticism will develop your ability to work with others.

Use Criticism to Improve Communication When you receive feedback about your own performance, keep an open mind and avoid being defensive. Consider the suggestions and ideas you get from others as ways to improve your communication. Although you need not follow all the suggestions, evaluate the feedback and consider revising to strengthen your performance. Remember that there is no single "right" way; what works for another might not work for you.

Apply the Strategies

Work with a small group to choose a short story and adapt it for a dramatic presentation. Each member should have a speaking part. Rehearse, critique one another's performance, and listen to praise as well as to suggestions about areas that need work. Decide which suggestions will help your presentation. When everyone feels reasonably confident, give a performance for the class.

Tips for Constructive Criticism

✔ To give tactful and constructive criticism:

▶ Begin with praise. An initial positive statement makes it easier to hear criticism that follows.

▶ Avoid negative language, such as, "That part was bad" or "I didn't like how you did that."

▶ Give specific examples that support your opinions.

▶ Give concrete suggestions.

Test Preparation Workshop

Reading Comprehension

Paired Passages

Strategies for Success

In standardized tests, you are sometimes asked to read paired passages and answer questions about literary elements in the two passages. Use the following strategies to help you answer these types of questions:

Paired Passages Read both passages quickly. Then read the first question. Scan the passages to identify the elements that the questions are addressing. Then answer the question.

Read these passages, and answer the question that follows:

Passage 1

Many people argue that hunters interfere with nature and disrupt the ecosystem. On the contrary, human hunters are not disruptive; they help keep animal populations healthy. In many areas, wild animals become too numerous because they lack natural predators. Hunting can be a humane practice that quickly kills animals who would otherwise die of starvation.

Passage 2

The number of game hunters has declined. About 20 percent of the hunters who stopped hunting quit because they believe it's wrong. Some former hunters object to the killing of animals for decorative purposes—especially the killing of animals that are not overpopulated. Other ex-hunters are concerned about possible hunting accidents and are repelled by the prevalence of guns and violence in society.

Which answer best expresses the relationship between the main ideas of these two passages?

A They offer opposing moral views on hunting.

B They address different aspects of hunting.

C They discuss people's positions on hunting.

D They support each other's positions on hunting.

E They contrast the motives of hunters and ex-hunters.

First identify the main ideas of the two passages—that hunting contributes to the health of the environment (Passage 1) and that people have stopped hunting for a variety of reasons (Passage 2). Evaluate the relationship between these main ideas. Answers **A** and **D** are incorrect because Passage 2 does not take a moral position on hunting; it explains the decline. **B** is too general and so is incorrect. **E** is incorrect because no motives are given in Passage 1. **C** best identifies the relationship and is correct.

Apply the Strategies

Refer to the sample passages to answer these questions:

1 Which answer best expresses the author's purpose in the two passages?

A Passage 1 is written to persuade; Passage 2 is written to inform.

B Both passages are written to entertain.

C Passage 1 is written to inform; Passage 2 is written to persuade.

D Both passages are written to inform.

E Both passages are written to persuade

2 Which answer best describes the tone of the passages?

A Both passages are serious and instructive.

B Both passages are morbid.

C The first passage is weak; the second passage is strong.

D Both passages are uplifting.

E The first passage is defiant; the second passage is appeasing.

The City Rises, 1911 (tempera on card), Umberto Boccioni, Jesi Collection, Milan

6

A Time of Rapid Change:

The Modern and Postmodern Periods (1901–Present)

We are living at one of the great turning points of history. . . . Yesterday, we split the atom. We assaulted that colossal citadel of power, the tiny unit of the substance of the universe. And because of this, the great dream and the great nightmare of centuries of human thought have taken flesh and walk beside us all, day and night.

—Doris Lessing,
from "The Small, Personal Voice"

Timeline

1901–Present

British Events

- **1901** Edward VII becomes king.
- **1902 Joseph Conrad** publishes *Heart of Darkness.*
- **1903** Emmeline Pankhurst founds women's suffrage organization.
- **1910** George V becomes king.
- **1913 D. H. Lawrence** publishes *Sons and Lovers.*
- **1914** Britain enters World War I. ▶
- **1918** Married women over thirty achieve right to vote.

- **1922** Irish Free State formed.
- **1922 T. S. Eliot** publishes *The Waste Land.*
- **1922 James Joyce** publishes *Ulysses.*
- **1924** First British airline begins regular operations.
- **1930 W. H. Auden** publishes *Poems.*
- **1936** First BBC television broadcast.
- **1939** Britain enters World War II. ▼
- **1940 Winston Churchill** becomes prime minister.

- **1945 George Orwell** publishes *Animal Farm.*
- **1947** Coal mines nationalized.
- **1947** India and Pakistan gain independence.
- **1949** Irish Free State becomes Republic of Ireland. ▶
- **1952** Elizabeth II becomes queen.
- **1954 William Golding** publishes *Lord of the Flies.*
- **1954** Roger Bannister breaks four-minute mile. ▶

World Events

- **1901** Germany: Thomas Mann publishes *Buddenbrooks.*
- **1903** Orville and Wilbur Wright build first successful airplane.
- **1904** Asia: Russo-Japanese War begins.
- **1905** Germany: Albert Einstein proposes theory of relativity. ▶
- **1917** Austria: Sigmund Freud publishes *Introduction to Psycho-analysis.*
- **1917** Russia: Czar overthrown; Bolsheviks seize power.

- **1920** India: **Mohandas Gandhi** leads nonviolent protests.
- **1925** Czechoslovakia: Franz Kafka publishes *The Trial.*
- **1927** United States: Charles Lindbergh flies solo to Paris. ▲
- **1936** Spain: Civil War begins.
- **1939** Europe: Hitler invades Poland; World War II begins.
- **1941** United States: Japan bombs Pearl Harbor; United States enters World War II.

- **1945** Japan: World War II ends as Japan surrenders. ▲
- **1947** Middle East: Palestine partitioned.
- **1948** Middle East: Israel established.
- **1949** China: Mao Zedong establishes People's Republic.
- **1954** United States: Jonas Salk begins polio inoculations.
- **1955** United States: Martin Luther King, Jr., leads civil rights bus boycott.
- **1957** Russia: Sputnik I, first spaceship launched.

British Events

- **1962 Doris Lessing** publishes *The Golden Notebook*.
- **1965** Miniskirt becomes fashionable.
- **1967** The Beatles release *Sgt. Pepper's Lonely Hearts Club Band*.
- **1972** Britain imposes direct rule on Northern Ireland.

- **1975** North Sea oil production begins. ▶

- **1977** John Fowles publishes *Daniel Martin*.
- **1979** Margaret Thatcher becomes first woman prime minister. ▼

- **1979 V. S. Naipaul** publishes *A Bend in the River*.
- **1980** Britain suffers worst recession since 1930's.
- **1982** British troops force Argentinians from Falkland Islands.
- **1985** Thatcher breaks coal miners' strike.
- **1985** Hillsborough Agreement gives Republic of Ireland voice in governing Northern Ireland.
- **1989** Parliament privatizes national electric and water companies.

- **1991 Nadine Gordimer** wins Nobel Prize for Literature.
- **1991** Great Britain participates in Persian Gulf War.
- **1992** Scandal-mongering about the royal family reaches new heights.
- **1994** Cease-fire agreed to between factions in Northern Ireland.
- **1997 Tony Blair** elected Prime Minister.
- **1997** Scotland and Wales gain right to form separate parliaments.

World Events

- **1960** Germany: Berlin Wall built.
- **1963** United States: President John F. Kennedy assassinated.
- **1964** Vietnam: American troops join fighting.
- **1966** India: Indira Gandhi becomes prime minister.
- **1967** Colombia: Gabriel García Márquez publishes *One Hundred Years of Solitude*.
- **1969** United States: Apollo 11 lands on moon. ▲

- **1977** Africa: Djibouti, last remaining European colony, granted independence.
- **1979** Iran: Ayatollah Khomeini overthrows Shah.
- **1980** United States: Ronald Reagan elected president.
- **1985** Ethiopia: warfare and drought result in great famine.
- **1989** Germany: Berlin Wall torn down; reunification of East and West Germany follows. ▼

- **1991** Eastern Europe: Soviet Union dissolved.
- **1991** Yugoslavia: Civil war breaks out.
- **1991** Europe: Maastricht Treaty providing for a common European currency signed.
- **1991** Middle East: Iraq defeated by United Nations forces in Persian Gulf War.
- **1993** Middle East: Israel and the PLO sign peace agreement.
- **1994** South Africa: Nelson Mandela elected president.
- **1997** China: Hong Kong returns from British to Chinese rule.

A Wolseley Six-Horsepower Two-Seater, 1904

▲ **Deduce** The spread of mass-produced automobiles eventually allowed the middle-classes to enjoy opportunities for travel. Judging from details of its appearance, what kind of driving—pleasure, work, or family-related—was this 1904 car designed for?

Gas Mask

▲ **Draw Conclusions** Gas masks such as this one were a standard part of a soldier's equipment during World War I, when the widespread use of mustard gas turned the very air hostile. Knowing that chemical warfare has since been banned, what conclusions can you draw about the effects of mustard gas?

The Story of the Times
(1901–Present)

Historical Background

The twentieth century dawned bright with promise. Progress in science and technology was helping to make life easier and the world more comprehensible. Yet while steady advances in communications and transportation drew the world closer together, the scourge of modern war soon wrenched it apart. The First World War (1914–1918) killed more than 8 million people, the Second World War (1939–1945), some 45 million more. British military and political power declined after the Second World War, yet British literary and artistic life remained vibrant. Disillusionment, though widespread, was accompanied by vigorous inventiveness.

The Edwardian Age The rigid class distinctions and moral certainties of Victorian times lingered on into the Edwardian Age (1901–1914), named for Victoria's successor, Edward VII. From the widespread use of electricity to the women's movement for the vote, rapid changes doomed the genteel life of the early twentieth century. By the time King George V came to the British throne in 1910, the nineteenth-century way of life was fading into memory.

The First World War In 1914, long-standing tensions among the nations of Europe exploded, ignited by the assassination of Austria-Hungary's Archduke Francis Ferdinand. When Germany invaded neutral Belgium, Britain joined with France to stem the tide of aggression.

The people of Great Britain went to war optimistically, expecting an easy victory. Soon, however, they recoiled with horror as the realities of poison gas, massive artillery barrages, and the terrible futility of trench warfare became evident.

In 1917, in the midst of war, revolution broke out in Russia, resulting in the overthrow of the czar and the establishment of the world's first communist state, the Soviet Union. By the time the Armistice was signed on November 11,

1918, other empires and monarchies had also been swept away, including imperial Germany and the Austro-Hungarian Empire. An uneasy peace, its harsh terms spelled out in the Treaty of Versailles, followed.

Between the Wars The disillusioned youth of postwar Europe were known as a "lost generation." Some young people masked their lack of purpose by the pursuit of pleasure—fast cars, wild jazz, giddy fads. Not all was disenchantment or frivolity, of course. Married British women over thirty won the right to vote in 1918.

The future, however, was being determined by political developments in Europe, exhausted and desperate after the Great War. Adolf Hitler began to aggressively expand Germany's borders. Only when Germany invaded Poland on September 1, 1939, did Britain admit that Hitler could not be stopped without violent intervention.

The Second World War World War II was even more destructive than World War I. Hitler's "final solution" to the "Jewish problem" brought death to 6 million Jews. The German invasion of Russia in 1941 killed soldiers and civilians by the millions. Fighting raged from Europe to North Africa, from the mountains of Burma and China to the Hawaiian Islands. Massive bombing raids turned London, Dresden, and Tokyo into infernos.

The darkest days for Britain came in 1940, when France had fallen and Britain alone bore the brunt of German air attacks. Inspired by Prime Minister Winston Churchill, and joined in 1941 by two powerful allies, the United States and the Soviet Union, Britain fought on.

Finally, in August of 1945, American atomic bombs blasted two Japanese cities, Hiroshima and Nagasaki, into cinder and ash, bringing the war to a brutal and abrupt end. The war's death toll by then had mounted to at least four times that of the First World War.

The End of an Empire The British Empire came undone after the Second World War. In addition to its domestic problems, like food shortages and cities lying in ruins, Britain began to lose its possessions and colonies. Part of Ireland had already won independence in 1921. In Asia and Africa, nationalist leaders challenged colonial rule and gained freedom. Ethnic, racial, and

Flapper Dancing the Charleston

▲ **Speculate** The flapper—a woman who cut her hair short, wore dresses without waists, and otherwise did as she pleased—appeared in the 1920's in Britain as well as in America. Why might this woman's clothing and the dance she is performing have shocked ladies of her mother's generation?

Scenes from the Blitz: Londoners Sheltering in Underground Station

▲ **Infer** During "the Blitz," which lasted from September, 1940, to May, 1941, German planes dropped bombs on London almost every night. Name two reasons why people would have taken shelter in subways during air raids.

▲ **Assess** The power of labor increased during the twentieth century. Unions had become legal in 1871. Their leaders helped form a political party, the Labor Party, in 1900. By 1914, unions were roughly four million members strong. What aspect of the worker's movement does the artist focus on in this painting?

▲ **Compare and Contrast** Though early reforms had instituted measures such as the labor exchange for job-seekers shown in the photo, workers such as the hunger marcher (see inset) continued to agitate for changes. Contrast the roles of the government in people's lives as shown by these two photographs.

border conflicts, however, led to bloodshed in many of the newly independent former colonies. On the Continent, British power declined sharply, and an "iron curtain" divided Eastern and Western Europe. The United States and the Soviet Union now dominated the world between them.

By the 1960's Britons had apparently put many of their troubles behind them. From rock music to "mod" clothing, Britain influenced fashion around the world. However, basic industries—textiles, steelmaking, shipbuilding—that had been vital to Britain were no longer competing successfully. Factories were forced to close their gates.

British society was also changing rapidly in a number of ways. Immigrants from Britain's former colonies, working-class people, and women were seizing opportunities from which they had formerly been excluded.

Contemporary Britain Margaret Thatcher, a member of the Conservative party, and the first woman prime minister, came to power in 1979 and dismantled much of the government's role in the economy. Prosperity resulted for some, but many Britons did not benefit from "Thatcherism." She resigned her office in 1990 to be replaced by her own handpicked Conservative party successor, John Major. In 1997, however, Major was defeated by Tony Blair, the Labor candidate.

Many problems and challenges remain as Britain adjusts to a rapidly changing world. Its participation in the European Economic Community—a trading bloc of some 300 million people—should be a benefit, but is still in its early stages. Intervals of cease-fire in Northern Ireland are interrupted by episodes of violence as negotiations continue. Wales and Scotland voted in 1997 to set up their own parliaments, and the nation ponders the monarchy's role in the twenty-first century.

Tradition has always been strong in Great Britain. As in previous times of trial, Britons can turn to the past as a source of pride and comfort while moving forward into the swirl and bustle of contemporary life.

Literature of the Period

Modernism and Poetry Modernism has been perhaps the most important artistic movement of the twentieth century, committed to creating new forms and styles. Many Modernists used images as symbols, leading to indirect, evocative work. They often presented experiences in fragments, rather than as a coherent whole.

Modernism lent itself to charting a world fragmented by war and increasingly removed from traditional sources of meaning. In his later poetry, William Butler Yeats (1865–1939) adopts the direct, more colloquial diction of Modernism, using images in powerful, symbolic ways and exploring troubling questions of modern life.

A few first-rate British poets died in the Great War, including Rupert Brooke (1887–1915) and Wilfred Owen (1893–1918). Others, such as Siegfried Sassoon (1886–1967), survived. Preeminent among the postwar poets was T. S. Eliot (1888–1965), whose poem "The Love Song of J. Alfred Prufrock" reflects the despair of the "lost generation."

The Auden Generation In the 1930's and 1940's, poets such as W. H. Auden (1907–1973), Louis MacNeice (1907–1963), and Stephen Spender (1909–1995) showed an increasing concern with political and social issues, though they did not abandon subtle symbolism and imagery. By contrast, Romanticism flared into wild brilliance in the poetry of Dylan Thomas (1914–1953).

The Movement During the 1950's and 1960's, British poets of "the Movement," such as Philip Larkin (1922–1985), Donald Davie (born 1922), and Thom Gunn (born 1929), tried to capture everyday experiences in common, yet tightly wrought, language.

Contemporary Poets Noteworthy British poets of recent years, such as Ted Hughes (born 1930), Peter Redgrove (born 1932), and the Irish-born Seamus Heaney (born 1939) have a visionary intensity. Two remarkable poets have appeared from former British colonies in the West Indies: James Berry (born 1925), a Jamaican, and Nobel Prize-winner Derek Walcott (born 1930), from the island of St. Lucia.

The Beatles

▲ **Compare and Contrast** The Beatles exploded as an international success in 1964. Compare this image of the Beatles with the image presented by a contemporary band you know.

A Model Wearing a Cheetah Print Miniskirt.

▲ **Speculate** During the 1960's, London's Carnaby Street set the pace for world fashion. Hemlines soared and plummeted with amazing speed. Fashion kept stepping into the future, and shock and outrage often followed. What kind of "statement" does the model's outfit in the photograph make?

The Cool Hearth

▲ **Speculate** British inventors pioneered television technology, yet from commercials to "Dallas," the United States contributed much of what is uniquely characteristic of the content of television. Why do you think this is so?

Airplane

▲ **Generalize** In 1952, the British de Haviland Comet—the world's first large commercial jet—began carrying passengers. British airlines at the time were owned by the government; they did not become private corporations until 1987. (a) Name two advantages of a nationalized airline. (b) Name two advantages of privately owned airlines, such as the United States has.

Twentieth-Century Drama George Bernard Shaw (1856–1950) dominated late Victorian, Edwardian, and early modern drama. His witty, socially conscious plays manage to evoke laughter while examining social issues. Influenced by the Irish Literary Revival, John Millington Synge (1871–1909) vividly captures Irish rural life in plays like *The Playboy of the Western World* (1907). In the depression years of the 1930's, Noel Coward (1899–1973) won attention with a series of smartly sophisticated dramas and musicals.

Angry Young Men and Absurdists In the 1950's and 1960's, a group of dramatists known as Britain's "angry young men," which included John Osborne, used realistic techniques in plays attacking the injustices of Britain's class system. A second strain of contemporary British drama, the theater of the absurd, uses disconnected dialogue and action to depict life itself as a pointless series of misfortunes. Dublin-born Samuel Beckett (1906–1989), author of *Waiting for Godot* (1952), pioneered this form, which has also influenced Harold Pinter (born 1930) and Tom Stoppard (born 1930).

Twentieth-Century Fiction The Edwardian Age produced a number of brilliant writers of realist and naturalist fiction. Joseph Conrad, one of the pioneers of psychological realism, examines the individual's struggle with the self in tales such as *Lord Jim* (1900) and *Heart of Darkness* (1902). D. H. Lawrence (1885–1930) unleashes a savage hatred of conventional British manners and morals in novels like *Sons and Lovers* (1913). E. M. Forster opposes the hypocrisies of society in a gentler fashion in novels such as *A Passage to India* (1924).

Perhaps the greatest pioneer of Modernist fiction was the Irish writer James Joyce (1882–1941). Joyce revolutionized the form and structure of both the short story and the novel. His brilliant novel *Ulysses* (1922), contains a great variety of innovative techniques—including stream of consciousness, symbolism, and disjointed typography. Another innovative Modernist novelist is Virginia Woolf (1882–1941), best known for stream-of-consciousness novels like *To the Lighthouse* (1927).

Political and social issues gained increasing attention among novelists in the 1930's and

1940's, when a new group of novelists emerged. Aldous Huxley's (1894–1963) *Brave New World* (1932) and George Orwell's (1903–1950) *1984* (1949) paint frightening pictures of the future based on the present. Two of Britain's most popular novelists are Graham Greene (1904–1991), author of novels such as *The Power and the Glory* (1940), and P. G. Wodehouse (1881–1975), a brilliant humorist. Among more recent British novelists are William Golding (1911–1993), Anthony Burgess (1917–1993), Kingsley Amis (1922–1995), John Fowles (born 1926), and Alan Sillitoe (born 1928).

In literature, as in other aspects of British life, women have been highly visible and productive in the latter half of the twentieth century. Irish-born Iris Murdoch (born 1919) is known for her intricate novels exploring human relationships, among them *The Message to the Planet* (1990). Doris Lessing (born 1919) grew up in Rhodesia (now Zimbabwe) and gained fame for a series of novels set in Africa, including *The Four-Gated City* (1969). Nobel Prize–winner Nadine Gordimer (born 1923) writes novels and short stories that examine the moral and political dilemmas of racially divided South Africa, where she lives.

From Former Colonies In recent years, a number of talented writers from what used to be the far-flung British Empire have added to the richness of English literature. Among these are Frank Sargeson (1903–1982) of New Zealand; Patrick White (1912–1990), the Nobel Prize-winner from Australia; Wilson Harris (born 1921) of Guyana; Chinua Achebe (born 1930) and Nobel Prize-winner Wole Soyinka (born 1934), both of Nigeria. A writer from the island of Trinidad, V. S. Naipaul (born 1932), has achieved success with both fiction and nonfiction. The award-winning novel *In a Free State* (1971) is one of his finest works.

These ex-colonial writers are busy making classics for a new age. Borrowing a famous line from Shakespeare's *The Tempest*, we can say that they are transforming English literature "into something rich and strange."

The Crossword Puzzle
David Hockney

▲ **Speculate** British-born David Hockney's paintings and art works are groundbreaking and influential. (a) How does Hockney's use of photographs in this piece "break up" images? (b) What does this "breaking up" suggest about the relation between still images and time? (c) Why did he match this technique with a crossword puzzle as his subject?

Canada Tower, London, Corbis

▲ **Speculate** This glass-and-steel office building has left its mark on the skyline of contemporary London. (a) What characteristics would you expect London to share with other major cities? (b) What characteristics would you expect to be particular to London?

The Changing English Language

BRITSPEAK, A TO ZED
by Richard Lederer

At the end of World War II, Winston Churchill tells us, the Allied leaders nearly came to blows over a single word during their negotiations when some diplomats suggested that it was time to "table" an important motion. For the British, *table* meant that the motion should be put on the table for discussion. For the Americans it meant just the opposite—that it should be put on the shelf and dismissed from discussion.

This confusion serves to illustrate the truth of George Bernard Shaw's pronouncement that "England and America are two countries divided by a common language." Or, as Oscar Wilde put it, "We have really everything in common with America nowadays, except, of course, language." Wilde made this comment when he heard that audiences in New York weren't queuing up to see his plays. Instead, they were waiting in line.

Separated by the Same Language

Many of the most beguiling misunderstandings can arise where identical words have different meanings in the two cultures and lingoes. When an American exclaims, "I'm mad about my flat," he is upset about his tire. When a Brit exclaims, "I'm mad about my flat," she is not bemoaning the "puncture" of her "tyre"; she is

British	American
gangway	aisle
hair grip	bobby pin
ironmonger	hardware store
serviette	napkin
fortnight	two weeks
zed	the letter $\underline{Z}$ [pronounced-zē]
prawn	shrimp

delighted with her apartment. When a Brit points out that you have "a ladder in your hose," the situation is not as bizarre as you might at first think. Quite simply, you have a run in your stocking.

Our buses are their coaches. When a hotel in the British Isles posts a large sign proclaiming, "No football coaches allowed," the message is not directed at the Don Shulas and Joe Paternos of the world. *No football coaches allowed* means "No soccer buses permitted."

With the increasing influence of film, radio, television, and international travel, the two main streams of the English language are rapidly converging like the streets of a circus (British for "traffic circle"). Nonetheless, there are scores of words, phrases, and spellings about which Brits and Yanks still don't agree.

Activities

1. If you choose to rent an automobile in the UK, with it will come a whole new vocabulary. Be sure to fill it with petrol, not gas. Investigate other differences between the words that Brits and Americans have for vehicles and roadways.
2. Define these words in American English first, then British English: biscuit, braces, chemist, chips, crisp, lift, plaster, pudding, spectacles, tin, torch.

PART **1** *Waking From the Dream*

The Children Enter the Palace of Luxury
Frederick Cayley Robinson, The Fine Art Society, London

Guide for Interpreting

Elizabeth Bowen *(1899–1973)*

The fiction of Elizabeth Bowen is distinguished by her subtle observation of landscape, by her innovative and believable use of the supernatural, and by her haunting portrayal of England during one of the darkest eras of the country's history.

A Troubled Childhood

Though she was born in comfortable circumstances —her parents were well-off, and she grew up on their country estate in County Cork, Ireland—Elizabeth Bowen's early life was marked by losses. Her father had a breakdown when she was seven years old and was confined to an institution. She and her mother moved to England, where her mother died of cancer when Elizabeth was thirteen.

Her family preferred to avoid or deny strong emotion. Bowen later said that she and her mother waged a "campaign of not noticing" her father's absence. Later, she was not allowed to attend her mother's funeral.

As an adult, Bowen was to write about the helplessness of the heart to understand itself or others in the absence of love.

In her characters' insecure lives, one can still trace the marks left by Bowen's own early abandonment.

Her Ambition to Write

After her mother's death, Bowen lived with her relatives, then attended boarding school until she was seventeen, when she moved to London. Her one ambition was to write, and her family's money was enough to support her as she wrote her first short stories.

A Writer's Life

Her first collection of short stories, published in 1923, received little attention. Through the 1930's, while living with her husband in Oxford, she perfected her craft, publishing regularly. During the war Bowen observed England's hardships keenly and with compassion. The brutal realities of the conflict were incorporated into some of her best stories. In 1938, she completed one of her best-known works, *The Death of the Heart*, a novel about the disillusionment of an innocent, teenage girl, taken in by uncaring relatives after her mother's death.

After the war, Bowen widened her literary activities to include literary criticism and book reviews. After 1952, Bowen returned to Ireland and wrote novels that exhibit a symbolic, poetic style.

Bowen defined the novel as the "non-poetic statement of poetic truth." Through her deceptively simple style, her explorations of human relationships, guided by the hardship she had undergone, she achieved this goal.

◆ Background for Understanding

HISTORY: BOWEN IN LONDON DURING THE BLITZ

Elizabeth Bowen lived in London during the Second World War, serving as an air-raid warden. War was a daily fact in 1940's London. After decisive victories in Europe, the Germans began a steady bombardment of Britain, with London as a focus. During "the Blitz," which lasted from September 1940 to May 1941, German planes dropped bombs on London almost every night. Warning sirens and blackouts were common; whole communities were evacuated periodically, leaving street after street of deserted buildings. Yet, amid the bombing, people continued to live in the city. The eeriness of Bowen's story stems from her experience of a time when war's unthinkable horrors had become all too "ordinary."

The Demon Lover

◆ *Literature and Your Life*

CONNECT YOUR EXPERIENCE

Becoming a "ghost" is easy; it's just a trick of time and place. Walk by your old elementary school . . . linger in your old home after the movers have come and emptied all the rooms. All becoming a ghost takes is a sideways step out of familiar routines into the past. When you are in a place where you no longer have a place, it is easy to feel like a ghost—or to meet one.

Elizabeth Bowen has a sharp sense of these tricks of time and place. In "The Demon Lover," Mrs. Drover returns like a ghost to her own shut-up house, only to find that it is, perhaps, haunted.

Journal Writing Describe a once-familiar place that made you feel like a "ghost."

THEMATIC FOCUS: WAKING FROM THE DREAM

As you read the story, notice how the dreamlike atmosphere that occurs during war makes everything seem out of place.

◆ Literary Focus

THE GHOST STORY

A **ghost story** is a tale that leaves you wondering whether there's a supernatural force at work. Some ghost stories allow either a supernatural or a natural explanation of the events they recount. By causing the mind to hesitate between these alternatives, a ghost story blurs the line between the familiar and the unfamiliar.

Elizabeth Bowen, for instance, makes us wonder whether the "ghost" in "The Demon Lover" is actually Mrs. Drover's dead fiancé or a hallucination, based on her unresolved feelings about him.

◆ Build Vocabulary

LATIN WORD ROOTS: *-loc-*

Before her marriage, Bowen writes, Kathleen experiences "a complete dislocation from everything." *Dislocation*—built on the Latin root *-loc-*, meaning "place"— refers to the condition of being out of place.

WORD BANK

Before you read, preview this list of words from the story.

spectral
dislocation
arboreal
circumscribed
aperture

◆ Grammar and Style

SENTENCE BEGINNINGS: PARTICIPIAL PHRASES

To add variety to her writing, Bowen begins some sentences with participial phrases. A **participle** is a verb form, usually ending in *-ed* or *-ing*, that is used as an adjective. A **participial phrase** is a participle, together with its modifiers and complements.

Shifting some parcels under her arm, she slowly forced round her latchkey . . .

A participial phrase can often be placed at the beginning of a sentence, as long as it is near the word it modifies. For example, *Shifting some parcels under her arm* appears next to the pronoun *she*, which it modifies.

Notice how Bowen adds a rhythm to her writing by occasionally beginning a sentence with a participial phrase. The sentence seems to start "in the middle" of an action or event that is already underway—an effect that helps draw the reader in.

Reading for Success

Strategies for Reading and Interpreting Fiction

When reading fiction, turn your mind into a kind of theater, in which the mind is the stage, the actors, and the director all at the same time. Use this theater to find the relationship between the details the author presents and the meaning of the piece. Here are a few strategies to help you find that meaning:

Identify with a character or the situation.

Short stories can take you through all kinds of experiences. When you identify with a situation, you live it with the character: You share the character's feelings and perceptions of the events. In this way, you may relate to experiences from your own life—or to experiences that you may never actually have had firsthand.

Draw inferences.

By implying meanings without stating them directly, writers offer us a world in which the mind can stretch itself, finding connections wherever it looks. As you read, look for significant word choices, patterns of events, and other clues to understand what a writer is saying between the lines.

Question and challenge the text.

A story will reveal its secrets only if you pursue them. Question as you read: What is happening? Why did he say that? You may not always find an answer right away, but pieces of the story will start to collect around your questions, and a larger picture will take shape. Then challenge the story: Are the characters and situations true? Do you accept the author's view of the world?

Draw conclusions about what you read.

Once you have understood and thought about the events and characters in a story, make judgments about the author's message—the overall picture the author is painting.

Respond to the story.

An important step in understanding a text is identifying your own reaction. Are you puzzled, thrilled, or scared? You may then judge whether your response was intended by the author and how he or she evoked it. Even the most sophisticated critical responses must start with these reactions.

As you read "The Demon Lover," notice the notes along the side. The notes demonstrate how to apply these strategies to your reading.

The DEMON Lover

ELIZABETH BOWEN

Toward the end of her day in London Mrs. Drover went round to her shut-up house to look for several things she wanted to take away. Some belonged to herself, some to her family, who were by now used to their country life. It was late August; it had been a steamy, showery day: at the moment the trees down the pavement glittered in an escape of humid yellow afternoon sun. Against the next batch of clouds, already piling up ink-dark, broken chimneys and parapets stood out. In her once familiar street, as in any unused channel, an unfamiliar queerness had silted up; a cat wove itself in and out of railings, but no human eye watched Mrs. Drover's return. Shifting some parcels under her arm, she slowly forced round her latchkey in an unwilling lock, then gave the door, which had warped, a push with her knee. Dead air came out to meet her as she went in.

The staircase window having been boarded up, no light came down into the hall. But one door, she could just see, stood ajar, so she went quickly through into the room and unshuttered the big window in there. Now the prosaic woman, looking about her, was more perplexed than she knew by everything that she saw, by traces of her long former habit of life—the yellow smoke stain up the white marble mantelpiece, the ring left by a vase on the top of the escritoire,[1] the bruise in the wallpaper where, on the door being thrown open widely, the china handle had always hit the wall. The piano, having gone away to be stored, had left what looked like claw marks on its part of the parquet.[2] Though not much dust had seeped in, each object wore a film of another kind; and, the only ventilation being the chimney, the whole drawing room smelled of the cold hearth. Mrs. Drover put down her parcels on the escritoire and left the room to proceed upstairs; the things she wanted were in a bedroom chest.

She had been anxious to see how the house was—the part-time caretaker she shared with some neighbors was away this week on his holiday, known to be not yet back. At the best of times he did not look in often, and she was never sure that she trusted him. There were some cracks in the structure, left by the last bombing, on which she was anxious to keep an eye. Not that one could do anything—

A shaft of refracted daylight now lay across the hall. She stopped dead and stared at the hall table—on this lay a letter addressed to her.

She thought first—then the caretaker *must* be back. All the same, who, seeing the house shuttered, would have dropped a letter in at the box? It was not a circular, it was not a bill. And the post office redirected, to the address in the country, everything for her that came through the post. The caretaker (even if he *were* back) did not know she was due in

> **Draw an inference** to detect the pattern that Bowen sets up in this passage. Stains, rings, bruises, and claw marks—all repeat the image of a trace—a mark left by a thing now absent.

---

1. **escritoire** (es´ krə twär´) *n*.: A writing desk or table.

2. **parquet** (pär kā´) *n*.: Flooring of inlaid woodwork in geometric forms.

London today—her call here had been planned to be a surprise—so his negligence in the manner of this letter, leaving it to wait in the dusk and the dust, annoyed her. Annoyed, she picked up the letter, which bore no stamp. But it cannot be important, or they would know . . . She took the letter rapidly upstairs with her, without a stop to look at the writing till she reached what had been her bedroom, where she let in light. The room looked over the garden and other gardens: the sun had gone in; as the clouds sharpened and lowered, the trees and rank lawns seemed already to smoke with dark. Her reluctance to look again at the letter came from the fact that she felt intruded upon—and by someone contemptuous of her ways. However, in the tenseness preceding the fall of rain she read it: it was a few lines.

DEAR KATHLEEN,

You will not have forgotten that today is our anniversary, and the day we said. The years have gone by at once slowly and fast. In view of the fact that nothing has changed, I shall rely upon you to keep your promise. I was sorry to see you leave London, but was satisfied that you would be back in time. You may expect me, therefore, at the hour arranged.

Until then . . . K.

As you read about the letter and Mrs. Drover's reaction to it, **note your own response.** Is it fear, curiosity, dread, or suspense?

Mrs. Drover looked for the date: it was today's. She dropped the letter onto the bedsprings, then picked it up to see the writing again—her lips, beneath the remains of lipstick, beginning to go white. She felt so much the change in her own face that she went to the mirror, polished a clear patch in it and looked at once urgently and stealthily in. She was confronted by a woman of forty-four, with eyes starting out under a hatbrim that had been rather carelessly pulled down. She had not put on any more powder since she left the shop where she ate her solitary tea. The pearls her husband had given her on their marriage hung loose round her now rather thinner throat, slipping into the V of the pink wool jumper her sister knitted last autumn as they sat round the fire. Mrs. Drover's most normal expression was one of controlled worry, but of assent. Since the birth of the third of her little boys, attended by a quite serious illness, she had had an intermittent muscular flicker to the left of her mouth, but in spite of this she could always sustain a manner that was at once energetic and calm.

Turning from her own face as precipitately as she had gone to meet it, she went to the chest where the things were, unlocked it, threw up the lid and knelt to search. But as rain began to come crashing down she could not keep from looking over her shoulder at the stripped bed on which the letter lay. Behind the blanket of rain the clock of the church that still stood struck six—with rapidly heightening apprehension she counted each of the slow strokes. "The hour arranged . . . My God," she said, "*What* hour? How should I . . . ? After twenty-five years. . . ."

Question the text to learn from the descriptive details how Mrs. Drover reacts to the letter.

The young girl talking to the soldier in the garden had not ever completely seen his face. It was dark; they were saying goodbye under a tree. Now and then—for it felt, from not seeing him at this intense moment, as though she had never seen him at all—she verified his presence for these few moments longer by putting out a hand, which he each time pressed, without very much kindness, and painfully, on to one of the breast buttons of his uniform. That cut of the button on the palm of her hand was, principally, what she was to carry away. This was so near the end of a leave from France that she could only wish him already gone. It was August 1916. Being not kissed, being drawn away from and looked at intimidated Kathleen till she imagined spectral glitters in the place of his eyes. Turning away and looking back up the lawn she saw, through branches of trees, the drawing-room window alight; she caught a breath for the moment when she could go running back there into the safe arms of her mother and sister, and cry: "What shall I do, what shall I do? He has gone."

Draw inferences to tie together the mark left in Kathleen's palm—a trace of her fiancé's button—with the earlier images of "traces." A ghost is itself a kind of trace—the present mark of a person now absent.

Hearing her catch her breath, her fiancé said, without feeling: "Cold?"

"You're going away such a long way."

"Not so far as you think."

"I don't understand?"

"You don't have to," he said. "You will. You know what we said."

"But that was—suppose you—I mean, suppose."

"I shall be with you," he said, "sooner or later. You won't forget that. You need do nothing but wait."

Draw inferences to understand this strange scene. The fiancé has neither left, nor is he truly, warmly present; Kathleen is ready to miss him, but feels frozen while he lingers. He is already a "ghost"—a trace of her past to which she cannot say goodbye.

Only a little more than a minute later she was free to run up the silent lawn. Looking in through the window at her mother and sister, who did not for the moment perceive her, she already felt that unnatural promise drive down between her and the rest of all humankind. No other way of having given herself could have made her feel so apart, lost and foresworn. She could not have plighted a more sinister troth.

Kathleen behaved well when, some months later, her fiancé was reported missing, presumed killed. Her family not only supported her but were able to praise her courage without stint because they could not regret, as a husband for her, the man they knew almost nothing about. They hoped she would, in a year or two, console herself—and had it been only a question of consolation things might have gone much straighter ahead. But her trouble, behind just a little grief, was a complete dislocation from everything. She did not reject other lovers, for these failed to appear: for years she failed to attract men—and with the approach of her thirties she became natural

enough to share her family's anxiousness on this score. She began to put herself out, to wonder; and at thirty-two she was very greatly relieved to find herself being courted by William Drover. She married him, and the two of them settled down in this quiet, arboreal part of Kensington; in this house the years piled up, her children were born and they all lived till they were driven out by the bombs of the next war. Her movements as Mrs. Drover were circumscribed, and she dismissed any idea that they were still watched.

When Bowen tells you that Kathleen "dismissed" any idea that her movements "were still watched," draw an inference to understand that, before she was married, she felt as if she were being watched.

As things were—dead or living the letter writer sent her only a threat. Unable, for some minutes, to go on kneeling with her back exposed to the empty room, Mrs. Drover rose from the chest to sit on an upright chair whose back was firmly against the wall. The desuetude[3] of her former bedroom, her married London home's whole air of being a cracked cup from which memory, with its reassuring power, had either evaporated or leaked away, made a crisis—and at just this crisis the letter writer had, knowledgeably, struck. The hollowness of the house this evening canceled years on years of voices, habits and steps. Through the shut windows she only heard rain fall on the roofs around. To rally herself, she said she was in a mood—and, for two or three seconds shutting her eyes, told herself that she imagined the letter. But she opened them—there it lay on the bed.

From this passage, you might draw conclusions about how fragile Bowen thinks our identity becomes when we are stripped of our habits and when familiar surroundings become foreign.

On the supernatural side of the letter's entrance she was not permitting her mind to dwell. Who, in London, knew she meant to call at the house today? Evidently, however, this had been known. The caretaker, *had* he come back, had had no cause to expect her: he would have taken the letter in his pocket, to forward it, at his own time, through the post. There was no other sign that the caretaker had been in—but, if not? Letters dropped in at doors of deserted

◆ Build Vocabulary

spectral (spek′ trəl) *adj*.: Ghostly

dislocation (dis′ lō kā′ shən) *n*.: Condition of being out of place; the event of becoming out of place

arboreal (är bôr′ ē′ əl) *adj*.: Of, near, or among trees

circumscribed (sur′ kəm skrībd′) *adj*.: Limited; having a definite boundary

---

3. **desuetude** (des′ wi tōōd′) *adj*.: Condition of not being used any more.

houses do not fly or walk to tables in halls. They do not sit on the dust of empty tables with the air of certainty that they will be found. There is needed some human hand—but nobody but the caretaker had a key. Under circumstances she did not care to consider, a house can be entered without a key. It was possible that she was not alone now. She might be being waited for, downstairs. Waited for—until when? Until "the hour arranged." At least that was not six o'clock; six has struck.

She rose from the chair and went over and locked the door.

The thing was, to get out. To fly? No, not that: she had to catch her train. As a woman whose utter dependability was the keystone of her family life she was not willing to return to the country, to her husband, her little boys and her sister, without the objects she had come up to fetch. Resuming work at the chest she set about making up a number of parcels in a rapid, fumbling-decisive way. These, with her shopping parcels, would be too much to carry; these meant a taxi—at the thought of the taxi her heart went up and her normal breathing resumed. I will ring up the taxi now; the taxi cannot come too soon; I shall hear the taxi out there running its engine, till I walk calmly down to it through the hall. I'll ring up—But no: the telephone is cut off . . . She tugged at a knot she had tied wrong.

> It is not hard to **identify with a character** like Mrs. Drover in this situation. When you are caught up in a panic, do you just run as fast as you can, or do you try to calm your mind and stick to your plans?

The idea of flight . . . He was never kind to me, not really. I don't remember him kind at all. Mother said he never considered me. He was set on me, that was what it was—not love. Not love, not meaning a person well. What did he do, to make me promise like that? I can't remember—But she found that she could.

She remembered with such dreadful acuteness that the twenty-five years since then dissolved like smoke and she instinctively looked for the weal[4] left by the button on the palm of her hand. She remembered not only all that he said and did but the complete suspension of *her* existence during that August week. I was not

4. **weal** *n*.: Raised mark, line, or ridge on the skin caused by an injury.

Ox House, Shaftsbury, 1932, John R. Biggs

▲ **Critical Viewing** Compare the suggestion of "life" this engraving gives to material objects with the role of objects in the story. Are they a threat, a consolation, or indifferent? [**Compare and Contrast**]

myself—they all told me so at the time. She remembered—but with one white burning blank as where acid has dropped on a photograph: *under no conditions* could she remember his face.

So wherever he may be waiting, I shall not know him. You have no time to run from a face you do not expect.

The thing was to get to the taxi before any clock struck what could be the hour. She would slip down the street and round the side of the square to where the square gave on the main road. She would return in the taxi, safe, to her own door, and bring the driver into the house with her to pick up the parcels from room to room. The idea of the taxi driver made her decisive, bold; she unlocked her door, went to the top of the staircase and listened down.

She heard nothing—but while she was hearing nothing the *passé*[5] air of the staircase was disturbed by a draft that traveled up to her face. It emanated from the basement: down there a door or window was being opened by someone who

> Mrs. Drover feels a draft from the basement—a door or window has opened. **Identify with** her feelings at this moment.

5. **passé** (pa sā´) *adj*.: Stale.

◆ Build Vocabulary

aperture (ap´ ər chər) *n*.: Opening

chose this moment to leave the house.

The rain had stopped; the pavements steamily shone as Mrs. Drover let herself out by inches from her own front door into the empty street. The unoccupied houses opposite continued to meet her look with their damaged stare. Making toward the thoroughfare and the taxi, she tried not to keep looking behind. Indeed, the silence was so intense—one of those creeks of London silence exaggerated this summer by the damage of war—that no tread could have gained on hers unheard. Where her street debouched on the square where people went on living, she grew conscious of, and checked, her unnatural pace. Across the open end of the square two buses impassively passed each other; women, a perambulator,[6] cyclists, a man wheeling a barrow signalized, once again, the ordinary flow of life. At the square's most populous corner should be—and was—the short taxi rank. This evening, only one taxi—but this, although it presented its blank rump, appeared already to be alertly waiting for her. Indeed, without looking round the driver started his engine as she panted up from behind and put

___

6. **perambulator** *n.*: Baby carriage.

her hand on the door. As she did so, the clock struck seven. The taxi faced the main road. To make the trip back to her house it would have to turn—she had settled back on the seat and the taxi *had* turned before she, surprised by its knowing movement, recollected that she had not "said where." She leaned forward to scratch at the glass panel that divided the driver's head from her own.

The driver braked to what was almost a stop, turned round and slid the glass panel back. The jolt of this flung Mrs. Drover forward till her face was almost into the glass. Through the aperture driver and passenger, not six inches between them, remained for an eternity eye to eye. Mrs. Drover's mouth hung open for some seconds before she could issue her first scream. After that she continued to scream freely and to beat with her gloved hands on the glass all round as the taxi, accelerating without mercy, made off with her into the hinterland of deserted streets.

> The end of the story might have you on the edge of your seat, or it may lead you to **challenge the text.** Does this scene spoil the story's effect by directly introducing the supernatural?

Guide for Responding

◆ Literature and Your Life

Reader's Response How effective was the ending of the story? Explain.

Thematic Focus In what sense has the war turned ordinary life into an illusion for Mrs. Drover?

☑ Check Your Comprehension

1. Why is Mrs. Drover's house empty?
2. (a) Who has written the letter Mrs. Drover discovers? (b) Why is she so upset by it?
3. Under what circumstances did she last meet the writer of the letter? What effect did their relationship have on her?
4. (a) How does Mrs. Drover plan to escape from the house? (b) Explain whether she succeeds.

◆ Critical Thinking

INTERPRET
1. (a) Identify three points where Mrs. Drover feels that she is being watched. (b) Describe what each adds to the story. **[Infer]**
2. (a) How does the author describe Mrs. Drover's reaction to the letter? (b) What feelings does this description prompt in you? **[Analyze]**
3. Contrast the young Kathleen with Mrs. Drover. **[Compare and Contrast]**
4. What does Mrs. Drover's fate suggest about the importance of habit and the familiar in human life? **[Draw Conclusions]**

APPLY
5. Name a place that is ripe for "haunting." Explain what it shares with wartime London. **[Relate]**

Guide for Responding (continued)

◆ Build Vocabulary

USING THE LATIN ROOT *-loc-*

Apply your knowledge that the Latin root *-loc-* means "place." Write the following sentences, filling in the blanks with a phrase that makes clear the meaning of the italicized word:

1. An animal's method of *locomotion* is its way of ____?____ .
2. The anesthetic is a *local* one; it affects only ____?____ .
3. His company is *relocating*. Will they pay for him to ____?____ ?

USING THE WORD BANK: Denotation

For each of the sentences below, write "correct" if the italicized word is used correctly. If the word is not used correctly, write "incorrect."

1. I was relieved when I reached out and touched, instead of a *spectral* presence, solid flesh and bone.
2. Given the pollution in the world's waterways, I am surprised that more *arboreal* species are not endangered.
3. Take whatever you wish; my generosity is strictly *circumscribed*.
4. The letter fit through the door's *aperture*.
5. The doctor has caused a permanent *dislocation* of your shoulder; you should feel fine in a day or so.

◆ Reading for Success

STRATEGIES FOR READING AND INTERPRETING FICTION

Reading a short story like "The Demon Lover" is like staging a play in your mind. Your "performance" of the story will be more powerful the more fully you explore the text and the wider the conclusions you draw about the author's message.

1. What was your response to the atmosphere Bowen creates at the beginning of the story?
2. (a) Describe Mrs. Drover's character. (b) Do you find her sympathetic? Explain why or why not.
3. (a) What did you expect would happen after Mrs. Drover left the house? (b) Were you surprised by the story's ending? Explain.
4. What conclusions can you draw from the story about Bowen's view of the damage done by war?

◆ Literary Focus

THE GHOST STORY

Ghost stories—tales in which the supernatural may be at work—often create a feeling of dread. This feeling arises from the appearance of the inexplicable or nameless in the midst of the ordinary. A good ghost story may also prevent you from deciding between a natural or a supernatural explanation of events.

1. Describe Mrs. Drover's conflict with the ghost.
2. (a) In the passage describing Mrs. Drover's last meeting with her soldier-lover, name two details suggesting there are supernatural influences at work. Explain your choice. (b) Name two details that make the parting seem psychologically realistic and not supernatural. Explain your choice.
3. Find two passages in the story that contrast the familiar with what is "outside" the familiar. (a) In these passages, what allows the strange to "leak into" the familiar? (b) What do these passages suggest about Bowen's view of the fragility of life?

◆ Grammar and Style

SENTENCE BEGINNINGS: PARTICIPIAL PHRASES

Bowen often begins sentences with **participial phrases,** a participle and all its modifiers and complements, to create variety. For clarity, she places the participial phrase next to the word it modifies.

Writing Application In your notebook, rewrite each of the following sentences so it begins with a participial phrase.

1. The staircase window, boarded up by the owner, let no light come into the hall.
2. The young girl, suddenly halting her conversation, ran from the soldier.
3. The piano, stored for many months, had left what looked like claw marks on the parquet.
4. The cracks in the structure, left by the last bombing, ran vertically down the side of the building.
5. The soldier, entering the lighted room, pulled his hat down to cover his face.

*B*uild *Y*our *P*ortfolio

 ## Idea Bank

Writing

1. **Journal Entry** Write a brief summary of a "ghost" story or movie that you found really scary. Explain which parts you found scariest, and examine what they had in common.

2. **Critical Evaluation** Write a critical review of a movie you have seen or a book you have read dealing with "ghostly" events. Spell out what makes such movies or books enjoyable, then discuss how well the one you are reviewing fits your criteria.

3. **Response to Criticism** "The fantastic," writes critic Tzvetan Todorov, "lasts only as long as a certain hesitation" between supernatural and natural explanations of events. Write an essay showing how Bowen produces this hesitation. **[Literature Link]**

Speaking, Listening, and Viewing

4. **Dramatic Retelling** Choose a ghost tale that you find especially effective. Dim the lights, and give a dramatic reading of this story for your class. **[Performing Arts Link]**

5. **Ballad** The title of Bowen's story comes from a ballad. Find a copy of this or another ballad about a lover and perform it for your class. **[Music Link; Performing Arts Link]**

Researching and Representing

6. **Portrait of the Demon Lover** In a drawing or painting, depict the demon lover, emphasizing the fact that he does not "belong" to this world. **[Visual Arts Link; Social Studies Link]**

7. **Blitz Report** Do library research about the London blitz during World War II. What was life like for the people who stayed in London? **[Social Studies Link]**

Online Activity www.phlit.phschool.com

 ## Guided Writing Lesson

Sequel

In a sense, "The Demon Lover" ends perfectly, yet the story leaves all sorts of loose ends. Write a sequel to "The Demon Lover," answering the question What happened next? An effective sequel weaves parts of the original story in with new events, filling in the reader about what happened in the original without simply retelling it. To ensure that your sequel is connected with the original, use a clear and logical organization.

Writing Skills Focus: Clear and Logical Organization

A sequel, like other kinds of fiction, must weave together past and present. To ensure your readers get a full picture of events, order information in your story using a **clear and logical organization.**

In "The Demon Lover," Bowen waits until Mrs. Drover looks in the mirror to tell us what Mrs. Drover looks like. Bowen's organization is clear— she does not clutter up her descriptions of place and action by telling us what Mrs. Drover looks like. It is also logical. Bowen tells the story from Mrs. Drover's point of view, so the best place to describe Mrs. Drover is when she is looking at herself.

Prewriting To get ideas for your sequel, jot down questions that "The Demon Lover" leaves unanswered. Then outline the events of your story. Note the parts of your story where readers will need to know what happened in Bowen's story in order to understand what is happening in yours.

Drafting As you draft, make sure that you order events in a clear and reasonable way. Choose logical places to give your reader the information about what happened in the original.

Revising Reread your story as if you had never read it. Look for points where only prior knowledge of Bowen's story can help you understand what is happening. Add necessary information.

Guide for Interpreting

William Butler Yeats
(1865–1939)

As the changes of the twentieth century swept away tradition, this poet delved into his nation's mythological past. William Butler Yeats was born in Dublin, Ireland, but his heart lay westward, in the Irish county of Sligo. Here he spent his childhood vacations with his grandparents. It was in the shadow of Sligo's barren mountains that he immersed himself in the magical mythology and legends of Ireland. This experience led to a lifelong enthusiasm for the roots of Irish culture.

Philosophical Influences
After three years of studying painting in Dublin, Yeats moved to London to pursue a literary career. He became a friend of the poet Arthur Symons, who awakened his interest in the symbolic poetry of William Blake and the French Symbolists. Yeats's early poems show the Symbolist influence as well as that of the Pre-Raphaelites, a group of painters and writers who strove for a medieval simplicity and beauty. Symbolism, Pre-Raphaelism, and Irish myth combined in Yeats's first important collection, *The Wanderings of Oisin,* published in 1889.

Political and Personal Influences
In the 1890's, Yeats led the Irish Literary Revival, helping to establish the Irish Literary Society in London and the Irish National Literary Society in Dublin. He also became involved in politics and was a fierce supporter of the movement for Irish independence from England. Perhaps some of this political activity was spurred by Yeats's love for a beautiful Irish actress and revolutionary named Maud Gonne. This attraction lasted his entire life, but it was never reciprocated. To his sorrow—after many refusals of his proposals—she chose a soldier, and Yeats, many years later, married another woman.

From Poetry to Plays to Poetry
As the century turned, Yeats became interested in drama. He joined his friend Lady Augusta Gregory in founding the Irish National Theatre Society. He began writing plays, among them *The Shadowy Waters* (1900) and *Deirdre* (1907). When Yeats returned to poetry, it was with a new voice, subtler and more powerful than the one he had used before. The poems in *The Tower* (1928) show Yeats at the height of his abilities.

Ireland's Hero
In 1922, Yeats was appointed a senator of the new Irish Free State, and on his seventieth birthday he was hailed by his nation as the greatest living Irishman. He kept writing poems until a day or two before his death in France. One of his last poems contains his famous epitaph: "Cast a cold eye / On life, on death. / Horseman, pass by!"

◆ Background for Understanding

CULTURE: YEATS'S IDEAS ABOUT CIVILIZATION AND CULTURE

In 1925, Yeats published *A Vision,* a serious prose work that explained the mythology, symbolism, and philosophy that he strove to express in his poetry. Yeats believed that history occurs in two-thousand-year cycles, during which a particular civilization passes through the stages of birth, growth, and decay. It then gives way to a new civilization that is the direct opposite of it. He thought that twentieth-century society was undergoing the final stages of decay. The birth of Christ had brought about a similar transition two thousand years ago, and Yeats believed that the society of the early twentieth century was in a state of decay that would lead to another sort of rebirth. These ideas appear vividly in the pageant of images in the poem "The Second Coming."

Poetry of William Butler Yeats

◆ *Literature and Your Life*

CONNECT YOUR EXPERIENCE

What transitions do you experience in life? New Year's Eves? Birthdays? Yeats believed that major civilizations occurred in cycles of two-thousand years. He viewed the twentieth century as a transition from one cycle into another.

Journal Writing List a few important dates in your journal and describe how they relate to your life.

THEMATIC FOCUS: WAKING FROM THE DREAM

As you read, notice the poetic dreams—and the historical nightmares—that Yeats describes.

◆ Literary Focus

SYMBOLISM

In literature, a **symbol** is a word, character, object, or action that stands for something beyond itself. The swans in "The Wild Swans at Coole," for example, may symbolize eternal, unchanging life, which the aging speaker knows is denied to him.

The use of symbols allows writers to achieve intensity and complexity in their work. Yeats embraced symbolism in his early poems, abandoned it for a while, then returned to it with enthusiasm, inventing an elaborate symbolic system of his own. In his best poems, the symbols do not require expertise in his system, but only the practiced eye of a careful reader.

◆ Grammar and Style

NOUN CLAUSES

In his poetry, Yeats often uses **noun clauses** to connect one image or complex thought to another. A noun clause is a subordinate clause that functions as a noun. It is used in a sentence in the same way a noun can be used. For example, it might be used as subject, direct object, or object of a preposition.

Noun Clause as Direct Object: Fish, flesh, or fowl, commend all summer long/*Whatever is begotten, born, and dies.*

Noun Clause as Object of a Preposition: To sing . . . / Of *what is past, or passing, or to come.*

◆ Build Vocabulary

LATIN WORD ROOTS: *-ques-*

The Latin root *-ques-* derives from a word meaning "seek." The word *conquest* refers to "a seeking for something by force."

WORD BANK

Preview this list of words from the poems before you read.

clamorous
conquest
anarchy
conviction
paltry
artifice

◆ Reading Strategy

APPLY LITERARY BACKGROUND

No poem is written in a vacuum. Poems are often inspired by a person, a landscape, an experience, or a memory. A writer's knowledge of literature may also become part of a poem and take the form of allusions, or references, to other works. As you read, apply your knowledge of **literary background**—including information about a writer's philosophical beliefs, reading, and personal history—to help you understand as you read.

For example, knowing that Yeats was an admirer of Thoreau may lead you to recognize that "The Lake Isle of Innisfree" was inspired by Yeats's appreciation of *Walden Pond.*

When You Are Old

WILLIAM BUTLER YEATS

When you are old and gray and full of sleep,
And nodding by the fire, take down this book,
And slowly read, and dream of the soft look
Your eyes had once, and of their shadows deep;

5 How many loved your moments of glad grace,
And loved your beauty with love false or true,
But one man loved the pilgrim soul in you,
And loved the sorrows of your changing face;

And bending down beside the glowing bars,
10 Murmur, a little sadly, how Love fled
And paced upon the mountains overhead
And hid his face amid a crowd of stars.

▶ **Critical Viewing** The mood in "When You Are Old" is gentle and bittersweet. What elements in this painting mirror that mood? **[Classify]**

Her Signal, Norman Garstin, The Royal Cornwall Museum, Truro

The Lake Isle of Innisfree

WILLIAM BUTLER YEATS

I will arise and go now, and go to Innisfree,
And a small cabin build there, of clay and wattles[1] made:
Nine bean-rows will I have there, a hive for the honeybee,
And live alone in the bee-loud glade.

5   And I shall have some peace there, for peace comes dropping slow,
Dropping from the veils of the morning to where the cricket sings;
There midnight's all a glimmer, and noon a purple glow,
And evening full of the linnet's wings.[2]

I will arise and go now, for always night and day
10   I hear lake water lapping with low sounds by the shore:
While I stand on the roadway, or on the pavements gray,
I hear it in the deep heart's core.

1. **wattles:** Stakes interwoven with twigs or branches.

2. **linnet's wings:** Wings of a European singing bird.

Guide for Responding

◆ Literature and Your Life

Reader's Response With which poem's speaker do you identify more? Explain.

Thematic Focus What outer forces might inspire a poet to long for the dreamlike serenity of these poems?

Journal Writing Are you attracted, like Yeats, to the solitude and "bee-loud" quiet of Innisfree? Explain why or why not.

☑ Check Your Comprehension

1. In "When You Are Old," what does the speaker ask the reader to do?
2. (a) In "The Lake Isle of Innisfree," what does the speaker want most to find at Innisfree?
   (b) How will each of the four times of day he mentions contribute to his goal?

◆ Critical Thinking

INTERPRET

1. Who is the "one man" in the second stanza of "When You Are Old"? Explain. **[Interpret]**
2. What does the phrase "pilgrim soul" in "When You Are Old" suggest about the person being addressed? **[Infer]**
3. In "Innisfree," does the speaker intend to leave for Innisfree immediately? Explain. **[Deduce]**
4. What does Innisfree offer that the speaker does not find where he is now? **[Infer]**
5. How do these poems suggest that devotion to art makes up for disappointments? **[Support]**

APPLY

6. Name a contemporary song that deals with the desire to leave for another place. Compare this place to Innisfree. **[Relate]**

The Wild Swans at Coole

WILLIAM BUTLER YEATS

The trees are in their autumn beauty,
The woodland paths are dry,
Under the October twilight the water
Mirrors a still sky;
5   Upon the brimming water among the stones
Are nine-and-fifty swans.

The nineteenth autumn has come upon me
Since I first made my count;
I saw, before I had well finished,
10   All suddenly mount
And scatter wheeling in great broken rings
Upon their <u>clamorous</u> wings.

I have looked upon those brilliant creatures,
And now my heart is sore.
15   All's changed since I, hearing at twilight,
The first time on this shore,
The bell-beat of their wings above my head,
Trod with a lighter tread.

Unwearied still, lover by lover,
20   They paddle in the cold
Companionable streams or climb the air;
Their hearts have not grown old;
Passion or <u>conquest</u>, wander where they will,
Attend upon them still.

25   But now they drift on the still water,
Mysterious, beautiful;
Among what rushes will they build,
By what lake's edge or pool
Delight men's eyes when I awake some day
30   To find they have flown away?

▶ **Critical Viewing**
Why might a poet like
Yeats describe swans
such as these as
"mysterious" and
"beautiful"? **[Infer]**

◆ **Build Vocabulary**

clamorous (klam´ ər əs) *adj*.: Loud
and confused; noisy

conquest (kän´ kwest´) *n*.: The
winning of another's affection or
favor

Guide for Responding

◆ Literature and Your Life

Reader's Response In what ways do beautiful, wild animals remind you, as the swans remind the speaker, of the mysteries of human life?

Thematic Focus How is the speaker's realization that time is passing like an awakening?

☑ Check Your Comprehension

1. For how many years has the speaker been coming to Coole and counting the swans?
2. What is different in the speaker's state since he first heard the "bell-beat" of swans' wings?
3. What may the speaker awaken to find one day?

◆ Critical Thinking

INTERPRET

1. For what thematic purpose does the speaker emphasize the setting in the first two stanzas? **[Interpret]**
2. (a) What is the speaker doing in the second stanza when the swans take flight? (b) How does their sudden flight affect him? **[Infer]**
3. According to stanza three, why is the speaker unhappy? **[Interpret]**
4. What might the swans symbolize to the speaker? **[Draw Conclusions]**

COMPARE LITERARY WORKS

5. Return to each of Yeats's poems and choose lines or symbols that suggest what is abiding or eternal. **[Connect]**

The Second Coming

WILLIAM BUTLER YEATS

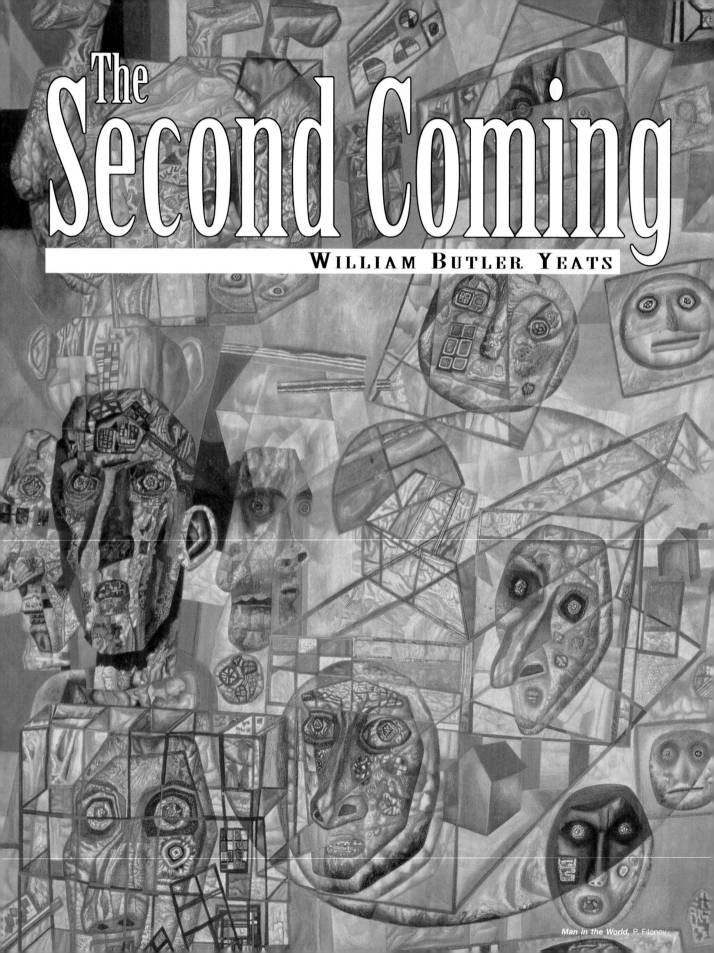

Man in the World, P. Filonov

Yeats believed that history occurs in two-thousand-year cycles. The birth of Christ ended one cycle and began another, and now a similar transition was about to occur.

Turning and turning in the widening gyre
The falcon cannot hear the falconer;
Things fall apart; the center cannot hold;
Mere anarchy is loosed upon the world,
5 The blood-dimmed tide is loosed, and everywhere
The ceremony of innocence is drowned;
The best lack all conviction, while the worst
Are full of passionate intensity.[1]

Surely some revelation is at hand;
10 Surely the Second Coming is at hand.
The Second Coming! Hardly are those words out
When a vast image out of Spiritus Mundi[2]
Troubles my sight: somewhere in sands of the desert
A shape with lion body and the head of a man,[3]
15 A gaze blank and pitiless as the sun,
Is moving its slow thighs, while all about it
Reel shadows of the indignant desert birds.
The darkness drops again; but now I know
That twenty centuries[4] of stony sleep
20 Were vexed to nightmare by a rocking cradle,[5]
And what rough beast, its hour come round at last,
Slouches towards Bethlehem to be born?

1. **Mere . . . intensity:** Refers to the Russian Revolution of 1917.

2. **Spiritus Mundi** (spir´ i təs moon´dē): Universal Spirit or Soul, in which the memories of the entire human race are forever preserved.
3. **A . . . man:** Sphinx.
4. **twenty centuries:** Historical cycle preceding the birth of Christ.
5. **rocking cradle:** Cradle of Jesus Christ.

◆ **Build Vocabulary**

anarchy (an´ ər kē) *n.*: Absence of government; confusion, disorder, and violence

conviction (kən´ vik´ shən) *n.*: Belief in something meaningful, such as a creed

Guide for Responding

◆ *Literature and Your Life*

Reader's Response Do you agree that in the modern world "things fall apart"?

Thematic Focus Explain how the first stanza can be said to represent "waking from a dream."

☑ Check Your Comprehension

1. Why does the falcon not return to the falconer, as it ordinarily would?
2. In the first stanza of "The Second Coming," what is happening to innocence?
3. What does the speaker believe is at hand?
4. (a) In stanza two, of "The Second Coming," what has begun to stir in the desert? (b) What is about to be born?

◆ Critical Thinking

INTERPRET
1. What imagery is used in lines 5–6 of "The Second Coming"? [Analyze]
2. When did the "twenty centuries of stony sleep" (line 19) occur? [Interpret]
3. (a) What would you expect to appear at the Second Coming? (b) How does that differ from what the speaker suggests will appear? [Draw Conclusions]

EXTEND
4. Chinua Achebe titled his novel *Things Fall Apart,* using the phrase from line 3 of "The Second Coming." What might the book be about, based on its title? [Literature Link]

SAILING to BYZANTIUM

WILLIAM BUTLER YEATS

I

That is no country for old men. The young
In one another's arms, birds in the trees
—Those dying generations—at their song,
The salmon-falls, the mackerel-crowded seas,
5   Fish, flesh, or fowl, commend all summer long
Whatever is begotten, born, and dies.
Caught in that sensual music all neglect
Monuments of unaging intellect.

II

An aged man is but a <u>paltry</u> thing,
10   A tattered coat upon a stick, unless
Soul clap its hands and sing, and louder sing
For every tatter in its mortal dress,
Nor is there singing school but studying
Monuments of its own magnificence;
15   And therefore I have sailed the seas and come
To the holy city of Byzantium.[1]

III

O sages standing in God's holy fire
As in the gold mosaic of a wall,[2]
Come from the holy fire, perne in a gyre,[3]
20   And be the singing-masters of my soul.
Consume my heart away; sick with desire
And fastened to a dying animal
It knows not what it is; and gather me
Into the <u>artifice</u> of eternity.

IV

25   Once out of nature I shall never take
My bodily form from any natural thing,
But such a form as Grecian goldsmiths make
Of hammered gold and gold enameling
To keep a drowsy Emperor awake;
30   Or set upon a golden bough to sing[4]
To lords and ladies of Byzantium
Of what is past, or passing, or to come.

1. Byzantium (bi zan´ shē əm): Ancient capital of the Eastern Roman (or Byzantine) Empire and the seat of the Greek Orthodox Church; today, Istanbul, Turkey. For Yeats, it symbolized the world of art as opposed to the world of time and nature.

2. sages . . . wall: Wise old men and saints portrayed in gold mosaic on the walls of Byzantine churches.

3. perne . . . gyre: Spin in a spiraling motion.

4. To . . . sing: Yeats wrote, "I have read somewhere that in the Emperor's palace at Byzantium was a tree made of gold and silver, and artificial birds that sang."

◆ Build Vocabulary

paltry (pôl´ trē) *adj.*: Practically worthless; insignificant

artifice (ärt´ə fis) *n.*: Skill or ingenuity

Ravenna: City and Port of Classis. Mosaic, late 6th century, from Basilica of St. Apollinare Nuovo

▲ **Critical Viewing** In what way do the colors and textures of this mosaic convey the idea that the ships have arrived at a wondrous place? [Interpret]

Guide for Responding

◆ *Literature and Your Life*

Reader's Response Do you think it is possible to escape the effects of time? Explain.

Thematic Focus In your view, which is a "dream," Byzantium or the world of begetting? Explain.

☑ Check Your Comprehension

1. (a) What do the people and things of the country referred to in the first stanza "commend"?
   (b) What do they neglect?
2. What does the speaker ask of the sages in the third stanza?

◆ Critical Thinking

INTERPRET

1. How does Byzantium contrast with the country described in the first two stanzas?
   [Compare and Contrast]
2. (a) What do stanzas 3 and 4 reveal about the speaker's attitude toward aging and death?
   (b) How does he hope to immortalize himself?
   [Interpret]
3. What does this poem suggest about the motives of artists and the purpose of art?
   [Draw Conclusions]

Guide for Responding (continued)

◆ Literary Focus

SYMBOLISM

Symbolism—the use of words, images, or characters to stand for something else—is found throughout many of Yeats's poems. The skillful use of symbolism gives literature complexity and allows the writer to show readers ways in which aspects of humanity and the world interrelate.

For example, in "The Second Coming," the falcon flying in circles represents, or symbolizes, something. To interpret this symbol, it helps to understand Yeats's theory about "gyres," or cycles, but the information is not necessary for an understanding.

1. Yeats does not only write about twenty centuries of stony sleep, he also symbolizes them.
(a) What symbol does he use? (b) Why do you think he presents it through a description of its features rather than by naming it directly?

2. (a) What symbolism, if any, do you find in line 6 of "The Second Coming"? (b) What might the "indignant desert birds" in line 17 represent?

3. (a) In "Sailing to Byzantium," Yeats refers to monuments, once in line 8 and again in line 14. What might the word *monument* symbolize? (b) Find two examples in this poem of Yeats using Byzantine art to symbolize perfection.

◆ Build Vocabulary

USING THE LATIN ROOT -ques-

Knowing that the Latin root -ques- means "to seek," write a definition for each word, showing how the root affects its meaning:

1. quest   3. request
2. inquest   4. question

USING THE WORD BANK: Synonyms

On your paper, write the letter of the word whose meaning is closest to that of the first word.
1. clamorous: (a) angry, (b) peaceful, (c) loud
2. conviction: (a) belief, (b) system, (c) violence
3. artifice: (a) greed, (b) beauty, (c) ingenuity
4. paltry: (a) magnificent, (b) trivial, (c) lying
5. anarchy: (a) peace, (b) cold, (c) disorder
6. conquest: (a) victory, (b) failure, (c) riches

◆ Reading Strategy

APPLY LITERARY BACKGROUND

As you read, apply your knowledge of **literary background** to help you to identify a poem's speaker, who is being addressed, references or allusions within the poem, a speaker's attitude, and other important information.

1. (a) What event in Yeats's life might have inspired him to write "When You Are Old"? (b) In line 2, the speaker advises the person being addressed to "take down this book." How might that advice furnish a clue to the speaker's identity?

2. (a) How does knowing the time period of "The Second Coming" help you to understand what's being referred to in stanza one? (b) In what ways do Yeats's ideas about cycles of civilization find their way into lines 18–22?

3. (a) How does knowing the age of Yeats at the time "Sailing to Byzantium" was written help you to understand its theme? (b) In what ways does Yeats's admiration for the "impersonal" qualities of Byzantine art find its way into this poem?

◆ Grammar and Style

NOUN CLAUSES

Noun clauses, subordinate clauses that function as nouns, help writers to vary sentence length and tie ideas together. Noun clauses can be used as the subject, direct object, or object of a preposition.

Practice Identify the noun clause and its function in each of the following passages.
1. Dropping from the veils of the morning to where the cricket sings . . .
2. It knows not what it is . . .
3. [D]ream . . . how many loved your moments of peace . . .

Writing Application Write a sentence using the given clause in the function indicated.
1. What the Irish National Movement sought . . . (subject)
2. . . . that the twentieth century was witnessing the decay of civilization. (direct object)

Build Your Portfolio

 Idea Bank

Writing

1. **Description** Yeats admired Byzantium, which is modern-day Istanbul. Write a brief description of a city or culture you admire, and explain why.

2. **Essay** Does the late twentieth century really signal the end of an era? Write an essay, using examples to support your opinion.

3. **Response to Criticism** Scholar Reuben A. Brower wrote that Yeats succeeded "by letting his dreamlike symbols materialize to express and connect conflict he could never resolve outside his poetry." This suggests that Yeats had no solutions for world problems. Write an essay in which you agree or disagree with this view.

Speaking, Listening, and Viewing

4. **Irish Poetry** Yeats led the Irish literary revival of the late nineteenth and early twentieth centuries. Research some Irish poets who were inspired by this rebirth and perform some of their poems for the class. **[Performing Arts Link]**

5. **Music and Swans** Yeats's fascination with swans was shared by many artists, including a number of composers. Play Tchaikovsky's *Swan Lake* and Saint-Saens's *Carnival of the Animals* for the class and explain how swans inspired these artists. **[Music Link]**

Researching and Representing

6. **Yeats Timeline** Create a bulletin board display of Yeats's life, unified by a timeline, with visuals representing some of the key events of his life. **[Social Studies Link]**

7. **Byzantium** Research and present a visual display showing Byzantium's treasures. **[Social Studies Link]**

Online Activity www.phlit.phschool.com

 Guided Writing Lesson

Prediction Essay

Yeats believed that the twentieth century would witness the end of one civilization (its 2,000-year span being up) and the twenty-first century would witness the birth of a new one. What will the twenty-first century, our new millennium, be like? Write an essay detailing your predictions. Before you begin, think about who will read your prediction.

Writing Skills Focus: Knowledge Level of Readers

Good writers always keep their **audience**, or readers, in mind as they write, choosing details that will interest them and that suit their knowledge of the subject. For example, if you were writing your prediction for very young readers, you'd use a different style and include different information than you would if you wrote this essay for your peers.

Yeats's "The Second Coming," for example, is appropriate for an audience that is familiar with Christianity, mythology, and the idea of the Second Coming of Christ.

Prewriting Before you write, jot down a list of ideas you have about the new millennium. Decide on your likely audience, and choose details that will grab their interest and suit their level of understanding.

Drafting Choose a format or organizational style and begin drafting. As you write, keep your audience in mind. Thoroughly explain any references or ideas with which they may not be familiar.

Revising Revise your prediction, adjusting your word choice where necessary to suit your audience. Then review your writing for style and consider combining some of your shorter sentences using noun clauses.

To learn more about **noun clauses** and how writers use them, see p. 897.

Guide for Interpreting

T. S. Eliot *(1888–1965)*

T. S. Eliot was the most famous English poet of his time. He also was the most influential. His style and his ideas influenced not only poets, but also critics, fiction writers, playwrights, and thinkers in many fields besides literature. From the 1920's on, he was the leader of what is called the Modernist movement. With fellow poet Ezra Pound, he rejected the outdated Romantic tradition. Together they transformed English poetry, making it more responsive to the nervous energy of a new era.

Crossing the Atlantic Eliot had ties to both the United States and Great Britain. Born Thomas Stearns Eliot in St. Louis, Missouri, he was educated at Harvard. However, he also studied at Oxford University in England and at the Sorbonne in Paris. The outbreak of World War I found Eliot in England, where he remained throughout most of his adult life, eventually becoming a British citizen.

Early Work Eliot's earliest work, owing to its unconventional style, was greeted with less than universal acclaim, although the poet Ezra Pound was a vocal supporter from the beginning. Pound saw, as many did not, that Eliot spoke in an authentic new voice and offered an original, if bleak, vision. From *Prufrock and Other Observations* (1917) through *The Waste Land* (1922) and "The Hollow Men" (1925), Eliot portrayed the fragmented, despairing modern world. In part, Eliot may have been responding to the events surrounding World War I. However, work like "Preludes" and "The Love Song of J. Alfred Prufrock" predated the war.

A Spiritual Rebirth Gradually, religion provided hope and led him in 1927 to join the Church of England. His faith shaped the writing of "Journey of the Magi" (1927), "Ash Wednesday" (1930), and the *Four Quartets* (1943), completed during World War II.

As he grew older, Eliot turned his attention to poetic drama and criticism. Although *Murder in the Cathedral* (1935) and *The Cocktail Party* (1950) are often performed, none of his plays have gained the critical admiration accorded his poetry. As a literary critic, Eliot had a profound influence on his contemporaries. His *Notes Towards the Definition of Culture* appeared in 1948, the year in which he received the Nobel Prize for Literature.

Poet's Corner On the second anniversary of Eliot's death (1967), a memorial was unveiled in Poet's Corner, Westminster Abbey. The descendant of Andrew Eliot, who had journeyed to America in the 1700's, was now home.

◆ Background for Understanding

LITERATURE: ELIOT'S ALLUSIONS

In his work, Eliot often uses allusions—indirect references to well-known people, places, or events from the past, or to works of literature. "Journey of the Magi," for instance, is a dramatic monologue spoken by one of the three "wise men" who visited the infant Jesus. In the poem, the speaker uses the conversational language of today to describe historic events. In this way, the spiritual agony of a man who lived long ago becomes vividly present.

In a different vein, Eliot's allusions at the beginning of "The Hollow Men" help him contrast the past and the present. "A penny for the Old Guy" is a traditional cry of children on Guy Fawkes Day. Fawkes (1570–1606) was executed for attempting to blow up the king and Parliament in 1605. He was one of the "lost/ Violent souls" (lines 15–16) of the past who contrast with "the hollow men" of the modern world.

Preludes ◆ Journey of the Magi
◆ The Hollow Men ◆

◆ Literature and Your Life

CONNECT YOUR EXPERIENCE

Suppose you want to make a short video to go with a song performed by a rock band. You try to remember mixed-up images from a dream so you can use them for your script—but putting them together so they make sense turns out to be hard work!

The use of quick-changing, dreamlike images is a technique modern poets invented long before movie special effects and MTV, as you'll see in T. S. Eliot's poems.

Journal Writing Write down the images you can recall from a music video. What links these images together?

THEMATIC FOCUS: WAKING FROM THE DREAM

How did Eliot's use of dreamlike images help readers awaken to the realities of twentieth-century life?

◆ Literary Focus

MODERNISM

Modernism in art began with the rejection of Realism. Modernists felt that democracy and industrialism had created a depressing, fragmented world. Rather than creating realistic pictures of this world, they treated it as mere raw material, to be made beautiful by art. Poetry would work on this "material" with its own suggestive language, full of images, musical and indirect.

In the "Preludes," for example, Eliot hints at his meanings through images like this one: "The showers beat/On broken blinds ..." Such images indirectly express his vision of a sad, ugly, modern world that results from a loss of spiritual life.

◆ Reading Strategy

INTERPRET

Because it often suggests themes rather than stating them directly, modernist literature makes greater demands on readers. It asks you to **interpret** meanings by linking different passages in a work and drawing conclusions from the patterns you find.

To interpret "The Hollow Men," you might consider the connotations of the words Eliot uses to describe these men—words like "hollow," "stuffed," "dried," and "broken." Ask yourself what the words suggest about the life these men are leading.

◆ Build Vocabulary

LATIN ROOTS: -fract-

In "Journey of the Magi," Eliot describes camels as *refractory*, meaning "stubborn" or "hard to control." The Latin root -fract- means "to break." A refractory animal is one that "breaks away" from the direction in which you want it to go.

WORD BANK

Before you read, preview this list of words from the poems.

galled
refractory
dispensation
supplication
tumid

◆ Grammar and Style

ADJECTIVAL MODIFIERS

Different types of structures act as adjectives. Among the structures that Eliot uses as **adjectival modifiers** are the following:

Prepositional Phrase:

The burnt-out ends *of smoky days*

The prepositional phrase *of smoky days* modifies *ends*.

Participial Phrase:

Headpiece *filled with straw*

The participial phrase *filled with straw* modifies *headpiece*.

Adjective Clause:

... hands *that are raising dingy shades*

The adjective clause *that are raising dingy shades* modifies *hands*.

Preludes

T. S. ELIOT

I

The winter evening settles down
With smell of steaks[1] in passageways.
Six o'clock.
The burnt-out ends of smoky days.
5   And now a gusty shower wraps
The grimy scraps
Of withered leaves about your feet
And newspapers from vacant lots;
The showers beat
10 On broken blinds and chimney-pots,
And at the corner of the street
A lonely cab-horse steams and stamps.
And then the lighting of the lamps.

II

The morning comes to consciousness
15 Of faint stale smells of beer
From the sawdust-trampled street
With all its muddy feet that press
To early coffee-stands.
With the other masquerades
20 That time resumes,
One thinks of all the hands
That are raising dingy shades
In a thousand furnished rooms.

---

1. **steaks:** In 1910, when this poem was composed, steaks were inexpensive and were commonly eaten by members of the lower class.

III

You tossed a blanket from the bed,
25　You lay upon your back, and waited;
You dozed, and watched the night revealing
The thousand sordid images
Of which your soul was constituted;
They flickered against the ceiling.
30　And when all the world came back
And the light crept up between the shutters
And you heard the sparrows in the gutters,
You had such a vision of the street
As the street hardly understands;
35　Sitting along the bed's edge, where
You curled the papers from your hair,
Or clasped the yellow soles of feet
In the palms of both soiled hands.

IV

His soul stretched tight across the skies
40　That fade behind a city block,
Or trampled by insistent feet
At four and five and six o'clock;
And short square fingers stuffing pipes,
And evening newspapers, and eyes
45　Assured of certain certainties,
The conscience of a blackened street
Impatient to assume the world.

I am moved by fancies that are curled
Around these images, and cling:
50　The notion of some infinitely gentle
Infinitely suffering thing.

Wipe your hands across your mouth, and laugh;
The worlds revolve like ancient women
Gathering fuel in vacant lots.

Journey of the Magi

T. S. ELIOT

*In this poem, the speaker, one of the three wise men
who traveled to Bethlehem to pay homage to the baby
Jesus, reflects upon the meaning of the journey.*

"A cold coming we had of it,
Just the worst time of the year
For a journey, and such a long journey:
The ways deep and the weather sharp,
5 The very dead of winter."[1]
And the camels galled, sore-footed, refractory,
Lying down in the melting snow.
There were times we regretted
The summer palaces on slopes, the terraces,
10 And the silken girls bringing sherbet.
Then the camel men cursing and grumbling
And running away, and wanting their liquor and women,
And the night-fires going out, and the lack of shelters,
And the cities hostile and the towns unfriendly
15 And the villages dirty and charging high prices:
A hard time we had of it.
At the end we preferred to travel all night,
Sleeping in snatches,
With the voices singing in our ears, saying
20 That this was all folly.

1. "A . . . winter":
Adapted from a part of a
sermon delivered by 17th-
century Bishop Lancelot
Andrews: "A cold coming
they had of it at this time
of year, just the worst time
of the year to take a journey, and specially a long
journey in. The ways deep,
the weather sharp, the
days short, the sun farthest
off . . . the very dead of
winter."

Then at dawn we came down to a temperate valley,
Wet, below the snow line, smelling of vegetation;
With a running stream and a water-mill beating the darkness,
And three trees on the low sky,
25 And an old white horse galloped away in the meadow.
Then we came to a tavern with vine-leaves over the lintel,
Six hands at an open door dicing for pieces of silver,
And feet kicking the empty wine-skins.
But there was no information, and so we continued
30 And arrived at evening, not a moment too soon
Finding the place; it was (you may say) satisfactory.

All this was a long time ago, I remember,
And I would do it again, but set down
This set down
35 This: were we led all that way for
Birth or Death? There was a Birth, certainly,
We had evidence and no doubt. I had seen birth and death,
But had thought they were different; this Birth was
Hard and bitter agony for us, like Death, our death.
40 We returned to our places, these Kingdoms,
But no longer at ease here, in the old dispensation,
With an alien people clutching their gods.
I should be glad of another death.

◆ **Build Vocabulary**

galled (gôld) *adj.*: Injured or made sore by rubbing or chafing

refractory (ri frak´ tər ē) *adj.*: Hard to manage; stubborn

dispensation (dis´ pən sā´ shən) *n.*: Religious system or belief

Guide for Responding

◆ Literature and Your Life

Reader's Response Does Eliot make beauty from ugliness in these poems? Explain.

Thematic Focus In what sense are the speakers in these poems awakened from a dream?

☑ Check Your Comprehension

1. In Prelude I, what is (a) the time of year, and (b) the time of day?
2. In Prelude II, what is taking place "in a thousand furnished rooms"?
3. Describe four problems encountered by the speaker in "Journey of the Magi."

◆ Critical Thinking

INTERPRET

1. What cycle of time do you find in the movement from Prelude I to Prelude IV? **[Connect]**
2. What is the "infinitely gentle/Infinitely suffering thing" (lines 50–51) in "Preludes"? Explain. **[Interpret]**
3. Consider the Magi's own religious traditions in "Journey." (a) Why is "this Birth . . . like Death" for them? (b) Why is the speaker "no longer at ease" (line 41) back home? **[Draw Conclusions]**

COMPARE LITERARY WORKS

4. Compare the first stanzas of "Preludes" and "The Gift of the Magi," and describe what you think Eliot was trying to achieve in each case with such gritty realism. **[Distinguish]**

The Hollow MEN

T. S. ELIOT

Mistah Kurtz[1]—he dead.

A penny for the Old Guy[2]

I

We are the hollow men
We are the stuffed men
Leaning together
Headpiece filled with straw. Alas!
5   Our dried voices, when
We whisper together
Are quiet and meaningless
As wind in dry grass
Or rats' feet over broken glass
10 In our dry cellar

Shape without form, shade without color,
Paralyzed force, gesture without motion;

Those who have crossed
With direct eyes, to death's other Kingdom[3]
15 Remember us—if at all—not as lost
Violent souls, but only
As the hollow men
The stuffed men.

1. **Mistah Kurtz:** Character in Joseph Conrad's "Heart of Darkness" who hopes to improve the lives of native Africans, but he finds instead that he is corrupted by his power over them.

2. **A . . . Guy:** Traditional cry used by children on Guy Fawkes Day (November 5), celebrating the execution of a famous English traitor of the same name. The "Old Guy" refers to stuffed dummies representing Fawkes.

3. **Those . . . kingdom:** Allusion to Dante's *Paradiso*, in which those "with direct eyes" are blessed by God in Heaven.

II

    Eyes I dare not meet in dreams
20 In death's dream kingdom
    These do not appear:
    There, the eyes are
    Sunlight on a broken column
    There, is a tree swinging
25 And voices are
    In the wind's singing
    More distant and more solemn
    Than a fading star.
    Let me be no nearer
30 In death's dream kingdom
    Let me also wear
    Such deliberate disguises
    Rat's coat, crowskin, crossed staves
    In a field[4]
35 Behaving as the wind behaves
    No nearer—

    Not that final meeting
    In the twilight kingdom

4. crossed . . . field: Scarecrows.

III

    This is the dead land
40 This is cactus land
    Here the stone images
    Are raised, here they receive
    The supplication of a dead man's hand
    Under the twinkle of a fading star.

45 Is it like this
    In death's other kingdom
    Waking alone
    At the hour when we are
    Trembling with tenderness
50 Lips that would kiss
    Form prayers to broken stone.

◆ **Build Vocabulary**

supplication (sup´ lə kā´ shən) *n*.: Act of praying

IV

The eyes are not here
There are no eyes here
In this valley of dying stars
55 In this hollow valley
This broken jaw of our lost kingdoms

In this last of meeting places
We grope together
And avoid speech
60 Gathered on this beach of the tumid river[5]

Sightless, unless
The eyes reappear
As the perpetual star[6]
Multifoliate rose[7]
65 Of death's twilight kingdom
The hope only
Of empty men.

V

Here we go round the prickly pear
Prickly pear prickly pear
70 Here we go round the prickly pear
At five o'clock in the morning.[8]

Between the idea
And the reality
Between the motion
75 And the act[9]
Falls the Shadow

For Thine is the Kingdom[10]

Between the conception
And the creation
80 Between the emotion
And the response
Falls the Shadow

5. **river:** From Dante's *Inferno*, the river Acheron, which the dead cross on the way to Hell.

6. **star:** Traditional symbol for Christ.

7. **Multifoliate rose:** Rose with many leaves. Dante describes paradise as such a rose in his *Paradiso*. The rose is a traditional symbol for the Virgin Mary.

8. **Here . . . morning:** Adaptation of a common nursery rhyme. A prickly pear is a cactus.

9. **Between . . . act:** Reference to *Julius Caesar*, Act II, Scene i, 63–65: "Between the acting of a dreadful thing/And the first motion, all the interim is/Like a phantasma or hideous dream."

10. **For . . . Kingdom:** From the ending of the Lord's Prayer.

11. **Life . . . long:** Quotation from Joseph Conrad's *An Outcast of the Islands*.

◆ **Build Vocabulary**

tumid (too′ mid) *adj.*: Swollen

Life is very long[11]

11. Life . . . long:
Quotation from Joseph
Conrad's *An Outcast of
the Islands*.

Between the desire
85   And the spasm
Between the potency
And the existence
Between the essence
And the descent
90   Falls the Shadow

For Thine is the Kingdom

For Thine is
Life is
For Thine is the

95   *This is the way the world ends*
This is the way the world ends
This is the way the world ends
Not with a bang but a whimper.

Guide for Responding

◆ Literature and Your Life

Reader's Response If you wanted to make a music video of this poem, what images from it would you use? Why?

Thematic Focus What do you think the hollow men fear in "death's dream kingdom"?

☑ Check Your Comprehension

1. What images describe the hollow men in the first ten lines?
2. Describe "death's dream kingdom" and "the dead land," the landscapes of this poem.
3. What is it that forever falls between idea and achievement, preventing the hollow men from accomplishing anything?
4. In the line, "Here we go round the prickly pear," what action is being described?
5. How does the poem's last line say the world will end?

◆ Critical Thinking

INTERPRET
1. What do the images of wind in parts I and II suggest about the hollow men? **[Infer]**
2. Why are Kurtz, a "hollow sham," and Guy Fawkes, a traitor, superior to the hollow men? **[Interpret]**
3. Why are the hollow men afraid of the "eyes" (lines 14, 19, 52)? **[Interpret]**
4. What do the fragments of prayer in the last part of the poem suggest about the hollow men? **[Draw Conclusions]**

EVALUATE
5. Is the nursery rhyme that Eliot uses in part V (lines 68–71, 95–98) effective in conveying the speakers' plight? Explain. **[Criticize]**

APPLY
6. What would you say makes someone a whole person rather than a hollow one? **[Apply]**

Critical Commentary on "The Hollow Men"

How It Was Written

T.S. Eliot had written a long poem called *The Waste Land*. He used sections that had been edited out of *The Waste Land* as the basis for "The Hollow Men." He often worked this way, building a poem from pieces that had been written independently and using discarded fragments of one poem to create the next.

He explained this process of working in a craft interview with Donald Hall (*The Paris Review*, No. 21). Hall begins this part of the interview by pointing out that two minor poems of Eliot's, probably "Eyes that last I saw in tears" and "The wind sprang up at four o'clock," sound to him like "The Hollow Men":

Interviewer. Are any of your minor poems actually sections cut out of longer works? There are two that sound like "The Hollow Men."

Eliot. Oh, those were the preliminary sketches. Those things were earlier. Others I published in periodicals but not in my collected poems . . .

Interviewer. You seem often to have written poems in sections. Did they begin as separate poems? I am thinking of "Ash Wednesday," in particular.

Eliot. Yes, like "The Hollow Men," it originated out of separate poems. As I recall, one or two early drafts of parts of "Ash Wednesday" appeared in *Commerce* [a magazine] and elsewhere. Then gradually I came to see it as a sequence. That's one way in which my mind does seem to have worked throughout the years poetically—doing things separately and then seeing the possibility of fusing them together, altering them, and making a kind of whole of them.

The Theme of "The Hollow Men"

It makes sense to assume that "The Hollow Men," which uses fragments discarded from *The Waste Land*, is thematically related to this earlier, longer poem. *The Waste Land*, as the word "waste" in its title suggests, deals with a sense of emotional and spiritual barrenness after the destruction wrought by World War I. (Eliot wrote the poem in 1921 and 1922.) Throughout the poem, however, Eliot uses allusions to past works of literature in order to compare the present with other historical moments. "The Hollow Men," published in 1925, also deals with a barren and empty (hollow) existence. Although it is quieter than *The Waste Land* and less rhythmically varied, it resembles the earlier poem in its use of literary allusions to convey this theme of barrenness and to compare the present with other historical eras.

Using Allusions to Interpret the Poem

Critics have identified four key allusions in the poem:

- Joseph Conrad's story "Heart of Darkness"
- A historical reference to the Gunpowder Plot of 1605, in which Guy Fawkes and other Catholics seeking revenge for the anti-Catholic laws of

James I plotted to blow up the king and Parliament

- Shakespeare's *Julius Caesar*, with its account of the assassination of Caesar
- Dante's *Divine Comedy*, a medieval Italian poem which describes the three realms of the afterlife according to Roman Catholic belief: inferno, purgatory, and paradise

More details about these allusions appear in specific footnotes to the poem. The following information explains how to use the allusions to build meaning from this difficult work.

Joseph Conrad's "Heart of Darkness"

Kurtz, referred to in a line introducing the poem, is a mysterious character in Conrad's "Heart of Darkness." He travels to the Belgian Congo on a mission to uplift and educate the Congolese people. However, he develops his own little kingdom in which he exercises absolute power over the people he intended to save. It is only when he is dying that he sees the "horror" of what he has done and how he has been, in Conrad's words, a "hollow sham," or fake. Yet Kurtz is in some ways the best of the white men that Conrad's narrator encounters. His tragic downfall, therefore, exposes the hollowness of his noble ideals and of the whole colonial enterprise. That enterprise is supported by a host of administrators and clerks who seem like ghosts wandering in a twilight world. It is these men who are most like the speakers in Eliot's poem, a chorus of paralyzed nonentities: "We are the hollow men. . . ." Eliot may also be suggesting that this chorus includes his readers.

The Gunpowder Plot

The hollow men are also like the effigies of Guy Fawkes burned to commemorate the uncovering of the Gunpowder Plot. Fawkes himself was tortured until he revealed the names of his co-conspirators. His dream of a powerful explosion that would destroy the government of England was therefore not realized. As Eliot writes at the end of the poem, "*This is the way the world ends,/Not with a bang but a whimper.*" Just as Fawkes is now only a straw figure to be burned, so the speakers of Eliot's poem are as helpless and ineffective as straw dummies: "Leaning together / Headpiece filled with straw. Alas!"

Shakespeare's Julius Caesar

This play deals with another conspiracy to commit violence. Brutus, a high-minded Roman, is lured by flattery into a plot to assassinate the Roman ruler Julius Caesar. Section V of "The Hollow Men" quotes lines from Shakespeare's play in which Brutus experiences the nightmarelike emptiness of the time before the deed. Like Kurtz in Conrad's story, Brutus is a tragic figure, a self-deluded man who commits murder in the name of high ideals. In this sense, he too is a hollow man.

Dante's Divine Comedy

Brutus is one of the betrayers that Dante punishes in the lowest circle of his inferno. The speakers in Eliot's poem are also being punished for their spiritual emptiness in a kind of inferno: a "dead land" (line 39); a "cactus land" (line 40); a "valley of dying stars" (line 54). It does not appear that these speakers will gain salvation, but Eliot uses images drawn from Dante's description of paradise to suggest the existence of higher realms: ". . . the perpetual star/Multifoliate rose . . ." (lines 63–64). "The Hollow Men" is therefore a poem about spiritual despair that contains only the slightest hints that such despair can be overcome. In terms of Dante's work, it is like an inferno (a realm of punishment) that is almost without the promise of a purgatory or a paradise.

Guide for Responding (continued)

◆ Reading Strategy

INTERPRET

You can **interpret** Eliot's poetry by linking images, statements, or phrases in the poem and figuring out the meanings they suggest. For example, Eliot uses images of "eyes" throughout "The Hollow Men." In part I, "Those who have crossed/With direct eyes, to death's other Kingdom" are unlike the hollow men. Then, in part II, one of the hollow men talks of "Eyes I dare not meet in dreams." Again, in part IV, "The eyes are not here," where the hollow men lead their "broken" existence. As a result, the hollow men are "Sightless."

These images suggest that the hollow men are unable to give or receive honest, direct looks. You might interpret this inability as evidence of their spiritual poverty.

Interpret these patterns from Eliot's poems:
1. Images in "Preludes" that focus on parts of bodies rather than whole people
2. In "Journey of the Magi," repetition of the journey's difficulties

◆ Build Vocabulary

USING THE LATIN ROOT -fract-

Explain how the Latin root -fract-, which means "to break," contributes to the meaning of each italicized word.
1. She was guilty of an *infraction* of the law.
2. This chore will take only a *fraction* of your time.
3. The *fractious* boys caused trouble at school.
4. Did you fall and *fracture* your wrist?
5. The *fracto-stratus* clouds were ragged and appeared in long, threadlike layers.

USING THE WORD BANK: Analogies

In your notebook, choose the word from the Word Bank that best completes the analogy.
1. burning : charred :: chafing : ____?____
2. category : group :: system : ____?____
3. contempt : insult :: humility : ____?____
4. knife : honed :: river : ____?____
5. prudent : thoughtless :: agreeable : ____?____

◆ Literary Focus

MODERNISM

One of the founders of **Modernism,** T. S. Eliot uses images and musical language to depict a chaotic, directionless world. The final image of "Preludes" summarizes the whole Modernist perspective: "The worlds revolve like ancient women/Gathering fuel in vacant lots." He compares something once thought of as large, grand, and orderly—"The worlds"—to something shabby, insignificant, and wandering—old women gathering things to burn.
1. How is Eliot's image a more effective expression of Modernism than a direct statement would be?
2. Find examples of these Modernist qualities in "The Hollow Men": use of images; musical, suggestive language; a world without meaning.
3. Explain how "Journey of the Magi," a later poem than the others, represents a departure from Modernist despair. How does it suggest that the world might have meaning after all?

◆ Grammar and Style

ADJECTIVAL MODIFIERS

Adjectival modifiers—prepositional phrases, participial phrases, and adjective clauses that act as adjectives—are a key part of Eliot's style. Often he places them together to suggest a meaning. For example, in lines 11–12 of "The Hollow Men," he uses a series of prepositional phrases to suggest the ineffectiveness of the speakers: "Shape *without form*, shade *without color*, / . . . gesture *without motion*."

Practice On your paper, identify the adjectival modifiers in these lines and explain their effect:
1. "Preludes," lines 1–4
2. "Preludes," lines 19–23
3. "Journey of the Magi," lines 10–12
4. "The Hollow Men," lines 43–44
5. "The Hollow Men," lines 54–55

Writing Application Write a brief profile of the speaker in "Journey of the Magi," using a variety of adjectival modifiers to describe your subject. Experiment with series of modifiers, as Eliot does.

Build Your Portfolio

 ## Idea Bank

Writing

1. **Analysis of an Image** Select an image you like from one of Eliot's poems. Indicate the senses to which it appeals and explain why you think it is effective.

2. **Critical Evaluation** Rate the Eliot poems you have read. Then explain and justify your ranking system, quoting specific passages from the poems to support your points.

3. **Response to Criticism** Bernard Bergonzi writes that a number of Eliot's poems, including "The Hollow Men," "were all put together out of fragments . . ." Do the poems you have read show evidence of this method of composition? Explain.

Speaking, Listening, and Viewing

4. **Choral Reading** With a small group, perform "The Hollow Men." Different sections should be read by different individuals or groups. Use a nursery-rhyme rhythm to recite lines 68–71 and 95–98. **[Performing Arts Link]**

5. **Debate** Does Eliot's view of modern life have truth in it, or is it distorted? Divide into two teams and debate this question. **[Social Studies Link]**

Researching and Representing

6. **Imagism** Using a book of Ezra Pound's essays, find what he says about his version of Modernism—Imagism. Then report on whether Eliot's poems are Imagist works. **[Literature Link]**

7. **Modern Dance** Modernism transformed dance as well as poetry. Research and report on a leading creator of modern dance, like Isadora Duncan. Explain how she can be considered a Modernist. **[Performing Arts Link]**

Online Activity www.phlit.phschool.com

 ## Guided Writing Lesson

Music Video Treatment

Modernist poetry conveys meaning largely through images, just as videos and movies do. Explaining the images you'll use, write a short descriptive plan (treatment) for a music video. Explain why you selected certain images and how you will coordinate them with the music. Draw on a variety of sources for your images.

Writing Focus: Variety of Sources

Many artistic expressions—from a Modernist poem to a music video—use a **variety of sources** to create fresh combinations of images. Here are some sources you might use to write your treatment:

- Music videos that you have enjoyed—what kinds of images do they use and how do they link them?
- Television commercials—what techniques of combining words and images do they use?
- Modern paintings—what strange combinations of images do they include?

Prewriting Research for images in a variety of sources. Then, use a flowchart like this one to organize your images and show how you will combine them.

Drafting Start with a striking image to get the audience's attention. For imagery, look at your notes on sources and your flowchart. Describe how the images you've selected match the song.

Revising As you review your treatment, listen to the song again. Be sure that your plan captures the spirit of the music. If your plan doesn't work for a section of the song, go back to your sources and choose other images.

*G*uide for Interpreting

W. H. Auden *(1907–1973)*

Born in York, England, Wystan Hugh Auden had early dreams of becoming an engineer but, instead, he gravitated to poetry. In 1939, Auden left England for the United States, where he taught in a number of universities and became an American citizen in 1946. From 1956 to 1961, he returned to Oxford as Professor of Poetry.

Achievements in Poetry Auden's poems first appeared in *Oxford Poetry*, a series of annual collections of verse by the university's undergraduates. The volumes in which his poems appear also contain poems by Stephen Spender and Louis MacNeice. Auden's first published collection, entitled simply *Poems,* appeared in 1930. Innovative and eloquent, Auden's verse struck many readers of the day as strange, even impenetrable. His second collection, *On This Island* (1937), is more down-to-earth and generated greater enthusiasm. Auden won a Pulitzer Prize in 1948 for his poetry collection *The Age of Anxiety.*

A Versatile Poet Auden wrote equally well in the idiom of the street or in the archaic measures of *Beowulf.* His output is remarkable for its variety, originality, and craftsmanship. He has been called "the most provocative as well as the most unpredictable poet of his generation." With Yeats and Eliot, he is among the most highly regarded British poets of the first half of the twentieth century.

Stephen Spender *(1909–1995)*

No poet of the 1930's provided a more honest picture of the era between the wars than did Stephen Spender. Born in London and educated at Oxford, Spender's first important book, *Poems* (1933), was published while he was living in Germany.

Spender, a political activist, promoted antifascist propaganda in Spain during its Civil War (1936–1939). He later co-edited the literary magazine *Horizon* and the political, cultural, and literary review *Encounter.*

Louis MacNeice *(1907–1963)*

Louis MacNeice was born the son of a Protestant clergyman in Belfast, Northern Ireland. A gifted youth, he began to write poetry at age seven. His first collection of poems, *Blind Fireworks,* appeared in 1929, followed six years later by *Poems,* the volume that established his reputation. During the 1930's, MacNeice taught Classics at university. In 1941, he joined the British Broadcasting Corporation as a feature writer and producer.

A lyric and reflective poet, MacNeice was modest about the aims of poetry, doubting that it could truly change the world. Today, many consider MacNeice second only to Auden among the poets of his generation.

◆ Background for Understanding

LITERATURE: THE AUDEN CIRCLE—THE WORLD AS POETIC INSPIRATION

The 1930's was a decade poised between a worldwide economic depression and the impending devastation of World War II. The complexity of this period is reflected in the poems of the Auden circle, which consisted of Auden himself, Spender, MacNeice, and C. Day Lewis. The political urgency of the times shaped much of the poetry they wrote then. Yet each of these poets had, at the same time, a deep sense of a specifically "poetic" vocation—to make something happen in language.

In Memory of W. B. Yeats ◆ Musée des Beaux Arts
Carrick Revisited ◆ Not Palaces

◆ Literature and Your Life

CONNECT YOUR EXPERIENCE

Things in life that make you pause and reflect—an object of exquisite beauty or a social injustice—might serve as sources of inspiration for creative pursuits such as art or music. The sources of inspiration for the following poems were world issues and events.

Journal Writing List a few memories, conversations, or events that might serve as inspiration for creative writing.

THEMATIC FOCUS: WAKING FROM THE DREAM

Between the world wars, some poets woke from their "dreams" to demand social justice. As you read writers who came of age during this period, notice their ideas of the poet's place in society.

◆ Literary Focus

THEME

The **theme** of a literary work is its central idea, concern, or purpose. A poem's theme may be directly stated or it may be implied by the poet's choice of words, comparisons, and images.

For example, in "In Memory of W. B. Yeats," Auden explores the role of the writer as artist. There are direct clues to this theme, as in line 36 ("poetry makes nothing happen") and in lines 50–51, which state that time "Worships language and forgives/Everyone by whom it lives." The vivid imagery of the "dark cold day" on which Yeats died and the overall tone, or attitude, of the poem are indirect clues to the poem's theme.

As you read these poems, look for clues that reveal their themes.

◆ Reading Strategy

PARAPHRASE

To follow concentrated expressions of ideas and emotions in poetry, it is often helpful to **paraphrase,** to restate the writer's words in your own words.

For example, you might paraphrase lines 4–6 of "In Memory of W. B. Yeats" this way: "It got colder as the day went on. There's no doubt that he died on a cold and dark day."

As you read these poems, check your understanding by choosing brief passages to paraphrase in your own words.

◆ Build Vocabulary

GREEK ROOTS: -top-

In "Carrick Revisited," you will encounter the word *topographical.* The Greek word root *-top-* means "place," and *topographical* means "relating to a map of the surface features of a place."

WORD BANK

Before you read, preview this list of words from the poems.

sequestered
topographical
affinities
prenatal
intrigues

◆ Grammar and Style

PARALLEL STRUCTURE

In both poetry and prose, writers create a natural rhythm and flow by using **parallel structure;** that is, they use the same grammatical form or pattern to express ideas of equal importance. In this example, Auden uses parallel pairs of prepositional phrases in the first and third lines:

In the deserts of the heart
Let the healing fountain
    start,
In the prison of his days
Teach the free man how to
    praise.

As you read the poems, look for other examples of parallel structure.

In Memory of
W. B. Yeats

W.H. AUDEN

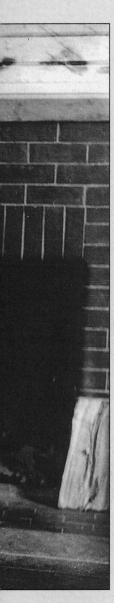

◄ **Critical Viewing** Does this photograph of Yeats
present him as the man described in part 1 of Auden's
poem or as the great writer eulogized in part 3?
[Interpret]

1

He disappeared in the dead of winter:
The brooks were frozen, the airports almost deserted,
And snow disfigured the public statues;
The mercury sank in the mouth of the dying day.
5   O all the instruments agree
The day of his death was a dark cold day.

Far from his illness
The wolves ran on through the evergreen forests,
The peasant river was untempted by fashionable quays;[1]
10   By mourning tongues
The death of the poet was kept from his poems.

But for him it was his last afternoon as himself,
An afternoon of nurses and rumors;
The provinces of his body revolted,
15   The squares of his mind were empty,
Silence invaded the suburbs,
The current of his feeling failed: he became his admirers.

Now he is scattered among a hundred cities
And wholly given over to unfamiliar affections;
20   To find his happiness in another kind of wood
And be punished by another code of conscience.
The words of a dead man
Are modified in the guts of the living.

But in the importance and noise of tomorrow
25   When the brokers are roaring like beasts on the floor of the Bourse,[2]
And the poor have the sufferings to which they are fairly accustomed,
And each in the cell of himself is almost convinced of his freedom;
A few thousand will think of this day
As one thinks of a day when one did something slightly unusual.

30   O all the instruments agree
The day of his death was a dark cold day.

---

1. **quays** (kēz): Wharfs with facilities for loading or unloading ships.
2. **Bourse** (boͮors): Paris Stock Exchange.

2

You were silly like us: your gift survived it all;
The parish of rich women, physical decay,
Yourself; mad Ireland hurt you into poetry.
35   Now Ireland has her madness and her weather still,
For poetry makes nothing happen: it survives
In the valley of its saying where executives
Would never want to tamper; it flows south
From ranches of isolation and the busy griefs,
40   Raw towns that we believe and die in; it survives,
A way of happening, a mouth.

3

Earth, receive an honored guest;
William Yeats is laid to rest:
Let the Irish vessel lie
45   Emptied of its poetry.

Time that is intolerant
Of the brave and innocent,
And indifferent in a week
To a beautiful physique,

50   Worships language and forgives
Everyone by whom it lives;
Pardons cowardice, conceit
Lays its honors at their feet.

Time with this strange excuse
55   Pardoned Kipling and his views,[3]
And will pardon Paul Claudel,[4]
Pardons him for writing well.

In the nightmare of the dark
All the dogs of Europe bark,
60   And the living nations wait,
Each sequestered in its hate;

---

3. **Kipling . . . views**: English writer Rudyard Kipling
(1865–1936) was a supporter of imperialism.
4. **pardon Paul Claudel** (klō del´): French poet, dramatist, and
diplomat. Paul Claudel (1868–1955) had antidemocratic political
views, which Yeats at times shared.

◆ **Build Vocabulary**

sequestered (si kwes´ tərd) *v.*: Kept apart from others

Intellectual disgrace
Stares from every human face,
And the seas of pity lie
65 Locked and frozen in each eye.

Follow, poet, follow right
To the bottom of the night,
With your unconstraining voice
Still persuade us to rejoice;

70 With the farming of a verse
Make a vineyard of the curse,
Sing of human unsuccess
In a rapture of distress;

In the deserts of the heart
75 Let the healing fountain start,
In the prison of his days
Teach the free man how to praise.

Guide for Responding

◆ Literature and Your Life

Reader's Response The speaker hopes that poetry will teach people "how to praise." What do you think the main role of poetry is?

Thematic Focus In what ways does Auden contrast Yeats the man and Yeats the poet?

Notes for a Profile Jot down some of the specific facts about Yeats that a reader can learn from this poem.

☑ Check Your Comprehension

1. On what kind of day did Yeats die?
2. What kept the poet's death from killing his poems?
3. What was it that "hurt" Yeats into writing poetry?
4. According to the third section of the poem, to whom is time (a) intolerant? (b) indifferent?
5. Whom does time forgive?
6. What does the speaker ask the poet to teach people?

◆ Critical Thinking

INTERPRET

1. Twice in the first section, the speaker uses the words "all the instruments agree." What might he mean (a) in a literal sense? (b) in a metaphorical sense? **[Interpret]**
2. What do you think the poet means by stating in line 18 that Yeats is now "scattered among a hundred cities"? **[Interpret]**
3. Whom is the speaker addressing (a) in the second section? (b) in the third section? **[Analyze]**
4. (a) How does the speaker view the situation in Europe? (b) How does he think the poet should react to it? Give evidence for your answer. **[Draw Conclusions]**

EVALUATE

5. This work is an elegy, or poem of mourning, for William Butler Yeats. Yet, in a sense, it could be addressed to any poet, for Auden sets down the responsibilities and rewards he thinks belong to every poet. Does this generalization diminish the effectiveness of the poem? **[Evaluate]**

Musée des Beaux Arts¹

W.H. AUDEN

▼ **Critical Viewing** In this poem, Auden comments on the indifference of humans to one another's misfortunes. How does this painting by Brueghel depict this indifference? **[Interpret]**

The Fall of Icarus, Pieter Brueghel, Musée Royaux des Beaux-Arts de Belgique, Bruxelles

About suffering they were never wrong,
The Old Masters: how well they understood
Its human position; how it takes place
While someone else is eating or opening a window or just
   walking dully along;
5   How, when the aged are reverently, passionately waiting
For the miraculous birth, there always must be
Children who did not specially want it to happen, skating
On a pond at the edge of the wood:
They never forgot
10 That even the dreadful martyrdom must run its course
Anyhow in a corner, some untidy spot
Where the dogs go on with their doggy life and the
   torturer's horse
Scratches its innocent behind on a tree.

In Brueghel's *Icarus*,[2] for instance: how everything turns away
15 Quite leisurely from the disaster; the ploughman may
Have heard the splash, the forsaken cry,
But for him it was not an important failure; the sun shone
As it had to on the white legs disappearing into the green
Water; and the expensive delicate ship that must have seen
20 Something amazing, a boy falling out of the sky,
Had somewhere to get to and sailed calmly on.

---

1. **Musée des Beaux Arts:** Museum of Fine Arts in Brussels, Belgium, which contains Brueghel's *Icarus*.
2. **Brueghel's** (brü´ gəlz) *Icarus* (ik´ ə rəs): *The Fall of Icarus*, a painting by Flemish painter Pieter Brueghel (1525?–1599). In Greek mythology, Icarus flies too close to the sun. The wax of his artificial wings melts, and he falls into the sea.

Guide for Responding

◆ Literature and Your Life

Reader's Response Does the poem express a kind of optimism, or is it pessimistic? Explain.

Thematic Focus What is the reality of human experience to which the poem awakens us?

Questions for Research Generate research questions about the mythical Icarus that would help you explore the meaning of his fall from the skies.

☑ Check Your Comprehension

1. Who are the "Old Masters"?
2. What do the Old Masters show "someone else" doing while suffering occurs?
3. (a) How does the ploughman react to the disaster? (b) How does the ship respond?

◆ Critical Thinking

INTERPRET

1. What do you think Auden intends the activities listed in line 4 to represent? **[Infer]**
2. What is the "miraculous birth" the aged are awaiting in line 6? **[Interpret]**
3. (a) What does Brueghel imply by calling his painting *The Fall of Icarus* but showing only Icarus' legs disappearing in the corner of the picture? (b) Does Auden's poem adhere to Brueghel's meaning? Explain. **[Analyze]**

APPLY

4. (a) In today's world, what examples can you find of indifference to suffering? (b) What might Auden say about your examples? **[Relate]**

CARRICK REVISITED

Louis MacNeice

Back to Carrick,[1] the castle as plumb assured
As thirty years ago—Which war was which?
Here are new villas, here is a sizzling grid
But the green banks are as rich and the lough[2] as hazily lazy
5 And the child's astonishment not yet cured.

Who was—and am—dumbfounded to find myself
In a topographical frame—here, not there—
The channels of my dreams determined largely
By random chemistry of soil and air;
10 Memories I had shelved peer at me from the shelf.

Fog-horn, mill-horn, corncrake and church bell
Half-heard through boarded time as a child in bed
Glimpses a brangle of talk from the floor below
But cannot catch the words. Our past we know
15 But not its meaning—whether it meant well.

Time and place—our bridgeheads into reality
But also its concealment! Out of the sea
We land on the Particular and lose
All other possible bird's-eye views, the Truth
20 That is of Itself for Itself—but not for me.

Torn before birth from where my fathers dwelt,
Schooled from the age of ten to a foreign voice,
Yet neither western Ireland nor southern England
Cancels this interlude; what chance misspelt
25 May never now be righted by my choice.

Whatever then my inherited or acquired
Affinities, such remains my childhood's frame
Like a belated rock in the red Antrim[3] clay
That cannot at this era change its pitch or name—
30 And the prenatal mountain is far away.

1. **Carrick:** Shortened form of Carrickfergus, a town in Northern Ireland.
2. **lough:** (läk): Lake, specifically Belfast Lough. Carrickfergus is situated on the northern shore of Belfast Lough.
3. **Antrim:** County in Northern Ireland in which Carrickfergus is located.

◆ Build Vocabulary

topographical (täp´ə graf´ i kəl) *adj*.: Relating to a map of the surface features of a region, including its elevations, rivers, mountains, and so on

affinities (ə fin´i tēz) *n*.: Family relationships; connections

prenatal (prē nāt´ əl) *adj*.: Before birth

◀ **Critical Viewing** In "Carrick Revisited," Mac-Neice explores the relationship between a person's childhood home and his or her identity. What might it be like to grow up in the setting shown in this photograph? **[Speculate]**

Guide for Responding

◆ Literature and Your Life

Reader's Response The poet uses the words "astonishment" and "dumbfounded" to describe his reaction when returning to his birthplace. Do you find these feelings understandable? Explain.

Thematic Focus How does the speaker's visit to Carrick help him better understand the reality of his identity?

☑ **Check Your Comprehension**

1. (a) Where does the speaker find himself at the beginning of the poem? (b) According to the first stanza, how has the place changed, and how does it remain the same?
2. According to the speaker, what three things contribute to his identity?

◆ Critical Thinking

INTERPRET

1. What does the speaker mean by the line "Memories I had shelved peer at me from the shelf"? **[Interpret]**
2. What distinction does the speaker draw when he says, "Our past we know/But not its meaning—whether it meant well"? **[Infer]**
3. The speaker draws attention to the random, chance influences on his development. How does he view people's ability to control their own destinies? **[Draw Conclusions]**

APPLY

4. MacNeice's poem discusses issues of national identity—Irish-born, he was educated in England. Name two ways in which issues of identity are even more complex in our day. **[Relate]**

Not Palaces

STEPHEN SPENDER

Not palaces, an era's crown
Where the mind dwells, <u>intrigues</u>, rests:
Architectural gold-leaved flower
From people ordered like a single mind,
5   I build: this only what I tell:
It is too late for rare accumulation,
For family pride, for beauty's filtered dusts;
I say, stamping the words with emphasis,
Drink from here energy and only energy
10 To will this time's change.
Eye, gazelle, delicate wanderer,
Drinker of horizon's fluid line;
Ear that suspends on a chord
The spirit drinking timelessness;
15 Touch, love, all senses;
Leave your gardens, your singing feasts,
Your dreams of suns circling before our sun,
Of heaven after our world.
Instead, watch images of flashing glass
20 That strike the outward sense, the polished will,
Flag of our purpose which the wind engraves.
No spirit seek here rest. But this: No one
Shall hunger: Man shall spend equally;
Our goal which we compel: Man shall be man.

◆ **Build Vocabulary**

intrigues (in trēgz´) *v.*: Plots or schemes secretly or underhandedly

Guide for Responding

◆ Literature and Your Life

Reader's Response Do you agree with Spender's ideas about art? Explain.

Thematic Focus In what way does Spender urge his readers to wake from a dream—to abandon illusions or outdated ideas about art?

Artwork Sketch a drawing of which Stephen Spender might approve.

☑ Check Your Comprehension

1. In lines 1–7, what ideas about art is the speaker rejecting?
2. What does the speaker urge the poem's audience to do in lines 9–10?
3. What is the "gazelle" in line 11?
4. (a) What does the speaker tell "all senses" to leave in lines 16? (b) What should they attend to instead (lines 19–21)?

◆ Critical Thinking

INTERPRET

1. In what cultures or periods in history have people lived "ordered like a single mind"? **[Interpret]**
2. In line 9, what is meant by the word *energy*? **[Interpret]**
3. To what real-life events might the speaker be referring in lines 19–21? **[Infer]**
4. (a) What does Spender think the job of poetry once was? (b) What does he think the job of poetry should be now? **[Analyze]**

APPLY

5. Auden writes that, while "poetry makes nothing happen," it teaches us a kind of joy in what is. Spender writes as if poetry could incite social change. Can art serve either function in our time? Explain. **[Relate]**

Guide for Responding (continued)

◆ Literary Focus

THEME

The central idea, concern, or purpose of a literary work is its **theme,** which may be expressed directly or indirectly. Clues to the theme of a work include elements such as its title, setting, word choice, tone, and atmosphere or mood.

1. How does the ploughman's response to the disaster in "Musée des Beaux Arts" help convey the poem's theme?
2. (a) What might be the theme of "Not Palaces"? (b) Was the theme stated directly or indirectly or both? Explain.
3. The theme of "Carrick Revisited" may be stated as "What creates an artist's identity?" (a) How does the setting of the poem help you identify the theme? (b) How does the speaker's attitude provide a clue to its theme?

◆ Reading Strategy

PARAPHRASE

By **paraphrasing,** restating a poet's words in your own words, you can ensure that you've understood the basic meaning of a poem. Once you've done that, you can interpret the poet's original work and appreciate how its language, imagery, and tone give it a deeper, more moving dimension.

For example, in "Musée des Beaux Arts," you can better understand the opening line by paraphrasing it as follows: "The Dutch painters of the sixteenth and seventeenth centuries were never wrong about suffering." When you reread the original line, however, you understand how Auden's word choice and phrasing make it sound as if the speaker is musing aloud, and by putting the word *suffering* second, Auden emphasizes its importance.

1. Paraphrase lines 32–41 of "In Memory of W. B. Yeats." (a) How did paraphrasing help you to understand the basic meaning of the passage? (b) Looking back at the original lines, what appreciation do you have now for the poet's craft?
2. (a) How would you paraphrase the final stanza of "Carrick Revisited"? (b) Do you find your paraphrase or MacNeice's poetry more memorable? Explain.

◆ Build Vocabulary

USING THE GREEK ROOT -top-

Knowing that the root -top- means "place," explain how it affects the meanings of these words.

1. topic   2. topographer   3. utopia

USING THE WORD BANK: Synonyms

Write the letter of the word or phrase whose meaning is closest to that of the first word.

1. sequestered: (a) convicted, (b) kept apart, (c) silent
2. intrigues: (a) schemes, (b) fails, (c) deceives
3. topographical: (a) representing a person's life, (b) atypical, (c) representing a place
4. affinities: (a) immensities, (b) ends, (c) attractions
5. prenatal: (a) natural, (b) naive, (c) before birth

◆ Grammar and Style

PARALLEL STRUCTURE

Poets at times may use **parallel structure**—repeated use of the same grammatical form or pattern—to make their writing memorable and effective. For example, lines 6–7 in "Not Palaces" contain parallel prepositional phrases.

> It is too late *for rare accumulation, /*
> *For family pride, for beauty's filtered dusts.*

Practice Rewrite each item in italics to make the sentence structure parallel.

1. Time worships language and is *pardoning* cowardice.
2. Suffering takes place while someone is likely to be eating or *opens* a window.
3. This is no time for collecting objects or *to admire* beautiful artifacts in museums.

Writing Application In your notebook, rewrite each sentence below, using parallel structure.

1. Auden and Brueghel both criticize people's self-centeredness and their being indifferent to the suffering of others.
2. The speaker in "Not Palaces" suggests that he is not interested in building palaces or the collection of rare objects.
3. Louis MacNeice tried his hand at various genres, including drama and translating in verse.

Build Your Portfolio

 ## Idea Bank

Writing

1. **Tribute** In "In Memory of W. B. Yeats," Auden pays tribute to the late, great poet. Write a tribute of your own in praise of someone whose work you particularly admire.

2. **Essay** In "Musée des Beaux Arts," Auden finds relevance in art of old; in "Not Palaces," Spender finds it irrelevant. With whom do you agree? Write a persuasive essay defending your ideas.

3. **Response to Criticism** David Perkins said of Auden's poetry, "By lessening the distance between 'poetry' and ordinary speech, it widens the range of possible subject matters." Using examples from Auden's poetry, write an essay in which you explain this quotation.

Speaking, Listening, and Viewing

4. **Museum Guide** Auden finds a basic human truth in a painting by Brueghel. Choose a painting with which you're familiar, and give a short talk to the class in which you explain the artist's craft and the significance of the work. **[Art Link]**

5. **Oral Interpretation** Perform an oral interpretation of "Carrick Revisited" in which you highlight the poem's musical qualities. **[Performing Arts Link]**

Researching and Representing

6. **Art Exhibition** With a group, discuss the type of art of which Spender would approve and find examples that fit the description. Display copies of the art you've found. **[Art Link]**

7. **Family Background** Like MacNeice, explore your family background. Create a map or chart that shows regions from which your ancestors came and where you yourself have lived.

Online Activity www.phlit.phschool.com

 ## Guided Writing Lesson

Poem About Art

Auden's poem "Musée des Beaux Arts" was inspired by Brueghel's painting *The Fall of Icarus*. Choose any painting or photograph that is reproduced in this book, and use the image as your inspiration for a poem. You may directly refer, as Auden does, to the specific work of art that serves as your inspiration, or you may choose to leave it unidentified.

Writing Skills Focus: Conveying a Main Impression

In "Not Palaces," Stephen Spender invokes "Eye . . . Ear . . . Touch, love, all senses." Heed his call as you write, and use sensory details to create a **main impression** of the art that inspired you. Rather than simply listing details in the painting, use details to capture the essence of the work.

No Main Impression: The painting is blue and yellow, with a large stripe in the middle . . .

Main Impression: A noisy, bold stripe down the center challenges the viewer to pick a side . . .

Prewriting Before you begin writing, study the art you have chosen. Freewrite for a few minutes about the feelings it prompts in you. Finally, jot down details that will help you to create a main impression for the reader.

Drafting As you draft your poem, you may decide to follow Auden's three-part structure, or you may choose another method of organization. Present your main idea in the most effective, vivid way.

Revising Exchange poems with a partner, and take turns reading them aloud. Showing each other the images you selected as inspiration may prompt helpful suggestions for revision. Display your poem along with the art that inspired it.

Guide for Interpreting

George Orwell (1903–1950)

Many television news reports today are on-the-scene broadcasts, showing people in the middle of an event. They give us not just facts but close-up personal experience, and bestselling "nonfiction novels" do the same. George Orwell pioneered this personal kind of reporting, using nonfiction and novels to expose truths covered up by prejudice or dishonest politics.

Starting as Eric Blair Orwell was born Eric Blair in colonial India, was educated in England, then joined the Imperial Police in Burma. After five years, he became disillusioned with his job and resigned. His first novel, *Burmese Days* (1934), describes his bitter years (1922–1927) as an imperial police officer. "Shooting an Elephant," one of his most famous essays, is based on a memorable experience from this period.

Becoming George Orwell Orwell seemed to have a talent for immersing himself in difficult situations and then writing about them with extraordinary insight. Each book that emerged from an Orwell experience was a one-of-a-kind classic. In *Down and Out in Paris and London* (1933), for example, Orwell describes what it's like to be poor in two big cities. In a strange way, his experience of life's shabbiness gave him a stronger sense of identity. He now published, and lived, under a new name: George Orwell.

During the 1930's, Orwell gave himself to political causes. In *The Road to Wigan Pier* (1937), he wrote about English coal miners with whom he had lived.

Then, during the Spanish Civil War (1936–1939), he fought with anarchists and democratic, socialist Republicans and directly experienced the infighting among them that enabled the Fascists to win. In his book on the Spanish Civil War, *Homage to Catalonia* (1938), Orwell blamed the interference of the Soviet Union for undermining the Republican cause—a charge that made him unpopular with his fellow leftists. The book is a gripping adventure story, one in which the narrator has so much presence of mind that he can describe in precise detail his own experience of being wounded.

A Political Prophet During World War II, Orwell wrote political and literary journalism, and in 1945 he published *Animal Farm,* a satirical fable attacking both Fascism and Communism. In 1949 appeared his famous futuristic novel *1984,* in which a dictator controls all thought and language.

The year 1984 has passed, but George Orwell's lifelong commitment to political freedom and to the honest use of language is as relevant as ever.

◆ Background for Understanding

HISTORY: GEORGE ORWELL, AN ENGLISH POLICEMAN IN BURMA

George Orwell's Burmese experiences, on which this essay is based, were typical for a special group of young Englishmen. Recruited as police officers for the British empire, they had no experience of police work and no knowledge of the country they would police. Some of them were barely out of their teens.

Their training in Burma consisted of memorizing laws and procedures and learning the native languages. They lived apart from the Burmese, who deeply resented being ruled by the British.

These police officers were a small contingent in a native-born police force of 13,000. Among the ninety officers, Englishmen held almost all the top ranks—a few white men governing 13 million Asians.

Police officers were at risk in this tense political situation. With many large public protests, rebellion was a constant threat.

◆ *Literature and Your Life*

CONNECT YOUR EXPERIENCE

One of the toughest things in the world is to put yourself on the line so that people can judge you. Even something as simple as giving an oral report at school can put you on the spot. Maybe you'll say something the wrong way or just say something silly.

In this essay, George Orwell describes a time when he had to perform in front of a crowd. Being a police officer for the British empire only made his situation more tense.

Journal Writing Describe how you would feel in Orwell's shoes—as a young police officer in a resentful country.

THEMATIC FOCUS: WAKING FROM THE DREAM

As you read, notice how Orwell's experiences awaken him from the colonial dream of a stable empire.

◆ Literary Focus

IRONY

Orwell uses **irony**, a device that brings out surprising or amusing contradictions, to describe the difficult situation he faced. In **verbal irony**, the intended meaning of words clashes with their usual meaning (as when you sarcastically call a bully "kind"). In **irony of situation**, events contradict what you expect to happen.

Orwell uses both kinds of irony in "Shooting an Elephant"—but especially irony of situation—to capture his peculiar dilemma. Watch carefully as what he wants and expects to do clash ironically with what he *has* to do.

◆ Reading Strategy

RECOGNIZE THE WRITER'S ATTITUDES

To understand what people say in a conversation, you must go beyond their words and recognize their attitudes. In the same way, to understand what you read, you must go beyond the words on the page and **recognize the writer's attitudes**.

Orwell's attitudes are not simple and clear-cut. For example, he feels that the Burmese are right, but at the same time, he hates them for tormenting him. Be aware of Orwell's clashing attitudes toward his situation as you read.

◆ Build Vocabulary

RELATED WORDS: WORDS ABOUT POLITICS

Orwell uses words relating to political power, such as *imperialism,* in his essay. *Imperialism* refers to "the system by which a powerful country dominates less powerful ones."

WORD BANK

Preview the list of words from the selection before you read.

| prostrate |
| imperialism |
| despotic |
| squalid |
| dominion |
| senility |

◆ Grammar and Style

PARTICIPIAL PHRASES: RESTRICTIVE AND NONRESTRICTIVE

Orwell uses **participial phrases**—a group of words with a participle—to modify nouns and pronouns. Such phrases are **restrictive** when they are essential to the sentence's meaning. They are **nonrestrictive** when they provide additional, but not necessary, information. Nonrestrictive phrases are separated from the noun or pronoun by commas; restrictive phrases are not:

Restrictive: The wretched prisoners *huddling in the stinking cages of the lockups* ....

Nonrestrictive: Some more women followed, *clicking their tongues and exclaiming* ....

SHOOTING AN

ELEPHANT

George Orwell

*I*n Moulmein, in lower Burma, I was hated by large numbers of people—the only time in my life that I have been important enough for this to happen to me. I was subdivisional police officer of the town, and in an aimless, petty kind of way anti-European feeling was very bitter. No one had the guts to raise a riot, but if a European woman went through the bazaars alone somebody would probably spit betel juice over her dress. As a police officer I was an obvious target and was baited whenever it seemed safe to do so. When a nimble Burman tripped me up on the football field and the referee (another Burman) looked the other way, the crowd yelled with hideous laughter. This happened more than once. In the end the sneering yellow faces of young men that met me everywhere, the insults hooted after me when I was at a safe distance, got badly on my nerves. The young Buddhist priests were the worst of all. There were several thousands of them in the town and none of them seemed to have anything to do except stand on street corners and jeer at Europeans.

All this was perplexing and upsetting. For at that time I had already made up my mind that imperialism was an evil thing and the sooner I chucked up my job and got out of it the better. Theoretically—and secretly, of course—I was all for the Burmese and all against their oppressors, the British. As for the job I was doing, I hated it more bitterly than I can

◆ **Reading Strategy**
Identify some of Orwell's conflicting **attitudes** in these early paragraphs.

◀ **Critical Viewing** Does this photograph depict a useful beast or a dangerous menace? Explain. **[Make a Judgment]**

perhaps make clear. In a job like that you see the dirty work of Empire at close quarters. The wretched prisoners huddling in the stinking cages of the lockups, the gray, cowed faces of the long-term convicts, the scarred buttocks of the men who had been flogged with bamboos—all these oppressed me with an intolerable sense of guilt. But I could get nothing into perspective. I was young and ill educated and I had had to think out my problems in the utter silence that is imposed on every Englishman in the East. I did not even know that the British Empire is dying, still less did I know that it is a great deal better than the younger empires that are going to supplant it. All I knew was that I was stuck between my hatred of the empire I served and my rage against the evil-spirited little beasts who tried to make my job impossible. With one part of my mind I thought of the British Raj[1] as an unbreakable tyranny, as something clamped down, *in saecula saeculorum,*[2] upon the will of prostrate peoples; with another part I thought that the greatest joy in the world would be to drive a bayonet into a Buddhist priest's guts. Feelings like these are the normal byproducts of imperialism; ask any Anglo-Indian official, if you can catch him off duty.

One day something happened which in a roundabout way was enlightening. It was a tiny incident in itself, but it gave me a better glimpse than I had had before of the real nature of imperialism—the real motives for which despotic governments act. Early one morning the subinspector at a police station the other end of the town rang me up on the phone and said that an elephant was ravaging the bazaar. Would I please come and do something about it? I did not know what I could do, but I wanted to see what was happening and I got onto a pony and started out. I took my rifle, an old .44 Winchester and much too small to kill an elephant, but I thought the noise might be

useful *in terrorem.*[3] Various Burmans stopped me on the way and told me about the elephant's doings. It was not, of course, a wild elephant, but a tame one which had gone "must."[4] It had been chained up, as tame elephants always are when their attack of "must" is due, but on the previous night it had broken its chain and escaped. Its mahout,[5] the only person who could manage it when it was in that state, had set out in pursuit, but had taken the wrong direction and was now twelve hours' journey away, and in the morning the elephant had suddenly reappeared in the town. The Burmese population had no weapons and were quite helpless against it. It had already destroyed somebody's bamboo hut, killed a cow and raided some fruit stalls and devoured the stock; also it had met the municipal rubbish van and, when the driver jumped out and took to his heels, had turned the van over and inflicted violences upon it.

The Burmese subinspector and some Indian constables were waiting for me in the quarter where the elephant had been seen. It was a very poor quarter, a labyrinth of squalid bamboo huts, thatched with palm leaf, winding all over a steep hillside. I remember that it was a cloudy, stuffy morning at the beginning of the rains. We began questioning the people as to where the ele-

---

3. *in terrorem:* For terror.
4. **must:** Into a dangerous, frenzied state.
5. **mahout** (mə hōōt′): Elephant keeper and rider.

◆ Build Vocabulary

prostrate (präs′ trāt) *adj.*: Defenseless; in a prone or lying position

imperialism (im pir′ ē əl iz′əm) *n.*: Policy and practice of forming and maintaining an empire in seeking to control raw materials and world markets by the conquest of other countries, the establishment of colonies, and so on

despotic (de spät′ ik) *adj.*: Tyrannical

squalid (skwäl′ id) *adj.*: Miserably poor; wretched

---

1. **Raj** (räj): Rule.
2. *in saecula saeculorum* (in sē′ kōō lə sē′ kōō lôr′ əm): Forever and ever.

▲ **Critical Viewing** At the story's beginning, Orwell describes how, as a police officer, he was a target for ridicule and baited by the Burmese. Judging from the details in this photograph, what made Orwell (third from left in back row) and his fellow officers conspicuous? **[Analyze]**

phant had gone and, as usual, failed to get any definite information. That is invariably the case in the East; a story always sounds clear enough at a distance, but the nearer you get to the scene of events the vaguer it becomes. Some of the people said that the elephant had gone in one direction, some said that he had gone in another, some professed not even to have heard of any elephant. I had almost made up my mind that the whole story was a pack of lies, when we heard yells a little distance away. There was a loud scandalized cry of "Go away, child! Go away this instant!" and an old woman with a switch in her hand came round the corner of a hut, violently shooing away a crowd of naked children. Some more women followed, clicking their tongues and exclaiming; evidently there was something that the children ought not to have seen. I rounded the hut and saw a man's dead body sprawling in the mud. He was an Indian, a black Dravidian[6] coolie,[7] almost naked, and he could not have been dead many minutes. The people said that the elephant had come suddenly upon him round the corner of the hut, caught him with its trunk, put its foot

6. **Dravidian** (drə vid´ ē ən): Belonging to the race of people inhabiting southern India.
7. **coolie:** Laborer.

on his back and ground him into the earth. This was the rainy season and the ground was soft, and his face had scored a trench a foot deep and a couple of yards long. He was lying on his belly with arms crucified and head sharply twisted to one side. His face was coated with mud, the eyes wide open, the teeth bared and grinning with an expression of unendurable agony. (Never tell me, by the way, that the dead look peaceful. Most of the corpses I have seen looked devilish.) The friction of the great beast's foot had stripped the skin from his back as neatly as one skins a rabbit. As soon as I saw the dead man I sent an orderly to a friend's house nearby to borrow an elephant rifle. I had already sent back the pony, not wanting it to go mad with fright and throw me if it smelled the elephant.

The orderly came back in a few minutes with a rifle and five cartridges, and meanwhile some Burmans had arrived and told us that the elephant was in the paddy fields[8] below, only a few hundred yards away. As I started forward practically the whole population of the quarter flocked out of the houses and followed me. They had seen the rifle and were all shouting excitedly that I was going to shoot the elephant. They had not shown much interest in the elephant when he was merely ravaging their homes, but it was different now that he was going to be shot. It was a bit of fun to them, as it would be to an English crowd; besides they wanted the meat. It made me vaguely uneasy. I had no intention of shooting the elephant— I had merely sent for the rifle to defend myself if necessary—and it is always unnerving to have a crowd following you. I marched down the hill, looking and feeling a fool, with the rifle over my shoulder and an ever-growing army of people jostling at my heels. At the bottom, when you got away from the huts, there was a metaled road[9] and beyond that a miry waste of paddy fields a thousand yards across, not yet plowed but soggy

◆ *Literature and Your Life*

If you were Orwell's friend, what would you counsel him to do: kill the elephant or spare its life? Why?

---

8. **paddy fields:** Rice fields.

9. **metaled road:** Road in which the pavement is reinforced with metal strips.

Beyond Literature

Cultural Connection

British Imperialism in Burma Orwell resented his position as an officer of the British empire whose responsibility it was to enforce a system of imperialism that he disliked, but the Burmese had even greater cause to resent the British for failing to recognize and respect the particularities of Burma's culture. The Burmese were profoundly insulted that, for the sake of administrative efficiency, the British treated Burma as a province of India. Not only was Burma different from India in language, race, religious traditions, and customs, but India had fought with the British in the wars that subjugated Burma to Britain's empire.

The British were especially inept in accommodating Burmese religious traditions. Great Britain had an imperial policy of strict neutrality in religious matters, yet instead of establishing government schools, it allowed Christian missionaries to develop mission schools that were staffed by teachers who were often ignorant of or hostile to Burma's Buddhist traditions and culture.

Activity Compare the relationship among religious groups in this country today to that of Christianity and Buddhism in Burma in 1930.

from the first rains and dotted with coarse grass. The elephant was standing eight yards from the road, his left side toward us. He took not the slightest notice of the crowd's approach. He was tearing up bunches of grass, beating them against his knees to clean them, and stuffing them into his mouth.

I had halted on the road. As soon as I saw the elephant I knew with perfect certainty that I ought not to shoot him. It is a serious matter to shoot a working elephant—it is comparable to destroying a huge and costly piece of machinery—and obviously one ought not to do it if it can possibly be avoided. And at that distance, peacefully eating, the elephant looked no more dangerous than a cow. I thought then and I think now that his attack of "must" was already passing off; in which case he would merely wander harmlessly about until the mahout came back and caught him. Moreover, I did not in the least want to shoot him. I decided that I would watch him for a little while to make sure that he did not turn savage again, and then go home.

But at that moment I glanced round at the crowd that had followed me. It was an immense crowd, two thousand at the least and growing every minute. It blocked the road for a long distance on either side. I looked at the sea of yellow faces above the garish clothes—faces all happy and excited over this bit of fun, all certain that the elephant was going to be shot. They were watching me as they would watch a conjurer about to perform a trick. They did not like me, but with the magical rifle in my hands I was momentarily worth watching. And suddenly I realized that I should have to shoot the elephant after all. The people expected it of me and I had got to do it; I could feel their two thousand wills pressing me forward, irresistibly. And it was at this moment, as I stood there with the rifle in my hands, that I first grasped the hollowness, the futility of the white man's <u>dominion</u> in the East. Here was I, the white man with his gun, standing in front of the unarmed native crowd—seemingly the leading actor of the piece; but in reality I was only an absurd puppet pushed to and fro by the will of those yellow faces behind. I perceived in this moment that when the white man turns tyrant it is his own freedom that he destroys. He becomes a sort of hollow, posing dummy, the conventionalized figure of a sahib.[10] For it is the condition of his rule that he shall spend his life in trying to impress the "natives," and so in every crisis he has got to do what the "natives" expect of him. He wears a mask, and his face grows to fit it. I had got to shoot the elephant. I had committed myself to doing it when I sent for the rifle. A sahib has got to act like a sahib; he has got to appear resolute, to know his own mind and do definite things. To come all that way, rifle in hand, with two thousand people marching at my heels, and then to trail feebly away, having done nothing—no, that was impossible. The crowd would laugh at me. And my whole life, every white man's life in the East, was one long struggle not to be laughed at.

But I did not want to shoot the elephant. I watched him beating his bunch of grass against his knees with that preoccupied grandmotherly air that elephants have. It seemed to me that it would be murder to shoot him. At that age I was not squeamish about killing animals, but I had never shot an elephant and never wanted to. (Somehow it always seems worse to kill a *large* animal.) Besides, there was the beast's owner to be considered. Alive, the elephant was worth at least a hundred pounds, dead, he would only be worth the value of his tusks, five pounds, possibly. But I had got to act quickly. I turned to some experienced-looking Burmans who had been there when we

◆ Literary Focus
What ironic observation is shared here?

◆ **Build Vocabulary**

dominion (də min′ yən) *n*.: Rule or power to rule; a governed territory

10. **sahib** (sä′ ib): Indian word for European gentleman.

arrived, and asked them how the elephant had been behaving. They all said the same thing: he took no notice of you if you left him alone, but he might charge if you went too close to him.

It was perfectly clear to me what I ought to do. I ought to walk up to within, say, twenty-five yards of the elephant and test his behavior. If he charged, I could shoot; if he took no notice of me, it would be safe to leave him until the mahout came back. But also I knew that I was going to do no such thing. I was a poor shot with a rifle and the ground was soft mud into which one would sink at every step. If the elephant charged and I missed him, I should have about as much chance as a toad under a steamroller. But even then I was not thinking particularly of my own skin, only of the watchful yellow faces behind. For at that moment, with the crowd watching me, I was not afraid in the ordinary sense, as I would have been if I had been alone. A white man mustn't be frightened in front of "natives"; and so, in general, he isn't frightened. The sole thought in my mind was that if anything went wrong those two thousand Burmans would see me pursued, caught, trampled on, and reduced to a grinning corpse like that Indian up the hill. And if that happened it was quite probable that some of them would laugh. That would never do. There was only one alternative. I shoved the cartridges into the magazine and lay down on the road to get a better aim.

The crowd grew very still, and a deep, low, happy sigh, as of people who see the theater curtain go up at last, breathed from innumerable throats. They were going to have their bit of fun, after all. The rifle was a beautiful German thing with cross-hair sights. I did not then know that in shooting an elephant one would shoot to cut an imaginary bar running from ear hole to ear hole. I ought, therefore, as the elephant was sideways on, to have aimed straight at his ear-hole; actually I aimed several inches in front of this, thinking the brain would be further forward.

When I pulled the trigger I did not hear the bang or feel the kick—one never does when a shot goes home—but I heard the devilish roar of glee that went up from the crowd. In that instant, in too short a time, one would have thought, even for the bullet to get there, a mysterious, terrible change had come over the elephant. He neither stirred nor fell, but every line of his body had altered. He looked suddenly stricken, shrunken, immensely old, as though the frightful impact of the bullet had paralyzed him without knocking him down. At last, after what seemed a long time—it might have been five seconds, I dare say—he sagged flabbily to his knees. His mouth slobbered. An enormous <u>senility</u> seemed to have settled upon him. One could have imagined him thousands of years old. I fired again into the same spot. At the second shot he did not collapse but climbed with desperate slowness to his feet and stood weakly upright, with legs sagging and head drooping. I fired a third time. That was the shot that did for him. You could see the agony of it jolt his whole body and knock the last remnant of strength from his legs. But in falling he seemed for a moment to rise, for as his hind legs collapsed beneath him he seemed to tower upward like a huge rock toppling, his trunk reaching skyward like a tree. He trumpeted, for the first and only time. And then down he came, his belly toward me, with a crash that seemed to shake the ground even where I lay.

I got up. The Burmans were already racing past me across the mud. It was obvious that the elephant would never rise again, but he was not dead. He was breathing very rhythmically with long rattling gasps, his great mound of a side painfully rising and falling. His mouth was wide open—I could see far down into caverns of pale pink throat. I waited a long time for him to die, but his breathing did not weaken. Finally I fired my two remaining shots into the spot where I

◆ Build Vocabulary

senility (si nil´ə tē) *n.*: Mental and physical decay due to old age

thought his heart must be. The thick blood welled out of him like red velvet, but still he did not die. His body did not even jerk when the shots hit him, the tortured breathing continued without a pause. He was dying, very slowly and in great agony, but in some world remote from me where not even a bullet could damage him further. I felt that I had got to put an end to that dreadful noise. It seemed dreadful to see the great beast lying there, powerless to move and yet powerless to die, and not even to be able to finish him. I sent back for my small rifle and poured shot after shot into his heart and down his throat. They seemed to make no impression. The tortured gasps continued as steadily as the ticking of a clock.

In the end I could not stand it any longer and went away. I heard later that it took him half an hour to die. Burmans were bringing dahs[11] and baskets even before I left, and I was told they had stripped his body almost to the bones by the afternoon.

Afterward, of course, there were endless discussions about the shooting of the elephant. The owner was furious, but he was only an Indian and could do nothing. Besides, legally I had done the right thing, for a mad elephant has to be killed, like a mad dog, if its owner fails to control it. Among the Europeans opinion was divided. The older men said I was right, the younger men said it was a shame to shoot an elephant for killing a coolie, because an elephant was worth more than any Coringhee[12] coolie. And afterward I was very glad that the coolie had been killed; it put me legally in the right and it gave me a sufficient pretext for shooting the elephant. I often wondered whether any of the others grasped that I had done it solely to avoid looking a fool.

---

11. **dahs** (däz): Knives.

12. **Coringhee** (cor in´ gē): Southern Indian.

Guide for Responding

◆ Literature and Your Life

Reader's Response If you were in the narrator's position, would you give up your job? Why or why not?

Thematic Focus Did Britain eventually awaken from the imperialist dream that Orwell describes? Explain.

☑ Check Your Comprehension

1. (a) Why was Orwell hated in Burma? (b) What were the mixed ways in which he reacted to this hatred?
2. What grisly evidence of the elephant's rampage does Orwell encounter?
3. Why do the Burmese get excited when they see Orwell has a rifle?
4. What reasons does Orwell give for not wanting to shoot the elephant?
5. According to Orwell, why did he shoot the elephant?

◆ Critical Thinking

INTERPRET

1. Being "hated by large numbers of people" provokes a conflict in Orwell. (a) What is that conflict? (b) What does it show about his character? **[Analyze]**
2. How does the crowd's excitement make Orwell see his position is absurd? **[Analyze Causes and Effects]**
3. How does the end show that "when the white man turns tyrant it is his own freedom that he destroys"? **[Draw Conclusions]**

EVALUATE

4. Does Orwell judge himself too harshly? Explain. **[Make a Judgment]**

APPLY

5. If Orwell hadn't shot the elephant, would that change the meaning of the essay? **[Modify]**

Guide for Responding (continued)

◆ Reading Strategy

RECOGNIZE THE WRITER'S ATTITUDES

The contradictory **attitudes** reflected in Orwell's essay are a clue to its meaning. When the crowd views the slaughter of a huge animal as "a bit of fun," Orwell seems to tolerate this. As he feels their pressure to shoot the elephant, however, his attitude becomes one of uneasiness and resistance.

1. Describe Orwell's attitude toward the Burmese people.
2. What was Orwell's attitude toward being a police officer?
3. Describe Orwell's conflicting attitudes in the paragraph beginning "It was perfectly clear ..."
4. What do Orwell's conflicting attitudes reveal about imperialism?

◆ Literary Focus

IRONY

In this essay, Orwell reveals his conflicts through the surprising contradictions of **irony**: the clash between a word's meaning and its use (**verbal irony**) or between what is expected and what actually exists or occurs (**irony of situation**). Irony enables Orwell to describe a complex and contradictory experience. Without using this literary device, he would not have been able to write about these events with such insight and bitter humor.

Describing a supposedly dangerous elephant as "grandmotherly" is an amusing example of verbal irony. As for irony of situation, Orwell says that it isn't necessary to kill the elephant for safety. Then, ironically, he kills it to avoid embarrassment.

Indicate what is ironic about each of the following descriptions, facts, or occurrences:

1. Orwell's attitude toward the British empire
2. His attitude toward the Burmese he supported
3. His lack of choice about whether or not to kill the elephant
4. The comparison of the dying elephant's blood to "red velvet"
5. The attitude of "the younger men" toward the shooting of the elephant

◆ Grammar and Style

PARTICIPIAL PHRASES: RESTRICTIVE AND NONRESTRICTIVE

Orwell uses **participial phrases**—groups of words with a participle—to modify nouns and pronouns. **Restrictive** participial phrases are essential to the meaning of the words they modify and aren't separated by commas. **Nonrestrictive** participial phrases are not essential and can be separated by commas.

Practice On your paper, underline the participial phrase in each sentence, say whether it is restrictive or nonrestrictive, and explain its effect.

1. It was a very poor quarter, a labyrinth of squalid bamboo huts, thatched with palm leaf ...
2. I ... saw a man's dead body sprawling in the mud.
3. I marched down the hill, looking and feeling a fool.
4. And at that distance, peacefully eating, the elephant looked no more dangerous than a cow.
5. ... in reality I was only an absurd puppet pushed to and fro by the will of those yellow faces ...

◆ Build Vocabulary

USING WORDS ABOUT POLITICS

Use your knowledge of the political words in this essay to answer these questions:

1. How was the relationship between Britain and Burma typical of *imperialism*?
2. Which nation had *dominion* over the other?
3. Name two specific examples of *despotic* power that Orwell mentions in the second paragraph.

USING THE WORD BANK: Context

Replace each italicized word or phrase with a word from the Word Bank.

As a seasoned veteran of summer camps, I can tell you a few things about the *wretched* conditions under which *tyrannical* counselors force you to live. In their *governed territory*, they have philosophies of *total control* that leave some campers totally *defenseless* in their fear. Before *mental decay* sets in, I plan to write of my incredible summer experiences.

Build Your Portfolio

 ## Idea Bank

Writing

1. Profile Orwell reveals a great deal about himself in this essay. Use what you learn to write a profile of the author as a young man. Include both his ideas and his personal traits.

2. Film Treatment Write a memo to a director suggesting how Orwell's essay could be adapted for film. Explain how you would shoot some of the key scenes. **[Media Link]**

3. Response to Criticism Lionel Trilling said of Orwell, "He told the truth, and told it in an exemplary way, quietly, simply, with due warning to the reader that it was only one man's truth." Does this comment also apply to "Shooting an Elephant"? Why or why not?

Speaking, Listening, and Viewing

4. Role Play With several classmates, act out a scene in which Orwell recounts the shooting incident to some younger and older Englishmen. Have them react as Orwell describes in the essay. **[Performing Arts Link]**

5. Oral Report Burma was one of many countries that had been subject to colonial rule but became independent in the post-World War II years. Prepare and deliver an oral report on the way Burma achieved independence from British colonial rule. **[Social Studies Link]**

Researching and Representing

6. Orwell in Film Orwell's books *1984* and *Animal Farm* have both inspired films. View one of these and report on it to the class. **[Media Link]**

7. Biography In 1991, a Burmese woman, Aung San Suu Kyi, won the Nobel Peace Prize. Research and report on her fight for freedom in Burma. **[Social Studies Link]**

Online Activity www.phlit.phschool.com

 ## Guided Writing Lesson

Police Report

As a police officer, Orwell probably had to write a report on the incident he describes. Review the essay and write the police report that he might have filed. Briefly summarize what happened, explain the events in order, and justify the shooting of the elephant. However, don't include observations on imperialism or the role of Britain in Burma. The officer who reads your report will just want to know the key facts.

Writing Skills Focus: Elaboration to Give Information

In all kinds of writing, you have to **elaborate to give information**—to add details and comments that give the reader a fuller understanding of your subject. For your report, keep in mind the facts that a police administrator might want to know:

- What happened?
- Where and when did the events occur?
- Why did they occur? For example, what caused the elephant to run wild, and why did you decide to shoot it?

Prewriting Jot down notes in response to the key questions listed above. Then figure out a format for your report: the order in which you will present information, the titles you'll give to the various sections, and the space you'll devote to each.

Drafting Begin with a quick summary of events. Often, busy administrators like to have an overview of what occurred, especially if they don't have time to read further. As you draft your report, refer to your notes and include only the key facts.

Revising Review the story to see if you have left out any essential information. Then review your report to see if you have included unimportant details that could be left out. Be sure you have justified killing the elephant and that the format is clear.

CONNECTIONS TO WORLD LITERATURE

The Diameter of the Bomb
Yehuda Amichai

Everything Is Plundered
Anna Akhmatova

Testament
Bei Dao

Cultural Connection

WAKING FROM THE DREAM

The writers in this section respond to the disconcerting, often violent, changes that mark the twentieth century. As their work shows, individuals caught up in these changes can feel as if they are trapped in a nightmare or are waking from an illusory dream to bitter disillusionment. Bowen, in "The Demon Lover," and Yeats, in "The Second Coming," stress the nightmarish aspects of war and of historical cycles. In "Preludes," T. S. Eliot portrays an awakening to a confused and fragmented world in which the soul suffers. Orwell depicts another kind of awakening in "To Shoot an Elephant." He shows how, as a young imperial police officer, he first understood the effects of colonialism on the oppressor and the oppressed alike.

"FROM STARRY BULLET-HOLES"

Yehuda Amichai (yə hōō′ də ä′ mi khī), Anna Akhmatova (äk mä′tō və) and Bei Dao (bä dou) also respond to the century's grim realities. Akhmatova, writing just after a bitter civil war in Russia (1918–1920), describes both the "misery" she sees around her and the "miraculous" that she senses. Amichai, himself a veteran of Israel's wars, shows the devastating and far-reaching effects of an act of terrorism. Bei Dao writes the "Testament" of a prisoner about to be executed by the oppressive Chinese government. Though soon to die, this man holds out the possibility that his death will be a source of renewal: "From starry bullet-holes / The blood-red dawn will flow."

YEHUDA AMICHAI (1924–)

Born in Germany, Amichai emigrated to Palestine prior to the start of World War II. Since then he has fought in nearly all of Israel's wars and has written poetry that expresses the thoughts and feelings of a whole generation of Israelis. He has also skillfully combined—in Hebrew—biblical phrases and down-to-earth, everyday language.

ANNA AKHMATOVA (1889–1966)

Russian poet Anna Akhmatova began writing poems at eleven. During her long life, she experienced and wrote about a host of devastating events, from the Russian Revolution to Stalin's oppression. Stalin banned her work for a time. In 1940, however, the ban was lifted, and she continued to write and publish until her death.

BEI DAO (1949–)

Bei Dao is a Chinese poet whose work is—in the words of one of his translators, Bonnie S. McDougall—a "complex reaction to the pressures of a brutalized and corrupt society." He was traveling abroad during the Tiananmen Square massacre (June 4, 1989), and since that time, he has lived in exile from China.

The Diameter of the **Bomb**

Yehuda Amichai

Translated by Chana Bloch

Thrust 1959, Adolph Gottlieb, The Metropolitain Museum of Art

▶ **Critical Viewing**
In what ways does this image illustrate Amichai's poem? **[Connect]**

The diameter of the bomb was thirty centimeters
and the diameter of its effective range about seven
  meters,
with four dead and eleven wounded.
And around these, in a larger circle
5   of pain and time, two hospitals are scattered
and one graveyard. But the young woman
who was buried in the city she came from,
at a distance of more than a hundred kilometers,
enlarges the circle considerably,
10 and the solitary man mourning her death
at the distant shores of a country far across the
  sea
includes the entire world in the circle.
And I won't even mention the crying of orphans
that reaches up to the throne of God and
15 beyond, making
a circle with no end and no God.

Everything Is Plundered

Anna Akhmatova
Translated by Stanley Kunitz

◀ **Critical Viewing** Does the Anna Akhmatova depicted in the portrait seem as if she could have written this poem? Why or why not? **[Compare and Contrast]**

Everything is plundered, betrayed, sold,
Death's great black wing scrapes the air,
Misery gnaws to the bone.
Why then do we not despair?

5   By day, from the surrounding woods,
cherries blow summer into town;
at night the deep transparent skies
glitter with new galaxies.

And the miraculous comes so close
10   to the ruined, dirty houses—
something not known to anyone at all,
but wild in our breast for centuries.

Testament[1]

Bei Dao

Translated by
Donald Finkel
and
Xueliang Chen

Perhaps the time has come.
I haven't left a will,
just one pen, for my mother.

I'm no hero, you understand.
5   This isn't the year for heroes.
I'd just like to be a man.

The horizon still divides
the living from the dead,
but the sky's all I need.

10   I won't kneel on the earth—
the firing squad might block
the last free breaths of air.

From starry bullet-holes
the blood-red dawn will flow.

1. **Testament** (Tes´ tə ment)
n.: Will; also, a statement of
one's beliefs.

Guide for Responding

◆ Literature and Your Life

Reader's Response Which poem did you find most disturbing? Which poem was most optimistic? Explain.

Thematic Connection What news of the twentieth century can you find in the work of these three poets?

☑ Check Your Comprehension

1. What does the circle include in Amichai's poem?
2. What sights help Akhmatova not "despair"?
3. Describe how the speaker in Bei Dao's poem pictures himself at his execution.

◆ Critical Thinking

INTERPRET

1. A paradox is an apparent contradiction. (a) What is paradoxical about the image in Amichai's poem of "a circle with no end"? (b) Why is a paradox well-suited to Amichai's ideas in this poem? **[Interpret]**
2. What is "the miraculous" Akhmatova refers to in line 9 of her poem? **[Interpret]**
3. What new insight about life does Akhmatova's poem reveal? **[Draw Conclusions]**
4. A testament is a will or a statement of belief. How do both meanings apply to "Testament"? **[Draw Conclusions]**

Cultural Connection

WAKING FROM THE DREAM

During the twentieth century, many writers in England and elsewhere had to find words to describe the realities of war and other upheavals. No longer could they rely on "poetic" language that depicted a dreamy, imaginary world.

1. How is the language that Amichai uses to describe the effects of a bomb different from that Akhmatova uses to describe the aftermath of a civil war?

2. Read Bei Dao's "Testament" together with part 3 of Auden's "In Memory of W. B. Yeats." Do you think that Bei Dao is—in Auden's terms—still persuading "us to rejoice"? Why or why not?

3. What do you think the speaker in Eliot's "Journey of the Magi" would say about the conclusion of Amichai's poem?

4. (a) Identify a contemporary song that deals with war or other political upheavals. (b) What thoughts and emotions does the song express?

 Idea Bank

Writing

1. **Narrative Essay** In a narrative essay, describe a time when you woke up to a certain reality or became aware of a truth.

2. **Personal Testament** Bei Dao's "Testament" is not only a last will and testament, but also a statement of his beliefs. Write your own testament, explaining your most important beliefs.

3. **Response to Criticism** Akhmatova told Isaiah Berlin "that the unending ordeal of her country in her own lifetime had generated poetry of wonderful depth and beauty." Apply this observation to her own poem "Everything Is Plundered."

Speaking, Listening, and Viewing

4. **Persuasive Speech** Prepare and deliver a persuasive speech arguing that poetry can preserve hope in times of upheaval. To support your position, quote from poems that appear in this section of the book. **[Performing Arts Link]**

Researching and Representing

5. **Historical Context** Research historical events that influenced one of these poets. One possible source, for instance, is the introduction to *The Complete Poems of Anna Akhmatova*, translated by Judith Hemschemeyer (Boston: Zephyr, 1992). Report on your findings to the class. **[Social Studies Link]**

Online Activity www.phlit.phschool.com

Writing Process Workshop

Just as poets like T. S. Eliot quote other writers in their poems, you can use facts and ideas from different sources in your research paper. Use these sources to support a thesis statement, which presents one or more key points about a topic. Your paper should have an introduction that presents your thesis, a body that includes supporting facts and arguments, and a conclusion. Source materials should be credited in footnotes, endnotes, or parenthetical notes.

Writing Skills Focus

▶ **Choose a clear and logical organization** that matches the content and purpose of your paper. (See p. 895.)

▶ **Use details and language** that suit your readers and help you achieve your purpose. (See pp. 907, 935.)

▶ **Research information using a variety of sources,** including databases and the Internet, when you gather ideas, facts, and data. (See p. 921.)

▶ **Elaborate** by including details that support your thesis. Details may be in chart, graph, or map form. (See p. 947.)

English Channel Tunnel

Margate
Herne Bay   Ramsgate
Canterbury
Deal
London 64 km / 40 mi
Folkstone Terminal
Terminal de Folkstone
Ashford
British Rail
Dover
Folkestone
Shakespeare Cliff
Service Tunnel
Running Tunnels
Undersea Crossover
Strait of Dover
Sangette
Calais
SNCF
Strait of Dover
Terminal de Coquelles
Coquelles Terminal
Paris 225 km / 140 mi
Area Enlarged
London
Atlantic
Ocean
Paris
Boulogne-sur-Mer
0   20 km
0   10 mi
©1994 MAGELLAN Geographix℠
Santa Barbara, CA (805) 685-3100

STUDENT MODEL

from *The Chunnel: The Tunnel That Builds Bridges*
by Dan Mahoney, Darien High School, Darien, Connecticut

The rivalry between England and France stems from centuries of war between these two countries. Although they were allies in both world wars, the animosity between England and France remains.① . . . [S]ince the tunnel was opened in 1994, however, it has helped to bring these two great cultures a little closer together.②

The greater ease of travel between Britain and France . . . has led to an increase in tourism between these two nations. ③ This is largely due to the efficiency of the Channel Tunnel. High-speed trains traverse the 23.6-mile tunnel in 35 minutes (Schmidt, E4).④ The boost in tourism has, in turn, led to greater mutual understanding. . . .⑤

① The writer provides background information for readers.

② This statement reveals the writer's thesis.

③ The writer supports his thesis with this fact.

④ The writer acknowledges the source of this fact by using a parenthetical note.

⑤ The writer elaborates with a cause-and-effect statement.

APPLYING LANGUAGE SKILLS: Citing Sources

Document your use of others' ideas or words with footnotes, endnotes, or parenthetical citations.

Text Citation: Footnote

Laura Wortley states, "The 'British' Impressionists translated the harsh facts of reality into a beautiful, fragile, fiction."[1]

Bottom of Page: Footnote

1. Laura Wortley, *British Impressionism: A Garden of Bright Images*. (London: The Studio Fine Art Publications, 1987) 285.

(For endnotes, number each cited passage like a footnote, but create a separate page for endnotes.)

Text Citation: Parenthetical

Laura Wortley states, "The 'British' Impressionists translated the harsh facts of reality into a beautiful, fragile, fiction" (Wortley 285).

Writing Application Refer to these examples as you document your sources.

Writer's Solution Connection Writing Lab

For help with Internet research, complete the interactive instruction dealing with on-line services in the Gathering Information section of the Research Writing tutorial.

Prewriting

Choose a Topic If your teacher has not assigned a topic and you're having trouble finding interesting subjects, consider using one of these topic ideas:

Topic Ideas

- Weapons and tactics in World War I
- Picasso's early years in Paris

Selection-Related Topic Ideas

- The Easter Rising in Ireland (1916)
- The influence of Keats on Wilfred Owen
- Yeats's ideas about historical cycles

Consider Your Audience and Purpose Identify your audience (your readers) and purpose (your reason for writing), and gather details that will suit both.

Research Information Collect information from a variety of credible resources, such as nonfiction books, almanacs, atlases, textbooks, anthologies, and technical sources, including databases and the Internet. On index cards, note the source (title, date, page number, author) from which each detail comes.

Organize Details Arrange your note cards in a clear and logical order. Here are some suggestions:

▶ **Chronological** Organize events in time order, especially if you will be giving a narrative account.
▶ **Order of importance** Organize details from least important to most important, or the other way around.
▶ **Cause and effect** Organize details according to causal relationships between them.
▶ **Pro and con** Arrange details in two categories: those that support an idea or point of view and those that contradict it.
▶ **Comparison and contrast** Arrange details in two categories: those showing similarities between two subjects and those showing differences between them.

Drafting

Draft a Thesis Statement Formulate a working thesis that can guide your writing. Modify this statement as you draft.

Work From Your Note Cards Work with prearranged note cards in front of you so that your thoughts are organized and you have facts at your fingertips to support your arguments.

Revising

Fact Check Review your draft, and highlight each fact you've used. Then verify each fact by checking it carefully against your sources.

Revision Tips Revise your research report, using the following tips to guide you:

▶ Check to be sure details and language are appropriate for your audience and purpose.

▶ Be sure you have maintained a consistent organization.

▶ Delete any details that do not support your thesis.

▶ Verify that you have properly credited sources for ideas and wording that are not your own.

▶ Proofread for errors in grammar, punctuation, capitalization, and spelling.

REVISION MODEL

①, undisputed leader of the Modernist movement in poetry,
Thomas Stearns Eliot was born and educated in the United

States. His conversion to the Anglican Church in 1927

marked a new phase in his life and in his writing.② When
③ Eliot was studying at Oxford University, and he chose to remain in
England, eventually acquiring British citizenship.
WWI broke out, Eliot chose to remain in England. In 1915,

the year he married, Eliot published *The Love Song of*

④, a bleak picture of a world fragmented by WWI and its aftermath.
J. Alfred Prufrock.

① This information strengthens the writer's purpose, which is to reveal the lasting influence Eliot has had on poetry.

② This statement must be deleted and moved because it is out of chronological order.

③ These details elaborate on the poet's background and nationality.

④ Taking into account the knowledge level of the reader, the author adds a brief description.

Publishing

▶ **Multimedia** Create a multimedia presentation that enhances the information in your report.

▶ **Internet** E-mail your work to interested people. For example, if you have written about Elizabethan clothing, send your paper to a site dedicated to costume design.

APPLYING LANGUAGE SKILLS: Creating a Bibliography

Complete your paper by creating a bibliography of the works you have cited in your writing.

Book:
Fussell, Paul. *The Great War and Modern Memory*. New York: Oxford University Press, 1975.

Magazine or newspaper article:
Roach, Margaret. "Wedgwood." *Martha Stewart Living*, April 1997: 134–139.

Reference book:
"Imagery." *The Oxford Companion to the English Language*. 1992 ed.

CD-ROM:
"World Wonders: Eiffel Tower." Planet Earth, Macmillan Digital: 1996.

Electronic journals/newsletters:
Engle-Cox, Glen. "The Life and Times of Macintosh." Book Review Resources: 3pp. On line. Internet. 21 July 1996.

Videotape:
King Richard II. Dir. William Woodman. With David Birney and Paul Shenar. Bennett Video Group, 1982.

Writing Application Refer to these examples as you create a bibliography for your research report. List all the important sources you consulted in your research.

Student Success Workshop

Real-World Reading Skills | Using Databases and the Internet

Strategies for Success

The Internet contains mountains of information. A great deal of it is accurate, but some pages include exaggerations or falsehoods. Use caution when collecting facts from the Internet.

Consider the Sponsor Every site on the Internet is sponsored by a group or an individual. Be wary if no author or sponsor is listed. Think about why this site was created. Evaluating a sponsor's motivation will help you detect bias.

Consider these questions:

▶ What purpose might the sponsor have in maintaining this site?

▶ Which facts and details might be biased?

▶ Which generalizations are too sweeping?

Verify Data Anyone can post anything to the Internet and claim it is factual. When possible, verify information by checking other Internet sources and reputable books and magazines.

Don't Be Fooled by Fancy Graphics An impressive look is no guarantee of truthfulness. Art and design programs make it simple to create a Web page that looks professional, but that doesn't mean the editing and research were careful and thorough. Use critical thinking skills and a healthy dose of skepticism to weed out Web sites that are unreliable.

Apply the Strategies

You are conducting a research report on George Orwell. While surfing the Internet, you find this site, full of writing by and opinions about the author. Use questions like the following to decide if the information is valid:

1. (a) Who sponsored the site? (b) What biases might this organization have?
2. What is questionable about the poll results that are quoted?
3. How could you verify that Orwell wrote the advice to writers on this page?

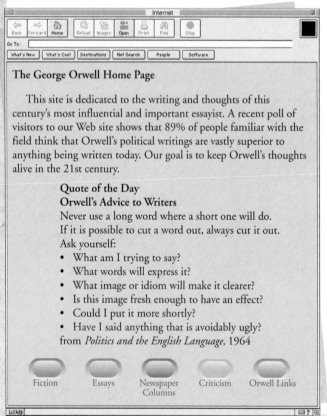

The George Orwell Home Page

This site is dedicated to the writing and thoughts of this century's most influential and important essayist. A recent poll of visitors to our Web site shows that 89% of people familiar with the field think that Orwell's political writings are vastly superior to anything being written today. Our goal is to keep Orwell's thoughts alive in the 21st century.

Quote of the Day
Orwell's Advice to Writers
Never use a long word where a short one will do.
If it is possible to cut a word out, always cut it out.
Ask yourself:
• What am I trying to say?
• What words will express it?
• What image or idiom will make it clearer?
• Is this image fresh enough to have an effect?
• Could I put it more shortly?
• Have I said anything that is avoidably ugly?
from *Politics and the English Language,* 1964

Fiction   Essays   Newspaper   Criticism   Orwell Links
Columns

✔ Here are other published materials that you should evaluate and question for factual truth:
▶ Pamphlets or leaflets distributed on the street
▶ Direct mail
▶ Posters and billboards

PART **2** *Conflicts Abroad
and at Home*

A Balloon Site, Coventry, 1940
Dame Laura Knight, Imperial War Museum

Britain had its share of conflicts during the twentieth century. It fought in two world wars, which cost many lives. Writers who fought and sometimes died in these struggles expressed their sense of patriotism, horror, or compassion. Britain won both wars, yet by mid-century had lost nearly all of Ireland, India, and most of its empire.

Guide for Interpreting

Rupert Brooke *(1887–1915)*

Rupert Brooke had striking good looks, personal charm, and high intelligence. Before World War I began, Brooke had already established himself as a serious poet. In 1914, when war broke out, he joined the Royal Naval Division. Tragically, he died from blood poisoning while on a mission to defeat the Turks. Brooke's war sonnets, traditional and idealistic, were among the last from the soldier-poets of World War I that expressed unalloyed patriotism.

Siegfried Sassoon *(1886–1967)*

Born into a wealthy family in Kent, England, Sassoon published a number of pastoral poems and parodies while still in his twenties. In 1914, he joined the army and showed such reckless courage in battle that he earned the nickname "Mad Jack," along with a medal for gallantry. By 1917, though, Sassoon's attitude toward war had changed. He began to write starkly realistic "trench poems" about war's agonies. In 1918, he was mistakenly shot by a sentry and spent the rest of the war in a hospital. Although he lived for nearly fifty years more, he wrote little to match his wartime verses.

Wilfred Owen *(1893–1918)*

Always interested in literature, but unable to win a university scholarship, Wilfred Owen joined the army in 1915 and became a respected officer. He was wounded three times in 1917, and he won a medal for outstanding bravery in 1918. One week before the end of the war, he was killed in battle. Owen was influenced by Siegfried Sassoon after the two met in an army hospital. Having published only four poems during his lifetime, Owen was unknown as a poet until Siegfried Sassoon published a collection of his work, *Poems*, in 1920.

Saki (H. H. Munro) *(1870–1916)*

Despite an unhappy childhood, Saki was known for his witty and humorous short stories. While conventional in some aspects, many of Saki's stories contain dark humor and cynical attitudes, as evidenced in the famous story "The Open Window." When the Great War broke out, Saki refused a commission, preferring to serve as an enlisted man. He was killed in the Battle of the Somme two years after he volunteered for service.

◆ Background for Understanding

HISTORY: WORLD WAR I

Called the "Great War," World War I was fought from 1914 to 1918. It began with the assassination of Archduke Ferdinand, heir to the throne of Austria, but quickly spread to nearly every country in the world. Nations fought either on the side of the Allies (Great Britain, France, Russia, and Italy) or with the Central Powers (Germany, Austria-Hungary, and the Ottoman Empire). The war was long, muddy, bloody, and complex, involving nationalist sentiments, hostile alliances, and arms races. By the time the Armistice, or peace treaty, was signed on November 11, 1918, about ten million people had been killed.

◆ *Literature and Your Life*

CONNECT YOUR EXPERIENCE

You're thigh-deep in mud, trembling in the darkness, on the alert for the whine of a grenade. Supplies are low, half your friends have died, and disease is beginning to affect "uninjured soldiers." Three more countries have joined the war, and no end is in sight.

World War I's unprecedented devastation and slaughter inspired millions of words—patriotic, indignant, or disillusioned, depending on who wrote them. As you read, look for details about the effects of war on people, animals, and the land.

THEMATIC FOCUS: CONFLICTS ABROAD AND AT HOME

The writers of these works were participants in the Great War. As you read, identify each writer's attitude about war.

Journal Writing Jot down some ideas that spring to mind when you think of war.

◆ Build Vocabulary

LATIN WORD ROOTS: *-laud-*

The word *laudable* comes from the Latin root *-laud-*, which means "praise." Knowing this, you can deduce that "laudable efforts," which Saki uses in his story, mean "praiseworthy efforts."

WORD BANK

Before you read, preview this list of words.

stealthy
desolate
mockeries
pallor
laudable
requisitioned
disconcerted

◆ Grammar and Style

USE OF *WHO* AND *WHOM* IN ADJECTIVE CLAUSES

Case is determined by the way a word is used. *Who,* in the subjective case, is used as a subject or a subject complement. *Whom,* in the objective case, is used as a direct object or as an object of a preposition. When *who* and *whom* are used in adjective clauses, the correct case is determined by the word's use in the clause.

Subject in Clause: What passing-bells for these *who die as cattle?*

Direct Object in Clause: A dust *whom England bore, shaped, made aware . . .*

◆ Literary Focus

TONE

The **tone** of a literary work is the writer's attitude toward the readers and toward the subject, which is primarily conveyed by his or her choice of words and details. In this passage, Rupert Brooke's recollection of England conveys a tone of patriotism and wistfulness:

> Her sights and sounds;
> dreams happy as her day; /
> And laughter, learnt of
> friends; and gentleness, / In
> hearts at peace, under an
> English heaven.

◆ Reading Strategy

DRAW INFERENCES

Because many elements of literature—tone, mood, theme—are implied, readers must **draw inferences,** educated guesses based on clues within the text.

For example, in "The Soldier," the phrase "foreign field" is a clue that the speaker is away from his native country. Within the poem, there are four direct references to England, giving the poem a patriotic tone. Finally, its theme can be inferred from several clues, including the speaker's observation that his foreign grave would be "forever England."

As you read, make inferences based on clues like these.

The Soldier

Rupert Brooke

If I should die, think only this of me:
    That there's some corner of a foreign field
That is forever England. There shall be
    In that rich earth a richer dust concealed;
5   A dust whom England bore, shaped, made aware,
    Gave, once, her flowers to love, her ways to roam,
A body of England's, breathing English air,
Washed by the rivers, blest by suns of home.

And think, this heart, all evil shed away,
10   A pulse in the eternal mind, no less
    Gives somewhere back the thoughts by England given;
Her sights and sounds; dreams happy as her day;
    And laughter, learnt of friends; and gentleness,
    In hearts at peace, under an English heaven.

▶ Critical Viewing How does the sentiment expressed in this poster relate to that in the poem? [Connect]

Beyond Literature

Community Connection

Showing Appreciation to War Veterans Citizens who fight in their nation's wars risk their own lives in the name of the entire community. Monuments are one important way that the community recognizes this sacrifice and expresses its gratitude to veterans. A monument may take any durable, public form, from plaques or statues to government buildings or opera houses to parks or museums. Usually there's a dedication to the veterans of a particular war. Often, memorials include a list of the names of the fallen, the most renowned of which is on the Vietnam War memorial in Washington.

If you were on a committee that had responsibility for paying tribute to returning soldiers, what would you suggest be done? What do you think is the best way of expressing gratitude to veterans?

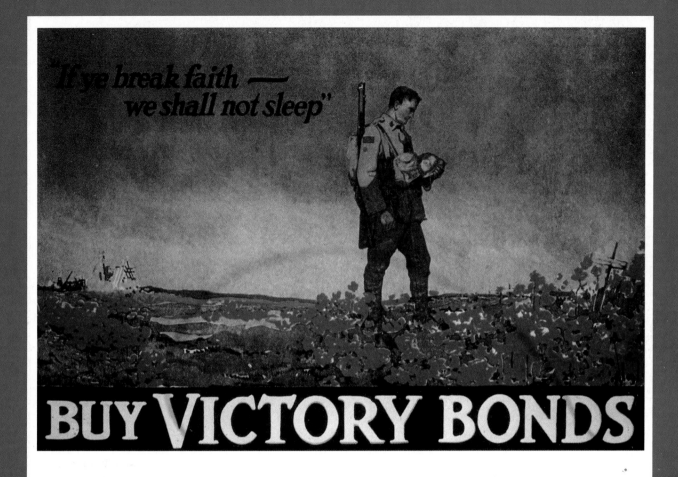

"If ye break faith —
we shall not sleep"

BUY VICTORY BONDS

Guide for Responding

◆ *Literature and Your Life*

Reader's Response Do you find the speaker's patriotism touching or sentimental? Why?

Thematic Focus How do conflicts such as World War I affect people's ideas about patriotism?

Questions for Research Generate research questions about Rupert Brooke's literary reputation and what it suggests about the outlook of the post-World War I era.

☑ Check Your Comprehension

1. How does the speaker ask his readers to remember him, should he die?
2. What three things has England given the speaker?

◆ Critical Thinking

INTERPRET

1. Why would the speaker go off to war, knowing he could be killed? **[Infer]**
2. What is the "richer dust" to which the speaker refers? **[Interpret]**
3. The speaker says his heart will become a "pulse in the eternal mind." Explain what he means. **[Interpret]**

EVALUATE

4. Brooke's attitude has been called a "ridiculous anachronism"—something outdated—in the face of modern warfare. Do you agree or disagree? **[Make a Judgment]**

Drawing of Tanks, World War I

◀ **Critical Viewing** How does the painter use color and line to convey the realities of war? [Analyze]

Wirers¹

Siegfried Sassoon

"Pass it along, the wiring party's going out"—
And yawning sentries mumble, "Wirers going out."
Unraveling; twisting; hammering stakes with muffled thud,
They toil with <u>stealthy</u> haste and anger in their blood.

5   The Boche² sends up a flare. Black forms stand rigid there,
Stock-still like posts; then darkness, and the clumsy ghosts
Stride hither and thither, whispering, tripped by clutching snare
Of snags and tangles.
            Ghastly dawn with vaporous coasts
10 Gleams <u>desolate</u> along the sky, night's misery ended.

Young Hughes was badly hit; I heard him carried away,
Moaning at every lurch; no doubt he'll die today.
But *we* can say the front-line wire's been safely mended.

---

1. **wirers:** Soldiers who were responsible for repairing the barbed-wire fences that protected the trenches in World War I.
2. **Boche** (bôsh): German soldier.

◆ **Build Vocabulary**

stealthy (stel´ *thē*) *adj*.: In a quiet, secretive way

desolate (des´ ə lit) *adj*.: Deserted; forlorn

mockeries (mäk´ ər ēz) *n*.: Ridicule; futile or disappointing efforts

pallor (pal´ ər) *n*.: Lack of color; paleness

Anthem for Doomed Youth

Wilfred Owen

What passing-bells for these who die as cattle?
Only the monstrous anger of the guns.
Only the stuttering rifles' rapid rattle
Can patter out their hasty orisons.[1]
5   No mockeries for them from prayers or bells,
Nor any voice of mourning save the choirs—
The shrill, demented choirs of wailing shells;
And bugles calling for them from sad shires.[2]

What candles may be held to speed them all?
10 Not in the hands of boys, but in their eyes
Shall shine the holy glimmers of good-byes.
The pallor of girls' brows shall be their pall;
Their flowers the tenderness of patient minds,
And each slow dusk a drawing-down of blinds.

◄ **Critical Viewing** Does the compassion Owen shows in the poem come through in this photograph of him? Explain. **[Analyze]**

---

1. **orisons** (or´ i zəns) *n*: Prayers.
2. **shires** (shīrz) *n*: Any of the counties of England.

Guide for Responding

◆ *Literature and Your Life*

Reader's Response Which poem conveys the horrors of war more effectively? Why?

Thematic Focus In times of conflict, what aspects of humanity are ignored?

☑ Check Your Comprehension

1. (a) What are the wirers getting ready to do at the beginning of the "Wirers"? (b) What happens when an enemy flare lights the scene?
2. What does the speaker in "Wirers" think will happen to the soldier named Hughes?
3. According to "Anthem for Doomed Youth," what are the only voices heard mourning the dying soldiers?
4. Where do the "holy glimmers of good-byes" shine in "Anthem for Doomed Youth"?

◆ Critical Thinking

INTERPRET
1. How do the soldiers in "Wirers" feel about the job they have to do? **[Infer]**
2. (a) Who is referred to as *we* in line 13 of "Wirers"? (b) What is the speaker's attitude towards this "we"? **[Draw Conclusions]**
3. Why does the speaker in "Anthem" refer to prayers and bells as mockeries? **[Interpret]**
4. (a) Name the four conventional signs of mourning in lines 9–14 of "Anthem." (b) What do Owen's suggested replacements for these signs have in common? **[Analyze]**
5. Explain how the last six lines of "Anthem" answer the first eight. **[Analyze]**

APPLY
6. Could the messages of these poems apply to other wars? Explain. **[Relate]**

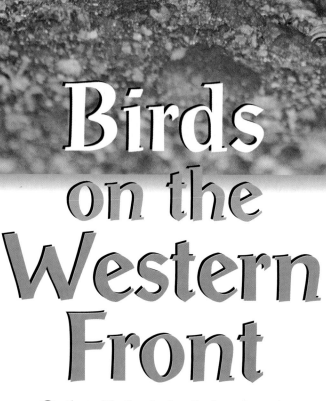

Birds on the Western Front

Saki (H. H. Munro)

Considering the enormous economic dislocation which the war operations have caused in the regions where the campaign[1] is raging, there seems to be very little corresponding disturbance in the bird life of the same districts. Rats and mice have mobilized and swarmed into the fighting line, and there has been a partial mobilization of owls, particularly barn owls, following in the wake of the mice, and making <u>laudable</u> efforts to thin out

---

1. **campaign:** Battles being fought against the Germans during World War I.

◀ **Critical Viewing** How does this photograph of an owl represent the separateness of nature from human existence that Saki stresses in this selection? [Draw Conclusions]

their numbers. What success attends their hunting one cannot estimate; there are always sufficient mice left over to populate one's dug-out and make a parade-ground and race-course of one's face at night. In the matter of nesting accommodation the barn owls are well provided for; most of the still intact barns in the war zone are requisitioned for billeting[2] purposes, but there is a wealth of ruined houses, whole streets and clusters of them, such as can hardly have been available at any previous moment of the world's history since Nineveh and Babylon[3] became humanly desolate. Without human occupation and cultivation there can have been no corn, no refuse, and consequently very few mice, and the owls of Nineveh cannot have enjoyed very good hunting; here in Northern France the owls have desolation and mice at their disposal in unlimited quantities, and as these birds breed in winter as well as in summer, there should be a goodly output of war owlets to cope with the swarming generations of war mice.

Apart from the owls one cannot notice that the campaign is making any marked difference in the bird life of the country-side. The vast flocks of crows and ravens that one expected to find in the neighborhood of the fighting line are non-existent, which is perhaps rather a pity. The obvious explanation is that the roar and crash and fumes of high explosives have driven the crow tribe in panic from the fighting area; like many obvious explanations, it is not a correct one. The crows of the locality are not at-tracted to the battlefield, but they certainly are not scared away from it. The rook is normally so gun-shy and nervous where noise is concerned that the sharp banging of a barn door or the report of a toy pistol will sometimes set an entire rookery in commotion; out here I have seen him sedately busy among the refuse heaps of a battered village, with shells bursting at no great distance, and the impatient-sounding, snapping rattle of machine-guns going on all round him; for all the notice that he took he might have been in some peaceful English meadow on a sleepy Sunday afternoon. Whatever else German frightfulness may have done it has not frightened the rook of North-Eastern France; it has made his nerves steadier than they have ever been before, and future genera-tions of small boys, em-ployed in scaring rooks away from the sown crops in this region, will have to invent something in the way of super-frightfulness to achieve their purpose. Crows and magpies are nesting well within the shell-swept area, and over a small beech-copse I once saw a pair of crows engaged in hot com-bat with a pair of sparrow-hawks, while con-siderably higher in the sky, but almost directly above them, two Allied battle-planes were en-gaging an equal number of enemy aircraft.

◆ **Literary Focus** What tone does Saki use in this description of the rook?

Unlike the barn owls, the magpies have had their choice of building sites considerably re-stricted by the ravages of war; the whole av-enues of poplars, where they were accustomed to construct their nests, have been blown to bits, leaving nothing but dreary-looking rows of shattered and splintered trunks to show where once they stood. Affection for a particular tree has in one case induced a pair of magpies to build their bulky, domed nest in the battered remnants[4] of a poplar of which so little re-mained standing that the nest looked almost bigger than the tree; the effect rather suggested an archiepiscopal enthronement[5] taking place in the ruined remains of Melrose Abbey. The magpie, wary and suspicious in his wild state,

---

2. **billeting** (bil´ it in) *adj.*: Designated for sleeping by written order as soldiers' quarters.
3. **Nineveh** (nin´ ə və) **and Babylon** (bab´ ə lən): Two great and prosperous ancient civilizations that fell to ruin and desolation.

◆ Build Vocabulary

laudable (lôd´ ə bəl) *adj.*: Worthy of praise

requisitioned (rek´ wə zish´ ənd) *v.*: To have requested or applied for with a formal written order

---

4. **remnants** (rem´ nənts) *n.*: Remainder; what is left over.
5. **archiepiscopal** (är´ kē ə pis´ kə pəl) **enthronement**: Ceremony during which the rank and duties of archbishop are conferred.

must be rather intrigued at the change that has come over the erst-while[6] fearsome not-to-be-avoided human, stalking everywhere over the earth as its possessor, who now creeps about in screened and sheltered ways, as chary of showing himself in the open as the shyest of wild creatures.

The buzzard, that earnest seeker after mice, does not seem to be taking any war risks, at least I have never seen one out here, but kestrels[7] hover about all day in the hottest parts of the line, not in the least <u>disconcerted</u>, apparently, when a promising mouse-area suddenly rises in the air in a cascade of black or yellow earth. Sparrow-hawks are fairly numerous, and a mile or two back from the firing line I saw a pair of hawks that I took to be red-legged falcons, circling over the top of an oak-copse. According to investigations made by Russian naturalists, the effect of the war on bird life on the Eastern front has been more marked than it has been over here. "During the first year of the war rooks disappeared, larks no longer sang in the fields, the wild pigeon disappeared also." The skylark in this region has stuck tenaciously to the meadows and crop-lands that have been seamed and bisected with trenches and honeycombed with shell-holes. In the chill, misty hour of gloom that precedes a rainy dawn, when nothing seemed alive except a few wary waterlogged sentries[8] and many scuttling rats, the lark would suddenly dash skyward and pour forth a song of ecstatic jubilation that sounded horribly forced and insincere. It seemed scarcely possible that the bird

168th Infantry French and American Raiding Party, Badonviller, France, March 1918

▲ **Critical Viewing** What does this photograph imply about soldiers' relationship with nature? Does Saki make the same point? Explain. **[Infer]**

could carry its insouciance[9] to the length of attempting to rear a brood in that desolate wreckage of shattered clods and gaping shell-holes, but once, having occasion to throw myself down with some abruptness on my face, I found myself nearly on the top of a brood of young larks. Two of them had already been hit by something, and were in rather a battered condition, but the survivors seemed as tranquil and comfortable as the average nestling.

At the corner of a stricken wood (which has had a name made for it in history, but shall be nameless here), at a moment when lyddite and shrapnel[10] and machine-gun fire swept and

◆ **Reading Strategy**
What can you infer about Saki's feelings about nature and war from his juxtaposition of images of peace and violence?

---

6. **erst-while** (ʉrst′hwīl′) *adv.*: Formerly.
7. **kestrel** (kes′ trəl) *n.*: Either of two small reddish-gray European falcons.
8. **sentries** (sen′ trēs) *n.*: Men of military guard that are posted to warn others of danger.

9. **insouciance** (in sōō′sē əns) *n.*: The state of being calm and untroubled.
10. **lyddite** (lid′ it) **and shrapnel** (shrap′ nəl) *n.*: Lyddite is a powerful explosive, and shrapnel is a collection of fragments scattered by an exploding shell or bomb.

raked and bespattered that devoted spot as though the artillery of an entire Division had suddenly concentrated on it, a wee hen-chaffinch flitted wistfully to and fro, amid splintered and falling branches that had never a green bough left on them. The wounded lying there, if any of them noticed the small bird, may well have wondered why anything having wings and no pressing reason for remaining should have chosen to stay in such a place. There was a battered orchard alongside the stricken wood, and the probable explanation of the bird's presence was that it had a nest of young ones whom it was too scared to feed, too loyal to desert. Later on, a small flock of chaffinches blundered into the wood, which they were doubtless in the habit of using as a highway to their feeding-grounds; unlike the solitary hen-bird, they made no secret of their desire to get away as fast as their dazed wits would let them. The only other bird I ever saw there was a magpie, flying low over the wreck-

age of fallen tree-limbs; "one for sorrow," says the old superstition. There was sorrow enough in that wood.

The English gamekeeper, whose knowledge of wild life usually runs on limited and perverted lines, has evolved a sort of religion as to the nervous debility[11] of even the hardiest game birds; according to his beliefs a terrier trotting across a field in which a partridge is nesting, or a mouse-hawking kestrel hovering over the hedge, is sufficient cause to drive the distracted bird off its eggs and send it whirring into the next county.

The partridge of the war zone shows no signs of such sensitive nerves. The rattle and rumble of transport, the constant coming and going of bodies of troops, the incessant rattle of musketry and deafening explosions of artillery, the night-long flare and flicker of star-shells, have not sufficed to scare the local birds away from their chosen feeding grounds, and to all appearances they have not been deterred from raising their broods. Gamekeepers who are serving with the colors might seize the opportunity to indulge in a little useful nature study.

---

11. **debility** (də bil′ ə tē) n.: Weakness or feebleness of body.

◆ Build Vocabulary

disconcerted (dis′ kən sʉrt′ əd) adj.: Embarassed and confused

Guide for Responding

◆ Literature and Your Life

Reader's Response Do you find the speaker's tone engaging? Why or why not?

Thematic Focus What effect does war have on wildlife?

Journal Writing How are humans and birds alike in their reactions to war? How do they differ?

☑ Check Your Comprehension

1. Where is the narrator? In what situation does he find himself?
2. How have the crows surprised the writer?
3. How does the war affect the birds in Russia?
4. What is the speaker's explanation of why the female chaffinch stayed on the battleground?

◆ Critical Thinking

INTERPRET

1. What effect has the "mobilization" of the rats and mice had on the owl population? **[Analyze Cause and Effect]**
2. (a) Describe the change that has occurred in human behavior, as witnessed by the magpie (paragraph 3). (b) What does this change imply about the state of humanity? **[Infer]**
3. What do you think is Saki's purpose in writing this description of wildlife in a war zone? **[Draw Conclusions]**

APPLY

4. How might various kinds of birds be affected by a modern war? **[Speculate]**

Guide for Responding (continued)

◆ Literary Focus

TONE

The **tone** in a work of literature is determined by the author's attitude toward the subject. Because a writer's tone is unstated or implied, examine the style of language and word choice to identify it. By identifying the tone, readers can understand and appreciate how it enhances the work or helps to convey the writer's purpose.

For example, after reading "The Soldier," you may identify the tone as patriotic, yet gentle and loving. Then, when you reflect about the poem's speaker, a soldier fighting on foreign soil, you gain a deeper understanding of the poignancy present in the speaker's tone.

1. (a) What is the speaker's attitude toward "Young Hughes" in "Wirers"? (b) How is this attitude revealed?
2. In "Anthem for Doomed Youth," Wilfred Owen contrasts customary funeral rituals with unceremonious death on the battlefield. In making this comparison, what tone does the poem take on?
3. (a) How would you describe the tone of "Birds on the Western Front"? (b) Explain how the tone reinforces the writer's purpose.

◆ Reading Strategy

DRAW INFERENCES

Draw inferences as you read to identify a work's tone, mood, theme, and any unstated but useful details. For example, in "Wirers" there are several details that suggest that the wirers' missions were dangerous. Phrases such as "ghastly dawn" and "night's misery" help create a mood of misery. Finally, the last three lines of the poem are cynical and ironic, revealing an attitude or tone of disgust.

1. (a) What can you infer about the speaker's situation in "The Soldier"? (b) What details lead you to this conclusion?
2. (a) In "Anthem for Doomed Youth," who are "these who die as cattle"? (b) How does this phrase help to set the tone of the poem?
3. (a) What is the tone of "Birds on the Western Front"? (b) How does the tone reinforce the theme of the story?

◆ Build Vocabulary

USING THE LATIN ROOT *-laud-*

With the knowledge that the Latin root *-laud-* means "praise," define each of these words. Incorporate the definition of *-laud-* into each answer.

1. applaud   2. plausible   3. laudatory   4. plaudit

USING THE WORD BANK: Context

Replace each italicized word or phrase with a word from the Word Bank.

Lying in the *deserted* trench, the wounded soldier's *paleness* became more pronounced. The *secretive* approach of a medic *unnerved* him. Although the medical supplies that had been *ordered* were *cheap imitations* of usable ones, the medic made *praiseworthy* efforts to save the wounded soldier.

◆ Grammar and Style

CORRECT USE OF *WHO* AND *WHOM* IN ADJECTIVE CLAUSES

When ***who*** and ***whom*** are used in **adjective clauses,** the correct case is determined by the word's use in the clause. *Who* is used for subjects and subject complements. *Whom* is used for objects of verbs and prepositions.

Practice In your notebook, write *who* or *whom* to complete each sentence.
1. Rupert Brooke, ____?____ wrote a poem thought of as his own epitaph, died before seeing battle.
2. Siegfried Sassoon, without ____?____ Wilfred Owen would be an unknown poet, was wounded twice in the war.
3. Wilfred Owen, ____?____ wrote about "the pity of war," was killed a week before the war ended.

Writing Application Rewrite each pair of sentences as one sentence, using an adjective clause with *who* or *whom*.
1. Rupert Brooke was born in 1887. He was the son of a housemaster at Rugby School.
2. At school, Brooke became involved in amateur acting. He attended King's College, Cambridge.
3. Brooke was a poet of remarkable promise. He wrote the line, "Blow out, you bugles, over the rich Dead!"

Build Your Portfolio

 Idea Bank

Writing

1. **Interview Questions** Prepare a set of questions about war that you'd like any of these writers to answer.

2. **Veterans Day** Veterans Day is celebrated on the anniversary of the signing of the armistice that ended World War I. In many places, there are no longer Veterans Day parades to honor war veterans. Write an editorial in which you express your views on such parades.

3. **Critical Response** Charles Sorley said of Rupert Brooke's patriotism, "He has clothed his attitude in fine words; but he has taken the sentimental attitude." Write an essay in response, using "The Soldier" to support your views. **[Literature Link]**

Speaking, Listening, and Viewing

4. **Debate** With three others, debate this statement: "Some issues are worth going to war over." Two people should take the pro side, and two should take the con side. **[Social Studies Link]**

5. **Skit** If birds could talk, what would they say? Put on a skit in which talking birds discuss how a war between humans is interfering with their everyday lives. **[Performing Arts Link]**

Researching and Representing

6. **Timeline** With a group, create an illustrated timeline beginning with the assassination of Archduke Ferdinand in 1914. **[Social Studies Link]**

7. **Trench Warfare** Learn more about trench warfare during World War I, focusing on a soldier's daily life, and present your findings to your class. Consult Paul Fussell's *The Great War and Modern Memory*. **[Social Studies Link]**

Online Activity www.phlit.phschool.com

 Guided Writing Lesson

Historical Letter

During World War I, soldiers maintained links with home by writing letters. In their letters, they no doubt talked about the past (their memories of home), the present (what it's like on the battlefront), and the future (how much they longed to get home). Put yourself in the place of a soldier at war, and write a letter home to a family member.

As you describe events, use transitions to show how these events are related in time.

Writing Skills Focus: Transitions to Show Time

All types of writing, from personal letters to legal documents, benefit from the use of **transitions** to connect and clarify the relationship of events in time. As you write your letter, use transitions—such as *first, then,* and *finally*—to link events in time.

Follow these strategies as you write.

Prewriting Decide on your character (are you an officer, a pilot, a wirer, a foot-soldier?) and on the recipient of your letter (a sibling, a friend, a parent). Make a three-column table with these headings: *Past, Present, Future.* Under each heading, jot down a few ideas for your letter.

Drafting Using a standard letter format, draft your letter home, describing events your character has seen and expressing hopes for the future. Use transition words—such as *first, next, then, after that,* and *later*—to indicate the order in which events happened or will happen.

Revising Show your letter to a classmate, and ask whether the time transitions are clear and if any sections need better development. Use the suggestions to make your letter easier to understand.

Guide for Interpreting

Winston Churchill *(1874–1965)*

"Never in the field of human conflict was so much owed by so many to so few." Winston Churchill spoke these words in tribute to the Royal Air Force in 1940. Prime Minister of England during a turbulent period in its history, Churchill was also one of the finest writers and speakers of his time.

Churchill the Warrior Directly descended from the dukes of Marlborough, Churchill was educated at Harrow and the Royal Military College at Sandhurst. After serving in Cuba, India, and South Africa, he was first elected to Parliament in 1900 and went on to play an important role in the government during World War I. During the 1930's, Churchill vigorously criticized government policies, warning against the ominous ambitions of Nazi Germany. He became Prime Minister in May 1940, after World War II had broken out, and went on to play a key role in the eventual victory of the Allies.

Churchill the Writer Amazingly, Churchill found time to write even within a busy public career. During the 1930's, he produced a four-volume historical work on his ancestor, the first Duke of Marlborough. His monumental history entitled *The Second World War* (1948–1954) is now regarded as a classic. In 1953, he was awarded the Nobel Prize in literature.

Mohandas K. Gandhi *(1869–1948)*

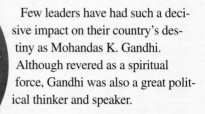

Few leaders have had such a decisive impact on their country's destiny as Mohandas K. Gandhi. Although revered as a spiritual force, Gandhi was also a great political thinker and speaker.

Finding a Mission Born in the northwestern Indian state of Gujarat, Ghandi went to London to study law when he was eighteen years old. From 1893 to 1914, he worked for an Indian law firm in South Africa. His experiences there as a victim of racial discrimination led him to join and lead protest campaigns. When he returned to India, he fought for independence from Britain.

Passive Resistance Working fearlessly for the cause of independence, Gandhi gradually developed the principles of his philosophy of *satyagraha,* or nonviolent resistance, which was to have worldwide influence, notably on the American Civil Rights leader Martin Luther King, Jr., and on South African freedom fighter Nelson Mandela. Gandhi devoted himself to improving the lot of India's lowest castes, or classes, and he worked ceaselessly for harmony between the country's two major religions, Hinduism and Islam. India gained independence in August 1947, but to Gandhi's distress Pakistan was established as a separate nation. A little more than five months afterwards, Gandhi was assassinated by a Hindu fanatic.

◆ Background for Understanding

HISTORY: CHURCHILL AND WORLD WAR II

When Churchill gave his first radio address as Prime Minister, France was Britain's only ally in opposing German aggression. Germany had already overrun several other countries. Soon after this speech was delivered, France would surrender. Through the dark days that followed, Churchill's speeches contributed powerfully to British morale.

HISTORY: GANDHI AND BRITISH POLICY

In response to Indian resistance, the British Empire imposed a series of repressive measures, known as the Rowlatt Acts, in 1919. Gandhi urged all Indians to refuse to obey such "unjust, subversive laws." Protest against the Rowlatt Acts led to the Amritsar massacre, in which British troops fired on an unarmed crowd, killing 400 Indians.

◆ Wartime Speech ◆
Defending Nonviolent Resistance

◆ *Literature and Your Life*

CONNECT YOUR EXPERIENCE

If you've ever stood up publicly for something you believed in, you took a risk. Even if you didn't risk injury, standing up for your beliefs—especially against prevailing opinion—could have caused you to lose popularity. In these selections, you'll see that the world leaders Churchill and Gandhi took substantial risks to assert their beliefs.

Journal Writing On a page in your notebook, freewrite about a person you admire, living or dead, who took a courageous stand for a cause or belief.

THEMATIC FOCUS: CONFLICTS ABROAD AND AT HOME

Notice what these speeches reveal about two of the most important conflicts Britain experienced during the twentieth century.

◆ Build Vocabulary

LATIN WORD ROOTS: *-dur-*

You will find the word *endurance* in Churchill's wartime speech. The Latin root *-dur-* means "hard." A synonym for *endurance* would be "toughness," the ability to withstand pain, fatigue, or wear.

WORD BANK

Before you read, preview this list of words from the speeches.

intimidated
endurance
formidable
invincible
retaliate
disaffection
diabolical
extenuating
excrescence

◆ Grammar and Style

PARALLEL STRUCTURE

Parallel structure is the use of the same grammatical form or pattern to express coordinate ideas. For example, Churchill uses parallel prepositional phrases early in his speech:

I speak to you for the first time as Prime Minister in a solemn hour for the life *of our country, of our Empire, of our Allies,* and, above all, *of the cause of* Freedom.

Parallel structure contributes to clarity and smoothness in writing. These qualities, in turn, make parallel structures easy to remember and therefore especially effective in persuasive writing or speaking. Look for other examples of parallelism in these speeches.

◆ Literary Focus

SPEECH

The general purpose of a **speech**, whether it sets out to inform, entertain, or persuade, is to get and maintain the interest of an audience. Organization and clarity are paramount in achieving this goal. The speaker's delivery—pitch, rate, rhythm, and inflection—also plays an important role in audience response.

Winston Churchill delivered his wartime speech over the radio, while Gandhi spoke in a packed Indian courtroom. The purpose of each speech was to persuade. Notice the different strategies each speaker used to achieve this purpose.

◆ Reading Strategy

IDENTIFY MAIN POINTS AND SUPPORT

Both Churchill and Gandhi deal with complex issues in their speeches. Both speakers, however, had a knack for presenting a few **main points** clearly and then using well-selected facts, examples, or reasons to **support** those points.

As you read these speeches, pause at the beginning of each paragraph to identify the speaker's main points. Then note the supporting details or arguments for each main idea.

Wartime Speech

Winston Churchill

**BBC, London,
19 May 1940**

I speak to you for the first time as Prime Minister in a solemn hour for the life of our country, of our Empire, of our Allies, and, above all, of the cause of Freedom. A tremendous battle is raging in France and Flanders.[1] The Germans, by a remarkable combination of air bombing and heavily armored tanks, have broken through the French defenses north of the Maginot Line,[2] and strong columns of their armored vehicles are ravaging the open country, which for the first day or two was without defenders. They have penetrated deeply and spread alarm and confusion in their track. Behind them there are now appearing infantry in lorries,[3] and behind them, again, the large masses are moving forward. The regroupment of the French armies to make head against,

▲ **Critical Viewing** In what ways does the presentation of a radio speech, such as Churchill's, differ from a speech given in person? **[Compare and Contrast]**

and also to strike at, this intruding wedge has been proceeding for several days, largely assisted by the magnificent efforts of the Royal Air Force.

We must not allow ourselves to be <u>intimidated</u> by the presence of these armored vehicles in unexpected places behind our lines. If they are behind our Front, the French are also at many points fighting actively behind theirs. Both sides are therefore in an extremely dangerous position. And if the French Army, and our own Army, are well handled, as I believe they will be; if the French retain that genius for recovery and counter-attack for which they have so long been famous; and if the British Army shows the dogged <u>endurance</u> and solid fighting power of which there have been so many exam-

---

1. **Flanders** (flan´ dərz): Region in Northwest Europe, on the North Sea, includes Northwest France and the provinces of East Flanders and West Flanders in Belgium.
2. **Maginot** (mazh´ ə nō) **Line:** Heavy fortifications built before World War II on the Eastern frontier of France; it did not prevent invasion during World War II.
3. **lorries** (lôr´ ēz) *n*.: British for "trucks."

ples in the past—then a sudden transformation of the scene might spring into being.

It would be foolish, however, to disguise the gravity of the hour. It would be still more foolish to lose heart and courage or to suppose that well-trained, well-equipped armies numbering three or four millions of men can be overcome in the space of a few weeks, or even months, by a scoop, or raid of mechanized vehicles, however <u>formidable</u>. We may look with confidence to the stabilization of the Front in France, and to the general engagement of the masses, which will enable the qualities of the French and British soldiers to be matched squarely against those of their adversaries. For myself, I have <u>invincible</u> confidence in the French Army and its leaders. Only a very small part of that splendid army has yet been heavily engaged; and only a very small part of France has yet been invaded. There is good evidence to show that practically the whole of the specialized and mechanized forces of the enemy have been already thrown into the battle; and we know that very heavy losses have been inflicted upon them. No officer or man, no brigade or division, which grapples at close quarters with the enemy, wherever encountered, can fail to make a worthy contribution to the general result. The Armies must cast away the idea of resisting behind concrete lines or natural obstacles, and must realize that mastery can only be regained by furious and unrelenting assault. And this spirit must not only animate the High Command, but must inspire every fighting man.

In the air—often at serious odds—often at odds hitherto[4] thought overwhelming—we have been clawing down three or four to one of our enemies; and the relative balance of the British and German Air Forces is now considerably more favorable to us than at the beginning of the battle. In cutting down the German

◆ Reading Strategy

What is the **main point** of this paragraph?

bombers, we are fighting our own battle as well as that of France. My confidence in our ability to fight it out to the finish with the German Air Force has been strengthened by the fierce encounters which have taken place and are taking place. At the same time, our heavy bombers are striking nightly at the taproot of German mechanized power, and have already inflicted serious damage upon the oil refineries on which the Nazi effort to dominate the world directly depends.

We must expect that as soon as stability is reached on the Western Front, the bulk of that hideous apparatus of aggression which gashed Holland into ruin and slavery in a few days, will be turned upon us. I am sure I speak for all when I say we are ready to face it; to endure it; and to <u>retaliate</u> against it—to any extent that the unwritten laws of war permit. There will be many men, and many women, in this island who when the ordeal comes upon them, as come it will, will feel comfort, and even a pride—that they are sharing the perils of our lads at the Front—soldiers, sailors and airmen, God bless them—and are drawing away from them a part at least of the onslaught they have to bear. Is not this the appointed time for all to make the utmost exertions in their power? If the battle is to be won, we must provide our men with ever-increasing quantities of the weapons and ammunition they need. We must have, and have quickly, more airplanes, more tanks, more shells, more guns. There is imperious need for these vital munitions. They increase our strength against the powerfully armed enemy. They replace the wastage of the obstinate struggle; and the knowledge that wastage will speedily be replaced enables us to draw more readily upon our reserves and throw them in now that everything counts so much.

Our task is not only to win the battle—but to win the War. After this battle in France abates[5] its force, there will come the battle for our island—for all that Britain is, and all that Britain

---

4. **hitherto** (hith´ ər too̅) *adv.*: Until this time.

◆ **Build Vocabulary**

intimidated (in tim´ə dāt´ əd) *v.*: Made afraid, frightened

endurance (en door´ əns) *n.*: Ability to withstand pain or fatigue

formidable (fôr´ mə də bəl) *adj.*: Causing fear or dread

invincible (in vin´ sə bəl) *adj.*: Unconquerable

retaliate (ri tal´ ē āt´) *v.*: Return an injury or wrong

---

5. **abates** (ə bāts´) *v.*: Makes less in amount.

means. That will be the struggle. In that supreme emergency we shall not hesitate to take every step, even the most drastic, to call forth from our people the last ounce and the last inch of effort of which they are capable. The interests of property, the hours of labor, are nothing compared with the struggle for life and honor, for right and freedom, to which we have vowed ourselves.

I have received from the Chiefs of the French Republic, and in particular from its indomitable Prime Minister, M. Reynaud, the most sacred pledges that whatever happens they will fight to the end, be it bitter or be it glorious. Nay, if we fight to the end, it can only be glorious.

Having received His Majesty's commission, I have found an administration of men and women of every party and of almost every point of view. We have differed and quarreled in the past; but now one bond unites us all—to wage war until victory is won, and never to surrender ourselves to servitude and shame, whatever the cost and the agony may be. This is one of the most awe-striking periods in the long history of France and Britain. It is also beyond doubt the most sublime. Side by side, unaided except by their kith and kin in the great Dominions and by the wide Empires which rest beneath their shield—side by side, the British and French peoples have advanced to rescue not only Europe but mankind from the foulest and most soul-destroying tyranny which has ever darkened and stained the pages of history. Behind them—behind us—behind the armies and fleets of Britain and France— gather a group of shattered States and bludgeoned races: the Czechs, the Poles, the Norwegians, the Danes, the Dutch, the Belgians—upon all of whom the long night of barbarism will descend, unbroken even by a star of hope, unless we conquer, as conquer we must; as conquer we shall.

Today is Trinity Sunday. Centuries ago words were written to be a call and a spur to the faithful servants of Truth and Justice; 'Arm yourselves, and be ye men of valor, and be in readiness for the conflict; for it is better for us to perish in battle than to look upon the outrage of our nation and our altar. As the Will of God is in Heaven, even so let it be.'

> ◆ **Literary Focus**
> What examples of parallelism can you find in the last sentence of this paragraph?

Guide for Responding

◆ Literature and Your Life

Reader's Response Do Churchill's words still have the power to stir a listener? Explain.

Thematic Focus How clear were right and wrong in Britain's conflict with Germany? Explain.

☑ Check Your Comprehension

1. What new development in the war does Churchill report at the beginning of his speech?
2. What evidence does he use to support his confidence in the French?
3. For what future crisis does Churchill prepare his audience?

◆ Critical Thinking

INTERPRET

1. What arguments does Churchill use to support his call for more weapons? **[Analyze]**
2. (a) Describe the tone of this speech. (b) Judging from this tone, how confident is Churchill in his public support? Explain. **[Infer]**
3. (a) Give two examples in which Churchill describes the terror of war. (b) In each case, explain how his words work persuasively. **[Interpret]**

EXTEND

4. Name a career in which one gives speeches to rally the support of others. Explain your answer. **[Career Link]**

Defending Nonviolent Resistance

Mohandas K. Gandhi

The following speech was given by Mohandas Gandhi before he was sentenced to six years in prison for stirring up rebellion. Gandhi, India's spiritual leader, worked to achieve political goals through nonviolent resistance. Through boycotts and passive refusal, he helped India gain freedom from British rule.

Before I read this statement, I would like to state that I entirely endorse the learned advocate general's remarks in connection with my humble self. I think that he was entirely fair to me in all the statements that he has made, because it is very true, and I have no desire whatsoever to conceal from this court the fact that to preach <u>disaffection</u> toward the existing system of government has become almost a passion with me; and the learned advocate general is also entirely in the right when he says that my preaching of disaffection did not commence with my connection with *Young India*, but that it commenced much earlier; and in the statement that I am about to read, it will be my painful duty to admit before this court that it commenced much earlier than the period stated by the advocate general. It is the most painful duty with me, but I have to discharge that duty knowing the responsibility that rests upon my shoulders, and I wish to endorse all the blame that the learned advocate general

has thrown on my shoulders, in connection with the Bombay occurrences, Madras occurrences, and the Chauri Chaura occurrences. Thinking over these deeply and sleeping over them night after night, it is impossible for me to dissociate myself from the <u>diabolical</u> crimes of Chauri Chaura or the mad outrages of Bombay. He is quite right when he says that as a man of responsibility, a man having received a fair share of education, having had a fair share of experience of this world, I should have known the consequences of every one of my acts. I know that I was playing with fire. I ran the risk, and if I was set free, I would still do the same. I have felt it this morning that I would have failed in my duty, if I did not say what I said here just now.

I wanted to avoid violence, I want to avoid violence. Nonviolence is the first article of my faith. It is also the last article of my creed. But

◆ **Reading Strategy**
Review the first paragraph of the speech and then sum up Gandhi's **main point** in a sentence.

◆ **Build Vocabulary**

disaffection (dis´ə fek´ shun) n.: Discontent; disillusionment

diabolical (dī´ə bäl´ i kəl) *adj.*: Evil

I had to make my choice. I had either to submit to a system which I considered had done an irreparable harm to my country, or incur the risk of the mad fury of my people bursting forth, when they understood the truth from my lips. I know that my people have sometimes gone mad. I am deeply sorry for it, and I am therefore here to submit not to a light penalty but to the highest penalty. I do not ask for mercy. I do not plead any <u>extenuating</u> act. I am here, therefore, to invite and cheerfully submit to the highest

▲ **Critical Viewing** How does this rendering of Gandhi reflect his beliefs about violence? **[Draw Conclusions]**

penalty that can be inflicted upon me for what in law is a deliberate crime and what appears to me to be the highest duty of a citizen. The only course open to you, the judge, is, as I am just going to say in my statement, either to resign your post or inflict on me the severest penalty, if you believe that the system and law you are assisting to administer are good for the people. I do not expect that kind of conversation, but by the time I have finished with my statement, you will perhaps have a glimpse of what is raging within my breast to run this maddest risk which a sane man can run.

I owe it perhaps to the Indian public and to the public in England to placate[1] which this prosecution is mainly taken up that I should explain why from a staunch loyalist and cooperator I have become an uncompromising disaffectionist and non-cooperator. To the court too I should say why I plead guilty to the charge of promoting disaffection toward the government established by law in India.

◆ **Reading Strategy**
What is the **main point** that Gandhi introduces in this section of the speech?

My public life began in 1893 in South Africa in troubled weather. My first contact with British authority in that country was not of a happy character. I discovered that as a man and as an Indian I had no rights. More correctly, I discovered that I had no rights as a man because I was an Indian.

But I was not baffled. I thought that this treatment of Indians was an <u>excrescence</u> upon a system that was intrinsically and mainly good. I gave the government my voluntary and hearty cooperation, criticizing it freely where I felt it was faulty but never wishing its destruction.

Consequently, when the existence of the empire was threatened in 1899 by the Boer challenge,[2] I offered my services to it, raised a volunteer ambulance corps, and served at several actions that took place for the relief of Ladysmith. Similarly in 1906, at the time of the Zulu revolt, I raised a stretcher-bearer party and served till the end of the "rebellion." On both these occasions I received medals and was even mentioned in dispatches. For my work in South Africa I was given by Lord Hardinge a Kaiser-i-Hind Gold Medal. When the war broke out in 1914 between England and Germany,[3] I raised a volunteer ambulance corps in London consisting of the then resident Indians in London, chiefly students. Its work was acknowledged by the authorities to be valuable. Lastly, in India, when a special appeal was made at the War Conference in Delhi in 1918 by Lord Chelmsford[4] for recruits, I struggled at the cost of my health to raise a corps in Kheda, and the response was being made when the hostilities ceased and orders were received that no more recruits were wanted. In all these efforts at service I was actuated by the belief that it was possible by such services to gain a status of full equality in the empire for my countrymen.

The first shock came in the shape of the Rowlatt Act,[5] a law designed to rob the people of all real freedom. I felt called upon to lead an intensive agitation against it. Then followed the Punjab horrors beginning with the massacre at Jallianwala Bagh[6] and culminating in crawling orders, public floggings, and other indescribable humiliations. I discovered too that the plighted word of the prime minister to the Mussulmans of India regarding the integrity of Turkey and the holy places of Islam was not likely to be fulfilled. But in spite of the forebodings and the grave warnings of friends, at the Amritsar Congress in 1919, I fought for cooperation and working with the Montagu-Chelmsford reforms,[7] hoping that the prime minister would redeem his promise to the Indian Mussulmans, that the Punjab wound would be healed, and that the re-

---

1. **placate** (plā´ kāt´) v.: To stop from being angry.
2. **Boer challenge:** Rebellion in South Africa against British rule; the British suppressed the rebellion in 1902 after resorting to guerrilla warfare.

◆ **Build Vocabulary**

extenuating (ek sten´ yoo āt´iŋ) adj.: Lessening the seriousness of; excusing

excrescence (eks kres´ ens) n.: Abnormal or disfiguring outgrowth

3. **the war . . . between England and Germany:** World War I.
4. **Lord Chelmsford:** Viceroy or governor as representative of Edwin Montagu, Secretary of State.
5. **Rowlatt Act:** Series of repressive acts that limited the powers of the Indian people.
6. **the massacre at Jallianwala Bagh:** Under orders of General R. H. Dyer, fifty British soldiers opened fire on a crowd of peaceful Indians, firing 1,650 rounds of ammunition. The general was dismissed from his duties.
7. **Montagu-Chelmsford reforms:** Formally known as The Government of India Act of 1919; an attempt to slowly place power in Indian hands.

forms, inadequate and unsatisfactory though they were, marked a new era of hope in the life of India.

But all that hope was shattered. The Khilafat promise was not to be redeemed. The Punjab crime was whitewashed, and most culprits went not only unpunished but remained in service and in some cases continued to draw pensions from the Indian revenue, and in some cases were even rewarded. I saw too that not only did the reforms not mark a change of heart, but they were only a method of further draining India of her wealth and of prolonging her servitude.

I came reluctantly to the conclusion that the British connection had made India more helpless than she ever was before, politically and economically. A disarmed India has no power of resistance against any aggressor if she wanted to engage in an armed conflict with him. So much is this the case that some of our best men consider that India must take generations before she can achieve the dominion status. She has become so poor that she has little power of resisting famines. Before the British advent, India spun and wove in her millions of cottages just the supplement she needed for adding to her meager agricultural resources. This cottage industry, so vital for India's existence, has been ruined by incredibly heartless and inhuman processes as described by English witnesses. Little do town dwellers know how the semistarved masses of India are slowly sinking to lifelessness. Little do they know that their miserable comfort represents the brokerage they get for the work they do for the foreign exploiter, that the profits and the brokerage are sucked from the masses. Little do they realize that the government established by law in British India is carried on for this exploitation of the masses. No sophistry,[8] no jugglery in figures can explain away the evidence that the skeletons in many villages present to the naked eye. I have no doubt whatsoever that both England and the town dwellers of India will have to answer, if there is a God above, for this crime against humanity which is perhaps unequaled in history. The law itself in this country has been used to serve the foreign exploiter. My un-

biased examination of the Punjab Martial Law cases has led me to believe that at least 95 percent of convictions were wholly bad. My experience of political cases in India leads me to the conclusion that in nine out of every ten the condemned men were totally innocent. Their crime consisted in the love of their country. In ninety-nine cases out of a hundred justice has been denied to Indians as against Europeans in the courts of India. This is not an exaggerated picture. It is the experience of almost every Indian who has had anything to do with such cases. In my opinion, the administration of the law is thus prostituted consciously or unconsciously for the benefit of the exploiter.

The greatest misfortune is that Englishmen and their Indian associates in the administration of the country do not know that they are engaged in the crime I have attempted to describe. I am satisfied that many Englishmen and Indian officials honestly believe that they are administering one of the best systems devised in the world and that India is making steady though slow progress. They do not know that a subtle but effective system of terrorism and an organized display of force, on the one hand, and the deprivation of all powers of retaliation or self-defense, on the other, have emasculated the people and induced in them the habit of simulation. This awful habit has added to the ignorance and the self-deception of the administrators. Section 124-A, under which I am happily charged, is perhaps the prince among the political sections of the Indian Penal Code[9] designed to suppress the liberty of the citizen. Affection cannot be manufactured or regulated by law. If one has an affection for a person or system, one should be free to give the fullest expression to his disaffection, so long as he does not contemplate, promote, or incite to violence. But the section under which Mr. Banker [a colleague in nonviolence] and I are charged is one under which mere promotion of disaffection is a crime. I have studied some of the cases tried under it, and I know that some of the most loved of India's patriots have been convicted under it. I consider it a privilege, therefore, to be charged under that section. I have endeavored to give in their briefest outline

---

8. **sophistry** (säf´is trē) *n*.: Unsound or misleading arguments.

9. **Section 124-A . . . Penal Code:** Gandhi was charged with sedition, inciting people to riot against British rule.

the reasons for my disaffection. I have no personal ill will against any single administrator, much less can I have any disaffection toward the king's person. But I hold it to be a virtue to be disaffected toward a government which in its totality has done more harm to India than any previous system. India is less manly under the British rule than she ever was before. Holding such a belief, I consider it to be a sin to have affection for the system. And it has been a precious privilege for me to be able to write what I have in the various articles, tendered in evidence against me.

In fact, I believe that I have rendered a service to India and England by showing in non-cooperation the way out of the unnatural state in which both are living. In my humble opinion, non-cooperation with evil is as much a duty as is cooperation with good. But in the past, non-cooperation has been deliberately expressed in violence to the evildoer. I am endeavoring to show to my countrymen that violent non-coop-

eration only multiplies evil and that as evil can only be sustained by violence, withdrawal of support of evil requires complete abstention from violence. Nonviolence implies voluntary submission to the penalty for non-cooperation with evil. I am here, therefore, to invite and submit cheerfully to the highest penalty that can be inflicted upon me for what in law is a deliberate crime and what appears to me to be the highest duty of a citizen. The only course open to you, the judge, is either to resign your post, and thus dissociate yourself from evil if you feel that the law you are called upon to administer is an evil and that in reality I am innocent, or to inflict on me the severest penalty if you believe that the system and the law you are assisting to administer are good for the people of this country and that my activity is therefore injurious to the public weal.[10]

> ◆ **Literary Focus**
> In what tone of voice do you think Gandhi may have delivered this final paragraph of the speech?

---

10. **weal** (wēl) *n.*: Well-being; welfare.

Guide for Responding

◆ *Literature and Your Life*

Reader's Response If you had been the judge, what impression would Gandhi's speech have made on you?

Thematic Focus What fundamental conflict motivated Gandhi to take a stand against the government established by law in India?

☑ Check Your Comprehension

1. How does Gandhi plead to the charges?
2. What does Gandhi say is the first article of his faith?
3. What did Gandhi discover in South Africa?
4. Identify three reasons for Gandhi's "disaffection" toward the British system of rule in India.
5. What response to British rule does Gandhi advocate?

◆ Critical Thinking

INTERPRET

1. In his speech, why does Gandhi resist the strategy of protesting his innocence? **[Analyze]**
2. Taking into account his ideals, why does Gandhi consider it a privilege to be charged for "promotion of disaffection"? **[Draw Conclusions]**
3. Explain how Gandhi's request that the judge either punish him fully or resign supports the ideals expressed in this speech. **[Support]**

APPLY

4. Is *satyagraha*, nonviolent resistance, a good strategy to take against enemies? Explain. **[Generalize]**

EXTEND

5. Explain why Gandhi's speech would not have been necessary in a society that protected his civil liberties. **[Social Studies Link]**

Guide for Responding (continued)

◆ Literary Focus

SPEECH

In a **speech,** a speaker addresses an audience with the purpose of informing, entertaining, or persuading. Churchill's and Gandhi's speeches have the dual purpose of informing ("The Germans . . . have broken through the French defenses north of the Maginot Line") and persuading ("Little do town dwellers know how the semi-starved masses of India are slowly sinking to lifelessness"). These purposes are strengthened by the fine writing and oratorical skills of these men—and by the passion that directs these skills.

1. Because Churchill spoke on radio, his listeners could not see him. Nevertheless, Churchill's capacity to forge a bond with his listeners became legendary. Analyze and comment upon his technique for emphasizing unity in the concluding paragraph of his speech.

2. On the surface, Gandhi addresses his statement to the court and the judge. Who is his real audience, in your opinion? Explain.

◆ Build Vocabulary

USING THE LATIN ROOT *-dur-*

Knowing that the Latin root *-dur-* means "hard" or "tough," write definitions for each of these words:

1. durable   2. duress   3. endure

USING THE WORD BANK: Synonyms

On your paper, write the letter of the term closest in meaning to that of the first word.

1. intimidated: (a) hinted, (b) frightened, (c) risked
2. endurance: (a) toughness, (b) length, (c) stretch
3. formidable: (a) shapely, (b) bullying, (c) fearsome
4. invincible: (a) insane, (b) timely, (c) unconquerable
5. retaliate: (a) surrender, (b) strike back, (c) refute
6. disaffection: (a) discontent, (b) anger, (c) rebellion
7. diabolical: (a) transparent, (b) foolish, (c) evil
8. extenuating: (a) widening, (b) excusing, (c) diminishing
9. excrescence: (a) waste, (b) abnormal outgrowth, (c) delay

◆ Reading Strategy

IDENTIFY MAIN POINTS AND SUPPORT

The **main points** of a speech or an essay are often found in the topic sentence of a paragraph. Topic sentences usually occur at the beginning of paragraphs. This is often the case in a speech, since a speaker needs to be particularly clear about identifying the main idea for an audience.

As you read these speeches, you paused to check your understanding by identifying the main points and supporting details. Now choose one of the speeches and outline three of its main points. Under each main point in your outline, list supporting points or examples.

◆ Grammar and Style

PARALLEL STRUCTURE

Sometimes parallel structures follow correlative conjunctions: "Our task is *not only* to win the battle—*but* to win the War."

> **Parallel structure** is the use of the same grammatical form or pattern to express similar ideas.

Practice In your notebook, rewrite each sentence below, correcting errors of faulty parallelism.

1. In Churchill's opinion, either to disguise the gravity of the hour or surrendering prematurely to despair would be a great mistake.
2. Churchill assembled an administration that represented every party and consisting of a complete spectrum of opinion.
3. Gandhi says that he faced the choice of submitting to a harmful system or to run the risk of his people's anger.
4. According to Gandhi, true affection cannot be manufactured or subjecting it to regulation by law.

Writing Application As the judge to whom Gandhi appeals, write a brief speech in response to his. Include two examples of parallel structures in your speech.

Build Your Portfolio

 Idea Bank

Writing

1. **Reporting on a Speech** Write a newspaper report on Churchill's speech. Create a suitable headline and a lead paragraph stating the main point of the speech.

2. **Dialogue** Based on what you know of their beliefs, write a brief conversation between Churchill and Gandhi set at a peace conference.

3. **Comparison-and-Contrast Essay** Churchill's and Gandhi's speeches were both meant to rally support, but they arose from different circumstances. Compare and contrast them.

Speaking, Listening, and Viewing

4. **Speech** Rehearse a part of either Churchill's or Gandhi's speech, experimenting with pacing and emphasis. Deliver the speech to your class. **[Performing Arts Link]**

5. **Panel Discussion** With several classmates, prepare to discuss how Gandhi might have responded in Churchill's position. Choose a moderator, and hold your "discussion" in front of the class. **[Social Studies Link]**

Researching and Representing

6. **Leaders on Film** With a small group of classmates, screen a film documenting Churchill's or Gandhi's life. (You might view *Gandhi,* directed by Richard Attenborough.) Write a group evaluation of the film. **[Performing Arts Link]**

7. **Gandhi's Legacy** Research the influence of Gandhi's philosophy of nonviolent resistance on Dr. Martin Luther King, Jr. Write a brief report comparing how the two leaders used this tactic. **[Social Studies Link]**

Online Activity www.phlit.phschool.com

 Guided Writing Lesson

Press Release

If you were a world leader like Churchill or Gandhi, you'd want your message to get out to the public accurately and in such a way as to encourage their support. To do this, you might write a **press release**—a statement to the news media.

Write a press release that announces a news development and how you are responding to it. The tone of your press release should reflect that you are in control of the situation and are acting on behalf of the people. Your press release should be brief and concise, yet answer any questions or comments you think the media might have.

Writing Skills Focus: Anticipating Questions

Anticipate questions by:
- presenting clear reasons that show you have considered all points of view.
- clearly refuting opposing arguments.
- conceding a point, if appropriate. Acknowledging the wisdom of opposing viewpoints establishes credibility with your audience.

Prewriting After you choose a real or imaginary news development and decide on your reaction, jot down questions the media would ask about your decision.

Drafting As you write your press release, keep in mind that your statement may be rapidly scanned or selectively summarized by reporters. Make every sentence count. Use devices like parallel structure where they are rhetorically effective.

Revising Read your statement aloud to a classmate. Encourage him or her to ask provocative or difficult questions. If your classmate comes up with a good question you haven't anticipated, revise your statement to address that question.

Guide for Interpreting

Alan Sillitoe (1928–)

Growing up poor left a permanent impression on Alan Sillitoe; much of his writing revolves around the struggles of the working poor, those whose labor leads to a hand-to-mouth existence.

A Short Military Career The son of an often unemployed tannery worker, Sillitoe grew up in Nottingham, an industrial city northwest of London. He left school at fourteen and worked in a bicycle plant and a plywood mill. At the same time, he enrolled in the Air Training Corps. World War II ended before he saw active duty, and after four years in the Royal Air Force, he was discharged because he had contracted tuberculosis. His illness entitled him to a pension, which he collected for thirteen years, lasting from age twenty-one until he was pronounced cured.

The Young Writer Sillitoe's small pension enabled him to survive without having to get a job. In his 1996 autobiography, *Life Without Armour*, he refers to this period in his life: "Such an extended period of cosseting merely for doing my duty turned into a much appreciated case of patronage." Sillitoe spent six years in France and Spain, writing and rewriting several books. He ended up scrapping the manuscripts of nine completed novels until he published *Saturday Night and Sunday Morning,* which met with instant success and was later made into a movie starring Albert Finney. For this work, Sillitoe was awarded the Author's Club Prize for the best English novel of 1958. Then, in 1959, he published the short story collection "The Loneliness of the Long Distance Runner,"—perhaps his most famous work. The title story—later adapted for film—tells of a young juvenile delinquent in an English reform school. Sillitoe's early works earned him a place among a group of writers known as the "Angry Young Men" who believed that British social and political traditions had become outmoded.

The scope of Sillitoe's subject matter has broadened to some extent in his later works, though he has remained primarily a chronicler of the working class. He is one of the more prolific British writers of our time, authoring more than forty books, including novels, short story collections, plays, a book of essays, books for children, and an autobiography.

The Story Behind the Story During his childhood, Alan Sillitoe lived for a time in a tiny cottage in Nottingham, England, near the River Leen. After a week of rain, the Sillitoes' cottage was flooded and had to be abandoned. The River Leen and the cottages on its banks make up the setting of "The Fiddle." Perhaps the people living in the houses served as inspiration for its characters.

◆ Background for Understanding

CULTURE: SILLITOE'S SETTING, THE COAL-MINING LIFE

This story is set in a town that revolves around coal-mining. The coal industry has been crucial to the British economy for generations, and the conditions in which miners work has been of concern. When coal mining began in England, working conditions were extremely dangerous. Until the mid-1600's, miners were often serfs or paroled convicts whose safety was of little concern to mine operators. The work was done entirely by hand; men crouched in narrow mine seams, digging the coal with picks. Women and children dragged the coal to the surface in baskets. Whole families settled near the mines and earned just enough to get by. In more recent years, both working conditions and wages have improved for miners. Yet, as this story reveals, the miners and their families still led difficult lives.

The Fiddle

◆ *Literature and Your Life*

CONNECT YOUR EXPERIENCE

Do you feel especially carefree on a sunny spring day—or especially gloomy when you pass down a particular dark side street? Some settings, such as the bleak coal mines in which a character in this story works, can have a profound effect on a person's outlook on life. As you read, think about how the setting of this story would affect *your* outlook on life.

Journal Writing Jot down the titles of some literary works with memorable settings. What moods do they evoke?

THEMATIC FOCUS: CONFLICTS ABROAD AND AT HOME

As you read, compare the conflicts faced by English laborers with those faced by laborers in the United States today.

◆ Reading Strategy

PREDICT THE EFFECT OF SETTING

A story's setting often has a major impact on the characters and the plot. The setting is likely to shape the characters' personalities and outlooks, and it may affect or limit the courses of action that characters can consider. As you read this story, predict how the **setting**—an English coal-mining town in the 1930's—will affect the characters' lives and shape the options they have available. You can use a chart like this to note your observations and your predictions.

Details of Setting	Effect on Characters	Predictions

◆ Build Vocabulary

LATIN WORD ORIGINS: *SUBLIME*

In his story, Sillitoe uses the expression "from ridiculousness to sublimity." The word *sublimity* is formed by combining the Latin roots *sub-*, meaning "up to" and *-limen-*, meaning "lintel," the piece of timber or stone over a door. *Sublimity* is therefore "the quality of being uplifted or noble."

WORD BANK

Before you read, preview these words from the story.

> persistent
> obliterate
> sublimity
> harried

◆ Literary Focus

SETTING AND ATMOSPHERE

The hardships faced by the characters in this story are directly related to the **setting,** or the time and place in which the characters live. In turn, the setting contributes to the **atmosphere**—the overall feeling or mood of a work. When Sillitoe describes the cottages as being "in a ruinous condition" and "isolated," he uses setting to evoke a bleak atmosphere. Be aware, as you read, of other details of setting that contribute to the atmosphere of this story.

◆ Grammar and Style

VARY SENTENCE BEGINNINGS

To make sentences flow together smoothly and to avoid monotony, good writers vary the way in which they begin their sentences. Look at some of the different ways Sillitoe begins his sentences:

Introductory Adverb *Sometimes they could almost paddle.*

Introductory Phrase *In that case there was no telling where you'd end up.*

Introductory Clause *When they did get Ted Griffin . . .*

The FIDDLE

Alan Sillitoe

On the banks of the sinewy River Leen, where it flowed through Radford, stood a group of cottages called Harrison's Row. There must have been six to eight of them, all in a ruinous condition, but lived in nevertheless.

They had been put up for stockingers[1] during the Industrial Revolution a hundred years before, so that by now the usual small red English housebricks had become weatherstained and, in some places, almost black.

Harrison's Row had a character all of its own, both because of its situation, and the people who lived there. Each house had a space of pebbly soil rising in front, and a strip of richer garden sloping away from the kitchen door down to the diminutive River Leen at the back. The front gardens had almost merged into one piece of common ground, while those behind had in most cases retained their separate plots.

As for the name of the isolated row of cottages, nobody knew who Harrison had been, and no one was ever curious about it. Neither did they know where the Leen came from, though some had a general idea as to where it finished up.

A rent man walked down cobblestoned Leen Place every week to collect what money he could. This wasn't much, even at the best of times which, in the "thirties," were not too good —though no one in their conversation was able to hark back to times when they had been any better.

From the slight rise on which the houses stood, the back doors and windows looked across the stream into green fields, out towards the towers and pinnacles of Wollaton Hall in one direction, and the woods of Aspley Manor in the other.

After a warm summer without much rain the children were able to wade to the fields on the other side. Sometimes they could almost paddle. But after a three-day downpour when the air was still heavy with undropped water, and colored a menacing gun-metal blue, it was best not to go anywhere near the river, for one false slip and you would get sucked in, and be dragged by the powerful current along to the Trent some miles away. In that case there was no telling where you'd end up. The water seemed to flow into the River Amazon[2] itself, indicated by the fact that Frankie Buller swore blind how one day he had seen a crocodile snapping left and right downstream with a newborn baby in its mouth. You had to be careful—and that was a fact. During the persistent rain of one autumn water came up over the gardens and almost in at the back doors.

Harrison's Row was a cut-off place in that not many people knew about it unless they were familiar with the district. You went to it along St. Peter's Street, and down Leen Place. But it was delightful for the kids who lived there because out of the back gardens they could go straight into the stream of the Leen. In summer an old tin hip bath would come from one of the

---

1. **stockingers** *n.*: Stocking weavers.

2. **River Amazon:** Largest, most powerful river in South America.

◄ Critical Viewing
What effect do you think this setting would have on residents? [Analyze Cause and Effect]

Hillside in Wales, (detail), L. S. Lowry, The Tate Gallery, London

houses. Using it for a boat, and stripped to their white skins, the children were happy while sun and weather lasted.

The youths and older kids would eschew this fun and set out in a gang, going far beyond, to a bend of the canal near Wollaton Pit where the water was warm—almost hot—due to some outlet from the mine itself. This place was known as "'otties," and they'd stay all day with a bottle of lemonade and a piece of bread, coming back late in the evening looking pink and tired as if out of a prolonged dipping in the ritual bath. But a swim in 'otties was only for the older ones, because a boy of four had once been drowned there.

Harrison's Row was the last of Nottingham where it met the countryside. Its houses were at the very edge of the city, in the days before those numerous housing estates had been built beyond. The line of dwellings called Harrison's Row made a sort of outpost bastion before the country began.

Yet the houses in the city didn't immediately start behind, due to gardens and a piece of wasteground, which gave to Harrison's Row a feeling of isolation. It stood somewhat on its own, as if the city intended one day to leapfrog over it and <u>obliterate</u> the country beyond.

On the other hand, any foreign army attacking from the west, over the green fields that glistened in front, would first have to flatten Harrison's Row before getting into the innumerable streets of houses behind.

Across the Leen, horses were sometimes to be seen in the fields and, in other fields beyond, the noise of combine harvesters could be heard at work in the summer. Children living there, and adults as well, had the advantage of both town and country. On a fine evening late in August one of the unemployed husbands might be seen looking across at the noise of some machinery working in a field, his cap on but wearing no shirt, as if wondering why he was here and not over there, and why in fact he had ever left those same fields in times gone by to be forced into this bit of a suburb where he now had neither work nor purpose in life. He was not bitter, and not much puzzled perhaps, yet he couldn't help being envious of those still out there in the sunshine.

◆ Literary Focus
What mood is created through these details or the setting?

In my visions of leaving Nottingham for good—and they were frequent in those days—I never reckoned on doing so by the high road or railway. Instead I saw myself wading or swimming the Leen from Harrison's Row, and setting off west once I was on the other side.

A tale remembered with a laugh at that time told about how young Ted Griffin, who had just started work, saw two policemen one day walking down Leen Place towards Harrison's Row.

◆ **Build Vocabulary**

persistent (pər sis´ tənt) *adj.*: Continuing
obliterate (ə blit´ ə rāt) *v.*: Destroy utterly

The Old Fiddle, Jefferson David Chalfant

▲ **Critical Viewing** Why might a fiddle like this one be a cherished possession? **[Speculate]**

Convinced they had come to arrest him for meter-breaking, he ran through the house and garden, went over the fence, jumped into the Leen—happily not much swollen—waded across to the field, then four-legged it over the railway, and made his way to Robins Wood a mile or so beyond. A perfect escape route. He stayed two days in hiding, and then crept home at night, famished and soaked, only to find that the police had not come for him, but to question Blonk next door, who was suspected of poaching. When they did get Ted Griffin he was pulled out of bed one morning even before he'd had time to open his eyes and think about a spectacular escape across the Leen.

Jeff Bignal was a young unmarried man of twenty-four. His father had been killed in the Great War,[3] and he lived with his mother at Number Six Harrison's Row, and worked down nearby Radford Pit. He was short in height, and plump, his white skin scarred back and front with livid blue patches where he had been knocked with coal at the mine face. When he went out on Saturday night he brilliantined his hair.

After tea in summer while it was still light and warm he would sit in his back garden playing the fiddle, and when he did everybody else came out to listen. Or they opened the doors and windows so that the sound of his music drifted in, while the woman stayed at the sink or wash-copper, or the man at his odd

---

3. **Great War:** World War I.

jobs. Anyone with a wireless would turn it down or off.

Even tall dark sallow-faced elderly Mrs. Deaffy (a kid sneaked into her kitchen one day and thieved her last penny-packet of cocoa and she went crying to tell Mrs. Atkin who, when her youngest came in, hit him so hard with her elbow that one of his teeth shot out and the blood washed away most of the cocoa-stains around his mouth)—old Mrs. Deaffy stood by her back door as if she weren't stone deaf any more and could follow each note of Jeffrey Bignal's exquisite violin. She smiled at seeing everyone occupied, fixed or entranced, and therefore no torment to herself, which was music enough to her whether she could hear it or not.

And Blonk, in the secretive dimness of the kitchen, went on mending his poaching nets before setting out with Arthur Bede next door on that night's expedition to Gunthorpe by the banks of the Trent, where the green escarpment between there and Kneeton was riddled with warrens and where, so it was said, if you stood sufficiently still the rabbits ran over your feet, and it was only necessary to make a quick grab to get one.

Jeff sat on a chair, oblivious to everybody, fed up with his day's work at the pit and only wanting to lose himself in his own music. The kids stopped splashing and shouting in the water, because if they didn't they might get hauled in and clouted with just the right amount of viciousness to suit the crime and the occasion. It had happened before, though Jeff had always been too far off to notice.

His face was long, yet generally cheerful—contrary to what one would expect—a smile settling on it whenever he met and passed anybody on the street, or on his way to the group of shared lavatories at the end of the Row. But his face was almost down and lost to the world as he sat on his chair and brought forth his first sweet notes of a summer's evening.

It was said that a neighbor in the last place they had lived had taught him to play like that. Others maintained it was an uncle who had shown him how. But nobody knew for sure because when someone asked directly he said that if he had any gift at all it must have come from

God above. It was known that on some Sundays of the year, if the sun was out, he went to the Methodist chapel on St. Peter's Street.

He could play anything from "Greensleeves" to "Mademoiselle from Armentières." He could do a beautiful heart-pulling version of Handel's *Largo,* and throw in bits from *The Messiah* as well. He would go from one piece to another with no rhyme or reason, from ridiculousness to sublimity, with almost shocking abruptness, but as the hour or so went by it all appeared easy and natural, part of a long piece coming from Jeff Bignal's fiddle while the ball of the sun went down behind his back.

To a child it seemed as if the songs lived in the hard collier's muscle at the top of his energetic arm, and that they queued one by to get out. Once free, they rushed along his flesh from which the shirtsleeves had been rolled up, and split into his fingertips, where they were played out with ease into the warm evening air.

The grass in the fields across the stream was livid and lush, almost blue, and a piebald horse stood with bent head, eating oats out of a large old pram whose wheels had long since gone. The breeze wafted across from places farther out, from Robins Wood and the Cherry Orchard, Wollaton Roughs and Bramcote Hills and even, on a day that was not too hot, from the tops of the Pennines in Derbyshire.

Jeff played for himself, for the breeze against his arm, for the soft hiss of the flowing Leen at the end of the garden, and maybe also for the horse in the field, which took no notice of anything and which, having grown tired of its oats in the pram, bent its head over the actual grass and began to roam in search of succulent pastures.

In the middle of the winter Jeff's fiddling was forgotten. He went into the coal mine before it was light, and came up only after it had got dark. Walking down Leen Place, he complained to Blonk that it was hard on a man not to see daylight for weeks at a time.

◆ Build Vocabulary

sublimity (sə blim′ ə tē) *n.*: Quality of being majestic or noble

"That's why I wain't go anywhere near the bleddy pit," Blonk said vehemently, though he had worked there from time to time, and would do so again when <u>harried</u> by his wife and children. "You'd do better to come out on a bit o' poaching with me and Arthur," he suggested.

It was virtually true that Jeff saw no daylight, because even on Sunday he stayed in bed most of the day, and if it happened to be dull there was little enough sky to be seen through his front bedroom window, which looked away from the Leen and up the hill.

The upshot of his complaint was that he would do anything to change such a situation. A man was less than an animal for putting up with it.

◆ **Reading Strategy**
What choice does Jeff have? Predict what he might do.

"I'd do anything," he repeated to his mother over his tea in the single room downstairs.

"But what, though?" she asked. "What can you do, Jeff?"

"Well, how do I know?" he almost snapped at her. "But I'll do summat,[4] you can be sure of that."

He didn't do anything till the weather got better and life turned a bit sweeter. Maybe this improvement finally got him going, because it's hard to help yourself towards better things when you're too far down in the dumps.

On a fine blowy day with both sun and cloud in the sky Jeff went out in the morning, walking up Leen Place with his fiddle under his arm. The case had been wiped and polished.

In the afternoon he came back without it.

"Where's your fiddle?" Ma Jones asked.

He put an awkward smile on to his pale face, and told her: "I sold it."

"Well I never! How much for?"

He was too shocked at her brazen question not to tell the truth: "Four quid."

"That ain't much."

"It'll be enough," he said roughly.

"Enough for what, Jeff?"

He didn't say, but the fact that he had sold his fiddle for four quid rattled up and down the line of cottages till everybody knew of it. Others swore he'd got ten pounds for it, because something that made such music must be worth more than a paltry four, and in any case Jeff would never say how much he'd really got for it, for fear that someone would go in and rob him.

They wondered why he'd done it, but had to wait for the answer, as one usually does. But there was nothing secretive about Jeff Bignal, and if he'd sold his music for a mess of pottage he saw no point in not letting them know why. They'd find out sooner or later, anyway.

All he'd had to do was make up his mind, and he'd done that lying on his side at the pit face while ripping coal out with his pick and shovel. Decisions made like that can't be undone, he knew. He'd brooded on it all winter, till the fact of having settled it seemed to have altered the permanent expression of his face, and given it a new look which caused people to wonder whether he would ever be able to play the fiddle again anyway—at least with his old spirit and dash.

With the four quid he paid the first week's rent on a butcher's shop on Denman Street, and bought a knife, a chopper, and a bit of sharpening stone, as well as a wooden block. Maybe he had a quid or two more knocking around, though if he had it couldn't have been much, but with four quid and a slice of bluff he got enough credit from a wholesaler at the meat market downtown to stock his shop with mutton and beef, and in a couple of days he was in trade. The people of Harrison's Row were amazed at how easy it was, though nobody had ever thought of doing it themselves.

Like a serious young man of business Mr. Bignal—as he was now known—parted his hair down the middle, so that he didn't look so young any more, but everyone agreed that it was better than being at Radford Pit. They'd seen how he had got fed up with selling the

---

4. **summat:** Something.

◆ **Build Vocabulary**

harried (har´ ēd) *v.*: Harassed

sweat of his brow.

No one could say that he prospered, but they couldn't deny that he made a living. And he didn't have to suffer the fact of not seeing daylight for almost the whole of the winter.

Six months after opening the shop he got married. The reception was held at the chapel on St. Peter's Street, which seemed to be a sort of halfway house between Harrison's Row on the banks of the Leen and the butcher's shop on Denman Street farther up.

Everybody from Harrison's Row was invited for a drink and something to eat; but he knew them too well to let any have either chops or chitterlings (or even black puddings) on tick[5] when they came into his shop.

The people of Harrison's Row missed the sound of his fiddle on long summer evenings, though the children could splash and shout with their tin bathtub undisturbed, floundering through shallows and scrambling up to grass on the other bank, and wondering what place they'd reach if they walked without stopping till it got dark.

Two years later the Second World War began, and not long afterwards meat as well as nearly everything else was put on the ration. Apart from which, Jeff was only twenty-six, so got called up into the army. He never had much chance to make a proper start in life, though people said that he came out all right in the end.

The houses of Harrison's Row were condemned as unfit to live in, and a bus depot stands on the site.

The packed mass of houses on the hill behind—forty years after Jeff Bignal sold his violin—is also vanishing, and high-rise hencoops (as the people call them) are put in their place. The demolition crew knock down ten houses a day—though the foreman told me there was still work for another two years.

Some of the houses would easily have lasted a few more decades, for the bricks were perfect, but as the foreman went on: "You can't let them stand in the way of progress"—whatever that means.

The people have known each other for generations but, when they are moved to their new estates and blocks of flats,[6] they will know each other for generations more, because as I listen to them talking, they speak a language which, in spite of everything and everyone, never alters.

---

5. **tick:** Credit.

6. **flats:** Apartments.

Guide for Responding

◆ Literature and Your Life

Reader's Response What advice would you have given Jeff about his decision?

Thematic Focus Is there always a conflict between pleasure and getting ahead?

☑ Check Your Comprehension

1. In what era does the story take place?
2. Tell the events that preceded Ted Griffin's arrest.
3. How did people react to Jeff's music?
4. (a) What does Jeff finally do with his fiddle? (b) For what purpose does he do this?

◆ Critical Thinking

INTERPRET

1. How is Jeff's attitude about the coal mines different from his friend's? **[Compare and Contrast]**
2. What is the connection between Jeff's fiddle and his standing in the town? **[Connect]**
3. (a) What does the fiddle symbolize? (b) How does this symbol reveal the story's theme? **[Draw Conclusions]**

EVALUATE

4. Do you think Jeff's decision to give up music is a good one? Explain. **[Make a Judgment]**

Guide for Responding (continued)

◆ Literary Focus

SETTING AND ATMOSPHERE

When a **setting** plays an important role in a story, as it does in "The Fiddle," it often evokes a certain **atmosphere**—a mood or feeling you get when you read the story. Sillitoe creates a forbidding atmosphere in this passage:

> But after a three-day downpour when the air was still heavy with undropped water and colored a menacing gun-metal blue, it was best not to go anywhere near the river, for one false step and you would get sucked in, and be dragged by the powerful current along to the Trent some miles away.

1. Find two examples from the story in which a description of the setting creates an ominous or depressing atmosphere. Explain each of your choices, citing individual words that contribute to the atmosphere.
2. Explain the effect the River Leen has on the atmosphere of this story. Support your explanation with examples from the story.
3. Describe the effect of the violin—an element of setting—on the atmosphere in this story, including how it changes the atmosphere at specific points.

◆ Reading Strategy

PREDICT THE EFFECT OF SETTING

The more you know about the setting of a particular story, the more accurately you may be able to **predict** the outcome of events.

The job of knowing about setting is a collaboration between the author and you; the author provides information and descriptions, and you add to that what you already know. For example, if you know about the difficulties of life in a coal-mining district, you can better appreciate Jeff Bignal's efforts to better his life in this story.

1. What effect did the violin, an important detail of setting, have on the outcome of events?
2. What was the effect of World War II, barely alluded to, on the outcome of events in this story?
3. Which elements of setting pointed most strongly to a particular outcome in this story? Why?

◆ Build Vocabulary

USING LATIN WORD ORIGINS: *SUBLIME*

The word *sublime* comes from roots meaning "up to" and "lintel." Use this knowledge to help you define these words:

1. sublimity   2. sublimate   3. sublimation

USING THE WORD BANK: Analogies

In your notebook, write the pair of words that has the same relationship as the pair given. Write a sentence explaining the relationship.

1. student : organized ::
   a. salesperson : persistent
   b. poet : persistent
2. faith : skepticism ::
   a. destroy : obliterate
   b. create : obliterate
3. story : predictability ::
   a. fondness : sublimity
   b. symphony : sublimity
4. ideas : inspired ::
   a. responsibilities : harried
   b. surprises : harried

◆ Grammar and Style

VARY SENTENCE BEGINNINGS

One way that writers sustain a reader's interest and establish a flow in their writing is by varying sentence beginnings.

Practice In your notebook, identify each of the italicized sentence beginnings as subject, introductory adverb, or introductory phrase or clause.
1. *Alan Sillitoe* grew up in Nottingham, England.
2. *By age fourteen,* he was earning enough to help his family.
3. *Fortunately,* he passed the necessary tests to join the Royal Air Force.
4. *When he was twenty-one,* he knew he wanted to be a writer.

Writing Application In your notebook, rewrite each Practice sentence so that it begins with a new part of speech, chosen from the following:
1. adverb 2. subject 3. clause 4. phrase

Build Your Portfolio

 ## Idea Bank

Writing

1. **Journal Entry** Put yourself in Jeff's place, and write a journal entry describing how you feel about having to sell your fiddle.

2. **Newspaper Report** As a reporter on the crime beat, write about Ted Griffin being pulled out of bed and arrested for meter-breaking. Tell *who, what, when, where,* and *why.* **[Career Link]**

3. **Response to Criticism** Critic Clancy Sigal has said no living English writer "can match Alan Sillitoe's sharp instinct for the grinding pain and convulsive joys of working-class life." Support or refute this view, using details from "The Fiddle."

Speaking, Listening, and Viewing

4. **Debate** Should the houses near Harrison's Row have been torn down so they wouldn't "stand in the way of progress"? In two teams of classmates, debate this issue. **[Social Studies Link]**

5. **Music Discussion** Find recordings of fiddle music from coal-mining regions in Appalachia and Great Britain. Present both to the class, comparing and contrasting the two. **[Music Link]**

Researching and Representing

6. **Performing Arts** With a group, write a script based on any scene in the story. Then rehearse it and perform it. **[Performing Arts Link]**

7. **Coal-Mining Report** Research and report on current conditions in the coal-mining industry in Great Britain. Broadly explain how coal is mined, and cover labor union or management's efforts to protect the safety and quality of life of coal miners. **[Social Studies Link; Health Link]**

Online Activity www.phlit.phschool.com

 ## Guided Writing Lesson

Favorite Setting

Alan Sillitoe creates a memorable impression of Harrison's Row and the surrounding area. His description of this setting just seems to ring true.

Whether the realistic setting in a story comes from the writer's memory or from his or her imagination, it must rely upon vivid details and clear, accurate description. Choose a favorite setting, and write a description of it. The setting could be one you come in contact with every day, one you remember, or just a place you've passed and admired. Following Sillitoe's example, use vivid details to describe this favorite setting.

Writing Skills Focus: Vivid Details

Once you've decided on a setting, you'll need to gather **vivid details** to capture how it looks, smells, sounds, tastes, and feels. To evoke these sensations:

- Choose exact nouns.
- Use vivid verbs: those that suggest as closely as possible the action being described.
- Use strong, precise modifiers to help your reader envision the scene.

Prewriting Make a five-column table like this one. Under the appropriate heading, organize and record the first few sensory details that come to mind.

Sight	Smell	Taste	Hearing	Touch

Drafting Choose an organizing principle for your description. You might organize your details in spatial order or order of importance. You might even mix organizing principles, such as organizing details by the sense to which they appeal and showing these in order of importance.

Revising Show your description to a classmate, and ask for a reaction. Can your classmate picture the setting clearly? Add any details that might help your reader envision the setting.

Guide for Interpreting

William Trevor (1928–)

Like his protagonists in "The Distant Past," William Trevor was born into a Protestant family in the largely Catholic Republic of Ireland. This experience of being outside the dominant culture—and the fact that his parents moved around constantly during his youth—gave him a sympathy for the outsiders about whom he writes in his short stories and novels. Trevor himself has said:

> *"I think the feeling of not belonging is very strong in me. In order to write about people, you have got actually to stand back quite a distance."*

Trevor admits that his view of life is pessimistic. The "villain" in his stories is usually circumstance. People's lives are troubled through no fault of their own.

Finding a Career Trevor attended Trinity College in Dublin and afterwards taught school to support his wife and young family while devoting his creative energies to sculpture. Eventually his sculpture became too abstract to interest him. "There weren't any people in it anymore, and I didn't like it," he says.

After abandoning sculpture, he took up writing, and became an immediate success, publishing short stories in magazines as fast as he could write them.

Acclaim Today William Trevor is recognized as one of the greatest living writers of short stories in the English language. In fact, critics have compared his stories to those of Anton Chekhov, Muriel Spark, and James Joyce. He has been praised for the "gritty detail" of his stories, his lack of sentimentality, and the subtle sense of humor that infuses his work.

◆ Background for Understanding

HISTORY: TROUBLE IN IRELAND

Between 1968 and 1994, in Northern Ireland—which has a population of about 1.6 million people—more than 40,000 people were wounded and 3,100 were killed in shootings and bombings as a result of a political dispute between Catholics and Protestants. Though 1968 is given as the starting date of "the Troubles," the source of the violence goes back about three hundred years to when the British government encouraged thousands of Scottish Protestants to emigrate to the north of Ireland and allowed them to confiscate land owned by Catholics. By 1703, Protestants owned 95 percent of the land in the six counties that make up present-day Northern Ireland. For the next two hundred years there was periodic violence between the two groups. More importantly, many Catholics left the six counties for the South and West of Ireland, where they joined others in agitating for independence from Britain.

When the Irish people finally won home rule in 1922, the six northern counties, with a firm majority of Protestants, remained part of Britain. The Catholics who still lived in the North experienced political and economic discrimination. In 1969 an incident occurred in which police fired on a group of Catholic demonstrators. Before long the troubles had escalated, leading to almost thirty years of violence between Catholics and Protestants and British troops, who were generally supportive of the Protestants. It wasn't until 1996 that a ceasefire was declared and negotiations began between the two parties in hope of resolving the conflict.

The Distant Past

◆ *Literature and Your Life*

CONNECT YOUR EXPERIENCE

Perhaps you'll soon join a political party and vote for its candidates. Joining a party means taking a stand with others, but it also means separating yourself from those who belong to a different party. In "The Distant Past," a brother and sister find themselves the only representatives of a very unpopular political viewpoint in the town in which they live.

Journal Writing How would you feel about being the only supporter of an unpopular political position in your school? Jot down your thoughts.

THEMATIC FOCUS: CONFLICTS AT HOME AND ABROAD

As you read, notice how people's alliances in the political conflict in Ireland affect their feelings toward one another.

◆ Build Vocabulary

LATIN SUFFIXES: *-ity (-ty)*

In "The Distant Past," two characters experience *adversity* ("misfortune") because they insist on the *sovereignty* ("ruling power") of the British crown. Both words contain the Latin suffix *-ity* (or *-ty*), meaning "the state of" or "the quality of."

WORD BANK

Preview these words from the story.

| countenance |
| adversity |
| sovereignty |
| anachronism |
| internment |

◆ Grammar and Style

RESTRICTIVE AND NONRESTRICTIVE ADJECTIVE CLAUSES

An adjective clause is a subordinate clause (a group of words that contains a subject and a verb but can't stand alone as a sentence) that modifies a noun or pronoun. A **restrictive adjective clause** contains information necessary to the meaning of the sentence. It is not separated by commas. A **nonrestrictive adjective clause** contains information that isn't necessary to the meaning of the sentence. It is separated by commas.

Nonrestrictive: Fat Driscoll, *who kept the butcher shop*, used even to joke about the past. . .

Restrictive: Mr. Healey doubled the number of girls *who served as waitresses in his dining room*. . .

◆ Literary Focus

SOCIAL CONFLICT

Conflict—a struggle between opposing forces—is at the heart of most stories. Some conflicts between people are individual and personal; others are on a larger scale. **Social conflict** refers to a struggle between those with opposing views about the society they live in. In "The Distant Past," notice how social conflict separates the two main characters from everyone else.

◆ Reading Strategy

CAUSE AND EFFECT

For years, a brother and sister are accepted as harmless eccentrics. Then suddenly they became outcasts. Why? Asking the question *why* is looking for a **cause,** the reason that something happens. An **effect** is the thing that happens as a result of the cause. When something unexpected happens in a story, ask yourself *why*. Sometimes, the author will explain. Other times, you will have to use your detective skills and examine events that come before and after the one in question for clues. Looking for causes and effects will make you more aware of the meaning behind the events in a story.

The Distant Past

William Trevor

In the town and beyond it they were regarded as harmlessly peculiar. Odd, people said, and in time this reference took on a burnish of affection.

They had always been thin, silent with one another, and similar in appearance: a brother and sister who shared a family face. It was a bony countenance, with pale blue eyes and a sharp, well-shaped nose and high cheekbones. Their father had had it too, but unlike them their father had been an irresponsible and careless man, with red flecks in his cheeks that they didn't have at all. The Middletons of Carraveagh the family had once been known as, but now the brother and sister were just the Middletons, for Carraveagh didn't count any more, except to them.

They owned four Herefords,[1] a number of hens, and the house itself, three miles outside the town. It was a large house, built in the reign of George II,[2] a monument that reflected in its glory and later decay the fortunes of a family. As the brother and sister aged, its roof increasingly ceased to afford protection, rust ate at its gutters, grass thrived in two thick channels all along its avenue. Their father had mortgaged his inherited estate, so local rumor claimed, in order to keep a Catholic Dublin woman in brandy and jewels. When he died, in 1924, his two children discovered that they possessed only a dozen acres. It was locally said also that this adversity hardened their will and that because of it they came to love the remains of Carraveagh more than they could ever have loved a husband or a wife. They blamed for their ill-fortune the Catholic Dublin woman whom they'd never met and they blamed as well the new national regime, contriving in their eccentric way to relate the two. In the days of the union jack[3] such women would have known their place—wasn't it all part and parcel?

Twice a week, on Fridays and Sundays, the Middletons journeyed into the town, first of all in a trap[4] and later in a Ford Anglia car. In the shops and elsewhere they made, quite gently, no secret of their continuing loyalty to the past. They attended on Sundays St. Patrick's Protestant Church, a place that matched their mood, for prayers were still said there for the King whose sovereignty their country had denied. The revolutionary regime would not last, they quietly informed the Reverend Packham—what sense was there in green-painted pillar boxes[5] and a language that nobody understood?

On Fridays, when they took seven or eight

> ◆ **Literary Focus**
> What social conflict is established in the opening paragraphs?

---

1. **Herefords** n.: Breed of cattle.
2. **reign of George II:** 1727–1760.
3. **union jack:** British flag; symbol of British rule.
4. **trap** n.: Two-wheeled, horse-drawn carriage.
5. **pillar boxes:** Mail collection boxes.

dozen eggs to the town, they dressed in pressed tweeds and were accompanied over the years by a series of red setters, the breed there had always been at Carraveagh. They sold the eggs in Keogh's grocery and then had a drink with Mrs. Keogh in the part of her shop that was devoted to the consumption of refreshment. They enjoyed the occasion, for they liked Mrs. Keogh and were liked by her in return. Afterwards they shopped, chatting to the shopkeepers about whatever news there was, and then they went to Healy's Hotel for a few more drinks before driving home.

. . . In spite of their loyalty to the past, they built up convivial relationships with the people of the town. Fat Driscoll, who kept the butcher's shop, used even to joke about the past when he stood with them in Healy's Hotel or stood behind his own counter cutting their slender chops or thinly slicing their liver. "Will you ever forget it, Mr. Middleton? I'd ha' run like a rabbit if you'd lifted a finger at me." Fat Driscoll would laugh then, rocking back on his heels with a glass of stout in his hand or banging their meat on to his weighing-scales. Mr. Middleton would smile. "There was alarm in your eyes, Mr. Driscoll," Miss Middleton would murmur, smil-

▲ **Critical Viewing** How does the image of the house illustrate the Middletons' relationship with the townspeople? **[Apply]**

ing also at the memory of the distant occasion.

Fat Driscoll, with a farmer called Maguire and another called Breen, had stood in the hall of Carraveagh, each of them in charge of a shotgun. The Middletons, children then, had been locked with their mother and father and an aunt into an upstairs room. Nothing else had happened: the expected British soldiers had not, after all, arrived and the men in the hall had eventually relaxed their vigil. "A massacre they wanted," the Middletons' father said after they'd gone. . . . "Bloody ruffians."

◆ **Reading Strategy**
Why was the family locked up?

◆ **Build Vocabulary**

countenance (koun´ tə nəns) *n.*: Face; facial features

adversity (ad vʉr´ sə tē) *n.*: Misfortune

sovereignty (säv´ rən tē) *n.*: Supreme political authority

The Second World War took place. Two Germans, a man and his wife called Winkelmann who ran a glove factory in the town, were suspected by the Middletons of being spies for the Third Reich.[6] People laughed, for they knew the Winkelmanns well and could lend no credence to the Middletons' latest fantasy—typical of them, they explained to the Winkelmanns, who had been worried. Soon after the War the Reverend Packham died and was replaced by the Reverend Bradshaw, a younger man who laughed also and regarded the Middletons as an <u>anachronism</u>. They protested when prayers were no longer said for the Royal Family in St. Patrick's, but the Reverend Bradshaw considered that their protests were as absurd as the prayers themselves had been. Why pray for the monarchy of a neighboring island when their own island had its chosen President now? The Middletons didn't reply to that argument. In the Reverend Bradshaw's presence they rose to their feet when the BBC played "God Save the King," and on the day of the coronation of Queen Elizabeth II they drove into the town with a small union jack propped up in the back window of their Ford Anglia. "Bedad, you're a holy terror, Mr. Middleton!" Fat Driscoll laughingly exclaimed, noticing the flag as he lifted a tray of pork steaks from his display shelf. The Middletons smiled. It was a great day for the Commonwealth of Nations, they replied, a remark which further amused Fat Driscoll and which he later repeated in Phelan's public house. "Her Britannic Majesty," guffawed his friend Mr. Breen.

Situated in a valley that was noted for its beauty and with convenient access to rich rivers and bogs over which gamebirds flew, the town benefited from post-war tourism. Healy's Hotel changed its title and became, overnight, the New Ormonde. Shopkeepers had their shopfronts painted and Mr. Healy organized an annual Salmon Festival. Even Canon Kelly, who had at first commented severely on the habits of the tourists, and in particular on the summertime dress of the women, was in the end obliged to confess that the morals of his flock remained unaffected. "God and good sense," he proclaimed, meaning God and his own teaching. In time he even derived pride from the fact that people with other values came briefly to the town and that the values esteemed by his parishioners were in no way diminished. . . .

From the windows of their convent the Loretto nuns observed the long, sleek cars with G.B. plates; English and American accents drifted on the breeze to them. Mothers cleaned up their children and sent them to the Golf Club to seek employment as caddies. Sweet shops sold holiday mementoes. The brown, soda and currant breads of Murphy-Flood's bakery were declared to be delicious. Mr. Healy doubled the number of local girls who served as waitresses in his dining room, and in the winter of 1961 he had the builders in again, working on an extension for which the Munster and Leinster Bank had lent him twenty-two thousand pounds.

But as the town increased its prosperity Carraveagh continued its decline. The Middletons were in their middle sixties now and were reconciled to a life that became more uncomfortable with every passing year. Together they roved the vast lofts of their house, placing old paint tins and flowerpot saucers beneath the drips from the roof. At night they sat over their thin chops in a dining room that had once been gracious and which in a way was gracious still, except for the faded appearance of furniture that was dry from lack of polish and of a wallpaper that time had rendered colorless. In the hall their father gazed down at them, framed in ebony and gilt, in the uniform of the Irish Guards. He had conversed with Queen Victoria, and even in their middle sixties they could still hear him saying that God and Empire and Queen formed a trinity unique in any worthy soldier's heart. In the hall hung the family crest, and on ancient Irish linen the Cross of St. George.[7]

The dog that accompanied the Middletons now was called Turloch, an animal whose death they dreaded for they felt they couldn't

◆ Build Vocabulary

anachronism (ə nak´ rə niz´ əm) *n*.: Something out of its proper time in history

---

6. **Third Reich** (rīk): German government under the Nazis (1933–1945).

7. **St. George:** Patron saint of England.

◀ **Critical Viewing** What do these flags symbolize to the characters in the story? **[Analyze]**

as far as they could see that was the result of living in a Christian country. That the Middletons bought their meat from a man who had once locked them into an upstairs room and had then waited to shoot soldiers in their hall was a fact that amazed the seasonal visitors. You lived and learned, they remarked to Mr. Healy.

The Middletons, privately, often considered that they led a strange life. Alone in their two beds at night they now and again wondered why they hadn't just sold Carraveagh forty-eight years ago when their father had died—why had the tie been so strong and why had they in perversity encouraged it? They didn't fully know, nor did they attempt to discuss the matter in any way. Instinctively they had remained at Carraveagh, instinctively feeling that it would have been cowardly to go. Yet often it seemed to them now to be no more than a game they played, this worship of the distant past. And at other times it seemed as real and as important as the remaining acres of land, and the house itself.

"Isn't that shocking?" Mr. Healy said one day in 1967. "Did you hear about that, Mr. Middleton, blowing up them post offices in Belfast?"

Mr. Healy, red-faced and short-haired, spoke casually in his Cocktail Room, making midday conversation. He had commented in much the same way at breakfast-time, looking up from the *Irish Independent*. Everyone in the town had said it too: that the blowing up of sub-post offices in Belfast was a shocking matter.

"A bad business," Fat Driscoll remarked, wrapping the Middletons' meat. "We don't want that old stuff all over again."

"We didn't want it in the first place," Miss Middleton reminded him. He laughed, and she laughed, and so did her brother. Yes, it was a game, she thought—how could any of it be as real or as important as the afflictions and problems of the old butcher himself, his rheumatism and his reluctance to retire? Did her

manage the antics of another pup. Turloch, being thirteen, moved slowly and was blind and a little deaf. He was a reminder to them of their own advancing years and of the effort it had become to tend the Herefords and collect the weekly eggs. More and more they looked forward to Fridays, to the warm companionship of Mrs. Keogh and Mr. Healy's chatter in the hotel. They stayed longer now with Mrs. Keogh and in the hotel, and idled longer in the shops, and drove home more slowly. Dimly, but with no less loyalty, they still recalled the distant past and were listened to without ill-feeling when they spoke of it and of Carraveagh as it had been, and of the Queen whose company their careless father had known.

The visitors who came to the town heard about the Middletons and were impressed. It was a pleasant wonder, more than one of them remarked, that old wounds could heal so completely, that the Middletons continued in their loyalty to the past and that, in spite of it, they were respected in the town. When Miss Middleton had been ill with a form of pneumonia in 1958 Canon Kelly had driven out to Carraveagh twice a week with pullets and young ducks that his housekeeper had dressed. "An upright couple," was the Canon's public opinion of the Middletons, and he had been known to add that eccentric views would hurt you less than malice. "We can disagree without guns in this town," Mr. Healy pronounced in his cocktail room, and his visitors usually replied that brother, she wondered, privately think so too?

"Come on, old Turloch," he said, stroking the flank of the red setter with the point of his shoe, and she reflected that you could never tell what he was thinking. Certainly it wasn't the kind of thing you wanted to talk about.

"I've put him in a bit of mince," Fat Driscoll said, which was something he often did these days, pretending the mince would otherwise be thrown away. There'd been a red setter about the place that night when he waited in the hall for the soldiers; Breen and Maguire had pushed it down into a cellar, frightened of it.

"There's a heart of gold in you, Mr. Driscoll," Miss Middleton murmured, nodding and smiling at him. He was the same age as she was, sixty-six—he should have shut up shop years ago. He would have, he'd once told them, if there'd been a son to leave the business to. As it was, he'd have to sell it and when it came to the point he found it hard to make the necessary arrangements. "Like us and Carraveagh," she'd said, even though on the face of it it didn't seem the same at all.

Every evening they sat in the big old kitchen, hearing the news. It was only in Belfast and Derry, the wireless said; outside Belfast and Derry you wouldn't know anything was happening at all. On Fridays they listened to the talk in Mrs. Keogh's bar and in the hotel. "Well, thank God it has nothing to do with the South," Mr. Healy said often, usually repeating the statement.

The first British soldiers landed in the North of Ireland, and soon people didn't so often say that outside Belfast and Derry you wouldn't know anything was happening. There were incidents in Fermanagh and Armagh, in border villages and towns. One Prime Minister resigned and then another one. The troops were unpopular, the newspapers said; internment became part of the machinery of government. In the town, in St. Patrick's Protestant Church and in the Church of the Holy Assumption, prayers for peace were offered, but no peace came.

"We're hit, Mr. Middleton," Mr. Healy said one Friday morning. "If there's a dozen visitors this summer it'll be God's own stroke of luck for us."

◆ Build Vocabulary

internment (in turn´ mənt) n.: Confinement during war

"Luck?"

"Sure, who wants to come to a country with all that malarkey in it?"

"But it's only in the North."

"Tell that to your tourists, Mr. Middleton."

The town's prosperity ebbed. The border was more than sixty miles away, but over that distance had spread some wisps of the fog of war. As anger rose in the town at the loss of fortune so there rose also the kind of talk there had been in the distant past. There was talk of atrocities and counteratrocities, and of guns and gelignite[8] and the rights of people. There was bitterness suddenly in Mrs. Keogh's bar because of the lack of trade, and in the empty hotel there was bitterness also.

◆ **Reading Strategy**
Why have tourists stopped coming to the town?

On Fridays, only sometimes at first, there was a silence when the Middletons appeared. It was as though, going back nearly twenty years, people remembered the union jack in the window of their car and saw it now in a different light. It wasn't something to laugh at any more, nor were certain words that the Middletons had gently spoken, nor were they themselves just an old, peculiar couple. Slowly the change crept about, all around them in the town, until Fat Driscoll didn't wish it to be remembered that he had ever given them mince for their dog. He had stood with a gun in the enemy's house, waiting for soldiers so that soldiers might be killed—it was better that people should remember that.

One day Canon Kelly looked the other way when he saw the Middletons' car coming and they noticed this movement of his head, although he hadn't wished them to. And on another day Mrs. O'Brien, who had always been keen to talk to them in the hotel, didn't reply when they addressed her.

The Middletons naturally didn't discuss these rebuffs but they each of them privately knew that there was no conversation they could have at this time with the people of the town. The stand they had taken and kept to for so many years no longer seemed ridiculous in the town. Had they driven with a union jack now they would, astoundingly, have been shot.

8. **gelignite** n.: Explosive.

"It will never cease." He spoke disconsolately one night, standing by the dresser where the wireless was.

She washed the dishes they'd eaten from, and the cutlery. "Not in our time," she said.

"It is worse than before."

"Yes, it is worse than before."

They took from the walls of the hall the portrait of their father in the uniform of the Irish Guards because it seemed wrong to them that at this time it should hang there. They took down also the crest of their family and the Cross of St. George, and from a vase on the drawing-room mantelpiece they removed the small union jack that had been there since the coronation of Queen Elizabeth II. They did not remove these articles in fear but in mourning for the *modus vivendi*[9] that had existed for so long between them and the people of the town. They had given their custom to a butcher who had planned to shoot down soldiers in their hall and he, in turn, had given them mince for their dog. For fifty years they had experienced, after suspicion had seeped away, a tolerance that never again in the years that were left to them would they know.

_____

9. ***modus vivendi*** (vi ven´ dī): Manner of getting along.

One November night their dog died and he said to her after he had buried it that they must not be depressed by all that was happening. They would die themselves and the house would become a ruin because there was no one to inherit it, and the distant past would be set to rest. But she disagreed: the *modus vivendi* had been easy for them, she pointed out, because they hadn't really minded the dwindling of their fortunes while the town prospered. It had given them a life, and a kind of dignity: you could take a pride out of living in peace.

He did not say anything and then, because of the emotion that both of them felt over the death of their dog, he said in a rushing way that they could no longer at their age hope to make a living out of the remains of Carraveagh. They must sell the hens and the four Herefords. As he spoke, he watched her nodding, agreeing with the sense of it. Now and again, he thought, he would drive slowly into the town, to buy groceries and meat with the money they had saved, and to face the silence that would sourly thicken as their own two deaths came closer and death increased in another part of their island. She felt him thinking that and she knew that he was right. Because of the distant past they would die friendless. It was worse than being murdered in their beds.

Guide for Responding

◆ Literature and Your Life

Reader's Response Would you describe the Middletons as odd, foolish, courageous, or with some other adjective? Explain.

Thematic Focus In this story, how does the "distant past" cause conflicts in the present?

Role-Play With a partner, role-play a scene in which Miss Middleton discusses openly and honestly with Fat Driscoll her feelings about how she and her brother are being treated.

☑ Check Your Comprehension

1. (a) Who is responsible for the Middletons' reduced economic position? (b) Whom do they blame?
2. Describe two ways in which the Middletons show their loyalty to the "distant past."
3. What kind of relationships do the Middletons have with the townspeople?
4. What changes occur in the town after World War II?
5. How is the town affected by the violence in the North?

Guide for Responding (continued)

◆ Critical Thinking

INTERPRET

1. How does the decline in the Middletons' fortunes parallel the decline of the British empire? **[Connect]**
2. What is ironic about the fact that throughout most of the story the townspeople respect the Middletons? **[Analyze]**
3. What does the change in the townspeople's attitude toward the Middletons reveal about human nature? **[Draw Conclusions]**
4. What message does this story convey? Support your answer. **[Draw Conclusions]**

EVALUATE

5. Are the Middletons to blame for their isolation at the end of the story? **[Make a Judgment]**

◆ Reading Strategy

CAUSE AND EFFECT

Noticing **cause and effect**—the reasons why things happen—can help you understand the theme of a story. Complete each sentence with a cause or an effect.

1. The Middletons displayed a union jack because . . .
2. As a result of the violence in the north, . . .
3. The townspeople began to shun the Middletons because . . .

◆ Literary Focus

SOCIAL CONFLICT

The plot of "The Distant Past" rises and falls around a central **social conflict,** a struggle between two different political views. Though the political events occur offstage, so to speak, they have a major effect on the characters in the story.

1. How is the Middletons' view of society different from that of everyone around them?
2. Why is the social conflict very mild at first?
3. What causes the social conflict to escalate?
4. How does the changing relationship between Fat Driscoll and the Middletons reflect the larger social conflict?
5. What connection is there between the social conflict and the theme of the story?

◆ Build Vocabulary

USING THE LATIN SUFFIX -ity

In your notebook, add -ity to each word and insert the new word in the sentence where it fits.

a. serene **b.** civil **c.** adverse

1. Though feelings ran high, the opposing factions maintained their ___?___ during negotiations.
2. The campers encountered one ___?___ after another, from ants to torrential rains.
3. The soothing music established a mood of ___?___ in the room.

USING THE WORD BANK: Sentence Completions

In your notebook, write the word from the Word Bank that best completes each sentence.

1. The townspeople regarded the brother and sister as an ___?___ .
2. They did not question the ___?___ of the English king.
3. Financial ___?___ bore down on them after their father's death.
4. Kindly eyes sparkled from the sister's careworn ___?___ .
5. They shuddered at news of the unjust ___?___ of innocent citizens.

◆ Grammar and Style

RESTRICTIVE AND NONRESTRICTIVE ADJECTIVE CLAUSES

A **restrictive adjective clause** is not separated from the rest of the sentence by commas. A **nonrestrictive adjective clause** is set off by commas.

Practice Rewrite the sentences, underlining each adjective clause and adding commas where needed.

1. The Middletons who had lived comfortably found themselves impoverished.
2. Twice a week they rode to town where they had friendly encounters with the townspeople.
3. The dog that accompanied them was always a red setter.
4. The shopkeepers with whom they did business considered them odd.
5. After a convivial afternoon, they made the trip back to their rundown home which they called Carraveagh.

Build Your Portfolio

Idea Bank

Writing

1. **Obituary** Write an obituary for either of the Middletons to appear in the local newspaper. Summarize the details of his or her life and comment on his or her position in the community.

2. **Poem** Write a poem that expresses the same theme as "The Distant Past." Your poem may be about the Middletons or any other topic that shows the effect of social conflict on individuals.

3. **Literary Analysis** Write an essay in which you analyze the effect of the story's social conflict on the characters. Support your points with details from the story.

Speaking, Listening, and Viewing

4. **Eulogy** Miss Middleton has died. As Fat Driscoll, give the eulogy at the funeral service. Present an honest portrait of the deceased and your relationship with her. **[Performing Arts Link]**

5. **Visual Presentation** Research and prepare a visual presentation that portrays the fading British presence in Hong Kong or some other former colony. In your presentation, include symbols of Great Britain, such as the union jack. **[History Link]**

Researching and Representing

6. **Portfolio** Create a series of sketches of the Middletons through the years. Put Carraveagh in the background and include a red setter, a trap or Ford Anglia, or other items that reflect the changes in their lives. **[Art Link]**

7. **A Celebration of Irish Culture** Stage a celebration of Irish culture that includes music, food, and storytelling. Tape Irish music, write out recipe cards for Irish dishes, and prepare Irish stories to tell. **[Social Studies Link; Music Link]**

Online Activity www.phlit.phschool.com

Guided Writing Lesson

Persuasive Letter

The political struggles in Northern Ireland is just one of many major social conflicts that have occurred in recent years. Think of a current social conflict—local, national, or international—about which you are concerned. Then write a persuasive letter to parties involved in the conflict, offering suggestions about how the conflict can be resolved.

Writing Skills Focus: Brevity and Clarity

To be effective, a persuasive letter must be **brief**—saying only what needs to be said—and **clear**—stating exactly what you propose.

- State your proposal for resolving the conflict in your introductory paragraph.
- Follow with a series of concise paragraphs supporting your opinion.
- Be as exact as possible when choosing words to present your case.
- Leave out any words or details that don't advance your argument.

Prewriting Start by charting out the causes and effects of the conflict. Then come up with possible solutions. List reasons you think the solutions would work. Review your notes, and decide on the strongest possible solutions.

Drafting In your opening paragraph, use some of the effects of the conflict to demonstrate why it is essential for the conflict to be resolved. Then present your ideas for resolving the conflict. Follow with a series of paragraphs that each focus on a single main point. End with a strong appeal to both parties to follow your advice.

Revising Show your letter to a classmate. Ask for suggestions about how you can make it more convincing and more direct. Use your peer's suggestions to help direct your revisions.

Guide for Interpreting

Seamus Heaney (1939–)

Born in County Derry, Northern Ireland, Seamus Heaney has devoted much of his poetry to the life and history of his homeland. He is a gifted traditionalist whom the American poet Robert Lowell called "the most important Irish poet since Yeats." Heaney has earned that high praise with visionary books of poetry like *Seeing Things* (1991) and *The Spirit Level* (1996), and with his brilliant lectures on poetry in *The Redress of Poetry* (1995).

The eldest of nine children, Heaney spent a happy childhood on a farm that had been in his family for generations. He has said that his deep regard for tradition and the past grew from his early experiences in the countryside.

He first published as an undergraduate at Queen's University in Belfast. Somewhat later, having struggled with the role of the artist in Northern Ireland's troubled political climate, he left Northern Ireland and settled in the Irish Republic in 1972. His departure was called by some an artistic necessity and by others, a betrayal. Heaney nevertheless remains the leading Irish poet, Republican or Northern.

Since 1984, he has been Boylston Professor of Rhetoric and Poetry at Harvard, and from 1989 to 1994 he held the chair of Professor of Poetry at Oxford. In 1995, Seamus Heaney received the Nobel Prize for Literature.

Eavan Boland (1944–)

Eavan Boland was born in Dublin, the capital of the Irish Republic. Her father was a diplomat who, she says, "recognized the importance of poetry to civilization." Her mother was a painter, who also "was totally in tune with what poetry tried to do."

During much of Boland's early life, she was away from Ireland. While her father was ambassador to Great Britain in the 1950's, she experienced anti-Irish hostility and felt "a great sense of isolation." Returning to Ireland in 1959, she found "a great imaginative release." Since 1967 she has published several acclaimed volumes of poetry, including *The War Horse, In Her Own Image, Night Feed,* and *Beyond History.*

Married to a novelist and the mother of two daughters, Boland often writes about domestic life, but she shuns the label "woman poet." She says poetry should create only statements that are "bound to be human."

◆ Background for Understanding

HISTORY: HEANEY IN THE CONTEXT OF NORTHERN IRELAND

For about 800 years before the twentieth century Ireland was, with the exception of a few brief periods, under English control. Since the 1920's, Ireland has been partitioned into the Irish Republic in the South and Ulster, or Northern Ireland, which remains allied with Great Britain.

Ulster has been a focus of conflict between Protestants and Catholics. The Ulster Protestants generally support British rule of Northern Ireland. For the most part, Northern Irish Catholics want "the British out" and Ireland united.

From the early 1970's on, this conflict has produced terrorism by Catholics and Protestants, with occasional cease-fires. It was just this strife—and the pressure it created to take sides—that Seamus Heaney turned from when he settled in the Irish Republic in 1972. In his poem "Two Lorries," he refers to a bombing incident from this struggle.

Follower ◆ Two Lorries ◆ Outside History

◆ Literature and Your Life

CONNECT YOUR EXPERIENCE

Try to go through a day without making a choice—it's impossible. Even if you spent the day in bed, under the covers, your mind would be roaming around the world—making choices.

These two Irish poets think about choices, and make them, in poems. "Deciding" in poetry lets these poets bring their deepest thoughts and feelings to their choices.

Journal Writing Briefly describe an important choice you made that turned out well.

THEMATIC FOCUS: CONFLICTS ABROAD AND AT HOME

What do these poets have to say, directly or indirectly, about the conflicts in Northern Ireland?

◆ Literary Focus

DICTION AND STYLE

Diction refers to a writer's typical choice of words—formal or informal, down-to-earth or intellectual. Word choice is an important part of **style,** which takes in a writer's whole manner of expression. Style also includes a poet's use of forms and rhythms (traditional or otherwise) and his or her typical themes and images.

Heaney's style is marked by his use of traditional forms like the **sestina** ("Two Lorries"), which recycles six words to end each line. He also has a love of precise and down-to-earth language. A farmer's son, he handles words as if they had the heft of potatoes.

◆ Reading Strategy

SUMMARIZE

No matter how you respond to individual images in a poem, when you reach the last line, it may seem as if you are left with nothing to hold onto. **Summarizing** a poem—briefly restating its key points—can help you hold it in your mind. You can even summarize individual stanzas like this one:

I wanted to grow up and plow,
To close one eye, stiffen my arm.
All I ever did was follow
In his broad shadow round the farm. ("Follower")
Summary I wanted to be a farmer, like my father.

◆ Build Vocabulary

LATIN ROOTS: -mort-

In "Outside History," Boland speaks about being *mortal,* meaning "subject to death." This word contains the Latin root -mort-, which means "death." The same root appears in words like *mortuary,* "a funeral home."

WORD BANK

Preview this list of words before you read the poems.

furrow
nuisance
inklings
mortal
ordeal

◆ Grammar and Style

CONCRETE AND ABSTRACT NOUNS

Both poets use **concrete nouns,** which name things that can be sensed, and **abstract nouns,** which name general things, like ideas and qualities. However, they use these two types of nouns in different proportions.

Heaney, as a farmer's son, fills his work with down-to-earth, concrete nouns—*shafts, furrow, horses.* Boland, at least in "Outside History," uses a greater proportion of abstract nouns, like *history* and *myth.*

As you read Heaney's and Boland's poems, notice the ratio of concrete to abstract nouns. This ratio is one measure of a writer's style.

FOLLOWER

Seamus Heaney

My father worked with a horse plow,
His shoulders globed like a full sail strung
Between the shafts and the furrow.
The horses strained at his clicking tongue.

5 An expert. He would set the wing
And fit the bright steel-pointed sock.
The sod rolled over without breaking.
At the headrig, with a single pluck

Of reins, the sweating team turned round
10 And back into the land. His eye
Narrowed and angled at the ground,
Mapping the <u>furrow</u> exactly.

I stumbled in his hobnailed wake,
Fell sometimes on the polished sod;
15 Sometimes he rode me on his back
Dipping and rising to his plod.

I wanted to grow up and plow,
To close one eye, stiffen my arm.
All I ever did was follow
20 In his broad shadow round the farm.

I was a <u>nuisance</u>, tripping, falling,
Yapping always. But today
It is my father who keeps stumbling
Behind me, and will not go away.

◆ **Build Vocabulary**

furrow (fʉr´ ō) *n*.: Narrow groove made in the ground by a plow

nuisance (no͞o´ səns) *n*.: Act, thing, or condition causing trouble

◀ **Critical Viewing** How does this photograph reveal the two sides of the father-son relationship that Heaney describes in his poem? How is it different? **[Evaluate]**

Two Lorries

Seamus Heaney

▲ **Critical Viewing**
In what way does the photograph suggest an event similar to one in the poem? [**Compare and Contrast**]

It's raining on black coal and warm wet ashes.
There are tire-marks in the yard, Agnew's old lorry[1]
Has all its cribs down and Agnew the coalman
With his Belfast accent's sweet-talking my mother.
5 Would she ever go to a film in Magherafelt?
But it's raining and he still has half the load

To deliver farther on. This time the lode
Our coal came from was silk-black, so the ashes
Will be the silkiest white. The Magherafelt
10 (Via Toomebridge) bus goes by. The half-stripped lorry
With its emptied, folded coal-bags moves my mother:
The tasty ways of a leather-aproned coalman!

And films no less! The conceit of a coalman . . .
She goes back in and gets out the black lead
15 And emery paper, this nineteen-forties mother,
All business round her stove, half-wiping ashes
With a backhand from her cheek as the bolted lorry
Gets revved and turned and heads for Magherafelt

---

1. lorry: Truck.

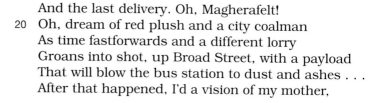

And the last delivery. Oh, Magherafelt!
20 Oh, dream of red plush and a city coalman
As time fastforwards and a different lorry
Groans into shot, up Broad Street, with a payload
That will blow the bus station to dust and ashes . . .
After that happened, I'd a vision of my mother,

25 A revenant on the bench where I would meet her
In that cold-floored waiting-room in Magherafelt,
Her shopping bags full up with shoveled ashes.
Death walked out past her like a dust-faced coalman
Refolding body-bags, plying his load
30 Empty upon empty, in a flurry

Of motes and engine-revs, but which lorry
Was it now? Young Agnew's or that other,
Heavier, deadlier one, set to explode
In a time beyond her time in Magherafelt . . .
35 So tally bags and sweet-talk darkness, coalman.
Listen to the rain spit in new ashes

As you heft a load of dust that was Magherafelt,
Then reappear from your lorry as my mother's
Dreamboat coalman filmed in silk-white ashes.

Guide for Responding

◆ Literature and Your Life

Reader's Response Have you ever felt about an adult the way the speaker feels about his father in "Follower"? Explain.

Thematic Focus What is the conflict between the world of each lorry? Explain.

☑ Check Your Comprehension

1. In "Follower," what is the father doing?
2. In "Follower," what does the speaker want to do in the future?
3. What are the two different incidents described in "Two Lorries"?
4. Which incident in "Two Lorries" comes before the other?

◆ Critical Thinking

INTERPRET
1. In "Follower," why does the boy want "To close one eye" and "stiffen" his "arm"? **[Interpret]**
2. Explain the reversal that occurs in lines 23–24 of "Follower." **[Draw Conclusions]**
3. Why does Heaney combine the two different incidents in "Two Lorries"? **[Interpret]**
4. From "Two Lorries," how would you describe Heaney's attitude toward violence in the Irish conflicts? **[Draw Conclusions]**

APPLY
5. "Follower" suggests that children never outgrow their parents. Do people's relations with their parents always leave lasting marks or burdens? Explain. **[Generalize]**

Outside History

Eavan Boland

Starry Night Over the Rhone River, Vincent van Gogh, Musée d'Orsay, Paris, France

▲ **Critical Viewing** How does this image depict outside and inside history as Boland does in her poem? **[Analyze]**

There are outsiders, always. These stars—
these iron <u>inklings</u> of an Irish January,
whose light happened

thousands of years before
5   our pain did: they are, they have always been
outside history.

They keep their distance. Under them remains
a place where you found
you were human, and

10   a landscape in which you know you are <u>mortal</u>.
And a time to choose between them.
I have chosen:

Out of myth into history I move to be
part of that <u>ordeal</u>
15   whose darkness is

only now reaching me from those fields,
those rivers, those roads clotted as
firmaments[1] with the dead.

How slowly they die
20   as we kneel beside them, whisper in their ear.
And we are too late. We are always too late.

_____

1. **firmaments** *n.*: The heavens.

◆ Build Vocabulary

inklings (iŋk´ liŋz) *n.*: Indirect suggestions

mortal (môr´ təl) *adj.*: That which must eventually die

ordeal (ôr dēl´) *n.*: Any difficult or painful experience

Guide for Responding

◆ *Literature and Your Life*

Reader's Response Is Boland too pessimistic when she writes, "We are always too late"? Explain.

Thematic Focus How might Boland's early years away from Ireland have contributed to the poem?

☑ Check Your Comprehension

1. What are the "iron inklings of an Irish January"?
2. What does the speaker learn under the stars?
3. What do the fields, rivers, and roads hold?
4. What does the speaker choose in this poem?
5. Whom does the poet "kneel beside" at the end of the poem?

◆ Critical Thinking

INTERPRET

1. Why are stars "outside" history? **[Interpret]**
2. What is the "ordeal" in line 14? **[Interpret]**
3. Who are "the dead" in line 18? **[Interpret]**
4. What does it mean to choose between myth and history? **[Draw Conclusions]**

EVALUATE

5. Does Boland really become part of a larger "ordeal," or is that itself a myth? Explain. **[Evaluate]**

APPLY

6. Defend the right to stay uninvolved in a conflict. **[Defend]**

Guide for Responding (continued)

◆ Reading Strategy

SUMMARIZE

It is often more difficult to **summarize** a poem, briefly restating its main idea, than to summarize an essay. However, it *is* possible to capture the essence of a poem while leaving out its many details and images. Sometimes a line or two near the end of a poem will point you toward a summary.

In "Follower," for example, the last two stanzas seem to sum up the many details from the poet's childhood relationship with his father: As a child, he followed his father as a hero, but now his aging or dead father follows him, as a memory.

1. Which three stanzas in "Outside History" seem to summarize the meaning of the poem?
2. Basing your answer on the stanzas you found but using your own words, summarize "Outside History."
3. A summary of "Two Lorries" would involve a brief comparison of the two incidents the poet recalls. Write such a summary.

◆ Build Vocabulary

USING THE LATIN ROOT -mort-

Keeping in mind that the Latin root *-mort-* means "death," briefly define the italicized words.
1. The head of the funeral home was a *mortician*.
2. The *mortality* rate for smokers is usually higher than it is for nonsmokers.
3. Some performers think that fame will make them *immortal*.
4. In sufficient amounts, arsenic is *mortiferous*.

USING THE WORD BANK: Sentence Completions

On your paper, fill in each blank with the most appropriate word from the Word Bank. Use each word only once.

When, as a child, Seamus Heaney followed his father around the farm, he may have made a ____?____ of himself. However, young Seamus's tripping over a ____?____ was probably more of a source of amusement than an ____?____ for his father. One thing is sure, that young Seamus Heaney had no ____?____ that his father was ____?____ .

◆ Literary Focus

DICTION AND STYLE

In poetry, **style** is a little word with a large meaning: It includes everything that is unique about a poet's **diction** (word choice), imagery, rhythms, forms, and themes. You can begin to understand these two poets' styles by comparing how they handle these elements. Be aware, however, that a style comparison based on a few poems is just a start.

Heaney tends to use images that help tell a story, and his diction is conversational and informal. He also uses well-crafted poetic forms: regular stanzas that rhyme *abab* ("Follower") and a sestina, built around six line-ending words ("Two Lorries").

By contrast, Boland uses an improvised, free-verse rhythm and only one partial rhyme ("found/ "and") in "Outside History." Her diction is abstract at first and then more concrete as she decides to become involved in the pain of life.

Use passages from the poems to help prove or disprove these claims about the poets' styles:
1. Boland is more of a gifted traditionalist than Heaney is.
2. Of these two gifted poets, Heaney writes more as the Irish insider and Boland as the outsider.

◆ Grammar and Style

CONCRETE AND ABSTRACT NOUNS

Both poets use **concrete nouns,** which name specific things, and **abstract nouns,** which name general things. In moving from abstract nouns like *myth* to concrete nouns like *fields,* Boland expresses her initial detachment from Irish suffering and her later acceptance of it. Heaney in "Two Lorries" makes concrete nouns gradually take on abstract meaning, as when the word *dust* changes its meaning from "coal-dust" into a noun referring to "death."

Practice On your paper, identify which italicized nouns are concrete and which are abstract.
1. My father worked with a *horse-plough* . . .
2. . . . the sweating *team* turned round . . .
3. The *conceit* of a coalman . . .
4. Dreamboat *coalman* filmed in silk-white ashes.
5. I move to be / part of that *ordeal* . . .

Build Your Portfolio

Idea Bank

Writing

1. Book Blurb Write a book blurb to appear on the jacket of a book by one of these poets. Describe the poet and the work in a way that will interest readers.

2. Comparison-and-Contrast Essay Compare and contrast the styles of Heaney and Boland. Consider such elements as word choice, imagery, poetic form, and theme.

3. Response to Criticism Dillon Johnston writes that Heaney's "poetry immediately attracts the reader: the images are vivid and precise; the speaking voice is reassuring . . ." Comment on this remark, citing passages from the poems.

Speaking, Listening, and Viewing

4. Monologue As Heaney's father, improvise a monologue in answer to the poem "Follower." Give your perspective on the experience described by your "son." **[Performing Arts Link]**

5. Oral Interpretation Choose a poem by Heaney or Boland, rehearse it, then recite it for the class. Be sure you know how to pronounce all the words, and note where you will pause. **[Performing Arts Link]**

Researching and Representing

6. Irish Folk Music Listen to recordings of Irish folk music made by groups like The Chieftains. Give an oral report on the recordings to your classmates, playing the music and explaining historical references in the songs. **[Music Link]**

7. The History of the "Troubles" Using books on recent Irish history, research and report on the causes of the strife in Northern Ireland. **[Social Studies Link]**

Online Activity www.phlit.phschool.com

Guided Writing Lesson

Conflict-Resolution Guidelines

Both Heaney and Boland refer to conflicts in Northern Ireland. You may not be able to suggest ways for settling that dispute, but you can probably give valuable advice for resolving conflicts in your own school. Work your ideas into a set of guidelines that students and teachers can follow in settling disagreements. Include specific procedures for putting your guidelines into action.

> ### Writing Skills Focus:
> ### Clear Explanation of Procedures
> Whether you're writing a manual for assembling a VCR or guidelines for settling conflicts, it's important to **explain procedures clearly.** Be sure that you give step-by-step instructions for part of the process you describe.

Prewriting Consider these questions: What kinds of conflicts arise in your school? Who, if anyone, tries to settle them? If necessary, create a new conflict-resolution group and diagram its authority using an organizational chart like this one:

Conflict-Resolution Committee

| Students | Faculty |

Drafting Devise and spell out step-by-step instructions for identifying, discussing, and resolving conflicts. Specify the rights and responsibilities of the disputing parties at each stage of the process.

Revising Test your procedures with several classmates by staging a mock conflict resolution. Note where procedures seem weak and brainstorm with your classmates to strengthen them.

Guide for Interpreting

Doris Lessing *(1919–)*

Freely admitting her desire to influence others through her fiction, Doris Lessing has said that publishing a story or novel is "an attempt to impose one's personality and beliefs on other people. If a writer accepts this responsibility, he must see himself . . . as an architect of the soul."

Exposing Injustice One of the ways that Doris Lessing fulfills this responsibility is by writing about social injustice. Her own experiences give her a unique perspective on the problems caused when cultures conflict.

She was born in Persia (now Iran), the daughter of a British bank clerk. When she was five, her family moved to the British colony of Rhodesia (now the independent country of Zimbabwe) in south-central Africa. Her memoir *Under My Skin* (1994) describes some ways in which Europeans mistreated the Africans, displacing them from their lands and ignoring their deeply held beliefs and traditions. Lessing's awareness of such injustice is reflected in her first novel, *The Grass is Singing* (1950), and in *African Stories* (1964).

Personal and Political Lessing's stories and novels often focus on how personal decisions can reflect and alter society. Martha Quest, the heroine of a five-novel series called *Children of Violence* (1952–1969), faces private battles that reflect global conflicts.

> *For Doris Lessing, the actions that people take every day are as political as government maneuvers.*

Lessing's best-known novel, *The Golden Notebook* (1962), highlights the social relevance of one woman's persistent search for identity. The dominant theme is that of the free woman who struggles for individuality and equality despite social and psychological conditioning.

Throughout her writing career, Doris Lessing has honored her responsibility to her audience. Her short stories and novels have explored the roles of women in modern society, the evils of racism, and the limits of idealism in solving the problems facing society. Her vision is broad and her voice is direct and challenging.

◆ Background for Understanding

HISTORY: LESSING AND THE BRITISH HOUSEHOLD IN RHODESIA

In 1890, a team of British explorers, settlers, hunters, and missionaries came to Africa seeking to expand the British Empire. Many of the British immigrants felt that colonization would be "good for Africa." Lessing suggests that this kind of idealism is enough to make us "wonder which of the idealisms that make our hearts beat faster will seem wrong-headed to people a hundred years from now."

By 1924, when Lessing's family moved to Rhodesia, the country had been under British rule for many years. Two cultures had met, clashed, and achieved an unequal balance. The British settlers were home-owners; native Africans became their servants. Although they were paid wages, salaries were so low they could not afford independence.

Christian missionaries converted many Africans in Rhodesia, but these conversions reflected the uneasy juxtapositions of widely divergent cultures. Many Africans incorporated a belief in Jesus Christ into their religious life without altering their traditional beliefs.

In "No Witchcraft for Sale," you will encounter native Africans who work for privileged British settlers. You'll also encounter two cultures, native and European, that coexist uneasily.

No Witchcraft for Sale

◆ Literature and Your Life

CONNECT YOUR EXPERIENCE

An anthropologist once described his nervousness as a foreigner approached him and, standing less than a foot away, started talking. The anthropologist became angrier and angrier at what he regarded as an invasion of his space. This incident shows how differences in the unwritten rules of cultures can spark a conflict.

In this story, Doris Lessing writes about a cultural conflict that arises between an English family and their African servant.

Journal Writing Jot down some unwritten cultural "rules" about matters like personal distance, privacy, or smiling.

THEMATIC FOCUS: CONFLICTS ABROAD AND AT HOME

As you read this story, consider what it suggests about the types of conflicts that arose in British colonies.

◆ Build Vocabulary

RELATED WORDS: FORMS OF *SKEPTICAL*

A character in this story smiles "with skeptical good humor." The word *skeptical* means "inclined to doubt or question." Other forms of this word include the nouns *skeptic* ("a person who doubts or disbelieves") and *skepticism* ("the tendency to doubt or disbelieve") and the adjective *skeptical* ("not believing readily").

WORD BANK

Before you read, preview these words from the story.

reverently
defiantly
efficacy
incredulously
skeptical

◆ Grammar and Style

CORRECT USE OF *LIKE* AND *AS*

Lessing correctly uses the subordinating conjunctions *as* or *as if* to introduce a subordinate clause, which has a subject and a verb. She uses the preposition *like* to introduce a prepositional phrase, which consists of an object and any words that modify it.

as if: subordinate clause
They congratulated Mrs. Farquar *as if she had achieved a very great thing.*

like: prepositional phrase
He spoke to Mr. Farquar *like an unwilling servant.*

◆ Literary Focus

CULTURAL CONFLICT

By bringing different peoples together, colonialism provided a new focus for writers: the **cultural conflicts** arising from differences in customs, beliefs, and values. Such conflicts could lead to misunderstandings, tension, and even violent confrontations.

In "No Witchcraft for Sale," Lessing helps you understand a cultural conflict by allowing you to see it from two different sides. Trace the conflict as it arises, and predict whether or not it will be resolved. You can even propose resolutions of your own.

◆ Reading Strategy

ANALYZE CULTURAL DIFFERENCES

You can better understand a story involving cultural conflicts by analyzing the **cultural differences** that create the problem in the first place.

To analyze the cultural differences in this story, use a diagram like the one below to compare the Farquars and Gideon. Where the circles intersect, jot down similarities in thinking. Where the circles are separate, jot down differences.

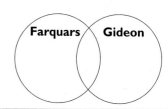

Farquars   Gideon

◀ **Critical Viewing**
Using this picture
and the title,
predict what this
story will be
about. **[Predict]**

NO WITCHCRAFT FOR SALE

Doris Lessing

The Farquars had been childless for years when little Teddy was born; and they were touched by the pleasure of their servants, who brought presents of fowls and eggs and flowers to the homestead when they came to rejoice over the baby, exclaiming with delight over his downy golden head and his blue eyes. They congratulated Mrs. Farquar as if she had achieved a very great thing, and she felt that she had—her smile for the lingering, admiring natives was warm and grateful.

Later, when Teddy had his first haircut, Gideon the cook picked up the soft gold tufts from the ground, and held them reverently in his hand. Then he smiled at the little boy and said: "Little Yellow Head." That became the native name for the child. Gideon and Teddy were great friends from the first. When Gideon had finished his work, he would lift Teddy on his shoulders to the shade of a big tree, and play with him there, forming curious little toys from twigs and leaves and grass, or shaping animals from wetted soil. When Teddy learned to walk it was often Gideon who crouched before him, clucking encouragement, finally catching him when he fell, tossing him up in the air till they both became breathless with laughter. Mrs. Farquar was fond of the old cook because of his love for her child.

There was no second baby; and one day Gideon said: "Ah, missus, missus, the Lord above sent this one; Little Yellow Head is the most good thing we have in our house." Because of that "we" Mrs. Farquar felt a warm impulse toward her cook; and at the end of the month she raised his wages. He had been with her now for several years; he was one of the few natives who had his wife and children in the compound and never wanted to go home to his kraal,[1] which was some hundreds of miles away.

---

1. kraal (kräl): Village of South African natives, usually fenced in with a stockade.

Sometimes a small piccanin who had been born the same time as Teddy, could be seen peering from the edge of the bush, staring in awe at the little white boy with his miraculous fair hair and Northern blue eyes. The two little children would gaze at each other with a wide, interested gaze, and once Teddy put out his hand curiously to touch the black child's cheeks and hair.

Gideon, who was watching, shook his head wonderingly, and said: "Ah, missus, these are both children, and one will grow up to be a baas, and one will be a servant"; and Mrs. Farquar smiled and said sadly, "Yes, Gideon, I was thinking the same." She sighed. "It is God's will," said Gideon, who was a mission boy. The Farquars were very religious people; and this shared feeling about God bound servant and masters even closer together.

Teddy was about six years old when he was given a scooter, and discovered the intoxications of speed. All day he would fly around the homestead, in and out of flowerbeds, scattering squawking chickens and irritated dogs, finishing with a wide dizzying arc into the kitchen door. There he would cry: "Gideon, look at me!" And Gideon would laugh and say: "Very clever, Little Yellow Head." Gideon's youngest son, who was now a herdsboy, came especially up from the compound to see the scooter. He was afraid to come near it, but Teddy showed off in front of him. "Piccanin," shouted Teddy, "get out of my way!" And he raced in circles around the black child until he was frightened, and fled back to the bush.

"Why did you frighten him?" asked Gideon, gravely reproachful.[2]

Teddy said defiantly: "He's only a black boy," and laughed. Then, when Gideon turned away from him without speaking, his face fell. Very soon he slipped into the house and found an orange and brought it to Gideon, saying: "This is for you." He could not bring himself to say he was sorry; but he could not bear to lose Gideon's affection either. Gideon took the orange unwillingly and sighed. "Soon you will be going away to school, Little Yellow Head," he said wonderingly, "and then you will be grown up." He shook his head gently and said, "And that is how our lives go." He seemed to be putting a distance between himself and Teddy, not because of resentment, but in the way a person accepts something inevitable. The baby had lain in his arms and smiled up into his face: the tiny boy had swung from his shoulders and played with him by the hour. Now Gideon would not let his flesh touch the flesh of the white child. He was kind, but there was a grave formality in his voice that made Teddy pout and sulk away. Also, it made him into a man: with Gideon he was polite, and carried himself formally, and if he came into the kitchen to ask for something, it was in the way a white man uses toward a servant, expecting to be obeyed.

But on the day that Teddy came staggering into the kitchen with his fists to his eyes, shrieking with pain, Gideon dropped the pot full of hot soup that he was holding, rushed to the child, and forced aside his fingers. "A snake!" he exclaimed. Teddy had been on his scooter, and had come to a rest with his foot on the side of a big tub of plants. A tree-snake, hanging by its tail from the roof, had spat full into his eyes. Mrs. Farquar came running when she heard the commotion. "He'll go blind," she sobbed, holding Teddy close against her. "Gideon, he'll go blind!" Already the eyes, with perhaps half an hour's sight left in them, were swollen up to the size of fists: Teddy's small white face was distorted by great purple oozing protuberances.[3] Gideon said: "Wait a minute, missus, I'll get some medicine." He ran off into the bush.

---

2. **reproachful** (ri prōch′ fəl) *adj.*: Expressing blame.

3. **protuberances** (prō tōō′ bər əns iz) *n.*: Bulges; swellings.

◆ Build Vocabulary

reverently (rev′ ər ənt lē) *adv.*: Respectfully

defiantly (di fī′ ənt lē) *adv.*: Disobediently; with resistance

Mrs. Farquar lifted the child into the house and bathed his eyes with permanganate.[4] She had scarcely heard Gideon's words; but when she saw that her remedies had no effect at all, and remembered how she had seen natives with no sight in their eyes, because of the spitting of a snake, she began to look for the return of her cook, remembering what she heard of the efficacy of native herbs. She stood by the window, holding the terrified, sobbing little boy in her arms, and peered helplessly into the bush. It was not more than a few minutes before she saw Gideon come bounding back, and in his hand he held a plant.

"Do not be afraid, missus," said Gideon, "this will cure Little Yellow Head's eyes." He stripped the leaves from the plant, leaving a small white fleshy root. Without even washing it, he put the root in his mouth, chewed it vigorously, and then held the spittle there while he took the child forcibly from Mrs. Farquar. He gripped Teddy down between his knees, and pressed the balls of his thumbs into the swollen eyes, so that the child screamed and Mrs. Farquar cried out in protest: "Gideon, Gideon!" But Gideon took no notice. He knelt over the writhing child, pushing back the puffy lids till chinks of eyeball showed, and then he spat hard, again and again, into first one eye, and then the other. He finally lifted Teddy gently into his mother's arms, and said: "His eyes will get better." But Mrs. Farquar was weeping with terror, and she could hardly thank him: it was impossible to believe that Teddy could keep his sight. In a couple of hours the swellings were gone: the eyes were inflamed and tender but Teddy could see. Mr. and Mrs. Farquar went to Gideon in the kitchen and thanked him over and over again. They felt helpless because of their gratitude: it seemed they could do nothing to express it. They gave Gideon presents for his wife and children, and a big increase in wages, but these things could not pay for Teddy's now completely cured eyes. Mrs. Farquar said: "Gideon, God chose you as an instrument for His goodness," and Gideon said: "Yes, missus, God is very good."

Now, when such a thing happens on a farm, it cannot be long before everyone hears of it. Mr. and Mrs. Farquar told their neighbors and the story was discussed from one end of the district to the other. The bush is full of secrets. No one can live in Africa, or at least on the veld,[5] without learning very soon that there is an ancient wisdom of leaf and soil and season—and, too, perhaps most important of all, of the darker tracts of the human mind—which is the black man's heritage. Up and down the district people were telling anecdotes, reminding each other of things that had happened to them.

"But I saw it myself, I tell you. It was a puff-adder bite. The kaffir's[6] arm was swollen to the elbow, like a great shiny black bladder. He was groggy after half a minute. He was dying. Then suddenly a kaffir walked out of the bush with his hands full of green stuff. He smeared something on the place, and next day my boy was back at work, and all you could see was two small punctures in the skin."

This was the kind of tale they told. And, as always, with a certain amount of exasperation, because while all of them knew that in the bush of Africa are waiting valuable drugs locked in bark, in simple-looking leaves, in roots, it was impossible to ever get the truth about them from the natives themselves.

The story eventually reached town; and perhaps it was at a sundowner party, or some such function, that a doctor, who happened to be there, challenged it. "Nonsense," he said. "These things get exaggerated in the telling. We are always checking up on this kind of story, and we draw a blank every time."

Anyway, one morning there arrived a strange

♦ **Reading Strategy**
When Teddy is injured, how do Gideon and Mrs. Farquar react differently? Jot your ideas in the diagram you are using to analyze cultural differences.

---

4. **permanganate** (pər maŋ´ gə nāt´): Salt of permanganic acid.

5. **veld:** In South Africa, open grassy country, with few bushes and almost no trees.
6. **kaffir's:** Belonging to a black African; in South Africa, a contemptuous term.

car at the homestead, and out stepped one of the workers from the laboratory in town, with cases full of test-tubes and chemicals.

Mr. and Mrs. Farquar were flustered and pleased and flattered. They asked the scientist to lunch, and they told the story all over again, for the hundredth time. Little Teddy was there too, his blue eyes sparkling with health, to prove the truth of it. The scientist explained how humanity might benefit if this new drug could be offered for sale; and the Farquars were even more pleased: they were kind, simple people, who liked to think of something good coming about because of them. But when the scientist began talking of the money that might result, their manner showed discomfort. Their feelings over the miracle (that was how they thought of it) were so strong and deep and religious, that it was distasteful to them to think of money. The scientist, seeing their faces, went back to his first point, which was the advancement of humanity. He was perhaps a trifle perfunctory:[7] it was not the first time he had come salting the tail of a fabulous bush secret.[8]

Eventually, when the meal was over, the Farquars called Gideon into their living room and explained to him that this baas, here, was a Big Doctor from the Big City, and he had come all that way to see Gideon. At this Gideon seemed afraid; he did not understand; and Mrs. Farquar explained quickly that it was because of the wonderful thing he had done with Teddy's eyes that the Big Baas had come.

Gideon looked from Mrs. Farquar to Mr. Farquar, and then at the little boy, who was showing great importance because of the occasion. At last he said grudgingly: "The Big Baas want to know what medicine I used?" He spoke incredulously, as if he could not believe his old friends could so betray him. Mr. Farquar began explaining how a useful medicine could be

▲ **Critical Viewing** In what ways does this man's expression and appearance illustrate the wisdom of Gideon's generation? [**Evaluate**]

made out of the root, and how it could be put on sale, and how thousands of people, black and white, up and down the continent of Africa, could be saved by the medicine when that spitting snake filled their eyes with poison. Gideon listened, his eyes bent on the ground, the skin of his forehead puckering in discomfort. When Mr. Farquar had finished he did not reply. The scientist, who all this time had been leaning back in a big chair, sipping his coffee and smiling with skeptical good humor,

---

7. perfunctory (pər fuŋk´ tə rē) *adj.*: Done without care or interest.

8. salting . . . bush secret: Allusion to the humororus and ironic advice given to children about how to catch a bird—by putting salt on its tail. In other words, the scientist does not really expect to capture a valuable bit of information.

◆ **Build Vocabulary**

efficacy (ef´ i kə sē) *n.*: Power to produce effects

incredulously (in krej´ ᴏᴏ ləs lē) *adv.*: In a doubting manner

skeptical (skep´ ti kəl) *adj.*: Not easily persuaded

chipped in and explained all over again, in different words, about the making of drugs and the progress of science. Also, he offered Gideon a present.

There was silence after this further explanation, and then Gideon remarked indifferently that he could not remember the root. His face was sullen and hostile, even when he looked at the Farquars, whom he usually treated like old friends. They were beginning to feel annoyed; and this feeling annulled[9] the guilt that had been sprung into life by Gideon's accusing manner. They were beginning to feel that he was unreasonable. But it was at that moment that they all realized he would never give in. The magical drug would remain where it was, unknown and useless except for the tiny scattering of Africans who had the knowledge, natives who might be digging a ditch for the municipality in a ragged shirt and a pair of patched shorts, but who were still born to healing, hereditary healers, being the nephews or sons of the old witch doctors whose ugly masks and bits of bone and all the uncouth[10] properties of magic were the outward signs of real power and wisdom.

The Farquars might tread on that plant fifty times a day as they passed from house to garden, from cow kraal to mealie field, but they would never know it.

But they went on persuading and arguing, with all the force of their exasperation; and Gideon continued to say that he could not remember, or that there was no such root, or that it was the wrong season of the year, or that it wasn't the root itself, but the spit from his mouth that had cured Teddy's eyes. He said all these things one after another, and seemed not to care they were contradictory. He was rude and stubborn. The Farquars could hardly recognize their gentle, lovable old servant in this ignorant, perversely obstinate African, standing there in front of them with lowered eyes, his hands twitching his cook's apron, repeating over and over whichever one of the stupid refusals that first entered his head.

And suddenly he appeared to give in. He lifted his head, gave a long blank angry look at the circle of whites, who seemed to him like a circle of yelping dogs pressing around him, and said: "I will show you the root."

They walked single file away from the homestead down a kaffir path. It was a blazing December afternoon, with the sky full of hot rain clouds. Everything was hot: the sun was like a bronze tray whirling overhead, there was a heat shimmer over the fields, the soil was scorching underfoot, the dusty wind blew gritty and thick and warm in their faces. It was a terrible day, fit only for reclining on a verandah with iced drinks, which is where they would normally have been at that hour.

From time to time, remembering that on the day of the snake it had taken ten minutes to find the root, someone asked: "Is it much further, Gideon?" And Gideon would answer over his shoulder, with angry politeness: "I'm looking for the root, baas." And indeed, he would frequently bend sideways and trail his hand among the grasses with a gesture that was insulting in its perfunctoriness. He walked them through the bush along unknown paths for two hours, in that melting destroying heat, so that the sweat trickled coldly down them and their heads ached. They were all quite silent: the Farquars because they were angry, the scientist because he was being proved right again; there was no such plant. His was a tactful[11] silence.

At last, six miles from the house, Gideon suddenly decided they had had enough; or perhaps his anger evaporated at that moment. He picked up, without an attempt at looking anything but casual, a handful of blue flowers from the grass, flowers that had been growing plentifully all down the paths they had come.

He handed them to the scientist without looking at him, and marched off by himself on the way home, leaving them to follow him if they chose.

◆ **Literary Focus**
What emotionally charged words does Lessing use to describe this scene? How do these words help her portray cultural conflict?

---

9. **annulled** (ə nuld´) v.: Did away with.
10. **uncouth** (un kōōth´) adj.: Uncultured; crude; strange.

11. **tactful** (takt´ fəl) adj.: Polite.

When they got back to the house, the scientist went to the kitchen to thank Gideon: he was being very polite, even though there was an amused look in his eyes. Gideon was not there. Throwing the flowers casually into the back of his car, the eminent visitor departed on his way back to his laboratory.

Gideon was back in his kitchen in time to prepare dinner, but he was sulking. He spoke to Mr. Farquar like an unwilling servant. It was days before they liked each other again.

The Farquars made inquiries about the root from their laborers. Sometimes they were answered with distrustful stares. Sometimes the natives said: "We do not know. We have never heard of the root." One, the cattle boy, who had been with them a long time, and had grown to trust them a little, said: "Ask your boy in the kitchen. Now, there's a doctor for you. He's the son of a famous medicine man who used to be in these parts, and there's nothing he cannot cure." Then he added politely: "Of course, he's not as good as the white man's doctor, we

know that, but he's good for us."

After some time, when the soreness had gone from between the Farquars and Gideon, they began to joke: "When are you going to show us the snake-root, Gideon?" And he would laugh and shake his head, saying, a little uncomfortably: "But I did show you, missus, have you forgotten?"

Much later, Teddy, as a schoolboy, would come into the kitchen and say: "You old rascal, Gideon! Do you remember that time you tricked us all by making us walk miles all over the veld for nothing? It was so far my father had to carry me!"

And Gideon would double up with polite laughter. After much laughing, he would suddenly straighten himself up, wipe his old eyes, and look sadly at Teddy, who was grinning mischievously at him across the kitchen: "Ah, Little Yellow Head, how you have grown! Soon you will be grown up with a farm of your own . . ."

◆ Literary Focus
Is the cultural conflict resolved? Why or why not?

Guide for Responding

◆ Literature and Your Life

Reader's Response Do you think Gideon is right to be so stubborn? Why or why not?

Thematic Focus What specific effects of colonial rule are demonstrated in this story?

Journal Writing When two cultures meet, is conflict inevitable? Write down your instinctive response and a few ideas that back it up.

☑ Check Your Comprehension

1. Who is "Little Yellow Head"?
2. How does Gideon save Teddy's sight?
3. Why does a scientist visit the Farquar's farm?
4. How does Gideon respond to the scientist's request?

◆ Critical Thinking

INTERPRET

1. Why are Teddy and Gideon closest during the period Teddy is under the age of six? **[Infer]**
2. Analyze the ultimate effect of the scientist's visit on the relationship between the Farquars and Gideon. **[Analyze Cause and Effect]**
3. Explain how the term "Little Yellow Head" gathers meaning as it reappears at different points. **[Interpret]**
4. Think about Gideon's last words to Teddy. What might they mean? **[Draw Conclusions]**

EXTEND

5. In what other countries or times could a story with the same theme be set? **[Social Studies Link]**

Guide for Responding (continued)

◆ Literary Focus

CULTURAL CONFLICT

In Lessing's short story, a **cultural conflict** arises when the Farquars want to use Gideon's medicine to benefit "thousands of people." They are surprised when Gideon feels betrayed by their efforts. The cultural conflict between the Farquars and Gideon stems from differing ideas about the way knowledge of medicines should be preserved and transmitted.

1. Summarize the point of view of each side in this cultural conflict.
2. In what way is this cultural conflict both resolved and not resolved?
3. In describing the conflict, does Lessing seem to assign blame to either side? Explain.
4. Journalists and nonfiction writers also write about cultural conflict. (a) Do you think that Lessing could have communicated the same message in a newspaper article or essay? Why or why not? (b) In what ways would a feature article on the incident with the snake differ from Lessing's story?

◆ Reading Strategy

ANALYZE CULTURAL DIFFERENCES

Lessing indicates **cultural differences** both in her portrayal of characters and in her description of the setting. For example, although the Farquars and Gideon share a "feeling about God," the Farquars seem to believe that their culture and ways are generally superior to Gideon's.

1. Explain how each of these episodes reveals the Farquars' sense of superiority over Gideon:
   (a) Teddy's frightening of Gideon's son, and
   (b) the Farquars' bringing the scientist to lunch.
2. In what ways do the Farquars and Gideon share universal human values?
3. How do the Farquars both know and fail to know Gideon?
4. In what ways does Lessing use the Farquars' farm and the bush to stand for different cultures and different values?
5. Considering the cultural differences this story brings out, explain the meaning of the story's title.

◆ Build Vocabulary

USING FORMS OF *SKEPTICAL*

The word *skeptical* means "doubting" or "not easily persuaded." Think about this definition as you answer each of the following questions.

1. In ancient Greece, some philosophers called themselves Skeptics. What do you think they believed about human knowledge?
2. Is skepticism an attitude appropriate for a modern scientist? Why or why not?
3. What might a *skeptical* store owner do when offered a personal check by a stranger?

WORD BANK: Synonyms

In your notebook, write the letter of the word that is the best synonym for the first word.

1. reverently: (a) politely, (b) respectfully, (c) shyly
2. defiantly: (a) disobediently, (b) wryly, (c) strongly
3. efficacy: (a) strength, (b) stamina, (c) effectiveness
4. incredulous: (a) disbelieving, (b) sincere, (c) flip
5. skeptical: (a) trusting, (b) angry, (c) suspicious

◆ Grammar and Style

CORRECT USE OF *LIKE* AND *AS*

Writers use the words *like* and *as* or *as if* to compare things and ideas. In making comparisons, however, don't confuse *like* with forms of *as*. As, *as if*, and *as though* are subordinating conjunctions. They introduce a clause with a subject and a verb. *Like* is a preposition, and it takes a noun or a pronoun as an object. Do not use *like* in place of *as*.

Practice In your notebook, complete each comparison with *as, as if, as though* or *like*.

1. Teddy's hair was colored ____?____ straw.
2. At first, Gideon stared ____?____ he didn't understand.
3. The scientist looked ____?____ he were skeptical.
4. The sun was ____?____ a bronze tray whirling overhead.
5. Teddy laughed ____?____ he had said something clever.

Writing Application In your notebook, write a paragraph describing Gideon's behavior during the medical crisis. Use *like* and *as* to make comparisons.

Build Your Portfolio

Idea Bank

Writing

1. **Review** For a class critic's file, write a review of "No Witchcraft for Sale." Prepare readers without giving away too much of the story.

2. **Proposal** Write a proposal for adapting this story as a short film. Explain which scenes would be particularly effective in a movie and why.

3. **Critical Response** Lessing has said that a responsible writer "must be a humanist, and must feel himself as an instrument of change for good or for bad." In an essay, explain how she meets or fails to meet this challenge in her story.

Speaking, Listening, and Viewing

4. **Debate** With two teams of classmates, debate the pros and cons of colonialism. Consider the economic, cultural, and medical effects of colonial rule. Use ideas from the story to support your main points. **[Social Studies Link]**

5. **Oral Report** Some medicines come from plants native to specific parts of the world. Research the way scientists have isolated medicines from the plants native to the Amazonian rain forest, and prepare an oral report on the subject for your class. **[Social Studies Link]**

Researching and Representing

6. **Book Cover Design** By hand or with a computer, create a book jacket for a collection that includes "No Witchcraft for Sale" and other stories about cultural conflict. Choose a title and cover design that reflect the content. **[Art Link]**

7. **Comparison Report** Pick an African nation, like Zimbabwe, and prepare a report on the aftermath of colonialism there. **[Social Studies Link]**

Online Activity www.phlit.phschool.com

Guided Writing Lesson

Problem-and-Solution Essay

Lessing's character Gideon knows many remedies. What is the most effective home remedy you and your family use? Your remedy might be a food (like chicken soup) or a method (like curing hiccups by holding your breath or taking steam baths to cure a cough). Write a problem-and-solution essay in which you state a problem (on illness or injury) and give a solution (a remedy with exact steps). Elaborate to give precise instructions.

Writing Skills Focus: Elaboration to Enhance Understanding

Elaborate to add information that will enhance a reader's understanding of the remedy you describe. Follow these steps to make sure readers will follow your explanations:

- Introduce the type and purpose of the remedy you're proposing, and elaborate with details so your reader will have no doubt *what* he or she is using and *why*.
- Be exact. Replace vague words with precise terms that describe your remedy exactly.
- Anticipate difficulties a reader might face and provide information to overcome them.
- Provide step-by-step instructions.

Prewriting Brainstorm for a list of home remedies you might write about. Choose two potential cures and write notes in support of each. Once you make a final decision, sketch out the steps you will describe.

Drafting Identify the remedy and its purpose. Then describe the materials needed and list the steps to follow in order. Use transition words, such as *first, then, next,* and *finally,* to clearly signal the order. End with a discussion of problems people might encounter, as well as possible solutions.

Revising Ask a classmate to read your description and tell you where your directions are unclear. Elaborate the details in those sections.

CONNECTIONS TO TODAY'S WORLD

The Rights We Enjoy, the Duties We Owe
from New Britain: My Vision of a Young Country
Tony Blair

Thematic Connection

CONFLICTS AT HOME AND ABROAD

In his speech "The Rights We Enjoy, the Duties We Owe," prime minister of England Tony Blair calls for a moral approach to social issues. As the writers in this section demonstrate, moral and social values have been tested by the many conflicts Britain has experienced in the twentieth century. The soldier-poets Siegfried Sassoon and Wilfred Owen, for example, show how traditional notions of patriotism were called into question by the horrors of trench warfare in World War I. Later, in World War II, Winston Churchill rallied the English to their traditional values in order to oppose the fascist tyranny of Hitler.

British belief in the value and permanence of empire was also tested during the twentieth century. Gandhi's speech illustrates the struggles of Indians to assert their own national identity in the face of British oppression. Also, stories by Lessing and Trevor and poems by Heaney and Boland address conflicts in South Africa and Ireland arising from the injustices of imperial rule.

A NEW BRITAIN

With many of Britain's major external conflicts settled, Tony Blair has expressed a new vision of British citizenship. Rejecting both the notion of doing one's "own thing" and the urge to look out only for oneself, he reaffirms the importance of rights and responsibilities. He argues for "practical policies" guided by "values" that stress "the good of all."

TONY BLAIR
(1953–   )

Tony Blair, Britain's youngest prime minister in the twentieth century, is a skillful orator and speech writer. Educated as an attorney, he became a member of Parliament in 1983. He went on to become leader of the Labor Party in 1994, transforming it into what became known as the "New Labor Party" In May 1997, Blair became the first Labor Party prime minister elected in eighteen years. He is also the first prime minister not to live at 10 Downing Street, traditional residence of the country's leader, because the home was too small to accommodate his wife and three young children.

The Rights We Enjoy, The Duties We Owe

TONY BLAIR

from New Britain: My Vision of a Young Country

Individuals prosper best within a strong and cohesive society. Especially in a modern world, we are interdependent. Unless we act together to provide common services, prepare our industry and people for industrial and technological challenge, and guarantee a proper system of law and government, we will be worse off as individuals. In particular, those without the best start in life through birth are unlikely to make up for it without access to the means of achievement. Furthermore—though this may be more open to debate—a society which is fragmented and divided, where people feel no sense of shared purpose, is unlikely to produce well-adjusted and responsible citizens.

But a strong society should not be confused with a strong state, or with powerful collectivist institutions. That was the confusion of early Left[1] thinking. It was compounded by a belief that the role of the state was to grant rights, with the language of responsibility spoken far less fluently. In a further strain of thinking, connected with the libertarian Left, there was a kind of social individualism espoused,[2] where you "did your own thing." In fact this had very little to do with any forms of left-of-center philosophy recognizable to the founders of the Labor Party.[3]

The reaction of the Right,[4] after the advent of Mrs. Thatcher, was to stress the notion of the individual as against the state. Personal responsibility was extolled.[5] But then a curious thing happened. In a mirror-image of the Left's confusion, the Right started to define personal responsibility as responsibility not just for yourself but to yourself. Outside of a duty not to break the law, responsibility appeared to exclude the broader notion of duty to others. It became narrowly acquisitive[6] and rather destructive. The economic message of enterprise—of the early 1980s—became a philosophy of "Get what you can."

All over the Western world, people are searching for a new political settlement which starts with the individual but sets him or her within the wider society. People don't want an overbearing state, but they don't want to live in a social vacuum either. It is in the search for this different, reconstructed, relationship between individual and society that ideas about "community" are found. "Community" implies a recognition of interdependence, but not overweening[7] government power. It accepts that we are better equipped to meet the forces of change and insecurity through working together. It provides a basis for the elements of our character that are cooperative as well as competitive, as part of a more enlightened view of self-interest.

People know they face a greater insecurity than ever before: a new global economy; massive and rapid changes in technology; a labor market where half the workers are women; a family life that has been altered drastically; telecommunications and media that visit a common culture upon us and transform our expectations and behavior.

This insecurity is not just about jobs or mortgages—though of course these are serious problems. It is about a world that in less than a lifetime has compressed the historical change

---

1. **Left:** Term used to describe liberal political views.
2. **espoused** (e spouzd´) *v*.: Supported a cause.
3. **Labor Party:** British political party.
4. **Right:** Term used to describe conservative political views.
5. **extolled** (eks tōld´) *v*.: Praised highly.

6. **acquisitive** (ə kwiz´ə tiv) *adj*.: Eager to acquire.
7. **overweening** (ō´vər wēn´ iŋ) *adj*.: Arrogant; excessively proud.

Labour

◀ **Critical Viewing** In what ways does Tony Blair present himself as a leader? **[Evaluate]**

allows it to develop healthily. It accords instinct with common sense. It draws on a broader and therefore more accurate notion of human nature than one formulated on insular[8] self-interest. The rights we receive should reflect the duties we owe. With power should come responsibility.

Duty is a Labor Value

The assertion that each of us is our brother's keeper has motivated the Labor movement since the mid nineteenth century. It is time to reassert what it really means.

The Left has always insisted that it is not enough to argue that our only duty is not to infringe on the lives and rights of others—what might be called negative duty. A minimal community creates a society of minimal citizens. It is a broader notion of duty that gives substance to the traditional belief of the Left in solidarity. This was well understood by the early pioneers of socialism. William Morris[9] put it colorfully: "Fellowship is life, and lack of fellowship is death."

But solidarity[10] and fellowship are the start of the story, and not the end, because they will be achieved only on the basis of both social equality and personal responsibility.

The historians of *English Ethical Socialism*, Norman Dennis and A.H. Halsey, argue that William Cobbett,[11] who lived before the word "socialism" achieved common currency, took it for granted that people stood a better chance of having a happy life if they were not selfish. They write that "a person matching Cobbett's ideal, therefore, was one who enjoyed the rights and performed the duties of citizenship."

Early socialists like Robert Owen understood very clearly that a society which did not encour-

of epochs. It is bewildering. Even religion—once a given—is now an exception. And of course the world has the nuclear weapons to destroy itself many times over. Look at our children and the world into which they are growing. What parent would not feel insecure?

People need rules which we all stand by, fixed points of agreement which impose order on chaos. That does not mean a return to the old hierarchy of deference. That is at best nostalgia, at worst reactionary. We do not want old class structures back. We do not want women chained to the sink. We do not want birth rather than merit to become once again the basis of personal advancement. Nor does it mean bureaucracy and regulation. Bad and foolish rules are bad and foolish rules, but they do not invalidate the need to have rules.

Duty is the cornerstone of a decent society. It recognizes more than self. It defines the context in which rights are given. It is personal; but it is also owed to society. Respect for others—responsibility to them—is an essential prerequisite of a strong and active community. It is the method through which we can build a society that does not subsume our individuality but

---

8. **insular** (in´ sə lər) *adj.*: Detached or isolated.
9. **William Morris** Early English socialist (1834–1896).
10. **solidarity** (säl´ə dar´ə tē) *n.*: Combination or agreement of all elements or individuals.
11. **William Cobbett** (käb´ it): English journalist and reformer (1762–1835).

age people voluntarily to carry out their responsibilities to others would always be in danger of slipping either into the anarchy[12] of mutual indifference—and its corollary, the domination of the powerless by the powerful—or the tyranny of collective coercion, where the freedom of all is denied in the name of the good of all.

Ethical socialists have long asserted that there was and is a distinctive socialist view of both human nature and social morality. R.H. Tawney[13] put it clearly in the 1920s: "Modern society is sick through the absence of a moral ideal," he wrote. "What we have been witnessing . . . both in international affairs and in industry, is the breakdown of society on the basis of rights divorced from obligations." And G.D.H

---

12. **anarchy** (an´ ər kē) *n.*: Complete absence of government.
13. **Robert Tawney** (tô´ nē): ; British economic historian (1880–1962).

Cole said that "A socialist society that is to be true to its egalitarian principles of human brotherhood must rest on the widest possible diffusion of power and responsibility, so as to enlist the active participation of as many of its citizens in the tasks of democratic self-government."

In his book *Liberals and Social Democrats*, the historian Peter Clarke drew a distinction between "moral reformers" and "mechanical reformers." The moral reformers were the ethical socialists like Tawney and Morris. They looked around the communities in which they lived, and called for a new moral impulse to guide them. The mechanical reformers, on the other hand, concentrated on the technicalities of social and economic reform. They were severely practical in their outlook.

Values without practical policies are useless; but policies without a set of values guiding them give no sense of meaning or direction to public life.

Guide for Responding

◆ *Literature and Your Life*

Reader's Response After reading this selection, did you feel optimistic or pessimistic about Britain's ability to solve its own problems? Explain.

Thematic Focus Do you see yourself as a member of a global community? Why or why not?

Journal Writing List some values that will help individuals and governments to achieve a just society.

☑ Check Your Comprehension

1. What are two beliefs of the Left that Blair rejects?
2. What is a "mirror-image" belief of the Right that Blair also rejects?
3. What changes in the world does Blair see as contributing to a sense of insecurity?
4. Blair sees solidarity and fellowship as dependent upon what two social principles?

◆ Critical Thinking

INTERPRET

1. This essay is entitled "The Rights We Enjoy, The Duties We Owe." (a) Do you think this title is appropriate? (b) What statements by Blair support or contradict the title of this selection? **[Support]**
2. Would you describe Blair as a "moral reformer," "mechanical reformer," or a combination of both? Explain. **[Analyze]**
3. (a) Explain what Tawney means by his statement "what we have been witnessing . . . is the breakdown of society on the basis of rights divorced from obligations." (b) Why would Blair have included this reference? **[Draw Conclusions]**

EVALUATE

4. How convincing and effective is Blair in getting his points across? **[Evaluate]**

Thematic Connection

CONFLICTS AT HOME AND ABROAD

Many of the poems and stories in this section deal with social and political conflicts that were resolved at great cost—or that have not yet been resolved. By contrast with the solemn, defiant, or pessimistic moods of these works, this speech by Tony Blair strikes a note of optimism. Blair seems to believe that, with rights and responsibilities in balance, Great Britain can meet the global challenges of a new century.

1. Why do you think Blair subtitles his speech "My Vision of a Young Country"?
2. Compare and contrast Blair's speech with those of Churchill and Gandhi. Pay special attention to tone, historical circumstances, and key ideas.
3. What do you think the election of Tony Blair suggests about the direction Britain will take in the twenty-first century?

 Idea Bank

Writing

1. **Campaign Poster** Using Tony Blair's key ideas, design a campaign poster that will help him in a future election.

2. **Persuasive Essay** Blair states that "The rights we receive should reflect the duties we owe." Write a persuasive essay in which you explain how this notion has relevance in your home, at work and school, and in your local community.

3. **Problem-Solution Essay** Apply Tony Blair's ideas about rights and responsibilities to resolve a conflict addressed in one of the stories and poems of this section.

Speaking, Listening, and Viewing

4. **Visual Presentation** Tony Blair mentions William Morris as an early British socialist, but Morris was also a poet, painter, and craftsman, whose works reflected his humanism. Present an oral report that uses examples of the home furnishings he designed to illustrate his belief that utility and beauty are compatible. **[Art Link]**

Researching and Representing

5. **Taking Responsibility** Many organizations, from local food banks to the International Red Cross, take responsibility for those who are less fortunate. Select one of these organizations and learn about how it functions. Present your findings in an article for your school newspaper. **[Social Studies Link]**

Online Activity www.phlit.phschool.com

Writing Process Workshop

How-to Essay

Literature inspired by World War I is intense and shocking. Writers who unflinchingly described trench warfare may have wished they could have given the world instructions on how to avoid warfare in the first place.

Choose a simpler process than solving global conflict, and write a traditional how-to essay in which you explain the ways in which readers can accomplish a specific task. After stating the task and giving necessary background information, take readers step by step through the process.

Use the following skills to guide you as you write:

Writing Skills Focus

▶ **Anticipate reader's questions** by considering what your readers will want or need to know, and providing adequate information. (See p. 981.)

▶ **Choose vivid, specific details** to clarify the steps in the process. (See p. 991.)

▶ **Maintain brevity and clarity** by providing information in the form of charts, outlines, or pictures. (See p. 1001.)

▶ **Elaborate to enhance understanding** by providing necessary details and explanations for each procedure. (See p. 1021.)

WORKPLACE WRITING MODEL

from "In Praise of the Kitchen Garden,"
Gardening How-To, May/June 1997

The history of the kitchen garden goes way back, as witnessed by this late-nineteenth-century walled kitchen garden in England. ① The walls kept predators at bay and created a microclimate ② more conducive to growing vegetables. To create your own special kitchen garden, follow these basic guidelines. Your kitchen garden should be: ③

1. Close to your house, preferably right next to your kitchen door. . . . It will be handiest there; besides, it will look wonderful ④. . . .

① Historical background creates interest and explains the origins of the task.

② The word *microclimate* is vivid and specific.

③ A numbered list, rather than a paragraph, keeps the explanation brief and clear.

④ The author anticipates and answers the reader's question, "Why next to the door?"

APPLYING LANGUAGE SKILLS: Avoiding Run-on Sentences

It is important to avoid confusing run-on sentences in how-to essays.Use the following strategies to correct run-on sentences.

- Form two sentences.

  Draft: Scrub the pot, pat it dry.

  Revision: Scrub the pot. Pat it dry.

- Separate independent clauses with a semicolon.

  Draft: Allow the paint to dry it should take two days.

  Revision: Allow the paint to dry; it should take two days.

- Use a comma and a coordinating conjunction to join the two sentences.

  Draft: Set the plant in the shelf give it lots of light.

  Revision: Set the plant in the shelf, and give it lots of light.

Practice Revise the following paragraph by correcting the run-on sentences.

To make linen by the traditional method, watch flax blooms carefully for the right moment to harvest them pull mature plants up by the roots. Bundle them loosely to dry soak the dry flax until the fibers separate. When the flax is dry again crush scrape, comb and split the stems wind the long fibers onto a distaff, ready for spinning.

Prewriting

Choose a Topic To choose a topic for a how-to essay, think about your areas of interest and expertise, anything from aerobics to guitar playing. Here are more ideas for topics:

Topic Ideas

- Training a dog to roll over
- Playing a computer game

Selection-Related Topic Ideas

- Playing a fiddle
- Bird-watching basics

List Vivid, Specific Details Gather precise, specific details about materials and tools needed to complete the project. Also, sketch or obtain any visual aids such as maps, charts, and diagrams that you plan to include in your how-to essay.

| **Vague:** | a saw | oil | fabric |
| **Specific:** | a hacksaw | olive oil | raw silk |

Develop Details by Anticipating Questions Jot down some questions your readers might ask, and gather information that will answer them. For example, if you are explaining how to brew herbal tea by infusion, provide answers to questions like the following:

▶ What types of kettles are best?
▶ How long should the herbs steep?
▶ What types of herbs can be blended?

Drafting

Provide Background Information At the beginning of your essay, engage readers by briefly noting the origins, historical significance, or relevance of the task you are explaining.

Provide Transitions As you draft, present the steps in time order. Use transitions such as *before, after, during,* and *next* to indicate the order in which steps should be performed.

Elaborate Details If you think of additional information that will enhance readers' understanding of the process you're describing, include it at this point.

Create Visual Aids Create graphs, diagrams, and charts to convey complex information in an easy-to-understand form. For example, diagrams can convey assembly instructions more effectively than numbered lists can.

Revising

Test-Run Ask a classmate to use your instructions to accomplish the task. Your classmate should use the following guidelines for reviewing:

▶ Does the background information help the reader better understand the task?

▶ Are any of the details vague and unspecific?

REVISION MODEL

Mrs. McCabe is the "uncrowned queen of the castle
① *on the Isle of Arran, Scotland*
bakehouse" at Brodick Castle. She bakes for the 50,000
∧
annual visitors to the Castle. Here is one of her recipes:

~~Place ten ounces of self rising flour in a bowl and make~~

~~a well in the center. Put three ounces of sugar and four~~
② *10 oz self-rising flour, 4 oz margarine, 3 oz sugar, 1 pt. milk*
~~ounces of margarine in the well...~~
∧

1. ~~Before mixing dough, generously grease a cookie sheet~~

and Preheat oven to 375 degrees.
③ *Generously grease a cookie sheet.*
2.
∧
④ *in the center*
3. Place 10 oz flour in a bowl and make a well.
∧
⑤ *Roughly combine*
4. Mix margarine and sugar . . .
∧

① *The author adds information to answer the question, "Where is Brodick Castle?"*
② *The author substitutes an ingredient list for a wordy and difficult-to-follow paragraph.*
③ *These steps were confusing and in the wrong order.*
④ *This detail is important for beginners to know.*
⑤ *The vague term* mix *was replaced by a more specific phrase.*

Publishing

▶ **How-to Fair** Organize a fair at which classmates can teach one another the procedures they have written about. Ask classmates to distribute copies of their essays at the fair.

▶ **Workshop** Use your how-to essay as the basis for a workshop. Teach friends and classmates the process you have explained.

APPLYING LANGUAGE SKILLS: Formatting Instructions

Maintain consistency as you format your instructions. Below is a list of tips.

▶ **Boldface:** Used for important information and warnings.

▶ **Capital letters:** Good for headings.

▶ **Italics:** Often used in chart labels.

▶ **Numbered Lists:** Organizes steps that should be performed in time order.

▶ **Bulleted Lists:** Handy way to list items or ingredients.

Practice Format the following directions.

When you determine you will need a passport, have a small picture made of yourself. You can call your local post office to get information on the cost and requirements. Take your materials to the post office and apply for the passport. Write a check and obtain a receipt. Bring forms of ID!

Writer's Solution Connection Writing Lab

For help in revising your essay, use the Revision checker for transition words in the Revising and Editing section of the tutorial on Exposition.

Student Success Workshop

Research Skills — Using Text Organizers for Research

Strategies for Success

Research skills are useful in everyday situations. If you want to buy a CD player, for example, you might first compare brands and prices by checking magazines, newspaper advertisements, and the Internet. To help you find the appropriate information quickly, you will need to learn how to use text organizers, such as overviews, headings, summaries, and graphics.

Use Text Organizers A search through books, magazines, databases, and the Internet on a topic can yield an overwhelming amount of material. To locate relevant information and categorize it, check for organizers in the text. Look at tables of contents, chapter headings and subheadings, photographs, illustrations, and captions. These organizers will help you determine the resources that will be most useful. Scan them to get the main ideas and key words that relate to your research.

Review Overviews and Summaries To preview research material, review overviews and summaries. An overview, often found at the beginning of a text, states key points and sometimes poses questions for you to consider as you read. In a book, the introduction and preface can provide an overview. A summary, which often appears toward the end of a text, also briefly restates the main points of a reading.

Examine Graphic Organizers Graphic organizers—such as maps, charts, diagrams, graphs, and timelines—often summarize complex information in the text. For example, if a text is describing the molecular structure of DNA, a diagram will clarify and simplify the information

for you. Examining a graphic organizer will help you determine at a glance whether the text material is relevant to your topic.

Apply the Strategies

Select a topic that interests you and locate relevant resources, such as books, journals, and Internet Web sites. Bring one of your resources to class, and apply these strategies about text organizers.

1. If there is a summary or overview, how do these text organizers help you locate information appropriate to your topic?

2. How is the text organized? Which chapter or section heads and subheads are most relevant to your topic?

3. What graphic organizers are found in your source? How are they helpful in locating and categorizing information in the text?

4. If you were going to write a paper on a topic you selected, would you use this source in your research? Why or why not?

✔ Here are some situations in which using text organizers for research can help you:
- ▶ Finding job listings in the newspaper
- ▶ Choosing a movie
- ▶ Reading college catalogs

Part 3 *Focus on Literary Forms:* *The Short Story*

The Snack Bar, 1930, Edward Burra, Tate Gallery, London

   The short story was the perfect form for a century in a hurry. It had all the elements of a novel—plot, setting, character, theme— but on a smaller scale. It could take you to the house next door, to Ireland, or to Southeast Asia, but wherever you went you got back quickly. It could also display the latest fictional techniques, sometimes taking you into a character's stream of thoughts.

Guide for Interpreting

Joseph Conrad *(1857–1924)*

It is accomplishment enough to become one of the most distinguished novelists in your age, but to do so in your third language is a true feat. Born in Poland, Joseph Conrad mastered English after his native language, Polish, and his second language, Russian.

At Sea in the World

Orphaned at the age of eleven, Conrad fled his Russian-occupied homeland when he was seventeen— landing first in France and later in England—and spent the next six years as an apprentice seaman. The voyages he made to Asia, Africa, and South America became the vivid settings of much of his fiction. In 1886, Conrad became a master mariner and an English citizen.

A Storytelling Life

Conrad published his first novel, *Almayer's Folly*, in his late thirties. In 1897, *The Nigger of the Narcissus* appeared. Three masterpieces followed: *Lord Jim* (1900); *Youth*, a collection of shorter pieces that includes his famous "Heart of Darkness" (1902); and *Nostromo* (1904).

Almost invariably, the notion of "voyage" in a tale by Conrad translates to a voyage of self-discovery. The menacing jungles, vast oceans, and exotic people that confront the characters become metaphors for the hidden depths of the self.

James Joyce *(1882–1941)*

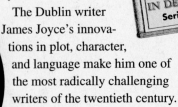

Featured in AUTHORS IN DEPTH Series

The Dublin writer James Joyce's innovations in plot, character, and language make him one of the most radically challenging writers of the twentieth century.

Experimentation

His family and teachers wanted him to become a priest. However, in 1907, he answered his true calling of writer by publishing the poetry collection *Chamber Music*.

Joyce moved to Zurich, Switzerland, in 1915, a year after the appearance of his landmark *Dubliners*, a short-story collection. Each of the main characters experiences a growth in self-awareness that leads to a climactic peak in the story. Joyce developed this process further in *A Portrait of the Artist as a Young Man* (1916), a fictionalized account of his life.

Mature Fiction

A heightened awareness of language and a deep immersion in the minds of characters were carried forward in *Ulysses* (1922). This stream-of-consciousness novel, originally banned in England and the United States, roughly parallels Homer's *Odyssey*. It presents a single day in the life of three Dubliners. Joyce's final novel, *Finnegans Wake* (1939), written in what one scholar terms "a dream language of Joyce's own invention," explores the author's view of human existence and its cycles.

◆ Background for Understanding

CULTURE: MALAY SETTING

Between 1883 and 1888, Conrad sailed the Far East in British merchant ships. He used his knowledge of the Malay language, details of setting, and facts about local people and customs to enrich his Far East tales. It is likely that Captain William Lingard, revered as a spellbinding storyteller among sailors of the Malay settlements, was the model for Marlow, who appears in many Conrad tales.

CULTURE: ANGLO-IRISH RELATIONS

James Joyce grew up during a turbulent time in Ireland, with demands for Irish home rule becoming ever louder. One of Ireland's most popular leaders was Charles Stewart Parnell (1846–1891), a Protestant who led the Irish members of the British House of Commons in the fight for Irish self-government. Home rule for the Irish Republic was achieved in 1922.

The Lagoon ◆ Araby

◆ *Literature and Your Life*

CONNECT YOUR EXPERIENCE

If you've ever had a sudden rush of insight—a moment when reasons for your behavior or basic truths about life seem to coalesce before your eyes—you know that gaining insight is an important part of growing up. Yet attaining these insights can be difficult or even painful—as these stories reveal.

Journal Writing Logan Pearsall Smith wrote, "All mirrors are magical mirrors; never can we see our faces in them." Write down your ideas about this in your journal.

THEMATIC FOCUS: CONFLICTS ABROAD AND AT HOME

These stories were influenced by the studies of Sigmund Freud and others who opened new frontiers by probing the human unconscious. As you read, notice how Conrad and Joyce explore conflicts and realizations within the protagonists' minds.

◆ Literary Focus

PLOT DEVICES

Both Conrad and Joyce use **plot devices** in these stories to achieve innovative effects. In "The Lagoon," Conrad uses a **story within a story**—a tale told by a character in a fictional narrative—to evoke the multi-faceted aspect of an experience. By using two or more fictional narrators, Conrad suggests various perspectives on the same events. In "Araby," Joyce employs an **epiphany**—a character's profound revelation—to heighten the climax of the story. This device generally occurs in stories that operate on a psychological level.

◆ Reading Strategy

ENVISION ACTION AND SITUATION

In modernist fiction, what characters *think* is often more important than what they *do*. To understand and appreciate this kind of storytelling, pause to **envision the action and situation** at different points in the narrative. Give at least equal weight to the characters' emotional state as you do to what is occurring at a given moment.

In "The Lagoon," for example, as you picture what is happening to Arsat during the last part of his journey with his brother and Diamelen, think about what is happening inside his mind.

◆ Build Vocabulary

LATIN ROOTS: *-vinc-*

Early in Conrad's "The Lagoon," you'll find the word *invincible*. The word root *-vinc-* comes from a Latin verb *vincere*, meaning "to conquer." Something *invincible* is not able to be conquered.

WORD BANK

Before you read, preview this list of words from the stories.

> portals
> invincible
> propitiate
> conflagration
> august
> imperturbable
> litanies
> garrulous
> derided

◆ Grammar and Style

An **adverb clause** is a subordinate clause that modifies a verb, an adjective, or an adverb. For example, Conrad uses this sentence to describe a sound:

> Astern of the boat the repeated call of some bird, a cry discordant and feeble, skipped along over the smooth water and lost itself, *before it could reach the other shore, in the breathless silence of the world.*

The adverb clause in italics modifies the verb *lost*. Like many other adverbs, it answers the question, *When?*

Look for other adverb clauses that add precision and vivid detail to these narratives.

The Lagoon

Joseph Conrad

The white man, leaning with both arms over the roof of the little house in the stern of the boat, said to the steersman—

"We will pass the night in Arsat's clearing. It is late."

The Malay[1] only grunted, and went on looking fixedly at the river. The white man rested his chin on his crossed arms and gazed at the wake of the boat. At the end of the straight avenue of forests cut by the intense glitter of the river, the sun appeared unclouded and dazzling, poised low over the water that shone smoothly like a band of metal. The forests, somber and dull, stood motionless and silent on each side of the broad stream. At the foot of big, towering trees trunkless nipa palms rose from the mud of the bank, in bunches of leaves enormous and heavy, that hung unstirring over the brown swirl of eddies. In the stillness of the air every tree, every leaf, every bough, every tendril of creeper and every petal of minute blossoms seemed to have been bewitched into an immobility perfect and final. Nothing moved on the river but the eight paddles that rose flashing regularly, dipped together with a single splash; while the steersman swept right and left with a periodic and sudden flourish of his blade describing a glinting semicircle above his head. The churned-up water frothed alongside with a confused murmur. And the white man's

canoe, advancing up stream in the short-lived disturbance of its own making, seemed to enter the portals of a land from which the very memory of motion had forever departed.

The white man, turning his back upon the setting sun, looked along the empty and broad expanse of the sea-reach. For the last three miles of its course the wandering, hesitating river, as if enticed irresistibly by the freedom of an open horizon, flows straight into the sea, flows straight to the east—to the east that harbors both light and darkness. Astern of the boat the repeated call of some bird, a cry discordant and feeble, skipped along over the smooth water and lost itself, before it could reach the other shore, in the breathless silence of the world.

The steersman dug his paddle into the stream, and held hard with stiffened arms, his body thrown forward. The water gurgled aloud; and suddenly the long straight reach seemed to pivot on its center, the forests swung in a semicircle, and the slanting beams of sunset touched the broadside of the canoe with a fiery glow, throwing the slender and distorted shadows of its crew upon the streaked glitter of the river. The white man turned to look ahead. The course of the boat had been altered at right-angles to the stream, and the carved dragon-onhead of its prow was pointing now at a gap in the fringing bushes of the bank. It glided through, brushing the overhanging twigs, and disappeared from the river like some slim and

---

1. **Malay** (mā´ lā): Native of the Malay peninsula in Southeast Asia.

amphibious creature leaving the water for its lair in the forests.

The narrow creek was like a ditch: tortuous, fabulously deep; filled with gloom under the thin strip of pure and shining blue of the heaven. Immense trees soared up, invisible behind the festooned draperies of creepers. Here and there, near the glistening blackness of the water, a twisted root of some tall tree showed amongst the tracery of small ferns, black and dull, writhing and motionless, like an arrested snake. The short words of the paddlers reverberated loudly between the thick and somber walls of vegetation. Darkness oozed out from between the trees, through the tangled maze of the creepers, from behind the great fantastic and unstirring leaves; the darkness, mysterious and <u>invincible</u>; the darkness scented and poisonous of impenetrable forests.

The men poled in the shoaling[2] water. The creek broadened, opening out into a wide sweep of a stagnant lagoon. The forests receded from the marshy bank, leaving a level strip of bright green, reedy grass to frame the reflected blueness of the sky. A fleecy pink cloud drifted high above, trailing the delicate coloring of its image under the floating leaves and the silvery blossoms of the lotus. A little house, perched on high piles, appeared black in the distance. Near it, two tall nibong palms, that seemed to have come out of the forests in the background, leaned slightly over the ragged roof, with a suggestion of sad tenderness and care in the droop of their leafy and soaring heads.

The steersman, pointing with his paddle, said, "Arsat is there. I see his canoe fast between the piles."

The polers ran along the sides of the boat glancing over their shoulders at the end of the day's journey. They would have preferred to spend the night somewhere else than on this lagoon of weird aspect and ghostly reputation. Moreover, they disliked Arsat, first as a stranger, and also because he who repairs a

_____
2. **shoaling:** Shallow.

ruined house, and dwells in it, proclaims that he is not afraid to live amongst the spirits that haunt the places abandoned by mankind. Such a man can disturb the course of fate by glances or words; while his familiar ghosts are not easy to <u>propitiate</u> by casual wayfarers upon whom they long to wreak the malice of their human master. White men care not for such things, being unbelievers and in league with the Father of Evil, who leads them unharmed through the invisible dangers of this world. To the warnings of the righteous they oppose an offensive pretense of disbelief. What is there to be done?

So they thought, throwing their weight on the end of their long poles. The big canoe glided on swiftly, noiselessly, and smoothly, toward Arsat's clearing, till, in a great rattling of poles thrown down, and the loud murmurs of "Allah[3] be praised!" it came with a gentle knock against the crooked piles below the house.

The boatmen with uplifted faces shouted discordantly, "Arsat! O Arsat!" Nobody came. The white man began to climb the rude ladder giving access to the bamboo platform before the house. The juragan[4] of the boat said sulkily, "We will cook in the sampan,[5] and sleep on the water."

"Pass my blankets and the basket," said the white man curtly.

He knelt on the edge of the platform to receive the bundle. Then the boat shoved off, and the white man, standing up, confronted Arsat, who had come out through the low door of his hut. He was a man young, powerful, with a broad chest and muscular arms. He had

_____
3. **Allah** (al′ ə): Muslim name for God.
4. **juragan** (jo͞o rä′ gän): Captain or master.
5. **sampan:** Small flat-bottomed boat with a cabin formed by mats.

◆ **Build Vocabulary**

portals (pôr′ təlz) *n*.: Doors; gateways

invincible (in vin′ sə bəl) *adj*.: Unconquerable

propitiate (prə pish′ ē āt) *v*.: Win the good will of; appease

nothing on but his sarong.[6] His head was bare. His big, soft eyes stared eagerly at the white man, but his voice and demeanor were composed as he asked, without any words of greeting—

◆ Reading Strategy
As Arsat and the white man meet for the first time in the story, envision the characters and the situation as vividly as you can.

"Have you medicine, Tuan?"[7]

"No," said the visitor in a startled tone. "No. Why? Is there sickness in the house?"

"Enter and see," replied Arsat, in the same calm manner, and turning short round, passed again through the small doorway. The white man, dropping his bundles, followed.

In the dim light of the dwelling he made out on a couch of bamboos a woman stretched on her back under a broad sheet of red cotton cloth. She lay still, as if dead; but her big eyes, wide open, glittered in the gloom, staring upward at the slender rafters, motionless and unseeing. She was in a high fever, and evidently unconscious. Her cheeks were sunk slightly, her lips were partly open, and on the young face there was the ominous and fixed expression—the absorbed, contemplating expression of the unconscious who are going to die. The two men stood looking down at her in silence.

"Has she been long ill?" asked the traveler.

"I have not slept for five nights," answered the Malay, in a deliberate tone. "At first she heard voices calling her from the water and struggled against me who held her. But since the sun of today rose she hears nothing—she hears not me. She sees nothing. She sees not me—me!"

He remained silent for a minute, then asked softly—

"Tuan, will she die?"

"I fear so," said the white man sorrowfully. He had known Arsat years ago, in a far country in times of trouble and danger, when no friendship is to be despised. And since his Malay friend had come unexpectedly to dwell in the hut on the lagoon with a strange woman, he had slept many times there, in his journeys up and down the river. He liked the man who knew how to keep faith in council and how to fight without fear by the side of his white friend. He liked him—not so much perhaps as a man likes his favorite dog—but still he liked him well enough to help and ask no questions, to think sometimes vaguely and hazily in the midst of his own pursuits, about the lonely man and the long-haired woman with audacious face and triumphant eyes, who lived together by the forests—alone and feared.

▲ **Critical Viewing** Judging from this photograph, would it be difficult to escape from an enemy in jungle territory? [Make a Judgment]

---

6. **sarong:** Long, brightly colored strip of cloth worn like a skirt.

7. **Tuan** (twan): Malayan for "sir."

The white man came out of the hut in time to see the enormous <u>conflagration</u> of sunset put out by the swift <u>and stealthy</u> shadows that, rising like a black and impalpable vapor above the treetops, spread over the heaven, extinguishing the crimson glow of floating clouds and the red brilliance of departing daylight. In a few moments all the stars came out above the intense blackness of the earth, and the great lagoon gleaming suddenly with reflected lights resembled an oval patch of night sky flung down into the hopeless and abysmal night of the wilderness. The white man had some supper out of the basket, then collecting

a few sticks that lay about the platform, made up a small fire, not for warmth, but for the sake of the smoke, which would keep off the mosquitos. He wrapped himself in his blankets and sat with his back against the reed wall of the house, smoking thoughtfully.

Arsat came through the doorway with noiseless steps and squatted down by the fire. The white man moved his outstretched legs a little.

"She breathes," said Arsat in a low voice, anticipating the expected question. "She breathes and burns as if with a great fire. She speaks not; she hears not—and burns!"

He paused for a moment, then asked in a quiet, incurious tone—

"Tuan . . . will she die?"

The white man moved his shoulders uneasily, and muttered in a hesitating manner—

"If such is her fate."

"No, Tuan," said Arsat calmly. "If such is my fate. I hear, I see, I wait. I remember . . . Tuan, do you remember the old days? Do you remember my brother?"

"Yes," said the white man. The Malay rose suddenly and went in. The other, sitting still outside, could hear the voice in the hut. Arsat said: "Hear me! Speak!" His words were succeeded by a complete silence. "O Diamelen!" he cried suddenly. After that cry there was a deep sigh. Arsat came out and sank down again in his old place.

They sat in silence before the fire. There was no sound within the house, there was no sound near them; but far away on the lagoon they could hear the voices of the boatmen ringing fitful and distinct on the calm water. The fire in the bows of the sampan shone faintly in the distance with a hazy red glow. Then it died out. The voices ceased. The land and the water slept invisible, unstirring and mute. It was as though there had been nothing left in the world but the glitter of stars streaming, ceaseless and vain, through the black stillness of the night.

The white man gazed straight before him into the darkness with wide-open eyes. The fear and fascination, the inspiration and the wonder of death—of death near, unavoidable,

◆ **Build Vocabulary**

conflagration (kän´ flə grā´ shən) *n.*: Great fire

and unseen, soothed the unrest of his race and stirred the most indistinct, the most intimate of his thoughts. The ever-ready suspicion of evil, the gnawing suspicion that lurks in our hearts, flowed out into the stillness round him—into the stillness profound and dumb, and made it appear untrustworthy and infamous, like the placid and impenetrable mask of an unjustifiable violence. In that fleeting and powerful disturbance of his being the earth enfolded in the starlight peace became a shadowy country of inhuman strife, a battlefield of phantoms terrible and charming, _august_ or ignoble, struggling ardently for the possession of our helpless hearts. An unquiet and mysterious country of inextinguishable desires and fears.

A plaintive murmur rose in the night; a murmur saddening and startling, as if the great solitudes of surrounding woods had tried to whisper into his ear the wisdom of their immense and lofty indifference. Sounds hesitating and vague floated in the air round him, shaped themselves slowly into words; and at last flowed on gently in a murmuring stream of soft and monotonous sentences. He stirred like a man waking up and changed his position slightly. Arsat, motionless and shadowy, sitting with bowed head under the stars, was speaking in a low and dreamy tone—

"... for where can we lay down the heaviness of our trouble but in a friend's heart? A man must speak of war and of love. You, Tuan, know what war is, and you have seen me in time of danger seek death as other men seek life! A writing may be lost; a lie may be written; but what the eye has seen is truth and remains in the mind!"

"I remember," said the white man quietly. Arsat went on with mournful composure—

"Therefore I shall speak to you of love. Speak in the night. Speak before both night and love are gone—and the eye of day looks upon my sorrow and my shame; upon my blackened face; upon my burnt-up heart."

◆ **Literary Focus**
What clues let you know that a story within a story begins here?

A sigh, short and faint, marked an almost imperceptible pause, and then his words flowed on, without a stir, without a gesture.

"After the time of trouble and war was over and you went away from my country in the pursuit of your desires, which we, men of the islands, cannot understand, I and my brother became again, as we had been before, the sword bearers of the Ruler. You know we were men of family, belonging to a ruling race, and more fit than any to carry on our right shoulder the emblem of power. And in the time of prosperity Si Dendring showed us favor, as we, in time of sorrow, had showed to him the faithfulness of our courage. It was a time of peace. A time of deer hunts and cock fights; of idle talks and foolish squabbles between men whose bellies are full and weapons are rusty. But the sower watched the young rice shoots grow up without fear, and the traders came and went, departed lean and returned fat into the river of peace. They brought news too. Brought lies and truth mixed together, so that no man knew when to rejoice and when to be sorry. We heard from them about you also. They had seen you here and had seen you there. And I was glad to hear, for I remembered the stirring times, and I always remembered you, Tuan, till the time came when my eyes could see nothing in the past, because they had looked upon the one who is dying there—in the house."

He stopped to exclaim in an intense whisper, "O Mara bahia! O Calamity!" then went on speaking a little louder.

"There's no worse enemy and no better friend than a brother, Tuan, for one brother knows another, and in perfect knowledge is strength for good or evil. I loved my brother. I went to him and told him that I could see nothing but one face, hear nothing but one voice. He told me: 'Open your heart so that she can see what is in it—and wait. Patience is wisdom. Inchi Midah may die or our Ruler may throw off his fear of a woman!'. . . I waited! . . . You remember the lady with the veiled face, Tuan, and the fear of our Ruler before her cunning and temper. And if she wanted her servant, what could

I do? But I fed the hunger of my heart on short glances and stealthy words. I loitered on the path to the bath houses in the daytime, and when the sun had fallen behind the forest I crept along the jasmine hedges of the women's courtyard. Unseeing, we spoke to one another through the scent of flowers, through the veil of leaves, through the blades of long grass that stood still before our lips; so great was our prudence, so faint was the murmur of our great longing. The time passed swiftly . . . and there were whispers amongst women—and our enemies watched—my brother was gloomy, and I began to think of killing and of a fierce death. . . . We are of a people who take what they want—like you whites. There is a time when a man should forget loyalty and respect. Might and authority are given to rulers, but to all men is given love and strength and courage. My brother said, 'You shall take her from their midst. We are two who are like one.' And I answered, 'Let it be soon, for I find no warmth in sunlight that does not shine upon her.' Our time came when the Ruler and all the great people went to the mouth of the river to fish by torchlight. There were hundreds of boats, and on the white sand, between the water and the forests, dwellings of leaves were built for the households of the Rajahs.[8] The smoke of cooking fires was like a blue mist of the evening, and many voices rang in it joyfully. While they were making the boats ready to beat up the fish, my brother came to me and said, 'Tonight!' I looked to my weapons, and when the time came our canoe took its place in the circle of boats carrying the torches. The lights blazed on the water, but behind the boats there was darkness. When the shouting began and the excitement made them like mad we dropped out. The water swallowed our fire, and we floated back to the shore that was dark with only here and there the glimmer of embers. We could hear the talk of slave girls amongst the sheds. Then we found a place deserted and silent. We waited there. She came. She came

running along the shore, rapid and leaving no trace, like a leaf driven by the wind into the sea. My brother said gloomily, 'Go and take her; carry her into our boat.' I lifted her in my arms. She panted. Her heart was beating against my breast. I said, 'I take you from those people. You came to the cry of my heart, but my arms take you into my boat against the will of the great!' 'It is right,' said my brother. 'We are men who take what we want and can hold it against many. We should have taken her in daylight.' I said, 'Let us be off'; for since she was in my boat I began to think of our Ruler's many men. 'Yes. Let us be off,' said my brother. 'We are cast out and this boat is our country now—and the sea is our refuge.' He lingered with his foot on the shore, and I entreated him to hasten, for I remembered the strokes of her heart against my breast and thought that two men cannot withstand a hundred. We left, paddling downstream close to the bank; and as we passed by the creek where they were fishing, the great shouting had ceased, but the murmur of voices was loud like the humming of insects flying at noonday. The boats floated, clustered together, in the red light of torches, under a black roof of smoke; and men talked of their sport. Men that boasted, and praised, and jeered—men that would have been our friends in the morning, but on that night were already our enemies. We paddled swiftly past. We had no more friends in the country of our birth. She sat in the middle of the canoe with covered face; silent as she is now; unseeing as she is now—and I had no regret at what I was leaving because I could hear her breathing close to me—as I can hear her now."

He paused, listened with his ear turned to the doorway, then shook his head and went on.

"My brother wanted to shout the cry of challenge—one cry only—to let the people know we were freeborn robbers who trusted our arms

---

8. **Rajahs** (ra´ jez): Malayan chiefs.

◆ **Build Vocabulary**

august (ô gust´) *adj.*: Worthy of great respect

◆ **Literary Focus**
Notice that the reader experiences the story within a story the same way the white man does, with pauses that allow a listener to observe changes in Arsat's emotional state.

and the great sea. And again I begged him in the name of our love to be silent. Could I not hear her breathing close to me? I knew the pursuit would come quick enough. My brother loved me. He dipped his paddle without a splash. He only said, 'There is half a man in you now—the other half is in that woman. I can wait. When you are a whole man again, you will come back with me here to shout defiance. We are sons of the same mother.' I made no answer. All my strength and all my spirit were in my hands that held the paddle—for I longed to be with her in a safe place beyond the reach of men's anger and of women's spite. My love was so great, that I thought it could guide me to a country where death was unknown, if I could only escape from Inchi Midah's fury and from our Ruler's sword. We paddled with haste, breathing through our teeth. The blades bit deep into the smooth water. We passed out of the river; we flew in clear channels amongst the shallows. We skirted the black coast; we skirted the sand beaches where the sea speaks in whispers to the land; and the gleam of white sand flashed back past our boat, so swiftly she ran upon the water. We spoke not. Only once I said, 'Sleep, Diamelen, for soon you may want all your strength.' I heard the sweetness of her voice, but I never turned my head. The sun rose and still we went on. Water fell from my face like rain from a cloud. We flew in the light and heat. I never looked back, but I knew that my brother's eyes, behind me, were looking steadily ahead, for the boat went as straight as a bushman's dart, when it leaves the end of the sumpitan.[9] There was no better paddler, no better steersman than my brother. Many times, together, we had won races in that canoe. But we never had put out our strength as we did then—then, when

9. **sumpitan** (sump´ ə tän): Malayan blowgun which discharges poisonous darts.

▲ **Critical Viewing** Why might a peninsula or an island such as this one be a bad choice as a hiding place? **[Deduce]**

for the last time we paddled together! There was no braver or stronger man in our country than my brother. I could not spare the strength to turn my head and look at him, every moment I heard the hiss of his breath getting louder behind me. Still he did not speak. The sun was high. The heat clung to my back like a flame of fire. My ribs were ready to burst, but I could no longer get enough air into my chest. And then I felt I must cry out with my last breath. 'Let us rest!' . . . 'Good!' he answered; and his voice was firm. He was strong. He was brave. He knew not fear and no fatigue . . . My brother!"

and through the jungle of that land there is a narrow path. We made a fire and cooked rice. Then we lay down to sleep on the soft sand in the shade of our canoe, while she watched. No sooner had I closed my eyes than I heard her cry of alarm. We leaped up. The sun was halfway down the sky already, and coming in sight in the opening of the bay we saw a prau[10] manned by many paddlers. We knew it at once; it was one of our Rajah's praus. They were watching the shore, and saw us. They beat the gong, and turned the head of the prau into the bay. I felt my heart become weak within my breast. Diamelen sat on the sand and covered her face. There was no escape by sea. My brother laughed. He had the gun you had given him, Tuan, before you went away, but there was only a handful of powder. He spoke to me quickly: 'Run with her along the path. I shall keep them back, for they have no firearms, and landing in the face of a man with a gun is certain death for some. Run with her. On the other side of that wood there is a fisherman's house—and a canoe. When I have fired all the shots I will follow. I am a great runner, and before they can come up we shall be gone. I will hold out as long as I can, for she is but a woman—that can neither run nor fight, but she has your heart in her weak hands.' He dropped behind the canoe. The prau was coming. She and I ran, and as we rushed along the path I heard shots. My brother fired—once — twice—and the booming of the gong ceased. There was silence behind us. That neck of land is narrow. Before I heard my brother fire the third shot I saw the shelving shore, and I saw the water again: the mouth of a broad river. We crossed a grassy glade. We ran down to the water. I saw a low hut above the black mud, and a small canoe hauled up. I heard another shot behind me. I thought, 'That is his last charge.' We rushed down to the canoe; a man came running from the hut, but I leaped on him, and we rolled together in the mud. Then I got up, and he lay still at my feet. I don't know whether I

A murmur powerful and gentle, a murmur vast and faint; the murmur of trembling leaves, of stirring boughs, ran through the tangled depths of the forests, ran over the starry smoothness of the lagoon, and the water between the piles lapped the slimy timber once with a sudden splash. A breath of warm air touched the two men's faces and passed on with a mournful sound—a breath loud and short like an uneasy sigh of the dreaming earth.

Arsat went on in an even, low voice:

"We ran our canoe on the white beach of a little bay close to a long tongue of land that seemed to bar our road; a long wooded cape going far into the sea. My brother knew that place. Beyond the cape a river has its entrance,

---

10. prau (prou): Swift Malayan boat with a large sail.

had killed him or not. I and Diamelen pushed the canoe afloat. I heard yells behind me, and I saw my brother run across the glade. Many men were bounding after him. I took her in my arms and threw her into the boat, then leaped in myself. When I looked back I saw that my brother had fallen. He fell and was up again, but the men were closing round him. He shouted, 'I am coming!' The men were close to him. I looked. Many men. Then I looked at her. Tuan, I pushed the canoe! I pushed it into deep water. She was kneeling forward looking at me, and I said, 'Take your paddle,' while I struck the water with mine. Tuan, I heard him cry. I heard him cry my name twice; and I heard voices shouting, 'Kill! Strike!' I never turned back. I heard him calling my name again with a great shriek, as when life is going out together with the voice—and I never turned my head. My own name! . . . My brother! Three times he called—but I was not afraid of life. Was she not there in that canoe? And could I not with her find a country where death is forgotten—where death is unknown!"

The white man sat up. Arsat rose and stood, an indistinct and silent figure above the dying embers of the fire. Over the lagoon a mist drifting and low had crept, erasing slowly the glittering images of the stars. And now a great expanse of white vapor covered the land; it flowed cold and gray in the darkness, eddied in noiseless whirls round the tree-trunks and about the platform of the house, which seemed to float upon a restless and impalpable illusion of a sea. Only far away the tops of the trees stood outlined on the twinkle of heaven, like a somber and forbidding shore—a coast deceptive, pitiless and black.

Arsat's voice vibrated loudly in the profound peace.

"I had her there! I had her! To get her I would have faced all mankind. But I had her—and—"

His words went out ringing into the empty distances. He paused, and seemed to listen to

♦ Reading Strategy
What expression do you think is on each character's face at the end of the story within a story?

them dying away very far—beyond help and beyond recall. Then he said quietly—

"Tuan, I loved my brother."

A breath of wind made him shiver. High above his head, high above the silent sea of mist the drooping leaves of the palms rattled together with a mournful and expiring sound. The white man stretched his legs. His chin rested on his chest, and he murmured sadly without lifting his head—

"We all love our brothers."

Arsat burst out with an intense whispering violence—

"What did I care who died? I wanted peace in my own heart."

He seemed to hear a stir in the house —listened—then stepped in noiselessly. The white man stood up. A breeze was coming in fitful puffs. The stars shone paler as if they had retreated into the frozen depths of immense space. After a chill gust of wind there were a few seconds of perfect calm and absolute silence. Then from behind the black and wavy line of the forests a column of golden light shot up into the heavens and spread over the semicircle of the eastern horizon. The sun had risen. The mist lifted, broke into drifting patches, vanished into thin flying wreaths; and the unveiled lagoon lay, polished and black, in the heavy shadows at the foot of the wall of trees. A white eagle rose over it with a slanting and ponderous flight, reached the clear sunshine and appeared dazzlingly brilliant for a moment, then soaring higher, became a dark and motionless speck before it vanished into the blue as if it had left the earth forever. The white man, standing gazing upward before the doorway, heard in the hut a confused and broken murmur of distracted words ending with a loud groan. Suddenly Arsat stumbled out with outstretched hands, shivered, and stood still for some time with fixed eyes. Then he said—

"She burns no more."

Before his face the sun showed its edge above the treetops, rising steadily. The breeze freshened; a great brilliance burst upon the lagoon, sparkled on the rippling water. The forests came out of the clear shadows of the morning, became distinct, as if they had rushed nearer—to stop short in a great stir of leaves, of nodding boughs, of swaying branches. In the merciless sunshine the whisper of unconscious life grew louder, speaking in an incomprehensible voice round the dumb darkness of that human sorrow. Arsat's eyes wandered slowly, then stared at the rising sun.

"I can see nothing," he said half aloud to himself.

"There is nothing," said the white man, moving to the edge of the platform and waving his hand to his boat. A shout came faintly over the lagoon and the sampan began to glide toward the abode of the friend of ghosts.

◆ **Reading Strategy**
What tone of voice do you think each character uses at this point?

"If you want to come with me, I will wait all the morning," said the white man, looking away upon the water.

"No, Tuan," said Arsat softly. "I shall not eat or sleep in this house, but I must first see my road. Now I can see nothing—see nothing! There is no light and no peace in the world; but there is death—death for many. We were sons of the same mother—and I left him in the midst of enemies; but I am going back now."

He drew a long breath and went on in a dreamy tone:

"In a little while I shall see clear enough to strike—to strike. But she has died, and . . . now . . . darkness."

He flung his arms wide open, let them fall along his body, then stood still with unmoved face and stony eyes, staring at the sun. The white man got down into his canoe. The polers ran smartly along the sides of the boat, looking over their shoulders at the beginning of a weary journey. High in the stern, his head muffled up in white rags, the juragon sat moody, letting his paddle trail in the water. The white man, leaning with both arms over the grass roof of the little cabin, looked back at the shining ripple of the boat's wake. Before the sampan passed out of the lagoon into the creek he lifted his eyes. Arsat had not moved. He stood lonely in the searching sunshine; and he looked beyond the great light of a cloudless day into the darkness of a world of illusions.

Guide for Responding

◆ Literature and Your Life

Reader's Response Do you think "The Lagoon" effectively dramatizes the idea that life is a "world of illusions"? Explain your view.

Thematic Focus What internal conflict rages within Arsat?

☑ Check Your Comprehension

1. Why do the members of the white man's crew want nothing to do with Arsat?
2. Why does Arsat ask the white man if he has medicine?
3. What happened to Arsat's brother?
4. At the end of the story, what does Arsat intend to do?

◆ Critical Thinking

INTERPRET

1. Compare and contrast the white man and Arsat. **[Compare and Contrast]**
2. Arsat abandons his brother to his death. (a) What motivates him to flee? (b) How else could he have responded, and what would have been the results? **[Analyze Cause and Effect]**
3. Following Diamelen's death, Arsat says, "I can see nothing," and the white man replies, "There is nothing." (a) What does each mean? (b) How might this dialogue relate to the story's final line? **[Infer]**
4. (a) Does Conrad present love or loyalty, or neither, as the worthier motive? Explain. (b) How would Conrad recommend people deal with past mistakes or regrets? Explain. **[Draw Conclusions]**

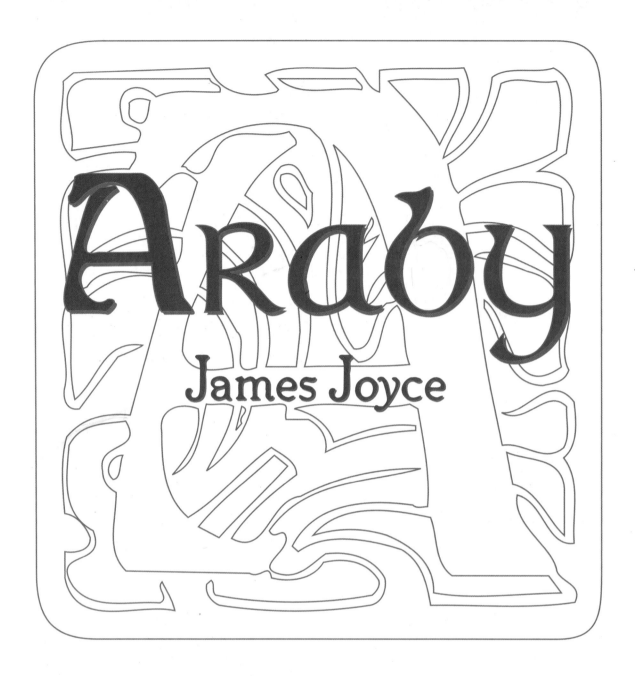

Araby

James Joyce

North Richmond Street, being blind,[1] was a quiet street except at the hour when the Christian Brothers' School set the boys free. An uninhabited house of two stories stood at the blind end, detached from its neighbors in a square ground. The other houses of the street, conscious of decent lives within them, gazed at one another with brown imperturbable faces.

The former tenant of our house, a priest, had died in the back drawing room. Air, musty from having been long enclosed, hung in all the rooms, and the waste room behind the kitchen was littered with old useless papers. Among these I found a few paper-covered books, the pages of which were curled and damp: *The Abbot*, by Walter Scott, *The Devout Communicant* and *The Memoirs of Vidocq*.[2] I liked the last best because its leaves were yellow. The wild garden behind the house contained a central apple tree

---

1. **blind:** Dead end.

2. ***The Abbot . . . Vidocq:*** A historical tale, a religious manual, and the remembrances of a French adventurer, respectively.

ENGLISH MONEY.

English or Sterling Money is the currency of Great Britain.

TABLE.

4 farthings (far. or qr.) make 1 penny,   marked d.
12 pence   " 1 shilling,   " s.
20 shillings   " 1 pound or sovereign, £, sov.
21 shillings   " 1 guinea, marked guin.

COINS.—The gold coins are the *sovereign* (£1), and the *half-sovereign* (10s.).

The silver coins are the *crown* (5s.), the *half-crown* (2s. 6d.), the *florin* (2s.), the *shilling* (12d.), *sixpenny-piece* (6d.), and *threepenny-piece* (3d.).

▶ **Critical Viewing** The narrator enters Araby at the shilling gate. Use this table to determine how many times less the price of entrance at the sixpence gate would be. **[Assess]**

and a few straggling bushes under one of which I found the late tenant's rusty bicycle pump. He had been a very charitable priest: in his will he had left all his money to institutions and the furniture of his house to his sister.

When the short days of winter came dusk fell before we had well eaten our dinners. When we met in the street the houses had grown somber. The space of sky above us was the color of ever-changing violet and toward it the lamps of the street lifted their feeble lanterns. The cold air stung us and we played till our bodies glowed. Our shouts echoed in the silent street. The career of our play brought us through the dark muddy lanes behind the houses where we ran the gantlet of the rough tribes from the cottages, to the back doors of the dark dripping gardens where odors arose from the ashpits, to the dark odorous stables where a coachman smoothed and combed the horse or shook music from the buckled harness. When we returned to the street, light from the kitchen windows had filled the areas. If my uncle was seen turning the corner we hid in the shadow until we had seen him safely housed. Or if Mangan's sister came out on the doorstep to call her brother in to his tea we watched her from our shadow peer up and down the street. We waited to see whether she

◆ **Build Vocabulary**

imperturbable (im´ pər tʉr´ bə bəl) *adj.*: Calm; not easily ruffled

would remain or go in and, if she remained, we left our shadow and walked up to Mangan's steps resignedly. She was waiting for us, her figure defined by the light from the half-opened door. Her brother always teased her before he obeyed and I stood by the railings looking at her. Her dress swung as she moved her body and the soft rope of her hair tossed from side to side.

Every morning I lay on the floor in the front parlor watching her door. The blind was pulled down to within an inch of the sash so that I could not be seen. When she came out on the doorstep my heart leaped. I ran to the hall, seized my books and followed her. I kept her brown figure always in my eye and, when we came near the point at which our ways diverged, I quickened my pace and passed her. This happened morning after morning. I had never spoken to her, except for a few casual words, and yet her name was like a summons to all my foolish blood.

Her image accompanied me even in places the most hostile to romance. On Saturday evenings when my aunt went marketing I had to go to carry some of the parcels. We walked through the flaring streets, jostled by drunken men and bargaining women, amid the curses of laborers, the shrill litanies of shop-boys who stood on guard by the barrels of pigs' cheeks, the nasal chanting of street singers, who sang a *come-all-you* about O'Donovan Rossa,[3] or a ballad about the troubles in our native land. These noises converged in a single sensation of life for me: I imagined that I bore my chalice safely through a throng of foes. Her name sprang to my lips at moments in strange prayers and praises which I myself did not understand. My eyes were often full of tears (I could not tell why) and at times a flood from my heart seemed to pour itself out into my bosom. I thought little of the future. I did not know whether I would ever speak to her or not or, if I spoke to her, how I could tell her of my confused adoration. But my body was like a harp

◆ **Reading Strategy**
Which vivid details in this passage help you to form a mental picture of the scene?

and her words and gestures were like fingers running upon the wires.

One evening I went into the back drawing room in which the priest had died. It was a dark rainy evening and there was no sound in the house. Through one of the broken panes I heard the rain impinge upon the earth, the fine incessant needles of water playing in the sodden beds. Some distant lamp or lighted window gleamed below me. I was thankful that I could see so little. All my senses seemed to desire to veil themselves and, feeling that I was about to slip from them, I pressed the palms of my hands together until they trembled, murmuring: *"O love! O love!"* many times.

At last she spoke to me. When she addressed the first words to me I was so confused that I did not know what to answer. She asked me was I going to *Araby*. I forget whether I answered yes or no. It would be a splendid bazaar, she said; she would love to go.

"And why can't you?" I asked.

While she spoke she turned a silver bracelet round and round her wrist. She could not go, she said, because there would be a retreat[4] that week in her convent.[5] Her brother and two other boys were fighting for their caps and I was alone at the railings. She held one of the spikes, bowing her head towards me. The light from the lamp opposite our door caught the white curve of her neck, lit up her hair that rested there and, falling, lit up the hand upon the railing. It fell over one side of her dress and caught the white border of a petticoat, just visible as she stood at ease.

"It's well for you," she said.

"If I go," I said, "I will bring you something."

What innumerable follies laid waste my waking and sleeping thoughts after that evening! I wished to annihilate the tedious intervening days. I chafed against the work of school. At night in my bedroom and by day in the classroom her image came between me and the page I strove to read. The syllables of the word *Araby* were called to me through the silence in which my soul luxuriated and cast an Eastern

3. **come-all-you . . . Rossa:** Opening of a ballad about an Irish hero.

4. **retreat** *n.*: Period of retirement or seclusion for prayer, religious study, and meditation.
5. **convent** *n.*: School run by an order of nuns.

enchantment over me. I asked for leave to go to the bazaar on Saturday night. My aunt was surprised and hoped it was not some Freemason[6] affair. I answered few questions in class. I watched my master's face pass from amiability to sternness; he hoped I was not beginning to idle. I could not call my wandering thoughts together. I had hardly any patience with the serious work of life which, now that it stood between me and my desire, seemed to me child's play, ugly monotonous child's play.

On Saturday morning I reminded my uncle that I wished to go to the bazaar in the evening. He was fussing at the hallstand, looking for the hat brush, and answered me curtly:

"Yes, boy, I know."

As he was in the hall I could not go into the front parlor and lie at the window. I left the house in bad humor and walked slowly toward the school. The air was pitilessly raw and already my heart misgave me.

When I came home to dinner my uncle had not yet been home. Still it was early. I sat staring at the clock for some time and, when its ticking began to irritate me, I left the room. I mounted the staircase and gained the upper part of the house. The high cold empty gloomy rooms liberated me and I went from room to room singing. From the front window I saw my companions playing in the street. Their cries reached me weakened and indistinct and, leaning my forehead against the cool glass, I looked over at the dark house where she lived. I may have stood there for an hour, seeing nothing but the brown-clad figure cast by my imagination, touched discreetly by the lamplight at the curved neck, at the hand upon the railings and at the border below the dress.

When I came downstairs again I found Mrs. Mercer sitting at the fire. She was an old garrulous woman, a pawnbroker's widow, who collected used stamps for some pious purpose. I had to endure the gossip of the tea table. The meal was prolonged beyond an hour and still my uncle did not come. Mrs. Mercer stood up to go: she was sorry she couldn't wait any longer, but it was after eight o'clock and she did not like to be out late, as the night air was bad for her. When she had gone I began to walk up and down the room, clenching my fists. My aunt said:

"I'm afraid you may put off your bazaar for this night of Our Lord."

At nine o'clock I heard my uncle's latchkey in the hall door. I heard him talking to himself and heard the hallstand rocking when it had received the weight of his overcoat. I could interpret these signs. When he was midway through his dinner I asked him to give me the money to go to the bazaar. He had forgotten.

"The people are in bed and after their first sleep now," he said.

I did not smile. My aunt said to him energetically:

"Can't you give him the money and let him go? You've kept him late enough as it is."

My uncle said he was very sorry he had forgotten. He said he believed in the old saying: *All work and no play makes Jack a dull boy.* He asked me where I was going and, when I had told him a second time he asked me did I know *The Arab's Farewell to His Steed.*[7] When I left the kitchen he was about to recite the opening lines of the piece to my aunt.

I held a florin[8] tightly in my hand as I strode down Buckingham Street toward the station. The sight of the streets thronged with buyers and glaring with gas recalled to me the purpose of my journey. I took my seat in a third-class carriage of a deserted train. After an intolerable delay the train moved out of the

◆ **Reading Strategy**
How do you envision the uncle, given the details in the paragraph above?

---

7. **The Arab's . . . His Steed:** Popular nineteenth-century poem.
8. **florin:** Two-shilling coin of the time.

◆ **Build Vocabulary**

litanies (lit′ən ēz) *n.*: Forms of prayer in which a congregation repeats a fixed response

garrulous (gar′ ə ləs) *adj.*: Talking continuously

---

6. **Freemason:** Free and Accepted Masons, an international secret society.

► Critical Viewing
Why might the
prospect of a fair
or bazaar be
appealing to
someone who
lived in a setting
such as this?
[Infer]

St. Patrick's Close, Walter Osborne, Courtesy of the National Gallery of Ireland

station slowly. It crept onward among ruinous houses and over the twinkling river. At West-land Row Station a crowd of people pressed to the carriage doors; but the porters moved them back, saying that it was a special train for the bazaar. I remained alone in the bare carriage. In a few minutes the train drew up beside an improvised wooden platform. I passed out onto the road and saw by the lighted dial of a clock that it was ten minutes to ten. In front of me was a large building which displayed the magical name.

I could not find any sixpenny entrance and, fearing that the bazaar would be closed, I passed in quickly through a turnstile, handing a shilling to a weary-looking man. I found my-self in a big hall girdled at half its height by a gallery. Nearly all the stalls were closed and the greater part of the hall was in darkness. I recognized a silence like that which pervades

◆ Literary Focus

In the remainder of this paragraph, Joyce leads directly to the epiphany of the story. What realization do you think the narrator is about to experience about himself and his situation?

a church after a service. I walked into the center of the bazaar timidly. A few people were gathered about the stalls which were still open. Before a curtain, over which the words *Café Chantant*[9] were written in colored lamps, two men were counting money on a salver.[10] I listened to the fall of the coins.

Remembering with difficulty why I had come I went over to one of the stalls and examined porcelain vases and flowered tea sets. At the door of the stall a young lady was talking and laughing with two young gentlemen. I remarked their English accents and listened vaguely to their conversation.

"O, I never said such a thing!"

"O, but you did!"

"O, but I didn't!"

"Didn't she say that?"

"Yes. I heard her."

"O, there's a . . . fib!"

---

9. *Café Chantant:* Café with musical entertainment.
10. **salver** *n.:* Tray usually used for the presentation of letters or visiting cards.

Observing me the young lady came over and asked me did I wish to buy anything. The tone of her voice was not encouraging; she seemed to have spoken to me out of a sense of duty. I looked humbly at the great jars that stood like Eastern guards at either side of the dark entrance to the stall and murmured:

"No, thank you."

The young lady changed the position of one of the vases and went back to the two young men. They began to talk of the same subject. Once or twice the young lady glanced at me over her shoulder.

I lingered before her stall, though I knew my stay was useless, to make my interest in her wares seem the more real. Then I turned away slowly and walked down the middle of the bazaar. I allowed the two pennies to fall against the sixpence in my pocket. I heard a voice call from one end of the gallery that the light was out. The upper part of the hall was now completely dark.

Gazing up into the darkness I saw myself as a creature driven and <u>derided</u> by vanity; and my eyes burned with anguish and anger.

◆ **Build Vocabulary**

derided (di rīd´ id) *v.:* Made fun of; ridiculed

Guide for Responding

◆ *Literature and Your Life*

Reader's Response Like the narrator in this story, do you ever have doubts or ambivalent feelings about a promise you've made?

Thematic Focus Why does the narrator feel conflict about the change he is experiencing?

☑ Check Your Comprehension

1. Why is going to the bazaar so important to the narrator?
2. Why is the narrator late getting to Araby?
3. Describe the narrator's experience at Araby.
4. How does the narrator feel at the end of the story?

◆ Critical Thinking

INTERPRET

1. What might have been the author's reason for not giving Mangan's sister a name? **[Analyze]**
2. Does Araby live up to the narrator's expectations? Describe his mood as he walks around Araby, and give reasons for that mood. **[Analyze Causes and Effects]**
3. (a) Why do you think the author chose "Araby" as the name for the bazaar? (b) As a title for the story? (c) How does this name relate to the narrator's experiences? **[Draw Conclusions]**

APPLY

4. Can reality ever live up to a person's dreams? Explain. **[Apply]**

Guide for Responding (continued)

◆ Literary Focus

PLOT DEVICES

A **story within a story** is a tale told by a character in a fictional narrative. Conrad uses this device in "The Lagoon" to enhance the meaning of Arsat's tale. The outer narrative provides a framework for Arsat's story.

An **epiphany** is a sudden recognition of an important truth by a character in a fictional work. An epiphany usually unmasks a truth that was present all along in a character's mind.

1. What specific information would you lack if "The Lagoon" had been narrated entirely by Arsat?
2. Why do you think Conrad chose to have Arsat narrate his own story?
3. Where in "Araby" does the epiphany occur?
4. What does the hero in "Araby" suddenly realize?

◆ Grammar and Style

ADVERB CLAUSES

Joseph Conrad and James Joyce often use **adverb clauses**—subordinate clauses that modify verbs, adjectives, and adverbs. As modifiers, adverb clauses add specificity and interest to writing.

Practice In your notebook, identify the word(s) that each adverb clause modifies.

1. And *since his Malay friend had come unexpectedly to dwell in the hut on the lagoon with a strange woman,* he had slept many times there. . . .
2. *Before the sampan passed out of the lagoon into the creek* he lifted his eyes.
3. *When we met in the street* the houses had grown somber.

Writing Application Rewrite each of the following items, using an adverb clause to combine the sentences.

1. Nothing moved on the river. The steersman swept right and left with periodic flourishes of his blade.
2. The sun had fallen behind the forest. I crept along the jasmine hedges.
3. We played during the cold, late afternoons. Our bodies glowed.

◆ Build Vocabulary

USING THE LATIN ROOT -*vinc*-

Knowing that the Latin root -*vinc*- means "conquer," write definitions for the following words. Within the definition, explain how the root's meaning affects the word's meaning.

1. convince
2. evince
3. invincibility

USING THE WORD BANK: Synonyms

In your notebook, write the letter of the word whose meaning is closest to that of the first word.

1. portals: (a) arteries, (b) doorways, (c) furniture
2. invincible: (a) unconquerable, (b) warriorlike, (c) facile
3. propitiate: (a) appease, (b) refuse, (c) resign
4. conflagration: (a) battle, (b) dispute, (c) fire
5. august: (a) portly, (b) virtuous, (c) awe-inspiring
6. imperturbable: (a) indifferent, (b) calm, (c) ruthless
7. litanies: (a) lawsuits, (b) prayers, (c) harangues
8. garrulous: (a) talkative, (b) extravagant, (c) suspicious
9. derided: (a) ejected, (b) ridiculed, (c) exaggerated

◆ Reading Strategy

ENVISION ACTION AND SITUATION

Your understanding of a story will be improved if you **envision its action and the characters' situations.** In modernist fiction like Conrad's and Joyce's, it's also helpful to focus in on the characters' internal responses to their situations.

Choose a moment in either "The Lagoon" or "Araby" in which the characters are involved in an especially intense or suspenseful dialogue. "Freeze" this moment in your mind's eye. Then write a paragraph in which you describe as vividly as you can your impression of what is happening, what each character looks like, and particularly any gestures, tones of voice, or facial expressions that are revealing of that character's inner thoughts or conflicts. Also describe changes in setting—in location or weather—that reflect the characters' inner states.

Build Your Portfolio

Idea Bank

Writing

1. **Recollection** In Conrad's story, Arsat reveals a confidence to the narrator. Write several paragraphs recalling a time you either (a) revealed a confidence or (b) listened to a confidence. Address your inner thoughts at the time.

2. **Extending a Story** Choose an episode from Joyce's "Araby" involving the narrator and Mangan's sister. Going beyond the events of the story, write a meaningful dialogue around this episode.

3. **Essay** A lagoon is a pool of brackish water separated from the sea by sandbars and reefs. In an essay, answer these questions: What does the lagoon represent in Conrad's story? What does a voyage to and from the lagoon symbolize?

Speaking, Listening, and Viewing

4. **Courtroom** Is Arsat in Conrad's "The Lagoon" responsible for the death of his brother? With a peer, argue for the defense and the prosecution. You may present your arguments to the class as "jury" and have them return a verdict.

5. **Panel Discussion** In "The Lagoon," Arsat betrays his brother, while in "Araby" the narrator's uncle breaks faith with him. With a panel of classmates, discuss the role of loyalty in these stories.

Researching and Representing

6. **Poster** Make a poster for the Araby bazaar. Research the design of turn-of-the century posters. Then design, write copy for, and illustrate your poster. **[Art Link]**

7. **Report on Colonialism** Choose a country that was formerly a British colony, such as India, Burma, or Malaysia. Investigate Britain's colonization in this area and the country's fight for independence. Present your findings to the class.

Online Activity www.phlit.phschool.com

Guided Writing Lesson

Personal Essay

The term *epiphany* was introduced by James Joyce to describe a moment of revelation or insight in which a literary character recognizes a truth. However, you've probably had an epiphany in your own life—a moment in which aspects of your experience just seem to come together in a sweep of truth or a charge of meaning.

Write a personal essay in which you describe an epiphany you've experienced. Use elaboration to build up to your final insight.

Writing Skills Focus: Elaboration to Entertain

To make your essay entertaining and suspenseful, work up gradually to the climactic moment at which you experienced your realization.

Joyce carefully builds towards his character's epiphany, fleshing out his situation by elaborating details. For instance, he does not begin the story with Mangan's sister; he leads up to her by first introducing the neighborhood boys. When he describes the narrator's crush on her, he elaborates by showing how the crush affects every part of the narrator's life, from the mornings he spends watching for her to the Saturday evenings he pretends to be carrying a "chalice" for her through the market crowd.

Prewriting Identify the situation that led to your epiphany, and then jot down the aspects of this situation that directly relate to the epiphany.

Drafting As you draft your essay, use vivid language and sensory details. Help your friend "see" your epiphany, then let him or her know how it changed your outlook.

Revising Read your essay aloud. Make sure it is clearly narrated and that it does not include irrelevant details. Be sure the written version of your essay corresponds to the way you would tell the story orally to a good friend.

Guide for Interpreting

Virginia Woolf (1882–1941)

Virginia Woolf revolutionized modern fiction by pioneering the use of the stream-of-consciousness technique. This device allows readers to tune in directly to the random flow of thoughts and images in a character's mind.

A Literary Life Woolf was a pioneer writer who came from a prim and proper Victorian family. Her father, the renowned editor Leslie Stephen, made sure his daughter grew up surrounded by books. This literary atmosphere had a strong effect. At the age of twenty-three, Woolf began contributing reviews to the *Times* of London. Later, she and her husband, Leonard, made their house in the Bloomsbury section of London, a meeting place for writers. This circle of thinkers became known as the Bloomsbury Group.

Revolutionizing Fiction Woolf's first two novels were not unusual, but *Jacob's Room* (1922) shattered the conventions of fiction by telling the story of a young man's life entirely through an examination of his room. (She also uses this device in "The Lady in the Looking Glass: A Reflection.") Woolf continued to refine her fluid, inward-looking style with three more stream-of-consciousness novels—*Mrs. Dalloway* (1925), *To the Lighthouse* (1927), and *The Waves* (1931). In her more revolutionary works, she virtually abolished the traditional concept of plot, preferring to concentrate on what she called "an ordinary mind on an ordinary day."

Depression and Tragedy Woolf suffered episodes of severe depression brought on by poor health and the turmoil of war. In 1941, two years after the outbreak of World War II, she drowned. Today she is recognized, along with James Joyce, as one of the shapers of modern fiction.

Muriel Spark (1918–)

The Scottish novelist Muriel Spark is best known for her novel *The Prime of Miss Jean Brodie* (1961), successfully adapted for both the stage and the screen.

A Prolific Career Born and educated in Edinburgh, Scotland, Spark began her literary career as an editor and biographer. She began to write fiction after she won a short story competition sponsored by the *Observer*, a Sunday newspaper.

In 1958, she published *The Go-Away Bird*, a collection of short stories. Some of these stories were set in central Africa, where she had spent several years in her youth. Her novels include *The Mandelbaum Gate* (1965), *Territorial Rights* (1979), and *The Only Problem* (1984).

Carefully crafted, suspenseful, and witty, Spark's fiction often raises serious moral issues. You will see all these qualities in "The First Year of My Life."

◆ Background for Understanding

HISTORY: SPARK'S ALLUSIONS TO WORLD WAR I

The title of Spark's story "The First Year of My Life" refers to 1918, the final year of World War I. For over three years, the nations of Europe had been locked in the bloodiest combat in history. Britain, allied with France, Italy, Russia, and the United States, fought against Germany, Austria-Hungary, and Turkey. Spark's story alludes to events in the final year of that war, like the collapse of the Russian effort on the Eastern Front and the German Spring Offensive, halted just short of Paris. British political leaders mentioned include Prime Ministers Herbert Asquith and David Lloyd George.

The Lady in the Looking Glass: A Reflection
◆ The First Year of My Life ◆

◆ *Literature and Your Life*

CONNECT YOUR EXPERIENCE

As you sit waiting in the dentist's office, you glance at a magazine cover featuring a model who looks like the woman who serves food in the cafeteria where you had an argument with your best friend yesterday who just got into college and, oh, no, did I forget to mail my application? The mind flows by such associations, which Virginia Woolf captures in her stream-of-consciousness narration.

Journal Writing Quickly jot down a series of linked thoughts as they enter your mind.

THEMATIC FOCUS: WAKING FROM THE DREAM

As you read, notice how both these stories end with a moment of disillusion, a waking into an unpleasant reality.

◆ Literary Focus

POINT OF VIEW: MODERN EXPERIMENTS

To capture the fragmentary quality of modern life, writers experimented with **point of view**, the perspective from which a story is told. **Stream-of-consciousness** narration, for example, reflects the random flow of thoughts in a character's mind. Other experiments involved surprising versions of **omniscient** narration, in which a narrator knows every character's thoughts.

Virginia Woolf pioneered the use of the stream-of-consciousness technique. As you read her story, don't confuse the narrator with Isabella Tyson. Muriel Spark plays with the traditional idea of the omniscient narrator. She pretends that, as a baby, her mind knew "everything . . . going on everywhere in the world."

◆ Reading Strategy

QUESTION

Experimental works, like Woolf's and Spark's, offer great rewards but also place great demands on readers. You must continually **ask questions** as you read, to find your way in the story.

In reading Woolf's story, ask how one thought leads to the next. Also ask: Who is the narrator and what is the reality mirrored in this character's mind? In reading Spark's story, ask why she combines her own early development with the events of World War I.

◆ Build Vocabulary

LATIN ROOTS: -*trans*-

You'll find the word *transient* in Woolf's story. This word, which means "passing through quickly," is built on the Latin root -*trans*-, meaning "through" or "across." A frequently used word with this same root is *transit*, as in *mass transit*.

WORD BANK

Before you read, preview this list of words from the stories.

suffused
transient
upbraidings
evanescence
reticent
omniscient
authenticity
discerned

◆ Grammar and Style

SUBJECT-VERB AGREEMENT IN INVERTED SENTENCES

Verbs must **agree** in number with subjects even when the verb precedes the subject, as it does in sentences beginning with *here* or *there*. In the following example, from "The Lady in the Looking Glass," the verb *were* precedes the plural subject and agrees with it in number:

There *were* her gray-green *dress*, and her *long shoes*, her *basket*, and *something* sparkling at her throat.

As you read these stories, note subject-verb agreement in other inverted sentences.

The Lady in the Looking Glass:
A Reflection

Virginia Woolf

People should not leave looking glasses hanging in their rooms any more than they should leave open checkbooks or letters confessing some hideous crime. One could not help looking, that summer afternoon, in the long glass that hung outside in the hall. Chance had so arranged it. From the depths of the sofa in the drawing room one could see reflected in the Italian glass not only the marble-topped table opposite, but a stretch of the garden beyond. One could see a long grass path leading between banks of tall flowers until, slicing off an angle, the gold rim cut it off.

The house was empty, and one felt, since one was the only person in the drawing room, like one of those naturalists who, covered with grass and leaves, lie watching the shyest animals—badgers, otters, king-fishers—moving about freely, themselves unseen. The room that afternoon was full of such shy creatures, lights and shadows, curtains blowing, petals falling—things that never happen, so it seems, if someone is looking. The quiet old country room with its rugs and stone chimney pieces, its sunken bookcases and red and gold lacquer cabinets, was full of such nocturnal creatures. They came pirouetting across the floor, stepping delicately with high-lifted feet and spread tails and pecking allusive beaks as if they had been cranes or flocks of elegant flamingoes whose pink was faded, or peacocks whose trains were veiled with silver. And there were obscure flushes and darkening too,

◆ Reading Strategy
What does this description reveal about the narrator? About the person the story is about?

as if a cuttlefish had suddenly suffused the air with purple; and the room had its passions and rages and envies and sorrows coming over it and clouding it, like a human being. Nothing stayed the same for two seconds together.

But, outside, the looking glass reflected the hall table, the sunflowers, the garden path so accurately and so fixedly that they seemed held there in their reality unescapably. It was a strange contrast—all changing here, all stillness there. One could not help looking from one to the other. Meanwhile, since all the doors and windows were open in the heat, there was a perpetual sighing and ceasing sound, the voice of the transient and the perishing, it seemed, coming and going like human breath, while in the looking glass things had ceased to breathe and lay still in the trance of immortality.

Half an hour ago the mistress of the house, Isabella Tyson, had gone down the grass path in her thin summer dress, carrying a basket, and had vanished, sliced off by the gilt rim of the looking glass. She had gone presumably into the lower garden to pick flowers; or as it seemed more natural to suppose, to pick something light and fantastic and leafy and trailing, traveler's-joy, or one of those elegant sprays of convolvulus that twine round ugly walls and burst here and there into white and violet blossoms. She suggested the fantastic and the tremulous convolvulus rather than the upright aster, the starched zinnia, or her own burning roses alight like lamps on the straight posts of their rose trees. The comparison showed how very little, after all these years, one knew about her; for it is impossible that any woman of flesh and blood of fifty-five or sixty should be really a wreath or a tendril. Such comparisons are worse than idle and superficial—they are cruel even, for they come like the convolvulus itself trembling between one's eyes and the truth. There must be truth; there must be a wall. Yet it was strange that after knowing her all these years one could not say what the truth about Isabella was; one still made up phrases like this about convolvulus and traveler's-joy. As for facts, it was a fact that she was a spinster; that she was rich; that she had bought this house and collected with her own hands—often in the most obscure corners of the world and at great risk from poisonous stings and Oriental diseases—the rugs, the chairs, the cabinets which now lived their nocturnal life before one's eyes. Sometimes it seemed as if they knew more about her than we, who sat on them, wrote at them, and trod on them so carefully, were allowed to know. In each of these cabinets were many little drawers, and each almost certainly held letters, tied with bows of ribbon, sprinkled with sticks of lavender or rose leaves. For it was another fact—if facts were what one wanted—that Isabella had known many people, had had many friends; and thus if one had the audacity to open a drawer and read her letters, one would find the traces of many agitations, of appointments to meet, of upbraidings for not having met, long letters

of intimacy and affection, violent letters of jealousy and reproach, terrible final words of parting—for all those interviews and assignations had led to nothing—that is, she had never married, and yet, judging from the masklike indifference of her face, she had gone through twenty times more of passion and experience than those whose loves are trumpeted forth for all the world to hear. Under the stress of thinking about Isabella, her room became more shadowy and symbolic; the corners seemed darker, the legs of chairs and tables more spindly and hieroglyphic.

Suddenly these reflections were ended violently and yet without a sound. A large black form loomed into the looking glass; blotted out everything, strewed the table with a packet of marble tablets veined with pink and gray, and was gone. But the picture was entirely altered. For the moment it was unrecognizable and irrational and entirely out of focus. One could not relate these tablets to any human purpose. And then by degrees some logical process set to work on them and

The Garden of Love, (detail), Walter Richard Sickert, The Fitzwilliam Museum, Cambridge

▲ **Critical Viewing** This story is a stream-of-consciousness narrative, in which thoughts, dreams, and ideas blend together to reveal a story. What aspects of this painting mirror this style of writing? **[Interpret]**

◆ **Build Vocabulary**

suffused (sə fyo͞ozd´) *v.:* Filled

transient (tran´ shənt) *adj.:* Temporary; passing through quickly

upbraidings (up brād´ iŋz) *n.:* Stern words of disapproval for an action

began ordering and arranging them and bringing them into the fold of common experience. One realized at last that they were merely letters. The man had brought the post.

There they lay on the marble-topped table, all dripping with light and color at first and crude and unabsorbed. And then it was strange to see how they were drawn in and arranged and composed and made part of the picture and granted that stillness and immortality which the looking glass conferred. They lay there invested with a new reality and significance and with a greater heaviness, too, as if it would have needed a chisel to dislodge them from the table. And, whether it was fancy or not, they seemed to have become not merely a handful of casual letters but to be tablets graven with eternal truth—if one could read them, one would know everything there was to be known about Isabella, yes, and about life, too. The pages inside those marble-looking envelopes must be cut deep and scored thick with meaning. Isabella would come in, and take them, one by one, very slowly, and open them, and read them carefully word by word, and then with a profound sigh of comprehension, as if she had seen to the bottom of everything, she would tear the envelopes to little bits and tie the letters together and lock the cabinet drawer in her determination to conceal what she did not wish to be known.

The thought served as a challenge. Isabella did not wish to be known—but she should no longer escape. It was absurd, it was monstrous. If she concealed so much and knew so much one must prize her open with the first tool that came to hand—the imagination. One must fix one's mind upon her at that very moment. One must fasten her down there. One must refuse to be put off any longer with sayings and doings such as the moment brought forth—with dinners and visits and polite conversations. One must put oneself in her shoes. If one took the phrase literally, it was easy to see the shoes in which she stood, down in the lower garden, at this moment. They were very narrow and long and fashionable —they were made of the softest and most flexible leather. Like everything she wore, they were

◆ Literary Focus
What elements in this paragraph reveal that the author uses a stream-of-consciousness technique?

exquisite. And she would be standing under the high hedge in the lower part of the garden, raising the scissors that were tied to her waist to cut some dead flower, some overgrown branch. The sun would beat down on her face, into her eyes; but no, at the critical moment a veil of cloud covered the sun, making the expression of her eyes doubtful—was it mocking or tender, brilliant or dull? One could only see the indeterminate outline of her rather faded, fine face looking at the sky. She was thinking, perhaps, that she must order a new net for the strawberries; that she must send flowers to Johnson's widow; that it was time she drove over to see the Hippesleys in their new house. Those were the things she talked about at dinner certainly. But one was tired of the things that she talked about at dinner. It was her profounder state of being that one wanted to catch and turn to words, the state that is to the mind what breathing is to the body, what one calls happiness or unhappiness. At the mention of those words it became obvious, surely, that she must be happy. She was rich; she was distinguished; she had many friends; she traveled—she bought rugs in Turkey and blue pots in Persia. Avenues of pleasure radiated this way and that from where she stood with her scissors raised to cut the trembling branches while the lacy clouds veiled her face.

Here with a quick movement of her scissors she snipped the spray of traveler's-joy and it fell to the ground. As it fell, surely some light came in too, surely one could penetrate a little farther into her being. Her mind then was filled with tenderness and regret. . . . To cut an overgrown branch saddened her because it had once lived, and life was dear to her. Yes, and at the same time the fall of the branch would suggest to her how she must die herself and all the futility and evanescence of things. And then again quickly catching this thought up, with her instant good sense, she thought life had treated her well; even if fall she must, it was to lie on the earth and molder sweetly into the roots of violets. So she stood thinking. Without making any thought precise—for she was one of those reticent people whose minds hold their thoughts enmeshed in clouds of silence—she was filled with thoughts. Her mind was like her room, in which lights advanced and retreated, came pirouetting and stepping delicately, spread their tails, pecked their way; and then her whole being was suffused, like the room again, with a cloud of some profound knowledge, some unspoken regret, and then she was full of locked drawers, stuffed with letters, like her cabinets. To talk of "prizing her open" as if she were an oyster, to use any but the finest and subtlest and most pliable tools upon her was impious and absurd. One must imagine—here was she in the looking glass. It made one start.

She was so far off at first that one could not see her clearly. She came lingering and pausing, here straightening a rose, there lifting a pink to smell it, but she never stopped; and all the time she became larger and larger in the looking glass, more and more completely the person into whose mind one had been trying to penetrate. One verified her by degrees—fitted the qualities one had discovered into this visible body. There were her gray-green dress, and her long shoes, her basket, and something sparkling at her throat. She came so gradually that she did not seem to derange the pattern in the glass, but only to bring in some new element which gently moved and altered the other objects as if asking them, courteously, to make room for her. And the letters and the table and the grass walk and the sunflowers which had been waiting in the looking glass separated and opened out so that

she might be received among them. At last there she was, in the hall. She stopped dead. She stood by the table. She stood perfectly still. At once the looking glass began to pour over her a light that seemed to fix her; that seemed like some acid to bite off the unessential and superficial and to leave only the truth. It was an enthralling spectacle. Everything dropped from her—clouds, dress, basket, diamond—all that one had called the creeper and convolvulus. Here was the hard wall beneath. Here was the woman herself. She stood naked in that pitiless light. And there was nothing. Isabella was perfectly empty. She had no thoughts. She had no friends. She cared for nobody. As for her letters, they were all bills. Look, as she stood there, old and angular, veined and lined, with her high nose and her wrinkled neck, she did not even trouble to open them.

People should not leave looking glasses hanging in their rooms.

◆ Reading Strategy
What is happening here? How does this description reveal the story's theme?

◆ Build Vocabulary

evanescence (ev´ ə nes´ əns) *n*.: Gradual disappearance, especially from sight

reticent (ret´ ə sənt) *adj*.: Silent; reserved

Guide for Responding

◆ Literature and Your Life

Reader's Response Do you think that knowledge about someone's true nature can be firmly "fastened down"? Explain.

Thematic Focus In what way does the narrator waken from a dream at the end of this story?

Sketch Do a quick drawing of the room described in the story.

☑ Check Your Comprehension

1. What has Isabella Tyson gone to do?
2. What arrives while she is out?
3. Briefly describe the room in the story.
4. What conclusion does the narrator reach about Isabella at the end of the story?

◆ Critical Thinking

INTERPRET

1. Who do you think the narrator is? **[Infer]**
2. (a) How does the looking glass "lead" the narrator to an understanding of Isabella? (b) What does the last sentence of the story, repeated from the beginning, mean? **[Interpret]**
3. In the story, what is the relation between imagination and "the hard wall" of the truth? **[Draw Conclusions]**

EVALUATE

4. Does Woolf succeed in creating a vivid portrait of Isabella? Why or why not? **[Criticize]**

EXTEND

5. How might free association give a psychologist insight into a patient's problems? **[Science Link]**

The First Year of My Life

Muriel Spark

I was born on the first day of the second month of the last year of the First World War, a Friday. Testimony abounds that during the first year of my life I never smiled. I was known as the baby whom nothing and no one could make smile. Everyone who knew me then has told me so. They tried very hard, singing and bouncing me up and down, jumping around, pulling faces. Many times I was told this later by my family and their friends; but, anyway, I knew it at the time.

You will shortly be hearing of that new school of psychology, or maybe you have heard of it already, which after long and far-adventuring research and experiment has established that all of the young of the human species are born omniscient. Babies, in their waking hours, know everything that is going on everywhere in the world; they can tune in to any conversation they choose, switch on to any scene. We have all experienced this power. It is only after the first year that it was brainwashed out of us; for it is demanded of us by our immediate environment that we grow to be of use to it in a practical way. Gradually, our know-all brain-cells are blacked out, although traces remain in some individuals in the form of E.S.P., and in the adults of some primitive tribes.

It is not a new theory. Poets and philosophers, as usual, have been there first. But scientific proof is now ready and to hand. Perhaps the final touches are being put to the new manifesto[1] in some cell at Harvard University. Any day now it will be given to the world, and the world will be convinced.

Let me therefore get my word in first, because I feel pretty sure, now, about the authenticity of my remembrance of things past. My autobiography, as I very well perceived at the time, started in the very worst year that the world had ever seen so far. Apart from being born bedridden and toothless, unable to raise myself on the pillow or utter anything but farmyard squawks or police-siren wails, my bladder and my bowels totally out of control, I was further depressed by the curious behavior of the two-legged mammals around me. There were those black-dressed people, females of the species to which I appeared to belong, saying they had lost their sons. I slept a great deal. Let them go and find their sons. It was like the special pin for my nappies[2] which my mother or some other hoverer dedicated to my care was always losing. These careless women in black lost their husbands and their brothers. Then they came to visit my mother and clucked and crowed over my cradle. I was not amused.

"Babies never really smile till they're three months old," said my mother. "They're not *supposed* to smile till they're three months old."

My brother, aged six, marched up and down

---

1. **manifesto** (man´ə fes´ tō) *n.:* Public declaration of motives and intentions.
2. **nappies** (nap´ ēz) *n.:* British term for diapers.

with a toy rifle over his shoulder:

The grand old Duke of York
He had ten thousand men;
He marched them up to the top of the hill
And he marched them down again.

And when they were up, they were up.
And when they were down, they were down.
And when they were neither down nor up
They were neither up nor down.

"Just listen to him!"
"Look at him with his rifle!"
I was about ten days old when Russia stopped fighting. I tuned in to the Czar,[3] a prisoner, with the rest of his family, since evidently the country had put him off his throne and there had been a revolution not long before I was born. Everyone was talking about it. I tuned in to the Czar. "Nothing would ever induce me to sign the treaty of Brest-Litovsk,"[4] he said to his wife. Anyway, nobody had asked him to.

At this point I was sleeping twenty hours a day to get my strength up. And from what I discerned in the other four hours of the day I knew I was going to need it. The Western Front on my frequency was sheer blood, mud, dismembered bodies, blistered crashes, hectic flashes of light in the night skies, explosions, total terror. Since it was plain I had been born into a bad moment in the history of the world, the future bothered me, unable as I was to raise my head from the pillow and as yet only twenty inches long. "I truly wish I were a fox or a bird," D. H. Lawrence[5] was writing to somebody. . . . I fell asleep.

Red sheets of flame shot across the sky. It was 21 March, the fiftieth day of my life, and the German Spring Offensive[6] had started

---

3. **Czar:** Czar Nicholas II of Russia, who was removed from power during the Russian Revolution of 1917.
4. **treaty of Brest-Litovsk:** Treaty in which Russia's new Communist government made peace with Germany and withdrew from WWI eight months before its end.
5. **D. H. Lawrence:** (1885–1930) English novelist and poet.
6. **German Spring Offensive:** After signing the peace treaty with Russia in March of 1918, Germany began to push to win the war along the western front.

before my morning feed. Infinite slaughter. I scowled at the scene, and made an effort to kick out. But the attempt was feeble. Furious, and impatient for some strength, I wailed for my feed. After which I stopped wailing but continued to scowl.

The grand old Duke of York
He had ten thousand men . . .

They rocked the cradle. I never heard a sillier song. Over in Berlin and Vienna the people were starving, freezing, striking, rioting and yelling in the streets. In London everyone was bustling to work and muttering that it was time the whole . . . business was over.

The big people around me bared their teeth; that meant a smile, it meant they were pleased or amused. They spoke of ration cards[7] for meat and sugar and butter.

"Where will it all end?"
I went to sleep. I woke and tuned into Bernard Shaw[8] who was telling someone to shut up. I switched over to Joseph Conrad[9] who, strangely enough, was saying precisely the same thing. I still didn't think it worth a smile, although it was expected of me any day now. I got on to Turkey. Women draped in black huddled and chattered in their harems; yak-yak-yak. This was boring, so I came back to home base.

In and out came and went the women in British black. My mother's brother, dressed in

◆ **Literary Focus**
What elements of omniscient narration can you find in this passage?

---

7. **ration cards:** Used to limit individuals' purchases of goods that were in short supply during the war.
8. **Bernard Shaw:** George Bernard Shaw (1856–1950), British dramatist and critic, born in Ireland.
9. **Joseph Conrad:** (1857–1924) English novelist, born in Poland.

◆ **Build Vocabulary**

omniscient (äm nish′ ənt) adj.: Having infinite knowledge; knowing all things

authenticity (ô′ thən tis′ə tē) n.: Quality or state of being authentic; genuineness

discerned (di zʉrnd′) v.: Recognized as separate or different

his uniform, came coughing. He had been poison-gassed in the trenches. *"Tout le monde à la bataille!"*[10] declaimed Marshal Foch[11] the old swine. He was now Commander-in-Chief of the Allied Forces. My uncle coughed from deep within his lungs, never to recover but destined to return to the Front. His brass buttons gleamed in the firelight. I weighed twelve pounds by now; I stretched and kicked for exercise, seeing that I had a lifetime before me, coping with this crowd. I took six feeds a day and kept most of them down by the time the *Vindictive* was sunk in Ostend harbor,[12] on which day I kicked with special vigor in my bath.

In France the conscripted[13] soldiers leapfrogged over the dead on the advance and littered the fields with limbs and hands, or drowned in the mud. The strongest men on all fronts were dead before I was born. Now the sentries[14] used bodies for barricades and the fighting men were unhealthy from the start. I checked my toes and fingers, knowing I was going to need them. *The Playboy of the Western World* was playing at the Court Theatre in London, but occasionally I beamed over to the House of Commons[15] which made me drop off gently to sleep. Generally, I preferred the Western Front[16] where one got the true state of affairs. It was essential to know the worst, blood and explosions and all, for one had to be prepared, as the boy scouts said. Virginia Woolf[17] yawned and reached for her diary. Really, I preferred the Western Front.

In the fifth month of my life I could raise my

---

10. *Tout le monde à la bataille* (tōō lə mônd′ ä lä bä tī′): The whole world into the battle!
11. **Marshal Foch** (fôsh): Ferdinand Foch, a French general who, after March 1918, became commander of all Allied forces on the Western Front.
12. *Vindictive* **was sunk in Ostend harbor:** Referring to a ship sunk in May 1918, by Allied forces, to block the harbor of Ostend, Belgium, used by the Germans as a submarine base.
13. **conscripted** (kən skript′ əd) *adj.*: Enrolled for compulsory service in the armed service.
14. **sentries** (sen′trēs) *n.*: Men of the military guard.
15. **House of Commons:** Lower house of British Parliament.
16. **Western Front:** 450-mile-long battlefront starting in Belgium and moving across France. This line is where the allies and Germany engaged in trench warfare from 1914 to 1918.
17. **Virginia Woolf:** (1882–1941) English novelist and critic.

▲ Critical Viewing This story takes place in 1918, the last year of World War I. Judging by this photograph, would you say the soldiers pictured were excited, weary, or numb? [Infer]

---

head from my pillow and hold it up. I could grasp the objects that were held out to me. Some of these things rattled and squawked. I gnawed on them to get my teeth started. "She hasn't smiled yet?" said the dreary old aunties. My mother, on the defensive, said I was probably one of those late smilers. On my wavelength Pablo Picasso[18] was getting married and early in that month of July the Silver Wedding of King George V and Queen Mary was celebrated in joyous pomp at St. Paul's Cathedral. They drove

---

18. **Pablo** (pä′ blō) **Picasso** (pi kä′ sō): (1881–1973) Spanish painter and sculptor.

Tout le monde à la bataille! That included my gassed uncle. My health had improved to the point where I was able to crawl in my playpen. Bertrand Russell[20] was still cheerily in prison for writing something seditious about pacifism. Tuning in as usual to the Front Lines it looked as if the Germans were winning all the battles yet losing the war. And so it was.

◆ **Reading Strategy**
How would you describe the narrator's tone up to this point in the story?

The upper-income people were upset about the income tax at six shillings to the pound. But all women over thirty got the vote. "It seems a long time to wait," said one of my drab old aunts, aged twenty-two. The speeches in the House of Commons always sent me to sleep which was why I missed, at the actual time, a certain oration by Mr. Asquith[21] following the armistice on 11 November.[22] Mr. Asquith was a greatly esteemed former prime minister later to be an Earl, and had been ousted by Mr. Lloyd George.[23] I clearly heard Asquith, in private, refer to Lloyd George as "that . . . Welsh goat."

The armistice was signed and I was awake for that. I pulled myself on to my feet with the aid of the bars of my cot. My teeth were coming through very nicely in my opinion, and well worth all the trouble I was put to in bringing them forth. I weighed twenty pounds. On all the world's fighting fronts the men killed in action or dead of wounds numbered 8,538,315 and the warriors wounded and maimed were 21,219,452. With these figures in mind I sat up in my high chair and banged my spoon on the table. One of my mother's black-draped friends recited:

> I have a rendezvous with Death
> At some disputed barricade,
> When spring comes back with rustling shade
> And apple blossoms fill the air—
> I have a rendezvous with Death.[24]

through the streets of London with their children. Twenty-five years of domestic happiness. A lot of fuss and ceremonial handing over of swords went on at the Guildhall where the King and Queen received a check for £53,000 to dispose of for charity as they thought fit. *Tout le monde à la bataille!* Income tax in England had reached six shillings in the pound. Everyone was talking about the Silver Wedding; yak-yak-yak, and ten days later the Czar and his family, now in Siberia, were invited to descend to a little room in the basement. Crack, crack, went the guns; screams and blood all over the place, and that was the end of the Romanoffs.[19] I flexed my muscles. "A fine healthy baby," said the doctor; which gave me much satisfaction.

---

19. Romanoff (rō′ mə nôf′): Name of the ruling family of Russia from 1613 to 1917.

---

20. Bertrand Russell: (1872–1970) British philosopher, mathematician, and writer.
21. Mr. Asquith (as′kwith): Henry Herbert Asquith (1852–1928), Prime Minister of Britain from 1908–1916.
22. armistice on 11 November: The agreement that brought World War I to an end.
23. Mr. Lloyd George: David Lloyd George (1863–1945), British Prime Minister from 1916 to 1922.
24. I . . . Death: From the poem "I Have a Rendezvous with Death" by American poet Alan Seeger, killed in war.

◀ Critical Viewing This story is narrated by a one-year-old girl who has an adult attitude about the bloodshed and devastation caused by World War I. Does the one-year-old in this photograph seem babylike or mature to you? Explain. [Evaluate]

Most of the poets, they said, had been killed. The poetry made them dab their eyes with clean white handkerchiefs.

Next February on my first birthday, there was a birthday-cake with one candle. Lots of children and their elders. The war had been over two months and twenty-one days. "Why doesn't she smile?" My brother was to blow out the candle. The elders were talking about the war and the political situation. Lloyd George and Asquith, Asquith and Lloyd George. I remembered recently having switched on to Mr. Asquith at a private party where he had been drinking a lot. He was playing cards and when he came to cut the cards he tried to cut a large box of matches by mistake. On another occasion I had seen him putting his arm around a lady's shoulder in a Daimler motor car, and generally behaving towards her in a very friendly fashion. Strangely enough she said, "If you don't stop this nonsense immediately, I'll order the chauffeur to stop and I'll get out." Mr. Asquith replied, "And pray, what reason will you give?" Well anyway it was my feeding time.

The guests arrived for my birthday. It was so sad, said one of the black widows, so sad about Wilfred Owen[25] who was killed so late in the war, and she quoted from a poem of his:

What passing-bells for these who die
as cattle?
Only the monstrous anger of the guns.[26]

The children were squealing and toddling around. One was sick and another wet the floor and stood with his legs apart gaping at the puddle. All was mopped up. I banged my spoon on the table of my high chair.

But I've a rendezvous with Death
At midnight in some flaming town;
When spring trips north again this year,
And I to my pledged word am true,
I shall not fail that rendezvous.

25. **Wilfred Owen:** (1893–1918) English poet.
26. **What . . . guns:** From Wilfred Owen's "Anthem for Doomed Youth" (see p. 963).

More parents and children arrived. One stout man who was warming his behind at the fire, said, "I always think those words of Asquith's after the armistice were so apt. . . ."

They brought the cake close to my high chair for me to see, with the candle shining and flickering above the pink icing. "A pity she never smiles."

"She'll smile in time," my mother said, obviously upset.

"What Asquith told the House of Commons just after the war," said that stout gentleman with his backside to the fire, "—so apt, what Asquith said. He said that the war has cleansed and purged the world. . . . I recall his actual words: 'All things have become new. In this great cleansing and purging it has been the privilege of our country to play her part. . . .'"

That did it. I broke into a decided smile and everyone noticed it, convinced that it was provoked by the fact that my brother had blown out the candle on the cake. "She smiled!" my mother exclaimed. And everyone was clucking away about how I was smiling. For good measure I crowed like a demented raven. "My baby's smiling," said my mother.

"It was the candle on her cake," they said.

. . . . Since that time I have grown to smile quite naturally, like any other healthy and house-trained person, but when I really mean a smile, deeply felt from the core, then to all intents and purposes it comes in response to the words uttered in the House of Commons after the First World War by the distinguished, the immaculately dressed and the late Mr. Asquith.

Guide for Responding

◆ Literature and Your Life

Reader's Response Did you find this story amusing, sad, or a combination of the two? Explain.

Thematic Focus In what way does Mr. Asquith's speech about the war reveal that he has not woken from a dream?

Interview Interview a classmate about his or her first year of life. Encourage your classmate to sort out what he or she has been told from actual recollections. Then reverse roles.

☑ Check Your Comprehension

1. What worldwide crisis corresponds with the first year of the narrator's life?
2. What special power does the narrator possess?
3. Briefly describe two examples that show the narrator's power.
4. (a) When does the narrator smile for the first time? (b) How do the guests explain this smile? (c) What is it that actually causes the narrator to smile?

◆ Critical Thinking

INTERPRET

1. (a) Sum up what you learn about the war from the narrator's "news briefs." (b) What do you learn about the war from the poems? **[Infer]**
2. Given the state of the world, what is amusing or surprising about the concern over the narrator's smile? **[Connect]**
3. What statement is the narrator making with her smile at the end of the story? **[Interpret]**
4. Summarize the central message of this story. **[Draw Conclusions]**

APPLY

5. How would the story have been different if it had been told by an adult? **[Speculate]**

EXTEND

6. Do you think the message about war in this story is relevant today? Explain. **[Social Studies Link]**

Guide for Responding *(continued)*

◆ Literary Focus

POINT OF VIEW: MODERN EXPERIMENTS

These authors experiment with **point of view,** the perspective from which they tell their stories, in order to surprise you into new insights. By immersing you in a narrator's **stream of consciousness,** Woolf makes you aware of your own random flow of thoughts. She also contrasts the fullness of the narrator's speculations about Isabella with the emptiness of Isabella's own mind. Reflected in the mirror of the narrator's thoughts, Isabella's material wealth becomes a sign of inner poverty.

Spark gets you to think about the war differently by reinventing herself as an **omniscient** baby who knows "everything." This device allows her to contrast the normal development of a baby with the abnormal destruction of war.

1. Using specific examples, show how Woolf's narrative is more a series of mental impressions than a chain of events in a normal plot.
2. (a) How does the literal reflection of Isabella in the mirror serve as a climax for the narrator's mental reflections? (b) What does this climax reveal about Isabella?
3. At the beginning of her story, how does Spark get you to accept her unusual point of view?
4. Find two examples in Spark's story where the baby's healthy development underscores the death and destruction going on in the world.

◆ Reading Strategy

QUESTION

Pausing to **question** as you read will help you understand works of literature, especially experimental stories like Woolf's or Spark's. Two types of questions relate to *who* is narrating a story and *why* the narrator emphasizes an incident. The first type of question helps you orient yourself in a story, and the second points you toward its meaning.

1. In Woolf's story, what questions about the narrator might you ask after reading the beginnings of the second and fourth paragraphs?
2. (a) What questions arise from the final paragraph of Spark's story? (b) Show how these questions lead you toward the story's meaning.

◆ Build Vocabulary

USING THE LATIN ROOT *-trans-*

Use your knowledge of the Latin root *-trans-* ("through" or "across") to guess what each of these companies or organizations does:
1. Transatlantic Shipping
2. City of Boston Mass Transit
3. Transitions to New Careers
4. Translations: German-English, English-German
5. Hotel for Transients

USING THE WORD BANK: Sentence Completions

On your paper, fill in each blank with the most suitable word from the Word Bank.

The ___?___ baby in Spark's story knew about everything. She may have been ___?___ with regard to her power, not telling the adults, but there is no doubt as to the ___?___ of her abilities. She could ___?___ events on remote battlefields, no matter how ___?___ they were. The ___?___ of human interactions, whether kisses or ___?___, did not protect them from her knowledge. She ___?___ with joy as she exercised her powers.

◆ Grammar and Style

SUBJECT-VERB AGREEMENT IN INVERTED SENTENCES

In inverted sentences, which often begin with *here* or *there*, the verb precedes the subject. However, the verb must still **agree** in number with its subject. Don't be misled into thinking that the subject is *here, there,* or any of the nouns or pronouns preceding the verb.

Practice On your paper, identify the subject in each sentence and choose the correct verb for it.
1. There (was,were) a perpetual sighing and ceasing sound.
2. In each of these cabinets (was,were) many little drawers.
3. There (was,were) her gray-green dress, and her long shoes, her basket, and something sparkling at her throat.
4. There (was,were) those people in black.
5. Next February on my first birthday, there (was,were) a birthday cake with one candle.

Build Your Portfolio

 ## Idea Bank

Writing

1. **Letter to the Author** Write a letter to either author responding to the unusual point of view in her story. Let her know your impressions of her narrative technique.

2. **Stream-of-Consciousness Narrative** List the contents of your own or a fictional character's room. Then write a brief stream-of-consciousness narrative about the room and its owner.

3. **Response to Criticism** Woolf has said, "The mind receives a myriad of impressions—trivial, fantastic, evanescent, or engraved with the sharpness of steel." In an essay, discuss how this observation relates to "The Lady in the Looking Glass."

Speaking, Listening, and Viewing

4. **Poetry Reading** Read aloud some poems that focus on World War I. Include poems by Alan Seeger and Wilfred Owen, whose work appears in Spark's story. **[Performing Arts Link]**

5. **Oral Interpretation** Choose one of these stories, and practice reading part or all of it aloud. Pay special attention to volume, rate, pitch, and tone of voice. Perform your oral interpretation for classmates. **[Performing Arts Link]**

Researching and Representing

6. **Report on World War I** Research the last year of World War I, referred to in Spark's story. Using maps, report to your classmates on the key developments of this year. **[Social Studies Link]**

7. **Freudian Psychology and Fiction** Freud used free association in therapy before Woolf wrote her stream-of-consciousness narratives. Research Freud's method, and compare and contrast it with Woolf's device. **[Science Link]**

Online Activity www.phlit.phschool.com

 ## Guided Writing Lesson

Narrative From an Unusual Perspective

In Muriel Spark's story, the omniscient infant narrator can "tune in" to people and events all over the world. Imitate Spark and write a narrative from the perspective of an omniscient one-year-old, either yourself or a fictional character. Like Spark, combine realistic details of a baby's life with current events of the time. Keep readers involved by creating suspense about the outcome of your "autobiography."

Writing Skills Focus: Suspense

Suspense is a feeling of growing curiosity or anxiety about the outcome of events in a narrative. To create suspense, writers play a cat-and-mouse game with readers. Spark, for example, keeps you guessing about whether the baby will smile. She finally answers the question, but with a surprising twist. You can also plant questions in the reader's mind about the outcome. Further, you can hint at the ending without giving it away—just enough to make readers nervous about it.

Prewriting Picture babies you know. What physical limitations and communication barriers will the baby-narrator encounter? Think of a realistic goal the narrator can strive for, one that will keep readers in suspense. Also, include suspenseful world events from the first year of this baby's life.

Drafting Remember that a good narrative involves a conflict (the war in Spark's tale) and rises to a climax, or turning point (the birthday party in Spark's story). Keep readers in suspense until the climax, and alternate between descriptions of the baby's life and accounts of outside events.

Revising Have a friend who knows about babies review your account and suggest ways to make it more realistic. Also, rewrite or remove any passages that reveal too much of the outcome before the climax. Only hints at the ending should remain.

Guide for Interpreting

D. H. Lawrence (1885–1930)

During his lifetime, D. H. Lawrence's literary achievements were overshadowed by explosive controversy. Like Shelley and Byron in their day, Lawrence took unorthodox positions on politics, society and morality.

Early Years David Herbert Lawrence was born in Eastwood, Nottinghamshire, the son of a coal miner. After attending local schools, Lawrence spent several years as a teacher. In 1913, he published his first major novel, *Sons and Lovers,* a thinly disguised autobiography. Two years later, *The Rainbow* (1915) was published.

Travels Abroad At the end of World War I, Lawrence and his wife, Frieda, traveled to Italy, Ceylon, Australia, Mexico, and the United States, and he later used many of these locales in his fiction. In 1921, while away from England, one of his greatest novels, *Women in Love,* was finally published. Ill from tuberculosis, Lawrence completed *Lady Chatterley's Lover* (1928), while living in Italy.

In over half a century since his death, society's views on Lawrence's writings have changed profoundly. Today his fiction is universally admired for its vivid settings, fine craftsmanship, and psychological insight.

Graham Greene (1904–1991)

The search for a source of inner peace, launched by such poets as Yeats and Eliot, continues in the novels and short stories of Graham Greene. A religious convert like Eliot, Greene wrote of pain, fear, despair, and alienation.

Reporting and Travel The son of a schoolmaster, Greene was born in Berkhamsted in Hertfordshire. Much of his early life was spent as a journalist and travel writer, and he developed the powers of observation, sensitivity to atmosphere, and simplicity of language that became hallmarks of his fiction. His trips to Africa inspired travelogues as well as two novels, *The Heart of the Matter* (1948) and *A Burnt-Out Case* (1961).

Psychological Insight Greene wrote children's books, as well as adventure stories, thrillers, and film scripts. However, his literary fiction focuses on the psychology of human character, rather than on plot. Many of his protagonists are people without roots or beliefs—people in pain. The characters in a Greene story are often unlikeable, but they almost always excite the reader's curiosity and pity—and, almost always, Greene treats them with compassion.

◆ Background for Understanding

CULTURE: WEALTH AND SOCIAL STATUS

The stories that follow touch on the subject of wealth. The British elite maintained their position by living at the "right addresses," attending the "right schools," and having the "right friends."

In "The Rocking-Horse Winner," Lawrence emphasizes the mother's persistent drive to live in style, despite the family's modest income. This need for wealth turns the house into a whispering gallery of voices: "There *must* be more money!"

Greene's "A Shocking Accident" concerns the fate of Jerome, whom we meet at "a rather expensive preparatory school." Because of the ludicrous way in which his father dies, Jerome faces ridicule from classmates and, later, from others who will not tolerate such abnormal occurrences.

Lawrence's story features "old money" and Greene's features more newly-acquired wealth, but, in both stories, money determines fate.

The Rocking-Horse Winner
◆ A Shocking Accident ◆

◆ Literature and Your Life

CONNECT YOUR EXPERIENCE

Have you ever had a relationship with someone who understood you completely? In each of these stories, the protagonist finds such a relationship. Paul in "The Rocking-Horse Winner" enjoys a special alliance with the gardener, and Jerome in "A Shocking Accident" discovers the healing power of having a true soul mate.

Journal Writing On a page in your journal, list several qualities that you value in a friend.

THEMATIC FOCUS: CONFLICTS AT HOME AND ABROAD

Although much of early twentieth-century literature is about war and its effects, some writers, like D. H. Lawrence and Graham Greene, explored conflicts at home in stories such as the following.

◆ Literary Focus

THEME

Most short stories contain a **theme,** or central idea, that the writer explores. One way in which a theme can be revealed is through symbols. A **symbol** is anything that represents something else. For example, a mask may symbolize deception or falsehood. As you read Lawrence's story, think about the symbolic meaning of the rocking horse.

Greene's "A Shocking Accident" highlights life's **absurdity**—the notion that human existence is irrational or meaningless. As you read the story, notice the ways in which Greene conveys his belief that life is absurd.

◆ Reading Strategy

IDENTIFY WITH A CHARACTER

In order to understand the author's purpose and the overall theme of a literary work, it helps to **identify with a character** —to put yourself in that character's place so you can truly understand his or her thoughts, feelings, problems, and motivations. When you identify with a character, you may feel as if you *are* that character. As you read these stories, for example, you may feel the anxiety of Paul in "The Rocking-Horse Winner" or the distress and embarrassment of Jerome in "A Shocking Accident."

◆ Build Vocabulary

LATIN PREFIXES: *ob-*

In "The Rocking-Horse Winner," you will encounter the word *obstinately*. The word contains the Latin prefix *ob-* which means "against, to, before, or on account of." *Obstinately* means "as if standing against" or "in an opposing manner"— "stubbornly."

WORD BANK

Before you read, preview this list of words from the stories.

discreet
brazening
careered
obstinately
uncanny
remonstrated
apprehension
embarked
intrinsically

◆ Grammar and Style

SUBJUNCTIVE MOOD

The **subjunctive mood** of a verb is used to state a wish or condition contrary to fact. It is most commonly expressed using the verb *were.* For example, in "The Rocking-Horse Winner," Paul's mother says to her son:

> If you *were* me and I *were* you . . . I wonder what we should do!

As you read, look for other examples of the subjunctive mood.

The Rocking-Horse Winner

D. H. Lawrence

There was a woman who was beautiful, who started with all the advantages, yet she had no luck. She married for love, and the love turned to dust. She had bonny children, yet she felt they had been thrust upon her, and she could not love them. They looked at her coldly, as if they were finding fault with her. And hurriedly she felt she must cover up some fault in herself. Yet what it was that she must cover up she never knew. Nevertheless, when her children were present, she always felt the center of her heart go hard. This troubled her, and in her manner she was all the more gentle and anxious for her children, as if she loved them very much. Only she herself knew that at the center of her heart was a hard little place that could not feel love, no, not for anybody. Everybody else said of her: "She is such a good mother. She adores her children." Only she herself, and her children themselves, knew it was not so. They read it in each other's eyes.

There were a boy and two little girls. They lived in a pleasant house, with a garden and they had discreet servants, and felt themselves superior to anyone in the neighborhood.

Although they lived in style, they felt always an anxiety in the house. There was never enough money. The mother had a small income and the father had a small income, but not nearly enough for the social position which they had to keep up. The father went into town to some office. But though he had good prospects, these prospects never materialized. There was always the grinding sense of the shortage of money, though the style was always kept up.

At last the mother said, "I will see if I can't make something." But she did not know where to begin. She racked her brains, and tried this thing and the other, but could not find anything successful. The failure made deep lines come into her face. Her children were growing up, they would have to go to school. There must be more money, there must be more money. The father, who was

◆ Build Vocabulary

discreet (dis krēt') *adj.*: Wise; prudent

always very handsome and expensive in his tastes, seemed as if he never *would* be able to do anything worth doing. And the mother, who had a great belief in herself, did not succeed any better, and her tastes were just as expensive.

And so the house came to be haunted by the unspoken phrase: *There must be more money! There must be more money!* The children could hear it all the time, though nobody said it aloud. They heard it at Christmas, when the expensive and splendid toys filled the nursery. Behind the shining modern rocking horse, behind the smart doll's house, a voice would start whispering: "There *must* be more money! There *must* be more money!" And the children would stop playing, to listen for a moment. They would look into each other's eyes to see if they had all heard. And each one saw in the eyes of the other two that they too had heard. "There *must* be more money! There *must* be more money!"

It came whispering from the springs of the still-swaying rocking horse, and even the horse, bending his wooden, champing head, heard it. The big doll, sitting so pink and smirking in her new pram,[1] could hear it quite plainly, and seemed to be smirking all the more self-consciously because of it. The foolish puppy, too, that took the place of the teddy bear, he was looking so extraordinarily foolish for no other reason but that he heard the secret whisper all over the house: "There *must* be more money."

Yet nobody ever said it aloud. The whisper was everywhere, and therefore no one spoke it. Just as no one ever says: "We are breathing!" in spite of the fact that breath is coming and going all the time.

"Mother!" said the boy Paul one day. "Why don't we keep a car of our own? Why do we always use uncle's, or else a taxi?"

"Because we're the poor members of the family," said the mother.

"But why *are* we, mother?"

"Well—I suppose," she said slowly and bitterly, "it's because your father has no luck."

The boy was silent for some time.

"Is luck money, mother?" he asked, rather timidly.

▲ **Critical Viewing** Lawrence's story comments on the unseen conflicts at work within a seemingly happy family. What aspects of this photograph seem too good to be true? **[Interpret]**

---

1. **pram:** Baby carriage.

"No, Paul! Not quite. It's what causes you to have money."

"Oh!" said Paul vaguely. "I thought when Uncle Oscar said *filthy lucker*, it meant money."

"*Filthy lucre* does mean money," said the mother. "But it's lucre, not luck."

"Oh!" said the boy. "Then what *is* luck, mother?"

"It's what causes you to have money. If you're lucky you have money. That's why it's better to be born lucky than rich. If you're rich, you may lose your money. But if you're lucky, you will always get more money."

"Oh! Will you! And is father not lucky?"

"Very unlucky, I should say," she said bitterly.

The boy watched her with unsure eyes.

"Why?" he asked.

"I don't know. Nobody ever knows why one person is lucky and another unlucky."

"Don't they? Nobody at all? Does *nobody* know?"

"Perhaps God! But He never tells."

"He ought to, then. And aren't you lucky either, mother?"

"I can't be, if I married an unlucky husband."

"But by yourself, aren't you?"

"I used to think I was, before I married. Now I think I am very unlucky indeed."

"Why?"

"Well—never mind! Perhaps I'm not really," she said.

The child looked at her, to see if she meant it. But he saw, by the lines of her mouth, that she was only trying to hide something from him.

"Well, anyhow," he said stoutly, "I'm a lucky person."

"Why?" said his mother, with a sudden laugh.

He stared at her. He didn't even know why he had said it.

"God told me," he asserted, <u>brazening</u> it out.

"I hope He did, dear!" she said, again with a laugh, but rather bitter.

"He did, mother!"

"Excellent!" said the mother, using one of her husband's exclamations.

The boy saw she did not believe him; or

rather, that she paid no attention to his assertion. This angered him somewhere, and made him want to compel her attention.

He went off by himself, vaguely, in a childish way, seeking for the clue to "luck." Absorbed, taking no heed of other people, he went about with a sort of stealth, seeking inwardly for luck. He wanted luck, he wanted it, he wanted it. When the two girls were playing dolls, in the nursery, he would sit on his big rocking horse, charging madly into space, with a frenzy that made the little girls peer at him uneasily. Wildly the horse <u>careered</u>, the waving dark hair of the boy tossed, his eyes had a strange glare in them. The little girls dared not speak to him.

When he had ridden to the end of his mad little journey, he climbed down and stood in front of his rocking horse, staring fixedly into its lowered face. Its red mouth was slightly open, its big eye was wide and glassy bright.

"Now!" he would silently command the snorting steed. "Now take me to where there is luck! Now take me!"

And he would slash the horse on the neck with the little whip he had asked Uncle Oscar for. He *knew* the horse could take him to where there was luck, if only he forced it. So he would mount again, and start on his furious ride, hoping at last to get there. He knew he could get there.

"You'll break your horse, Paul!" said the nurse.

"He's always riding like that! I wish he'd leave off!" said his elder sister Joan.

But he only glared down on them in silence. Nurse gave him up. She could make nothing of him. Anyhow he was growing beyond her.

One day his mother and his Uncle Oscar came in when he was on one of his furious rides. He did not speak to them.

"Hallo! you young jockey! Riding a winner?" said his uncle.

"Aren't you growing too big for a rocking

◆ **Build Vocabulary**

brazening (brā´ zən iŋ) *v.*: Daring boldly or shamelessly

careered (kə rird´) *v.*: Rushed wildly

horse? You're not a very little boy any longer, you know," said his mother.

But Paul only gave a blue glare from his big, rather close-set eyes. He would speak to nobody when he was in full tilt. His mother watched him with an anxious expression on her face.

At last he suddenly stopped forcing his horse into the mechanical gallop, and slid down.

"Well, I got there!" he announced fiercely, his blue eyes still flaring, and his sturdy long legs straddling apart.

"Where did you get to?" asked his mother.

"Where I wanted to go to," he flared back at her.

"That's right, son!" said Uncle Oscar. "Don't you stop till you get there. What's the horse's name?"

"He doesn't have a name," said the boy.

"Gets on without all right?" asked the uncle.

"Well, he has different names. He was called Sansovino last week."

"Sansovino, eh? Won the Ascot.[2] How did you know his name?"

"He always talks about horse races with Bassett," said Joan.

The uncle was delighted to find that his small nephew was posted with all the racing news. Bassett, the young gardener who had been wounded in the left foot in the war, and had got his present job through Oscar Cresswell, whose batman[3] he had been, was a perfect blade of the "turf."[4] He lived in the racing events, and the small boy lived with him.

Oscar Cresswell got it all from Bassett.

"Master Paul comes and asks me, so I can't do more than tell him, sir," said Bassett, his face terribly serious, as if he were speaking of religious matters.

"And does he ever put anything on a horse he fancies?"

"Well—I don't want to give him away—he's a young sport, a fine sport, sir. Would you mind asking him yourself? He sort of takes a plea-

sure in it, and perhaps he'd feel I was giving him away, sir, if you don't mind."

Bassett was serious as a church.

The uncle went back to his nephew, and took him off for a ride in the car.

"Say, Paul, old man, do you ever put anything on a horse?" the uncle asked.

The boy watched the handsome man closely.

"Why, do you think I oughtn't to?" he parried.

"Not a bit of it! I thought perhaps you might give me a tip for the Lincoln."[5]

The car sped on into the country, going down to Uncle Oscar's place in Hampshire.

"Honor bright?" said the nephew.

"Honor bright, son!" said the uncle.

"Well, then, Daffodil."

"Daffodil! I doubt it, sonny. What about Mirza?"

"I only know the winner," said the boy. "That's Daffodil!"

"Daffodil, eh?"

There was a pause. Daffodil was an obscure horse comparatively.

"Uncle!"

"Yes, son?"

"You won't let it go any further, will you? I promised Bassett."

"Bassett be hanged, old man! What's he got to do with it?"

"We're partners! We've been partners from the first! Uncle, he lent me my first five shillings, which I lost. I promised him, honor bright, it was only between me and him: only you gave me that ten-shilling note I started winning with, so I thought you were lucky. You won't let it go any further, will you?"

The boy gazed at his uncle from those big, hot, blue eyes, set rather close together. The uncle stirred and laughed uneasily.

"Right you are, son! I'll keep your tip private. Daffodil, eh! How much are you putting on him?"

"All except twenty pounds," said the boy. "I keep that in reserve."

The uncle thought it a good joke.

"You keep twenty pounds in reserve, do you,

◆ **Reading Strategy**
What does this exchange indicate about Paul's sense of loyalty?

---

2. **Ascot:** Major English horse race.
3. **batman:** British military officer's orderly.
4. **blade . . . "turf":** Horse-racing fan.

5. **Lincoln:** Major English horse race.

you young romancer? What are you betting, then?"

"I'm betting three hundred," said the boy gravely. "But it's between you and me, Uncle Oscar! Honor bright?"

The uncle burst into a roar of laughter.

"It's between you and me all right, you young Nat Gould,"[6] he said, laughing. "But where's your three hundred?"

"Bassett keeps it for me. We're partners."

"You are, are you! And what is Bassett putting on Daffodil?"

"He won't go quite as high as I do, I expect. Perhaps he'll go a hundred and fifty."

"What, pennies?" laughed the uncle.

"Pounds," said the child, with a surprised look at his uncle. "Bassett keeps a bigger reserve than I do."

Between wonder and amusement, Uncle Oscar was silent. He pursued the matter no further, but he determined to take his nephew with him to the Lincoln races.

"Now, son," he said, "I'm putting twenty on Mirza, and I'll put five for you on any horse you fancy. What's your pick?"

"Daffodil, uncle!"

"No, not the fiver on Daffodil!"

"I should if it was my own five," said the child.

"Good! Good! Right you are! A fiver for me and a fiver for you on Daffodil."

The child had never been to a race meeting before, and his eyes were blue fire. He pursed his mouth tight, and watched. A Frenchman just in front had put his money on Lancelot. Wild with excitement, he flayed his arms up and down, yelling *Lancelot! Lancelot!* in his French accent.

Daffodil came in first, Lancelot second, Mirza third. The child, flushed and with eyes blazing, was curiously serene. His uncle brought him five five-pound notes: four to one.

"What am I to do with these?" he cried, waving them before the boy's eyes.

"I suppose we'll talk to Bassett," said the boy. "I expect I have fifteen hundred now; and twenty in reserve; and this twenty."

---

6. **Nat Gould:** Famous English sportswriter and authority on horse racing.

His uncle studied him for some moments.

"Look here, son!" he said. "You're not serious about Bassett and that fifteen hundred, are you?"

"Yes, I am. But it's between you and me, uncle! Honor bright!"

"Honor bright all right, son! But I must talk to Bassett."

"If you'd like to be a partner, uncle, with Bassett and me, we could all be partners. Only you'd have to promise, honor bright, uncle, not to let it go beyond us three. Bassett and I are lucky, and you must be lucky, because it was your ten shillings I started winning with. . . ."

Uncle Oscar took both Bassett and Paul into Richmond Park for an afternoon, and there they talked.

"It's like this, you see, sir," Bassett said. "Master Paul would get me talking about racing events, spinning yarns, you know, sir. And he was always keen on knowing if I'd made or if I'd lost. It's about a year since, now, that I put five shillings on Blush of Dawn for him— and we lost. Then the luck turned, with that ten shillings he had from you, that we put on Singhalese. And since that time, it's been pretty steady, all things considering. What do you say, Master Paul?"

"We're all right when we're *sure*," said Paul. "It's when we're not quite sure that we go down."

"Oh, but we're careful then," said Bassett.

"But when are you *sure*?" smiled Uncle Oscar.

"It's Master Paul, sir," said Bassett, in a secret, religious voice. "It's as if he had it from heaven. Like Daffodil now, for the Lincoln. That was as sure as eggs."

"Did you put anything on Daffodil?" asked Oscar Cresswell.

"Yes, sir. I made my bit."

"And my nephew?"

Bassett was <u>obstinately</u> silent, looking at Paul.

"I made twelve hundred, didn't I, Bassett? I told uncle I was putting three hundred on Daffodil."

◆ Build Vocabulary

obstinately (äb´ stə nət lē) *adv.*: In a determined way; stubbornly

"That's right," said Bassett, nodding.

"But where's the money?" asked the uncle.

"I keep it safe locked up, sir. Master Paul, he can have it any minute he likes to ask for it."

"What, fifteen hundred pounds?"

"And twenty! And *forty*, that is, with the twenty he made on the course."

"It's amazing!" said the uncle.

"If Master Paul offers you to be partners, sir, I would, if I were you; if you'll excuse me," said Bassett.

Oscar Cresswell thought about it.

▲ **Critical Viewing** Although Paul, the young protagonist of the story, rides a rocking horse, he acts years older than he is. Which elements in this photograph make the child seem old and serious? Which elements emphasize the child's youth? **[Classify]**

"I'll see the money," he said.

They drove home again, and sure enough, Bassett came round to the garden house with fifteen hundred pounds in notes. The twenty pounds reserve was left with Joe Glee, in the Turf Commission deposit.

"You see, it's all right, uncle, when I'm *sure*! Then we go strong, for all we're worth. Don't we, Bassett?"

"We do that, Master Paul."

"And when are you sure?" said the uncle, laughing.

"Oh, well, sometimes I'm *absolutely* sure, like about Daffodil," said the boy, "and sometimes I have an idea; and sometimes I haven't even an idea, have I, Bassett? Then we're careful, because we mostly go down."

"You do, do you! And when you're sure, like about Daffodil, what makes you sure, sonny?"

"Oh, well, I don't know," said the boy uneasily. "I'm sure, you know, uncle; that's all."

"It's as if he had it from heaven, sir," Bassett reiterated.

"I should say so!" said the uncle.

But he became a partner. And when the Leger was coming on, Paul was "sure" about Lively Spark, which was a quite inconsiderable horse. The boy insisted on putting a thousand on the horse, Bassett went for five hundred, and Oscar Cresswell two hundred. Lively Spark came in first, and the betting had been ten to one against him. Paul had made ten thousand.

"You see," he said. "I was absolutely sure of him."

Even Oscar Cresswell had cleared two thousand.

"Look here, son," he said, "this sort of thing makes me nervous."

"It needn't, uncle! Perhaps I shan't be sure again for a long time."

"But what are you going to do with your money?" asked the uncle.

"Of course," said the boy, "I started it for mother. She said she had no luck, because father is unlucky, so I thought if *I* was lucky, it might stop whispering."

"What might stop whispering?"

"Our house! I *hate* our house for whispering."

"What does it whisper?"

"Why—why"—the boy fidgeted—"why, I don't know! But it's always short of money, you know, uncle."

"I know it, son, I know it."

"You know people send mother writs, don't you, uncle?"

"I'm afraid I do," said the uncle.

"And then the house whispers like people laughing at you behind your back. It's awful, that is! I thought if I was lucky . . ."

"You might stop it," added the uncle.

The boy watched him with big blue eyes, that had an uncanny cold fire in them, and he said never a word.

"Well then!" said the uncle. "What are we doing?"

"I shouldn't like mother to know I was lucky," said the boy.

"Why not, son?"

"She'd stop me."

"I don't think she would."

"Oh!"—and the boy writhed in an odd way—"I *don't* want her to know, uncle."

"All right, son! We'll manage it without her knowing."

They managed it very easily. Paul, at the other's suggestion, handed over five thousand pounds to his uncle, who deposited it with the family lawyer, who was then to inform Paul's mother that a relative had put five thousand pounds into his hands, which sum was to be paid out a thousand pounds at a time, on the mother's birthday, for the next five years.

"So she'll have a birthday present of a thousand pounds for five successive years," said Uncle Oscar. "I hope it won't make it all the harder for her later."

Paul's mother had her birthday in November. The house had been "whispering" worse than ever lately, and even in spite of his luck, Paul could not bear up against it. He was very anxious to see the effect of the birthday letter, telling his mother about the thousand pounds.

When there were no visitors, Paul now took his meals with his parents, as he was beyond the nursery control. His mother went into town nearly every day. She had discovered that she had an odd knack of sketching furs and dress materials, so she worked secretly in the studio of a friend who was the chief "artist" for the leading drapers. She drew the figures of ladies in furs and ladies in silk and sequins for the newspaper advertisements. This young woman artist earned several thousand pounds a year, but Paul's mother only made several hundreds, and she was again dissatisfied. She so wanted to be first in something, and she did not succeed, even in making sketches for drapery advertisements.

She was down to breakfast on the morning of her birthday. Paul watched her face as she read her letters. He knew the lawyer's letter. As his mother read it, her face hardened and became more expressionless. Then a cold, determined look came on her mouth. She hid the letter under the pile of others, and said not a word about it.

"Didn't you have anything nice in the post for your birthday, mother?" said Paul.

"Quite moderately nice," she said, her voice cold and absent.

She went away to town without saying more.

But in the afternoon Uncle Oscar appeared. He said Paul's mother had had a long interview with the lawyer, asking if the whole five thousand could not be advanced at once, as she was in debt.

"What do you think, uncle?" said the boy.

"I leave it to you, son."

"Oh, let her have it, then! We can get some more with the other," said the boy.

"A bird in the hand is worth two in the bush, laddie!" said Uncle Oscar.

"But I'm sure to *know* for the Grand National; or the Lincolnshire; or else the Derby.[7] I'm sure to know for *one* of them," said Paul.

So Uncle Oscar signed the agreement, and Paul's mother touched the whole five thousand. Then something very curious happened. The voices in the house suddenly went mad, like a chorus of frogs on a spring evening. There were

---

7. **Grand National . . . Derby:** Major English horse races.

◆ **Literary Focus**

In what way does the personification of the house help you to identify the theme of the story?

certain new furnishings, and Paul had a tutor. He was *really* going to Eton,[8] his father's school, in the following autumn. There were flowers in the winter, and a blossoming of the luxury Paul's mother had been used to. And yet the voices in the house, behind the sprays of mimosa and almond blossom, and from under the piles of iridescent cushions, simply trilled and screamed in a sort of ecstasy: "There *must* be more money! Oh-h-h! There *must* be more money! Oh, now, now-w! now-w-w—there *must* be more money!—more than ever! More than ever!"

It frightened Paul terribly. He studied away at his Latin and Greek with his tutors. But his intense hours were spent with Bassett. The Grand National had gone by: he had not "known," and had lost a hundred pounds. Summer was at hand. He was in agony for the Lincoln. But even for the Lincoln he didn't "know," and he lost fifty pounds. He became wild-eyed and strange, as if something were going to explode in him.

"Let it alone, son! Don't you bother about it!" urged Uncle Oscar. But it was as if the boy couldn't really hear what his uncle was saying.

"I've got to know for the Derby! I've *got* to know for the Derby!" the child reiterated, his big blue eyes blazing with a sort of madness.

His mother noticed how overwrought he was.

"You'd better go to the seaside. Wouldn't you like to go now to the seaside, instead of waiting? I think you'd better," she said, looking down at him anxiously, her heart curiously heavy because of him.

But the child lifted his uncanny blue eyes.

"I couldn't possibly go before the Derby, mother!" he said. "I couldn't possibly!"

"Why not?" she said, her voice becoming heavy when she was opposed. "Why not? You can still go from the seaside to see the Derby with your Uncle Oscar, if that's what you wish. No need for you to wait here. Besides, I think you care too much about these races. It's a bad sign. My family has been a gambling family, and you won't know till you grow up how much damage it has done. But it has done damage. I shall have to send Bassett away, and ask Uncle Oscar not to talk racing to you, unless you promise to be reasonable about it; go away to the seaside and forget it. You're all nerves!"

"I'll do what you like, mother, so long as you don't send me away till after the Derby," the boy said.

"Send you away from where? Just from this house?"

"Yes," he said, gazing at her.

"Why, you curious child, what makes you care about this house so much, suddenly? I never knew you loved it!"

He gazed at her without speaking. He had a secret within a secret, something he had not divulged, even to Bassett or to his Uncle Oscar.

But his mother, after standing undecided and a little bit sullen for some moments, said:

"Very well, then! Don't go to the seaside till after the Derby, if you don't wish it. But promise me you won't let your nerves go to pieces! Promise you won't think so much about horse racing and *events*, as you call them!"

"Oh, no!" said the boy, casually. "I won't think much about them, mother. You needn't worry. I wouldn't worry, mother, if I were you."

"If you were me and I were you," said his mother, "I wonder what we *should* do!"

"But you know you needn't worry, mother, don't you?" the boy repeated.

"I should be awfully glad to know it," she said wearily.

"Oh, well, you *can*, you know. I mean you *ought* to know you needn't worry!" he insisted.

"Ought I? Then I'll see about it," she said.

Paul's secret of secrets was his wooden horse, that which had no name. Since he was emancipated from a nurse and a nursery governess, he had had his rocking horse removed to his own bedroom at the top of the house

"Surely you're too big for a rocking horse!" his mother had <u>remonstrated</u>.

"Well, you see, mother, till I can have a *real* horse, I like to have *some* sort of animal

---

8. **Eton:** Prestigious private school in England.

◆ **Build Vocabulary**

uncanny (un kan´ ē) *adj.*: Mysterious; hard to explain

remonstrated (ri män´ strāt id) *v.*: Objected strongly

about," had been his quaint answer.

"Do you feel he keeps you company?" she laughed.

"Oh, yes! He's very good, he always keeps me company, when I'm there," said Paul.

So the horse, rather shabby, stood in an arrested prance in the boy's bedroom.

The Derby was drawing near, and the boy grew more and more tense. He hardly heard what was spoken to him, he was very frail, and his eyes were really uncanny. His mother had sudden strange seizures of uneasiness about him. Sometimes, for half an hour, she would feel a sudden anxiety about him that was almost anguish. She wanted to rush to him at once, and know he was safe.

Two nights before the Derby, she was at a big party in town, when one of her rushes of anxiety about her boy, her firstborn, gripped her heart till she could hardly speak. She fought with the feeling, might and main, for she believed in common sense. But it was too strong. She had to leave the dance and go downstairs to telephone to the country. The children's nursery governess was terribly surprised and startled at being rung up in the night.

"Are the children all right, Miss Wilmot?"

"Oh yes, they are quite all right."

"Master Paul? Is he all right?"

"He went to bed as right as a trivet.[9] Shall I run up and look at him?"

"No!" said Paul's mother reluctantly. "No! Don't trouble. It's all right. Don't sit up. We shall be home fairly soon." She did not want her son's privacy intruded upon.

"Very good," said the governess.

It was about one o'clock when Paul's mother and father drove up to their house. All was still. Paul's mother went to her room and slipped off her white fur cloak. She had told her maid not to wait up for her. She heard her husband downstairs, mixing a whisky-and-soda.

And then, because of the strange anxiety at her heart, she stole upstairs to her son's room. Noiselessly she went along the upper corridor. Was there a faint noise? What was it?

She stood, with arrested muscles, outside his door, listening. There was a strange, heavy, and yet not loud noise. Her heart stood still.

---

9. **right as a trivet:** Perfectly right.

It was a soundless noise, yet rushing and powerful. Something huge, in violent, hushed motion. What was it? What in God's name was it? She ought to know. She felt that she *knew* the noise. She knew what it was.

Yet she could not place it. She couldn't say what it was. And on and on it went, like madness.

Softly, frozen with anxiety and fear, she turned the door handle.

The room was dark. Yet in the space near the window, she heard and saw something plunging to and fro. She gazed in fear and amazement.

Then suddenly she switched on the light, and saw her son, in his green pajamas, madly surging on his rocking horse. The blaze of light suddenly lit him up, as he urged the wooden horse, and lit her up, as she stood, blond, in her dress of pale green and crystal, in the doorway.

"Paul!" she cried. "Whatever are you doing?"

"It's Malabar!" he screamed, in a powerful, strange voice. "It's Malabar!"

His eyes blazed at her for one strange and senseless second, as he ceased urging his wooden horse. Then he fell with a crash to the ground, and she, all her tormented motherhood flooding upon her, rushed to gather him up.

But he was unconscious, and unconscious he remained, with some brain fever. He talked and tossed, and his mother sat stonily by his side.

"Malabar! It's Malabar! Bassett, Bassett, I *know* it's Malabar!"

So the child cried, trying to get up and urge the rocking horse that gave him his inspiration.

"What does he mean by Malabar?" asked the heart-frozen mother.

"I don't know," said the father, stonily.

"What does he mean by Malabar?" she asked her brother Oscar.

"It's one of the horses running for the Derby," was the answer.

And, in spite of himself, Oscar Cresswell spoke to Bassett, and himself put a thousand on Malabar: at fourteen to one.

The third day of the illness was critical: they were watching for a change. The boy, with his rather long, curly hair, was tossing ceaselessly on the pillow. He neither slept nor regained consciousness, and his eyes were like blue stones. His mother sat, feeling her heart had gone, turned actually into a stone.

In the evening, Oscar Cresswell did not come, but Bassett sent a message, saying could he come up for one moment, just one moment? Paul's mother was very angry at the intrusion, but on second thoughts she agreed. The boy was the same. Perhaps Bassett might bring him to consciousness.

The gardener, a shortish fellow with a little brown moustache and sharp little brown eyes, tiptoed into the room, touched his imaginary cap to Paul's mother, and stole to the bedside, staring with glittering, smallish eyes at the tossing, dying child.

"Master Paul!" he whispered. "Master Paul! Malabar came in first all right, a clean win. I did as you told me. You've made over seventy thousand pounds, you have; you've got over eighty thousand. Malabar came in all right, Master Paul."

"Malabar! Malabar! Did I say Malabar, mother? Did I say Malabar? Do you think I'm lucky, mother? I knew Malabar, didn't I? Over eighty thousand pounds! I call that lucky, don't you, mother? Over eighty thousand pounds! I knew, didn't I know I knew? Malabar came in all right. If I ride my horse till I'm sure, then I tell you, Bassett, you can go as high as you like. Did you go for all you were worth, Bassett?"

"I went a thousand on it, Master Paul."

"I never told you, mother, that if I can ride my horse, and *get there*, then I'm absolutely sure—oh, absolutely! Mother, did I ever tell you? I *am* lucky!"

"No, you never did," said the mother.

But the boy died in the night.

And even as he lay dead, his mother heard her brother's voice saying to her: "My God, Hester, you're eighty-odd thousand to the good, and a poor devil of a son to the bad. But, poor devil, poor devil, he's best gone out of a life where he rides his rocking horse to find a winner."

Guide for Responding

◆ Literature and Your Life

Reader's Response What is your impression of Paul's relationship with (a) his mother? (b) his Uncle Oscar?

Thematic Focus To what extent do you think that the family problems that Lawrence addresses in this story—lack of communication, social snobbery, and greed—reflect conflicts in the larger world? Explain your answer.

☑ Check Your Comprehension

1. Why is the family in the story always short of money?
2. How does Paul try to change the family's luck?
3. Why is Paul sometimes "careful" when he bets on horses?
4. (a) What secret birthday present does Paul give his mother? (b) How does she react to it?
5. What does Paul's mother discover upon returning from the big party?

◆ Critical Thinking

INTERPRET

1. (a) What do you think Paul's mother means when she describes her husband as unlucky? (b) What does the description reveal about her as a person? **[Infer]**
2. (a) Over the course of the story, how is Paul affected by the house's "whispers?" (b) Why is he affected as he is? **[Analyze Cause and Effect]**
3. What comment about life do you think the author is suggesting by Uncle Oscar's statement on Paul's death at the story's close? **[Draw Conclusions]**

APPLY

4. (a) Identify Lawrence's theme in this story. (b) Do you think the theme is still relevant today? Explain. **[Relate]**

EXTEND

5. What other stories do you know of in which a perceived lack of money has driven characters to extremes? Explain. **[Literature Link]**

A Shocking Accident

Graham Greene

1

Jerome was called into his housemaster's room in the break between the second and the third class on a Thursday morning. He had no fear of trouble, for he was a warden—the name that the proprietor and headmaster of a rather expensive preparatory school had chosen to give to approved, reliable boys in the lower forms (from a warden one became a guardian and finally before leaving, it was hoped for Marlborough or Rugby, a crusader). The housemaster, Mr. Wordsworth, sat behind his desk with an appearance of perplexity and apprehension. Jerome had the odd impression when he entered that he was a cause of fear.

"Sit down, Jerome," Mr. Wordsworth said. "All going well with the trigonometry?"

"Yes, sir."

"I've had a telephone call, Jerome. From your aunt. I'm afraid I have bad news for you."

"Yes, sir?"

"Your father has had an accident."

"Oh."

Mr. Wordsworth looked at him with some surprise. "A serious accident."

"Yes, sir?"

Jerome worshipped his father: the verb is exact. As man re-creates God, so Jerome re-created his father—from a restless widowed author into a mysterious adventurer who traveled in far places—Nice, Beirut, Majorca, even the Canaries. The time had arrived about his eighth birthday when Jerome believed that his father either "ran guns" or was a member of the British Secret Service. Now it occurred to him that his father might have been wounded in "a hail of machine-gun bullets."

Mr. Wordsworth played with the ruler on his desk. He seemed at a loss how to continue. He said, "You knew your father was in Naples?"

"Yes, sir."

"Your aunt heard from the hospital today."

"Oh."

Mr. Wordsworth said with desperation, "It was a street accident."

"Yes, sir?" It seemed quite likely to Jerome that they would call it a street accident. The police, of course, had fired first; his father would not take human life except as a last resort.

"I'm afraid your father was very seriously hurt indeed."

"Oh."

"In fact, Jerome, he died yesterday. Quite without pain."

"Did they shoot him through the heart?"

"I beg your pardon. What did you say, Jerome?"

"Did they shoot him through the heart?"

◆ **Build Vocabulary**

apprehension (ap´ rē hen´ shən) *n.*: Anxious feeling of foreboding; dread

embarked (em bärkt´) *v.*: Engaged in conversation

"Nobody shot him, Jerome. A pig fell on him." An inexplicable convulsion took place in the nerves of Mr. Wordsworth's face; it really looked for a moment as though he were going to laugh. He closed his eyes, composed his features, and said rapidly, as though it were necessary to expel the story as rapidly as possible, "Your father was walking along a street in Naples when a pig fell on him. A shocking accident."

◆ Literary Focus
How does the manner in which Jerome's father died convey the idea that life is absurd?

Apparently in the poorer quarters of Naples they keep pigs on their balconies. This one was on the fifth floor. It had grown too fat. The balcony broke. The pig fell on your father."

Mr. Wordsworth left his desk rapidly and went to the window, turning his back on Jerome. He shook a little with emotion.

Jerome said, "What happened to the pig?"

2

This was not callousness on the part of Jerome as it was interpreted by Mr. Wordsworth to his colleagues (he even discussed with them whether, perhaps, Jerome was not yet fitted to be a warden). Jerome was only attempting to visualize the strange scene and to get the details right. Nor was Jerome a boy who cried; he was a boy who brooded, and it never occurred to him at his preparatory school that the circumstances of his father's death were comic—they were still part of the mystery of life. It was later in his first term at his public school, when he told the story to his best friend, that he began to realize how it affected others. Naturally, after that disclosure he was known, rather unreasonably, as Pig.

Unfortunately his aunt had no sense of humor. There was an enlarged snap-shot

▲ **Critical Viewing** In this story, Jerome becomes orphaned and suffers humiliation because of the way in which his father died. How well does this photograph convey a young man's loneliness and sadness? **[Evaluate]**

of his father on the piano: a large sad man in an unsuitable dark suit posed in Capri with an umbrella (to guard him against sunstroke), the Faraglioni rocks forming the background. By the age of sixteen Jerome was well aware that the portrait looked more like the author of *Sunshine and Shade* and *Rambles in the Balearics* than an agent of the Secret Service. All the same, he loved the memory of his father: he still possessed an album filled with picture-postcards (the stamps had been soaked off long ago for his other collection), and it pained him when his aunt embarked with strangers on the story of his father's death.

"A shocking accident," she would begin, and the stranger would compose his or her features into the correct shape for interest and commiseration. Both reactions, of course, were false, but it was terrible for Jerome to see how suddenly, midway in her rambling discourse, the interest would become genuine. "I can't think how such things can be allowed in a civilized country," his aunt would say. "I suppose one has to regard Italy as civilized. One is prepared for all kinds of things abroad, of course, and my brother was a great traveler. He always carried a water-filter with him. It was far less expensive, you know, than buying all those bottles of mineral water. My brother always said that his filter paid for his dinner wine. You can see from that what a careful man he was, but who could possibly have expected when he was walking along the Via Dottore Manuele Panucci on his way to the Hydrographic Museum that a pig would fall on him?" That was the moment when the interest became genuine.

Jerome's father had not been a distinguished writer, but the time always seems to come, after an author's death, when somebody thinks it worth his while to write a letter to *The Times Literary Supplement* announcing the preparation of a biography and asking to see any letters or documents or receive any anecdotes from friends of the dead man. Most of the biographies, of course, never appear—one wonders whether the whole thing may not be an obscure form of blackmail and whether many a potential writer of a biography or thesis finds the means in this way to finish his education at Kansas or Nottingham. Jerome, however, as a chartered accountant, lived far from the literary world. He did not realize how small the menace really was, nor that the danger period for someone of his father's obscurity had long passed. Sometimes he rehearsed the method of recounting his father's death so as to reduce the comic element to its smallest dimensions—it would be of no use to refuse information, for in that case the biographer would undoubtedly visit his aunt, who was living to a great old age with no sign of flagging.

It seemed to Jerome that there were two possible methods—the first led gently up to the accident, so well prepared that the death came really as an anticlimax. The chief danger of laughter in such a story was always surprise. When he rehearsed this method Jerome began boringly enough.

"You know Naples and those high tenement buildings? Somebody once told me that the Neapolitan always feels at home in New York just as the man from Turin feels at home in London because the river runs in much the same way in both cities. Where was I? Oh, yes, Naples, of course. You'd be surprised in the poorer quarters what things they keep on the balconies of those skyscraping tenements—not washing, you know, or bedding, but things like livestock, chickens or even pigs. Of course the pigs get no exercise whatever and fatten all the quicker." He could imagine how his hearer's eyes would have glazed by this time. "I've no idea, have you, how heavy a pig can be, but those old buildings are all badly in need of repair. A balcony on the fifth floor gave way under one of those pigs. It struck the third-floor balcony on its way down and sort of ricocheted into the street. My father was on the way to the Hydrographic Museum when the pig hit him. Coming from that height and that angle it broke his neck." This was really a masterly attempt to make an intrinsically interesting subject boring.

The other method Jerome rehearsed had the virtue of brevity.

"My father was killed by a pig."

"Really? In India?"

"No, in Italy."

"How interesting. I never realized there was pig-sticking in Italy. Was your father keen on polo?"

In course of time, neither too early nor too late, rather as though, in his capacity as a chartered accountant, Jerome had studied the statistics and taken the average, he became engaged to be married: to a pleasant fresh-faced girl of twenty-five whose father was a doctor in Pinner. Her name was Sally, her favorite author was still Hugh Walpole, and she had adored babies ever since she had been given a doll at the age of five which moved its eyes and made water. Their relationship was contented rather than exciting, as became the love affair of a chartered accountant; it would never have done if it had interfered with the figures.

One thought worried Jerome, however. Now that within a year he might himself become a father, his love for the dead man increased; he realized what affection had gone into the picture-postcards. He felt a longing to protect his memory, and uncertain whether this quiet love of his would survive if Sally were so insensitive as to laugh when she heard the story of his father's death. Inevitably she would hear it when Jerome brought her to dinner with his aunt. Several times he tried to tell her himself, as she was naturally anxious to know all she could that concerned him.

"You were very small when your father died?"

"Just nine."

"Poor little boy," she said.

◆ Build Vocabulary

intrinsically (in trin´ sik lē) *adv.*: At its core; inherently; innately

"I was at school. They broke the news to me."

"Did you take it very hard?"

"I can't remember."

"You never told me how it happened."

"It was very sudden. A street accident."

"You'll never drive fast, will you, Jemmy?" (She had begun to call him "Jemmy.") It was too late then to try the second method—the one he thought of as the pig-sticking one.

They were going to marry quietly at a registry-office and have their honeymoon at Torquay. He avoided taking her to see his aunt until a week before the wedding, but then the night came, and he could not have told himself whether his apprehension was more for his father's memory or the security of his own love.

The moment came all too soon. "Is that Jemmy's father?" Sally asked, picking up the portrait of the man with the umbrella.

"Yes, dear. How did you guess?"

"He has Jemmy's eyes and brow, hasn't he?"

"Has Jerome lent you his books?"

"No."

"I will give you a set for your wedding. He wrote so tenderly about his travels. My own favorite is *Nooks and Crannies*. He would have had a great future. It made that shocking accident all the worse."

"Yes?"

How Jerome longed to leave the room and not see that loved face crinkle with irresistible amusement.

"I had so many letters from his readers after the pig fell on him." She had never been so abrupt before.

And then the miracle happened. Sally did not laugh. Sally sat with open eyes of horror while his aunt told her the story, and at the end, "How horrible," Sally said. "It makes you think, doesn't it? Happening like that. Out of a clear sky."

Jerome's heart sang with joy. It was as though she had appeased his fear forever. In the taxi going home he kissed her with more passion than he had ever shown, and she returned it. There were babies in her pale blue pupils, babies that rolled their eyes and made water.

"A week today," Jerome said, and she squeezed his hand. "Penny for your thoughts, my darling."

"I was wondering," Sally said, "what happened to the poor pig?" "They almost certainly had it for dinner," Jerome said happily and kissed the dear child again.

◆ **Literary Focus**
How does Sally's reaction to this news support the story's theme that life is absurd?

Guide for Responding

◆ Literature and Your Life

Reader's Response Did you anticipate the way in which this story ended? Why or why not?

Thematic Focus After the "shocking accident" occurred to Jerome's father, what conflicts does Jerome experience?

☑ Check Your Comprehension

1. What roles in life does Jerome assign his father in his imagination?
2. What is the "accident" of the title?
3. (a) How does Sally react when she hears the story about the accident? (b) How does Sally's reaction affect her relationship with Jerome?

◆ Critical Thinking

INTERPRET

1. Keeping in mind that Jerome worshiped his father, explain his reaction to news of his father's death—"What happened to the pig?" **[Interpret]**
2. Compare and contrast Jerome's attitude towards the circumstances of his father's death with that of his aunt. Support your points with examples from the story. **[Compare and Contrast]**
3. (a) What are some inner conflicts Jerome experiences after his father's death? (b) Are Jerome's conflicts resolved at the end of the story? Why or why not? **[Draw Conclusions]**

Guide for Responding (continued)

◆ Literary Focus

THEME

Most short stories revolve around a single **theme**, which conveys a main idea or message about life to the reader.

A **symbol** in a literary work may often enhance that work's theme by suggesting multiple meanings, references, and associations. Similarly, the notion of **absurdity**, or the belief that human existence is irrational or meaningless, is another literary element that adds dimension to the theme of a literary work.

1. What do you think Paul's rocking horse and his attachment to it may symbolize in Lawrence's story?
2. What does this symbolism reveal about Paul's family and the society in which Paul and his family live? Explain.
3. In "A Shocking Accident," what events suggest that life is fundamentally absurd? Explain your choices.

◆ Build Vocabulary

USING THE LATIN PREFIX *ob-*

The Latin prefix *ob-* means "against, to, before, or on account of." Write definitions for the following words.

1. object (verb)   4. obstruction
2. obstacle   5. obnoxious
3. obligation

USING THE WORD BANK: Antonyms

On your paper, write the letter of the word that is the best antonym of the first word.

1. discreet: (a) multiple, (b) imprudent, (c) invisible
2. brazening: (a) flinching, (b) shouting, (c) insisting
3. obstinately: (a) boldly, (b) concisely, (c) agreeably
4. uncanny: (a) eerie, (b) funny, (c) explainable
5. remonstrated: (a) praised, (b) scolded, (c) scorned
6. apprehension: (a) turmoil, (b) confidence, (c) fear
7. embark: (a) emphasize, (b) hesitate, (c) conclude
8. intrinsically: (a) emphatically, (b) uncharacteristically, (c) richly
9. careered: (a) advanced, (b) stayed still, (c) tipped over

◆ Reading Strategy

IDENTIFY WITH A CHARACTER

Understanding a story is often easier if you **identify with characters** by putting yourself in their situation and "trying it on for size." By doing this, you sympathize with their struggles and experiences and get an idea how you might respond in their circumstances.

1. In "The Rocking-Horse Winner," Paul hears his house's desperate but silent plea, "There *must* be more money!" What might you do in response to such a message?
2. In "A Shocking Accident," Jerome feels the degradation of having his father's death ridiculed. How would you respond if you found yourself in a similar position?
3. Did you identify with any other character? If so, which actions and events led you to identify with that character?

◆ Grammar and Style

SUBJUNCTIVE MOOD

To state a wish or condition contrary to fact, writers use the **subjunctive mood**. They also use the subjunctive in *that* clauses of recommendation, command, or demand. The subjunctive form, used with third-person singular subjects, is the present form of the verb without *s*. For the verb *to be*, the present subjunctive form is *be* and the past is *were*.
Recommendation: It is important that he *speak* up.
Demand: The teacher insisted that students *be* on time.

Practice In your notebook, write the correct verb for each sentence.

1. Paul's mother insisted that the child (goes, go) to a first-class boarding school.
2. Bassett and Paul thought it essential that they (are, be) sure of a winner before placing a bet.
3. Paul often wished that his mother (wasn't, weren't) so worried.
4. It really looked for a moment as though he (was, were) going to laugh.
5. Jerome thought that, if Sally (was, were) insensitive, their engagement might end.

Build **Y**our **P**ortfolio

 Idea Bank

Writing

1. **Notes for a Screenplay** Make some notes for a screenplay based on "A Shocking Accident." Your notes might include a list of settings, costume descriptions, and casting suggestions.

2. **Retelling a Passage** Select a portion of "The Rocking-Horse Winner" and retell it from Paul's perspective. Maintain a consistent point of view.

3. **Response to Criticism** E. M. Forster called Lawrence "the only prophetic novelist" writing at that time. Keeping in mind the meaning of "prophetic," write a response, evaluating whether or not you find Lawrence's story prophetic.

Speaking, Listening, and Viewing

4. **Soliloquy** A play has been made of "A Shocking Accident," and you are playing Jerome. Deliver a soliloquy—a speech made by a character who is alone—about other people's reactions to your father's death. **[Performing Arts Link]**

5. **Movie Discussion** Together with a small group, find and screen the film *The Rocking-Horse Winner* (1949). Then present a round table discussion in which you compare and contrast the film with Lawrence's story. **[Media Link]**

Researching and Representing

6. **Social Research** At the time these stories were set, the British class system was rigidly stratified. Research the classes and their effect on British society in general. Present your findings in a report to the class. **[Social Studies Link]**

7. **Multimedia Travelogue** Research Graham Greene's travels. Compile your results in a multimedia exhibit that guides your audience in the footsteps of the novelist. **[Social Studies Link]**

Online Activity www.phlit.phschool.com

 Guided Writing Lesson

Product Description

From the moment it is first mentioned as an example of the "expensive and splendid toys [that] filled the nursery," the rocking horse in Lawrence's tale occupies a central role in the narrative.

In their own way, many toys *do* possess a magical dimension for children. Write a description of an amazing toy. Think of it as a product description intended to sell the toy. Try to convey the wonder and happiness that this toy inspires in children.

Writing Skills Focus: Climax and Resolution

Even a product description can build to a high point of interest, a **climax,** and present a **resolution**—the point at which all pieces of description come together. To achieve this:

- Present your points in order of interest. Start by describing what a customer would *expect* of this particular toy, then present increasingly amazing details about it.
- Conclude with an irresistible argument as to why your reader should buy your toy. Restate your strongest points and leave no question in your reader's mind that your toy possesses unique qualities.

Prewriting Before you begin your description, visualize your toy. Sketch it, and make notes about its size, sounds, color, texture, moving parts, as well as its function.

Drafting As you draft, remember that the aim of your description is to sell the toy. Your audience is children and their parents. Describe the amazing features of your toy, but make the description believable, too.

Revising Exchange the description with a partner. Ask: Do my points build to a peak of interest? Is my description persuasive? Did I do an effective job of making my toy seem like an object of wonder?

CONNECTIONS TO WORLD LITERATURE

The Book of Sand
Jorge Luis Borges

Literary Connection

THE SHORT STORY

A short story is a brief work of fiction; it resembles the longer novel but generally has a simpler plot and setting. In addition, a short story tends to reveal character at a crucial moment rather than develop it through many incidents. The writers in this section helped make the story an important literary form in the twentieth century, and they pioneered the use of bold new fictional techniques.

MASTERS OF STORYTELLING

In "The Lagoon" Conrad uses elements that appear in much of his fiction: a tale of betrayal set in an exotic, dreamlike place and a story-within-a-story narrative. As in many of his other stories, Joyce builds to an epiphany in "Araby"—a character's flash of awareness that illuminates the story's meaning. In their stories, Woolf and Spark use unusual narrative devices—a stream-of-consciousness narration that mirrors the random thoughts in a character's mind and an omniscient point of view attributed to an infant!

Argentine writer Jorges Luis Borges's uses story-telling techniques as original as those of the early twentieth-century English writers. His tale "The Book of Sand," for example, is a fantastic story filled with symbolism and inspired by philosophical ideas. Told by a first-person narrator, it gains in strangeness what it lacks in conventional action. It may be brief, but it will cause you to think about its narrator's discovery and dilemma for a long time.

JORGE LUIS BORGES

(1899 – 1986)

Jorge Luis Borges (hōr′ he loo ēs′ bōr′ hes) is an Argentine writer known for his inventive, poetic, and fantastic short stories and poetry. The strangeness of his tales recalls the fiction of Edgar Allan Poe. Despite their strangeness, however, these stories deal with universal themes like the meaning of time and infinity, and the nature of personal identity. Often Borges de-emphasizes the usual fictional elements of plot and character as he pursues meaning and fantastic effects. For many years, his work was not widely known. However, he received the International Publisher's Prize in 1961, finally gaining the recognition he deserved. His book Labyrinths (1962), which contains a number of his best stories, has influenced the work of many American writers.

The Book of Sand

JORGE LUIS BORGES

Translated by Norman Thomas Di Giovanni

Thy rope of sands ...—George Herbert

The line is made up of an infinite number of points; the plane of an infinite number of lines; the volume of an infinite number of planes; the hypervolume of an infinite number of volumes. . . . No, unquestionably this is not— *more geometrico*[1]—the best way of beginning my story. To claim that it is true is nowadays the convention of every made-up story. Mine, however, is true.

I live alone in a fourth-floor apartment on Belgrano Street, in Buenos Aires.[2] Late one evening, a few months back, I heard a knock at my door. I opened it and a stranger stood there. He was a tall man, with nondescript features—or perhaps it was my myopia[3] that made them seem that way. Dressed in gray and carrying a gray suitcase in his hand, he had an unassuming look about him. I saw at once that he was a foreigner. At first, he struck me as old; only later did I realize that I had been misled by his thin blond hair, which was, in a Scandinavian sort of way, almost white. During the course of our conversation, which was not to last an hour, I found out that he came from the Orkneys.[4]

▲ **Critical Viewing** What words would you use to describe the books in this photograph? **[Interpret]**

I invited him in, pointing to a chair. He paused awhile before speaking. A kind of gloom emanated from him—as it does now from me.

"I sell Bibles," he said.

Somewhat pedantically,[5] I replied, "In this house are several English Bibles, including the first—John Wiclif's.[6] I also have Cipriano de Valera's, Luther's—which, from a literary viewpoint, is the worst—and a Latin copy of the Vulgate.[7] As you see, it's not exactly Bibles I stand in need of."

After a few moments of silence, he said, "I don't only sell Bibles. I can show you a holy book I came across on the outskirts of Bikaner.[8] It may interest you."

He opened the suitcase and laid the book on a table. It was an octavo volume, bound in cloth. There was no doubt that it had passed through many hands. Examining it, I was surprised by its unusual weight. On the spine were the words "Holy Writ" and, below them, "Bombay.[9]"

"Nineteenth century, probably," I remarked.

"I don't know," he said. "I've never found out."

---

1. *more geometrico* (môr´ ā gā´ ō me´ tri cō): By the method of geometry; a learned Latin phrase.
2. **Buenos Aires** (bwā´ nəs er´ ēz): Capital of Argentina.
3. **myopia** (mī ō´ pē ə) *n*.: Abnormal eye condition in which objects are not seen distinctly; nearsightedness.
4. **Orkneys** (ôrk´ nēs): Orkney Islands; group of islands north of Scotland.

5. **pedantically** (pe dan´ ti clklē) *adv*.: Putting unnecessary stress on minor or trivial points of learning.
6. **John Wiclif** (wĭk´ lif): (1330–1380) English religious reformer who made the first translation of the Bible into English from the Vulgate, a Latin version of the Bible authorized as the official Bible in the fourth century.
7. **Capriano de Valera's, Luther's . . . Vulgate:** Different translations of the Holy Bible.
8. **Bikaner** (bē kə nir´): City in Northwest India.
9. **Bombay** (bäm´ bā): Seaport in West India.

I opened the book at random. The script was strange to me. The pages, which were worn and typographically poor, were laid out in double columns, as in a Bible. The text was closely printed, and it was ordered in versicles. In the upper corners of the pages were Arabic numbers. I noticed that one left-hand page bore the number (let us say) 40,514 and the facing right-hand page 999. I turned the leaf; it was numbered with eight digits. It also bore a small illustration, like the kind used in dictionaries— an anchor drawn with pen and ink, as if by a schoolboy's clumsy hand.

It was at this point that the stranger said, "Look at the illustration closely. You'll never see it again."

I noted my place and closed the book. At once, I reopened it. Page by page, in vain, I looked for the illustration of the anchor. "It seems to be a version of Scriptures in some Indian language, is it not?" I said to hide my dismay.

"No," he replied. Then, as if confiding a secret, he lowered his voice. "I acquired the book in a town out on the plain in exchange for a handful of rupees and a Bible. Its owner did not know how to read. I suspect that he saw the Book of Books as a talisman. He was of the lowest caste;[10] nobody but other untouchables could tread his shadow without contamination. He told me his book was called the Book of Sand, because neither the book nor the sand has any beginning or end."

The stranger asked me to find the first page.

I laid my left hand on the cover and, trying to put my thumb on the flyleaf, I opened the book. It was useless. Every time I tried, a number of pages came between the cover and my thumb. It was as if they kept growing from the book.

"Now find the last page."

Again I failed. In a voice that was not mine, I barely managed to stammer, "This can't be."

Still speaking in a low voice, the stranger said, "It can't be, but it *is*. The number of pages in this book is no more or less than infinite. None is the first page, none the last. I don't know why they're numbered in this arbitrary way. Perhaps to suggest that the terms of an infinite series admit any number."

Then, as if he were thinking aloud, he said,

"If space is infinite, we may be at any point in space. If time is infinite, we may be at any point in time."

His speculations irritated me. "You are religious, no doubt?" I asked him.

"Yes, I'm a Presbyterian. My conscience is clear. I am reasonably sure of not having cheated the native when I gave him the word of God in exchange for his devilish book."

I assured him that he had nothing to reproach himself for, and I asked if he were just passing through this part of the world. He replied that he planned to return to his country in a few days. It was then that I learned that he was a Scot from the Orkney Islands. I told him I had a great personal affection for Scotland, through my love of Stevenson[11] and Hume.[12]

"You mean Stevenson and Robbie Burns,"[13] he corrected.

While we spoke, I kept exploring the infinite book. With feigned indifference, I asked, "Do you intend to offer this curiosity to the British Museum?"

"No. I'm offering it to you," he said, and he stipulated a rather high sum for the book.

I answered, in all truthfulness, that such a sum was out of my reach, and I began thinking. After a minute or two, I came up with a scheme.

"I propose a swap," I said. "You got this book for a handful of rupees and a copy of the Bible. I'll offer you the amount of my pension check, which I've just collected, and my black-letter Wiclif Bible. I inherited it from my ancestors."

"A black-letter Wiclif!" he murmured.

I went to my bedroom and brought him the money and the book. He turned the leaves and studied the title page with all the fervor of a true bibliophile.[14]

"It's a deal," he said.

It amazed me that he did not haggle. Only later was I to realize that he had entered my house with his mind made up to sell the book. Without counting the money, he put it away.

We talked about India, about Orkney, and

---

10. **lowest caste** (kast) *n*.: Member of the lowest social class; an "untouchable."

11. **Stevenson:** Robert Louis Stevenson, (1850–1894); Scottish novelist, poet, and essayist.
12. **Hume** (hyo͞om): David Hume, (1711–1776); Scottish philosopher and historian.
13. **Robbie Burns:** Robert Burns, (1759–1796); Scottish poet.
14. **bibliophile** (bib´ lē ə fīl´) *n*.: Person who loves or admires books.

about the Norwegian jarls[15] who once ruled it. It was night when the man left. I have not seen him again, nor do I know his name.

I thought of keeping the Book of Sand in the space left on the shelf by the Wiclif, but in the end I decided to hide it behind the volumes of a broken set of The Thousand and One Nights. I went to bed and did not sleep. At three or four in the morning, I turned on the light. I got down the impossible book and leafed through its pages. On one of them I saw engraved a mask. The upper corner of the page carried a number, which I no longer recall, elevated to the ninth power.

I showed no one my treasure. To the luck of owning it was added the fear of having it stolen, and then the misgiving that it might not truly be infinite. These twin preoccupations intensified my old misanthropy.[16] I had only a few friends left; I now stopped seeing even them. A prisoner of the book, I almost never went out anymore. After studying its frayed spine and covers with a magnifying glass, I rejected the possibility of a contrivance of any sort. The

---

15. **jarls** (yärlz) *n.*: In early Scandinavia, a chieftain or nobleman.
16. **misanthropy** (mis an´*thr*ə pē) *n.*: Hatred or distrust of all people.

small illustrations, I verified, came two thousand pages apart. I set about listing them alphabetically in a notebook, which I was not long in filling up. Never once was an illustration repeated. At night, in the meager intervals my insomnia granted, I dreamed of the book.

Summer came and went, and I realized that the book was monstrous. What good did it do me to think that I, who looked upon the volume with my eyes, who held it in my hands, was any less monstrous? I felt that the book was a nightmarish object, an obscene thing that affronted and tainted reality itself.

I thought of fire, but I feared that the burning of an infinite book might likewise prove infinite and suffocate the planet with smoke. Somewhere I recalled reading that the best place to hide a leaf is in a forest. Before retirement, I worked on Mexico Street, at the Argentine National Library, which contains nine hundred thousand volumes. I knew that to the right of the entrance a curved staircase leads down into the basement, where books and maps and periodicals are kept. One day I went there and, slipping past a member of the staff and trying not to notice at what height or distance from the door, I lost the Book of Sand on one of the basement's musty shelves.

Guide for Responding

◆ *Literature and Your Life*

Reader's Response Do you believe that a chance encounter, like the one in the story, can change a person's life? Why or why not?

Thematic Focus In what ways does the character's experience have a dreamlike quality?

☑ Check Your Comprehension

1. How did the Bible salesman acquire the Book of Sand?
2. Name everything that is unique about the Book of Sand.
3. How does the main character dispose of the Book of Sand?

◆ Critical Thinking

INTERPRET

1. (a) What is the meaning of the title of the story? (b) What does it suggest about the book? **[Interpret]**
2. How does owning the Book of Sand change the narrator's life? **[Analyze]**
3. (a) In what way is the book "devilish"? (b) How does the book affront and taint reality? **[Draw Conclusions]**

EVALUATE

4. Does Borges effectively blend elements of fantasy and elements of reality? Explain. **[Evaluate]**

Literary Connection

THE SHORT STORY

Short story writers often use the shorthand of symbolism to convey their meaning in a brief work of fiction. For D. H. Lawrence, a child's rocking horse becomes a means of summing up and criticizing a whole society's materialism. For Virginia Woolf, a looking glass symbolizes the skin-deep, superficial personality of a character. Like these authors, Borges centers his narrative on a single symbolic object. For him it is a mysterious book that appears to sum up life's infinite meaning and possibility.

1. Which writer is more effective in using symbolism—Woolf, Lawrence, or Borges? Why?
2. If you were to write story about a symbolic object, what would it be? Explain.
3. Do you think that in the next hundred years, the short story will continue to be as important a literary form as it has been in the last hundred years? Why or why not?

Idea Bank

Writing

1. **New Ending** How would you end this story if you were its author? Continue the story and develop a new ending. However, maintain Borges's use of suspense and the fantastic.

2. **Comparison and Contrast** Compare and contrast this story with one of the British stories from this section. Consider such elements as point of view, setting, plot, and theme.

3. **Response to Criticism** James E. Irby writes of Borges's tales that "The insight they provide is ironic, pathetic: a painful sense of inevitable limits that block total aspirations." Is this remark true of "The Book of Sand"? Why or why not?

Researching and Representing

4. **Model of the Book of Sand** Scan the story for descriptions of The Book of Sand. Then, using the details you find, create a model of the book that you can display in your classroom. **[Art Link]**

5. **Geometry and the Short Story** Borges begins the story with geometric principles. Research those principles and then apply them in order to understand the story. Write a brief essay, with mathematical diagrams, in which you present your conclusions to the class. **[Math Link]**

Online Activity www.phlit.phschool.com

Writing Process Workshop

During the twentieth century, the short story came into its own as a literary form. Its brevity and its focus on a few characters and settings were appropriate for an intense and fast-paced world.

Write a short story of your own. Your brief fictional narrative should include a limited number of characters and settings, with a plot centered on a conflict involving the main character. The narrator who tells your story may or may not be a character in the story. If possible, your story should convey a central message about life or human nature.

These writing skills, introduced in the Mini-Lessons in this section, will help you write your story.

Writing Skills Focus

▶ **Elaborate to entertain** by including interesting and unusual details. (See p. 1051.)

▶ **Create suspense** by raising questions in the mind of your reader; create a feeling of growing curiosity. (See p. 1065.)

▶ **Develop the story to a climax and resolution** by advancing the conflict to a high point, then explaining how it is resolved. (See p. 1083.)

This brief passage from Conrad's "The Lagoon" contains or suggests many elements of a short story.

Joseph Conrad

MODEL FROM LITERATURE

from "The Lagoon" by Joseph Conrad

Arsat went on in an even, low voice ①:

"We ran our canoe on the white beach of a little bay close to a long tongue of land that seemed to bar our road; a long wooded cape going far into the sea. ② My brother knew that place. . . . No sooner had I closed my eyes than I heard her cry of alarm ③. We leaped up. . . and coming in sight in the opening of the bay we saw a prau manned by many paddlers. We knew it at once; it was one of our Rajah's praus." ④

① The action and dialogue in this passage are building to a high point.

② This sentence creates suspense. It makes the reader wonder what will happen next.

③ This detail heightens the suspense.

④ An unusual detail, the Malayan boat, adds interest to the story.

Applying LANGUAGE SKILLS:
Writing Dialogue

Through dialogue, a character's own words reveal his or her personality. Dialogue can also do the following:

- **Enhance setting.**
  Narration: It was a starry night.
  Dialogue: "I've never seen so many stars in the sky."

- **Advance the plot.**
  Narration: She sent Charlie to get the police.
  Dialogue: "Charlie! Get the police!"

- **Create a mood.**
  Narration: The team felt depressed and grim.
  Dialogue: "Who cares, anymore?"

Practice Rewrite the following, using dialogue.

It was a stormy night. Gerry's mother called for him to come inside. Gerry pretended not to hear and continued telling his friend Jack about last night's big game. Suddenly, a bolt of lighting struck near them and sent Jack flying. Gerry screamed to his mother to get help.

Writer's Solution Connection
Writing Lab

For help in finding story ideas, use the Story Wheel in the Choosing a Topic section of the Narration tutorial.

Prewriting

Choose a Topic Using a real series of events or your own imagination as inspiration, decide on a character and a situation for your short story. If you're having trouble coming up with ideas, try one of these:

Topic Ideas

- A servant is accused of stealing.
- A series of misunderstandings occurs.

Selection-Related Topic Ideas

- A person comes to a painful realization.
- A mysterious woman appears.
- A boy develops special abilities.

Develop Character Decide on the characters for your story and take notes about their personalities, habits, desires, as well as about their appearance, income level, and background.

Plot Diagram Rough out the events for your short story by filling in a plot diagram such as this one. Identify the major events that form the story's exposition, the events that build conflict, the climax, and the resolution of the conflict.

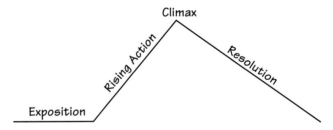

Drafting

Draft the Climax and Resolution Some writers find it easier to write the high point of the story first, then backtrack to the exposition. With your story ending in place, you can focus on creating suspense and interest.

Develop Setting Although most short stories contain only one setting, that setting may have a significant impact on the story and help to create mood and atmosphere. As you draft your story, bring the setting to life through vivid descriptions or dialogue.

Revising

Follow these Tips for Revising:

▶ **Character** Give a boring character a quirk or endearing habit to make him or her more interesting. Revise dialogue to make your characters more believable and sympathetic. Eliminate unnecessary characters from the story.

▶ **Plot** Examine plot events to ensure that they make sense and build suspense. To build suspense, try hinting at an ominous event before it happens.

▶ **Setting** Make the setting a part of the story by adding vivid sensory details to enhance your description. Consider using details from the setting to hint at the story's outcome.

REVISION MODEL

① *glowered*
The sun ~~shone down on me~~ at me as I biked down the desert

highway. Head down, I hunched my shoulders and felt the

② *"Nobody but me in this crazy old world,"*
sweat trickle down my back. I suddenly shouted at the top of

my lungs. No one looked at me or yelled back because there

③ *Literally.*
was no one. ④ *With a loud squawk and a battering of wings, a desert*
bird flew directly over my shoulder and headed for the sun.
It turned around in midair and poised as if to attack, then,
silently and suddenly, it dropped like a stone out of the sky
and smashed to the ground.

① To make the setting more dynamic, the verb *glowered* replaced a standard descriptive phrase.

② This dialogue reveals the character's situation and his attitude.

③ This fragment adds interest and will make readers feel slightly uneasy.

④ This passage was added to foreshadow the danger that is to come.

Publishing

▶ **Festival** Hold a storytelling festival in which students read their short stories to an invited audience.

▶ **Videotape** Adapt your short story for film. Create a video-script and ask your classmates to serve as the cast and crew.

▶ **Contest** Enter a student fiction contest, for example, the *Seventeen Magazine* Fiction Contest. Ask your teacher or librarian for contest information.

APPLYING LANGUAGE SKILLS: Using Active Voice

Your short story will be more exciting if you use the active voice. The active voice indicates that the subject of the sentence performs an action; the passive voice indicates that the subject receives the action, or is acted upon.

Passive Voice:
The candle was lit by Brian.

Active Voice:
Brian lit the candle.

Practice Rewrite this paragraph, using the active voice.

After the award was won by Stephanie, she was given a ride home by her friend, Marvin. The car ride was felt by them to be too bumpy. The car was then stopped by Marvin and Stephanie was asked by him to get out and see if the tires were okay.

Writing Application As you revise your story, replace the passive voice with the active voice—unless you want to disguise who or what performed an action.

Writer's Solution Connection Writing Lab

For help in punctuating dialogue, complete the Semicolons, Colons, and Quotation Marks lesson in the Punctuation unit.

Student Success Workshop

Research Skills — Organizing Information Gathered Through Research

Strategies for Success

Organizing and recording information that you've gathered through research can be a daunting task. The strategies of summarizing and condensing text by note taking, outlining, and creating graphic organizers will help you remember information and allow you to refer back to it easily.

Take Notes and Summarize When you take notes, identify and write down the main ideas and supporting details. Be selective in choosing details. Leave space under your main points to add more details. Summarizing is another useful organizational tool. When you write a summary, use complete sentences and paragraphs and include the main ideas in the text.

Outline An outline organizes information by arranging it in a structure that shows main ideas or topics, subtopics, and supporting facts. The organization of information in an outline is easy to understand because successively less important information is indented. Whether you create a formal or an informal outline, include only the important and relevant information.

Use Graphic Organizers Graphic organizers— such as diagrams, maps, and charts—are especially effective in showing relationships among ideas and concepts. A comparison chart, for example, will show you how two or more things are alike and different. A cause-and-effect diagram shows how events can cause other events to occur. Be precise, because you will have limited space.

Apply the Strategies

Read the sample text, and answer the questions that follow:

> Whatever happened to the cozy neighborhood bookstore? The days of privately owned, small bookstores seem to be ending. In 1986, 54 percent of the U.S. population purchased books from small, unpretentious bookstores. By 1998, this number had plummeted to 17 percent. The reason? Huge chain stores can afford to offer discount prices and provide features, such as cafes and music sections. Many small stores, unable to compete, have been forced into bankruptcy. Some small stores have survived only because they provide customers with personal services, author readings, and book clubs. Owners and patrons of these stores don't believe that bigger is better.

1. If you were taking notes, how would you organize the main ideas and details in the text?
2. How would you summarize it?
3. If you were outlining this text, what main heads and subheads would you use?
4. What kind of graphic organizers would best represent the text? Why?

✔ Here are situations in which to organize researched information:
▶ Writing a term paper
▶ Comparing the positions of two political candidates
▶ Choosing between two products you might buy
▶ Noting key events in a biography

PART 4

From the National to the Global

Political World, Kenneth Eward

Guide for Interpreting

Dylan Thomas *(1914–1953)*

Playful with language and exuberant about life, Thomas also had a darker side, evident in his poems of death and the loss of childhood innocence. Dylan Thomas was born in Swansea, Wales, and wrote many of his best-known poems before he turned twenty. As a teenager, he also produced source books of ideas that served as a basis for later works.

Visits to America At the age of twenty, Thomas went to London, where he worked in journalism, broadcasting, and filmmaking. In 1950, he made the first of four trips to the United States. Audiences here embraced him not only for his theatrical readings of his poems but for the freshness of his poetic voice.

An Artist's Problems Though acclaimed at an early age, Thomas struggled with poverty and alcoholism. In later years, he had difficulty achieving the focus needed to write poetry and turned instead to prose, producing two of the works for which he is best known, *Under Milkwood*, a play for voices, and *A Child's Christmas in Wales*, a memoir. Dylan Thomas died while on a trip to the United States, where he planned to collaborate on an opera with Igor Stravinsky.

Ted Hughes *(1930–1998)*

Born in rural West Yorkshire, Hughes spent much of his youth hunting and fishing with his brother. These experiences contributed to his lifelong interest in the beauty and violence of nature, recurring themes in his work.

Hughes and His Father It would be a mistake, however, to ignore the violence of World War I as an influence on Hughes. He was born well after that war, but his father had had terrible experiences in it. Hughes once said that, as a child, he was strongly affected by his father's silence about those experiences.

Hughes himself served in the Royal Air Force and then studied archaeology and anthropology at Pembroke College, Cambridge, where he met the American poet Sylvia Plath. He married Plath in 1956, but they later separated.

A Variety of Work Best known for volumes of poetry like *Hawk in the Rain*, *Crow*, and *Moortown*, Hughes wrote a variety of works. These include books for children, a play in an invented language, and fiction like "The Rain Horse." In 1984, he was named poet laureate of England.

◆ Background for Understanding

LITERATURE: THOMAS, HUGHES, AND WRITERS' ATTITUDES TOWARD NATURE

Is nature an arena of bloody competition, "red in tooth and claw," as Tennyson writes? Is it something in which we can trust, as Wordsworth suggests: "Nature never did betray/The heart that loved her"? The answer is that different poets "see" different things in the natural world.

Dylan Thomas was fascinated by nature's double face: life and death. He refers to both creation and destruction in the title of one of his most famous poems, "The Force That Through the Green Fuse Drives the Flower." The color green suggests life and vitality, but the word *fuse*—a figure of speech for the flower's stem—suggests a bomb's fuse. In "Fern Hill," the double face of nature is also evident: "Time held me green and dying." Through most of the poem, however, Thomas stresses nature's sweet greenness, associated with childhood.

Ted Hughes was attuned to nature's violence. In "Hawk Roosting," a poem not included here, he has the hawk say, "I kill where I please . . ." This violence may be present in "The Rain Horse," but does it come from nature or from the human mind?

Do Not Go Gentle into That Good Night
Fern Hill ◆ The Horses ◆ The Rain Horse

◆ *Literature and Your Life*

CONNECT YOUR EXPERIENCE

Maybe you live on a mountain and can step out your door into a glorious sunset or sunrise. Perhaps you live in the suburbs, where houses have neat lawns but crows, raccoons, and deer are shy or feisty neighbors. Maybe you're a big-city person who finds nature in a park—pigeons, squirrels, and starlings—but can occasionally spot a peregrine falcon mistaking a church for a cliff. Wherever you live, nature is all around you. In fact, it's your home.

These poets reflect on what a strangely familiar home nature is, rocking us *awake* in its cradle or haunting us with memories.

Journal Writing Describe a memorable encounter you had with nature. Include as many specific details as you can.

THEMATIC FOCUS: FROM THE NATIONAL TO THE GLOBAL

Notice how these writers describe scenes that are local but address concerns that are universal.

◆ Literary Focus

VOICE

In the same way you recognize a friend's voice, you can recognize the **voices** of different poets, their "sound" on the page. This distinctive voice is based on word choice and combinations, sound devices, pace of "speaking," attitude, and even patterns of vowels and consonants.

Dylan Thomas, for example, tends to tumble words out, "speaking" in a rush: "All the sun long it was running, it was lovely . . ." Hughes, however, speaks in a different voice, giving you little separate blips of images: "Not a leaf, not a bird." People who knew him claim that he really did speak that way!

◆ Grammar and Style

SENTENCE BEGINNINGS: ADVERB CLAUSES

To add variety to their writing, Dylan Thomas and Ted Hughes sometimes begin sentences with **adverb clauses,** subordinate clauses that modify verbs, adverbs, and adjectives and answer the questions *when, why,* or *under what conditions.*

Example: *As he watched it,* the horse ran up to that crest . . .

◆ Reading Strategy

JUDGE THE MESSAGE

Reading involves not only understanding a **writer's message** but also **judging** it. In this process, you test what a writer says against your own experience and your past reading. Such testing helps you to keep and use ideas that make sense to you and to discard ones that don't.

The message of "Do Not Go Gentle into That Good Night" is that dying people should fight against death. Don't simply ignore this idea or accept it blindly. Use what you know to judge it. Would you give Thomas's advice to a person, real or imaginary, who was very sick? Why or why not?

◆ Build Vocabulary

LATIN ROOTS: -vol-

In "The Rain Horse," the narrator suspects the horse of having malevolent intentions. The word *malevolent* contains the root -vol-, meaning "wish." Combined with the prefix *mal-,* meaning "evil," the root offers a clue to the word's definition, "wishing evil."

WORD BANK

Before you read, preview this list of words from the poems.

| grieved |
| transfiguring |
| exasperated |
| nondescript |
| malevolent |

Do Not Go Gentle into That Good Night

Dylan Thomas

Fisherman at Sea off the Needles, J. M. W. Turner, Tate Gallery

Do not go gentle into that good night,
Old age should burn and rave at close of day:
Rage, rage against the dying of the light.

Though wise men at their end know dark is right,
5 Because their words had forked no lightning they
Do not go gentle into that good night.

Good men, the last wave by, crying how bright
Their frail deeds might have danced in a green bay,
Rage, rage against the dying of the light.

10 Wild men who caught and sang the sun in flight,
And learn, too late, they grieved it on its way,
Do not go gentle into that good night.

Grave men, near death, who see with blinding sight
Blind eyes could blaze like meteors and be gay,
15 Rage, rage against the dying of the light.

And you, my father, there on the sad height,
Curse, bless, me now with your fierce tears, I pray.
Do not go gentle into that good night.
Rage, rage against the dying of the light.

◆ **Build Vocabulary**

grieved (grēvd) *v.*: Caused to feel deep grief;
mourned, felt deep grief for

�◀ Critical Viewing In what ways is the main boat in this
painting an apt image of the soul's struggle against the
"good night"? [Analyze]

Fern Hill

Dylan Thomas

Now as I was young and easy under the apple boughs
About the lilting house and happy as the grass was green,
    The night above the dingle starry,
      Time let me hail and climb
5   Golden in the heydays of his eyes,
And honored among wagons I was prince of the apple towns
And once below a time I lordly had the trees and leaves
      Trail with daisies and barley
    Down the rivers of the windfall light.

10 And as I was green and carefree, famous among the barns
About the happy yard and singing as the farm was home,
    In the sun that is young once only,
      Time let me play and be
    Golden in the mercy of his means,
15 And green and golden I was huntsman and herdsman, the calves
Sang to my horn, the foxes on the hills barked clear and cold,
      And the sabbath rang slowly
    In the pebbles of the holy streams.

All the sun long it was running, it was lovely, the hay
20 Fields high as the house, the tunes from the chimneys, it was air
     And playing, lovely and watery
       And fire green as grass.
     And nightly under the simple stars
As I rode to sleep the owls were bearing the farm away,
25 All the moon long I heard, blessed among stables, the nightjars[1]
      Flying with the ricks,[2] and the horses
       Flashing into the dark.

And then to awake, and the farm, like a wanderer white
With the dew, come back, the cock on his shoulder; it was all
30   Shining, it was Adam and maiden,
      The sky gathered again
    And the sun grew round that very day.
So it must have been after the birth of the simple light
In the first, spinning place, the spellbound horses walking warm
35   Out of the whinnying green stable
      On to the fields of praise.

---

1. nightjars *n.*: Common nocturnal birds, named for the
whirring sound that the male makes.
2. ricks *n.*: Haystacks.

And honored among foxes and pheasants by the gay house
Under the new made clouds and happy as the heart was long,
   In the sun born over and over,
40   I ran my heedless ways,
   My wishes raced through the house-high hay
And nothing I cared, at my sky blue trades, that time allows
In all his tuneful turning so few and such morning songs
   Before the children green and golden
45   Follow him out of grace,

Nothing I cared, in the lamb white days, that time would take me
Up to the swallow thronged loft by the shadow of my hand,
   In the moon that is always rising,
     Nor that riding to sleep
50   I should hear him fly with the high fields
And wake to the farm forever fled from the childless land.
Oh as I was young and easy in the mercy of his means,
   Time held me green and dying
Though I sang in my chains like the sea.

Guide for Responding

◆ Literature and Your Life

Reader's Response Which poem do you like better? Why?

Thematic Focus Does Thomas succeed in moving beyond his own personal concerns in these poems? Explain.

☑ Check Your Comprehension

1. (a) What is the "good night" mentioned in the title of "Do Not Go Gentle into That Good Night"? (b) Who are the four kinds of men the poet describes in the poem?
2. (a) To whom is the "Do not go gentle" addressed? (b) What does the poet tell the person he is addressing?
3. Use Thomas's images in "Fern Hill" to describe the farm he used to visit there.
4. In "Fern Hill," what two colors does the speaker use to describe himself in his youth?
5. In the last stanza of "Fern Hill," where does the speaker suggest that time has taken him?

◆ Critical Thinking

INTERPRET

1. (a) In "Fern Hill," how would you describe the speaker's feelings about his childhood? (b) What are some of the words and phrases that convey this feeling? **[Analyze]**
2. The mood in the last stanza of "Fern Hill" changes from that in the preceding stanzas. (a) What is the change? (b) What lines or phrases earlier in the poem foreshadow that change? **[Interpret]**
3. In "Do Not Go Gentle into That Good Night," why do you think Thomas wants his father to "rage against the dying of the light"? **[Infer]**
4. Basing your answer on these two poems and using your own words, summarize Thomas's attitudes toward the different stages of life. **[Draw Conclusions]**

APPLY

5. Which of the four kinds of men mentioned in "Do Not Go Gentle into That Good Night" do you think Thomas saw himself as? Why? **[Speculate]**

The Horses

Ted Hughes

I climbed through woods in the hour-before-dawn dark.
Evil air, a frost-making stillness,

Not a leaf, not a bird—
A world cast in frost. I came out above the wood

5   Where my breath left tortuous statues in the iron light.
But the valleys were draining the darkness

Till the moorline—blackening dregs of the brightening gray—
Halved the sky ahead. And I saw the horses:

Huge in the dense gray—ten together—
10   Megalith-still.[1] They breathed, making no move,

With draped manes and tilted hind-hooves,
Making no sound.

I passed: not one snorted or jerked its head.
Gray silent fragments

15   Of a gray silent world.

I listened in emptiness on the moor-ridge.
The curlew's[2] tear turned its edge on the silence.

Slowly detail leafed from the darkness. Then the sun
Orange, red, red erupted

20   Silently, and splitting to its core tore and flung cloud,
Shook the gulf open, showed blue,

And the big planets hanging—
I turned

Stumbling in the fever of a dream, down towards
25   The dark woods, from the kindling tops.

---

1. **Megalith-still:** Still as the huge stones left by ancient peoples, such as those at Stonehenge.
2. **curlew** (kʉr´ lōō) *n*.: Large, brownish wading bird with long legs.

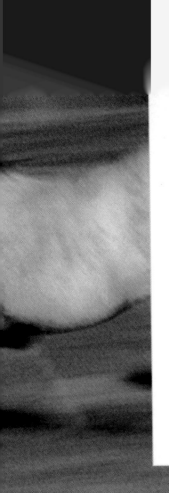

And came to the horses.
                                There, still they stood,
But now steaming and glistening under the flow of light,

Their draped stone manes, their tilted hind-hooves
30   Stirring under a thaw while all around them

The frost showed its fires. But still they made no sound.
Not one snorted or stamped,

Their hung heads patient as the horizons,
High over valleys, in the red leveling rays—

35   In din of the crowded streets, going among the years, the faces,
May I still meet my memory in so lonely a place

Between the streams and the red clouds, hearing curlews,
Hearing the horizons endure.

◀ **Critical Viewing** Contrast the horses in the poem with those in the picture. Do both convey the power of the horse? Explain. **[Compare and Contrast]**

Guide for Responding

◆ Literature and Your Life

Reader's Response What kind of place or scene would you like to remember later, in "the crowded streets, going among the years"? Why?

Thematic Focus In what way does this poem touch upon issues that ecologists discuss?

Sketch Briefly sketch one of the scenes that Hughes describes in the poem.

☑ Check Your Comprehension

1. What is the setting of the poem (time, place, weather)?
2. What are the horses doing?
3. What wish does the speaker make near the end of the poem?

◆ Critical Thinking

INTERPRET

1. Compare and contrast the horses in the first and second sighting. **[Compare and Contrast]**
2. (a) What figure of speech is found in line 33? (b) How do you explain the comparison? **[Analyze]**
3. What view of nature does this poem express? **[Draw Conclusions]**

EVALUATE

4. Are horses a good symbol for what the poet is expressing about nature? Explain. **[Criticize]**

APPLY

5. What are some of the reasons people might have for cherishing memories of solitary experiences? **[Generalize]**

The Rain Horse

Ted Hughes

s the young man came over the hill the first thin blowing of rain met him. He turned his coat-collar up and stood on top of the shelving rabbit-riddled hedgebank, looking down into the valley.

He had come too far. What had set out as a walk along pleasantly-remembered tarmac[1] lanes had turned dreamily by gate and path and hedge-gap into a cross-ploughland trek, his shoes ruined, the dark mud of the lower fields inching up the trouser legs of his gray suit where they rubbed against each other. And now there was a raw, flapping wetness in the air that would be downpour again at any minute. He shivered, holding himself tense against the cold.

This was the view he had been thinking of. Vaguely, without really directing his walk, he had felt he would get the whole thing from this point. For twelve years, whenever he had re-called this scene, he had imagined it as it looked from here. Now the valley lay sunken in front of him, utterly deserted, shallow, bare fields, black and sodden as the bed of an an-cient lake after the weeks of rain.

Nothing happened. Not that he had looked forward to any very transfiguring experience. But he had expected something, some plea-sure, some meaningful sensation, he didn't quite know what.

So he waited, trying to nudge the right feel-ings alive with the details—the surprisingly familiar curve of the hedges, the stone gate-pillar and iron gatehook let into it that he had used as a target, the long bank of the rabbit-warren on which he stood and which had been the first thing he ever noticed about the hill when twenty years ago, from the distance of the village, he had said to himself "That looks like rabbits."

Twelve years had changed him. This land no longer recognized him, and he looked back at it coldly, as at a finally visited home-country, known only through the stories of a grandfather; felt nothing but the dullness of feeling nothing. Boredom. Then, suddenly, impatience, with a whole exasperated swarm of little anxieties about his shoes, and the spitting rain and his new suit and that sky and the two-mile trudge through the mud back to the road.

It would be quicker to go straight forward to the farm a mile away in the valley and behind which the road looped. But the thought of meeting the farmer—to be embarrassingly remembered or shouted at as a trespasser—deterred him. He saw the rain pulling up out of the distance, dragging its gray broken columns, smudging the trees and the farms.

A wave of anger went over him: anger against himself for blundering into this mud-trap and anger against the land that made him feel so outcast, so old and stiff and stupid. He wanted nothing but to get away from it as quickly as possible. But as he turned, something moved in his eye-corner. All his senses startled alert. He stopped.

Over to his right a thin, black horse was running across the ploughland to-wards the hill, its head down, neck stretched out. It seemed to be running on its toes like a cat, like a dog up to no good.

> ◆ **Reading Strategy**
> Here the author begins to set up his message. What is the man's relation to the land? In what way is the horse an "answer" to his anger and impatience? What does the phrase "nightmarish leop-ard" suggest?

---

1. **tarmac:** Material used for paving.

From the high point on which he stood the hill dipped slightly and rose to another crested point fringed with the tops of trees, three hundred yards to his right. As he watched it, the horse ran up to that crest, showed against the sky—for a moment like a nightmarish leopard—and disappeared over the other side.

For several seconds he stared at the skyline, stunned by the unpleasantly strange impression the horse had made on him. Then the plastering beat of icy rain on his bare skull brought him to himself. The distance had vanished in a wall of gray. All around him the fields were jumping and streaming.

Holding his collar close and tucking his chin down into it he ran back over the hilltop towards the town-side, the lee-side, his feet sucking and splashing, at every stride plunging to the ankle.

This hill was shaped like a wave, a gently rounded back lifting out of the valley to a sharply crested, almost concave front hanging over the river meadows towards the town. Down this front, from the crest, hung two small woods separated by a fallow field. The near wood was nothing more than a quarry, circular, full of stones and bracken,[2] with a few thorns and nondescript saplings, foxholes and rabbit holes. The other was rectangular, mainly a planting of scrub oak trees. Beyond the river smoldered the town like a great heap of blue cinders.

He ran along the top of the first wood and finding no shelter but the thin, leafless thorns of the hedge, dipped below the crest out of the

---

2. **bracken:** Large, coarse ferns.

◆ Build Vocabulary

transfiguring (trans fig´ yər iŋ) *adj.*: Changing the appearance of a thing or person, especially so as to glorify it

exasperated (eg zas´ pər āt´ id) *adj.*: Extremely annoyed; out of patience

nondescript (nän´ di skript´) *adj.*: Lacking identifying characteristics; bland

wind and jogged along through thick grass to the wood of oaks. In blinding rain he lunged through the barricade of brambles at the wood's edge. The little crippled trees were small choice in the way of shelter, but at a sudden fierce thickening of the rain he took one at random and crouched down under the leaning trunk.

Still panting from his run, drawing his knees up tightly, he watched the bleak lines of rain, gray as hail, slanting through the boughs into

Rearing Horse, Kazuyuki Hashimoto

▲ **Critical Viewing** The horse in the photograph, like the horse in the story, is a symbol of untamed natural power. How does the photographer emphasize the energy and wildness of horses? **[Apply]**

the clumps of bracken and bramble. He felt hidden and safe. The sound of the rain as it rushed and lulled in the wood seemed to seal him in. Soon the chilly sheet lead of his suit became a tight, warm mold, and gradually he sank into a state of comfort that was all but trance, though the rain beat steadily on his exposed shoulders and trickled down the oak trunk on to his neck.

All around him the boughs angled down, glistening, black as iron. From their tips and elbows the drops hurried steadily, and the channels of the bark pulsed and gleamed. For a time he amused himself calculating the variation in the rainfall by the variations in a dribble of water from a trembling twig-end two feet in front of his nose. He studied the twig, bringing dwarfs and continents and animals out of its scurfy bark. Beyond the boughs the blue shoal of the town was rising and falling, and darkening and fading again, in the pale, swaying backdrop of rain.

He wanted this rain to go on forever. Whenever it seemed to be drawing off he listened anxiously until it closed in again. As long as it lasted he was suspended from life and time. He didn't want to return to his sodden shoes and his possibly ruined suit and the walk back over that land of mud.

All at once he shivered. He hugged his knees to squeeze out the cold and found himself thinking of the horse. The hair on the nape of his neck prickled slightly. He remembered how it had run up to the crest and showed against the sky.

He tried to dismiss the thought. Horses wander about the countryside often enough. But the image of the horse as it had appeared against the sky stuck in his mind. It must have come over the crest just above the wood in which he was now sitting. To clear his mind, he twisted around and looked up the wood between the tree stems, to his left.

At the wood top, with the silvered gray light coming in behind it, the black horse was standing under the oaks, its head high and alert, its ears pricked, watching him.

A horse sheltering from the rain generally goes into a sort of stupor, tilts a hind hoof and hangs its head and lets its eyelids droop, and so it stays as long as the rain lasts. This horse was nothing like that. It was watching him intently, standing perfectly still, its soaked neck and flank shining in the hard light.

◆ *Literature and Your Life*

Think of a moment when you were alone and suddenly came upon an animal. How did it behave? Were you alarmed?

He turned back. His scalp went icy and he shivered. What was he to do? Ridiculous to try driving it away. And to leave the wood, with the rain still coming down full pelt, was out of the question. Meanwhile the idea of being watched became more and more unsettling until at last he had to twist around again, to see if the horse had moved. It stood exactly as before.

This was absurd. He took control of himself and turned back

deliberately, determined not to give the horse one more thought. If it wanted to share the wood with him, let it. If it wanted to stare at him, let it. He was nestling firmly into these resolutions when the ground shook and he heard the crash of a heavy body coming down the wood. Like lightning his legs bounded him upright and about face. The horse was almost on top of him, its head stretching forwards, ears flattened and lips lifted back from the long yellow teeth. He got one snapshot glimpse of the red-veined eyeball as he flung himself backwards around the tree. Then he was away up the slope, whipped by oak twigs as he leapt the brambles and brushwood, twisting between the close trees till he tripped and sprawled. As he fell the warning flashed through his head that he must at all costs keep his suit out of the leaf-mold, but a more urgent instinct was already rolling him violently sideways. He spun around, sat up and looked back, ready to scramble off in a flash to one side. He was panting from the sudden excitement and effort. The horse had disappeared. The wood was empty except for the drumming, slant gray rain, dancing the bracken and glittering from the branches.

He got up, furious. Knocking the dirt and leaves from his suit as well as he could he looked around for a weapon. The horse was evidently mad, had an abscess on its brain or something of the sort. Or maybe it was just spiteful. Rain sometimes puts creatures into queer states. Whatever it was, he was going to get away from the wood as quickly as possible, rain or no rain.

Since the horse seemed to have gone on down the wood, his way to the farm over the hill was clear. As he went, he broke a yard length of wrist-thick dead branch from one of the oaks, but immediately threw it aside and wiped the slime of rotten wet bark from his hands with his soaked handkerchief. Already he was thinking it incredible that the horse could have meant to attack him. Most likely it was just going down the wood for better shelter and had made a feint[3] at him in passing—as much out of curiosity or playfulness as anything. He recalled the way horses menace each other when they are galloping around in a paddock.

---

3. **feint:** Pretend attack.

The wood rose to a steep bank topped by the hawthorn hedge that ran along the whole ridge of the hill. He was pulling himself up to a thin place in the hedge by the bare stem of one of the hawthorns when he ducked and shrank down again. The swelling gradient of fields lay in front of him, smoking in the slowly crossing rain. Out in the middle of the first field, tall as a statue, and a ghostly silver in the under-cloud light, stood the horse, watching the wood.

He lowered his head slowly, slithered back down the bank and crouched. An awful feeling of helplessness came over him. He felt certain the horse had been looking straight at him. Waiting for him? Was it clairvoyant?[4] Maybe a mad animal can be clairvoyant. At the same time he was ashamed to find himself acting so inanely, ducking and creeping about in this way just to keep out of sight of a horse. He tried to imagine how anybody in their senses would just walk off home. This cooled him a little, and he retreated farther down the wood. He would go back the way he had come, along under the hill crest, without any more nonsense.

The wood hummed and the rain was a cold weight, but he observed this rather than felt it. The water ran down inside his clothes and squelched in his shoes as he eased his way carefully over the bedded twigs and leaves. At every instant he expected to see the prick-eared black head looking down at him from the hedge above.

At the woodside he paused, close against a tree. The success of this last manoeuvre was restoring his confidence, but he didn't want to venture out into the open field without making sure that the horse was just where he had left it. The perfect move would be to withdraw quietly and leave the horse standing out there in the rain. He crept up again among the trees to the crest and peeped through the hedge.

The gray field and the whole slope were empty. He searched the distance. The horse was quite likely to have forgotten him altogether and wandered off. Then he raised himself and leaned out to see if it had come in close to the hedge. Before he was aware of anything the ground shook. He twisted around wildly to see how he had been caught. The

black shape was above him, right across the light. Its whinnying snort and the spattering whack of its hooves seemed to be actually inside his head as he fell backwards down the bank, and leapt again like a madman, dodging among the oaks, imagining how the buffet would come and how he would be knocked headlong. Half-way down the wood the oaks gave way to bracken and old roots and stony rabbit diggings. He was well out into the middle of this before he realized that he was running alone.

Gasping for breath now and cursing mechanically, without a thought for his suit he sat down on the ground to rest his shaking legs, letting the rain plaster the hair down over his forehead and watching the dense flashing lines disappear abruptly into the soil all around him as if he were watching through thick plate glass. He took deep breaths in the effort to steady his heart and regain control of himself. His right trouser turn-up was ripped at the seam and his suit jacket was splashed with the yellow mud of the top field.

Obviously the horse had been farther along the hedge above the steep field, waiting for him to come out at the woodside just as he had intended. He must have peeped through the hedge—peeping the wrong way—within yards of it.

However, this last attack had cleared up one thing. He need no longer act like a fool out of mere uncertainty as to whether the horse was simply being playful or not. It was definitely after him. He picked up two stones about the size of goose eggs and set off towards the bottom of the wood, striding carelessly.

A loop of the river bordered all this farm-land. If he crossed the little level meadow at the bottom of the wood, he could follow the three-mile circuit, back to the road. There were deep hollows in the river-bank, shoaled with pebbles, as he remembered, perfect places to defend himself from if the horse followed him out there.

The hawthorns that choked the bottom of the wood—some of them good-sized trees—

◆ Literary Focus
Consider the writer's use of phrases such as "whinnying snort" and "spattering whack." Describe the voice such word choices create—is it distant or engaged, slow or rapid?

---

4. **clairvoyant:** Having the supernatural ability to see what is not present or to read minds.

knitted into an almost impassable barrier. He had found a place where the growth thinned slightly and had begun to lift aside the long spiny stems, pushing himself forward, when he stopped. Through the bluish veil of bare twigs he saw the familiar shape out in the field below the wood.

But it seemed not to have noticed him yet. It was looking out across the field towards the river. Quietly, he released himself from the thorns and climbed back across the clearing towards the one side of the wood he had not yet tried. If the horse would only stay down there he could follow his first and easiest plan, up the wood and over the hilltop to the farm.

Now he noticed that the sky had grown much darker. The rain was heavier every second, pressing down as if the earth had to be flooded before nightfall. The oaks ahead blurred and the ground drummed. He began to run. And as he ran he heard a deeper sound running with him. He whirled around. The horse was in the middle of the clearing. It might have been running to get out of the terrific rain except that it was coming straight for him, scattering clay and stones, with an immensely supple and powerful motion. He let out a tearing roar and threw the stone in his right hand. The result was instantaneous. Whether at the roar or the stone the horse reared as if against a wall and shied to the left. As it dropped back on its fore-feet he flung his second stone, at ten yards' range, and saw a bright mud blotch suddenly appear on the glistening black flank. The horse surged down the wood, splashing the earth like water, tossing its long tail as it plunged out of sight among the hawthorns.

He looked around for stones. The encounter had set the blood beating in his head and given him a savage energy. He could have killed the horse at that moment. That this brute should pick him and play with him in this malevolent fashion was more than he could bear. Whoever owned it, he thought, deserved to have its neck broken for letting the dangerous thing loose.

He came out at the woodside, in open battle now, still searching for the right stones. There were plenty here, piled and scattered where they had been ploughed out of the field. He selected two, then straightened and saw the horse twenty yards off in the middle of the steep field, watching him calmly. They looked at each other.

"Out of it!" he shouted, brandishing his arm. "Out of it! Go on!" The horse twitched its pricked ears. With all his force he threw. The stone soared and landed beyond with a soft thud. He re-armed and threw again. For several minutes he kept up his bombardment without a single hit, working himself into a despair and throwing more and more wildly, till his arm began to ache with the unaccustomed exercise. Throughout the performance the horse watched him fixedly. Finally he had to stop and ease his shoulder muscle. As if the horse had been waiting for just this, it dipped its head twice and came at him.

He snatched up two stones and roaring with all his strength flung the one in his right hand. He was astonished at the crack of the impact. It was as if he had struck a tile—and the horse actually stumbled. With another roar he jumped forward and hurled his other stone. His aim seemed to be under superior guidance. The stone struck and rebounded straight up into the air, spinning fiercely, as the horse swirled away and went careering down towards the far bottom of the field, at first with great, swinging leaps, then at a canter,[5] leaving deep churned holes in the soil.

It turned up the far side of the field, climbing till it was level with him. He felt a little surprise of pity to see it shaking its head, and once it paused to lower its head and paw over its ear with its fore-hoof as a cat does.

"You stay there!" he shouted. "Keep your distance and you'll not get hurt."

And indeed the horse did stop at that moment, almost obediently. It watched him as he climbed to the crest.

The rain swept into his face and he realized that he was freezing, as if his very flesh were sodden. The farm seemed miles away over the dreary fields. Without another glance at the horse—he felt too exhausted to care now what it did—he loaded the crook of his left arm with stones and plunged out on to the waste of mud.

He was half-way to the first hedge before the horse appeared, silhouetted against the sky at

---

5. **canter:** Gait like a slow gallop.

the corner of the wood, head high and attentive, watching his laborious retreat over the three fields.

The ankle-deep clay dragged at him. Every stride was a separate, deliberate effort, forcing him up and out of the sucking earth, burdened as he was by his sogged clothes and load of stone and limbs that seemed themselves to be turning to mud. He fought to keep his breathing even, two strides in, two strides out, the air ripping his lungs. In the middle of the last field he stopped and looked around. The horse, tiny on the skyline, had not moved.

At the corner of the field he unlocked his clasped arms and dumped the stones by the gatepost, then leaned on the gate. The farm was in front of him. He became conscious of the rain again and suddenly longed to stretch out full-length under it, to take the cooling, healing drops all over his body and forget himself in the last wretchedness of the mud. Making an effort, he heaved his weight over the gate-top. He leaned again, looking up at the hill.

Rain was dissolving land and sky together like a wet water-color as the afternoon darkened. He concentrated raising his head, searching the skyline from end to end. The horse had vanished. The hill looked lifeless and desolate, an island lifting out of the sea, awash with every tide.

Under the long shed where the tractors, plough, binders and the rest were drawn up, waiting for their seasons, he sat on a sack thrown over a petrol drum, trembling, his lungs heaving. The mingled smell of paraffin, creosote,[6] fertilizer, dust—all was exactly as he had left it twelve years ago. The ragged swallows' nests were still there tucked in the angles of the rafters. He remembered three dead foxes hanging in a row from one of the beams, their teeth bloody.

The ordeal with the horse had already sunk from reality. It hung under the surface of his mind, an obscure confusion of fright and shame, as after a narrowly-escaped street accident. There was a solid pain in his chest, like a spike of bone stabbing, that made him wonder if he had strained his heart on that last stupid burdened run. Piece by piece he began to take off his clothes, wringing the gray water out of them, but soon he stopped that and just sat staring at the ground, as if some important part had been cut out of his brain.

---

6. **petrol . . . paraffin, creosote** (krē′ ə sōt′): Petrol is gasoline; paraffin, wax; creosote, an oily liquid made from tar and used to preserve wood.

◆ **Build Vocabulary**

malevolent (mə lev′ ə lent) *adj.*: Wishing harm to others

Guide for Responding

◆ Literature and Your Life

Reader's Response Describe a time when you have seen an animal behave as the "rain horse" does.

Thematic Focus What elements of this story are purely English? Which are universal?

☑ Check Your Comprehension

1. (a) What expectations does the man have when he starts the walk? (b) What are his reactions when he arrives at his destination?
2. What is the man's first impression of the horse?
3. Briefly describe what the horse does and how the man finally gets free of it.

◆ Critical Thinking

INTERPRET

1. What do you learn about the man? **[Analyze]**
2. Why is the weather significant? **[Analyze]**
3. (a) What is the relationship between the behavior of the horse and the man's feelings about nature? (b) What is the meaning of the last line of the story? **[Connect]**

COMPARE LITERARY WORKS

2. Compare the character of the speaker of "The Horses" to the protagonist of "The Rain Horse." Do they bring to their encounter with horses the same attitude? Explain. **[Compare and Contrast]**

Guide for Responding (continued)

◆ Reading Strategy

JUDGE THE MESSAGE

A final step in reading a poem is using your own experience and knowledge to **judge its message.** Poets don't always neatly sum up their messages, but Thomas offers a kind of summary at the end of "Fern Hill": "Time held me green and dying/Though I sang in my chains like the sea."

1. (a) Explain how, as a child, the poet was both "green and dying." (b) What is the meaning of the poem's final line?
2. Use your knowledge of children and of your own childhood to judge the poet's message. Do children "sing" while unaware they are in "chains"?

◆ Literary Focus

VOICE

A poet's **voice** is the distinct "sound" of his or her work. Once you know a poet's writing, you can identify this sound even if the author's name is missing—just as you can identify a friend's voice in a crowd. For example, imagine coming across lines 1–15 of "The Horses" without a name or title attached. The clipped couplets, spoken as if through held breath, might suggest you were "hearing" Hughes's voice. Also typical of his voice is the sense of wonder at nature, an almost whispered reverence. Still another sign is the use of phrases and fragments to give information: "Huge in the dense gray—ten together—/Megalith-still."

1. One sign of Thomas's voice is his use of sound devices like rhyme, alliteration (repetition of initial consonant sounds), and assonance (repetition of vowel sounds). Also, he "speaks" in a rush, crowding together images and perceptions even as he uses complex poetic forms. Find an example to demonstrate each of these qualities.
2. Identify the voice in this passage as belonging to Thomas or Hughes, and explain your choice:

> Dawn—a smoldering fume of dry frost,
> Sky-edge of red-hot iron.
> Daffodils motionless—some fizzled out.
> The birds—earth-brim simmering.
> Sycamore buds unsticking—the leaf out-
>   crumpling, purplish . . .

◆ Build Vocabulary

USING THE LATIN ROOT *-vol-*

Use your knowledge of the Latin root *-vol-* ("wish") to define each word in these pairs of antonyms.

1. benevolent—malevolent
2. voluntary—involuntary
3. volunteer—conscript
4. volitional—fated

USING THE WORD BANK: Sentence Completions

On your paper, write the word from the Word Bank that best fits in each blank.

At first the young man walking in the rain was merely ____?____ . His clothes were soaked and the meadow was dull and ____?____—that is, until the moment the ____?____ horse showed up and tried to attack him. His flight from the "rain horse" became a disturbing experience but also a(n) ____?____ one. As he thought about it later, he ____?____ . Nature, once friendly toward him, had become hostile.

◆ Grammar and Style

SENTENCE BEGINNINGS: ADVERB CLAUSES

Both Hughes and Thomas employ **adverb clauses** at the beginning of sentences to increase sentence variety.

Practice In your notebook, combine each pair of sentences to create a single sentence that begins with an adverb clause. Add subordinating conjunctions like *as, as if, after, because, when,* and *since.* Insert a comma after the adverb clause to separate it from the main clause. If necessary, use pronouns to avoid repeating nouns.

1. The young man came over the hill. The first thin blowing of rain met him.
2. He went. He broke a yard length of wrist-thick dead branch from one of the oaks.
3. The horse seemed to have gone on down the wood. His way to the farm was clear.
4. He fell. The warning flashed through his head that he must keep his suit out of the leaf-mold.
5. The horse had been waiting for just this. It dipped its head twice and came at him.

Build Your Portfolio

 ## Idea Bank

Writing

1. **Description** Describe a place you went as a child or a scene from nature that has haunted your memory. Use language that appeals to a variety of senses, as Hughes and Thomas do.

2. **Reflective Essay** Both Thomas and Hughes describe memories that are important to them. Using their poems as examples, write a reflective essay on memory and the gifts it gives us.

3. **Response to Criticism** William York Tindall writes of "Fern Hill": "Waking to death, the poet still sings green and golden songs." Comment on the truth of this remark, citing specific passages from the poem.

Speaking, Listening, and Viewing

4. **Oral Interpretation** Read one of these poems aloud to the class. As part of your rehearsal, listen to a recorded reading of the poem. Note instances in which the speaker pauses or emphasizes words. **[Performing Arts Link]**

5. **Research** The power and beauty of horses have long impressed the human imagination. Research the cave paintings from Lascaux or early depictions of horses in other cultures, and prepare a brief report comparing those depictions to the view of horses in Ted Hughes's writings. **[Art Link]**

Researching and Representing

6. **The Laureateship** Ted Hughes was the poet laureate of England. Research his duties, and compare and contrast them with those of the American poet laureate. **[Literature Link]**

7. **The Voice of Dylan Thomas** Thomas's poetry readings made him a star. Treat classmates to recordings of his performances. Then lead a discussion on what makes his readings so powerful. **[Performing Arts Link]**

Online Activity www.phlit.phschool.com

 ## Guided Writing Lesson

Nature Journal

Dylan Thomas and Ted Hughes are both keen observers of nature, and it shows in their writing. Train your powers of observation by writing an entry for a nature journal. Choose a place to observe, and record your observations. You may write one long entry or several shorter ones showing changes over time. Whether you observe nature in the city, the suburbs, or the country, be sure to describe specific details in your journal entry.

Writing Skills Focus: Use of Specific Details

A nature journal is a record of fleeting moments. The more **specific** the **details** you use, the more readers can experience those moments. "A beautiful day" tells almost nothing. Was it blazing hot, steamy and muggy, or cool and crisp? Did a butterfly flit, float, or flutter? Notice the specific details that Ted Hughes includes in this description from "The Rain Horse":

Model From Literature

The horse was almost on top of him, its head stretching forwards, ears flattened and lips lifted back from the long yellow teeth.

Prewriting Choose a place to observe, and make yourself inconspicuous. If you are noisy or obvious, you may frighten animals and distract yourself from what you want to see. Be prepared to take notes so that you don't forget specific details.

Drafting Refer to the notes you took, and organize them systematically: chronologically, from earliest to latest; spatially, from top to bottom or left to right; or by order of importance.

Revising Check to be sure you've included details that appeal to the senses of touch, smell, and taste, which are often neglected. If you haven't, add them. Replace general words like *beautiful* with more specific ones like *purple-and-yellow striped*.

Guide for Interpreting

Philip Larkin (1922–1985)

Larkin turned what could have been a discouragement into a reason for developing poetic skill and emotional restraint. As a child in Coventry, England, his home life was dominated by a father who held him accountable to rigid standards. Larkin escaped from these pressures by building a private childhood world, rich in creativity and imagination. He began a lifelong interest in jazz, which he came to love "even more than poetry." However, it was his clear-eyed, honest poetry, combining conversational language with well-crafted forms, that won him international fame. His poetry speaks of everyday realities, sometimes discouragingly, but is quietly haunted by realities beyond everyday life.

Stevie Smith (1902–1971)

Stevie Smith's poems, which cannot easily be classified, are modeled on nineteenth-century British and American poems, hymns, and popular songs. The author of this unusual body of work was born Florence Margaret Smith in Hull, Yorkshire. Due to her mother's ill health, she was raised mostly by her beloved Auntie Lion, whom she continued to live with even as an adult. While working for a magazine, she wrote three novels and ten collections of poetry.

Peter Redgrove (1932–   )

Like William Blake, a visionary poet with whom he is sometimes compared, Peter Redgrove does not fit into the usual categories. He lives at a distance from the literary hub of London—in Falmouth, Cornwall, the southwestern tip of England. He lives at an imaginative distance from London as well, rejecting the drab dailiness so prevalent in many post-World War II British poems. In his own poems, novels, television scripts, and nonfiction works, he celebrates our power to reimagine and transform our lives. His poems of celebration have been widely acclaimed in England, and he is the recipient of the 1996 Queen's Medal for Poetry, an honor that was also accorded the late Philip Larkin.

◆ Background for Understanding

SCIENCE: BODY LANGUAGE

In the past two centuries, scientists have discovered much about the role of body language in communication. Biologists have studied how animals use different postures to communicate messages like "threat" and "submission." Also, anthropologists have examined differences in human body language from culture to culture.

For example, people from Latin American and Arab cultures generally stand closer together when they talk than do people from the United States. In addition, people from Japanese and Native American cultures consider it disrespectful to look a person in the eye in some situations. Finally, if you "read" body language, you can occasionally detect differences between what people say with words and what they say with posture and gestures.

Poets have long recognized the importance of body language. Each of these poems includes a gesture that "comments" on what is happening. In Larkin's "Explosion," wives who are remembering an explosion that killed their husbands imagine one man holding miraculously "unbroken" eggs in his outstretched hand. Stevie Smith, in "Not Waving but Drowning," shows how a misinterpreted gesture can tell the story of a person's life. Meanwhile, Redgrove sums up a whole attitude toward life in a single gesture.

Read these poems for their body language as well as for their words.

An Arundel Tomb ◆ The Explosion
On the Patio ◆ Not Waving but Drowning

◆ *Literature and Your Life*

CONNECT YOUR EXPERIENCE

You look at your friend's tense shoulders and clenched fist and know immediately that something is wrong. However, when you ask what it is, your friend denies that there is a problem, claiming that he or she couldn't be in a better mood.

There are many reasons for hiding feelings, but in some cases, our body language betrays the truth. These poems play on body language as an essential indicator of human thought and emotion. In each case, a striking gesture stands out, offering itself as the central image of the poem, holding the secret to the poem's meaning.

Journal Writing Describe a scene from a movie or from life in which body language revealed a person's true feelings.

THEMATIC FOCUS: FROM THE NATIONAL TO THE GLOBAL

As you read these poems, notice how they go beyond specific settings and situations to arrive at universal meanings.

◆ Build Vocabulary

LATIN WORD ROOTS: *-fid-*

Larkin uses the word *fidelity* in "An Arundel Tomb." It means "faithfulness" and contains the Latin root *-fid-*, based on a word that means "faith." Think about other words that use this root, like *confide*.

effigy
supine
fidelity
larking

WORD BANK

Before you read, preview this list of words from the poems.

◆ Grammar and Style

SEQUENCE OF TENSES

These poets use different **verb tenses** to show the relationship of events in time. The present tense indicates events in the present or ongoing conditions. The past tense shows events that occurred and ended in the past, while the present perfect tense shows events that began in the past and have continued into the present. Following are examples from Larkin's "An Arundel Tomb," which describes a sculpture of an "earl and countess":

Present Tense: The earl and countess *lie* in stone.
Past Tense: Rigidly they/*Persisted, linked* . . .
Present Perfect Tense: Time *has transfigured* them . . .

◆ Literary Focus

FREE VERSE AND METER

Free verse is rhymed or unrhymed poetry without any of the regular rhythms called **meter**. Widely used in twentieth-century poetry, free verse has lines of different lengths and an invented rhythm that suits its meaning.

Smith and Redgrove use varying free-verse rhythms to reinforce their meanings. Larkin uses trochaic tetrameter in "The Explosion" and iambic tetrameter in "An Arundel Tomb" (a trochee is a stressed followed by an unstressed syllable ´ ˘; an iamb is an unstressed followed by a stressed syllable ˘ ´; and *tetrameter* means four feet per line):

On the day of the explosion
("The Explosion")

Untruth the stone fidelity
("An Arundel Tomb")

◆ Reading Strategy

READ IN SENTENCES

Poets often run sentences past the ends of lines. Therefore, when you're reading a poem for meaning, rather than for rhyme or sound devices, **read sentences** and not lines.

If you stop after the first line of "The Explosion," for example—"On the day of the explosion"—you don't find out *what* happened on that day.

Philip Larkin

An Arundel Tomb

Side by side, their faces blurred,
The earl and countess lie in stone,
Their proper habits vaguely shown
As jointed armour, stiffened pleat,
5 And that faint hint of the absurd—
The little dogs under their feet.

Such plainness of the pre-baroque
Hardly involves the eye, until
It meets his left-hand gauntlet,[1] still
10 Clasped empty in the other; and
One sees, with a sharp tender shock,
His hand withdrawn, holding her hand.

They would not think to lie so long.
Such faithfulness in effigy
15 Was just a detail friends would see:
A sculptor's sweet commissioned grace
Thrown off in helping to prolong
The Latin names around the base.

They would not guess how early in
20 Their supine stationary voyage
The air would change to soundless damage,
Turn the old tenantry[2] away;
How soon succeeding eyes begin
To look, not read. Rigidly they

25 Persisted, linked, through lengths and breadths
Of time. Snow fell, undated. Light
Each summer thronged the glass. A bright
Litter of birdcalls strewed the same
Bone-riddled ground. And up the paths
30 The endless altered people came,

Washing at their identity.
Now, helpless in the hollow of
An unarmorial age, a trough
Of smoke in slow suspended skeins[3]
35 Above their scrap of history,
Only an attitude remains:

Time has transfigured them into
Untruth. The stone fidelity
They hardly meant has come to be
40 Their final blazon,[4] and to prove
Our almost-instinct almost true:
What will survive of us is love.

---

1. **gauntlet:** Armored glove.
2. **tenantry:** Peasants farming the nobles' land.
3. **skeins:** Loosely coiled bunches of thread or yarn.
4. **blazon:** Coat of arms; a noble family's symbol.

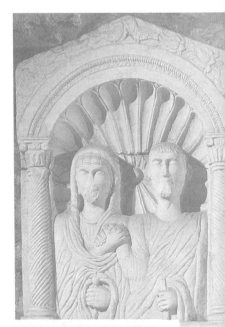

Tombstones of Tiberius Julius Rufus and his son Petronius Rufus and their wives.

▲ **Critical Viewing** Do engraved images and messages such as the ones on these tombstones always become an "untruth" in relation to life—as Larkin's poem seems to claim? Explain. **[Relate]**

The Explosion
Philip Larkin

On the day of the explosion
Shadows pointed towards the pithead:
In the sun the slagheap slept.

Down the lane came men in pitboots
5 Coughing oath-edged talk and pipe-smoke,
Shouldering off the freshened silence.

One chased after rabbits; lost them;
Came back with a nest of lark's eggs;
Showed them; lodged them in the grasses.

10 So they passed in beards and moleskins,[1]
Fathers, brothers, nicknames, laughter,
Through the tall gates standing open.

At noon, there came a tremor; cows
Stopped chewing for a second; sun,
15 Scarfed as in a heat-haze, dimmed.

The dead go on before us, they
Are sitting in God's house in comfort,
We shall see them face to face—

Plain as lettering in the chapels
20 It was said, and for a second
Wives saw men of the explosion

Larger than in life they managed—
Gold as on a coin, or walking
Somehow from the sun towards them,

25 One showing the eggs unbroken.

---

1. **moleskins:** Garments, especially trousers, of heavy cotton.

Guide for Responding

◆ Literature and Your Life

Reader's Response Which of these poems do you prefer? Why?

Thematic Focus Larkin has sometimes been called an especially British poet. (a) What, if anything, is British about these poems? (b) What, if anything, has universal meaning?

☑ Check Your Comprehension

1. (a) In "An Arundel Tomb," what is the sculpture on the tomb? (b) What detail of the sculpture catches the eye?
2. What is the "final blazon" of the couple on the tomb?
3. (a) Where is "The Explosion" set? (b) What immediate effect does the explosion have on life above ground?
4. What do the widows of the miners see "for a second" at the funeral service?

◆ Critical Thinking

INTERPRET

1. (a)In "An Arundel Tomb," what is the "supine stationary voyage" of the couple? (b) How has time "transfigured them into / Untruth"? **[Interpret]**
2. What two things in "The Explosion" last "for a second"? **[Connect]**
3. (a) How does the final gesture in the poem seem to "undo" everything? (b) Does it really "undo" everything? Explain. **[Draw Conclusions]**
4. Each of these poems has a central gesture. (a) Compare and contrast those gestures. (b) What does each symbolize? **[Draw Conclusions]**

APPLY

5. (a) How do these poems show the imagination ranging freely in time, zeroing in on an instant or observing the effects of centuries? (b) What gives the imagination this power? **[Generalize]**

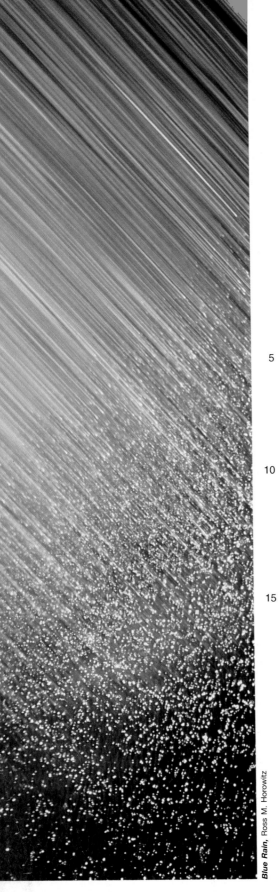

Blue Rain, Ross M. Horowitz

On the Patio

Peter Redgrove

A wineglass overflowing with thunderwater
Stands out on the drumming steel table

Among the outcries of the downpour
Feathering chairs and rethundering on the awnings.

5   How the pellets of water shooting miles
Fly into the glass of swirl, and slop

Over the table's scales of rust
Shining like chained sores,

Because the rain eats everything except the glass
10   Of spinning water that is clear down here

But purple with rumbling depths above, and this cloud
Is transferring its might into a glass

In which thunder and lightning come to rest,
The cloud crushed into a glass.

15   Suddenly I dart out into the patio,
Snatch the bright glass up and drain it,

Bang it back down on the thundery steel table for a
refill.

◀ **Critical Viewing** Does this photograph
convey the power of the "thunderwater" in
the poem? Explain your answer. **[Evaluate]**

Not Waving but Drowning

Stevie Smith

Nobody heard him, the dead man,
But still he lay moaning:
I was much further out than you thought
And not waving but drowning.

5   Poor chap, he always loved <u>larking</u>
And now he's dead
It must have been too cold for him his heart gave way,
They said.

     Oh, no no no, it was too cold always
10 (Still the dead one lay moaning)
I was much too far out all my life
And not waving but drowning.

◆ **Build Vocabulary**

larking (lärk´ iŋ) *n.*: Free-spirited, whimsical fun

Guide for Responding

◆ Literature and Your Life

Reader's Response When have you seen a gesture completely misinterpreted, as in "Not Waving but Drowning"?

Thematic Focus Does the way in which these poems focus on gestures make them accessible to a wider audience? Why or why not?

Danger Signals If you know special signs or signals for danger, draw or perform them for a group of classmates.

☑ Check Your Comprehension

1. Describe the scene in "On the Patio."
2. At the end of "On the Patio," what does the speaker do?
3. In "Not Waving but Drowning," what do "They" say about "the dead man"?
4. What does "the dead man" say about himself?

◆ Critical Thinking

INTERPRET

1. What do you think is the meaning of Redgrove's gesture in "On the Patio"? **[Interpret]**
2. How does "On the Patio" transform the ordinary into the extraordinary? **[Draw Conclusions]**
3. In "Not Waving but Drowning," how do "They" misinterpret the gesture and the whole life of "the dead man"? **[Interpret]**
4. (a) What does "the dead man" in "Not Waving but Drowning" mean by the statement in line 11? (b) In what way is the "drowning" in the poem a figure of speech? **[Draw Conclusions]**

EXTEND

5. To what extent can animals and humans communicate by gesture? **[Science Link]**

Guide for Responding (continued)

◆ Reading Strategy

READ IN SENTENCES

Even in poetry, where line breaks and rhymes can distract your eye and ear, the sentence is the unit of meaning. When you read a poem for meaning, therefore, you must **read in sentences.** Train your eye to continue past line endings where there are no marks of punctuation. Also, identify the sentences in a poem, noticing how they fall in relation to lines and stanzas. The first stanza of "The Explosion," for example, is one complete sentence.

1. (a) How many other stanzas in this poem represent complete sentences? (b) Where does the last sentence in the poem begin and end? (c) What is the relation of its length to the pace of the poem?
2. (a) How many complete sentences are there in "On the Patio"? (b) Which sentence describes a scene, which elaborates on the description, and which describes an action?

◆ Literary Focus

FREE VERSE AND METER

Smith and Redgrove use **free verse,** improvising the rhythms and line lengths that will best convey their meanings. Larkin uses regular **meters,** the set rhythms of trochaic tetrameter ("The Explosion") and iambic tetrameter ("An Arundel Tomb"). However, he varies these meters to suit his meanings. For example, the downbeat of trochaic tetrameter creates the feeling of a measured procession: "Down the lane came men in pitboots." However, Larkin introduces variations in this rhythm at key points: "One showing the eggs unbroken."

1. (a) What is the effect of breaking the rhythm for this final image and gesture? (b) What is the relation between the rhythmic variation in lines 13–14 and the event being described?
2. In lines 5–9 of "Not Waving but Drowning," how do the alternating long and short lines (a) first stress the finality of the death, (b) then seem to bring "the dead man" back to life?
3. How do the sometimes long free-verse lines of "On the Patio" relate to the setting?

◆ Build Vocabulary

USING THE LATIN ROOT -*fid*-

Use your knowledge of the Latin root -*fid*- ("faith") to paraphrase this paragraph:

> In "An Arundel Tomb," Larkin *confides* to us that the *fidelity* of the earl and countess is a facade. Their loving gesture, which at first seems *bona fide,* is revealed as a sculptor's invention.

USING THE WORD BANK: Antonyms

On your paper, write the word from the Word Bank that is the opposite of each numbered word.
1. original
2. standing
3. working
4. treachery

◆ Grammar and Style

SEQUENCE OF TENSES

Like all writers, these poets use **verb tenses** to to show the relationship of events in time. Further, the skillful use of tenses by these expert writers produces desirable stylistic effects.

Stevie Smith, for example, uses the past tense to describe the mysterious "moaning" of an already "dead man" and the discussion of his life by a mysterious "They." However, her use of the present participle *moaning* gives the dead man's complaint the sense of an ongoing action. This moaning mysteriously continues even though someone says, shifting to the present tense, "now *he's* dead" (line 6).

Practice On your paper, answer these questions about tenses:

1. (a) What tense does Larkin use in lines 1–12 of "An Arundel Tomb"? (b) How does this tense help put you face to face with the sculpture?
2. (a) Where in "An Arundel Tomb" does Larkin use the past tense to describe what happened to the sculpture over the years? (b) In which line does the poem shift from past back to present? (c) How does the use of the present perfect tense in lines 37–39 help Larkin sum up his message?
3. (a) Which tense does Redgrove use in "On the Patio"? (b) Why is this tense a good choice for the poem?

Build Your Portfolio

 ## Idea Bank

Writing

1. **Description** Each of these poems focuses on a gesture. In your own words, describe these four different gestures.

2. **Comparison and Contrast** Compare and contrast poems by two of these poets. Consider such elements as rhythm, form, imagery, and theme.

3. **Response to Criticism** David Perkins describes Larkin's "pervading emotional state . . . as low-grade psychological depression." In an essay, explain whether "The Explosion" and "An Arundel Tomb" confirm that description.

Speaking, Listening, and Viewing

4. **Eulogy** Drawing on images and descriptions from "The Explosion," deliver a speech in praise of the miners killed in the accident. **[Performing Arts Link]**

5. **Poetry Reading** With a small group, organize a reading of these poems for your class. Remember not to pause automatically at line endings as you read a poem aloud. **[Performing Arts Link]**

Researching and Representing

6. **Pantomime of a Poem** Create a series of gestures without words to capture the action, spirit, and meaning of one of these poems. Then perform your pantomime for the class. **[Performing Arts Link]**

7. **Film Review** View the film *Stevie,* which is based on the life of poet Stevie Smith, and report on it to the class. Consider reading a biography about Smith so you can explain whether the film is accurate. **[Media Link]**

Online Activity www.phlit.phschool.com

 ## Guided Writing Lesson

How-to Guide for an Interview

The poems you have read show the importance of body language. Gesture and posture can also be important in everyday situations. When you interview for a job or for a college, your body language can convey confidence or insecurity, honesty or evasiveness. Write a how-to guide for students going on interviews, explaining how to read and control body language. Support the points you make with stories, facts, and examples.

Writing Skills Focus: Elaboration to Prove a Point

In writing a how-to guide or a critical evaluation, you must **elaborate to prove the points** you make. A guide, for example, should do more than mention the steps of a process. It should support what it says with anecdotes, facts, examples, and statistics. This elaboration will help readers understand the *why* behind the *how*.

Prewriting Jot down some typical body language mistakes that occur at interviews. Using a graphic organizer with three columns labeled *Nervous, Uninterested,* and *Frivolous,* list examples of typical body language that suggests each mistaken attitude. Also, freewrite about your own interview experiences and those you have heard from others. Note some of the lessons that these experiences teach.

Drafting Use humor to engage readers and support the points you make about body language. Draw on your prewriting notes to give some purposely exaggerated examples of what *not* to do. Consider including sketches of postures and gestures as part of your elaboration.

Revising Have several classmates use your how-to guide to stage a mock job or college interview. As you watch them, you may think of additional negative examples, anecdotes, or statistics that you can include to support your points.

Guide for Interpreting

V. S. Naipaul (1932–   )

Do you live in the country of your ancestors? Can you feel removed from the government in power and still be part of that country? These questions of cultural identification are central to the writing of V. S. Naipaul; he explores them in novels and his nonfiction works about India.

A "Many-Sided Background"

Naipaul, whose family came from India, was born in Trinidad, then a part of the British West Indies. There he grew up in the Hindu culture and attended British schools. These experiences, combined with the experience of living in England as a young man and traveling all over the world since, make up what Naipaul calls his "many-sided background."

An excellent writer even as a student, he won a scholarship to Oxford University. When his father died, his family wanted him to return to Trinidad, but Naipaul decided to remain in Britain. Yet his choice of subject matter clearly indicates his strong ties to the country where he was raised. Few writers are better suited than Naipaul to examine the results of British colonialism.

Explorations in Writing

In his 1959 collection of short stories, *Miguel Street*, a young narrator's tales celebrate the comic and absurd elements of growing up in the West Indies. Comedy remains a key element in *A House for Mr. Biswas* (1961), but Naipaul adds poignant and universal themes to this story of a man similar to his father, a popular journalist with the main Trinidadian newspaper. Naipaul returns to his own youth in the novelistic memoir *A Way in the World* (1994).

Reports on Rootlessness

Naipaul is drawn to writing about people living on the margins of the modern world, people who have to struggle against rootlessness and overwhelming change. His 1971 novel *In a Free State*, about self-exiles who meet in Africa, won the prestigious Booker Prize.

Naipaul has written several books detailing his changing feelings about India. *An Area of Darkness* (1964) has a light, confident tone while *India: A Wounded Civilization* (1977) darkens toward pessimism. Naipaul's doubt reverses again into optimism in *India: A Million Mutinies Now* (1990).

◆ Background for Understanding

CULTURE: NAIPAUL'S EXPERIENCE AS RESIDENT IN A BRITISH COLONY

Imagine that a foreign country takes control of your country, changes the language spoken, the holidays celebrated, and the religion observed. How would you feel? These changes occurred in British colonies, creating feelings of alienation in the native people of each colonized region.

Naipaul recognizes the feelings of displacement caused by unjust colonialism. Writing about displaced Indians in Trinidad, Naipaul says "they were people who had been, as in a fairy story, lifted up from the peasantry of India and set down thousands of miles away …"

Writers living in former British colonies, such as Indian writers R. K. Narayan, Anita Desai, and Salman Rushdie, have explored how people have adjusted to post-colonial life, and Nobel-Prize-winning poet Derek Walcott often deals with the Jamaicans' struggle for identity. Naipaul feels that the key post-colonial challenge is to find a way to accept the past and continue to grow.

As you read "B. Wordsworth," keep in mind that the characters are living their daily lives against the ever-present feelings of displacement brought about by colonialism.

B. Wordsworth

◆ *Literature and Your Life*

CONNECT YOUR EXPERIENCE

What does your name say about you? Many names come from Latin, Greek, and Hebrew, and they have specific meanings. For example, *Richard* means "strong." If you could choose a name for yourself, what would it be? A character in "B. Wordsworth" chooses a name for himself, taking inspiration from a famous British poet.

Journal Writing Jot down four names you might choose if you decided to change your name. Add a few notes about what inspired you to select each name.

THEMATIC FOCUS: FROM THE NATIONAL TO THE GLOBAL

Although Trinidad gained its independence in 1962, the events in "B. Wordsworth" take place in a British-ruled Trinidad. As you read, imagine what it would be like to come under the rule of a such a geographically and culturally removed "mother country."

◆ Literary Focus

FIRST-PERSON NARRATOR

When you read a story, consider the point of view from which the story is told. A **first-person narrator** is one who participates in the events described in a story and is identified by the first-person pronoun *I*. However, an *I* narrator, just as a *he* or *she* third-person narrator, is a fictional creation and does not necessarily express the author's views or experiences.

In "B. Wordsworth," Naipaul uses a first-person narrator to recreate an environment he knows well from his own childhood—Trinidad in the 1940's. Why might Naipaul have chosen as narrator a boy roughly Naipaul's own age at the time?

◆ Grammar and Style

PRONOUN CASE IN COMPOUND CONSTRUCTIONS

When writers use pronouns in compound constructions, such as compound objects of prepositions, they use the case that would be correct if the pronoun were used alone. Notice the **pronoun case** in these compound constructions that the narrator of "B. Wordsworth" uses:

Subjective Case: We became friends, B. Wordsworth and *I*.

(appositive of subject, *we*)

Objective Case: This is just between you and *me*, remember.

(object of preposition *between*)

◆ Build Vocabulary

RELATED WORDS: FORMS OF *PATRON*

A character in "B. Wordsworth" asks "Which café shall we patronize?" *Patronize* means "to be a customer of a store or merchant." It contains the word *patron*, meaning "customer." Other related words include *patronage*, "the support of a customer," and *patronizing*, "to treat as a customer of" or "condescending to."

WORD BANK

Preview this list of words from the story before you read.

rogue
patronize
distill
keenly

◆ Reading Strategy

RESPOND TO CHARACTER

It will help you be an active reader, one who fully envisions the word created by a writer, if you **respond to character** as you read. For example, when the title character first appears in "B. Wordsworth," he is a stranger with an odd request: He wants to watch bees in the narrator's yard. How do you feel about this unusual request? As you continue to read, jot down your personal responses to the behavior and comments of each of the main characters.

B. Wordsworth

V. S. Naipaul

Three beggars called punctually every day at the hospitable houses in Miguel Street. At about ten an Indian came in his dhoti[1] and white jacket, and we poured a tin of rice into the sack he carried on his back. At twelve an old woman smoking a clay pipe came and she got a cent. At two a blind man led by a boy called for his penny.

Sometimes we had a rogue. One day a man called and said he was hungry. We gave him a meal. He asked for a cigarette and wouldn't go until we had lit it for him. That man never came again.

The strangest caller came one afternoon about four o'clock. I had come back from school and was in my home-clothes. The man said to me, "Sonny, may I come inside your yard?"

He was a small man and he was tidily dressed. He wore a hat, a white shirt and black trousers.

I asked, "What do you want?"

He said, "I want to watch your bees."

We had four small gru-gru palm trees[2] and they were full of uninvited bees.

I ran up the steps and shouted, "Ma, it have a man outside here. He say he want to watch the bees."

My mother came out, looked at the man and asked in an unfriendly way, "What you want?"

The man said, "I want to watch your bees."

His English was so good, it didn't sound natural, and I could see my mother was worried.

She said to me, "Stay here and watch him while he watch the bees."

The man said, "Thank you, Madam. You have done a good deed today."

He spoke very slowly and very correctly as though every word was costing him money.

We watched the bees, this man and I, for about an hour, squatting near the palm trees.

The man said, "I like watching bees. Sonny, do you like watching bees?"

I said, "I ain't have the time."

He shook his head sadly. He said, "That's what I do, I just watch. I can watch ants for days. Have you ever watched ants? And scorpions, and centipedes, and congorees[3]—have you watched those?"

I shook my head.

I said, "What you does do, mister?"

He got up and said, "I am a poet."

I said, "A good poet?"

He said, "The greatest in the world."

"What your name, mister?"

"B. Wordsworth."

"B for Bill?"

"Black. Black Wordsworth. White Wordsworth[4] was my brother. We share one heart. I can watch a small flower like the morning glory and cry."

I said, "Why you does cry?"

"Why, boy? Why? You will know when you grow up. You're a poet, too, you know. And when you're a poet you can cry for everything."

I couldn't laugh.

He said, "You like your mother?"

"When she not beating me."

He pulled out a printed sheet from his

---

1. dhoti (dō′ tē): Traditional loincloth worn by Hindu men.
2. gru-gru (grōō′ grōō′) **palm trees**: West Indian palms that yield edible nuts.

3. congorees (kän′ gər ēz): Conger or Congo eels; large, scaleless eels found in the warm waters of the West Indies.
4. White Wordsworth: English Romantic poet William Wordsworth (1770–1850).

Man From the Village, Carlton Murrell

◀ **Critical Viewing** Compare the attitude of the man in the painting with that of B. Wordsworth. How might the man in the painting appear to a young boy such as the narrator? [**Compare and Contrast**]

hip-pocket and said, "On this paper is the greatest poem about mothers and I'm going to sell it to you at a bargain price. For four cents."

I went inside and I said, "Ma, you want buy a poetry for four cents?"

My mother said, "Tell that blasted man I haul his tail away from my yard, you hear."

I said to B. Wordsworth, "My mother say she ain't have four cents."

B. Wordsworth said, "It is the poet's tragedy."

And he put the paper back in his pocket. He didn't seem to mind.

I said, "Is a funny way to go round selling poetry like that. Only calypsonians[5] do that sort of thing. A lot of people does buy?"

He said, "No one has yet bought a single copy."

"But why you does keep on going round, then?"

He said, "In this way I watch many things, and I always hope to meet poets."

I said, "You really think I is a poet?"

"You're as good as me," he said.

And when B. Wordsworth left, I prayed I would see him again.

About a week later, coming back from school one afternoon, I met him at the corner of Miguel Street.

---

5. **calypsonians** (kə lip sō′ nē ənz): Those who sing songs, the characteristic satirical street singers of Trinidad.

◆ **Build Vocabulary**

rogue (rōg) *n.*: Scoundrel; wandering beggar

He said, "I have been waiting for you for a long time."

I said, "You sell any poetry yet?"

He shook his head.

He said, "In my yard I have the best mango tree in Port-of-Spain.[6] And now the mangoes are ripe and red and very sweet and juicy. I have waited here for you to tell you this and to invite you to come and eat some of my mangoes."

He lived in Alberto Street in a one-roomed hut placed right in the center of the lot. The yard seemed all green. There was the big mango tree. There was a coconut tree and there was a plum tree. The place looked wild, as though it wasn't in the city at all. You couldn't see all the big concrete houses in the street.

He was right. The mangoes were sweet and juicy. I ate about six, and the yellow mango juice ran down my arms to my elbows and down my mouth to my chin and my shirt was stained.

My mother said when I got home, "Where you was? You think you is a man now and could go all over the place? Go cut a whip for me."

She beat me rather badly, and I ran out of the house swearing that I would never come back. I went to B. Wordsworth's house. I was so angry, my nose was bleeding.

B. Wordsworth said, "Stop crying, and we will go for a walk."

I stopped crying, but I was breathing short. We went for a walk. We walked down St. Clair Avenue to the Savannah and we walked to the race-course.

B. Wordsworth said, "Now, let us lie on the grass and look up at the sky, and I want you to think how far those stars are from us."

I did as he told me, and I saw what he meant. I felt like nothing, and at the same time I had never felt so big and great in all my life. I forgot all my anger and all my tears and all the blows.

When I said I was better, he began telling me the names of the stars, and I particularly remembered the constellation of Orion the

▶ **Critical Viewing** The house in the painting, like B. Wordsworth's hut, seems to be a world of its own; our attention is focused on the question of what is inside. What methods does the artist use to achieve this effect? [**Analyze**]

Hunter,[7] though I don't really know why. I can spot Orion even today, but I have forgotten the rest.

Then a light was flashed into our faces, and we saw a policeman. We got up from the grass.

The policeman said, "What you doing here?"

B. Wordsworth said, "I have been asking myself the same question for forty years."

We became friends, B. Wordsworth and I. He told me, "You must never tell anybody about me and about the mango tree and the coconut tree and the plum tree. You must keep that a secret. If you tell anybody, I will know, because I am a poet."

I gave him my word and I kept it.

I liked his little room. It had no more furniture than George's front room,[8] but it looked cleaner and healthier. But it also looked lonely.

One day I asked him, "Mister Wordsworth, why you does keep all this bush in your yard? Ain't it does make the place damp?"

He said, "Listen, and I will tell you a story. Once upon a time a boy and girl met each other and they fell in love. They loved each other so much they got married. They were both poets. He loved words. She loved grass and flowers and trees. They lived happily in a single room, and then one day, the girl poet said to the boy poet, 'We are going to have another poet in the family.' But this poet was never born, because the girl died, and the young poet died with her, inside her. And the girl's husband was very sad, and he said he would never touch a thing in the girl's garden. And so the garden

◆ **Reading Strategy** Describe how the star-gazing scene contributes to your response to B. Wordsworth.

---

6. **Port-of-Spain:** Seaport capital of Trinidad and Tobago.

7. **Constellation of Orion** (ō rī′ ən) **the Hunter:** Group of stars named after a mythological giant who was killed accidentally by the goddess of hunting, Diana.

8. **George's front room:** George is a character in one of the companion stories in Naipaul's book, *Miguel Street*.

remained, and grew high and wild."

I looked at B. Wordsworth, and as he told me this lovely story, he seemed to grow older. I understood his story.

We went for long walks together. We went to the Botanical Gardens and the Rock Gardens. We climbed Chancellor Hill in the late afternoon and watched the darkness fall on Port-of-Spain, and watched the lights go on in the city and on the ships in the harbor.

He did everything as though he were doing it for the first time in his life. He did everything as though he were doing some church rite.

He would say to me, "Now, how about having some ice cream?"

And when I said, yes, he would grow very serious and say, "Now, which café shall we patronize?" As though it were a very important thing. He would think for some time about it, and finally say, "I think I will go and negotiate the purchase with that shop."

The world became a most exciting place.

One day, when I was in his yard, he said to me, "I have a great secret which I am now going to tell you."

I said, "It really secret?"

"At the moment, yes."

I looked at him, and he looked at me. He said, "This is just between you and me, remember. I am writing a poem."

"Oh." I was disappointed.

He said, "But this is a different sort of poem. This is the greatest poem in the world."

I whistled.

He said, "I have been working on it for more than five years now. I will finish it in about twenty-two years from now, that is, if I keep on writing at the present rate."

"You does write a lot, then?"

He said, "Not any more. I just write one line a month. But I make sure it is a good line."

I asked, "What was last month's good line?"

He looked up at the sky, and said, *"The past is deep."*

I said, "It is a beautiful line."

B. Wordsworth said, "I hope to distill the experiences of a whole month into that single line of poetry. So, in twenty-two years, I shall have written a poem that will sing to all humanity."

I was filled with wonder.

Our walks continued. We walked along the sea-wall at Docksite one day, and I said, "Mr. Wordsworth, if I drop this pin in the water, you think it will float?"

He said, "This is a strange world. Drop your pin, and let us see what will happen."

The pin sank.

I said, "How is the poem this month?"

But he never told me any other line. He merely said, "Oh, it comes, you know. It comes."

Or we would sit on the sea-wall and watch the liners come into the harbor.

But of the greatest poem in the world I heard no more.

I felt he was growing older.

"How you does live, Mr. Wordsworth?" I asked him one day.

He said, "You mean how I get money?"

When I nodded, he laughed in a crooked way.

He said, "I sing calypsoes in the calypso season."

"And that last you the rest of the year?"

"It is enough."

"But you will be the richest man in the world when you write the greatest poem?"

He didn't reply.

One day when I went to see him in his little house, I found him lying on his little bed. He looked so old and so weak, that I found myself wanting to cry.

He said, "The poem is not going well."

He wasn't looking at me. He was looking through the window at the coconut tree, and he was speaking as though I wasn't there. He said, "When I was twenty I felt the power within myself." Then, almost in front of my eyes, I could see his face growing older and more tired. He said, "But that—that was a long time ago."

And then—I felt it so keenly, it was as though I had been slapped by my mother. I could see it clearly on his face. It was there for everyone to see. Death on the shrinking face.

He looked at me, and saw my tears and sat up.

◆ **Literary Focus**
Would the story have the same impact if told by a third-person narrator? Explain.

He said, "Come." I went and sat on his knees.

He looked into my eyes, and he said, "Oh, you can see it, too. I always knew you had the poet's eye."

He didn't even look sad, and that made me burst out crying loudly.

He pulled me to his thin chest, and said, "Do you want me to tell you a funny story?" and he smiled encouragingly at me.

But I couldn't reply.

He said, "When I have finished this story, I want you to promise that you will go away and never come back to see me. Do you promise?"

I nodded.

He said, "Good. Well, listen. That story I told you about the boy poet and the girl poet, do you remember that? That wasn't true. It was something I just made up. All this talk about poetry and the greatest poem in the world, that wasn't true, either. Isn't that the funniest thing you have heard?"

But his voice broke.

I left the house, and ran home crying, like a poet, for everything I saw.

I walked along Alberto Street a year later, but I could find no sign of the poet's house. It hadn't vanished, just like that. It had been pulled down, and a big, two-storied building had taken its place. The mango tree and the plum tree and the coconut tree had all been cut down, and there was brick and concrete everywhere.

It was just as though B. Wordsworth had never existed.

◆ Build Vocabulary

patronize (pā´ trə nīz) v.: To be a customer of a particular merchant or store

distill (dis til´) v.: To obtain the essential part

keenly (kēn´ lē) adv.: Sharply; intensely

Guide for Responding

◆ Literature and Your Life

Reader's Response What simple things make the world a more exciting place for you? Why?

Thematic Focus In what way does the title of the story reflect the challenge of developing an identity in a colonial society?

Questions for Research Generate research questions that would help you learn how the land and traditions of Trinidad shaped V. S. Naipaul.

☑ Check Your Comprehension

1. What reason does B. Wordsworth give for wanting to come into the boy's yard?
2. What does the "B" in the title character's name stand for?
3. How does B. Wordsworth explain his overgrown yard?
4. What happens to B. Wordsworth's house?

◆ Critical Thinking

INTERPRET

1. What does the opening description tell you about the city in which the story is set? **[Infer]**
2. How is B. Wordsworth different from the other visitors described? **[Compare and Contrast]**
3. B. Wordsworth says that he thinks the boy is a "poet." How do you think he would define that term? **[Interpret]**
4. What is B. Wordsworth's motivation for spending time with the boy? **[Infer]**
5. Why does B. Wordsworth ask the boy to promise not to return after their last visit? **[Infer]**
6. B. Wordsworth "did everything as though he was doing it for the first time." What does this mean? **[Draw Conclusions]**

EVALUATE

7. Why did Naipaul choose the character of B. Wordsworth as the focal point of a story? **[Evaluate]**

Guide for Responding (continued)

◆ Literary Focus

FIRST-PERSON NARRATOR

A **first-person narrator** conveys a limited perspective. We know only what the narrator knows. For example, when the narrator describes the beggars, we believe him because he presents himself as an eyewitness. However, when B. Wordsworth tells the narrator that he earns a living as a calypso singer, neither we nor the boy think that this is true.

1. How would the story be different if it were told from B. Wordsworth's point of view?
2. What would you like to know about events in this story that the first-person narrator, with his limited viewpoint, cannot convey?
3. (a) How is the narrator's voice different from the boy's dialogue? (b) Explain how this difference emphasizes B. Wordsworth's effect on the boy.

◆ Reading Strategy

RESPOND TO CHARACTER

After finishing a story, reflect on your **response to the characters.** Think about the qualities and behaviors they display. Then note how *other* characters respond to them. For example, when the narrator reflects that B. Wordsworth "did everything as though he were doing it for the first time," he is revealing an important part of B. Wordsworth's character—an insight that will ultimately help you respond to him.

Once you have looked at a character from all angles, including other characters' reactions to him or her, draw from your own experience and set of values to respond personally to that character—as if he or she were entering your life for the first time.

1. Based on your observations about him, how do you think B. Wordsworth would sum up his philosophy of life?
2. Why do you think B. Wordsworth repeatedly tells the narrator that he, too, is a poet?
3. Which of the two main characters do you identify with more strongly? Why?

◆ Build Vocabulary

USING FORMS OF *PATRON*

The word *patronize* means "be a customer of." Use this knowledge to help you complete each sentence using one of the following words.

patron   patronage   patronizing

1. The continued ____?____ of a core group of loyal customers helped to keep the small bookstore in business.
2. I enjoy ____?____ that fruit store because its owner has a wonderful sense of humor.
3. Every time I go to that restaurant some loud and obnoxious ____?____ makes a scene.

USING THE WORD BANK: Connotation

In your notebook, answer the following.

1. Would a *keenly* observant poet be more likely to describe, or gloss over, details?
2. If you *distill* the meaning in a passage, do you concentrate it or expand upon it?
3. Does a *rogue* ignore or promote society's rules?
4. Would you *patronize* a forest or a cafe?

◆ Grammar and Style

PRONOUN CASE IN COMPOUND CONSTRUCTIONS

In a compound construction, use the **correct pronoun case,** depending on the pronoun's function in the sentence. For example, because the pronoun "I" is an appositive of the subject "We," the subjective case is used in the compound construction: "*We* watched the bees, this man and *I*, for about an hour."

Practice In your notebook, write each sentence, using the correct pronoun.

1. The poet and (I/me) shared a mango.
2. It was a secret between (he/him) and (I/me).
3. It was as if the stars glowed for (he/him) and (I/me).
4. A calypsonian sang my friend and (I/me) a song.

Writing Application In your notebook, write a paragraph featuring the adventures of you and a friend. Use the subjective and objective cases one time each in compound constructions.

Build Your Portfolio

 ## Idea Bank

Writing

1. **Memorial Plaque** Write the text of a memorial plaque that the narrator of "B. Wordsworth" might have created to honor his friend. Consider using a quotation from the story on your plaque.

2. **First-Person Narrative** Write a story using a first-person narrator. You may use a series of events that you actually experienced, but choose a narrator who is different from you.

3. **Critical Evaluation** Naipaul once said, "I think I look for the seeds of regeneration in a situation; I long to find what is good and hopeful . . ." Write an essay in which you explain whether or not this philosophy is reflected in "B. Wordsworth."

Speaking, Listening, and Viewing

4. **Poetry Reading** Select three poems from British literature that you think B. Wordsworth would enjoy. Read the poems aloud to the class and explain why you chose each selection.

5. **Music Appreciation** Find and play for the class several calypso songs. As a class, discuss your responses to the Trinidadian music. **[Music Link]**

Researching and Representing

6. **Exhibit** Investigate the history of the British colonialism in the West Indies through independence. Create a classroom exhibit that reflects the British influence on the West Indies. **[Social Studies Link]**

7. **Fashion Design** Research traditional Indian clothing such as *saris* and *dhotis*. Then choose an article of clothing to design. You can just sketch it or carry your design from sketch through pattern and finished piece. **[Art Link]**

Online Activity www.phlit.phschool.com

 ## Guided Writing Lesson

Description of a Person

The narrator of Naipaul's story will never forget B. Wordsworth for his remarkable qualities. Think about the most remarkable person you have ever met, and write a description in which you share your perceptions of this person with your readers. Your goal is to make readers feel as if they actually know this outstanding person.

Writing Skills Focus: Types of Support—Details

Choose **specific details** that show readers why this person is so memorable.

- Choose details that are unique to the person you are describing.
- Support generalizations with specific, precise details.
- Use figurative language to create fresh details that will capture your readers' attention.
- Use a variety of sensory details to create a full portrait.
- Bring your character to life by writing dialogue appropriate to his or her personality.

Prewriting Think about the traits and actions that make this person special, and choose a situation to describe in which your character displays his or her memorable personality. Then brainstorm for sensory words and phrases that apply to your character. Also, jot down ideas for dialogue that capture the character's way of speaking.

Drafting As you draft, weave together the details you've gathered to create a memorable portrait.

Revising Review your description critically. Replace vague, generalized details with ones specific to the person you're describing. Add dialogue whenever the description seems flat or unlively. Read your description aloud to a friend to get more suggestions for revision.

Guide for Interpreting

Nadine Gordimer (1923–)

The fiction of Nadine Gordimer has been shaped by her life in South Africa and by her firm opposition to the former government's policy of apartheid (ə pär´ tīd´)—racial separation and prejudice. Initially honored for her short fiction, she says that in time she found the short story "too delicate for what I have to say." In her longer works, and in short stories as well, she has had a great deal to say about racial prejudice and its harmful effects on oppressed and oppressor alike.

Born in a Small Town Gordimer was born in Springs, South Africa, a small town near Johannesburg. Her mother took her out of the local private school when she was eleven, and from then until she was sixteen, she "read tremendously," wrote much fiction, and published her first adult short story, "Come Again Tomorrow," when she was fifteen. She studied for a year at the University of Witwatersrand, continuing to write short stories.

Literary Successes *The Soft Voice of the Serpent* (1952) was the first collection of her stories to be published in the United States. Following the critical success of that book, Gordimer's stories began appearing in well-known American magazines. These stories often describe the entrapment of whites who have inherited power in South Africa's closed society. Frequently, as in "The Train from Rhodesia," she builds a tale around a fleeting but sharply focused moment of insight.

Compassionate Observer In all her fiction—including novels like *A Guest of Honor* (1970), *The Conservationist* (1974), and *Burger's Daughter* (1979)—she shows an ability to write from different vantage points. She portrays the Anglos (South Africans of English ancestry), Afrikaners (South Africans of Dutch ancestry), and black South Africans, describing her characters in a variety of economic and social settings. She writes as a compassionate observer, stressing the themes of understanding, adjustment, and forgiveness.

"Luminous Symbol" Until she was thirty, Gordimer had never been outside South Africa. Since then, however, she has traveled widely and lectured in a number of universities. She has also won a great many literary awards, including the Nobel Prize for Literature in 1991. Called "a luminous symbol of at least one white person's understanding of the black man's burden," she is also one of the leading novelists writing in English.

◆ Background for Understanding

HISTORY: GORDIMER, COLONIALISM, AND APARTHEID

This story takes place at a small train station somewhere on the line from Rhodesia (now the African nation of Zimbabwe) to South Africa. It occurs at a time when South Africa, and Rhodesia to its north, were dominated by policies of racial separation and prejudice called apartheid. This word itself means "apartness" in Afrikaans, the language of Dutch South Africans.

Racial prejudice and apartheid were a legacy of European colonial domination of Africa. In the late nineteenth century, the major European powers carved up the African continent for their own economic and political gain: Much of Central Africa was controlled by the Belgians, North and Northwestern Africa by the French, and Eastern and Southern Africa by the British.

Whites lived as privileged rulers in Rhodesia and South Africa, as they did elsewhere in the continent. The native black people, however, lived for the most part in poverty.

The Train from Rhodesia

◆ *Literature and Your Life*

CONNECT YOUR EXPERIENCE

You've seen movies in which a honeymoon, instead of bringing a couple together, reveals the differences that will eventually tear them apart. Often the clue to these differences is something small, a single harsh word or even a false gesture.

The woman in this story seems to be coming back from her honeymoon. Her train stops at a station in the middle of nowhere, and a minor incident occurs—or is it minor?

Journal Writing Describe a movie you've seen or a story you've read in which a small difference of opinion revealed a major difference in personality or belief.

THEMATIC FOCUS: FROM THE NATIONAL TO THE GLOBAL

As you read this story, consider the global importance of an incident at an out-of-the-way train station.

◆ Build Vocabulary

LATIN PREFIXES: *a-*

The word *atrophy*, which appears in this story, means "waste away." It combines the Latin prefix *a-*, meaning "without or not," with a word that means "to nourish." As you can see from this example, the prefix negates the root it precedes, like a negative sign in front of a number.

WORD BANK

Before you read, preview this list of words from the story.

impressionistic
elongated
segmented
splaying
atrophy

◆ Grammar and Style

ABSOLUTE PHRASES

Throughout her story, Gordimer piles up details so that you can experience the tension of the situation. One grammatical device she uses to create this effect is the **absolute phrase**, a group of words containing a participle and the words the participle modifies. An absolute phrase does not have a grammatical link with any single word in the sentence. Instead, it modifies the whole clause to which it is attached:

"The old native stood, *breath blowing out the skin between his ribs* . . ."

As you come across absolute phrases, delete them in your mind and see how tension and immediacy drain from the description.

◆ Literary Focus

CONFLICT AND THEME

Writers often dramatize their **themes**, their central insights, by showing a character in the midst of a **conflict**, an inner or outer struggle. The way in which the character resolves, or fails to resolve, this conflict helps communicate the writer's message.

In this story, a young woman reacts to a conflict as if she were focusing a lens. At first the conflict is totally out of focus. Gradually, however, she turns a dial in her mind and the conflict becomes clearer. By the end of the story, the conflict and its meaning will be painfully clear—to her and to you.

◆ Reading Strategy

READ BETWEEN THE LINES

In fiction, characters sometimes react to things without understanding them. You have to **read between the lines** in order to make the connections that the character is missing.

In Gordimer's story, for example, a young woman wants to buy a carved lion. However, she does not understand at first the powerful effect of a seemingly insignificant object: The lion's mouth "opened in an endless roar too terrible to be heard." You can read between the lines by asking yourself what is so "terrible" about the lion or the situation in which the woman finds herself.

Warp-printed cotton, Arthur Sanderson & Sons, 1930, The Victoria and Albert Museum, London

The Train from Rhodesia[1]

Nadine Gordimer

The train came out of the red horizon and bore down toward them over the single straight track.

The stationmaster came out of his little brick station with its pointed chalet roof, feeling the creases in his serge uniform in his legs as well. A stir of preparedness rippled through the squatting native vendors waiting in the dust; the face of a carved wooden animal, eternally surprised, stuck out of a sack. The stationmaster's barefoot children wandered over. From the gray mud huts with the untidy heads that stood within a decorated mud wall, chickens, and dogs with their skin stretched like parchment over their bones, followed the piccanins[2] down to the track. The flushed and perspiring west cast a reflection, faint, without heat, upon the station, upon the tin shed marked "Goods," upon the walled kraal,[3] upon the gray tin house of the stationmaster and upon the sand, that lapped all around, from sky to sky, cast little rhythmical cups of

shadow, so that the sand became the sea, and closed over the children's black feet softly and without imprint.

The stationmaster's wife sat behind the mesh of her veranda. Above her head the hunk of a sheep's carcass moved slightly, dangling in a current of air.

They waited.

The train called out, along the sky; but there was no answer; and the cry hung on: I'm coming . . . I'm coming . . .

The engine flared out now, big, whisking a dwindling body behind it; the track flared out to let it in.

Creaking, jerking, jostling, gasping, the train filled the station.

Here, let me see that one—the young woman curved her body further out of the corridor window. Missus? smiled the old boy, looking at the creatures he held in his hand. From a piece of string on his gray finger hung a tiny woven basket; he lifted it, questioning. No, no, she urged, leaning down toward him, across the height of the train, toward the man in the piece of old rug; that one, that one, her hand commanded. It was a lion, carved out of soft dry wood that looked like spongecake; heraldic, black and, white, with impressionistic detail

---

1. **Rhodesia** (rō dē′ zhə): Former name of Zimbabwe (zim bä′ bwā), a country in southern Africa.
2. **piccanins** *n.*: Native children.
3. **kraal** (kräl) *n.*: Fenced-in enclosure for cattle or sheep.

burnt in. The old man held it up to her still smiling, not from the heart, but at the customer. Between its Vandyke[4] teeth, in the mouth opened in an endless roar too terrible to be heard, it had a black tongue. Look, said the young husband, if you don't mind! And round the neck of the thing, a piece of fur (rat? rabbit? meerkat?); a real mane, majestic, telling you somehow that the artist had delight in the lion.

◆ **Reading Strategy**
What conflict is suggested by the contrast between the "bent" artists, moving like performing animals, and the "elongated" statues of lion-hunting warriors?

All up and down the length of the train in the dust the artists sprang, walking bent, like performing animals, the better to exhibit the fantasy held toward the faces on the train. Buck, startled and stiff, staring with round black and white eyes. More lions, standing erect, grappling with strange, thin, elongated warriors who clutched spears and showed no fear in their slits of eyes. How much, they asked from the train, how much?

Give me penny, said the little ones with nothing to sell. The dogs went and sat, quite still, under the dining car, where the train breathed out the smell of meat cooking with onion.

A man passed beneath the arch of reaching arms meeting gray-black and white in the exchange of money for the staring wooden eyes, the stiff wooden legs sticking up in the air; went along under the voices and the bargaining, interrogating the wheels. Past the dogs; glancing up at the dining car where he could stare at the faces, behind glass, drinking beer, two by two, on either side of a uniform railway vase with its pale dead flower. Right to the end, to the guard's van, where the stationmaster's children had just collected their mother's two loaves of bread; to the engine itself, where the stationmaster and the driver stood talking against the steaming complaint of the resting beast.

The man called out to them, something loud and joking. They turned to laugh, in a twirl of steam. The two children careered over the sand, clutching the bread, and burst through the iron gate and up the path through the garden in which nothing grew.

Passengers drew themselves in at the corridor windows and turned into compartments to fetch money, to call someone to look. Those sitting inside looked up: suddenly different, caged faces, boxed in, cut off, after the contact of outside. There was an orange a piccanin would like. . . . What about that chocolate? It wasn't very nice. . . .

A young girl had collected a handful of the hard kind, that no one liked, out of the chocolate box, and was throwing them to the dogs, over at the dining car. But the hens darted in, and swallowed the chocolates, incredibly quick and accurate, before they had even dropped in the dust, and the dogs, a little bewildered, looked up with their brown eyes, not expecting anything.

—No, leave it, said the girl, don't take it. . . .

Too expensive, too much, she shook her head and raised her voice to the old boy, giving up the lion. He held it up where she had handed it to him. No, she said, shaking her head. Three-and-six?[5] insisted her husband, loudly. Yes baas! laughed the boy. *Three-and-six?*—the young man was incredulous. Oh leave it—she said. The young man stopped. Don't you want it? he said, keeping his face closed to the boy. No, never mind, she said, leave it. The old native kept his head on one side, looking at them sideways, holding the lion. Three-and-six, he murmured, as old people repeat things to themselves.

The young woman drew her head in. She went into the coupé[6] and sat down. Out of the

---

5. **three-and-six:** Three shillings and sixpence.
6. **coupé** (ko͞o pā´) *n.:* Half-compartment at the end of a train, with seats on only one side.

◆ **Build Vocabulary**

impressionistic (im presh´ ə nis´ tik) *adj.:* Conveying a quick, overall picture

elongated (i lôŋ´ gāt id) *adj.:* Lengthened; stretched

---

4. **Vandyke** (van dīk´) *adj.:* Tapering to a point, like a Vandyke beard.

window, on the other side, there was nothing; sand and bush; a thorn tree. Back through the open doorway, past the figure of her husband in the corridor, there was the station, the voices, wooden animals waving, running feet. Her eye followed the funny little valance of scrolled wood that outlined the chalet roof of the station; she thought of the lion and smiled. That bit of fur round the neck. But the wooden buck, the hippos, the elephants, the baskets that already bulked out of their brown paper under the seat and on the luggage rack! How will they look at home? Where will you put them? What will they mean away from the places you found them? Away from the unreality of the last few weeks? The man outside. But he is not part of the unreality; he is for good now. Odd . . . somewhere there was an idea that he, that living with him, was part of the holiday, the strange places.

Outside, a bell rang. The stationmaster was leaning against the end of the train, green flag rolled in readiness. A few men who had got down to stretch their legs sprang on to the train, clinging to the observation platforms, or perhaps merely standing on the iron step, holding the rail; but on the train, safe from the one dusty platform, the one tin house, the empty sand.

There was a grunt. The train jerked. Through the glass the beer drinkers looked out, as if they could not see beyond it. Behind the fly-screen, the stationmaster's wife sat facing back at them beneath the darkening hunk of meat.

There was a shout. The flag drooped out. Joints not yet coordinated, the segmented body of the train heaved and bumped back against itself. It began to move; slowly the scrolled chalet moved past it, the yells of the natives, running alongside, jetted up into the air, fell back at different levels. Staring wooden faces waved drunkenly, there, then gone, questioning for the last time at the windows. Here, one-and-six baas!—As one automatically opens a hand to catch a thrown ball, a man fumbled wildly down his pocket, brought up the shilling and sixpence and threw them out; the old native, gasping, his skinny toes splaying the sand, flung the lion.

The piccanins were waving, the dogs stood, tails uncertain, watching the train go: past the mud huts, where a woman turned to look, up from the smoke of the fire, her hand pausing on her hip.

The stationmaster went slowly in under the chalet.

The old native stood, breath blowing out the skin between his ribs, feet tense, balanced in the sand, smiling and shaking his head. In his opened palm, held in the attitude of receiving, was the retrieved shilling and sixpence.

The blind end of the train was being pulled helplessly out of the station.

The young man swung in from the corridor, breathless. He was shaking his head with laughter and triumph. Here! he said. And waggled the lion at her. One-and-six!

What? she said.

He laughed. I was arguing with him for fun, bargaining—when the train had pulled out already, he came tearing after. . . . One-and-six baas! So there's your lion.

She was holding it away from her, the head with the open jaws, the pointed teeth, the black tongue, the wonderful ruff of fur facing her. She was looking at it with an expression of not seeing, of seeing something different. Her face was drawn up, wryly, like the face of a discomforted child. Her mouth lifted nervously at the corner. Very slowly, cautious, she lifted her finger and touched the mane, where it was joined to the wood.

But how could you, she said. He was shocked by the dismay of her face.

Good heavens, he said, what's the matter?

If you wanted the thing, she said, her voice rising and breaking with the shrill impotence of anger, why didn't you buy it in the first place? If you wanted it, why didn't you pay for it? Why didn't you take it decently, when he offered it? Why did you have to wait for him to run after the train with it, and give him one-and-six? One-and-six!

She was pushing it at him, trying to force him to take it. He stood astonished, his hands hanging at his sides.

But you wanted it! You liked it so much?

—It's a beautiful piece of work, she said fiercely, as if to protect it from him.

◆ **Literary Focus**
Analyze the conflict between the husband and wife. What connections does the man see between "liking," "wanting," and "buying"? What connections does the woman see?

You liked it so much! You said yourself it was too expensive—

Oh *you*—she said, hopeless and furious. *You* . . . . She threw the lion onto the seat.

He stood looking at her.

She sat down again in the corner and, her face slumped in her hand, stared out of the window. Everything was turning around inside her. One-and-six. One-and-six. One-and-six for the wood and the carving and the sinews of the legs and the switch of the tail. The mouth open like that and the teeth, the black tongue, rolling, like a wave. The mane round the neck. To give one-and-six for that. The heat of shame mounted through her legs and body and sounded in her ears like the sound of sand pouring, pouring, pouring. She sat there, sick. A weariness, a tastelessness, the discovery of a void made her hands slacken their grip, atrophy emptily, as if the hour was not worth their grasp. She was feeling like this again. She had thought it was something to do with singleness, with being alone and belonging too much to oneself.

She sat there not wanting to move or speak, or to look at anything, even; so that the mood should be associated with nothing, no object, word or sight that might recur and so recall the feeling again. . . . Smuts blew in grittily, settled on her hands. Her back remained at exactly the same angle, turned against the young man sitting with his hands drooping between his sprawled legs, and the lion, fallen on its side in the corner.

The train had cast the station like a skin. It called out to the sky, I'm coming, I'm coming; and again, there was no answer.

◆ **Build Vocabulary**

segmented (seg´ ment id) *adj.*: Separated into parts
splaying (splā´ iŋ) *v.*: Spreading
atrophy (a´ trə fē) *v.*: Waste away

Guide for Responding

◆ *Literature and Your Life*

Reader's Response What do you think of the bargaining custom described in the story? Is it an example of exploitation? Explain.

Thematic Focus Suppose you are an American television reporter on vacation, and you witness the scene in the station. Would you report it as a local incident or one that reflects global issues?

Research In the years since "The Train from Rhodesia" was written, the nations of Rhodesia and South Africa have undergone momentous changes. Research their recent histories, and discuss with classmates how each society is coping with change.

☑ Check Your Comprehension

1. Who comes to meet the train from Rhodesia?
2. (a) How much money does the vendor want for the carved lion? (b) How much does he finally accept?
3. Describe what kinds of things the young couple have already bought on their holiday.
4. How does the "old native" get paid by the young man as the train pulls away?
5. Briefly summarize the interaction between the young woman and her husband at the end of the story.

Guide for Responding (continued)

◆ Critical Thinking

INTERPRET

1. Why is the arrival of the train important to the people of the town? **[Infer]**
2. Why do you think the young woman wants the carved lion? **[Analyze]**
3. Why is the young woman angry when her husband bargains for and obtains the lion at a low price? **[Interpret]**
4. How does the final description of the train help disclose the story's meaning? **[Draw Conclusions]**

EVALUATE

5. Do you think the woman is being too harsh on her husband? Explain. **[Make a Judgment]**

APPLY

6. What issues would this couple have to discuss to reconcile their differences? **[Resolve]**

◆ Reading Strategy

READ BETWEEN THE LINES

Because Gordimer doesn't spell out the underlying conflict between blacks and whites, you must **read between the lines** to discover it. Find evidence of this conflict between the lines of the following descriptions:

1. "... the artists sprang, walking bent, like performing animals, the better to exhibit the fantasy held toward the faces on the train."
2. "A man passed beneath the arch of reaching arms meeting gray-black and white in the exchange of money ..."

◆ Build Vocabulary

USING THE LATIN PREFIX a-

Use your knowledge of the Latin prefix a- to explain each of these terms:

1. *atypical* situation
2. *asymmetrical* design
3. *amoral* person
4. *atonal* music

USING THE WORD BANK: Context

As the woman in the story, write a diary entry about the incident at the station. Use all the words from the Word Bank in your entry.

◆ Literary Focus

CONFLICT AND THEME

As the **conflicts** in the story become clearer—the woman's inner struggle and her struggle with her husband—so does its central idea, its **theme**. You can trace the stages by which the woman understands her conflicts and their meaning. First she vaguely senses something "terrible" about the unheard roar of the carved lion. Then she is dimly aware that her relationship with her husband has an "unreality ... that living with him ... was part of the holiday, the strange places."

1. Why does her conflict with her husband flare up when he buys the lion so cheaply?
2. (a) How does the "shame" she feels relate to an inner conflict? (b) Why might she explain her inner "void" differently from the way she once did?
3. Are the woman's conflicts resolved at the end of the story? Why or why not?
4. In a thematic statement, explain the link between the woman's conflicts and those in the society.

◆ Grammar and Style

ABSOLUTE PHRASES

Gordimer uses **absolute phrases,** which contain a participle and the word the participle modifies, to add details to descriptions. These details bring scenes to life, heighten suspense, and point out conflicts.

Practice On your paper, identify the absolute phrase in each sentence and describe its effect.

1. A man passed beneath the arch of reaching arms meeting ... in the exchange of money for the staring wooden eyes, the stiff wooden legs sticking up in the air.
2. The stationmaster was leaning against the end of the train, green flag rolled in readiness.
3. Joints not yet coordinated, the segmented body of the train ... bumped back against itself.
4. If you wanted the thing, she said, her voice rising and breaking with the shrill impotence of anger, why didn't you buy it in the first place?
5. She sat down again in the corner and, her face slumped in her hand, stared out of the window.

Build Your Portfolio

 ## Idea Bank

Writing

1. Letter of Advice Suppose you are a friend of the young woman in the story. Write her a letter advising her what to do about her new feelings of "shame" and "weariness."

2. Interpretation Why does Gordimer say at the end, "The train had cast the station like a skin"? Explain the meaning of this image by connecting it to other passages in the story.

3. Evaluation Do you think the story is pessimistic or optimistic about the relations of blacks and whites in Southern Africa? Use specific passages to support the points you make.

Speaking, Listening, and Viewing

4. Debate Divide into teams and debate this proposition: Colonialism brought little or nothing of value to the native peoples of Africa. **[Social Studies Link]**

5. Nobel Prize Address Find the speech that Gordimer made on receiving the Nobel Prize for Literature in 1991. Then rehearse it, choosing the words you will emphasize, and present it to the class. **[Literature Link; Performing Arts Link]**

Researching and Representing

6. Retelling Find a book or a recording of folk tales that come from Southern Africa. Choose one of these and retell it to the class. Keep the main story line, but add details if you like. **[Performing Arts Link; Social Studies Link]**

7. African Art What might the carved lion in the story look like? In an art book, find examples of sculpture from Southern Africa. Show the class pictures of this sculpture, and share what you've learned about it. **[Art Link]**

Online Activity www.phlit.phschool.com

 ## Guided Writing Lesson

Wedding Speech

In "The Train from Rhodesia," Gordimer uses a minor incident to reveal the personalities of her characters. You can use the same device to reveal a friend's personality. Imagine that you must write and deliver a speech about a friend at his or her wedding. To help people appreciate your friend, focus on an incident that discloses the real person. Be sure to use the right level of formality for the occasion.

Writing Skills Focus: Level of Formality

No matter what you write, you can decide on the **level of formality** to use by considering your audience. You can be very casual in a letter to a good friend. However, in speaking to a wedding crowd, you will be addressing a variety of people who know your friend in different ways. It is therefore appropriate to be a bit more formal than you would in a letter to someone who knows you well. However, you can be conversational and humorous.

Prewriting To bring to mind your friend's traits and stories that illustrate them, use a cluster diagram like this to organize your thoughts.

Julia

Drafting Choose one story that illustrates your friend's personality. Before telling it, introduce yourself, describe your relationship with your friend, and provide any background that listeners will need to understand the story. As you tell the anecdote, help yourself reach the right level of formality by picturing your audience in front of you.

Revising Read your speech aloud to several friends who know your subject. Use their comments and suggestions to improve your speech.

Guide for Interpreting

Derek Walcott *(1930–   )*

Both Derek Walcott's grandmothers were descended from African slaves, and both of his grandfathers were white. Throughout his life, the poet has had to reflect upon these contrasting elements in his heritage. These reflections have propelled his poems, which may lead the reader from Trinidad to ancient Greece, sometimes in a single line of poetry.

Early Success Walcott was born on the Caribbean Island of St. Lucia and attended university in Jamaica, where he now lives. He published the first of his many books of poetry, *Twenty-five Poems*, when he was just a teenager. His subsequent books of poetry include, among others, *The Gulf* (1970), *Sea Grapes* (1976), and *Collected Poems* 1948–1984 (1986).

Playwright In addition to being a poet, Walcott is also an accomplished playwright. He was the founding director of the Trinidad Theatre Workshop (1959), which staged a number of his plays. In these dramas, he explores his Caribbean roots even more deeply than he does in his poetry. His most famous play is *Dream on Monkey Mountain*, which won an Obie award (1971) when it was produced in New York. Walcott recently collaborated with composer Paul Simon on a Broadway musical, *The Capeman* (1997).

Walcott has taught at a number of American colleges, including Boston University, and is just as at home in the United States as he is in the Caribbean.

Most critics agree that it was his 1990 book, *Omeros*, which draws on the epics of the ancient Greek poet Homer, that ensured his winning the Nobel Prize for Literature in 1992. The Swedish Academy granting the award concluded that "West Indian culture has found its great poet."

James Berry *(1925–   )*

Born in a small village in Jamaica and finally settling in Britain, Berry draws upon the imagery and rhythms of his rural West Indian background as well as the excitement and personal freedom of urban London.

Experiences of Poverty Berry's childhood experiences of poverty are common in the West Indies. He

had to leave school at age fourteen to help support his family. During World War II, he left Jamaica for the United States to find work. After living in several places, including Harlem, he returned to Jamaica, discouraged by the prejudice he encountered. Then, in 1948, he left for England and began to write.

His books include collections of stories for children like *A Thief in the Village*, which was a Coretta Scott King Honor Book in 1989. Among his volumes of poetry are *Fractured Circles* (1979) and *Lucy's Letters and Loving* (1982), from which "From Lucy: Englan' Lady" comes.

◆ Background for Understanding

HISTORY: WALCOTT, BERRY, AND THE BRITISH EMPIRE

Several island groups in the West Indies were part of the British Empire, and colonial settlers brought enslaved Africans to work on their plantations. These slaves were set free in the 1830's and, in the 1960's and 1970's, the islands won their political independence. A lasting legacy of British rule, however, is a British system of education and the use of the English language. Because of that legacy,

Walcott and Berry write in English but bring a Caribbean flavor and perspective to their work.

Many West Indians, including Berry, have emigrated to the United Kingdom in search of a better life. West Indians in Britain have suffered from racial prejudice and economic hardship. Sometimes frustrations erupt in violence, as in the April 1981 riots in the West Indian neighborhood of Brixton.

from Midsummer, XXIII ◆ from Omeros, from Chapter XXVIII ◆ From Lucy: Englan' Lady

◆ Literature and Your Life

CONNECT YOUR EXPERIENCE

Like Walcott's St. Lucia and Berry's Jamaica, the United States was once a British colony. In its struggle for independence, it adopted British principles and gave them eloquent expression in *The Declaration of Independence*.

Walcott and Berry, whose island nations won independence in their lifetimes, are also giving gifts to the English language, infusing it with a new Caribbean vision.

THEMATIC FOCUS: FROM THE NATIONAL TO THE GLOBAL

As you read, find the new words, rhythms, and perspectives that Walcott and Berry are contributing to the language.

◆ Literary Focus

THEME AND CONTEXT

The central insight expressed in a literary work is its **theme**. Often such insights are universal, applying to people who live in different places and times. No matter how global a theme is, however, you can better understand it by appreciating the local conditions from which it comes, its **context**.

The context of these poems is the colonial history of the Caribbean region and the experience of Caribbean immigrants in Britain. As a result, the insights these poets express come from a dialogue between British culture and Afro-Caribbean culture.

Journal Writing Jot down some interesting cultural combinations you have observed, in food, language, or customs.

◆ Grammar and Style

COMMONLY CONFUSED WORDS: *AFFECT* AND *EFFECT*

Two commonly confused words are *affect* and *effect*. In a poem that re-creates Jamaican English, Berry abbreviates the verb *affect*, which means "influence": "She *affec'* the place / like the sun." Keep these definitions in mind:

Affect most often means "to influence" (verb); it can also mean "mood; feeling" (noun).

Effect most often means "result" (noun); it can also mean "bring about" (verb).

◆ Reading Strategy

APPLY BACKGROUND INFORMATION

Sometimes you must **apply background information** to understand a poem. For example, the more you know about the history of the West Indies and the lives of Walcott and Berry, the better you will understand the language and attitudes of these poets.

It's especially helpful to apply background information to the excerpts from Walcott's *Midsummer* and *Omeros*. You can find this information on p. 1136 and in the footnotes to the poems. Also, keep in mind Walcott's mixed European and African heritage. This key detail helps explain his guilt and anger at the Brixton riots (*Midsummer*) and his fascination with his African roots (*Omeros*).

◆ Build Vocabulary

LATIN ROOTS: *-duc-*

In Walcott's *Midsummer*, you'll encounter the verb *inducted*, which means "to bring or lead formally into a group." Its Latin root, *-duc-*, which means "to lead," appears in such words as *conduct* and *education*.

WORD BANK

Before you read, preview this list of words from the poems.

antic
rancor
eclipse
inducted

from Midsummer XXIII

Derek Walcott

With the stampeding hiss and scurry of green lemmings,
midsummer's leaves race to extinction like the roar
of a Brixton riot[1] tunneled by water hoses;
they seethe towards autumn's fire—it is in their nature,

5   being men as well as leaves, to die for the sun.
The leaf stems tug at their chains, the branches bending
like Boer cattle under Tory whips that drag every wagon
nearer to apartheid.[2] And, for me, that closes
the child's fairy tale of an <u>antic</u> England—fairy rings,

10 thatched cottages fenced with dog roses,
a green gale lifting the hair of Warwickshire.
I was there to add some color to the British theater.
"But the blacks can't do Shakespeare, they have no experience."
This was true. Their thick skulls bled with <u>rancor</u>

15 when the riot police and the skinheads exchanged quips
you could trace to the Sonnets, or the Moor's <u>eclipse</u>.
Praise had bled my lines white of any more anger,
and snow had <u>inducted</u> me into white fellowships,
while Calibans howled down the barred streets of an empire

20 that began with Caedmon's raceless dew,[3] and is ending
in the alleys of Brixton, burning like Turner's ships.[4]

---

1. Brixton riot: Residents of the South London district of Brixton rioted in April 1981 to protest racial prejudice and economic disadvantage.

2. Boer (bōor) **cattle . . . apartheid:** In the seventeenth century, the Boers, people of Dutch descent, colonized a portion of what is now South Africa. The Tories, members of a political party in Britain, held power when the Boer War (1899–1902) resulted in British control of South Africa. The system of apartheid was established by the Boers when South Africa became a republic.

3. Caedmon's (kad´ mənz) **raceless dew:** Poetry written by the earliest known English poet, Caedmon, who lived in the seventh century.

4. Turner's ships: British artist J.M.W. Turner (1775–1851) painted atmospheric canvases of ships burning in battle.

◆ **Build Vocabulary**

antic (an´ tik) *adj.*: Odd and funny

rancor (raŋ´ kər) *n.*: Continuing, bitter hate or ill will

eclipse (ē klips´) *n.*: Dimming or extinction of fame or glory

inducted (in dukt´ id) *v.*: Brought formally into a society or organization; provided with knowledge or experience of something

Revolution Is Change, Change Is Life, 1988, Jean Patrick Icart-Pierre, The Bronx Museum of the Arts, New York

◀ **Critical Viewing** How does the painter suggest violence similar to "the roar/of a Brixton riot"? What details suggest that the rage of "Calibans" might express the desire for a more meaningful existence? **[Compare and Contrast]**

Guide for Responding

◆ *Literature and Your Life*

Reader's Response Does the tone and language of this poem make you feel as if you were listening to a British or West Indian person? Explain.

Thematic Focus What makes the issues Walcott discusses in this poem global rather than national?

☑ Check Your Comprehension

1. To what things does Walcott compare midsummer's leaves?

2. (a) What references to British history does Walcott make? (b) What event, recent at the time, does he include in those references?

◆ Critical Thinking

INTERPRET

1. What "closes" for the speaker "the child's fairy tale of an antic England"? Why? **[Interpret]**

2. What does the speaker mean when he says that the "empire ... is ending / in the alleys of Brixton"? **[Draw Conclusions]**

EVALUATE

3. From reading this poem, would you say that Walcott has come to terms with his dual heritage? Why or why not? **[Make a Judgment]**

APPLY

4. How does this poem affect your attitude toward racial prejudice? **[Relate]**

from Omeros

from Chapter XXVIII

Derek Walcott

Now he heard the griot[1] muttering his prophetic song
of sorrow that would be the past. It was a note, long-drawn
and endless in its winding like the brown river's tongue:

"We were the color of shadows when we came down
5   with tinkling leg-irons to join the chains of the sea,
for the silver coins multiplying on the sold horizon,

and these shadows are reprinted now on the white sand
of antipodal[2] coasts, your ashen ancestors
from the Bight of Benin, from the margin of Guinea.[3]

10   There were seeds in our stomachs, in the cracking pods
of our skulls on the scorching decks, the tubers[4]
withered in no time. We watched as the river-gods

changed from snakes into currents. When inspected,
our eyes showed dried fronds[5] in their brown irises,
15   and from our curved spines, the rib-cages radiated

---

1. griot (grē´ ō) *n.*: In West African cultures, a poet/historian/performer who preserves and passes on the oral tradition.
2. antipodal (an tip´ ə dəl) *adj.*: Situated on opposite sides of the earth.
3. the Bight (bīt) **of Benin** (be nēn´) **. . . Guinea** (gin´ ē): Area of west central Africa that came to be known as the Slave Coast.
4. tubers (to͞o´ bərz) *n.*: Thick, fleshy parts of underground stems, such as potatoes.
5. fronds (frändz) *n.*: Leaves of a palm; also the leaflike parts of seaweed.

like fronds from a palm-branch. Then, when the dead
palms were heaved overside, the ribbed corpses
floated, riding, to the white sand they remembered,

to the Bight of Benin, to the margin of Guinea.
20 So, when you see burnt branches riding the swell,
trying to reclaim the surf through crooked fingers,

after a night of rough wind by some stone-white hotel,
past the bright triangular passage of the windsurfers,
remember us to the black waiter bringing the bill."

25 But they crossed, they survived. There is the epical splendor.
Multiply the rain's lances, multiply their ruin,
the grace born from subtraction as the hold's iron door

rolled over their eyes like pots left out in the rain,
and the bolt rammed home its echo, the way that thunder-
30 claps perpetuate their reverberation.

So there went the Ashanti one way, the Mandingo another,
the Ibo another, the Guinea.[6] Now each man was a nation
in himself, without mother, father, brother.

---

6. **the Ashanti** (ə shan′ tĭ) . . . **the Mandingo** (man dĭn′ gō) . . .
the Ibo (ē′ bō′) . . . **the Guinea** (gĭn′ ē): Names of West African peoples.

Guide for Responding

◆ Literature and Your Life

Reader's Response How does the tone of
this poem affect you? Explain.

Thematic Focus What other factors besides
nationality determine people's identity, according to
the griot?

Group Activity In the excerpt from *Omeros*,
Walcott refers to the slave trade. With several
classmates, discuss what you know about the
process that brought enslaved Africans to
America and the Caribbean islands.

☑ Check Your Comprehension

1. In this excerpt from *Omeros*, what does the
speaker describe in lines 4 through 24?
2. What happens to members of the different
West African peoples once they cross the sea?

◆ Critical Thinking

INTERPRET

1. In this excerpt from *Omeros*, who is speaking
in lines 4 through 24? **[Infer]**
2. What does Walcott mean when he says, "Now
each man was a nation / in himself"? **[Interpret]**
3. Does anything positive come from the suffering
caused by the slave trade? Explain. **[Draw
Conclusions]**

EVALUATE

4. Would you say that Walcott has effectively
portrayed the condition of the enslaved
peoples? Explain. **[Assess]**

APPLY

5. What movies or television presentations have
you seen that explore the history of slavery?
[Relate]

From Lucy: Englan' Lady

James Berry

You ask me 'bout the lady. Me dear,
old center here still shine
with Queen. She affec' the place
like the sun: not comin' out oft'n
5   an' when it happ'n everybody's out
smilin' as she wave a han'
like a seagull flyin' slow slow.

An' you know she come from
dust free rooms an' velvet
10   an' diamond. She make you feel
this on-an'-on[1] town, London,
where long long time deeper than mind.[2]
An' han's after han's[3] die away,
makin' streets, putt'n' up bricks,
15   a piece of brass, a piece of wood
an' plantin' trees: an' it give
a car a halfday job gett'n' through.

An' Leela, darlin', no, I never
meet the Queen in flesh. Yet
20   sometimes, deep deep, I sorry for her.

Elizabeth II

▲ **Critical Viewing** Does Queen Elizabeth show the "strain keepin' good graces" referred to in the poem? Explain. **[Analyze]**

---

1. **on-an'-on:** Extraordinary.
2. **deeper . . . mind:** More than can be comprehended.
3. **han's after han's:** Many generations.

Everybody expec' a show
from her, like she a space touris'
on earth. An' darlin', unless
you can go home an' scratch up[4]
25   you' husban', it mus' be hard
strain keepin' good graces for
all hypocrite faces.

Anyhow, me dear, you know what
ole time people say,
30   "Bird sing sweet for its nest."[5]

---

4. **scratch up:** Lose your temper at.
5. **"Bird . . . nest":** Jamaican proverb, referring to
the nightingale's habit of singing loudest near its
nest. It means, "Those closest to home are the
most contented."

Elizabeth II at Age 18 at Sandringham

▲ **Critical Viewing** What details in this
photograph suggest the "human" side
of the queen, the side alluded to by
the poem's speaker? **[Analyze]**

Guide for Responding

◆ Literature and Your Life

Reader's Response How did you react to
Lucy's description of Queen Elizabeth?

Thematic Focus What is distinctively Jamaican
about Lucy's comments on the Queen?

Proverbs and Sayings Lucy closes her letter
with a Jamaican proverb. In a small group, brainstorm to come up with other proverbs similar
to Lucy's.

☑ Check Your Comprehension

1. Where is the speaker of this poem?
2. To whom is the poem addressed?
3. According to Lucy, how is the Queen
   like the sun?

◆ Critical Thinking

INTERPRET

1. What problems does Lucy think the Queen
   has as a result of her position? **[Interpret]**
2. What perception of the Queen does Lucy
   illustrate by quoting the proverb in line 30?
   [Connect]
3. What can you infer about Lucy's character
   from her "letter"? **[Draw Conclusions]**

EVALUATE

4. Is this poem effective in conveying the rhythm
   and feel of Jamaican dialect? Explain. **[Evaluate]**

APPLY

5. How do you think Lucy would react to life
   in the United States? **[Hypothesize]**

Guide for Responding *(continued)*

◆ Reading Strategy

APPLY BACKGROUND INFORMATION

By **applying background information** from the writers' biographies, the Background for Understanding, and the footnotes, you can better understand the poems. For example, Walcott's divided heritage—part European, part African—explains why he seems to accuse himself of not sharing the rioters' fury: "Praise had bled my lines white of any more anger." It's as if he's saying that his own white heritage and British "praise" for his work have led him to betray his African origins.

1. If Walcott expresses the conflict of a divided heritage in *Midsummer*, how does he deal with that heritage in the excerpt from *Omeros*?
2. How do Berry's rural Jamaican background and longtime residence in London help explain the word choice, form, and subject matter of his poem?

◆ Literary Focus

THEME AND CONTEXT

The **themes** of these poems, their central insights, cannot be separated from their **context**: the history of British colonization in the Caribbean and the recent immigration of West Indians to Britain. Because of this history, the key ideas in these poems relate to the collision of cultures. In *Midsummer*, XXIII, that collision sparks a riot, while in "From Lucy: Englan' Lady," it lights a twinkle in the eye of a Jamaican woman.

1. In *Midsummer*, explain how a clash between cultures ignites a conflict in the poet's mind.
2. (a) What is the conflict between cultures that Walcott brings to life in the excerpt from *Omeros*? (b) Is there also an internal conflict? Why or why not?
3. (a) In Berry's poem, what does Lucy find impressive about London, her new home? (b) As a rural Jamaican, why might she be especially impressed by this aspect of London?
4. (a) Identify two ways in which Lucy brings a humorous Jamaican twist to her observations of an English queen. (b) Overall, would you say that Lucy appreciates British culture? Explain.

◆ Build Vocabulary

USING THE LATIN ROOT *-duc-*

Briefly explain how the meaning of the Latin root -duc- ("to lead") contributes to the definition of each italicized word:

I'm here to *conduct* the tour of a typical West Indian sugar plantation that will be very *educational*. Please, don't bump into the *ducts* that transport the juice from the pressed sugarcane stalks. In this room, the juice is concentrated by evaporation into a dark, sticky sugar, a *product* that can be sold locally —it can be further refined by eliminating nonsugar elements. Under British colonialism, the plantation was owned by the *Duchess* of Devonshire. Perhaps I can *induce* you to donate to our museum on the way out.

USING THE WORD BANK: Synonyms

On your paper write the lettered word closest in meaning to the first word.

1. rancor: (a) pleasure, (b) hate, (c) music
2. inducted: (a) initiated, (b) cried, (c) lost
3. antic: (a) zany, (b) dangerous, (c) helpful
4. eclipse: (a) burst, (b) fire, (c) extinction

◆ Grammar and Style

COMMONLY CONFUSED WORDS: *AFFECT* AND *EFFECT*

You can usually avoid confusing **affect** and **effect** by deciding whether you want a verb meaning "to influence" (*affect*) or a noun meaning "result" (*effect*). Other forms of these words—*affect* as a noun ("mood") and *effect* as a verb ("bring about") are less common.

Practice On your paper, insert the correct word.
1. Berry's stay in Harlem had a great (affect, effect) upon his ideas about prejudice.
2. Walcott's multiracial background has (effected, affected) the kind of poetry he writes.
3. The (affect, effect) of Berry's poetry is to change the way West Indians view themselves.
4. Was Walcott less (effected, affected) by the Brixton riot when it happened than he was later?
5. Readers respond strongly to the (effect, affect) of Berry's use of Jamaican dialect in his Lucy poems.

Build Your Portfolio

Idea Bank

Writing

1. **Personal Letter** Write a letter to Lucy giving her some recent news about the queen and other members of Britain's royal family. Respond to some of the ideas she expresses in her letter.

2. **Literary Analysis** Choose one of these poems and show how its author brings Caribbean language, rhythms, and perspectives to English.

3. **Response to Criticism** Louis James writes that in *Midsummer*, Derek Walcott tries "to reconcile his divided heritage." Show how Walcott makes this attempt in *Midsummer*, XXIII.

Speaking, Listening, and Viewing

4. **Oral Interpretation of Dialect** Perform Berry's dialect poem for the class. In rehearsing, follow the poet's own advice for reading a poem in Jamaican dialect: "Feel out the rhythms. . . . Then express it with your own easy natural voice." **[Performing Arts Link]**

5. **Debate** Are Caribbean immigrants better off shedding their culture and adapting fully to their new British home, or is there value in holding on to traditions? Organize a debate about the issue. **[Social Studies Link]**

Researching and Representing

6. **Black Roots** What happened to the Ashanti and other African cultures transplanted to the Caribbean by slavery? Research the answer in books on Caribbean history and write a report on your findings. **[Social Studies Link]**

7. **Caribbean Festival** Prepare a festival of Caribbean culture. Highlight the language, food, and music of Jamaica, St. Lucia, and other countries in the region. **[Social Studies Link]**

Online Activity www.phlit.phschool.com

Guided Writing Lesson

Pro-and-Con Editorial

"From Lucy: Englan' Lady" offers a humorous, endearingly biased portrait of the Queen. Today, however, the royal family is a controversial issue. Some think it is an expensive symbol of the past that should be eliminated. Others think it is an important tradition that must be maintained. Discuss this subject in an editorial written for a local newspaper. Give the arguments on both sides, the pros and cons, before expressing your own opinion.

Writing Skills Focus: Transitions to Show Comparisons

In giving pro-and-con arguments, you'll want to use **transitions to show comparisons**. Such transitions help readers find their way among different arguments. Following are some commonly used transitions:

on the one hand	however
on the other hand	nevertheless
while	

Prewriting Jot down a sentence or phrase that sums up the main point of your editorial. Under it, summarize arguments for and against your point of view.

Drafting Begin with a question, image, or anecdote that will surprise readers, get their attention, and possibly even support your main point. As you move from arguments for to arguments against, use transitions to show comparisons.

Revising If possible, choose as a peer editor someone who has taken the opposite point of view. Have this person carefully read your editorial and suggest any strong arguments against your position that you may have left out. Include and respond to these arguments, making sure you use transitions to show comparisons.

Guide for Interpreting

Anita Desai *(1937–   )*

Anita Desai's unusual heritage—her father was Indian and her mother German—may have contributed to her understanding of people from different cultures. She displays that understanding in finely-crafted novels and short stories about conflicts among people of different generations and backgrounds. These works of fiction have gained her a reputation as one of the most gifted Indian novelists writing in English.

Early Life Desai was born in the northern Indian town of Mussoorie, located at the foot of the Himalayan mountains. She grew up in a large house in the old section of Delhi, India's capital city.

> *"There were a great many books in the house and we were all book-worms," Desai recalls.*

Because of her unique heritage, her family spoke three languages—Hindi, English, and German. However, English became Desai's literary language.

Early Work and Recognition After graduating from Delhi University, Desai, newly married, joined the Writers Workshop in Calcutta. In 1963, she published her first novel, *Cry the Peacock*, a portrayal of the despair of a young married woman. This novel was followed by *Bye-Bye, Blackbird* (1968), *Fire on the Mountain* (1977), and *Clear Light of Day* (1980).

This last novel, a study of complex family relationships, was nominated for England's prestigious Booker Prize. The critic Victoria Glendinning said of this work, "Quiet writing, like Anita Desai's, can be more impressive than stylistic fireworks."

Teaching Career After winning success as a writer, Desai pursued a teaching career, too. She has taught, for example, at Cambridge University in England and at Smith College in Massachusetts.

Recent Fiction In her recent novels, Desai examines the gulf between reality and the delusions of her characters. Another theme of her work, evident in *Baumgartner's Bombay* (1989) and in *Journey to Ithaca* (1995), is the contrast between Indian and modern European perspectives. *Journey to Ithaca*, for example, features a European couple who travel to India on a quest for spiritual meaning. "A Devoted Son," which first appeared in the collection of short stories *Games at Twilight* (1978), also shows a clash between modern and traditional Indian values.

◆ Background for Understanding

CULTURE: DESAI'S PORTRAIT OF INDIA, OLD AND NEW

Ever since India won its independence from Britain in 1947, increasing modernization has resulted in dramatic contrasts between the old and the new. For example, it's not unusual to see a camel pulling a cart filled with brand-new motorcycles or a fax sign at a traditional marketplace.

In her story, Anita Desai alludes to traditional customs of Indian family life, as when children show their father respect by touching his feet. Desai also shows the customary way in which several generations live in the same household.

However, Desai contrasts these traditions with features of the new India: travel for study in the United States, a scientific attitude toward public health, and a challenge to the older generation's household authority. The title "A Devoted Son" is, therefore, a bit ironic. It suggests the India of old, while the story captures the poignant contradictions of old and new. In the new India, devotion may not be all that it seems.

A Devoted Son

◆ Literature and Your Life

CONNECT YOUR EXPERIENCE

Computers, VCRs, cellular phones, the Internet, fax machines: Are you more "plugged in" to the latest technology than your parents are? When it comes to gadgets, do you feel that the older generation is just a little slow to pick up on things?

In "A Devoted Son," a major theme is the difference between generations, especially in their reactions to what is new.

Journal Writing Freewrite about some of the ways in which your generation differs from your parents' generation.

THEMATIC FOCUS: FROM THE NATIONAL TO THE GLOBAL

As you read this story, notice that Desai is not simply a "regional" author. The conflicts she depicts are universal.

◆ Literary Focus

STATIC AND DYNAMIC CHARACTERS

A **static character** is a figure in a literary work who does not change. In contrast, a figure who undergoes significant change is called a **dynamic character.** Often readers feel that a dynamic character is more lifelike—the basis of life is change—and therefore more appealing.

In "A Devoted Son," only one character is dynamic. Consider whether the character who changes is someone who *believes* in change or someone who is committed to traditional ways.

◆ Grammar and Style

SENTENCE VARIETY

Sentence variety makes for lively, interesting writing. Sentences can vary by length, type (declarative, interrogative, imperative), structure (simple, compound, complex), and placement of elements like appositives and participial phrases.

Notice how Desai uses sentence variety in the fourth paragraph of her story to dramatize a family's joy. Two short, simple sentences are followed by a longer sentence and then by a very long sentence, with parallel phrases and clauses, ending with the words "golden and glorious." Be alert to other passages in which sentence variety heightens the suspense or drama.

◆ Reading Strategy

EVALUATE CHARACTERS' DECISIONS

Like people in life, characters in literary works make choices. You can **evaluate** their choices just as you would assess your own decisions: Was the decision based on logic or emotion? Were the results worth the risks, and why? Also, just as you might celebrate or regret a decision you have made, you can respond emotionally to the choices that literary characters make.

Each time a character in this story makes a choice, evaluate it and trace its effects on future actions. In making such judgments, however, don't forget to mourn and rejoice with characters as they live out the results of their decisions.

◆ Build Vocabulary

LATIN ROOTS: -fil-

In "A Devoted Son," you will find the word *filial.* This word contains the Latin root -*fil*-, meaning "son or daughter," and means "suitable to, or due from, a son or daughter." Look for other words with this root, like *affiliation.*

WORD BANK

Before you read, preview this list of words from the story.

| exemplary |
| filial |
| encomiums |
| complaisant |
| fathom |

A DEVOTED SON

Anita Desai

When the results appeared in the morning papers, Rakesh scanned them barefoot and in his pajamas, at the garden gate, then went up the steps to the verandah where his father sat sipping his morning tea and bowed down to touch his feet.

"A first division, son?" his father asked, beaming, reaching for the papers.

"At the top of the list, papa," Rakesh murmured, as if awed. "First in the country."

Bedlam broke loose then. The family whooped and danced. The whole day long visitors streamed into the small yellow house at the end of the road to congratulate the parents of this *Wunderkind*,[1] to slap Rakesh on the back and fill the house and garden with the sounds and colors of a festival. There were garlands and halwa,[2] party clothes and gifts (enough fountain pens to last years, even a watch or two), nerves and temper and joy, all in a multicolored whirl of pride and great shining vistas newly opened: Rakesh was the first son in the family to receive an education, so much had been sacrificed in order to send him to school and then medical college, and at last the fruits of their sacrifice had arrived, golden and glorious.

To everyone who came to him to say "*Mubarak*, Varmaji, your son has brought you glory," the father said, "Yes, and do you know what is the first thing he did when he saw the results this morning? He came and touched my feet. He bowed down and touched my feet." This moved many of the women in the crowd so much that they were seen to raise the ends of their saris and dab at their tears while the men reached out for the betel-leaves[3] and sweetmeats that were offered around on trays and shook their heads in wonder and approval of such exemplary filial behavior. "One does not often see such behavior in sons any more," they all agreed, a little enviously perhaps. Leaving the house, some of the women said, sniffing, "At least on such an occasion they might have served pure *ghee*[4] sweets," and some of the men said, "Don't you think old Varma was giving himself airs? He needn't think we don't remember that he comes from the vegetable

---

1. *Wunderkind:* Person who achieves remarkable success at an early age.
2. **halwa (also halva):** Middle Eastern sweet confection made of sesame flour and honey.

3. **betel-leaves:** Leaves of a climbing evergreen shrub which are chewed in the East with betel nut parings and a little lime.
4. *ghee:* Clarified butter, often used in Indian cooking.

market himself, his father used to sell vegetables, and he has never seen the inside of a school." But there was more envy than rancor[5] in their voices and it was, of course, inevitable—not every son in that shabby little colony at the edge of the city was destined to shine as Rakesh shone, and who knew that better than the parents themselves?

And that was only the beginning, the first step in a great, sweeping ascent to the radiant heights of fame and fortune. The thesis he wrote for his M.D. brought Rakesh still greater glory, if only in select medical circles. He won a scholarship. He went to the USA (that was what his father learnt to call it and taught the whole family to say—not America, which was what the ignorant neighbors called it, but, with a grand familiarity, "the USA") where he pursued his career in the most prestigious of all hospitals and won <u>encomiums</u> from his American colleagues which were relayed to his admiring and glowing family. What was more, he came *back*, he actually returned to that small yellow house in the once-new but increasingly shabby colony, right at the end of the road where the rubbish vans tipped out their stinking contents for pigs to nose in and rag-pickers to build their shacks on, all steaming and smoking just outside the neat wire fences and well-tended gardens. To this Rakesh returned and the first thing he did on entering the house was to slip out of the embraces of his sisters and brothers and bow down and touch his father's feet.

As for his mother, she gloated chiefly over the strange fact that he had not married in America, had not brought home a foreign wife as all her neighbors had warned her he would, for wasn't that what all Indian boys went abroad for? Instead he agreed, almost without argument, to marry a girl she had picked out for him in her own village, the daughter of a childhood friend, a plump and uneducated girl, it was true, but so old-fashioned, so placid, so <u>complaisant</u> that she slipped into the household and settled in like a charm, seemingly too

lazy and too good-natured to even try and make Rakesh leave home and set up independently, as any other girl might have done. What was more, she was pretty—really pretty, in a plump, pudding way that only gave way to fat—soft, spreading fat, like warm wax—after the birth of their first baby, a son, and then what did it matter?

For some years Rakesh worked in the city hospital, quickly rising to the top of the administrative organization, and was made a director before he left to set up his own clinic. He took his parents in his car—a new, sky-blue Ambassador with a rear window full of stickers and charms revolving on strings—to see the clinic when it was built, and the large sign-board over the door on which his name was printed in letters of red, with a row of degrees and qualifications to follow it like so many little black slaves of the regent.[6] Thereafter his fame seemed to grow just a little dimmer—or maybe it was only that everyone in town had grown accustomed to it at last—but it was also the beginning of his fortune for he now became known not only as the best but also the richest doctor in town.

However, all this was not accomplished in the wink of an eye. Naturally not. It was the achievement of a lifetime and it took up Rakesh's whole life. At the time he set up his clinic his father had grown into an old man and retired from his post at the kerosene dealer's depot at which he had worked for forty

◆ **Reading Strategy**
What seems to be guiding the decisions Rakesh is making about his life? What kind of character do these decisions show him to be?

◆ **Build Vocabulary**

exemplary (eg zem´ plə rē) *adj.*: Serving as a model or example; of that which should be imitated

filial (fil´ ē əl) *adj.*: Suitable to, of, or from a son or daughter

encomiums (en kō´ mē əmz) *n.*: Formal expressions of great praise

complaisant (kəm plā´ zənt) *adj.*: Agreeable; willing to please

years, and his mother died soon after, giving up the ghost with a sigh that sounded positively happy, for it was her own son who ministered to her in her last illness and who sat pressing her feet at the last moment—such a son as few women had borne.

For it had to be admitted—and the most unsuccessful and most rancorous of neighbors eventually did so—that Rakesh was not only a devoted son and a miraculously good-natured man who contrived somehow to obey his parents and humor his wife and show concern equally for his children and his patients, but there was actually a brain inside this beautifully polished and formed body of good manners and kind nature and, in between ministering to his family and playing host to many friends and coaxing them all into feeling happy and grateful and content, he had actually trained his hands as well and emerged an excellent doctor, a really fine surgeon. How one man—and a man born to illiterate parents, his father having worked for a kerosene dealer and his mother having spent her life in a kitchen—had achieved, combined and conducted such a medley of virtues, no one could <u>fathom</u>, but all acknowledged his talent and skill.

It was a strange fact, however, that talent and skill, if displayed for too long, cease to dazzle. It came to pass that the most admiring of all eyes eventually faded and no longer blinked at his glory. Having retired from work and having lost his wife, the old father very quickly went to pieces, as they say. He developed so many complaints and fell ill so frequently and with such mysterious diseases that even his son could no longer make out when it was something of significance and when it was merely a peevish whim. He sat huddled on his string bed most of the day and developed an exasperating habit of stretching out suddenly and lying absolutely still, allowing the whole family to fly around him in a flap, wailing and weeping, and then suddenly sitting up, stiff and gaunt, and spitting out a big gob of betel-juice as if to mock their behavior.

He did this once too often: there had been a big party in the house, a birthday party for the youngest son, and the celebrations had to be suddenly hushed, covered up and hustled out of the way when the daughter-in-law discovered, or thought she discovered, that the old man, stretched out from end to end of his string bed, had lost his pulse; the party broke up, dissolved, even turned into a band of mourners, when the old man sat up and the distraught daughter-in-law received a gob of red spittle right on the hem of her organza sari.[7] After that no one much cared if he sat up crosslegged on his bed, hawking and spitting, or lay down flat and turned gray as a corpse. Except, of course, for that pearl amongst pearls, his son Rakesh.

It was Rakesh who brought him his morning tea, not in one of the china cups from which the rest of the family drank, but in the old man's favorite brass tumbler, and sat at the edge of his bed, comfortable and relaxed with the string of his pajamas dangling out from under his fine lawn night-shirt, and discussed or, rather, read out the morning news to his father. It made no difference to him that his father made no response apart from spitting. It was Rakesh, too, who, on returning from the clinic in the evening, persuaded the old man to come out of his room, as bare and desolate as a cell, and take the evening air out in the garden, beautifully arranging the pillows and bolsters on the *divan* in the corner of the open verandah. On summer nights he saw to it that the servants carried out the old man's bed onto the lawn and himself helped his father down the steps and onto the bed, soothing him and settling him down for a night under the stars.

All this was very gratifying for the old man. What was not so gratifying was that he even undertook to supervise his father's diet. One day when the father was really sick, having

---

7. **organza sari:** Saris are traditional garments worn by Indian women, consisting of lengths of cotton, silk, or other cloth wrapped around the waist and draped over one shoulder; organza is a sheer, stiffened fabric.

▲ **Critical Viewing** How comfortable do you imagine it is for a man such as Rakesh or the businessman in the photograph to dwell among those less fortunate than themselves? [Speculate]

ordered his daughter-in-law to make him a dish of *soojie halwa* and eaten it with a saucerful of cream, Rakesh marched into the room, not with his usual respectful step but with the confidant and rather contemptuous stride of the famous doctor, and declared, "No more *halwa* for you, papa. We must be sensible, at your age. If you must have something sweet, Veena will cook you a little *kheer*,[8] that's light, just a little rice and milk. But nothing fried, nothing rich. We can't have this happening again."

The old man who had been lying stretched out on his bed, weak and feeble after a day's illness, gave a start at the very sound, the tone of these

> ◆ **Literary Focus**
> Does Rakesh's "rather contemptuous stride" show a change in his character? In what way is he still the ideal son in this scene?

words. He opened his eyes—rather, they fell open with shock—and he stared at his son with disbelief that darkened quickly to reproach. A son who actually refused his father the food he craved? No, it was unheard of, it was incredible. But Rakesh had turned his back to him and was cleaning up the litter of bottles and packets on the medicine shelf and did not notice while Veena slipped silently out of the room with a little smirk that only the old man saw, and hated.

Halwa was only the first item to be crossed off the old man's diet. One delicacy after the other went—everything fried to begin with, then everything sweet, and eventually everything, everything that the old man enjoyed. The meals that arrived for him on the shining

---

8. **kheer:** Rice pudding traditionally served as a dessert in Southern India.

◀ **Critical Viewing** Name three details in this photograph that illustrate the story's theme of ambition and the conflict between the modern and the traditional. **[Interpret]**

stainless steel tray twice a day were frugal to say the least—dry bread, boiled lentils, boiled vegetables and, if there were a bit of chicken or fish, that was boiled too. If he called for another helping—in a cracked voice that quavered theatrically—Rakesh himself would come to the door, gaze at him sadly and shake his head, saying, "Now, papa, we must be careful, we can't risk another illness, you know," and although the daughter-in-law kept tactfully out of the way, the old man could just see her smirk sliding merrily through the air. He tried to bribe his grand-children into buying him sweets (and how he missed his wife now, that generous, indulgent and illiterate cook), whispering, "Here's fifty paise," as he stuffed the coins into a tight, hot fist. "Run down to the shop at the crossroads and buy me thirty paise worth of *jalebis*,[9] and you can spend the remaining twenty paise on yourself. Eh? Understand? Will you do that?" He got away with it once or twice but then was found out, the conspirator was scolded by his father and smacked by his mother and Rakesh came storming into the room, almost tearing his hair as he shouted through compressed lips, "Now papa, are you

---

9. **jalebis:** Indian sweet made by frying a coil of batter and then soaking it in syrup.

trying to turn my little son into a liar? Quite apart from spoiling your own stomach, you are spoiling him as well—you are encouraging him to lie to his own parents. You should have heard the lies he told his mother when she saw him bringing back those jalebis wrapped up in filthy newspaper. I don't allow anyone in my house to buy sweets in the bazaar, papa, surely you know that. There's cholera in the city, typhoid, gastroenteritis[10]—I see these cases daily in the hospital, how can I allow my own family to run such risks?" The old man sighed and lay down in the corpse position. But that worried no one any longer.

There was only one pleasure left in the old man now (his son's early morning visits and readings from the newspaper could no longer be called that) and those were visits from elderly neighbors. These were not frequent as his contemporaries were mostly as decrepit and helpless as he and few could walk the length of the road to visit him any more. Old Bhatia, next door, however, who was still spry enough to refuse, adamantly, to bathe in the tiled bathroom indoors and to insist on carrying out his brass mug and towel, in all seasons and usually at impossible hours, into the yard and bathe noisily under the garden tap, would look over the hedge to see if Varma were out on his verandah and would call to him and talk while he wrapped his *dhoti*[11] about him and dried the sparse hair on his head, shivering with enjoyable exaggeration. Of course these conversations, bawled across the hedge by two rather deaf old men conscious of having their entire households overhearing them, were not very satisfactory but Bhatia occasionally came out of his yard, walked down the bit of road and came in at Varma's gate to collapse onto the stone plinth built under the temple tree. If Rakesh was at home he would help his father down the steps into the garden and arrange him on his night bed under the tree and leave the two old men to chew betel-leaves and discuss the ills of their individual bodies with combined passion.

"At least you have a doctor in the house to look after you," sighed Bhatia, having vividly described his martyrdom to piles.

"Look after me?" cried Varma, his voice cracking like an ancient clay jar. "He—he does not even give me enough to eat."

"What?" said Bhatia, the white hairs in his ears twitching. "Doesn't give you enough to eat? Your own son?"

"My own son. If I ask him for one more piece of bread, he says no, papa, I weighed out the *ata* myself and I can't allow you to have more than two hundred grams of cereal a day. He *weighs* the food he gives me, Bhatia—he has scales to weigh it on. That is what it has come to."

"Never," murmured Bhatia in disbelief. "Is it possible, even in this evil age, for a son to refuse his father food?"

"Let me tell you," Varma whispered eagerly. "Today the family was having fried fish—I could smell it. I called to my daughter-in-law to bring me a piece. She came to the door and said no. . . ."

"Said no?" It was Bhatia's voice that cracked. A *drongo*[12] shot out of the tree and sped away. *"No?"*

"No, she said no, Rakesh has ordered her to give me nothing fried. No butter, he says, no oil. . . ."

"No butter? No oil? How does he expect his father to *live?*"

Old Varma nodded with melancholy triumph. "That is how he treats me—after I have brought him up, given him an education, made him a great doctor. Great doctor! This is the way great doctors treat their fathers, Bhatia," for the son's sterling personality and character now underwent a curious sea change. Outwardly all might be the same but the interpretation had altered: his masterly efficiency was nothing but cold heartlessness, his authority was only tyranny in disguise.

There was cold comfort in complaining to neighbors and, on such a miserable diet,

---

10. cholera...typhoid, gastroenteritis: Dangerous infectious diseases causing fever or intestinal problems.

11. *dhoti:* Cloth worn by male Hindus, the ends being passed through the legs and tucked in at the waist.

12. *drongo:* Any of several black birds with long forked tails, native to Africa, Southern Asia, and Australia.

Varma found himself slipping, weakening and soon becoming a genuinely sick man. Powders and pills and mixtures were not only brought in when dealing with a crisis like an upset stomach but became a regular part of his diet—became his diet, complained Varma, supplanting the natural foods he craved. There were pills to regulate his bowel movements, pills to bring down his blood pressure, pills to deal with his arthritis and, eventually, pills to keep his heart beating. In between there were panicky rushes to the hospital, some humiliating experience with the stomach pump and enema, which left him frightened and helpless. He cried easily, shriveling up on his bed, but if he complained of a pain or even a vague, gray fear in the night, Rakesh would simply open another bottle of pills and force him to take one. "I have my duty to you papa," he said when his father begged to be let off.

"Let me be," Varma begged, turning his face away from the pills on the outstretched hand. "Let me die. It would be better. I do not want to live only to eat your medicines."

"Papa, be reasonable."

"I leave that to you," the father cried with sudden spirit. "Leave me alone, let me die now, I cannot live like this."

"Lying all day on his pillows, fed every few hours by his daughter-in-law's own hand, visited by every member of his family daily—and then he says he does not want to live 'like this,'" Rakesh was heard to say, laughing, to someone outside the door.

"Deprived of food," screamed the old man on the bed, "his wishes ignored, taunted by his daughter-in-law, laughed at by his grand-children—*that* is how I live." But he was very old and weak and all anyone heard was an incoherent croak, some expressive grunts and cries of genuine pain. Only once, when old Bhatia had come to see him and they sat together under the temple tree, they heard him cry, "God is calling me—and they won't let me go."

The quantities of vitamins and tonics he was made to take were not altogether useless. They kept him alive and even gave him a kind of strength that made him hang on long after he ceased to wish to hang on. It was as though he were straining at a rope, trying to break it, and it would not break, it was still strong. He only hurt himself, trying.

In the evening, that summer, the servants would come into his cell, grip his bed, one at each end, and carry it out to the verandah, there sitting it down with a thump that jarred every tooth in his head. In answer to his agonized complaints they said the doctor sahib had told them he must take the evening air and the evening air they would make him take—thump. Then Veena, that smiling, hypocritical pudding in a rustling sari, would appear and pile up the pillows under his head till he was propped up stiffly into a sitting position that made his head swim and his back ache.

"Let me lie down," he begged. "I can't sit up any more."

"Try, papa, Rakesh said you can if you try," she said, and drifted away to the other end of the verandah where her transistor radio vibrated to the lovesick tunes from the cinema that she listened to all day.

So there he sat, like some stiff corpse, terrified, gazing out on the lawn where his grandsons played cricket,[13] in danger of getting one of their hard-spun balls in his eye, and at the gate that opened onto the dusty and rubbish-heaped lane but still bore, proudly, a newly touched-up signboard that bore his son's name and qualifications, his own name having vanished from the gate long ago.

At last the sky-blue Ambassador arrived, the cricket game broke up in haste, the car drove in smartly and the doctor, the great doctor, all in white, stepped out. Someone ran up to take his bag from him, others to escort him up the steps. "Will you have tea?" his wife called, turning down the transistor set. "Or a Coca-Cola? Shall I fry you some *samosas*?"[14] But he did not reply or even

◆ **Literary Focus**
Compare the father's character at the end of the story with the proud father and the betel-juice spitter of earlier scenes. Is he more sympathetic? Explain.

---

13. cricket: Open-air game played between two teams and utilizing a ball, bats, and wicket.

glance in her direction. Ever a devoted son, he went first to the corner where his father sat gazing, stricken, at some undefined spot in the dusty yellow air that swam before him. He did not turn his head to look at his son. But he stopped gobbling air with his uncontrolled lips and set his jaw as hard as a sick and very old man could set it.

"Papa," his son said, tenderly, sitting down on the edge of the bed and reaching out to press his feet.

Old Varma tucked his feet under him, out of the way, and continued to gaze stubbornly into the yellow air of the summer evening.

"Papa, I'm home."

Varma's hand jerked suddenly, in a sharp, derisive movement, but he did not speak.

"How are you feeling, papa?"

Then Varma turned and looked at his son. His face was so out of control and all in pieces, that the multitude of expressions that crossed it could not make up a whole and convey to the famous man exactly what his father thought of him, his skill, his art.

"I'm dying," he croaked. "Let me die, I tell you."

---

14. **samosas:** Triangular pastries fried in clarified butter or oil, containing spiced vegetables or meat.

"Papa, you're joking," his son smiled at him, lovingly. "I've brought you a new tonic to make you feel better. You must take it, it will make you feel stronger again. Here it is. Promise me you will take it regularly, papa."

Varma's mouth worked as hard as though he still had a gob of betel in it (his supply of betel had been cut off years ago). Then he spat out some words, as sharp and bitter as poison, into his son's face. "Keep your tonic—I want none—I want none—I won't take any more of—of your medicines. None. Never," and he swept the bottle out of his son's hand with a wave of his own, suddenly grand, suddenly effective.

His son jumped, for the bottle was smashed and thick brown syrup had splashed up, staining his white trousers. His wife let out a cry and came running. All around the old man was hubbub once again, noise, attention.

He gave one push to the pillows at his back and dislodged them so he could sink down on his back, quite flat again. He closed his eyes and pointed his chin at the ceiling, like some dire prophet, groaning, "God is calling me—now let me go."

◆ **Reading Strategy**

How does the father's situation at the end of the story reflect on the family's decision, referred to at the beginning, to educate Rakesh?

Guide for Responding

◆ Literature and Your Life

Reader's Response At the end of the story, with whom do you sympathize more—Rakesh or his father? Explain your answer.

Thematic Focus Would you consider Anita Desai to be a British author, an Indian author, or a combination of the two? Explain.

Monologue Improvise a brief monologue in which the elderly Varma expresses his deepest feelings about his son and about his own future.

☑ Check Your Comprehension

1. According to the father's boast, what is the first thing Rakesh did when he saw the exam results?
2. Why does Rakesh's marriage surprise his family?
3. By the time his father has grown old, what has Rakesh achieved in his professional career?
4. What does Rakesh's father complain of to Bhatia, the neighbor?
5. At the end of the story, what does Varma do when his son tries to persuade him to take a new medicine?

Guide for Responding (continued)

◆ Critical Thinking

INTERPRET

1. Name three things that qualify Rakesh as a devoted son. **[Classify]**
2. (a) What is the central conflict of this story? (b) Is this conflict a struggle between different generations? Explain. **[Interpret]**
3. In what ways is the conflict in this story specifically Indian, and in what ways is it universal? **[Distinguish]**

EVALUATE

4. Do you think the title of this story is suitable and effective? Why or why not? **[Criticize]**

EXTEND

5. From the evidence presented in this story, how would you describe attitudes toward the elderly in India? **[Social Studies Link]**

◆ Reading Strategy

EVALUATE CHARACTERS' DECISIONS

Evaluate the wisdom of each of the following choices by considering whether it was based on emotion or logic, sympathy or selfishness. Also consider the consequences or later effects of the choice as you make your evaluation.

1. The family sacrifices for Rakesh's education.
2. Rakesh marries a young woman from the village.
3. Rakesh supervises his father's diet.

◆ Build Vocabulary

USING THE LATIN ROOT -fil-

Explain how the Latin root -fil- ("son or daughter") contributes to the meanings of these words:

1. filial   2. affiliate (noun)   3. affiliate (verb)

USING THE WORD BANK: Sentence Completions

On your paper, write the word from the Word Bank that fits best in each sentence.

1. Rakesh won ____?____ for his superior talents.
2. Rakesh felt he had fulfilled his ____?____ obligations.
3. The town considered Rakesh an ____?____ son.
4. Varma could not ____?____ the change in his relationship with Rakesh.
5. People who are____?____ aim to please.

◆ Literary Focus

STATIC AND DYNAMIC CHARACTERS

Desai's use of **static** and **dynamic characters,** characters who remain the same and those who change, is essential to her theme. Strangely, it is the tradition-bound father who is dynamic while his forward-looking son is static. Varma is dynamic even in his defeat, as his attitude toward Rakesh changes. Varma sees that by sacrificing to create a "modern" son, he has lost in old age all that he hoped to gain.

1. After the conversation between Old Bhatia and Varma, Desai summarizes in a paragraph how Varma has changed. In what way has Varma developed a new perspective on his "devoted son"?
2. Cite evidence from the story to support the idea that Rakesh is a static character.
3. What does the relationship between dynamic father and static son reveal about the fate of traditional beliefs in the modern world?

◆ Grammar and Style

SENTENCE VARIETY

Desai uses **sentence variety**—sentences of different lengths, types, and structures—to heighten drama and reinforce meanings. For example, in the paragraph beginning "However, all this was not accomplished ..." Desai sums up Rakesh's achievements with a simple sentence, a fragment, and a compound sentence, all of which are brief. By contrast, she uses a long compound-complex sentence to describe his father's retirement and his mother's death. This contrast suggests the emptiness of Rakesh's life, even though it is filled with triumphs, and the fullness of his mother's feelings about him.

Practice On your paper, vary these sentences to make them more lively and interesting.

Rakesh's mother gloated over his decision to marry an Indian village girl. Rakesh was not like most Indian boys who went abroad, she thought. He agreed almost without argument to his mother's choice of bride. The new wife was the daughter of a childhood friend. She was old-fashioned, placid, and complaisant. She was too good-natured to make Rakesh leave home and set up independently.

Build Your Portfolio

 ## Idea Bank

Writing

1. **Character Sketch** Write a character sketch of Rakesh or his father. Include information on your subject's appearance, opinions, and habits.

2. **Memorial Tribute** Write a memorial tribute—a speech in praise of someone who has died—that Rakesh might deliver for his father.

3. **Response to Criticism** Desai has said she's interested in discovering "the truth that is nine-tenths of the iceberg that lies submerged beneath the one-tenth visible portion we call Reality." Write an essay discussing how this statement relates to "A Devoted Son."

Speaking, Listening, and Viewing

4. **Role Play** Choose a scene from the story. Together with a partner, role-play the scene for an audience of classmates, adding dialogue where necessary. **[Performing Arts Link]**

5. **Panel Discussion** In India, elderly parents often live with the family of one of their children. In a panel with classmates, discuss the potential advantages and conflicts of such an arrangement. **[Social Studies Link]**

Researching and Representing

6. **India's Public Health** Rakesh mentions cholera and typhoid as infectious diseases in India. Research India's major infectious diseases and the ways doctors are treating them. Present your findings to the class. **[Health Link]**

7. **Cross-Cultural Survey** Research and compare how India and two other countries provide for their elderly. Present your findings to the class, using graphs to illustrate comparative statistics. **[Social Studies Link; Math Link]**

Online Activity www.phlit.phschool.com

 ## Guided Writing Lesson

Proposal

As Anita Desai's story shows, people are often blind or indifferent to the feelings of elders. Help remedy that situation. Write a proposal to your principal in which you plan for regular student contact with elders. First, state two or three major objectives for your program. Then develop a specific program calling for visits to elders. Such visits might include socializing, conducting oral-history interviews, and giving performances. In writing your proposal, use language that will help "sell" your idea.

Writing Skills Focus: Connotations

The associations that words have beyond their dictionary meaning, their **connotations**, create an emotional "music." If you're tone-deaf to this music, you may be playing sour notes that spoil the effects of your good ideas. One such sour note is the term *old folks' home,* which has depressing associations and is condescending to the residents. A term that's more on key is *residence for elders,* which suggests a more positive environment. Throughout the writing process, be sure the emotional music of your words supports your message.

Prewriting Brainstorm with a group about the benefits that a program for visiting elders might offer to *everyone* concerned. Including benefits to students and to the school will help convince your most important reader, the principal.

Drafting Be especially careful in drafting your objectives. Use active verbs with positive associations, like *broaden*, *teach*, and *serve*. Also, include upbeat quotations from students and elders enthusiastic about your project.

Revising Trade papers with a classmate and read over each other's proposals. Watch out for—and replace—words that sour your positive tone that suggest the benefits are all one way.

Guide for Interpreting

Arthur C. Clarke (1917–)

With more than one hundred million copies of his books in print worldwide, Arthur C. Clarke may be the most successful science fiction writer of all time. The appeal of his books may result from the way he combines technical expertise with touches of poetry.

Early Career Clarke discovered science fiction at the age of twelve when he started to read a mass-circulation magazine called *Amazing Stories*. His interest in scientific matters led to his service as a radar instructor in the Royal Air Force during World War II.

After the war, he graduated from the University of London with honors in science. Even before he graduated, he had published a prophetic article exploring the possibility of a communications satellite.

Success as a Writer Since the early 1950's, Clarke has worked full-time as a writer producing more than seventy works of fiction and nonfiction. Among his famous novels are *Childhood's End* (1953) and *The City and the Stars* (1956).

His story "The Sentinel" served as the basis for the epic film *2001: A Space Odyssey* (1968). Clarke worked on this film with British director Stanley Kubrick.

Clarke and Science Fiction Like his distinguished contemporaries Isaac Asimov and Ray Bradbury, Clarke has established credibility with his audience by means of an impressive command of aeronautics, astronautics, and undersea exploration. Clarke has also contributed a lyrical, romantic _____ tion.

_____ hallenging the concept that _____ pism, Clarke has asserted that _____ the only kind of writing that's _____ lems and possibilities. . . ."

apid Change (1901–Present)

◆ Background for Understanding

HISTORY: A TIMELINE OF SPACE EXPLORATION

In reading Arthur C. Clarke's assessment of the future of space travel, keep these milestones in mind.

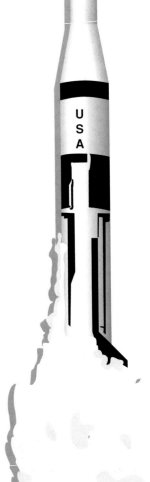

1997 Landing of *Pathfinder* on Mars

1995 Docking of American space shuttle *Atlantis* with Russian space station *Mir*

1981 First space shuttle flight

1976 Missions of *Viking 1* and *Viking 2* to Mars

1969 First landing of men on moon

1961 Alan Shepard is first American in space

1957 *Sputnik* launched by former USSR

1945 Clarke's essay predicting space satellites

from We'll Never Conquer Space

◆ Literature and Your Life

CONNECT YOUR EXPERIENCE

Focus on an object that is five feet away from you. Then imagine that there is no other object for a thousand miles, about the distance from New York City to Kansas City, Missouri. You have just formed a picture of the distance to the nearest planet, as compared with the distance to the nearest star.

Arthur C. Clarke uses such comparisons to help you picture the vastness of the universe. Because the universe will be "forever too large," he argues, "We'll Never Conquer Space."

Journal Writing Briefly freewrite about your fantasies, associations, or opinions on the conquest of space.

THEMATIC FOCUS: FROM THE NATIONAL TO THE GLOBAL

Notice how Clarke gives his own twist to the theme of the shrinking globe as he discusses an unshrinkable universe.

◆ Literary Focus

PROPHETIC ESSAY

All of us make guesses about the future. In a **prophetic essay**, however, a writer uses a brief work of nonfiction to make bold statements about the future of a nation or of our entire planet. Like the statements of prophets in the Bible, these predictions can serve as a kind of warning.

The title of the prophetic essay "We'll Never Conquer Space" contains a prediction that is also a warning against overconfidence.

◆ Grammar and Style

LINKING VERBS AND SUBJECT COMPLEMENTS

Clarke often uses **linking verbs** like *seem* or *be* to connect the subject of a sentence with nouns, pronouns, or adjectives that are called **subject complements**. The connection between a subject and a subject complement is so close that the sentence is like an equation: the subject = the complement. This grammatical device helps Clarke to make definite statements that will convince you of his predictions:

subject   linking verb subject complement

. . . the vastness of the earth *was* a dominant fact.

◆ Build Vocabulary

LATIN SUFFIXES: -ible AND -able

In Clarke's essay, you will find the words *incredible* and *irrevocable*. The suffixes of these words, *-ible* and *-able,* both mean "able to, having qualities of, worthy of, or capable of." Something that is *incredible* is "not able to be believed." Something that is *irrevocable* is "not able to be altered."

WORD BANK

Preview this list of words before you read the essay.

ludicrous
irrevocable
instantaneous
enigma
inevitable
zenith

◆ Reading Strategy

CHALLENGE THE TEXT

By **challenging a text**, you call into question the statements it makes. You treat it like a friend you can argue with rather than like an authority whose words you must accept. As a result, you will start to feel more friendly toward what you read.

Don't be bullied by the definite statements that Clarke makes, including the assertion in his title: "We'll Never Conquer Space." Be suspicious of generalizations with *never* and *always*—just one counter-example proves them wrong. Check to see that his comparisons really prove what he s... they do.

We'll Never Conquer Space

Arthur C. Clarke

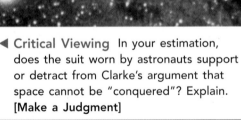

◀ **Critical Viewing** In your estimation, does the suit worn by astronauts support or detract from Clarke's argument that space cannot be "conquered"? Explain. **[Make a Judgment]**

an will never conquer space. Such a statement may sound <u>ludicrous</u>, now that ... e already 100 million miles ... the first human travelers ... e the atmosphere. Yet it ex- ... our forefathers knew, one ... d our descendants must ... reak and loneliness. ... ways unique, full of

events and phenomena which never occurred before and can never happen again. They distort our thinking, making us believe that what is true now will be true forever, though perhaps on a larger scale. Because we have annihilated distance on this planet, we imagine that we can do it once again. The facts are far otherwise, and we will see them more clearly if we forget the present and turn our minds towards the past.

To our ancestors, the vastness of the earth was a dominant fact controlling their thoughts and lives. In all earlier ages than ours, the world was wide indeed, and no man could ever see more than a tiny fraction of its immensity. A few hundred miles—a thousand, at the most—was infinity. Only a lifetime ago, parents waved farewell to their emigrating children in the virtual certainty that they would never meet again.

And now, within one incredible generation, all this has changed. Over the seas where Odysseus wandered for a decade, the Rome-Beirut Comet whispers its way within the hour. And above that, the closer satellites span the distance between Troy and Ithaca[1] in less than a minute.

Psychologically as well as physically, there are no longer any remote places on earth. When a friend leaves for what was once a far country, even if he has no intention of returning, we cannot feel that same sense of <u>irrevocable</u> separation that saddened our forefathers. We know that he is only hours away by jet liner, and that we have merely to reach for the telephone to hear his voice.

◆ **Reading Strategy**
Name an event or trend in the contemporary world that you could use in challenging Clarke's statement that the world is "shrinking." (Think of things that separate people besides distance.)

In a very few years, when the satellite communication network is established, we will be able to see friends on the far side of the earth as easily as we talk to them on the other side of the town. Then the world will shrink no more, for it will have become a dimensionless point.

Forever Too Large

But the new stage that is opening up for the human drama will never shrink as the old one has done. We have abolished space here on the little earth; we can never abolish the space that yawns between the stars. Once again we are face to face with immensity and must accept its grandeur and terror, its inspiring possibilities and its dreadful restraints. From a world that has become too small, we are moving out into one that will be forever too large, whose frontiers will recede from us always more swiftly than we can reach out towards them.

Consider first the fairly modest solar, or planetary, distances which we are now preparing to assault. The very first Lunik[2] made a substantial impression upon them, traveling more than 200 million miles from the earth—six times the distance to Mars. When we have harnessed nuclear energy for spaceflight, the solar system will contract until it is little larger than the earth today. The remotest of the planets will be perhaps no more than a week's travel from the earth, while Mars and Venus will be only a few hours away.

This achievement, which will be witnessed within a century, might appear to make even the solar system a comfortable, homely place, with such giant planets as Saturn and Jupiter playing much the same role in our thoughts as do Africa or Asia today. (Their qualitative differences of climate, atmosphere and gravity, fundamental though they are, do not concern us at the moment.) To some extent this may be true, yet as soon as we pass beyond the orbit of the moon, a mere quarter-million miles away, we will meet the first of the barriers that will separate the earth from her scattered children.

The marvelous telephone and television network that will soon enmesh the whole world, making all men neighbors, cannot be extended into space. It will never be possible to converse with anyone on another planet.

Do not misunderstand this statement. Even with today's radio equipment, the problem of sending speech to the other planets is almost trivial. But the messages will take minutes—sometimes hours—on their journey, because radio and light waves travel at the same limited speed of 186,000 miles a second.

---

2. **Lunik:** Name given by American journalists to Luna I, an unmanned Soviet space probe of 1959.

---

1. **Odysseus . . . Troy and Ithaca:** Odysseus was the King of Ithaca and hero of Homer's *Odyssey*. The distance between Troy and Ithaca, the cities marking the beginning and end of Odysseus' wanderings in the Odyssey, are about equal to the route flown by the Comet airplane between Rome and Beirut.

◆ **Build Vocabulary**

ludicrous (lōō´ di krəs): Absurd; ridiculous

irrevocable (ir rev´ ə kə bəl): That which cannot be undone or canceled

Twenty years from now you will be able to listen to a friend on Mars, but the words you hear will have left his mouth at least three minutes earlier, and your reply will take a corresponding time to reach him. In such circumstances, an exchange of verbal messages is possible—but not a conversation.

Even in the case of the nearby moon, the 2½ second time-lag will be annoying. At distances of more than a million miles, it will be intolerable.

◆ **Reading Strategy**
How important do you judge conversation to be in conducting human affairs across a distance?

"Time Barrier"

To a culture which has come to take <u>instantaneous</u> communication for granted, as part of the very structure of civilized life, this "time barrier" may have a profound psychological impact. It will be a perpetual reminder of universal laws and limitations against which not all our technology can ever prevail. For it seems as certain as anything can be that no signal—still less any material object—can ever travel faster than light.

The velocity of light is the ultimate speed limit, being part of the very structure of space and time. Within the narrow confines of the solar system, it will not handicap us too severely, once we have accepted the delays in communication which it involves. At the worst, these will amount to 20 hours—the time it takes a radio signal to span the orbit of Pluto, the outermost planet.

Between the three inner worlds the earth, Mars, and Venus, it will never be more than 20 minutes—not enough to interfere seriously with commerce or administration, but more than sufficient to shatter those personal links of sound or vision that can give us a sense of direct contact with friends on earth, wherever they may be.

It is when we move out beyond the confines of the solar system that we come face to face with an altogether new order of cosmic reality. Even today, many otherwise educated men—like those savages who can count to three but lump together all numbers beyond four—cannot grasp the profound distinction between solar and stellar space. The first is the space enclosing our neighboring worlds, the planets; the second is that which embraces those distant suns, the stars, and it is literally millions of times greater.

There is no such abrupt change of scale in terrestrial affairs. To obtain a mental picture of the distance to the nearest star, as compared with the distance to the nearest planet, you must imagine a world in which the closest object to you is only five feet away—and then there is nothing else to see until you have traveled a thousand miles.

Many conservative scientists, appalled by these cosmic gulfs, have denied that they can ever be crossed. Some people never learn; those who 60 years ago scoffed at the possibility of flight, and ten (even five!) years ago laughed at the idea of travel to the planets, are now quite sure that the stars will always be beyond our reach. And again they are wrong, for they have failed to grasp the great lesson of our age—that if something is possible in theory, and no fundamental scientific laws oppose its realization, then sooner or later it will be achieved.

One day, it may be in this century, or it may be a thousand years from now, we shall discover a really efficient means of propelling our space vehicles. Every technical device is always developed to its limit (unless it is superseded by something better) and the ultimate speed for spaceships is the velocity of light. They will never reach that goal, but they will get very close to it. And then the nearest star will be less than five years' voyaging from the earth.

Our exploring ships will spread outwards from their home over an ever-expanding sphere of space. It is a sphere which will grow at almost—but never quite—the speed of light. Five years to the triple system of Alpha Centauri, 10 to the strangely-matched doublet Sirius A and B, 11 to the tantalizing <u>enigma</u> of 61 Cygni,[3] the first star suspected to possess a planet. These journeys are long, but they are not impossible. Man has always accepted whatever price was necessary for his explorations and discoveries, *and the price of Space is Time.*

---

3. Alpha Centauri . . . 61 Cygni: Alpha Centauri is a system of three stars in the constellation of the Centaur; one of these, Proxima Centauri, is the star closest to Earth besides the sun. Sirius, known as the Dog Star, is the brightest star in Earth's sky; it is actually two stars orbiting each other, one of which (Sirius B), is only as big as the earth. 61 Cygni is a binary star in the constellation Cygnus, the Swan.

Even voyages which may last for centuries or millennia will one day be attempted. Suspended animation has already been achieved in the laboratory, and may be the key to interstellar travel. Self-contained cosmic arks which will be tiny traveling worlds in their own right may be another solution, for they would make possible journeys of unlimited extent, lasting generation after generation.

The famous Time Dilation effect predicted by the Theory of Relativity,[4] whereby time appears to pass more slowly for a traveler moving at almost the speed of light, may be yet a third. And there are others.

Looking far into the future, therefore, we must picture a slow (little more than half a billion miles an hour!) expansion of human activities outwards from the solar system, among the suns scattered across the region of the galaxy in which we now find ourselves. These suns are on the average five light-years apart; in other words, we can never get from one to the next in less than five years.

To bring home what this means, let us use a down-to-earth analogy. Imagine a vast ocean, sprinkled with islands—some desert, others perhaps inhabited. On one of these islands an energetic race has just discovered the art of building ships. It is preparing to explore the ocean, but must face the fact that the very nearest island is five years' voyaging away, and that no possible improvement in the technique of ship-building will ever reduce this time.

In these circumstances (which are those in which we will soon find ourselves) what could

Large spiral galaxy, Andromeda with two small companion galaxies, NASA

▲ **Critical Viewing** Think about your reponse to Clarke's comparison of distances within the solar system to galactic distance. Does this picture convey a sense of these immense distances as clearly as Clarke's prose? Explain. **[Analyze]**

the islanders achieve? After a few centuries, they might have established colonies on many of the nearby islands and have briefly explored many others. The daughter colonies might themselves have sent out further pioneers, and so a kind of chain reaction would spread the original culture over a steadily expanding area of the ocean.

But now consider the effects of the <u>inevitable</u>, unavoidable time-lag. There could be only the most tenuous contact between the home island and its offspring. Returning messengers could report what had happened on the nearest colony—five years ago. They could never bring information more up to date than

◆ **Reading Strategy**
In his arguments about information-lag, what is Clarke quietly assuming about the length of human life? Formulate a challenge to his argument by making the opposite assumption.

---

4. **Theory of Relativity:** In physics, the theory that measurements of an object's physical properties (and thus the measurement of time) will vary depending on the relative motion of the observer and the observed object—only the speed of light is constant when measured in any frame of reference. One of the consequences of the theory is that speeds faster than the speed of light are impossible.

◆ **Build Vocabulary**

instantaneous (in′ stən tā′ nē əs) *adj.*: Done or happening in an instant

enigma (e nig′ mə) *n.*: Riddle; a perplexing statement, person, or situation

inevitable (in ev′ i tə bəl) *adj.*: Unavoidable; certain to happen

that, and dispatches from the more distant parts of the ocean would be from still further in the past—perhaps centuries behind the times. There would never be news from the other islands, but only history.

Independent "Colonies"

All the star-borne colonies of the future will be independent, whether they wish it or not. Their liberty will be inviolably protected by Time as well as Space. They must go their own way and achieve their own destiny, with no help or hindrance from Mother Earth.

At this point, we will move the discussion on to a new level and deal with an obvious objection. Can we be sure that the velocity of light is indeed a limiting factor? So many "impassible" barriers have been shattered in the past; perhaps this one may go the way of all the others.

We will not argue the point, or give the reasons why scientists believe that light can never be outraced by any form of radiation or any material object. Instead, let us assume the contrary and see just where it gets us. We will even take the most optimistic possible case and imagine that the speed of transportation may eventually become infinite.

Picture a time when, by the development of techniques as far beyond our present engineering as a transistor is beyond a stone axe, we can reach anywhere we please instantaneously, with no more effort than by dialing a number. This would indeed cut the universe down to size and reduce its physical immensity to nothingness. What would be left?

Everything that really matters. For the universe has two aspects—its scale, and its overwhelming, mind-numbing complexity. Having abolished the first, we are now face-to-face with the second.

What we must now try to visualize is not size, but quantity. Most people today are familiar with the simple notation which scientists use to describe large numbers; it consists merely of counting zeroes, so that a hundred becomes 10^2, a million, 10^6, a billion, 10^9 and so on. This useful trick enables us to work with quantities of any magnitude, and even defense budget totals look modest when expressed as $\$5.76 \times 10^9$ instead of $\$5,760,000,000$.

The number of other suns in our own galaxy (that is, the whirlpool of stars and cosmic dust

of which our sun is an out-of-town member, lying in one of the remoter spiral arms) is estimated at about 10^{11}—or written in full, 100,000,000,000. Our present telescopes can observe something like 10^9 other galaxies, and they show no sign of thinning out even at the extreme limit of vision.

There are probably at least as many galaxies in the whole of creation as there are stars in our own galaxy, but let us confine ourselves to those we can see. They must contain a total of about 10^{11} times 10^9 stars, or 10^{20} stars altogether. 1 followed by 20 other digits is, of course, a number beyond all understanding.

Before such numbers, even spirits brave enough to face the challenge of the light-years must quail. The detailed examination of all the grains of sand on all the beaches of the world

Beyond Literature

Technology Connection

Clarke and COMSAT Arthur C. Clarke is one of the few writers to have had the pleasure of making the future happen even as they predict it. At end of World War II, Clarke combined his wartime experience of radar operation with his passion for space and wrote an article for *Wireless World* magazine. The piece, entitled "Extra Terrestrial Relays," explained how television and telephone signals could be bounced off relay stations— satellites—sent into orbit by rocket. Clarke described, in essence, the methods used to this day for television and other broadcasting. Nearly twenty years later, in 1962, the Communications Satellite Corporation (COMSAT) was authorized by Congress to manage commercial communication satellite systems. Clarke modestly believed that the article advanced telecommunications by "15 minutes." Even a genius can be wrong about his own work, though. Many consider Clarke "the godfather of global communications."

Make your own prediction about communications in the future. What contemporary trends support your prediction?

is a far smaller task than the exploration of the universe.

And so we return to our opening statement. Space can be mapped and crossed and occupied without definable limit; but it can never be conquered. When our race has reached its ultimate achievements, and the stars themselves are scattered no more widely than the seed of Adam, even then we shall still be like ants crawling on the face of the earth. The ants have covered the world but have they conquered it—for what do their countless colonies know of it, or of each other?

So it will be with us as we spread outwards from Mother Earth, loosening the bonds of kinship and understanding, hearing faint and belated rumors at second—or third—or thousandth-hand of an ever-dwindling fraction of the entire human race.

Though Earth will try to keep in touch with her children, in the end all the efforts of her archivists and historians will be defeated by time

and distance, and the sheer bulk of material. For the number of distinct societies or nations, when our race is twice its present age, may be far greater than the total number of all the men who have ever lived up to the present time.

We have left the realm of human comprehension in our vain effort to grasp the scale of the universe; so it must always be, sooner rather than later.

When you are next outdoors on a summer night, turn your head towards the zenith. Almost vertically above you will be shining the brightest star of the northern skies—Vega of the Lyre,[5] 26 years away at the speed of light, near enough the point-of-no-return for us short-lived creatures. Past this blue-white beacon, 50 times as brilliant as our sun, we may send our minds and bodies, but never our hearts.

For no man will ever turn homewards from beyond Vega, to greet again those he knew and loved on the earth.

> ♦ **Literary Focus**
> In what ways is this a prophetic statement?

♦ Build Vocabulary

zenith (zē´ nəth) *n.*: Highest point of something, especially of the sky or celestial sphere

---

5. **Vega of the Lyre:** Star in the northern constellation, Lyra. Fourth brightest of the stars in Earth's night sky.

Guide for Responding

♦ *Literature and Your Life*

Reader's Response What questions would you like to ask the author of this essay?

Thematic Focus In what ways is our world still vast? In what ways is it small?

☑ Check Your Comprehension

1. Why will it never be possible to have a true conversation with someone on another planet?
2. What is the ultimate speed limit, which is part of the very structure of space and time?
3. What achievement will be reached within a century, according to Clarke?

♦ Critical Thinking

INTERPRET

1. (a) What distinction does Clarke make between exchanging verbal messages and having a conversation? (b) Why is this distinction crucial to his thesis? **[Classify; Draw Conclusions]**
2. At the end of "Time Barrier," why does Clarke use the analogy of an ocean sprinkled with islands? **[Compare and Contrast]**
3. What implications does Clarke seem to suggest conquering space would have for human relations? **[Infer]**

EVALUATE

4. Has Clarke made a persuasive argument about the impossibility of conquering space? Explain. **[Assess]**

Guide for Responding (continued)

◆ Literary Focus

PROPHETIC ESSAY

In his **prophetic essay**, Clarke predicts that humans will never dominate outer space as we have dominated the Earth. As is often true in prophetic essays, his prediction may also suggest a moral lesson: We need to be more humble about ourselves and our place in the universe.

To convince you of his prediction, Clarke includes such pieces of information as the speed of light and a description of the Lunik space probe. However, he also uses two effective persuasive devices. First, he writes in memorable phrases and sentences, like "... the price of Space is Time." Second, he uses comparisons to help you visualize the vastness of space.

1. Find two memorable phrases or sentences in the essay, and explain why they are effective.
2. Identify a comparison Clarke uses, and tell why it does or does not help you "see" the point he is making.
3. (a) Do you agree or disagree with Clarke's prophecy concerning space travel? Explain.
   (b) Do you think that Clarke is asking readers to rethink their behavior or attitudes? Why or why not?

◆ Reading Strategy

CHALLENGE THE TEXT

Challenging a text means giving yourself the freedom to argue with it as you would with a friend. Often key words like *always, never, ever,* or *may* give you a clue about which statements to test against your own knowledge. *Never, always,* or *ever* signal a sweeping generalization: "Man has *always* accepted whatever price was necessary for his explorations." You can challenge such generalizations by looking for a single exception that would disprove them.

Also, look for the word *may,* which indicates that Clarke is guessing rather than giving facts: "this 'time barrier' *may* have a profound psychological impact." Test such statements by determining whether they suggest other results or explanations.

1. Find another *always* or *never* statement, challenge it, and then decide whether you agree with it.
2. Find and challenge one of Clarke's guesses.

◆ Build Vocabulary

USING THE LATIN SUFFIXES -ible AND -able

Use the Latin suffixes *-ible* and *-able* to form words with the following definitions:

1. able to be defined
2. able to be tolerated
3. showing hospitality
4. able to be resisted

USING THE WORD BANK: Synonyms

On your paper, write the letter of the word or words closest in meaning to the first word.

1. ludicrous: (a) frisky, (b) fun-loving, (c) absurd
2. irrevocable: (a) rapid, (b) unalterable, (c) fickle
3. instantaneous: (a) immediate, (b) faulty, (c) risky
4. enigma: (a) beverage, (b) riddle, (c) archive
5. inevitable: (a) unavoidable, (b) incomprehensible, (c) direct
6. zenith: (a) point on the horizon, (b) point directly overhead, (c) bending of light rays

◆ Grammar and Style

LINKING VERBS AND SUBJECT COMPLEMENTS

Clarke uses **linking verbs** like *seem* or *be* to equate subjects with their **complements**, nouns, pronouns, or adjectives that describe them. The effect of this grammatical structure is to make sentences seem like equations that must be true.

Practice In your notebook, identify the linking verb and subject complement in each sentence.

1. Our age is in many ways unique.
2. To our ancestors, the vastness of the Earth was a dominant fact.
3. A few hundred miles was infinity.
4. The problem of sending speech to other planets is almost trivial.
5. The detailed examination of all the grains of sand on all the beaches of the world is a far smaller task than the exploration of the universe.

Writing Application Find five well-known proverbs or sayings, like "Home is where the heart is," and determine whether or not they use linking verbs and subject complements. If you find that many of them do have this grammatical structure, explain why this might be so.

Build Your Portfolio

 ## Idea Bank

Writing

1. **E-mail Response** Write an e-mail message to Arthur C. Clarke responding to his message in "We'll Never Conquer Space." Tell him about passages you liked or disliked and ask him any questions you may have.

2. **Reflective Essay** Using Clarke's piece as a launching pad, write your own reflective essay on space exploration. Speculate about future developments and what they might teach us.

3. **Literary Analysis** Clarke is known for combining scientific knowledge with a philosophical outlook. Write a literary analysis of "We'll Never Conquer Space," finding evidence of both these qualities.

Speaking, Listening, and Viewing

4. **Panel Discussion** In a small group, discuss the implications of Clarke's essay. If Clarke is correct that space will never be conquered, what are the practical and philosophical uses of space exploration? **[Science Link]**

5. **Introduction** Arthur C. Clarke is appearing on your television talk show to discuss "We'll Never Conquer Space." Using the biographical information on page 1158, introduce him to viewers. **[Media Link; Performing Arts Link]**

Researching and Representing

6. **Film Review** View *2001: A Space Odyssey* and write a review of it for your classmates. Focus on its plot, music, and special effects. **[Media Link]**

7. **Museum Exhibit** Create a museum exhibit that will dramatize Clarke's ideas about space for high-school students. Contact your local science museum or university for advice. **[Science Link]**

Online Activity www.phlit.phschool.com

 ## Guided Writing Lesson

Astronaut's Diary

Arthur C. Clarke is convinced that we will continue to explore space, although we can never conquer it. Imagine that you are an astronaut on a mission of exploration and discovery sometime in the future. Write a series of diary entries recording your experiences. Be consistent in giving your impressions from an astronaut's perspective.

Writing Skills Focus: Consistent Perspective

In writing diary entries, and other types of narration and description, you should keep a **consistent perspective.** Your astronaut should always refer to himself or herself as "I." Also, avoid having your astronaut describe scenes that he or she could not have actually seen. Still another way to maintain consistency is to keep the details of the mission the same in all your entries. Such details might include the ones in the chart below.

Prewriting Review Clarke's essay for information you can use for diary entries. Then make a prewriting chart like this one, listing items that you can refer to for consistency:

Purpose of Mission	Duration	Type of ship	Gear and clothing

Drafting Imagine the day-to-day concerns your astronaut would have, even in outer space, and incorporate these into the entries. In addition, always write from your astronaut's point of view and refer to your chart so that details remain consistent.

Revising Have a peer editor review your entries and suggest where you can include more sensory details to bring descriptions to life. Also have your editor check for consistency in the use of the pronoun "I" and in descriptions of details.

Writing Process Workshop

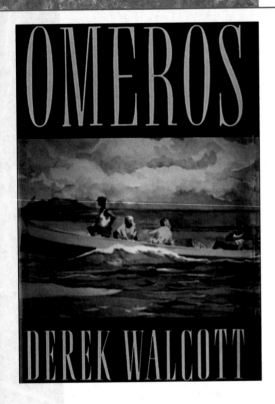

The works of modern writers, like the ones in this section, have yet to stand the test of time. However, they have undergone, and will continue to undergo, evaluation—by literary scholars, historians, students, and everyday people who discuss books in informal groups. Write a critical evaluation in which you focus on the positive and negative characteristics of a literary work. In your evaluation, include an examination of various literary elements, with specific examples, and a summary of the work. The writing-skills focus points, introduced in the Guided Writing Lessons in this section, will help you write your evaluation.

Writing Skills Focus

▶ **Use specific examples** by including direct quotations from the work that support your opinion. (See p. 1109.)

▶ **Maintain a level of formality** that suits a critical evaluation. (See p. 1135.)

▶ **Use transitions to show comparisons and connections** among your ideas and details. (See p. 1145.)

▶ **Choose words with positive and negative connotations** to help convey your purpose. (See p. 1157.)

The following passage from a critical evaluation contains many elements appropriate to this type of writing.

① The positive connotations of *dignity* and *humanity* convey the writer's approval of Walcott's work.

② The transition *what is common to* introduces a similarity between *Omeros* and the ancient work that inspired it.

③ The writer uses appropriately formal language throughout his evaluation.

MODEL FROM LITERATURE

from A Critical Evaluation of *Omeros* by John Figueroa

In *Omeros* the grand names are given to simple folk, some of whom had the kind of problems the noble heroes had in Homer's poems. With these problems they struggled, as with the "loud sounding sea," with no less dignity and humanity ① than all the heroes in the bloody wars . . . . But what is common to ② Homer and *Omeros* is not only struggle and coming to terms with death and violence and separation from home, but the sea . . . and its moods and sounds. ③

Prewriting

Choose a Topic To find a topic for your critical evaluation, think about books or poems you've read, such as a current best seller, something you read for class, or even a children's book. Following are additional topic ideas:

Topic Ideas

- A drama you loved
- A short story you hated

Selection-Related Topic Ideas

- "From Lucy: Englan' Lady" by James Berry
- A work by Arthur C. Clarke

Support Your Ideas with Specific Examples Write your thesis statement, then list specific references from the work that support your point. You may use specific words, lines, or entire stanzas to support your arguments.

Experiment with Connotations Think of the words you might use in your evaluation. Then use a thesaurus or dictionary to identify similar words with slightly different meanings. The following sentences convey different ideas because of the different connotations of the underlined words.

▶ The poetry of Ted Hughes reveals a *fascination* with nature.

▶ The poetry of Ted Hughes reveals an *over-absorption* with nature.

▶ The poetry of Ted Hughes reveals a *fondness* for nature.

Drafting

Develop a Consistent Level of Formality A scholarly work, such as a critical evaluation, should be formal and serious in tone. As you draft, maintain this tone by choosing formal vocabulary and creating balanced and complex sentences.

▶ **Informal:** *The story really rocks.*

▶ **Formal:** *The narrative is gripping and involving.*

Connect Your Ideas and Examples While drafting, use transitions to connect your ideas and examples. Refer to the following word list for suggestions:

Transitions: all, alike, both, most, similar, either, neither, equal, identical, same, like, other, closely related, common to, also, likewise, too, similarly, therefore, however, thus.

APPLYING LANGUAGE SKILLS: Avoiding Incomplete and Illogical Comparisons

Critical evaluation often involves comparing works. Avoid illogical comparisons that do not match similar items.

Example:
Walcott's hero Achille is very different from the *Iliad*.

Revision:
Walcott's hero Achille is very different from the hero Achilleus in the *Iliad*.

Avoid incomplete comparisons by clearly indicating the group of items with which you are comparing a work.

Example:
Dylan Thomas's work is more powerful than others.

Revision:
Dylan Thomas's work is more powerful than that of any other modern poet.

Practice Rewrite the following sentences to make the comparisons logical and complete.

1. Derek Walcott's *Omeros* has more precise sea imagery.
2. The dialect in Berry's work is more accurate than Walcott's poetry.
3. The imagery in Walcott's *Omeros* is more convincing.

Applying Language Skills: Avoiding Clichés

Clichés are expressions that were once fresh and vivid but through overuse now lack force and appeal. Replace any clichés you find with original observations.

First Draft:
Until I studied British history, I found reading poetry to be as dull as dishwater.

Revision:
Until I studied British history, I found reading poetry to be as tedious as counting out pennies.

Practice Rewrite the following statements, using fresh, interesting images in place of the highlighted clichés.

1. In her story, the train *roars like thunder* through the countryside.
2. According to A. E. Housman, *time flies.*
3. The leading character is *as pretty as a picture.*

Writing Application Search for and delete clichés in your own writing.

Writer's Solution Connection
Language Lab

For help in using quotation marks in titles of literary works or in punctuating passages from literature, see the Semicolons, Colons, and Quotation Marks lesson in the Punctuation unit.

Revising

Revision Checklist Use the following questions to develop a revision checklist:

▶ Is the level of formality consistent throughout?
▶ What words can you replace to clarify your meaning?
▶ Have you used transitions to connect details and ideas?
▶ What details from the work can you add as support?

REVISION MODEL

① In comparison to descriptions in other poetry,
the description of an event from three perspectives

distinguishes "Not Waving but Drowning." Stevie Smith uses
② Notice the unusual shift in perspective from line two to line three:
"But still he lay moaning: /I was much further out than you thought . . . "
a literary element, point of view, to create depth. ~~When you~~
③ On first reading the deceptively simple piece,
read this ~~simple poem,~~ the reader might be confused by the
④ stratagem
change in speaker, but Smith uses this ~~deception~~ to force the

reader to read again. It is in the careful, subsequent

readings that one moves beyond the apparent meanings to

the metaphorical meanings.

① This transition signals to the reader that the writer is linking this piece to poetry in general.
② By adding a direct quotation from the poem, the writer supports his prior statement.
③ This phrase was revised to better match the formal, academic tone set in the rest of the evaluation.
④ Because the word *deception* creates a negative connotation that was unintended by the writer, the word *stratagem* was substituted.

Publishing

▶ **Discussion** Organize a literary discussion group. Let members read and discuss the critical evaluations they have written.

▶ **Internet** Submit your work to an Internet site that is dedicated to literary reviews.

Student Success Workshop

Research Skills — Drawing Questions for Study From Research Findings

Strategies for Success

Research can be a quick drive down a dead-end road or a lifelong journey of exploration in which every road leads to another. Begin such a journey by learning how to draw questions for further study from your research findings. The following strategies will help you identify unanswered questions in your research, save questions that occur to you, and transform your conclusions into questions for additional study:

Identify Unanswered Questions Your research may have been originally motivated by more than one question. For example, you may have wanted to discover why young poets enlisted in the British army during World War I and how the war influenced their poetry. As you researched this topic, you may have devoted more time to the second question. By comparing your findings to your notes, you can determine that you have not fully answered the first question. Then you can use this question as the basis for another research project.

Save the Questions That Occur to You While doing research, you may think of additional questions related to your inquiry. A study of George Orwell's essay "Shooting an Elephant" may prompt you to wonder why Eric Blair used the pen name George Orwell. To avoid forgetting such a question, jot it down or record it in a special computer file. Returning to it later, you may be inspired to do further research on Eric Blair's psychology or on the reasons that authors use pen names.

Find the Questions in Your Answers Those who are lifelong learners know that every question suggests an answer and every answer suggests more

questions. In keeping with this idea, practice generating new questions from your conclusions. Use words like *how, when, where, why,* and *to what extent* in order to turn a conclusion into a new question. Here's an example:

▶ *Conclusion:* The main theme in Mary Wollstonecraft Shelley's *Frankenstein* (1818) is that creativity can be dangerous when separated from morality.

▶ *New Questions:* To what extent is this theme reflected in modern films based on *Frankenstein?* What is another important theme in the novel?

Apply the Strategies

Use the work in your writing portfolio to answer the following questions:

1. Scan the notes you made while working on a report. Identify a question that occurred to you during the research process but was not answered in your conclusion.

2. Review the conclusion of one of your reports. Then use words like *how, why, where, when, to what extent,* and *why* to generate two questions based on your conclusion.

✔ Here are other situations in which you might have to draw relevant questions for further study from your research findings:

▶ Proposing a solution to a problem you have discovered in the workplace

▶ Learning more about a sport or hobby that interests you

▶ Deciding whether a new product is as good as one you have already researched

Speaking, Listening, and Viewing Workshop

Evaluating an Oral Report

A student government representative explains a proposed change in election procedures. A club treasurer delivers an annual financial report. A classmate reports on a research project. Knowing how to evaluate oral presentations like these will help you improve your own listening and speaking abilities.

Be an active listener by asking questions about the content of the speech. Does the report answer all of your questions? What other questions would you like to have answered? If you've listened carefully but still don't understand the report, analyze the presentation to find the reasons for its weakness. A strong presentation should be engaging and should clearly and accurately inform the listener.

Analyze and Evaluate the Report When you listen to an oral report, create a mental outline of the key points to help you remember them. You may want to take notes as you listen. Consider the source of the information and whether it is accurate and unbiased. Analyze the organization and structure. Is there an introduction and body text with main ideas and supporting facts and examples? Does the summary or conclusion make sense? Is the report interesting?

Judge the Visuals Visual aids—such as maps, charts, diagrams, and photos—should support, not detract from, the presentation. Are the visuals relevant? Do they clearly illustrate difficult concepts? If a report includes statistics, a graph or chart might be appropriate. If the presentation follows definite steps or a sequence, a flowchart or sequence chart might be helpful. Has the speaker chosen appropriate visual aids to support the report?

Make Praise and Criticism Count An important part of critiquing an oral report is sharing your thoughts with others in a constructive way. In your evaluation, point out the strong parts of the presentation as well as the weak ones. For instance, you might want to praise the speaker for using effective visual aids but suggest that he or she speak more slowly next time. Criticism is easier to accept if it's coupled with thoughtful advice and constructive suggestions.

Apply the Strategies

Listen to an oral report in one of your classes.

1. Respond to the report's organization. Is the report well organized with an introduction, body, and conclusion? Do the facts support the main ideas and the conclusion?

2. Evaluate the visual aids. How well do they support the information? Do the visual aids help explain key points? Are they relevant? Do they clarify the report?

3. Give constructive feedback to the report giver. Which parts of the report are strong? What areas are weak? What constructive suggestions can you make for improvements?

Tips for Evaluating an Oral Report

▶ Make sure you can hear and understand the information.

▶ Check that the visual aids help to explain the information.

▶ Consider whether the report ends with an interesting, clear conclusion.

Test Preparation Workshop

Writing Skills

Strategy, Organization, and Style

Strategies for Success

Some standardized tests ask you to read a passage and answer multiple-choice questions about revision strategies and the effective use of language. Use these strategies to help you answer test questions about these skills.

Strategy Questions Strategy questions ask whether a given device is useful or appropriate. Read this example, and answer the question:

> Today, doctors issued warnings that long-term exposure to the harmful rays of the sun can promote skin cancer.

I To add information about the dangers of sun exposure, which of the following statements would be most suitable?

A Those who don't wear sunscreen are more likely to develop cancerous lesions.

B The suns rays travel at the speed of light.

C Depletion of the ozone layer has increased the intensity of sunlight.

D Sloan Institute doctors are experts on skin conditions.

Answer **A** is correct because it's the only answer that contains information about dangers.

Organization Questions These questions ask you about the logical sequence of ideas in a written passage. Read the following passage, and answer the question:

> (1) Millions of people communicate over the Internet. (2) Some choose a custom-made home entertainment center. (3) Technology certainly has made the world seem smaller. (4) As communication technologies advance, consumers can choose among devices designed to make their lives easier. (5) Many people carry cell phones.

2 Choose the sentence sequence that is most logical.

A NO CHANGE **C** 3, 1, 4, 2, 5

B 4, 2, 5, 1, 3 **D** 1, 4, 2, 3, 5

The correct answer is **B**. It's the most logical because (4) is the topic of the passage.

Style Questions These questions deal with the use of appropriate and effective language for an intended audience. Reread the passage about communication, and answer the question:

3 The tone of this passage may best be described as:

A informational. **C** negative.

B emotional. **D** whimsical.

Answer **A** is correct; the passage provides information in a neutral tone.

Apply the Strategies

Read the passage, and answer the questions:

> (1) It's time for everyone to realize that these laws make sense. (2) Several cities have enacted laws prohibiting the playing of boom boxes in public. (3) When will people learn to turn off those obnoxious boom boxes in public places? (4) Such laws have returned peace to city streets. (5) Too often citizens are assaulted by high-volume noise.

I Choose the most logical sentence sequence:

A 3, 5, 2, 4, 1 **C** 5, 3, 1, 2, 4

B 1, 2, 3, 5, 4 **D** 4, 2, 1, 3, 5

2 The tone of this passage is

A emotional. **C** persuasive.

B funny. **D** neutral.

Analyzing Real-World Texts

Background

James Joyce is famous for his literary re-creations of Dublin; William Wordsworth, for his love of the Lake District. This map places important authors in the locations with which they are identified.

◆ Reading Strategy

Generate Researchable Questions A map can answer a particular question. It can also lead you to **generate researchable questions.**

Hidden among the facts on this literary map are any number of questions. The note along the English–Scottish border— "Setting of many early ballads" —suggests the following question: What historical facts make this border a good setting for a ballad? Research in an encyclopedia suggests an answer: Border conflicts between the Scots and the English provided ballads with dramas of bravery, loyalty, and betrayal.

Use a graphic organizer like the one below to note five questions suggested by the map.

Literary Map of Great Britain and Ireland

*Cambridge
Authors who studied here include:
- Bacon 1561–1626
- Brooke 1887–1915
- Byron 1788–1824
- Coleridge 1772–1834
- Dryden 1631–1700
- Forster 1879–1970
- Gray 1716–1771
- Herbert 1593–1633
- Herrick 1591–1674
- Marlowe 1564–1593
- Marvell 1621–1678
- Pepys 1633–1703
- Sassoon 1886–1967
- Spenser 1552?–1599
- Tennyson 1809–1892
- Wordsworth 1770–1850
- Wyatt 1503–1542

**Oxford
Authors who studied here include:
- Addison 1672–1719

- Arnold 1822–1888
- Donne 1572–1631
- T. S. Eliot 1888–1965
- Hopkins 1844–1889
- Housman 1859–1936
- Johnson 1709–1784
- Lovelace 1618–1657
- MacNeice 1907–1963
- Raleigh 1552–1618
- Shelley, Percy Bysshe 1792–1822
- Sidney 1554–1586
- Steele 1672–1729

†Dublin
Authors associated with the city include:
- Joyce 1882–1941
- Steele 1672–1729
- Shaw 1856–1950
- Swift 1667–1745
- Wilde 1854–1900
- Yeats 1865–1939

Fact of Interest	Question	How to Research
English–Scottish border was setting for many ballads.	What historical facts made the border a good setting?	Encyclopedia: Check entry for "Ballad"; "Scotland"
Wordsworth set one poem at Tintern Abbey, hundreds of miles from his home.	What was transportation like at the time that Wordsworth wrote?	

◆ Apply the Reading Strategy

Give five questions suggested by the map that could make the basis of a report. Describe the way you would do research into each.

◆ Compare Literary Forms

Read or review Bede's "History," p. 78. (a) What united the region in his time? (b) Judging from the map, what unites past and present there today?

LITERARY MAP OF GREAT BRITAIN AND IRELAND

0   50 miles

0   50 kilometers

N

Outer Hebrides

Isle of Skye

SCOTTISH HIGHLANDS

Inner Hebrides

Johnson and Boswell toured Hebrides, 1773

King Duncan's palace
Macbeth, 1623

Macbeth's castle

Dunsinane
Macbeth slain

Loch Ness

North Sea

SCOTLAND

Atlantic Ocean

Loch Lomond

Dumferling
Sir Patrick Spens and Scottish lords drown, "Sir Patrick Spens," *c.* 1285

Ayshire
Burns's "To a Mouse," 1786

English–Scottish border
Setting of many early ballads

NORTHERN IRELAND

Kelloe
E.B. Browning born, 1806

LAKE DISTRICT
Wordsworth (1770–1850) lived, set many of his poems

Whitby
Caedmon's hymns, *c.* 650

Sligo
Yeats's "Lake of Innisfree," 1890

Isle of Man

Irish Sea

Haworth Moor
Setting of *Jane Eyre,* 1847

Wakefield
Medieval mystery and morality plays

Humberside
Marvell, (1621–78) lived, wrote

IRELAND

Dublin†

Forest of Wirral
Gawain journeys to meet the Green Knight (poem composed c. 1375–1400)

SHROPSHIRE
Shropshire Lad, Housman, 1896

Lichfield
Samuel Johnson born, 1709

ENGLAND

Kilcolman
Spenser composed *The Fairie Queene,* 1589, 1596

Stratford-on-Avon
Shakespeare (1564–1616)

Cambridge*

WALES

Tintern Abbey
Setting for Wordsworth's poem

Thames River

Oxford**

London

Canterbury
Destination of Chaucer's (1345–1400) pilgrims; Marlowe born, 1564

Swansea
Dylan Thomas's (1914–53) poetry

Route of Chaucer's pilgrims

Stonehenge

Salisbury
Geo. Herbert's *Temple* (1633, posthumous)

Dover
Arnold's "Dover Beach," 1867

Tintagel
Legendary birthplace of King Arthur

DORSET
Hardy's Wessex

Portsmouth
Dickens born, 1812

Dean Prior
Herrick (1591–1674) a country parson here

English Channel

FRANCE

The Defense of Poesy

Sir Philip Sidney

Literary theory

About the Author
Famed as a soldier and courtier as well as a poet, **Sir Philip Sidney** (1554–1586) died of battle wounds. His *Defense of Poesy* is the first work of literary criticism in English.

◆ Reading Strategy

Analyze Aspects of Texts: Allusions Through the use of **allusions**—indirect references to literary works and historical figures—writers propose and draw on a world of readings shared with their readers.

In *The Defense of Poesy*, Sidney alludes to the "Cyclops," a mythological giant described by the ancient Greek poet Homer. The allusion assumes the reader has read Homer; it implies a common bond that helps a reader to feel "friendly" toward Sidney. Also, ancient works carried great authority for sixteenth-century writers. By alluding to such works, writers gave their own writing weight.

Use a graphic organizer like the one below to record each allusion in the *Defense*, noting the work to which he refers (consult reference works where necessary).

Allusion	Source/Reference
Cyclops	Greek mythology; Homer's *Odyssey*
Chimeras	
Aristotle	

There is no art delivered unto mankind that has not the works of Nature for his principal object, without which they could not consist, and on which they so depend, as they become actors and players, as it were, of what Nature will have set forth. So does the astronomer look upon the stars, and, by that he sees set down what order Nature has taken therein. So do the geometrician and arithmetician in their diverse sorts of quantities. . . .

Only the poet, disdaining to be tied to any such subjection,[1] lifted up with the vigor of his own invention, grows in effect into another Nature, in making things either better than Nature brings forth, or, quite anew, forms such as never were in Nature, as the Heroes, Demigods, Cyclops, Chimeras, Furies, and such like: so as he goes hand in hand with Nature, not enclosed within the narrow warrant[2] of her gifts, but freely ranging within the zodiac of his own wit.

Nature never set forth the earth in so rich tapestry as divers poets have done, neither with so pleasant rivers, fruitful trees, sweet-smelling flowers, nor whatsoever else may make the too much loved earth more lovely. Her world is brazen,[3] the poets only deliver a golden. But let those things alone, and go to man (for whom as the other things are, so it seems in him her uttermost cunning is employed), and know whether she have brought forth so true

---

1. **subjection** (sub jek´ shən) *n.*: Condition of being ruled by or at the mercy of another.
2. **warrant** (wôr´ ənt) *n.*: Authorization; proper sphere of activity.
3. **brazen** (brā´ zən) *adj.*: Made of brass, a metal alloy of inferior value to gold; possibly an allusion to the ancient Greek writer Hesiod (active in the eighth century B.C.) who tells of a golden age preceding ages of silver, bronze, and iron.

a lover as Theagenes,[4] so constant a friend as Pylades,[5] so valiant a man as Orlando, so right a prince as Xenophon's Cyrus, and so excellent a man every way as Virgil's Aeneas. Neither let this be jestingly conceived because the works of the one be essential, the other in imitation or fiction, for every understanding knows the skill of each artificer stands in that Idea or foreconceit[6] of the work, and not in the work itself. And that the poet has that Idea is manifest, by delivering them forth in such excellency as he had imagined them. Which delivering forth also is not wholly imaginative, as we are wont to say by them that build castles in the air, but so far substantially it works, not only to make a Cyrus, which had been but a particular excellence, as Nature might have done, but to bestow a Cyrus upon the world to make many Cyruses, if they will learn aright why and how that maker made him.

. . .

[Definition] Poesy, therefore, is an art of imitation, for so Aristotle terms it in the word *mimesis*;[7] that is to say, a representing, counterfeiting, or figuring forth—to speak metaphorically, a speaking picture—with this end, to teach and delight.

. . .

This purifying of wit, this enriching of memory, enabling of judgment, and enlarging of conceit, which commonly we call learning, under what name soever it comes forth, or to what immediate end soever it be directed,

the final end is to lead and draw us to as high a perfection as our degenerate souls, made worse by their clay lodgings,[8] can be capable of. This, according to the inclination of the man, bred many formed impressions. For some that thought this felicity[9] principally to be gotten by knowledge and no knowledge to be so high of heavenly as acquaintance with the stars, gave themselves to astronomy; others, persuading themselves to be demigods if they knew the causes of things, became natural and supernatural philosophers; some an admirable delight drew to music; and some the certainty of demonstration to the mathematics. But all, one and other, having this scope—to know, and by knowledge to lift up the mind from the dungeon of the body to the enjoying his own divine essence.

But when by the balance of experience it was found that the astronomer looking to the stars might fall in a ditch, that the inquiring philosopher might be blind in himself, and the mathematician might draw forth a straight line with a crooked heart, then, lo, did proof, the overruler of opinions, make manifest that all these are but serving sciences, which, as they have a private end in themselves, so yet are they all directed to the highest end of the mistress knowledge, by the Greeks [called] *architektonike*,[10] which stands (as I think) in the knowledge of a man's self, in the ethic and politic consideration, with the end of well doing and not of well knowing only; even as the saddler's next end is to make a good saddle, but his further end to serve a nobler faculty, which is horsemanship; so the horseman's to soldiery, and the soldier not only to have the skill, but to perform the practice of a soldier. So that, the ending end of all earthly learning being virtuous action, those skills that most serve to bring forth that, have a

---

4. Theagenes (thē aj´ e nēz): Hero of *Ethiopica,* a romance by Heliodorus, a Greek writer, about 400 A.D.
5. Pylades (pī´ la dēz´) *adj.*: Friend of the mythological figure Orestes; he appears in *Iphigenia Among the Taurians,* a tragedy by the ancient Greek playwright Euripides (yōō rip´ i dēz´) (484–406 B.C.).
6. Idea or foreconceit: The Greek philosopher Plato (428/27–348/47 B.C.) held that the Idea of a thing, which does not change, is greater than the thing itself, which can change or be destroyed. His Renaissance interpreters held that artists draw directly on the Idea in representing things.
7. *mimesis* (mim ē´ sis) *n.*: Greek for "act of imitation," especially one that shows the essence of the thing represented.

---

8. clay lodgings: That is, "bodies."
9. felicity (fə lis´ i tē) *n.*: Happiness; good fortune.
10. *architektonike* (är kə tek tän´ ik ā) *n.*: Greek for "construction." The ancient Greek philosophers Aristotle (384–322 B.C.) and Plato used the term to refer to purposeful, knowledgeable activity.

Analyzing Real-World Texts

most just title to be princes over all the rest. Wherein we can show the poet is worthy to have it before any other competitors.

. . .

The philosopher . . . and the historian are they which would win the goal, the one by precept,[11] the other by example. But both, not having both, do both halt. For the philosopher, setting down with thorny arguments the bare rule, is so hard of utterance, and so misty to be conceived, that one that has no other guide but him shall wade in him till he be old before he shall find sufficient cause to be honest: for his knowledge stands so upon the abstract and general, that happy is that man who may understand him, and more happy that can apply what he does understand. On the other side, the historian, wanting the precept, is so tied, not to what should be but to what is, to the particular truth of things and not to the general reason of things, that his example draws no necessary consequence, and therefore a less fruitful doctrine.

Now does the peerless poet perform both: for whatsoever the philosopher says should be done, he gives a perfect picture of it by some one by whom he presupposes it was done; so as he couples the general notion with the particular example. A perfect picture, I say, for he yields to the powers of the mind an image of that whereof the philosopher bestows but a wordish description, which does neither strike, pierce, nor possess the sight of the soul so much as that other does. For, as in outward things, to a man that had never seen an elephant or a rhinoceros, who should tell him most exquisitely all their shape[s], color, bigness, and particular marks, or of a gorgeous palace [the] architecture, who declaring the full beauties might well make the hearer able to repeat, as it were by rote, all he had heard, yet should never satisfy his inward conceit[12] with being witness to itself of a true lively knowledge; but the same man, as soon as he might see those beasts well painted, or that house well in model, should straightways grow, without need of any description, to a judicial[13] comprehending of them: so no doubt the philosopher with his learned definitions, be it of virtues or vices, matters of public policy or private government, replenishes the memory with many infallible grounds of wisdom, which, notwithstanding, lie dark before the imaginative and judging power, if they be not illuminated, or figured forth, by the speaking picture of poesy.

---

11. **precept** (prē′ sept′) *n.*: Rule of action or conduct.

12. **conceit** (kän sēt′) *n.*: Consciousness or imagination (obsolete usage).

13. **judicial** (jo͞o dish′ əl) *adj.*: That is, "judicious"; showing sound judgment.

◆ Apply the Reading Strategy

1. Note five allusions found in the *Defense*. For each, explain the reference.
2. Sidney's argument that there must be an ultimate end of knowledge served by other activities alludes to arguments found in the works of Plato and Aristotle. Explain why this allusion would make Sidney's point seem strong to his readers.

◆ Compare Literary Forms

Read or review Sidney's Sonnet 31, p. 212. Explain whether Sidney the poet fulfills the ideal proposed by Sidney the critic—to "deliver a golden" world and to "teach and delight."

Sir Isaac Newton (1642–1727) revolutionized science with his *Principia Mathematica*, in which he set forth new laws of motion and gravity.

◆ **Reading Strategy**

Recognize Logical Modes of Persuasion To persuade readers, writers **anticipate and rule out alternative explanations.** Newton is struck by the width of the rectangular spectrum produced by passing light through a prism. Before he concludes that this shape reflects a characteristic of light, he anticipates an alternative explanation—unevenness in the glass causes the shape. He then passes the light through two prisms. The second prism exactly cancels the effect of the first, ruling out the possibility that uneven glass is a factor.

Use a graphic organizer like the one below to list each variable that Newton eliminates.

Effect	Variable	How Eliminated	Reason for Eliminating
Spectrum cast by prism has rectangular shape.	Possibly caused by unevenness in glass of prism	Shine through second prism; spectrum returned to round beam.	Effect of unevenness would not be exactly canceled by second prism.
[same]	Possibly caused by different thickness along the prism.		

Letter on Light and Color

Sir Isaac Newton

Letter sent to the Royal Society

February 6, 1672

Sir,

To perform my late promise to you, I shall without further ceremony acquaint you that in the beginning of the year 1666 (at which time I applied myself to the grinding of optic glasses of other figures than spherical) I procured me a triangular glass prism to try therewith the celebrated phenomena of colors. And in order thereto having darkened my chamber and made a small hole in my window-shuts to let in a convenient quantity of the sun's light, I placed my prism at his entrance that it might be thereby refracted[1] to the opposite wall. It was at first a very pleasing divertissement to view the vivid and intense colors produced thereby; but after a while, applying myself to consider more circumspectly, I became surprised to see them in an *oblong*[2] form, which according to the received laws of refraction I expected should have been *circular*.

They were terminated at the sides with straight lines, but at the ends the decay of light was so gradual that it was difficult to determine justly what was their figure; yet they seemed *semicircular*.

Comparing the length of this colored spectrum with its breadth, I found it about five times greater, a disproportion so extravagant that it excited me to a more than ordinary curiosity of examining from whence it might proceed. I could scarce think that the various thickness of the glass or the termination with shadow or darkness could have any influence on light to produce such an effect; yet I thought it not amiss first to examine those circumstances, and so tried what would happen by transmitting light through parts of the glass of divers

---

1. **refracted** (ri frakt´ id) *v*.: Bent when passing from one medium to another (as from air to glass).
2. **oblong** (äb´ lôŋ´) *adj*.: Rectangular.

Analyzing Real-World Texts

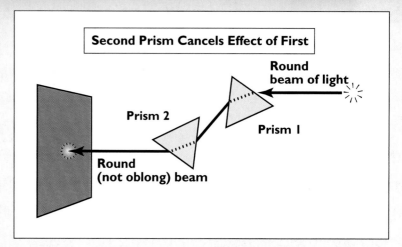

Second Prism Cancels Effect of First

Prism 2

Prism 1

Round
beam of light

Round
(not oblong) beam

thicknesses, or by setting the prism without so that the light might pass through it and be refracted before it was terminated by the hole. But I found none of those circumstances material. The fashion of the colors was in all these cases the same.

Then I suspected whether by any unevenness in the glass or other contingent[3] irregularity these colors might be thus dilated.[4] And to try this, I took another prism like the former and so placed it that the light, passing through them both, might be refracted contrary ways, and so by the latter returned into that course from which the former had diverted it. For by this means I thought the regular effects of the first prism would be destroyed by the second prism but the irregular ones more augmented[5] by the multiplicity of refractions. The event was that the light which by the first prism was diffused[6] into an oblong form was by the second reduced into an orbicular[7] one with as much regularity as when it did not at all pass through them. So that, whatever was the cause of that length, 'twas not any contingent irregularity.[8]

. . .

The gradual removal of these suspicions at length led me to the *experimentum crucis*,[9] which was this: I took two boards, and placed one of them close behind the prism at the window, so that the light might pass through a small hole made in it for the purpose and fall on the other board, which I placed at about 12 feet distance, having first made a small hole in it also, for some of that incident light to pass through. Then I placed another prism behind

this second board so that the light, trajected through both the boards, might pass through that also, and be again refracted before it arrived at the wall. This done, I took the first prism in my hand, and turned it to and fro slowly about its axis, so much as to make the several parts of the image cast on the second board successively pass through the hole in it, that I might observe to what places on the wall the second prism would refract them. And I saw by the variation of those places that the light tending to that end of the image towards which the refraction of the first prism was made did in the second prism suffer a refraction considerably greater than the light tending to the other end. And so the true cause of the length of that image was detected to be no other than that light consists of *rays differently refrangible*,[10] which, without any respect to a difference in their incidence,[11] were, according to their degrees of refrangibility, transmitted towards divers parts of the wall.

. . .

I shall now proceed to acquaint you with another more notable difformity in its rays, wherein the *origin of color* is unfolded: concerning which I shall lay down the doctrine first and then for its examination give you an instance or two of the experiments, as a specimen of the rest.

---

3. **contingent** (kən tin´ jənt) *adj.*: Chance; accidental.
4. **dilated** (dī´ lāt´ id) *v.*: Made wider; expanded
5. **augmented** (ôg ment´ id) *v.*: Increased.
6. **diffused**: (di fyo͞ozd´) *v.*: Spread out.
7. **orbicular** (ôr bik´ yo͞o lər) *adj.*: Circular.
8. Newton here considers a few other variables, including the origin of rays from different parts of the sun.
9. ***experimentum crucis*** (ek sper´ ə ment´ o͞om kro͞ok´ is) *n.*: Latin for "crucial experiment."

---

10. **refrangible** (ri fran´ jə bəl) *adj.*: Able to be refracted (bent).
11. **incidence** (in´ sə dəns) *n.*: The falling of a ray, object, etc., in a straight line onto a surface.

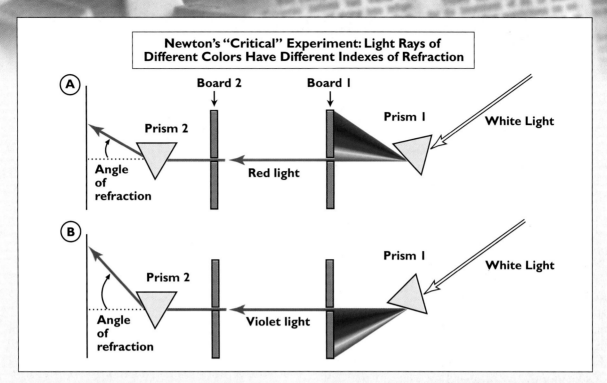

Newton's "Critical" Experiment: Light Rays of Different Colors Have Different Indexes of Refraction

The doctrine you will find comprehended and illustrated in the following propositions.

1. As the rays of light differ in degrees of refrangibility, so they also differ in their disposition to exhibit this or that particular color. Colors are not qualifications of light, derived from refractions or reflections of natural bodies (as 'tis generally believed), but original and connate properties which in divers rays are divers. Some rays are disposed to exhibit a red color and no other; some a yellow and no other, some a green and no other, and so of the rest. Nor are there only rays proper and particular to the more eminent colors, but even to all their intermediate gradations.

2. To the same degree of refrangibility ever belongs the same color, and to the same color ever belongs the same degree of refrangibility. The least refrangible rays are all disposed to exhibit a red color, and contrarily those rays which are disposed to exhibit a red color are all the least refrangible. So the most refrangible rays are all disposed to exhibit a deep violet color, and contrarily those which are apt to exhibit such a violet color are all the most refrangible. And so to all the intermediate colors in a continued series belong intermediate degrees of refrangibility. And this analogy 'twixt colors and refrangibility is very precise and strict; the rays always exactly agreeing in both or proportionally disagreeing in both.

◆ Apply the Reading Strategy

1. List three alternative explanations that Newton rules out. Explain the reasoning he uses.
2. How does Newton explain the phenomena of refraction that he considers—the oblong shape of the spectrum and the effect of passing different parts of the spectrum through a second prism?

◆ Compare Literary Forms

Read or review Samuel Johnson's "Preface" to *A Dictionary of the English Language,* p. 505. (a) What does Johnson's project of bringing order to a language "energetic without rule" have in common with Newton's project of finding a rule behind what he sees? (b) What are the differences between the two?

Analyzing Real-World Texts

About the Author

In his journal, *The Edinburgh Review*, **Francis Jeffrey** (1773–1850) panned the poetry of William Wordsworth.

◆ Reading Strategy

Analyze Aspects of Text: Sentence Structure Writers **gain emphasis** by placing groups of words at the beginning or end of a sentence, by balancing phrases, or by delaying the main clause. Jeffrey emphasizes "With Mr. Wordsworth and his friends" by placing it at the beginning of a sentence. Later, he balances the phrases "be gained in freedom and originality" and "be lost in allusion and authority." By delaying the main clause in the sentence beginning "That its flights should be graceful . . . ," he makes it seem that his ideas inevitably flow toward that clause.

Using a graphic organizer like the one below, list examples from the reviews of these three ways of gaining emphasis.

Means of Emphasis	Position	Effect
Placement: beginning or end	1. "With Mr. Wordsworth and his friends,"	Emphasizes the contrast between Wordsworth and traditional poets
	2.	
Balanced Clauses		
Delayed Main Clause		

Early Reviews of Wordsworth

Francis Jeffrey

Book reviews, *The Edinburgh Review*, 1807 and 1814

With Mr. Wordsworth and his friends, it is plain that their peculiarities of diction[1] are things of choice, and not of accident. They write as they do, upon principle and system; and it evidently costs them much pains to keep *down* to the standard which they have proposed to themselves. They are, to the full, as much mannerists,[2] too, as the poetasters[3] who ring changes on the commonplaces of magazines versification; and all the difference between them is, that they borrow their phrases from a different and scantier *gradus ad Parnassum.*[4] If they were, indeed, to discard all imitation and set phraseology, and to bring in no words merely for show or for meter—as much, perhaps, might be gained in freedom and originality, as would infallibly be lost in allusion and authority; but, in point of fact, the new poets are just as great borrowers as the old; only that, instead of borrowing from the more popular passages of their illustrious predecessors, they have preferred furnishing themselves from vulgar ballads and plebeian nurseries.

. . .

Long habits of seclusion, and an excessive ambition of originality, can alone account for the disproportion which seems to exist between this author's taste and his genius; or for the devotion with which he has sacrificed so many precious gifts at the shrine of those paltry idols which he has set up for himself among his lakes and his mountains. Solitary musings, amidst such scenes, might no doubt be expected to nurse up the mind to the majesty of poetical conception (though

---

1. **diction** (dik´ shən) *n.*: Choice of words; style of expression.
2. **mannerists**: Artists using an exaggerated or artificial style.
3. **poetasters** (pō´ ət as´ tərz) *n.*: Inferior poets.
4. *gradus ad Parnassum* (grā´ dəs ad Pär nas´ oom) *n.*: Dictionary for writing poetry (Latin for "step to Parnassus" [mountain of Apollo and the Muses, Greek deities of the arts]).

it is remarkable, that all the greater poets lived, or had lived, in the full current of society), but the collision of equal minds—the admonition of prevailing impressions—seems necessary to reduce its redundancies, and repress that tendency to extravagance or puerility, into which the self-indulgence and self-admiration of genius is so apt to be betrayed, when it is allowed to wanton, without awe or restraint, in the triumph and delight of its own intoxication. That its flights should be graceful and glorious in the eyes of men, it seems almost to be necessary that they should be made in the consciousness that men's eyes are to behold them,—and that the inward transport[5] and vigor by which they are inspired, should be tempered by an occasional reference to what will be thought of them by those ultimate dispensers of glory. An habitual and general knowledge of the few settled and permanent maxims, which form the canon[6] of general taste in all large and polished societies—a certain tact, which informs us at once that many things, which we still love and are moved by in secret, must necessarily be despised as childish, or derided as absurd, in all such societies—though it will not stand in the place of genius, seems necessary to the success of its exertions; and though it will never enable anyone to produce the higher beauties of art, can alone secure the talent which does produce them, from errors that must render it useless. Those who have most of the talent, however, commonly acquire this knowledge with the greatest facility; and if Mr. Wordsworth, instead of confining himself almost entirely to the society of the dalesmen[7] and cottagers and little children, who form the subjects of his book, had condescended to mingle a little more with the people that were to read and judge of it, we cannot help thinking that its texture might have been considerably improved: at least it appears to us to be absolutely impossible, that anyone who had lived or mixed familiarly with men of literature and ordinary judgment in poetry, (of course we exclude the coadjutors[8] and disciples of his own school) could ever have fallen into such gross faults, or so long mistaken them for beauties. His first essays we looked upon in a good degree as poetical paradoxes—maintained experimentally, in order to display talent, and court notoriety;—and so maintained, with no more serious belief in their truth, than is usually generated by an ingenious and animated defense of other paradoxes. But when we find that he has been for twenty years exclusively employed upon articles of this very fabric, and that he has still enough of raw material on hand to keep him so employed for twenty years to come, we cannot refuse him the justice of believing that he is a sincere convert to his own system, and must ascribe the peculiarities of his composition, not to any transient affectation, or accidental caprice of imagination, but to a settled perversity of taste or understanding, which has been fostered, if not altogether created, by the circumstances to which we have already alluded.

---

5. **transport** (trans´ pôrt´) *n.*: Rapture; strong emotion.
6. **canon** (kan´ ən) *n.*: Group of established, basic rules.

7. **dalesmen**: Simple farmers.
8. **coadjutors** (ko aj´ ə tərz) *n.*: Assistants.

◆ **Apply the Reading Strategy**

1. (a) Give an instance in these reviews in which several clauses precede the main clause of a sentence. (b) Explain the "feel" the delay gives.
2. (a) Give an example of the use of balanced clauses. (b) The use of balanced clauses makes the reviewer's opinions seem more decisive. Explain.

◆ **Compare Literary Forms**

Read or review William Wordsworth's "Lines Composed a Few Miles Above Tintern Abbey," p. 616. Does the poem suffer from the faults ascribed to the Romantics by Jeffrey, or does it show that Jeffrey was unable to appreciate the good in Wordsworth? Explain.

About the Author

George P. Landow (1940–) is professor of English and Art History at Brown University.

◆ Reading Strategy

Evaluate Credibility of Sources To evaluate the credibility of sources, ask what the authors' motives are. If they wish to support a particular viewpoint, they may focus on certain details at the expense of others. Are they experts in the field? If so, they will be careful with facts, if only to protect their reputations.

You can find out about the authors of "The Victorian Web" by clicking on *Who created the Victorian Web?* The author providing information on Victorian public health is a history professor, so you can probably trust his claims. You might want to find out more about Glenn Everett before using his work.

Using a graphic organizer like the one below, list each link on the site, and evaluate the information you find there.

Link	Credibility	My Reasoning
Victorianism	Mixed	Link probably discusses historical issues, but site is created largely by people studying literature and the arts.
Gender Matters		
Social Context		

The Victorian Web

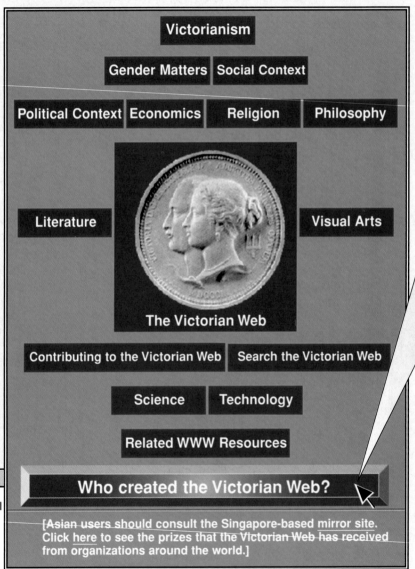

Credits: Who Created the Victorian Web?

George P. Landow, Professor of English and Art History, Brown University

The Victorian Web

The Victorian Web and *Context32*

The Victorian Web is the WWW translation of Brown University's **Context 61,** which serves as a resource for courses in Victorian literature [follow for syllabus of one such course]. These materials ultimately derive from **Context 32,** the Intermedia web that provided contextual information for English 32, "Survey of English Literature From 1700 to the Present." **Context 32** was begun in Spring 1985 as part of Brown University's Institute for Research in Information and Scholarship (IRIS) Intermedia project, which IBM, Apple Computers, the Annenberg/CPB Project, and other sources funded.

George P. Landow designed and edited the entire web, made many of the links, and is responsible for most of the materials on the individual authors and works as well as those on Biblical typology. He authored multiple lexias throughout the web and selected both the external criticism cited and most of the visual images. All captions for images are his. Under his direction David Cody wrote many of the general materials and chose many of the original digitized images, and Glenn Everett wrote some of the basic materials on Romantic and Victorian poets including timelines. The following year Kathryn Stockton created many of the documents on feminism and literary theory.

Anthony S. Wohl, Professor of History at Vassar College, generously contributed much of the material on Victorian public health, race and class issues, and anti-Catholic prejudice in Victorian England. This work draws upon both his published and unpublished writings.

Transferring the Intermedia Materials to Eastgate Systems Storyspace

In 1992 Robert Arellano '90 transferred most of the documents from the Intermedia system (which ceased operating in 1992) into Storyspace and relinked them. **The Victorian Web** also draws upon several other hypertext webs developed under Landow's direction. In particular, most of the Dickens materials come originally from the Intermedia **Dickens Web,** which Julie Launhardt, Paul Kahn, and he assembled. (It won the 1990 EDUCOM/NCRIPTAL award for best software in the humanities and has been published in Storyspace by Eastgate Systems); similarly, most of the Tennyson materials are taken from the **In Memoriam Web,** developed by him and Jon Lanestedt, University of Oslo, Norway (also published by Eastgate Systems).

In 1993 David Stevenson '96 rearranged this wealth of materials approximately into the form in which you now encounter them. He reorganized many of the materials on authors, imported and wrote most of the biographical materials, built and linked all works' overviews, and developed several of the contextual overviews. He was responsible for importing a significant amount of the web's materials. In one month's work over the summer of 1993 at IRIS, the web grew from one to three megabytes, gained over a thousand links, and acquired the structure and form that you see it in now.

◆ Apply the Reading Strategy

1. Which documents did Professor Landow write? Which were written by his students and edited by him? Explain whether you would give higher credibility to his own work.
2. Name two links to information you would be inclined to trust. Name two links to information you would consider more cautiously. Explain.

◆ Compare Literary Forms

Read or review Sydney Smith's "Progress in Personal Comfort," p. 805. Write a paragraph in Smith's style extolling the amazing virtues of the World Wide Web.

Analyzing Real-World Texts

About the Author
John G. Blair (1934–) has taught literature at the University of Geneva in Switzerland.

◆Reading Strategy

Use Elements of Text to Support Interpretations
To arrive at or judge an interpretation of a work, you must test whether it is supported by **elements of text**—from word choice to images to theme.

To assess critic John G. Blair's claims about W. H. Auden's poems, you must return to Auden's texts (pp. 924, 928). For instance, Blair claims that "[Auden's] characters appear not as recognizably complex human beings, but as personified human types...." You might find confirmation of this point in the image "The provinces of his body revolted ..." ("In Memory of W. B. Yeats," l. 14)—a comparison of the dying poet to a country.

Using a chart like the one below, list elements of Auden's poems that do or do not support each of Blair's claims.

Claim	Text Element	Conclusion
Characters are "personified human types."	"The provinces of his body revolted...." ("In Memory of W.B. Yeats," l.14)	Though Yeats is not exactly a "personified type" in the poem, Auden carefully avoids creating a sense of the man.
"[A]bstract concepts [are] made palpable in mountains, lakes, and streams."		

Auden's Impersonal Poetry

John G. Blair

Critical commentary

Auden's[1] "now-ness"[2] we are in a better position to estimate. The danger of universally applicable insights is that they may seem unrelated to any particular time or place and hence fail to make contact with the reader. Indeed, most of Auden's mature poetry has inclined toward allegory,[3] which is particularly liable to this fault. His characters appear not as recognizably complex human beings, but as personified human types or philosophical attitudes. His landscapes are ordered not by Nature, but by an Intelligence that finds its abstract concepts made palpable in mountains, lakes, or streams. Auden's poems sparkle with striking particulars, but his images derive their aptness from the precision and, frequently, the unexpectedness with which they embody an idea. The "now-ness" that Auden achieves, then, is not based on a new insight into what the world around him can mean, but on a new perception of the immediacy and relevance of a generalized human attitude or concept. This allegorical habit of mind has cut Auden off from the kind of poetic particularity that has been most often admired in this century. Allegory, however, has received less respect than it deserves, as Auden's character types, at their best, can demonstrate. For example, the power of his insight and his control over rhetoric have enabled him to particularize for all time, as it were, two antipodal[4] aberrations of

---

1. **Auden's** (ô´ denz): W(ystan) H(ugh) Auden (1907–1973) was a leading British and American poet.
2. **"now-ness":** As defined by Auden, the mark of an author's personality and times on his or her poems.
3. **allegory** (al´ ə gôr´ ē) n.: Use of characters, events, places, and so on to stand for abstract ideas or principles.
4. **antipodal** (an tip´ ō dəl) adj.: Directly opposite.

mind which every human being must fear in others and in himself. One is embodied in the self-appointed divine scourge of the world (most notably the Vicar in *The Dog Beneath the Skin)* and the other, in the self-defeated disciple of progress who, out of his lack of spiritual commitment, cannot perform any significant action (Herod in *For the Time Being).*[5]

"Now-ness," as Auden describes it, is a quality a poem derives from being the product of a unique person at a unique moment in time, but his own poems, as we have seen, refuse to assert his personal uniqueness. By avoiding a recognizably individual style and by presenting his poems impersonally, Auden has separated his work from the usual ways of identifying a unique vision. His poems as much as those of any other poet are the products of a particular individual, but he does not ask acceptance of his vision because it is unique or because it is his. The vision of humanity articulated in his poems, he seems to imply, would be available to any perceptive and rigorously honest pair of eyes. To put it another way, Auden's reader is rarely allowed the comfortable feeling that the poem puts him in contact with a fellow human being who is revealing his innermost feelings. Instead, the reader is confronted with a verbal mirror which lays bare some aspect of his human nature. Usually the sight is anything but comforting. Auden has found poetry a discipline which measures and controls his impulses; he asks the reader as well to ponder self-critically what "the luck of verbal playing" reveals of his hidden nature.

The combination of Auden's impersonal presentation of poetry and his serious moral and didactic[6] purpose in writing it places him in a paradoxical situation. He very rightly rejects the self-assertion implicit in preaching at the reader. Yet Auden wants to lead his reader to measure himself against the mirror of the poem, not to treat it simply as an aesthetic[7] performance. The resources available to the poet to trap the reader, such as satire, the rhetorical pyrotechnics[8] of riddling, or the upsetting of a reader's nostalgia, all have one great disadvantage. While they may direct the reader toward the unflattering reflection of himself, every additional complexity in the poetic performance makes it easier for him to feel satisfied with himself for perceiving that brilliance of technique. The artifice[9] of Auden's poetry reflects his consciousness of himself as an actor and his desire to lead the reader to similar self-awareness. The same artifice, unfortunately, offers the reader a way to escape real self-examination, not merely by understanding the ingenious mechanics of the trap, but by entertaining satisfaction at his power to do so. In fact, an awareness of such a paradox may have supported Auden's recent views on the impossibility of being serious in poetry.

---

5. ***The Dog Beneath the Skin . . . For the Time Being:*** Respectively, a play written by Auden and Christopher Isherwood, published in 1935, and a collection of Auden's poems, published in 1945.

6. **didactic** (dī dak´ tik) *adj*.: Intended to teach.
7. **aesthetic** (es thet´ ik) *adj*.: For the sake of beauty.
8. **pyrotechnics** (pī´ rō tek´ niks) *n*.: Fireworks; displays.
9. **artifice** (ärt´ ə fis) *n*.: Device; clever means of creating an effect.

◆ Apply the Reading Strategy

1. Cite the points on which you disagree with Blair and the ones on which you agree, giving examples from Auden's work.
2. Do you think Blair touches on something essential about Auden's work? Explain.

◆ Compare Literary Forms

Read or review W. B. Yeats's "Sailing to Byzantium," p. 904. (a) Explain the speaker's pleas "Consume my heart away" (l. 21) and "gather me / Into the artifice of eternity" (ll. 23–24) in relation to writing poetry. (b) Explain whether, according to Blair, Auden would join in these pleas.

Suggestions for Sustained Reading

Sustained Reading and Its Benefits

Novels, plays, short-story collections, and full-length nonfiction works all provide a great opportunity for sustained reading—reading that takes place over an extended period of time. Through any of these types of writing, you can travel to new and distant worlds, follow a character's life from birth through adulthood, and experience events unlike anything that happens in your everyday life.

The Keys to Successful Sustained Reading

Reading longer works can be more challenging than reading brief pieces because longer works usually involve more characters and plot events and because it is unlikely that you will read a longer work in a single sitting. Following are a few of the keys to successful sustained reading:

- **Set aside extended periods of time.** It is very hard to follow a longer work if you read it in short intervals of a few minutes at a time. Read in periods of a half hour or more. Do not allow yourself to be distracted by the television set or the telephone.
- **Make yourself comfortable.** You'll concentrate better if you make yourself comfortable each time you sit down to read. Choose a comfortable chair in a place you like.
- **Take notes as you read.** Jot down details of the settings, note information about the characters, and record important events.

- **Hold book-circle discussions.** Get together with classmates who are reading the same work. Share your reactions. Discuss what you learn about the characters, and try to analyze the message the writer is trying to convey.

The Prentice Hall Literature Library

The Prentice Hall Literature Library includes many longer works that fit in well with the literature included in this book. Your teacher can provide you with access to many of these titles. In addition, you can find an unlimited array of other extended reading possibilities in bookstores and in your local libraries.

Suggested Works and Connections to Unit Themes

Following are some suggestions for longer works that will give you the opportunity to experience the fun of sustained reading. Each of the suggestions further explores one of the themes in this book. Many of the titles are included in the Prentice Hall Literature Library.

Suggested Titles Related to Units

Unit One

Grendel
John Gardner

Once again we meet Beowulf's foe, but this time we get the story from Grendel's point of view. This retelling of the epic poem begins with the monster attacking Hrothgar's meadhall and men and ends right after his fight with Beowulf, as Grendel is about to die. *Grendel* is a funny, intriguing examination of the way we look at monsters, heroes, and the world we create with both.

The Once and Future King
T. H. White

This novel is a magical retelling of the legend of Arthur—from the adventure-filled days of Arthur's youth, to the golden age of Camelot, to the final scene in which the old, broken king lies alone on the battlefield at Salisbury. In this unforgettable tale, the characters of the legend step out of the book's pages and into your life, as they experience the wonders and horrors of magic, suffer victory and defeat in battle, and grapple with matters of love, betrayal, and honor.

Unit Two

Hamlet
William Shakespeare

One of Shakespeare's greatest tragedies, *Hamlet* is the tale of a young man forced to confront and question all he formerly believed as true. As the play begins, Prince Hamlet is mourning the death of his father, the King of Denmark. In addition, he must accept the new marriage of his mother to his uncle, who now rules Denmark. As Hamlet struggles with these changes, the ghost of his father appears to him. The king tells Hamlet that he was poisoned by his brother and urges Hamlet to avenge his murder.

The Tempest
William Shakespeare

This drama is a tale of magic, mystery, and love that takes place on what at first appears to be a deserted island. Prospero, the rightful Duke of Milan, his daughter Miranda, the spirit Ariel, and the man-monster Caliban inhabit the island. Through his magic and the aid of Ariel, Prospero is able to lure a boat to the island that contains his brother Antonio, who dispossessed him of his throne. Prospero works his magic to arrive at a wonderful marriage for his daughter and the prince of Naples and to reclaim his rightful title.

Unit Three

Robinson Crusoe
Daniel Defoe

Defoe's *Robinson Crusoe* marked the beginning of the modern English novel. It is, however, a novel populated mostly by a single character. In 1659, Crusoe is shipwrecked on an island off the coast of South America and begins a twenty-eight-year stay on the island. Although specific history is not alluded to, Crusoe is very much a product of his time—he grew up during England's Civil War and its restoration. Crusoe's attempts to create a decent society and improve his own moral character echo England's struggles to restore itself after the political turmoil of the Civil War.

Gulliver's Travels
Jonathan Swift

Swift's *Gulliver's Travels* is a children's story, a fantasy, a parody of travel books, and a sophisticated satire of English politics all in one. This masterpiece describes four voyages of Lemuel Gulliver, a ship's physician, to exotic lands. Gulliver begins in Lilliput, where the inhabitants are one twelfth the size of human beings. By the story's end, the playful elements have yielded to a bitter indictment of humankind's corruption of reason. Swift's unique combination of allegory—using settings, objects, or characters to stand for ideas and qualities beyond themselves—has made his work appeal to all audiences.

Unit Four

Pride and Prejudice
Jane Austen

With her usual comic flair and common sense, Jane Austen explores the pressure on women to succeed in the marriage market. Mrs. Bennet, all too aware of this market's demands, shamelessly pursues marriage for each of her daughters. Although one of those daughters, Elizabeth, is socially inferior to the arrogant Fitzwilliam Darcy, he loses his heart to her all the same. This victory of romance shows that feelings are at least as important as the shrewd calculations of amateur matchmakers. Austen's common sense prevails over pounds and shillings.

Emma
Jane Austen

Austen has great fun with her busybody heroine Emma Woodhouse. Emma has appointed herself matchmaker for her whole community, meddling in just about everyone's affairs. Though her friend Mr. Knightly cautions her against the reckless pursuit of marital bliss for others, she learns the folly of her ways only through bitter experience. Also, she realizes almost too late that her frantic activity has led her to ignore her own happiness and the person best suited to guarantee it: the same Mr. Knightly who has been her loyal friend.

Unit Five

Wuthering Heights
Emily Brontë

The setting of *Wuthering Heights* is the wild and windy moors of northern Yorkshire. Central to the story is the romantic and brooding Heathcliff, a gypsy adopted into a family and mistreated by his foster-brother. The story revolves around Heathcliff's thwarted love for Catherine and his revenge on those who mistreated him. By the end of the tale, Heathcliff's passion is spent, and happiness becomes possible for two of the younger members of the family, who are able to make a new beginning.

The Importance of Being Earnest
Oscar Wilde

Mocking the social conventions of the Victorian period, *The Importance of Being Earnest* is one of the wittiest comedies ever written. Jack Worthing invents a mischievous younger brother named Ernest to allow him to adventure in London. Algernon Moncrieff appears at Jack's home assuming the identity of Ernest Worthing to meet Jack's attractive ward, Cecily Cardew. Both men have told their romantic interests that their names are Ernest because the women want to marry men named Ernest!

Unit Six

Heart of Darkness
Joseph Conrad

Conrad explores the human mind and the effects of colonialism in this great novel that has inspired many other writers. Conrad's narrator, the river steamer captain Marlow, tells a group of friends about an ominous journey into the heart of the African jungle. Mysterious, grotesque tales about the white ivory trader Kurtz pale in comparison with the reality Marlow finds when he meets the man. In Conrad's classic tale, the "heart of darkness" is both the human heart and the oppressive colonial system.

Pygmalion
George Bernard Shaw

Like his professor of phonetics, Henry Higgins, Shaw believed in the power of language to break down class barriers. In Shaw's play, the overbearing Higgins transforms Eliza Doolittle, a cockney flower girl, into an elegant woman. Neither character foresees, however, that falling in love may complicate the process of Eliza's transformation. Nearly half a century after it was written, Shaw's comedy became the basis of the enormously successful musical *My Fair Lady*.

A Passage to India
E. M. Forster

Forster's novel is a classic portrayal of clashing cultures. Adela Quested, a young British visitor to India, falsely accuses Aziz, a likable Indian doctor, of assaulting her on a tour of the Malabar Caves. As the British and Indian characters react to this accusation, the reader sees the cultural differences between them. Forster shows that in a colonial situation, these differences inevitably lead to misunderstandings.

Test Practice Bank

Reading Comprehension

Sequential Order and Complex Written Directions

Read the passage, and then answer the questions that follow. Mark the letter of your answer on a bubble sheet if your teacher provides one; otherwise, number from 1 to 6 on a separate sheet of paper, and write the letter of the correct answer next to each number.

You can patch a small area of damaged carpet yourself. You need a piece of matching carpet for the repair. Check with the store where you bought your carpet. If the same carpet is not available through your dealer, cut a piece from the back of a closet.

To begin the repair, use a sharp knife to cut a rectangle around the damaged area. Cut through the carpet backing only—do not cut through the pad. Remove the damaged piece, but be sure to save it. Then cut the replacement carpet in an identical rectangle. Trim this patch so it fits the cutout area exactly. Spread adhesive on the back of the patch, and carefully fit it into place. Rub the carpet until the new and old edges merge and the seams are concealed. Finally, if your patch came from the back of a closet, glue the saved piece of damaged carpet in its place.

1 When should you fit the new patch into the carpet?
 A before trimming it
 B before spreading adhesive on it
 C after spreading adhesive on it
 D after cutting through the pad

2 What is the first thing you should do when patching a carpet?
 A find a piece of matching carpet
 B cut out the damaged area
 C find a piece of different carpet
 D spread adhesive on the patch

3 What do you use to cut the carpet?
 A adhesive
 B scissors
 C a sharp knife
 D a screwdriver

4 Which action should you avoid?
 A cutting out the damaged area
 B trimming the patch
 C inserting the patch
 D cutting through the padding

5 What do you do with the damaged piece of carpet you have removed?
 A save it
 B throw it away
 C glue it on top of the new patch
 D take it to the carpet store

6 What is the final repair step?
 A go to the carpet store
 B cut out the damaged area
 C fit the new patch into the damaged area
 D glue the damaged piece into the hole in the closet

See the Test Preparation Workshop on page 193 for tips on answering questions about sequential order and complex written directions.

Test Practice Bank

Reading Comprehension

Propaganda; Fact and Opinion

Read the passage, and then answer the questions that follow. Mark the letter of your answer on a bubble sheet if your teacher provides one; otherwise, number from 1 to 6 on a separate sheet of paper, and write the letter of the correct answer next to each number.

(1) *Calling All Clowns*, the Green Blackbirds' newest CD, hit the stores yesterday and immediately sold out. (2) It has been five years since the release of the band's popular CD *Lazy Days*. (3) Impatient fans waited overnight in long lines outside record stores; some even braved snow and sleet in Chicago. (4) Unfortunately, *Calling All Clowns* isn't worth the wait; you'd be better off spending your money on almost any other CD. (5) Lead guitarist Les Izmore has contributed six songs to the CD, which is six songs too many. (6) As you know, drummer Karla T. left the Green Blackbirds four years ago to form her own band, the Velvet Tonsils. (7) Karla T. *was* the Green Blackbirds; without her, the Blackbirds are just another garage band. (8) Check out Karla T. and the Velvet Tonsils at the Hightop Club on Wednesday, and you'll see what I mean.

1 Which of the statements in the passage might be labeled as propaganda?
 A Statements 1 and 2
 B Statements 2 and 5
 C Statements 4 and 5
 D Statements 3 and 6

2 Which of the following statements in the passage represent an opinion?
 A Statements 1 and 3
 B Statements 2 and 3
 C Statements 1 and 6
 D Statements 4 and 7

3 Which of the following represents a statement of fact?
 A Statement 2
 B Statement 4
 C Statement 5
 D Statement 7

4 How would you characterize Statement 3?
 A fact
 B propaganda
 C opinion
 D unreliable source

5 Which of the following may be considered factual?
 A "isn't worth the wait"
 B "six songs too many"
 C "*was* the green Blackbirds"
 D "has contributed six songs"

6 Which sentence is a fact?
 A Statement 4
 B Statement 5
 C Statement 6
 D Statement 7

See the Test Preparation Workshop on page 377 for tips on answering questions about forms of propaganda and fact and opinion.

Test Practice Bank

Reading Comprehension

Writer's Purpose and Point of View

Read the passage, and then answer the questions that follow. Mark the letter of your answer on a bubble sheet if your teacher provides one; otherwise, number from 1 to 6 on a separate sheet of paper, and write the letter of the correct answer next to each number.

Are you sick and tired of being taxed, taxed, and taxed again? Raise your voices! Let's not fool ourselves. If the bond issue for a new town library is passed, it will raise our taxes. Some homeowners will pay a great deal more every year. And that's just the beginning. Hidden maintenance costs may triple the annual tax bite within three to five years. The old library has served our town well and can continue to do so. Vote against the spendthrift library bond issue on October 19!

1 What is the writer's main purpose?
  A to entertain
  B to persuade
  C to inform
  D to provide statistics

2 What is the writer's point of view regarding the bond issue?
  A approval
  B indifference
  C disapproval
  D agreement

3 What point of view does the writer express in the passage?
  A Taxes should be raised.
  B The old library is falling apart.
  C The bond issue will save the town money.
  D The bond issue will raise taxes unfairly.

4 Which of the following describes the writer's tone?
  A lighthearted
  B angry
  C humorous
  D positive

5 Which statement best represents the writer's specific point of view?
  A Vote against the bond issue.
  B Remodel the old library.
  C Vote for the bond issue.
  D Stay home on October 19.

6 In this passage, the writer's purpose is to—
  A present information objectively
  B present information humorously
  C argue both sides of the issue
  D urge people to act

See the Test Preparation Workshop on page 563 for tips on answering questions about a writer's purpose and point of view.

Test Practice Bank

Reading Comprehension

Critical Reasoning

Read the passage, and then answer the questions that follow. Mark the letter of your answer on a bubble sheet if your teacher provides one; otherwise, number from 1 to 4 on a separate sheet of paper, and write the letter of the correct answer next to each number.

Although no written record of Shakespeare's boyhood exists, we know some details about his childhood and early life. Given his father's status as a wealthy glove maker, it is almost certain that young Shakespeare attended the Stratford Grammar School, where he undoubtedly achieved high marks in Latin. Stratford is northwest of London.

In November 1582, Shakespeare received a license to marry Anne Hathaway. The couple had a daughter, Susanna, in 1583, and twins, Judith and Hamnet, in 1585. Beyond their names and the years in which they were born, we know little about Shakespeare's family. Some writers have made much of the fact that Shakespeare left his wife and children behind when he went to London not long after the twins were born.

1 Which fact is irrelevant?
  A Shakespeare married Anne Hathaway.
  B Shakespeare had three children.
  C Shakespeare left Stratford for London.
  D Stratford is northwest of London.

2 What potentially invalid assumption does the writer make?
  A No written record of Shakespeare's boyhood exists.
  B He undoubtedly achieved high marks in Latin.
  C He married Anne Hathaway in 1582.
  D Their daughter Susanna was born in 1583.

3 Which of the following facts is most relevant to the main idea?
  A Shakespeare had three children.
  B He almost certainly attended Stratford Grammar School.
  C We know little about Shakespeare's family.
  D Stratford is northwest of London.

4 Which of the following assumptions is invalid?
  A Shakespeare was married and had three children.
  B Shakespeare purposefully abandoned his family and went to London.
  C Shakespeare lived in Stratford before moving to London.
  D No written record of Shakespeare's boyhood exists.

See the Test Preparation Workshop on page 735 for tips on answering questions about critical reasoning.

Test Practice Bank

Reading Comprehension

Paired Passages

Read the passage, and then answer the questions that follow. Mark the letter of your answer on a bubble sheet if your teacher provides one; otherwise, number from 1 to 4 on a separate sheet of paper, and write the letter of the correct answer next to each number.

Passage 1

Strong and clever, Elizabeth I was probably England's ablest monarch since William the Conqueror. She had received a Renaissance education and had read widely in the Greek and Latin classics.

Passage 2

I know I have but the body of a weak and feeble woman; but I have the heart of a king, and of a king of England, too: and think foul scorn that Parma or Spain, or any prince of Europe, should dare to invade the borders of my realms to which rather than dishonor should grow by me, I myself will take arms: I myself will be your general, judge and rewarder of every one of your virtues in the field.

1 Which answer best describes the tones of the passages?
  A Both passages are humorous.
  B The first is humorous; the second is serious.
  C The first is instructive; the second is emphatic.
  D The first is negative; the second is positive.

2 Which answer best expresses the relationship between these two passages?
  A They present different views on Elizabeth I.
  B They show why Elizabeth I was not fit to be queen.
  C They show that Elizabeth I was a strong ruler.
  D They illustrate different aspects of Elizabeth I's education.

3 Which answer best describes the authors' purposes in the two passages?
  A Passage 1 is written to inform; Passage 2 is written to persuade.
  B Both passages are written to urge action.
  C Both passages are written to entertain.
  D Passage 1 is written to persuade; Passage 2 is written to inform.

4 What is the main idea in the passages?
  A Elizabeth I was a strong and well-educated queen.
  B Elizabeth I was an ineffectual and weak queen.
  C Elizabeth I was a meek ruler.
  D Elizabeth I was against war.

See the Test Preparation Workshop on page 873 for tips on answering questions about paired passages.

Test Practice Bank

Reading Comprehension

Combined Skills

Read the passage, and then answer the questions that follow. Mark the letter of your answer on a bubble sheet if your teacher provides one; otherwise, number from 1 to 6 on a separate sheet of paper, and write the letter of the correct answer next to each number.

Passage 1

VCRs were designed to drive the average consumer crazy! Today, almost every home in America has a VCR. How many of you can successfully record one television program while you watch another program? It's almost easier to go out and buy a second television!

Passage 2

Here's a method for recording a television program on a VCR while watching another program. First, check all the connections. Make sure the VCR is plugged in. Turn on the TV, and set it to channel 3 or 4. Now you're ready to program. Insert a videocassette. Select the channel you want to record. Press the SPEED button to choose the recording speed. Then, press the RECORD button. Finally, to stop recording, press the STOP button.

1 Which best describes the tones of the passages?
   A Both are humorous.
   B Both are instructional.
   C Passage 1 is humorous; Passage 2 is instructional.
   D Passage 1 is persuasive; Passage 2 is argumentative.

2 When do you press RECORD?
   A before you turn on the TV
   B before you plug in the VCR
   C after you press the STOP button
   D after you select the speed

3 Which statement is propaganda?
   A Statement 1 in Passage 1
   B Statement 2 in Passage 1
   C Statement 2 in Passage 2
   D Statement 4 in Passage 2

4 Which is a statement of fact?
   A Statement 1 in Passage 1
   B Statement 3 in Passage 1
   C Statement 4 in Passage 1
   D Statement 5 in Passage 2

5 What are the writers' points of view in the two passages?
   A Passage 1, neutral; Passage 2, frustrated
   B Passage 1, frustrated; Passage 2, neutral
   C Passage 1, approving; Passage 2, disapproving
   D Passage 1, sorrowful; Passage 2, merry

6 What is the writer's purpose in Passage 1?
   A to inform
   B to persuade
   C to provide statistics
   D to entertain

Test Practice Bank

Reading Comprehension

Combined Skills

Read the passage, and then answer the questions that follow. Mark the letter of your answer on a bubble sheet if your teacher provides one; otherwise, number from 1 to 6 on a separate sheet of paper, and write the letter of the correct answer next to each number.

(1) Also, different styles of trousers—loose or tight, slit at the ankle or with belt loops—were not just a matter of personal taste but often indicated a tribal tradition. (2) Societies that encouraged the wearing of pants were undoubtedly more productive. (3) Before the Anglo-Saxon period, trousers distinguished Germanic tribes from Romans, who wore loose, gownlike garments called togas. (4) I prefer loose pants with belt loops. (5) By examining the clothing of the Anglo-Saxons, we can learn more about Anglo-Saxon society, especially its various social groups and the types of work done by men and women.

1 Choose the sentence sequence that is most logical.
 A 1, 4, 2, 3, 5
 B 3, 1, 4, 5, 2
 C 4, 1, 5, 2, 3
 D NO CHANGE

2 The tone of this passage is
 A envious
 B admiring
 C informational
 D negative

3 Which fact is irrelevant?
 A Greeks wore togas.
 B Germanic settlers wore pants.
 C Trousers and traditions were related.
 D The writer prefers loose pants.

4 Which potentially invalid assumption does the writer make?
 A Trouser-wearing societies were more productive.
 B There were different styles of pants.
 C Romans wore togas.
 D Clothing tells us about a society.

5 To add information about togas, which of the following statements would be most suitable?
 A Nobody wears togas anymore.
 B Climate affects the type of clothing that people wear.
 C The word *toga* comes from the Latin *tegere*, which means "to cover."
 D Roman women spun and wove cloth.

6 What is the writer's purpose?
 A to entertain
 B to persuade
 C to inform
 D to argue an issue

Test Practice Bank

Reading Comprehension

Combined Skills

Read each passage. Then read each question that follows the passage. Decide which is the best answer to each question. Mark the letter of your answer on a bubble sheet if your teacher provides one; otherwise, number from 1 to 19 on a separate sheet of paper, and write the letter of the correct answer next to each number.

Passage I

Though elephants can be dangerous to people, people have turned out to be much more dangerous to elephants. By clearing land in forestry and for farming, (5) as well as by hunting elephants for their valuable ivory tusks, human beings have brought the elephant close to extinction. Since the late 1970's and early 1980's, the elephant population in Africa has (10) declined severely, dropping from 1.3 million to 600,000 in little more than a decade. Many countries have set aside parklands and preserves to protect elephants and other endangered species.

(15) In 1989, the Convention on International Trade in Endangered Species of Wild Fauna and Flora (CITES) banned any trade in ivory. Illegal hunting continues, though. Some countries attempt to (20) discourage poaching by turning profits from the use of wildlife—from tourism to sport hunting—to the benefit of local communities. They also practice culling—selectively killing individual (25) elephants—to keep elephants from destroying people's crops in their quest for food.

1. You can tell from the passage that *culling* in line 24 means—
   A. selecting
   B. cooking
   C. creating
   D. cornering

2. According to this passage, CITES in line 17 is—
   F. an international organization set up to assist third-world countries
   G. an international organization set up to protect endangered species
   H. a local organization set up to design parklands and preserves
   J. a local organization set up to assist third-world countries

3. How many elephants died between the late 1970's and early 1980's?
   A. approximately 200,000
   B. approximately 600,000
   C. approximately 300,000
   D. approximately 700,000

4. You can tell from the passage that *poaching* in line 20 means—
   F. helping wild animals
   G. stealing wild game
   H. helping hunters
   J. trespassing

5. What point does the writer make about parklands and preserves?
   A. They are unnecessary.
   B. They haven't been created yet.
   C. They helped people hunt animals.
   D. They are being set aside.

Test Practice Bank

Passage II

The first Tudor monarch, Henry VII, inherited an England that had been depleted and exhausted by years of civil war. By the time he died in 1509, he
(5) had rebuilt the nation's treasury and established law and order. In doing so, he had restored the prestige of the monarchy and had set the stage for his successors.
(10) Henry VII was succeeded by his handsome and athletic son, Henry VIII. Like his father, Henry VIII was a practicing Catholic. He even wrote a book against Martin Luther, for which a grateful Pope granted
(15) him the title "Defender of the Faith."

Henry VIII's good relationship with the Pope did not last, however. Because his marriage with Catherine of Aragon had not produced a son, Henry tried to
(20) obtain an annulment from the Pope so that he could marry Anne Boleyn. When the Pope refused, Henry remarried anyway. This defiance of papal authority led to an open break with the Roman Catholic
(25) Church. Henry seized the Catholic Church's English property and dissolved the powerful monasteries. He even had his former friend and leading advisor, Thomas More, executed because More
(30) had refused to renounce his faith.

Henry married six times in all. His first two marriages produced two daughters, Mary and Elizabeth. His third wife, Jane Seymour, bore a son, Edward,
(35) who was but a frail child when Henry died in 1547.

6. Which of these is the main purpose of this passage?
   F. To explain the power of the Roman Catholic Church
   G. To explain the power of King Henry VIII
   H. To describe Henry VIII's wives
   J. To provide historical information about the Tudors

7. You can tell from the passage that *depleted* in line 3 means—
   A. severe
   B. unreal
   C. drained
   D. overrun

8. According to the passage, Henry VIII was—
   F. a kind ruler
   G. a practicing Catholic
   H. a cruel ruler
   J. twenty-one years old

9. According to the passage, who was responsible for the conflict between the English throne and the Roman Catholic Church?
   A. Anne Boleyn
   B. Henry VIII
   C. Henry VII
   D. Jane Seymour

10. You can infer from the passage, that *papal* in line 23 means—
    F. of the English crown
    G. of Catholicism
    H. of the Pope
    J. of power

Test Practice Bank

Passage III

from The First Year of My Life
by Muriel Spark

I was born on the first day of the second month of the last year of the First World War, a Friday. Testimony abounds that during the first year of my
(5) life I never smiled. I was known as the baby whom nothing and no one could make smile. Everyone who knew me then has told me so. They tried very hard, singing and bouncing me up and
(10) down, jumping around, pulling faces. Many times I was told this later by my family and their friends; but, anyway, I knew it at the time.

You will shortly be hearing of that
(15) new school of psychology, or maybe you have heard of it already, which after long and far-adventuring research and experiment has established that all of the young of the human species are born
(20) omniscient. Babies, in their waking hours, know everything that is going on everywhere in the world; they can tune in to any conversation they choose, switch on to any scene. We have all experienced
(25) this power. It is only after the first year that it is brainwashed out of us; for it is demanded of us by our immediate environment that we grow to be of use to it in a practical way. Gradually, our
(30) know-all brain-cells are blacked out, although traces remain in some individuals in the form of E.S.P., and in the adults of some primitive tribes.

11. Which of these best summarizes the main idea of this passage?
    A. Research is being done that will prove babies are born with the ability to know everything.
    B. A new school of psychology is being established.
    C. Brainwashing children is society's way of making children conform.
    D. Many individuals have E.S.P.

12. You can infer from this passage that *omniscient* in line 20 most likely means—
    F. unsmiling
    G. knowing all things
    H. very powerful
    J. primitive

13. In what month was the writer born?
    A. January
    B. February
    C. March
    D. April

14. According to the passage, when do most babies lose their ability to "know everything that is going on everywhere in the world"?
    F. after the second year of life
    G. when they start walking
    H. when they start talking
    J. after the first year of life

15. As it is used in this passage, the word *practical* in line 29 means—
    A. unusual
    B. creative
    C. boring
    D. useful

16. Which of the following is NOT mentioned in the passage?
    F. the First World War
    G. the environments of some primitive tribes
    H. babies' waking hours
    J. a new school of psychology

Test Practice Bank

Passage IV

By Shakespeare's time, the story of the eleventh-century Scottish king Macbeth was a mixture of fact and legend. Shakespeare and his contemporaries, however, probably (5) regarded the account of Macbeth in Raphael Holinshed's *Chronicles of England, Scotland, and Ireland* as completely factual. The playwright drew on the *Chronicles* as a source for the play. Yet he freely adapted (10) the material for his own purposes, as the chart below indicates. Although Shakespeare may have consulted other Scottish histories, it is probable that he primarily relied on Holinshed's *Chronicles* for his "facts."

Holinshed's *Chronicles*	Shakespeare's *Macbeth*
• Macbeth meets the witches. • Duncan is slain in an ambush set up by Macbeth and his friends, who are angry at the naming of Malcolm as Prince of Cumberland. Macbeth's claim to the throne has some basis. • Banquo is Macbeth's accomplice in the slaying, and Lady Macbeth does not have a prominent role in the narrative.	• Shakespeare uses this account. • Duncan is slain while he is a guest at Macbeth's castle. Macbeth and his wife are the only conspirators, and Macbeth apparently does not have a legitimate claim to the throne. • Banquo is not an accomplice. Using a different story from the *Chronicles*, in which a wife urges her husband to kill a friend and guest, Shakespeare creates Lady Macbeth.

17. You can tell from the passage that *adapted* in line 9 means—
   A. created
   B. edited
   C. changed
   D. named

18. According to this passage, Shakespeare probably used which of the following sources for the basis of *Macbeth*?
   F. Holinshed's *Chronicles* and other Scottish histories
   G. only Holinshed's *Chronicles*
   H. Scottish myths and news accounts
   J. only Scottish myths

19. Which statement best summarizes the main idea of the passage?
   A. Shakespeare believed that the story of Macbeth in Holinshed's *Chronicles* was true.
   B. Shakespeare probably used several sources to write his play *Macbeth*.
   C. King James figured prominently in *Macbeth* because Shakespeare knew the king thought Banquo was one of his ancestors.
   D. Shakespeare drew on information in only Holinshed's *Chronicles* to write *Macbeth*.

20. In the *Chronicles*, Banquo is—
   F. Macbeth's accomplice
   G. Lady Macbeth's lover
   H. Duncan's friend
   J. a witch

21. According to the chart, which of the following is true?
   A. In Shakespeare's *Macbeth*, Duncan is slain in an ambush.
   B. In *Macbeth*, Lady Macbeth does not have a major role.
   C. Holinshed doesn't describe Banquo as an accomplice.
   D. Shakespeare uses Holinshed's mention of the witches.

Test Practice Bank

Vocabulary Development

Antonyms, Analogies, Sentence Completion

Read the instructions and answer the questions in each segment below. Mark the letter of your answer on a bubble sheet if your teacher provides one; otherwise, number from 1 to 17 on a separate sheet of paper, and write the letter of the correct answer next to each number.

For items 1–6, choose the word that *best* answers the question.

1 Which of the following is an antonym for the word *frugal*?
   (A) thrifty
   (B) parsimonious
   (C) cheap
   (D) extravagant
   (E) economical

2 An antonym for the word *wary* is
   (A) reckless
   (B) alert
   (C) conscientious
   (D) cautious
   (E) vigilant

3 Identify the antonym for the word *novice*.
   (A) apprentice
   (B) debutante
   (C) expert
   (D) amateur
   (E) rookie

4 The word *censure* is the opposite of
   (A) reprove
   (B) condemn
   (C) denounce
   (D) sanction
   (E) chastise

5 Which of the following is an antonym for the word *intrepid*?
   (A) fearless
   (B) cowardly
   (C) audacious
   (D) courageous
   (E) brazen

6 Identify the antonym for the word *jubilation*.
   (A) satisfaction
   (B) celebration
   (C) sorrow
   (D) exultation
   (E) euphoria

For items 7–12, choose the pair of words whose relationship is most similar to the relationship expressed by the pair of words in all capitals.

7 ARID : DESERT ::
   (A) high : mountain
   (B) deep : ocean
   (C) shallow : river
   (D) ancient : glacier
   (E) wet : rain forest

8 METER : LENGTH ::
   (A) clock : time
   (B) odometer : car
   (C) liter : volume
   (D) feather : weight
   (E) ruler : length

9 PARCHED : THIRST ::
   (A) starved : hunger
   (B) hungry : food
   (C) cold : snow
   (D) tired : exercise
   (E) thirsty : water

10 OPULENT : WEALTHY ::
   (A) mansion : hovel
   (B) diligent : careless
   (C) sickly : healthy
   (D) frugal : wasteful
   (E) indigent : poor

11 ARTIST : CREATIVITY ::
   (A) doctor : hospital
   (B) architect : skyscraper
   (C) gardener : soil
   (D) martyr : sacrifice
   (E) musician : silence

12 MARATHON : DISTANCE ::
   (A) skiing : mountain
   (B) sprint : speed
   (C) sailing : wind
   (D) football : team
   (E) skating : ice rink

For items 14–17, choose the word or pair of words that *best* completes the sentence.

13 The two sides were able to discuss the border dispute and agree to a _____ ; the agreement was _____ until the people voted on it.
   (A) renovation; inconsequential
   (B) dispute; incompatible
   (C) congregation; prudent
   (D) situation; pretentious
   (E) compromise; conditional

14 Unable to _____ the rumors, the reporter sought more information.
   (A) substantiate
   (B) emulate
   (C) enhance
   (D) convert
   (E) dictate

15 The donor who gave one million dollars to the museum wanted to remain _____ because of her _____ nature.
   (A) benevolent; condescending
   (B) nonchalant; ostentatious
   (C) prudent; unrestrained
   (D) anonymous; reclusive
   (E) venerable; perfidious

16 To stir the passions of their supporters, _____ often _____ information that would calm the people's fears.
   (A) demagogues; suppress
   (B) orators; provide
   (C) lobbyists; reveal
   (D) scientists; ignore
   (E) hermits; divulge

17 Many cultures _____ older people; their longer life experience bestows _____.
   (A) disdain; wisdom
   (B) venerate; sagacity
   (C) impute; longevity
   (D) scrutinize; nonchalance
   (E) discredit; exasperation

Test Practice Bank

Writing

Strategy, Organization, and Style

Read the passage, and then answer the questions that follow. Mark the letter of your answer on a bubble sheet if your teacher provides one; otherwise, number from 1 to 5 on a separate sheet of paper, and write the letter of the correct answer next to each number.

(1) Whites lived as privileged rulers in Rhodesia and South Africa, as they did elsewhere on the continent. (2) This word means "apartness" in Afrikaans, the language of Dutch South Africans. (3) Black Africans, however, lived for the most part in poverty. (4) South Africa, and Rhodesia to its north, were dominated by policies of racial separation and prejudice called *apartheid*. (5) Racial prejudice and apartheid were a legacy of European colonial domination of Africa. (6) Much of Central Africa was controlled by the Belgians, North and Northwestern Africa by the French, and Eastern and Southern Africa by the British. (7) In the late nineteenth century, the major European powers carved up the African continent for their own economic and political gain.

1 The tone of this passage is
  A emotional
  B informative
  C humorous
  D persuasive

2 Choose the most logical sentence sequence.
  A 4, 2, 5, 7, 6, 1, 3
  B 5, 2, 1, 4, 7, 6, 3
  C 3, 7, 6, 2, 1, 5, 4
  D 7, 1, 2, 6, 4, 3, 5

3 What is the main idea of the passage?
  A Native people and Europeans lived together in harmony in Africa.
  B Native Africans were unaffected by European colonization.
  C Apartheid led to understanding between Africans and Europeans.
  D Africa was greatly affected by European colonization.

4 To add information about the history of apartheid in South Africa, which of the following statements would be most suitable?
  A The Nile is the longest river in Africa.
  B One of South Africa's natural resources is gold.
  C Apartheid ended in South Africa in 1992.
  D Rhodesia was divided into two countries—Zambia and Zimbabwe.

5 The phrase "carved up the African continent" means—
  A claimed various African territories as their own
  B mined and farmed the African land excessively
  C dug canals across Africa
  D mapped and labeled new areas of Africa

See the Test Preparation Workshop on page 1173 for tips on answering questions about strategy, organization, and style.

Test Practice Bank

Writing

Combined Skills

The following passage is written in the form of a press release. Read the text and answer the questions. Mark the letter of your answer on a bubble sheet if your teacher provides one; otherwise, number from 1 to 6 on a separate sheet of paper, and write the letter of the correct answer next to each number.

[1]Tracy Chapman grew up in a working-class neighborhood in Cleveland Ohio. [2]At an early age, she ____ herself to play the guitar and began to write music. [3]chapman's love of music and knowledge motivated her to seek the best education possible. [4]Chapman attained a scholarship to a prestigious prep school. _____
[5]Chapman has used their music to combat ignorance and raise social awareness of issues from spirituality to racism. [6]She says, _____

1. Which of the following changes is needed in Part 1?
   A. Capitalize "neighborhood."
   B. Change "grew" to "grows."
   C. Insert a comma after "Cleveland."
   D. Insert a period after "Chapman."

2. Which of the following words best fits in the blank in Part 2?
   A. teach
   B. taught
   C. was taught
   D. will teach

3. Which of the following changes is needed in Part 3?
   A. Change "chapman's" to "chapmans."
   B. Change "chapman's" to "Chapman's."
   C. Place a comma after "knowledge."
   D. Change "motivated" to "motivating"

4. Which of the following, if used in place of the blank in Part 4, best fits the development of the passage?
   A. Prep school is a very exciting and challenging experience.
   B. An exceptionally bright pupil, she was fully deserving of the scholarship.
   C. She observed that her wealthy classmates were often ignorant of the harshness of poverty.
   D. Many people have a negative image of prep schools as places where class prejudice runs rampant.

5. Which of the following should be substituted for the underlined word in Part 5?
   A. his
   B. she
   C. hers
   D. her

6. Which quotation best fits in the blank in Part 6?
   A. "I want to stay close to home and use musicians from San Francisco."
   B. "We're at a place right now where we could find new solutions to old problems that still plague society."
   C. "Some songs deal with the degradation of the natural environment."
   D. "Many of my songs share the themes of change and growth."

Test Practice Bank

Writing

Combined Skills

The following passage is written in the form of a letter to a newspaper. Read the text and answer the questions. Mark the letter of your answer on a bubble sheet if your teacher provides one; otherwise, number from 1 to 6 on a separate sheet of paper, and write the letter of the correct answer next to each number.

[1]Knuckling under to a few misguided state legislators, the school board _____ that it plans to condemn private property and homes worth $10 million for expansion of school facilities. [2]One homeowner effected by this measure declared, "We never had a chance to state our case." [3]The deal would be part of a $25 million school bond issue going before voters this November. [4]Opponents of the bond issue urges voters to express their displeasure at the polls. [5]_____.

1. Which of the following, if used in the blank in Part 1, best completes the meaning of the sentence?
   A. revealed
   B. reveal
   C. had been revealed
   D. was revealing

2. Which of the following changes is needed?
   A. Part 1: Capitalize "legislator."
   B. Part 1: Change "expansion" to "expantion."
   C. Part 2: Change "effected" to "affected."
   D. Part 2: Delete the comma after "declared."

3. Which of the following words, underlined in Part 3, needs to be replaced by a more precise word?
   A. million
   B. issue
   C. part
   D. deal

4. Which of the following would help the focus of the main idea of the passage?
   A. Delete Part 1.
   B. Reverse the order of Parts 1 and 2.
   C. Delete Part 3.
   D. Add a sentence after Part 1 telling how many homes would be condemned.

5. Which of the following should be substituted for the underlined word in Part 4?
   A. urging
   B. urged
   C. urgent
   D. urge

6. Which of the following, if used in place of the blank labeled Part 5, best supports the main idea of the paragraph?
   A. Our schools deserve all that we can give them.
   B. The fate of our property is at stake.
   C. Voting is one or our most important rights.
   D. Nobody likes legislators.

Test Practice Bank

Writing

Combined Skills

The following passage is written in the form of an English textbook. Read the text and answer the questions. Mark the letter of your answer on a bubble sheet if your teacher provides one; otherwise, number from 1 to 6 on a separate sheet of paper, and write the letter of the correct answer next to each number.

[1]Conflict. A struggle between opposing forces. [2]sometimes this struggle is internal, or within a character. [3]The outside force being another character, nature, or some element of society, such as a custom. [4]At other times the struggle is external, or between the character and some outside force. [5]For instance, I fight with my brother a lot. [6]Often, the conflict in a work combines several of ____ possibilities.

1. Which of the following is the best way to rewrite Part 1?
   A. Conflict is a struggle between opposing forces.
   B. Conflict, a struggle between opposing forces.
   C. Conflict, which is a struggle between opposing forces.
   D. A struggle between opposing forces. Conflict.

2. Which of the following changes is needed in Part 2?
   A. Delete the comma after "internal."
   B. Insert a comma after "or."
   C. Capitalize "sometimes."
   D. Change "struggle" to "strugle."

3. Which of the following makes the sequence of ideas clearer in the passage?
   A. Delete Part 1
   B. Reverse the order of Parts 1 and 2.
   C. Delete Part 4.
   D. Reverse the order of Parts 3 and 4.

4. Which of the following changes is need in Part 3?
   A. Capitalize "nature."
   B. Place a comma after "force."
   C. Delete "or."
   D. Change "being" to "may be."

5. Which of the following, if used in place of the blank in Part 6, best completes the meaning of the sentence?
   A. them
   B. their
   C. these
   D. its

6. Which of the following is the LEAST consistent with the author's purpose and audience?
   A. Part 5
   B. Part 4
   C. Part 3
   D. Part 1

Test Practice Bank

Writing

Combined Skills

The following passage is written in the form of a magazine article. Read the text and answer the questions. Mark the letter of your answer on a bubble sheet if your teacher provides one; otherwise, number from 1 to 6 on a separate sheet of paper, and write the letter of the correct answer next to each number.

[1]What to do after high school is one of the ___ decisions of your life, although I took my time about it and I turned out fine. [2]You probably have definite ideas about what you are interested in and weather you would like to pursue a college education or jump directly into the job market. [3]The challenge you ___ is getting admitted to the right college or land the right job. [4]You can begin the process. Identify your options.

1. Which of the following, if used in place of the blank in Part 1, best completes the meaning of the sentence?
   A. importantly
   B. importanter
   C. importantest
   D. most important

2. Which of the following is needed in Part 2?
   A. Change "weather" to "whether."
   B. Change "definite" to "definate."
   C. Capitalize "college."
   D. Change "job market" to "job-market."

3. Which of the following would help the focus of the main idea?
   A. Delete the phrase "or jump directly into the job market" in Part 2.

B. Change the comma after "life" in Part 1 to a semicolon.
C. Delete the phrase "although I took my time about it and I turned out fine" in Part 1.
D. Insert a comma before "or" in Part 2.

4. Which of the following, if used in place of the blank in Part 3, best completes the meaning of the sentence?
   A. have faced
   B. will never face
   C. will face
   D. had been faced

5. Which of the following is needed in Part 3?
   A. Place a comma after "admitted."
   B. Delete "or land the right job."
   C. Change "admitted" to "admited."
   D. Change "land" to "landing."

6. Which of the following should be substituted for Part 4?
   A. You can begin the process. How? Identify your options.
   B. You can begin the process by identifying your options.
   C. You can, begin the process. Identify your options.
   D. Identify your options.

Test Practice Bank

Writing Sample

DIRECTIONS: Write an essay that is between 300 and 600 words on one of the following writing topics. You should expect to spend approximately **60 minutes** on your writing sample. During this time, you should organize your ideas, write a rough draft, and proofread and revise your draft essay.

Make sure to read your topic carefully, and consider what your position will be before you start writing. After you are confident in what you have written, copy your essay onto clean notebook pages or the lined pages of the Writing Sample answer sheet if your teacher provides one.

Your essay will be scored according to the following criteria:

1. **Appropriateness**—how completely you respond to the prompt; how well you explore the topic; and how suitably you address your audience.
2. **Unity and focus**—how clearly you state your main idea; how well you maintain and support your main idea.
3. **Development**—the relevance and specificity of your supporting ideas and details.
4. **Organization**—the logical arrangement of your ideas.
5. **Sentence structure**—how successfully you use sentences and how varied your sentence forms are.
6. **Usage**—the effectiveness and proper implementation of your word usage.
7. **Mechanical conventions**—your proper use of spelling, punctuation, and capitalization.

Your essay must be written on one of the topics given and must employ numerous paragraphs. Make sure it is legible—if it cannot be read, it cannot be graded.

Writing Sample Topics

Currently, sport utility vehicles are classified as trucks—such as those used for commercial businesses—and they are allowed to emit more carbon monoxide and other fumes than are automobiles. However, most sport utility vehicles are used by commuters, and more and more people are driving these popular trucks in city traffic.

Your purpose is to write an essay, to be read by a classroom instructor, in which you take a position on whether or not sport utility vehicles should have their emissions standards increased.

Some people believe that gun ownership is a right guaranteed under the Constitution. Others think that the only way to curb violence is by severely limiting, or even banning, guns in our society.

Your purpose is to write an essay, to be read by a peer who has recently immigrated to this country, explaining the various sides of the issue.

Although the president of the United States may serve no more than two terms, U.S. representatives and senators are not restricted by term limits. Some people argue that term limits are unnecessary because the representative or senator can always be voted out of office. Others insist that imposing term limits will guarantee that Congress remains a vital and responsive governing body.

Your purpose is to write a letter, to be published in a local newspaper, in which you take a position on congressional term limits.

Should volunteerism become a mandatory part of the school curriculum? If students are required to volunteer their time to causes, doesn't that negate the voluntary aspect? On the other hand, won't volunteering their efforts to worthy causes broaden the students' perception of the world?

Your purpose is to write an essay, to be read by a classroom instructor, in which you take a position on student volunteerism.

GLOSSARY

abasement (ə bās´ mənt) n.: Condition of being put down or humbled

abated (ə bāt´ id) v.: Lessened

abrogated (ab´rō gāt´ id) v.: Repealed; annulled

absolution (ab sə loo´ shən) n.: Act of freeing someone of a sin or of a criminal charge

acceded (ak sēd´ id) v.: Yielded to; agreed upon

adjure (ə joor´) v.: Appeal earnestly

admonish (ad män´ ish) v.: Advise; caution

adroitly (ə droit´ lē) adv: Physically or mentally skillful

adulterations (ə dul´ tər ā´ shənz) n.: Impurities; added ingredients that are improper or inferior

adversary (ad´ vər ser´ ē) n.: Opponent

adversity (ad vʉr´ sə tē) n.: Misfortune

affinities (ə fin´ i tēz) n.: Family relationships; connections

affluence (af´ loo əns) n.: Abundant wealth

aldermen (ôl´ dər mən) n.: Chief officers in a shire, or district

alters (ôl´ tərs) v.: Changes

amiable (ā´ mē ə bəl) adj.: Friendly

amorous (am´ ə rəs) adj.: Full of love

anachronism (ə nak´ rə niz´ əm) n.: Something out of its proper time in history

anarchy (an´ ər kē) n.: Absence of government; confusion, disorder, and violence

anatomize (ə nat´ ə mīz´) v.: To dissect in order to examine structure

antic (an´ tik) adj.: Odd and funny

aperture (ap´ ər chər´) n.: Opening

appendage (ə pen´ dij) n.: Something added on

apprehension (ap´ rē hen´ shən) n.: Anxious feeling of foreboding; dread

approbation (ap´ rə bā´ shən) n.: Official approval, sanction, or commendation

arbiter (är´ bət ər) n.: Judge; umpire

arboreal (är bôr´ ē əl) adj.: Of, near, or among trees

artifice (ärt´ ə fis) n.: Skill or ingenuity

aspire (ə spir´) v.: Rise high, yearn, or seek after

assault (ə sôlt´) v.: Violently attack

assay (a sā´) v.: Try or attempt

assignations (as´ ig nā´ shənz) n.: Appointments to meet

asunder (ə sun´ dər) adv.: Into parts or pieces

atrophy (a´ trə fē) v.: Waste away

augment (ôg ment´) v.: To make greater; enlarge

august (ô gust´) adj.: Worthy of great respect

authenticity (ô´ thən tis´ ə tē) n.: Quality or state of being authentic; genuineness

avarice (av´ ər is) n.: Greed

averred (ə vʉrd´) v.: Stated to be true

avouches (ə vouch´ ez) v.: Asserts positively; affirms

balm (bäm) n.: Anything healing or soothing

barricaded (ber´ i ka´ did) v.: Blocked

blight (blīt) n.: Condition of withering

blithe (blīth) adj.: Cheerful

brazening (brā´ zən iŋ) v.: Daring boldly or shamelessly

breach (brēch) n.: Breaking open; the opening created by a break

cadence (kād´ əns) n.: Measured movement

cant (kant) n.: Insincere or meaningless talk

capital (kap´ ət əl) n.: Wealth in money or property

caprices (kə prē´ sis) n.: Whims

careered (kə rird´) v.: Rushed wildly

certify (sʉrt´ ə fī´) v.: Declare a thing true or accurate; verify; attest

chronicle (krän´ i kəl) n.: Historical record of annals or facts

churls (chʉrlz) n.: Farm laborers; peasants

circumscribed (sʉr´ kəm skrībd´) adj.: Limited; having a definite boundary

clamorous (klam´ ər əs) adj.: Noisy

combustible (kəm bus´ tə bəl) adj.: Capable of igniting and burning; flammable

commission (kə mish´ ən) n.: Authorization; act of giving authority to an individual

compassionate (kəm pash´ ən it) adj.: Sympathizing; pitying

complaisant (kəm plā´ zənt) adj.: Agreeable; willing to please

comprised (kəm prīzd´) v.: Consisted of; to include or contain

confiscation (kän´ fis kā´ shən) n.: Act of seizing private property for the public treasury or for personal gain, usually as a penalty

conflagration (kän´ flə grā´ shən) n.: Great fire

confounded (kən found´ id) adj.: Confused; bewildered

conjecture (kən jek´ chər) v.: Guess

conquest (kän´ kwest) n.: The winning of another's affection or favor

contention (kən ten´ shən) n.: Dispute; argument

contentious (kən ten´ shus) adj.: Quarrelsome

contrite (kən trīt´) adj.: Willing to repent or atone

conviction (kən vik´ shən) n.: Belief in something meaningful, such as a creed

copious (kō´ pē əs) adj.: Abundant; plentiful

countenance (koun´ tə nəns) n.: Face

covetousness (kuv´ ət əs ness) n.: Greediness

coyness (koi´ nis) n.: Reluctance to make a commitment

credulity (krə doo´ lə tē) n.: Tendency to believe too readily

credulous (krej´ oo ləs) adj.: Tending to believe too readily

dauntless (dônt´ lis) adj.: Fearless; cannot be intimidated

decimation (des´ ə mā´ shun) n.: Destruction or killing of one in ten or of any large group

defiantly (di fī´ ənt lē) adv.: Disobediently; with resistance

deign (dān) v.: Condescend; lower oneself

depredation (dep´ rə dā´ shən) n.: Act or instance of robbing, plundering or laying waste

derided (di rīd´ id) v.: Made fun of; ridiculed

derision (di rizh´ ən) n.: Contempt or ridicule

desolate (des´ ə lit) adj.: Deserted; forlorn

despotic (de spät´ ik) adj.: Tyrannical

destitute (des´ tə toot) adj.: Lacking

devise (de vīz´) v.: Work out or create; plan

diabolical (dī´ ə bäl´ i kəl) adj.: Evil

diffusive (di fyoo´ siv) adj.: Spread out

disabused (dis´ ə byoozd´) v.: Freed from false ideas

disaffection (dis´ ə fek´ shun) n.: Discontent; disillusionment

discerned (di zʉrnd´) v.: Recognized as separate or different

disconcerted (dis´ kən sʉrt´ əd) adj.: Embarrassed and confused

discoursing (dis kôrs´ iŋ) v.: Talking about; discussing

discreet (dis krēt´) adj.: Wise; prudent

discretion (di skresh´ ən) n.: Good judgment; prudence

dislocation (dis´ lō kā´ shən) n.: Condition of being out of place; the event of becoming out of place

dispensation (dis´ pən sā´ shən) n.: Religious system or belief

distemper (dis tem´ pər) n.: Infectious disease such as the plague

distill (dis til´) v.: To obtain the essential part

divert (de vʉrt´) v.: Amuse; entertain; distract

dominion (də min´ yən) n.: Rule or power to rule; a governed territory

dowry (dou´ rē) n.: Property that a woman brings to her husband at marriage

eclipse (ē klips´) n.: Dimming or extinction of fame or glory

efficacious (ef´ i kā´ shəs) adj.: Producing the desired result; effective

efficacy (ef´ i kə sē) n.: Power to produce effects

effigy (ef´ i jē) n.: Image of a person

elongated (i lôŋ´ gāt id) adj.: Lengthened; stretched

eludes (ē loodz´) v.: Avoids or escapes

emancipate (ē man´ sə pāt) v.: To free from slavery or oppression

embarked (em bärkt´) v.: Engaged in conversation

embellishments (em bel´ ish məntz) n.: Decorative touches; ornamentation

encomiums (en kō´ mē əmz) n.: Formal expressions of great praise

endurance (en door´ əns) n.: Ability to withstand pain or fatigue

enigma (e nig´ mə) n.: Riddle; a perplexing statement, person, or situation

enquiry (en kwīr´ ē) n.: Question

entreated (in trēt´ id) v.: Begged; pleaded

equivocate: (ē kwiv´ə kāt) v.: To use terms that have two or more meanings to mislead purposely or deceive

evanescence (ev´ ə nes´ əns) *n.*: Gradual disappearance, especially from sight

exasperated (eg zas´ pər āt´ id) *adj.*: Extremely annoyed; out of patience

excrescence (eks kres´ əns) *n.*: Abnormal or disfiguring outgrowth

exemplary (eg zem´ plə rē) *adj.*: Serving as a model or example; of that which should be imitated

exonerate (eg zän´ ər āt´) *v.*: Free from a charge of guilt; declare or prove blameless

expedient (ik spē´ dē ənt) *n.*: Device used in an emergency

expiated (ēk´ spē āt´ əd) *v.*: Forgiven; absolved

expostulate (ik späs´ chə lāt´) *v.*: Reason earnestly with

extenuating (ek sten´ yōō āt´ iŋ) *adj.*: Lessening the seriousness of; excusing

fastidious (fas tid´ ē əs) *adj.*: Difficult to please

fathom (fath´ əm) *v.*: To understand thoroughly

fathomless (fath´ əm lis) *adj.*: Too deep to be measured or understood

feigned (fānd) *v.*: Made a false show of; pretended

fervent (fur´ vənt) *adj.*: Having or showing great warmth of feeling

fidelity (fə del´ ə tē) *n.*: Faithfulness

filial (fil´ ē əl) *adj.*: Suitable to, of, or from a son or daughter

forage (fôr´ ij) *n.*: Food for farm animals, especially that found by grazing outdoors

forfeited (fôr´ fit id) *v.*: Gave up, as a penalty

formidable (fôr´ mə də bəl) *adj.*: Causing fear or dread

fortitude (fôrt´ ə tōōd) *n.*: Strength of mind that allows one to endure courageously

fraudulent (frô´ jə lənt) *adj.*: Characterized by deceit or trickery

furrow (fur´ ō) *n.*: Narrow groove made in the ground by a plow

galled (gôld) *adj.*: Injured or made sore by rubbing or chafing

garnished (gär´ nisht) *adj.*: Decorated; trimmed

garrulous (gar´ ə ləs) *adj.*: Talking continuously

gaunt (gônt) *adj.*: Very thin and angular

gleaned (glēnd) *v.*: Picked or gathered, as one does with fruit or crops

grandeur (gran´ jər) *n.*: Splendor; magnificence

gravity (grav´ i tē) *n.*: Seriousness

grieved (grēvd) *v.*: Caused to feel deep grief; mourned; felt deep grief for

grievous (grēv´ əs) *adj.*: Causing sorrow; hard to bear

guile (gīl) *n.*: Artful trickery; cunning

habituate (hə bich´ ōō āt´) *v.*: Make used to

harbingers (här´ bin jərs) *n.*: Forerunners

harried (har´ ēd) *v.*: Harassed

ignoble (ig nō´ bəl) *adj.*: Not noble; common

ignominy (ig´ nə min´ ē) *n.*: Humiliation; dishonor; disgrace

illumine (i lōō´ mən) *v.*: Light up

impediments (im ped´ə mənts) *n.*: Hindrances; obstructions

imperial (im pir´ ē əl) *adj.*: Of an empire; having supreme authority

imperialism (im pir´ ē əl iz´ əm) *n.*: Policy and practice of forming and maintaining an empire in seeking to control raw materials and world markets through the conquest of other countries, the establishment of colonies, and so on

imperturbable (im´ pər tur´ bə bəl) *adj.*: Calm; not easily ruffled

importuning (im´ pôr tōōn´ iŋ) *v.*: Pleading

impressionistic (im presh´ ə nis´ tik) *adj.*: Conveying a quick, overall picture

impudence (im´ pyōō dəns) *n.*: Lack of shame; rudeness

impulse (im´ puls) *n.*: Driving force forward

inauspicious (in´ ô spish´əs) *adj.*: Not promising a good outcome; unfavorable

incitement (in sīt´ mənt) *n.*: Cause to perform; encouragement

inconstancy (in kän´ stən sē) *n.*: Fickleness; changeableness

inconstantly (in kän´ stənt lē) *adv.*: Changeably; in a fickle way

incredulously (in krej´ ōō ləs lē) *adv.*: In a doubting manner

inculcated (in kul´ kāt id) *v.*: Impressed upon the mind by frequent repetition

indignant (in dig´nənt) *v.*: Be displeased about

indissoluble (in´ di säl´ yōō bəl) *adj.*: Not able to be dissolved or undone

indolence (in´ də lens) *n.*: Idleness; laziness

inducted (in dukt´ id) *v.*: Brought formally into a society or organization; provided with knowledge or experience of something

inevitable (in ev´ i tə bəl) *adj.*: Unavoidable; certain to happen

infirmity (in fur´ mə tē) *n.*: Physical or mental defect; illness

ingenuous (in jen´ yōō əs) *adj.*: Naive; simple

inklings (iŋk´ linz) *n.*: Indirect suggestions

innumerable (i nōō´ mər ə bəl) *adj.*: Too many to count

insensible (in sen´ sə bəl) *adj.*: Unable to feel or sense anything; numb

instantaneous (in´ stən tā´ nē əs) *adj.*: Done or happening in an instant

intemperance (in tem´ pər əns) *n.*: Lack of restraint

intermit (in´ tər mit´) *v.*: Stop for a time

internment (in turn´ mənt) *n.*: Confinement during war

interred (in turd´) *v.*: Buried

intimidated (in tim´ ə dāt´ əd) *v.*: Made afraid; frightened

intrigues (in trēgz´) *v.*: Plots or schemes secretly or underhandedly

intrinsically (in trin´ sik lē) *adv.*: At its core; inherently; innately

invincible (in vin´ sə bəl) *adj.*: Unconquerable

irrevocable (ir rev´ ə kə bəl): That which cannot be undone or canceled

judicious (jōō dish´ əs) *adj.*: Showing good judgment

keenly (kēn´ lē) *adv.*: Sharply; intensely

ken (ken) *n.*: Range of sight or knowledge

laity (lā´ ət ē) *n.*: Those not initiated into the priesthood or other profession

lamentable (lam´ mən tə bəl) *adj.*: Distressing

languish (laŋ´ gwish) *v.*: To become weak; droop

languished (laŋ´ gwisht) *adj.*: Weak or sickly looking

largesse (lär jes´) *n.*: Nobility of spirit

larking (lark´ iŋ) *n.*: Free-spirited, whimsical fun

laudable (lôd´ ə bəl) *adj.*: Worthy of praise

liege (lēj) *n.*: Lord or king

litanies (lit´ ən ēz) *n.*: Forms of prayer in which a congregation repeats a fixed response

loathsome (lōth´ səm) *adj.*: Disgusting

ludicrous (lōō´ di krəs): Absurd; ridiculous

malevolence (mə lev´ ə ləns) *n.*: Ill will; spitefulness

malevolent (mə lev´ ə lent) *adj.*: Wishing harm to others

malicious (mə lish´ əs) *adj.*: Deliberately harmful; destructive

malignity (mə lig´ nə tē) *n.*: Strong desire to harm others

massive (mas´ iv) *adj.*: Big and solid

maxim (maks´ im) *n.*: Briefly expressed general truth or rule of conduct

melancholy (mel´ ən käl´ ē) *adj.*: Sad and depressed

minions (min´ yənz) *n.*: Attendants or agents

mockeries (mäk´ ər ēz) *n.*: Ridicule; futile or disappointing efforts

monotonous (mə nät´ ən əs) *adj.*: Having little or no variation or variety

mortal (môr´ təl) *adj.*: That which must eventually die

multitudinous (mul´ tə tōōd´ ən əs) *adj.*: Existing in great numbers

munificence (myōō nif´ə səns) *n.*: State of being very generous in giving; lavish

nocturnal (näk tur´ nəl) *adj.*: Occurring at night

nondescript (nän´ di skript´) *adj.*: Lacking identifying characteristics; bland

nuisance (nōō´ səns) *n.*: Act, thing, or condition causing trouble

obdurate (äb´ door it) *adj.*: Stubborn; unyielding

obliquely (ə blēk´ lē) *adv.*: At a slant; indirect

obliterate (ə blit´ ə rāt) *v.*: Destroy utterly

obscure (əb skyoor´) *adj.*: Not easily understood; vague or undefined

obstinate (äb´ stə nət) *adj.*: Stubborn; dogged; mulish

odious (ō´ dē əs) *adj.*: Hateful; disgusting

officious (ə fish´ əs) *adj.*: Overly eager to please

omniscient (äm nish´ ənt) *adj.*: Having infinite knowledge; knowing all things

ordeal (ôr dēl´) *n.*: Any difficult or painful experience

pallor (pal´ ər) *n.*: Lack of color; paleness

palpable (pal´ pə bəl) *adj.*: Capable of being touched or felt

paltry (pôl´ trē) *adj.*: Practically worthless; insignificant

patronize (pā´ trə nīz´) *v.*: To be a customer of a particular merchant or store

penury (pen´ yōō rē) *n.*: Poverty

peril (per´ əl) *n.*: Exposure to harm

pernicious (pər nish´ əs) *adj.*: Causing serious injury; deadly

persistent (pər sis´ tənt) *adj.*: Continuing

perturbation (pur´ tər bā´ shən) *n.*: Disturbance

phantasm (fan´ taz əm) *n.*: Supernatural form or shape; ghost; figment of the mind

piety (pī´ ə tē) *n.*: Devotion or loyalty

platitude (plat´ ə tōōd) *n.*: Statement lacking originality

plebeian (pli bē´ ən) *adj.*: Common; ordinary

portals (pôr´ təlz) *n.*: Doors; gateways

predominance (pri däm´ ə nəns) *n.*: Superiority

prefiguring (prē fig´ yer iŋ) *v.*: Suggesting beforehand

prenatal (prē nāt´ əl) *adj.*: Before birth

preponderates (prē pän´ də rāts) *v.*: Becomes larger or heavier than something else

presumption (prē zump´ shən) *n.*: Audacity; tending to assume certain things

prevarication (pri var´ i kā´ shən) *n.*: Evasion of truth

prime (prīm) *n.*: Best stage of time

pristine (pris tēn´) *adj.*: Original; unspoiled

procured (prō kyoord´) *v.*: Obtained; found

prodigal (präd´ i gəl) *adj.*: Addicted to wasteful expenditure

prodigious (prō´dij´ əs) *adj.*: Enormous

profanation (präf´ ə nā´ shən) *n.*: Action showing disrespect for something sacred

profuse (prō fyōōs´) *adj.*: Abundant; pouring out

promontories (prä´ mən tôr´ ēz) *n.*: Parts of high land sticking out into the sea or other body of water

propagators (präp´ ə gā´ tərz) *n.*: Those who cause something to happen or to spread

propitiate (prə pish´ ē āt) *v.*: Win the good will of; appease

prostrate (präs´ trāt) *adj.*: Defenseless; in a prone or lying position

purge (pʉrj) *v.*: Purify; cleanse

rancor (raŋ´ kər) *n.*: Ill will

ransacked (ran´ sakt´) *v.*: Searched through for plunder; pillaged; robbed

rapture (rap´ chər) *n.*: Expression of joy or pleasure

rapturous (rap´ chər us) *adj.*: Ecstatic

ravaged (rav´ ijd) *v.*: Destroyed

recompense (rek´əm pens´) *n.*: Reward; payment

redress (ri dres´) *n.*: Compensation, as for a wrong

refractory (ri frak´ tər ē) *adj.*: Hard to manage; stubborn

remnant (rem´ nənt) *n.*: What is left over

remonstrated (ri män´ strāt id) *v.*: Objected strongly

reparation (rep´ ə rā´ shən) *n.*: Making up for wrong or injury

requiem (rek´ wē əm) *n.*: Musical composition honoring the dead

requisites (rek´wə zits) *n.*: Things necessary for a given purpose

requisitioned (rek´ wə zish´ ənd) *v.*: To have requested or applied for with a formal written order

retaliate (ri tal´ ē āt´) *v.*: Return an injury or wrong

reticent (ret´ ə sənt) *adj.*: Silent; reserved

retort (ri tôrt´) *v.*: Respond with a clever answer or wisecrack

reverence (rev´ər əns) *n.*: Respect

reverently (rev´ ər ənt lē) *adv.*: Respectfully

righteous (rī´chəs) *adj.*: Acting in a just, upright manner; doing what is right

rogue (rōg) *n.*: Scoundrel; wandering beggar

roused (rouzd) *v.*: Stirred up; risen from cover

rue (rōō) *n.*: Sorrow

sanction (saŋk´ shən) *n.*: Authorized approval or permission

sanguine (saŋ´ gwin) *adj.*: Confident; cheerful

satiety (sə tī´ ə tē) *n.*: State of being filled to excess

schism (siz´ əm) *n.*: Division into groups or factions

scope (skōp) *n.*: Range of perception or understanding

scruple (skrōō´ pəl) *n.*: Hesitation caused by one's conscience or principles; uneasy feeling; qualm

segmented (seg´ ment id) *adj.*: Separated into parts

semblance (sem´ bləns) *n.*: Appearance; image

senility (si nil´ə tē) *n.*: Mental and physical decay due to old age

sentinel (sen´ ti nəl) *n.*: Person or animal that guards or watches over

sequestered (si kwes´ tərd) *v.*: Kept apart from others

sinuous (sin´ yōō əs) *adj.*: Bending, winding, or curving in and out

skeptical (skep´ ti kəl) *adj.*: Not easily persuaded

sloth (slôth) *n.*: Laziness; idleness

sojourn (sō´ jʉrn) *v.*: Stay for a while

solace (säl´ is) *n.*: Comfort; relief

solicitous (sə lis´ ə təs) *adj.*: Showing care or concern

solicitude (sə lis´ ə tōōd) *n.*: Care; concern

sordid (sôr´ did) *adj.*: Unclean; dirty

sovereign (säv´ rən) *adj.*: Supreme in power, rank, or authority

sovereignty (säv´ rən tē) *n.*: Supreme political authority

specious (spē´ shəs) *adj.*: Deceptively attractive; seeming valid but actually illogical or untrue

spectral (spek´ trəl) *adj.*: Ghostly

speculation (spek´ yoo lā´ shən) *n.*: Train of thought on a subject, especially one using hypotheses or guesses

splaying (splā´ iŋ) *v.*: Spreading

squalid (skwäl´ id) *adj.*: Miserably poor; wretched

stagnant (stag´ nənt) *adj.*: Motionless; stale

stature (stach´ ər) *n.*: Height of a person standing; development, growth, or level of achievement

stead (sted) *n.*: Position of a person as filled by a replacement or substitute

stealthy (stel´ thē) *adj.*: Sly; furtive

stoic (stō´ ik) *n.*: Person indifferent to joy, grief, pleasure, or pain

stranded (stran´ did) *v.*: Forced into shallow water or onto a beach, reef, or other land; left helpless

stringent (strin´ jənt) *adj.*: Strict

sublime (sə blīm´) *adj.*: Inspiring admiration through greatness or beauty

sublimity (sə blim´ ə tē) *n.*: Quality of being majestic or noble

subsequently (sub´ si kwənt lī) *adv.*: At a later time

succor (suk´ ər) *n.*: Help; aid; relieve

suffused (sə fyōōzd´) *v.*: Filled

sullen (sul´ ən) *adj.*: Gloomy; dismal

sundry (sun´ drē) *adj.*: Various; miscellaneous

supine (sōō pīn´) *adj.*: Lying on the back

suppliant (sup´ lē ənt) *adj.*: Beseeching prayerfully; imploring

supplication (sup´ lə kā´ shən) *n.*: Act of praying

surmise (sər mīz´) *n.*: Guess; assumption

symmetry (sim´ ə trē) *n.*: Beauty resulting from balance of forms

teeming (tēm´ iŋ) *adj.*: Filled to overflowing

temperate (tem´ pər it) *adj.*: Mild

tempests (tem´ pists) *n.*: Storms

tempestuous (tem pes´ choo wəs) *adj.*: Turbulent; violently stormy

terrestrial (tə res´ trē əl) *adj.*: Relating to the Earth

timorous (tim´ ər əs) *adj.*: Timid

topographical (täp´ə graf´ i kəl) *adj.*: Relating to a map of the surface features of a region, including its elevations, rivers, mountains, and so on

torrid (tôr´ id) *adj.*: Very hot; scorching

tranquil (traŋ´ kwil) *adj.*: Calm; serene

transcendent (tran sen´ dənt) *adj.*: Surpassing; exceeding beyond all limits

transfiguring (trans fig´ yər iŋ) *adj.*: Changing the appearance of a thing or person, especially so as to glorify it

transgress (trans gres´) *v.*: Violate a law or command

transient (tran´ shənt) *adj.*: Temporary; passing through quickly

treachery (trech´ ər ē) *n.*: Betrayal of trust, faith, or allegiance

treasons (trē´ zenz) *n.*: Betrayals of one's country or oath of loyalty

trepidation (trep´ ə dā´ shən) *n.*: Trembling

trifles (trī´ fəlz) *n.*: Things of little value or importance; trivial matters

tumid (tōō´ mid) *adj.*: Swollen

tumult (tōō´ mult) *n.*: Noisy commotion

turbid (tʉr´ bid) *adj.*: Confused; perplexed

uncanny (un kan´ ē) *adj.*: Mysterious; hard to explain

ungenial (un jēn´ yəl) *adj.*: Unfriendly

upbraidings (up brād´ iŋz) *n.*: Stern words of disapproval for an action

vales (vāls) *n.*: Hollows or depressions in the ground

valor (val´ ər) *n.*: Marked courage or bravery

venerable (ven´ ər ə bəl) *adj.*: Commanding respect by virtue of age, character, or rank

vernal (vʉrn´ əl) *adj.*: Relating to spring

vestige (ves´ tij) *n.*: Trace; bit

vindication (vin´ də kā´ shən) *n.*: Act of providing justification or support for

vintage (vin´ tij) *n.*: Wine of fine quality

visage (viz´ ij) *n.*: Person's face or expression

wan (wän) *adj.*: Sickly; pale

waning (wān´ iŋ) *v.*: Gradually becoming dimmer

winsome (win´ səm) *adj.*: Having a charming, attractive appearance or manner

writhing (rīth´ iŋ) *adj.*: Making twisting or turning motions

zenith (zē´ nəth) *n.*: Highest point of something, especially of the sky

LITERARY TERMS HANDBOOK

ALLEGORY An *allegory* is a literary work with two or more levels of meaning—a literal level and one or more symbolic levels. The events, settings, objects, or characters in an allegory—the literal level—stand for ideas or qualities such as goodness, tyranny, salvation, and so on. Allegorical writing was common in the Middle Ages. Spenser revived the form in *The Faerie Queene*, and John Bunyan revived it yet again in *The Pilgrim's Progress*. Some modern novels, such as George Orwell's *Animal Farm*, can be read as allegories.

ALLITERATION *Alliteration* is the repetition of initial consonant sounds in accented syllables. Coleridge uses the alliteration of both *b* and *f* sounds in this line from *The Rime of the Ancient Mariner*:

> The fair *breeze blew*, the white *foam flew*.

Especially in poetry, alliteration is often used to emphasize and to link words, as well as to create pleasing, musical sounds.

See also Anglo-Saxon Poetry.

ALLUSION *Allusion* is a reference to a well-known person, place, event, literary work, or work of art.

ANAPEST *See* Meter.

ANGLO-SAXON POETRY The rhythmic poetry composed in the Old English language before A.D. 1100 is known as Anglo-Saxon poetry. It generally has four accented syllables and an indefinite number of unaccented syllables in each line. Each line is divided in half by a caesura, or pause, and the halves are linked by the alliteration of two or three of the accented syllables. The following translation from "Wulf and Eadwacer" shows the alliteration and caesuras used in Anglo-Saxon poetry:

> I waited for my Wulf // with far-Wandering yearnings,
>
> When it was rainy weather // and I sat weeping.

Anglo-Saxon poetry was sung or chanted to the accompaniment of a primitive harp; it was not written but was passed down orally.

See also Alliteration, Caesura, *and* Kenning.

ASSONANCE *Assonance* is the repetition of vowel sounds in stressed syllables containing dissimilar consonant sounds. Robert Browning uses assonance in this line in "Andrea del Sarto":

> Ah, but man's reach should exceed his grasp . . .

The long e sound is repeated in the words *reach* and *exceed*. The syllables containing these sounds are stressed and contain different consonants: *r-ch* and *c-d*.

See also Consonance.

BALLAD A *ballad* is a song that tells a story, often dealing with adventure or romance, or a poem imitating such a song. Most ballads are divided into four- or six-line stanzas, are rhymed, use simple language, and depict dramatic action. Many ballads employ a repeated refrain. Some use incremental repetition, in which the refrain is varied slightly each time it appears.

Folk ballads are songs that originated among illiterate peoples and were passed from singer to singer by word of mouth. *Literary ballads,* written by more sophisticated writers, are not usually set to music. "Barbara Allan," on page 176, is a folk ballad. Samuel Taylor Coleridge's *The Rime of the Ancient Mariner*, on page 630, is a literary ballad.

BLANK VERSE *Blank verse* is unrhymed poetry written in iambic pentameter (see Meter). Usually, occasional variations in rhythm are introduced in blank verse to create emphasis, variety, and naturalness of sound. Because blank verse sounds much like ordinary spoken English, it is often used in drama, as by Shakespeare, and in poetry. The following lines come from Wordsworth's blank-verse poem "Lines Composed a Few Miles Above Tintern Abbey," on page 616:

> For thou / art with / me here / upon / the banks
>
> Of this / fair riv / er; thou / my dear / est Friend

See also Meter.

CAESURA A *caesura* is a natural pause, or break, in the middle of a line of poetry. In Anglo-Saxon poetry, a caesura divides each four-stress line in half and thus is essential to the rhythm.

See also Anglo-Saxon Poetry.

CARPE DIEM A Latin phrase, *carpe diem* means "seize the day" or "make the most of passing time." Many great literary works have been written with the *carpe diem* theme, presenting arguments for enjoying life in the present. One of the best-known poems on this theme is Robert Herrick's "To the Virgins, to Make Much of Time," on page 416.

CHARACTER A person (though not necessarily a human being) who takes part in the action of a literary work is known as a *character*. Characters can be classified in different ways:

1. In terms of their significance: A character who plays an important role is called a *major character*. A character who does not play an important role is called a *minor character*.

2. In terms of their roles: A character who plays the central role in a story is called the *protagonist*. A character who opposes the protagonist is called the *antagonist*.

3. In terms of their complexity: A character with many aspects to his or her personality, possibly including internal conflicts, is called *round*; a character defined by only a few qualities is called *flat*.

4. In terms of the degree to which they change: A character who changes is called *dynamic*; a character who does not change is called *static*.

Character types that readers recognize easily, such as the hard-boiled detective or the wicked stepmother, are called *stereotypes*, or *stock characters*.

See *also* Characterization.

CHARACTERIZATION *Characterization* is the act of creating and developing a character. A writer uses *direct characterization* when he or she describes a character's traits explicitly. Writers also use *indirect characterization*. A character's traits can be revealed indirectly by means of what he or she says, thinks, or does; by means of a description of his or her appearance; or by means of the statements, thoughts, or actions of other characters.

See *also* Character.

CLIMAX The *climax* is the high point of interest or suspense in a literary work. Often the climax is also the *crisis* in the plot, the point at which the protagonist changes his or her understanding or situation. Sometimes the climax coincides with the *resolution*, the point at which the central conflict is ended. In a story, the climax generally occurs near the end. In a play, the climax often falls close to the middle, marking the end of the rising action and the beginning of the falling action.

See *also* Plot.

COMEDY A *comedy* is a literary work, especially a play, that has a happy ending. Comedies often show ordinary characters in conflict with their societies. These conflicts, which result in misunderstandings, deceptions, and concealed identities, are resolved with the correction of moral faults or social wrongs. Types of comedy include *romantic comedy*, which involves problems among lovers, and the *comedy of manners*, which satirically challenges the social customs of a sophisticated society. Comedy is often contrasted with tragedy, in which the protagonist meets an unfortunate end.

See *also* Drama *and* Tragedy.

CONCEIT A *conceit* is an unusual and surprising comparison between two very different things. This special kind of metaphor or complicated analogy is often the basis for a whole poem. During the Elizabethan period, sonnets commonly included *Petrarchan conceits*. Petrarchan conceits make extravagant claims about the beloved's beauty or the speaker's suffering, with comparisons to divine beings, powerful natural forces, and objects that contain a given quality in the highest degree. Spenser uses a Petrarchan conceit when he claims in Sonnet 1, on page 209, that the "starry light" of his beloved's eyes will make his book happy when she reads it.

Seventeenth-century metaphysical poets were fond of elaborate, unusual, highly intellectual conceits. For example, in "Valediction: Forbidding Mourning," on page 398, John Donne compares two separated lovers to the two legs of a drawing compass, which are united even when they are apart.

See *also* Metaphor.

CONFLICT A *conflict* is a struggle between opposing forces. Sometimes, this struggle is internal, or within a character. At other times, the struggle is external, or between the character and some outside force. The outside force may be another character, nature, or some element of society such as a custom or a political institution. Often the conflict in a work combines several of these possibilities. For example, in Shakespeare's *Macbeth*, beginning on page 270, Macbeth struggles against the better parts of his own nature, against Banquo and Fleance, against fate, and against the forces led by Malcolm, Macduff, and Siward.

See *also* Plot.

CONNOTATION *Connotation* refers to the associations that a word calls to mind in addition to its dictionary meaning. For example, the words *home* and *domicile* have the same dictionary meaning. However, the first has positive connotations of warmth and security, whereas the second does not.

See *also* Denotation.

CONSONANCE *Consonance* is the repetition of final consonant sounds in stressed syllables containing dissimilar vowel sounds. Samuel Taylor Coleridge uses consonance in these lines from *The Rime of the Ancient Mariner,* on page 645:

a frightful fie**nd** / Doth close behi**nd** him tread.

Fiend and the stressed syllable in *behind* have the same final consonant sounds but different vowel sounds.

See also Assonance.

COUPLET A *couplet* is a pair of rhyming lines written in the same meter. A *heroic couplet* is a rhymed pair of iambic pentameter lines. In a *closed couplet,* the meaning and grammar is completed within the two lines. These lines from Alexander Pope's *An Essay on Criticism* illustrate the closed heroic couplet:

True ease in writing comes from art, not chance,
As those move easiest who have learned to dance.

Sonnets written in the English, or Shakespearean, style usually end with heroic couplets.

See also Sonnet.

DACTYL *See* Meter.

DENOTATION *Denotation* is the objective meaning of a word—that to which the word refers, independent of other associations the word calls to mind. Dictionaries list the denotative meanings of words.

See also Connotation.

DIALECT *Dialect* is the form of a language spoken by people in a particular region or group. Dialects differ from one another in grammar, vocabulary, and pronunciation. Robert Burns used a Scots dialect in poems like "Auld Lang Syne":

Should auld acquaintance be forgot,
And never brought to min'?
Should auld acquaintance be forgot,
And days o' auld lang syne?

Dialect is sometimes used as a part of characterization, as in V. S. Naipul's "B. Wordsworth," on page 1118, in which B. Wordsworth's "educated" English contrasts with the island dialect of other characters.

DIALOGUE *Dialogue* is a conversation between characters. Writers use dialogue to reveal character, to present events, to add variety to narratives, and to interest readers. Dialogue in a story is usually set off by quotation marks and paragraphing. Dialogue in a play script generally follows the name of the speaker.

DIARY A *diary* is a personal record of daily events, usually written in prose. Most diaries are not written for publication; sometimes, however, interesting diaries or diaries written by influential people are published. One example of a published diary is that of Samuel Pepys, a selection from which appears on page 462.

See also Journal.

DICTION *Diction* is a writer's word choice. It can be a major determinant of the writer's style. Diction can be described as formal or informal, abstract or concrete, plain or ornate, ordinary or technical.

See also Style.

DIMETER *See* Meter.

DRAMA A *drama* is a story written to be performed by actors. It may consist of one or more large sections, called acts, which are made up of any number of smaller sections, called scenes.

Drama originated in the religious rituals and symbolic reenactments of primitive peoples. The ancient Greeks, who developed drama into a sophisticated art form, created such dramatic forms as tragedy and comedy.

The first dramas in England were the miracle plays and morality plays of the Middle Ages. Miracle plays told biblical stories. Morality plays, such as *Everyman,* were allegories dealing with personified virtues and vices. The English Renaissance saw a great flowering of drama in England, culminating in the works of William Shakespeare, who wrote many of the world's greatest comedies, tragedies, histories, and romances. During the Neoclassical Age, English drama turned to witty, satirical comedies of manners that probed the virtues of upper-class society, such as Goldsmith's *She Stoops to Conquer* and Congreve's *The Way of the World.* The Romantic and Victorian ages were not great periods for drama in England. However, a few good verse plays were written, including Percy Bysshe Shelley's *The Cenci* and *Prometheus Unbound* as well as Robert Browning's *Pippa Passes.* The end of the nineteenth and beginning of the twentieth centuries saw a resurgence of the drama in England and throughout the English-speaking world. Great plays of the Modern period include plays by Bernard Shaw, William Butler Yeats, John Millington Synge, Christopher Fry, T. S. Eliot, Harold Pinter, and Samuel Beckett.

DRAMATIC MONOLOGUE A *dramatic monologue* is a poem in which an imaginary character speaks to a silent listener. During the monologue, the speaker reveals his or her personality, usually at a moment of crisis. Examples of dramatic monologues in this text are

Robert Browning's "My Last Duchess," on page 766, and Alfred, Lord Tennyson's "Ulysses," on page 757.

ELEGY   An *elegy* is a solemn and formal lyric poem about death. It may mourn a particular person or reflect on a serious or tragic theme, such as the passing of youth, beauty, or a way of life. See Thomas Gray's "Elegy Written in a Country Churchyard," on page 520.

See also Lyric Poem.

END-STOPPED LINE   An *end-stopped line* is a line of poetry concluding with a break in the meter and in the meaning. This pause at the end of a line is often punctuated by a period, comma, dash, or semi-colon. These lines from "Away, Melancholy," by Stevie Smith, are end-stopped:

> Are not the trees green,
> The earth as green?
> Does not the wind blow,
> Fire leap and the rivers flow?
> Away melancholy.

See also Run-on Line.

EPIC   An *epic* is a long narrative poem about the adventures of gods or of a hero. *Beowulf,* on page 40, is a *folk epic,* one that was composed orally and passed from storyteller to storyteller. The ancient Greek epics attributed to Homer—the *Iliad* and the *Odyssey*—are also folk epics. The *Aeneid,* by the Roman poet Virgil, and *The Divine Comedy,* by the Italian poet Dante Alighieri, are examples of literary epics from the Classical and Medieval periods, respectively. John Milton's *Paradise Lost,* a selection from which appears on page 434, is also a literary epic. Milton's goal in creating *Paradise Lost* was to write a Christian epic similar in form and equal in value to the great epics of antiquity. Serious and wide-ranging, an epic presents an encyclopedic portrait of the culture in which it was produced.

Epic conventions are traditional characteristics of epic poems, including an opening statement of the theme; an appeal for supernatural help in telling the story (an invocation); a beginning *in medias res* (Latin: "in the middle of things"); long lists, or catalogs, of people and things; accounts of past events; and descriptive phrases such as kennings, Homeric similes, and Homeric epithets (a word or phrase that states a characteristic quality of a person or thing, such as "wide-wayed city" or "clear-voiced heralds" in the *Iliad*).

See also Kenning.

EPIGRAM   An *epigram* is a brief, pointed statement in prose or in verse. The concluding couplet in an English sonnet may be epigrammatic. An essay may be written in an epigrammatic style, one characterized by the use of epigrams.

EPIPHANY   An *epiphany* is a term introduced by James Joyce to describe a moment of insight in which a character recognizes some truth. In Joyce's "Araby," beginning on page 1042, the boy's epiphany comes at the end of the story, when he recognizes the falsity of his dream.

EPITAPH   An *epitaph* is an inscription written on a tomb or burial place. In literature, epitaphs include serious or humorous lines written as if intended for such use, like the epitaph in Thomas Gray's "Elegy Written in a Country Churchyard," on page 520.

EPITHET   See Epic.

ESSAY   An *essay* is a short, nonfiction work about a particular subject. Essays are of many types but may be classified by tone or style as formal or informal. Addison's breezy style and tongue-in-cheek descriptions make "The Aims of the Spectator," on page 550, an instance of an informal essay. An essay is often classed by its main purpose as descriptive, narrative, expository, argumentative, or persuasive. Jonson's "On Spring,"on page 546, mixes a variety of purposes but is in the end an attempt to persuade us of one means to happiness.

EXTENDED METAPHOR   See Metaphor.

FICTION   *Fiction* is prose writing about imaginary characters and events. Some writers of fiction base their stories on real people and events, whereas others rely solely on their imaginations.

See also Narration *and* Prose.

FIGURATIVE LANGUAGE   *Figurative language* is writing or speech not meant to be interpreted literally. Poets and other writers use figurative language to create vivid word pictures, to make their writing emotionally intense and concentrated, and to state their ideas in new and unusual ways.

Among the figures of speech making up figurative language are apostrophe, hyperbole, irony, metaphor, metonymy, oxymoron, paradox, personification, simile, and synecdoche.

See also the entries for individual figures of speech.

FOLKLORE   The stories, legends, myths, ballads, riddles, sayings, and other traditional works produced orally by illiterate or semiliterate peoples is known as *folklore.*

It influences written literature in many ways. Examples include the beheading contest in *Sir Gawain and the Green Knight,* on page 142, and the fiancé in Elizabeth Bowen's "The Demon Lover," on page 887, a creation inspired by the ghostly lover in the old ballad of the same title.

FOOT *See Meter.*

FREE VERSE *Free verse* is poetry not written in a regular, rhythmical pattern, or meter. Instead of having metrical feet and lines, free verse has a rhythm that suits its meaning and that uses the sounds of spoken language in lines of different lengths. Free verse has been widely used in twentieth-century poetry. An example is "The Galloping Cat," by Steve Smith:

> All the same I
> Intend to go on being
> A cat that likes to
> Gallop about doing good
> So
> Now with my bald head I go,
> Chopping the untidy flowers down, to and fro.

GOTHIC *Gothic* is a term used to describe literary works that make extensive use of primitive, medieval, wild, mysterious, or natural elements. Gothic novels, such as Mary Wollstonecraft Shelley's *Frankenstein,* a selection from which appears on page 579, often depict horrifying events set in gloomy castles.

HEPTAMETER *See Meter.*

HEXAMETER *See Meter.*

HYPERBOLE *Hyperbole* is a deliberate exaggeration or overstatement. In "Song," John Donne uses this figure of speech:

> When thou sigh'st, thou sigh'st not wind,
> but sigh'st my soul away

However much pain his beloved's unhappiness causes him—and however intertwined their fates are by love—her sighs surely do not bring him near death. Such an excessive claim is an example of hyperbole.

See also Figurative Language.

IAMBIC PENTAMETER *See Meter.*

IMAGE An *image* is a word or phrase that appeals to one or more of the senses—sight, hearing, touch, taste, or smell. In a famous essay on *Hamlet,* T. S. Eliot explained how a group of images can be used as an "objective correlative." By this phrase, Eliot meant that a complex emotional state can be suggested by images that are carefully chosen to evoke this state.

See also Imagery.

IMAGERY *Imagery* is the descriptive language used in literature to re-create sensory experiences. Imagery enriches writing by making it more vivid, setting a tone, suggesting emotions, and guiding readers' reactions.

IRONY *Irony* is the general name given to literary techniques that involve surprising, interesting, or amusing contradictions. In *verbal irony,* words are used to suggest the opposite of their usual meaning. In *dramatic irony,* there is a contradiction between what a character thinks and what the reader or audience knows to be true. In *irony of situation,* an event occurs that directly contradicts expectations.

JOURNAL A *journal* is a daily autobiographical account of events and personal reactions. Daniel Defoe adapted this form to fictional use in *A Journal of the Plague Year,* an excerpt from which appears on page 468.

See also Diary.

KENNING A *kenning* is a metaphorical phrase, used in Anglo-Saxon poetry to replace a concrete noun. In "The Seafarer," on page 15, the cuckoo is called "summer's sentinel" and the sea, "the whale's home."

See also Anglo-Saxon Poetry *and* Epic.

LEGEND A *legend* is a widely told story about the past that may or may not be based in fact. A legend often reflects a people's identity or cultural values, generally with more historical truth than in a myth. English legends include the stories of King Arthur (retold in *Morte d'Arthur,* a selection from which appears on page 156) and Robin Hood.

See also Myth.

LYRIC POEM A *lyric poem* is a poem expressing the observations and feelings of a single speaker. Unlike a narrative poem, it presents an experience or a single effect, but it does not tell a full story. Types of lyrics include the elegy, the ode, and the sonnet. The lyric flourished in the songs and sonnets of the Renaissance, was revived by the Romantic poets, and remained the most common poetic form in the nineteenth and twentieth centuries. Alfred, Lord Tennyson; Robert Browning; Elizabeth Barrett Browning; Matthew Arnold; William Butler Yeats; W. H. Auden; Dylan Thomas; and Stevie Smith all wrote great lyric poems.

MEMENTO MORI *Memento mori* is a Latin phrase meaning "remember that you must die." Many literary works have dealt with the *memento mori* theme, including Marvell's "To His Coy Mistress," on page 414, and

Gray's "Elegy Written in a Country Churchyard," on page 520.

METAPHOR A *metaphor* is a figure of speech in which one thing is spoken of as though it were something else, as in "death that long sleep." Through this identification of dissimilar things, a comparison is suggested or implied. Emily Brontë uses the following metaphor in her poem "Remembrance," on page 846: "my thoughts no longer hover . . . resting their wings." The metaphor suggests similarities between the speaker's thoughts and the wings of a bird.

An *extended metaphor* is developed at length and involves several points of comparison. A *mixed metaphor* occurs when two metaphors are jumbled together. For example, thorns and rain are illogically mixed in "The thorns of life rained down on him."

A *dead metaphor* is one that has been so overused that its original metaphorical impact has been lost. Examples of dead metaphors include "the foot of the bed" and "toe the line."

See *also* Figurative Language.

METAPHYSICAL POETRY The term *metaphysical poetry* is used to describe the works of such seventeenth-century English poets as Richard Crashaw, John Donne, George Herbert, Andrew Marvell, Thomas Traherne, and Henry Vaughan. The term was first used by Samuel Johnson in an attack on writers who fill their works with far-fetched conceits and who make poetry a vehicle for displays of learning. Characteristic features of metaphysical poetry include intellectual playfulness, argument, paradoxes, irony, elaborate and unusual conceits, incongruity, and the rhythms of ordinary speech. Examples of metaphysical poems in this text include Donne's "Song," on page 396, and Marvell's "To His Coy Mistress," on page 414.

METER *Meter* is the rhythmical pattern of a poem. This pattern is determined by the number and types of stresses, or beats, in each line. To describe the meter of a poem, you must scan its lines. Scanning involves marking the stressed and unstressed syllables, as follows:

I weén / that, when / the grave's / dark wall

Did first / her form / retain,

They thought / their hearts / could ne'er / recall

The light / of joy / again.

—Emily Brontë, "Song"

As you can see, each stressed syllable is marked with a slanted line (´) and each unstressed syllable with a horseshoe symbol (ˇ) . The stresses are then divided by

vertical lines into groups called feet. The following types of feet are common in English poetry:

1. *Iamb:* a foot with one unstressed syllable followed by one stressed syllable, as in the word "afraid"

2. *Trochee:* a foot with one stressed syllable followed by one unstressed syllable, as in the word "heather"

3. *Anapest:* a foot with two unstressed syllables followed by one stressed syllable, as in the word "disembark"

4. *Dactyl:* a foot with one stressed syllable followed by two unstressed syllables, as in the word "solitude"

5. *Spondee:* a foot with two stressed syllables, as in the word "workday"

6. *Pyrrhic:* a foot with two unstressed syllables, as in the last foot of the word "unspeak / ably"

7. *Amphibrach:* a foot with an unstressed syllable, one stressed syllable, and another unstressed syllable, as in the word "another"

8. *Amphimacer:* a foot with a stressed syllable, one unstressed syllable, and another stressed syllable, as in "up and down"

A line of poetry is described as *iambic, trochaic, anapestic,* or *dactylic* according to the kind of foot that appears most often in the line. Lines are also described in terms of the number of feet that occur in them, as follows:

1. *Monometer:* verse written in one-foot lines:
    Sound the Flute!
    Now it's mute.
    Birds delight
    Day and Night.
         —William Blake, "Spring"

2. *Dimeter:* verse written in two-foot lines:
    O Rose / thou art sick.
    The invis / ible worm.
    That flies / in the night
    In the how / ling storm:
    Has found / out thy bed
    Of crim / son joy:
    And his dark / secret love
    Does thy life / destroy.
         —William Blake, "The Sick Rose"

3. *Trimeter:* verse written in three-foot lines:

> Ĭ went / tŏ the Gárd / en ŏf Lóve
> Ănd sáw / whăt Ĭ név / er hăd séen:
> Ă Cháp / ĕl wăs búilt / ĭn the mídst,
> Whĕre Ĭ úsed / tŏ pláy / ŏn the gréen.
>> —William Blake, "The Garden of
>> Love"

4. *Tetrameter:* verse written in four-foot lines:

> Ĭ wánd / er thró' / eăch chárt / er'd strĕet
> Néar whĕre / the chárt / er'd Thámes /
>> dŏes flów
> Ănd márk / ĭn év / erў fáce / Ĭ méet
> Márks ŏf / wéakness, / márks ŏf / wóe.
>> —William Blake, "The Little Black
>> Boy"

A six-foot line is called a *hexameter.* A line with seven feet is a *heptameter.*

A complete description of the meter of a line tells both how many feet there are in the line and what kind of foot is most common. Thus, the stanza from Emily Brontë's poem, quoted at the beginning of this entry, would be described as being made up of alternating iambic tetrameter and iambic trimeter lines. Poetry that does not have a regular meter is called *free verse.*

See also Free Verse.

METONYMY *Metonymy* is a figure of speech that substitutes something closely related for the thing actually meant. In the opening line of "The Lost Leader," Robert Browning says, "Just for a handful of silver he left us," using "silver" to refer to money paid for a betrayal.

See also Figurative Language.

MIRACLE PLAY See Drama.

MOCK EPIC A *mock epic* is a poem about a trivial matter written in the style of a serious epic. The incongruity of style and subject matter produces comic effects. Alexander Pope's *The Rape of the Lock,* on page 488, is a mock epic.

See also Epic.

MODERNISM *Modernism* is the name given to an international movement in the arts during the early twentieth century. Modernists rejected old forms and experimented with the new, which often led to controversy. Literary modernists such as James Joyce, W. B. Yeats, and T. S. Eliot used images as symbols. They presented human experiences in fragments, rather than as

a coherent whole, which led to new experiments in the forms of poetry and fiction. Often, Modernists took on trivial or shocking subject matter—subject matter not traditionally the focus of art.

MONOLOGUE A *monologue* is a speech or performance given entirely by one person or by one character.

See also Dramatic Monologue *and* Soliloquy.

MOOD *Mood,* or *atmosphere,* is the feeling created in the reader by a literary work or passage. Mood may be suggested by the writer's choice of words, by events in the work, or by the physical setting. Nadine Gordimer begins "The Train from Rhodesia," on page 1128, with a mood-evoking description of the brick, mud, and tin buildings at the hot, sandy train station. Everyone there awaits the train, the only relief in this inactive and restricted environment.

See also Setting *and* Tone.

MORALITY PLAY See Drama.

MYTH A *myth* is a fictional tale, originally with religious significance, that explains the actions of gods or heroes, the causes of natural phenomena, or both. Allusions to characters and motifs from Greek, Roman, Norse, and Celtic myths are common in English literature. In addition, mythological stories are often retold or adapted.

See also Legend.

NARRATION *Narration* is writing that tells a story. The act of telling a story is also called narration. The *narrative,* or story, is told by a storyteller called the *narrator.* Narration is one of the major forms of discourse, and it appears in many guises. Biographies, autobiographies, journals, reports, novels, short stories, plays, narrative poems, anecdotes, fables, parables, myths, legends, folk tales, ballads, and epic poems are all narratives, or types of narration.

See also Point of View.

NARRATIVE POEM A *narrative poem* is a poem that tells a story in verse. Three traditional types of narrative poems include ballads, such as "Barbara Allan," on page 176; epics, such as *Beowulf,* on page 40; and metrical romances, such as *Sir Gawain and the Green Knight,* on page 142. Other narrative poems in this text include the selection from Milton's *Paradise Lost,* on page 434; Coleridge's *The Rime of the Ancient Mariner,* on page 630; and Tennyson's "The Lady of Shalott," on page 752.

NATURALISM *Naturalism* was a literary movement among writers at the end of the nineteenth century and during the early decades of the twentieth century. The Naturalists depicted life in its grimmer details and tended to view people as hopeless victims of immutable natural laws.

See also Realism.

NEOCLASSICISM *Neoclassicism* was a literary movement of the Restoration and the eighteenth century in which writers turned to classical Greek and Roman literary models and standards. Like the ancients, Neoclassicists, such as Alexander Pope, stressed order, harmony, restraint, and the ideal. Much Neoclassical literature dealt with themes related to proper human conduct. The most popular literary forms of the day—essays, letters, early novels, epigrams, parodies, and satires—reflected this emphasis on society as a subject. Just as the Neoclassicists rejected the individualism and extravagance of the Renaissance in favor of classical restraint, so the nineteenth-century Romantics rejected Neoclassicism in favor of imagination, emotion, and the individual.

See also Romanticism.

NOVEL A *novel* is an extended work of fiction that often has a complicated plot, many major and minor characters, a unifying theme, and several settings. Novels can be grouped in many ways, based on the historical periods in which they are written (such as Romantic or Victorian), on the subjects and themes that they treat (such as Gothic or regional), on the techniques used in them (such as stream-of-consciousness), or on their debts to literary movements (such as Naturalism or Realism). Among the early novels were Samuel Richardson's *Pamela* and *Clarissa* and Henry Fielding's *Tom Jones*. Other classic English novels include Jane Austen's *Pride and Prejudice*, Sir Walter Scott's *Waverley*, Charles Dickens's *David Copperfield*, and George Eliot's *The Mill on the Floss*. Major twentieth-century novelists include James Joyce, Virginia Woolf, D. H. Lawrence, Henry James, Graham Greene, and Patrick White. A *novella*, for example, Joseph Conrad's *Heart of Darkness*, is not as long as a novel but is longer than a short story.

OBJECTIVE CORRELATIVE *See* Image.

OCTAVE *See* Stanza.

ODE An *ode* is a long, formal lyric poem with a serious theme. It may have a traditional structure with three alternating stanza patterns, called the *strophe,* the *antistrophe,* and the *epode.* An ode may be written for a private occasion, as was John Keats's "Ode to a Nightingale," on page 686, or it may be prepared for a public ceremony. Odes often honor people, commemorate events, or respond to natural scenes.

See also Lyric Poem.

ONOMATOPOEIA *Onomatopoeia* is the use of words that imitate sounds. Examples of such words are *buzz, hiss, murmur,* and *rustle.* Seamus Heaney uses onomatopoeia in "Churning Day" to suggest the sounds of making butter:

> My mother took first turn, set up rhythms
> that slugged and thumped for hours. Arms
> ached.
> Hands blistered. Cheeks and clothes were
> splattered
> with flabbymilk.

Onomatopoeia is used to create musical effects and to reinforce meaning.

ORAL TRADITION *Oral tradition* is the body of songs, stories, and poems preserved by being passed from generation to generation by word of mouth. Among the many materials composed or preserved through oral tradition in Great Britain are *Beowulf,* on page 40, and the folk ballads on pages 170–176. In his *Morte d'Arthur,* a selection from which appears beginning on page 156, Sir Thomas Malory drew on written French sources and on Arthurian legends from the oral tradition. Shakespeare drew on materials from the oral tradition to create the sprites and fairies of *A Midsummer Night's Dream* and the witches of *Macbeth,* on page 270. Folk epics, ballads, myths, legends, folk tales, folk songs, proverbs, nursery rhymes—all products of the oral tradition—were originally spoken or sung rather than written down.

See also Ballad, Folklore, Legend, *and* Myth.

OXYMORON An *oxymoron* is a figure of speech that fuses two contradictory or opposing ideas, such as "freezing fire" or "happy grief," thus suggesting a paradox in just a few words. In Book I of *Paradise Lost,* which begins on page 434, Milton uses the oxymoron "darkness visible" to describe the pit into which Satan and the other rebellious angels have been thrown.

See also Figurative Language *and* Paradox.

PARABLE A *parable* is a short, simple story from which a moral or religious lesson can be drawn. The most famous parables are those in the New Testament, an example of which appears on page 248.

PARADOX A *paradox* is a statement that seems to be contradictory but that actually presents a truth. In "Love's Growth," John Donne presents the following paradox:

> Methinks I lied all winter, when I swore
> My love was infinite, if spring make it more.

Because a paradox is surprising or even shocking, it draws the reader's attention to what is being said.

See also Figurative Language *and* Oxymoron.

PASTORAL *Pastoral* refers to the quality of literary works that deal with the pleasures of a simple, rural life or with escape to a simpler place and time. The tradition of pastoral literature began in ancient Greece with the poetic idylls of Theocritus, who wrote about the simple lives of shepherds and goatherds. The Roman poet Virgil also wrote a famous collection of pastoral poems, the *Eclogues,* in imitation of Theocritus. Virgil's characters were also idealized rustics.

During the European Renaissance, pastoral writing became quite popular. One famous example of the genre is *The Countess of Pembroke's Arcadia*, by Sir Phillip Sidney. Another example is Christopher Marlowe's "The Passionate Shepherd to His Love," on page 217.

Today, the term *pastoral* is commonly applied to any work in which a speaker longs to escape to a simpler, rural life. By this definition, both William Wordsworth's "The World Is Too Much with Us," on page 624, and William Butler Yeats's "The Lake Isle of Innisfree," on page 897, are pastoral poems.

PENTAMETER See Meter.

PERSONIFICATION *Personification* is a figure of speech in which a nonhuman subject is given human characteristics. Percy Bysshe Shelley uses personification in these lines from "To Night":

> Swiftly walk o'er the western wave,
> Spirit of the Night!
> Out of the misty eastern cave
> Where, all the long and lone daylight
> Thou wovest dreams of joy and fear,
> Which makes thee terrible and dear,
> Swift be thy flight!

Effective personification of things or ideas makes them vital, as if they were human.

See also Figurative Language *and* Metaphor.

PLOT *Plot* is the sequence of events in a literary work. The two primary elements of any plot are characters and a conflict. Most plots can be analyzed into many or all of the following parts:

1. The *exposition* introduces the setting, the characters, and the basic situation.
2. The *inciting incident* introduces the central conflict.
3. During the *development,* the conflict runs its course and usually intensifies.
4. At the *climax,* the conflict reaches a high point of interest or suspense.
5. At the *resolution,* the conflict is ended.
6. The *denouement* ties up loose ends that remain after the resolution of the conflict.

There are many variations on the standard plot structure. Some stories begin *in medias res* ("in the middle of things"), after the inciting incident has already occurred. In some stories, the expository material appears toward the middle, in flashbacks. In many stories, there is no denouement. Occasionally, though not often, the conflict is left unresolved.

POETRY *Poetry* is one of the three major types, or genres, of literature, the others being prose and drama. Poetry defies simple definition because there is no single characteristic that is found in all poems and not found in all nonpoems.

Often, poems are divided into lines and stanzas. Poems such as sonnets, odes, villanelles, and sestinas are governed by rules regarding the number of lines, the number and placement of stressed syllables in each line, and the rhyme scheme. In the case of villanelles and sestinas, the repetition of words at the ends of lines or of entire lines is required. (An example of a sestina, Seamus Heaney's "Two Lorries," appears on page 1004. An example of a villanelle, Dylan Thomas's "Do Not Go Gently into That Dark, Dark Night," appears on page 1094.) However, some poems are written in free verse. Most poems make use of highly concise, musical, and emotionally charged language. Many also use imagery, figurative language, and devices of sound like rhyme.

Types of poetry include *narrative poetry* (ballads, epics, and metrical romances); *dramatic poetry* (dramatic monologues and dramatic dialogues); *lyrics* (sonnets, odes, elegies, and love poems); and *concrete poetry* (a poem presented on the page in a shape that suggests its subject).

POINT OF VIEW The perspective, or vantage point, from which a story is told is its *point of view*. If a character within the story tells the story, then it is told from the *first-person point of view*. If a voice from outside the story tells it, then the story is told from the *third-person point of view*. If the knowledge of the storyteller is limited to the internal states of one character, then the storyteller has a *limited point of view*. If the storyteller's knowledge extends to the internal states of all of the characters, then the storyteller has an *omniscient point of view*. The point of view from which a story is told determines what view of events will be presented.

PROSE *Prose* is the ordinary form of written language and one of the three major types of literature. Most writing that is not poetry, drama, or song is considered prose. Prose occurs in two major forms: fiction and nonfiction.

PSALM A *psalm* is a song or hymn of praise, like those in the Book of Psalms in the Bible.

PYRRHIC *See Meter.*

QUATRAIN *See Stanza.*

REALISM *Realism* is the presentation in art of details from actual life. Another term for Realism, one that derives from Aristotle's *Poetics*, is *mimesis*, the Greek word for "imitation." During the last part of the nineteenth century and the first part of the twentieth, Realism enjoyed considerable popularity among writers in the English-speaking world. Novels often dealt with grim social realities and presented realistic portrayals of the psychological states of characters. The most common sort of stage setting during this period was one in which a room was presented as though one wall had been removed and the audience were peering inside.

REFRAIN A *refrain* is a regularly repeated line or group of lines in a poem or song.

See also Ballad.

REGIONALISM *Regionalism* is the tendency to confine one's writing to the presentation of materials drawn from a particular geographical area. For example, the Brontës wrote about Yorkshire, Thomas Hardy wrote about Dorset and Wessex, and D. H. Lawrence wrote about Nottinghamshire. A Regionalist writer presents the distinct culture of an area, including its speech, customs, landscape, and history.

RHYME *Rhyme* is the repetition of sounds at the ends of words. *End rhyme* occurs when rhyming words appear at the ends of lines. *Internal rhyme* occurs when rhyming words fall within a line. *Exact rhyme* is the use of identical rhyming sounds, as in *love* and *dove*. *Approximate,* or *slant rhyme,* is the use of sounds that are similar but not identical, as in *prove* and *glove*.

RHYME SCHEME *Rhyme scheme* is the regular pattern of rhyming words in a poem or stanza. To

indicate a rhyme scheme, assign each final sound in the poem or stanza a different letter. The following lines from Charlotte Brontë's "On the Death of Anne Brontë" have been marked:

There's little joy in life for me,	a
And little terror in the grave;	b
I've lived the parting hour to see	a
Of one I would have died to save.	b

The rhyme scheme of this stanza is *abab*.

RHYTHM *See Meter.*

ROMANCE A *romance* is a story that presents remote or imaginative incidents rather than ordinary, realistic experience. The term *romance* was originally used to refer to medieval tales of the deeds and loves of noble knights and ladies. These early romances, or tales of chivalry and courtly love, are exemplified by *Sir Gawain and the Green Knight*, on page 142, and by Malory's *Morte d'Arthur*, on page 156. During the Renaissance in England, many writers, such as Edmund Spenser in *The Faerie Queene*, drew heavily on the romance tradition. From the eighteenth century on, the term *romance* has been used to describe sentimental novels about love.

ROMANTICISM *Romanticism* was a literary and artistic movement of the eighteenth and nineteenth centuries. In reaction to Neoclassicism, the Romantics emphasized imagination, fancy, freedom, emotion, wildness, the beauty of the untamed natural world, the rights of the individual, the nobility of the common man, and the attractiveness of pastoral life. Important figures in the Romantic movement included William Wordsworth; Samuel Taylor Coleridge; Percy Bysshe Shelley; John Keats; and George Gordon, Lord Byron.

RUN-ON LINE A *run-on line* is a line that does not contain a pause or a stop at the end. It ends in the middle of a statement and a grammatical unit, and the reader must read the next line to find the end of the statement and the completion of the grammatical unit. The beginning of Molly Holden's "The Double Nature of White" illustrates the run-on line:

White orchards are the earliest, stunning
the spirit resigned to winter's black, white thorn
sprays first the bare wet branches of the hedge.

See also End-Stopped Line.

SATIRE *Satire* is writing that ridicules or holds up to contempt the faults of individuals or of groups. A satirist may use a sympathetic tone or an angry, bitter tone. Some satire, like Jonathan Swift's *Gulliver's Travels*, an excerpt from which appears beginning on page 476, is written in prose. Other satire, such as Alexander Pope's *The Rape of the Lock*, on page 488, is written in poetry. Although a satire is often humorous, its purpose is not simply to make readers laugh but also to correct the flaws and shortcomings that it points out.

SCANSION *Scansion* is the process of analyzing the metrical pattern of a poem.

See also Meter.

SERMON A *sermon* is a speech offering religious or moral instruction. Given by Jesus on a mountainside in Galilee, the Sermon on the Mount, on page 247, contains the basic teachings of Christianity.

SESTET See Stanza.

SETTING The *setting* is the time and place of the action of a literary work. A setting can serve many different purposes. It can provide a backdrop for the action. It can be the force that the protagonist struggles against and thus the source of the central conflict. It can also be used to create an atmosphere. In many works, the setting symbolizes a point that the author wishes to emphasize.

See also Mood *and* Symbol.

SHORT STORY A *short story* is a brief work of fiction. The short story resembles the longer novel, but it generally has a simpler plot and setting. In addition, a short story tends to reveal character at a crucial moment, rather than to develop it through many incidents.

SIMILE A *simile* is a figure of speech that compares two apparently dissimilar things by using a key word such as *like* or *as*. Christina Rossetti uses simile in "Goblin Market" to describe two sisters:

> Like two blossoms on one stem,
> Like two flakes of new-fallen snow,
> Like two wands of ivory
> Tipped with gold for awful kings.

By comparing apparently dissimilar things, the writer of a simile surprises the reader into an appreciation of the hidden similarities of the things being compared.

See also Figurative Language.

SOLILOQUY A *soliloquy* is a long speech in a play or in a prose work made by a character who is alone and thus reveals private thoughts and feelings to the audience or reader. William Shakespeare opens Act III of *Macbeth* with a soliloquy in which Banquo speculates on Macbeth's reaction to the witches' prophecy.

See also Monologue.

SONNET A *sonnet* is a fourteen-line lyric poem with a single theme. Sonnets vary, but they are usually written in iambic pentameter, following one of two traditional patterns.

The *Petrarchan,* or *Italian, sonnet* is divided into two parts, an eight-line octave and a six-line sestet. The octave rhymes *abba abba*, while the sestet generally rhymes *cde cde* or uses some combination of *cd* rhymes. The two parts of this sonnet work together. The octave raises a question, states a problem, or presents a brief narrative, and the sestet answers the question, solves the problem, or comments on the narrative.

The *Shakespearean,* or *English, sonnet* has three four-line quatrains plus a concluding two-line couplet. The rhyme scheme of such a sonnet is usually *abab cdcd efef gg*. Each of the three quatrains usually explores a different variation of the main theme. Then the couplet presents a summarizing or concluding statement.

See also Lyric Poem *and* Sonnet Sequence.

SONNET SEQUENCE A *sonnet sequence* is a series or group of sonnets written to one person or on one theme. Although each sonnet can stand alone as a separate poem, the sequence lets the poet trace the development of a relationship or examine different aspects of a single subject. Examples of sonnet sequences are Sir Philip Sidney's *Astrophel and Stella*, Edmund Spenser's *Amoretti*, and Elizabeth Barrett Browning's *Sonnets from the Portuguese*.

See also Sonnet.

SPEAKER The *speaker* is the imaginary voice assumed by the writer of the poem; the character who "tells" the poem. This character is often not identified by name. The title of William Blake's poem "The Chimney Sweeper," on page 600, identifies the speaker, a child who gives an account of his life. The child tells us in the poem, for instance, that "When my mother died I was very young."

Although this speaker matter-of-factly accepts his life, the poem is ironic because the poet expects readers to have a different view of the child's situation. Recognizing the speaker and thinking about his or her characteristics are often central to interpreting a lyric poem.

See also Point of View.

SPONDEE See Meter.

SPRUNG RHYTHM The term *sprung rhythm* was used by Gerard Manley Hopkins to describe the idiosyncratic meters of his poems. Discovering the underlying metrical pattern of a poem written in sprung rhythm is difficult. The rhythm is quite varied and contains such violations of traditional metrical rules as several strong stresses in a row or feet containing more than two weak stresses.

STANZA A *stanza* is a group of lines in a poem, seen as a unit. Many poems are divided into stanzas that are separated by spaces. Stanzas often function like paragraphs in prose. Each stanza states and develops one main idea.

Stanzas are commonly named according to the number of lines found in them, as follows:

1. *Couplet:* a two-line stanza
2. *Tercet:* a three-line stanza
3. *Quatrain:* a four-line stanza
4. *Cinquain:* a five-line stanza
5. *Sestet:* a six-line stanza
6. *Heptastich:* a seven-line stanza
7. *Octave:* an eight-line stanza

See also Sonnet.

STYLE *Style* is a writer's typical way of writing. Determinants of a writer's style include formality, use of figurative language, use of rhythm, typical grammatical patterns, typical sentence lengths, and typical methods of organization. John Milton is noted for a grand, heroic style that contrasts with John Keats's rich, sensory style and with T. S. Eliot's allusive, ironic style.

See also Diction.

SYMBOL A *symbol* is a sign, word, phrase, image, or other object that stands for or represents something else. Thus, a flag can symbolize a country, a spoken word can symbolize an object, a fine car can symbolize wealth, and so on. In literary criticism, a distinction is often made between *traditional* or *conventional symbols*—those that are part of our general cultural inheritance—and personal symbols—those that are created by particular authors for use in particular works. For example, the lamb in William Blake's poem "The Lamb," on page 598, is a conventional symbol for peace, gentleness, and innocence, one that Blake inherited from the Bible and from the pastoral tradition. However, the tiger in Blake's poem "The Tyger," on page 599, is not a conventional or inherited symbol. Blake created this symbol specifically for this poem.

Conventional symbolism is often based on elements of nature. For example, youth is often symbolized by greenery or springtime, middle age by summer, and old age by autumn or winter. Conventional symbols are also borrowed from religion and politics. For example, a cross may be a symbol of Christianity or the color red, a symbol of Marxist ideology.

SYNECDOCHE *Synecdoche* is a figure of speech in which a part of something is used to stand for the whole. In the preface to his long poem entitled *Milton*, William Blake includes these lines: "And did those feet in ancient time/ Walk upon England's mountains green?" The "feet" stand for the whole body, and "England's mountains green" stand for England.

See also Figurative Language.

TETRAMETER See Meter.

THEME *Theme* is the central idea, concern, or purpose in a literary work. In an essay, the theme might be directly stated in what is known as a thesis statement. In a serious literary work, the theme is usually expressed indirectly rather than directly. A light work, one written strictly for entertainment, may not have a theme.

TONE *Tone* is the writer's attitude toward the readers and toward the subject. It may be formal or informal, friendly or distant, personal or pompous. For example, John Keats's tone in his poem "On First Looking into Chapman's Homer," on page 684, is earnest and respectful, while James Boswell's tone in *The Life of Samuel Johnson*, which begins on page 510, is familiar and engaging.

See also Mood.

TRAGEDY *Tragedy* is a type of drama or literature that shows the downfall or destruction of a noble or outstanding person, traditionally one who possesses a character weakness called a *tragic flaw*. Macbeth, for example, is a brave and noble figure led astray by ambition. The *tragic hero* is caught up in a sequence of events that inevitably results in disaster. Because the protagonist is neither a wicked villain nor an innocent victim, the audience reacts with mixed emotions—both pity and fear, according to the Greek philosopher Aristotle, who defined tragedy in the *Poetics*. The outcome of a tragedy, in which the protagonist is isolated from society, contrasts with the happy resolution of a comedy, in which the protagonist makes peace with society.

See also Comedy *and* Drama.

TRIMETER See Meter.

TROCHEE See Meter.

WRITING HANDBOOK

THE WRITING PROCESS

A polished piece of writing can seem to have been effortlessly created, but most good writing is the result of a process of writing, rethinking, and rewriting. The process can roughly be divided into stages: prewriting, drafting, revising, editing, proofreading, and publishing.

It's important to remember that the writing process is one that moves backward as well as forward. Even while you are moving forward in the creation of your composition, you may still return to a previous stage—to rethink or rewrite.

Following are stages of the writing process, with key points to address during each stage.

Prewriting

In this stage, you plan out the work to be done. You prepare to write by exploring ideas, gathering information, and working out an organization plan. Following are the key steps to take at this stage:

Step 1: Analyze the writing situation. Start by clarifying your assignment, so that you know exactly what you are supposed to do.

- *Focus your topic.* If necessary, narrow the topic—the subject you are writing about—so that you can write about it fully in the space you have.
- *Know your purpose.* What is your goal for this paper? What do you want to accomplish? Your purpose will determine what you include in the paper.
- *Know your audience.* Knowing who will read your paper should influence what you say and how you say it.

Step 2: Gather ideas and information. You can do this in a number of ways:

- *Brainstorm.* Brainstorm, either alone or with others, to come up with possible ideas to use in your paper. Not all of the ideas that occur to you will be useful or suitable. You'll need to evaluate them later.
- *Consult other people about your subject.* Speaking informally with others may suggest an idea or approach you did not see at first.
- *Make a list of questions about your topic.* When your list is complete, find the answers to your questions.

- *Do research.* Your topic may require information that you don't have, so you will need to go to other sources to find information. There are numerous ways to find information on a topic. See the Research Handbook, p. 1239, for suggestions.

The ideas and information you gather will become the content of your paper. Not all of the information you gather will be needed. As you develop and revise your paper, you will make further decisions about what to include and what to leave out.

Step 3: Organize. First, make a rough plan for presenting your information. Sort your ideas and notes; decide what goes with what and which points are the most important. You can make an outline to show the order of ideas, or you can use some other organizing plan that works for you.

There are many ways in which you can organize and develop your material. Use a method that works for your topic. Following are common methods of organizing information in the development of a paper:

- *Chronological Order* You can present events in the order in which they occurred. This organization works best for presenting narrative material or explaining a process in a "how to."
- *Spatial Order* You can present details as they appear in space; for example, from left to right or from foreground to background. This order helps in descriptive writing.
- *Order of Importance* By presenting ideas from most to least important or from least to most important, you help your reader grasp your priorities.
- *Main Idea and Details* This logical organization works well to support an idea or opinion.

Drafting

When you draft, you put down your ideas on paper in rough form. Working from your prewriting notes and your outline or plan, you develop and present your ideas in sentences and paragraphs.

Don't worry about getting everything perfect at the drafting stage. Concentrate on getting your ideas down.

Draft in a way that works for you. Some writers work best by writing a quick draft—putting down all their ideas without stopping to evaluate them. Other writers prefer to develop each paragraph carefully and thoughtfully, making sure that each main idea is supported by details.

As you are developing a draft, keep in mind your purpose and your audience. These determine what you say and how you say it.

Don't be afraid to change your original plans during drafting. Some of the best ideas are those that were not planned at the beginning. Write as many drafts as you like. You can draft over and over until you're happy with the results.

Most papers, regardless of the topic, are developed with an introduction, a body, and a conclusion. Here are tips for developing these parts.

Introduction In the introduction to a paper, you want to engage your readers' attention and let them know the purpose of your paper. You may use the following strategies in your introduction:

- State your main idea.
- Use an anecdote.
- Startle your readers.
- Take a stand.
- Quote someone.

Body of the paper In the body of your paper, you present your information and make your points. Your **organization** is an important factor in leading readers through your ideas. Your elaboration on your main ideas is also important. **Elaboration** is the development of ideas to make your written work precise and complete. You can use the following kinds of details to elaborate your main ideas:

- Facts and statistics
- Sensory details
- Explanation and definition
- Anecdotes
- Examples
- Quotations

Conclusion The ending of your paper will determine the final impression you leave with your readers. Your conclusion should give readers the sense that you have pulled everything together. Following are some effective ways to end your paper:

- Summarize and restate.
- State an opinion.
- Call for action.
- Ask a question.
- Tell an anecdote.

Revising

Once you have a draft, you can look at it critically or have others review it. This is the time to make changes—on many levels. Revising is the process of reworking what you have written to make it as good as it can be. You may change some details so that your ideas flow smoothly and are clearly supported. You may

discover that some details don't work, and you'll need to discard them. Two strategies may help you start the revising process:

1. Read your work aloud. This is an excellent way to catch any ideas or details that have been left out and to notice errors in logic.
2. Ask someone else to read your work. Choose someone who can point out its strengths and suggest how to improve it.

How do you know what to check for and what to change? Here is a checklist of major writing issues. If the answer to any of these questions is "no," then that is an area that needs revision.

1. Does the writing achieve your purpose?
2. Does the paper have unity? That is, does it have a single focus, with all details and information contributing to that focus?
3. Is the arrangement of information clear and logical?
4. Have you elaborated enough to give your audience sufficient information?

Editing

When you edit, look more closely at the language you have used to ensure that the way you express your ideas is most effective.

- Replace dull language with vivid, precise words.
- Cut or change redundant expressions (unnecessary repetition).
- Cut empty words and phrases—those that do not add anything to the writing.
- Check for passive voice. Usually active voice is more effective.
- Replace wordy expressions with shorter, more precise ones.

Proofreading

After you finish your final draft, you must proofread it, either on your own or with the help of a partner.

It's useful to have both a dictionary and a usage handbook to help you check for correctness. Here are the tasks in proofreading:

- Correct errors in grammar and usage.
- Correct errors in punctuation and capitalization.
- Correct errors in spelling.

Publishing

Now your paper is ready to be shared by others.

THE MODES OF WRITING

Description

Description is writing that creates a vivid picture, draws readers into a scene, and makes readers feel as if they are meeting a character or experiencing an event firsthand. A description may stand on its own or be part of a longer work, such as a short story.

When you write a description, bring it to life with sensory details, which tell how your subject looks, smells, sounds, tastes, or feels. You'll want to choose your details carefully so that you create a single main impression of your subject. Avoid language and details that don't contribute to this main impression. Keep these guidelines in mind whenever you are assigned one of the following types of description:

Observation In an observation, you describe an event that you have witnessed firsthand, often over an extended period of time. You may focus on an aspect of daily life or on a scientific phenomenon, such as a storm or an eclipse.

Remembrance When you write a remembrance, you use vivid, descriptive details to bring to life memorable people, places, or events from your past.

Reflective Essay A reflective essay is more than just a description of personal experiences or pivotal events from your life; it also describes your thoughts and feelings about the significance of those events.

Character Profile In a character profile, you capture a person's appearance and personality traits and reveal information about his or her life. Your subject may be a real person or a fictional character.

Travel Brochure In a travel brochure, you present details about the culture, architecture, food, and scenery of a vacation destination to appeal to potential visitors.

Narration

Whenever writers tell any type of story, they are using **narration.** While there are many kinds of narration, most narratives share certain elements—characters, a setting, a sequence of events (or plot, in fiction), and, often, a theme. You might be asked to write one of these types of narration:

Personal Narrative A personal narrative is a true story about a memorable experience or period in your life. In a personal narrative, your feelings about events shape the way you tell the story—even the way you describe people and places.

Historical Narrative A historical narrative recounts an event or series of events from the past. It may be partially fictional, as when a writer creates a character who witnesses the actions of real historical characters up close. In your historical narrative, you draw on research to create accurate settings and authentic characters from the time.

Firsthand Biography A firsthand biography tells about the life (or a period in the life) of someone whom you know personally. Use your close relationship with the person to help you include insights not found in biographies based solely on research.

Short Story Short stories are brief fictional, or made-up, narratives in which a main character faces a conflict that is resolved by the end of the story. In planning a short story, you focus on developing the plot, the setting, and the characters. You must also decide on a point of view: Will your story be told by a character who participates in the action or by someone who describes the action as an outside observer?

Exposition

Exposition is writing that informs or explains. The information you include in expository writing is factual or (when you're expressing an opinion) based on fact.

Your expository writing should reflect a well-thought-out organization—one that includes a clear introduction, body, and conclusion and is appropriate for the type of exposition you are writing. Here are some types of exposition you may be asked to write:

Cause-and-Effect Essay In a cause-and-effect essay, you consider the reasons something did happen or might happen. You may examine several causes of a single effect or several effects of a single cause.

Comparison-and-Contrast Essay When you write a comparison-and-contrast essay, you consider the similarities and differences between two or more subjects. You may organize your essay point by point—moving from one aspect of your subjects to the next—or subject by subject—discussing the qualities of one subject first, and then the qualities of the next subject.

Problem-and-Solution Essay In a problem-and-solution essay, you identify a conflict or problem and offer a resolution. Begin by clearly stating the problem, and follow with a reasoned path to a solution.

How-to Essay A how-to essay provides explicit instructions for accomplishing a specific task. To aid readers, provide background (such as a list of materials) at the beginning of your piece, and then break down the task into smaller, logical steps. Use diagrams, photographs, and other visual aids for clarity.

Consumer Report A consumer report presents up-to-date information and relevant statistical data about one or more products in a given category. You might also rate the product or products you profile, and discuss the advantages or disadvantages of each.

Persuasion

Persuasion is writing or speaking that attempts to convince people to agree with a position or to take a desired action. When used effectively, persuasive writing has the power to change people's lives. As a reader and a writer, you will find yourself engaged in many forms of persuasion. Here are a few of them:

Persuasive Essay In writing a persuasive essay, you build an argument, supporting your opinions with a variety of evidence: facts, statistics, examples, statements from experts. You also anticipate and develop counterarguments to opposing opinions.

Advertisement Advertisements are probably the most common type of persuasion. When you write an advertisement, you present information in an appealing way to make the product or service seem desirable.

Position Paper In a position paper, you try to persuade readers to accept your views on a controversial issue. Most often, your audience will consist of people who have some power to shape policy related to the issue. Your views in a position paper should be supported with evidence.

Persuasive Speech A persuasive speech is a piece of persuasion that you present orally instead of in writing. As a persuasive speaker, you use a variety of techniques, such as repetition of key points, to capture your audience's interest and to add force to your argument.

Editorial An editorial expresses an opinion or a position on a current issue or concern. When you write an editorial, you state and then defend your opinion with logical reasons, facts, examples, and other details.

Research Writing

Writers often use outside research to gather information and explore subjects of interest. The product of that research is called **research writing.** In connection with your reading, you may occasionally be assigned one of the following types of research writing:

Research Paper A research paper uses information gathered from a variety of outside sources to explore a topic. In your research paper, you will usually include an introduction, in which you state your thesis, or main point; a body, in which you present support for the thesis; and a conclusion that summarizes, or restates, your main points. You should credit the sources of information, using footnotes or other types of citation, and include a bibliography, or general list of sources, at the end.

Multimedia Presentation In preparing a multimedia presentation, you will gather and organize information in a variety of media, or means of communication. You may present your information using written materials, slides, videos, audiocassettes, sound effects, art, photographs, models, charts, and diagrams.

Annotated Bibliography An annotated bibliography is a list of materials about a certain topic. For each entry, you must provide source information (title, author, date of publication, etc.), as well as a summary of the material that includes your personal review or comments.

Statistical Report A statistical report uses numbers to support a thesis, or main idea. Before drafting your report, you must first interpret and draw conclusions from the numerical data you've gathered. Then present and support your findings in the report.

Creative Writing

Creative writing blends imagination, ideas, and emotions and allows you to present your own unique view of the world. Poems, plays, short stories, dramas, and even some cartoons are examples of creative writing. Many are found in this anthology; use them as an inspiration to produce your own creative works, such as the following:

Poem In a poem, you use sensory images, figurative language, and sound devices to communicate ideas, tell a story, describe feelings, or create a mood. Using exact and highly charged language will help you convey meaning and create vivid images for your readers.

Drama When you write a drama or a dramatic scene, you are writing a story that is intended to be performed. Since a drama consists largely of the words and actions of the characters, be sure to write dialogue that clearly shows the characters' personalities, emotions, and thoughts, as well as stage directions that convey your ideas about sets, props, sound effects, and the speaking style and movements of the characters.

Monologue A monologue is a speech delivered by a single character. You may create a monologue within the context of a longer drama or as a work to be read or performed in its own right.

Video Script A video script or screenplay is a drama written for television, film, or a video production. In addition to dialogue and stage directions, you must also include detailed stage and camera directions. These instructions indicate the specific actions or effects necessary in telling the story clearly.

Imitation of an Author's Style In this type of creative writing, you take the recognizable elements of an author's style and use them to create your own piece of writing. You may write your imitation in a true attempt to replicate a writer's style or in the spirit of a humorous parody.

Response to Literature

In a **response to literature,** you express your thoughts and feelings about a work and often, in so doing, gain a better understanding of what the work is all about. Your response to literature can take many forms—oral or written, formal or informal. During the course of your reading, you may be asked to respond to a work of literature in one of these forms:

Critical Review In a critical review of a literary work, you discuss various elements in the work and offer opinions about them. You may also give a summary of the work and a recommendation to readers.

Comparative Analysis of Two Literary Works A comparative analysis shows the similarities and differences between several elements—such as characters and plot—of two literary works. You might compare the works on a point-by-point basis or analyze one work before moving on to the next. Use quotations and specific details from the works to support your points.

Response to a Short Story In your response to a short story, you present your reactions to elements of the story—such as the setting, a particular character, or a plot twist—that made a strong impression on you. Include supporting quotations from the story, as well as a brief summary and personal evaluation of the work.

Literary Analysis In a literary analysis, you take a critical look at various important elements in the work. You then attempt to explain how the author has used those elements and how they work together to convey the author's message.

Parody A parody is a piece imitating the style of another work in a humorous or satirical manner. You

can often get a good start on a parody by applying an author's serious style to an inappropriate subject.

Practical and Technical Writing

Practical writing is fact-based writing that people do in the workplace or in their day-to-day lives. Business letters, memos, school forms, and job applications are examples of practical writing. **Technical writing,** which is also based on facts, explains procedures, provides instructions, or presents specialized information. You encounter technical writing every time you read a manual or a set of instructions.

In the following descriptions, you'll find tips for tackling several types of practical and technical writing.

Résumé A résumé is a written summary of your educational background, work experience, and job qualifications presented in a concise, consistent format. Keep your descriptions brief and to the point. A résumé should be limited to one page. Each section should be appropriately labeled. Include a centered heading giving your name, address, and phone number.

Cover and Follow-up Letters Accompany a résumé with a cover letter in which you introduce yourself and briefly explain your qualifications for the position. It's also a good idea to send a brief thank-you letter to follow up an interview. Use proper business letter format for both types of correspondence.

College-Application Essay College applications usually ask for an essay. The question can require a descriptive, narrative, or expository approach. Often, these essays give you the chance to describe an experience that had a profound effect on who you are. Since the point of such essays is to give the college admissions staff a little insight into who you are, make sure that your introduction captures their attention and that your conclusion is memorable. Focus on a subject that is of genuine interest to you. Your own enthusiasm or concern for your subject will help you find words your readers will remember.

Test Essay Good organization is the key to writing an effective essay under test conditions. Adhering to an organizational plan will help you create a coherent essay, even under tight time restrictions. Your introduction should include a thesis statement, a one-sentence summary of your response to the test essay question. Make sure that each paragraph in the body of the essay supports this main idea, and conclude with a restatement of the thesis and a summary of your main points.

GRAMMAR AND MECHANICS HANDBOOK

Summary of Grammar

Nouns A **noun** names a person, place, or thing. A **common noun,** such as *country,* names any one of a class of people, places, or things. A **proper noun,** such as *Great Britain,* names a specific person, place, or thing.

Pronouns Pronouns are words that stand for nouns or for words that take the place of nouns. **Personal pronouns** refer to the person speaking; the person spoken to; or the person, place, or thing spoken about.

	Singular	**Plural**
First Person	I, me, my, mine	we, us, our, ours
Second Person	you, your, yours	you, your, yours
Third Person	he, him, his, she, her, hers, it, its	they, them, their, theirs

A **reflexive pronoun** ends in *-self* or *-selves* and names the person or thing receiving an action when that person or thing is the same as the one performing the action.

> I pray you, school *yourself.* (Shakespeare, p. 334)

An **intensive pronoun** also ends in *-self* or *-selves.* It adds emphasis to a noun or pronoun.

> The raven *himself* is hoarse
> That croaks the fatal entrance of Duncan
> Under my battlements. (Shakespeare, p. 285)

Demonstrative pronouns—such as *this, that, these,* and *those*—single out specific people, places, or things.

A **relative pronoun** begins a subordinate clause and connects it to another idea in the sentence.

> Annoyed, she picked up the letter, *which* bore no stamp. (Bowen, p. 890)

Interrogative pronouns are used to begin questions.

> *Who* casts not up his eye to the sun when it rises? (Donne, p. 394)

Indefinite pronouns refer to people, places, or things, often without specifying which ones.

> *Nought's* had, *all's* spent,
> Where our desire is got without content: . . .
> (Shakespeare, p. 314)

Verbs A **verb** is a word or group of words that expresses an action, a condition, or the fact that something exists, while indicating the time of the action, condition, or fact. An **action verb** tells what action someone or something is performing. An action verb is **transitive** if it directs action toward someone or something named in the same sentence.

> *Gather* ye rosebuds while ye may, . . . (Herrick, p. 416)

An action verb is **intransitive** if it does not direct action toward something or someone named in the same sentence.

> The thought *served* as a challenge. (Woolf, p. 1056)

A **linking verb** expresses its subject's condition by connecting the subject with another word.

> But after some time that order *was* more necessary, . . . (Defoe, p. 470)

Helping verbs are verbs added to another verb to make a single verb phrase. They indicate the time at which an action takes place or whether it actually happens, could happen, or should happen.

> Nothing but an extreme love of truth *could have* hindered me from concealing this part of my story. (Swift, p. 482)

Adjectives An **adjective** is a word used to describe what is named by a noun or pronoun or to give a noun or pronoun a more specific meaning. Adjectives answer these questions:

> What kind? *purple* hat, *happy* face
> Which one? *this* bowl, *those* cameras
> How many? *three* cars, *several* dishes
> How much? *less* attention, *enough* food

The **articles** *the, a,* and *an* are adjectives. *An* is used before a word beginning with a vowel sound. *This, that, these,* and *those* are used as **demonstrative adjectives** when they appear directly before a noun.

> Perhaps he for whom *this* bell tolls may be so ill as that he knows not it tolls for him. . . . (Donne, p. 393)

A noun may sometimes be used as an adjective:

> *language* lesson   *chemistry* book

Adverbs An **adverb** is a word that modifies a verb, an adjective, or another adverb. Adverbs answer the questions *where, when, how,* or *to what extent.*

> She will answer *soon.* (modifies verb *will answer*)
>
> I was *extremely* sad. (modifies adjective *sad*)
>
> You called *more* often than I. (modifies adverb *often*)

Prepositions A **preposition** is a word that relates a noun or pronoun that appears with it to another word in the sentence. It can indicate relations of time, place, causality, responsibility, and motivation. Prepositions are almost always followed by nouns or pronouns.

> *around* the fire   *for* us
>
> *in* sight   *till* sunrise

Conjunctions A conjunction is used to connect other words or groups of words.

Coordinating conjunctions connect similar kinds or groups of words:

> bread *and* wine
>
> brief *but* powerful

Correlative conjunctions are used in pairs to connect similar words or groups of words:

> *both* Luis *and* Rosa
>
> *neither* you *nor* I

Subordinating conjunctions indicate the connection between two ideas by placing one below the other in rank or importance:

> The Count your master's known munificence
> Is ample warrant *that* no one just pretense
> Of mine for dowry will be disallowed; . . .
> (Browning, p. 770)

Interjections An **interjection** is a word or phrase that expresses feeling or emotion and functions independently of a sentence.

> *Ah,* love, let us be true
> To one another! . . . . (Arnold, p. 793)

Sentences A **sentence** is a group of words with a subject and predicate expressing a complete thought.

Phrases A **phrase** is a group of words without a subject and verb that functions as one part of speech. A **prepositional phrase** is a group of words that includes a preposition and a noun or pronoun.

> *before* dawn   *on account of* the rain

An **adjective phrase** is a prepositional phrase that modifies a noun or pronoun.

> The space of sky above us was the color *of ever-changing violet.* . . . (Joyce, p. 1045)

An **adverb phrase** is a prepositional phrase that modifies a verb, an adjective, or an adverb.

> Arsat came *through the doorway with noiseless steps* . . . (Conrad, p. 1037)

An **appositive phrase** is a noun or pronoun with modifiers, placed next to a noun or pronoun to add information and details.

> How soon hath Time, *the subtle thief of youth,*
> Stolen on his wing my three and twentieth year.
> (Milton, p. 432)

A **participial phrase** is a participle that is modified by an adjective or adverb phrase or that has a complement (a group of words that completes the participle's meaning). The entire phrase acts as an adjective.

> The boy gazed at his uncle from those big, hot, blue eyes, *set rather close together.* (Lawrence, p. 1071)

A **gerund** is a noun formed from the present participle of a verb (ending in *-ing*). A **gerund phrase** is a gerund with modifiers or a complement (words that complete its meaning), all acting together as a noun.

> Neither can we call this *a begging of misery* or *a borrowing of misery* . . . (Donne, p. 394)

An **infinitive phrase** is an infinitive with modifiers, complements (words completing its meaning), or a subject, all acting together as a single part of speech.

> . . . let baser things devise To die in dust . . .
> (Spenser, p. 211)

Clauses A **clause** is a group of words with its own subject and verb. An **independent clause** can stand by itself as a complete sentence. A **subordinate clause** cannot stand by itself as a complete sentence.

> Mr. Thomas Davies the actor, *who then kept a bookseller's shop in Russell Street, Covent Garden,* told me that Johnson was very much his friend. . . .
> (Boswell, p. 510)

An **adjective clause** is a subordinate clause that modifies a noun or pronoun by telling *what kind* or *which one.*

> . . . coffins were not to be had for the prodigious numbers *that fell in such a calamity as this.*
> (Defoe, p. 471)

Subordinate adverb clauses modify verbs, adjectives, adverbs, or verbals by telling *where, when, in what way, to what extent, under what condition,* or *why.*

> *As soon as I saw the dead man* I sent an orderly to a friend's house nearby . . . (Orwell, p. 942)

Subordinate noun clauses act as nouns.

> To confirm *what I have now said,* . . . I shall here insert a passage which will hardly obtain belief.
> (Swift, p. 482)

Summary of Capitalization and Punctuation

CAPITALIZATION

Capitalize the first word in sentences, interjections, and complete questions. Also capitalize the first word in a quotation if the quotation is a complete sentence.

> I asked, "What do you want?" (Naipul, p. 1120)

Capitalize all proper nouns and adjectives.

> Trinidadian   Thames River

Capitalize titles showing family relationships when they refer to a specific person unless they are preceded by a possessive noun or pronoun.

> Uncle Oscar   Mangan's sister

Capitalize the first word and all other key words in the titles of books, periodicals, poems, stories, plays, songs, and other works of art.

> *Frankenstein*   "Shooting an Elephant"

PUNCTUATION

End Marks Use a **period** to end a declarative sentence, imperative sentence, an indirect question, and most abbreviations.

> This tale is true, and mine. ("The Seafarer," p. 15)
> Let me not to the marriage of true minds
> Admit impediments. (Shakespeare, p. 222)
> At last she spoke to me. (Joyce, p. 1046)
> Mrs. Drover

Use a **question mark** to end an interrogative sentence or an incomplete question.

> Sent he to Macduff? (Shakespeare, p. 325)
> what ignorance of pain? (Shelley, p. 678)

Use an **exclamation mark** after an exclamatory sentence, a forceful imperative sentence, or an interjection expressing strong emotion.

> "Hold off! unhand me, graybeard loon!"
> (Coleridge, p. 630)

Commas Use a **comma** before the conjunction to separate two independent clauses in a compound sentence.

> My heart aches, and a drowsy numbness pains
> My sense, . . . (Keats, p. 686)

Use commas to separate three or more words, phrases, or clauses in a series.

> Daffodil came in first, Lancelot second, Mirza third. (Lawrence, p. 1072)

Use commas to separate adjectives unless they must stay in a specific order.

> His *big, soft* eyes stared . . . (Conrad, p. 1036)
> And *each slow* dusk a drawing-down of blinds. (Owen, p. 963)

Use a comma after an introductory word, phrase, or clause.

> *When I nodded,* he laughed in a crooked way. (Naipul, p. 1124)

Use commas to set off nonessential expressions.

> "Only you'd have to promise, *honor bright, uncle,* not to let it go beyond us three." (Lawrence, p. 1072)

Use commas with places, dates, and titles.

> Coventry, England
> September 1, 1939
> Reginald Farrars, M. P.

Use commas after items in addresses, after the salutation in a personal letter, after the closing in all letters, and in numbers of more than three digits.

> Hull Crescent, Dorchester
> Dear Randolph,
> Yours faithfully,
> 9,744

Use a comma to indicate words left out of parallel clauses, to set off a direct quotation, and to prevent a sentence from being misunderstood.

> In Tennyson's poetry, I admire the music; in Browning's, the sentiments.
> "Well—I suppose," she said slowly and bitterly, "it's because your father has no luck." (Lawrence, p. 1069)

Semicolons Use a **semicolon** to join independent clauses that are not already joined by a conjunction.

> He had been a very charitable priest; in his will he had left all his money to institutions . . . . (Joyce, p. 1045)

Use semicolons to avoid confusion when independent clauses or items in a series already contain commas.

> The Emperor concluded me to be drowned, and that the enemy's fleet was approaching in a

hostile manner; but he was soon eased of his fears; for, the channel growing shallower every step I made, I came in a short time within hearing, . . . (Swift, p. 479)

Colons   Use a **colon** before a list of items following an independent clause.
> Notable Victorian poets include the following: Tennyson, Browning, Arnold, Housman, and Hopkins.

Use a colon to introduce a formal or lengthy quotation.
> And on the pedestal these words appear:
> "My name is Ozymandias, king of kings: . . ." (Shelley, p. 670)

Use a colon to introduce an independent clause that summarizes or explains the sentence before it.
> The third day of the illness was critical: they were waiting for a change. (Lawrence, p. 1076)

Quotation Marks   A **direct quotation** represents a person's exact speech or thoughts and is enclosed within quotation marks.
> "If I go," I said, "I will bring you something." (Joyce, p. 1046)

An **indirect quotation** reports only the general meaning of what a person said or thought and does not require quotation marks.
> Mother said he never considered me. (Bowen, p. 892)

Always place a comma or a period inside the final quotation mark.
> "We will each write a ghost story," said Lord Byron . . . (Shelley, p. 580)

Always place a question mark or an exclamation mark inside the final quotation mark if the end mark is part of the quotation; if it is not part of the quotation, place it outside the final quotation mark.
> The man said to me, "Sonny, may I come inside your yard?" (Naipul, p. 1120)

Use single quotation marks for a quotation within a quotation.
> "Lying all day on his pillows, . . . and then he says he does not want to live 'like this,'" Rakesh was heard to say . . . . (Desai, p. 1154)

Italicize the titles of long written works, movies, television and radio shows, lengthy works of music, paintings, and sculpture. Also italicize foreign words not yet accepted into English and words you wish to stress.

Underline such titles and words.
> *Howards End*   *60 Minutes*
> *Guernica*   *déjà vu*

Use quotation marks around the titles of short written works, episodes in a series, songs, and titles of works mentioned as parts of collections.
> "The Lagoon"   "Boswell Meets Johnson"

Parentheses   Use **parentheses** to set off asides and explanations only when the material is not essential or when it consists of one or more sentences.

> My eyes were often full of tears (I could not tell why) and at times a flood from my heart seemed to pour itself out into my bosom. (Joyce, p. 1046)

Hyphens   Use a **hyphen** with certain numbers, after certain prefixes, with two or more words used as one word, with a compound modifier, and within a word when a combination of letters might otherwise be confusing.

> twenty-nine   re-create
> pre-Romantic   brother-in-law

Apostrophe   Add an **apostrophe** and an s to show the possessive case of most singular nouns and of plural nouns that do not end in -s or -es.

> Blake's poems   the mice's whiskers

Add an apostrophe to show the possessive case of plural nouns ending in -s and -es.
> the girls' songs   the Ortizes' car

Use an apostrophe in a contraction to indicate the position of the missing letter or letters.
> His English was so good, it *didn't* seem natural. . . . (Naipul, p. 1120)

Use an apostrophe and an -s to write the plurals of numbers, symbols, letters, and words used to name themselves.
> the 1890's   no *if*'s or *but*'s
> five *a*'s

Glossary of Common Usage

among, between

Among is generally used with three or more items. *Between* is generally used with only two items.

> *Among* Chaucer's characters, my favorite has always been the Wife of Bath.

> The ballad "Get Up and Bar the Door" consists largely of a dialogue *between* a man and his wife.

amount, number

Amount refers to quantity or a unit, whereas *number* refers to individual items that can be counted. *Amount* generally appears with a singular noun, and *number* appears with a plural noun.

> The *amount* of attention that great writers have paid to the Faust legend is remarkable.

> A considerable *number* of important English writers have been fascinated by the legend of King Arthur.

as, because, like, as to

To avoid confusion, use *because* rather than *as* when you want to indicate cause and effect.

> *Because* the narrator of Joyce's "Araby" is infatuated with Mangan's sister, he cannot see that he is driven by vanity.

Do not use the preposition *like* to introduce a clause that requires the conjunction *as*.

> *As* we might expect in a story by Joseph Conrad, there are two narrators in "The Lagoon."

The use of *as to* for *about* is awkward and should be avoided.

bad, badly

Use the predicate adjective *bad* after linking verbs such as *feel*, *look*, and *seem*. Use *badly* when an adverb is required.

> In "My Last Duchess," the Duke of Ferrara does not seem to feel *bad* about the death of his wife.

> The announcement of Lady Macbeth's death *badly* unnerves Macbeth.

because of, due to

Use *due to* if it can logically replace the phrase *caused by*. In introductory phrases, however, *because of* is better usage than *due to*.

> The classical allusions in *Paradise Lost* may be *due to* the poet's ambition to imitate the epics of Homer and Virgil.

> *Because of* the expansion of the reading public, eighteenth-century writers became less dependent on wealthy patrons.

compare, contrast

The verb *compare* can involve both similarities and differences. The verb *contrast* always involves differences. Use *to* or *with* after compare. Use *with* after contrast.

> Denise's report compared Shelley's style in "To a Skylark" *with* that of Keats in "Ode to a Nightingale."

> In Conrad's "The Lagoon," Arsat's point of view in the narration of his "story within a story" contrasts *with* the more detached, third-person point of view that the author uses for the rest of the tale.

continual, continuous

Continual means "occurring again and again in succession," while *continuous* means "occurring without interruption."

> In "The Seafarer" the speaker describes *continual* hailstorms at sea.

> The white-hot fervor of "Ode to the West Wind" suggests that Shelley wrote the poem in a single *continuous* burst of inspiration.

different from, different than

The preferred usage is *different from*.

> In its simple, precise language, Housman's style is *different from* that of many other Victorian poets, including Tennyson and Hopkins.

farther, further

Use *farther* when you refer to distance. Use *further* when you mean "to a greater degree" or "additional."

> Although the sexton tries to persuade him to go no *farther*, Defoe is determined to enter the churchyard.

> Boswell *further* illustrates Johnson's conversation by quoting his opinions of Sheridan and Derrick.

fewer, less

Use *fewer* for things that can be counted. Use *less* for amounts or quantities that cannot be counted.

> Wordsworth uses *fewer* end-stopped lines than Pope does.

> At the beginning of Luke's parable, the prodigal son shows *less* respect for the father than the older son does.

just, only

Only should appear directly before the word it modifies. *Just,* used as an adverb meaning "no more than," also belongs directly before the word it modifies.

> The form of the villanelle allows a poet to use *just* two rhymes.

> John Keats was *only* twenty-four when he wrote some of his greatest poems.

lay, lie

Lay is a transitive verb meaning "to set or put something down." Its principal parts are *lay, laying, laid, laid. Lie* is an intransitive verb meaning "to recline." Its principal parts are *lie, lying, lay, lain.*

> Coleridge implies that the mariner's reckless act of killing the albatross *lays* a curse on the crew.

> As Paul *lies* dead at the end of D. H. Lawrence's story, his Uncle Oscar sadly comments that the boy may be better off.

plurals that do not end in -s

The plurals of certain nouns from Greek and Latin are formed as they were in their original language. Words such as *data, criteria, media,* and *phenomena* are plural and should be treated as such. Each has its own distinctive singular form: *datum, criterion, medium, phenomenon.*

> Are the electronic *media* of the twentieth century contributing to the death of literature?

raise, rise

Raise is a transitive verb that usually takes a direct object. *Rise* is intransitive and never takes a direct object.

> In "Musée des Beaux Arts," W. H. Auden *raises* the question of our insensitivity to suffering.

> In Tennyson's poem, when Lancelot passes, the Lady of Shallot *rises* from her loom and paces.

that, which, who

Use the relative pronoun *that* to refer to things or people. Use *which* only for things and *who* only for people. Use *that* when introducing a subordinate clause that singles out a particular thing or person.

> The contemporary poet *that* I most enjoy reading is James Berry.

Which is usually used to introduce a subordinate clause that is not essential to identifying the thing or person in question:

> "Fern Hill," *which* reflects Dylan Thomas's brilliant ability to evoke emotional response, plays on the connotations of words.

Who can be used to introduce either essential or nonessential subordinate clauses:

> Two writers *who* helped redefine the essay are Addison and Steele. (essential)

> Addison and Steele, *who* were close friends for most of their lives, had very different personalities and careers. (nonessential)

when, where

Do not directly follow a linking verb with *when* or *where.* Also be careful not to use *where* when your context requires *that.*

> Evaluation is ~~when you make~~ *the process of making* a judgment about the quality or value of something.

> Sandy read ~~where~~ *that* after the Brownings eloped to Italy, they spent most of their married life in Florence.

who, whom

Remember to use *who* only as a subject in clauses and sentences and *whom* only as an object.

> V. S. Naipul, *who* wrote "B. Wordsworth," has also written some well-received novels.

> V. S. Naipaul, *whom* many critics have praised as one of the best contemporary writers in English, was born and raised in Trinidad.

SPEAKING, LISTENING, AND VIEWING HANDBOOK

You use many different forms of communication every day. The literature in this book is written, which is one way to communicate, but most of your communication is probably oral, which involves speaking, listening, and viewing, usually in face-to-face situations.

Communication

You use oral and visual communication in ordinary conversation as well as in class discussions, speeches, interviews, debates, and other presentations and performances. Having strong communication skills will benefit you both in and out of school.

Many assignments accompanying the literature in this textbook involve speaking, listening, and viewing skills. The following terms will give you a better understanding of the many elements that are a part of communication.

ARTICULATION is the process of forming sounds into words by using the tongue, teeth, lower jaw, and soft palate to produce speech sounds.

AUDIENCE Your audience is the person or persons to whom you direct your message. An audience can be a group of people sitting in a classroom observing a performance or just one person to whom you address a comment. When preparing for any speaking situation, analyze your audience so you can tailor your message to their background, interests, and attitudes.

BODY LANGUAGE refers to the use of facial expressions, eye contact, gestures, posture, and movement to communicate a feeling or an idea.

CONNOTATION is the set of associations a word calls to mind. The connotations of the words you choose influence the message you send. For example, most people respond more favorably to being described as "slim" rather than as "skinny." The connotation of *slim* is more appealing than that of *skinny.*

EYE CONTACT is direct visual contact with another person's eyes.

FEEDBACK is the set of verbal and nonverbal reactions that indicate to a speaker that a message has been received and understood.

GESTURES are the movements made with arms, hands, face, and fingers to communicate.

INFLECTION refers to the rise and fall in the pitch of the voice in speaking; it is also called **intonation.**

LISTENING is understanding and interpreting sound in a meaningful way. You listen differently for different purposes.

Listening for key information: For example, when a teacher gives an assignment or when someone gives you directions to a place, you listen for key information.

Listening for main points: In a classroom exchange of ideas or information or while watching a television documentary, you listen for main points.

Listening critically: When you evaluate a performance, song, or a persuasive or political speech, you listen critically, questioning and judging the speaker's message.

NONVERBAL COMMUNICATION is communication without the use of words. People communicate nonverbally through gestures, facial expressions, posture, and body movements. Sign language is an entire language based on nonverbal communication.

PROJECTION is speaking in such a way that the voice carries clearly to an audience. It's important to project your voice when speaking in a large space like a classroom or an auditorium.

VOCAL DELIVERY is the way in which you present a message. Your vocal delivery involves all of the following elements:

Volume: the loudness or quietness of your voice
Pitch: the high or low quality of your voice
Rate: the speed at which you speak; also called pace
Stress: the amount of emphasis placed on different syllables in a word or on different words in a sentence

All of these elements individually and in combination contribute to the meaning of a spoken message.

Speaking, Listening, and Viewing Situations

The following terms apply to speaking, listening, and viewing situations:

DEBATE is a formal event in which participants prepare and present arguments on opposing sides of a question, stated as a **proposition.** The proposition must be controversial: It must concern an issue on which there are two serious positions.

The two sides in a debate are the *affirmative* (pro) and the *negative* (con). The affirmative side begins the debate. The opposing sides take turns presenting their arguments, and each side has an opportunity for *rebuttal,* in which they may challenge or question the other side's argument.

DOCUMENTARY is a TV program or a film that dramatically presents or analyzes people, places, events, or ideas in a factual way.

INTERVIEW is a form of interaction in which one person, the interviewer, asks questions of another person, the interviewee. Interviews may take place for many purposes: to obtain information, to discover a person's suitability for a job or a college, or to inform the public of a notable person's opinions.

MEDIA PRESENTATION provides current news and entertainment by means of radio, TV, films, videos, the Internet, newspapers, or news magazines.

ORAL INTERPRETATION is the reading or speaking of a work of literature aloud for an audience. Oral interpretation involves giving expression to the ideas, meaning, or even the structure of a work of literature. The speaker interprets the work through his or her vocal delivery. **Storytelling,** in which a speaker reads or tells a story, is a form of oral interpretation.

PANEL DISCUSSION is a group discussion on a topic of interest common to all members of a panel and to a listening audience. A panel is usually composed of four to six experts on a particular topic who are brought together to share information and opinions.

PARLIAMENTARY PROCEDURE refers to the set of rules used to conduct a meeting in an orderly manner. Parliamentary procedure makes discussions at meetings more efficient and productive and protects the rights of individuals attending the meeting.

All of the business conducted according to parliamentary procedure is handled through motions. **Motions** are proposals for action made by participants.

For example, besides main motions that set forth the items of business that will be considered, a motion can be made to adjourn (end the meeting) or to amend (alter the wording of) another motion.

The following are the main principles of parliamentary procedure:

1. Only one item of business may be considered at a time.
2. Everyone has a right to express an opinion.
3. Every member of the group has the right to vote, and each vote is counted as equal.
4. The group follows the decision of the majority.

PERFORMANCE ELEMENTS combine to make a literary or dramatic presentation, a persuasive speech, oral report, or other performance. Elements such as delivery, visual representation, intonation, organization, imagery, and language are all part of a performance.

ROLE-PLAY is the acting out of a part in a given situation, speaking, acting, and responding in the manner of a particular person or character.

SPECIAL EFFECTS are artificial sounds or images that create realistic or fantastic effects in films, videos, or TV shows.

SPEECH is a talk or an address given to an audience. A speech may be **impromptu**—delivered on the spur of the moment with no preparation—or formally prepared and delivered for a specific purpose or occasion.

- *Purposes:* The most common purposes of speeches are to persuade, to entertain, to explain, and to inform.
- *Occasions:* The following are common occasions for speeches:

    Introduction: Introducing a speaker or presenter at a meeting or assembly

    Presentation: Giving an award or acknowledging the contributions of someone

    Acceptance: Accepting an award or a tribute

    Keynote: Giving an inspirational address at a large meeting or convention

    Commencement: A celebration honoring the graduates of a school or university

RESEARCH HANDBOOK

Many of the assignments and activities in this literature book require you to find out more about your topic. Whenever you need ideas, details, or information, you must conduct research. You can find information by using library resources and computer resources, as well as by interviewing experts in a field.

Before you begin, create a research plan that lists the questions you want answered about your topic. Then decide which sources will best provide answers to those questions. When gathering information, it is important to use a variety of sources and not to rely on one main source of information. It is also important to document where you find different pieces of information you use so that you can cite those sources in your work.

The suggestions that follow can help you locate your sources.

Library Resources

Libraries contain many sources of information in both print and electronic form. You'll save time if you plan your research before actually going to the library. Make a list of the information you think you will need, and for each item list possible sources for the information. Here are some sources to consider:

NONFICTION BOOKS An excellent starting point for researching your topic, nonfiction books can provide either broad coverage or specific details, depending on the book. To find appropriate nonfiction books, use the library catalog, which may be in card files or in electronic form on computers. In either case, you can search by author, title, or subject; in a computer catalog, you can also search by key word. When you find the listing for a book you want, print it out or copy down the title, author, and call number. The call number, which also appears on the book's spine, will help you locate the book in the library.

NEWSPAPERS AND MAGAZINES Books are often not the best places for finding up-to-the-minute information. Instead, you might try newspapers and magazines. To find information about an event that occurred on a specific date, go directly to newspapers and magazines for that date. To find articles on a particular topic, use indexes like the *Readers' Guide to Periodical Literature*, which lists magazine articles under subject headings. For each article that you want, jot down the title, author (if given), page number or numbers, and the name and date of the magazine in which the article appears. If your library does not have the magazine you need, either as a separate issue or on microfilm, you may still be able to obtain photocopies of the article through an interlibrary loan.

REFERENCE WORKS The following important reference materials can also help you with your research.

- *General encyclopedias* have articles on thousands of topics and are a good starting point for your research, although they shouldn't be used as primary sources.
- *Specialized encyclopedias* contain articles in particular subject areas, such as science, music, or art.
- *Biographical dictionaries and indexes* contain brief articles on people and often suggest where to find more information.
- *Almanacs* provide statistics and data on current events and act as a calendar for the upcoming year.
- *Atlases*, or books of maps, usually include geographical facts and may also include information like population and weather statistics.
- *Indexes and bibliographies*, such as the *Readers' Guide to Periodical Literature*, tell you in what publications you can find specific information, articles, or shorter works (such as poems or essays).
- *Vertical files* (drawers in file cabinets) hold pamphlets, booklets, and government publications that often provide current information.

Computer Research

The Internet Use the Internet to get up-to-the-minute information on virtually any topic. The Internet provides access to a multitude of resource-rich sources such as news media, museums, colleges and universities, and government institutions. There are a number of indexes and directories organized by subject to help you locate information on the Internet, including Yahoo!, the World Wide Web Virtual Library, the Kids Web, and the Webcrawler. These indexes and directories will help you find direct links to information related to your topic.

Internet Sources and Addresses

- *Yahoo! Directory* allows you to do word searches or link directly to your topic by clicking on such subjects as the arts, computers, entertainment, or government.
  http://www.yahoo.com
- *World Wide Web Virtual Library* is a comprehensive and easy-to-use subject catalog that provides direct links to academic subjects in alphabetical order.
  http://celtic.stanford.edu/vlib/Overview.html
- *Kids Web* supplies links to reference materials, such as dictionaries, *Bartlett's Familiar Quotations*, a thesaurus, and a world fact book.
  http://www.npac.syr.edu/textbook/kidsweb/
- *Webcrawler* helps you to find links to information about your topic that are available on the Internet when you type in a concise term or key word.
  http://www.webcrawler.com

CD-ROM References

Other sources that you can access using a computer are available on CD-ROM. The Wilson Disk, Newsquest, the *Readers' Guide to Periodical Literature,* and many other useful indexes are available on CD-ROM, as are encyclopedias, almanacs, atlases, and other reference works. Check your library to see which are available.

Interviews as Research Sources

People who are experts in their field or who have experience or knowledge relevant to your topic are excellent sources for your research. If such people are available to you, the way to obtain information from them is through an interview. Follow these guidelines to make your interview successful and productive:

- Make an appointment at a time convenient to the person you want to interview, and arrange to meet in a place where he or she will feel comfortable talking freely.
- If necessary, do research in advance to help you prepare the questions you will ask.
- Before the interview, list the questions you will ask, wording them so that they encourage specific answers. Avoid questions that can be answered simply with *yes* or *no.*
- Make an audiotape or videotape of the interview

if possible. If not, write down the answers as accurately as you can.
- Include the date of the interview at the top of your notes or on the tape.
- Follow up with a thank-you note or phone call to the person you interviewed.

Sources for a Multimedia Presentation

When preparing a multimedia presentation, keep in mind that you'll need to use some of your research findings to illustrate or support your main ideas when you actually give the presentation. Do research to find media support, such as visuals, CD's, and so on—in addition to those media you might create yourself. Here are some media that may be useful as both sources and illustrations:

- Musical recordings on audiocassette or compact disc (CD), often available at libraries
- Videos that you prepare yourself
- Fine art reproductions, often available at libraries and museums
- Photographs that you or others have taken
- Computer presentations using slide shows, graphics, and so on
- Video or audiocassette recordings of interviews that you conduct.

Crediting Sources

Whatever form you use to present your research results, remember to credit your sources for any ideas you use that are not common knowledge and are not your own. In addition, be sure that you acknowledge passages or distinctive phrases that come from a source. In written work, credit others' ideas or words with footnotes, endnotes, or parenthetical notes.

Failure to credit sources properly is **plagiarism,** the presenting of someone else's words or ideas as your own. Plagiarism is a form of stealing. Words and ideas may not seem as tangible as physical property, but they are forms of intellectual property. As you know from your own experience, it takes hard work to formulate a new idea or to find just the right phrase to describe something. Acknowledge this work.

COLLEGE AND CAREER HANDBOOK

BEYOND GRADUATION

Deciding what to do after high school is one of the most important decisions of your life. You probably have definite ideas about what you are interested in and whether you would like to pursue a college education or enter the job market. The challenge you face is getting admitted to the right college or landing the right job. The following tips can help you prepare for life after high school.

Tips for the College-Bound

CHOOSING A COLLEGE

To create a list of schools to which to apply, narrow your choices step by step. You will find helpful information in guidebooks such as *Barron's, Lovejoy's,* and *Peterson's.* Make an appointment with your guidance counselor to match your interests and high-school record with the most likely college choices. Draw up a list of schools, and then start narrowing them down.

Step 1: Identify Your Options

• *Be realistic.* Focus on schools that are in the range of competitiveness—and expense—suited to you.

If you are in the top quarter of your high-school class and have combined SAT scores of at least 1,000 or ACT scores starting at 25, you have a good chance of being accepted at a very selective college. If your scores and standing are lower, you would do better to focus your application efforts on less selective schools.

• *Identify a "safety" school.* The college admissions process is affected by many factors, and schools turn down many qualified candidates. To ensure that you can start college when you would like, apply to at least one less competitive school.

• *Identify a "wish list" school.* Even if your academic performance is not outstanding, you may have other assets that a highly competitive school finds valuable. Apply to a "wish list" school that you would enjoy attending if you were accepted.

Step 2: Identify Your Needs

• *Special interests* Not every college has the same academic strengths. If you think you might specialize in a particular field, look for schools with a strong department in that field.

• *General experience* Consider the kind of life a college can offer you. Will you be happier amid the bustle of a large university in a big city or the intimate atmosphere of a small college in a quiet town? Do you want to live in a dorm or off campus? Keep your answers to these questions in mind as you narrow your list.

Step 3: Evaluate Your Choices

Once you have narrowed your list down to about half a dozen choices, write or call the admissions office of each school to request an application and catalog. The catalogs, along with the college guidebooks you consult, will give you the information you need to evaluate your choices. In addition to general rankings of colleges, pay attention to the following:

• *Facilities* Consider the athletic facilities, computer labs, libraries, and other facilities at the school. What hours are they open? How up to date are they?

• *Special areas of study* If you are interested in a special area of study, find out the size of the department in that area. What degrees do the teachers have? What courses are required to major in that area?

Step 4: Do a Reality Check

After you have looked through the catalogs of promising schools, consider visiting them.

• *Visit when school is in session.* Pick up the school newspaper, look at the bulletin boards, talk to students in the cafeteria. Are there activities on campus in which you are interested? Do you think you will fit in with the other students? If there is a special subject you are interested in, speak to one of the professors teaching in that area, and sit in on a class.

• *Speak to alumni.* Talk to alumni—graduates of the school—about their experiences. The school may be able to provide the names of alumni in your area.

APPLYING TO COLLEGES

The College Application

There are usually two parts to a college application. The first includes basic questions about who you are, with special attention to your educational background and outside interests. Keep your answers to these questions accurate, specific, and clear.

The essay portion of the application often asks you to describe an experience that played an important role in shaping your character. To help your essay stay in the reader's mind, write from your heart—from what interests or excites you.

It's a good idea to make a photocopy of the blank application and draft your answers on the photocopy. Save the original for your final draft.

For more tips, see the Writing Process Workshop on the College-Application Essay on page 135.

Interviewing

An interview with a school representative is a good chance for you to learn more about the school, as well as to make a good impression. Expect questions about your in-school and extracurricular interests and activities, your strengths and weaknesses (both academic and personal), and what makes you a good candidate for admission.

Recommendations

Written recommendations are a required part of your application. Look to family friends, co-workers, and community leaders as well as teachers for recommendations. People are often happy to write on behalf of others. Indicate to your recommendation writers what qualities, interests, or accomplishments of yours you feel are worth emphasizing.

SUCCESS IN COLLEGE

Once you have chosen and been accepted by a college, you face a new challenge—surviving the next four years. The following two tips may help you orient yourself in your new life.

- *Get the most out of your classes.* Arrive to class on time, prepared to participate actively. Consistent lateness is a sign of disrespect, and participation is often weighed as part of your grade.

Getting the most out of class also means meeting with your instructors during their office hours or by appointment to clarify difficult concepts, to get project ideas approved, and to resolve any questions you may have about your grades.

- *Manage your time.* At college, you will have large amounts of time that you must manage for yourself. Maintain a weekly schedule. Note which activities in your routine cannot change, and then plan your study and social time around them.

Many college courses require long-term assignments. Keep a calendar on which you mark the due date for each paper or project. Begin researching your topic choices early on.

A schedule should not imprison you; rather, it should give your life a healthy rhythm. Leave enough time open to stay flexible. Successful scheduling will help you avoid long periods of little work followed by frantic "all-nighters"—an unnecessary source of stress.

Tips for a Career Search

You may decide that you want to move directly into the job market after high school. Your first step is to identify your skills and interests and try to match them to an appropriate job. For example, if you have excellent interpersonal skills, don't apply for a job that will keep you alone in an office doing paperwork.

FINDING WORK

- *Check job listings.* The "Help Wanted" section of a newspaper is a good place to start. If you want to move, call the papers in the area you are considering and ask if they will send you copies of their want ads. Some towns sponsor career centers that post information about jobs. You may want to find out more about training programs that are available for specific kinds of work, such as computer support or clerical jobs.

- *Send out your résumé to companies in your field.* Even if they have no job openings when they receive your résumé, businesses may keep it on file for a period of time and contact candidates when an opportunity does arise.

- *Network.* Many people report that they got their jobs by talking to a neighbor, a family friend, a person for whom they caddied on the golf course, a teacher, or a business associate of their mother's—a person who knew someone in the business.

Make a list of people you can contact. Call them and let them know that you are looking for a job of a particular sort. Ask if they know of anyone in that line of work and if they would be willing to give you that person's name and number. When you call these new contacts, mention the name of the person who gave you their name and explain your reason for calling. Even though you are a stranger, the person you call may be helpful.

ASSEMBLING THE RÉSUMÉ

Assembling a polished, professional résumé and cover letter is the most important part of your job search. The following tips can help:

- *Limit your résumé to one page.* Employers must review hundreds of résumés and will not have time to read lengthy documents.

- *Format your résumé.* Allow employers to find important facts easily. Use boldface, capitalization, bullets, underlining and other devices to highlight your résumé's organization. For professional effect, though, do not use different typefaces or sizes.

- *Clearly indicate the contents.* Your résumé should begin with a heading, centered in the middle of the top of the page, and should include your name, address, and phone number near the top. It should also include the following sections, each with an appropriate label:

Objective: In a single phrase, let your prospective employer know what position interests you.

Employment history: List jobs and the dates you held them. Include a description of the responsibilities that you held in each position, emphasizing those that would make you an excellent candidate for the new job.

Education: Include your educational history up to this point. List any special training you have received that would make you a desirable candidate for the position for which you are applying.

Skills and talents; clubs and organizations: List any additional skills that may be helpful in the new job, such as computer knowledge or fluency in a language. Your membership in clubs and other organizations indicates social skills and an ability to work well with people.

For more tips, see the Writing Process Workshop on the Job Portfolio, on page 730.

WRITING THE COVER LETTER

A cover letter, tailored to the specific job for which you are applying, should accompany each résumé you send out. It should be as brief as possible; the recipient can read the enclosed résumé for more details. If possible, find out who will be reviewing your résumé and address the letter to that person.

- *Use a standard business letter form.* The body of your letter may be divided as follows:

First paragraph: The letter should start by explaining how you came to apply for a job with that particular company. If you are answering an ad, refer to its place and date of appearance. If you are sending out résumés "cold," explain how the company came to your attention.

Second paragraph: The next paragraph should briefly and forcefully explain how your experience, qualities, and skills fit the employer's needs.

Third paragraph: In the third and last paragraph, thank the reader, note that you are available for an interview at his or her convenience, and mention that you look forward to a meeting.

For more tips, see the Writing Process Workshop on the Job Portfolio, on page 730.

PREPARING FOR THE INTERVIEW

Once you get an appointment for an interview, prepare yourself with answers and questions for your interviewer.

- *Practice answering questions.* Your interviewer will ask about your work experience, skills and talents, strengths and weaknesses, and desire for the job. Practice answering such questions with a friend.

- *List questions you want to ask.* Asking questions based on your knowledge of the company shows your interest in the job.

- *Dress appropriately.* Arrive neatly groomed.

- *Speak clearly, politely, grammatically, and loudly enough to be heard.* If you are asked an unexpected question, relax and give yourself time to think.

After your interview, write your interviewer a follow-up letter mentioning that you enjoyed your conversation and thanking him or her for the opportunity.

For more tips, see the Speaking, Listening, and Viewing Workshop on Handling a Job Interview, on page 734.

INDEX OF AUTHORS AND TITLES

Page numbers in *italics* refer to biographical information.

INDEX OF SKILLS

GRAMMAR AND STYLE

WRITING

Writing Opportunities

Writing Skills

Town crier, 473
Visual presentation, 63, 371, 443, 531, 608, 779, 799, 1001, 1026
Visual research, 243
Vocal delivery, elements of, 1237
Weather report, 681

LIFE AND WORK SKILLS

Advertisements, evaluating, 191
Bias in writing, identifying, 458
Career Link, 23, 70, 155, 169
College-application essay, 135
Consumer reports, reading of, 818
Contracts, evaluating, 234
Following written directions, 375, 1030
Heads and text structure, 1171
Historical accounts, evaluating, 733
Identifying main ideas, 788
Information sources, evaluation of, 74
Instructions, reading of, 1030
Internet, evaluating information on, 956
Job application, 138
Job interview, 734
Main ideas in article, 788
Manuals, reading of, 1092
Political persuasion, evaluation of, 262
Reading an application, 138
Reading novels and extended works, 844
Reading rate, 871
Reading for specific information, 612
Reading visual information, 542
Résumé, 163, 187, 730, 731
Speech-making, 974
Visual cues, 702
Writer's purpose, judging, 428

BACKGROUND FOR UNDERSTANDING

Culture
Anglo-Irish relations, 1032
Desai's portrait of India, old and new, 1146
Elizabethan ideas of design and order, 206
Malay setting, 1032
Meaning of exile, 12
Naipaul's experience as resident in British colony, 1118
Perils of everyday life, in Middle Ages, 164
Newspapers and magazines, 544
Robert Burns's use of language, 586
Role of women, 714
Sillitoe's setting, the coal-mining life, 982
Systematizing knowledge, 502
Wealth and social status, 1066
Yeats's ideas about civilization and culture, 896
History
Aftermath of the Civil War, 444
Bowen in London during the Blitz, 886
Churchill and World War II, 970
Dickens and utilitarianism, 820
Donne and the system of patronage, 390
Fight to preserve learning, 76
Gandhi and British policy, 970
Gordimer, colonialism, and apartheid, 1128
Heaney in context of Northern Ireland, 1002
Impact of Bible, 244
Influence of ancient Greece on Keats's poetry, 682
Legends of King Arthur, 140
Lessing and the British household in Rhodesia, 1012
Milton's epic response to conflict, 430
More, Elizabeth I, and religious conflict, 236

George Orwell, an English policeman in Burma, 936
Paganism and Christianity, 38
Pilgrimages, 86
Political uncertainty, 164
Reform in Britain, 704
Spark's allusions to World War I, 1052
Swift's targets for satire, 474
Timeline of space exploration, 1158
Tribute to the King, A, 270
Trouble in Ireland, 992
Twin disasters, 460
Walcott, Berry, and the British empire, 1136
Wordsworth, the French Revolution, and Romanticism, 614
World War I, 958
Humanities
Blake as an artist, 596
Nature in Romantic poetry and art, 668
Language, word play and wit, 412
Literature
Auden circle—the world as poetic inspiration, 922
Brontë's Romanticism; Hardy's naturalism, 846
Browning legend, 766
Byronic hero, 656
Coleridge's Dreamscapes, 628
Daylight of reason, nighttime of feeling, 518
Eliot's allusions, 908
Gerard Manley Hopkins, from obscurity to fame, 856
Shakespeare's sources, 270
Shelley, Frankenstein, and the Prometheus myth, 576
Sons of Ben, 404
Story behind the poem, 486
Story behind Shakespeare's sonnets, 218
Tennyson's sources of inspiration, 748
Thomas, Hughes, and writers' attitudes toward nature, 1094
Science
Body language, 1110
Progress and potatoes, 800

RESEARCHING AND REPRESENTING

Art exhibition, 935
Art presentation, 681, 1135
Biographical report, 411, 779, 855, 863, 947
Book cover design, 1021
Brain study, 531
Byzantium display, 907
Caribbean festival, 1145
Caricature, 835
Charter/constitution, 538
Collage, 230, 454, 655
Comic book, mock-heroic, 129
Comic strip, 595
Conflict resolution, with multimedia presentation, 814
Costume design, 308
Cross-cultural survey, 1157
Dance, modern, 921
Diagram, 517
and tour, 85
Drawing of group, 411
Ecological material, Romantic elements of, 627
Elizabethan fashions, 225
Elizabethan music, 225
Evening newscast, 85
Exhibit, 1127
Family background, 935
Fashion design, 1127

Film review, 243, 799, 1117, 1167
Films
about Brownings, 779
about leaders, 981
about Orwell, 947
about Poe, 608
First-person biography, 517
Freudian psychology and fiction, 1065
Geometric principles, applied to short story, 1088
Glossary of classical terms, 501
Greek mask, 371
Help Wanted page, 27
Historical account, 729
Historical background, report on, 230, 627, 835, 952, 969, 991, 1011, 1145
Holidays chart, 179
Illuminated manuscript, 163
Illustration, 443, 603
Imagism, 921
Irish festival, 1001
Irish folk music, 1011
Magazine article, compared to past article, 809
Magazines, 553
Map, 32, 129, 187, 403, 473
Model, of Book of Sand, 1088
Multimedia presentation, 63, 595, 814, 863, 867
travelogue, 1083
Museum catalog, 693
Museum exhibit, 1167
Newsletter, 557
Nighttime walk, 531
Novelist, study of, 840
Observation Journal, 681
Opera, analysis of, 363
Pantomime of poem, 1117
Past glory, report on lesser-known person, 867
Poem
illustrating a poem, 603
setting to music, 713
writing music for, 667
Poetry reading, 784
Poets, laureateship, 1109
Political cartoon, 713
Portfolio, 1001
Portrait, 27, 110, 667, 723, 895
Poster, 451, 1051
Recordings of Dylan Thomas, 1109
Research project, 655, 907, 1065
royal family tree, 134
Research report, 443, 451, 485, 501, 603, 681, 698, 809, 895, 921, 969, 981, 991, 1021, 1051, 1065, 1135, 1145, 1157
Retelling, 1135
Satire, with illustrations, 485
Satirical cartoon, 553
Scale model, 179
Science display, 693
Scientific paper, 215
Scientific research, 585
Script and performance, 991
Sculpture, 63, 403
Set design, 363, 585, 765
Social organization, learning about, 1026
Social research, 1083
Song, 251, 419, 713
Tennyson, taped recording of, 765
Time experiment, 424
Timeline, 32, 243, 473, 723, 855, 907, 969
Tour of a Castle, 799
Visual history, 258
Visual sonnet, 215
Wedding plan, 419

ACKNOWLEDGMENTS (continued)

Carol Publishing Group

"The Lorelei" by Heinrich Heine from *The Poetry and Prose of Heinrich Heine,* edited by Frederic Ewen. Copyright © 1948, 1976 by The Citadel Press. Used by arrangement with Carol Publishing Group.

Cassell PLC

"Be Ye Men of Valor" (retitled Wartime Speech), BBC, London, May 19, 1940, from *Blood, Toil, Tears and Sweat: The Speeches of Winston Churchill* edited and with an Introduction by David Cannadine. Speeches Copyright © 1989 by Winston Churchill, MP. All rights reserved.

Darhansoff & Verrill Literary Agency

"Everything Is Plundered" by Anna Akhmatova from *Poems of Akhmatova,* selected, translated and introduced by Stanley Kunitz and Max Hayward. Copyright © 1967, 1968, 1972, 1973 by Stanley Kunitz and Max Hayward. Reprinted by permission of Darhansoff & Verrill Literary Agency.

Doubleday & Company, Inc.

"The Tyger" by William Blake from *The Poetry and Prose of William Blake,* edited by David V. Erdman, published by Doubleday & Company, Inc. "The Lagoon" from *Tales of Unrest* by Joseph Conrad (Doubleday, Page & Company). Reprinted by permission of Doubleday & Company, Inc. "Poverty's child" and "Clouds come from time to time" by Bashō, translated by Harold G. Henderson, from *An Introduction to Haiku* by Harold G. Henderson. Copyright © 1958 by Harold G. Henderson. Used by permission of Doubleday, a division of Bantam Doubleday Dell Publishing Group, Inc.

Dutton Signet, a division of Penguin Books USA Inc.

"The Book of Sand," from *The Book of Sand,* by Jorge Luis Borges, translated by Norman Thomas di Giovanni. Translation copyright © 1971, 1975, 1976, 1977 by Emece Editores, S.A., and Norman Thomas di Giovanni. From *Beowulf* by Burton Raffel, translator. Translation copyright © 1963 by Burton Raffel, Afterword © 1963 by New American Library. Used by permission of Dutton Signet, a division of Penguin Books USA Inc.

Faber and Faber Ltd.

"The Horses" from *New Selected Poems* by Ted Hughes. Copyright © 1957, 1960 by Ted Hughes. Published in the UK in *The Hawk in the Rain* by Ted Hughes. "The Rain Horse" by Ted Hughes from *Wodwo.* Copyright © 1967. Reprinted by permission of Faber and Faber Ltd.

Faber and Faber Ltd. and Random House, Inc.

"Not Palaces" by Stephen Spender. In the UK, from *Collected Poems 1928–1985.* Copyright © 1986 by Stephen Spender. In the US, from *Collected Poems 1928–1953* by Stephen Spender. Copyright 1934 by The Modern Library, Inc. and renewed 1962 by Stephen Spender. Reprinted by permission of Faber and Faber Ltd., and Random House, Inc.

Faber and Faber Ltd. for Seamus Heaney

"The Funeral of Beowulf" from *Beowulf,* lines 3137–3182, translated by Seamus Heaney. Appeared in *The Times Literary Supplement,* 9/19/97, No. 4929, page 4.

Farrar, Straus & Giroux, Inc.

Excerpt from *Omeros* by Derek Walcott. Copyright © 1990 by Derek Walcott. Excerpt from "Midsummer" from *Collected Poems 1948–1984* by Derek Walcott. Copyright © 1986 by Derek Walcott. Excerpt from *Gilgamesh: A New Rendering in English Verse* by David Ferry. Copyright © 1992 by David Ferry. Reprinted by permission of Farrar, Straus & Giroux, Inc.

Farrar, Straus & Giroux, Inc., and Faber and Faber, Ltd.

"The Explosion" and "An Arundel Tomb" from *Collected Poems* by Philip Larkin. Copyright © 1988, 1989 by the Estate of Philip Larkin. "Follower" from *Poems 1965–1975* by Seamus Heaney. Copyright © 1980 by Seamus Heaney. Published in London in *Death of a Naturalist* by Seamus Heaney. "Two Lorries" from *The Spirit Level* by Seamus Heaney. Copyright © 1996 by Seamus Heaney. Reprinted by permission.

Estate of Angel Flores

"Eternity" by Arthur Rimbaud, translated by Francis Golffing, from *An Anthology of French Poetry From Nerval to Valéry in English Translation With French Originals,* edited by Angel Flores. Reprinted by permission of the Estate of Angel Flores.

Fourth Estate Ltd.

"The Rights We Enjoy, the Duties We Owe" reprinted by permission of Fourth Estate Ltd. from *New Britain: My Vision of a Young Country* by Tony Blair © 1996 by The Office of Tony Blair.

Gardening: How-to

From "In Praise of the Kitchen Garden" from *Gardening: How-To,* May/June 1997, published by the National Home Gardening Club. Used by permission of *Gardening: How-to* magazine.

Hal Leonard Corporation

"New Beginning," words and music by Tracy Chapman. © 1996 EMI APRIL MUSIC INC. and PURPLE RABBIT MUSIC. All rights controlled and administered by EMI APRIL MUSIC INC. All Rights Reserved. International copyright secured. Used by permission.

Harcourt Brace & Company

"L'Invitation au Voyage" by Charles Baudelaire, translated by Richard Wilbur from *Things of This World,* copyright © 1956 and renewed 1984 by Richard Wilbur. Reprinted by permission of Harcourt Brace & Company. From "Modern Fiction" by Virginia Woolf from *The Common Reader.* Published by The Hogarth Press.

Harcourt Brace & Company, the Executors of the Virginia Woolf Estate, and the Hogarth Press

"The Lady in the Looking Glass: A Reflection" from *A Haunted House and Other Short Stories* by Virginia Woolf, copyright 1944 and renewed 1972 by Harcourt Brace & Company. Reprinted by permission.

Harcourt Brace & Company, and Faber and Faber Ltd.

"The Hollow Men," "Preludes" and "Journey of the Magi" from *Collected Poems 1909–1962* by T. S. Eliot, copyright 1936 by Harcourt Brace & Company, copyright © 1964, 1963 by T. S. Eliot. Reprinted by permission of the publishers, Harcourt Brace & Company, and Faber and Faber Limited.

Harcourt Brace & Company, and A. M. Heath & Co. Ltd.

"Shooting an Elephant" from *Shooting an Elephant and Other*

Essays by George Orwell, copyright 1950 by Sonia Brownell Orwell and renewed 1978 by Sonia Pitt-Rivers. Copyright © Mark Hamilton as the Literary Executor of the Estate of the Late Sonia Brownell Orwell and Martin Secker and Warburg Ltd. Reprinted by permission of Harcourt Brace & Company and A. M. Heath & Co. Ltd.

Harlan Davidson, Inc. / Forum Press Inc.
Excerpt from "Book I" of *Utopia* by Thomas More, edited and translated by H. V. S. Ogden, pp. 21, 22 (Crofts Classics Series). Copyright © 1949 by Harlan Davidson, Inc. Reprinted by permission.

HarperCollins Publishers, Inc., and Rogers, Coleridge & White Ltd.
"The Devoted Son" from *Games at Twilight and Other Stories* by Anita Desai. Copyright © 1978 by Anita Desai. Reprinted by permission of HarperCollins Publishers, Inc., and the author c/o Rogers, Coleridge & White Ltd., 20 Powis Mews, London W11 1JN.

Henry Holt & Co., Inc.
"To an Athlete Dying Young" (from "A Shropshire Lad," authorized edition) and "When I Was One-and-Twenty" from *The Collected Poems of A. E. Housman* by A. E. Housman. Copyright 1939, 1940, © 1965 by Henry Holt and Company, Inc., © 1967, 1968 by Robert E. Symons. Reprinted by permission of Henry Holt and Company, Inc.

David Higham Associates
"On the Patio" from *Poems 1954–1987* by Peter Redgrove. Copyright © Peter Redgrove, 1959, 1961, 1963, 1966, 1972, 1973, 1975, 1977, 1979, 1981, 1985, 1986, 1987. All rights reserved. Reprinted by permission.

Houghton Mifflin Company
From "Childe Harold's Pilgrimage" ("Apostrophe to the Ocean"), lines from "Don Juan" and "She Walks in Beauty" reprinted from *The Complete Poetical Words of Lord Byron*. From "A Voyage to Brobdingnag" and from "A Voyage to Lilliput" reprinted from *Gulliver's Travels and Other Writings* by Jonathan Swift, edited by Louis A. Landa. Riverside Edition. Copyright © 1960 by Houghton Mifflin Company. Used by permission.

John Johnson Ltd. for Dr. A. L. Rowse
Emilia Lanier: "Eves Apologie" from *The Poems of Shakespeare's Dark Lady: Salve Deus Rex Judaeorum* by Emilia Lanier, introduced by A. L. Rowse. Reprinted by permission of John Johnson Ltd. for Dr. A. L. Rowse.

Alfred A. Knopf, Inc.
"The Demon Lover" from *Collected Stories* by Elizabeth Bowen. Copyright 1946 and renewed 1974 by Elizabeth Bowen. Reprinted by permission of Alfred A. Knopf, Inc.

L. R. Lind
From *Ovid: Tristia* translated by L. R. Lind. Published by The University of Georgia Press. Copyright © 1975 by L. R. Lind. All rights reserved.

Methuen & Company Ltd.
Lines from "An Essay on Man," Canto III and lines from Canto V from *The Rape of the Lock,* reprinted from *The Poems of Alexander Pope* edited by John Butt. Published by Methuen & Co., Ltd, London.

New Beacon Books Ltd.
"From Lucy: Englan' Lady" from *Lucy's Letters and Loving* by James Berry. © 1982 by James Berry. Reprinted by permission of the publisher, New Beacon Books Ltd.

New Directions Publishing Co.
"Not Waving but Drowning" from Stevie Smith, *The Collected Poems of Stevie Smith.* Copyright © 1972 by Stevie Smith. "Far Corners of the Earth" by Tu Fu, translated by David Hinton, from *The Selected Poems of Tu Fu.* Copyright ©1989 by David Hinton. "Anthem for Doomed Youth" by Wilfred Owen, from *The Collected Poems of Wilfred Owen,* edited by C. Day Lewis. Copyright © Chatto & Windus Ltd. 1946, 1963. Reprinted by permission of New Directions Publishing Co.

New Directions Publishing Corporation, and David Higham Associates Ltd.
"Do Not Go Gentle into That Good Night" by Dylan Thomas, from *The Poems of Dylan Thomas.* Copyright © 1952 by The Trustees for the Copyrights of Dylan Thomas. "Fern Hill" by Dylan Thomas, from *The Poems of Dylan Thomas.* Copyright © 1945 by The Trustees for the Copyrights of Dylan Thomas. Reprinted by permission of New Directions Publishing Corporation, and David Higham Associates Ltd.

Newmarket Press
From *The Sense and Sensibility Screenplay & Diaries,* by Emma Thompson. Screenplay Copyright © 1995 Columbia Pictures Industries, Inc. All Rights Reserved. Reprinted by permission of Newmarket Press, 18 East 48th Street, New York, NY 10017.

News International Syndication
Articles "Death of a King" and "The New Queen" reprinted from Times Newspapers Limited, 7 February 1952. Copyright © Times Newspapers Limited, 1952. Used by permission of News International Syndication.

North Point Press, a division of Farrar, Straus & Giroux, Inc.
"Testament" by Bei Dao from *A Splintered Mirror: Chinese Poetry From the Democracy Movement,* translated by Donald Finkel. Translation copyright © 1991 by Donald Finkel. Reprinted by permission of North Point Press, a division of Farrar, Straus & Giroux, Inc.

W. W. Norton & Company, Inc.
"Sonnet 35" by Edmund Spenser, from *Edmund Spenser's Poetry: Authoritative Texts Criticism,* selected and edited by Hugh Maclean, copyright © 1968 by W. W. Norton & Company, Inc. "Outside History" reprinted from *Outside History, Selected Poems, 1980–1990,* by Eavan Boland, by permission of W. W. Norton & Company, Inc. Copyright © 1990 by Eavan Boland. Reprinted from *Sir Gawain and the Green Knight: A New Verse Translation* by Marie Borroff, translator. Copyright © 1967 by W. W. Norton & Company, Inc. Reprinted by permission of W. W. Norton & Company, Inc.

Oakland Press
"Clinton, Dole need to focus on making college more accessible to public" by Myles Brand from *The Oakland Press,* June 6, 1996. Reprinted by permission of *The Oakland Press,* Pontiac, MI.

Oxford University Press, Inc.
From "The Wanderer," translated by Charles W. Kennedy, from *An Anthology of Old English Poetry.* Copyright © 1960 by Charles W. Kennedy. Used by permission of Oxford University Press, Inc.

Oxford University Press, London
"God's Grandeur" and "Spring and Fall" from *Poems of Gerard Manley Hopkins,* 4th edition, edited by W. H. Gardner and N. H. MacKenzie. "The Lamb," "The Chimney Sweeper," and "Infant Sorrow" from *The Poetical Works of William Blake,* edited by John Sampson. "Sonnet 43" from *The Poetical Works of Elizabeth Barrett Browning,* Oxford Edition. "To Althea" and "To Lucasta, on Going to the Wars" from *The Poems of Richard Lovelace,* edited by C. H. Wilkinson, copyright © 1953. "Kubla Khan" and "The Rime of the Ancient Mariner" from *The Poems of Samuel Taylor Coleridge.* Lines from "In Memoriam, A. H. H.," "Tears, Idle Tears," "The Lady of Shalott," lines from "The Princess," and "Ulysses" from *Alfred Tennyson: Poetical Works.* "To the Virgins, to Make Much of Time" from *The Poems of Robert Herrick,* edited by L. C. Martin. From "The Life of Samuel Johnson" in *Boswell's Life of Johnson* by James Boswell, edited by C. B. Tinker. "Sonnet 31" and "Sonnet 39" from *The Poems of Sir Philip Sidney,* edited by William A. Ringler, Jr. "The Passionate Shepherd to His Love" from *Marlow's Poems,* edited by Roma Gill, Volume 1, © Roma Gill 1987, Clarendon Press, Oxford. Reprinted by permission of the publisher, Oxford University Press. "Sonnet 1" and "Sonnet 75" from *The Poetical Works of Edmund Spenser,* edited by J. C. Smith and E. de Selincourt. "On Making an Agreeable Marriage" from *Jane Austen's Letters,* collected and edited by Deirdre Le Faye, copyright Deirdre Le Faye 1995. Permission granted by the publisher, Oxford University Press Ltd.

Penguin Books Ltd.
"How Seigfried Was Slain" from *The Nibelungenlied,* translated by A. T. Hatto (Penguin Classics, Revised Edition, 1969), copyright © A. T. Hatto, 1965, 1969. From *A History of the English Church and People* by Bede, translated by Leo Sherley-Price, revised by R. E. Latham (Penguin Classics 1955, Revised edition 1968). Copyright © Leo Sherley-Price, 1955, 1968. "The Nun's Priest's Tale" and "The Prologue" to *The Canterbury Tales* by Geoffrey Chaucer, translated by Nevill Coghill (Penguin Classics 1951, fourth revised edition 1977), copyright © 1951 by Nevill Coghill. Copyright, © Nevil Coghill 1958, 1960, 1975, 1977. Reprinted by permission of Penguin Books Ltd. From "Parsons Prologue" from *The Canterbury Tales* by Geoffrey Chaucer, translated by Nevill Coghill. Copyright © Nevill Coghill, 1952.

Phoebe Phillips Editions
Excerpt from *The Anglo-Saxon Chronicle,* translated and collated by Anne Savage. Copyright © 1983 by Phoebe Phillips. All rights reserved.

Princeton University Press
"Auden's Impersonal Poetry" from *The Poetic Art of W. H. Auden* by John G. Blair. Copyright © 1965 Princeton University Press. Reprinted by permission of Princeton University Press.

Random House, Inc.
From "That English Weather" from *Parodies: An Anthology from Chaucer to Beerbohm—and After,* edited by Dwight Macdonald. © Copyright, 1960, by Dwight Macdonald. From *War and Peace* by Leo Tolstoy, translated from the Russian by Constance Garnett, published by Modern Library, Random House, Inc. "Holy Sonnet 10", "A Valediction: Forbidding Mourning," "Meditation 17," and "Song" from *Complete Poetry and Selected Prose of John Donne* by John Donne, edited by John Hayward. "Musée des Beaux Arts" and "In Memory of W. B. Yeats" from *W. H. Auden: Collected Poems* by W. H. Auden, edited by Edward Mendelson. Copyright 1940 and renewed 1968 by W. H. Auden. "Homeless" from *Living Out Loud* by Anna Quindlen. Copyright © 1987 by Anna Quindlen. Reprinted by permission of Random House, Inc.

Random House, Inc., and Heinemann Educational Publishers, a division of Reed Educational & Professional Publishing Limited
From *A Man For All Seasons* by Robert Bolt, published by Heinemann Educational Books. Copyright © 1960, 1962 by Robert Bolt; copyright renewed 1988, 1990 by Robert Bolt. Reprinted by permission of Random House, Inc. and Heinemann Educational Publishers, a division of Reed Educational & Professional Publishing Limited.

Tessa Sayle Agency
"The Fiddle" from The *Second Chance and Other Stories* by Alan Sillitoe. Copyright © 1981 by Alan Sillitoe. First appeared in The Nottingham Press.

Scovil Chichak Galen Literary Agency, Inc.
"We'll Never Conquer Space" by Arthur C. Clarke, published in *Science Digest,* June 1960, © 1960 by Popular Mechanics Company. Reprinted by permission of the author and the author's agents, Scovil Chichak Galen Literary Agency, Inc., New York.

Simon & Schuster, Inc.
"Ah, Are You Digging on My Grave?" and "The Darkling Thrush" from *The Complete Poems of Thomas Hardy,* edited by James Gibson (New York: Macmillan, 1978). This collection was published outside the U.S. by Macmillan (London) Ltd. in 1976. Reprinted with permission of Simon & Schuster, Inc. from *The Poems of W. B. Yeats: A New Edition,* edited by Richard J. Finneran: "The Lake Isle at Innisfree," "When You are Old" and "The Wild Swans at Coole," copyright 1919 by Macmillan Publishing Company, renewed 1947 by Bertha Georgie Yeats; "The Second Coming," copyright © 1924 by Macmillan Publishing Company, renewed 1952 by Bertha Georgie Yeats; "Sailing to Byzantium," copyright 1928 by Macmillan Publishing Company, copyright renewed © 1956 by Bertha Georgie Yeats.

Simon & Schuster, Inc., and Jonathan Clowes Ltd.
"No Witchcraft for Sale" for USA rights from *African Short Stories* by Doris Lessing. Copyright © 1951, 1953, 1954, 1957, 1958, 1962, 1963, 1964, 1965, 1972, 1981 by Doris Lessing. Used by permission of Simon & Schuster, Inc. For Canadian rights, from *This Was the Old Chief's Country* by Doris Lessing. Copyright 1951 Doris Lessing. Reprinted by kind permission of Jonathan Clowes, Ltd., London, on behalf of Doris Lessing.

Simon & Schuster, and HarperCollins Publishing Ltd.
Excerpts from *The Analects of Confucius,* translated and annotated by Arthur Waley, is reprinted with the permission Simon & Schuster and HarperCollins Publishing Ltd. Copyright © 1938 by George Allen and Unwin Ltd.

University of California Press

Excerpts from "An Essay on Dramatic Poesy" by John Dryden, from *The Works of John Dryden, Prose 1668–1691*, General Editor H. T. Swedenberg, Jr. Copyright © 1971 by The Regents of the University of California. "You Know the Place, Then" from *Sappho: A New Translation* by Mary Barnard. Copyright © 1958 The Regents of the University of California; © renewed 1984 Mary Barnard. "The Diameter of the Bomb," translated by Chana Bloch, from *The Selected Poetry of Yehuda Amichai*, translated/edited by Chana Bloch and Stephen Mitchell. Translation Copyright © 1986 by Chana Bloch and Stephen Mitchell. Reprinted by permission of the University of California Press.

University of Chicago Press

From "Oedipus the King," Sophocles, translated by David Grene, from *Complete Greek Tragedies*, edited by David Grene and Richmond Lattimore. Copyright 1954 by The University of Chicago. Excerpt from *The Iliad of Homer*, translated by Richmond Lattimore. Copyright © 1951, The University of Chicago. Reprinted by permission of the publisher, University of Chicago Press.

University of Texas Press

"Sonnet LXXXIX" on page 189 and "Sonnet LXIX" on page 147 from *100 Love Sonnets: Cien Sonetos de Amor*, by Pablo Neruda, translated by Stephen Tapscott. © Pablo Neruda, 1959. Copyright © 1986 by The University of Texas Press. Reprinted by permission.

The University of Wisconsin Press

Excerpts from "The Defense of Poesy" from *Sir Philip Sidney: Selected Prose and Poetry*, edited by Robert Kimbrough. Copyright © 1969, 1983 Robert Kimbrough. Reprinted by permission of The University of Wisconsin Press.

Viking Penguin, a division of Penguin Books USA Inc.

"Birds on the Western Front" from *The Complete Works of Saki* by H. H. Munro, published by Barnes & Noble by arrangement with Doubleday & Company, Inc. "Araby," from *Dubliners*, by James Joyce. Copyright 1916 by B. W. Heubsch. Definitive text copyright © 1967 by The Estate of James Joyce. "The Rocking-Horse Winner" by D. H. Lawrence. Copyright © 1933 by the Estate of D. H. Lawrence, renewed © 1961 by Angelo Ravagli and C. M. Weekley, Executors of the Estate of Trieda Lawrence, from *Complete Short Stories of D. H. Lawrence* by D. H. Lawrence. "The Train from Rhodesia," copyright 1952 by Nadine Gordimer, from *Selected Stories* by Nadine Gordimer. Used by permission of Viking Penguin, a division of Penguin Books USA Inc.

Viking Penguin, a division of Penguin Books USA Inc., and John Johnson (Authors' Agent) Limited

"The Distant Past" from *Angels at the Ritz and Other Stories* by William Trevor. Copyright © 1975 by William Trevor, published in England by The Bodley Head. Used by permission.

Viking Penguin, a division of Penguin Books USA Inc., and George Sassoon

"Wirers" from *Collected Poems of Siegfried Sassoon* by Siegfried Sassoon. Copyright 1918, 1920 by E. P. Dutton. Copyright 1936, 1946, 1947, 1948 by Siegfried Sassoon. Reprinted by permission.

Viking Penguin, a division of Penguin Books USA Inc., and The Wylie Agency

"B. Wordsworth" by V. S. Naipaul, from *Miguel Street* by V. S. Naipaul. Copyright © 1959 by V. S. Naipaul. Used by permission of Viking Penguin, a division of Penguin Books USA Inc., and The Wylie Agency.

Viking Penguin, a division of Penguin Books USA Inc. and David Higham Associates Ltd.

"A Shocking Accident," copyright © 1957 by Graham Greene. In the USA from *Collected Stories of Graham Greene* by Graham Greene. In England from *Twenty-One Stories* by Graham Greene. Used by permission of Viking Penguin, a division of Penguin Books USA Inc. and David Higham Associates Ltd.

Viking Press, a division of Penguin Putnam Inc.

From *On Social Plays*, an extract from *A View from the Bridge* by Arthur Miller. Copyright © 1955 by Arthur Miller.

Vital Speeches of the Day

From "The New Atlantic Initiative" by Margaret Thatcher, delivered at the John Findley Green Foundation Lecture, Westminster College, Fulton, MO, March 9, 1996. Used by permission.

Wake Forest University Press

"Carrick Revisited" from *Selected Poems of Louis MacNeice*, edited by Michael Longley. © Wake Forest University Press, 1990. Reprinted by permission of Wake Forest University Press.

Warner Chappell Music

"Freeze Tag" written by Suzanne Vega. Song copyright © 1985 by Waifersongs Ltd. and AGF Music Ltd. (ASCAP)

Washington Post Writers' Group

From "A Farewell to the 'People's Princess'" by Dan Balz, Washington Post Foreign Service, Sunday, September 7, 1997; Page A01. Copyright © 1997 Washington Post. Reprinted by permission.

The Wylie Agency, Inc.

Excerpt from "Chatwin Revisited" by Paul Theroux. First published in *Granta*. Copyright © 1993 by Paul Theroux. Reprinted with the permission of The Wylie Agency, Inc.

Yale University Press

"The Seafarer" from *Poems From the Old English*, translated by Burton Raffel. Copyright © 1960, 1964; renewed 1988, 1992 by the University of Nebraska Press. Copyright © 1994 by Burton Raffel. Reprinted by permission of Yale University Press.

Note: Every effort has been made to locate the copyright owner of material reprinted in this book. Omissions brought to our attention will be corrected in subsequent editions.

ART CREDITS

Cover: viii: (top) *Susanna in Bath* (detail), Albrecht Altdorfer, Wasserholendes, Madchen, Munchen, Alte Pinakothek, Munich. Photo: Blauel/Artothek; (bottom) *Golden Horn* (detail), The National Museet, Copenhagen, Photo by Lennart Larsen; **ix:** The Granger Collection, New York; **xi:** Photofest; **xiv:** Corel Professional Photos CD-ROM™; **xvi:** Greek Vase, Terracotta c. 460 B.C., Attributed to the Orchard Painter, Column Krater (called the "Orchard Vase"), Side A: *Women Gathering Apples,* The Metropolitan Museum of Art, Rogers Fund, 1907, (07.286.74) **xviii:** Springer/Corbis-Bettmann; **xix** © Gregory C. Dimijian/Photo Researchers, Inc.; **xx:** Photri; **xxi:** *The Garden of Love* by Walter Richard Sickert. Fitzwilliam Museum, Cambridge; **xxii:** Grace Davies/Omni-Photo Communications, Inc.; **A 3:** The Master and Fellows of Corpus Christi College, Cambridge; **A 6:** The Granger Collection, New York; **A 9:** Scala/Art Resource, NY; **A 11:** Harris Museum and Art Gallery, Preston, Lancashire, UK/The Bridgeman Art Library, London/New York; **A 16:** *Ben Johnson* (1573–1637), English playwright (engraving) (b&w photo) by English School (18th century). Private Collection/Bridgeman Art Library, London/New York; **A 17:** *The Taking of the Bastille, 14th July 1789,* Jean-Pierre Houel, Musée Carnavalet, Paris, France/The Bridgeman Art Library, London/New York; **A 18:** National Gallery, London, UK/The Bridgeman Art Library, London/New York; **A 22:** *Hampstead Heath,* John Constable, Victoria & Albert Museum, London, UK/Bridgeman Art Library, London/New York; **A 25:** Bradford Art Galleries and Museums, West Yorkshire, UK/The Bridgeman Art Library, London/New York; **A 27:** The Science Museum/Science & Society Picture Library; **A 31:** *Day Dream,* 1880, Dante Gabriel Rossetti, Victoria & Albert Museum, London, UK/Bridgeman Art Library, London/New York; **A 33:** Culver Pictures, Inc.; **A 35:** Prado, Madrid, Spain/The Bridgeman Art Library, London/New York; **A 40:** *Head of a Woman* (possibly Fernande Olivier), 1909–10 Pablo Picasso, © 1999 Estate of Pablo Picasso/Artists Rights Society (ARS), NY. Fitzwilliam Museum, University of Cambridge, UK/Bridgeman Art Library, London/New York; **1:** *Sir Gawain and the Green Knight,* MS Douce 199, folio 157 verso, Bodleian Library, Oxford; **2:** (449) Richard Nowitz/Corbis; (552) Art Resource, NY; (771) *King Charlemagne – Jewelled Gold Reliquary Bust,* c.1350, Domschatz, Aachen, Art Resource, NY; (792) *Arrival of William at Penvesy* (detail from Bayeux Tapestry) Giraudon/Art Resource, NY; (871) Michael Nicholson/Corbis; (1066) The Granger Collection, New York; **3:** (1170) & (1348) & (1408) The Granger Collection, New York; (1327) Art Resource, NY; (1386) Superstock; **4:** (top) Richard Nowitz/Corbis; (bottom) The Granger Collection, New York; **6:** (top) Art Resource, NY; (bottom) *Viking Sword, Iron, Copper, and Silver,* The Metropolitan Museum of Art, Rogers Fund, 1955, © Copyright 1980/87 By The Metropolitan Museum of Art; **8:** (top) & (bottom) The Granger Collection, New York; **9:** (top) Lauros-Giraudon/Art Resource, NY; (bottom) The Granger Collection, New York; **10:** *Sampler* (detail), 1797 by Mary Wiggin. 18 x 21 1/2." Philadelphia Museum of Art, Whitman Sampler Collection/Given by Pet, Incorporated; **11:** *Arrival of William at Penvesy* (detail from Bayeux Tapestry) Giraudon/Art Resource, NY; **12:** Corel Professional Photos CD-ROM™; **15:** *Ships with Three Men, Fish,* Ms. Ashmole, 1511, Folio 86 verso, Bodleian Library, Oxford; **18:** *Arthur Going To Avalon for "The High Kings"* (detail), George Sharp, Courtesy of the artist; **20:** The Granger Collection, New York; **24:** *Susanna in Bath,* detail, Albrecht Altdorfer, Wasserholendes, Madchen, Munchen, Alte Pinakothek, Munich. Photo: Blauel/Artothek; **28:** (background) NASA; (top) Corbis-Bettmann; (bottom) New York Public Library Picture Collection; **30:** The Granger Collection, New York; **31:** Fan mounted as an album leaf: *Evening in Spring Hills,* Ink and color on silk. H. 9-3/4 in. W. 10-1/4 in. (24.8 x 26.1 cm.) Chinese, The Metropolitan Museum of Art, Gift of John M. Crawford, Jr., in honor of Alfreda Murck, 1986, (1986.493.1) Photograph © 1987 The Metropolitan Museum of Art; **32:** (background) NASA; **33:** Corel Professional Photos CD-ROM™; **37:** The Granger Collection, New York; **38:** (top) Statens Historiska Museet, Stockholm, Werner Forman Archive/Art Resource, NY; (bottom) Werner Forman Archive, National Museum, Copenhagen, Art Resource, NY; **41:** *Grendel, Frontispiece from Beowulf,* 1908, Patten Wilson, Courtesy of the Trustees of British Library; **44:** Werner Forman Archive, Viking Ship Museum, Bygdoy, Oslo, Art Resource, NY; **46:** Werner Forman Archive, Statens Historiska Museet, Stockholm, Art Resource, NY; **50:** *Golden Horn* (detail), The National Museet, Copenhagen, Photo by Lennart Larsen; **52:** Silver Pendant Showing the Helmet of the Vendel, 10th century, Swedish-Ostergotland, Viking, Werner Forman Archive, Statens Historiska Museet, Stockholm, Art Resource, NY; **55:** Courtesy of the artist; **56:** Werner Forman Archive, National Museum, Copenhagen, Art Resource, NY; **57:** Gilt-Bronze Winged Dragon-Bridle Mounting, 8th century, Swedish Artifact, Statens Historiska Museet, Stockholm, Werner Forman Archive/Art Resource, NY; **60:** Head of Carved Post from the Ship Burial at Oseberg, Werner Forman Archive/Art Resource, NY; **64:** (background) NASA; (bl) © British Museum; (br) Corbis-Bettmann; **65:** The Granger Collection, New York; **67–69:** (background) Red-figured crater, Eucharides Painter, *Running warriors with shields and spears.* Louvre, Paris, France, Erich Lessing/Art Resource, NY; **69:** (tl) The Granger Collection, New York; **70:** (background) NASA; **71:** Culver Pictures, Inc.; **75:** *Four Kings of England* (left to right): Henry II, Richard I, John, Henry III, from Historia Anglorum, 13th c. Roy 14 C VII f. 9. British Library, London, Great Britain, Bridgeman/ Art Resource, NY; **76:** (left) Snark/Art Resource, NY; **79:** Cotton Ms. Tiberius C II Folio 5 Verso Page of Bede's History, Courtesy of the Trustees of British Library; **80:** *Monks,* Ms. University College 165 pii, Bodleian Library, Oxford; **86:** Image Select/Art Resource, NY; **89:** *The Tabard Inn,* Arthur Szyk for *The Canterbury Tales,* The George Macy Companies; **91:** *The Yeoman,* Arthur Szyk for *The Canterbury Tales,* The George Macy Companies; **93:** *The Monk,* Arthur Szyk for *The Canterbury Tales,* The George Macy Companies; **96:** *The Student,* Arthur Szyk for *The Canterbury Tales,* The George Macy Companies; **100:** *The*

Wife of Bath, Arthur Szyk for *The Canterbury Tales*, The George Macy Companies; **106:** *The Pardoner*, Arthur Szyk for *The Canterbury Tales*, The George Macy Companies; **114:** Courtesy of the Trustees of British Library; **117:** *Woman Feeding Chickens*, From an Italian Manuscript (c. 1385), Osterreichische National Bibliothek, Vienna; **121:** *Chaucer Reciting Troilus and Cressida Before a Court Gathering* (Frontispiece), Corpus Christi College; **122:** *The Nun's Priest* (detail), from The Ellesmere Manuscript, Chaucer's The Canterbury Tales, The Huntington Library, San Marino, California; **124:** *Chaucer's Canterbury Pilgrims*, by William Blake, The Huntington Library, San Marino, California; **130:** (background) & (tl) NASA; (tr) C. Beaton/Camera Press London; **134:** (background) NASA; **135:** Bob Daemmrich/Stock, Boston; **139:** *St. George and the Dragon*, c. 1506, Raphael, oil on panel, 11 1/8 x 8 1/2" © Board of Trustees, National Gallery of Art, Washington, D.C. Andrew W. Mellon Collection; **143:** From *The Romance of King Arthur and His Knights of the Round Table*, Arthur Rackham, Weathervane Books; **145:** *Three Knights Returning from a Tournament*. French miniature from "Recueil de Traites de Devotion." Ms. 137/1687, fol. 144 r.c.1371–78, Giraudon/Art Resource, NY; **149:** *Sir Gawain and the Green Knight*, MS Douce 199, folio 157 verso, Bodleian Library, Oxford; **154:** *Gawain Receiving The Green Girdle*, Fritz Kredel, Woodcut, From John Gardner's *The Complete Works of the Gawain Poet*, © 1965, The University of Chicago; **157:** Art Resource, NY; **158:** *The Nine Heroes Tapestries: Christian Heroes: Arthur* (Detail), Probably Nicolas Bataille, Paris, The Metropolitan Museum of Art; **167:** Nicholas Sapieha/Stock, Boston; **168:** Culver Pictures, Inc.; **171 & 172:** The Granger Collection, New York; **175:** ©Michael Giannechini/Photo Researchers, Inc.; **177:** *Veronica Veronese*, Dante Gabriel Rossetti, Delaware Art Museum, Samuel and Mary Bancroft Memorial Collection; **180:** (background) & (tl) NASA; **182:** The Granger Collection, New York; **185:** *Siegfried's Death*, Handschriftenabteilung, Staatsbibliothek Preussischer Kulturbesitz, Berlin, photo Bildarchiv Preussicher Kulturbesitz; **187:** (background) NASA; **188:** UPI/Corbis-Bettmann; **194:** The Granger Collection, New York; **196:** (1503) Scala/Art Resource, NY; (1532) & (1534) & (1535) & (1564) The Granger Collection, New York; (1558) National Portrait Gallery, London/Superstock; **197:** (1558) & (1594) & (1611) & (1620) The Granger Collection, New York; (1582) Library of Congress/Corbis; (1609) Scala/Art Resource, NY; **198:** Hornbook dating from Shakespeare's lifetime, By permission of the Folger Shakespeare Library; **199:** (top) Marquess of Bath Collection, Longleat House, Wilts/ET Archive, London/Superstock; (center) & (bottom) The Granger Collection, New York; **200:** (top) The Granger Collection, New York; (bottom) *The Hireling Shepherd*, William Holman Hunt, The Manchester City Art Galleries; **201:** (top) National Trust/Art Resource, NY; (bottom) National Portrait Gallery, London/Superstock; **202:** (top) Corbis-Bettmann; (bottom) The Granger Collection, New York; **203:** (top) *The Launching of Fireships Against the Spanish Armada* (detail), National Maritime Museum, Greenwich, England; (bottom) Collection of Plymouth City Museum and Art Gallery; **204:** *Sampler* (detail), 1797 by Mary Wiggin. 18 x 21 1/2." Philadelphia Museum of Art, Whitman Sampler Collection/Given by Pet, Incorporated; **205:** Victoria and Albert Museum/Art Resource, NY; **206:** (left) The Granger Collection,

New York; (right) *Sir Philip Sidney* (detail), c.1576, Artist Unknown, by courtesy of the National Portrait Gallery, London; **209–211:** Corel Professional Photos CD-ROM™; **212:** Chad Ehlers, 1987/PNI; **216:** The Granger Collection, New York; **218:** *William Shakespeare*, (detail), Artist Unknown, by courtesy of the National Portrait Gallery, London; **219:** Corel Professional Photos CD-ROM™; **220:** *Autumn, 1865*, Frederick Walker, Victoria & Albert Museum/Art Resource, NY; **222:** Corel Professional Photos CD-ROM™; **226:** (background) NASA; (top) The Granger Collection, New York; (bottom) Sergio Larrain/Magnum Photos, Inc.; **227:** *Portrait of Laura*, Biblioteca Laurenziana, Firenze, Scala/Art Resource, NY; **228–229:** *Man and Woman*, 1981, Rufino Tamayo, Tate Gallery, London/Art Resource, NY; **230:** NASA; **231:** Ken Karp/Omni-Photo Communications, Inc.; **235:** (left) & (right) The Granger Collection, New York; (bottom) Scala/Art Resource, NY; **236:** (left) The Granger Collection, New York; (right) North Wind Picture Archives; **237:** Petrified Colle/The Image Bank; **238–239:** *Gardens at Llanerch, Denbigshire*, c. 1662–72, British School, 17th c., oil on canvas, 45 x 59 3/4 in. (114.1 x 151.7 cm) B1976.7.115. Yale Center for British Art, New Haven, Connecticut, Paul Mellon Collection; **240:** *Portrait of Queen Elizabeth I*, Bridgeman/Art Resource, NY; **241:** "Dangers Averted" medal celebrating the defeat of the Spanish Armada, c. 1589, gold cast and chased by Nicholas Hilliard (1537–1619), Fitzwilliam Museum, University of Cambridge/The Bridgeman Art Library International Ltd., London/New York; **244:** © Mark N. Boulton/Photo Researchers, Inc.; **246:** The Folger Shakespeare Library, Washington, D.C.; **252:** (background) NASA; (br) AP/Wide World Photos; **254–255:** Photofest; **258:** NASA; **259:** *Portrait of Queen Elizabeth I*, Bridgeman/Art Resource, NY; **263 & 265:** The Granger Collection, New York; **266:** (tl) Hulton-Deutsch/Corbis; (rc) Photofest; (bl) New York Public Library at Lincoln Center; **267:** (tl) *Mrs. Siddons as Lady Macbeth*, (detail), G.H. Harlow, Garrick Club/ET Archive; (rc) *Ellen Terry (as Lady Macbeth)*, 1889, oil on canvas, 87x45", Tate Gallery on loan to National Portrait Gallery, London, Art Resource, NY; (bl) Photofest; **268:** *William Shakespeare*, (detail), Artist Unknown, by courtesy of the National Portrait Gallery, London; **273:** *The Three Witches*, 1783, Henry Fuseli, oil on canvas, 65 x 91.5 cm, Kunsthaus Zurich © 1997 Copyright Kunsthaus Zurich. All rights reserved.; **277:** *Macbeth and the Witches*, Clarkson Stanfield, Leicestershire Museums, Art Galleries and Records Service; **283:** Anne Van De Vaeken/The Image Bank; **287:** Photofest; **289:** Hans Neleman/The Image Bank; **297:** *Ellen Terry (as Lady Macbeth)*, 1889, oil on canvas 87x45", Tate Gallery on loan to National Portrait Gallery, London, Art Resource, NY; **304:** *Lady Macbeth Seizing the Daggers*, Henry Fuseli, The Tate Gallery, London/Art Resource, NY; **315:** *Mrs. Siddons as Lady Macbeth*, G.H. Harlow, Garrick Club/ET Archive; **321:** *Scene from Macbeth and the Witches*, Cattermole, The Folger Shakespeare Library, Washington, D.C.; **329:** e.t.archive; **337:** The Granger Collection, New York; **349:** *Lady Macbeth Sleepwalking*, Henry Fuseli, Louvre, Paris, Scala/Art Resource, NY; **364:** (background) NASA; (br) Vatican Museum/Scala/Art Resource, NY; **367 & 368:** Photofest; **371:** NASA; **372:** The Granger Collection, New York; **378–379:** The Granger Collection, New York; **380:** (1600) & (1614) & (1627)

& (1649) & (1650) The Granger Collection, New York; (1644) Chinese Porcelain Jar Hsuan-te (Xuande) Period, 1426–1435. Ming dynasty porcelain painted in underglaze blue, 19 inches in height. The Metropolitan Museum of Art, Gift of Robert E. Tod, 1937. (37.191.1); (1661) Dave G. Houser/Corbis; (1663) Historical Picture Archive/Corbis; (1667) Corbis-Bettmann; **381:** (1680) Erich Lessing/Art Resource, NY; (1690) & (1721) & (1773) The Granger Collection, New York; (1719) *Marylebone Cricket Club,* London/The Bridgeman Art Library, London; (1775) *Mrs. Siddons,* Thomas Gainsborough, National Gallery, London/The Bridgeman Art Library, London; **382:** The Granger Collection, New York; **383 & 384:** (bottom) Archiv für Kunst und Geschichte, Berlin; **384:** (top) *Haycarting* by George Stubbs, 1785, Board of Trustees of the National Museums and Galleries on Merseyside (Lady Lever Art Gallery, Port Sunlight); **385:** (top) The Granger Collection, New York; (bottom) © British Museum; **386:** (top) The Bettmann Archive; (tl) Archiv für Kunst und Geschichte, Berlin; (tr) Burghley House Collection, Lincolnshire/The Bridgeman Art Library International Ltd., London/New York; (lc) Philip Mould, Historical Portraits, Ltd./The Bridgeman Art Library International Ltd., London/New York; (rc) Division of Rare and Manuscript Collections, Carl A. Kroch Library, Cornell University; (bl) © Roger-Viollet; (br) © Editions Tallandier; **387:** (top) *Marriage á la Mode: The Marriage Contract,* 1743, William Hogarth, Reproduced by courtesy of the Trustees, National Gallery of Art, London; (bottom) *View of The River Dee,* c. 1761, (oil on canvas) by Richard Wilson (1714–82), National Gallery, London/Bridgeman Art Library, London/New York; **388:** *Sampler* (detail), 1797 by Mary Wiggin. 18 x 21 1/2." Philadelphia Museum of Art, Whitman Sampler Collection/Given by Pet, Incorporated; **389:** *A Musical Garden Party* (detail), colored silk on canvas, very fine tent stitch. H. 13 in. W. 20-1/2 in. Metropolitan Museum of Art, Gift of Irwin Untermyer, 1964. (64.101.1314) Photograph Copyright © 1991 By the Metropolitan Museum of Art; **390:** The Granger Collection, New York; **391:** Corel Professional Photos CD-ROM™; **393:** Romilly Lockyer/The Image Bank; **397:** *Fair is My Love* (detail), Edwin A. Abbey, Harris Museum and Art Gallery, Preston; **399:** The Granger Collection, New York; **401:** *Sir Thomas Aston at the Deathbed of His Wife,* John Souch, Manchester City Art Galleries; **404:** The Granger Collection, New York; **409:** *The Interrupted Sleep,* oil on canvas. Oval 29-1/2 x 25-1/2 in., Francois Boucher, The Metropolitan Museum of Art, The Jules Bache Collection, 1949. (49.7.46) Photograph © 1984 The Metropolitan Museum of Art; **412:** (top) & (bottom) The Granger Collection, New York; (center) New York Public Library; **416:** *Three Ladies Adorning a Term of Hymen, 1773,* Sir Joshua Reynolds, The Tate Gallery, London/Art Resource, NY; **420:** (background) NASA; (top) Jane Bowr/Camera Press London/Globe Photos; (bottom) AP/Wide World Photos; **421:** Jules Zalon/The Image Bank; **422–423:** (background) Corel Professional Photos CD-ROM™; **424:** (background) NASA; **425:** Bill Bachmann/PNI; **429:** *Whitehall, January 30th, 1649 (Execution of Charles I),* Ernest Crofts, Forbes Magazine Collection, Bridgeman/Art Resource, NY; **430:** Corbis-Bettmann; **433:** The Granger Collection, New York; **437 & 440:** *Paradsise Lost,* 1688, John Milton, British Library; **444:** The Granger Collection, New York; **446:** *Dorothy Seton—A Daughter of Eve, 1903,* James McNeil Whistler, oil on canvas, 20 3/8 x 12 1/2", Hunterian Art Gallery, University of Glasgow, Scotland; **448:** *Going to the Battle, 1858,* Edward Burne-Jones, Fitzwilliam Museum, Cambridge; **452:** (background) NASA; (br) Henrieta Butler/Globe Photos; **454:** (background) NASA; **455 & 459 & 460 & 463:** The Granger Collection, New York; **464:** Last page of Samuel Pepys's Diary 31 May 1669, Pepys Library, Magdalene College, Cambridge, England; **466–467:** *The Great Fire, 1666,* (coloured engraving) by Marcus Willemsz Doornik, (17th century), Guildhall Library, Corporation of London/Bridgeman Art Library International Ltd., London/New York; **468:** *Journal of the Plague Year: the Dead Cart,* The British Library; **474 & 477 & 478 & 481 & 486:** The Granger Collection, New York; **489:** *The Barge,* (detail) *1895–1896,* Aubrey Beardsley from "The Rape of the Lock," Smithers, 1896 from *The Best of Beardsley,* Collected and edited by R. A. Walker, ©1948 by The Bodley Head, Published in the U.S.A. by Excalibur Books, plate 63; **491:** *The Rape of the Lock, 1895–1896,* Aubrey Beardsley, from "The Rape of the Lock," Smithers, 1896 from *The Best of Beardsley,* Collected and edited by R. A. Walker, ©1948 by The Bodley Head, Published in the U.S.A. by Excalibur Books, plate 64; **493:** *The Battle of the Beaux and Belles,* Aubrey Beardsley, The Barber Institute of Fine Arts, The University of Birmingham; **498–499:** Corel Professional Photos CD-ROM™; **502 & 504:** The Granger Collection, New York; **513:** *Johnson and Boswell,* ©Trustees of the British Museum; **518:** The Granger Collection, New York; **520–521:** Lenore Weber/Omni-Photo Communications, Inc.; **526–527:** Alan Becker/The Image Bank; **528:** *Cottage and Pond, Moonlight,* Thomas Gainsborough, Art Resource, NY/Victoria and Albert Museum, London; **532:** (background) NASA; (top) AP/Wide World Photos; (bottom) The Granger Collection, New York; **533:** *The Thirteen Emperors,* (view: overall of 7th emperor) second half of 7th century (with later replacement), Yan Liben (attributed to) d. 673, China, Tang Dynasty, handscroll; ink and color on silk 51.3x531.0 cm (pictorial section), Denman Waldo Ross Collection, Courtesy, Museum of Fine Arts, Boston; **536:** *Thomas Jefferson,* Gilbert Stuart, National Portrait Gallery, Smithsonian Institution; gift of the Regents of the Smithsonian Institution, the Thomas Jefferson Memorial Foundation, and the Enid and Crosby Kemper Foundation; owned jointly with Monticello, Art Resource, NY; **538:** (background) NASA; **539:** The Granger Collection, New York; **542:** "Cover" from GULLIVER'S TRAVELS by Jonathan Swift foreword by Marcus Cunliffe. Copyright © 1960 Foreword by New American Library. Used by permission of Dutton Signet, a division of Penguin Books USA Inc.; **543:** *Girl Writing by Lamplight,* © 1850, by William Henry Hunt, (1790–1864), The Maas Gallery London/Bridgeman Art Library, London; **544:** The Granger Collection, New York; **546–549:** Corel Professional Photos CD-ROM™; **554:** (br) John Barrett/Globe Photos; **556:** Mary Kate Denny/Photo Edit/PNI; **557:** (background) NASA; **558:** Gayna Hoffman/PNI; **562:** Ken Karp Photography; **564–565:** *Two Men Observing the Moon,* Caspar David Friedrich, oil on canvas, 35 x 44.5 cm, (1819–1820), Staatl, Kunstsammlungen, Neue Meister, Dresden, Germany, Erich Lessing/Art Resource, NY; **566:** (1799) Art Resource, NY; (1801) Corel Professional

Photos CD-ROM™; (1802) Gianni Dagli Orti/Corbis; (1805) & (1807) & (1813) & (1814) The Granger Collection, New York; **567:** (1818) ©Barson Collection/Archive Photos; (1819) © Archive Photos; (1825) ©Brian Yarvin, 1994/PNI; (1830) & (1831) The Granger Collection, New York; **568 & 569:** (top) The Granger Collection, New York; **570:** (top) Christie's, London/SuperStock; (bottom) Private Collection/The Bridgeman Art Library, London; **571:** (top) The Granger Collection, New York; **572:** (top) SEF/Art Resource, NY; (bottom) IBM; **573:** (top) & (bottom) The Granger Collection, New York; **574:** (top) *Sampler* (detail), 1797 by Mary Wiggin. 18 x 21 1/2." Philadelphia Museum of Art, Whitman Sampler Collection/Given by Pet, Incorporated; **575:** *Hummingbird Holders,* 1884, James Farrington Gookins, Collection of the Shelden Swope Art Museum, Terre Haute, Indiana; **576:** (top) *Mary Shelley* (detail), c.1840, Richard Rothwell, by courtesy of the National Portrait Gallery, London; (bottom) John Lei/Omni-Photo Communications, Inc.; **577:** Photofest; **580–581:** *A View of Chamonix and Mt. Blanc,* Julius Schnon von Carolsfeld, Austrian Gallery, Vienna; **586:** (top) *Robert Burns,* A. Nasmyth, by courtesy of the National Portrait Gallery, London; (bottom) The Granger Collection, New York; **589:** ©R. J. Erwin/Photo Researchers, Inc.; **590:** Warrington Museum & Art Gallery, Great Britain, Bridgeman/Art Resource, NY; **592:** *The Village Wedding,* detail, Sir Luke Fildes, (1844–1927) Christopher Wood Gallery, London/The Bridgeman Art Library/London; **596:** The Granger Collection, New York; **598:** From a Manuscript of "The Lamb" by William Blake, Lessing J. Rosenwald Collection, Courtesy of the Library of Congress, Washington, D.C.; **599:** *The Tiger,* A Page from "Songs of Innocence and Experience," William Blake, The Metroplitan Museum of Art, Rogers Fund, 1917 © Copyright 1984 By The Metropolitan Museum of Art; **600–601:** The Granger Collection, New York; **604:** (background) NASA; (br) Corbis-Bettmann; **605:** *Elizabeth Beale Bordley,* ca. 1797, Gilbert Stuart, Oil on canvas, 29 1/4 x 24", 1886.2, Courtesy of the Museum of American Art of the Pennsylvania Academy of the Fine Arts, Philadelphia. Bequest of Elizabeth Mifflin.; **608:** (background) NASA; **609:** Superstock; **613:** *The Wanderer Over the Sea of Clouds,* 1818, by Caspar-David Friedrich, (1774–1840) Kunsthalle, Hamburg/Bridgeman Art Library; **614:** The Granger Collection, New York; **616–617:** The Granger Collection, New York; **618:** (tc) *Tintern Abbey,* J.M.W. Turner, Courtesy of the Trustees of the British Museum; **618–619 & 620:** (background) The Granger Collection, New York; **622:** *Storming of the Bastille 14 July 1789,* Anonymous, Chateau, Versailles, France; **623:** *Execution of King Louis XVI on January 21, 1793,* Musee de la Ville de Paris, Musee Carnavalet, Paris, France, Erich Lessing/Art Resource, NY; **624:** Corel Professional Photos CD-ROM™; **628:** *Samuel Taylor Coleridge* (detail), by courtesy of the National Portrait Gallery, London; **633, 635, 636, 642:** Engraving by Gustáve Doré for *The Rime of the Ancient Mariner* by Samuel Taylor Coleridge ©1970 by Dover Publications, Inc.; **646 & 649:** The Granger Collection, New York; **652:** *Box and Cover,* Ming Dynasty, first half of 16th century, lacquer, black; mother-of-pearl; wood; fabric. H. 4 in. The Seattle Art Museum, Gift of Mr. and Mrs. Louis Brechemin, Photo by Paul Macapia; **656:** The Granger Collection, New York; **659:** *In the Garden* (detail), ca.1889,

Thomas Wilmer Dewing, oil on canvas, 20 5/8 x 35" National Museum of American Art, Washington, D.C./Art Resource, NY; **660–661:** *Shipwreck,* J.C.C. Dahl, Munich Neue Pinakothek/Kavaler/Art Resource, NY; **663, 664, 665:** *Lord Byron, shaking the dust of England from his shoes,* from "The Poet's Corner" pub. by William Heinemann, 1904 (engraving) by Max Beerbohm (1872–1956), Central Saint Martins College of Art and Design/The Bridgeman Art Library International Ltd., London/New York; **668:** The Granger Collection, New York; **671:** ©Diane Rawson/Photo Researchers, Inc.; **673:** *Cirrus Cloud Study,* John Constable, Victoria and Albert Museum Trustees/Art Resource, NY; **676:** *Cloud Study,* 1821, John Constable, Yale Center for British Art, Paul Mellon Collection; **682:** (top) The Granger Collection, New York; (bottom) Greek Vase, Terracotta c. 460 B.C., Attributed to the Orchard Painter, Column Krater (called the "Orchard Vase"), Side A: *Women Gathering Apples,* The Metropolitan Museum of Art, Rogers Fund, 1907, (07.286.74); **684:** Frontspiece, Homer's *Iliad* and *Odyssey,* 1612, William Hole, By permission of the British Library; **685:** *John Keats,* 1821, Joseph Severn, by courtesy of the National Portrait Gallery, London; **687:** *Small Bird on a Flowering Plum Branch,* attributed to Ma Lin, The Goto Museum; **690–691:** Greek Vase, Terracotta c. 460 B.C., Attributed to the Orchard Painter, Column Krater (called the "Orchard Vase"), Side A: *Women Gathering Apples,* The Metropolitan Museum of Art, Rogers Fund, 1907, (07.286.74); **694:** (background) NASA; (top) Corbis-Bettmann; (center) The Granger Collection, New York; (bottom) Yosa Buson, Heibonsha/Pacific Press Service; **696:** *Crows Taking Flight through Spring Haze,* (1782–1846) hanging scroll, Edo period, dated 1841; Toyama Kinenkan, Saitama prefecture, Okada Hanko, Foundation Toyama Memorial Museum; **698:** (background) NASA; **699:** Chris Steele-Perkins/PNI; **703:** *Forging the Anchor,* 1831, William James Muller, (1812–45) City of Bristol Museum and Art Gallery/Bridgeman Art Library, London; **704:** The Granger Collection, New York; **709:** *The Workshops at the Gobelins Factory,* 1840, Jean-Charles Develly, (1876–1958) watercolor, Musée Carnavalet, Paris/Giraudon/Bridgeman Art Library, London; **710:** © British Museum; **714:** (top) Jane Austen (detail), c. 1801—C. Auston., by courtesy of the National Portrait Gallery, London; (bottom) The Granger Collection, New York; **716–717:** *Marriage à la Mode: The Marriage Contract,* 1743, William Hogarth, Reproduced by courtesy of the Trustees, National Gallery of Art, London; **724:** (background) NASA; (br) Globe Photos; **726:** Photofest; **729:** (background) NASA; **730:** Bob Daemmrich/Stock, Boston; **736–737:** *The Railway Station,* 1862, by William Powell Frith, (1819–1909), Royal Holloway and Bedford New College, Surrey/Bridgeman Art Library International Ltd., London/New York; **738:** (1837) © British Museum; (1844) Corbis-Bettmann; (1845) Illustrated London News/Corbis; (1854) The Granger Collection, New York; (1860) Library of Congress/Corbis; (1861) Chicago Historical Society, 1920.691; **739:** (1865—Alice) & (1880) & (1888) The Granger Collection, New York; (1865—Stamp) Gary J. Shulfer; (1876) Corbis-Bettmann; (1898) National Institutes of Health/Corbis; **740:** The Royal Collection © Her Majesty Queen Elizabeth II; **741:** (bottom) Hulton-Deutsch Collection/Corbis; **742:** (top) The Granger Collection, New

York; (bottom) London Museum/E.T. Archive; **743:** (top) © Museum of London; (bottom) *Bayswater Omnibus*, G.W. Joy, Museum of London; **744:** (top) Christopher Wood Gallery, London/The Bridgeman Art Library, London; (bottom) Science Museum, London/The Bridgeman Art Library, London; **745:** (top) Erich Lessing/Art Resource, NY; (bottom) Historical Picture Archive/Corbis; **746:** *Sampler* (detail), 1797 by Mary Wiggin. 18 x 21 1/2." Philadelphia Museum of Art, Whitman Sampler Collection/Given by Pet, Incorporated; **747:** *Faustine*, 1904, Maxwell Armfield, Musée d'Orsay, Paris, France/Erich Lessing/Art Resource, NY; **748:** *Alfred Lord Tennyson* (detail), c.1840, S. Laurence, by courtesy of the National Portrait Gallery, London; **751:** *The Stages of Life* by Caspar-David Friedrich, (1774–1840), Museum der Bildenden Kunst, Leipzig/Bridgeman Art Library International Ltd., London/New York; **755:** *The Lady of Shalott* by John W. Waterhouse, Tate Gallery, London/E.T. Archive, London/SuperStock; **760:** *Ulysses Mourning for Home*, carved gem of light brown sardonyx, Roman 3rd to 2nd century B.C., Staatliche Museen zu Berlin; **762:** *Beach at Heist (Belgium)*, 1891–1892, Georges Lemmen, Musée d'Orsay, Paris, France/Erich Lessing/Art Resource, NY; **766:** The Granger Collection, New York; **769:** *Antea (Portrait of a Lady)*, Parmigianino, Museo Nazionale di Capodimonte, Naples/Art Resource, NY; **771:** Culver Pictures, Inc.; **772:** Victoria and Albert Museum/Art Resource, NY; **773 & 774–775:** Corel Professional Photos CD-ROM™; **776:** Corbis-Bettmann; **777:** Archive Photos; **780:** (background) NASA; (top) & (bottom) Corbis-Bettmann; **781:** Walters Art Gallery, Baltimore; **782:** *Marine*, Marcel Mouillot, Galleria d'arte Moderna, Nancy/Art Resource, NY; **785:** Jean-Philippe Varin/JACANA/Photo Researchers, Inc.; **789:** e.t.archive; **790:** (left) *Matthew Arnold* (detail), 1888, G.J. Watts, by courtesy of the National Portrait Gallery, London; (right) *Rudyard Kipling* (detail), 1899, P. Burne Jones, by courtesy of the National Portrait Gallery, London; **792:** Andrea Pistolesi/The Image Bank; **794:** The Granger Collection, New York; **796:** Culver Pictures, Inc.; **802:** *Woman Begging at Clonakilty*, James Mahony, *The Illustrated London News*, 1847. Photo by Grace Davies/ Omni-Photo Communications, Inc.; **805 & 806:** Culver Pictures, Inc.; **810:** (left) NASA; (br) Derek Speirs/Report Ltd.; **812:** Derek Speirs/Report Ltd.; **814:** (left) NASA; **815:** The Granger Collection, New York; **819:** *Music and Literature*, 1878, William H. Harnett, oil on canvas, 24 x 32-1/8", Albright-Knox Art Gallery Buffalo, New York, Gift of Seymour H. Knox, 1941; **820 & 823:** The Granger Collection, New York; **824:** "Horses" design #5, page 301 from the book *Textile Designs*, ©The Design Library, New York; **831:** Springer/Corbis-Bettmann; **836:** (background) NASA; (br) *L. N. Tolstoi*, I. E. Repin, Sovfoto/Eastfoto; **838:** *Portrait of Koutouzov, Prince of Smolensk*, George Dawe, Hermitage, St. Petersburg, Russia/Giraudon/Art Resource, NY; **841:** The Granger Collection, New York; **844:** M.K. Denny/PhotoEdit; **845:** *Past and Present (no.2)*, Augustus Leopold Egg, Tate Gallery, London/Art Resource, NY; **846:** (top) The Granger Collection, New York; (bottom) *Thomas Hardy* (detail), R.G. Eres, by courtesy of the National Portrait Gallery, London; **848:** *My Sweet Rose*, John William Waterhouse, Roy Miles Gallery, London/Bridgeman/Art Resource, NY; **850–851:** ©Gregory K. Scott/Photo Researchers, Inc.; **852 & 853:**

Lenore Weber/Omni-Photo Communications, Inc.; **856:** (left) *Gerard Manley Hopkins* (detail), 1859, A.E. Hopkins, by Courtesy of the National Portrait Gallery, London; (right) The Granger Collection, New York; **858:** *Bird's Nest*, Ros W. Jenkins. Warrington Museum and Art Gallery, Bridgeman/Art Resource, NY; **860–861:** Springer/Corbis-Bettmann; **864:** (left) NASA; (br) Art Resource, NY; **865 & 866:** Corel Professional Photos CD-ROM™; **868:** © M. L. Miller/Stock South/PNI; **874–875:** *The City Rises*, 1911 (tempera on card), Umberto Boccioni (1882–1916), Jesi Collection, Milan/The Bridgeman Art Library International Ltd., London/New York; **876:** (1905) UPI/Corbis-Bettmann; (1914) Imperial War Museum, London; (1927) Wood River Gallery/PNI; (1939) The National Archives/Corbis; (1945) SuperStock; (1949) Corel Professional Photos CD-ROM™; (1954) Corbis-Bettmann; **877:** (1969) NASA; (1975) Michael St. Maur Shell/Corbis; (1979) © Peter Marlow/Sygma; (1989) © Reggis Bossu/Sygma; **878:** (top) Corel Professional Photos CD-ROM™; (bottom) Musée de Verdun/Luc Joubert/Tallandier; **879:** (top) Culver Pictures, Inc.; (bottom) UPI/Corbis-Bettmann; **880:** (top) Domenica del Corriere/ET Archive, London/SuperStock; (center) & (bottom) AP/Wide World Photos; **881:** (top) AP/Wide World Photos; (bottom) UPI/Corbis-Bettmann; **882:** (top) Culver Pictures, Inc.; (bottom) Erik Schaffer, Ecoscene/Corbis; **883:** (top) David Hockney Studio; (bottom) Martin Jones/Corbis; **884:** *Sampler* (detail), 1797 by Mary Wiggin. 18 x 21 1/2." Philadelphia Museum of Art, Whitman Sampler Collection/Given by Pet, Incorporated; **885:** *The Children Enter the Palace of Luxury*, probably from "The Bluebird" by Maeterlinck, 1911 (oil on card) by Frederick Cayley Robinson, (1862–1927), The Fine Art Society, London/Bridgeman Art Library International Ltd., London/New York; **886:** (top) Alfred A. Knopf; (bottom) Hulton-Deutsch Collection/Corbis; **892:** *Ox House, Shaftesbury*, 1932, John R. Biggs, Wood Engraving; **896:** The Granger Collection, New York; **898:** *Her Signal*, c. 1892, Norman Garstin, (1847–1926) The Royal Cornwall Museum, Truro/Bridgeman Art Library International Ltd., London/New York; **901:** Dennis Stock/Magnum Photos, Inc.; **902:** *Man in the World*, P. Filonov, Russian State Museum, St. Petersburg, Russia/Superstock; **905:** The Granger Collection, New York; **908:** *T. S. Eliot* (detail), 1888–1965, Sir Gerald Kelly, National Portrait Gallery, Smithsonian Institution, Art Resource, New York; **922:** (tl) BBC Hulton/Corbis-Bettmann; (tr) The Granger Collection, New York; (br) *Louis MacNeice* (detail), H. Loster, by Courtesy of the National Portrait Gallery, London; **924:** The Granger Collection, New York; **928:** *The Fall of Icarus*, Pieter Brueghel, Musées Royaux des Beaux-Arts de Belgique, Bruxelles; **931:** Simon Wilkinson/The Image Bank; **932–933:** Richard Nowitz/Corbis; **936:** The Granger Collection, New York; **938–939:** ©Gregory C. Dimijian/Photo Researchers, Inc.; **941:** © Orwell Archive; **948:** (background) NASA; (tl) Inge Morath/Magnum Photos, Inc.; (tr) The Granger Collection, New York; (bottom) Dorothy Alexander; **949:** *Thrust*, 1959, Adolph Gottlieb, The Metropolitan Museum of Art, George A. Hearn Fund, 1959, Photography by Malcolm Varon, ©1987/1989 Copyright by the Metropolitan Museum of Art, © Adolph and Esther Gottlieb Foundation/Licensed by VAGA, New York, NY; **950:** The Granger Collection, New York; **952:** (background)